AC
INTERNA
CRICKET
YEAR
BOOK
1998

Compiled by Philip Bailey

Published by The Association of Cricket Statisticians and Historians, West Bridgford,
Nottingham
Typeset by Limlow Books from the compiler's disks
Printed by Tranters, Derby

ISBN: 0 947774 97 1

INTRODUCTION

This book lists every cricketer who appeared in a first-class match and/or important limited overs match in the 1997 English season or in the 1996-97 season in Australia, Canada, India, Kenya, New Zealand, Pakistan, Sharjah, South Africa, Sri Lanka, West Indies and Zimbabwe: thus the book includes every current major cricketer in the world. The 1996-97 season is deemed to have ended in the West Indies in June, so matches played outside England from August will be included as part of the 1997-98 season.

The English section is divided up into the 18 first-class counties, followed by the first-class touring teams to England and then English players who did not appear for a first-class county. If a player appeared in major cricket overseas in 1996-97 a note appears directly after the player's name and his record there can be found in the section for the appropriate country. English players who previously represented counties other than their current club have a note at the end of the biographical line, giving the county and seasons involved.

In countries other than England, players are listed alphabetically with their current first-class side(s) in brackets after their name. If they toured abroad in 1996-97 or 1997, this is also noted.

The lines of statistics after the players biographical details are as follows:

Test	Appearances in Test Cricket in England in 1997
FC	Appearances in First-Class Cricket in England in 1997 (including Tests)
Int	Appearances in One-Day Internationals in England in 1997
SL	Appearances in the Sunday League in 1997
BH	Appearances in the Benson and Hedges Cup in 1997
NW	Appearances in the National Westminster Bank Trophy in 1997

These are followed by similar lines showing the full career record in the appropriate competition, with the year of debut. If a player only appeared in a particular competition in 1997, then no career line is printed. A similar pattern is followed for overseas countries. In limited overs matches the 5i column gives instances of exactly 4 wickets in an innings, and the 10m column gives instances of 5 or more wickets in an innings.

STATUS of MATCHES in SOUTH AFRICA

The matches played on 'rebel' tours from 1981-82 to 1989-90 in South Africa are still included as first-class in this book, as they were regarded as such at the time they were played.

ACKNOWLEDGEMENTS

David Baggett (Derbyshire), Brian Hunt (Durham), Michael Smith (Essex), Andrew Hignell (Glamorgan), Keith Gerrish (Gloucestershire), Vic Isaacs (Hampshire), Howard Milton (Kent), Malcolm Lorimer (Lancashire), Dennis Lambert (Leicestershire), David Kendix (Middlesex), Tony Kingston (Northamptonshire), Peter Wynne-Thomas (Nottinghamshire), Michael Hill (Somerset), Keith Booth (Surrey), Len Chandler (Sussex), Robert Brooke (Warwickshire), Les Hatton (Worcestershire and Sunday League), Roy Wilkinson (Yorkshire), Ken Trushell (Minor Counties), Neil Leitch (Scotland), Gerry Byrne (Ireland), Alex de la Mar (Holland), Allan Miller and Tony Lalley (Australia), Mohan Menon, Ashim Kumar Sarkar, Rajesh Kumar, Sudhir Vaidya, I.U.Khan (India), Francis Payne and Ian Smith (New Zealand), Ghulam Mustafa Khan and Nauman Bader (Pakistan), Andrew Samson and Robin Isherwood (South Africa), Sa'adi Thawfeeq (Sri Lanka), Craig Cozier (West Indies), John Ward (Zimbabwe), Bill Frindall and Harriet Monkhouse. Special thanks are due to Brian Croudy and Geoffrey Saulez for their assistance in compiling and checking the figures.

CONTENTS

TEST MATCHES

Test Series 1996-97 and 1997

Sri Lanka v Zimbabwe: Sri Lanka won 2
India v Australia: drawn 1
Pakistan v Zimbabwe: Pakistan won 1, drawn 1
India v South Africa: India won 2, South Africa won 1
Pakistan v New Zealand: Pakistan won 1, New Zealand won 1
Australia v West Indies: Australia won 3, West Indies 2
Zimbabwe v England: drawn 2
South Africa v India: South Africa won 2, drawn 1
New Zealand v England: England won 2, drawn 1
South Africa v Australia: Australia won 2, South Africa 1
West Indies v India: West Indies won 1, drawn 4
New Zealand v Sri Lanka: New Zealand won 2
Sri Lanka v Pakistan: drawn 2
West Indies v Sri Lanka: West Indies won 1, drawn 1
England v Australia: Australia won 3, England won 2, drawn 1

Test Match Table of Results 1996-97 and 1997

	P	W	L	D	% wins
Australia	15	8	5	2	53.33
South Africa	9	4	4	1	44.44
New Zealand	7	3	3	1	42.85
England	11	4	3	4	36.36
Pakistan	6	2	1	3	33.33
West Indies	12	4	3	5	33.33
Sri Lanka	8	2	3	3	25.00
India	12	2	4	6	16.66
Zimbabwe	6	0	3	3	0.00

Test Match Table of Results 1876-77 to 1997

	P	W	L	D	T	% wins
Australia	572	240	161	169	2	41.95
West Indies	334	129	80	124	1	38.62
England	740	251	210	279	0	33.91
Pakistan	237	66	54	117	0	27.84
South Africa	209	53	86	70	0	25.35
India	310	56	102	151	1	18.06
New Zealand	252	36	104	112	0	14.28
Sri Lanka	74	9	34	31	0	12.16
Zimbabwe	22	1	10	11	0	4.54

TEST RECORDS

Highest Team Total: 903-7d England v Australia (Oval) 1938
Highest in 1996-97: 628-8d Australia v South Africa (Cape Town); 586-7d New Zealand v Sri Lanka (Dunedin); 553 Pakistan v Zimbabwe (Sheikhupura); 529-7d South Africa v India (Cape Town); 521 England v New Zealand (Auckland)

Lowest Team Total: 26 New Zealand v England (Auckland) 1954-55
Lowest in 1996-97: 97 66 India v South Africa (Durban); 77 England v Australia (Lord's); 81 India v West Indies (Bridgetown); 100 India v South Africa (Durban); 104 Australia v England (Oval)

Highest Individual Innings: 375 B.C.Lara West Indies v England (St John's) 1993-94
Highest in 1996-97: 267* B.A.Young New Zealand v Sri Lanka (Dunedin); 257* Wasim Akram Pakistan v Zimbabwe (Sheikhupura); 214 G.S.Blewett Australia v South Africa (Johannesburg); 207 N.Hussain England v Australia (Edgbaston); 201 N.S.Sidhu India v West Indies (Port of Spain)

Most Runs in Series: 974 (av 139.14) D.G.Bradman Australia v England 1930
Most in 1996-97: 556 (av 55.60) M.T.G.Elliott Australia v England; 453 (av 50.33) G.P.Thorpe England v Australia; 443 (av 73.83) S.Chanderpaul West Indies v India; 431 (av 39.18) N.Hussain England v Australia; 391 (av 48.87) B.C.Lara West Indies v India

Most Runs in Career: 11,174 (av 50.56) A.R.Border (Australia) 1978-79 to 1993-94
Most by Current Batsman: 6,116 (av 41.89) M.A.Taylor (Australia) 1988-89 to date; 5,960 (av 49.66) S.R.Waugh (Australia) 1985-86 to date; 5,528 (av 45.68) Saleem Malik (Pakistan) 1981-82 to date; 5,243 (av 40.64) M.A.Atherton (England) 1989 to date; 5,011 (av 43.95) M.Azharuddin (India) 1984-85 to date

Best Innings Analysis: 10-53 J.C.Laker England v Australia (Old Trafford) 1956
Best in 1996-97: 8-38 G.D.McGrath Australia v England (Lord's); 8-64 L.Klusener South Africa v India (Calcutta); 7-36 M.S.Kasprowicz Australia v England (Oval); 7-37 J.N.Gillespie Australia v England (Headingley)

Most Wickets in Series: 49 (av 10.93) S.F.Barnes England v South Africa 1913-14
Most in 1996-97: 36 (av 19.47) G.D.McGrath Australia v England; 26 (av 17.42) G.D.McGrath Australia v West Indies; 24 (av 26.41) A.R.Caddick England v Australia; 24 (av 24.04) S.K.Warne Australia v England; 22 (av 27.00) S.K.Warne Australia v West Indies

Most Wickets in Career: 434 (av 29.64) Kapil Dev (India) 1978-79 to 1993-94
Most by Current Bowler: 339 (av 25.95) C.A.Walsh (West Indies) 1984-85 to date; 311 (av 22.68) Wasim Akram (Pakistan) 1984-85 to date; 306 (av 21.45) C.E.L.Ambrose (West Indies) 1987-88 to date; 264 (av 23.95) S.K.Warne (Australia) 1991-92 to date; 227 (av 21.33) Waqar Younis (Pakistan) 1989-90 to date

Record Wicket Partnerships

1st	413	M.H.Mankad & P.Roy	India v New Zealand (Madras)	1955-56
2nd	451	W.H.Ponsford & D.G.Bradman	Australia v England (Oval)	1934
3rd	467	A.H.Jones & M.D.Crowe	New Zealand v Sri Lanka (Wellington)	1990-91
4th	411	P.B.H.May & M.C.Cowdrey	England v West Indies (Edgbaston)	1957
5th	405	S.G.Barnes & D.G.Bradman	Australia v England (Sydney)	1946-47
6th	346	J.H.W.Fingleton & D.G.Bradman	Australia v England (Melbourne)	1936-37
7th	347	D.S.Atkinson & C.C.Depeiaza	West Indies v Australia (Bridgetown)	1954-55
8th	313	Wasim Akram & Saqlain Mushtaq	Pakistan v Zimbabwe (Sheikhupura)	1996-97
9th	190	Asif Iqbal & Intikhab Alam	Pakistan v England (Oval)	1967
10th	151	B.F.Hastings & R.O.Collinge	New Zealand v Pakistan (Auckland)	1972-73

Highest Partnerships in 1996-97

1st	236	A.C.Hudson & G.Kirsten	South Africa v India (Calcutta)
2nd	262	Saeed Anwar & Ijaz Ahmed	Pakistan v New Zealand (Rawalpindi)
3rd	268	R.G.Samuels & B.C.Lara	West Indies v Australia (Perth)
4th	288	N.Hussain & G.P.Thorpe	England v Australia (Edgbaston)
5th	385	S.R.Waugh & G.S.Blewett	Australia v South Africa (Johannesburg)
6th	222	S.R.Tendulkar & M.Azharuddin	India v South Africa (Cape Town)
7th	137	R.S.Kaluwitharana & W.P.U.J.C.Vaas	Sri Lanka v New Zealand (Dunedin)
8th	313	Wasim Akram & Saqlain Mushtaq	Pakistan v Zimbabwe (Sheikhupura)
9th	87	P.A.Strang & B.C.Strang	Zimbabwe v Pakistan (Sheikhupura)
10th	106*	N.J.Astle & D.K.Morrison	New Zealand v England (Auckland)

Most Wicketkeeping Dismissals in Innings: 7 (7ct) Wasim Bari Pakistan v New Zealand (Auckland) 1978-79; 7 (7ct) R.W.Taylor England v India (Bombay) 1979-80; 7 (7ct) I.D.S.Smith New Zealand v Sri Lanka (Hamilton) 1990-91
Most in 1996-97: 6 (6ct) I.A.Healy Australia v England (Edgbaston); 6 (6ct) A.J.Stewart England v Australia (Old Trafford); 5 (5ct) I.A.Healy Australia v South Africa (Johannesburg); 5 (5ct) N.R.Mongia India v South Africa (Durban)

Most Wicketkeeping Dismissals in Match: 11 (11ct) R.C.Russell England v South Africa (Johannesburg) 1995-96
Most in 1996-97: 8 (8ct) N.R.Mongia India v South Africa (Durban); 8 (8ct) A.J.Stewart England v Australia (Old Trafford); 7 (7ct) I.A.Healy Australia v South Africa (Johannesburg); 7 (7ct) I.A.Healy Australia v England (Trent Bridge)

Most Wicketkeeping Dismissals in Series: 28 (28ct) R.W.Marsh Australia v England 1982-83
Most in 1996-97: 227 (25ct 2st) I.A.Healy Australia v England; 23 (23ct) A.J.Stewart England v Australia

Most Wicketkeeping Dismissals in Career: 355 (343ct 12st) R.W.Marsh (Australia) 1970-71 to 1983-84
Most by Current Wicketkeeper: 329 (307ct 22st) I.A.Healy (Australia) 1988-89 to date; 135 (134ct 1st)

D.J.Richardson (South Africa) 1991-92 to date; 119 (112ct 7st) A.J.Stewart (England) 1989-90 to date; 95 (92ct 3st) J.R.Murray (West Indies) 1992-93 to date; 71 (69ct 2st) A.C.Parore (New Zealand) 1990-91 to date

Most Catches by Fielder in Innings: 5 V.Y.Richardson Australia v South Africa (Durban) 1935-36; 5 Yajuvindra Singh India v England (Bangalore) 1976-77; 5 M.Azharuddin India v Pakistan (Karachi) 1989-90; 5 K.Srikkanth India v Australia (Perth) 1991-92
Most in 1996-97: 4 N.V.Knight England v New Zealand (Christchurch); 4 R.S.Mahanama Sri Lanka v Zimbabwe (Colombo); 4 R.S.Mahanama Sri Lanka v New Zealand (Dunedin); 4 Saleem Elahi Pakistan v Sri Lanka (Colombo)

Most Catches by Fielder in Match: 7 G.S.Chappell Australia v England (Perth) 1970-71; 7 Yajuvindra Singh India v England (Bangalore) 1976-77; 7 H.P.Tillakaratne Sri Lanka v New Zealand (Colombo) 1992-93
Most in 1996-97: 5 R.S.Mahanama Sri Lanka v Zimbabwe (Colombo)

Most Catches by Fielder in Series: 15 J.M.Gregory Australia v England 1920-21
Most in 1996-97: 9 M.Azharuddin India v West Indies; 9 G.S.Blewett Australia v South Africa; 9 C.L.Hooper West Indies v Australia; 9 N.V.Knight England v New Zealand; 9 M.A.Taylor Australia v West Indies

Most Catches by Fielder in Career: 156 A.R.Border (Australia) 1978-79 to 1993-94
Most by Current Fielder: 123 M.A.Taylor (Australia) 1988-89 to date; 88 M.Azharuddin (India) 1981-82 to date; 87 M.E.Waugh (Australia) 1990-91 to date; 72 C.L.Hooper (West Indies) 1987-88 to date; 70 S.R.Waugh (Australia) 1985-86 to date

Most Appearances in Career: 156 A.R.Border (Australia) 1978-79 to 1993-94
Most by Current Player: 96 Saleem Malik (Pakistan) 1981-82 to date; 95 S.R.Waugh (Australia) 1985-86 to date; 94 I.A.Healy (Australia) 1988-89 to date; 93 C.A.Walsh (West Indies) 1984-85 to date; 87 M.A.Taylor (Australia) 1988-89 to date

ONE-DAY INTERNATIONAL MATCHES

RESULTS OF THE MAJOR COMPETITIONS

Prudential/Texaco Trophy
The Prudential Trophy series between England and Touring teams to England commenced in 1972, matches being 55 overs per side. The number of matches played each season was either 3 or 4 depending on the number of teams touring England except in 1992 when 5 matches were played. The sponsors changed to Texaco in 1984.

1972 England 2, Australia 1
1973 England 1, New Zealand 0, no result 1
1973 West Indies 1, England 1 (West Indies won series on faster scoring rate)
1974 England 2, India 0
1974 Pakistan 2, England 0
1976 West Indies 3, England 0
1977 England 2, Australia 1
1978 England 2, Pakistan 0
1978 England 2, New Zealand 0
1980 West Indies 1, England 1 (West Indies won series on faster scoring rate)
1980 England 2, Australia 0
1981 Australia 2, England 1
1982 England 2, India 0
1982 England 2, Pakistan 0
1984 West Indies 2, England 1
1985 Australia 2, England 1
1986 India 1, England 1 (India won series on faster scoring rate)
1986 New Zealand 1, England 1 (New Zealand won series on faster scoring rate)
1987 England 2, Pakistan 1
1988 England 3, West Indies 0
1988 England 1, Sri Lanka 0
1989 England 1, Australia 1, tied 1 (England won series by losing fewer wickets in tied match)
1990 England 1, New Zealand 1 (England won series on faster scoring rate)
1990 India 2, England 0
1991 England 3, West Indies 0
1992 England 4, Pakistan 1

1993 Australia 3, England 0
1994 England 1, New Zealand 0 (abandoned 1)
1994 England 2, South Africa 0
1995 England 2, West Indies 1
1996 England 2, India 0 (abandoned 1)
1996 England 2, Pakistan 1
1997 England 3, Australia 0

World Cup

The World Cup was introduced in 1975, a 60 overs per side competition played between the six full members of the ICC together with Sri Lanka and East Africa. Two qualifying groups of four teams each played a round-robin with the top two teams in each group contesting the semi-finals and final. The same format was used in 1979, when Sri Lanka and Canada qualified by reaching the final of the ICC Associate Members Trophy. In 1983 a double round-robin was played in the qualifying stages. Sri Lanka, having been elected as a full member of the ICC, automatically participated and the eighth place went to Zimbabwe, who won the ICC Trophy. The same format was used in 1987 except that the over limit was reduced to 50. In 1992 South Africa were admitted and the nine teams, including Zimbabwe as ICC Trophy winners, played a single round robin. In 1996 Zimbabwe, having been elected as a full member of the ICC, automatically participated and with the three leading teams from the ICC Trophy formed two groups of six teams for the qualifying round. Results of the finals:

1975 West Indies 291-8 (60 overs) beat Australia 274 (58.4 overs) by 17 runs
1979 West Indies 286-9 (60 overs) beat England 194 (51 overs) by 92 runs
1983 India 183 (54.4 overs) beat West Indies 140 (52 overs) by 43 runs
1987 Australia 253 (50 overs) beat England 246-8 (50 overs) by 7 runs
1992 Pakistan 249-6 (50 overs) beat England 227 (49.2 overs) by 22 runs
1996 Sri Lanka 245-3 (46.2 overs) beat Australia 241-7 (50 overs) by 7 wkts

World Series Cup

The World Series Cup has been staged in Australia each season since 1979-80 between Australia and two invited countries. In 1994-95, only a fourth team, Australia A, competed but their matches were ruled as not official One-Day Internationals by the ICC. A qualifying group, currently of 12 matches, is played to decide the two teams to contest a final series, currently the best of three matches. The sponsors changed from Benson and Hedges to Carlton and United in 1996-97. The overs limit has been 50 throughout. Results of the final matches:

1979-80 West Indies 2, England 0 (3rd Australia)
1980-81 Australia 3, New Zealand 1 (3rd India)
1981-82 West Indies 3, Australia 1 (3rd Pakistan)
1982-83 Australia 2, New Zealand 0 (3rd England)
1983-84 West Indies 2, Australia 0, tied 1 (3rd Pakistan)
1984-85 West Indies 2, Australia 1 (3rd Sri Lanka)
1985-86 Australia 2, India 0 (3rd New Zealand)
1986-87 England 2, Australia 0 (3rd West Indies)
1987-88 Australia 2, New Zealand 0 (3rd Sri Lanka)
1988-89 West Indies 2, Australia 1 (3rd Pakistan)
1989-90 Australia 2, Pakistan 0 (3rd Sri Lanka)
1990-91 Australia 2, New Zealand 0 (3rd England)
1991-92 Australia 2, India 0 (3rd West Indies)
1992-93 West Indies 2, Australia 0 (3rd Pakistan)
1993-94 Australia 2, South Africa 1 (3rd New Zealand)
1994-95 Australia 2, Australia A 0 (3rd England, 4th Zimbabwe)
1995-96 Australia 2, Sri Lanka 0 (3rd West Indies)
1996-97 Pakistan 2, West Indies 0 (3rd Australia)

Asia Cup

The Asia Cup was introduced in 1983-84, a 45 overs per side competition played between the Asian Countries (India, Pakistan and Sri Lanka). From 1985-86 Bangladesh also competed, their matches now being recognised by the ICC as official One-Day Internationals. The overs limit was increased to 50 in 1994-95. Results of the finals:

1983-84 India won a round-robin competition, Sri Lanka being runner-up
1985-86 Sri Lanka 195-5 (42.2 overs) beat Pakistan 191-9 (45 overs) by 5 wkts

1988-89 India 180-4 (37.1 overs) beat Sri Lanka 176 (43.2 overs) by 6 wkts
1990-91 India 205-3 (42.1 overs) beat Sri Lanka 204-9 (45 overs) by 7 wkts
1994-95 India 233-2 (41.5 overs) beat Sri Lanka 230-7 (50 overs) by 8 wkts

Table of Results 1996-97 and 1997

	P	W	L	T	NR	% wins
South Africa	27	19	7	0	1	73.07
Sri Lanka	24	17	6	1	0	70.83
Pakistan	40	24	16	0	0	60.00
West Indies	15	9	6	0	0	60.00
England	11	5	5	1	0	45.45
India	31	10	19	1	1	33.33
Australia	27	9	18	0	0	33.33
New Zealand	18	6	10	2	0	33.33
Zimbabwe	20	5	14	1	0	25.00
Kenya	3	0	3	0	0	0.00

Table of Results 1970-71 to 1997

	P	W	L	T	NR	% wins
West Indies	338	213	115	4	6	64.15
South Africa	120	68	49	0	3	58.11
Australia	377	203	160	3	11	55.46
Pakistan	370	192	165	5	8	53.03
England	264	135	119	2	8	52.73
India	319	141	165	3	10	45.63
New Zealand	281	116	152	3	10	42.80
Sri Lanka	245	86	147	1	11	36.75
Zimbabwe	77	12	60	3	2	16.00
United Arab Emirates	7	1	6	0	0	14.28
Kenya	9	1	7	0	1	12.50
Canada	3	0	3	0	0	0.00
East Africa	3	0	3	0	0	0.00
Holland	5	0	5	0	0	0.00
Bangladesh	12	0	12	0	0	0.00

The percentage calculations exclude no-result games

One-Day International Records

Highest Team Totals: 398-5 (50 overs) Sri Lanka v Kenya (Kandy) 1995-96; 371-9 (50 overs) Pakistan v Sri Lanka (Nairobi) 1996-97; 363-7 (55 overs) England v Pakistan (Trent Bridge) 1992

Lowest Team Totals: 43 (19.5 overs) Pakistan v West Indies (Cape Town) 1992-93; 45 (40.3 overs) Canada v England (Old Trafford) 1979; 55 (28.3 overs) Sri Lanka v West Indies (Sharjah) 1986-87
Lowest in 1996-97: 94 (31.4 overs) Zimbabwe v Pakistan (Sharjah)

Highest Individual Innings: 194 Saeed Anwar Pakistan v India (Madras) 1996-97; 189* I.V.A.Richards West Indies v England (Old Trafford) 1984; 188* G.Kirsten South Africa v United Arab Emirates (Rawalpindi) 1995-96
344 centuries have been scored in One-Day Internationals, D.L.Haynes (West Indies) scoring 17

Most Runs in Year: 1,351 (av 38.60) Ijaz Ahmed (Pakistan) 1996-97

Most Runs in Career: 8,648 (av 41.37) D.L.Haynes (West Indies) 1977-78 to 1993-94; 7,381 (av 41.70) Javed Miandad (Pakistan) 1975 to 1995-96; 6,721 (av 47.00) I.V.A.Richards (West Indies) 1975 to 1991
Most by Current Batsman: 6,701 (av 36.22) M.Azharuddin (India) 1984-85 to date

Best Innings Analyses: 7-37 Aaqib Javed Pakistan v India (Sharjah) 1991-92; 7-51 W.W.Davis West Indies v Australia (Headingley) 1983; 6-12 A.Kumble India v West Indies (Calcutta) 1993-94
Best in 1996-97: 6-23 A.A.Donald South Africa v Kenya (Nairobi)
Five wickets in an innings has been achieved on 122 occasions, 9 times by Waqar Younis (Pakistan)

Most Economical Bowling: 10-8-3-4 P.V.Simmons West Indies v Pakistan (Sydney) 1992-93
Most Economical in 1996-97: 10-3-13-2 W.P.U.J.C.Vaas Sri Lanka v India (Mumbai)

Most Expensive Bowling: 12-1-105-2 M.C.Snedden New Zealand v England (Oval) 1983
Most Expensive in 1996-97: 10-0-94-3 S.T.Jayasuriya Sri Lanka v Pakistan (Nairobi)

Most Wickets in Year: 86 (av 17.09) Saqlain Mushtaq (Pakistan) 1996-97

Most Wickets in Career: 333 (av 22.57) Wasim Akram (Pakistan) 1984-85 to date; 265 (av 21.74) Waqar Younis (Pakistan) 1989-90 to date; 253 (av 27.45) Kapil Dev (India) 1978-79 to 1994-95

Record Wicket Partnerships

1st	212	G.R.Marsh & D.C.Boon	Australia v India (Jaipur)	1986-87
2nd	263	Aamer Sohail & Inzamam-ul-Haq	Pakistan v New Zealand (Sharjah)	1993-94
3rd	224*	D.M.Jones & A.R.Border	Australia v Sri Lanka (Adelaide)	1984-85
4th	232	D.J.Cullinan & J.N.Rhodes	South Africa v Pakistan (Nairobi)	1996-97
5th	159	R.T.Ponting & M.G.Bevan	Australia v Sri Lanka (Melbourne)	1995-96
6th	154	R.B.Richardson & P.J.L.Dujon	West Indies v Pakistan (Sharjah)	1991-92
7th	115	P.J.L.Dujon & M.D.Marshall	West Indies v Pakistan (Gujranwala)	1986-87
	115	A.C.Parore & L.K.Germon	New Zealand v Pakistan (Sharjah)	1996-97
8th	119	P.R.Reiffel & S.K.Warne	Australia v South Africa (Port Elizabeth)	1993-94
9th	126*	Kapil Dev & S.M.H.Kirmani	India v Zimbabwe (Tunbridge Wells)	1983
10th	106*	I.V.A.Richards & M.A.Holding	West Indies v England (Old Trafford)	1984

Highest Partnerships in 1996-97

1st	200*	S.Chanderpaul & S.C.Williams	West Indies v India (Bridgetown)
2nd	145	M.E.Waugh & S.G.Law	Australia v West Indies (Brisbane)
3rd	184	M.S.Atapattu & P.A.de Silva	Sri Lanka v Pakistan (Sharjah)
4th	232	D.J.Cullinan & J.N.Rhodes	South Africa v Pakistan (Nairobi)
5th	135*	G.P.Thorpe & A.J.Hollioake	England v Australia (Headingley)
6th	137	W.J.Cronje & S.M.Pollock	South Africa v Zimbabwe (Johannesburg)
7th	115	A.C.Parore & L.K.Germon	New Zealand v Pakistan (Sharjah)
8th	91	H.D.P.K.Dharmasena & D.K.Liyanage	Sri Lanka v West Indies (Port of Spain)
9th	89	H.S.Modi & Asif Karim	Kenya v Sri Lanka (Nairobi)
10th	33	A.Kumble & B.K.Venkatesh Prasad	India v Pakistan (Toronto)

Most Wicketkeeping Dismissals in Innings: 5 (5ct) R.W.Marsh Australia v England (Headingley) 1981; 5 (5ct) R.G.De Alwis Sri Lanka v Australia (Colombo) 1982-83; 5 (5ct) S.M.H.Kirmani India v Zimbabwe (Tunbridge Wells); 5 (3ct 2st) S.Viswanath India v England (Sydney) 1984-85; 5 (3ct 2st) K.S.More India v New Zealand (Sharjah) 1987-88; 5 (5ct) H.P.Tillakaratne Sri Lanka v Pakistan (Sharjah) 1990-91; 5 (3ct 2st) N.R.Mongia India v New Zealand (Auckland) 1993-94; 5 (4ct 1st) R.S.Kaluwitharana Sri Lanka v Pakistan (Sharjah) 1994-95; 5 (5ct) Moin Khan Pakistan v Zimbabwe (Harare) 1994-95; 5 (3ct 2st) A.C.Parore New Zealand v West Indies (Margao) 1994-95; 5 (5ct) D.J.Richardson South Africa v Pakistan (Johannesburg) 1994-95; 5 (5ct) C.O.Browne West Indies v Sri Lanka (Brisbane) 1995-96; 5 (5ct) A.Flower Zimbabwe v South Africa (Harare) 1995-96; 5 (4ct 1st) Rashid Latif Pakistan v New Zealand (Lahore) 1995-96; 5 (5ct) D.J.Richardson South Africa v Zimbabwe (Harare) 1995-96; 5 (5ct) A.Flower Zimbabwe v England (Harare) 1996-97; 5 (3ct 2st) N.R.Mongia India v Pakistan (Toronto) 1996-97

Most Wicketkeeping Dismissals in Year: 52 (34ct 18st) Moin Khan (Pakistan) 1996-97

Most Wicketkeeping Dismissals in Career: 234 (195ct 39st) I.A.Healy (Australia) 1988-89 to date; 204 (183ct 21st) P.J.L.Dujon (West Indies) 1980-81 to 1991-92; 146 (131ct 15st) D.J.Richardson (South Africa) 1991-92 to date

Most Catches by Fielder in Innings: 5 J.N.Rhodes South Africa v West Indies (Bombay) 1993-94
Most in 1996-97: no fielder held more than 3

Most Catches by Fielder in Year: 22 Ijaz Ahmed (Pakistan) 1996-97

Most Catches by Fielder in Career: 127 A.R.Border (Australia) 1978-79 to 1993-94; 106 M.Azharuddin (India) 1984-85 to date; 101 I.V.A.Richards (West Indies) 1975 to 1991

Most Appearances in Career: 273 A.R.Border (Australia) 1978-79 to 1993-94; 259 Saleem Malik (Pakistan) 1981-82 to date; 245 M.Azharuddin (India) 1984-85 to date; 239 D.L.Haynes (West Indies) 1977-78 to 1993-94

Note: records 'in a year' include the English season and the preceding overseas season

The records and averages include abandoned One Day Internationals which were replayed the following day in accordance with the ICC ruling. Similar matches in domestic competitions are, however, not included in accordance with the ECB (formerly TCCB) ruling.

ENGLAND

First First-Class Match: England v Surrey 1801 is the first 'important' match listed in the ACS Guide to matches in England before 1864

First Test Match: England v Australia (Oval) 1880

Present First-Class Teams: Derbyshire, Durham, Essex, Glamorgan, Gloucestershire, Hampshire, Kent, Lancashire, Leicestershire, Middlesex, Northamptonshire, Nottinghamshire, Somerset, Surrey, Sussex, Warwickshire, Worcestershire, Yorkshire (County Championship). Cambridge University and Oxford University matches are also first-class, as also is the annual Ireland v Scotland match.

First-Class Competition: Britannic Assurance County Championship

County Champions 1997: Glamorgan

FIRST-CLASS RECORDS

Highest Team Total: 903-7d England v Australia (Oval) 1938
Highest in 1997: 631-7d Warwickshire v Hampshire (Southampton); 597-8d Glamorgan v Durham (Cardiff); 592-4d Lancashire v Surrey (Oval); 581-7d Surrey v Northamptonshire (Northampton); 569-8d Lancashire v Hampshire (Southampton)

Lowest Team Total: 6 The Bs v England (Lord's) 1810; 12 Oxford Univ v MCC (Oxford) 1877; 12 Northamptonshire v Gloucestershire (Gloucester) 1907
Lowest in 1997: 31 Glamorgan v Middlesex (Cardiff); 51 Lancashire v Glamorgan (Liverpool); 54 Sussex v Glamorgan (Swansea); 63 Sussex v Warwickshire (Edgbaston); 67 Sussex v Glamorgan (Swansea)

Highest Individual Innings: 501* B.C.Lara Warwickshire v Durham (Edgbaston) 1994
Highest in 1997: 303* G.A.Hick Worcestershire v Hampshire (Southampton); 271* A.J.Stewart Surrey v Yorkshire (Oval); 237 S.Young Gloucestershire v Derbyshire (Cheltenham); 235* M.L.Hayden Hampshire v Warwickshire (Southampton); 233* H.Morris Glamorgan v Warwickshire (Cardiff)

Most Runs in Season: 3,816 (av 90.85) D.C.S.Compton (Middlesex) 1947
Most in 1997: 1,775 (av 68.26) S.P.James (Glamorgan); 1,575 (av 63.00) D.S.Lehmann (Yorkshire); 1,524 (av 69.27) G.A.Hick (Worcestershire); 1,482 (av 57.00) S.G.Law (Essex); 1,453 (av 55.88) M.R.Ramprakash (Middlesex)

Most Runs in Career: 61,760 (av 50.66) J.B.Hobbs (Surrey) 1905 to 1934
Most by Current Batsman: 44,841 (av 49.11) G.A.Gooch (Essex, Western Province) 1973 to date; 35,410 (av 49.73) M.W.Gatting (Middlesex) 1975 to date; 28,473 (av 56.27) G.A.Hick (Worcestershire, Zimbabwe, Queensland, Northern Districts) 1983-84 to date; 26,493 (av 42.93) R.T.Robinson (Nottinghamshire) 1978 to date; 25,453 (av 35.69) C.W.J.Athey (Yorkshire, Gloucestershire, Sussex) 1976 to date

Best Innings Analysis: 10-10 H.Verity Yorkshire v Nottinghamshire (Headingley) 1932
Best in 1997: 9-64 M.M.Betts Durham v Northamptonshire (Northampton); 8-17 Waqar Younis Glamorgan v Sussex (Swansea); 8-32 P.J.Martin Lancashire v Middlesex (Uxbridge); 8-38 G.D.McGrath Australia v England (Lord's); 8-49 K.D.James Hampshire v Somerset (Basingstoke)

Most Wickets in Season: 304 (av 18.05) A.P.Freeman (Kent) 1928
Most in 1997: 83 (av 17.63) A.M.Smith (Gloucestershire); 81 (av 19.37) D.R.Brown (Warwickshire); 81 (av 26.61) A.R.Caddick (Somerset); 75 (av 23.48) D.E.Malcolm (Derbyshire); 68 (av 22.80) Waqar Younis (Glamorgan)

Most Wickets in Career: 4,204 (av 16.72) W.Rhodes (Yorkshire) 1898 to 1930
Most by Current Bowler: 1,608 (av 27.96) J.E.Emburey (Middlesex, Northamptonshire, Western Province) 1973 to date; 916 (av 27.96) P.A.J.DeFreitas (Leicestershire, Lancashire, Derbyshire, Boland) 1985 to date; 852 (av 28.62) G.C.Small (Warwickshire, South Australia) 1979 to date; 813 (av 27.17) P.J.Newport (Worcestershire, Boland) 1982 to date. A.A.Donald, 945 (av 22.39), played for Warwickshire, and Wasim Akram, 829 (av 21.39), played for Lancashire in 1997.

Record Wicket Partnerships

1st	555	P.Holmes & H.Sutcliffe	Yorkshire v Essex (Leyton)	1932
2nd	465*	J.A.Jameson & R.B.Kanhai	Warwickshire v Gloucestershire (Edgbaston)	1974
3rd	438*	G.A.Hick & T.M.Moody	Worcestershire v Hampshire (Southampton)	1997
4th	470	A.I.Kallicharran & G.W.Humpage	Warwickshire v Lancashire (Southport)	1982
5th	393	E.G.Arnold & W.B.Burns	Worcestershire v Warwickshire (Edgbaston)	1909
6th	428	W.W.Armstrong & M.A.Noble	Australians v Sussex (Hove)	1902
7th	344	K.S.Ranjitsinhji & W.Newham	Sussex v Essex (Leyton)	1902

8th	292	R.Peel & Lord Hawke	Yorkshire v Warwickshire (Edgbaston)	1896
9th	283	A.Warren & J.Chapman	Derbyshire v Warwickshire (Blackwell)	1910
10th	249	C.T.Sarwate & S.N.Banerjee	Indians v Surrey (Oval)	1946

Highest Partnerships in 1997

1st	291	J.J.B.Lewis & P.D.Collingwood	Durham v Oxford University (Oxford)
2nd	417	K.J.Barnett & T.A.Tweats	Derbyshire v Yorkshire (Derby)
3rd	438*	G.A.Hick & T.M.Moody	Worcestershire v Hampshire (Southampton)
4th	288	N.Hussain & G.P.Thorpe	England v Australia (Edgbaston)
5th	268	M.T.G.Elliott & R.T.Ponting	Australia v England (Headingley)
6th	205	M.W.Alleyne & R.C.Russell	Gloucestershire v Durham (Cheltenham)
7th	279	R.J.Harden & G.D.Rose	Somerset v Sussex (Taunton)
8th	186	N.M.K.Smith & D.R.Brown	Warwickshire v Gloucestershire (Edgbaston)
9th	171	M.A.Ealham & P.A.Strang	Kent v Nottinghamshire (Trent Bridge)
10th	183	S.A.Marsh & B.J.Phillips	Kent v Sussex (Horsham)

Most Wicketkeeping Dismissals in Innings: 8 (8ct) D.E.East Essex v Somerset (Taunton) 1985; 8 (8ct) S.A.Marsh Kent v Middlesex (Lord's) 1991; 8 (6ct 2s) T.J.Zoehrer Australians v Surrey 1993
Most in 1997: 6 (6ct) I.A.Healy Australia v England (Edgbaston); 6 (6ct) S.A.Marsh Kent v Nottinghamshire (Trent Bridge); 6 (6ct) W.M.Noon Nottinghamshire v Derbyshire (Trent Bridge); 6 (6ct) A.J.Stewart England v Australia (Old Trafford)

Most Wicketkeeping Dismissals in Match: 12 (8ct 4st) E.Pooley Surrey v Sussex (Oval) 1868
Most in 1997: 9 (9ct) Javed Qadeer Pakistan A v Nottinghamshire (Trent Bridge); 9 (9ct) P.A.Nixon Leicestershire v Nottinghamshire (Leicester); 8 (8ct) P.A.Nixon ECB First Class Counties XI v Pakistan A (Chelmsford); 8 (8ct) A.J.Stewart England v Australia (Old Trafford)

Most Wicketkeeping Dismissals in Season: 128 (79ct 49st) L.E.G.Ames (Kent) 1929
Most in 1997: 63 (61ct 2st) S.A.Marsh (Kent); 61 (57ct 4st) P.A.Nixon (Leicestershire); 57 (52ct 5st) R.C.Russell (Gloucestershire); 55 (53ct 2st) K.M.Krikken (Derbyshire)

Most Wicketkeeping Dismissals in Career: 1,649 (1,473ct 176st) R.W.Taylor (Derbyshire) 1960 to 1988
Most by Current Wicketkeeper: 1,002 (893ct 109st) R.C.Russell (Gloucestershire) 1981 to date; 929 (821ct 108st) S.J.Rhodes (Yorkshire, Worcestershire) 1981 to date; 668 (618ct 50st) S.A.Marsh (Kent) 1982 to date; 611 (560ct 51st) C.P.Metson (Middlesex, Glamorgan) 1981 to date; 599 (525ct 74st) D.Ripley (Northamptonshire) 1984 to date

Most Catches by Fielder in Innings: 7 M.J.Stewart Surrey v Northamptonshire (Northampton) 1957; 7 A.S.Brown Gloucestershire v Nottinghamshire (Trent Bridge) 1966
Most in 1997: 4 G.F.Archer Nottinghamshire v Lancashire (Old Trafford); 4 C.W.J.Athey Sussex v Essex (Hove); 4 D.Byas Yorkshire v Essex (Ilford); 4 M.W.Gatting Middlesex v Kent (Lord's); 4 M.Newell Sussex v Yorkshire (Scarborough); 4 T.R.Ward Kent v Essex (Canterbury); 4 R.J.Warren Northamptonshire v Worcestershire (Northampton)

Most Catches by Fielder in Match: 10 W.R.Hammond Gloucestershire v Surrey (Cheltenham) 1928
Most in 1997: 6 T.R.Ward Kent v Essex (Canterbury)

Most Catches by Fielder in Season: 78 W.R.Hammond (Gloucestershire) 1928
Most in 1997: 30 T.R.Ward (Kent); 29 D.P.Ostler (Warwickshire); 28 M.A.Butcher (Surrey); 24 M.C.J.Ball (Gloucestershire); 24 D.Byas (Yorkshire)

Most Catches by Fielder in Career: 1,018 F.E.Woolley (Kent) 1906 to 1938
Most by Current Fielder: 555 G.A.Gooch (Essex, Western Province) 1973 to date; 474 M.W.Gatting (Middlesex) 1975 to date; 459 J.E.Emburey (Middlesex, Western Province) 1973 to date; 429 C.W.J.Athey (Yorkshire, Gloucestershire, Sussex) 1976 to date; 417 G.A.Hick (Worcestershire, Zimbabwe, Queensland, Northern Districts) 1983-84 to date

DOMESTIC LIMITED OVERS RECORDS

AXA Life Sunday League

Highest Team Totals: 375-4 (40 overs) Surrey v Yorkshire (Scarborough) 1994; 360-3 (40 overs) Somerset v Glamorgan (Neath) 1990; 344-6 (40 overs) Leicestershire v Durham (Chester-le-Street) 1996; 344-5 (40 overs) Surrey v Hampshire (Guildford) 1997

Lowest Team Totals: 23 (19.4 overs) Middlesex v Yorkshire (Headingley) 1974; 36 (25.4 overs) Leicestershire v Sussex (Leicester) 1973; 41 (32 overs) Northamptonshire v Middlesex (Northampton) 1972
Lowest in 1997: 93 (16.5 overs) Derbyshire v Warwickshire (Edgbaston)

Highest Individual Innings: 203 A.D.Brown Surrey v Hampshire (Guildford) 1997; 176 G.A.Gooch Essex v Glamorgan (Southend) 1983; 175* I.T.Botham Somerset v Northamptonshire (Wellingborough) 1986
578 centuries have been scored in the competition, W.Larkins scoring 14

Most Runs in Season: 917 (av 70.53) T.M.Moody (Worcestershire) 1991
Most in 1997: 654 (av 43.60) M.L.Hayden (Hampshire)

Most Runs in Career: 8,573 (av 34.99) G.A.Gooch (Essex) 1973 to date; 7,504 (av 31.93) C.W.J.Athey (Yorkshire, Gloucestershire, Sussex) 1976 to date; 7,499 (av 28.84) W.Larkins (Northamptonshire, Durham) 1972 to 1995

Best Innings Analyses: 8-26 K.D.Boyce Essex v Lancashire (Old Trafford) 1971; 7-15 R.A.Hutton Yorkshire v Worcestershire (Headingley) 1969; 7-39 A.Hodgson Northamptonshire v Somerset (Northampton) 1976; 7-41 A.N.Jones Sussex v Nottinghamshire (Trent Bridge) 1986
Best in 1997: 6-21 D.G.Cork Derbyshire v Glamorgan (Chesterfield)
Five wickets in an innings has been achieved on 329 occasions, 6 times by D.L.Underwood

Most Economical Bowling: 8-8-0-0 B.A.Langford Somerset v Essex (Yeovil) 1969
Most Economical in 1997: 8-2-10-3 A.R.C.Fraser Middlesex v Sussex (Lord's)

Most Expensive Bowling: 8-0-96-1 D.G.Cork Derbyshire v Nottinghamshire (Trent Bridge) 1993
Most Expensive in 1997: 8-0-81-0 C.A.Connor Hampshire v Surrey (Guildford)

Most Wickets in Season: 39 (av 12.15) A.J.Hollioake (Surrey) 1996
Most in 1997: 31 (av 12.64) P.J.Martin (Lancashire)

Most Wickets in Career: 386 (av 19.73) J.K.Lever (Essex) 1969 to 1989; 368 (av 23.47) J.E.Emburey (Middlesex, Northamptonshire) 1975 to date; 346 (av 16.89) D.L.Underwood (Kent) 1969 to 1987

Record Wicket Partnerships

1st	239	G.A.Gooch & B.R.Hardie	Essex v Nottinghamshire (Trent Bridge)	1985
2nd	273	G.A.Gooch & K.S.McEwan	Essex v Nottinghamshire (Trent Bridge)	1983
3rd	223	S.J.Cook & G.D.Rose	Somerset v Glamorgan (Neath)	1990
4th	219	C.G.Greenidge & C.L.Smith	Hampshire v Surrey (Southampton)	1987
5th	190	R.J.Blakey & M.J.Foster	Yorkshire v Leicestershire (Leicester)	1993
6th	137	M.P.Speight & I.D.K.Salisbury	Sussex v Surrey (Guildford)	1996
7th	132	K.R.Brown & N.F.Williams	Middlesex v Somerset (Lord's)	1988
8th	110*	C.L.Cairns & B.N.French	Nottinghamshire v Surrey (Oval)	1993
9th	105	D.G.Moir & R.W.Taylor	Derbyshire v Kent (Derby)	1984
10th	82	G.Chapple & P.J.Martin	Lancashire v Worcestershire (Old Trafford)	1996

The highest partnership in 1997 was 200 for the 3rd wicket P.Johnson & G.F.Archer Nottinghamshire v Derbyshire (Trent Bridge)

Most Wicketkeeping Dismissals in Innings: 7 (6ct 1st) R.W.Taylor Derbyshire v Lancashire (Old Trafford) 1975
Most in 1997: 5 (5ct) B.J.Hyam Essex v Middlesex (Chelmsford)

Most Wicketkeeping Dismissals in Season: 29 (26ct 3st) S.J.Rhodes (Worcestershire) 1987
Most in 1997: 26 (18ct 8st) W.K.Hegg (Lancashire)

Most Wicketkeeping Dismissals in Career: 264 (206ct 58st) S.J.Rhodes (Worcestershire) 1985 to date; 257 (234ct 23st) D.L.Bairstow (Yorkshire) 1970 to 1990; 236 (187ct 49st) R.W.Taylor (Derbyshire)1969 to 1984

Most Catches by Fielder in Innings: 5 J.M.Rice Hampshire v Warwickshire (Southampton) 1978
Most in 1997: no fielder held more than 3

Most Catches by Fielder in Season: 16 J.M.Rice (Hampshire) 1978
Most in 1997: 15 W.S.Kendall (Hampshire)

Most Catches by Fielder in Career: 103 V.P.Terry (Hampshire) 1978 to 1995; 101 J.F.Steele (Leicestershire, Glamorgan) 1970 to 1986; 100 G.A.Gooch (Essex) 1973 to date

Most Appearances in Competition: 303 D.P.Hughes (Lancashire) 1969 to 1991; 301 J.Simmons (Lancashire) 1969 to 1989; 291 J.K.Lever (Essex) 1969 to 1989
Most by Current Player: 277 J.E.Emburey (Middlesex, Northamptonshire) 1975 to date

Benson and Hedges Cup

Highest Team Totals: 388-7 (55 overs) Essex v Scotland (Chelmsford) 1992; 371-6 (50 overs) Leicestershire v Scotland (Leicester) 1997; 369-8 (50 overs) Warwickshire v Minor Counties (Jesmond) 1996

Lowest Team Totals: 50 (27.2 overs) Hampshire v Yorkshire (Headingley) 1991; 56 (26.2 overs) Leicestershire v Minor Counties (Wellington) 1982; 59 (34 overs) Combined Universities v Glamorgan (Cambridge) 1983
Lowest in 1997: 63 (30.3 overs) Hampshire v Surrey (Southampton)

Highest Individual Innings: 198* G.A.Gooch Essex v Sussex (Hove) 1982; 177 S.J.Cook Somerset v Sussex (Hove) 1990; 173* C.G.Greenidge Hampshire v Minor Counties South (Amersham) 1973
Highest in 1997: 138 C.J.Adams Derbyshire v Minor Counties (Lakenham)
298 centuries have been scored in the competition, G.A.Gooch scoring 15

Most Runs in Season: 591 (av 84.42) G.A.Gooch (Essex) 1979
Most in 1997: 335 (av 55.83) M.J.Walker (Kent)

Most Runs in Career: 5,176 (av 52.28) G.A.Gooch (Essex) 1973 to date; 2,921 (av 40.56) M.W.Gatting (Middlesex) 1976 to date; 2,761 (av 32.48) C.J.Tavaré (Universities, Kent, Somerset) 1975 to 1993

Best Innings Analyses: 7-12 W.W.Daniel Middlesex v Minor Counties East (Ipswich) 1978; 7-22 J.R.Thomson Middlesex v Hampshire (Lord's) 1981; 7-24 Mushtaq Ahmed Somerset v Ireland (Taunton) 1997
Five wickets in an innings has been achieved 148 times, 4 times by M.J.Procter

Most Economical Bowling: 11-9-3-1 C.M.Old Yorkshire v Middlesex (Lord's) 1979
Most Economical in 1997: 10-2-13-2 S.J.E.Brown Durham v Scotland (Forfar)

Most Expensive Bowling: 11-0-103-0 G.Welch Warwickshire v Lancashire (Edgbaston) 1995
Most Expensive in 1997: 6-0-82-2 J.A.R.Blain Scotland v Leicestershire (Leicester)

Most Wickets in Season: 19 (av 13.05) J.K.Lever (Essex) 1979; 19 (av 7.73) C.E.H.Croft (Lancashire) 1982
Most in 1997: 17 (av 15.11) M.V.Fleming (Kent)

Most Wickets in Career: 149 (av 18.71) J.K.Lever (Essex) 1972 to 1989; 132 (av 21.35) I.T.Botham (Somerset, Worcestershire, Durham) 1974 to 1993; 107 (av 20.96) S.Turner (Essex, Minor Counties) 1972 to 1988; 107 (av 22.75) D.L.Underwood (Kent) 1972 to 1987
Most by Current Bowler: 98 (av 27.20) J.E.Emburey (Middlesex, Northamptonshire) 1975 to date

Record Wicket Partnerships

1st	252	V.P.Terry & C.L.Smith	Hampshire v Universities (Southampton)	1990
2nd	285*	C.G.Greenidge & D.R.Turner	Hampshire v Minor Co South (Amersham)	1973
3rd	269*	P.M.Roebuck & M.D.Crowe	Somerset v Hampshire (Southampton)	1987
4th	184*	D.Lloyd & B.W.Reidy	Lancashire v Derbyshire (Chesterfield)	1980
5th	160	A.J.Lamb & D.J.Capel	Northants v Leicestershire (Northampton)	1986
6th	167*	M.G.Bevan & R.J.Blakey	Yorkshire v Lancashire (Old Trafford)	1996
7th	149*	J.D.Love & C.M.Old	Yorkshire v Scotland (Bradford)	1981
8th	109	R.E.East & N.Smith	Essex v Northamptonshire (Chelmsford)	1977
9th	83	P.G.Newman & M.A.Holding	Derbyshire v Nottinghamshire (Trent Bridge)	1985
10th	80*	D.L.Bairstow & M.Johnson	Yorkshire v Derbyshire (Derby)	1981

There were 31 hundred partnerships in 1997, the highest being 208 for the 3rd wicket A.Habib & V.J.Wells Leicestershire v Durham (Chester-le-Street).

Most Wicketkeeping Dismissals in Innings: 8 (8ct) D.J.S.Taylor Somerset v Combined Universities (Taunton) 1982
Most in 1997: 5 (3ct 2st) R.J.Rollins Essex v Glamorgan (Chelmsford)

Most Wicketkeeping Dismissals in Season: 19 (16ct 3st) W.K.Hegg (Lancashire) 1996
Most in 1997: 13 (11ct 2st) P.A.Nixon (Leicestershire)

Most Wicketkeeping Dismissals in Career: 122 (117 ct 5st) D.L.Bairstow (Yorkshire) 1972 to 1990; 94 (85ct 9st) S.J.Rhodes (Worcestershire) 1985 to date; 88 (78ct 10st) A.P.E.Knott (Kent) 1972 to 1985

Most Catches by Fielder in Innings: 5 V.J.Marks Combined Universities v Kent (Oxford) 1976
Most in 1997: 4 G.P.Thorpe Surrey v Leicestershire (Oval)

Most Catches by Fielder in Season: 12 C.J.Tavaré (Kent) 1986
Most in 1997: 7 G.P.Thorpe (Surrey)

Most Catches by Fielder in Career: 68 G.A.Gooch (Essex) 1973 to date; 55 C.J.Tavaré (Universities, Kent, Somerset) 1975 to 1993; 53 I.T.Botham (Somerset, Worcestershire, Durham) 1974 to 1993

Most Appearances in Competition: 115 G.A.Gooch (Essex) 1973 to date; 98 D.W.Randall (Nottinghamshire) 1972 to 1993; 94 C.J.Tavare (Universities, Kent, Somerset) 1975 to 1993

National Westminster Bank Trophy

Highest Team Totals: 413-4 (60 overs) Somerset v Devon (Torquay) 1990; 406-5 (60 overs) Leicestershire v Berkshire (Leicester) 1996; 404-3 (60 overs) Worcestershire v Devon (Worcester) 1987
Highest in 1997: 367-5 (60 overs) Somerset v Herefordshire (Taunton)

Lowest Team Totals: 39 (26.4 overs) Ireland v Sussex (Hove) 1985; 41 (20 overs) Cambridgeshire v Buckinghamshire (Cambridge) 1972; 41 (19.4 overs) Middlesex v Essex (Westcliff) 1972; 41 (36.1 overs) Shropshire v Essex (Wellington) 1974
Lowest in 1997: 53 (18.5 overs) Ireland v Yorkshire (Headingley)

Highest Individual Innings: 206 A.I.Kallicharran Warwickshire v Oxfordshire (Edgbaston) 1984; 201 V.J.Wells Leicestershire v Berkshire (Leicester) 1996; 180* T.M.Moody Worcestershire v Surrey (Oval) 1994
Highest in 1997: 177 A.J.Wright Gloucestershire v Scotland (Bristol)
309 centuries have been scored in the competition, C.L.Smith scoring 7

Most Runs in Season: 417 (av 104.25) R.T.Robinson (Nottinghamshire) 1985
Most in 1997: 333 (av 83.25) S.G.Law (Essex)

Most Runs in Career: 2,547 (av 48.98) G.A.Gooch (Essex) 1973 to 1996; 2,113 (av 43.12) M.W.Gatting (Middlesex) 1975 to date; 1,950 (av 39.00) D.L.Amiss (Warwickshire) 1963 to 1987

Best Innings Analyses: 8-21 M.A.Holding Derbyshire v Sussex (Hove) 1988; 8-31 D.L.Underwood Kent v Scotland (Edinburgh) 1987; 7-15 A.L.Dixon Kent v Surrey (Oval) 1967; 7-15 R.P.Lefebvre Somerset v Devon (Torquay) 1990
Best in 1997: 7-27 D.Gough Yorkshire v Ireland (Headingley)
Five wickets in an innings has been achieved 148 times, 4 times by R.D.Jackman and J.Garner

Most Economical Bowling: 12-9-3-1 J.Simmons Lancashire v Suffolk (Bury St Edmunds) 1985
Most Economical in 1997: 12-7-13-3 S.D.Udal Hampshire v Cambridgeshire (Wisbech)

Most Expensive Bowling: 12-0-107-2 C.C.Lovell Cornwall v Warwickshire (St Austell) 1996
Most Expensive in 1997: 12-0-81-1 D.M.Owen Buckinghamshire v Essex (Beaconsfield)

Most Wickets in Season: 17 (av 5.41) J.Garner (Somerset) 1979; 17 (av 7.88) R.D.Jackman (Surrey) 1980
Most in 1997: 15 (av 14.86) A.A.Donald (Warwickshire)

Most Wickets in Career: 81 (av 14.85) G.G.Arnold (Surrey, Sussex) 1963 to 1980; 79 (av 22.72) J.Simmons (Lancashire) 1970 to 1989; 78 (av 17.12) P.Lever (Lancashire) 1963 to 1976
Most by Current Bowler: 71 (av 26.85) J.E.Emburey (Middlesex, Northamptonshire) 1975 to date

Record Wicket Partnerships

1st	311	A.J.Wright & N.J.Trainor	Gloucestershire v Scotland (Bristol)	1997
2nd	286	I.S.Anderson & A.Hill	Derbyshire v Cornwall (Derby)	1986
3rd	309*	T.S.Curtis & T.M.Moody	Worcestershire v Surrey (Oval)	1994
4th	234*	D.Lloyd & C.H.Lloyd	Lancashire v Gloucestershire (Old Trafford)	1978
5th	166	M.A.Lynch & G.R.J.Roope	Surrey v Durham (Oval)	1982
6th	178	J.P.Crawley & I.D.Austin	Lancashire v Sussex (Hove)	1997
7th	160*	C.J.Richards & I.R.Payne	Surrey v Lincolnshire (Sleaford)	1983
8th	112	A.L.Penberthy & J.E.Emburey	Northamptonshire v Lancashire (Old Trafford)	1996
9th	87	M.A.Nash & A.E.Cordle	Glamorgan v Lincolnshire (Swansea)	1974
10th	81	S.Turner & R.E.East	Essex v Yorkshire (Headingley)	1982

There were 23 hundred partnerships in 1997, the highest being the new 1st wicket record.

Most Wicketkeeping Dismissals in Innings: 7 (7ct) A.J.Stewart Surrey v Glamorgan (Swansea) 1994
Most in 1997: 5 (5ct) K.R.Brown Middlesex v Kent (Lord's)

Most Wicketkeeping Dismissals in Season: 12 (10ct 2st) R.W.Taylor (Derbyshire) 1981
Most in 1997: 8 (8ct) K.R.Brown (Middlesex)

Most Wicketkeeping Dismissals in Career: 66 (58ct 8st) R.W.Taylor (Derbyshire) 1963 to 1984; 65 (59ct 6st) A.P.E.Knott (Kent) 1965 to 1985; 61 (54ct 7st) P.R.Downton (Kent, Middlesex) 1978 to 1990
Most by Current Wicketkeeper: 60 (51ct 9st) R.C.Russell (Gloucestershire) 1982 to date

Most Catches by Fielder in Innings: 4 A.S.Brown (Gloucestershire) 1963; 4 G.Cook (Northamptonshire) 1972; 4 C.G.Greenidge (Hampshire) 1981; 4 D.C.Jackson (Durham) 1984; 4 T.S.Smith (Hertfordshire) 1984; 4 H.Morris (Glamorgan) 1988; 4 C.C.Lewis (Nottinghamshire) 1992
Most in 1997: 3 M.B.Loye Northamptonshire v Derbyshire (Derby); 3 G.P.Thorpe Surrey v Nottinghamshire (Oval)

Most Catches by Fielder in Season: 6 M.J.K.Smith (Warwickshire) 1964; 6 D.Wilson (Yorkshire) 1969; 6 C.G.Greenidge (Hampshire) 1981; 6 G.W.Johnson (Kent) 1983; 6 R.A.Smith (Hampshire) 1988; 6 G.A.Hick (Worcestershire) 1994; 6 N.H.Fairbrother (Lancashire) 1996
Most in 1997: 4 A.P.Grayson (Essex)

Most Catches by Fielder in Career: : 26 G.A.Gooch (Essex) 1973 to 1996; 26 J.Simmons (Lancashire) 1970 to 1989; 25 G.Cook (Northamptonshire, Durham) 1972 to 1992

Most Appearances in Competition: 64 M.W.Gatting (Middlesex) 1975 to date; 61 D.P.Hughes (Lancashire) 1969 to 1991; 61 J.E.Emburey (Middlesex, Northamptonshire) 1977 to date

CHAMPION TEAMS

Britannic Assurance County Championship

Since newspaper coverage of cricket matches in England became commonplace, the major games until the advent of Test Cricket were inter-county matches, or matches between a county and the rest of England. There was in the 18th century great rivalry between the South-Eastern counties, but the modern County Championship gradually evolved during the 19th century. Sussex were proclaimed Champions in 1827, but a continuous list of County Champions did not commence until 1864. The methods by which the Champion County was determined have varied, but currently 16 points are awarded for a win with up to 4 bonus points available for both batting and bowling in the first innings. From 1977 the Championship was sponsored by Schweppes, but in 1984 they were replaced by Britannic Assurance.

Championship Table 1997

	P	W	L	D	T	Bat	Bwg	Pts
1 Glamorgan (10)	17	8	2	7	0	50	57	256
2 Kent (4)	17	8	4	5	0	44	60	252
3 Worcestershire (7)	17	6	3	8	0	49	54	228
4 Middlesex (9)	17	7	4	6	0	33	56	219
Warwickshire (8)	17	7	2	8	0	32	51	219
6 Yorkshire (6)	17	6	3	8	0	41	54	215
7 Gloucestershire (13)	17	6	6	5	0	35	60	206
8 Surrey (3)	17	5	5	7	0	39	52	192
Essex (5)	17	5	6	6	0	39	55	192
10 Leicestershire (1)	17	4	1	12	0	37	54	191
11 Lancashire (15)	17	5	6	6	0	34	54	186
12 Somerset (11)	17	3	3	11	0	38	64	183
13 Nottinghamshire (17)	17	4	3	10	0	26	55	175
14 Hampshire (14)	17	3	5	9	0	42	41	158
15 Northamptonshire (16)	17	3	5	9	0	33	48	156
16 Derbyshire (4)	17	2	9	6	0	32	59	141
17 Durham (17)	17	2	8	7	0	22	56	131
18 Sussex (12)	17	1	10	6	0	24	57	115

Kent and Worcestershire records include eight points in a drawn match when the scores finished level and they were batting.

County Champions since 1864

1864 Surrey	1903 Middlesex	1956 Surrey
1865 Nottinghamshire	1904 Lancashire	1957 Surrey
1866 Middlesex	1905 Yorkshire	1958 Surrey
1867 Yorkshire	1906 Kent	1959 Yorkshire
1868 Nottinghamshire	1907 Nottinghamshire	1960 Yorkshire
1869 Nottinghamshire,	1908 Yorkshire	1961 Hampshire
Yorkshire	1909 Kent	1962 Yorkshire
1870 Yorkshire	1910 Kent	1963 Yorkshire
1871 Nottinghamshire	1911 Warwickshire	1964 Worcestershire
1872 Nottinghamshire	1912 Yorkshire	1965 Worcestershire
1873 Gloucestershire,	1913 Kent	1966 Yorkshire
Nottinghamshire	1914 Surrey	1967 Yorkshire
1874 Gloucestershire	1919 Yorkshire	1968 Yorkshire
1875 Nottinghamshire	1920 Middlesex	1969 Glamorgan
1876 Gloucestershire	1921 Middlesex	1970 Kent
1877 Gloucestershire	1922 Yorkshire	1971 Surrey
1878 undecided	1923 Yorkshire	1972 Warwickshire
1879 Nottinghamshire,	1924 Yorkshire	1973 Hampshire
Lancashire	1925 Yorkshire	1974 Worcestershire
1880 Nottinghamshire	1926 Lancashire	1975 Leicestershire
1881 Lancashire	1927 Lancashire	1976 Middlesex
1882 Nottinghamshire,	1928 Lancashire	1977 Kent,
Lancashire	1929 Nottinghamshire	Middlesex
1883 Nottinghamshire	1930 Lancashire	1978 Kent
1884 Nottinghamshire	1931 Yorkshire	1979 Essex
1885 Nottinghamshire	1932 Yorkshire	1980 Middlesex
1886 Nottinghamshire	1933 Yorkshire	1981 Nottinghamshire
1887 Surrey	1934 Lancashire	1982 Middlesex
1888 Surrey	1935 Yorkshire	1983 Essex
1889 Surrey,	1936 Derbyshire	1984 Essex
Lancashire,	1937 Yorkshire	1985 Middlesex
Nottinghamshire	1938 Yorkshire	1986 Essex
1890 Surrey	1939 Yorkshire	1987 Nottinghamshire
1891 Surrey	1946 Yorkshire	1988 Worcestershire
1892 Surrey	1947 Middlesex	1989 Worcestershire
1893 Yorkshire	1948 Glamorgan	1990 Middlesex
1894 Surrey	1949 Middlesex,	1991 Essex
1895 Surrey	Yorkshire	1992 Essex
1896 Yorkshire	1950 Lancashire,	1993 Middlesex
1897 Lancashire	Surrey	1994 Warwickshire
1898 Yorkshire	1951 Warwickshire	1995 Warwickshire
1899 Surrey	1952 Surrey	1996 Leicestershire
1900 Yorkshire	1953 Surrey	1997 Glamorgan
1901 Yorkshire	1954 Surrey	
1902 Yorkshire	1955 Surrey	

Domestic Limited Overs Competitions

AXA Life Sunday League

This competition, played on Sundays, is a 40 overs per side League between the English first-class counties. Four points are awarded for a win and two points for a no result match or a tie. In the event of a tie for 1st place in the League, the rules since 1975 have stipulated most wins as being the deciding factor. The 1977 title was won on this factor. If teams are still equal, then most away wins decided (up to 1991), as was the case in 1983. If these methods fail to establish an outright winner then higher run rate during the season will decide. This happened in 1976 (when five counties were equal on points at the top), 1978 and 1995. Before 1975, run rate was the only criterion used to separate top teams with equal points. Warwickshire won the title in 1971 under this rule. Positions for teams level on points are now decided by most wins and then run rate.

The bowlers run-ups were restricted to 15 yards, although for 1989 only this was increased to 22. Fielding circles were introduced in 1982 to limit the number of outfielders. The League was sponsored by John Player from 1969 to 1986, and by Refuge Assurance from 1987 to 1991. For 1993 the competition was changed to 50 overs per side with coloured clothing, white ball and black sightscreens and no restriction on bowlers run-ups, and sponsored by AXA Equity and Law. From 1994 the overs limit returned to 40.

AXA Life Sunday League Table 1997

	P	W	L	T	NR	Pts
1 Warwickshire (4)	17	13	4	0	0	52
2 Kent (10)	17	12	4	0	1	50
3 Lancashire (9)	17	10	4	1	2	46
4 Leicestershire (12)	17	9	5	1	2	42
5 Surrey (1)	17	9	5	0	3	42
6 Somerset (5)	17	9	6	0	2	40
7 Essex (17)	17	9	6	1	1	40
8 Worcestershire (8)	17	8	6	1	2	38
9 Northamptonshire (6)	17	8	6	0	3	38
10 Yorkshire (3)	17	8	7	1	1	36
11 Gloucestershire (16)	17	7	6	0	4	36
12 Nottinghamshire (2)	17	7	7	0	3	34
13 Glamorgan (13)	17	5	9	0	3	26
14 Derbyshire (11)	17	4	9	0	4	24
15 Hampshire (15)	17	5	11	0	1	22
16 Middlesex (7)	17	3	10	1	3	20
17 Durham (18)	17	3	13	0	1	14
18 Sussex (14)	17	2	13	0	2	12

League Champions

1969 Lancashire	1979 Somerset	1989 Lancashire
1970 Lancashire	1980 Warwickshire	1990 Derbyshire
1971 Worcestershire	1981 Essex	1991 Nottinghamshire
1972 Kent	1982 Sussex	1992 Middlesex
1973 Kent	1983 Yorkshire	1993 Glamorgan
1974 Leicestershire	1984 Essex	1994 Warwickshire
1975 Hampshire	1985 Essex	1995 Kent
1976 Kent	1986 Hampshire	1996 Surrey
1977 Leicestershire	1987 Worcestershire	1997 Warwickshire
1978 Hampshire	1988 Worcestershire	

Table of Results 1969 to 1997

	P	W	L	T	NR	Winner	R-up
Kent	470	256	165	6	42	4	4
Essex	470	243	180	8	39	3	5
Lancashire	470	239	171	9	51	3	2
Worcestershire	470	230	188	10	42	3	3
Hampshire	470	223	200	7	40	3	1
Somerset	470	222	199	2	47	1	6
Surrey	470	212	203	4	51	1	0
Middlesex	470	210	203	7	50	1	1
Yorkshire	470	210	209	3	48	1	1
Leicestershire	470	202	206	3	59	2	2
Warwickshire	470	202	213	6	50	3	1
Nottinghamshire	470	199	225	3	43	1	3
Sussex	470	198	217	5	50	1	2
Derbyshire	470	198	219	4	49	1	0
Northamptonshire	470	184	232	5	49	0	0
Glamorgan	470	166	248	4	52	1	0
Gloucestershire	470	161	248	4	57	0	1
Durham	102	29	58	2	13	0	0

Four counties shared the runners-up position in 1976

Benson and Hedges Cup

Established in 1972, the competition was restricted to twenty teams which are divided into four groups of five playing a round-robin. The top two teams in each group then compete on a knock-out basis. The overs limit is 55 per innings. Fielding circles were introduced in 1981 to restrict the number of outfielders. The teams competing are the first-class counties and three other sides. These three have varied; originally there were two representative Minor Counties sides (either North and South, or East and West) and the third place alternated between Oxford and Cambridge Universities. In 1975, the two Universities combined to form one team. In 1980, the Minor Counties were restricted to one team, with the vacant place being given to Scotland. In 1987, the Combined Universities team was expanded to include other members of the UAU. In 1992 Durham became the 21st team and one group increased to six teams. In 1993 and 1994 the groups were replaced by knockout throughout. In 1994 Ireland became the 22nd team. Results of the finals:

1972 Leicestershire 140-5 (46.5 overs) beat Yorkshire 136-9 (55 overs) by 5 wkts
1973 Kent 225-7 (55 overs) beat Worcestershire 186 (51.4 overs) by 39 runs
1974 Surrey 170 (54.1 overs) beat Leicestershire 143 (54 overs) by 27 runs
1975 Leicestershire 150-5 (51.2 overs) beat Middlesex 146 (54.2 overs) by 5 wkts
1976 Kent 236-7 (55 overs) beat Worcestershire 193 (52.4 overs) by 43 runs
1977 Gloucestershire 237-6 (55 overs) beat Kent 173 (47.3 overs) by 64 runs
1978 Kent 151-4 (41.4 overs) beat Derbyshire 147 (54.4 overs) by 6 wkts
1979 Essex 290-6 (55 overs) beat Surrey 255 (51.4 overs) by 35 runs
1980 Northamptonshire 209 (54.5 overs) beat Essex 203-8 (55 overs) by 6 runs
1981 Somerset 197-3 (44.3 overs) beat Surrey 194-8 (55 overs) by 7 wkts
1982 Somerset 132-1 (33.1 overs) beat Nottinghamshire 130 (50.1 overs) by 9 wkts
1983 Middlesex 196-8 (55 overs) beat Essex 192 (54.1 overs) by 4 runs
1984 Lancashire 140-4 (42.4 overs) beat Warwickshire 139 (50.4 overs) by 6 wkts
1985 Leicestershire 215-5 (52 overs) beat Essex 213-8 (55 overs) by 5 wkts
1986 Middlesex 199-7 (55 overs) beat Kent 197-8 (55 overs) by 2 runs
1987 Yorkshire 244-6 (55 overs) beat Northamptonshire 244-7 (55 overs) by losing fewer wkts
1988 Hampshire 118-3 (31.5 overs) beat Derbyshire 117 (46.3 overs) by 7 wkts
1989 Nottinghamshire 244-7 (55 overs) beat Essex 243-7 (55 overs) by 3 runs
1990 Lancashire 241-8 (55 overs) beat Worcestershire 172 (54 overs) by 69 runs
1991 Worcestershire 236-8 (55 overs) beat Lancashire 171 (47.2 overs) by 65 runs
1992 Hampshire 253-5 (55 overs) beat Kent 212 (52.3 overs) by 41 runs
1993 Derbyshire 252-6 (55 overs) beat Lancashire 246-7 (55 overs) by 6 runs
1994 Warwickshire 172-4 (44.2 overs) beat Worcestershire 170-9 (55 overs) by 6 wkts
1995 Lancashire 274-7 (55 overs) beat Kent 239 (52.1 overs) by 35 runs
1996 Lancashire 245-9 (50 overs) beat Northamptonshire 214 (48.3 overs) by 31 runs
1997 Surrey 215-2 (45 overs) beat Kent 214-9 (50 overs) by 8 wkts

Group Tables 1997

GROUP A	P	W	L	NR	Pts
Yorkshire	5	4	1	0	8
Warwickshire	5	3	2	0	6
Derbyshire	5	3	2	0	6
Lancashire	5	3	2	0	6
Worcestershire	5	2	3	0	4
Minor Counties	5	0	5	0	0

GROUP C	P	W	L	NR	Pts
Kent	5	4	0	1	9
Surrey	5	4	1	0	8
Gloucestershire	5	2	2	1	5
Sussex	5	2	3	0	4
Hampshire	5	1	4	0	2
British Univs	5	1	4	0	2

GROUP B	P	W	L	NR	Pts
Leicestershire	4	3	1	0	6
Northamptonshire	4	3	1	0	6
Durham	4	2	2	0	4
Nottinghamshire	4	1	2	1	3
Scotland	4	0	3	1	1

GROUP D	P	W	L	NR	Pts
Essex	4	3	0	1	7
Somerset	4	3	1	0	6
Glamorgan	4	2	2	0	4
Ireland	4	1	2	1	3
Middlesex	4	0	4	0	0

Where counties are equal on points net run-rate determines the final position

Quarter-Finals: Kent beat Warwickshire by 4 wkts; Surrey beat Essex by 6 wkts; Leicestershire beat Somerset by 20 runs; Northamptonshire beat Yorkshire by 7 wkts.

Semi-Finals: Kent beat Northamptonshire by 66 runs; Surrey beat Leicestershire by 130 runs.

Table of Results 1972 to 1997

	P	W	L	NR	Winner	R-up
Kent	139	90	45	4	3	5
Lancashire	134	86	41	7	4	2
Essex	129	79	47	3	1	4
Surrey	125	71	50	4	2	2
Nottinghamshire	120	69	44	7	1	1
Somerset	122	67	52	3	2	0
Leicestershire	123	67	49	7	3	1
Warwickshire	124	67	49	8	1	1
Worcestershire	127	66	57	4	1	4
Yorkshire	118	63	48	7	1	1
Middlesex	124	62	53	9	2	1
Hampshire	120	61	54	5	2	0
Derbyshire	117	61	47	9	1	2
Northamptonshire	118	57	53	8	1	2
Sussex	111	54	56	1	0	0
Gloucestershire	111	54	52	5	1	0
Glamorgan	110	49	57	4	0	0
British Universities	90	8	79	3	0	0
Durham	21	8	11	2	0	0
Minor Counties	70	6	60	4	0	0
Scotland	66	2	60	4	0	0
Ireland	13	1	11	1	0	0
Oxford University	4	1	3	0	0	0
Cambridge University	8	0	8	0	0	0
Minor Counties East	12	0	12	0	0	0
Minor Counties North	20	0	20	0	0	0
Minor Counties South	20	0	19	1	0	0
Minor Counties West	12	0	12	0	0	0

Matches decided by a bowl-out are included as no result matches

National Westminster Bank Trophy

Inaugurated in 1963 as a knock-out competition under the sponsorship of Gillette, it was the first limited overs competition involving all the first-class counties. In 1964, the competition was expanded to include the five leading Minor Counties. In 1980, Ireland was added, making a total of 23 teams. When National Westminster Bank took over the sponsorship in 1981, the company requested a further expansion to 32 teams. Scotland was therefore added as well as 8 more Minor Counties. Holland replaced one of the Minor Counties from 1995. In 1963 the overs limit per innings was 65, but since 1964 it has been 60. Fielding circles to limit the number of out-fielders were introduced in 1982. Results of the finals:

Gillette Cup
1963 Sussex 168 (60.2 overs) beat Worcestershire 154 (63.2 overs) by 14 runs
1964 Sussex 131-2 (43 overs) beat Warwickshire 127 (48 overs) by 8 wkts
1965 Yorkshire 317-4 (60 overs) beat Surrey 142 (40.4 overs) by 175 runs
1966 Warwickshire 159-5 (56.4 overs) beat Worcestershire 155-8 (60 overs) by 5 wkts
1967 Kent 193 (59.4 overs) beat Somerset 161 (54.5 overs) by 32 runs
1968 Warwickshire 215-6 (57 overs) beat Sussex 214-7 (60 overs) by 4 wkts
1969 Yorkshire 219-8 (60 overs) beat Derbyshire 150 (54.4 overs) by 69 runs
1970 Lancashire 185-4 (55.1 overs) beat Sussex 184-9 (60 overs) by 6 wkts
1971 Lancashire 224-7 (60 overs) beat Kent 200 (56.2 overs) by 24 runs
1972 Lancashire 235-6 (56.4 overs) beat Warwickshire 234-9 (60 overs) by 4 wkts

1973 Gloucestershire 248-8 (60 overs) beat Sussex 208 (56.5 overs) by 40 runs
1974 Kent 122-6 (56.4 overs) beat Lancashire 118 (60 overs) by 4 wkts
1975 Lancashire 182-3 (57 overs) beat Middlesex 180-8 (60 overs) by 7 wkts
1976 Northamptonshire 199-6 (58.1 overs) beat Lancashire 195-7 (60 overs) by 4 wkts
1977 Middlesex 178-5 (55.4 overs) beat Glamorgan 177-9 (60 overs) by 5 wkts
1978 Sussex 211-5 (53.1 overs) beat Somerset 207-7 (60 overs) by 5 wkts
1979 Somerset 269-8 (60 overs) beat Northamptonshire 224 (56.3 overs) by 45 runs
1980 Middlesex 202-3 (53.5 overs) beat Surrey 201 (60 overs) by 7 wkts

National Westminster Bank Trophy
1981 Derbyshire 235-6 (60 overs) beat Northamptonshire 235-9 (60 overs) by losing fewer wkts
1982 Surrey 159-1 (34.4 overs) beat Warwickshire 158 (57.2 overs) by 9 wkts
1983 Somerset 193-9 (50 overs) beat Kent 169 (47.1 overs) by 24 runs
1984 Middlesex 236-6 (60 overs) beat Kent 232-6 (60 overs) by 4 wkts
1985 Essex 280-2 (60 overs) beat Nottinghamshire 279-5 (60 overs) by 1 run
1986 Sussex 243-3 (58.2 overs) beat Lancashire 242-8 (60 overs) by 7 wkts
1987 Nottinghamshire 231-7 (49.3 overs) beat Northamptonshire 228-3 (50 overs) by 3 wkts
1988 Middlesex 162-7 (55.3 overs) beat Worcestershire 161-9 (60 overs) by 3 wkts
1989 Warwickshire 211-6 (59.4 overs) beat Middlesex 210-5 (60 overs) by 4 wkts
1990 Lancashire 173-3 (45.4 overs) beat Northamptonshire 171 (60 overs) by 7 wkts
1991 Hampshire 243-6 (59.4 overs) beat Surrey 240-5 (60 overs) by 4 wkts
1992 Northamptonshire 211-2 (49.4 overs) beat Leicestershire 208-7 (60 overs) by 8 wkts
1993 Warwickshire 322-5 (60 overs) beat Sussex 321-6 (60 overs) by 5 wkts
1994 Worcestershire 227-2 (49.1 overs) beat Warwickshire 223-9 (60 overs) by 8 wkts
1995 Warwickshire 203-6 (58.5 overs) beat Northamptonshire 200 (59.5 overs) by 4 wkts
1996 Lancashire 186 (60 overs) beat Essex 59 (27.2 overs) by 127 runs
1997 Essex 171-1 (26.3 overs) beat Warwickshire 170-8 (60 overs) by 9 wkts

Results 1997: *First Round*: Hampshire beat Cambridgeshire by 239 runs; Glamorgan beat Bedfordshire by 7 wkts; Gloucestershire beat Scotland by 101 runs; Lancashire beat Berkshire by 169 runs; Derbyshire beat Lincolnshire by 8 wkts; Surrey beat Durham by 5 wkts; Nottinghamshire beat Staffordshire by 10 wkts; Somerset beat Herefordshire by 231 runs; Sussex beat Shropshire by 10 wkts; Yorkshire beat Ireland by 196 runs; Middlesex beat Kent by 3 wkts; Worcestershire beat Holland by 111 runs; Essex beat Buckinghamshire by 89 runs; Warwickshire beat Norfolk by 83 runs; Northamptonshire beat Cumberland by 36 runs; Leicestershire beat Devon by 53 runs. *Second Round*: Nottinghamshire beat Surrey by 22 runs; Sussex beat Lancashire by 7 wkts; Warwickshire beat Somerset by 11 runs; Essex beat Somerset by 7 wkts; Derbyshire beat Northamptonshire by 144 runs; Glamorgan beat Hampshire by 2 wkts; Yorkshire beat Leicestershire by 128 runs; Middlesex beat Gloucestershire by 4 wkts. *Quarter-Finals*: Sussex beat Derbyshire by 5 wkts; Essex beat Nottinghamshire by 3 wkts; Warwickshire beat Middlesex by 28 runs; Glamorgan beat Yorkshire by 1 wkt. *Semi-Finals*: Essex beat Glamorgan by 1 wkt; Warwickshire beat Sussex by 105 runs.

Table of Results 1963 to 1997

	P	W	L	NR	Winner	R-up
Warwickshire	101	72	29	0	5	5
Lancashire	98	69	29	0	6	3
Middlesex	95	64	31	0	4	2
Sussex	92	61	31	0	4	4
Northamptonshire	90	57	33	0	2	5
Hampshire	88	54	34	0	1	0
Surrey	88	53	34	1	1	3
Somerset	84	51	33	0	2	2
Kent	80	47	33	0	2	3
Worcestershire	80	46	34	0	1	3
Essex	79	45	34	0	2	1
Yorkshire	75	42	33	0	2	0
Nottinghamshire	73	39	34	0	1	1
Glamorgan	74	39	35	0	0	1
Gloucestershire	72	38	34	0	1	0
Leicestershire	71	36	35	0	0	1
Derbyshire	70	36	33	1	1	1
Durham	39	12	27	0	0	0

Buckinghamshire	19	3	16	0	0	0
Hertfordshire	22	3	18	1	0	0
Cheshire	18	2	16	0	0	0
Lincolnshire	14	2	12	0	0	0
Staffordshire	21	2	19	0	0	0
Bedfordshire	12	1	11	0	0	0
Berkshire	18	1	17	0	0	0
Cambridgeshire	18	1	17	0	0	0
Devon	19	1	18	0	0	0
Northumberland	9	1	8	0	0	0
Oxfordshire	19	1	17	1	0	0
Shropshire	14	1	13	0	0	0
Suffolk	17	1	16	0	0	0
Cornwall	7	0	7	0	0	0
Cumberland	11	0	11	0	0	0
Dorset	11	0	11	0	0	0
Herefordshire	2	0	2	0	0	0
Holland	3	0	3	0	0	0
Minor Counties Wales	2	0	2	0	0	0
Ireland	18	0	18	0	0	0
Norfolk	16	0	16	0	0	0
Scotland	15	0	15	0	0	0
Wiltshire	12	0	12	0	0	0

Matches decided by a bowl-out are included as no result matches

1997 AND CAREER FIGURES FOR DERBYSHIRE PLAYERS

ADAMS, Christopher John (Rest of England) b Whitwell 6.5.1970 RHB OB

Cmp	Debut	M	I	NO	Runs	HS	Avge	100	50	Balls	Runs	Wkts	Avge	BB	5i	10m	RpO	ct	st
FC		15	25	1	767	108	31.95	2	3		17	16	0					5.64	18	
SL		11	11	1	427	121	42.70	2	1		60	85	1	85.00	1-49	0	0	8.50	9	
BH		5	5	0	260	138	52.00	1	1										1	
NW		3	3	2	301	129*	301.00	2	1										0	
FC	1988	155	253	20	8431	239	36.18	21	39		1637	1088	18	60.44	4-29	0	0	3.98	172	
SL	1989	120	113	19	3417	141*	36.35	4	22		238	266	3	88.66	2-15	0	0	6.70	65	
BH	1990	32	29	4	866	138	34.64	2	5		24	21	0					5.25	10	
NW	1990	18	17	5	883	129*	73.58	4	4		18	15	1	15.00	1-15	0	0	5.00	7	

ALDRED, Paul b Chellaston 4.2.1969 RHB RM

Cmp	Debut	M	I	NO	Runs	HS	Avge	100	50	Balls	Runs	Wkts	Avge	BB	5i	10m	RpO	ct	st
FC		8	8	2	133	83	22.16	0	1	1086	454	12	37.83	3-28	0	0	2.50	7	
SL		10	6	1	53	17	10.60	0	0	330	290	7	41.42	3-40	0	0	5.27	1	
NW		3	2	1	4	4	4.00	0	0	140	99	4	24.75	4-30	1	0	4.24	1	
FC	1995	20	25	4	280	83	13.33	0	1	2575	1366	35	39.02	3-28	0	0	3.18	13	
SL	1995	27	11	4	87	17	12.42	0	0	861	826	23	35.91	4-41	1	0	5.75	5	
BH	1996	2	1	0	7	7	7.00	0	0	54	53	2	26.50	2-35	0	0	5.88	6	

BARNETT, Kim John b Stoke-on-Trent 17.7.1960 RHB LB

Cmp	Debut	M	I	NO	Runs	HS	Avge	100	50	Balls	Runs	Wkts	Avge	BB	5i	10m	RpO	ct	st
FC		15	24	3	1055	210*	50.23	3	5										3	
SL		8	7	0	297	99	42.42	0	1		12	20	2	10.00	2-20	0	0	10.00	1	
BH		5	5	1	325	112*	81.25	1	2		60	52	3	17.33	3-52	0	0	5.20	0	
NW		3	2	0	129	111	64.50	1	0		60	48	0					4.80	1	
Test	1988	4	7	0	207	80	29.57	0	2		36	32	0					5.33	1	
FC	1979	414	670	62	24327	239*	40.01	52	131	13422	6717	180	37.31	6-28	3	0	3.00	242	
Int	1988	1	1	0	84	84	84.00	0	1											
SL	1979	263	251	39	7389	131*	34.85	6	40	1189	1106	38	29.10	3-26	0	0	5.58	88	
BH	1979	81	72	5	2595	115	38.73	4	18	439	294	10	29.40	3-52	0	0	4.01	30	
NW	1979	39	37	3	1253	113*	36.85	2	8	544	369	21	17.57	6-24	0	2	4.06	15	

BLACKWELL, Ian David b Chesterfield 10.6.1978 LHB SLA

Cmp	Debut	M	I	NO	Runs	HS	Avge	100	50	Balls	Runs	Wkts	Avge	BB	5i	10m	RpO	ct	st
FC		4	5	0	51	42	10.20	0	0	312	227	2	113.50	1-27	0	0	4.36	0	
SL		4	4	0	54	29	13.50	0	0										0	
BH		1									30	38	0					7.60	0	

CASSAR, Matthew Edward b Sydney, Australia 16.10.1972 RHB RFM

Cmp	Debut	M	I	NO	Runs	HS	Avge	100	50	Balls	Runs	Wkts	Avge	BB	5i	10m	RpO	ct	st
FC		7	8	1	227	78	32.42	0	2	313	224	8	28.00	3-31	0	0	4.29	2	
SL		4	3	0	36	33	12.00	0	0	66	85	2	42.50	1-15	0	0	7.72	2	
FC	1994	10	12	1	361	78	32.81	0	3	641	409	16	25.56	4-54	0	0	3.82	4	

CLARKE, Vincent Paul b Liverpool 11.11.1971 RHB LB (Somerset 1994, Leicestershire 1995-96)

Cmp	Debut	M	I	NO	Runs	HS	Avge	100	50	Balls	Runs	Wkts	Avge	BB	5i	10m	RpO	ct	st
FC		19	30	6	847	99	35.29	0	5	1343	835	13	64.23	3-47	0	0	3.73	9	
SL		13	13	3	244	77*	24.40	0	2	312	292	9	31.33	2-28	0	0	5.61	4	
BH		5	5	1	81	52	20.25	0	1	168	142	7	20.28	4-49	1	0	5.07	2	
NW		3	2	1	35	24*	35.00	0	0	162	92	2	46.00	1-38	0	0	3.40	2	
FC	1994	26	43	7	991	99	27.52	0	5	1988	1276	20	63.80	3-47	0	0	3.85	11	
SL	1994	23	23	3	304	77*	15.20	0	2	452	428	12	35.66	2-28	0	0	5.68	6	
BH	1994	12	12	4	103	52	20.60	0	1	168	142	7	20.28	4-49	1	0	5.07	2	

CORK, Dominic Gerald (England to New Zealand) b Newcastle-under-Lyme 7.8.1971 RHB RFM

Cmp	Debut	M	I	NO	Runs	HS	Avge	100	50	Balls	Runs	Wkts	Avge	BB	5i	10m	RpO	ct	st
FC		6	9	1	192	55*	24.00	0	2	792	457	11	41.54	4-48	0	0	3.46	4	
SL		3	3	0	67	33	22.33	0	0	102	80	6	13.33	6-21	0	1	4.70	0	
NW		1	1	0	16	16	16.00	0	0	68	67	1	67.00	1-67	0	0	5.91	0	
Test	1995	19	27	4	482	59	20.95	0	2	4345	2249	74	30.39	7-43	3	0	3.10	10	
FC	1990	137	201	30	4216	104	24.65	2	24	22974	11468	429	26.73	9-43	12	2	2.99	86	
Int	1992	25	15	2	132	31*	10.15	0	0	1440	1071	35	30.60	3-27	0	0	4.46	6	
SL	1991	69	55	6	867	66	17.69	0	2	2874	2293	79	29.02	6-21	1	1	4.78	26	
BH	1992	18	14	5	281	92*	31.22	0	2	1076	712	20	35.60	5-49	1	1	3.97	8	
NW	1992	12	10	0	290	62	29.00	0	3	757	481	26	18.50	5-18	2	2	3.81	3	

DEAN, Kevin James b Derby 16.10.1975 LHB LFM

Cmp	Debut	M	I	NO	Runs	HS	Avge	100	50	Balls	Runs	Wkts	Avge	BB	5i	10m	RpO	ct	st
FC		10	12	5	79	21*	11.28	0	0	1408	811	28	28.96	4-39	0	0	3.45	2	
SL		10	3	2	2	1*	2.00	0	0	417	329	10	32.90	3-24	0	0	4.73	3	
BH		5	1	0	6	6	6.00	0	0	180	149	3	49.66	1-16	0	0	4.96	0	
NW		1								54	24	1	24.00	1-24	0	0	2.66	0	
FC	1996	18	20	6	112	21*	8.00	0	0	2273	1282	44	29.13	4-39	0	0	3.38	3	
SL	1996	22	4	3	10	8*	10.00	0	0	879	688	23	29.91	5-32	0	1	4.69	7	
NW	1996	4	1	1	0	0*		0	0	222	189	6	31.50	3-52	0	0	5.10	1	

DE FREITAS, Phillip Anthony Jason (England) b Scotts Head, Dominica 18.2.1966 RHB RFM (Leicestershire 1985-88, Lancashire 1989-93)

Cmp	Debut	M	I	NO	Runs	HS	Avge	100	50	Balls	Runs	Wkts	Avge	BB	5i	10m	RpO	ct	st
FC		19	24	1	484	96	21.04	0	2	3445	1810	67	27.01	7-64	5	2	3.15	5	
Int		2								102	82	0					4.82	0		
SL		12	10	1	140	45	15.55	0	0	383	309	10	30.90	3-19	0	0	4.84	4	
BH		5	3	1	44	32*	22.00	0	0	294	171	5	34.20	2-43	0	0	3.48	1	

Cmp	Debut	M	I	NO	Runs	HS	Avge	100	50	Balls	Runs	Wkts	Avge	BB	5i	10m	RpO	ct	st
NW		3	2	0	50	26	25.00	0	0	186	102	2	51.00	1-20	0	0	3.29	1	
Test	1986	44	68	5	934	88	14.82	0	4	9838	4700	140	33.57	7-70	4	0	2.86	14	
FC	1985	273	385	35	7624	113	21.78	6	38	52368	25616	916	27.96	7-21	47	5	2.93	96	
Int	1986	103	66	23	690	67	16.04	0	1	5712	3775	115	32.82	4-35	1	0	3.96	26	
SL	1985	154	113	22	1692	72*	18.59	0	3	6099	4578	172	26.61	5-26	6	1	4.50	29	
BH	1985	55	36	7	593	75*	20.44	0	2	3145	1767	81	21.81	5-16	4	1	3.37	14	
NW	1986	32	22	4	323	69	17.94	0	1	2015	976	48	20.33	5-13	0	4	2.90	7	

GRIFFITHS, Steven Paul b Hereford 31.5.1973 RHB WK

Cmp	Debut	M	I	NO	Runs	HS	Avge	100	50	Balls	Runs	Wkts	Avge	BB	5i	10m	RpO	ct	st
FC		1	1	0	1	1	1.00	0	0									3	
SL		1																1	
FC	1995	6	10	0	76	20	7.60	0	0									17	

HARRIS, Andrew James (England A, England A to Australia) b Ashton-under-Lyne 26.6.1973 RHB RM

Cmp	Debut	M	I	NO	Runs	HS	Avge	100	50	Balls	Runs	Wkts	Avge	BB	5i	10m	RpO	ct	st
FC		18	24	4	171	36	8.55	0	0	2889	1694	35	48.40	3-66	0	0	3.51	9	
SL		13	7	4	27	10*	9.00	0	0	530	479	21	22.80	4-22	1	0	5.42	2	
BH		5	2	1	6	4*	6.00	0	0	287	234	8	29.25	3-41	0	0	4.89	0	
NW		2	1	1	5	5*		0	0	108	79	3	26.33	2-12	0	0	4.38	0	
FC	1993	37	51	11	335	36	8.37	0	0	5961	3647	107	34.08	6-40	2	1	3.67	12	
SL	1993	35	12	6	31	10*	5.16	0	0	1398	1207	51	23.66	4-22	1	0	5.18	9	
BH	1995	7	3	1	11	5	5.50	0	0	395	322	10	32.20	3-41	0	0	4.89	1	
NW	1996	4	2	2	16	11*		0	0	234	156	6	26.00	3-58	0	0	4.00	1	

HAYHURST, Andrew Neil b Davyhulme 23.11.1962 RHB RM (Lancashire 1985-89, Somerset 1990-96)

Cmp	Debut	M	I	NO	Runs	HS	Avge	100	50	Balls	Runs	Wkts	Avge	BB	5i	10m	RpO	ct	st
FC		2	2	0	6	6	3.00	0	0	54	30	1	30.00	1-12	0	0	3.33	3	
SL		2	2	0	20	12	10.00	0	0	42	37	2	18.50	2-37	0	0	5.28	0	
FC	1985	166	265	34	7825	172*	33.87	14	40	8961	4991	110	45.37	4-27	0	0	3.34	56	
SL	1985	121	103	24	2253	84	28.51	0	12	2958	2607	74	35.22	4-37	2	0	5.28	16	
BH	1987	34	30	5	736	95	29.44	0	6	1114	770	32	24.06	4-50	1	0	4.14	3	
NW	1985	22	20	4	588	91*	36.75	0	3	809	543	24	22.62	5-60	2	1	4.02	4	

JONES, Dean Mervyn (Victoria) b Coburg, Australia 24.3.1961 RHB RM/OB (Durham 1992)

Cmp	Debut	M	I	NO	Runs	HS	Avge	100	50	Balls	Runs	Wkts	Avge	BB	5i	10m	RpO	ct	st
FC		7	12	1	458	99*	41.63	0	5	36	20	0					3.33	8	
SL		5	5	0	189	58	37.80	0	1	24	45	0					11.25	1	
BH		5	5	0	105	35	21.00	0	0									5	
Test	1983	52	89	11	3631	216	46.55	11	14	198	64	1	64.00	1-5	0	0	1.93	34	
FC	1981	234	394	41	18292	324*	51.81	52	83	2704	1533	27	56.77	5-112	1	0	3.40	182	
Int	1983	164	161	25	6068	145	44.61	7	46	106	81	3	27.00	2-34	0	0	4.58	54	
SL	1992	31	30	5	1594	118	63.76	6	7	224	246	5	49.20	2-15	0	0	6.58	13	
BH	1992	14	14	0	432	142	30.85	1	2	54	52	2	26.00	2-34	0	0	5.77	11	
NW	1992	4	3	1	171	100*	85.50	1	0	14	16	2	8.00	2-0	0	0	6.85	5	

KHAN, Gul Abbass b Gujrat, Pakistan 31.12.1973 RHB LB

Cmp	Debut	M	I	NO	Runs	HS	Avge	100	50	Balls	Runs	Wkts	Avge	BB	5i	10m	RpO	ct	st
FC		3	5	1	95	62*	23.75	0	1									0	
SL		7	6	1	124	71*	24.80	0	1									1	
BH		5	5	1	88	33	22.00	0	0									1	
NW		2	2	0	19	19	9.50	0	0									1	
FC	1996	16	23	3	703	101*	35.15	1	5	174	190	3	63.33	2-48	0	0	6.55	7	
SL	1996	14	12	2	205	71*	20.50	0	1									3	
BH	1996	10	10	1	320	147	35.55	1	0									2	
NW	1996	3	3	0	34	19	11.33	0	0									2	

KRIKKEN, Karl Matthew b Bolton 9.4.1969 RHB WK

Cmp	Debut	M	I	NO	Runs	HS	Avge	100	50	Balls	Runs	Wkts	Avge	BB	5i	10m	RpO	ct	st
FC		19	27	4	558	72	24.26	0	3									53	2
SL		12	11	3	153	39	19.12	0	0									11	3
BH		5	4	3	123	42*	123.00	0	0									3	
NW		3	2	0	39	38	19.50	0	0									1	
FC	1988	151	221	46	4057	104	23.18	1	15	36	40	0					6.66	382	25
SL	1987	91	61	21	719	44*	17.97	0	0									98	13
BH	1992	23	16	7	252	42*	28.00	0	0									25	2
NW	1992	14	9	4	156	55	31.20	0	1									12	

LACEY, Simon James b Nottingham 9.3.1975 RHB OB

Cmp	Debut	M	I	NO	Runs	HS	Avge	100	50	Balls	Runs	Wkts	Avge	BB	5i	10m	RpO	ct	st
FC		6	8	4	129	50	32.25	0	1	564	291	7	41.57	3-97	0	0	3.09	1	
SL		3	1	0	9	9	9.00	0	0	66	62	1	62.00	1-38	0	0	5.63	0	

MALCOLM, Devon Eugene (England) b Kingston, Jamaica 22.2.1963 RHB RF

Cmp	Debut	M	I	NO	Runs	HS	Avge	100	50	Balls	Runs	Wkts	Avge	BB	5i	10m	RpO	ct	st
Test		4	5	1	12	12	3.00	0	0	558	307	6	51.16	3-100	0	0	3.30	2	
FC		19	24	9	92	21*	6.13	0	0	3157	1761	75	23.48	6-23	5	2	3.34	2	
SL		1	1	0	3	3	3.00	0	0	48	51	1	51.00	1-51	0	0	6.37	0	
BH		3	3	0	16	13	5.33	0	0	161	116	5	23.20	2-38	0	0	4.32	0	
NW		3								169	95	10	9.50	7-35	0	1	3.37	0	
Test	1989	40	58	19	236	29	6.05	0	0	8480	4748	128	37.09	9-57	5	2	3.35	7	
FC	1984	232	277	86	1524	51	7.97	0	1	40562	24247	793	30.57	9-57	31	7	3.58	33	
Int	1990	10	5	2	9	4	3.00	0	0	526	404	16	25.25	3-40	0	0	4.60	1	
SL	1986	64	25	10	134	42	8.93	0	0	2827	2428	87	27.90	4-21	4	0	5.15	7	

Cmp	Debut	M	I	NO	Runs	HS	Avge	100	50	Balls	Runs	Wkts	Avge	BB	5i	10m	RpO	ct	st
BH	1988	32	17	4	88	15	6.76	0	0	1799	1320	50	26.40	5-27	3	1	4.40	3	
NW	1987	21	10	1	29	10*	3.22	0	0	1307	847	33	25.66	7-35	0	1	3.88	1	

MAY, Michael Robert b Chesterfield 22.7.1971 RHB OB

Cmp	Debut	M	I	NO	Runs	HS	Avge	100	50	Balls	Runs	Wkts	Avge	BB	5i	10m	RpO	ct	st
FC		9	17	2	588	116	39.20	2	3	25	50	0					12.00	2	
NW		1	1	0	5	5	5.00	0	0									0	
FC	1996	12	21	4	748	116	44.00	2	4	43	69	0					9.62	3	

OWEN, John Edward Houghton b Derby 7.8.1971 RHB OB

Cmp	Debut	M	I	NO	Runs	HS	Avge	100	50	Balls	Runs	Wkts	Avge	BB	5i	10m	RpO	ct	st
FC		4	6	0	83	22	13.83	0	0									3	
SL		2	1	0	5	5	5.00	0	0									0	
NW		1	1	0	10	10	10.00	0	0									0	
FC	1995	17	29	0	782	105	26.96	2	4									6	
SL	1995	13	11	1	191	45	19.10	0	0									2	
BH	1996	2	2	0	70	49	35.00	0	0									0	
NW	1996	3	3	0	20	10	6.66	0	0									1	

ROBERTS, Glenn Martin b Huddersfield 4.11.1973 LHB SLA

Cmp	Debut	M	I	NO	Runs	HS	Avge	100	50	Balls	Runs	Wkts	Avge	BB	5i	10m	RpO	ct	st
FC		2	3	1	45	30*	22.50	0	0	36	8	0					1.33		
SL		6	5	2	19	9	6.33	0	0	195	195	0					6.00	1	
BH		5	3	1	15	12	7.50	0	0	276	228	9	25.33	3-45	0	0	4.95	2	
FC	1996	3	4	1	97	52	32.33	0	1	252	81	1	81.00	1-55	0	0	1.92	1	
SL	1996	11	7	4	25	9	8.33	0	0	423	393	6	65.50	2-28	0	0	5.57	3	

ROLLINS, Adrian Stewart b Barking 8.2.1972 RHB RM WK

Cmp	Debut	M	I	NO	Runs	HS	Avge	100	50	Balls	Runs	Wkts	Avge	BB	5i	10m	RpO	ct	st
FC		17	29	3	1142	210	43.92	3	6	18	21	0					7.00	11	
SL		8	8	2	212	36	35.33	0	0	12	15	0					7.50	3	
BH		1	1	0	0	0	0.00	0	0									0	
NW		3	3	0	67	40	22.33	0	0									0	
FC	1993	76	140	15	4438	210	35.50	8	24	90	122	1	122.00	1-19	0	0	8.13	61	1
SL	1993	45	39	4	739	126*	21.11	1	1	12	15	0					7.50	21	
BH	1994	7	7	0	159	70	22.71	0	1									2	
NW	1994	7	7	0	131	56	18.71	0	1									3	

SMITH, Trevor Mark b Derby 18.1.1977 LHB RM

Cmp	Debut	M	I	NO	Runs	HS	Avge	100	50	Balls	Runs	Wkts	Avge	BB	5i	10m	RpO	ct	st
FC		1								108	51	1	51.00	1-27	0	0	2.83	1	

SPENDLOVE, Benjamin Lee b Belper 4.11.1978 RHB OB

Cmp	Debut	M	I	NO	Runs	HS	Avge	100	50	Balls	Runs	Wkts	Avge	BB	5i	10m	RpO	ct	st
FC		2	3	1	27	15*	13.50	0	0									2	
SL		1	1	0	4	4	4.00	0	0									0	

STUBBINGS, Stephen David b Huddersfield 31.3.1978 LHB OB

Cmp	Debut	M	I	NO	Runs	HS	Avge	100	50	Balls	Runs	Wkts	Avge	BB	5i	10m	RpO	ct	st
FC		1	2	0	27	22	13.50	0	0									0	

TWEATS, Timothy Andrew b Stoke-on-Trent 18.4.1974 RHB RM

Cmp	Debut	M	I	NO	Runs	HS	Avge	100	50	Balls	Runs	Wkts	Avge	BB	5i	10m	RpO	ct	st
FC		7	13	2	590	189	53.63	1	1									7	
SL		4	4	1	40	19	13.33	0	0									2	
NW		1	1	1	5	5*		0	0									0	
FC	1992	20	37	5	1052	189	32.87	1	4	280	208	4	52.00	1-23	0	0	4.45	19	
SL	1995	14	10	2	100	19	12.50	0	0	24	27	0					6.75	9	
BH	1996	2	1	0	10	10	10.00	0	0									2	
NW	1995	2	2	1	21	16	21.00	0	0									1	

VANDRAU, Matthew James b Epsom 22.7.1969 RHB OB

Cmp	Debut	M	I	NO	Runs	HS	Avge	100	50	Balls	Runs	Wkts	Avge	BB	5i	10m	RpO	ct	st
FC		5	8	1	186	54	26.57	0	1	270	182	4	45.50	3-78	0	0	4.04	1	
SL		3	2	0	16	10	8.00	0	0	60	63	2	31.50	2-32	0	0	6.30	1	
FC	1990	59	94	18	1567	66	20.61	0	5	8420	4440	132	33.63	6-34	7	2	3.16	29	
SL	1993	26	12	4	175	32*	21.87	0	0	855	800	22	36.36	3-25	0	0	5.61	11	
BH	1993	4	3	1	23	12*	11.50	0	0	186	158	3	52.66	1-46	0	0	5.09	1	
NW	1993	7	5	1	55	27	13.75	0	0	294	163	7	23.28	2-36	0	0	3.32	1	

1997 AND CAREER FIGURES FOR DURHAM PLAYERS

BETTS, Melvyn Morris b Sacriston 26.3.1975 RHB RFM

Cmp	Debut	M	I	NO	Runs	HS	Avge	100	50	Balls	Runs	Wkts	Avge	BB	5i	10m	RpO	ct	st
FC		13	19	1	207	35	11.50	0	0	1974	1085	49	22.14	9-64	3	1	3.29	1	
SL		6	5	2	35	21	11.66	0	0	240	193	5	38.60	3-22	0	0	4.82	1	
BH		2	2	1	6	5*	6.00	0	0	84	65	1	65.00	1-44	0	0	4.64	0	
NW		1	1	0	3	3	3.00	0	0	54	73	1	73.00	1-73	0	0	8.11	0	
FC	1993	37	57	10	574	57*	12.21	0	0	5518	3710	111	33.42	9-64	5	1	4.03	7	
SL	1995	23	16	11	96	21	19.20	0	0	949	811	22	36.86	3-22	0	0	5.12	3	
BH	1996	4	2	1	6	5*	6.00	0	0	138	101	3	33.66	2-36	0	0	4.39	1	
NW	1995	4	4	1	24	11	8.00	0	0	258	240	7	34.28	3-33	0	0	5.57	0	

BOILING, James b Delhi, India 8.4.1968 RHB OB (Surrey 1988-94)

Cmp	Debut	M	I	NO	Runs	HS	Avge	100	50	Balls	Runs	Wkts	Avge	BB	5i	10m	RpO	ct	st
FC		17	26	4	334	62	15.18	0	1	2016	925	21	44.04	3-21	0	0	2.75	13	
SL		16	10	5	54	19*	10.80	0	0	609	530	11	48.18	3-33	0	0	5.22	8	
BH		4	1	0	11	11	11.00	0	0	222	152	4	38.00	2-26	0	0	4.10	3	
NW		1	1	1	6	6*		0	0	72	54	0					4.50	0	

Cmp	Debut	M	I	NO	Runs	HS	Avge	100	50	Balls	Runs	Wkts	Avge	BB	5i	10m	RpO	ct	st
FC	1988	88	125	38	1160	69	13.33	0	2	14806	6633	140	47.37	6-84	4	1	2.68	70	
SL	1991	99	47	22	305	27	12.20	0	0	4029	3188	96	33.20	5-24	1	1	4.74	39	
BH	1988	38	22	13	99	15	11.00	0	0	2020	1391	33	42.15	3-9	0	0	4.13	16	
NW	1991	16	7	3	112	46*	28.00	0	0	1024	558	13	42.92	4-22	1	0	3.26	8	

BOON, David Clarence (Tasmania) b Launceston, Australia 29.12.1960 RHB OB

Cmp	Debut	M	I	NO	Runs	HS	Avge	100	50	Balls	Runs	Wkts	Avge	BB	5i	10m	RpO	ct	st
FC		18	30	3	1144	117	42.37	3	8	74	39	2	19.50	2-18	0	0	3.16	19	
SL		16	16	3	448	76	34.46	0	2	42	46	0					6.57	3	
BH		4	3	1	171	103	85.50	1	1									1	
NW		1	1	0	57	57	57.00	0	1									1	
Test	1984	107	190	20	7422	200	43.65	21	32	36	14	0					2.33	99	
FC	1978	296	496	44	20583	227	45.53	63	95	951	569	12	47.41	2-18	0	0	3.58	251	
Int	1983	181	177	16	5964	122	37.04	5	37	82	86	0					6.29	45	

BROWN, Simon John Emmerson (Rest of England) b Cleadon 29.6.1969 RHB LMF (Northamptonshire 1987-90)

Cmp	Debut	M	I	NO	Runs	HS	Avge	100	50	Balls	Runs	Wkts	Avge	BB	5i	10m	RpO	ct	st
FC		17	24	5	121	30	6.36	0	0	3543	1855	67	27.68	5-58	4	1	3.14	2	
SL		12	8	1	25	8	3.57	0	0	495	420	13	32.30	2-34	0	0	5.09	4	
BH		4	1	1	8	8*		0	0	230	130	10	13.00	6-30	0	1	3.39	3	
NW		1								60	42	2	21.00	2-42	0	0	4.20	0	
Test	1996	1	2	1	11	10*	11.00	0	0	198	138	2	69.00	1-60	0	0	4.18	1	
FC	1987	124	172	50	1490	69	12.21	0	2	22243	12692	408	31.10	7-70	25	2	3.42	36	
SL	1987	72	34	12	152	18	6.90	0	0	3099	2586	79	32.73	4-20	1	0	5.00	15	
BH	1988	19	8	4	38	12	9.50	0	0	1031	626	27	23.18	6-30	0	1	3.64	4	
NW	1988	10	6	3	12	7*	4.00	0	0	640	450	18	25.00	5-22	0	1	4.21	1	

CAMPBELL, Colin Lockey b Newcastle upon Tyne 11.8.1977 RHB RFM

Cmp	Debut	M	I	NO	Runs	HS	Avge	100	50	Balls	Runs	Wkts	Avge	BB	5i	10m	RpO	ct	st
FC		1								72	92	1	92.00	1-92	0	0	7.66	0	
FC	1996	2	1	0	7	7	7.00	0	0	164	136	2	68.00	1-29	0	0	4.97	0	
SL	1996	2	1	0	0	0	0.00	0	0	96	89	3	29.66	2-45	0	0	5.56	0	

COLLINGWOOD, Paul David b Shotley Bridge 26.5.1976 RHB RM/OB

Cmp	Debut	M	I	NO	Runs	HS	Avge	100	50	Balls	Runs	Wkts	Avge	BB	5i	10m	RpO	ct	st
FC		8	13	1	316	107	26.33	1	1	288	203	6	33.83	3-46	0	0	4.22	11	
SL		8	7	0	63	19	9.00	0	0	124	104	3	34.66	1-2	0	0	5.03	3	
BH		4	4	0	123	49	30.75	0	0	84	64	2	32.00	1-12	0	0	4.57	1	
NW		1	1	0	15	15	15.00	0	0									0	
FC	1996	19	33	1	780	107	24.37	1	3	620	384	9	42.66	3-46	0	0	3.71	17	
SL	1995	24	23	3	368	61*	18.40	0	2	262	210	4	52.50	1-2	0	0	4.80	11	
BH		9	8	1	165	49	23.57	0	0	265	224	7	32.00	3-28	0	0	5.07	2	
NW	1996	3	3	0	69	28	23.00	0	0	12	20	0					10.00	0	

COX, David Mathew b Southall 2.3.1972 LHB SLA

Cmp	Debut	M	I	NO	Runs	HS	Avge	100	50	Balls	Runs	Wkts	Avge	BB	5i	10m	RpO	ct	st
FC		4	3	0	46	24	15.33	0	0	417	202	7	28.85	3-72	0	0	2.90	1	
FC	1994	17	25	5	535	95*	26.75	0	4	3481	1852	45	41.15	5-97	2	1	3.19	4	
SL	1994	6	2	0	7	7	3.50	0	0	264	195	3	65.00	2-34	0	0	4.43	1	

DALEY, James Arthur b Sunderland 24.9.1973 RHB RM

Cmp	Debut	M	I	NO	Runs	HS	Avge	100	50	Balls	Runs	Wkts	Avge	BB	5i	10m	RpO	ct	st
FC		2	2	0	46	39	23.00	0	0									2	
FC	1992	46	79	8	2224	159*	31.32	1	13	12	9	0					4.50	26	
SL	1993	20	18	6	461	98*	38.41	0	3	1	4	0					24.00	5	
BH	1995	6	5	0	72	33	14.40	0	0	12	19	0					9.50	0	

FOSTER, Michael James b Leeds 17.9.1972 RHB RFM (Yorkshire 1993-94, Northamptonshire 1995)

Cmp	Debut	M	I	NO	Runs	HS	Avge	100	50	Balls	Runs	Wkts	Avge	BB	5i	10m	RpO	ct	st
FC		14	24	0	575	129	23.95	1	3	1654	1027	30	34.23	4-58	0	0	3.72	2	
SL		10	8	0	66	18	8.25	0	0	300	315	8	39.37	3-52	0	0	6.30	1	
BH		2	2	1	74	73*	74.00	0	1	96	91	1	91.00	1-27	0	0	5.68	0	
NW		1	1	1	56	56*		0	1	48	37	2	18.50	2-37	0	0	4.62	0	
FC	1993	22	37	1	807	129	22.41	1	4	2544	1488	44	33.81	4-21	0	0	3.50	8	
SL	1993	38	29	2	375	118	13.88	1	0	990	955	20	47.75	3-52	0	0	5.78	8	
BH	1996	7	7	3	179	73*	44.75	0	2	332	274	5	54.80	2-52	0	0	4.95	0	

HUTTON, Stewart b Stockton-on-Tees 30.11.1969 LHB RM

Cmp	Debut	M	I	NO	Runs	HS	Avge	100	50	Balls	Runs	Wkts	Avge	BB	5i	10m	RpO	ct	st
FC		7	13	1	258	95	21.50	0	1									1	
SL		7	7	0	188	57	26.85	0	1									3	
FC	1992	65	118	6	3241	172*	28.93	3	13	25	18	0					4.32	34	
SL	1992	56	53	5	1219	81	25.39	0	4									16	
BH	1994	2	2	0	44	36	22.00	0	0									0	
NW	1993	8	8	1	287	125	41.00	1	1									3	

KILLEEN, Neil b Shotley Bridge 17.10.1975 RHB RMF

Cmp	Debut	M	I	NO	Runs	HS	Avge	100	50	Balls	Runs	Wkts	Avge	BB	5i	10m	RpO	ct	st
FC		3	3	2	24	15	24.00	0	0	384	205	7	29.28	4-50	0	0	3.20	2	
SL		7	4	1	2	1*	0.66	0	0	286	259	11	23.54	4-46	1	0	5.43	0	
BH		4	1	0	3	3	3.00	0	0	216	139	1	139.00	1-43	0	0	3.86	0	
FC	1995	15	23	6	201	48	11.82	0	0	2246	1406	36	39.05	5-118	1	0	3.75	7	
SL	1995	29	19	4	85	32	5.66	0	0	1247	1077	39	27.61	5-26	1	1	5.18	5	
BH	1995	13	7	1	21	8	3.50	0	0	718	526	9	58.44	2-43	0	0	4.39	2	
NW	1996	1								72	46	1	46.00	1-46	0	0	3.83	1	

Cmp	Debut	M	I	NO	Runs	HS	Avge	100	50	Balls	Runs	Wkts	Avge	BB	5i	10m	RpO	ct	st

LEWIS, Jonathan James Benjamin (ECB First Class Counties XI) b Isleworth 21.5.1970 RHB RM (Essex 1990-96)

Cmp	Debut	M	I	NO	Runs	HS	Avge	100	50	Balls	Runs	Wkts	Avge	BB	5i	10m	RpO	ct	st
FC		18	32	4	1252	210*	44.71	3	5									10	
SL		16	15	4	469	102	42.63	1	3									5	
BH		4	4	0	119	47	29.75	0	0									1	
NW		1	1	0	1	1	1.00	0	0									0	
FC	1990	76	133	18	4211	210*	36.61	7	25	72	48	0					4.00	59	
SL	1991	58	48	12	915	102	25.41	1	5	2	4	0					12.00	14	
BH	1995	9	9	1	171	47	21.37	0	0									3	
NW	1992	7	7	1	76	24*	12.66	0	0									1	

LUGSDEN, Steven b Gateshead 10.7.1976 RHB RFM

Cmp	Debut	M	I	NO	Runs	HS	Avge	100	50	Balls	Runs	Wkts	Avge	BB	5i	10m	RpO	ct	st
FC		1	2	1	4	4	4.00	0	0	101	88	1	88.00	1-88	0	0	5.22	0	
FC	1993	10	13	5	30	9	3.75	0	0	1318	847	17	49.82	3-45	0	0	3.85	1	
SL	1994	1								48	55	1	55.00	1-55	0	0	6.87	0	

MORRIS, John Edward b Crewe 1.4.1964 RHB RM (Derbyshire 1982-93)

Cmp	Debut	M	I	NO	Runs	HS	Avge	100	50	Balls	Runs	Wkts	Avge	BB	5i	10m	RpO	ct	st
FC		17	30	1	1009	149	34.79	2	4	6	1	0					1.00	7	
SL		15	15	0	376	110	25.06	1	0	6	1	0					1.00	4	
BH		1	1	0	62	62	62.00	0	1									0	
NW		1	1	0	75	75	75.00	0	1									1	
Test	1990	3	5	2	71	32	23.66	0	0									3	
FC	1982	313	527	31	18739	229	37.78	44	92	998	913	7	130.42	1-6	0	0	5.48	134	
Int	1990	8	8	1	167	63*	23.85	0	1									2	
SL	1982	197	188	12	4530	134	25.73	5	19	9	8	0					5.33	44	
BH	1984	55	51	6	1441	145	32.02	3	7	24	14	0					3.50	12	
NW	1983	27	26	3	812	109	35.30	1	5									9	

PRATT, Andrew b Helmington Row 4.3.1975 LHB WK

Cmp	Debut	M	I	NO	Runs	HS	Avge	100	50	Balls	Runs	Wkts	Avge	BB	5i	10m	RpO	ct	st
FC		1																0	

ROSEBERRY, Michael Anthony b Sunderland 28.11.1966 RHB RM (Middlesex 1985-94)

Cmp	Debut	M	I	NO	Runs	HS	Avge	100	50	Balls	Runs	Wkts	Avge	BB	5i	10m	RpO	ct	st
FC		4	8	1	97	45	13.85	0	0									3	
SL		7	6	4	202	91*	101.00	2	2									3	
BH		3	3	1	50	27*	25.00	0	0									0	
FC	1986	196	332	37	10203	185	34.58	19	51	511	406	4	101.50	1-1	0	0	4.76	144	
SL	1985	118	112	14	3226	119*	32.91	3	23	4	7	0					10.50	45	
BH	1987	30	28	3	688	84	27.52	0	6	6	2	0					2.00	7	
NW	1989	16	16	0	680	121	42.50	3	1	36	42	1	42.00	1-22	0	0	7.00	7	

SAGGERS, Martin John b King's Lynn 23.5.1972 RHB RFM

Cmp	Debut	M	I	NO	Runs	HS	Avge	100	50	Balls	Runs	Wkts	Avge	BB	5i	10m	RpO	ct	st
FC		3	4	2	14	10*	7.00	0	0	384	177	7	25.28	5-57	1	0	2.76	2	
SL		4	1	1	5	5*		0	0	168	141	6	23.50	4-35	1	0	5.03	1	
FC	1996	8	13	3	103	18	10.30	0	0	990	620	20	31.00	6-65	2	0	3.75	2	
SL	1996	7	2	1	18	13	18.00	0	0	288	200	9	22.22	4-35	1	0	4.16	1	
BH	1996	5	5	3	58	34*	29.00	0	0	246	247	5	49.40	2-49	0	0	6.02	2	
NW	1996	1	1	0	0	0	0.00	0	0	60	56	0					5.60	0	

SPEAK, Nicholas Jason b Manchester 21.11.1966 RHB LB (Lancashire 1986-96)

Cmp	Debut	M	I	NO	Runs	HS	Avge	100	50	Balls	Runs	Wkts	Avge	BB	5i	10m	RpO	ct	st
FC		12	21	3	426	124*	23.66	1	1	24	14	0					3.50	6	
SL		9	9	1	192	74*	24.00	0	1									3	
BH		4	3	0	90	59	30.00	0	1									1	
NW		1	1	0	4	4	4.00	0	0									0	
FC	1986	135	235	24	7826	232	37.09	13	44	169	178	2	89.00	1-0	0	0	6.31	90	
SL	1987	77	71	8	1675	102*	26.58	1	7									16	
BH	1991	20	18	2	516	82	32.25	0	4									1	
NW	1992	8	8	0	223	83	27.87	0	2	24	31	0					7.75	2	

SPEIGHT, Martin Peter b Walsall 24.10.1967 RHB WK (Sussex 1986-96)

Cmp	Debut	M	I	NO	Runs	HS	Avge	100	50	Balls	Runs	Wkts	Avge	BB	5i	10m	RpO	ct	st
FC		17	28	3	573	73*	22.92	0	3									54	
SL		16	16	1	407	64*	27.13	0	3									10	1
BH		4	3	1	82	42*	41.00	0	0									4	
NW		1	1	0	9	9	9.00	0	0									2	
FC	1986	140	234	18	7387	184	34.19	13	38	21	32	2	16.00	1-2	0	0	9.14	154	
SL	1986	112	103	6	2882	126	29.71	3	15									39	2
BH	1987	35	32	1	738	83	23.80	0	3									24	1
NW	1989	17	16	1	359	50	23.93	0	1									6	

SYMINGTON, Marc Joseph b Newcastle upon Tyne 10.1.1980 RHB RM

Cmp	Debut	M	I	NO	Runs	HS	Avge	100	50	Balls	Runs	Wkts	Avge	BB	5i	10m	RpO	ct	st
SL		1	1	0	7	7	7.00	0	0	42	51	1	51.00	1-51	0	0	7.28	1	

WALKER, Alan b Emley 7.7.1962 LHB RFM (Northamptonshire 1983-93)

Cmp	Debut	M	I	NO	Runs	HS	Avge	100	50	Balls	Runs	Wkts	Avge	BB	5i	10m	RpO	ct	st
FC		12	20	8	92	16	7.66	0	0	2047	1063	33	32.21	7-56	2	0	3.11	0	
SL		16	5	3	25	11	12.50	0	0	618	538	14	38.42	4-18	1	0	5.22	5	
BH		4	1	1	3	3*		0	0	222	159	5	31.80	2-32	0	0	4.29	0	
NW		1								59	32	0					3.25	0	
FC	1983	127	140	61	917	41*	11.60	0	0	18547	11063	298	32.26	8-118	6	1	3.11	43	
SL	1983	150	44	19	278	30	11.12	0	0	6138	4885	168	29.07	4-18	5	0	4.77	35	
BH	1985	37	16	11	55	15*	11.00	0	0	1955	1418	44	32.22	4-42	2	0	4.35	7	
NW	1984	22	7	1	52	13	8.66	0	0	1311	770	24	32.08	4-7	1	0	3.52	5	

Cmp	Debut	M	I	NO	Runs	HS	Avge	100	50	Balls	Runs	Wkts	Avge	BB	5i	10m	RpO	ct	st

WESTON, Robin Michael Swann b Durham 7.6.1975 RHB LB

Cmp	Debut	M	I	NO	Runs	HS	Avge	100	50	Balls	Runs	Wkts	Avge	BB	5i	10m	RpO	ct	st
FC		5	8	0	137	36	17.12	0	0	6	5	0					5.00	5	
SL		2	2	0	19	13	9.50	0	0									1	
FC	1995	11	19	0	181	36	9.52	0	0	151	81	1	81.00	1-41	0	0	3.21	11	
SL	1996	3	3	0	32	13	10.66	0	0									1	

WOOD, John b Crofton, Wakefield 22.7.1970 RHB RFM

Cmp	Debut	M	I	NO	Runs	HS	Avge	100	50	Balls	Runs	Wkts	Avge	BB	5i	10m	RpO	ct	st
FC		6	8	4	72	21*	18.00	0	0	672	541	11	49.18	4-73	0	0	4.83	4	
SL		8	6	1	27	11*	5.40	0	0	348	278	11	25.27	4-17	1	0	4.79	2	
FC	1992	51	76	15	779	63*	12.77	0	2	7039	4880	129	37.82	6-110	4	0	4.15	14	
SL	1992	32	23	7	165	28	10.31	0	0	1356	1191	32	37.21	4-17	1	0	5.26	4	
BH	1993	6	4	0	36	27	9.00	0	0	348	224	5	44.80	3-50	0	0	3.86	0	
NW	1991	5	1	1	1	1	1.00	0	0	228	168	4	42.00	2-22	0	0	4.42	0	

1997 AND CAREER FIGURES FOR ESSEX PLAYERS

ANDREW, Stephen Jon Walter b Marylebone 27.1.1966 RHB RMF (Hampshire 1984-89)

Cmp	Debut	M	I	NO	Runs	HS	Avge	100	50	Balls	Runs	Wkts	Avge	BB	5i	10m	RpO	ct	st
FC		3	3	0	27	24	9.00	0	0	408	223	4	55.75	1-16	0	0	3.27	0	
SL		2	2	1	12	7	12.00	0	0	84	42	3	14.00	3-20	0	0	3.00	0	
FC	1984	132	112	42	499	35	7.12	0	0	19487	10679	317	33.68	7-47	7	0	3.28	26	
SL	1984	63	22	8	140	32	10.00	0	0	2468	2030	53	38.30	4-40	2	0	4.93	3	
BH	1984	11	3	3	5	4*		0	0	654	363	20	18.15	5-24	0	1	3.33	1	
NW	1985	9	2	2	1	1*		0	0	471	308	11	28.00	2-34	0	0	3.92	2	

COUSINS, Darren Mark b Cambridge 24.9.1971 RHB RMF

Cmp	Debut	M	I	NO	Runs	HS	Avge	100	50	Balls	Runs	Wkts	Avge	BB	5i	10m	RpO	ct	st
SL		1	1	0	1	1	1.00	0	0	48	42	1	42.00	1-42	0	0	5.25	0	
NW		1								18	28	0					9.33	0	
FC	1993	14	23	5	145	18*	8.05	0	0	1890	1086	26	41.76	6-35	1	0	3.44	5	
SL	1993	29	11	4	18	6	2.57	0	0	1203	930	38	24.47	3-18	0	0	4.63	2	
BH	1995	6	2	1	22	12*	22.00	0	0	239	171	2	85.50	1-33	0	0	4.29	1	
NW	1994	4	2	1	1	1*	1.00	0	0	150	145	1	145.00	1-33	0	0	5.80	0	

COWAN, Ashley Preston b Hitchin 7.5.1975 RHB RFM

Cmp	Debut	M	I	NO	Runs	HS	Avge	100	50	Balls	Runs	Wkts	Avge	BB	5i	10m	RpO	ct	st
FC		16	26	6	447	77	22.35	0	1	2520	1334	52	25.65	5-45	3	0	3.17	7	
SL		16	12	4	113	22	14.12	0	0	656	560	23	24.34	4-31	2	0	5.12	5	
BH		4	2	1	10	8	10.00	0	0	222	196	5	39.20	2-35	0	0	5.29	1	
NW		5	3	2	22	17*	22.00	0	0	336	220	8	27.50	3-29	0	0	3.92	2	
FC	1995	33	50	13	682	77	18.43	0	1	5120	2911	93	31.30	5-45	4	0	3.41	14	
SL	1995	26	19	7	161	22*	13.41	0	0	964	797	27	29.51	4-31	2	0	4.96	8	
BH	1996	6	2	1	10	8	10.00	0	0	336	262	6	43.66	2-35	0	0	4.67	1	
NW	1996	7	4	2	33	17*	16.50	0	0	456	297	9	33.00	3-29	0	0	3.90	4	

FLANAGAN, Ian Nicholas b Colchester 5.6.1980 LHB OB

Cmp	Debut	M	I	NO	Runs	HS	Avge	100	50	Balls	Runs	Wkts	Avge	BB	5i	10m	RpO	ct	st
FC		2	3	1	72	40	36.00	0	0									0	

GOOCH, Graham Alan b Leytonstone 23.7.1953 RHB RM

Cmp	Debut	M	I	NO	Runs	HS	Avge	100	50	Balls	Runs	Wkts	Avge	BB	5i	10m	RpO	ct	st
FC		10	17	1	369	56	23.06	0	2	12	3	0					1.50	12	
SL		1	1	0	28	28	28.00	0	0									0	
BH		4	4	1	70	40	23.33	0	0									0	
Test	1975	118	215	6	8900	333	42.58	20	46	2655	1069	23	46.47	3-39	0	0	2.41	103	
FC	1973	580	988	75	44841	333	49.11	128	217	18785	8457	246	34.37	7-14	3	0	2.70	555	
Int	1976	125	122	6	4290	142	36.98	8	23	2066	1516	36	42.11	3-19	0	0	4.40	45	
SL	1973	274	268	23	8573	176	34.99	12	58	5576	4244	143	29.67	4-33	1	0	4.56	100	
BH	1973	115	114	15	5176	198*	52.28	15	30	3770	2195	69	31.81	3-24	0	0	3.49	68	
NW	1973	57	56	4	2547	144	48.98	6	17	1655	855	33	25.90	5-8	0	1	3.09	26	

GRAYSON, Adrian Paul (ECB First Class Counties XI) b Ripon 31.3.1971 RHB SLA (Yorkshire 1990-95)

Cmp	Debut	M	I	NO	Runs	HS	Avge	100	50	Balls	Runs	Wkts	Avge	BB	5i	10m	RpO	ct	st
FC		19	28	3	1022	105	40.88	1	6	2369	1009	28	36.03	4-53	0	0	2.55	20	
SL		16	15	1	333	69*	23.78	0	1	600	572	19	30.10	4-63	1	0	5.72	4	
BH		4	3	1	70	49*	35.00	0	0	228	166	7	23.71	3-39	0	0	4.36	2	
NW		5	4	1	179	82*	59.66	0	2	252	207	7	29.57	3-40	0	0	4.92	4	
FC	1990	88	138	16	3919	140	32.12	4	21	5759	2614	59	44.30	4-53	0	0	2.72	75	
SL	1991	82	65	10	878	69*	15.96	0	2	2420	2224	69	32.23	4-25	3	0	5.51	25	
BH	1992	18	14	4	222	49*	22.20	0	0	630	440	15	29.33	3-30	0	0	4.19	6	
NW	1993	17	14	1	301	82*	23.15	0	2	809	629	20	31.45	3-24	0	0	4.66	7	

HIBBERT, Andrew James Edward b Harold Wood 17.12.1974 RHB

Cmp	Debut	M	I	NO	Runs	HS	Avge	100	50	Balls	Runs	Wkts	Avge	BB	5i	10m	RpO	ct	st
FC		1	1	0	17	17	17.00	0	0	6	1	0					1.00	3	
FC	1995	4	7	1	151	85	25.16	0	1	6	1	0					1.00	3	
SL	1996	6	6	2	45	25	11.25	0	0									1	

HODGSON, Timothy Philip (British Universities) b Guildford 27.3.1975 LHB

Cmp	Debut	M	I	NO	Runs	HS	Avge	100	50	Balls	Runs	Wkts	Avge	BB	5i	10m	RpO	ct	st
FC		3	6	0	101	44	16.83	0	0									0	
SL		1	1	0	12	12	12.00	0	0									0	
BH		5	5	0	237	113	47.40	1	1									1	
NW		1	1	0	2	2	2.00	0	0									0	
SL	1996	5	4	0	39	21	9.75	0	0									0	

Cmp	Debut	M	I	NO	Runs	HS	Avge	100	50	Balls	Runs	Wkts	Avge	BB	5i	10m	RpO	ct	st

HUSSAIN, Nasser (England, England to Zimbabwe, England to New Zealand) b Madras, India 28.3.1968 RHB LB

Cmp	Debut	M	I	NO	Runs	HS	Avge	100	50	Balls	Runs	Wkts	Avge	BB	5i	10m	RpO	ct	st
Test		6	11	0	431	207	39.18	2	0									8	
FC		16	28	0	1081	207	38.60	4	3									17	
SL		12	12	2	206	45*	20.60	0	0									3	
BH		3	2	1	84	52	84.00	0	1									3	
NW		5	5	2	221	89*	73.66	0	2									2	
Test	1989	23	40	3	1391	207	37.59	5	3									23	
FC	1987	210	331	34	13107	207	44.13	35	61	276	307	2	153.50	1-38	0	0	6.67	261	
Int	1989	12	12	4	155	49*	19.37	0	0									5	
SL	1987	122	111	17	2837	83	30.18	0	17									48	
BH	1987	40	36	8	1238	118	44.21	1	11									18	
NW	1989	23	22	3	857	108	45.10	2	4									14	

HYAM, Barry James b Romford 9.9.1975 RHB WK

Cmp	Debut	M	I	NO	Runs	HS	Avge	100	50	Balls	Runs	Wkts	Avge	BB	5i	10m	RpO	ct	st
FC		7	10	2	79	26	9.87	0	0									15	
SL		4	2	1	4	3	4.00	0	0									6	
FC	1993	10	16	2	153	49	10.92	0	0									20	1
SL	1996	5	3	1	4	3	2.00	0	0									6	

ILOTT, Mark Christopher b Watford 27.8.1970 LHB LMF

Cmp	Debut	M	I	NO	Runs	HS	Avge	100	50	Balls	Runs	Wkts	Avge	BB	5i	10m	RpO	ct	st
FC		13	20	5	290	47	19.33	0	0	1992	946	43	22.00	7-59	1	0	2.84	1	
SL		12	8	3	65	15*	13.00	0	0	504	432	9	48.00	2-10	0	0	5.14	0	
BH		4	2	0	4	4	2.00	0	0	234	182	9	20.22	3-28	0	0	4.66	0	
NW		3	1	1	1	1*		0	0	216	113	2	56.50	1-29	0	0	3.13	0	
Test	1993	5	6	2	28	15	7.00	0	0	1042	542	12	45.16	3-48	0	0	3.12	0	
FC	1988	137	168	39	1883	60	14.59	0	4	25869	13008	468	27.79	9-19	23	3	3.01	32	
SL	1989	86	56	18	404	56*	10.63	0	1	3680	2757	99	27.84	4-15	4	0	4.49	14	
BH	1990	26	9	1	69	21	8.62	0	0	1409	813	41	19.82	5-21	2	1	3.46	3	
NW	1990	18	10	5	111	54*	22.20	0	1	1153	728	18	40.44	2-23	0	0	3.78	5	

IRANI, Ronald Charles (England to Zimbabwe, England to New Zealand) b Leigh 26.10.1971 RHB RM (Lancashire 1990-93)

Cmp	Debut	M	I	NO	Runs	HS	Avge	100	50	Balls	Runs	Wkts	Avge	BB	5i	10m	RpO	ct	st
FC		16	24	1	793	123*	34.47	3	3	1571	695	18	38.61	3-51	0	0	2.65	5	
SL		15	15	3	321	52	26.75	0	1	530	421	20	21.05	3-23	0	0	4.76	3	
BH		4	3	1	165	82*	82.50	0	1	192	169	6	28.16	3-42	0	0	5.28	0	
NW		5	4	1	168	79*	56.00	0	2	314	207	5	41.40	2-61	0	0	3.95	0	
Test	1996	2	3	0	76	41	25.33	0	0	126	74	2	37.00	1-22	0	0	3.52	0	
FC	1990	86	139	16	4334	123*	35.23	7	29	8578	4547	135	33.68	5-19	3	0	3.18	37	
Int	1996	10	10	2	78	45*	9.75	0	0	329	246	4	61.50	1-23	0	0	4.48	2	
SL	1992	68	63	6	1306	101*	22.91	1	6	2099	1702	68	25.02	3-22	0	0	4.86	14	
BH	1994	16	11	2	391	82*	43.44	0	2	768	580	24	24.16	4-30	1	0	4.53	2	
NW	1994	14	13	2	461	124	41.90	1	4	854	578	14	41.28	4-59	1	0	4.06	2	

LAW, Danny Richard b Lambeth 15.7.1975 RHB RFM (Sussex 1993-96)

Cmp	Debut	M	I	NO	Runs	HS	Avge	100	50	Balls	Runs	Wkts	Avge	BB	5i	10m	RpO	ct	st
FC		19	29	0	492	81	16.96	0	2	1623	969	31	31.25	5-93	1	0	3.58	11	
SL		15	14	3	339	82	30.81	0	3	132	139	2	69.50	2-29	0	0	6.31	4	
BH		4	3	0	38	28	12.66	0	0									1	
NW		5	3	0	40	17	13.33	0	0	18	18	0					6.00	2	
FC	1993	47	72	0	1370	115	19.02	1	5	4346	2709	84	32.25	5-33	3	0	3.73	24	
SL	1995	42	37	8	821	82	28.31	0	4	725	705	22	32.04	3-34	0	0	5.83	10	
BH	1996	6	5	0	46	28	9.20	0	0	96	76	1	76.00	1-44	0	0	4.75	1	
NW	1995	9	6	0	65	18	10.83	0	0	81	80	1	80.00	1-2	0	0	5.92	3	

LAW, Stuart Grant (Queensland, Australia, Australia to Sri Lanka, Australia to India, Australia to South Africa) b Herston, Australia 18.10.1968 RHB RM/LBG

Cmp	Debut	M	I	NO	Runs	HS	Avge	100	50	Balls	Runs	Wkts	Avge	BB	5i	10m	RpO	ct	st
FC		17	28	2	1482	175	57.00	5	8	696	356	5	71.20	3-27	0	0	3.12	19	
SL		16	16	0	574	123	35.87	1	3	341	298	10	29.80	4-37	1	0	5.24	8	
BH		4	4	0	181	88	45.25	0	2	72	58	0					4.83	3	
NW		5	5	1	333	100	83.25	1	2	226	180	3	60.00	2-54	0	0	4.77	3	
Test	1995	1	1	1	54	54*		0	1	18	9	0					3.00	1	
FC	1988	133	224	23	9522	179	47.37	27	50	6152	2963	64	46.29	5-39	1	0	2.88	135	
Int	1988	44	42	3	1145	110	29.35	1	7	747	572	12	47.66	2-22	0	0	4.59	10	
SL	1996	29	29	1	1075	123	38.39	4	3	742	660	19	34.73	4-37	2	0	5.33	12	
BH	1996	9	9	0	406	116	45.11	1	2	262	241	4	60.25	2-57	0	0	5.51	3	
NW	1996	9	9	1	624	107	78.00	3	3	367	290	7	41.42	2-36	0	0	4.74	6	

NAPIER, Graham Richard b Colchester 6.1.1980 RHB RM

Cmp	Debut	M	I	NO	Runs	HS	Avge	100	50	Balls	Runs	Wkts	Avge	BB	5i	10m	RpO	ct	st
FC		2	2	2	39	35*		0	0	102	65	3	21.66	2-25	0	0	3.82	0	
SL		3	2	0	17	12	8.50	0	0	66	79	0					7.18	1	

PETERS, Stephen David b Harold Wood 10.12.1978 RHB

Cmp	Debut	M	I	NO	Runs	HS	Avge	100	50	Balls	Runs	Wkts	Avge	BB	5i	10m	RpO	ct	st
FC		3	3	1	135	102*	67.50	1	0									3	
SL		3	2	0	17	15	8.50	0	0									0	
FC	1996	7	10	2	277	110	34.62	2	0									8	
SL	1996	4	3	0	18	15	6.00	0	0									0	

	Cmp	Debut	M	I	NO	Runs	HS	Avge	100	50	Balls	Runs	Wkts	Avge	BB	5i	10m	RpO	ct	st

POWELL, Jonathan Christopher b Harold Wood 13.6.1979 RHB OB

	Cmp	Debut	M	I	NO	Runs	HS	Avge	100	50	Balls	Runs	Wkts	Avge	BB	5i	10m	RpO	ct	st
FC			1	1	1	4	4*		0	0	234	109	1	109.00	1-109	0	0	2.79	0	
SL			5	3	1	4	2	2.00	0	0	66	63	2	31.50	2-10	0	0	5.72	1	
SL		1996	6	3	1	4	2	2.00	0	0	114	125	4	31.25	2-10	0	0	6.57	1	

PRICHARD, Paul John b Billericay 7.1.1965 RHB

	Cmp	Debut	M	I	NO	Runs	HS	Avge	100	50	Balls	Runs	Wkts	Avge	BB	5i	10m	RpO	ct	st
FC			17	27	2	1184	224	47.36	3	9									10	
SL			12	12	0	349	103	29.08	1	1									3	
BH			4	4	0	173	114	43.25	1	0									3	
NW			4	4	0	156	58	39.00	0	2									1	
FC		1982	280	454	46	14769	245	36.19	29	86	289	497	2	248.50	1-28	0	0	10.31	178	
SL		1982	169	151	9	3743	107	26.35	4	17									49	
BH		1985	55	52	8	1388	114	31.54	2	7									14	
NW		1985	32	31	4	1057	94	39.14	0	8									13	

ROBINSON, Darren David John b Braintree 2.3.1973 RHB RMF

	Cmp	Debut	M	I	NO	Runs	HS	Avge	100	50	Balls	Runs	Wkts	Avge	BB	5i	10m	RpO	ct	st
FC			14	22	1	735	148	35.00	2	3									13	
SL			14	14	2	300	38	25.00	0	0	5	7	1	7.00	1-7	0	0	8.40	7	
BH			1	1	0	8	8	8.00	0	0									0	
NW			5	3	0	74	62	24.66	0	1									1	
FC		1993	46	82	3	2335	148	29.55	4	13	36	31	0					5.16	47	
SL		1993	46	46	6	973	80	24.32	0	3	17	26	1	26.00	1-7	0	0	9.17	14	
BH		1995	11	10	2	200	36	25.00	0	0									2	
NW		1995	12	10	0	202	62	20.20	0	2									4	

ROLLINS, Robert John b Plaistow 30.1.1974 RHB WK

	Cmp	Debut	M	I	NO	Runs	HS	Avge	100	50	Balls	Runs	Wkts	Avge	BB	5i	10m	RpO	ct	st
FC			13	19	1	452	82	25.11	0	4									24	2
SL			12	9	0	124	38	13.77	0	0									9	7
BH			4	3	1	43	18*	21.50	0	0									5	2
NW			5	3	1	85	67*	42.50	0	1									2	
FC		1992	58	95	9	2022	133*	23.51	1	11									139	20
SL		1993	55	44	9	443	38	12.65	0	0									51	13
BH		1995	12	6	2	46	18*	11.50	0	0									12	2
NW		1995	12	10	4	248	67*	41.33	0	3									4	3

SUCH, Peter Mark (England A, ECB First Class Counties XI) b Helensburgh, Scotland 12.6.1964 RHB OB (Nottinghamshire 1982-86, Leicestershire 1987-89)

	Cmp	Debut	M	I	NO	Runs	HS	Avge	100	50	Balls	Runs	Wkts	Avge	BB	5i	10m	RpO	ct	st
FC			21	22	11	63	14	5.72	0	0	4351	1739	66	26.34	6-55	6	1	2.39	5	
SL			16	7	6	25	15*	25.00	0	0	596	459	21	21.85	5-29	0	1	4.62	3	
BH			4	2	1	3	3	3.00	0	0	204	126	3	42.00	2-34	0	0	3.70	1	
NW			5	1	1	4	4*		0	0	348	211	3	70.33	1-27	0	0	3.63	1	
Test		1993	8	11	4	65	14*	9.28	0	0	2177	805	22	36.59	6-67	1	0	2.21	2	
FC		1982	239	240	81	1206	54	7.58	0	2	44922	19800	684	28.94	8-93	39	7	2.64	98	
SL		1983	114	45	27	167	19*	9.27	0	0	4511	3522	114	30.89	5-29	2	3	4.68	31	
BH		1985	31	12	6	31	10*	5.16	0	0	1632	999	30	33.30	4-43	1	0	3.67	4	
NW		1991	22	8	4	18	8*	4.50	0	0	1422	806	23	35.04	3-56	0	0	3.40	3	

WILLIAMS, Neil FetzGerald b Hope Well, St Vincent 2.7.1962 RHB RFM (Middlesex 1982-94)

	Cmp	Debut	M	I	NO	Runs	HS	Avge	100	50	Balls	Runs	Wkts	Avge	BB	5i	10m	RpO	ct	st
FC			4	5	1	66	23	16.50	0	0	606	336	13	25.84	5-55	1	0	3.32	3	
NW			1								72	41	1	41.00	1-41	0	0	3.41	1	
Test		1990	1	1	0	38	38	38.00	0	0	246	148	2	74.00	2-148	0	0	3.60	0	
FC		1982	246	286	57	4286	77	18.71	0	13	36004	19599	649	30.19	8-75	22	2	3.26	65	
SL		1982	125	55	20	455	43	13.00	0	0	5159	3860	137	28.17	4-39	3	0	4.48	31	
BH		1982	56	31	7	259	29*	10.79	0	0	2940	1879	58	32.39	3-16	0	0	3.83	7	
NW		1983	23	13	6	73	11*	10.42	0	0	1151	778	18	43.22	4-36	1	0	4.05	5	

WILSON, Daniel Graeme b Paddington 18.2.1977 RHB RM

	Cmp	Debut	M	I	NO	Runs	HS	Avge	100	50	Balls	Runs	Wkts	Avge	BB	5i	10m	RpO	ct	st
FC			1								93	67	2	33.50	1-31	0	0	4.32	1	
SL		1996	2	1	0	7	7	7.00	0	0	48	40	3	13.33	3-40	0	0	5.00	1	

1997 AND CAREER FIGURES FOR GLAMORGAN PLAYERS

BUTCHER, Gary Paul b Clapham 11.3.1975 RHB RM

	Cmp	Debut	M	I	NO	Runs	HS	Avge	100	50	Balls	Runs	Wkts	Avge	BB	5i	10m	RpO	ct	st
FC			11	11	2	296	101*	32.88	1	1	685	466	12	38.83	3-87	0	0	4.08	1	
SL			13	10	2	192	47	24.00	0	0	244	305	6	50.83	2-28	0	0	7.50	1	
BH			4	3	1	27	17	13.50	0	0	85	76	1	76.00	1-20	0	0	5.36	0	
NW			3	2	1	29	18*	29.00	0	0	84	72	3	24.00	2-33	0	0	5.14	0	
FC		1994	31	44	8	1046	101*	29.05	1	6	2282	1559	35	44.54	7-77	1	0	4.09	11	
SL		1994	25	17	4	251	47	19.30	0	0	456	513	14	36.64	4-32	1	0	6.75	2	
BH		1995	9	6	2	39	17	9.75	0	0	169	136	3	45.33	2-21	0	0	4.82	0	
NW		1996	4	3	1	77	48	37.50	0	0	120	122	4	30.50	2-33	0	0	6.10	0	

COSKER, Dean Andrew (Rest of England) b Weymouth 7.1.1978 RHB SLA

	Cmp	Debut	M	I	NO	Runs	HS	Avge	100	50	Balls	Runs	Wkts	Avge	BB	5i	10m	RpO	ct	st
FC			16	9	5	16	7	4.00	0	0	2252	1100	29	37.93	4-64	0	0	2.93	4	
SL			7	2	0	5	5	2.50	0	0	312	250	6	41.66	2-40	0	0	4.80	2	
BH			1	1	0	0	0	0.00	0	0	36	38	1	38.00	1-38	0	0	6.33	0	

Cmp	Debut	M	I	NO	Runs	HS	Avge	100	50	Balls	Runs	Wkts	Avge	BB	5i	10m	RpO	ct	st
NW		1	1	1	3	3*		0	0	72	26	3	8.66	3-26	0	0	2.16	0	
FC	1996	21	15	6	61	24	6.77	0	0	3186	1722	45	38.26	4-60	0	0	3.24	7	
SL	1996	8	3	0	9	5	3.00	0	0	360	288	8	36.00	2-38	0	0	4.80	2	

COTTEY, Phillip Anthony b Swansea 2.6.1966 RHB OB

Cmp	Debut	M	I	NO	Runs	HS	Avge	100	50	Balls	Runs	Wkts	Avge	BB	5i	10m	RpO	ct	st
FC		17	21	4	475	83	27.94	0	2	21	19	0					5.42	15	
SL		13	12	2	327	61	32.70	0	2	132	127	2	63.50	1-29	0	0	5.77	3	
BH		4	4	1	45	21*	15.00	0	0									0	
NW		4	4	1	92	56	30.66	0	1	48	37	1	37.00	1-9	0	0	4.62	2	
FC	1986	184	297	46	9607	203	38.27	19	54	1100	767	13	59.00	4-49	0	0	4.18	122	
SL	1986	117	97	19	1957	92*	25.08	0	10	455	456	13	35.07	4-56	1	0	6.01	39	
BH	1988	29	27	5	462	68	21.00	0	1	66	50	1	50.00	1-49	0	0	4.54	8	
NW	1990	23	22	6	439	61*	27.43	0	3	150	96	3	32.00	1-9	0	0	3.84	8	

CROFT, Robert Damien Bale (England, England to Zimbabwe, England to New Zealand) b Morriston 25.5.1970 RHB OB

Cmp	Debut	M	I	NO	Runs	HS	Avge	100	50	Balls	Runs	Wkts	Avge	BB	5i	10m	RpO	ct	st
Test		5	8	0	75	24	9.37	0	0	971	439	8	54.87	3-125	0	0	2.71	1	
FC		18	26	1	652	86	26.08	0	4	3997	1698	62	27.38	5-33	1	0	2.54	14	
Int		3								180	106	2	53.00	1-39	0	0	3.53	0	
SL		10	9	0	230	50	25.55	0	1	456	339	8	42.37	2-31	0	0	4.46	3	
BH		4	4	0	89	43	22.25	0	0	240	172	4	43.00	2-38	0	0	4.30	1	
NW		4	4	0	133	64	33.25	0	2	288	136	4	34.00	2-45	0	0	2.83	0	
Test	1996	10	14	1	138	31	10.61	0	0	2350	904	28	32.28	5-95	1	0	2.30	6	
FC	1989	185	269	49	5621	143	25.55	2	24	39260	18172	497	36.56	8-66	20	2	2.77	93	
Int	1996	14	9	3	89	30*	14.83	0	0	780	516	15	34.40	2-26	0	0	3.96	4	
SL	1989	100	75	22	1155	68	21.79	0	3	4012	3020	90	33.55	6-20	0	1	4.51	25	
BH	1991	23	19	7	327	50*	27.25	0	1	1337	841	29	29.00	4-30	1	0	3.77	7	
NW	1990	22	18	5	339	64	26.07	0	3	1336	730	20	36.50	3-30	0	0	3.27	4	

DALE, Adrian b Germiston, South Africa 24.10.1968 RHB RM

Cmp	Debut	M	I	NO	Runs	HS	Avge	100	50	Balls	Runs	Wkts	Avge	BB	5i	10m	RpO	ct	st
FC		19	27	4	860	142*	37.39	2	5	427	261	0					3.66	6	
SL		13	13	1	400	65	33.33	0	3	401	350	13	26.92	2-18	0	0	5.23	2	
BH		4	4	0	199	100	49.75	1	0	200	155	8	19.37	3-30	0	0	4.65	2	
NW		4	3	0	122	71	40.66	0	1	102	100	1	100.00	1-61	0	0	5.88	0	
FC	1989	146	240	23	7129	214*	32.85	14	34	9897	5358	132	40.59	6-18	1	0	3.24	57	
SL	1989	114	99	13	2408	67*	28.00	0	14	3555	3212	99	32.44	6-22	1	1	5.42	27	
BH	1989	29	28	4	709	100	29.54	1	1	1220	867	36	24.08	5-41	0	1	4.26	10	
NW	1989	24	21	2	565	110	29.73	1	2	1036	730	21	34.76	3-54	0	0	4.22	6	

DAVIES, Andrew Philip b Neath 7.11.1976 LHB RM

Cmp	Debut	M	I	NO	Runs	HS	Avge	100	50	Balls	Runs	Wkts	Avge	BB	5i	10m	RpO	ct	st
SL		1	1	0	3	3	3.00	0	0	48	25	2	12.50	2-25	0	0	3.12	0	
FC	1995	3	2	1	19	11*	19.00	0	0	174	135	1	135.00	1-25	0	0	4.65	0	

EDWARDS, Gareth John Maldwyn b St Asaph 13.11.1976 RHB OB

Cmp	Debut	M	I	NO	Runs	HS	Avge	100	50	Balls	Runs	Wkts	Avge	BB	5i	10m	RpO	ct	st
FC		1								54	49	0					5.44	0	

EVANS, Alun Wyn b Glanamman 20.8.1975 RHB RM

Cmp	Debut	M	I	NO	Runs	HS	Avge	100	50	Balls	Runs	Wkts	Avge	BB	5i	10m	RpO	ct	st
FC		2	3	0	61	31	20.33	0	0									1	
SL		7	6	1	70	25	14.00	0	0									1	
FC	1996	9	16	3	437	71*	33.61	0	2									6	
SL	1996	13	12	3	169	50*	18.77	0	1									3	

JAMES, Stephen Peter b Lydney 7.9.1967 RHB RM

Cmp	Debut	M	I	NO	Runs	HS	Avge	100	50	Balls	Runs	Wkts	Avge	BB	5i	10m	RpO	ct	st
FC		18	30	4	1775	162	68.26	7	8									14	
SL		11	10	4	230	75*	38.33	0	1									5	
BH		4	4	1	30	15	10.00	0	0									2	
NW		4	3	0	178	109	59.33	1	1									3	
FC	1985	168	296	25	10485	235	38.69	31	38	2	3	0					9.00	133	
SL	1989	89	86	11	2763	107	36.84	2	20									22	
BH	1989	29	29	2	984	135	36.44	2	8									10	
NW	1987	19	18	1	708	123	41.64	2	4									5	

LAW, Wayne Lincoln b Swansea 4.9.1978 RHB OB

Cmp	Debut	M	I	NO	Runs	HS	Avge	100	50	Balls	Runs	Wkts	Avge	BB	5i	10m	RpO	ct	st
FC		1	1	1	38	38*		0	0									0	
SL		2	2	0	23	15	11.50	0	0									1	

MAYNARD, Matthew Peter (Otago) b Oldham 21.3.1966 RHB RM

Cmp	Debut	M	I	NO	Runs	HS	Avge	100	50	Balls	Runs	Wkts	Avge	BB	5i	10m	RpO	ct	st
FC		18	25	7	1170	161*	65.00	3	7	83	66	0					4.77	21	
SL		12	12	2	426	132	42.60	1	1	4	2	0					3.00	7	
BH		4	4	0	106	50	26.50	0	1	6	6	0					6.00	4	
NW		4	4	1	159	62	53.00	0	1	18	8	0					2.66	3	
Test	1988	4	8	0	87	35	10.87	0	0									3	
FC	1985	288	473	52	18516	243	43.98	43	101	966	783	6	130.50	3-21	0	0	4.86	274	5
Int	1993	10	10	1	153	41	17.00	0	0									3	
SL	1985	175	167	13	4727	132	30.69	4	30	22	31	0					8.45	67	
BH	1986	46	46	6	1737	151*	43.42	4	8	30	38	0					7.60	17	
NW	1986	34	33	3	1374	151*	45.80	2	11	18	8	0					2.66	13	

Cmp	Debut	M	I	NO	Runs	HS	Avge	100	50	Balls	Runs	Wkts	Avge	BB	5i	10m	RpO	ct	st
METSON, Colin Peter b Goffs Oak 2.7.1963 RHB WK (Middlesex 1981-86)
FC		1	1	0	0	0	0.00	0	0									3	1
FC	1981	231	302	71	4059	96	17.57	0	7	6	0	0					0.00	560	51
SL	1981	156	87	42	647	30*	14.37	0	0									153	48
BH	1987	38	22	4	189	23	10.50	0	0									31	5
NW	1987	28	16	2	90	21	6.42	0	0									27	2
MORRIS, Hugh b Cardiff 5.10.1963 LHB RM
FC		17	28	4	1262	233*	52.58	4	3									14	
SL		10	10	1	180	66*	20.00	0	1									4	
BH		4	4	0	169	76	42.25	0	2									0	
NW		4	4	0	79	53	19.75	0	1									3	
Test	1991	3	6	0	115	44	19.16	0	0									3	
FC	1981	314	544	53	19785	233*	40.29	53	98	348	380	2	190.00	1-6	0	0	6.55	197	
SL	1983	182	176	19	5447	127*	34.69	5	36									62	
BH	1984	45	45	3	1361	143*	33.19	4	5	18	15	1	15.00	1-14	0	0	5.00	15	
NW	1985	36	35	4	1361	154*	43.90	4	5	12	12	0					6.00	13	
PARKIN, Owen Thomas b Coventry 24.9.1972 RHB RM
FC		1	1	1	0	0*		0	0	204	116	3	38.66	3-38	0	0	3.41	1	
SL		8	5	3	2	1*	1.00	0	0	276	262	7	37.42	4-45	1	0	5.69	1	
BH		4	2	0	15	8	7.50	0	0	192	149	5	29.80	3-42	0	0	4.65	1	
FC	1994	13	15	10	67	14	13.40	0	0	1876	1030	24	42.91	3-22	0	0	3.29	5	
SL	1996	13	5	3	2	1*	1.00	0	0	504	435	16	27.18	5-28	1	1	5.17	1	
NW	1992	3	2	1	1	1*	1.00	0	0	120	77	3	25.66	3-23	0	0	3.85	2	
POWELL, Michael John b Abergavenny 3.2.1977 RHB
FC		5	8	3	286	200*	57.20	1	0	6	3	0					3.00	1	
SL		3	3	0	85	42	28.33	0	0									0	
SHAW, Adrian David b Neath 17.2.1972 RHB WK
FC		18	21	5	389	53*	24.31	0	1									52	2
SL		14	9	2	73	48	10.42	0	0									7	1
BH		4	3	0	26	15	8.66	0	0									5	1
NW		4	4	1	64	34*	21.33	0	0									4	
FC	1994	36	46	8	708	74	18.63	0	3									89	9
SL	1992	26	16	5	178	48	16.18	0	0									10	5
THOMAS, Stuart Darren b Morriston 25.1.1975 LHB RFM
FC		18	19	5	301	75*	21.50	0	1	2433	1444	53	27.24	5-24	3	0	3.56	8	
SL		10	7	0	53	15	7.57	0	0	373	307	10	30.70	3-30	0	0	4.93	3	
BH		2	2	2	14	13*		0	0	96	107	4	26.75	2-47	0	0	6.68	0	
NW		4	3	0	15	13	5.00	0	0	258	226	8	28.25	5-74	0	1	5.25	0	
FC	1992	53	69	20	929	78*	18.95	0	4	8096	5252	149	35.24	5-24	8	0	3.89	17	
SL	1992	21	12	3	102	20*	11.33	0	0	669	585	15	39.00	3-30	0	0	5.24	4	
BH	1995	9	5	3	41	27*	20.50	0	0	428	371	17	21.82	6-20	1	1	5.20	5	
NW	1995	5	3	0	15	13	5.00	0	0	312	262	8	32.75	5-74	0	1	5.03	0	
WAQAR YOUNIS (United Bank, Pakistan, Pakistan to Canada, Pakistan to Kenya, Pakistan to Sharjah, Pakistan to Australia)   b Vehari 16.11.1971 RHB RF (Surrey 1990-93)
FC		16	17	1	289	47	18.06	0	0	2650	1551	68	22.80	8-17	3	1	3.51	3	
SL		9	4	2	12	11*	6.00	0	0	348	285	14	20.35	4-14	1	0	4.91	0	
BH		1								60	42	1	42.00	1-42	0	0	4.20	1	
NW		4	2	2	42	34*		0	0	258	203	4	50.75	2-35	0	0	4.72	1	
Test	1989	44	57	11	429	34	9.32	0	0	9071	4844	227	21.33	7-76	19	4	3.20	6	
FC	1987	151	168	41	1683	55	13.25	0	2	27115	14501	688	21.07	8-17	54	13	3.20	37	
Int	1989	156	78	29	463	37	9.44	0	0	7707	5762	265	21.74	6-26	11	9	4.48	18	
SL	1990	49	20	6	116	39	8.28	0	0	2202	1583	92	17.20	5-26	6	1	4.31	7	
BH	1990	7	5	2	15	5*	5.00	0	0	401	264	9	29.33	3-29	0	0	3.95	1	
NW	1990	13	5	2	75	34*	25.00	0	0	859	557	29	19.20	5-40	1	1	3.89	2	
WARREN, Paul Michael (Devon) b Plymouth 18.1.1978 RHB RM
FC		1								114	60	0					3.15	1	
NW		1	1	1	12	12*		0	0	36	24	1	24.00	1-24	0	0	4.00	0	
WATKIN, Steven Llewellyn b Duffryn Rhondda 15.9.1964 RHB RMF
FC		17	16	3	138	39	10.61	0	0	3050	1393	61	22.83	7-41	2	0	2.74	3	
SL		11	4	1	22	15	7.33	0	0	462	348	10	34.80	4-15	1	0	4.51	3	
BH		4	2	1	11	10*	11.00	0	0	240	134	8	16.75	3-26	0	0	3.35	2	
NW		4	1	0	1	1	1.00	0	0	282	169	7	24.14	3-23	0	0	3.59	0	
Test	1991	3	5	0	25	13	5.00	0	0	534	305	11	27.72	4-65	0	0	3.42	1	
FC	1986	210	232	74	1531	41	9.68	0	0	42108	20720	726	28.53	8-59	24	4	2.95	54	
Int	1993	4	2	0	4	4	2.00	0	0	221	193	7	27.57	4-49	1	0	5.23	0	
SL	1986	124	46	15	239	31*	7.70	0	0	5426	3912	148	26.43	5-23	4	1	4.32	20	
BH	1988	33	18	9	72	15	8.00	0	0	1971	1278	46	27.78	4-31	1	0	3.89	8	
NW	1989	27	12	4	53	13	6.62	0	0	1740	904	37	24.43	4-26	1	0	3.11	2	

31

1997 AND CAREER FIGURES FOR GLOUCESTERSHIRE PLAYERS

ALLEYNE, Mark Wayne b Tottenham 23.5.1968 RHB RM WK

Cmp	Debut	M	I	NO	Runs	HS	Avge	100	50	Balls	Runs	Wkts	Avge	BB	5i	10m	RpO	ct	st
FC		19	30	4	1059	169	40.73	1	8	2161	1148	44	26.09	6-64	3	0	3.18	14	
SL		15	14	3	339	58	30.81	0	1	487	430	16	26.87	3-24	0	0	5.29	10	
BH		5	4	1	74	32	24.66	0	0	210	206	4	51.50	2-39	0	0	5.88	4	
NW		2	1	0	43	43	43.00	0	0	108	75	3	25.00	3-47	0	0	4.16	0	
FC	1986	219	359	37	10239	256	31.79	13	54	15132	8007	256	31.27	6-64	6	0	3.17	169	2
SL	1986	175	159	38	3740	134*	30.90	3	15	5483	4686	148	31.66	5-28	1	1	5.12	65	
BH	1987	43	35	7	596	75	21.28	0	1	1681	1255	37	33.91	5-27	1	1	4.47	17	
NW	1987	27	22	4	416	73	23.11	0	1	953	615	22	27.95	5-30	0	1	3.87	9	

AVERIS, James Maxwell Michael (Oxford University) b Bristol 28.5.1974 RHB RM

Cmp	Debut	M	I	NO	Runs	HS	Avge	100	50	Balls	Runs	Wkts	Avge	BB	5i	10m	RpO	ct	st
FC		10	15	4	276	42	25.09	0	0	1635	1104	16	69.00	5-98	1	0	4.05	2	
SL		2									54	53	2	26.50	2-43	0	0	5.88	0	
SL	1994	5	2	2	3	2*		0	0	174	175	6	29.16	2-35	0	0	6.03	1	

BALL, Martyn Charles John b Bristol 26.4.1970 RHB OB

Cmp	Debut	M	I	NO	Runs	HS	Avge	100	50	Balls	Runs	Wkts	Avge	BB	5i	10m	RpO	ct	st
FC		18	27	3	587	50	24.45	0	1	2876	1271	29	43.82	5-66	1	0	2.65	24	
SL		15	10	2	54	12	6.75	0	0	516	402	12	33.50	4-26	1	0	4.67	3	
BH		5	2	0	37	28	18.50	0	0	258	197	6	32.83	4-23	1	0	4.58	2	
NW		2	1	1	9	9*		0	0	144	99	1	99.00	1-51	0	0	4.12	2	
FC	1988	103	158	28	2231	71	17.16	0	4	15304	7337	195	37.62	8-46	8	1	2.87	122	
SL	1989	83	57	18	383	28*	9.82	0	0	2786	2389	58	41.18	4-26	1	0	5.14	23	
BH	1990	22	13	1	138	28	11.50	0	0	1140	738	20	36.90	4-23	1	0	3.88	10	
NW	1989	10	5	2	72	31	24.00	0	0	558	347	10	34.70	3-42	0	0	3.73	7	

CHURCH, Matthew John b Guildford 26.7.1972 RHB RM (Worcestershire 1994-96)

Cmp	Debut	M	I	NO	Runs	HS	Avge	100	50	Balls	Runs	Wkts	Avge	BB	5i	10m	RpO	ct	st
FC		2	4	0	73	53	18.25	0	1									0	
SL		1	1	0	25	25	25.00	0	0									0	
FC	1994	16	29	1	544	152	19.42	1	1	241	163	9	18.11	4-50	0	0	4.05	8	
SL	1994	15	11	0	98	25	8.90	0	0	6	12	0					12.00	7	
BH	1995	1																0	
NW	1996	1	1	0	35	35	35.00	0	0	30	34	0					6.80	0	

CUNLIFFE, Robert John b Oxford 8.11.1973 RHB RM

Cmp	Debut	M	I	NO	Runs	HS	Avge	100	50	Balls	Runs	Wkts	Avge	BB	5i	10m	RpO	ct	st
FC		9	14	1	273	61	21.00	0	1									4	
SL		9	9	1	225	56	28.12	0	2									0	
BH		5	5	1	181	113	45.25	1	0									2	
NW		2	1	0	33	33	33.00	0	0									0	
FC	1994	29	46	5	1291	190*	31.48	2	5									15	
SL	1993	14	14	1	328	56	25.23	0	3									2	
BH	1996	10	10	3	534	137*	76.28	3	1									3	
NW	1995	5	4	0	110	40	27.50	0	0									1	

DAVIS, Richard Peter b Westbrook 18.3.1966 RHB SLA (Kent 1986-93, Warwickshire 1994-95)

Cmp	Debut	M	I	NO	Runs	HS	Avge	100	50	Balls	Runs	Wkts	Avge	BB	5i	10m	RpO	ct	st
FC		9	12	0	135	39	11.25	0	0	1446	607	17	35.70	4-35	0	0	2.51	9	
SL		6	4	2	24	12*	12.00	0	0	114	139	5	27.80	2-29	0	0	7.31	3	
BH		4	1	1	8	8*		0	0	240	190	3	63.33	2-48	0	0	4.75	3	
NW		1	1	1	1*			0	0	72	44	0					3.66	0	
FC	1986	169	208	46	2452	67	15.13	0	4	30998	14543	414	35.12	7-64	16	2	2.81	155	
SL	1987	95	47	19	255	40*	9.10	0	0	3506	2768	100	27.68	5-52	1	1	4.73	31	
BH	1988	27	11	5	65	18*	10.83	0	0	1466	1018	20	50.90	2-26	0	0	4.16	12	
NW	1988	14	7	2	47	22	9.40	0	0	801	436	15	29.06	3-19	0	0	3.26	10	

DAWSON, Robert Ian b Exmouth 29.3.1970 RHB RM

Cmp	Debut	M	I	NO	Runs	HS	Avge	100	50	Balls	Runs	Wkts	Avge	BB	5i	10m	RpO	ct	st
FC		8	14	0	329	100	23.50	1	1	18	22	0					7.33	3	
SL		7	5	1	116	45	29.00	0	0									1	
BH		4	3	0	38	24	12.66	0	0									0	
FC	1992	55	98	7	2375	127*	26.09	3	12	308	132	3	44.00	2-38	0	0	2.57	27	
SL	1992	68	60	6	1138	85	21.07	0	4	38	59	1	59.00	1-19	0	0	9.31	11	
BH	1995	14	13	0	258	38	19.84	0	0	18	12	0					4.00	1	
NW	1990	5	4	0	73	60	18.25	0	1	24	37	1	37.00	1-37	0	0	9.25	0	

HANCOCK, Timothy Harold Coulter b Reading 20.4.1972 RHB RM

Cmp	Debut	M	I	NO	Runs	HS	Avge	100	50	Balls	Runs	Wkts	Avge	BB	5i	10m	RpO	ct	st
FC		19	31	3	854	100*	30.50	1	5	599	386	5	77.20	1-24	0	0	3.86	10	
SL		15	13	0	332	57	25.53	0	2	124	94	2	47.00	1-22	0	0	4.54	8	
BH		5	4	1	69	24*	23.00	0	0	139	99	2	49.50	2-34	0	0	4.27	0	
NW		2	1	0	4	4	4.00	0	0	72	58	6	9.66	6-58	0	1	4.83	0	
FC	1991	94	165	13	4015	123	26.41	4	24	1485	945	18	52.50	3-10	0	0	3.81	58	
SL	1991	68	62	1	984	57	16.13	0	2	375	343	9	38.11	2-6	0	0	5.48	29	
BH	1992	21	18	3	357	71*	23.80	0	1	217	150	6	25.00	3-13	0	0	4.14	2	
NW	1993	6	5	0	88	45	17.60	0	0	113	97	8	12.12	6-58	0	1	5.15	3	

HEWSON, Dominic Robert b Cheltenham 3.10.1974 RHB RM

Cmp	Debut	M	I	NO	Runs	HS	Avge	100	50	Balls	Runs	Wkts	Avge	BB	5i	10m	RpO	ct	st
FC		3	4	0	56	42	14.00	0	0									3	
SL		1																	0	

Cmp	Debut	M	I	NO	Runs	HS	Avge	100	50	Balls	Runs	Wkts	Avge	BB	5i	10m	RpO	ct	st
FC	1996	9	16	1	317	87	21.13	0	3									5	
SL	1996	2	1	0	3	3	3.00	0	0									0	

LAWRENCE, Dave Valentine b Gloucester 28.1.1964 RHB RF

Cmp	Debut	M	I	NO	Runs	HS	Avge	100	50	Balls	Runs	Wkts	Avge	BB	5i	10m	RpO	ct	st
FC		4	6	3	32	23*	10.66	0	0	516	359	8	44.87	2-28	0	0	4.17	1	
Test	1988	5	6	0	60	34	10.00	0	0	1089	676	18	37.55	5-106	1	0	3.72	0	
FC	1981	185	211	38	1851	66	10.69	0	2	26930	16521	515	32.07	7-47	21	1	3.68	45	
Int	1991	1								66	67	4	16.75	4-67	1	0	6.09	0	
SL	1983	59	23	8	179	38*	11.93	0	0	2430	2115	75	28.20	5-18	4	1	5.22	15	
BH	1983	29	12	6	94	23	15.66	0	0	1614	1050	44	23.86	6-20	2	2	3.90	6	
NW	1983	20	10	5	11	5*	2.20	0	0	1108	763	28	27.25	5-17	2	1	4.13	3	

LEWIS, Jonathan b Aylesbury 26.8.1975 RHB RM

Cmp	Debut	M	I	NO	Runs	HS	Avge	100	50	Balls	Runs	Wkts	Avge	BB	5i	10m	RpO	ct	st
FC		15	19	8	193	30	17.54	0	0	2513	1401	54	25.94	6-50	3	0	3.34	2	
SL		12	5	3	16	8	8.00	0	0	498	389	14	27.78	3-39	0	0	4.68	2	
BH		1								54	74	1	74.00	1-74	0	0	8.22	0	
NW		1								54	38	0					4.22	1	
FC	1995	28	38	10	315	30	11.25	0	0	4575	2456	84	29.23	6-50	3	0	3.22	6	
SL	1995	29	14	10	47	9*	11.75	0	0	1173	979	29	33.75	3-27	0	0	5.00	5	
BH	1996	2								114	105	4	26.25	3-31	0	0	5.52	0	
NW	1996	3	2	1	7	6*	7.00	0	0	152	84	5	16.80	3-27	0	0	3.31	1	

LYNCH, Monte Alan b Georgetown, Guyana 21.5.1958 RHB RM/OB (Surrey 1977-94)

Cmp	Debut	M	I	NO	Runs	HS	Avge	100	50	Balls	Runs	Wkts	Avge	BB	5i	10m	RpO	ct	st
FC		12	19	1	465	64	25.83	0	3									9	
SL		14	13	2	356	88*	32.36	0	3									5	
BH		5	5	1	133	87	33.25	0	1									2	
NW		2	2	1	100	100	100.00	1	0									1	
FC	1977	359	585	64	18325	172*	35.17	39	88	2195	1398	26	53.76	3-6	0	0	3.82	367	
Int	1988	3	3	0	8	6	2.66	0	0									1	
SL	1977	248	228	29	5593	136	28.10	2	34	167	205	8	25.62	2-2	0	0	7.36	85	
BH	1979	68	63	4	1521	112*	25.77	2	8	132	121	0					5.50	34	
NW	1979	43	38	6	988	129	30.67	2	4	304	179	7	25.57	2-28	0	0	3.53	20	

READ, Christopher Mark Wells (Devon) b Paignton 10.8.1978 RHB WK

Cmp	Debut	M	I	NO	Runs	HS	Avge	100	50	Balls	Runs	Wkts	Avge	BB	5i	10m	RpO	ct	st
SL		1	1	0	0	0	0.00	0	0									0	
NW		1	1	0	3	3	3.00	0	0									1	1
NW	1995	3	2	0	'40	37	20.00	0	0									1	1

RUSSELL, Robert Charles (England to New Zealand) b Stroud 15.8.1963 LHB OB WK

Cmp	Debut	M	I	NO	Runs	HS	Avge	100	50	Balls	Runs	Wkts	Avge	BB	5i	10m	RpO	ct	st
FC		19	29	6	1049	103*	45.60	1	8	18	15	0					5.00	52	5
SL		13	10	1	156	59*	17.33	0	1									13	1
BH		5	4	1	143	66	47.66	0	1									4	2
NW		2	1	0	20	20	20.00	0	0									4	1
Test	1988	49	77	15	1807	128*	29.14	2	6									141	11
FC	1981	367	536	118	12934	129*	30.94	7	70	56	68	1	68.00	1-4	0	0	7.28	893	109
Int	1987	38	29	7	383	50	17.40	0	1									41	6
SL	1982	195	148	34	2599	108	22.79	1	10									158	29
BH	1983	61	44	16	776	66	27.71	0	2									58	12
NW	1982	38	26	7	454	59*	23.89	0	1									51	9

SHEERAZ, Kamran Pasha b Wellington, Shropshire 28.12.1973 RHB RMF

Cmp	Debut	M	I	NO	Runs	HS	Avge	100	50	Balls	Runs	Wkts	Avge	BB	5i	10m	RpO	ct	st
FC		2	2	2	15	12*		0	0	42	40	0					5.71	0	
SL		5	3	2	9	7*	9.00	0	0	119	87	3	29.00	2-34	0	0	4.38	0	
NW		1								60	30	0					3.00	0	
FC	1994	13	16	9	27	12*	3.85	0	0	1717	1104	27	40.88	6-67	2	1	3.85	4	
SL	1994	17	8	5	35	14*	11.66	0	0	611	486	12	40.50	2-20	0	0	4.77	2	

SMITH, Andrew Michael (England) b Dewsbury 1.10.1967 RHB LFM

Cmp	Debut	M	I	NO	Runs	HS	Avge	100	50	Balls	Runs	Wkts	Avge	BB	5i	10m	RpO	ct	st
Test		1	2	1	4	4*	4.00	0	0	138	89	0					3.86	0	
FC		18	26	9	165	41*	9.70	0	0	3074	1464	83	17.63	6-45	5	3	2.85	4	
SL		14	8	4	46	10	11.50	0	0	534	386	16	24.12	2-14	0	0	4.33	1	
BH		5	2	1	5	3*	5.00	0	0	300	180	8	22.50	3-24	0	0	3.60	0	
NW		1	1	0	4	4	4.00	0	0	72	62	2	31.00	2-62	0	0	5.16	0	
FC	1991	92	115	24	1044	55*	11.47	0	2	15006	7916	299	26.47	8-73	13	5	3.16	15	
SL	1991	94	48	28	261	26*	13.05	0	0	3645	2914	101	28.85	4-38	2	0	4.79	13	
BH	1988	32	20	10	81	15*	8.10	0	0	1838	1247	43	29.00	6-39	1	1	4.07	7	
NW	1991	14	7	4	44	13	14.66	0	0	775	490	16	30.62	3-21	0	0	3.79	3	

TRAINOR, Nicholas James b Gateshead 29.6.1975 RHB OB

Cmp	Debut	M	I	NO	Runs	HS	Avge	100	50	Balls	Runs	Wkts	Avge	BB	5i	10m	RpO	ct	st
FC		14	25	1	484	121	20.16	1	1	126	89	0					4.23	3	
SL		3	2	0	26	22	13.00	0	0	24	12	0					3.00	1	
BH		3	3	0	98	62	32.66	0	1	36	26	0					4.33	1	
NW		2	2	0	172	143	86.00	1	0	48	49	2	24.50	2-25	0	0	6.12	1	
FC	1996	22	39	2	745	121	20.13	1	3	132	93	0					4.22	8	
SL	1996	4	3	0	46	22	15.33	0	0	24	12	0					3.00	1	
BH	1996	4	4	0	123	62	30.75	0	1	36	26	0					4.33	1	
NW	1996	3	3	0	186	143	62.00	1	0	48	49	2	24.50	2-25	0	0	6.12	1	

Cmp	Debut	M	I	NO	Runs	HS	Avge	100	50	Balls	Runs	Wkts	Avge	BB	5i	10m	RpO	ct	st

WILLIAMS, Richard Charles James b Southmead 8.8.1969 LHB WK

Cmp	Debut	M	I	NO	Runs	HS	Avge	100	50	Balls	Runs	Wkts	Avge	BB	5i	10m	RpO	ct	st
SL		1	1	0	0	0	0.00	0	0									0	
FC	1990	35	44	8	640	90	17.77	0	4									94	14
SL	1990	18	7	2	76	19	15.20	0	0									19	4

WINDOWS, Matthew Guy Newman b Bristol 5.4.1973 RHB SLA

Cmp	Debut	M	I	NO	Runs	HS	Avge	100	50	Balls	Runs	Wkts	Avge	BB	5i	10m	RpO	ct	st
FC		8	15	0	369	84	24.60	0	2	42	51	0					7.28	7	
SL		5	2	0	13	8	6.50	0	0									0	
FC	1992	40	75	4	2064	184	29.07	2	11	93	90	2	45.00	1-6	0	0	5.80	35	
SL	1993	38	34	2	610	72	19.06	0	2	48	49	0					6.12	7	
BH	1994	1	1	1	16	16*		0	0									0	
NW	1994	3	3	0	42	33	14.00	0	0									0	

WRIGHT, Anthony John b Stevenage 27.6.1962 RHB RM

Cmp	Debut	M	I	NO	Runs	HS	Avge	100	50	Balls	Runs	Wkts	Avge	BB	5i	10m	RpO	ct	st
FC		13	22	3	416	79	21.89	0	1									11	
SL		12	12	0	236	69	19.66	0	1									5	
BH		3	3	0	76	41	25.33	0	0									0	
NW		2	2	0	178	177	89.00	1	0									1	
FC	1982	276	484	38	13095	193	29.36	18	66	74	68	1	68.00	1-16	0	0	5.51	213	
SL	1980	183	172	17	3853	96	24.85	0	25	26	22	0					5.07	67	
BH	1984	47	44	0	1350	123	30.68	1	8									10	
NW	1982	30	29	2	1260	177	46.66	3	9									11	

YOUNG, Shaun (Tasmania, Australia to England) b Burnie, Australia 13.6.1970 LHB RFM

Cmp	Debut	M	I	NO	Runs	HS	Avge	100	50	Balls	Runs	Wkts	Avge	BB	5i	10m	RpO	ct	st
Test		1	2	1	4	4*	4.00	0	0	48	13	0					1.62	0	
FC		19	31	4	985	237	36.48	2	5	2379	1104	32	34.50	4-26	0	0	2.78	10	
SL		14	14	2	457	146*	38.08	1	2	480	444	15	29.60	3-32	0	0	5.55	4	
BH		5	4	0	140	67	35.00	0	2	254	196	9	21.77	4-54	1	0	4.62	0	
NW		2	2	1	14	14*	14.00	0	0	87	63	1	63.00	1-20	0	0	4.34	0	
FC	1991	90	147	25	4951	237	40.58	10	30	15125	7300	214	34.11	7-64	8	1	2.89	56	

1997 AND CAREER FIGURES FOR HAMPSHIRE PLAYERS

AYMES, Adrian Nigel b Southampton 4.6.1964 RHB-WK

Cmp	Debut	M	I	NO	Runs	HS	Avge	100	50	Balls	Runs	Wkts	Avge	BB	5i	10m	RpO	ct	st
FC		18	23	4	442	96*	23.26	0	1	54	76	0					8.44	35	7
SL		17	11	4	107	30	15.28	0	0									14	6
BH		5	4	1	57	22*	19.00	0	0									6	2
NW		2	1	1	11	11*		0	0									4	
FC	1987	145	212	56	4771	113	30.58	3	23	96	151	1	151.00	1-75	0	0	9.43	321	31
SL	1987	109	76	33	1127	54	26.20	0	1									103	27
BH	1991	31	17	5	226	38	18.83	0	0									31	9
NW	1991	15	5	1	75	34	18.75	0	0									22	2

BOVILL, James Noel Bruce b High Wycombe 2.6.1971 RHB RFM

Cmp	Debut	M	I	NO	Runs	HS	Avge	100	50	Balls	Runs	Wkts	Avge	BB	5i	10m	RpO	ct	st
FC		9	9	2	65	27	9.28	0	0	1402	902	23	39.21	4-62	0	0	3.86	5	
SL		4	1	0	2	2	2.00	0	0	150	180	5	36.00	4-44	1	0	7.20	1	
FC	1993	38	49	16	324	31	9.81	0	0	5717	3384	104	32.53	6-29	4	1	3.55	7	
SL	1993	16	6	2	16	7*	4.00	0	0	587	558	15	37.20	4-44	1	0	5.70	2	
BH	1992	7	1	1	14	14*		0	0	373	249	5	49.80	2-21	0	0	4.00	1	

CONNOR, Cardigan Adolphus b The Valley, Anguilla 24.3.1961 RHB RFM

Cmp	Debut	M	I	NO	Runs	HS	Avge	100	50	Balls	Runs	Wkts	Avge	BB	5i	10m	RpO	ct	st
FC		5	4	2	34	12*	17.00	0	0	737	430	13	33.07	7-46	1	0	3.50	0	
SL		8	3	2	1	1*	1.00	0	0	335	300	6	50.00	2-35	0	0	5.37	0	
BH		1	1	0	2	2	2.00	0	0	60	61	1	61.00	1-61	0	0	6.10	0	
NW		2								118	66	3	22.00	2-55	0	0	3.35	0	
FC	1984	217	205	53	1814	59	11.93	0	2	37091	19338	612	31.59	9-38	18	4	3.12	61	
SL	1984	187	55	18	239	25	6.45	0	0	8243	6196	228	27.17	5-25	6	1	4.51	33	
BH	1985	55	15	7	39	11	4.87	0	0	3091	2063	80	25.78	4-19	4	0	4.00	10	
NW	1984	34	7	4	37	13	12.33	0	0	2196	1299	69	18.82	4-11	5	0	3.54	10	

FRANCIS, Simon Richard George b Bromley 15.8.1978 RHB RMF

Cmp	Debut	M	I	NO	Runs	HS	Avge	100	50	Balls	Runs	Wkts	Avge	BB	5i	10m	RpO	ct	st
FC		1	2	0	8	4	4.00	0	0	114	97	0					5.10	0	
SL		1								48	31	2	15.50	2-31	0	0	3.87	0	

HANSEN, Thomas Munkholt b Glostrup, Denmark 25.3.1976 RHB LFM

Cmp	Debut	M	I	NO	Runs	HS	Avge	100	50	Balls	Runs	Wkts	Avge	BB	5i	10m	RpO	ct	st
FC		1	2	1	31	19	31.00	0	0	156	75	0					2.88	0	

HAYDEN, Matthew Lawrence (Queensland, Australia, Australia to South Africa) b Kingaroy 29.10.1971 LHB RM

Cmp	Debut	M	I	NO	Runs	HS	Avge	100	50	Balls	Runs	Wkts	Avge	BB	5i	10m	RpO	ct	st
FC		17	30	3	1446	235*	53.55	4	7	198	166	3	55.33	2-17	0	0	5.03	13	
SL		16	15	0	654	118	43.60	2	3	81	78	2	39.00	2-38	0	0	5.77	8	
BH		5	5	1	216	120*	54.00	1	0	54	45	2	22.50	2-45	0	0	5.00	3	
NW		2	2	0	110	90	55.00	0	1									1	
Test	1993	7	12	0	261	125	21.75	1	0									8	
FC	1991	108	194	23	9280	235*	54.26	28	39	371	282	4	70.50	2-17	0	0	4.56	92	
Int	1993	13	12	1	286	67	26.00	0	2									4	

Cmp	Debut	M	I	NO	Runs	HS	Avge	100	50	Balls	Runs	Wkts	Avge	BB	5i	10m	RpO	ct	st

JAMES, Kevan David b Lambeth 18.3.1961 LHB LMF (Middlesex 1980-84)

Cmp	Debut	M	I	NO	Runs	HS	Avge	100	50	Balls	Runs	Wkts	Avge	BB	5i	10m	RpO	ct	st
FC		10	15	2	359	85	27.61	0	5	967	504	27	18.66	8-49	2	1	3.12	5	
SL		8	3	0	57	50	19.00	0	1	240	221	8	27.62	3-16	0	0	5.52	0	
BH		3	2	1	23	13*	23.00	0	0	120	112	1	112.00	1-48	0	0	5.60	1	
FC	1980	205	307	48	7928	162	30.61	10	39	22316	11323	357	31.71	8-49	11	1	3.04	70	
SL	1980	159	107	31	1590	66	20.92	0	5	6331	4671	157	29.75	6-35	3	2	4.42	43	
BH	1980	42	29	6	430	56	18.69	0	1	2017	1364	32	42.62	3-31	0	0	4.05	10	
NW	1985	23	14	3	159	42	14.45	0	0	1426	896	34	26.35	4-42	1	0	3.76	4	

KEECH, Matthew b Hampstead 21.10.1970 RHB RM (Middlesex 1991-93)

Cmp	Debut	M	I	NO	Runs	HS	Avge	100	50	Balls	Runs	Wkts	Avge	BB	5i	10m	RpO	ct	st
FC		10	16	4	518	127	43.16	2	1	72	51	1	51.00	1-12	0	0	4.25	10	
SL		11	11	3	295	53*	36.87	0	2	36	40	2	20.00	2-29	0	0	6.66	1	
BH		3	3	0	63	32	21.00	0	0									1	
NW		2	2	0	59	34	29.50	0	0	6	6	0					6.00	1	
FC	1991	49	84	11	2136	127	29.26	3	11	756	383	8	47.87	2-28	0	0	3.03	36	
SL	1991	66	61	9	1217	98	23.40	0	4	492	393	9	43.66	2-22	0	0	4.79	11	
BH	1991	9	8	0	191	47	23.87	0	0	66	47	1	47.00	1-37	0	0	4.27	7	
NW	1993	4	3	0	62	34	20.66	0	0	66	47	0					4.27	3	

KENDALL, William Salwey b Wimbledon 18.12.1973 RHB RM

Cmp	Debut	M	I	NO	Runs	HS	Avge	100	50	Balls	Runs	Wkts	Avge	BB	5i	10m	RpO	ct	st
FC		12	19	2	413	76	24.29	0	1	30	46	0					9.20	6	
SL		16	13	0	235	55	18.07	0	1	12	22	0					11.00	15	
BH		4	4	0	67	26	16.75	0	0									0	
NW		2	2	1	16	16	16.00	0	0									0	
FC	1994	44	68	11	2168	145*	38.03	4	10	630	383	10	38.30	3-37	0	0	3.64	32	
SL	1996	24	21	1	365	55	18.25	0	1	12	22	0					11.00	18	
BH	1995	7	7	0	121	26	17.28	0	0									0	

KENWAY, Derek Anthony b Fareham 12.6.1978 RHB WK

Cmp	Debut	M	I	NO	Runs	HS	Avge	100	50	Balls	Runs	Wkts	Avge	BB	5i	10m	RpO	ct	st
FC		1	2	1	22	20*	22.00	0	0	54	58	2	29.00	1-5	0	0	6.44	1	

LANEY, Jason Scott (Rest of England) b Winchester 27.4.1973 RHB OB

Cmp	Debut	M	I	NO	Runs	HS	Avge	100	50	Balls	Runs	Wkts	Avge	BB	5i	10m	RpO	ct	st
FC		15	27	1	848	95	32.61	0	6	30	19	0					3.80	6	
SL		14	14	0	371	69	26.50	0	2									4	
BH		4	4	0	39	17	9.75	0	0									1	
NW		2	2	0	75	40	37.50	0	0									1	
FC	1995	43	78	2	2584	112	34.00	4	14	132	83	0					3.77	28	
SL	1993	31	31	0	832	69	26.83	0	4									8	
BH	1996	8	8	0	148	41	18.50	0	0									1	
NW	1996	5	5	0	340	153	68.00	1	1									2	

MARU, Rajesh Jamandass b Nairobi, Kenya 28.10.1962 RHB SLA (Middlesex 1980-82)

Cmp	Debut	M	I	NO	Runs	HS	Avge	100	50	Balls	Runs	Wkts	Avge	BB	5i	10m	RpO	ct	st
FC		4	4	1	67	36*	22.33	0	0	762	336	3	112.00	2-60	0	0	2.64	6	
SL		7	4	2	15	6*	7.50	0	0	270	231	7	33.00	4-29	1	0	5.13	5	
BH		3	2	2	19	10*		0	0	180	114	3	38.00	2-51	0	0	3.80	1	
NW		2								66	55	0					5.00	0	
FC	1980	227	229	57	2938	74	17.08	0	7	39750	17547	525	33.42	8-41	15	1	2.64	252	
SL	1980	71	32	19	184	33*	14.15	0	0	2527	2192	55	39.85	4-29	1	0	5.20	27	
BH	1990	15	6	3	38	10*	12.66	0	0	771	511	15	34.06	3-46	0	0	3.97	6	
NW	1987	16	6	2	44	22	11.00	0	0	948	586	13	45.07	3-46	0	0	3.70	12	

MASCARENHAS, Adrian Dimitri b Chiswick 30.10.1977 RHB RFM

Cmp	Debut	M	I	NO	Runs	HS	Avge	100	50	Balls	Runs	Wkts	Avge	BB	5i	10m	RpO	ct	st
FC		6	7	1	50	21	8.33	0	0	760	417	8	52.12	5-63	1	0	3.29	0	
SL		3	2	0	17	10	8.50	0	0	66	96	0					8.72	1	
BH		2	2	0	21	20	10.50	0	0	102	92	0					5.41	0	
FC	1996	8	10	1	74	21	8.22	0	0	1312	714	24	29.75	6-88	2	0	3.26	0	
SL	1996	6	4	1	24	10	8.00	0	0	194	220	5	44.00	2-34	0	0	6.80	2	

MILBURN, Stuart Mark b Harrogate 29.9.1972 RHB RFM (Yorkshire 1992-95)

Cmp	Debut	M	I	NO	Runs	HS	Avge	100	50	Balls	Runs	Wkts	Avge	BB	5i	10m	RpO	ct	st
FC		11	8	2	90	23	15.00	0	0	1992	1127	22	51.22	4-38	0	0	3.39	1	
SL		4	3	1	1	1	0.50	0	0	162	137	4	34.25	1-27	0	0	5.07	0	
BH		1	1	0	1	1	1.00	0	0	34	32	1	32.00	1-32	0	0	5.64	0	
FC	1992	27	28	6	292	54*	13.27	0	1	4369	2497	53	47.11	4-38	0	0	3.42	1	
SL	1995	13	7	3	24	13*	6.00	0	0	546	454	11	41.27	2-18	0	0	4.98	3	
BH	1996	3	2	0	3	2	1.50	0	0	119	93	3	31.00	2-7	0	0	4.68	1	
NW	1996	2	1	0	27	27	27.00	0	0	120	108	0					5.40	0	

PATEL, Chetan Morar (Oxford University) b Islington 12.4.1972 LHB RM

Cmp	Debut	M	I	NO	Runs	HS	Avge	100	50	Balls	Runs	Wkts	Avge	BB	5i	10m	RpO	ct	st
FC		12	22	5	420	63*	24.70	0	3	1962	1326	27	49.11	6-110	1	0	4.05	2	
SL		1								24	25	0					6.25	1	

RENSHAW, Simon John b Bebington 6.3.1974 RHB RMF

Cmp	Debut	M	I	NO	Runs	HS	Avge	100	50	Balls	Runs	Wkts	Avge	BB	5i	10m	RpO	ct	st
FC		13	19	7	269	56	22.41	0	1	2139	1278	37	34.54	5-110	1	0	3.58	3	
SL		17	12	7	104	25	20.80	0	0	690	621	22	28.22	3-45	0	0	5.40	1	
BH		5	4	1	3	2*	1.00	0	0	294	202	13	15.53	6-25	0	1	4.12	1	
NW		2								114	88	2	44.00	2-71	0	0	4.63	1	
FC	1995	21	27	12	279	56	18.60	0	1	3620	2212	54	40.96	5-110	1	0	3.66	6	
SL	1996	22	14	9	111	25	22.20	0	0	828	730	25	29.20	3-45	0	0	5.28	1	

Cmp	Debut	M	I	NO	Runs	HS	Avge	100	50	Balls	Runs	Wkts	Avge	BB	5i	10m	RpO	ct	st
BH	1995	10	6	2	3	2*	0.75	0	0	588	412	18	22.88	6-25	0	1	4.20	2	
NW	1994	4	2	0	5	4	2.50	0	0	186	133	4	33.25	2-20	0	0	4.29	1	

SAVIDENT, Lee b Guernsey 22.10.1976 RHB RM

Cmp	Debut	M	I	NO	Runs	HS	Avge	100	50	Balls	Runs	Wkts	Avge	BB	5i	10m	RpO	ct	st
FC		3	4	1	15	6	5.00	0	0	336	247	4	61.75	2-86	0	0	4.41	1	
SL		3	2	2	8	7*		0	0	115	104	6	17.33	3-41	0	0	5.42	0	

SMITH, Robin Arnold b Durban, South Africa 13.9.1963 RHB LB

Cmp	Debut	M	I	NO	Runs	HS	Avge	100	50	Balls	Runs	Wkts	Avge	BB	5i	10m	RpO	ct	st
FC		14	23	1	918	154	41.72	2	4	31	75	0					14.51	4	
SL		14	13	0	229	49	17.61	0	0									4	
BH		5	5	0	166	92	33.20	0	1									0	
NW		2	2	0	245	126	122.50	2	0									0	
Test	1988	62	112	15	4236	175	43.67	9	28	24	6	0					1.50	39	
FC	1980	333	568	78	21645	209*	44.17	53	107	955	768	12	64.00	2-11	0	0	4.82	192	
Int	1988	71	70	8	2419	167*	39.01	4	15									26	
SL	1983	154	147	16	5231	131	39.93	9	32	2	0	1	0.00	1-0	0	0	0.00	64	
BH	1983	52	49	8	2105	155*	51.34	5	9	6	2	0					2.00	21	
NW	1985	35	35	10	1954	158	78.16	7	8	17	13	2	6.50	2-13	0	0	4.58	20	

STEPHENSON, John Patrick b Stebbing 14.3.1965 RHB RM (Essex 1985-94)

Cmp	Debut	M	I	NO	Runs	HS	Avge	100	50	Balls	Runs	Wkts	Avge	BB	5i	10m	RpO	ct	st
FC		17	26	3	784	140	34.08	2	1	2573	1480	37	40.00	6-54	1	0	3.45	7	
SL		16	13	4	251	38*	27.88	0	0	605	544	24	22.66	6-33	2	1	5.39	7	
BH		5	5	1	124	65	31.00	0	1	294	252	8	31.50	2-34	0	0	5.14	2	
NW		2	1	0	1	1	1.00	0	0	140	83	8	10.37	5-34	0	1	3.55	2	
Test	1989	1	2	0	36	25	18.00	0	0									0	
FC	1985	237	405	41	12517	202*	34.38	21	66	15681	8771	254	34.53	7-51	9	0	3.35	135	
SL	1986	148	130	18	3218	110*	28.73	4	13	4328	3389	137	24.73	6-33	3	2	4.69	63	
BH	1987	42	37	5	1398	142	43.68	2	10	1342	965	38	25.39	3-22	0	0	4.31	9	
NW	1986	23	21	1	770	107	38.50	1	7	829	677	20	33.85	5-34	0	1	4.89	9	

UDAL, Shaun David b Farnborough 18.3.1969 RHB OB

Cmp	Debut	M	I	NO	Runs	HS	Avge	100	50	Balls	Runs	Wkts	Avge	BB	5i	10m	RpO	ct	st
FC		18	24	3	600	117*	28.57	1	4	3763	1810	34	53.23	4-17	0	0	2.88	3	
SL		17	14	3	342	78	31.09	0	4	756	590	29	20.34	3-26	0	0	4.68	5	
BH		5	4	0	40	34	10.00	0	0	288	199	7	28.42	2-28	0	0	4.14	5	
NW		2	2	2	45	39*		0	0	144	69	3	23.00	3-13	0	0	2.87	1	
FC	1989	126	180	30	3352	117*	22.34	1	16	25837	12934	356	36.33	8-50	20	4	3.00	60	
Int	1994	10	6	4	35	11*	17.50	0	0	570	371	8	46.37	2-37	0	0	3.90	1	
SL	1989	111	69	23	797	78	17.32	0	5	4805	4017	131	30.66	4-51	2	0	5.01	33	
BH	1991	30	15	4	142	34	12.90	0	0	1848	1181	40	29.52	4-40	1	0	3.83	9	
NW	1991	17	8	4	102	39*	25.50	0	0	1134	621	22	28.22	3-13	0	0	3.28	7	

WHITAKER, Paul Robert b Keighley 28.6.1973 LHB OB

Cmp	Debut	M	I	NO	Runs	HS	Avge	100	50	Balls	Runs	Wkts	Avge	BB	5i	10m	RpO	ct	st
FC		3	5	1	132	73	33.00	0	1	148	89	1	89.00	1-31	0	0	3.60	1	
SL		3	2	0	6	6	3.00	0	0	72	54	1	54.00	1-37	0	0	4.50.	1	
BH		3	2	0	28	28	14.00	0	0	48	50	0					6.25	1	
FC	1994	30	51	4	1425	119	30.31	1	9	919	546	12	45.50	3-36	0	0	3.56	8	
SL	1994	29	27	2	460	97	18.40	0	2	332	303	10	30.30	3-44	0	0	5.47	8	
BH	1995	9	8	0	149	53	18.62	0	1	216	155	4	38.75	2-33	0	0	4.30	1	
NW	1995	4	4	1	23	13	7.66	0	0	120	99	3	33.00	3-48	0	0	4.95	0	

WHITE, Giles William b Barnstaple 23.3.1972 RHB LB (Somerset 1991-93)

Cmp	Debut	M	I	NO	Runs	HS	Avge	100	50	Balls	Runs	Wkts	Avge	BB	5i	10m	RpO	ct	st
FC		10	17	2	681	145	45.40	1	4	65	49	0					4.52	8	
SL		7	7	0	154	67	22.00	0	1	12	14	0					7.00	0	
BH		1	1	0	56	56	56.00	0	1									0	
FC	1991	50	86	8	2396	145	30.71	2	15	257	189	1	189.00	1-30	0	0	4.41	47	
SL	1993	35	33	3	754	67	25.13	0	4	12	14	0					7.00	8	
BH	1995	7	6	0	125	56	20.83	0	1									0	
NW	1992	3	3	0	12	11	4.00	0	0	72	45	1	45.00	1-45	0	0	3.75	2	

1997 AND CAREER RECORDS FOR KENT PLAYERS

COWDREY, Graham Robert b Farnborough 27.6.1964 RHB RM

Cmp	Debut	M	I	NO	Runs	HS	Avge	100	50	Balls	Runs	Wkts	Avge	BB	5i	10m	RpO	ct	st
FC		9	15	0	442	101	29.46	1	1	30	31	0					6.20	7	
SL		13	11	2	354	82	39.33	0	3	48	35	2	17.50	2-35	0	0	4.37	2	
BH		7	7	1	200	77	33.33	0	1									1	
FC	1984	179	284	29	8858	147	34.73	17	46	1206	872	12	72.66	1-5	0	0	4.33	97	
SL	1985	165	146	23	3529	105*	28.69	3	17	690	544	24	22.66	4-15	2	0	4.73	56	
BH	1986	55	50	4	1064	77	23.13	0	6	202	139	2	69.50	1-6	0	0	4.12	19	
NW	1986	23	20	4	416	65	26.00	0	1	303	157	4	39.25	2-4	0	0	3.10	3	

EALHAM, Mark Alan (England, England A, England A to Australia) b Willesborough 27.8.1969 RHB RMF

Cmp	Debut	M	I	NO	Runs	HS	Avge	100	50	Balls	Runs	Wkts	Avge	BB	5i	10m	RpO	ct	st
Test		4	6	3	105	53*	35.00	0	1	352	191	8	23.87	3-60	0	0	3.25	3	
FC		18	30	10	1055	139	52.75	3	6	2446	1238	40	30.95	4-47	0	0	3.03	12	
Int		3								162	108	4	27.00	2-21	0	0	4.00	1	
SL		12	10	1	201	61	22.33	0	2	374	280	12	23.33	5-41	0	1	4.49	3	
BH		8	8	3	185	52	37.00	0	1	372	284	10	28.40	2-31	0	0	4.58	5	

Cmp	Debut	M	I	NO	Runs	HS	Avge	100	50	Balls	Runs	Wkts	Avge	BB	5i	10m	RpO	ct	st
NW		1	1	0	46	46	46.00	0	0	72	45	1	45.00	1-45	0	0	3.75	0	
Test	1996	6	9	3	186	53*	31.00	0	2	832	383	15	25.53	4-21	0	0	2.76	4	
FC	1989	106	171	28	4689	139	32.79	4	32	14234	7037	236	29.81	8-36	8	1	2.96	44	
Int	1996	5	1	0	40	40	40.00	0	0	198	131	4	32.75	2-21	0	0	3.96	1	
SL	1989	105	85	23	1535	112	24.75	1	7	4023	3087	98	31.50	6-53	1	2	4.60	24	
BH	1990	34	31	8	618	75	26.86	0	4	1775	1195	49	24.38	4-29	3	0	4.03	14	
NW	1992	14	14	4	298	58*	29.80	0	2	767	387	16	24.18	4-10	1	0	3.02	4	

FLEMING, Matthew Valentine b Macclesfield 12.12.1964 RHB RM

Cmp	Debut	M	I	NO	Runs	HS	Avge	100	50	Balls	Runs	Wkts	Avge	BB	5i	10m	RpO	ct	st
FC		18	31	4	790	138	29.25	1	4	2390	1145	37	30.94	5-51	2	0	2.87	5	
SL		17	14	2	192	40	16.00	0	0	647	530	26	20.38	3-14	0	0	4.91	2	
BH		8	8	0	167	63	20.87	0	1	370	257	17	15.11	5-27	1	2	4.16	3	
NW		1	1	0	41	41	41.00	0	0	72	22	1	22.00	1-22	0	0	1.83	0	
FC	1989	149	244	27	6689	138	30.82	9	36	14168	6726	173	38.87	5-51	2	0	2.84	60	
SL	1988	140	129	15	2706	112	23.73	1	12	5181	4567	174	26.24	4-13	5	0	5.28	36	
BH	1989	42	39	2	922	72	24.91	0	5	2046	1449	58	24.98	5-27	1	2	4.24	12	
NW	1989	18	18	1	326	53	19.17	0	1	693	428	18	23.77	3-28	0	0	3.70	10	

FULTON, David Paul b Lewisham 15.11.1971 RHB SLA

Cmp	Debut	M	I	NO	Runs	HS	Avge	100	50	Balls	Runs	Wkts	Avge	BB	5i	10m	RpO	ct	st
FC		16	29	3	953	110	36.65	1	4									23	
SL		3	3	0	19	9	6.33	0	0									0	
BH		1	1	0	17	17	17.00	0	0									2	
NW		1	1	0	9	9	9.00	0	0									0	
FC	1992	59	106	8	3105	134*	31.68	4	16	67	65	1	65.00	1-37	0	0	5.82	90	
SL	1993	12	12	0	96	29	8.00	0	0									4	
BH	1995	2	2	0	42	25	21.00	0	0									3	
NW	1994	4	4	0	50	19	12.50	0	0	6	9	0					9.00	0	

HEADLEY, Dean Warren (England, England A, England A to Australia) b Norton 27.1.1970 RHB RFM (Middlesex 1991-92)

Cmp	Debut	M	I	NO	Runs	HS	Avge	100	50	Balls	Runs	Wkts	Avge	BB	5i	10m	RpO	ct	st
Test		3	6	2	39	22	9.75	0	0	788	444	16	27.75	4-72	0	0	3.38	1	
FC		12	17	5	166	40	13.83	0	0	2552	1419	46	30.84	5-92	1	0	3.33	3	
Int		1								48	36	1	36.00	1-36	0	0	4.50	0	
SL		8	5	3	12	7*	6.00	0	0	354	220	12	18.33	4-27	1	0	3.72	1	
BH		8	1	1	3	3*		0	0	414	294	8	36.75	3-36	0	0	4.26	1	
NW		1	1	0	1	1	1.00	0	0	72	31	3	10.33	3-31	0	0	2.58	0	
FC	1991	98	127	33	1655	91	17.60	0	4	18108	9419	318	29.61	8-98	18	2	3.12	38	
Int	1996	3	1	1	3	3*		0	0	150	120	1	120.00	1-36	0	0	4.80	0	
SL	1991	74	25	14	129	29*	11.72	0	0	3131	2477	92	26.92	6-42	3	1	4.74	15	
BH	1991	23	8	3	60	26	12.00	0	0	1301	859	25	34.36	4-19	1	0	3.96	5	
NW	1991	12	6	4	44	24*	22.00	0	0	733	454	21	21.61	5-20	0	1	3.71	0	

HOUSE, William John (Cambridge University, British Universities) b Sheffield 16.3.1976 LHB RMF

Cmp	Debut	M	I	NO	Runs	HS	Avge	100	50	Balls	Runs	Wkts	Avge	BB	5i	10m	RpO	ct	st
FC		10	14	1	331	94	25.46	0	2	413	284	0					4.12	11	
SL		1	1	0	0	0	0.00	0	0									0	
BH		5	5	0	155	93	31.00	0	1	18	14	0					4.66	0	
FC	1996	18	29	6	857	136	37.26	2	4	947	696	2	348.00	1-44	0	0	4.40	13	
SL	1996	5	5	1	46	19*	11.50	0	0									1	
BH	1996	6	6	0	177	93	29.50	0	1	18	14	0					4.66		

IGGLESDEN, Alan Paul b Farnborough 8.10.1964 RHB RFM

Cmp	Debut	M	I	NO	Runs	HS	Avge	100	50	Balls	Runs	Wkts	Avge	BB	5i	10m	RpO	ct	st
FC		6	8	3	6	3	1.20	0	0	912	538	18	29.88	4-67	0	0	3.53	1	
SL		6								258	195	9	21.66	3-29	0	0	4.53	0	
Test	1989	3	5	3	6	3*	3.00	0	0	555	329	6	54.83	2-91	0	0	3.55	1	
FC	1986	151	166	62	868	41	8.34	0	0	26159	13286	501	26.51	7-28	23	4	3.04	38	
Int	1993	4	3	1	20	18	10.00	0	0	168	122	2	61.00	2-12	0	0	4.35	1	
SL	1987	87	27	17	93	13*	9.30	0	0	3954	2632	113	23.29	5-13	3	2	3.99	19	
BH	1987	25	10	7	43	26*	14.33	0	0	1457	892	35	25.48	3-24	0	0	3.67	5	
NW	1987	14	4	3	23	12*	23.00	0	0	728	375	18	20.83	4-29	1	0	3.09	3	

LLONG, Nigel James b Ashford, Kent 11.2.1969 LHB OB

Cmp	Debut	M	I	NO	Runs	HS	Avge	100	50	Balls	Runs	Wkts	Avge	BB	5i	10m	RpO	ct	st
FC		8	14	0	256	99	18.28	0	2	315	200	4	50.00	2-33	0	0	3.80	9	
SL		15	9	0	123	52	13.66	0	1	160	162	5	32.40	1-1	0	0	6.07	4	
BH		8	7	0	266	75	38.00	0	2	114	106	0					5.57	3	
NW		1	1	0	68	68	68.00	0	1	56	49	2	24.50	2-49	0	0	5.25	0	
FC	1990	66	104	10	2992	130	31.82	6	16	2273	1259	35	35.97	5-21	2	0	3.32	57	
SL	1989	87	71	15	1126	70	20.10	0	5	619	611	23	26.56	4-24	1	0	5.92	26	
BH	1993	17	14	1	320	75	24.61	0	2	204	175	3	58.33	2-38	0	0	5.14	4	
NW	1992	6	6	3	261	115*	87.00	1	1	134	96	6	16.00	3-36	0	0	4.29	3	

McCAGUE, Martin John b Larne, Ireland 24.5.1969 RHB RF

Cmp	Debut	M	I	NO	Runs	HS	Avge	100	50	Balls	Runs	Wkts	Avge	BB	5i	10m	RpO	ct	st
FC		11	17	6	190	53*	17.27	0	1	1876	1125	48	23.43	7-50	4	0	3.59	3	
SL		12	8	1	41	11	5.85	0	0	434	377	14	26.92	3-50	0	0	5.21	3	
BH		8	4	3	24	12*	24.00	0	0	402	326	10	32.60	4-41	1	0	4.86	0	
NW		1	1	1	4	4*		0	0	12	8	0					4.00	0	
Test	1993	3	5	0	21	11	4.20	0	0	593	390	6	65.00	4-121	0	0	3.94	1	
FC	1990	106	146	36	1691	63*	15.37	0	4	19163	10369	392	26.45	9-86	24	2	3.24	58	

37

Cmp	Debut	M	I	NO	Runs	HS	Avge	100	50	Balls	Runs	Wkts	Avge	BB	5i	10m	RpO	ct	st
SL	1991	77	42	13	252	22*	8.68	0	0	3000	2634	109	24.16	5-40	6	1	5.26	15	
BH	1991	30	19	8	169	30	15.36	0	0	1532	1186	39	30.41	5-43	1	1	4.64	7	
NW	1991	12	10	6	100	31*	25.00	0	0	654	437	21	20.80	5-26	0	1	4.00	2	

MARSH, Steven Andrew b Westminster 27.1.1961 RHB WK

Cmp	Debut	M	I	NO	Runs	HS	Avge	100	50	Balls	Runs	Wkts	Avge	BB	5i	10m	RpO	ct	st
FC		18	27	6	837	142	39.85	1	3									61	2
SL		16	12	6	107	39*	17.83	0	0									10	1
BH		8	4	2	79	27*	39.50	0	0									6	1
NW		1	1	0	0	0	0.00	0	0									1	
FC	1982	260	379	63	9012	142	28.51	9	48	202	240	2	120.00	2-20	0	0	7.12	618	50
SL	1984	178	129	39	1763	59	19.58	0	4									168	22
BH	1986	59	44	11	584	71	17.69	0	1									67	4
NW	1986	23	16	3	209	55	16.07	0	1	3	3	1	3.00	1-3	0	0	6.00	34	4

PATEL, Minal Mahesh b Bombay, India 7.7.1970 RHB SLA

Cmp	Debut	M	I	NO	Runs	HS	Avge	100	50	Balls	Runs	Wkts	Avge	BB	5i	10m	RpO	ct	st
FC		1	2	0	38	30	19.00	0	0	18	12	0					4.00	1	
Test	1996	2	2	0	45	27	22.50	0	0	276	180	1	180.00	1-101	0	0	3.91	2	
FC	1989	80	114	25	1231	56	13.83	0	2	18191	8118	250	32.47	8-96	15	7	2.67	43	
SL	1994	6	2	0	6	5	3.00	0	0	176	191	6	31.83	3-50	0	0	6.51	1	
BH	1995	8	6	5	39	18*	39.00	0	0	456	327	6	54.50	2-29	0	0	4.30	3	
NW	1990	6	2	1	9	5*	9.00	0	0	386	200	7	28.57	2-29	0	0	3.10	5	

PHILLIPS, Ben James b Lewisham 30.9.1974 RHB RFM

Cmp	Debut	M	I	NO	Runs	HS	Avge	100	50	Balls	Runs	Wkts	Avge	BB	5i	10m	RpO	ct	st
FC		13	19	4	376	100*	25.06	1	1	1693	877	44	19.93	5-47	2	0	3.10	6	
SL		2	1	1	1	1*		0	0	60	34	2	17.00	1-17	0	0	3.40	2	
FC	1996	16	22	4	381	100*	21.16	1	1	1933	986	48	20.54	5-47	2	0	3.06	7	
SL	1996	6	5	2	34	29	11.33	0	0	185	146	5	29.20	2-42	0	0	4.73	5	

PRESTON, Nicholas William b Dartford 22.1.1972 RHB RFM

Cmp	Debut	M	I	NO	Runs	HS	Avge	100	50	Balls	Runs	Wkts	Avge	BB	5i	10m	RpO	ct	st
FC		1	1	0	8	8	8.00	0	0	48	21	1	21.00	1-21	0	0	2.62	0	
FC	1996	9	12	4	71	17*	8.87	0	0	833	373	12	31.08	4-68	0	0	2.68	3	
SL	1996	5	2	1	11	7*	11.00	0	0	78	83	0					6.38	0	
NW	1996	1								36	6	0					1.00	1	

SMITH, Edward Thomas (Cambridge University, British Universities) b Pembury 19.7.1977 RHB RMF

Cmp	Debut	M	I	NO	Runs	HS	Avge	100	50	Balls	Runs	Wkts	Avge	BB	5i	10m	RpO	ct	st
FC		18	30	3	1163	190	43.07	2	6	12	22	0					11.00	7	
SL		4	3	2	146	72*	146.00	0	2									2	
BH		4	4	0	61	43	15.25	0	0									3	
FC	1996	25	42	3	1739	190	44.58	4	10	12	22	0					11.00	8	

STANFORD, Edward John b Dartford 21.1.1971 LHB SLA

Cmp	Debut	M	I	NO	Runs	HS	Avge	100	50	Balls	Runs	Wkts	Avge	BB	5i	10m	RpO	ct	st
FC		1	1	0	32	32	32.00	0	0	30	10	1	10.00	1-10	0	0	2.00	0	
FC	1995	5	6	4	48	32	24.00	0	0	902	388	9	43.11	3-84	0	0	2.58	2	

STRANG, Paul Andrew (Mashonaland, Zimbabwe, Zimbabwe to Pakistan, Zimbabwe to Sri Lanka, Zimbabwe to Sharjah, Zimbabwe to South Africa) b Bulawayo, Rhodesia 28.7.1970 RHB LBG

Cmp	Debut	M	I	NO	Runs	HS	Avge	100	50	Balls	Runs	Wkts	Avge	BB	5i	10m	RpO	ct	st
FC		17	26	2	590	82	24.58	0	5	4399	1929	63	30.61	7-118	4	1	2.63	17	
SL		17	12	1	165	40	15.00	0	0	669	531	16	33.18	3-31	0	0	4.76	5	
BH		8	7	5	86	38*	43.00	0	0	411	222	12	18.50	4-27	2	0	3.24	4	
NW		1	1	0	6	6	6.00	0	0	72	62	0					5.16	0	
Test	1994	13	21	5	505	106*	31.56	1	1	2894	1278	32	39.93	5-106	3	0	2.64	6	
FC	1992	61	91	19	2050	106*	28.47	2	11	13777	6424	200	32.12	7-75	15	2	2.79	50	
Int	1994	38	34	10	603	47	25.12	0	0	1872	1355	37	36.62	5-21	1	1	4.34	12	

THOMPSON, Julian Barton de Courcy b Cape Town, South Africa 28.10.1968 RHB RFM

Cmp	Debut	M	I	NO	Runs	HS	Avge	100	50	Balls	Runs	Wkts	Avge	BB	5i	10m	RpO	ct	st
FC		9	10	3	106	59*	15.14	0	1	1340	890	31	28.70	5-89	1	0	3.98	3	
SL		11	5	3	27	18*	13.50	0	0	424	322	11	29.27	3-17	0	0	4.55	1	
FC	1994	18	23	6	281	59*	16.52	0	1	2314	1503	47	31.97	5-72	2	0	3.89	4	
SL	1994	27	15	8	74	30	10.57	0	0	862	696	20	34.80	3-17	0	0	4.84	3	
BH	1996	4	3	2	17	12*	17.00	0	0	180	114	6	19.00	3-29	0	0	3.80	0	

WALKER, Matthew Jonathan b Gravesend 2.1.1974 LHB OB

Cmp	Debut	M	I	NO	Runs	HS	Avge	100	50	Balls	Runs	Wkts	Avge	BB	5i	10m	RpO	ct	st
FC		10	19	0	369	62	19.42	0	2									4	
SL		13	13	0	374	80	28.76	0	3									2	
BH		7	7	1	335	117	55.83	1	3									3	
NW		1	1	0	13	13	13.00	0	0									0	
FC	1992	33	55	5	1415	275*	28.30	2	5	6	19	0					19.00	16	
SL	1994	47	45	6	807	80	20.69	0	4									12	
BH	1995	18	17	3	611	117	43.64	1	4									8	
NW	1996	3	3	1	105	51	52.50	0	1									0	

WARD, Trevor Robert b Farningham 18.1.1968 RHB OB

Cmp	Debut	M	I	NO	Runs	HS	Avge	100	50	Balls	Runs	Wkts	Avge	BB	5i	10m	RpO	ct	st
FC		18	32	2	1018	161*	33.93	1	8	30	34	0					6.80	30	
SL		17	16	1	566	68*	37.73	0	4									5	
BH		8	8	0	182	78	22.75	0	1									3	
NW		1	0	0	0	0	0.00	0	0									0	
FC	1986	186	320	19	11241	235*	37.34	23	69	1071	643	8	80.37	2-10	0	0	3.60	180	
SL	1988	144	142	6	4150	131	30.51	3	26	228	187	6	31.16	3-20	0	0	4.92	33	

Cmp	Debut	M	I	NO	Runs	HS	Avge	100	50	Balls	Runs	Wkts	Avge	BB	5i	10m	RpO	ct	st
BH	1989	45	45	3	1522	125	36.23	2	10	12	10	0					5.00	11	
NW	1988	20	20	0	845	120	42.25	1	7	156	129	2	64.50	1-28	0	0	4.96	2	

WELLS, Alan Peter   b Newhaven 2.10.1961   RHB RM   (Sussex 1981-96)

Cmp	Debut	M	I	NO	Runs	HS	Avge	100	50	Balls	Runs	Wkts	Avge	BB	5i	10m	RpO	ct	st
FC		18	31	1	1120	109	37.33	1	9	108	55	0					3.05	16	
SL		16	15	2	321	56*	24.69	0	2									10	
BH		8	8	0	110	40	13.75	0	0									5	
NW		1	1	0	9	9	9.00	0	0									0	
Test	1995	1	2	1	3	3*	3.00	0	0									0	
FC	1981	339	568	78	19628	253*	40.04	44	93	1171	820	10	82.00	3-67	0	0	4.20	220	
Int	1995	1	1	0	15	15	15.00	0	0									0	
SL	1981	234	216	24	5803	127	30.22	3	36	62	69	4	17.25	1-0	0	0	6.67	69	
BH	1982	62	59	7	1528	74	29.38	0	14	60	72	3	24.00	1-17	0	0	7.20	15	
NW	1981	35	32	6	961	119	36.96	3	4	6	1	0					1.00	13	

WILLIS, Simon Charles   b Greenwich 19.3.1974   RHB WK

Cmp	Debut	M	I	NO	Runs	HS	Avge	100	50	Balls	Runs	Wkts	Avge	BB	5i	10m	RpO	ct	st
FC		1	2	1	37	19	37.00	0	0									1	
SL		1																0	1
FC	1993	10	13	3	331	82	33.10	0	3									24	
SL	1994	8	6	2	80	31*	20.00	0	0									11	1
BH	1995	1																0	
NW	1995	1	1	1	19	19*		0	0									1	

WREN, Timothy Neil   b Folkestone 26.3.1970   RHB LMF

Cmp	Debut	M	I	NO	Runs	HS	Avge	100	50	Balls	Runs	Wkts	Avge	BB	5i	10m	RpO	ct	st
FC		1	1	1	11	11*		0	0	52	22	2	11.00	2-22	0	0	2.53	0	
SL		3								102	96	0					5.64	1	
BH		1																0	
FC	1990	30	34	13	141	23	6.71	0	0	4024	2416	66	36.60	6-48	3	0	3.60	12	
SL	1989	35	12	9	34	7*	11.33	0	0	1329	1080	22	49.09	3-20	0	0	4.87	6	
BH	1995	8	3	1	11	7	5.50	0	0	324	256	13	19.69	6-41	0	1	4.74	2	
NW	1994	2	2	1	1	1*	1.00	0	0	120	92	1	92.00	1-51	0	0	4.60	0	

1997 AND CAREER FIGURES FOR LANCASHIRE PLAYERS

ATHERTON, Michael Andrew   (England, England to Zimbabwe, England to New Zealand)   b Manchester 23.3.1968   RHB LB

Cmp	Debut	M	I	NO	Runs	HS	Avge	100	50	Balls	Runs	Wkts	Avge	BB	5i	10m	RpO	ct	st
Test		6	12	1	257	77	23.36	0	2									2	
FC		16	28	2	853	149	32.80	2	5	6	7	0					7.00	8	
Int		3	3	1	118	113*	59.00	1	0									1	
SL		10	10	1	260	90*	28.88	0	1									2	
BH		4	4	0	61	24	15.25	0	0									3	
NW		2	2	0	10	8	5.00	0	0									1	
Test	1989	73	134	5	5243	185*	40.64	11	33	408	302	2	151.00	1-20	0	0	4.44	49	
FC	1987	249	431	39	16725	199	42.66	44	84	8981	4733	108	43.82	6-78	3	0	3.16	196	
Int	1990	53	53	3	1727	127	34.54	2	11									15	
SL	1987	83	81	6	2630	111	35.06	4	13	216	248	7	35.42	3-33	0	0	6.88	28	
BH	1987	54	53	4	1807	121*	36.87	3	11	252	228	7	32.57	4-42	1	0	5.42	29	
NW	1989	22	22	2	790	115	39.50	2	4	188	154	6	25.66	2-15	0	0	4.91	8	

AUSTIN, Ian David   b Haslingden 30.5.1966   LHB RM

Cmp	Debut	M	I	NO	Runs	HS	Avge	100	50	Balls	Runs	Wkts	Avge	BB	5i	10m	RpO	ct	st
FC		17	25	4	825	95	39.28	0	8	2692	1218	45	27.06	4-44	0	0	2.71	6	
SL		16	13	4	119	27*	13.22	0	0	635	432	19	22.73	3-25	0	0	4.08	2	
BH		5	5	0	138	35	27.60	0	0	294	172	9	19.11	3-33	0	0	3.51	3	
NW		2	2	0	99	97	49.50	0	1	138	67	3	22.33	2-45	0	0	2.91	0	
FC	1987	105	146	31	3349	115*	29.12	2	18	14143	6501	215	30.23	5-23	5	1	2.75	26	
SL	1986	155	97	38	1069	48	18.11	0	0	6408	4879	167	29.21	5-56	4	1	4.56	31	
BH	1987	50	32	9	549	80	23.86	0	2	2925	1867	63	29.63	4-8	3	0	3.82	12	
NW	1987	23	17	8	321	97	35.66	0	2	1503	920	27	34.07	3-32	0	0	3.67	1	

CHAPPLE, Glen   (England A, England A to Australia)   b Skipton 23.1.1974   RHB RMF

Cmp	Debut	M	I	NO	Runs	HS	Avge	100	50	Balls	Runs	Wkts	Avge	BB	5i	10m	RpO	ct	st
FC		11	14	4	237	66	23.70	0	2	1655	900	27	33.33	4-80	0	0	3.26	2	
SL		11	4	3	26	13*	26.00	0	0	402	382	10	38.20	3-22	0	0	5.70	3	
BH		1								30	23	0					4.60	0	
NW		2	1	1	2	2*		0	0	61	46	1	46.00	1-28	0	0	4.52	0	
FC	1992	74	102	38	1386	109*	21.65	1	3	12256	6470	214	30.23	6-48	8	0	3.16	24	
SL	1993	53	19	10	146	43	16.22	0	0	1968	1582	50	31.64	3-22	0	0	4.82	9	
BH	1994	14	4	3	20	8	20.00	0	0	750	584	13	44.92	3-31	0	0	4.67	2	
NW	1994	9	5	2	6	4	2.00	0	0	480	355	12	29.58	6-18	0	1	4.43	2	

CHILTON, Mark James   (British Universities)   b Sheffield 2.10.1976   RHB RM

Cmp	Debut	M	I	NO	Runs	HS	Avge	100	50	Balls	Runs	Wkts	Avge	BB	5i	10m	RpO	ct	st
FC		1	1	0	9	9	9.00	0	0	24	23	0					5.75	0	
SL		3	3	0	31	22	10.33	0	0	96	80	3	26.66	2-27	0	0	5.00	0	
BH		5	5	0	104	43	20.80	0	0	171	159	8	19.87	5-26	0	1	5.57	0	

CRAWLEY, John Paul (England, England to Zimbabwe, England to New Zealand) b Maldon 21.9.1971 RHB RM WK

Cmp	Debut	M	I	NO	Runs	HS	Avge	100	50	Balls	Runs	Wkts	Avge	BB	5i	10m	RpO	ct	st
Test		5	9	1	243	83	30.37	0	2									3	
FC		16	25	2	1141	133	49.60	3	7									11	
Int		1	1	0	52	52	52.00	0	1									0	
SL		11	11	1	267	83	26.70	0	2									3	
BH		5	5	0	39	37	7.80	0	0									3	
NW		2	2	1	124	113*	124.00	1	0	6	4	0					4.00	0	
Test	1994	22	35	4	1028	112	33.16	2	7									21	
FC	1990	154	252	26	11111	286	49.16	22	69	78	108	1	108.00	1-90	0	0	8.30	126	
Int	1994	10	9	0	180	73	20.00	0	2									1	
SL	1992	58	56	2	1368	91	25.33	0	10									17	
BH	1991	30	29	1	957	114	34.17	1	4									10	
NW	1994	11	11	1	362	113*	36.20	1	2	6	4	0					4.00	2	

FAIRBROTHER, Neil Harvey b Warrington 9.9.1963 LHB LM

Cmp	Debut	M	I	NO	Runs	HS	Avge	100	50	Balls	Runs	Wkts	Avge	BB	5i	10m	RpO	ct	st
FC		16	24	2	887	132	40.31	2	4									19	
SL		15	15	5	546	88	54.60	0	6									3	
BH		5	5	2	246	75*	82.00	0	3									1	
Test	1987	10	15	1	219	83	15.64	0	1	12	9	0					4.50	4	
FC	1982	303	483	68	17182	366	41.40	37	93	673	440	5	88.00	2-91	0	0	3.92	220	
Int	1986	56	54	13	1539	113	37.53	1	11	6	9	0					9.00	24	
SL	1982	200	186	45	5552	116*	39.37	4	36	48	48	1	48.00	1-33	0	0	6.00	60	
BH	1984	69	66	21	2471	116*	54.91	1	20	54	67	1	67.00	1-17	0	0	7.44	34	
NW	1984	34	33	5	1254	93*	44.78	0	9	48	44	1	44.00	1-28	0	0	5.50	18	

FLINTOFF, Andrew b Preston 6.12.1977 RHB RM

Cmp	Debut	M	I	NO	Runs	HS	Avge	100	50	Balls	Runs	Wkts	Avge	BB	5i	10m	RpO	ct	st
FC		5	8	0	243	117	30.37	1	1	60	11	1	11.00	1-11	0	0	1.10	4	
SL		4	4	0	83	31	20.75	0	0									2	
BH		1	1	0	0	0	0.00	0	0	24	17	0					4.25	0	
NW		1	1	0	2	2	2.00	0	0	35	21	0					3.60	0	
FC	1995	7	11	0	252	117	22.90	1	1	126	50	1	50.00	1-11	0	0	2.38	7	
SL	1995	7	7	0	119	31	17.00	0	0									2	
BH	1995	2	1	0	0	0	0.00	0	0	60	27	1	27.00	1-10	0	0	2.70	0	

GALLIAN, Jason Edward Riche (England A, England A to Australia) b Manly, Australia 25.6.1971 RHB RM

Cmp	Debut	M	I	NO	Runs	HS	Avge	100	50	Balls	Runs	Wkts	Avge	BB	5i	10m	RpO	ct	st
FC		11	19	2	506	106	29.76	1	3	500	375	8	46.87	3-51	0	0	4.50	12	
SL		10	10	3	424	104	60.57	2	2	168	144	4	36.00	1-23	0	0	5.14	5	
BH		5	5	0	151	59	30.20	0	2	72	60	1	60.00	1-13	0	0	5.00	1	
NW		1	1	0	1	1	1.00	0	0	42	37	0					5.28	0	
Test	1995	3	6	0	74	28	12.33	0	0	84	62	0					4.42	1	
FC	1990	91	159	13	5728	312	39.23	12	28	5657	3332	82	40.63	6-115	1	0	3.53	62	
SL	1994	46	45	7	1402	104	36.89	2	9	694	653	26	25.11	2-10	0	0	5.64	18	
BH	1992	25	24	1	763	134	33.17	2	5	479	383	13	29.46	5-15	0	1	4.79	4	
NW	1994	8	8	1	212	101*	30.28	1	0	120	88	1	88.00	1-11	0	0	4.40	3	

GREEN, Richard James b Warrington 13.3.1976 RHB RM

Cmp	Debut	M	I	NO	Runs	HS	Avge	100	50	Balls	Runs	Wkts	Avge	BB	5i	10m	RpO	ct	st
FC		4	5	2	93	51	31.00	0	1	614	320	5	64.00	3-66	0	0	3.12	1	
SL		5									156	150	6	25.00	3-18	0	0	5.76	1	
BH		5	3	1	13	7	6.50	0	0	249	231	6	38.50	2-33	0	0	5.56	1	
FC	1995	12	16	5	185	51	16.81	0	1	1861	1006	30	33.53	6-41	1	0	3.24	3	
SL	1995	12	1	1	0	0*		0	0	462	405	17	23.82	3-18	0	0	5.25	1	

HARVEY, Mark Edward b Burnley 26.6.1974 RHB RM

Cmp	Debut	M	I	NO	Runs	HS	Avge	100	50	Balls	Runs	Wkts	Avge	BB	5i	10m	RpO	ct	st
FC		2	4	0	49	25	12.25	0	0									1	
SL		2	1	0	8	8	8.00	0	0									0	
NW		1	1	0	86	86	86.00	0	1									1	
FC	1994	5	8	0	116	25	14.50	0	0									2	
BH	1995	4	4	0	9	5	2.25	0	0									3	

HAYNES, Jamie Jonathan b Bristol 5.7.1974 RHB WK

Cmp	Debut	M	I	NO	Runs	HS	Avge	100	50	Balls	Runs	Wkts	Avge	BB	5i	10m	RpO	ct	st
FC		2	3	0	41	21	13.66	0	0									12	
FC	1996	3	5	0	67	21	13.40	0	0									12	1
SL	1996	1																1	

HEGG, Warren Kevin (England A, England A to Australia) b Whitefield 23.2.1968 RHB WK

Cmp	Debut	M	I	NO	Runs	HS	Avge	100	50	Balls	Runs	Wkts	Avge	BB	5i	10m	RpO	ct	st
FC		17	23	5	456	77*	25.33	0	5									37	2
SL		15	11	3	141	31*	17.62	0	0									18	8
BH		5	5	2	83	54*	27.66	0	1									5	
NW		2	1	0	37	37	37.00	0	0									2	
FC	1986	223	325	63	6745	134	25.74	4	31	6	7	0					7.00	536	63
SL	1987	159	92	42	1120	52	22.40	0	1									160	24
BH	1988	54	24	10	371	81	26.50	0	2									74	5
NW	1988	27	16	1	288	37	19.20	0	0									35	2

KEEDY, Gary b Sandal, Wakefield 27.11.1974 LHB SLA

Cmp	Debut	M	I	NO	Runs	HS	Avge	100	50	Balls	Runs	Wkts	Avge	BB	5i	10m	RpO	ct	st
FC		8	8	7	11	6*	11.00	0	0	1756	917	27	33.96	6-79	1	1	3.13	1	
SL		1									31	47	0					9.09	0	

Cmp	Debut	M	I	NO	Runs	HS	Avge	100	50	Balls	Runs	Wkts	Avge	BB	5i	10m	RpO	ct	st
FC	1994	38	40	27	158	26	12.15	0	0	7805	3703	89	41.60	6-79	1	1	2.84	10	
SL	1995	5								175	175	1	175.00	1-40	0	0	6.00	0	

LLOYD, Graham David (England) b Accrington 1.7.1969 RHB RM

Cmp	Debut	M	I	NO	Runs	HS	Avge	100	50	Balls	Runs	Wkts	Avge	BB	5i	10m	RpO	ct	st
FC		16	24	2	1073	225	48.77	4	5	71	101	0					8.53	17	
Int		3	2	0	22	22	11.00	0	0									1	
SL		15	14	0	461	134	32.92	1	1									4	
BH		5	5	0	91	36	18.20	0	0	12	8	0					4.00	1	
NW		2	2	0	100	96	50.00	0	1	12	12	0					6.00	0	
FC	1988	145	236	24	8306	241	39.17	18	48	234	291	2	145.50	1-4	0	0	7.46	95	
Int	1996	5	4	1	39	22	13.00	0	0									2	
SL	1990	126	116	16	3222	134	32.22	3	19	12	18	0					9.00	27	
BH	1991	35	29	9	612	81*	30.60	0	3	30	50	0					10.00	5	
NW	1990	16	15	0	428	96	28.53	0	3	30	35	1	35.00	1-23	0	0	7.00	3	

McKEOWN, Patrick Christopher b Liverpool 1.6.1976 RHB OB

Cmp	Debut	M	I	NO	Runs	HS	Avge	100	50	Balls	Runs	Wkts	Avge	BB	5i	10m	RpO	ct	st
FC		4	6	0	135	46	22.50	0	0									2	
SL		4	4	0	39	37	9.75	0	0									2	
BH		1	1	0	10	10	10.00	0	0									0	
NW		1	1	0	42	42	42.00	0	0	60	51	0					5.10	0	
FC	1996	6	8	0	208	64	26.00	0	1									3	
SL	1996	9	9	0	156	69	17.33	0	1									5	

MARTIN, Peter James (England) b Accrington 15.11.1968 RHB RFM

Cmp	Debut	M	I	NO	Runs	HS	Avge	100	50	Balls	Runs	Wkts	Avge	BB	5i	10m	RpO	ct	st
Test		1	2	0	23	20	11.50	0	0	114	51	0					2.68	1	
FC		17	19	4	281	78*	18.73	0	1	2846	1342	58	23.13	8-32	3	1	2.82	4	
SL		16	5	2	17	11*	5.66	0	0	578	392	31	12.64	5-21	0	2	4.06	3	
BH		5	2	1	10	10*	10.00	0	0	291	197	11	17.90	3-31	0	0	4.06	1	
NW		2								129	60	1	60.00	1-14	0	0	2.79	0	
Test	1995	8	13	0	115	29	8.84	0	0	1452	580	17	34.11	4-60	0	0	2.39	6	
FC	1989	134	154	38	2316	133	19.96	1	5	22339	10414	341	30.53	8-32	7	1	2.79	34	
Int	1995	16	10	6	33	6	8.25	0	0	838	610	25	24.40	4-44	1	0	4.36	1	
SL	1990	81	25	15	149	35*	14.90	0	0	3120	2341	102	22.95	5-21	1	3	4.50	12	
BH	1993	19	6	5	28	10*	28.00	0	0	1053	719	25	28.76	3-31	0	0	4.09	5	
NW	1990	14	4	3	27	16	27.00	0	0	825	443	23	19.26	4-36	1	0	3.22	1	

RIDGWAY, Paul Matthew b Airedale 13.2.1977 RHB RFM

Cmp	Debut	M	I	NO	Runs	HS	Avge	100	50	Balls	Runs	Wkts	Avge	BB	5i	10m	RpO	ct	st
FC		2	2	1	0	0*	0.00	0	0	234	163	2	81.50	2-46	0	0	4.17	0	

SHADFORD, Darren James b Oldham 4.3.1975 RHB RMF

Cmp	Debut	M	I	NO	Runs	HS	Avge	100	50	Balls	Runs	Wkts	Avge	BB	5i	10m	RpO	ct	st
FC		8	10	3	106	30	15.14	0	0	894	786	19	41.36	5-80	1	0	5.27	5	
SL		7	3	2	3	2	3.00	0	0	251	246	11	22.36	3-30	0	0	5.88	3	
NW		1								42	31	0					4.42	0	
FC	1995	10	12	4	107	30	13.37	0	0	1073	893	22	40.59	5-80	1	0	4.99	5	
SL	1996	10	3	2	3	2	3.00	0	0	299	288	11	26.18	3-30	0	0	5.77	4	

TITCHARD, Stephen Paul b Warrington 17.12.1967 RHB RM

Cmp	Debut	M	I	NO	Runs	HS	Avge	100	50	Balls	Runs	Wkts	Avge	BB	5i	10m	RpO	ct	st
FC		6	9	0	180	79	20.00	0	1	90	47	3	15.66	1-11	0	0	3.13	2	
FC	1990	75	131	8	3945	163	32.07	4	25	312	171	4	42.75	1-11	0	0	3.28	52	
SL	1992	29	29	3	705	96	27.11	0	3									4	
BH	1992	3	3	0	101	82	33.66	0	1									1	
NW	1992	3	3	0	116	92	38.66	0	1									1	

WASIM AKRAM (Pakistan, PIA, Pakistan to Australia, Pakistan to Canada, Pakistan to Kenya, Pakistan to Sharjah) b Lahore 3.6.1966 LHB LF

Cmp	Debut	M	I	NO	Runs	HS	Avge	100	50	Balls	Runs	Wkts	Avge	BB	5i	10m	RpO	ct	st
FC		1	2	0	16	13	8.00	0	0	216	86	3	28.66	3-74	0	0	2.38	1	
SL		3	2	0	29	28	14.50	0	0	138	89	6	14.83	3-39	0	0	3.86	2	
BH		3	3	1	84	52*	42.00	0	0	168	120	5	24.00	2-31	0	0	4.28	0	
Test	1984	72	100	13	1944	257*	22.34	2	4	16464	7054	311	22.68	7-119	21	4	2.57	28	
FC	1984	197	271	31	5380	257*	22.41	5	18	39728	17731	829	21.39	8-30	63	15	2.67	67	
Int	1984	232	181	33	2180	86	14.72	0	4	11954	7517	333	22.57	5-15	13	5	3.77	56	
SL	1988	94	75	19	1250	51*	22.32	0	2	4060	2914	151	19.29	5-41	7	1	4.30	20	
BH	1988	31	24	5	538	64	28.31	0	3	1841	1208	59	20.47	5-10	2	2	3.93	2	
NW	1988	17	14	3	192	50	17.45	0	1	1090	681	23	29.60	4-27	2	0	3.74	5	

WATKINSON, Michael b Westhoughton 1.8.1961 RHB RMF/OB

Cmp	Debut	M	I	NO	Runs	HS	Avge	100	50	Balls	Runs	Wkts	Avge	BB	5i	10m	RpO	ct	st
FC		12	19	1	520	135	28.88	1	2	1390	805	20	40.25	3-35	0	0	3.47	5	
SL		12	11	0	162	66	14.72	0	1	228	224	8	28.00	3-23	0	0	5.89	6	
NW		1	1	0	36	36	36.00	0	0	42	41	1	41.00	1-41	0	0	5.85	0	
Test	1995	4	6	1	167	82*	33.40	0	1	672	348	10	34.80	3-64	0	0	3.10	1	
FC	1982	290	434	47	10276	161	26.55	10	48	45932	23940	709	33.76	8-30	26	3	3.12	146	
Int	1995	1								54	43	0					4.77	0	
SL	1982	214	169	37	2865	121	21.70	1	8	8208	6744	212	31.81	5-46	4	1	4.92	55	
BH	1983	70	50	12	785	76	20.65	0	4	3656	2565	86	29.82	5-44	3	2	4.20	21	
NW	1982	40	34	7	891	90	33.00	0	7	2411	1581	42	37.64	3-14	0	0	3.93	11	

Cmp	Debut	M	I	NO	Runs	HS	Avge	100	50	Balls	Runs	Wkts	Avge	BB	5i	10m	RpO	ct	st
WOOD, Nathan Theodore b Thornhill Edge 4.10.1974 LHB OB																			
FC		10	15	2	469	155	36.07	1	2	25	38	0					9.12	3	
FC	1996	11	16	2	470	155	33.57	1	2	25	38	0					9.12	3	
YATES, Gary b Ashton-under-Lyne 20.9.1967 RHB OB																			
FC		11	13	3	194	39	19.40	0	0	1816	963	29	33.20	5-59	1	0	3.18	7	
SL		16	10	7	85	18	28.33	0	0	552	455	15	30.33	3-29	0	0	4.94	4	
BH		5	4	1	32	14	10.66	0	0	300	214	6	35.66	2-36	0	0	4.28	2	
NW		2	1	1	34	34*		0	0	132	88	2	44.00	2-15	0	0	4.00	0	
FC	1990	66	87	34	1496	134*	28.22	3	3	11063	5821	137	42.48	5-34	3	0	3.15	26	
SL	1991	74	31	16	252	38	16.80	0	0	2640	2215	76	29.14	4-34	2	0	5.03	19	
BH	1991	26	10	2	97	26	12.12	0	0	1260	862	28	30.78	3-42	0	0	4.10	6	
NW	1994	12	7	4	69	34*	23.00	0	0	780	457	11	41.54	2-15	0	0	3.51	1	

1997 AND CAREER FIGURES FOR LEICESTERSHIRE PLAYERS

Cmp	Debut	M	I	NO	Runs	HS	Avge	100	50	Balls	Runs	Wkts	Avge	BB	5i	10m	RpO	ct	st
BRIMSON, Matthew Thomas (Leicestershire to South Africa) b Plumstead 1.12.1970 RHB SLA																			
FC		7	7	2	59	30*	11.80	0	0	1025	451	11	41.00	3-49	0	0	2.64	3	
SL		6	1	1	12	12*		0	0	234	201	7	28.71	3-37	0	0	5.15	2	
BH		5	1	0	0	0	0.00	0	0	287	186	6	31.00	2-36	0	0	3.88	1	
NW		1								72	16	2	8.00	2-16	0	0	1.33	0	
FC	1993	34	36	15	217	30*	10.33	0	0	4898	2384	67	35.58	5-12	2	0	2.92	6	
SL	1993	12	2	2	16	12*		0	0	492	383	13	29.46	3-23	0	0	4.67	2	
BH	1996	6	1	0	0	0	0.00	0	0	347	242	7	34.57	2-36	0	0	4.18	1	
NW	1996	2	1	0	9	9	9.00	0	0	136	50	5	10.00	3-34	0	0	2.20	0	
DAKIN, Jonathan Michael (Leicestershire to South Africa) b Hitchin 28.2.1973 LHB RM																			
FC		4	5	1	311	190	77.75	2	0	408	204	5	40.80	2-12	0	0	3.00	2	
SL		14	13	2	224	41*	20.36	0	0	336	330	13	25.38	3-38	0	0	5.89	3	
BH		5	5	2	115	45*	38.33	0	0	186	176	7	25.14	2-16	0	0	5.67	5	
NW		1	1	0	6	6	6.00	0	0									0	
FC	1993	16	24	3	706	190	33.61	3	2	1332	733	17	43.11	4-45	0	0	3.30	9	
SL	1993	51	46	6	570	45	14.25	0	0	1206	1190	39	30.51	3-23	0	0	5.92	12	
BH	1995	8	8	3	251	108*	50.20	1	0	198	203	7	29.00	2-16	0	0	6.15	5	
NW	1995	4	4	0	63	26	15.75	0	0	144	100	1	100.00	1-63	0	0	4.16	0	
HABIB, Aftab b Reading 7.2.1972 RHB RMF (Middlesex 1992-94)																			
FC		9	14	4	397	175*	39.70	1	1	24	37	0					9.25	4	
SL		6	6	3	114	45*	38.00	0	0									2	
BH		6	6	1	249	111	49.80	1	1									3	
FC	1992	29	45	9	1438	215	39.94	3	3	24	37	0					9.25	14	
SL	1993	18	16	6	338	99*	33.80	0	2	1	4	0					24.00	5	
NW	1995	2	2	0	38	35	19.00	0	0									0	
JOHNSON, Neil Clarkson (Natal) b Salisbury, Rhodesia 24.1.1970 LHB RFM																			
FC		12	18	5	819	150	63.00	2	5	696	420	8	52.50	3-61	0	0	3.62	13	
SL		11	11	1	300	79*	30.00	0	2	284	325	14	23.21	3-37	0	0	6.86	6	
BH		5	5	1	73	58	18.25	0	1	216	205	6	34.16	2-38	0	0	5.69	1	
NW		2	2	0	19	15	9.50	0	0	18	19	0					6.33	1	
FC	1989	64	97	14	2777	150	33.45	4	18	6608	3308	110	30.07	5-79	2	0	3.00	73	
MACMILLAN, Gregor Innes b Guildford 7.8.1969 RHB OB																			
FC		5	7	1	99	34	16.50	0	0	66	41	0					3.72	3	
SL		4	4	0	33	15	8.25	0	0									3	
BH		4	3	1	43	16*	21.50	0	0	18	28	0					9.33	1	
FC	1993	48	76	9	1848	122	27.58	3	9	2081	1203	23	52.30	3-13	0	0	3.46	51	
SL	1994	23	22	2	378	58	18.90	0	1	96	76	3	25.33	2-37	0	0	4.75	7	
BH	1992	15	14	2	339	77	28.25	0	2	107	109	2	54.50	1-18	0	0	6.11	4	
NW	1995	1	1	0	9	9	9.00	0	0	18	13	1	13.00	1-13	0	0	4.33	0	
MADDY, Darren Lee (Rest of England, ECB First Class Counties XI, Leicestershire to South Africa) b Leicester 23.5.1974 RHB RM																			
FC		19	30	1	1047	103	36.10	3	5	284	122	2	61.00	1-2	0	0	2.57	18	
SL		15	15	0	515	85	34.33	0	5	184	184	9	20.44	3-11	0	0	6.00	4	
BH		6	6	0	253	101	42.16	1	1	48	31	1	31.00	1-23	0	0	3.87	3	
NW		2	2	0	15	15	7.50	0	0	24	15	0					3.75	1	
FC	1994	52	85	4	2401	131	29.64	5	10	578	298	6	49.66	2-21	0	0	3.09	53	
SL	1993	58	50	5	1414	106*	31.42	1	12	738	739	24	30.79	3-11	0	0	6.00	23	
BH	1995	14	14	1	497	101	38.23	1	3	126	112	5	22.40	3-32	0	0	5.33	4	
NW	1995	5	5	0	62	34	12.40	0	0	132	109	4	27.25	2-38	0	0	4.95	1	
MASON, Timothy James b Leicester 12.4.1975 RHB OB																			
FC		1	1	0	4	4	4.00	0	0	34	22	2	11.00	2-21	0	0	3.88	1	
SL		10	9	4	56	17*	11.20	0	0	262	247	8	30.87	2-15	0	0	5.65	2	
BH		1	1	0	30	30	30.00	0	0	60	55	1	55.00	1-55	0	0	5.50	0	
NW		2	2	0	66	36	33.00	0	0	144	92	3	30.66	3-29	0	0	3.91	0	

Cmp	Debut	M	I	NO	Runs	HS	Avge	100	50	Balls	Runs	Wkts	Avge	BB	5i	10m	RpO	ct	st
FC	1994	3	2	0	7	4	3.50	0	0	226	123	3	41.00	2-21	0	0	3.26	4	
SL	1995	22	13	5	85	17*	10.62	0	0	700	635	14	45.35	2-15	0	0	5.44	3	
BH	1995	5	4	2	61	30	30.50	0	0	264	186	5	37.20	2-35	0	0	4.22	1	
NW	1995	4	3	0	71	36	23.66	0	0	288	164	3	54.66	3-29	0	0	3.41	3	

MILLNS, David James (Boland, Leicestershire to South Africa) b Clipstone 27.2.1965 LHB RF (Nottinghamshire 1988-89)

Cmp	Debut	M	I	NO	Runs	HS	Avge	100	50	Balls	Runs	Wkts	Avge	BB	5i	10m	RpO	ct	st
FC		15	15	2	449	121	34.53	2	1	2452	1341	49	27.36	6-61	2	1	3.28	2	
SL		3	2	2	6	3*		0	0	108	67	2	33.50	1-9	0	0	3.72	0	
BH		6	4	2	23	12	11.50	0	0	306	216	6	36.00	3-36	0	0	4.23	3	
NW		2	2	1	9	6*	9.00	0	0	114	81	1	81.00	1-25	0	0	4.26	0	
FC	1988	145	171	51	2455	121	20.45	3	6	22747	12973	465	27.89	9-37	21	4	3.42	64	
SL	1988	40	19	10	104	20*	11.55	0	0	1512	1323	31	42.67	2-11	0	0	5.25	9	
BH	1991	22	13	7	100	39*	16.66	0	0	1064	756	27	28.00	4-26	2	0	4.26	5	
NW	1991	11	5	3	49	29*	24.50	0	0	648	423	12	35.25	3-22	0	0	3.91	2	

MULLALLY, Alan David (England to Zimbabwe, England to New Zealand) b Southend-on-Sea 12.7.1969 RHB LFM (Hampshire 1988)

Cmp	Debut	M	I	NO	Runs	HS	Avge	100	50	Balls	Runs	Wkts	Avge	BB	5i	10m	RpO	ct	st
FC		13	12	6	43	13*	7.16	0	0	2299	1302	37	35.18	5-52	4	0	3.39	2	
SL		6	1	0	6	6	6.00	0	0	228	207	7	29.57	3-36	0	0	5.44	1	
BH		6	4	2	6	4	3.00	0	0	330	235	10	23.50	3-33	0	0	4.27	0	
NW		1	1	1	0	0*		0	0	72	59	0					4.91	0	
Test	1996	9	12	4	79	24	9.87	0	0	2379	927	28	33.10	3-44	0	0	2.33	1	
FC	1987	142	159	42	1034	75	8.83	0	2	26115	12608	393	32.08	7-72	13	2	2.89	28	
Int	1996	8	3	0	22	20	7.33	0	0	396	276	10	27.60	3-29	0	0	4.18	3	
SL	1990	80	34	16	181	38	10.05	0	0	3491	2663	83	32.08	5-15	0	1	4.57	16	
BH	1990	32	14	5	33	11	3.66	0	0	1780	1131	29	39.00	3-33	0	0	3.81	0	
NW	1990	14	8	5	42	19*	14.00	0	0	864	497	18	27.61	2-22	0	0	3.45	2	

NIXON, Paul Andrew (ECB First Class Counties XI, Leicestershire to South Africa) b Carlisle 21.10.1970 LHB WK

Cmp	Debut	M	I	NO	Runs	HS	Avge	100	50	Balls	Runs	Wkts	Avge	BB	5i	10m	RpO	ct	st
FC		19	25	9	708	96	44.25	0	4	12	4	0					2.00	57	4
SL		15	14	2	181	33	15.08	0	0									11	3
BH		6	5	1	98	53	24.50	0	1									11	2
NW		2	2	0	15	14	7.50	0	0									2	1
FC	1989	144	206	48	4803	131	30.39	8	19	12	4	0					2.00	382	31
SL	1989	109	91	15	1498	84	19.71	0	6									83	21
BH	1992	18	16	2	223	53	15.92	0	1									17	4
NW	1990	16	14	4	219	39	21.90	0	0									18	5

ORMOND, James (ECB First Class Counties XI) b Wallsgrave, Coventry 20.8.1977 RHB RMF

Cmp	Debut	M	I	NO	Runs	HS	Avge	100	50	Balls	Runs	Wkts	Avge	BB	5i	10m	RpO	ct	st
FC		13	12	2	69	35	6.90	0	0	2073	1162	44	26.40	6-54	3	0	3.36	2	
SL		8	7	4	70	18	23.33	0	0	234	167	9	18.55	3-30	0	0	4.28	1	
FC	1995	14	12	2	69	35	6.90	0	0	2175	1227	46	26.67	6-54	3	0	3.38	3	
SL	1995	12	8	5	72	18	24.00	0	0	336	271	10	27.10	3-30	0	0	4.83	1	

PARSONS, Gordon James (Leicestershire to South Africa) b Slough 17.10.1959 LHB RMF (Warwickshire 1986-88)

Cmp	Debut	M	I	NO	Runs	HS	Avge	100	50	Balls	Runs	Wkts	Avge	BB	5i	10m	RpO	ct	st
FC		6	6	1	113	69*	22.60	0	1	1094	500	13	38.46	4-22	0	0	2.74	1	
SL		11	6	4	70	41*	35.00	0	0	456	345	8	43.12	2-9	0	0	4.53	3	
BH		1	1	0	4	4	4.00	0	0	60	39	1	39.00	1-39	0	0	3.90	2	
NW		2	2	0	17	9	8.50	0	0	144	102	3	34.00	3-68	0	0	4.25	0	
FC	1978	338	449	100	6763	76	19.37	0	29	49923	24509	809	30.29	9-72	19	1	2.94	147	
SL	1979	207	129	55	1183	41*	15.98	0	0	8545	6332	203	31.19	4-19	5	0	4.44	31	
BH	1981	61	35	14	357	63*	17.00	0	1	3300	1985	72	27.56	4-12	2	0	3.60	13	
NW	1980	34	23	6	189	25*	11.11	0	0	1928	1199	28	42.82	3-68	0	0	3.73	7	

PIERSON, Adrian Roger Kirshaw (Leicestershire to South Africa) b Enfield 21.7.1963 RHB OB (Warwickshire 1985-91)

Cmp	Debut	M	I	NO	Runs	HS	Avge	100	50	Balls	Runs	Wkts	Avge	BB	5i	10m	RpO	ct	st
FC		16	16	0	266	59	16.62	0	1	2995	1478	38	38.89	6-56	1	0	2.96	8	
SL		1								6	11	0					11.00	1	
FC	1985	147	180	60	1948	59	16.23	0	3	23313	11815	322	36.69	8-42	13	0	3.04	72	
SL	1985	68	35	14	202	29*	9.61	0	0	2547	2094	61	34.32	5-36	1	1	4.93	31	
BH	1986	17	12	8	47	11	11.75	0	0	866	530	12	44.16	3-34	0	0	3.67	5	
NW	1988	11	6	2	33	20*	8.25	0	0	668	345	9	38.33	3-20	0	0	3.09	2	

SMITH, Benjamin Francis (Leicestershire to South Africa) b Corby 3.4.1972 RHB RM

Cmp	Debut	M	I	NO	Runs	HS	Avge	100	50	Balls	Runs	Wkts	Avge	BB	5i	10m	RpO	ct	st
FC		13	19	5	624	131*	44.57	2	2	6	4	0					4.00	3	
SL		12	12	1	275	71	25.00	0	2									4	
BH		2	2	0	72	61	36.00	0	1									1	
NW		1	1	0	4	4	4.00	0	0									1	
FC	1990	109	167	25	4726	190	33.28	7	23	231	194	2	97.00	1-5	0	0	5.03	41	
SL	1990	96	94	11	2197	115	26.46	1	8	18	15	0					5.00	23	
BH	1992	19	17	0	418	61	24.58	0	3									9	
NW	1991	9	8	1	170	63*	24.28	0	1									3	

STEVENS, Darren Ian b Leicester 30.4.1976 RHB RM

Cmp	Debut	M	I	NO	Runs	HS	Avge	100	50	Balls	Runs	Wkts	Avge	BB	5i	10m	RpO	ct	st
FC		2	2	0	35	27	17.50	0	0	12	5	1	5.00	1-5	0	0	2.50	1	
SL		2	2	0	7	6	3.50	0	0									1	

Cmp	Debut	M	I	NO	Runs	HS	Avge	100	50	Balls	Runs	Wkts	Avge	BB	5i	10m	RpO	ct	st

SUTCLIFFE, Iain John (Leicestershire to South Africa) b Leeds 20.12.1974 LHB OB

Cmp	Debut	M	I	NO	Runs	HS	Avge	100	50	Balls	Runs	Wkts	Avge	BB	5i	10m	RpO	ct	st
FC		13	20	2	727	130	40.38	2	3	6	12	0					12.00	6	
SL		7	7	1	182	96	30.33	0	1									2	
BH		3	3	0	85	59	28.33	0	1									0	
NW		2	2	1	193	103*	193.00	1	1									0	
FC	1994	41	62	7	2036	163*	37.01	3	13	198	149	4	37.25	2-21	0	0	4.51	18	
SL	1995	8	8	1	196	96	28.00	0	1									4	
BH	1995	6	6	0	155	59	25.83	0	1									0	
NW	1995	4	4	1	276	103*	92.00	1	2									1	

WELLS, Vincent John (Leicestershire to South Africa) b Dartford 6.8.1965 RHB RM WK (Kent 1987-93)

Cmp	Debut	M	I	NO	Runs	HS	Avge	100	50	Balls	Runs	Wkts	Avge	BB	5i	10m	RpO	ct	st
FC		18	27	0	1200	224	44.44	3	6	1224	671	17	39.47	2-8	0	0	3.28	10	
SL		15	15	0	376	69	25.06	0	2	419	366	12	30.50	3-33	0	0	5.24	3	
BH		5	5	0	211	90	42.20	0	2	250	170	8	21.25	3-35	0	0	4.08	0	
NW		2	2	0	0	0	0.00	0	0	132	70	4	17.50	3-30	0	0	3.18	0	
FC	1988	115	182	14	5735	224	34.13	9	29	9563	4851	174	27.87	5-43	2	0	3.04	75	
SL	1987	93	87	12	2046	101	27.28	2	9	2922	2416	86	28.09	5-10	2	1	4.96	22	
BH	1988	29	26	3	609	90	26.47	0	3	1126	867	28	30.96	4-37	1	0	4.61	8	
NW	1990	13	13	3	427	201	42.70	2	0	521	314	14	22.42	3-30	0	0	3.61	0	

WHITAKER, John James (Leicestershire to South Africa) b Skipton 5.5.1962 RHB OB

Cmp	Debut	M	I	NO	Runs	HS	Avge	100	50	Balls	Runs	Wkts	Avge	BB	5i	10m	RpO	ct	st
FC		16	23	2	919	133*	43.76	3	4	2	0	0					0.00	5	
SL		14	14	0	400	74	28.57	0	4									8	
BH		5	5	1	115	51	28.75	0	2									1	
NW		2	2	0	17	12	8.50	0	0									0	
Test	1986	1	1	0	11	11	11.00	0	0									1	
FC	1983	309	490	51	17068	218	38.87	38	80	178	268	2	134.00	1-29	0	0	9.03	171	
Int	1986	2	2	1	48	44*	48.00	0	0									1	
SL	1983	183	171	18	5025	132	32.84	4	31	2	4	0					12.00	52	
BH	1984	58	53	3	1490	100	29.80	1	10									10	
NW	1984	30	29	2	1077	155	39.88	1	6	24	9	0					2.25	1	

WILLIAMSON, Dominic b Durham 15.11.1975 RHB RM

Cmp	Debut	M	I	NO	Runs	HS	Avge	100	50	Balls	Runs	Wkts	Avge	BB	5i	10m	RpO	ct	st
FC		1	1	0	3	3	3.00	0	0	107	40	4	10.00	3-19	0	0	2.24	0	
SL		5	4	2	28	17	14.00	0	0	196	147	8	18.37	5-32	0	1	4.50	3	
FC	1996	2	1	0	3	3	3.00	0	0	281	135	5	27.00	3-19	0	0	2.88	0	
SL	1996	18	12	7	53	17	10.60	0	0	531	442	15	29.46	5-32	0	1	4.99	6	
BH	1996	2	1	0	6	6	6.00	0	0	84	91	1	91.00	1-64	0	0	6.50	0	

1997 AND CAREER RECORDS FOR MIDDLESEX PLAYERS

BLANCHETT, Ian Neale b Melbourne, Australia 2.10.1975 RHB RFM

Cmp	Debut	M	I	NO	Runs	HS	Avge	100	50	Balls	Runs	Wkts	Avge	BB	5i	10m	RpO	ct	st
SL		5	2	1	2	1*	2.00	0	0	162	184	1	184.00	1-51	0	0	6.81	2	
BH		1								36	44	1	44.00	1-44	0	0	7.33	0	

BLOOMFIELD, Timothy Francis b Ashford 31.5.1973 RHB RMF

Cmp	Debut	M	I	NO	Runs	HS	Avge	100	50	Balls	Runs	Wkts	Avge	BB	5i	10m	RpO	ct	st
FC		4	3	2	4	4	4.00	0	0	510	258	13	19.84	5-77	1	0	3.03	2	
SL		6	1	0	1	1	1.00	0	0	234	198	6	33.00	2-8	0	0	5.07	1	
NW		1								48	25	1	25.00	1-25	0	0	3.12	0	

BROWN, Keith Robert b Edmonton 18.3.1963 RHB RM WK

Cmp	Debut	M	I	NO	Runs	HS	Avge	100	50	Balls	Runs	Wkts	Avge	BB	5i	10m	RpO	ct	st
FC		19	29	9	601	144*	30.05	1	2									47	3
SL		13	12	4	159	44*	19.87	0	0									11	2
BH		4	4	1	91	42*	30.33	0	0									5	2
NW		3	3	0	88	50	29.33	0	1									8	
FC	1984	230	348	69	9911	200*	35.52	13	54	321	276	6	46.00	2-7	0	0	5.15	425	28
SL	1985	162	137	41	2805	102	29.21	1	10	28	29	0					6.21	101	28
BH	1988	39	36	7	726	75	25.03	0	2	6	0	0					0.00	28	9
NW	1987	24	21	3	536	103*	29.77	1	1	6	8	0					8.00	23	6

COOK, Simon James b Oxford 15.1.1977 RHB RFM

Cmp	Debut	M	I	NO	Runs	HS	Avge	100	50	Balls	Runs	Wkts	Avge	BB	5i	10m	RpO	ct	st
BH		1	1	0	6	6	6.00	0	0	54	71	0					7.88	0	

DUTCH, Keith Philip b Harrow 21.3.1973 RHB OB

Cmp	Debut	M	I	NO	Runs	HS	Avge	100	50	Balls	Runs	Wkts	Avge	BB	5i	10m	RpO	ct	st
FC		7	9	2	138	79	19.71	0	1	529	289	9	32.11	3-79	0	0	3.27	2	
SL		14	10	3	114	58	16.28	0	1	455	375	10	37.50	2-19	0	0	4.94	1	
BH		4	4	0	30	20	7.50	0	0	96	85	6	14.16	4-42	1	0	5.31	0	
NW		2	2	1	9	6*	9.00	0	0	132	78	1	78.00	1-24	0	0	3.54	1	
FC	1993	12	13	2	177	79	16.09	0	1	781	416	12	34.66	3-25	0	0	3.19	8	
SL	1995	26	20	5	181	58	12.06	0	1	684	581	17	34.17	3-10	0	0	5.09	6	
BH	1996	5	5	0	43	20	8.60	0	0	126	118	6	19.66	4-42	1	0	5.61	0	

FAY, Richard Anthony b Kilburn 14.5.1974 RHB RM

Cmp	Debut	M	I	NO	Runs	HS	Avge	100	50	Balls	Runs	Wkts	Avge	BB	5i	10m	RpO	ct	st
SL		2								96	50	3	16.66	2-23	0	0	3.12	0	
BH		1	1	1	3	3*		0	0	60	63	1	63.00	1-63	0	0	6.30	0	
FC	1995	16	25	3	164	26	7.45	0	0	2178	1146	31	36.96	4-53	0	0	3.15	5	
SL	1995	22	8	5	36	12*	12.00	0	0	906	656	22	29.81	4-33	1	0	4.34	2	

Cmp	Debut	M	I	NO	Runs	HS	Avge	100	50	Balls	Runs	Wkts	Avge	BB	5i	10m	RpO	ct	st
BH	1996	5	3	1	4	3*	2.00	0	0	264	186	4	46.50	1-13	0	0	4.22	0	
NW	1996	2	1	0	0	0	0.00	0	0	102	63	3	21.00	2-43	0	0	3.70	2	

FRASER, Angus Robert Charles b Billinge 8.8.1965 RHB RFM

Cmp	Debut	M	I	NO	Runs	HS	Avge	100	50	Balls	Runs	Wkts	Avge	BB	5i	10m	RpO	ct	st
FC		19	23	6	244	35	14.35	0	0	3431	1460	47	31.06	6-77	2	0	2.55	4	
SL		14	7	2	65	33	13.00	0	0	648	430	20	21.50	3-10	0	0	3.98	2	
BH		4	4	2	35	30*	17.50	0	0	222	114	4	28.50	1-23	0	0	3.08	0	
NW		3	1	1	9	9*		0	0	210	103	3	34.33	2-22	0	0	2.94	1	
Test	1989	32	46	10	265	29	7.36	0	0	7967	3509	119	29.48	8-75	8	0	2.64	7	
FC	1984	220	258	63	2175	92	11.15	0	1	42138	18208	660	27.58	8-75	26	3	2.59	42	
Int	1989	33	14	6	80	38*	10.00	0	0	1876	1132	38	29.78	4-22	1	0	3.62	1	
SL	1985	145	56	24	366	33	11.43	0	0	6392	4277	151	28.32	5-32	3	1	4.01	21	
BH	1985	39	22	11	100	30*	9.09	0	0	2295	1313	49	26.79	4-49	1	0	3.43	7	
NW	1987	28	10	8	65	19	32.50	0	0	1833	927	41	22.60	4-34	2	0	3.03	4	

GATTING, Michael William b Kingsbury 6.6.1957 RHB RM

Cmp	Debut	M	I	NO	Runs	HS	Avge	100	50	Balls	Runs	Wkts	Avge	BB	5i	10m	RpO	ct	st
FC		19	29	2	1053	160*	39.00	2	4	42	46	1	46.00	1-46	0	0	6.57	23	
SL		11	10	1	164	82*	18.22	0	1									5	
BH		4	4	0	62	23	15.50	0	0									2	
NW		3	3	0	30	20	10.00	0	0									1	
Test	1977	79	138	14	4409	207	35.55	10	21	752	317	4	79.25	1-14	0	0	2.52	59	
FC	1975	534	832	120	35410	207	49.73	92	174	10031	4694	157	29.89	5-34	2	0	2.80	474	
Int	1977	92	88	17	2095	115*	29.50	1	9	392	336	10	33.60	3-32	0	0	5.14	22	
SL	1975	268	241	30	6671	124*	31.61	6	40	3196	2730	90	30.33	4-30	3	0	5.12	90	
BH	1976	96	90	18	2921	143*	40.56	3	18	1382	940	41	22.92	4-49	1	0	4.08	30	
NW	1975	64	62	13	2113	132*	43.12	2	15	1004	643	19	33.84	2-14	0	0	3.84	25	

HEWITT, James Peter b Southwark 26.2.1976 LHB LM

Cmp	Debut	M	I	NO	Runs	HS	Avge	100	50	Balls	Runs	Wkts	Avge	BB	5i	10m	RpO	ct	st
FC		18	21	4	264	75	15.52	0	1	2622	1389	60	23.15	6-14	2	0	3.17	6	
SL		14	6	2	69	32*	17.25	0	0	618	435	17	25.58	2-24	0	0	4.22	2	
BH		4	4	0	22	14	5.50	0	0	210	178	4	44.50	2-49	0	0	5.08	1	
NW		3	2	2	18	14*		0	0	150	117	2	58.50	1-37	0	0	4.68	1	
FC	1996	28	36	8	576	75	20.57	0	2	3699	2070	84	24.64	6-14	2	0	3.35	11	
SL	1995	27	13	4	118	32*	13.11	0	0	999	737	29	25.41	3-26	0	0	4.42	8	

JOHNSON, Richard Leonard b Chertsey 29.12.1974 RHB RMF

Cmp	Debut	M	I	NO	Runs	HS	Avge	100	50	Balls	Runs	Wkts	Avge	BB	5i	10m	RpO	ct	st
FC		18	24	1	320	39	13.91	0	0	2576	1429	50	28.58	4-26	0	0	3.32	6	
SL		10	7	2	72	29	14.40	0	0	378	366	12	30.50	3-35	0	0	5.80	0	
BH		3	3	0	39	19	13.00	0	0	174	154	3	51.33	2-50	0	0	5.31	0	
NW		3	2	0	8	8	4.00	0	0	156	130	8	16.25	5-50	0	1	5.00	0	
FC	1992	56	77	8	1005	50*	14.56	0	1	8370	4417	158	27.95	10-45	4	2	3.16	23	
SL	1993	51	31	12	256	29	13.47	0	0	2089	1872	50	37.44	4-66	1	0	5.37	6	
BH	1994	9	8	0	58	19	7.25	0	0	456	380	5	76.00	2-50	0	0	5.00	1	
NW	1993	11	9	2	106	33	15.14	0	0	600	416	17	24.47	5-50	0	1	4.16	0	

KALLIS, Jacques Henry (Western Province, South Africa) b Newlands, South Africa 16.10.1975 RHB RM

Cmp	Debut	M	I	NO	Runs	HS	Avge	100	50	Balls	Runs	Wkts	Avge	BB	5i	10m	RpO	ct	st
FC		16	25	3	1034	172*	47.00	4	4	1407	655	32	20.46	5-54	1	0	2.79	15	
SL		11	10	0	140	24	14.00	0	0	206	124	5	24.80	2-19	0	0	3.61	4	
BH		2	2	0	82	72	41.00	0	1	90	79	2	39.50	2-49	0	0	5.26	0	
NW		3	3	0	116	100	38.66	1	0	138	107	5	21.40	4-47	1	0	4.65	1	
Test	1995	5	7	0	57	39	8.14	0	0	376	136	5	27.20	3-29	0	0	2.17	1	
FC	1993	54	80	8	3271	186*	45.43	8	19	4523	2079	76	27.35	5-54	2	0	2.75	36	
Int	1995	25	24	6	700	82	38.88	0	6	570	459	8	57.37	3-21	0	0	4.83	5	

MARTIN, Neil Donald b Enfield 19.8.1979 RHB RFM

Cmp	Debut	M	I	NO	Runs	HS	Avge	100	50	Balls	Runs	Wkts	Avge	BB	5i	10m	RpO	ct	st
SL		1								36	29	1	29.00	1-29	0	0	4.83	0	

MOFFAT, Scott Park b Germiston, South Africa 1.2.1973 RHB OB

Cmp	Debut	M	I	NO	Runs	HS	Avge	100	50	Balls	Runs	Wkts	Avge	BB	5i	10m	RpO	ct	st
FC		4	6	1	122	47	24.40	0	0									2	
SL		6	5	0	77	29	15.40	0	0									1	
BH		2	2	0	62	60	31.00	0	1									1	
FC	1996	5	7	1	122	47	20.33	0	0									2	

NASH, David Charles b Chertsey 19.1.1978 RHB WK

Cmp	Debut	M	I	NO	Runs	HS	Avge	100	50	Balls	Runs	Wkts	Avge	BB	5i	10m	RpO	ct	st
FC		6	8	2	332	100	55.33	1	1	18	19	1	19.00	1-8	0	0	6.33	4	
SL		6	5	0	69	23	13.80	0	0									5	
SL	1995	7	5	0	69	23	13.80	0	0									7	1

POOLEY, Jason Calvin b Hammersmith 8.8.1969 LHB OB

Cmp	Debut	M	I	NO	Runs	HS	Avge	100	50	Balls	Runs	Wkts	Avge	BB	5i	10m	RpO	ct	st
FC		18	28	1	619	98	22.92	0	3									21	
SL		13	12	3	438	94*	48.66	0	5									5	
BH		4	4	1	82	50*	27.33	0	1									0	
NW		3	3	1	125	79*	62.50	0	1									0	
FC	1989	81	137	12	3811	138*	30.48	8	17	60	68	0					6.80	81	
SL	1991	57	54	6	1354	109	28.20	1	10									18	
BH	1991	18	18	1	351	50*	20.64	0	2									5	
NW	1994	8	8	1	204	79*	29.14	0	1									1	

Cmp	Debut	M	I	NO	Runs	HS	Avge	100	50	Balls	Runs	Wkts	Avge	BB	5i	10m	RpO	ct	st

RAMPRAKASH, Mark Ravin (England, Rest of England) b Bushey 5.9.1969 RHB RM/OB

Cmp	Debut	M	I	NO	Runs	HS	Avge	100	50	Balls	Runs	Wkts	Avge	BB	5i	10m	RpO	ct	st
Test		1	2	0	52	48	26.00	0	0									0	
FC		19	30	4	1453	190	55.88	6	7	212	126	2	63.00	1-30	0	0	3.56	9	
SL		12	11	1	329	90	32.90	0	3	27	28	1	28.00	1-26	0	0	6.22	3	
BH		3	3	0	155	77	51.66	0	1									4	
NW		3	3	0	212	98	70.66	0	2	78	45	0					3.46	3	
Test	1991	20	35	1	585	72	17.20	0	2	265	149	0					3.37	13	
FC	1987	224	364	47	14596	235	46.04	39	72	1925	1151	18	63.94	3-91	0	0	3.58	120	
Int	1991	10	10	3	184	32	26.28	0	0	12	14	0					7.00	5	
SL	1987	130	123	23	4289	147*	42.89	4	30	289	309	13	23.76	5-38	0	1	6.41	39	
BH	1989	35	34	7	1130	119*	41.85	2	6	126	94	3	31.33	3-35	0	0	4.47	14	
NW	1988	24	23	1	734	104	33.36	1	3	282	169	6	28.16	2-15	0	0	3.59	9	

SHAH, Owais Alam (England A to Australia) b Karachi, Pakistan 22.10.1978 RHB OB

Cmp	Debut	M	I	NO	Runs	HS	Avge	100	50	Balls	Runs	Wkts	Avge	BB	5i	10m	RpO	ct	st
FC		11	16	2	548	104*	39.14	1	2	12	19	0					9.50	14	
SL		7	7	2	201	66*	40.20	0	2	12	29	0					14.50	1	
NW		3	3	1	46	27*	23.00	0	0									1	
FC	1996	18	28	3	813	104*	32.52	1	4	42	43	1	43.00	1-24	0	0	6.16	16	
SL	1995	23	20	5	448	66*	29.86	0	3	19	33	1	33.00	1-4	0	0	10.42	6	
BH	1996	3	3	1	52	42*	26.00	0	0									0	
NW	1996	4	4	1	57	27*	19.00	0	0									0	

STRAUSS, Andrew John (British Universities) b Johannesburg, South Africa 2.3.1977 LHB

Cmp	Debut	M	I	NO	Runs	HS	Avge	100	50	Balls	Runs	Wkts	Avge	BB	5i	10m	RpO	ct	st
SL		2	2	0	7	4	3.50	0	0									1	
BH		1	1	0	1	1	1.00	0	0									0	

TUFNELL, Philip Clive Roderick (England, England to Zimbabwe, England to New Zealand) b Barnet 29.4.1966 RHB SLA

Cmp	Debut	M	I	NO	Runs	HS	Avge	100	50	Balls	Runs	Wkts	Avge	BB	5i	10m	RpO	ct	st
Test		1	2	0	1	1	0.50	0	0	286	93	11	8.45	7-66	1	1	1.95	0	
FC		17	21	6	101	21	6.73	0	0	3371	1205	55	21.90	7-66	3	1	2.14	4	
SL		2	1	0	7	7	7.00	0	0	96	103	1	103.00	1-56	0	0	6.43	0	
BH		2	2	0	12	10	6.00	0	0	96	72	2	36.00	1-35	0	0	4.50	0	
Test	1990	28	39	20	112	22*	5.89	0	0	7953	3198	93	34.38	7-47	5	2	2.41	11	
FC	1986	222	235	95	1445	67*	10.32	0	1	54457	22265	767	29.02	8-29	40	5	2.45	93	
Int	1990	20	10	9	15	5*	15.00	0	0	1020	699	19	36.78	4-22	1	0	4.11	4	
SL	1988	33	10	5	30	13*	6.00	0	0	1392	1064	41	25.95	5-28	2	1	4.58	3	
BH	1990	15	8	4	56	18	14.00	0	0	809	591	15	39.40	3-32	0	0	4.38	2	
NW	1988	8	1	0	8	8	8.00	0	0	570	323	10	32.30	3-29	0	0	3.40	4	

WEEKES, Paul Nicholas b Hackney 8.7.1969 LHB OB

Cmp	Debut	M	I	NO	Runs	HS	Avge	100	50	Balls	Runs	Wkts	Avge	BB	5i	10m	RpO	ct	st
FC		15	24	0	439	101	18.29	1	0	858	432	6	72.00	2-35	0	0	3.02	18	
SL		15	14	1	306	53*	23.53	0	2	438	369	17	21.70	4-38	2	0	5.05	4	
BH		4	4	0	158	77	39.50	0	1	162	143	1	143.00	1-47	0	0	5.29	2	
NW		3	3	0	46	34	15.33	0	0	168	136	3	45.33	1-35	0	0	4.85	1	
FC	1990	103	157	15	4425	171*	31.16	8	18	10312	4905	120	40.87	8-39	3	0	2.85	84	
SL	1990	108	87	12	2004	119*	26.72	1	10	3767	3201	119	26.89	4-29	9	0	5.09	43	
BH	1990	26	23	3	588	77	29.40	0	4	1118	817	21	38.90	3-32	0	0	4.38	6	
NW	1991	12	12	1	380	143*	34.54	2	1	701	494	14	35.28	3-35	0	0	4.22	4	

WELLINGS, Peter Edward b Wolverhampton 5.3.1970 RHB RM

Cmp	Debut	M	I	NO	Runs	HS	Avge	100	50	Balls	Runs	Wkts	Avge	BB	5i	10m	RpO	ct	st
FC		2	2	1	141	128*	141.00	1	0	18	18	0					6.00	1	
SL		1	1	0	12	12	12.00	0	0	6	9	0					9.00	1	
BH		1	1	0	23	23	23.00	0	0									0	
FC	1996	6	10	2	378	128*	47.25	1	0	18	18	0					6.00	2	
SL	1996	9	8	1	82	42	11.71	0	0	48	81	2	40.50	1-22	0	0	10.12	4	
BH	1996	2	2	1	37	23	37.00	0	0	35	45	1	45.00	1-45	0	0	7.71	1	
NW	1996	1	1	1	9	9*		0	0	36	20	1	20.00	1-20	0	0	3.33	0	

1997 AND CAREER RECORDS FOR NORTHAMPTONSHIRE PLAYERS

BAILEY, Robert John b Biddulph 28.10.1963 RHB OB

Cmp	Debut	M	I	NO	Runs	HS	Avge	100	50	Balls	Runs	Wkts	Avge	BB	5i	10m	RpO	ct	st
FC		17	30	5	1078	117*	43.12	3	5	675	367	10	36.70	4-10	0	0	3.26	19	
SL		13	12	2	381	75	38.10	0	5	126	121	3	40.33	1-18	0	0	5.76	2	
BH		6	6	2	282	73*	70.50	0	3	30	17	1	17.00	1-1	0	0	3.40	3	
NW		2	2	0	33	23	16.50	0	0	72	67	3	22.33	3-55	0	0	5.58	2	
Test	1988	4	8	0	119	43	14.87	0	0									0	
FC	1982	317	537	80	19099	224*	41.79	42	99	8468	4561	105	43.43	5-54	2	0	3.23	241	
Int	1984	4	4	2	137	43*	68.50	0	0	36	25	0					4.16	1	
SL	1983	210	198	31	6016	125*	36.02	4	41	1294	1229	38	32.34	3-23	0	0	5.69	54	
BH	1984	64	61	10	2538	134	49.76	4	19	390	260	3	86.66	1-1	0	0	4.00	18	
NW	1983	46	46	12	1562	145	45.94	1	10	654	407	16	25.43	3-47	0	0	3.73	17	

BAILEY, Tobin Michael Barnaby (British Universities) b Kettering 28.8.1976 RHB WK

Cmp	Debut	M	I	NO	Runs	HS	Avge	100	50	Balls	Runs	Wkts	Avge	BB	5i	10m	RpO	ct	st
SL		3																4	1
BH		5	4	0	74	52	18.50	0	1									3	3
FC	1996	2	2	1	33	31*	33.00	0	0									4	

Cmp	Debut	M	I	NO	Runs	HS	Avge	100	50	Balls	Runs	Wkts	Avge	BB	5i	10m	RpO	ct	st

BLAIN, John Angus Rae (Scotland) b Edinburgh, Scotland 4.1.1979 RHB RFM

Cmp	Debut	M	I	NO	Runs	HS	Avge	100	50	Balls	Runs	Wkts	Avge	BB	5i	10m	RpO	ct	st
FC		1	1	0	0	0	0.00	0	0	180	105	2	52.50	1-18	0	0	3.50	1	
SL		3								144	110	7	15.71	5-24	0	1	4.58	1	
BH		1								36	82	2	41.00	2-82	0	0	13.66	0	
FC	1996	2	1	0	0	0	0.00	0	0	312	208	2	104.00	1-18	0	0	4.00	2	
BH	1996	3	2	1	14	10*	14.00	0	0	90	140	3	46.66	2-82	0	0	9.33	0	
NW	1996	1								66	56	2	28.00	2-56	0	0	5.09	1	

BOSWELL, Scott Antony John (British Universities) b Fulford 11.9.1974 RHB RM

Cmp	Debut	M	I	NO	Runs	HS	Avge	100	50	Balls	Runs	Wkts	Avge	BB	5i	10m	RpO	ct	st
FC		9	12	3	122	35	13.55	0	0	1115	769	15	51.26	5-94	1	0	4.13	2	
BH		4	1	0	3	3	3.00	0	0	207	177	3	59.00	3-39	0	0	5.13	0	
FC	1996	12	16	5	127	35	11.54	0	0	1557	1012	22	46.00	5-94	1	0	3.89	4	
SL	1995	4	1	0	2	2	2.00	0	0	138	104	3	34.66	1-20	0	0	4.52	0	
BH	1995	10	6	1	24	14	4.80	0	0	536	485	6	80.83	3-39	0	0	5.42	1	

BROWN, Jason Fred b Newcastle-under-Lyme 10.10.1974 RHB OB

Cmp	Debut	M	I	NO	Runs	HS	Avge	100	50	Balls	Runs	Wkts	Avge	BB	5i	10m	RpO	ct	st
FC		6	8	4	25	16*	6.25	0	0	1222	651	20	32.55	4-50	0	0	3.19	2	
SL		1								42	26	4	6.50	4-26	1	0	3.71	0	
FC	1996	7	9	5	25	16*	6.25	0	0	1354	715	20	35.75	4-50	0	0	3.16	3	

CAPEL, David John b Northampton 6.2.1963 RHB RMF

Cmp	Debut	M	I	NO	Runs	HS	Avge	100	50	Balls	Runs	Wkts	Avge	BB	5i	10m	RpO	ct	st
FC		4	7	0	140	57	20.00	0	1	234	180	2	90.00	1-22	0	0	4.61	1	
SL		7	6	0	79	54	13.16	0	1	192	195	5	39.00	2-42	0	0	6.09	2	
BH		5	5	0	182	68	36.40	0	2	210	154	10	15.40	5-51	0	1	4.40	3	
Test	1987	15	25	1	374	98	15.58	0	2	2000	1064	21	50.66	3-88	0	0	3.19	6	
FC	1981	311	477	66	12202	175	29.68	16	72	32992	17507	545	32.12	7-44	14	0	3.18	156	
Int	1986	23	19	2	327	50*	19.23	0	1	1038	805	17	47.35	3-38	0	0	4.65	6	
SL	1982	185	167	33	3981	121	29.70	3	16	5485	4453	133	33.48	4-30	4	0	4.87	46	
BH	1982	61	55	5	1181	97	23.62	0	5	2632	1699	64	26.54	5-51	3	1	3.87	15	
NW	1982	39	34	8	916	101	35.23	1	4	1702	1120	33	33.93	3-21	0	0	3.94	10	

CURRAN, Kevin Malcolm b Rusape, Rhodesia 7.9.1959 RHB RMF (Gloucestershire 1985-90)

Cmp	Debut	M	I	NO	Runs	HS	Avge	100	50	Balls	Runs	Wkts	Avge	BB	5i	10m	RpO	ct	st
FC		15	26	4	1032	159	46.90	2	6	1292	715	24	29.79	4-32	0	0	3.32	8	
SL		12	12	2	440	78*	44.00	0	3	294	292	9	32.44	4-36	1	0	5.95	3	
BH		6	6	1	96	49*	19.20	0	0	186	137	0					4.41	2	
NW		2	2	0	30	21	15.00	0	0	96	54	2	27.00	2-31	0	0	3.37	0	
FC	1980	297	467	78	14722	159	37.84	25	76	30787	16234	586	27.70	7-47	15	4	3.16	179	
Int	1983	11	11	0	287	73	26.09	0	2	506	398	9	44.22	3-65	0	0	4.71	1	
SL	1985	185	175	37	4569	119*	33.10	1	26	5691	4693	169	27.76	5-15	4	1	4.94	38	
BH	1985	53	48	8	1002	57	25.05	0	6	2448	1701	52	32.71	4-38	3	0	4.16	10	
NW	1985	41	35	7	809	78*	28.89	0	3	2123	1204	41	29.36	4-34	1	0	3.40	11	

DAVIES, Michael Kenton (British Universities) b Ashby-de-la-Zouch 17.7.1976 RHB SLA

Cmp	Debut	M	I	NO	Runs	HS	Avge	100	50	Balls	Runs	Wkts	Avge	BB	5i	10m	RpO	ct	st
FC		6	9	4	49	17	9.80	0	0	1406	674	23	29.30	5-46	1	0	2.87	2	
BH		1	1	1	1	1*		0	0	50	69	1	69.00	1-69	0	0	8.28	0	

EMBUREY, John Ernest b Peckham 20.8.1952 RHB OB (Middlesex 1973-95)

Cmp	Debut	M	I	NO	Runs	HS	Avge	100	50	Balls	Runs	Wkts	Avge	BB	5i	10m	RpO	ct	st
FC		3	3	0	39	39	13.00	0	0	663	259	4	64.75	2-36	0	0	2.34	1	
SL		11	7	2	25	8	5.00	0	0	435	350	13	26.92	4-28	1	0	4.82	3	
BH		6	3	1	33	19*	16.50	0	0	330	187	6	31.16	3-34	0	0	3.40	3	
NW		2	2	0	2	1	1.00	0	0	144	83	1	83.00	1-61	0	0	3.45	0	
Test	1978	64	96	20	1713	75	22.53	0	10	15391	5646	147	38.40	7-78	6	0	2.20	34	
FC	1973	513	644	130	12021	133	23.38	7	55	112862	41958	1608	26.09	8-40	72	12	2.23	459	
Int	1979	61	45	10	501	34	14.31	0	0	3425	2346	76	30.86	4-37	2	0	4.10	19	
SL	1975	277	179	61	1901	50	16.11	0	1	11789	8640	368	23.47	5-23	15	2	4.39	85	
BH	1975	93	62	19	679	50	15.79	0	1	5032	2666	98	27.20	5-37	3	1	3.17	45	
NW	1975	61	39	11	521	46	18.60	0	0	4082	1907	71	26.85	3-11	0	0	2.80	21	

FOLLETT, David b Newcastle-under-Lyme 14.10.1968 RHB RFM (Middlesex 1995-96)

Cmp	Debut	M	I	NO	Runs	HS	Avge	100	50	Balls	Runs	Wkts	Avge	BB	5i	10m	RpO	ct	st
FC		1	2	0	3	3	1.50	0	0	147	123	2	61.50	2-123	0	0	5.02	0	
SL		4	2	1	2	1*	2.00	0	0	156	138	5	27.60	2-28	0	0	5.30	2	
BH		2	1	0	4	4	4.00	0	0	90	69	6	11.50	4-39	1	0	4.60	0	
FC	1995	8	10	6	30	17	7.50	0	0	1211	807	26	31.03	8-22	3	1	3.99	3	
SL	1995	7	2	1	2	1*	2.00	0	0	294	260	10	26.00	2-27	0	0	5.30	4	
BH	1995	9	3	0	8	4	2.66	0	0	408	302	12	25.16	4-39	1	0	4.44	0	

FORDHAM, Alan b Bedford 9.11.1964 RHB RM

Cmp	Debut	M	I	NO	Runs	HS	Avge	100	50	Balls	Runs	Wkts	Avge	BB	5i	10m	RpO	ct	st
FC		9	17	2	673	85*	44.86	0	6	27	8	0					1.77	10	
SL		5	5	0	114	43	22.80	0	0									2	
FC	1986	167	297	24	10939	206*	40.06	25	54	431	297	4	74.25	1-0	0	0	4.13	117	
SL	1988	112	105	1	2731	111	26.25	1	17	6	10	0					10.00	31	
BH	1987	27	26	1	732	108	29.28	2	4									6	
NW	1990	24	24	1	1158	132*	50.34	3	6	21	6	1	6.00	1-3	0	0	1.71	4	

HUGHES, John Gareth b Wellingborough 3.5.1971 RHB RM

Cmp	Debut	M	I	NO	Runs	HS	Avge	100	50	Balls	Runs	Wkts	Avge	BB	5i	10m	RpO	ct	st
FC		2	1	1	5	5*		0	0	276	141	4	35.25	2-15	0	0	3.06	0	
FC	1990	20	26	2	128	17	5.33	0	0	2725	1622	37	43.83	5-69	1	0	3.57	5	
SL	1990	6	5	2	31	21	10.33	0	0	174	127	3	42.33	2-39	0	0	4.37	1	
BH	1994	4	3	0	11	9	3.66	0	0	116	106	2	53.00	2-47	0	0	5.48	1	

Cmp	Debut	M	I	NO	Runs	HS	Avge	100	50	Balls	Runs	Wkts	Avge	BB	5i	10m	RpO	ct	st
INNES, Kevin John b Wellingborough 24.9.1975 RHB RM																			
FC		1	1	1	8	8*		0	0	120	49	0					2.45	0	
SL		4	2	2	26	19*		0	0	24	36	0					9.00	1	
NW		1	1	0	25	25	25.00	0	0									0	
FC	1994	6	8	1	116	63	16.57	0	1	534	275	8	34.37	4-61	0	0	3.08	3	
SL	1994	11	4	2	34	19*	17.00	0	0	256	309	3	103.00	1-35	0	0	7.24	4	
BH	1994	1								36	25	1	25.00	1-25	0	0	4.16	0	
LOYE, Malachy Bernard b Northampton 27.9.1972 RHB OB																			
FC		8	15	3	412	86	34.33	0	2									2	
SL		6	6	0	151	68	25.16	0	1									1	
BH		5	5	1	120	47	30.00	0	0									0	
NW		2	2	0	21	19	10.50	0	0									3	
FC	1991	82	133	15	4107	205	34.80	7	21	1	1	0					6.00	48	
SL	1992	61	57	6	1500	122	29.41	1	8									12	
BH	1993	17	17	4	406	68*	31.23	0	2									6	
NW	1993	12	11	3	218	65	27.25	0	1									4	
MOHAMMAD AKRAM (Rawalpindi, Allied Bank, Pakistan) b Islamabad, Pakistan 10.9.1974 RHB RFM																			
FC		11	14	2	116	28	9.66	0	0	1722	1135	30	37.83	5-72	2	0	3.95	1	
SL		5	3	3	3	2*		0	0	204	141	6	23.50	4-19	1	0	4.14	1	
BH		4	2	1	4	4	4.00	0	0	222	158	6	26.33	4-47	1	0	4.27	0	
NW		1	1	1	0	0*		0	0	72	42	1	42.00	1-42	0	0	3.50	0	
Test	1995	6	9	3	8	5	1.33	0	0	1033	522	10	52.20	3-39	0	0	3.03	4	
FC	1992	37	47	12	258	28	7.37	0	0	5777	3294	113	29.15	7-51	7	0	3.42	13	
Int	1995	8	5	3	11	7*	5.50	0	0	342	307	9	34.11	2-36	0	0	5.38	2	
MONTGOMERIE, Richard Robert b Rugby 3.7.1971 RHB OB																			
FC		10	18	3	504	73	33.60	0	4	6	1	0					1.00	7	
SL		5	5	1	204	86*	51.00	0	2									2	
BH		1	1	0	39	39	39.00	0	0									0	
FC	1991	88	154	16	4675	192	33.87	9	26	102	66	0					3.88	80	
SL	1993	35	34	1	1040	86*	31.51	0	10									10	
BH	1992	15	14	2	412	75	34.33	0	2	6	0	0					0.00	2	
NW	1995	7	7	1	300	109	50.00	1	2									3	
PENBERTHY, Anthony Leonard b Troon 1.9.1969 LHB RM																			
FC		13	19	0	499	96	26.26	0	3	1140	722	9	80.22	2-52	0	0	3.80	8	
SL		14	14	2	317	81*	26.41	0	3	414	307	16	19.18	3-32	0	0	4.44	3	
BH		6	5	1	102	38	25.50	0	0	138	112	1	112.00	1-34	0	0	4.86	0	
NW		2	2	0	119	62	59.50	0	2	78	79	5	15.80	5-56	0	1	6.07	2	
FC	1989	101	151	19	3010	101*	22.80	1	17	10527	5848	154	37.97	5-37	3	0	3.33	58	
SL	1989	95	73	13	1261	81*	21.01	0	6	3015	2673	88	30.37	5-36	1	1	5.31	18	
BH	1990	24	18	3	315	41	21.00	Q	0	996	725	18	40.27	3-38	0	0	4.36	6	
NW	1992	19	12	1	320	79	29.09	0	3	817	583	17	34.29	5-56	0	1	4.28	7	
RIPLEY, David b Leeds 13.9.1966 RHB WK																			
FC		17	24	6	772	92	42.88	0	6									29	7
SL		3	3	0	35	20	11.66	0	0									1	
BH		5	2	1	20	11*	20.00	0	0									7	2
FC	1984	247	323	87	6249	134*	26.47	6	21	60	103	2	51.50	2-89	0	0	10.30	525	74
SL	1984	137	83	36	867	52*	18.44	0	1									96	13
BH	1986	42	27	10	325	36*	19.11	0	0									44	6
NW	1984	35	20	9	130	27*	11.81	0	0									36	3
ROBERTS, David James b Truro 29.12.1976 RHB RM																			
FC		7	13	0	385	117	29.61	1	0									1	
FC	1996	11	20	0	639	117	31.95	1	2									1	
SALES, David John Grimwood (ECB First Class Counties XI) b Carshalton 3.12.1977 RHB RM																			
FC		14	21	1	548	103	27.40	1	2	48	28	0					3.50	4	
SL		10	10	1	168	42*	18.66	0	0									2	
BH		1	1	0	15	15	15.00	0	0									1	
NW		2	2	0	53	53	26.50	0	1									1	
FC	1996	18	29	2	828	210*	30.66	2	2	48	28	0					3.50	8	
SL	1994	18	16	4	284	70*	23.66	0	1									4	
SNAPE, Jeremy Nicholas b Stoke-on-Trent 27.4.1973 RHB OB																			
FC		11	16	3	306	66	23.53	0	3	1519	724	15	48.26	4-46	0	0	2.85	9	
SL		9	6	2	95	33	23.75	0	0	312	261	9	29.00	4-31	1	0	5.01	2	
BH		6	4	1	45	27*	15.00	0	0	252	163	8	20.37	5-32	0	1	3.88	4	
NW		2	2	0	59	54	29.50	0	1	144	72	1	72.00	1-22	0	0	3.00	1	
FC	1992	39	56	11	1139	87	25.31	0	7	5498	2931	65	45.09	5-65	1	0	3.19	34	
SL	1992	39	23	10	242	33	18.61	0	0	1182	968	34	28.47	4-31	1	0	4.91	11	
BH	1992	15	12	4	210	52	26.25	0	1	798	521	18	28.94	5-32	0	1	3.91	7	
NW	1992	7	6	2	99	54	24.75	0	1	289	188	5	37.60	2-43	0	0	3.90	3	

Cmp	Debut	M	I	NO	Runs	HS	Avge	100	50	Balls	Runs	Wkts	Avge	BB	5i	10m	RpO	ct	st
SWANN, Alec James b Northampton 26.10.1976 RHB OB																		
FC		2	3	0	162	136	54.00	1	0									0	
FC	1996	5	8	1	262	136	37.42	1	1	30	15	0					3.00	1	
SWANN, Graeme Peter b Northampton 24.3.1979 RHB OB																		
SL		4	2	1	0	0*	0.00	0	0	192	128	5	25.60	2-28	0	0	4.00	0	
TAYLOR, Jonathan Paul b Ashby-de-la-Zouch 8.8.1964 LHB LFM (Derbyshire 1984-86)																		
FC		16	21	4	216	36	12.70	0	0	2734	1532	54	28.37	7-87	3	1	3.36	7	
SL		13	4	3	33	20	33.00	0	0	516	369	9	41.00	2-13	0	0	4.29	2	
BH		6	2	0	13	7	6.50	0	0	342	195	7	27.85	2-31	0	0	3.42	1	
NW		2	2	1	9	6	9.00	0	0	114	98	2	49.00	2-58	0	0	5.15	0	
Test	1992	2	4	2	34	17*	17.00	0	0	288	156	3	52.00	1-18	0	0	3.25	0	
FC	1984	132	145	56	1197	86	13.44	0	4	22822	11969	404	29.62	7-23	16	3	3.14	45	
Int	1992	1	1	0	1	1	1.00	0	0	18	20	0					6.66	0	
SL	1984	96	32	16	160	24	10.00	0	0	4176	3241	108	30.00	3-14	0	0	4.65	17	
BH	1991	29	11	7	36	7*	9.00	0	0	1617	931	39	23.87	5-45	1	1	3.45	5	
NW	1989	26	10	5	31	9	6.20	0	0	1581	1016	35	29.02	4-34	1	0	3.85	6	
WALTON, Timothy Charles b Low Head 8.11.1972 RHB RM																		
FC		7	10	1	231	60	25.66	0	2	48	45	0					5.37	1	
SL		13	11	1	163	42	16.30	0	0									1	
BH		6	4	1	105	35*	35.00	0	0									4	
NW		2	2	0	6	6	3.00	0	0									1	
FC	1994	19	29	3	653	71	25.11	0	7	390	282	4	70.50	1-26	0	0	4.33	5	
SL	1992	47	40	6	821	72	24.14	0	4	240	197	6	32.83	2-27	0	0	4.92	12	
BH	1995	11	8	2	238	70*	39.66	0	1	36	27	1	27.00	1-27	0	0	4.50	5	
NW	1996	3	2	0	6	6	3.00	0	0									1	
WARREN, Russell John (Rest of England) b Northampton 10.9.1971 RHB OB WK																		
FC		10	17	2	664	174*	44.26	1	4									12	1
SL		9	8	3	144	44	28.80	0	0									9	2
BH		1	1	0	4	4	4.00	0	0									2	
NW		2	2	0	3	3	1.50	0	0									3	1
FC	1992	56	92	12	2713	201*	33.91	3	15									75	3
SL	1993	52	42	9	689	71*	20.87	0	3									44	8
BH	1995	12	11	1	95	23	9.50	0	0									11	
NW	1994	12	10	2	251	100*	31.37	1	0									17	1

1997 AND CAREER FIGURES FOR NOTTINGHAMSHIRE PLAYERS

Cmp	Debut	M	I	NO	Runs	HS	Avge	100	50	Balls	Runs	Wkts	Avge	BB	5i	10m	RpO	ct	st
AFFORD, John Andrew (Nottinghamshire to South Africa) b Crowland 12.5.1964 RHB SLA																		
FC	1984	170	167	72	398	22*	4.18	0	0	33757	15436	468	32.98	6-51	16	2	2.74	57	
SL	1976	19	5	3	1	1	0.50	0	0	690	576	15	38.40	3-33	0	0	5.00	7	
BH	1987	24	2	2	2	1*		0	0	1504	943	25	37.72	4-38	1	0	3.76	3	
NW	1989	7	4	3	2	2*	3.00	0	0	486	218	6	36.33	3-32	0	0	2.69	0	
AFZAAL, Usman (Nottinghamshire to South Africa) b Rawalpindi, Pakistan 9.6.1977 LHB SLA																		
FC		17	29	2	720	80	26.66	0	5	1195	689	14	49.21	3-79	0	0	3.45	9	
SL		2	2	0	29	20	14.50	0	0	12	21	0					10.50	0	
NW		1																1	
FC	1995	31	53	5	1159	80	24.14	0	7	2719	1537	25	61.48	3-62	0	0	3.39	15	
SL	1995	8	4	1	31	20	10.33	0	0	216	186	8	23.25	2-25	0	0	5.16	3	
NW	1995	2	1	1	26	26*		0	0	66	57	0					5.18	1	
ARCHER, Graeme Francis (Nottinghamshire to South Africa) b Carlisle 26.9.1970 RHB RM																		
FC		12	22	2	375	81	18.75	0	2	318	188	4	47.00	1-24	0	0	3.54	15	
SL		11	10	3	319	104*	45.57	1	1	54	70	2	35.00	1-28	0	0	7.77	5	
BH		3	3	1	125	111*	62.50	1	0	78	73	1	73.00	1-34	0	0	5.61	1	
NW		3	2	0	45	33	22.50	0	0	30	17	1	17.00	1-17	0	0	3.40	2	
FC	1992	72	128	13	4072	168	35.40	8	20	1053	648	14	46.28	3-18	0	0	3.69	77	
SL	1992	50	44	7	798	104*	21.56	1	2	222	216	8	27.00	2-16	0	0	5.83	17	
BH	1994	8	7	1	259	111*	43.16	1	1	114	117	1	117.00	1-34	0	0	6.15	1	
NW	1993	6	5	0	99	39	24.75	0	0	30	17	1	17.00	1-17	0	0	3.40	3	
ASTLE, Nathan John (Canterbury, New Zealand) b Christchurch, New Zealand 15.9.1971 RHB RM																		
FC		10	16	0	644	100	40.25	2	3	1254	525	22	23.86	5-46	1	0	2.51	11	
SL		6	6	0	192	75	32.00	0	2	234	203	9	22.55	3-22	0	0	5.20	3	
NW		3	2	0	83	56	41.50	0	1	162	61	4	15.25	3-20	0	0	2.25	0	
Test	1995	11	21	1	633	125	31.65	3	2	654	264	8	33.00	2-26	0	0	2.42	8	
FC	1991	48	77	7	2635	191	37.64	8	10	5258	1869	61	30.63	6-22	2	0	2.13	33	
Int	1995	46	46	1	1460	120	32.44	4	8	1523	1130	37	30.54	4-43	1	0	4.45	13	
BATES, Richard Terry b Stamford 17.6.1972 RHB OB																		
FC		8	12	5	69	21	9.85	0	0	1354	576	11	52.36	3-89	0	0	2.55	6	
SL		13	9	1	32	9	4.00	0	0	395	349	9	38.77	3-33	0	0	5.30	4	
BH		3	2	1	8	4*	8.00	0	0	179	155	2	77.50	2-40	0	0	5.19	0	

Cmp	Debut	M	I	NO	Runs	HS	Avge	100	50	Balls	Runs	Wkts	Avge	BB	5i	10m	RpO	ct	st
NW		1	1	0	11	11	11.00	0	0	54	38	0					4.22	2	
FC	1993	30	43	10	433	34	13.12	0	0	4675	2339	50	46.78	5-88	1	0	3.00	18	
SL	1993	38	19	4	108	16	7.20	0	0	1276	1134	36	31.50	3-30	0	0	5.33	15	
BH	1996	7	5	1	53	27	13.25	0	0	401	283	9	31.44	3-21	0	0	4.23	4	
NW	1990	3	3	0	17	11	5.66	0	0	120	94	0					4.70	2	

BOWEN, Mark Nicholas (Nottinghamshire to South Africa) b Redcar 6.12.1967 RHB RM (Northamptonshire 1991-95)

Cmp	Debut	M	I	NO	Runs	HS	Avge	100	50	Balls	Runs	Wkts	Avge	BB	5i	10m	RpO	ct	st
FC		15	19	6	145	32	11.15	0	0	2804	1394	41	34.00	7-75	3	1	2.98	5	
SL		11	6	3	44	14	14.66	0	0	398	429	17	25.23	4-29	1	0	6.46	2	
NW		2	1	1	8	8*		0	0	90	55	3	18.33	3-38	0	0	3.66	0	
FC	1991	42	52	13	462	32	11.84	0	0	7156	3970	111	35.76	7-75	5	1	3.32	11	
SL	1992	45	20	10	182	27*	18.20	0	0	1730	1548	47	32.93	4-29	1	0	5.36	8	
BH	1994	1	1	0	0	0	0.00	0	0	60	39	1	39.00	1-39	0	0	3.90	0	
NW	1996	3	2	2	8	8*		0	0	126	97	3	32.33	3-38	0	0	4.61	1	

DOWMAN, Mathew Peter b Grantham 10.5.1974 LHB RMF

Cmp	Debut	M	I	NO	Runs	HS	Avge	100	50	Balls	Runs	Wkts	Avge	BB	5i	10m	RpO	ct	st
FC		19	33	1	1091	149	34.09	3	5	486	260	6	43.33	3-10	0	0	3.20	11	
SL		13	13	0	222	71	17.07	0	1	269	254	4	63.50	2-31	0	0	5.66	3	
BH		3	3	0	151	92	50.33	0	1	126	115	3	38.33	2-46	0	0	5.47	0	
NW		1	1	0	14	14	14.00	0	0									0	
FC	1994	40	70	3	2087	149	31.14	6	7	804	457	8	57.12	3-10	0	0	3.41	22	
SL	1993	37	37	2	638	74*	18.22	0	3	533	524	11	47.63	2-31	0	0	5.89	9	
BH	1995	10	7	2	190	92	38.00	0	1	242	201	8	25.12	3-21	0	0	4.98	3	

EVANS, Kevin Paul b Nottingham 10.9.1963 RHB RMF

Cmp	Debut	M	I	NO	Runs	HS	Avge	100	50	Balls	Runs	Wkts	Avge	BB	5i	10m	RpO	ct	st
FC		15	18	1	208	47	12.23	0	0	2747	1277	45	28.37	6-40	2	0	2.78	6	
SL		12	10	2	74	20	9.25	0	0	516	436	12	36.33	4-26	1	0	5.06	3	
BH		3	2	0	20	13	10.00	0	0	162	127	4	31.75	3-61	0	0	4.70	2	
NW		3	1	0	11	11	11.00	0	0	184	78	5	15.60	2-22	0	0	2.88	0	
FC	1984	151	207	44	4069	104	24.96	3	21	23047	11292	334	33.80	6-40	8	0	2.93	108	
SL	1984	133	81	31	776	30	15.52	0	0	5456	4613	141	32.71	5-29	4	1	5.07	26	
BH	1985	33	21	5	243	47	15.18	0	0	1838	1261	45	28.02	4-19	2	0	4.11	10	
NW	1985	22	15	2	126	21	9.69	0	0	1346	724	31	23.35	6-10	2	1	3.22	6	

FRANKS, Paul John b Mansfield 3.2.1979 LHB RFM

Cmp	Debut	M	I	NO	Runs	HS	Avge	100	50	Balls	Runs	Wkts	Avge	BB	5i	10m	RpO	ct	st
FC		14	19	6	280	50	21.53	0	1	2236	1158	30	38.60	4-47	0	0	3.10	7	
SL		4	2	1	15	8	15.00	0	0	162	163	4	40.75	2-46	0	0	6.03	0	
NW		3	1	0	4	4	4.00	0	0	162	115	5	23.00	3-80	0	0	4.25	2	
FC	1996	15	19	6	280	50	21.53	0	1	2482	1260	33	38.18	4-47	0	0	3.04	7	

GIE, Noel Addison b Pretoria, South Africa 12.4.1977 RHB RM

Cmp	Debut	M	I	NO	Runs	HS	Avge	100	50	Balls	Runs	Wkts	Avge	BB	5i	10m	RpO	ct	st
FC		3	6	0	85	50	14.16	0	1									4	
SL		8	6	1	149	75*	29.80	0	1									3	
BH		3	3	0	61	47	20.33	0	0									0	
FC	1995	7	12	0	183	50	15.25	0	1									4	

HINDSON, James Edward b Huddersfield 13.9.1973 RHB SLA

Cmp	Debut	M	I	NO	Runs	HS	Avge	100	50	Balls	Runs	Wkts	Avge	BB	5i	10m	RpO	ct	st
FC		3	4	2	54	42*	27.00	0	0	580	287	11	26.09	4-28	0	0	2.96	2	
SL		1	1	1	3	3*		0	0									0	
NW		1								30	37	0					7.40	0	
FC	1992	28	36	7	384	53*	13.24	0	1	5827	3045	93	32.74	5-42	7	2	3.13	14	
SL	1994	21	8	4	61	21	15.25	0	0	768	639	16	39.93	4-19	1	0	4.99	5	
BH	1995	1	1	1	41	41*		0	0	60	69	1	69.00	1-69	0	0	6.90	0	
NW	1995	3	1	1	16	16*		0	0	150	120	2	60.00	2-57	0	0	4.80	0	

JOHNSON, Paul (Nottinghamshire to South Africa) b Newark 24.4.1965 RHB RM

Cmp	Debut	M	I	NO	Runs	HS	Avge	100	50	Balls	Runs	Wkts	Avge	BB	5i	10m	RpO	ct	st
FC		16	27	5	942	96*	42.81	0	8	84	34	0					2.42	12	
SL		12	12	1	467	117	42.45	2	2	1	1	0					6.00	7	
BH		3	3	0	60	34	20.00	0	0									0	
NW		2	2	0	110	106	55.00	1	0									3	
FC	1982	301	501	49	16755	187	37.06	34	98	634	595	6	99.16	1-9	0	0	5.63	188	1
SL	1981	202	191	24	5554	167*	33.25	8	31	1	1	0					6.00	70	
BH	1983	53	50	11	1364	104*	34.97	2	9									15	
NW	1985	31	31	2	879	146	30.31	3	1	12	16	0					8.00	10	

METCALFE, Ashley Anthony (Nottinghamshire to South Africa) b Horsforth 25.12.1963 RHB OB (Yorkshire 1983-95)

Cmp	Debut	M	I	NO	Runs	HS	Avge	100	50	Balls	Runs	Wkts	Avge	BB	5i	10m	RpO	ct	st
FC		9	12	1	262	79	23.81	0	2									4	
SL		5	5	1	133	70*	33.25	0	1									0	
NW		1																0	
FC	1983	216	369	21	11938	216*	34.30	26	57	428	362	4	90.50	2-18	0	0	5.07	82	
SL	1984	157	149	11	3887	116	28.16	2	25									36	
BH	1986	35	35	4	1438	114	46.38	1	10									11	
NW	1984	22	21	3	742	127*	41.22	1	5	42	44	2	22.00	2-44	0	0	6.28	5	

NOON, Wayne Michael (Nottinghamshire to South Africa) b Grimsby 5.2.1971 RHB WK (Northamptonshire 1988-93)

Cmp	Debut	M	I	NO	Runs	HS	Avge	100	50	Balls	Runs	Wkts	Avge	BB	5i	10m	RpO	ct	st
FC		18	25	4	542	83	25.80	0	3	6	12	0					12.00	34	4
SL		13	10	5	89	31	17.80	0	0									9	5
BH		3	2	1	31	24	31.00	0	0									1	1

Cmp	Debut	M	I	NO	Runs	HS	Avge	100	50	Balls	Runs	Wkts	Avge	BB	5i	10m	RpO	ct	st
NW		3	2	1	32	19	32.00	0	0									2	
FC	1989	81	128	21	2423	83	22.64	0	12	30	34	0					6.80	168	20
SL	1988	74	46	14	421	38	13.15	0	0									54	14
BH	1989	13	8	2	94	24	15.66	0	0									7	4
NW	1994	7	4	1	73	34	24.33	0	0									4	2

ORAM, Andrew Richard b Northampton 7.3.1975 RHB RM

Cmp	Debut	M	I	NO	Runs	HS	Avge	100	50	Balls	Runs	Wkts	Avge	BB	5i	10m	RpO	ct	st
FC		8	9	5	14	5*	3.50	0	0	1360	684	26	26.30	4-53	0	0	3.01	6	
SL		9	2	2	0	0*		0	0	353	283	10	28.30	4-45	1	0	4.81	0	
NW		1								66	51	1	51.00	1-51	0	0	4.63	0	

PICK, Robert Andrew (Nottinghamshire to South Africa) b Nottingham 19.11.1963 LHB RFM

Cmp	Debut	M	I	NO	Runs	HS	Avge	100	50	Balls	Runs	Wkts	Avge	BB	5i	10m	RpO	ct	st
FC		4	2	1	15	8*	15.00	0	0	584	307	5	61.40	2-23	0	0	3.15	0	
SL		3	1	0	8	8	8.00	0	0	107	67	1	67.00	1-30	0	0	3.75	1	
BH		3	2	1	3	2	3.00	0	0	150	153	1	153.00	1-43	0	0	6.12	0	
NW		1								54	17	3	5.66	3-17	0	0	1.88	0	
FC	1983	195	206	55	2259	65*	14.96	0	5	30238	16454	495	33.24	7-128	16	3	3.26	50	
SL	1983	121	43	19	370	58*	15.41	0	1	5258	4375	128	34.17	4-32	3	0	4.99	28	
BH	1985	44	19	12	117	25*	16.71	0	0	2593	1861	48	38.77	4-42	1	0	4.30	5	
NW	1985	29	16	11	121	34*	24.20	0	0	1867	1186	50	23.72	5-22	0	2	3.81	5	

POLLARD, Paul Raymond (Nottinghamshire to South Africa) b Nottingham 24.9.1968 LHB RM

Cmp	Debut	M	I	NO	Runs	HS	Avge	100	50	Balls	Runs	Wkts	Avge	BB	5i	10m	RpO	ct	st
FC		10	17	5	480	115*	40.00	1	1									8	
SL		6	5	0	129	87	25.80	0	1									4	
BH		3	3	0	70	38	23.33	0	0									0	
NW		2	2	1	44	42*	44.00	0	0									1	
FC	1987	153	268	20	8226	180	33.16	13	39	274	268	4	67.00	2-79	0	0	5.86	145	
SL	1987	95	85	9	2666	132*	35.07	4	13									38	
BH	1989	27	26	2	746	104	31.08	1	6									9	
NW	1989	13	13	2	369	96	33.54	0	2	18	9	0					3.00	4	

ROBINSON, Robert Timothy (Nottinghamshire to South Africa) b Sutton-in-Ashfield 21.11.1958 RHB RM

Cmp	Debut	M	I	NO	Runs	HS	Avge	100	50	Balls	Runs	Wkts	Avge	BB	5i	10m	RpO	ct	st
FC		17	29	4	812	143*	32.48	1	5									7	
SL		7	7	1	240	58	40.00	0	2									2	
BH		3	3	0	36	25	12.00	0	0									0	
NW		3	3	1	94	52	47.00	0	1									1	
Test	1984	29	49	5	1601	175	36.38	4	6	6	0	0					0.00	8	
FC	1978	402	699	82	26493	220*	42.93	62	133	259	289	4	72.25	1-22	0	0	6.69	241	
Int	1984	26	26	0	597	83	22.96	0	3									6	
SL	1978	229	223	27	6568	119*	33.51	4	44									72	
BH	1981	74	72	9	2531	120	40.17	3	18									16	
NW	1980	41	41	3	1595	139	41.97	2	8									17	

TOLLEY, Christopher Mark (Nottinghamshire to South Africa) b Kidderminster 30.12.1967 RHB LMF (Worcestershire 1989-95)

Cmp	Debut	M	I	NO	Runs	HS	Avge	100	50	Balls	Runs	Wkts	Avge	BB	5i	10m	RpO	ct	st
FC		12	22	4	479	73*	26.61	0	3	2178	1005	35	28.71	6-61	1	0	2.76	6	
SL		11	10	2	196	43	24.50	0	0	384	328	15	21.86	4-24	2	0	5.12	4	
BH		3	3	1	62	23*	31.00	0	0	156	104	1	104.00	1-33	0	0	4.00	0	
NW		2	2	1	30	18	30.00	0	0	126	55	4	13.75	3-21	0	0	2.61	0	
FC	1989	85	112	28	1963	84	23.36	0	8	10913	5357	146	36.69	6-61	2	0	2.94	35	
SL	1989	60	34	10	368	43	15.33	0	0	1960	1616	62	26.06	5-16	3	1	4.94	20	
BH	1989	20	17	2	355	77	23.66	0	3	978	633	9	70.33	1-12	0	0	3.88	3	
NW	1990	8	5	3	67	18	33.50	0	0	432	258	11	23.45	3-21	0	0	3.58	0	

WALKER, Lyndsay Nicholas Paton b Armidale, Australia 22.6.1974 RHB WK

Cmp	Debut	M	I	NO	Runs	HS	Avge	100	50	Balls	Runs	Wkts	Avge	BB	5i	10m	RpO	ct	st
FC		4	5	2	97	42*	32.33	0	0									1	
SL		2	2	0	24	22	12.00	0	0									0	
FC	1994	12	15	3	233	42*	19.41	0	0									19	3
NW	1996	1	1	0	1	1	1.00	0	0									0	

WELTON, Guy Edward b Grimsby 4.5.1978 RHB OB

Cmp	Debut	M	I	NO	Runs	HS	Avge	100	50	Balls	Runs	Wkts	Avge	BB	5i	10m	RpO	ct	st
FC		6	11	0	295	95	26.81	0	1									1	
SL		5	5	0	96	68	19.20	0	1									2	

1997 AND CAREER FIGURES FOR SOMERSET PLAYERS

BOULTON, Nicholas Ross b Johannesburg, South Africa 22.3.1979 LHB RM

Cmp	Debut	M	I	NO	Runs	HS	Avge	100	50	Balls	Runs	Wkts	Avge	BB	5i	10m	RpO	ct	st
FC		1	2	0	15	14	7.50	0	0									0	

BOWLER, Peter Duncan b Plymouth 30.7.1963 RHB OB WK (Leicestershire 1986-87, Derbyshire 1988-94)

Cmp	Debut	M	I	NO	Runs	HS	Avge	100	50	Balls	Runs	Wkts	Avge	BB	5i	10m	RpO	ct	st
FC		16	26	1	666	123	26.64	1	5	266	145	3	48.33	2-48	0	0	3.27	20	
SL		14	13	2	353	61	32.09	0	2	42	56	1	56.00	1-33	0	0	8.00	4	
BH		5	5	0	159	79	31.80	0	1	36	24	1	24.00	1-24	0	0	4.00	2	
NW		2	2	0	101	87	50.50	0	1									2	
FC	1986	212	368	33	13438	241*	40.11	29	75	2962	1901	27	70.40	3-41	0	0	3.85	140	
SL	1986	158	153	17	4700	138*	34.55	2	38	284	293	8	36.62	3-31	0	0	6.19	61	1

Cmp	Debut	M	I	NO	Runs	HS	Avge	100	50	Balls	Runs	Wkts	Avge	BB	5i	10m	RpO	ct	st
BH	1988	46	45	1	1364	109	31.00	2	11	309	182	5	36.40	1-15	0	0	3.53	21	1
NW	1988	18	18	0	510	111	28.33	1	3	36	26	0					4.33	8	

BURNS, Michael b Barrow-in-Furness 2.6.1969 RHB RM WK (Warwickshire 1992-96)

Cmp	Debut	M	I	NO	Runs	HS	Avge	100	50	Balls	Runs	Wkts	Avge	BB	5i	10m	RpO	ct	st
FC		14	21	1	510	82	25.50	0	4	372	266	5	53.20	2-18	0	0	4.29	8	1
SL		15	14	1	362	115*	27.84	1	2	349	324	13	24.92	4-39	1	0	5.57	5	
BH		5	5	0	256	91	51.20	0	3	130	95	5	19.00	3-18	0	0	4.38	0	
NW		2	2	0	9	6	4.50	0	0	36	27	0					4.50	0	
FC	1992	34	55	3	1150	82	22.11	0	8	432	287	5	57.40	2-18	0	0	3.98	49	6
SL	1992	46	40	5	699	115*	19.97	1	2	349	324	13	24.92	4-39	1	0	5.57	33	8
BH	1991	13	11	0	311	91	28.27	0	3	130	95	5	19.00	3-18	0	0	4.38	6	2
NW	1996	4	4	1	46	37*	15.33	0	0	36	27	0					4.50	0	

CADDICK, Andrew Richard (England, England to Zimbabwe, England to New Zealand) b Christchurch, New Zealand 21.11.1968 RHB RFM

Cmp	Debut	M	I	NO	Runs	HS	Avge	100	50	Balls	Runs	Wkts	Avge	BB	5i	10m	RpO	ct	st
Test		5	8	2	59	26*	9.83	0	0	1079	634	24	26.41	5-42	2	0	3.52	1	
FC		18	22	4	321	56*	17.83	0	1	4216	2156	81	26.61	6-65	6	0	3.06	5	
SL		10	3	0	13	8	4.33	0	0	444	375	21	17.85	4-19	1	0	5.06	4	
BH		5	3	2	47	38	47.00	0	0	279	214	9	23.77	3-43	0	0	4.60	1	
NW		2	1	0	5	5	5.00	0	0	113	57	2	28.50	1-27	0	0	3.02	0	
Test	1993	16	26	4	272	29*	12.36	0	0	3890	2006	61	32.88	6-65	4	0	3.09	6	
FC	1991	103	132	23	1797	92	16.48	0	5	21325	11187	415	26.95	9-32	26	8	3.14	37	
Int	1993	9	5	4	35	20*	35.00	0	0	522	398	15	26.53	3-35	0	0	4.57	2	
SL	1992	58	20	6	192	39	13.71	0	0	2475	1953	80	24.41	4-18	3	0	4.73	12	
BH	1992	17	12	8	114	38	28.50	0	0	999	669	25	26.76	5-51	0	1	4.01	3	
NW	1992	14	8	2	26	8	4.33	0	0	848	458	29	15.79	6-30	1	2	3.24	2	

DIMOND, Mathew b Taunton 24.9.1975 RHB RFM

Cmp	Debut	M	I	NO	Runs	HS	Avge	100	50	Balls	Runs	Wkts	Avge	BB	5i	10m	RpO	ct	st
FC		1	1	0	4	4	4.00	0	0	66	30	0					2.72	0	
FC	1994	5	5	1	71	26	17.75	0	0	483	316	6	52.66	4-73	0	0	3.92	4	
SL	1994	3								60	76	0					7.60	0	
BH	1996	1								18	26	0					8.66	0	

ECCLESTONE, Simon Charles b Great Dunmow 16.7.1971 LHB RM

Cmp	Debut	M	I	NO	Runs	HS	Avge	100	50	Balls	Runs	Wkts	Avge	BB	5i	10m	RpO	ct	st
FC		13	23	2	951	133	45.28	3	4	6	0	0					0.00	12	
SL		12	11	1	236	96*	23.60	0	1									1	
BH		5	5	0	130	92	26.00	0	1									1	
NW		2	2	0	188	101	94.00	1	1									0	
FC	1994	41	67	9	2091	133	36.05	3	11	2427	1208	33	36.60	4-66	0	0	2.98	18	
SL	1994	42	41	4	997	130	26.94	1	3	590	593	18	32.94	4-31	1	0	6.03	7	
BH	1994	14	13	2	465	112*	42.27	1	3	210	155	3	51.66	2-44	0	0	4.42	4	
NW	1992	7	7	0	295	101	42.14	1	2	66	53	0					4.81	0	

HARDEN, Richard John b Bridgwater 16.8.1965 RHB SLA

Cmp	Debut	M	I	NO	Runs	HS	Avge	100	50	Balls	Runs	Wkts	Avge	BB	5i	10m	RpO	ct	st
FC		7	11	2	395	136*	43.88	2	1									3	
SL		8	8	2	244	85	40.66	0	3									7	
BH		5	5	0	235	68	47.00	0	3									3	
FC	1985	229	374	58	12596	136*	39.86	28	65	1454	1011	20	50.55	2-7	0	0	4.17	172	
SL	1985	160	154	28	4130	100*	32.77	1	26	1	0	0					0.00	51	
BH	1985	52	50	4	1036	76	22.52	0	6									14	
NW	1986	21	19	2	733	108*	43.11	3	2	18	23	0					7.66	12	

HERZBERG, Steven b Carshalton 25.5.1967 RHB OB (Worcestershire 1990, Kent 1995)

Cmp	Debut	M	I	NO	Runs	HS	Avge	100	50	Balls	Runs	Wkts	Avge	BB	5i	10m	RpO	ct	st
FC		7	8	3	207	56	41.40	0	1	612	281	10	28.10	3-100	0	0	2.75	2	
SL		2								30	37	1	37.00	1-37	0	0	7.40	1	
BH		1								18	20	0					6.66	0	
FC	1991	21	26	8	394	57*	21.88	0	2	3568	1813	47	38.57	5-33	1	0	3.04	6	
SL	1990	3								60	65	1	65.00	1-37	0	0	6.50	1	

HOLLOWAY, Piran Charles Laity b Helston 1.10.1970 LHB WK (Warwickshire 1988-93)

Cmp	Debut	M	I	NO	Runs	HS	Avge	100	50	Balls	Runs	Wkts	Avge	BB	5i	10m	RpO	ct	st
FC		19	34	4	905	106	30.16	1	5									12	
SL		11	10	2	267	117	33.37	1	0									3	
NW		2	2	0	128	90	64.00	0	1									1	
FC	1988	59	99	18	2921	168	36.06	5	17	40	46	0					6.90	54	1
SL	1988	54	45	11	769	117	22.61	1	2									28	7
BH	1991	6	6	1	67	27	13.40	0	0									7	
NW	1991	6	5	1	196	90	49.00	0	2									4	1

JONES, Philip Steffan (Cambridge University, British Universities) b Llanelli 9.2.1974 RHB RFM

Cmp	Debut	M	I	NO	Runs	HS	Avge	100	50	Balls	Runs	Wkts	Avge	BB	5i	10m	RpO	ct	st
FC		10	13	3	142	36	14.20	0	0	1247	739	23	32.13	6-67	1	0	3.55	4	
SL		1								12	19	0					9.50	1	
BH		5	3	2	26	12	26.00	0	0	258	188	5	37.60	2-51	0	0	4.37	2	
NW	1994	1	1	1	26	26*		0	0	18	30	0					10.00	0	

KERR, Jason Ian Douglas b Bolton 7.4.1974 RHB RMF

Cmp	Debut	M	I	NO	Runs	HS	Avge	100	50	Balls	Runs	Wkts	Avge	BB	5i	10m	RpO	ct	st
FC		5	6	1	133	35	26.60	0	0	618	374	10	37.40	4-83	0	0	3.63	1	
SL		12	6	3	75	33	25.00	0	0	491	485	16	30.31	4-28	1	0	5.92	2	
BH		5	3	0	31	17	10.33	0	0	186	138	5	27.60	3-34	0	0	4.45	0	

Cmp	Debut	M	I	NO	Runs	HS	Avge	100	50	Balls	Runs	Wkts	Avge	BB	5i	10m	RpO	ct	st
NW		2	1	0	0	0	0.00	0	0	90	73	5	14.60	3-32	0	0	4.86	0	
FC	1993	32	47	9	730	80	19.21	0	3	3866	2590	64	40.46	5-82	1	0	4.01	10	
SL	1993	40	24	8	174	33	10.87	0	0	1597	1477	50	29.54	4-28	1	0	5.54	5	
BH	1995	6	3	0	31	17	10.33	0	0	234	173	7	24.71	3-34	0	0	4.43	0	
NW	1994	4	3	0	3	3	1.00	0	0	156	147	7	21.00	3-32	0	0	5.65	0	

LATHWELL, Mark Nicholas   b Bletchley 26.12.1971   RHB RM

Cmp	Debut	M	I	NO	Runs	HS	Avge	100	50	Balls	Runs	Wkts	Avge	BB	5i	10m	RpO	ct	st
FC		20	34	1	912	95	27.63	0	6	30	60	1	60.00	1-60	0	0	12.00	11	
SL		15	15	2	316	72	24.30	0	3									4	
BH		5	5	0	103	77	20.60	0	1									4	
NW		2	2	0	43	42	21.50	0	0									1	
Test	1993	2	4	0	78	33	19.50	0	0									0	
FC	1991	122	218	9	7194	206	34.42	11	43	1102	684	13	52.61	2-21	0	0	3.72	85	
SL	1991	90	89	3	2300	117	26.74	1	14	102	85	0					5.00	22	
BH	1992	21	21	0	821	121	39.09	2	6	25	50	0					12.00	7	
NW	1991	16	16	0	459	103	28.68	1	2	66	23	1	23.00	1-23	0	0	2.09	5	

MacGILL, Stuart Charles Glyndwr   (Devon, New South Wales)   b Mount Lawley, Australia 25.2.1971   RHB LBG

Cmp	Debut	M	I	NO	Runs	HS	Avge	100	50	Balls	Runs	Wkts	Avge	BB	5i	10m	RpO	ct	st
FC		1	2	0	32	25	16.00	0	0	216	123	4	30.75	2-49	0	0	3.41	0	
NW		1	1	0	4	4	4.00	0	0	72	30	1	30.00	1-30	0	0	2.50	0	
FC	1993	9	14	6	90	25	11.25	0	0	1533	806	20	40.30	4-72	0	0	3.15	3	

MUSHTAQ AHMED (Lahore, Pakistan, Pakistan to Australia, Pakistan to Sri Lanka, Pakistan to Canada, Pakistan to Sharjah)
b Sahiwal, Pakistan 28.6.1970   RHB LBG

Cmp	Debut	M	I	NO	Runs	HS	Avge	100	50	Balls	Runs	Wkts	Avge	BB	5i	10m	RpO	ct	st
FC		14	16	2	174	33	12.42	0	0	3078	1407	50	28.14	6-70	3	0	2.74	3	
SL		12	5	2	15	7*	5.00	0	0	535	348	12	29.00	3-36	0	0	3.90	3	
BH		3	2	0	41	31	20.50	0	0	134	81	7	11.57	7-24	0	1	3.62	0	
NW		2	1	1	10	10*		0	0	144	61	6	10.16	4-27	1	0	2.54	1	
Test	1989	28	42	1	355	42	10.14	0	0	7172	3309	117	28.28	7-56	7	2	2.76	10	
FC	1986	150	189	22	2345	90	14.04	0	7	35086	17052	671	25.41	9-93	47	13	2.91	73	
Int	1988	124	64	27	332	26	8.97	0	0	6431	4638	141	32.89	5-36	2	1	4.32	27	
SL	1993	46	35	10	251	32	10.04	0	0	2057	1428	45	31.73	3-17	0	0	4.16	5	
BH	1993	11	8	0	87	31	10.87	0	0	606	324	17	19.05	7-24	1	1	3.20	0	
NW	1993	9	6	2	92	35	23.00	0	0	610	313	15	20.86	4-27	1	0	3.07	3	

PARSONS, Keith Alan   b Taunton 2.5.1973   RHB RM

Cmp	Debut	M	I	NO	Runs	HS	Avge	100	50	Balls	Runs	Wkts	Avge	BB	5i	10m	RpO	ct	st
FC		10	15	3	437	74	36.41	0	3	473	204	7	29.14	2-4	0	0	2.58	12	
SL		11	7	3	125	52*	31.25	0	1	384	300	7	42.85	2-18	0	0	4.68	8	
BH		3	3	2	32	22*	32.00	0	0	60	74	1	74.00	1-74	0	0	7.40	1	
NW		2	2	1	1	1	1.00	0	0	66	34	3	11.33	3-34	0	0	3.09	0	
FC	1992	43	74	8	1839	105	27.86	1	14	1361	851	15	56.73	2-4	0	0	3.75	32	
SL	1993	44	33	6	560	56	20.74	0	3	948	780	23	33.91	3-36	0	0	4.93	22	
BH	1996	6	5	3	68	33*	34.00	0	0	138	171	3	57.00	2-60	0	0	7.43	3	
NW	1993	8	8	3	347	116	51.61	1	1	264	190	8	23.75	3-34	0	0	4.31	1	

ROSE, Graham David   b Tottenham 12.4.1964   RHB RM   (Middlesex 1983-86)

Cmp	Debut	M	I	NO	Runs	HS	Avge	100	50	Balls	Runs	Wkts	Avge	BB	5i	10m	RpO	ct	st
FC		18	26	9	852	191	50.11	2	3	2933	1563	63	24.80	5-53	1	0	3.19	7	
SL		15	13	5	181	37*	22.62	0	0	682	436	24	18.16	3-15	0	0	3.83	5	
BH		5	5	0	46	24	9.20	0	0	244	214	9	23.77	3-31	0	0	5.26	2	
NW		2	1	0	18	18	18.00	0	0	126	88	4	22.00	2-43	0	0	4.19	1	
FC	1985	204	284	54	7170	191	31.17	8	35	27664	14749	503	29.32	7-47	12	1	3.19	107	
SL	1983	165	144	28	3232	148	27.86	1	17	6402	4803	164	29.28	4-26	3	0	4.50	44	
BH	1984	50	44	4	814	79	20.35	0	4	2740	1830	64	28.59	4-21	2	0	4.00	11	
NW	1987	22	19	3	347	110	21.68	1	1	1187	786	25	31.44	3-11	0	0	3.97	4	

SHINE, Kevin James   b Bracknell 22.2.1969   RHB RF   (Hampshire 1989-93, Middlesex 1994-95)

Cmp	Debut	M	I	NO	Runs	HS	Avge	100	50	Balls	Runs	Wkts	Avge	BB	5i	10m	RpO	ct	st
FC		18	20	5	96	18	6.40	0	0	2661	1678	55	30.50	7-43	3	1	3.78	5	
SL		5	1	0	3	3	3.00	0	0	182	182	6	30.33	2-25	0	0	6.00	0	
FC	1989	99	91	35	520	40	9.28	0	0	13551	8772	245	35.80	8-47	12	2	3.88	21	
SL	1991	23	5	4	8	3	8.00	0	0	913	846	26	32.53	4-31	1	0	5.55	2	
BH	1990	7	2	1	38	38*	38.00	0	0	308	329	6	54.83	4-68	1	0	6.40	0	
NW	1993	2								129	92	3	30.66	3-31	0	0	4.27	0	

SLADDIN, Richard William   b Halifax 8.1.1969   RHB SLA   (Derbyshire 1991-94)

Cmp	Debut	M	I	NO	Runs	HS	Avge	100	50	Balls	Runs	Wkts	Avge	BB	5i	10m	RpO	ct	st
FC		1								228	105	6	17.50	5-60	1	0	2.76	1	
FC	1991	34	42	9	372	51*	11.27	0	0	8089	3910	99	39.49	6-58	3	0	2.90	15	
SL	1992	11	3	2	24	16	24.00	0	0	456	378	8	47.25	2-26	0	0	4.97	3	

SUTTON, Luke David   b Keynsham 4.10.1976   RHB WK

Cmp	Debut	M	I	NO	Runs	HS	Avge	100	50	Balls	Runs	Wkts	Avge	BB	5i	10m	RpO	ct	st
FC		1	2	1	17	11*	17.00	0	0									5	

TRESCOTHICK, Marcus Edward   b Keynsham 25.12.1975   LHB RM

Cmp	Debut	M	I	NO	Runs	HS	Avge	100	50	Balls	Runs	Wkts	Avge	BB	5i	10m	RpO	ct	st
FC		13	19	1	390	83*	21.66	0	4	90	69	1	69.00	1-18	0	0	4.60	6	
SL		5	4	1	50	28	16.66	0	0	42	52	0					7.42	2	
FC	1993	54	93	2	2465	178	27.08	4	15	426	309	6	51.50	4-36	0	0	4.35	48	
SL	1993	41	37	2	705	74	20.14	0	3	96	107	2	53.50	1-13	0	0	6.68	13	
BH	1995	7	7	1	266	122	44.33	1	2									5	
NW	1994	4	4	0	189	116	47.25	1	0	18	28	0					9.33	2	

53

Cmp	Debut	M	I	NO	Runs	HS	Avge	100	50	Balls	Runs	Wkts	Avge	BB	5i	10m	RpO	ct	st
TROTT, Benjamin James b Wellington 14.3.1975 RHB RF																			
FC		2	2	1	1	1*	1.00	0	0	162	128	5	25.60	3-74	0	0	4.74	1	
SL		1								24	29	1	29.00	1-29	0	0	7.25	0	
TRUMP, Harvey Russell John b Taunton 11.10.1968 RHB OB																			
SL		2	1	0	0	0	0.00	0	0	60	70	0					7.00	1	
BH		3	2	2	3	2*		0	0	84	80	4	20.00	4-51	1	0	5.71	2	
FC	1988	107	121	41	991	48	12.38	0	0	19146	9424	243	38.78	7-52	9	2	2.95	76	
SL	1988	90	28	14	131	19	9.35	0	0	3608	2837	78	36.37	3-19	0	0	4.71	33	
BH	1992	21	9	3	27	11	4.50	0	0	984	668	22	30.36	4-51	1	0	4.07	9	
NW	1989	10	6	2	19	10*	4.75	0	0	547	342	7	48.85	3-15	0	0	3.75	4	
TURNER, Robert Julian b Malvern 25.11.1967 RHB WK																			
FC		17	28	7	1069	144	50.90	1	7									51	2
SL		14	12	1	220	67	20.00	0	1									13	1
BH		5	5	2	129	42	43.00	0	0									7	
NW		2	2	1	15	14*	15.00	0	0									3	
FC	1988	119	186	40	4431	144	30.34	5	21	19	29	0					9.15	272	36
SL	1993	63	52	17	737	67	21.05	0	1									57	10
BH	1990	21	19	9	475	70	47.50	0	1									22	1
NW	1994	9	7	2	100	40	20.00	0	0									17	1
VAN TROOST, Adrianus Petrus b Schiedam, Holland 2.10.1972 RHB RF																			
FC		6	8	3	20	12*	4.00	0	0	473	496	7	70.85	3-79	0	0	6.29	1	
FC	1991	66	78	26	400	35	7.69	0	0	7743	5199	131	39.68	6-48	4	0	4.02	10	
SL	1993	17	6	3	29	9*	9.66	0	0	639	532	17	31.29	4-23	1	0	4.99	2	
BH	1993	3	3	1	19	9*	9.50	0	0	172	172	4	43.00	2-38	0	0	6.00	0	
NW	1993	7	3	1	27	17*	13.50	0	0	366	274	12	22.83	5-22	0	1	4.49	0	

1997 AND CAREER FIGURES FOR SURREY PLAYERS

Cmp	Debut	M	I	NO	Runs	HS	Avge	100	50	Balls	Runs	Wkts	Avge	BB	5i	10m	RpO	ct	st
AMIN, Rupesh Mahesh b Clapham 20.8.1977 RHB SLA																			
FC		4	6	3	11	4*	3.66	0	0	807	348	8	43.50	3-58	0	0	2.58	2	
SL		1								48	43	2	21.50	2-43	0	0	5.37	1	
BATTY, Jonathan Neil b Chesterfield 18.4.1974 RHB WK																			
FC		3	3	1	54	23*	27.00	0	0	24	9	0					2.25	7	1
SL		4	3	1	15	8	7.50	0	0									1	
FC	1994	15	19	5	396	56	28.28	0	2	24	9	0					2.25	18	3
BH	1994	10	8	3	65	26*	13.00	0	0									9	
NW	1996	1	1	0	1	1	1.00	0	0									0	
BENJAMIN, Joseph Emmanuel b Christ Church, St Kitts 2.2.1961 RHB RFM (Warwickshire 1988-91)																			
FC		11	15	6	152	35	16.88	0	0	1266	759	13	58.38	3-52	0	0	3.59	0	
SL		12	3	1	18	13*	9.00	0	0	414	321	7	45.85	2-40	0	0	4.65	1	
BH		6	2	2	5	5*		0	0	348	228	10	22.80	4-19	1	0	3.93	0	
Test	1994	1	1	0	0	0	0.00	0	0	168	80	4	20.00	4-42	0	0	2.85	0	
FC	1988	116	134	40	1095	49	11.64	0	0	21427	10884	364	29.90	6-19	16	1	3.04	23	
Int	1994	2	1	0	0	0	0.00	0	0	72	47	1	47.00	1-22	0	0	3.91	0	
SL	1989	91	36	15	190	24	9.04	0	0	3873	2895	89	32.52	4-44	1	0	4.48	16	
BH	1990	24	6	4	32	20	16.00	0	0	1458	939	31	30.29	4-19	2	0	3.86	6	
NW	1986	18	8	3	64	25	12.80	0	0	1086	652	21	31.04	4-20	1	0	3.60	3	
BICKNELL, Darren John b Guildford 24.6.1967 LHB SLA																			
FC		9	15	0	594	162	39.60	2	1	72	38	1	38.00	1-12	0	0	3.16	1	
SL		4	4	1	79	49*	26.33	0	0									3	
FC	1987	200	352	34	12696	235*	39.92	30	59	1232	789	23	34.30	3-7	0	0	3.84	75	
SL	1988	96	93	13	2915	125	36.43	4	17	36	39	2	19.50	1-11	0	0	6.50	24	
BH	1987	33	32	3	1241	119	42.79	2	9									12	
NW	1989	20	20	4	778	135*	48.62	1	5									1	
BICKNELL, Martin Paul b Guildford 14.1.1969 RHB RFM																			
FC		15	20	5	305	74	20.33	0	2	2312	1174	44	26.68	5-34	1	0	3.04	8	
SL		14	7	5	107	57*	53.50	0	1	504	389	18	21.61	4-28	1	0	4.63	4	
BH		8	4	3	26	13	26.00	0	0	450	316	15	21.06	4-41	1	0	4.21	0	
NW		2	1	0	24	24	24.00	0	0	132	53	3	17.66	2-28	0	0	2.40	0	
Test	1993	2	4	0	26	14	6.50	0	0	522	263	4	65.75	3-99	0	0	3.02	0	
FC	1986	181	215	58	2979	88	18.97	0	10	34387	16405	630	26.03	9-45	27	2	2.86	63	
Int	1990	7	6	2	96	31*	24.00	0	0	413	347	13	26.69	3-55	0	0	5.04	2	
SL	1986	137	60	30	485	57*	16.16	0	1	5821	4200	165	25.45	5-12	6	1	4.32	33	
BH	1987	44	23	7	208	43	13.00	0	0	2568	1692	69	24.52	4-41	2	0	3.95	8	
NW	1986	28	14	6	126	66*	15.75	0	1	1779	984	38	25.89	4-35	2	0	3.31	13	
BROWN, Alistair Duncan b Beckenham 11.2.1970 RHB LB																			
FC		14	21	1	848	170*	42.40	3	2	96	37	0					2.31	11	
SL		14	14	1	558	203	42.92	2	2									1	
BH		8	8	0	256	71	32.00	0	2									4	

Cmp	Debut	M	I	NO	Runs	HS	Avge	100	50	Balls	Runs	Wkts	Avge	BB	5i	10m	RpO	ct	st
NW		2	2	0	63	44	31.50	0	0									1	
Int	1996	3	3	0	155	118	51.66	1	0									1	
FC	1992	93	150	14	5628	187	41.38	14	23	324	176	0					3.25	92	
SL	1990	107	103	4	3419	203	34.53	8	15									26	
BH	1991	30	30	6	987	117*	41.12	1	5									9	
NW	1993	15	12	1	377	72	34.27	0	2									3	

BUTCHER, Mark Alan (England, England A, England A to Australia) b Croydon 23.8.1972 LHB RM

Cmp	Debut	M	I	NO	Runs	HS	Avge	100	50	Balls	Runs	Wkts	Avge	BB	5i	10m	RpO	ct	st
Test		5	10	0	254	87	25.40	0	2	12	14	0					7.00	8	
FC		19	34	1	1068	153	32.36	1	7	246	97	7	13.85	3-24	0	0	2.36	28	
SL		10	10	1	227	81	25.22	0	1	48	35	1	35.00	1-24	0	0	4.37	6	
BH		6	5	1	124	48	31.00	0	0									2	
NW		2	2	0	35	35	17.50	0	0									3	
FC	1992	78	139	11	5029	167	39.28	7	37	4311	2494	68	36.67	4-31	0	0	3.47	91	
SL	1991	52	40	11	682	81	23.51	0	2	1381	1305	28	46.60	3-23	0	0	5.66	17	
BH	1993	15	11	3	187	48	23.37	0	0	343	291	6	48.50	3-37	0	0	5.09	4	
NW	1992	10	10	2	370	91	46.25	0	3	216	127	3	42.33	2-57	0	0	3.52	6	

HOLLIOAKE, Adam John (England, England A, England A to Australia) b Melbourne, Australia 5.9.1971 RHB RMF

Cmp	Debut	M	I	NO	Runs	HS	Avge	100	50	Balls	Runs	Wkts	Avge	BB	5i	10m	RpO	ct	st
Test		2	4	0	51	45	12.75	0	0	114	55	2	27.50	2-31	0	0	2.89	4	
FC		16	25	1	891	182	37.12	1	6	796	458	15	30.53	4-22	0	0	3.45	15	
Int		3	3	3	123	66*		0	2	92	82	4	20.50	2-22	0	0	5.34	1	
SL		12	12	0	288	63	24.00	0	2	348	375	16	23.43	5-38	0	1	6.46	3	
BH		8	6	0	217	80	36.16	0	2	242	209	11	19.00	3-40	0	0	5.18	2	
NW		2	2	0	41	34	20.50	0	0	78	66	0					5.07	0	
FC	1993	76	123	12	4691	182	42.26	11	28	6017	3324	82	40.53	4-22	0	0	3.31	63	
Int	1996	5	5	3	151	66*	75.50	0	2	185	150	12	12.50	4-23	2	0	4.86	1	
SL	1992	70	61	10	1510	93	29.60	0	8	2519	2445	105	23.28	5-38	5	3	5.82	13	
BH	1994	21	15	1	318	80	22.71	0	2	692	602	21	28.66	4-34	1	0	5.21	6	
NW	1994	12	10	2	302	60	37.75	0	2	500	388	14	27.71	4-53	1	0	4.65	6	

HOLLIOAKE, Benjamin Caine (England, Rest of England) b Melbourne, Australia 11.11.1977 RHB RMF

Cmp	Debut	M	I	NO	Runs	HS	Avge	100	50	Balls	Runs	Wkts	Avge	BB	5i	10m	RpO	ct	st
Test		1	2	0	30	28	15.00	0	0	90	83	2	41.50	1-26	0	0	5.53	1	
FC		14	22	1	559	76	26.61	0	3	1286	782	23	34.00	4-54	0	0	3.64	13	
Int		1	1	0	63	63	63.00	0	1	42	36	0					5.14	0	
SL		11	10	1	213	61	23.66	0	1	462	444	13	34.15	3-47	0	0	5.76	1	
BH		8	8	0	259	98	32.37	0	2	308	271	6	45.16	2-15	0	0	5.27	1	
NW		2	1	0	0	0	0.00	0	0	96	70	1	70.00	1-39	0	0	4.37	1	
FC	1996	17	26	1	622	76	24.88	0	3	1676	1034	33	31.33	4-54	0	0	3.70	16	
SL	1996	22	18	3	283	61	18.86	0	1	814	712	26	27.38	5-10	0	1	5.24	6	
BH	1996	9	8	0	259	98	32.37	0	2	350	296	7	42.28	2-15	0	0	5.07	1	
NW	1996	3	1	0	0	0	0.00	0	0	120	95	1	95.00	1-39	0	0	4.75	3	

KENNIS, Gregor John b Yokohama, Japan 9.3.1974 RHB OB

Cmp	Debut	M	I	NO	Runs	HS	Avge	100	50	Balls	Runs	Wkts	Avge	BB	5i	10m	RpO	ct	st
FC		3	5	0	49	24	9.80	0	0	6	4	0					4.00	3	
FC	1994	6	11	1	140	29	14.00	0	0	24	4	0					1.00	6	
SL	1995	1	1	0	5	5	5.00	0	0									0	

KNOTT, James Alan b Canterbury 14.6.1975 RHB RM WK

Cmp	Debut	M	I	NO	Runs	HS	Avge	100	50	Balls	Runs	Wkts	Avge	BB	5i	10m	RpO	ct	st
FC		5	9	3	118	27*	19.66	0	0									8	1
SL		4	3	0	23	22	7.66	0	0									5	
BH		2	1	0	10	10	10.00	0	0									6	
FC	1995	7	11	4	170	49*	24.28	0	0									11	2

LEWIS, Clairmonte Christopher b Georgetown, Guyana 14.2.1968 RHB RFM (Leicestershire 1987-91, Nottinghamshire 1992-95)

Cmp	Debut	M	I	NO	Runs	HS	Avge	100	50	Balls	Runs	Wkts	Avge	BB	5i	10m	RpO	ct	st
FC		13	19	2	389	76	22.88	0	1	1750	970	33	29.39	5-42	1	0	3.32	10	
SL		12	11	5	182	68*	30.33	0	1	477	345	16	21.56	4-21	1	0	4.33	8	
BH		7	4	1	102	35*	34.00	0	0	342	217	12	18.08	3-39	0	0	3.80	3	
NW		2	2	1	18	15	18.00	0	0	120	49	3	16.33	2-37	0	0	2.45	1	
Test	1990	32	51	3	1105	117	23.02	1	4	6852	3490	93	37.52	6-111	3	0	3.05	25	
FC	1987	161	241	29	6439	247	30.37	7	28	28667	14366	481	29.86	6-22	18	3	3.00	131	
Int	1989	51	38	13	348	33	13.92	0	0	2513	1854	65	28.52	4-30	4	0	4.42	20	
SL	1987	101	86	21	1777	93*	27.33	0	8	3932	2861	110	26.00	4-13	4	0	4.36	33	
BH	1988	35	26	10	494	48*	30.87	0	0	1869	1245	53	23.49	5-46	0	1	3.99	13	
NW	1987	19	17	2	361	89	24.06	0	2	1062	626	24	26.08	3-24	0	0	3.53	11	

PEARSON, Richard Michael b Batley 27.1.1972 RHB OB (Northamptonshire 1992, Essex 1994-95)

Cmp	Debut	M	I	NO	Runs	HS	Avge	100	50	Balls	Runs	Wkts	Avge	BB	5i	10m	RpO	ct	st
FC		1	1	0	1	1	1.00	0	0	156	90	2	45.00	2-90	0	0	3.46	1	
FC	1991	51	56	16	475	37	11.87	0	0	10356	5516	100	55.16	5-108	2	0	3.19	15	
SL	1992	29	13	10	46	9*	15.33	0	0	901	828	23	36.00	3-33	0	0	5.51	3	
BH	1991	13	3	2	22	12*	22.00	0	0	749	556	11	50.54	3-46	0	0	4.45	1	
NW	1994	5	1	0	11	11	11.00	0	0	276	188	3	62.66	1-39	0	0	4.08	0	

RATCLIFFE, Jason David b Solihull 19.6.1969 RHB RM (Warwickshire 1988-94)

Cmp	Debut	M	I	NO	Runs	HS	Avge	100	50	Balls	Runs	Wkts	Avge	BB	5i	10m	RpO	ct	st
FC		15	26	2	759	135	31.62	1	4	348	177	1	177.00	1-14	0	0	3.05	3	
SL		13	10	0	290	82	29.00	0	3	114	92	2	46.00	1-16	0	0	4.84	5	

Cmp	Debut	M	I	NO	Runs	HS	Avge	100	50	Balls	Runs	Wkts	Avge	BB	5i	10m	RpO	ct	st
BH		3	2	1	13	13*	13.00	0	0	48	42	2	21.00	2-42	0	0	5.25	1	
NW		2	2	0	42	39	21.00	0	0									0	
FC	1988	111	203	11	5666	135	29.51	4	34	943	578	10	57.80	2-26	0	0	3.67	58	
SL	1989	34	30	3	567	82	21.00	0	3	277	271	7	38.71	2-11	0	0	5.87	11	
BH	1991	5	4	1	56	29	18.66	0	0	48	42	2	21.00	2-42	0	0	5.25	1	
NW	1989	11	11	1	379	105	37.90	1	2	30	20	0					4.00	1	

SALISBURY, Ian David Kenneth b Northampton 21.1.1970 RHB LB (Sussex 1989-96)

FC		13	17	2	159	30*	10.60	0	0	1885	936	30	31.20	6-19	2	0	2.97	7	
SL		10	5	4	43	23*	43.00	0	0	336	310	10	31.00	3-56	0	0	5.53	5	
BH		8	5	1	31	14	7.75	0	0	383	292	8	36.50	4-53	1	0	4.57	4	
NW		2	1	0	5	5	5.00	0	0	144	68	5	13.60	3-36	0	0	2.83	0	
Test	1992	9	17	2	255	50	17.00	0	1	1773	1154	18	64.11	4-163	0	0	3.90	3	
FC	1989	178	234	50	3335	86	18.12	0	10	32883	17285	509	33.95	8-75	26	4	3.15	131	
Int	1992	4	2	1	7	5	7.00	0	0	186	177	5	35.40	3-41	0	0	5.70	1	
SL	1989	102	65	20	623	48*	13.84	0	0	3894	3224	94	34.29	5-30	2	1	4.96	32	
BH	1990	26	16	5	129	19	11.72	0	0	1448	1027	31	33.12	4-53	1	0	4.25	12	
NW	1990	19	13	3	102	33	10.20	0	0	1212	662	23	28.78	3-28	0	0	3.27	5	

SAQLAIN MUSHTAQ (Pakistan, Pakistan to Australia, Pakistan to Sri Lanka, Pakistan to Canada, Pakistan to Kenya, Pakistan to Sharjah, Pakistan to India) b Lahore 27.11.1976 RHB OB

FC		8	10	4	149	41*	24.83	0	0	1529	617	32	19.28	5-17	4	2	2.42	1	
SL		9	4	1	61	29*	20.33	0	0	333	276	12	23.00	3-31	0	0	4.97	2	
BH		2								102	54	2	27.00	2-33	0	0	3.17	0	
NW		2	1	1	6	6*		0	0	121	93	4	23.25	3-30	0	0	4.61	0	
Test	1995	9	14	4	256	79	25.60	0	2	3045	1387	38	36.50	5-89	1	0	2.73	4	
FC	1994	41	61	17	716	79	16.27	0	4	9405	4011	172	23.31	7-66	13	3	2.55	21	
Int	1995	56	37	10	255	30*	9.44	0	0	2971	2115	109	19.40	5-29	4	2	4.27	17	

SHAHID, Nadeem b Karachi, Pakistan 23.4.1969 RHB LB (Essex 1989-94)

FC		7	11	0	198	34	18.00	0	0	30	14	0					2.80	4	
SL		9	8	2	97	34*	16.16	0	0									1	
BH		6	6	3	122	52	40.66	0	1									1	
FC	1989	98	154	21	4195	139	31.54	5	23	2914	1927	41	47.00	3-91	0	0	3.96	89	
SL	1989	77	65	11	1307	101	24.20	1	2	36	43	0					7.16	24	
BH	1991	18	12	4	238	65*	29.75	0	2	150	131	1	131.00	1-59	0	0	5.24	2	
NW	1991	7	5	1	151	85*	37.75	0	1	18	0	1	0.00	1-0	0	0	0.00	5	

STEWART, Alec James (England, England to Zimbabwe, England to New Zealand) b Merton 8.4.1963 RHB RM WK

Test		6	12	1	268	87	24.36	0	1									23	
FC		15	26	2	994	271*	41.41	2	3									39	
Int		3	3	0	126	79	42.00	0	1									2	1
SL		8	8	1	141	67*	20.14	0	1									7	2
BH		8	8	2	384	87	64.00	0	5									10	
NW		2	2	1	116	90*	116.00	0	1									3	
Test	1989	69	123	8	4701	190	40.87	10	23	20	13	0					3.90	112	7
FC	1981	333	551	62	19965	271*	40.82	41	110	469	417	3	139.00	1-7	0	0	5.33	456	17
Int	1989	90	85	7	2452	103	31.43	1	14									77	8
SL	1981	162	146	16	4093	125	31.48	7	23	4	8	0					12.00	127	10
BH	1984	58	58	10	2321	167*	48.35	3	18									44	4
NW	1984	36	33	6	1356	125*	50.22	3	9									40	2

THORPE, Graham Paul (England, England to Zimbabwe, England to New Zealand) b Farnham 1.8.1969 LHB RM

Test		6	11	2	453	138	50.33	1	3									8	
FC		14	23	4	1160	222	61.05	3	6	24	13	0					3.25	17	
Int		3	3	2	127	75*	127.00	0	1									3	
SL		6	6	1	225	100*	45.00	1	0									2	
BH		8	8	1	327	79	46.71	0	3									7	
NW		2	2	0	0	0	0.00	0	0									3	
Test	1993	43	78	8	2964	138	42.34	5	22	138	37	0					1.60	39	
FC	1988	215	362	49	14048	222	44.88	30	82	2219	1235	25	49.40	4-40	0	0	3.33	167	
Int	1993	39	39	6	1349	89	40.87	0	12	120	97	2	48.50	2-15	0	0	4.85	21	
SL	1988	108	99	14	3088	115*	36.32	4	21	318	307	8	38.37	3-21	0	0	5.79	41	
BH	1989	37	36	3	1239	103	37.54	1	8	168	131	4	32.75	3-35	0	0	4.67	19	
NW	1989	23	22	4	807	145*	44.83	1	6	13	12	0					5.53	13	

TUDOR, Alex Jeremy (Rest of England) b Kensington 23.10.1977 RHB RFM

FC		9	11	6	109	35*	21.80	0	0	963	607	17	35.70	6-101	1	0	3.78	0	
SL		2								54	49	2	24.50	1-23	0	0	5.44	2	
FC	1995	14	20	6	232	56	16.57	0	1	1464	927	31	29.90	6-101	2	0	3.79	1	
SL	1995	4	2	1	40	29*	40.00	0	0	96	97	3	32.33	1-19	0	0	6.06	4	
NW	1995	1								60	27	1	27.00	1-27	0	0	2.70	0	

WARD, Ian James b Plymouth 30.9.1972 LHB RM

FC		3	4	0	102	56	25.50	0	1									6	
SL		10	9	3	81	31	13.50	0	0									1	
FC	1992	5	7	0	121	56	17.28	0	1	102	84	0					4.94	7	

Cmp	Debut	M	I	NO	Runs	HS	Avge	100	50	Balls	Runs	Wkts	Avge	BB	5i	10m	RpO	ct	st
SL	1996	13	11	4	83	31	11.85	0	0	23	41	0					10.69	2	
NW	1996	1	1	0	14	14	14.00	0	0									0	

1997 AND CAREER FIGURES FOR SUSSEX PLAYERS

ATHEY, Charles William Jeffrey b Middlesbrough 27.9.1957 RHB RM (Yorkshire 1976-83, Gloucestershire 1984-92)

Cmp	Debut	M	I	NO	Runs	HS	Avge	100	50	Balls	Runs	Wkts	Avge	BB	5i	10m	RpO	ct	st
FC		12	21	2	682	138*	35.89	1	5	42	21	0					3.00	9	
SL		9	9	1	252	109*	31.50	1	1									0	
BH		5	4	0	121	66	30.25	0	1									0	
NW		4	4	1	95	30	31.66	0	0									1	
Test	1980	23	41	1	919	123	22.97	1	4									13	
FC	1976	467	784	71	25453	184	35.69	55	126	4810	2673	48	55.68	3-3	0	0	3.33	429	2
Int	1980	31	30	3	848	142*	31.40	2	4	6	10	0					10.00	16	
SL	1976	269	258	23	7504	121*	31.93	7	47	913	857	30	28.56	5-35	1	1	5.63	97	
BH	1976	84	79	11	2551	118	37.51	1	20	478	364	16	22.75	4-48	2	0	4.56	34	1
NW	1976	53	52	9	1860	115	43.25	2	14	199	168	1	168.00	1-18	0	0	5.06	22	

BATES, Justin Jonathan b Farnborough, Hampshire 9.4.1976 RHB OB

Cmp	Debut	M	I	NO	Runs	HS	Avge	100	50	Balls	Runs	Wkts	Avge	BB	5i	10m	RpO	ct	st
FC		7	9	2	113	47	16.14	0	0	1364	525	19	27.63	5-89	1	0	2.30	6	
SL		3	3	1	8	5*	4.00	0	0	60	53	1	53.00	1-24	0	0	5.30	1	
SL	1996	4	4	1	16	8	5.33	0	0	78	99	1	99.00	1-24	0	0	7.61	2	

BATT, Christopher James b Taplow 22.9.1976 LHB LMF

Cmp	Debut	M	I	NO	Runs	HS	Avge	100	50	Balls	Runs	Wkts	Avge	BB	5i	10m	RpO	ct	st
FC		1								240	100	6	16.66	4-56	0	0	2.50	1	

CARPENTER, James Robert b Birkenhead 20.10.1975 LHB SLA

Cmp	Debut	M	I	NO	Runs	HS	Avge	100	50	Balls	Runs	Wkts	Avge	BB	5i	10m	RpO	ct	st
FC		3	6	0	153	63	25.50	0	1	129	81	1	81.00	1-50	0	0	3.76	2	
SL		2	2	1	35	18	35.00	0	0	6	15	0					15.00	0	

DRAKES, Vasbert Conniel (Barbados, Border) b St James, Barbados 5.8.1969 RHB RF

Cmp	Debut	M	I	NO	Runs	HS	Avge	100	50	Balls	Runs	Wkts	Avge	BB	5i	10m	RpO	ct	st
FC		10	18	1	221	48	13.00	0	0	1800	1043	31	33.64	4-55	0	0	3.47	7	
SL		9	8	2	48	12*	8.00	0	0	342	282	7	40.28	2-21	0	0	4.94	0	
BH		4	3	0	75	58	25.00	0	1	186	146	4	36.50	3-46	0	0	4.70	0	
NW		4	1	0	15	15	15.00	0	0	258	148	9	16.44	4-62	1	0	3.44	0	
FC	1991	63	100	15	2048	180*	24.09	4	6	10463	6027	198	30.43	8-59	6	1	3.45	17	
Int	1994	5	2	0	25	16	12.50	0	0	239	204	3	68.00	1-36	0	0	5.12	1	
SL	1996	23	20	4	213	37	13.31	0	0	962	862	24	35.91	4-50	1	0	5.37	2	
BH	1996	8	6	1	130	58	26.00	0	1	396	289	11	26.27	5-19	0	1	4.37	0	
NW	1996	7	4	1	104	35	34.66	0	0	441	250	15	16.66	4-62	1	0	3.40	0	

EDWARDS, Alexander David (British Universities) b Cuckfield 2.8.1975 RHB RFM

Cmp	Debut	M	I	NO	Runs	HS	Avge	100	50	Balls	Runs	Wkts	Avge	BB	5i	10m	RpO	ct	st
FC		6	10	2	66	20	8.25	0	0	620	389	17	22.88	5-34	1	0	3.76	5	
SL		4	4	1	11	9*	3.66	0	0	107	82	3	27.33	2-44	0	0	4.59	1	
BH		2	2	1	9	9	9.00	0	0	120	109	0					5.45	0	
FC	1995	9	13	2	104	22	9.45	0	0	980	699	20	34.95	5-34	1	0	4.27	7	
SL	1994	5	4	1	11	9*	3.66	0	0	137	106	3	35.33	2-44	0	0	4.64	1	
BH	1995	7	6	2	30	9	7.50	0	0	444	341	5	68.20	2-51	0	0	4.60	5	

GREENFIELD, Keith b Brighton 6.12.1968 RHB RM

Cmp	Debut	M	I	NO	Runs	HS	Avge	100	50	Balls	Runs	Wkts	Avge	BB	5i	10m	RpO	ct	st
FC		11	21	0	372	108	17.71	1	0	60	45	0					4.50	12	
SL		15	15	2	426	69*	32.76	0	4	42	38	0					5.42	3	
BH		5	5	0	123	44	24.60	0	0	30	27	1	27.00	1-17	0	0	5.40	1	
NW		4	4	1	223	129	74.33	1	1	120	121	0					6.05	2	
FC	1987	78	135	15	3550	154*	29.58	9	13	814	524	5	104.80	2-40	0	0	3.86	65	
SL	1987	111	109	10	2634	102	26.60	1	16	964	954	21	45.42	3-34	0	0	5.93	34	
BH	1989	23	22	2	518	62	25.90	0	3	432	354	2	177.00	1-17	0	0	4.91	8	
NW	1992	15	14	3	431	129	39.18	1	2	402	303	3	101.00	2-35	0	0	4.52	7	

HUMPHRIES, Shaun b Horsham 11.1.1973 RHB WK

Cmp	Debut	M	I	NO	Runs	HS	Avge	100	50	Balls	Runs	Wkts	Avge	BB	5i	10m	RpO	ct	st
FC		2	3	1	52	41*	26.00	0	0									6	
FC	1993	4	3	1	52	41*	26.00	0	0									9	

JARVIS, Paul William (Wellington) b Redcar 29.6.1965 RHB RFM (Yorkshire 1981-93)

Cmp	Debut	M	I	NO	Runs	HS	Avge	100	50	Balls	Runs	Wkts	Avge	BB	5i	10m	RpO	ct	st
FC		11	18	2	374	64	23.37	0	4	1913	1091	30	36.36	5-44	2	0	3.42	5	
SL		11	11	0	51	14	4.63	0	0	440	355	12	29.58	3-32	0	0	4.84	1	
BH		5	5	3	144	63	72.00	0	1	288	221	10	22.10	4-60	1	0	4.60	0	
NW		2	1	0	16	16	16.00	0	0	114	129	0					6.78	0	
Test	1987	9	15	2	132	29*	10.15	0	0	1912	965	21	45.95	4-107	0	0	3.02	2	
FC	1981	201	252	66	3189	80	17.14	0	10	33444	17786	621	28.64	7-55	22	3	3.19	59	
Int	1987	16	8	2	31	16*	5.16	0	0	879	672	24	28.00	5-35	1	1	4.58	1	
SL	1981	138	83	28	592	43	10.76	0	0	5804	4326	197	21.95	6-27	5	4	4.47	30	
BH	1985	45	25	9	336	63	21.00	0	1	2582	1553	74	20.98	4-34	3	0	3.60	4	
NW	1982	21	13	3	139	34*	13.90	0	0	1325	890	22	40.45	4-41	1	0	4.03	4	

KHAN, Aamer Ali b Lahore, Pakistan 5.11.1969 RHB LB (Middlesex 1995)

Cmp	Debut	M	I	NO	Runs	HS	Avge	100	50	Balls	Runs	Wkts	Avge	BB	5i	10m	RpO	ct	st
FC		15	24	5	291	52	15.31	0	1	2667	1397	33	42.33	5-137	1	0	3.14	4	
SL		13	9	3	48	22*	8.00	0	0	545	474	15	31.60	5-40	0	1	5.21	2	

Cmp	Debut	M	I	NO	Runs	HS	Avge	100	50	Balls	Runs	Wkts	Avge	BB	5i	10m	RpO	ct	st
BH		5	3	0	15	8	5.00	0	0	294	217	8	27.12	3-31	0	0	4.42	2	
NW		4	1	0	4	4	4.00	0	0	240	196	2	98.00	1-13	0	0	4.90	1	
FC	1987	19	24	5	291	52	15.31	0	1	3147	1557	41	37.97	5-137	1	0	2.96	5	

KIRTLEY, Robert James (Mashonaland, Mashonaland to South Africa) b Eastbourne 10.1.1975 RHB RFM

Cmp	Debut	M	I	NO	Runs	HS	Avge	100	50	Balls	Runs	Wkts	Avge	BB	5i	10m	RpO	ct	st
FC		11	16	7	49	15*	5.44	0	0	1659	1094	31	35.29	6-60	1	0	3.95	4	
SL		7	4	2	14	7	7.00	0	0	289	300	7	42.85	2-36	0	0	6.22	2	
NW		2								144	100	7	14.28	5-39	0	1	4.16	0	
FC	1995	23	31	13	76	15*	4.22	0	0	3475	2125	74	28.71	6-60	4	0	3.66	11	
SL	1995	16	7	4	17	7	5.66	0	0	571	554	12	46.16	2-36	0	0	5.82	2	

LENHAM, Neil John b Worthing 17.12.1965 RHB RMF

Cmp	Debut	M	I	NO	Runs	HS	Avge	100	50	Balls	Runs	Wkts	Avge	BB	5i	10m	RpO	ct	st
FC		7	12	0	290	93	24.16	0	2									2	
SL		4	4	0	71	41	17.75	0	0	12	14	1	14.00	1-14	0	0	7.00	0	
BH		3	3	0	6	6	2.00	0	0									1	
NW		1	1	1	28	28*		0	0									0	
FC	1984	192	332	29	10135	222*	33.44	20	49	3637	1847	42	43.97	4-13	0	0	3.04	73	
SL	1985	98	85	16	1861	86	26.97	0	11	894	884	30	29.46	5-28	0	1	5.93	19	
BH	1986	28	26	6	606	82	30.30	0	4	264	223	4	55.75	1-3	0	0	5.06	4	
NW	1986	15	14	4	601	129*	60.10	1	3	411	240	10	24.00	2-12	0	0	3.50	0	

MARTIN-JENKINS, Robin Simon Christopher (British Universities) b Guildford 28.10.1975 RHB RM

Cmp	Debut	M	I	NO	Runs	HS	Avge	100	50	Balls	Runs	Wkts	Avge	BB	5i	10m	RpO	ct	st
FC		3	6	1	77	36*	15.40	0	0	342	184	5	36.80	3-26	0	0	3.22	2	
SL		2	2	0	5	3	2.50	0	0	96	90	1	90.00	1-32	0	0	5.62	0	
BH		3	2	0	20	10	10.00	0	0	138	140	5	28.00	4-57	1	0	6.08	0	
FC	1995	7	9	2	147	50	21.00	0	1	708	353	6	58.83	3-26	0	0	2.99	2	
SL	1995	12	8	1	17	10	2.42	0	0	420	382	6	63.66	2-41	0	0	5.45	0	
BH	1994	6	5	0	36	12	7.20	0	0	304	276	9	30.66	4-57	1	0	5.44	0	

MOORES, Peter b Macclesfield 18.12.1962 RHB WK (Worcestershire 1983-84)

Cmp	Debut	M	I	NO	Runs	HS	Avge	100	50	Balls	Runs	Wkts	Avge	BB	5i	10m	RpO	ct	st
FC		17	31	4	571	102*	21.14	1	2									36	
SL		15	15	1	182	32	13.00	0	0									10	1
BH		5	5	1	54	21*	13.50	0	0									7	1
NW		4	2	1	64	45	64.00	0	0									4	1
FC	1983	228	342	41	7295	185	24.23	7	31	18	16	0					5.33	500	44
SL	1983	168	136	37	1927	89*	19.46	0	7									145	23
BH	1987	35	27	4	329	76	14.30	0	1									29	5
NW	1985	28	19	4	231	45	15.40	0	0									36	3

NEWELL, Keith b Crawley 25.3.1972 RHB RM

Cmp	Debut	M	I	NO	Runs	HS	Avge	100	50	Balls	Runs	Wkts	Avge	BB	5i	10m	RpO	ct	st
FC		17	31	2	827	112	28.51	2	3	829	436	11	39.63	4-61	0	0	3.15	2	
SL		13	12	0	152	35	12.66	0	0	318	222	7	31.71	2-22	0	0	4.18	4	
BH		3	3	0	45	34	15.00	0	0	66	58	1	58.00	1-35	0	0	5.27	1	
NW		4	2	1	52	29*	52.00	0	0	210	148	2	74.00	1-61	0	0	4.22	1	
FC	1995	33	61	5	1625	135	29.01	4	6	1195	647	12	53.91	4-61	0	0	3.24	6	
SL	1993	34	29	2	449	76*	16.62	0	1	474	418	8	52.25	2-22	0	0	5.29	8	
BH	1995	7	6	0	126	46	21.00	0	0	145	115	2	57.50	1-25	0	0	4.75	1	
NW	1995	6	4	1	152	52	50.66	0	1	210	148	2	74.00	1-61	0	0	4.22	1	

NEWELL, Mark b Crawley 19.12.1973 RHB OB

Cmp	Debut	M	I	NO	Runs	HS	Avge	100	50	Balls	Runs	Wkts	Avge	BB	5i	10m	RpO	ct	st
FC		12	22	1	471	100	22.42	1	3									9	
SL		13	13	1	258	60	21.50	0	1									4	
BH		2	2	0	147	87	73.50	0	2									0	
NW		4	3	1	186	79	93.00	0	2									0	
FC	1996	13	24	1	471	100	20.47	1	3									10	
SL	1996	18	18	2	423	69	26.43	0	2									7	

PEIRCE, Michael Toby Edward b Maidenhead 14.6.1973 LHB SLA

Cmp	Debut	M	I	NO	Runs	HS	Avge	100	50	Balls	Runs	Wkts	Avge	BB	5i	10m	RpO	ct	st
FC		12	23	0	576	104	25.04	1	3	121	76	0					3.76	10	
SL		1	1	0	7	7	7.00	0	0									0	
FC	1994	19	35	0	819	104	23.40	1	4	175	106	0					3.63	15	
SL	1994	3	3	0	20	7	6.66	0	0									2	
BH	1995	5	5	0	134	44	26.80	0	0									1	

PHILLIPS, Nicholas Charles b Pembury 10.5.1974 RHB OB

Cmp	Debut	M	I	NO	Runs	HS	Avge	100	50	Balls	Runs	Wkts	Avge	BB	5i	10m	RpO	ct	st
FC		3	2	1	7	6	7.00	0	0	156	114	1	114.00	1-47	0	0	4.38	0	
SL		5	4	0	31	21	7.75	0	0	96	79	1	79.00	1-17	0	0	4.93	0	
BH		5	4	1	11	11	3.66	0	0	205	161	5	32.20	3-48	0	0	4.80	2	
FC	1993	19	26	10	450	53	28.12	0	3	2903	1643	27	60.85	3-39	0	0	3.39	9	
SL	1994	19	13	5	110	38*	13.75	0	0	521	464	7	66.28	2-19	0	0	5.34	3	
BH	1996	6	5	1	21	11	5.25	0	0	235	210	5	42.00	3-48	0	0	5.36	2	

PYEMONT, James Patrick b Eastbourne 10.4.1978 RHB OB

Cmp	Debut	M	I	NO	Runs	HS	Avge	100	50	Balls	Runs	Wkts	Avge	BB	5i	10m	RpO	ct	st
FC		1	1	0	22	22	22.00	0	0									2	
SL		4	4	1	23	18*	7.66	0	0									1	

RADFORD, Toby Alexander b Caerphilly 31.12.1971 RHB OB (Middlesex 1993-95)

Cmp	Debut	M	I	NO	Runs	HS	Avge	100	50	Balls	Runs	Wkts	Avge	BB	5i	10m	RpO	ct	st
FC		2	4	2	131	69*	65.50	0	2									3	
FC	1994	14	24	6	476	69*	26.44	0	5	6	0	1	0.00	1-0	0	0	0.00	13	

Cmp	Debut	M	I	NO	Runs	HS	Avge	100	50	Balls	Runs	Wkts	Avge	BB	5i	10m	RpO	ct	st
SL	1993	4	4	1	73	38	24.33	0	0									0	
NW	1995	1	1	0	82	82	82.00	0	1									0	

RAO, Rajesh Krishnakant   b Park Royal 9.12.1974   RHB LBG

Cmp	Debut	M	I	NO	Runs	HS	Avge	100	50	Balls	Runs	Wkts	Avge	BB	5i	10m	RpO	ct	st
FC		11	20	1	375	89	19.73	0	3	168	100	2	50.00	1-14	0	0	3.57	6	
SL		12	12	0	266	60	22.16	0	2	30	34	0					6.80	5	
BH		2	2	0	76	61	38.00	0	1									1	
NW		2	2	0	158	158	79.00	1	0									2	
FC	1996	13	23	2	462	89	22.00	0	3	198	107	2	53.50	1-14	0	0	3.24	6	
SL	1996	23	23	1	559	91	25.40	0	5	84	82	3	27.33	3-31	0	0	5.85	9	

ROBINSON, Mark Andrew   b Hull 23.11.1966   RHB RFM   (Northamptonshire 1987-90, Yorkshire 1991-95)

Cmp	Debut	M	I	NO	Runs	HS	Avge	100	50	Balls	Runs	Wkts	Avge	BB	5i	10m	RpO	ct	st
FC		17	25	9	114	27	7.12	0	0	2690	1426	48	29.70	6-78	2	0	3.18	4	
SL		14	10	5	39	9*	7.80	0	0	540	365	9	40.55	1-15	0	0	4.05	2	
BH		5	3	2	0	0*	0.00	0	0	276	173	4	43.25	2-34	0	0	3.76	2	
NW		4	1	1	3	3*		0	0	281	175	6	29.16	3-59	0	0	3.73	1	
FC	1987	172	186	77	426	27	3.90	0	0	27966	13485	417	32.33	9-37	9	2	2.89	35	
SL	1987	111	42	19	77	9*	3.34	0	0	4720	3512	94	37.36	4-23	2	0	4.46	13	
BH	1989	24	11	6	6	3*	1.20	0	0	1336	764	27	28.29	3-20	0	0	3.43	5	
NW	1989	22	8	6	7	3*	3.50	0	0	1500	833	32	26.03	4-32	1	0	3.33	3	

STRONG, Michael Richard   b Cuckfield 28.6.1974   LHB RFM

Cmp	Debut	M	I	NO	Runs	HS	Avge	100	50	Balls	Runs	Wkts	Avge	BB	5i	10m	RpO	ct	st
SL		1	1	0	1	1	1.00	0	0	18	23	0					7.66	0	
SL	1996	3	3	1	4	2*	2.00	0	0	92	97	0					6.32	0	

TAYLOR, Neil Royston   b Orpington 21.7.1959   RHB OB   (Kent 1979-95)

Cmp	Debut	M	I	NO	Runs	HS	Avge	100	50	Balls	Runs	Wkts	Avge	BB	5i	10m	RpO	ct	st
FC		16	28	1	1033	127	38.25	3	5									3	
SL		8	8	1	139	47	19.85	0	0									3	
BH		5	5	0	250	116	50.00	1	1									3	
NW		4	3	0	68	48	22.66	0	0									1	
FC	1979	319	543	69	18804	204	39.67	45	89	1575	891	16	55.68	2-20	0	0	3.39	154	
SL	1981	155	149	15	4026	95	30.04	0	24									40	
BH	1982	56	53	2	2122	137	41.60	6	8	12	5	0					2.50	14	
NW	1982	35	34	1	890	86	26.96	0	5	143	86	6	14.33	3-29	0	0	3.60	7	

THURSFIELD, Martin John   b South Shields 14.12.1971   RHB RM   (Middlesex 1990, Hampshire 1992-96)

Cmp	Debut	M	I	NO	Runs	HS	Avge	100	50	Balls	Runs	Wkts	Avge	BB	5i	10m	RpO	ct	st
FC		2	2	1	32	32*	32.00	0	0	177	108	3	36.00	2-36	0	0	3.66	1	
BH		1	1	0	2	2	2.00	0	0	48	49	2	24.50	2-49	0	0	6.12	1	
NW		1																0	
FC	1990	24	26	6	309	47	15.45	0	0	2844	1539	38	40.50	6-130	1	0	3.24	2	
SL	1993	23	11	3	34	9	4.25	0	0	948	805	16	50.31	3-31	0	0	5.09	4	
BH	1995	7	5	3	26	19	13.00	0	0	360	291	8	36.37	2-33	0	0	4.85	2	
NW	1996	2								60	34	1	34.00	1-34	0	0	3.40	0	

1997 AND CAREER FIGURES FOR WARWICKSHIRE PLAYERS

ALTREE, Darren Anthony   b Rugby 30.9.1974   RHB LFM

Cmp	Debut	M	I	NO	Runs	HS	Avge	100	50	Balls	Runs	Wkts	Avge	BB	5i	10m	RpO	ct	st
FC		1								150	119	2	59.50	2-108	0	0	4.76	0	
FC	1996	4	5	2	0	0*	0.00	0	0	552	386	8	48.25	3-41	0	0	4.19	1	

BELL, Michael Anthony Vincent   b Birmingham 19.12.1966   RHB LMF

Cmp	Debut	M	I	NO	Runs	HS	Avge	100	50	Balls	Runs	Wkts	Avge	BB	5i	10m	RpO	ct	st
FC		3	2	0	30	30	15.00	0	0	477	232	3	77.33	1-12	0	0	2.91	1	
FC	1992	20	23	10	109	30	8.38	0	0	3012	1565	49	31.93	7-48	3	0	3.11	8	
SL	1993	13	5	2	27	8*	9.00	0	0	570	411	22	18.68	5-19	0	2	4.32	1	
BH	1994	2								66	34	2	17.00	2-34	0	0	3.09	1	
NW	1995	1								53	41	2	20.50	2-41	0	0	4.64	0	

BROWN, Douglas Robert   (ECB First Class Counties XI)   b Stirling, Scotland 29.10.1969   RHB RFM

Cmp	Debut	M	I	NO	Runs	HS	Avge	100	50	Balls	Runs	Wkts	Avge	BB	5i	10m	RpO	ct	st
FC		17	24	3	504	79	24.00	0	4	3135	1569	81	19.37	8-89	4	1	3.00	9	
SL		17	17	1	374	68	23.37	0	2	576	432	17	25.41	4-42	1	0	4.50	4	
BH		6	6	0	194	62	32.33	0	2	297	216	8	27.00	5-31	0	1	4.36	1	
NW		5	4	0	46	37	11.50	0	0	282	163	3	54.33	2-34	0	0	3.46	0	
FC	1989	64	97	11	2143	85	24.91	0	12	9197	4813	201	23.94	8-89	8	3	3.13	34	
SL	1991	59	52	7	929	78	20.64	0	4	1797	1378	48	28.70	4-42	2	0	4.60	12	
BH	1990	18	13	1	336	62	28.00	0	2	903	609	20	30.45	5-31	0	1	4.04	5	
NW	1995	11	10	1	216	67	24.00	0	2	510	339	6	56.50	2-34	0	0	3.98	1	

DONALD, Allan Anthony   (South Africa, Free State, South Africa to India, South Africa to Kenya)   b Bloemfontein, South Africa 20.10.1966   RHB RF

Cmp	Debut	M	I	NO	Runs	HS	Avge	100	50	Balls	Runs	Wkts	Avge	BB	5i	10m	RpO	ct	st
FC		11	13	6	140	29	20.00	0	0	2327	938	60	15.63	6-55	3	1	2.41	5	
SL		14	2	2	5	5*		0	0	515	336	30	11.20	5-10	2	1	3.91	4	
BH		6	4	3	28	17*	28.00	0	0	288	159	8	19.87	5-25	0	1	3.31	1	
NW		5	3	2	4	3*	4.00	0	0	313	223	15	14.86	5-37	1	1	4.27	1	
Test	1991	33	44	18	334	33	12.84	0	0	7609	3621	155	23.36	8-71	8	2	2.85	7	
FC	1985	241	279	107	2126	46*	12.36	0	0	44768	21160	945	22.39	8-37	51	8	2.83	92	
Int	1991	87	21	10	40	7*	3.63	0	0	4710	3211	147	21.84	6-23	5	2	4.09	12	

Cmp	Debut	M	I	NO	Runs	HS	Avge	100	50	Balls	Runs	Wkts	Avge	BB	5i	10m	RpO	ct	st
SL	1987	71	24	12	139	18*	11.58	0	0	3109	2074	102	20.33	6-15	4	2	4.00	16	
BH	1987	26	15	8	87	23*	12.42	0	0	1489	996	38	26.21	5-25	2	1	4.01	4	
NW	1995	29	10	6	32	14*	8.00	0	0	1829	1023	73	14.01	5-12	4	5	3.35	4	

EDMOND, Michael Denis b Barrow-in-Furness 30.7.1969 RHB RM

Cmp	Debut	M	I	NO	Runs	HS	Avge	100	50	Balls	Runs	Wkts	Avge	BB	5i	10m	RpO	ct	st
FC		3	3	1	35	21	17.50	0	0	348	175	4	43.75	2-26	0	0	3.01	1	
SL		5	3	1	34	19	17.00	0	0	185	146	9	16.22	2-4	0	0	4.73	1	
FC	1996	4	4	2	43	21	21.50	0	0	449	254	5	50.80	2-26	0	0	3.39	1	
SL	1996	8	5	2	43	19	14.33	0	0	311	233	12	19.41	2-4	0	0	4.49	2	
NW	1996	1	1	1	0	0	0.00	0	0	48	24	1	24.00	1-24	0	0	3.00	0	

FROST, Tony b Stoke-on-Trent 17.11.1975 RHB WK

Cmp	Debut	M	I	NO	Runs	HS	Avge	100	50	Balls	Runs	Wkts	Avge	BB	5i	10m	RpO	ct	st
FC		9	11	2	158	56	17.55	0	1									27	2
SL		7	2	1	2	2*	2.00	0	0									7	
NW		1	1	0	0	0	0.00	0	0									2	1

GILES, Ashley Fraser (ECB First Class Counties XI, England, England A to Australia) b Chertsey 19.3.1973 RHB SLA

Cmp	Debut	M	I	NO	Runs	HS	Avge	100	50	Balls	Runs	Wkts	Avge	BB	5i	10m	RpO	ct	st
FC		16	20	4	624	97	39.00	0	5	3037	1225	38	32.23	4-54	0	0	2.42	4	
Int		1								54	48	0					5.33	0	
SL		15	9	3	159	57	26.50	0	1	457	398	18	22.11	4-25	1	0	5.22	2	
BH		6	5	2	93	29	31.00	0	0	308	211	7	30.14	2-26	0	0	4.11	4	
NW		5	3	0	103	69	34.33	0	1	297	195	10	19.50	5-21	0	1	3.93	0	
FC	1993	44	60	14	1427	106*	31.02	1	9	8522	3521	127	27.72	6-45	4	0	2.47	15	
SL	1995	34	17	5	269	57	22.41	0	1	931	751	40	18.77	5-36	2	1	4.83	11	
BH	1996	10	7	2	110	29	22.00	0	0	422	316	8	39.50	2-26	0	0	4.49	6	
NW	1995	8	5	1	127	69	31.75	0	1	429	278	14	19.85	5-21	0	1	3.88	0	

HEMP, David Lloyd (ECB First Class Counties XI) b Hamilton, Bermuda 8.11.1970 LHB RM (Glamorgan 1991-96)

Cmp	Debut	M	I	NO	Runs	HS	Avge	100	50	Balls	Runs	Wkts	Avge	BB	5i	10m	RpO	ct	st
FC		18	31	4	1107	138	41.00	3	5	138	120	0					5.21	9	
SL		17	17	4	370	70*	28.46	0	2									7	
BH		6	6	0	59	23	9.83	0	0									0	
NW		5	5	1	273	112	68.25	2	0									2	
FC	1991	94	164	16	4984	157	33.67	9	27	516	450	10	45.00	3-23	0	0	5.23	59	
SL	1991	64	53	6	947	74	20.14	0	5	38	43	1	43.00	1-14	0	0	6.78	32	
BH	1995	13	12	0	294	121	24.50	1	1									1	
NW	1994	11	10	1	435	112	48.33	2	1									3	

KHAN, Wasim Gulzar b Birmingham 26.2.1971 LHB LB

Cmp	Debut	M	I	NO	Runs	HS	Avge	100	50	Balls	Runs	Wkts	Avge	BB	5i	10m	RpO	ct	st
FC		3	5	0	102	43	20.40	0	0	6	0	0					0.00	2	
SL		3	3	0	33	27	11.00	0	0									0	
FC	1995	31	56	7	1687	181	34.42	4	8	61	24	0					2.36	30	
SL	1992	10	10	0	65	27	6.50	0	0									2	
BH	1996	1	1	1	0	0*		0	0									1	

KNIGHT, Nicholas Verity (England, England to Zimbabwe, England to New Zealand) b Watford 28.11.1969 LHB RM (Essex 1990-94)

Cmp	Debut	M	I	NO	Runs	HS	Avge	100	50	Balls	Runs	Wkts	Avge	BB	5i	10m	RpO	ct	st
FC		11	17	3	689	119*	49.21	2	3	36	71	0					11.83	8	
Int		2	2	0	16	12	8.00	0	0									0	
SL		8	8	0	252	102	31.50	1	0									3	
BH		2	2	0	74	69	37.00	0	1									0	
NW		2	2	0	0	0	0.00	0	0									1	
Test	1995	11	19	0	573	113	30.15	1	4									21	
FC	1991	107	180	21	6412	174	40.32	16	31	148	176	1	176.00	1-61	0	0	7.13	148	
Int	1996	12	12	3	428	125*	47.55	2	1									3	
SL	1991	75	66	9	1667	134	29.24	2	5	84	85	2	42.50	1-14	0	0	6.07	29	
BH	1990	25	22	3	605	104	31.84	1	3	6	4	0					4.00	7	
NW	1992	12	12	1	419	151	38.09	1	3									5	

MOLES, Andrew James b Solihull 12.2.1961 RHB RM

Cmp	Debut	M	I	NO	Runs	HS	Avge	100	50	Balls	Runs	Wkts	Avge	BB	5i	10m	RpO	ct	st
FC		12	22	3	635	168	33.42	1	2									10	
SL		1	1	0	19	19	19.00	0	1									0	
BH		4	4	0	72	60	18.00	0	1									2	
NW		4	4	0	159	64	39.75	0	2									1	
FC	1986	230	416	40	15305	230*	40.70	29	89	3396	1882	40	47.05	3-21	0	0	3.32	146	
SL	1986	100	95	5	2268	96*	25.20	0	15	446	415	7	59.28	2-24	0	0	5.58	26	
BH	1987	36	34	0	1036	89	30.47	0	12	300	224	4	56.00	1-11	0	0	4.48	11	
NW	1986	35	35	3	1155	127	36.09	2	7	90	81	0					5.40	6	

OSTLER, Dominic Piers b Solihull 15.7.1970 RHB RM

Cmp	Debut	M	I	NO	Runs	HS	Avge	100	50	Balls	Runs	Wkts	Avge	BB	5i	10m	RpO	ct	st
FC		15	22	1	419	65	19.95	0	3	36	66	0					11.00	29	
SL		17	16	4	466	70	38.83	0	4									3	
BH		6	6	1	132	44	26.40	0	0									4	
NW		4	4	0	197	58	49.25	0	3									3	
FC	1990	147	246	20	7659	208	33.88	9	50	179	188	0					6.30	179	
SL	1990	118	110	15	3012	91*	31.70	0	22	6	4	0					4.00	29	
BH	1991	30	29	4	1055	87	42.20	0	9									16	
NW	1990	30	29	3	848	104	32.61	1	6	9	4	1	4.00	1-4	0	0	2.66	16	

Cmp	Debut	M	I	NO	Runs	HS	Avge	100	50	Balls	Runs	Wkts	Avge	BB	5i	10m	RpO	ct	st
PENNEY, Trevor Lionel b Salisbury, Rhodesia 12.6.1968 RHB RM																			
FC		16	24	5	784	99	41.26	0	6									11	
SL		17	15	3	268	57	22.33	0	1									4	
BH		6	6	1	182	55	36.40	0	1									3	
NW		5	5	1	100	45	25.00	0	0	3	4	0					8.00	2	
FC	1986	114	180	34	6268	151	42.93	13	29	247	183	6	30.50	3-18	0	0	4.44	67	
SL	1992	92	79	27	1499	83*	28.82	0	6	6	2	0					2.00	36	
BH	1992	23	20	4	443	55	27.68	0	2									8	1
NW	1992	24	22	5	459	90	27.00	0	2	13	16	1	16.00	1-8	0	0	7.38	13	
PIPER, Keith John b Leicester 18.12.1969 RHB WK																			
FC		8	11	3	111	34*	13.87	0	0									24	1
SL		10	4	1	53	29*	17.66	0	0									13	1
BH		4	3	0	8	7	2.66	0	0									3	
NW		4	2	1	28	15*	28.00	0	0									4	
FC	1989	138	191	29	3197	116*	19.73	2	9	28	57	1	57.00	1-57	0	0	12.21	372	24
SL	1989	77	42	20	302	30	13.72	0	0									77	18
BH	1991	19	13	4	62	11*	6.88	0	0									23	1
NW	1989	25	12	6	104	16*	17.33	0	0									37	2
POWELL, Michael James b Bolton 5.4.1975 RHB RM																			
FC		1	1	0	20	20	20.00	0	0									2	
FC	1996	5	9	0	202	39	22.44	0	0	24	18	1	18.00	1-18	0	0	4.50	4	
SHEIKH, Mohamed Avez b Birmingham 2.7.1973 LHB LM																			
FC		1	1	0	24	24	24.00	0	0	87	24	3	8.00	2-14	0	0	1.65	0	
SL		2	1	0	1	1	1.00	0	0									0	
SINGH, Anurag (Cambridge University, British Universities) b Kanpur, India 9.9.1975 RHB OB																			
FC		10	14	1	355	134	27.30	1	1	18	10	0					3.33	5	
SL		5	5	0	112	86	22.40	0	1									1	
BH		5	5	1	78	53*	19.50	0	1									0	
FC	1995	23	38	3	1085	157	31.00	3	2	42	24	0					3.42	12	
SL	1996	6	6	0	114	86	19.00	0	1									1	
BH	1996	10	10	1	338	123	37.33	1	2									1	
SMALL, Gladstone Cleophas b St George, Barbados 18.10.1961 RHB RFM																			
FC		3	4	1	13	11	4.33	0	0	300	158	3	52.66	3-51	0	0	3.16	1	
SL		15	3	2	11	9*	11.00	0	0	575	462	21	22.00	5-26	0	1	4.82	3	
BH		6	2	1	15	14*	15.00	0	0	282	195	15	13.00	5-23	0	1	4.14	0	
NW		5	2	1	36	32*	36.00	0	0	224	121	5	24.20	3-22	0	0	3.24	0	
Test	1986	17	24	7	263	59	15.47	0	1	3927	1871	55	34.01	5-48	2	0	2.85	9	
FC	1979	315	404	97	4409	70	14.36	0	7	49567	24392	852	28.62	7-15	29	2	2.95	95	
Int	1986	53	24	9	98	18*	6.53	0	0	2793	1942	58	33.48	4-31	1	0	4.17	7	
SL	1980	191	85	31	429	40*	7.94	0	0	8006	5924	240	24.68	5-26	6	3	4.43	40	
BH	1980	64	37	10	184	22	6.81	0	0	3572	2084	79	26.37	5-23	2	1	3.50	11	
NW	1980	48	30	9	256	33	12.19	0	0	2828	1491	53	28.13	3-22	0	0	3.16	8	
SMITH, Neil Michael Knight b Birmingham 27.7.1967 RHB OB																			
FC		15	22	3	642	148	33.78	1	3	1910	930	23	40.43	4-32	0	0	2.92	7	
SL		17	17	0	532	60	31.29	0	5	420	329	10	32.90	3-20	0	0	4.70	10	
BH		6	6	0	212	125	35.33	1	1	217	181	3	60.33	2-42	0	0	5.00	0	
NW		5	5	0	85	72	17.00	0	1	78	57	1	57.00	1-30	0	0	4.38	2	
FC	1982	127	182	25	4084	161	26.01	2	18	19933	9964	265	37.60	7-42	15	0	2.99	44	
Int	1995	7	6	1	100	31	20.00	0	0	261	190	6	31.66	3-29	0	0	4.36	1	
SL	1982	139	113	18	2428	111*	25.55	1	15	4536	3520	130	27.07	6-33	3	2	4.65	52	
BH	1990	30	24	2	548	125	24.90	1	3	1112	863	27	31.96	3-29	0	0	4.65	5	
NW	1989	32	28	6	479	72	21.77	0	3	1342	813	36	22.58	5-17	1	1	3.63	11	
WAGH, Mark Anant (Oxford University, British Universities) b Birmingham 20.10.1976 RHB OB																			
FC		18	31	2	1156	125*	39.86	4	5	1182	669	6	111.50	2-45	0	0	3.39	14	
BH		1	1	1	7	7*		0	0	54	39	1	39.00	1-39	0	0	4.33	0	
FC	1996	29	44	5	1354	125*	34.71	4	5	2307	1301	16	81.31	3-82	0	0	3.38	18	
BH	1996	3	3	1	36	23	18.00	0	0	174	119	3	39.66	1-39	0	0	4.10	0	
WELCH, Graeme (ECB First Class Counties XI) b Durham 21.3.1972 RHB RM																			
FC		18	26	6	455	75	22.75	0	2	3245	1625	65	25.00	6-115	3	1	3.00	3	
SL		17	15	8	195	32*	27.85	0	0	587	439	12	36.58	2-18	0	0	4.48	3	
BH		6	5	2	129	55*	43.00	0	1	204	156	2	78.00	1-18	0	0	4.58	0	
NW		5	4	1	38	20	12.66	0	0	282	191	3	63.66	1-18	0	0	4.06	0	
FC	1994	45	62	10	1121	84*	21.55	0	6	6700	3749	125	29.99	6-115	3	1	3.35	18	
SL	1992	39	30	14	421	54	26.31	0	1	1347	1097	28	39.17	3-37	0	0	4.88	7	
BH	1995	14	10	3	190	55*	27.14	0	1	612	524	8	65.50	2-43	0	0	5.13	0	
NW	1994	8	6	2	52	20	13.00	0	0	408	243	4	60.75	1-11	0	0	3.57	0	

1997 AND CAREER FIGURES FOR WORCESTERSHIRE PLAYERS

BRINKLEY, James Edward b Helensburgh, Scotland 13.3.1974 RHB RFM

Cmp	Debut	M	I	NO	Runs	HS	Avge	100	50	Balls	Runs	Wkts	Avge	BB	5i	10m	RpO	ct	st
SL		1	1	0	7	7	7.00	0	0	18	26	0					8.66	0	
BH		4	2	2	7	7*		0	0	137	122	3	40.66	2-35	0	0	5.34	0	
FC	1993	14	16	4	89	29	7.41	0	0	2229	1115	34	32.79	6-35	2	0	3.00	5	
SL	1995	4	2	0	7	7	3.50	0	0	138	106	3	35.33	2-26	0	0	4.60	0	
BH	1996	7	2	2	7	7*		0	0	287	258	7	36.85	2-35	0	0	5.39	0	

CHAPMAN, Robert James (Worcestershire to Zimbabwe) b Nottingham 28.7.1972 RHB RFM (Nottinghamshire 1992-96)

Cmp	Debut	M	I	NO	Runs	HS	Avge	100	50	Balls	Runs	Wkts	Avge	BB	5i	10m	RpO	ct	st
FC		6	4	1	10	7*	3.33	0	0	621	468	13	36.00	3-26	0	0	4.52	2	
SL		9	2	0	0	0	0.00	0	0	294	214	7	30.57	3-27	0	0	4.36	0	
BH		1	1	0	0	0	0.00	0	0	36	27	0					4.50	0	
NW		1																0	
FC	1992	21	21	5	131	25	8.18	0	0	2450	1759	38	46.28	4-109	0	0	4.30	5	
SL	1994	20	5	2	6	4*	2.00	0	0	663	582	14	41.57	3-27	0	0	5.26	0	
NW	1995	2								72	40	0					3.33	0	

CURTIS, Timothy Stephen (Worcestershire to Zimbabwe) b Chislehurst 15.1.1960 RHB LB

Cmp	Debut	M	I	NO	Runs	HS	Avge	100	50	Balls	Runs	Wkts	Avge	BB	5i	10m	RpO	ct	st
FC		13	21	1	742	160	37.10	4	1	72	65	1	65.00	1-55	0	0	5.41	9	
SL		5	5	0	195	93	39.00	0	1									3	
NW		2	2	0	69	41	34.50	0	0									0	
Test	1988	5	9	0	140	41	15.55	0	0	18	7	0					2.33	3	
FC	1979	339	579	67	20832	248	40.68	43	103	1133	813	14	58.07	2-17	0	0	4.30	192	
SL	1980	192	186	28	6423	124	40.65	2	54									62	
BH	1983	62	62	5	1936	97	33.96	0	18	2	4	0					12.00	14	
NW	1981	42	41	5	1761	136*	48.91	4	11	36	31	2	15.50	1-6	0	0	5.16	11	

DAWOOD, Ismail b Dewsbury 23.7.1976 RHB WK (Northamptonshire 1994)

Cmp	Debut	M	I	NO	Runs	HS	Avge	100	50	Balls	Runs	Wkts	Avge	BB	5i	10m	RpO	ct	st
FC		1	2	1	10	10*	10.00	0	0									1	2
SL		1	1	0	1	1	1.00	0	0									0	
FC	1994	3	4	2	13	10*	6.50	0	0									4	2
SL	1994	2	2	0	3	2	1.50	0	0									0	

HAYNES, Gavin Richard (Worcestershire to Zimbabwe) b Stourbridge 29.9.1969 RHB RM

Cmp	Debut	M	I	NO	Runs	HS	Avge	100	50	Balls	Runs	Wkts	Avge	BB	5i	10m	RpO	ct	st
FC		17	25	3	794	70	36.09	0	6	1723	875	31	28.22	3-46	0	0	3.04	5	
SL		13	12	3	355	64*	39.44	0	1	432	326	15	21.73	4-13	1	0	4.52	1	
BH		5	5	0	112	39	22.40	0	0	276	160	3	53.33	1-15	0	0	3.47	0	
NW		1	1	0	32	32	32.00	0	0	54	18	1	18.00	1-18	0	0	2.00	1	
FC	1991	80	122	9	3464	158	30.65	3	19	5108	2558	67	38.17	4-33	0	0	3.00	37	
SL	1992	63	52	6	1141	83	24.80	0	3	1810	1246	45	27.68	4-13	2	0	4.13	17	
BH	1992	17	15	3	303	65	25.25	0	1	719	423	15	28.20	3-17	0	0	3.52	4	
NW	1992	9	7	1	309	116*	51.50	1	1	318	204	5	40.80	1-9	0	0	3.84	3	

HICK, Graeme Ashley (Worcestershire to Zimbabwe) b Salisbury, Rhodesia 23.5.1966 RHB OB

Cmp	Debut	M	I	NO	Runs	HS	Avge	100	50	Balls	Runs	Wkts	Avge	BB	5i	10m	RpO	ct	st
FC		18	28	6	1524	303*	69.27	6	4	1158	629	9	69.88	4-70	0	0	3.25	20	
SL		16	16	2	549	119*	39.21	1	1	292	251	9	27.88	2-12	0	0	5.15	7	
BH		5	5	0	89	40	17.80	0	0	162	139	3	46.33	1-26	0	0	5.14	0	
NW		2	2	0	153	146	76.50	1	0	98	54	2	27.00	2-14	0	0	3.30	1	
Test	1991	46	80	6	2672	178	36.10	4	15	2973	1247	22	56.68	4-126	0	0	2.51	62	
FC	1983	346	565	59	28473	405*	56.27	96	107	18695	9218	210	43.89	5-18	5	1	2.95	417	
Int	1991	62	61	7	2105	105*	38.98	2	16	840	696	18	38.66	3-41	0	0	4.97	32	
SL	1985	168	162	30	6128	130	46.42	8	46	2403	2050	74	27.70	4-21	2	0	5.11	44	
BH	1986	58	57	11	2589	127*	56.28	7	16	732	562	12	46.83	3-36	0	0	4.60	37	
NW	1986	35	35	6	1532	172*	52.82	4	8	1193	716	22	32.54	4-54	2	0	3.60	19	

ILLINGWORTH, Richard Keith (Worcestershire to Zimbabwe) b Bradford 23.8.1963 RHB SLA

Cmp	Debut	M	I	NO	Runs	HS	Avge	100	50	Balls	Runs	Wkts	Avge	BB	5i	10m	RpO	ct	st
FC		5	4	2	157	112	78.50	1	0	1236	442	18	24.55	7-79	1	1	2.14	3	
SL		4	1	1	2	2*		0	0	162	119	3	39.66	2-29	0	0	4.40	0	
Test	1991	9	14	7	128	28	18.28	0	0	1485	615	19	32.36	4-96	0	0	2.48	5	
FC	1982	330	368	108	5818	120*	22.37	4	16	59927	23794	780	30.50	7-50	27	6	2.38	146	
Int	1991	25	11	5	68	14	11.33	0	0	1501	1059	30	35.30	3-33	0	0	4.23	8	
SL	1982	181	80	42	542	31	14.26	0	0	6964	5013	211	23.75	5-24	4	2	4.31	40	
BH	1983	54	26	15	214	36*	19.45	0	0	2794	1619	51	31.74	4-27	2	0	3.47	12	
NW	1983	33	16	6	139	29*	13.90	0	0	1969	1014	28	36.21	4-20	1	0	3.08	10	

LAMPITT, Stuart Richard (Worcestershire to Zimbabwe) b Wolverhampton 29.7.1966 RHB RM

Cmp	Debut	M	I	NO	Runs	HS	Avge	100	50	Balls	Runs	Wkts	Avge	BB	5i	10m	RpO	ct	st
FC		15	17	7	277	52	27.70	0	1	2008	1302	35	37.20	5-39	1	0	3.89	16	
SL		15	8	5	130	38*	43.33	0	0	552	460	21	21.90	4-49	1	0	5.00	5	
BH		4	4	2	57	23	28.50	0	0	174	109	3	36.33	2-17	0	0	3.75	0	
NW		2	2	1	28	28*	28.00	0	0	72	72	0					6.00	1	
FC	1985	176	224	49	4219	122	24.10	1	17	24134	13164	432	30.47	5-32	13	0	3.27	117	
SL	1987	138	79	30	1039	41*	21.20	0	0	4788	3875	153	25.32	5-67	7	1	4.85	40	
BH	1990	35	19	7	242	41	20.16	0	0	1882	1230	60	20.50	6-26	4	1	3.92	10	
NW	1989	22	15	4	163	29	14.81	0	0	1151	841	33	25.48	5-22	0	1	4.38	7	

Cmp	Debut	M	I	NO	Runs	HS	Avge	100	50	Balls	Runs	Wkts	Avge	BB	5i	10m	RpO	ct	st

LEATHERDALE, David Antony (Worcestershire to Zimbabwe) b Bradford 26.11.1967 RHB RM

Cmp	Debut	M	I	NO	Runs	HS	Avge	100	50	Balls	Runs	Wkts	Avge	BB	5i	10m	RpO	ct	st
FC		17	25	8	886	129	52.11	2	5	1317	742	26	28.53	5-56	1	0	3.38	15	
SL		15	12	5	301	58*	43.00	0	3	351	315	18	17.50	3-13	0	0	5.38	9	
BH		5	5	1	51	25	12.75	0	0	210	126	9	14.00	4-13	2	0	3.60	0	
NW		2	2	0	51	42	25.50	0	0	72	61	0					5.08	0	
FC	1988	125	193	24	5777	157	34.18	8	32	2889	1647	47	35.04	5-56	1	0	3.42	111	
SL	1988	111	90	15	1395	62*	18.60	0	6	611	517	29	17.82	4-31	1	0	5.07	56	
BH	1990	24	19	4	267	66	17.80	0	1	282	188	9	20.88	4-13	2	0	4.00	4	
NW	1988	19	16	1	297	43	19.80	0	0	136	106	3	35.33	3-14	0	0	4.67	5	

MIRZA, Maneer Mohammed b Birmingham 1.4.1978 RHB RFM

Cmp	Debut	M	I	NO	Runs	HS	Avge	100	50	Balls	Runs	Wkts	Avge	BB	5i	10m	RpO	ct	st
FC		6	7	4	17	10*	5.66	0	0	916	620	19	32.63	4-51	0	0	4.06	1	
SL		4								96	113	1	113.00	1-31	0	0	7.06	1	

MOODY, Thomas Masson (Western Australia, Australia) b Adelaide, Australia 2.10.1965 RHB RM (Warwickshire 1990)

Cmp	Debut	M	I	NO	Runs	HS	Avge	100	50	Balls	Runs	Wkts	Avge	BB	5i	10m	RpO	ct	st
FC		14	21	1	973	272	48.65	3	4	1282	829	19	43.63	5-148	1	0	3.87	14	
SL		15	15	0	529	112	35.26	1	3	318	241	8	30.12	2-29	0	0	4.54	7	
BH		5	5	0	259	92	51.80	0	3									6	
NW		2	2	0	114	108	57.00	1	0	48	35	0					4.37	0	
Test	1989	8	14	0	456	106	32.57	2	3	432	147	2	73.50	1-17	0	0	2.04	9	
FC	1985	258	429	35	18555	272	47.09	56	84	18288	8424	269	31.31	7-38	7	2	2.76	258	
Int	1987	40	36	4	766	89	23.93	0	7	1163	854	21	40.66	3-56	0	0	4.40	11	
SL	1990	106	104	10	4222	160	44.91	10	28	2331	1648	59	27.93	4-46	1	0	4.24	33	
BH	1990	34	32	7	1459	110*	58.36	2	13	786	460	15	30.66	4-59	1	0	3.51	17	
NW	1990	15	15	3	856	180*	71.33	3	3	559	308	9	34.22	2-33	0	0	3.30	10	

NEWPORT, Philip John (Worcestershire to Zimbabwe) b High Wycombe 11.10.1962 RHB RFM

Cmp	Debut	M	I	NO	Runs	HS	Avge	100	50	Balls	Runs	Wkts	Avge	BB	5i	10m	RpO	ct	st
FC		8	6	0	91	45	15.16	0	0	1064	444	19	23.36	7-37	1	0	2.50	0	
SL		5	1	0	7	7	7.00	0	0	180	107	8	13.37	3-18	0	0	3.56	0	
BH		5	4	1	42	15*	14.00	0	0	282	161	11	14.63	4-37	1	0	3.42	1	
NW		2	1	0	2	2	2.00	0	0	108	84	3	28.00	2-52	0	0	4.66	1	
Test	1988	3	5	1	110	40*	27.50	0	0	669	417	10	41.70	4-87	0	0	3.73	1	
FC	1982	266	307	87	5445	98	24.75	0	20	42693	22097	813	27.17	8-52	35	3	3.10	72	
SL	1983	161	68	25	440	26*	10.23	0	0	6310	4446	170	26.15	5-32	2	1	4.22	32	
BH	1986	52	26	7	206	28	10.84	0	0	3089	1675	79	21.20	5-22	2	2	3.25	10	
NW	1984	31	16	5	134	25	12.18	0	0	1665	1040	41	25.36	4-30	3	0	3.74	4	

RAWNSLEY, Matthew James b Birmingham 8.6.1976 RHB SLA

Cmp	Debut	M	I	NO	Runs	HS	Avge	100	50	Balls	Runs	Wkts	Avge	BB	5i	10m	RpO	ct	st
FC		4	4	1	64	26	21.33	0	0	519	218	6	36.33	3-67	0	0	2.52	0	
SL		2	1	1	1	1*		0	0	90	83	4	20.75	2-29	0	0	5.53	0	
NW		1								66	50	2	25.00	2-50	0	0	4.54	0	
FC	1996	8	5	2	68	26	22.66	0	0	975	437	11	39.72	3-67	0	0	2.68	1	
SL	1996	5	4	1	12	7	4.00	0	0	167	152	4	38.00	2-29	0	0	5.46	0	

RHODES, Steven John (Worcestershire to Zimbabwe) b Bradford 17.6.1964 RHB WK (Yorkshire 1981-84)

Cmp	Debut	M	I	NO	Runs	HS	Avge	100	50	Balls	Runs	Wkts	Avge	BB	5i	10m	RpO	ct	st
FC		18	23	6	584	78	34.35	0	4									44	3
SL		16	7	4	38	19	12.66	0	0									20	4
BH		5	4	0	44	37	11.00	0	0									6	
NW		2	2	2	7	7*		0	0									2	
Test	1994	11	17	5	294	65*	24.50	0	1									46	3
FC	1981	328	450	126	10837	122*	33.44	9	57	6	30	0					30.00	821	108
Int	1989	9	8	2	107	56	17.83	0	1									9	2
SL	1984	198	119	31	1612	48*	18.31	0	0									206	58
BH	1985	62	44	7	525	51*	14.18	0	1									85	9
NW	1985	39	30	11	394	61	20.73	0	2	6	1	0					1.00	47	7

SHERIYAR, Alamgir b Birmingham 15.11.1973 RHB LFM (Leicestershire 1993-95)

Cmp	Debut	M	I	NO	Runs	HS	Avge	100	50	Balls	Runs	Wkts	Avge	BB	5i	10m	RpO	ct	st
FC		18	13	4	94	21	10.44	0	0	2677	1575	62	25.40	6-19	3	1	3.53	4	
SL		12	2	1	1	1	1.00	0	0	299	272	11	24.72	4-18	1	0	5.45	1	
BH		1								60	65	1	65.00	1-65	0	0	6.50	0	
NW		2	1	0	0	0	0.00	0	0	90	74	2	37.00	1-35	0	0	4.93	0	
FC	1994	46	43	16	219	21	8.11	0	0	7159	4435	139	31.90	6-19	6	2	3.71	11	
SL	1993	29	8	6	36	19	18.00	0	0	767	718	20	35.90	4-18	2	0	5.61	3	
BH	1996	4	1	1	1	1*		0	0	211	173	6	28.83	3-40	0	0	4.91	0	
NW	1996	3	2	0	10	10	5.00	0	0	120	109	2	54.50	1-35	0	0	5.45	0	

SOLANKI, Vikram Singh (Rest of England, Worcestershire to Zimbabwe) b Udaipur, India 1.4.1976 RHB OB

Cmp	Debut	M	I	NO	Runs	HS	Avge	100	50	Balls	Runs	Wkts	Avge	BB	5i	10m	RpO	ct	st
FC		14	18	1	478	128*	28.11	1	2	534	309	2	154.50	1-33	0	0	3.47	10	
SL		16	13	1	239	58	19.91	0	1	24	18	1	18.00	1-9	0	0	4.50	5	
BH		5	5	0	90	21	18.00	0	0	18	17	1	17.00	1-17	0	0	5.66	1	
NW		1	1	0	6	6	6.00	0	0	63	51	1	51.00	1-51	0	0	4.85	0	
FC	1995	35	53	5	1517	128*	31.60	1	9	2366	1550	32	48.43	5-69	3	1	3.93	29	
SL	1993	40	28	5	418	58	18.17	0	2	132	141	4	35.25	1-9	0	0	6.40	12	
NW	1995	5	4	0	94	50	23.50	0	1	183	142	2	71.00	1-48	0	0	4.65	1	

SPIRING, Karl Reuben b Southport 13.11.1974 RHB OB

Cmp	Debut	M	I	NO	Runs	HS	Avge	100	50	Balls	Runs	Wkts	Avge	BB	5i	10m	RpO	ct	st
FC		17	28	3	876	150	35.04	1	4	12	10	0					5.00	7	
SL		13	12	6	235	58*	39.16	0	1									5	

Cmp	Debut	M	I	NO	Runs	HS	Avge	100	50	Balls	Runs	Wkts	Avge	BB	5i	10m	RpO	ct	st
BH		5	5	1	82	33	20.50	0	0									1	
NW		2	2	0	100	53	50.00	0	1									2	
FC	1994	37	64	9	2072	150	37.67	4	13	12	10	0					5.00	19	
SL	1993	29	25	10	518	58*	34.53	0	1									9	
BH	1995	12	10	1	202	35	22.44	0	0									4	
NW	1996	4	4	0	141	53	35.25	0	1									2	

THOMAS, Paul Anthony   b Perry Bar, Birmingham 3.6.1971   RHB RM

Cmp	Debut	M	I	NO	Runs	HS	Avge	100	50	Balls	Runs	Wkts	Avge	BB	5i	10m	RpO	ct	st
FC		2	2	1	16	16*	16.00	0	0	258	166	4	41.50	3-43	0	0	3.86	0	
FC	1995	21	24	5	119	25	6.26	0	0	3304	2295	49	46.83	5-70	1	0	4.16	1	
SL	1996	1			•					36	30	0					5.00	0	
BH	1996	2	1	0	3	3	3.00	0	0	112	85	1	85.00	1-34	0	0	4.55	0	
NW	1992	2	1	1	12	12*		0	0	108	84	2	42.00	2-30	0	0	4.66	0	

WESTON, William Philip Christopher (Worcestershire to Zimbabwe)   b Durham 16.6.1973   LHB LM

Cmp	Debut	M	I	NO	Runs	HS	Avge	100	50	Balls	Runs	Wkts	Avge	BB	5i	10m	RpO	ct	st
FC		17	29	5	1190	205	49.58	4	3	54	63	0					7.00	7	
SL		14	11	1	93	28	9.30	0	0									2	
BH		5	5	0	37	16	7.40	0	0									3	
FC	1991	106	182	20	6033	205	37.24	13	29	907	579	4	144.75	2-39	0	0	3.83	58	
SL	1993	50	42	7	872	80*	24.91	0	4	6	2	1	2.00	1-2	0	0	2.00	10	
BH	1993	17	16	2	201	54*	14.35	0	1									7	
NW	1993	7	7	0	97	31	13.85	0	0									1	

1997 AND CAREER FIGURES FOR YORKSHIRE PLAYERS

BATTY, Gareth Jon   b Bradford 13.10.1977   RHB OB

Cmp	Debut	M	I	NO	Runs	HS	Avge	100	50	Balls	Runs	Wkts	Avge	BB	5i	10m	RpO	ct	st
FC		1	2	0	18	18	9.00	0	0	66	70	2	35.00	1-11	0	0	6.36	0	

BLAKEY, Richard John   b Huddersfield 15.1.1967   RHB WK

Cmp	Debut	M	I	NO	Runs	HS	Avge	100	50	Balls	Runs	Wkts	Avge	BB	5i	10m	RpO	ct	st
FC		18	24	6	680	92	37.77	0	6									49	4
SL		16	15	3	231	56	19.25	0	1									18	4
BH		6	6	3	60	23*	20.00	0	0									5	2
NW		3	3	2	23	20*	23.00	0	0									2	
Test	1992	2	4	0	7	6	1.75	0	0									2	
FC	1985	258	413	65	11364	221	32.65	10	67	63	68	1	68.00	1-68	0	0	6.47	517	46
Int	1992	3	2	0	25	25	12.50	0	0									2	1
SL	1986	150	134	26	4055	130*	37.54	3	24									122	22
BH	1987	46	40	8	914	80*	28.56	0	6									39	4
NW	1986	27	21	6	388	75	25.86	0	2									30	2

BYAS, David   b Kilham 26.8.1963   LHB RM

Cmp	Debut	M	I	NO	Runs	HS	Avge	100	50	Balls	Runs	Wkts	Avge	BB	5i	10m	RpO	ct	st
FC		20	33	4	1319	128	45.48	3	9									24	
SL		16	16	0	409	83	25.56	0	2									7	
BH		6	6	0	142	72	23.66	0	1									1	
NW		3	3	0	17	10	5.66	0	0									3	
FC	1986	200	337	32	11232	213	36.82	20	64	1092	719	12	59.91	3-55	0	0	3.95	247	
SL	1985	156	151	22	3936	111*	30.51	3	20	529	463	19	24.36	3-19	0	0	5.25	44	
BH	1985	36	33	2	933	116*	30.09	1	4	283	155	5	31.00	2-38	0	0	3.28	9	
NW	1989	23	21	2	625	73*	32.89	0	6	18	23	1	23.00	1-23	0	0	7.66	12	

CHAPMAN, Colin Anthony   b Bradford 8.6.1971   RHB WK

Cmp	Debut	M	I	NO	Runs	HS	Avge	100	50	Balls	Runs	Wkts	Avge	BB	5i	10m	RpO	ct	st
FC		2	4	0	139	80	34.75	0	1									3	1
FC	1990	6	11	1	211	80	21.10	0	1									8	3
SL	1990	7	6	3	89	36*	29.66	0	0									2	
NW	1995	1																1	

FISHER, Ian Douglas   b Bradford 31.3.1976   LHB SLA

Cmp	Debut	M	I	NO	Runs	HS	Avge	100	50	Balls	Runs	Wkts	Avge	BB	5i	10m	RpO	ct	st
FC		2	4	0	75	37	18.75	0	0	234	103	1	103.00	1-26	0	0	2.64	0	
SL		2								96	47	4	11.75	2-23	0	0	2.93	0	
FC	1995	5	5	1	75	37	18.75	0	0	624	285	12	23.75	5-35	1	0	2.74	0	

GOUGH, Darren   (England, England to Zimbabwe, England to New Zealand)   b Barnsley 18.9.1970   RHB RF

Cmp	Debut	M	I	NO	Runs	HS	Avge	100	50	Balls	Runs	Wkts	Avge	BB	5i	10m	RpO	ct	st
Test		4	6	0	17	10	2.83	0	0	852	511	16	31.93	5-149	1	0	3.59	0	
FC		12	16	1	196	58	13.06	0	1	2008	1149	43	26.72	5-56	3	0	3.43	0	
Int		3								180	119	7	17.00	5-44	0	1	3.96	0	
SL		9	7	3	69	23*	17.25	0	0	378	325	14	23.21	3-21	0	0	5.15	2	
BH		6	4	3	40	22*	40.00	0	0	318	223	7	31.85	3-38	0	0	4.20	4	
NW		3	2	0	50	46	25.00	0	0	185	85	13	6.53	7-27	0	1	2.75	0	
Test	1994	21	30	4	363	65	13.96	0	2	4522	2401	85	28.24	6-49	3	0	3.18	8	
FC	1989	136	182	31	2475	121	16.39	1	9	24023	12625	463	27.26	7-28	19	3	3.15	34	
Int	1994	38	24	7	203	45	11.94	0	0	2120	1438	58	24.79	5-44	2	2	4.06	4	
SL	1990	88	57	14	571	72*	13.27	0	1	3770	2833	105	26.98	5-13	3	1	4.50	18	
BH	1990	24	14	5	130	48*	14.44	0	0	1260	786	26	30.23	3-38	0	0	3.74	7	
NW	1990	21	11	0	183	46	16.63	0	0	1338	735	41	17.92	7-27	0	1	3.29	3	

	Cmp	Debut	M	I	NO	Runs	HS	Avge	100	50	Balls	Runs	Wkts	Avge	BB	5i	10m	RpO	ct	st

HAMILTON, Gavin Mark b Broxburn, Scotland 16.9.1974 LHB RMF

FC			11	16	2	240	49	17.14	0	0	1446	907	27	33.59	5-89	1	0	3.76	3	
SL			6	3	3	28	18*		0	0	186	222	5	44.40	3-30	0	0	7.16	0	
FC	1993		25	32	7	476	61	19.04	0	1	3569	2033	59	34.45	5-65	2	0	3.41	10	
SL	1994		22	12	5	74	18*	10.57	0	0	775	772	25	30.88	4-27	2	0	5.97	2	
BH	1993		2	1	1	8	8*		0	0	78	42	0					3.23	0	
NW	1993		2	1	0	2	2	2.00	0	0	120	86	4	21.50	2-42	0	0	4.30	1	

HARTLEY, Peter John b Keighley 18.4.1960 RHB RMF (Warwickshire 1982)

FC			9	10	0	121	39	12.10	0	0	1020	532	23	23.13	5-34	1	0	3.12	3	
SL			14	12	2	200	48*	20.00	0	0	514	490	12	40.83	3-42	0	0	5.71	7	
BH			6	6	1	65	22	13.00	0	0	298	239	8	29.87	3-31	0	0	4.81	1	
NW			3	2	0	86	83	43.00	0	1	132	81	3	27.00	2-49	0	0	3.68	1	
FC	1982		198	241	52	3875	127*	20.50	2	13	31401	17653	581	30.38	9-41	21	2	3.37	62	
SL	1982		146	102	31	1164	52	16.39	0	2	6201	4797	174	27.56	5-36	2	2	4.64	26	
BH	1986		43	26	10	195	29*	12.18	0	0	2343	1539	61	25.22	5-43	1	1	3.94	12	
NW	1986		28	17	8	250	83	27.77	0	2	1715	1108	45	24.62	5-46	0	1	3.87	2	

HOGGARD, Matthew James b Leeds 31.12.1976 RHB RFM

| FC | | | 1 | 2 | 1 | 2 | 1* | 2.00 | 0 | 0 | 162 | 155 | 2 | 77.50 | 1-45 | 0 | 0 | 5.74 | 0 | |
| FC | 1996 | | 2 | 3 | 1 | 12 | 10 | 6.00 | 0 | 0 | 252 | 196 | 3 | 65.33 | 1-41 | 0 | 0 | 4.66 | 0 | |

HUTCHISON, Paul Michael b Leeds 9.6.1977 LHB LFM

| FC | | | 7 | 8 | 7 | 29 | 15* | 29.00 | 0 | 0 | 1399 | 741 | 37 | 20.02 | 7-38 | 3 | 1 | 3.17 | 1 | |
| FC | 1995 | | 10 | 10 | 7 | 29 | 15* | 9.66 | 0 | 0 | 1812 | 1028 | 49 | 20.97 | 7-38 | 3 | 1 | 3.40 | 2 | |

KETTLEBOROUGH, Richard Allan b Sheffield 15.3.1973 LHB RM

FC			3	5	0	22	10	4.40	0	0	78	74	1	74.00	1-74	0	0	5.69	2	
SL			1	1	0	9	9	9.00	0	0									0	
FC	1994		13	19	2	446	108	26.23	1	2	198	153	3	51.00	2-26	0	0	4.63	9	
SL	1994		10	6	3	71	28	23.66	0	0	66	72	3	24.00	2-43	0	0	6.54	4	

LEHMANN, Darren Scott (South Australia, Australia, Australia to Sri Lanka) b Gawler 5.2.1970 LHB SLA

FC			17	27	2	1575	182	63.00	4	10	123	71	2	35.50	1-0	0	0	3.46	9	
SL			16	16	3	643	78*	49.46	0	6	76	85	4	21.25	3-43	0	0	6.71	4	
BH			5	5	0	166	67	33.20	0	1	18	22	0					7.33	1	
NW			3	3	0	132	105	44.00	1	0	6	5	0					5.00	0	
FC	1987		115	200	11	9792	255	51.80	29	48	1454	730	12	60.83	2-15	0	0	3.01	67	
Int	1996		3	3	0	27	15	9.00	0	0	78	65	1	65.00	1-29	0	0	5.00	2	

McGRATH, Anthony (England A, England A to Australia) b Bradford 6.10.1975 RHB OB

FC			15	25	1	832	141	34.66	2	3	77	59	1	59.00	1-19	0	0	4.59	5	
SL			13	11	3	281	63	35.12	0	2									5	
BH			6	6	1	223	109*	44.60	1	0									2	
NW			3	3	0	35	24	11.66	0	0									0	
FC	1995		49	84	4	2436	141	30.45	5	9	203	129	2	64.50	1-6	0	0	3.81	29	
SL	1995		31	27	6	608	72	28.95	0	4									10	
BH	1995		13	12	1	331	109*	30.09	1	0	12	10	2	5.00	2-10	0	0	5.00	2	
NW	1996		7	7	1	115	34	19.16	0	0									3	

MORRIS, Alexander Corfield b Barnsley 4.10.1976 LHB RM

FC			7	9	0	117	37	13.00	0	0	468	289	4	72.25	2-62	0	0	3.70	4	
SL			10	7	2	102	35	20.40	0	0	204	209	9	23.22	4-49	1	0	6.14	2	
FC	1995		16	23	2	362	60	17.23	0	1	846	508	9	56.44	2-62	0	0	3.60	12	
SL	1995		23	15	3	208	48*	17.33	0	0	402	362	15	24.13	4-49	1	0	5.40	4	
BH	1996		1								6	4	0					4.00	1	
NW	1995		1	1	1	1	1*		0	0	48	43	1	43.00	1-43	0	0	5.37	0	

MOXON, Martyn Douglas b Stairfoot 4.5.1960 RHB RM

FC			12	18	0	589	155	32.72	1	5									3	
SL			2	2	0	14	13	7.00	0	0									0	
BH			3	3	0	97	52	32.33	0	1									0	
NW			3	3	0	108	74	36.00	0	1									0	
Test	1986		10	17	1	455	99	28.43	0	3	48	30	0					3.75	10	
FC	1981		317	541	47	21161	274*	42.83	45	116	2650	1481	28	52.89	3-24	0	0	3.35	218	
Int	1984		8	8	0	174	70	21.75	0	1									5	
SL	1980		151	143	8	4128	129*	30.57	3	24	984	868	21	41.33	3-29	0	0	5.29	46	
BH	1981		50	50	7	1863	141*	43.32	2	14	342	242	9	26.88	5-31	0	1	4.24	19	
NW	1981		34	34	6	1316	137	47.00	2	10	132	68	4	17.00	2-19	0	0	3.09	12	

PARKER, Bradley b Mirfield 30.1.1966 RHB RM

FC			19	30	5	806	138*	32.24	1	4	6	3	0					3.00	6	
SL			16	14	2	193	42	16.08	0	0									1	
BH			4	2	0	73	58	36.50	0	1									0	
NW			2	2	0	69	69	34.50	0	1									0	
FC	1992		36	61	8	1659	138*	31.30	2	9	6	3	0					3.00	16	
SL	1993		38	33	5	480	42	17.14	0	0									6	
NW	1995		3	2	0	69	69	34.50	0	1									0	

Cmp	Debut	M	I	NO	Runs	HS	Avge	100	50	Balls	Runs	Wkts	Avge	BB	5i	10m	RpO	ct	st

SIDEBOTTOM, Ryan Jay b Huddersfield 15.1.1978 LHB LFM

FC		1	1	1	2	2*		0	0	100	71	3	23.66	3-71	0	0	4.26	0	
SL		3								114	103	1	103.00	1-41	0	0	5.42	1	

SILVERWOOD, Christopher Eric Wilfred (Rest of England, England, England to Zimbabwe, England to New Zealand) b Pontefract 5.3.1975 RHB RFM

FC		18	23	6	365	58	21.47	0	1	2872	1531	58	26.39	7-93	4	1	3.19	0	
Int		1								36	44	0					7.33	0	
SL		14	8	4	21	7*	5.25	0	0	537	452	14	32.28	3-12	0	0	5.05	2	
BH		6	2	0	8	8	4.00	0	0	300	225	10	22.50	3-22	0	0	4.50	0	
NW		3	1	0	3	3	3.00	0	0	134	95	4	23.75	3-24	0	0	4.25	0	
Test	1996	1	1	0	0	0	0.00	0	0	150	71	4	17.75	3-63	0	0	2.84	1	
FC	1993	55	77	18	829	58	14.05	0	2	8440	4849	168	28.86	7-93	8	1	3.44	14	
Int	1996	6	4	0	17	12	4.25	0	0	252	201	3	67.00	2-27	0	0	4.78	0	
SL	1993	47	22	13	86	14*	9.55	0	0	1860	1449	57	25.42	4-26	1	0	4.67	4	
BH	1993	11	4	0	11	8	2.75	0	0	568	402	22	18.27	5-28	0	1	4.24	2	
NW	1994	8	3	2	11	8*	11.00	0	0	416	264	8	33.00	3-24	0	0	3.80	3	

STEMP, Richard David b Erdington, Birmingham 11.12.1967 RHB SLA (Worcestershire 1990-92)

FC		17	20	6	154	33*	11.00	0	0	2838	1379	42	32.83	6-77	1	0	2.91	7	
SL		13	6	2	13	9*	3.25	0	0	528	437	18	24.27	3-29	0	0	4.96	3	
BH		6	1	0	2	2	2.00	0	0	330	195	9	21.66	3-22	0	0	3.54	0	
NW		3	1	1	0	0*		0	0	144	89	4	22.25	4-54	1	0	3.70	0	
FC	1990	124	145	44	1292	65	12.79	0	2	23064	9867	292	33.79	6-37	12	1	2.56	53	
SL	1990	59	19	6	108	23*	8.30	0	0	2271	1848	64	28.87	4-25	1	0	4.88	15	
BH	1990	19	4	1	3	2	1.00	0	0	1062	679	19	35.73	3-22	0	0	3.83	0	
NW	1993	10	2	2	1	1*		0	0	606	369	14	26.35	4-45	2	0	3.65	1	

VAUGHAN, Michael Paul (England A, England A to Australia) b Manchester 29.10.1974 RHB OB

FC		15	27	2	839	161	33.56	3	2	883	619	5	123.80	2-3	0	0	4.20	3	
SL		9	9	0	309	66	34.33	0	2	210	229	7	32.71	3-48	0	0	6.54	2	
BH		6	6	0	325	88	54.16	0	2	75	57	3	19.00	1-0	0	0	4.56	0	
NW		1	1	0	22	22	22.00	0	0	30	17	1	17.00	1-17	0	0	3.40	0	
FC	1993	80	146	6	4679	183	33.42	10	22	5373	3121	61	51.16	4-39	0	0	3.48	31	
SL	1993	45	44	3	1027	71*	25.04	0	4	252	273	7	39.00	3-48	0	0	6.50	9	
BH	1994	16	16	1	623	88	41.53	0	5	141	104	4	26.00	1-0	0	0	4.42	4	
NW	1994	11	11	0	185	64	16.81	0	1	30	17	1	17.00	1-17	0	0	3.40	2	

WHARF, Alexander George b Bradford 4.6.1975 RHB RMF

FC		2	3	0	19	14	6.33	0	0	258	155	4	38.75	2-37	0	0	3.60	1	
SL		1								18	34	0					11.33	0	
FC	1994	7	9	1	186	62	23.25	0	1	754	454	11	41.27	4-29	0	0	3.61	2	
SL	1994	4	1	1	2	2*		0	0	84	87	3	29.00	3-39	0	0	6.21	1	
BH	1996	2								114	89	5	17.80	4-29	1	0	4·68	0	

WHITE, Craig (England to Zimbabwe, England to New Zealand, England A to Australia) b Morley Hall 16.12.1969 RHB RMF

FC		17	24	2	639	172*	29.04	1	2	2122	1236	41	30.14	5-31	1	0	3.49	17	
SL		15	13	0	408	148	31.38	1	2	540	462	20	23.10	4-18	1	0	5.13	9	
BH		6	6	2	111	36*	27.75	0	0	312	226	7	32.28	3-22	0	0	4.34	2	
NW		3	3	1	180	96*	90.00	0	2	120	79	1	79.00	1-43	0	0	3.95	1	
Test	1994	8	12	0	166	51	13.83	0	1	811	452	11	41.09	3-18	0	0	3.34	3	
FC	1990	135	204	30	5582	181	32.08	7	30	10622	5902	205	28.79	6-66	5	0	3.33	87	
Int	1994	15	13	0	187	38	14.38	0	0	608	446	15	29.73	4-37	1	0	4.40	2	
SL	1990	90	77	14	1758	148	27.90	1	6	2546	2011	73	27.54	4-18	2	0	4.73	33	
BH	1990	22	19	5	329	57*	23.50	0	1	906	716	19	37.68	3-22	0	0	4.74	5	
NW	1992	18	15	5	569	113	56.90	1	4	845	511	17	30.05	3-38	0	0	3.62	8	

WOOD, Matthew James b Huddersfield 6.4.1977 RHB OB

FC		1	2	0	102	81	51.00	0	1									1	

AUSTRALIA IN ENGLAND 1997

BERRY, D.S.

FC		2	2	0	21	12	10.50	0	0									9	1

BEVAN, M.G.

Test		3	5	0	43	24	8.60	0	0	208	121	2	60.50	1-14	0	0	3.49	1	
FC		11	16	3	463	104*	35.61	1	3	916	606	11	55.09	3-73	0	0	3.96	6	
Int		3	3	1	146	108*	73.00	1	0	72	70	1	70.00	1-43	0	0	5.83	0	

BICHEL, A.J.

FC		1								30	28	0					5.60	0	

Cmp Debut	M	I	NO	Runs	HS	Avge	100	50	Balls	Runs	Wkts	Avge	BB	5i	10m	RpO	ct	st
BLEWETT, G.S.																		
Test	6	10	0	381	125	38.10	1	2	18	17	0					5.66	9	
FC	12	18	1	686	125	40.35	2	4	120	93	0					4.65	17	
Int	1	1	0	28	28	28.00	0	0	18	12	0					6.00	0	
ELLIOTT, M.T.G.																		
Test	6	10	0	556	199	55.60	2	2									4	
FC	12	19	0	1091	199	57.42	4	5	54	43	0					4.77	7	
Int	1	1	0	1	1	1.00	0	0									0	
GILCHRIST, A.C.																		
FC	1	1	1	9	9*		0	0									3	
Int	2	2	0	86	53	43.00	0	1									0	
GILLESPIE, J.N.																		
Test	4	7	2	57	28*	11.40	0	0	550	332	16	20.75	7-37	1	0	3.62	3	
FC	8	9	2	67	28*	9.57	0	0	1192	692	29	23.86	7-37	2	0	3.48	5	
Int	3	2	1	9	6	9.00	0	0	157	136	1	136.00	1-55	0	0	5.19	0	
HEALY, I.A.																		
Test	6	10	1	225	63	25.00	0	1									25	2
FC	12	16	4	407	63	33.91	0	1									39	4
Int	3	3	0	51	27	17.00	0	0									1	
JULIAN, B.P.																		
FC	5	5	1	162	71	40.50	0	2	648	455	9	50.55	3-88	0	0	4.21	4	
KASPROWICZ, M.S.																		
Test	3	4	0	21	17	5.25	0	0	561	310	14	22.14	7-36	1	0	3.31	2	
FC	10	8	3	56	17	11.20	0	0	1604	1010	39	25.89	7-36	1	0	3.77	8	
Int	3	2	2	45	28*		0	0	146	125	3	41.66	1-27	0	0	5.13	0	
LANGER, J.L.																		
FC	6	10	3	312	152*	44.57	1	1									5	
Int	1	1	0	29	29	29.00	0	0									1	
LEE, S.																		
FC	1	1	0	1	1	1.00	0	0	213	113	8	14.12	4-27	0	0	3.18	1	
McGRATH, G.D.																		
Test	6	8	6	25	20*	12.50	0	0	1499	701	36	19.47	8-38	2	0	2.80	2	
FC	11	10	6	25	20*	6.25	0	0	2182	1012	49	20.65	8-38	2	0	2.78	4	
Int	3	1	0	1	1	1.00	0	0	168	125	3	41.66	2-34	0	0	4.46	0	
PONTING, R.T.																		
Test	3	5	0	241	127	48.20	1	0									1	
FC	8	12	3	571	127	63.44	2	2	18	9	0					3.00	7	
REIFFEL, P.R.																		
Test	4	6	3	179	54*	59.66	0	1	673	293	11	26.63	5-49	1	0	2.61	1	
FC	8	9	4	242	56	48.40	0	2	1132	520	28	18.57	5-49	2	0	2.75	2	
SLATER, M.J.																		
FC	5	8	0	159	47	19.87	0	0									3	
Int	2	2	0	18	17	9.00	0	0									0	
TAYLOR, M.A.																		
Test	6	10	0	317	129	31.70	1	1									6	
FC	12	19	0	680	129	35.78	2	4									8	
Int	2	2	0	18	11	9.00	0	0									0	
WARNE, S.K.																		
Test	6	10	0	188	53	18.80	0	1	1423	577	24	24.04	6-48	1	0	2.43	2	
FC	12	17	1	293	53	18.31	0	1	2602	1154	57	20.24	7-103	4	0	2.66	5	
Int	3	3	1	20	11*	10.00	0	0	174	129	1	129.00	1-39	0	0	4.44	1	
WAUGH, M.E.																		
Test	6	10	0	209	68	20.90	0	2	42	16	1	16.00	1-16	0	0	2.28	6	
FC	13	20	3	746	173	43.88	2	3	282	150	4	37.50	1-16	0	0	3.19	11	
Int	3	3	0	131	95	43.66	0	1	48	44	1	44.00	1-28	0	0	5.50	0	
WAUGH, S.R.																		
Test	6	10	0	390	116	39.00	2	1	120	76	0					3.80	4	
FC	13	17	0	924	154	54.35	4	4	156	97	1	97.00	1-13	0	0	3.73	9	
Int	3	3	0	60	24	20.00	0	0	42	42	0					6.00	2	
YOUNG, S. (Gloucestershire - see main section)																		
Test	1	2	1	4	4*	4.00	0	0	48	13	0					1.62	0	
FC	2	3	1	4	4*	2.00	0	0	204	99	2	49.50	1-40	0	0	2.91	0	

PAKISTAN A IN ENGLAND 1997

ABDUR RAZZAQ

Cmp	Debut	M	I	NO	Runs	HS	Avge	100	50	Balls	Runs	Wkts	Avge	BB	5i	10m	RpO	ct	st
FC		6	9	2	216	62	30.85	0	2	1124	753	23	32.73	5-106	1	0	4.01	0	

ALI HUSSAIN RIZVI

FC		8	13	1	77	28	6.41	0	0	1836	822	24	34.25	5-68	1	0	2.68	5	

ALI NAQVI

FC		8	13	0	362	114	27.84	1	1	36	20	1	20.00	1-11	0	0	3.33	4	

AZHAR MAHMOOD

FC		8	13	1	379	92	31.58	0	3	1745	829	40	20.72	5-66	1	0	2.85	2	

FARHAN ADIL

FC		5	9	0	198	50	22.00	0	1									3	

FAZL-E-AKBAR

FC		2	3	1	11	6	5.50	0	0	270	181	4	45.25	2-47	0	0	4.02	0	

HASAN RAZA

FC		6	10	0	349	96	34.90	0	4	114	50	1	50.00	1-36	0	0	2.63	3	

IRFAN FAZIL

FC		3	5	2	43	19	14.33	0	0	336	234	7	33.42	3-51	0	0	4.17	0	

JAVED QADEER

FC		9	15	4	277	61	25.18	0	2									26	1

MOHAMMAD WASIM

FC		9	15	0	390	155	26.00	1	1	42	21	0					3.00	17	

MUJAHID JAMSHED

FC		9	15	0	230	59	15.33	0	1	19	18	0					5.68	3	

QAYYUM-UL-HASSAN, Rana

FC		8	13	1	320	97	26.66	0	2									0	

SALEEM ELAHI

FC		8	13	0	625	229	48.07	1	3									6	

SHOAIB AKHTAR

FC		7	10	4	32	10	5.33	0	0	1167	747	25	29.88	5-62	2	0	3.84	6	

SHOAIB MALIK

FC		3	4	0	18	9	4.50	0	0	738	333	12	27.75	3-49	0	0	2.70	0	

PLAYERS WHO DID NOT APPEAR FOR THE FIRST-CLASS COUNTIES OR TOURISTS IN 1997

ADAMS, Nicholas Jack (Norfolk) b Bedford 1.3.1967 RHB RM

Cmp	Debut	M	I	NO	Runs	HS	Avge	100	50	Balls	Runs	Wkts	Avge	BB	5i	10m	RpO	ct	st
NW		1	1	0	0	0	0.00	0	0	18	13	0					4.33	0	
BH	1993	1	1	0	11	11	11.00	0	0									0	
NW	1987	7	7	1	212	104*	35.33	1	1	109	103	1	103.00	1-52	0	0	5.66	2	

AJAZ AKHTAR (Cambridgeshire) b Banghipur, Pakistan 1.9.1968 RHB RM

NW		1	1	0	5	5	5.00	0	0	66	44	0					4.00	1	
NW	1991	6	5	0	37	15	7.40	0	0	384	241	8	30.12	4-28	1	0	3.76	1	

ALLINGHAM, Michael James de Grey (Scotland) b Inverness 6.1.1965 RHB RM

FC		1	2	0	13	13	6.50	0	0	6	3	0					3.00	1	
FC	1996	2	4	2	99	50*	49.50	0	1	138	101	4	25.25	3-53	0	0	4.39	2	
BH	1996	3	3	1	37	30	18.50	0	0	48	60	0					7.50	1	
NW	1995	1	1	0	13	13	13.00	0	0	21	24	0					6.85	0	

AMOS, Carl (Norfolk) b King's Lynn 30.3.1973 LHB

NW		1	1	0	13	13	13.00	0	0									2	
NW	1994	3	3	0	38	21	12.66	0	0									2	

ANDERS, Jonathan Victor (Shropshire) b Tunbridge Wells 25.1.1971 RHB OB

NW		1	1	0	8	8	8.00	0	0	22	2	0					0.54	0	

ANTHONY, Hamish Arbeb Gervais (MCC, Leeward Islands) b Urlings Village, Antigua 16.1.1971 RHB RFM (Glamorgan 1990-95)

FC		1	1	0	0	0	0.00	0	0	252	113	10	11.30	6-34	1	1	2.69	1	
FC	1989	74	108	9	1707	91	17.24	0	7	11344	6303	222	28.39	6-22	6	1	3.33	28	
Int	1995	3	3	0	23	21	7.66	0	0	156	143	3	47.66	2-47	0	0	5.50	0	
SL	1995	11	8	2	22	7	3.66	0	0	450	404	11	36.72	3-40	0	0	5.38	0	
BH	1995	1	1	0	2	2	2.00	0	0	66	40	3	13.33	3-40	0	0	3.63	0	
NW	1995	4	2	0	12	8	6.00	0	0	197	111	5	22.20	4-25	1	0	3.38	1	

ARTHURTON, Keith Lloyd Thomas (MCC, Buckinghamshire, Leeward Islands) b Charlestown, Nevis 21.2.1965 LHB SLA

FC		1	1	0	200	200*		1	0	18	5	0					1.66	1	
NW		1	1	0	18	18	18.00	0	0	72	53	4	13.25	4-53	1	0	4.41	1	
Test	1988	33	50	5	1382	157*	30.71	2	8	473	183	1	183.00	1-17	0	0	2.32	22	

Cmp	Debut	M	I	NO	Runs	HS	Avge	100	50	Balls	Runs	Wkts	Avge	BB	5i	10m	RpO	ct	st
FC	1985	115	180	25	7171	200*	46.26	19	39	2242	926	27	34.29	3-14	0	0	2.47	61	
Int	1988	86	76	15	1652	84	27.08	0	9	797	666	22	30.27	3-31	0	0	5.01	21	

ASIF DIN (MCC, Shropshire) b Kampala, Uganda 21.9.1960 RHB LB (Warwickshire 1981-95)

Cmp	Debut	M	I	NO	Runs	HS	Avge	100	50	Balls	Runs	Wkts	Avge	BB	5i	10m	RpO	ct	st
FC		1	2	1	16	12*	16.00	0	0									0	
NW		1	1	0	1	1	1.00	0	0	72	20	0					1.66	0	
FC	1981	211	343	46	9074	217	30.55	9	42	6573	4393	79	55.60	5-61	2	0	4.01	114	
SL	1981	171	155	27	3792	132*	29.62	4	16	230	261	4	65.25	1-11	0	0	6.80	32	
BH	1981	43	40	5	1211	137	34.60	2	6	126	102	1	102.00	1-26	0	0	4.85	5	
NW	1981	31	28	7	807	104	38.42	1	3	241	119	7	17.00	5-40	0	1	2.96	6	

BADENHORST, Alan (MCC, Eastern Province) b Cape Town, South Africa 10.7.1970 RHB RF

Cmp	Debut	M	I	NO	Runs	HS	Avge	100	50	Balls	Runs	Wkts	Avge	BB	5i	10m	RpO	ct	st
FC		1	1	0	0	0	0.00	0	0	186	72	5	14.40	3-48	0	0	2.32	0	
FC	1993	24	27	10	86	21*	5.05	0	0	2134	76		28.07	5-49	2	0	2.91	7	

BAGGS, Richard James (Devon) b Eastbourne 19.11.1974 LHB RMF

Cmp	Debut	M	I	NO	Runs	HS	Avge	100	50	Balls	Runs	Wkts	Avge	BB	5i	10m	RpO	ct	st
NW		1	1	0	5	5	5.00	0	0									0	

BAILEY, Matthew Richard Kelland (Cambridge University) b Cambridge 6.10.1977 RHB WK

Cmp	Debut	M	I	NO	Runs	HS	Avge	100	50	Balls	Runs	Wkts	Avge	BB	5i	10m	RpO	ct	st
FC		1	1	1	6	6*		0	0									1	1

BARLOW, Richard Guy Ross (Herefordshire) b Epsom 28.6.1972 RHB LB

Cmp	Debut	M	I	NO	Runs	HS	Avge	100	50	Balls	Runs	Wkts	Avge	BB	5i	10m	RpO	ct	st
NW		1	1	0	15	15	15.00	0	0									0	

BARROW, James Keith (Berkshire) b Haslemere 16.12.1964 RHB RFM

Cmp	Debut	M	I	NO	Runs	HS	Avge	100	50	Balls	Runs	Wkts	Avge	BB	5i	10m	RpO	ct	st
NW		1									54	32	1	32.00	1-32	0	0	3.55	0	
NW	1994	3									198	178	1	178.00	1-32	0	0	5.39	0	

BATTARBEE, Christopher Mark (Oxford University) b Sidcup 11.4.1975 RHB RM

Cmp	Debut	M	I	NO	Runs	HS	Avge	100	50	Balls	Runs	Wkts	Avge	BB	5i	10m	RpO	ct	st
FC		7	8	6	29	10*	14.50	0	0	904	627	11	57.00	2-56	0	0	4.16	1	

BEECH, Paul (Cumberland) b Hailsham 2.10.1965 RHB RFM

Cmp	Debut	M	I	NO	Runs	HS	Avge	100	50	Balls	Runs	Wkts	Avge	BB	5i	10m	RpO	ct	st
NW		1	1	0	5	5	5.00	0	0	30	21	1	21.00	1-21	0	0	4.20	0	
NW	1996	2	2	0	47	42	23.50	0	0	96	81	2	40.50	1-21	0	0	5.06	0	

BENSON, Justin David Ramsay (Ireland) b Dublin 1.3.1967 RHB RM (Leicestershire 1988-93)

Cmp	Debut	M	I	NO	Runs	HS	Avge	100	50	Balls	Runs	Wkts	Avge	BB	5i	10m	RpO	ct	st
FC		1	2	1	61	61*	61.00	0	1	55	44	3	14.66	2-38	0	0	4.80	1	
BH		3	3	0	51	23	17.00	0	0	105	96	5	19.20	3-45	0	0	5.48	1	
NW		1	1	0	0	0	0.00	0	0	66	55	1	55.00	1-55	0	0	5.00	1	
FC	1988	57	85	9	2158	153	28.39	4	6	824	532	11	48.36	2-24	0	0	3.87	66	
SL	1988	66	59	9	1010	67	20.20	0	2	1017	991	33	30.03	4-27	1	0	5.84	25	
BH	1988	23	22	3	335	43	17.63	0	0	376	324	11	29.45	3-45	0	0	5.17	8	
NW	1986	11	11	1	192	85	19.20	0	1	252	212	9	23.55	3-13	0	0	5.04	7	

BEVINS, Stuart Roy (Herefordshire) b Solihull 8.3.1967 RHB WK (Worcestershire 1989-91)

Cmp	Debut	M	I	NO	Runs	HS	Avge	100	50	Balls	Runs	Wkts	Avge	BB	5i	10m	RpO	ct	st
NW		1	1	0	8	8	8.00	0	0									0	
FC	1989	6	6	2	34	10	8.50	0	0									18	
SL	1989	4																4	1
BH	1990	2	1	1	0	0*		0	0									2	1
NW	1995	2	2	0	34	26	17.00	0	0									0	

BLAKEMORE, Ian Paul Corbett (Herefordshire) b Ironbridge 13.5.1965 LHB SLA

Cmp	Debut	M	I	NO	Runs	HS	Avge	100	50	Balls	Runs	Wkts	Avge	BB	5i	10m	RpO	ct	st
NW		1	1	0	7	7	7.00	0	0	12	19	0					9.50	0	

BOON, Timothy James (Norfolk) b Doncaster 1.11.1961 RHB RM (Leicestershire 1980-95)

Cmp	Debut	M	I	NO	Runs	HS	Avge	100	50	Balls	Runs	Wkts	Avge	BB	5i	10m	RpO	ct	st
NW		1	1	0	12	12	12.00	0	0									0	
FC	1980	248	419	42	11821	144	31.35	14	68	667	563	11	51.18	3-40	0	0	2.53	124	
SL	1980	115	102	11	2175	135*	23.90	1	9	42	55	1	55.00	1-23	0	0	7.85	25	
BH	1980	34	31	7	866	103	36.08	1	6									9	
NW	1984	21	19	4	518	117	34.53	1	2	72	65	1	65.00	1-63	0	0	5.41	9	

BOWETT, Duncan John (Shropshire) b Perth, Australia 7.12.1971 RHB RFM

Cmp	Debut	M	I	NO	Runs	HS	Avge	100	50	Balls	Runs	Wkts	Avge	BB	5i	10m	RpO	ct	st
NW		1	1	1	11	11*		0	0	42	15	0					2.14	0	

BOWYER, Matthew (Buckinghamshire) b Eastbourne 25.7.1973 RHB

Cmp	Debut	M	I	NO	Runs	HS	Avge	100	50	Balls	Runs	Wkts	Avge	BB	5i	10m	RpO	ct	st
NW		1	1	0	43	43	43.00	0	0									0	

BOYDEN, Matthew Kavan Leslie (Norfolk) b King's Lynn 24.2.1979 RHB WK

Cmp	Debut	M	I	NO	Runs	HS	Avge	100	50	Balls	Runs	Wkts	Avge	BB	5i	10m	RpO	ct	st
NW		1	1	1	8	8*		0	0									1	

BRADSHAW, Paul John (Norfolk) b Chelmsford 1.5.1978 RHB RFM

Cmp	Debut	M	I	NO	Runs	HS	Avge	100	50	Balls	Runs	Wkts	Avge	BB	5i	10m	RpO	ct	st
NW		1	1	0	0	0	0.00	0	0	69	42	3	14.00	3-42	0	0	3.65	0	

BRADFORD, Stephen Alvin (Lincolnshire) b Lincoln 15.7.1963 LHB SLA

Cmp	Debut	M	I	NO	Runs	HS	Avge	100	50	Balls	Runs	Wkts	Avge	BB	5i	10m	RpO	ct	st
NW		1	1	1	15	15*		0	0	24	18	1	18.00	1-18	0	0	4.50	0	
NW	1996	2	2	1	26	15*	26.00	0	0	96	70	3	23.33	2-52	0	0	4.37	0	

BROCK, Denton John (Staffordshire) b Newcastle-under-Lyme 10.7.1971 RHB RFM

Cmp	Debut	M	I	NO	Runs	HS	Avge	100	50	Balls	Runs	Wkts	Avge	BB	5i	10m	RpO	ct	st
NW		1	1	0	3	3	3.00	0	0	48	31	0					3.87	0	
NW	1996	2	2	0	22	19	11.00	0	0	84	64	1	64.00	1-33	0	0	4.57	0	

BUCHANAN, Laurence George (Oxford University) b Perivale 9.3.1976 RHB

Cmp	Debut	M	I	NO	Runs	HS	Avge	100	50	Balls	Runs	Wkts	Avge	BB	5i	10m	RpO	ct	st
FC		8	14	4	168	43*	16.80	0	0									1	

Cmp	Debut	M	I	NO	Runs	HS	Avge	100	50	Balls	Runs	Wkts	Avge	BB	5i	10m	RpO	ct	st

BULL, James Jonathan (Oxford University) b Leicester 22.12.1976 RHB OB

Cmp	Debut	M	I	NO	Runs	HS	Avge	100	50	Balls	Runs	Wkts	Avge	BB	5i	10m	RpO	ct	st
FC		3	5	1	49	30	12.25	0	0									0	
FC	1996	5	6	1	53	30	10.60	0	0									0	

BULLEN, Christopher Keith (Bedfordshire) b Clapham 5.11.1962 RHB OB (Surrey 1982-91)

Cmp	Debut	M	I	NO	Runs	HS	Avge	100	50	Balls	Runs	Wkts	Avge	BB	5i	10m	RpO	ct	st
NW		1	1	0	2	2	2.00	0	0	12	9	0					4.50	0	
FC	1982	31	36	7	665	65	22.93	0	4	2469	1150	40	28.75	6-119	1	0	2.79	31	
SL	1985	73	39	20	344	28*	18.10	0	0	2582	2055	67	30.67	5-31	0	1	4.37	42	
BH	1987	18	11	5	168	35*	28.00	0	0	995	637	15	42.46	2-14	0	0	3.84	13	
NW	1987	13	10	4	173	93*	28.83	0	1	840	487	11	44.27	3-58	0	0	3.47	5	

BURNS, Neil David (Buckinghamshire) b Chelmsford 19.9.1965 LHB WK (Essex 1986, Somerset 1987-93)

Cmp	Debut	M	I	NO	Runs	HS	Avge	100	50	Balls	Runs	Wkts	Avge	BB	5i	10m	RpO	ct	st
NW		1	1	0	51	51	51.00	0	1									2	
FC	1985	156	234	52	5349	166	29.39	5	26	3	8	0					16.00	316	32
SL	1986	103	81	22	1056	58	17.89	0	3									103	17
BH	1987	32	25	9	441	51	27.56	0	1									29	6
NW	1987	17	13	3	185	51	18.50	0	1									19	6

BYRAM, Adam Bramley (Shropshire) b Wellington 17.3.1971 RHB SLA

Cmp	Debut	M	I	NO	Runs	HS	Avge	100	50	Balls	Runs	Wkts	Avge	BB	5i	10m	RpO	ct	st
NW		1	1	0	5	5	5.00	0	0	72	29	0					2.41	0	
NW	1990	5	5	1	66	22	16.50	0	0	288	182	3	60.66	2-41	0	0	3.91	2	

BYRAM, Gavin James (Shropshire) b Shrewsbury 15.2.1974 RHB RFM

Cmp	Debut	M	I	NO	Runs	HS	Avge	100	50	Balls	Runs	Wkts	Avge	BB	5i	10m	RpO	ct	st
NW		1	1	0	0	0	0.00	0	0	42	22	0					3.14	0	

BYRNE, Byron Walter (Oxford University) b Sydney, Australia 15.2.1972 RHB OB

Cmp	Debut	M	I	NO	Runs	HS	Avge	100	50	Balls	Runs	Wkts	Avge	BB	5i	10m	RpO	ct	st
FC		11	20	0	354	49	17.70	0	0	588	439	3	146.33	1-19	0	0	4.47	2	

BYRNE, John Edward (Ireland) b Dublin 17.1.1972 RHB

Cmp	Debut	M	I	NO	Runs	HS	Avge	100	50	Balls	Runs	Wkts	Avge	BB	5i	10m	RpO	ct	st
FC		1	2	1	19	12*	19.00	0	0									0	

CHRISTMAS, David Anthony (Lincolnshire) b Bourne 1.4.1969 RHB RM

Cmp	Debut	M	I	NO	Runs	HS	Avge	100	50	Balls	Runs	Wkts	Avge	BB	5i	10m	RpO	ct	st
NW		1	1	0	0	0	0.00	0	0	24	30	0					7.50	0	
NW	1991	3	3	0	15	11	5.00	0	0	168	177	1	177.00	1-67	0	0	6.32	0	

CHURTON, David Richard Harding (Cambridge University) b Salisbury 29.3.1975 RHB WK

Cmp	Debut	M	I	NO	Runs	HS	Avge	100	50	Balls	Runs	Wkts	Avge	BB	5i	10m	RpO	ct	st
FC		7	7	1	177	44	29.50	0	0									9	1
FC	1995	20	24	1	329	44	14.30	0	0									23	7

CLARKE, Andrew Russell (Buckinghamshire) b Brighton 23.12.1961 RHB LB (Sussex 1988-90)

Cmp	Debut	M	I	NO	Runs	HS	Avge	100	50	Balls	Runs	Wkts	Avge	BB	5i	10m	RpO	ct	st
NW		1	1	0	0	0	0.00	0	0	66	70	1	70.00	1-70	0	0	6.36	0	
FC	1988	26	37	9	406	68	14.50	0	1	4194	1872	53	35.32	5-60	2	0	2.67	7	
SL	1988	31	12	5	25	9*	3.57	0	0	1327	1013	42	24.11	4-24	1	0	4.58	6	
BH	1989	6	2	0	1	1	0.50	0	0	390	278	5	55.60	1-17	0	0	4.27	1	
NW	1988	7	5	1	29	24	7.25	0	0	414	276	6	46.00	3-41	0	0	4.00	1	

CLARKE, Grahame Jeffrey (Cumberland) b Lancaster 1.8.1965 RHB

Cmp	Debut	M	I	NO	Runs	HS	Avge	100	50	Balls	Runs	Wkts	Avge	BB	5i	10m	RpO	ct	st
NW		1	1	0	9	9	9.00	0	0									1	
NW	1985	7	7	0	132	61	18.85	0	1									1	

COCKBAIN, Ian (Minor Counties) b Bootle 19.4.1958 RHB SLA (Lancashire 1979-83)

Cmp	Debut	M	I	NO	Runs	HS	Avge	100	50	Balls	Runs	Wkts	Avge	BB	5i	10m	RpO	ct	st
BH		5	5	0	54	30	10.80	0	0									1	
FC	1979	47	80	10	1483	98	21.18	0	7	48	14	0					1.75	22	
SL	1980	23	17	1	246	53*	15.37	0	1									4	
BH	1980	19	16	2	345	65*	24.64	0	3									8	
NW	1985	11	11	0	187	57	17.00	0	1									5	

COCKROFT, Jonathan Richard (Oxford University) b Bradford 28.5.1977 RHB LB

Cmp	Debut	M	I	NO	Runs	HS	Avge	100	50	Balls	Runs	Wkts	Avge	BB	5i	10m	RpO	ct	st
FC		1	1	0	1	1	1.00	0	0									0	

COOKE, Gordon (Ireland) b Londonderry 24.7.1975 RHB RMF

Cmp	Debut	M	I	NO	Runs	HS	Avge	100	50	Balls	Runs	Wkts	Avge	BB	5i	10m	RpO	ct	st
FC		1	1	0	0	0	0.00	0	0	102	63	2	31.50	1-31	0	0	3.70	1	
BH		2	2	1	19	12*	19.00	0	0	72	101	1	101.00	1-76	0	0	8.41	0	
FC	1994	2	1	0	0	0	0.00	0	0	240	128	4	32.00	1-26	0	0	3.20	1	
BH	1995	4	4	1	19	12*	6.33	0	0	138	163	2	81.50	1-21	0	0	7.08	1	
NW	1994	1								72	48	0					4.00	0	

COOPER, Kevin Edward (Herefordshire) b Sutton-in-Ashfield 27.12.1957 LHB RFM (Nottinghamshire 1970-92, Gloucestershire 1993-96)

Cmp	Debut	M	I	NO	Runs	HS	Avge	100	50	Balls	Runs	Wkts	Avge	BB	5i	10m	RpO	ct	st
NW		1	1	0	4	4	4.00	0	0	72	63	0					5.25	2	
FC	1976	305	330	83	2484	52	10.05	0	1	49492	22010	817	26.94	8-44	26	1	2.66	93	
SL	1976	167	60	21	248	31	6.35	0	0	6994	5170	141	36.66	4-25	3	0	4.43	28	
BH	1976	75	27	17	143	25*	14.30	0	0	4429	2415	81	29.81	4-9	3	0	3.27	13	
NW	1976	28	10	1	54	11	6.00	0	0	1886	877	41	21.39	4-49	1	0	2.79	9	

COTTAM, Andrew Colin (Devon) b Northampton 14.7.1973 RHB SLA (Somerset 1992-96, Derbyshire 1995)

Cmp	Debut	M	I	NO	Runs	HS	Avge	100	50	Balls	Runs	Wkts	Avge	BB	5i	10m	RpO	ct	st
NW		1	1	1	22	22*		0	0	72	41	0					3.41	0	
FC	1992	13	16	1	153	36	10.20	0	0	1708	819	13	63.00	2-5	0	0	2.87	1	
SL	1993	1								36	24	0					4.00	0	
BH	1991	1								42	34	0					4.85	0	
NW	1993	3	2	1	24	22*	24.00	0	0	210	133	1	133.00	1-45	0	0	3.80	1	

Cmp	Debut	M	I	NO	Runs	HS	Avge	100	50	Balls	Runs	Wkts	Avge	BB	5i	10m	RpO	ct	st

CRONJE, Wessel Johannes (Ireland, Free State, South Africa to India, South Africa to Kenya) b Bloemfontein, South Africa 25.9.1969 RHB RM (Leicestershire 1995)

Cmp	Debut	M	I	NO	Runs	HS	Avge	100	50	Balls	Runs	Wkts	Avge	BB	5i	10m	RpO	ct	st
BH		3	3	1	180	94*	90.00	0	2	132	134	6	22.33	3-38	0	0	6.09	0	
Test	1991	36	63	7	2012	135	35.92	5	7	2411	768	17	45.17	2-11	0	0	1.91	12	
FC	1987	128	226	23	8496	251	41.85	22	39	7000	2816	70	40.22	4-47	0	0	2.41	83	
Int	1991	115	107	20	3473	112	39.91	2	22	3554	2559	69	37.08	5-22	1	1	4.32	46	
SL	1995	13	13	3	357	93*	35.70	0	2	588	466	11	42.36	3-37	0	0	4.75	4	
BH	1995	8	8	1	408	158	58.28	1	2	396	299	10	29.90	3-38	0	0	4.53	2	

CURRY, Desmond John (Ireland) b Strabane 20.12.1966 LHB OB

Cmp	Debut	M	I	NO	Runs	HS	Avge	100	50	Balls	Runs	Wkts	Avge	BB	5i	10m	RpO	ct	st
FC		1	2	0	9	6	4.50	0	0									0	
BH		1	1	0	75	75	75.00	0	1									0	
NW		1	1	0	4	4	4.00	0	0	36	24	0					4.00	0	
FC	1993	2	4	0	54	41	13.50	0	0	60	16	1	16.00	1-12	0	0	1.60	0	
BH	1994	6	6	1	107	75	21.40	0	1	48	32	0					4.00	2	
NW	1993	2	2	0	26	22	13.00	0	0	72	52	1	52.00	1-28	0	0	4.33	1	

DALTON, Richard Neil (Minor Counties, Bedfordshire) b Portsmouth 11.8.1965 RHB RM

Cmp	Debut	M	I	NO	Runs	HS	Avge	100	50	Balls	Runs	Wkts	Avge	BB	5i	10m	RpO	ct	st
BH		5	5	0	170	76	34.00	0	2	235	222	6	37.00	3-33	0	0	5.66	2	
NW		1	1	0	8	8	8.00	0	0	36	32	2	16.00	2-32	0	0	5.33	0	
NW	1994	2	2	0	8	8	4.00	0	0	60	66	4	16.50	2-32	0	0	6.60	0	

DAVIES, Alec George (Scotland) b Rawalpindi, Pakistan 18.4.1962 RHB WK (Surrey 1985)

Cmp	Debut	M	I	NO	Runs	HS	Avge	100	50	Balls	Runs	Wkts	Avge	BB	5i	10m	RpO	ct	st
FC		1	1	0	10	10	10.00	0	0									2	
BH		3	3	1	41	35*	20.50	0	0									2	
NW		1	1	0	16	16	16.00	0	0									0	
FC	1985	3	4	2	65	26*	32.50	0	0									8	2
BH	1994	8	7	1	71	35*	11.83	0	0									7	
NW	1996	2	2	0	19	16	9.50	0	0									1	

DAVIES, Mark Robert (Shropshire) b Shrewsbury 24.9.1962 RHB RM

Cmp	Debut	M	I	NO	Runs	HS	Avge	100	50	Balls	Runs	Wkts	Avge	BB	5i	10m	RpO	ct	st
NW		1	1	0	9	9	9.00	0	0									0	
NW	1985	7	7	0	141	89	20.14	0	1									0	

DAVY, John Oliver (Ireland) b Dublin 1.7.1974 RHB LFM

Cmp	Debut	M	I	NO	Runs	HS	Avge	100	50	Balls	Runs	Wkts	Avge	BB	5i	10m	RpO	ct	st
FC		1	2	1	53	51*	53.00	0	1	114	93	0					4.89	0	

DAWSON, Mark William (Cambridge University) b Clifton 28.3.1974 LHB SLA

Cmp	Debut	M	I	NO	Runs	HS	Avge	100	50	Balls	Runs	Wkts	Avge	BB	5i	10m	RpO	ct	st
FC		4	7	0	35	23	5.00	0	0	356	240	0					4.04	1	

DEAN, Steven John (Minor Counties, Staffordshire) b Cosford 16.11.1960 RHB (Warwickshire 1993)

Cmp	Debut	M	I	NO	Runs	HS	Avge	100	50	Balls	Runs	Wkts	Avge	BB	5i	10m	RpO	ct	st
BH		5	5	0	126	56	25.20	0	1									0	
NW		1	1	0	4	4	4.00	0	0									0	
FC	1994	1	2	0	73	39	36.50	0	0									1	
SL	1993	1	1	0	17	17	17.00	0	0									0	
BH	1982	22	21	0	531	56	25.28	0	1									5	
NW	1986	12	12	0	238	72	19.83	0	1									4	

DONELAN, Bradleigh Thomas Peter (Cambridgeshire) b Park Royal 3.1.1968 RHB OB (Sussex 1989-93, Somerset 1994)

Cmp	Debut	M	I	NO	Runs	HS	Avge	100	50	Balls	Runs	Wkts	Avge	BB	5i	10m	RpO	ct	st
NW		1	1	0	3	3	3.00	0	0	42	44	0					6.28	0	
FC	1989	53	66	21	1105	68*	24.55	0	5	8626	4627	106	43.65	6-62	4	1	3.21	14	
SL	1989	13	6	2	71	19	17.75	0	0	426	322	7	46.00	2-39	0	0	4.53	1	
BH	1991	3	3	3	25	9*		0	0	174	127	1	127.00	1-41	0	0	4.37	1	
NW	1995	3	3	0	64	32	21.33	0	0	180	154	2	77.00	1-52	0	0	5.13	1	

DONOHUE, Keith (Devon) b Chatham 11.10.1963 RHB RMF

Cmp	Debut	M	I	NO	Runs	HS	Avge	100	50	Balls	Runs	Wkts	Avge	BB	5i	10m	RpO	ct	st
NW		1	1	0	5	5	5.00	0	0	72	44	2	22.00	2-44	0	0	3.66	0	
NW	1986	9	8	3	87	31	17.40	0	0	614	505	11	45.90	3-41	0	0	4.93	2	

DUNLOP, Angus Richard (Ireland) b Dublin 17.3.1967 RHB OB

Cmp	Debut	M	I	NO	Runs	HS	Avge	100	50	Balls	Runs	Wkts	Avge	BB	5i	10m	RpO	ct	st
BH		3	2	1	31	31*	31.00	0	0									1	
NW		1	1	0	5	5	5.00	0	0									0	
FC	1990	3	5	0	166	57	33.20	0	2	240	143	2	71.50	1-8	0	0	3.57	2	
BH	1994	9	8	1	96	50	13.71	0	1	24	29	0					7.25	2	
NW	1990	4	4	0	14	8	3.50	0	0	48	45	3	15.00	3-45	0	0	5.62	1	

DURANT, Cristian Dominic (Cambridgeshire) b Leicester 23.1.1977 RHB WK

Cmp	Debut	M	I	NO	Runs	HS	Avge	100	50	Balls	Runs	Wkts	Avge	BB	5i	10m	RpO	ct	st
NW		1	1	0	1	1	1.00	0	0									0	

DUTTON, Simon Michael (Cumberland) b Barrow-in-Furness 17.3.1964 RHB WK

Cmp	Debut	M	I	NO	Runs	HS	Avge	100	50	Balls	Runs	Wkts	Avge	BB	5i	10m	RpO	ct	st
NW		1	1	0	38	38	38.00	0	0									3	
NW	1987	8	8	2	192	61	32.00	0	1									13	

DYER, Nicholas Rayner (Scotland) b Edinburgh 10.6.1969 RHB OB

Cmp	Debut	M	I	NO	Runs	HS	Avge	100	50	Balls	Runs	Wkts	Avge	BB	5i	10m	RpO	ct	st
FC		1	1	1	0	0*		0	0	126	59	2	29.50	1-29	0	0	2.80	1	

EAGLESON, Ryan Logan (Ireland) b Carrickfergus 17.12.1974 RHB RFM

Cmp	Debut	M	I	NO	Runs	HS	Avge	100	50	Balls	Runs	Wkts	Avge	BB	5i	10m	RpO	ct	st
BH		1	1	0	9	9	9.00	0	0	42	50	0					7.14	1	
NW		1	1	0	10	10	10.00	0	0	60	40	2	20.00	2-40	0	0	4.00	0	
FC	1996	1	2	2	91	50*		0	1	187	149	3	49.66	2-50	0	0	4.78	2	
BH	1996	4	4	0	40	13	10.00	0	0	137	209	1	209.00	1-51	0	0	9.15	2	
NW	1995	3	3	2	25	15*	25.00	0	0	198	179	5	35.80	2-40	0	0	5.42	1	

Cmp	Debut	M	I	NO	Runs	HS	Avge	100	50	Balls	Runs	Wkts	Avge	BB	5i	10m	RpO	ct	st

ECCLESTONE, Giles William (Minor Counties, Cambridgeshire) b Lambeth 17.10.1968 LHB RM

Cmp	Debut	M	I	NO	Runs	HS	Avge	100	50	Balls	Runs	Wkts	Avge	BB	5i	10m	RpO	ct	st
BH		1	1	0	0	0	0.00	0	0									1	
NW		1	1	0	0	0	0.00	0	0									0	
NW	1992	5	5	0	109	92	21.80	0	1	36	20	0					3.33	2	

EVANS, Russell John (Lincolnshire) b Calverton 1.10.1965 RHB RM (Nottinghamshire 1985-90)

Cmp	Debut	M	I	NO	Runs	HS	Avge	100	50	Balls	Runs	Wkts	Avge	BB	5i	10m	RpO	ct	st
NW		1	1	0	3	3	3.00	0	0									0	
FC	1987	7	11	3	201	59	25.12	0	2	198	97	3	32.33	3-40	0	0	2.93	5	
SL	1985	6	5	1	55	20	13.75	0	0									0	
BH	1995	7	6	0	135	56	22.50	0	1									1	
NW	1994	3	3	0	21	15	7.00	0	0									0	

FELL, Mark Andrew (Minor Counties, Lincolnshire) b Newark 17.11.1960 RHB SLA (Nottinghamshire 1981-83, Derbyshire 1985)

Cmp	Debut	M	I	NO	Runs	HS	Avge	100	50	Balls	Runs	Wkts	Avge	BB	5i	10m	RpO	ct	st
BH		3	3	1	104	67	52.00	0	1	78	74	3	24.66	2-55	0	0	5.69	0	
NW		1	1	0	17	17	17.00	0	0									0	
FC	1982	20	35	0	506	108	14.45	1	0	288	157	1	157.00	1-20	0	0	3.27	13	
SL	1981	18	15	2	109	28	8.38	0	0	156	131	4	32.75	2-39	0	0	5.09	9	
BH	1982	8	7	1	146	67	24.33	0	1	144	112	5	22.40	2-38	0	0	4.66	1	
NW	1982	6	6	0	132	39	22.00	0	0	318	210	4	52.50	3-50	0	0	3.96	3	

FELTHAM, Christopher Glen (Staffordshire) b Sydney, Australia 8.9.1972 RHB OB

Cmp	Debut	M	I	NO	Runs	HS	Avge	100	50	Balls	Runs	Wkts	Avge	BB	5i	10m	RpO	ct	st
NW		1	1	1	6	6*		0	0	5	1	0					1.20	0	
NW	1996	2	2	1	24	18	24.00	0	0	11	8	0					4.36	0	

FIELDING, Jonathan Mark (Minor Counties, Cumberland) b Bury 13.3.1973 RHB SLA (Lancashire 1994)

Cmp	Debut	M	I	NO	Runs	HS	Avge	100	50	Balls	Runs	Wkts	Avge	BB	5i	10m	RpO	ct	st
BH		3	3	0	15	14	5.00	0	0	168	157	4	39.25	2-47	0	0	5.60	2	
NW		1	1	0	5	5	5.00	0	0	72	24	1	24.00	1-24	0	0	2.00	0	
FC	1994	1	1	1	27	27*		0	0	118	53	2	26.50	1-15	0	0	2.69	0	
NW	1996	2	2	0	6	5	3.00	0	0	138	76	2	38.00	1-24	0	0	3.30	0	

FLOWER, Andrew (MCC, Mashonaland, Zimbabwe, Zimbabwe to Pakistan, Zimbabwe to Sri Lanka, Zimbabwe to Sharjah, Zimbabwe to South Africa) b Cape Town, South Africa 28.4.1968 LHB OB WK

Cmp	Debut	M	I	NO	Runs	HS	Avge	100	50	Balls	Runs	Wkts	Avge	BB	5i	10m	RpO	ct	st
FC		1	1	0	14	14	70.00	0	0									0	
Test	1992	22	37	5	1330	156	41.56	3	9	1	0	0					0.00	50	4
FC	1986	63	103	19	3912	156	46.57	10	24	390	163	4	40.75	1-1	0	0	2.50	111	10
Int	1991	65	63	4	1711	115*	29.00	1	12	30	23	0					4.60	52	10

FLOWER, Grant William (MCC, Mashonaland, Zimbabwe, Zimbabwe to Pakistan, Zimbabwe to Sri Lanka, Zimbabwe to Sharjah, Zimbabwe to South Africa) b Salisbury 20.12.1970 RHB SLA

Cmp	Debut	M	I	NO	Runs	HS	Avge	100	50	Balls	Runs	Wkts	Avge	BB	5i	10m	RpO	ct	st
FC		1	1	0	78	78	78.00	0	1	30	10	0					2.00	1	
Test	1992	22	38	1	1175	201*	31.75	2	6	672	322	3	107.33	1-4	0	0	2.87	11	
FC	1989	65	116	9	4501	243*	42.06	8	29	3890	1834	43	42.65	3-20	0	0	2.82	57	
Int	1992	55	53	3	1526	91	30.52	0	11	863	719	16	44.93	3-15	0	0	4.99	27	

FOLEY, Geoffrey Ian (MCC, Queensland) b Jandowae, Australia 11.10.1967 LHB RM

Cmp	Debut	M	I	NO	Runs	HS	Avge	100	50	Balls	Runs	Wkts	Avge	BB	5i	10m	RpO	ct	st
FC		1	1	0	4	4	4.00	0	0	114	53	0					2.78	1	
FC	1989	29	48	5	1322	155	30.74	1	7	2985	1566	29	54.00	3-64	0	0	3.14	27	

FOLLAND, Nicholas Arthur (Devon) b Bristol 17.9.1963 LHB RM (Somerset 1992-94)

Cmp	Debut	M	I	NO	Runs	HS	Avge	100	50	Balls	Runs	Wkts	Avge	BB	5i	10m	RpO	ct	st
NW		1	1	0	17	17	17.00	0	0									1	
FC	1990	32	56	5	1755	108*	34.41	2	10									20	
SL	1992	25	24	1	671	107*	29.17	1	4									10	
BH	1989	19	19	3	781	100*	48.81	1	7									11	
NW	1984	17	17	0	511	104	30.05	1	4	26	55	1	55.00	1-52	0	0	12.69	12	

FORD, James Antony (British Universities) b Pembury 30.3.1976 RHB SLA (Kent 1996)

Cmp	Debut	M	I	NO	Runs	HS	Avge	100	50	Balls	Runs	Wkts	Avge	BB	5i	10m	RpO	ct	st
BH		4	4	0	63	38	15.75	0	0	30	27	0					5.40	3	
FC	1996	1								68	54	0					4.76	1	

FOWLES, Mitchell Graham (Herefordshire) b Worcester 18.12.1970 RHB RM

Cmp	Debut	M	I	NO	Runs	HS	Avge	100	50	Balls	Runs	Wkts	Avge	BB	5i	10m	RpO	ct	st
NW		1	1	0	0	0	0.00	0	0	60	73	1	73.00	1-73	0	0	7.30	0	
NW	1995	2	2	1	2	2*	2.00	0	0	132	146	3	48.66	2-73	0	0	6.63	1	

FOX, Neil (Norfolk) b Norwich 10.2.1962 RHB OB

Cmp	Debut	M	I	NO	Runs	HS	Avge	100	50	Balls	Runs	Wkts	Avge	BB	5i	10m	RpO	ct	st
NW		1	1	0	21	21	21.00	0	0	30	22	0					4.40	0	
NW	1993	5	5	0	121	68	24.20	0	1	54	45	1	45.00	1-23	0	0	5.00	0	

FRANCIS, Nigel Bernard (MCC, Trinidad, West Indies A to Sri Lanka) b Trinidad 6.9.1971 RHB RF

Cmp	Debut	M	I	NO	Runs	HS	Avge	100	50	Balls	Runs	Wkts	Avge	BB	5i	10m	RpO	ct	st
FC		1	1	0	1	1	1.00	0	0	108	56	0					3.11	1	
FC	1992	25	34	3	251	26	8.09	0	0	3067	1863	50	37.26	4-32	0	0	3.64	12	

FREETH, James William Owen (Cambridge University) b Bournemouth 9.4.1974 RHB OB

Cmp	Debut	M	I	NO	Runs	HS	Avge	100	50	Balls	Runs	Wkts	Avge	BB	5i	10m	RpO	ct	st
FC		7	5	2	9	7*	3.00	0	0	894	609	11	55.36	4-101	0	0	4.08	2	
FC	1995	14	11	3	44	18	5.50	0	0	2157	1330	19	70.00	4-101	0	0	3.69	4	

FULTON, James Anthony Gervase (Oxford University) b Plymouth 21.9.1977 LHB RM

Cmp	Debut	M	I	NO	Runs	HS	Avge	100	50	Balls	Runs	Wkts	Avge	BB	5i	10m	RpO	ct	st
FC		10	19	0	451	78	23.73	0	4	30	18	0					3.60	6	

GADSBY, Nigel Timothy (Cambridgeshire) b Wimpole 1.2.1961 RHB LB

Cmp	Debut	M	I	NO	Runs	HS	Avge	100	50	Balls	Runs	Wkts	Avge	BB	5i	10m	RpO	ct	st
NW		1	1	0	1	1	1.00	0	0	42	41	0					5.85	0	
NW	1992	12	12	1	189	63	17.18	0	1	48	48	0					6.00	3	

Cmp	Debut	M	I	NO	Runs	HS	Avge	100	50	Balls	Runs	Wkts	Avge	BB	5i	10m	RpO	ct	st

GARAWAY, Mark (MCC) b Swindon 20.7.1973 RHB WK (Hampshire 1996)

Cmp	Debut	M	I	NO	Runs	HS	Avge	100	50	Balls	Runs	Wkts	Avge	BB	5i	10m	RpO	ct	st
FC		1	1	0	5	5	5.00	0	0									5	
FC	1996	2	2	0	49	44	24.50	0	0									9	1

GAYWOOD, Nicholas Richard (Minor Counties, Devon) b Newton Abbot 30.4.1963 LHB SLA

Cmp	Debut	M	I	NO	Runs	HS	Avge	100	50	Balls	Runs	Wkts	Avge	BB	5i	10m	RpO	ct	st
BH		2	2	0	48	30	24.00	0	0									2	
NW		1	1	0	5	5	5.00	0	0									0	
BH	1993	3	3	0	52	30	17.33	0	0									2	
NW	1985	7	7	0	157	69	22.42	0	1	2	5	0					15.00	1	

GILLESPIE, Peter Gerard (Ireland) b Strabane 11.5.1974 RHB RM

Cmp	Debut	M	I	NO	Runs	HS	Avge	100	50	Balls	Runs	Wkts	Avge	BB	5i	10m	RpO	ct	st
BH		2	1	0	4	4	4.00	0	0	72	64	0					5.33	2	
FC	1996	1	2	0	53	53	26.50	0	1	180	136	5	27.20	3-93	0	0	4.53	0	
BH	1996	3	2	0	4	4	2.00	0	0	102	81	0					4.76	2	
NW	1995	1	1	0	5	5	5.00	0	0	6	10	0					10.00	0	

GOLDSMITH, Steven Clive (Norfolk) b Ashford, Kent 19.12.1964 RHB RM (Kent 1986-87, Derbyshire 1988-92)

Cmp	Debut	M	I	NO	Runs	HS	Avge	100	50	Balls	Runs	Wkts	Avge	BB	5i	10m	RpO	ct	st
NW		1	1	0	22	22	22.00	0	0	36	13	0					2.16	0	
FC	1987	75	118	12	2646	127	24.96	2	12	2898	1571	29	54.17	3-42	0	0	3.25	37	
SL	1986	54	47	11	866	67*	24.05	0	3	764	751	14	53.64	3-48	0	0	5.89	16	
BH	1988	18	13	3	195	45*	19.50	0	0	151	123	6	20.50	3-38	0	0	4.88	9	
NW	1988	12	11	0	194	47	17.63	0	0	366	249	6	41.50	4-64	1	0	4.08	4	

GOULDSTONE, Mark Roger (Lincolnshire) b Bishops Stortford 3.2.1963 RHB RM (Northamptonshire 1986-88)

Cmp	Debut	M	I	NO	Runs	HS	Avge	100	50	Balls	Runs	Wkts	Avge	BB	5i	10m	RpO	ct	st
NW		1	1	0	37	37	37.00	0	0									1	
FC	1986	8	13	1	274	71	22.83	0	2									4	
SL	1986	6	6	0	38	11	6.33	0	0									0	
NW	1991	4	4	1	119	68*	39.66	0	1									3	

GOURLAY, Scott (Scotland) b Kirkcaldy 8.1.1971 RHB RM

Cmp	Debut	M	I	NO	Runs	HS	Avge	100	50	Balls	Runs	Wkts	Avge	BB	5i	10m	RpO	ct	st
BH		3	3	0	20	16	6.66	0	0	93	95	1	95.00	1-37	0	0	6.12	2	
BH	1996	6	5	1	40	18	10.00	0	0	197	168	2	84.00	1-31	0	0	5.11	3	

GOVAN, James Walter (Scotland) b Dunfermline 6.5.1966 RHB OB (Northamptonshire 1989-90)

Cmp	Debut	M	I	NO	Runs	HS	Avge	100	50	Balls	Runs	Wkts	Avge	BB	5i	10m	RpO	ct	st
BH		3	3	2	47	22*	47.00	0	0	102	94	1	94.00	1-17	0	0	5.52	1	
FC	1987	13	15	1	142	50	10.14	0	1	2433	1153	42	27.45	6-70	2	0	2.84	6	
SL	1989	4	3	2	23	9*	23.00	0	0	138	101	4	25.25	3-23	0	0	4.39	1	
BH	1988	22	19	5	293	38*	20.92	0	0	1039	799	13	61.46	4-55	2	0	4.61	4	
NW	1988	4	3	0	5	5	1.66	0	0	239	130	4	32.50	2-29	0	0	3.26	0	

GRAHAM, David Alexander (Herefordshire) b Moreton-in-Marsh 21.5.1971 RHB

Cmp	Debut	M	I	NO	Runs	HS	Avge	100	50	Balls	Runs	Wkts	Avge	BB	5i	10m	RpO	ct	st
NW		1	1	0	2	2	2.00	0	0									0	

HALL, Harry Mark (Berkshire) b Wokingham 19.11.1970 RHB SLA

Cmp	Debut	M	I	NO	Runs	HS	Avge	100	50	Balls	Runs	Wkts	Avge	BB	5i	10m	RpO	ct	st
NW		1	1	0	17	17	17.00	0	0									0	
NW	1996	2	2	0	125	108	62.50	1	0	24	31	0					7.75	2	

HALL, Robert (Herefordshire) b Andover 1.11.1963 RHB WK

Cmp	Debut	M	I	NO	Runs	HS	Avge	100	50	Balls	Runs	Wkts	Avge	BB	5i	10m	RpO	ct	st
NW		1	1	0	29	29	29.00	0	0									0	

HARDING, Richard John (Herefordshire) b Bristol 14.10.1966 RHB OB

Cmp	Debut	M	I	NO	Runs	HS	Avge	100	50	Balls	Runs	Wkts	Avge	BB	5i	10m	RpO	ct	st
NW		1	1	0	17	17	17.00	0	0	72	53	0					4.41	0	
NW	1995	2	2	0	27	17	13.50	0	0	132	109	0					4.95	0	

HARTLEY, David James Benedict (Berkshire) b Ruscombe 28.8.1963 RHB LB

Cmp	Debut	M	I	NO	Runs	HS	Avge	100	50	Balls	Runs	Wkts	Avge	BB	5i	10m	RpO	ct	st
NW		1									54	64	0					7.11	0
NW	1988	7	3	0	8	8	2.66	0	0	368	301	4	75.25	2-35	0	0	4.90	0	

HAYNES, James Edward (Oxford University) b Nottingham 29.9.1972 RHB OB

Cmp	Debut	M	I	NO	Runs	HS	Avge	100	50	Balls	Runs	Wkts	Avge	BB	5i	10m	RpO	ct	st
FC		2	4	0	13	9	3.25	0	0									0	

HEASLEY, Derek (Ireland) b Lisburn 15.1.1972 RHB RM

Cmp	Debut	M	I	NO	Runs	HS	Avge	100	50	Balls	Runs	Wkts	Avge	BB	5i	10m	RpO	ct	st
BH		3	2	0	12	12	6.00	0	0	94	89	3	29.66	2-30	0	0	5.68	1	
NW		1	1	0	18	18	18.00	0	0	58	41	3	13.66	3-41	0	0	4.24	0	
BH	1996	4	3	0	48	36	16.00	0	0	136	121	4	30.25	2-30	0	0	5.33	2	
NW	1996	2	2	0	23	18	11.50	0	0	124	107	7	15.28	4-66	1	0	5.17	0	

HOARE, Philip David Baxter (Bedfordshire) b Bedford 29.11.1962 RHB RM

Cmp	Debut	M	I	NO	Runs	HS	Avge	100	50	Balls	Runs	Wkts	Avge	BB	5i	10m	RpO	ct	st
NW		1	1	0	12	12	12.00	0	0									0	
NW	1985	4	3	0	24	12	8.00	0	0	72	64	2	32.00	2-64	0	0	5.33	1	

HODGSON, James (Berkshire) b Reading 28.3.1972 RHB LB

Cmp	Debut	M	I	NO	Runs	HS	Avge	100	50	Balls	Runs	Wkts	Avge	BB	5i	10m	RpO	ct	st
NW		1	1	1	53	53*		0	1									1	

HORSFALL, Simon Daniel (Staffordshire) b Leeds 4.3.1976 LHB LB

Cmp	Debut	M	I	NO	Runs	HS	Avge	100	50	Balls	Runs	Wkts	Avge	BB	5i	10m	RpO	ct	st
NW		1	1	0	0	0	0.00	0	0	36	15	0					2.50	0	

HOW, Edward Joseph (Cambridge University) b Amersham 16.5.1974 RHB LMF

Cmp	Debut	M	I	NO	Runs	HS	Avge	100	50	Balls	Runs	Wkts	Avge	BB	5i	10m	RpO	ct	st
FC		8	4	1	0	0*	0.00	0	0	1162	685	12	57.08	5-59	1	0	3.53	1	
FC	1995	14	10	5	7	7*	1.40	0	0	1774	1145	13	88.07	5-59	1	0	3.87	2	

HUDSON, Roger Douglas (Oxford University) b Selly Oak 8.6.1967 RHB RM

Cmp	Debut	M	I	NO	Runs	HS	Avge	100	50	Balls	Runs	Wkts	Avge	BB	5i	10m	RpO	ct	st
FC		11	20	2	202	62	11.22	0	1	246	184	0					4.48	2	

HUGHES, Quentin John (Cambridge University) b Durham 17.10.1974 LHB OB

Cmp	Debut	M	I	NO	Runs	HS	Avge	100	50	Balls	Runs	Wkts	Avge	BB	5i	10m	RpO	ct	st
FC		8	12	3	197	47*	21.88	0	0	198	128	3	42.66	2-73	0	0	3.87	1	

Cmp	Debut	M	I	NO	Runs	HS	Avge	100	50	Balls	Runs	Wkts	Avge	BB	5i	10m	RpO	ct	st

HUMPHRIES, Mark Ian (Staffordshire) b Highley 4.10.1965 LHB WK

Cmp	Debut	M	I	NO	Runs	HS	Avge	100	50	Balls	Runs	Wkts	Avge	BB	5i	10m	RpO	ct	st
NW		1	1	0	2	2	2.00	0	0									0	
FC	1994	1	1	0	0	0	0.00	0	0									3	
BH	1992	8	7	1	124	27	20.66	0	0									6	1
NW	1990	8	8	1	54	21	7.71	0	0									4	

HURD, Richard Brian (Buckinghamshire) b Amersham 18.12.1970 RHB

Cmp	Debut	M	I	NO	Runs	HS	Avge	100	50	Balls	Runs	Wkts	Avge	BB	5i	10m	RpO	ct	st
NW		1	1	0	18	18	18.00	0	0									1	

HURLBATT, Graeme Peter (Scotland) b Bulawayo, Rhodesia 9.3.1964 RHB RMF

Cmp	Debut	M	I	NO	Runs	HS	Avge	100	50	Balls	Runs	Wkts	Avge	BB	5i	10m	RpO	ct	st
BH		3	2	1	40	28	40.00	0	0	114	123	2	61.50	1-28	0	0	6.47	1	
FC	1983	4	4	2	14	8	7.00	0	0	457	251	12	20.91	4-36	0	0	3.29	1	
NW	1994	1	1	0	2	2	2.00	0	0	54	30	1	30.00	1-30	0	0	3.33	1	

JAGGARD, Charles Milne (Buckinghamshire) b Chalfont St Peter 22.5.1973 LHB

Cmp	Debut	M	I	NO	Runs	HS	Avge	100	50	Balls	Runs	Wkts	Avge	BB	5i	10m	RpO	ct	st
NW		1	1	0	28	28	28.00	0	0									0	

JANISCH, Adam Nicholas (Cambridge University) b Hammersmith 21.10.1975 RHB RM

Cmp	Debut	M	I	NO	Runs	HS	Avge	100	50	Balls	Runs	Wkts	Avge	BB	5i	10m	RpO	ct	st
FC		4	3	0	18	11	6.00	0	0	479	299	9	33.22	4-71	0	0	3.74	0	
FC	1995	14	14	5	85	25	9.44	0	0	2009	1285	23	55.86	4-71	0	0	3.83	2	

JEH, Michael Pradeep Williams (MCC) b Colombo, Ceylon 21.4.1968 RHB RFM

Cmp	Debut	M	I	NO	Runs	HS	Avge	100	50	Balls	Runs	Wkts	Avge	BB	5i	10m	RpO	ct	st
FC		1	1	0	30	30	30.00	0	0	113	61	5	12.20	3-37	0	0	3.23	0	
FC	1992	20	22	6	137	30	8.56	0	0	3298	2047	46	44.50	5-63	1	0	3.72	5	
BH	1992	2	2	2	28	20*		0	0	96	71	1	71.00	1-37	0	0	4.43	0	

JOHNSON, Andy Neil (Shropshire) b Wolverhampton 30.8.1964 RHB

Cmp	Debut	M	I	NO	Runs	HS	Avge	100	50	Balls	Runs	Wkts	Avge	BB	5i	10m	RpO	ct	st
NW		1	1	0	15	15	15.00	0	0									0	
NW	1989	4	4	0	47	20	11.75	0	0									1	

JONES, John Bryan Richardson (Shropshire) b Shrewsbury 21.5.1961 LHB RM

Cmp	Debut	M	I	NO	Runs	HS	Avge	100	50	Balls	Runs	Wkts	Avge	BB	5i	10m	RpO	ct	st
NW		1	1	0	14	14	14.00	0	0									0	
NW	1983	11	11	0	264	83	24.00	0	2									3	

JONES, Robin Owen (Cambridge University) b Crewe 4.10.1973 RHB OB

Cmp	Debut	M	I	NO	Runs	HS	Avge	100	50	Balls	Runs	Wkts	Avge	BB	5i	10m	RpO	ct	st
FC		8	11	2	325	60	36.11	0	3	892	580	9	64.44	3-116	0	0	3.90	4	
FC	1996	16	24	3	530	61	25.23	0	4	2006	1240	18	68.88	3-116	0	0	3.70	8	

JOYCE, Edmund Christopher (Ireland) b Dublin 22.9.1978 LHB RM

Cmp	Debut	M	I	NO	Runs	HS	Avge	100	50	Balls	Runs	Wkts	Avge	BB	5i	10m	RpO	ct	st
FC		1	2	0	56	43	28.00	0	0	12	20	0					10.00	1	

KELLETT, Simon Andrew (Cambridgeshire) b Mirfield 16.10.1967 RHB RM (Yorkshire 1989-95)

Cmp	Debut	M	I	NO	Runs	HS	Avge	100	50	Balls	Runs	Wkts	Avge	BB	5i	10m	RpO	ct	st
NW		1	1	0	10	10	10.00	0	0									0	
FC	1989	87	149	10	4234	125*	30.46	2	29	30	19	0					3.80	77	
SL	1990	30	30	2	697	118*	24.89	1	3	18	16	0					5.33	6	
BH	1990	14	12	1	239	45	21.72	0	0									0	
NW	1990	11	9	0	259	107	28.77	1	1									6	

KENDRICK, Neil Michael (Berkshire) b Bromley 11.11.1967 RHB SLA (Surrey 1988-94, Glamorgan 1995-96)

Cmp	Debut	M	I	NO	Runs	HS	Avge	100	50	Balls	Runs	Wkts	Avge	BB	5i	10m	RpO	ct	st
NW		1								72	46	1	46.00	1-46	0	0	3.83	0	
FC	1988	81	106	30	1206	59	15.86	0	4	14109	6891	179	38.49	7-115	6	1	2.93	58	
SL	1990	6	4	3	17	13*	17.00	0	0	237	215	4	53.75	2-48	0	0	5.44	2	
BH	1992	2	2	1	25	24	25.00	0	0	132	98	3	32.66	2-47	0	0	4.45	1	
NW	1992	2								144	97	2	48.50	1-46	0	0	4.04	0	

KENNEDY, Stuart Robert (Scotland) b Paisley 9.1.1965 RHB RM

Cmp	Debut	M	I	NO	Runs	HS	Avge	100	50	Balls	Runs	Wkts	Avge	BB	5i	10m	RpO	ct	st
NW		1	1	1	7	78		0	0	60	62	0					6.20	1	

KIPPAX, Simon Alexander Jonathan (Cumberland) b Leeds 8.5.1964 RHB LBG

Cmp	Debut	M	I	NO	Runs	HS	Avge	100	50	Balls	Runs	Wkts	Avge	BB	5i	10m	RpO	ct	st
NW		1	1	0	5	5	5.00	0	0	54	50	2	25.00	2-50	0	0	5.55	1	
NW	1995	2	2	0	15	10	7.50	0	0	96	85	3	28.33	2-50	0	0	5.31	2	

KNOX, Steven Thomas (Cumberland) b Barrow-in-Furness 16.2.1974 RHB RM

Cmp	Debut	M	I	NO	Runs	HS	Avge	100	50	Balls	Runs	Wkts	Avge	BB	5i	10m	RpO	ct	st
NW		1	1	0	0	0	0.00	0	0									1	
NW	1996	2	2	0	8	8	4.00	0	0									2	

LANE, Mark Geoffrey (Berkshire) b Aldershot 26.1.1968 RHB WK

Cmp	Debut	M	I	NO	Runs	HS	Avge	100	50	Balls	Runs	Wkts	Avge	BB	5i	10m	RpO	ct	st
NW		1	1	1	18	18*		0	0									0	1
NW	1996	2	2	2	19	18*		0	0									1	1

LARKINS, Wayne (Minor Counties, Bedfordshire) b Roxton 22.11.1953 RHB RM (Northamptonshire 1972-91, Durham 1992-96)

Cmp	Debut	M	I	NO	Runs	HS	Avge	100	50	Balls	Runs	Wkts	Avge	BB	5i	10m	RpO	ct	st
BH		5	5	0	58	26	11.60	0	0									3	
NW		1	1	0	1	1	1.00	0	0									1	
Test	1979	13	25	1	493	64	20.54	0	3									8	
FC	1972	482	842	54	27142	252	34.44	59	116	3517	1915	42	45.59	5-59	1	0	3.26	306	
Int	1979	25	24	0	591	124	24.62	1	0	15	22	0					8.80	8	
SL	1972	290	278	18	7499	172*	28.84	14	36	2033	1679	57	29.45	5-32	1	1	4.95	91	
BH	1972	87	83	4	2718	132	34.40	7	11	675	444	16	27.75	4-37	1	0	3.94	24	
NW	1976	53	52	3	1774	121*	36.20	2	13	455	274	4	68.50	2-38	0	0	3.61	22	

Cmp	Debut	M	I	NO	Runs	HS	Avge	100	50	Balls	Runs	Wkts	Avge	BB	5i	10m	RpO	ct	st
LAUDAT, Stewart Vernon (Minor Counties) b Oxford 25.2.1971 RHB RM																			
BH		4	4	1	49	43*	16.33	0	0	208	202	2	101.00	1-46	0	0	5.82	0	
BH	1996	7	7	1	95	43*	15.83	0	0	340	308	5	61.60	2-40	0	0	5.43	0	
NW	1992	4	4	1	122	57	40.66	0	1	198	162	1	162.00	1-44	0	0	4.90	1	
LAUGHTON, Nigel Ewan Felix (Oxford University) b Aldershot 12.10.1965 RHB OB																			
FC		1	2	0	6	5	3.00	0	0									1	
LAVENDER, Mark Philip (MCC, Western Australia) b Madras, India 28.8.1967 RHB RM																			
FC		1	2	1	6	6*	6.00	0	0									3	
FC	1990	52	98	8	3079	173*	34.21	6	14	42	15	0					2.14	47	
LEWIS, David Alan (Ireland) b Cork 1.6.1964 RHB RM																			
BH		3	3	0	64	34	21.33	0	0									0	
NW		1	1	0	0	0	0.00	0	0	18	23	0					7.66	1	
FC	1988	8	15	3	640	122*	53.33	2	3	354	276	5	55.20	2-39	0	0	4.67	5	
BH	1994	12	12	1	266	67*	24.18	0	2	144	145	1	145.00	1-22	0	0	6.04	2	
NW	1984	11	11	0	82	28	7.45	0	0	313	252	6	42.00	4-47	1	0	4.83	2	
LIGHTFOOT, Charles Gordon Rufus (Oxford University) b Amersham 25.2.1976 LHB SLA																			
FC		9	16	0	289	61	18.06	0	1	126	126	0					6.00	2	
FC	1996	13	20	1	304	61	16.00	0	1	293	255	2	127.50	2-65	0	0	5.22	2	
LOCKHART, Douglas Ross (Scotland) b Glasgow 19.1.1976 RHB																			
FC		1	2	1	96	77*	96.00	0	1									1	
BH		3	3	0	13	7	4.33	0	0									1	
FC	1996	2	4	1	136	77*	45.33	0	1									2	
LOVEDAY, Gary Edward (Berkshire) b Windsor 15.4.1964 RHB																			
NW		1	1	0	11	11	11.00	0	0									0	
NW	1988	9	9	0	182	38	20.22	0	0									2	
McCALLAN, William Kyle (Ireland) b Carrickfergus 27.8.1975 RHB OB																			
FC		1	2	0	112	65	56.00	0	1	120	59	1	59.00	1-10	0	0	2.95	1	
BH		2	2	0	17	17	8.50	0	0									0	
NW		1	1	0	2	2	2.00	0	0									0	
FC	1996	2	4	0	174	65	43.50	0	2	210	123	1	123.00	1-10	0	0	3.51	1	
NW	1996	2	2	0	19	17	9.50	0	0									0	
McCRUM, Paul (Ireland) b Waringstown 11.8.1962 RHB RFM																			
FC		1	1	1	44	44*		0	0	144	88	1	88.00	1-27	0	0	3.66	0	
BH		3	2	1	6	5	6.00	0	0	132	114	3	38.00	2-58	0	0	5.18	0	
NW		1	1	0	0	0	0.00	0	0	72	26	3	8.66	3-26	0	0	2.16	0	
FC	1990	4	5	2	49	44*	16.33	0	0	588	343	5	68.60	3-56	0	0	3.50	0	
BH	1996	7	5	2	17	9	5.66	0	0	312	248	5	49.60	2-10	0	0	4.76	2	
NW	1984	6	5	1	26	16	6.50	0	0	342	232	11	21.09	3-26	0	0	4.07	2	
MACKLEWORTH, Andrew Nicholas (Shropshire) b Wolverhampton 15.5.1963 RHB WK																			
NW		1	1	0	0	0	0.00	0	0									0	
NW	1989	2	2	0	2	2	1.00	0	0									0	
MARC, Kervin (Berkshire) b Mon Repos, St Lucia 9.1.1975 RHB RF (Middlesex 1994-95)																			
NW		1								54	61	1	61.00	1-61	0	0	6.77	0	
FC	1994	3	3	0	17	9	5.66	0	0	426	275	6	45.83	3-91	0	0	3.87	0	
BH	1996	4	4	0	19	13	4.75	0	0	204	214	4	53.50	2-30	0	0	6.29	1	
MATHER, David Peter (Oxford University) b Bebington 20.11.1975 LHB LM																			
FC		2	3	1	10	5*	5.00	0	0	270	190	2	95.00	2-38	0	0	4.22	0	
FC	1995	18	11	4	31	8*	4.42	0	0	2459	1436	29	49.51	4-65	0	0	3.50	2	
MAWSON, Andrew David (Cumberland) b Workington 27.10.1974 RHB LB																			
NW		1	1	0	77	77	77.00	0	1									1	
NW	1996	2	2	0	118	77	59.00	0	1									1	
MERRIMAN, Richard Peter (Cambridgeshire) b Loughborough 12.10.1958 RHB LB																			
NW		1	1	0	11	11	11.00	0	0									0	
NW	1986	5	5	0	64	25	12.80	0	0	18	32	2	16.00	2-32	0	0	10.66	0	
MOHAMMAD, Imraan (Cambridge University) b Solihull 31.12.1976 RHB OB																			
FC		1	1	0	12	12	12.00	0	0									0	
MOHAMMAD, Salim (Cambridgeshire) b Peterborough 5.7.1968 RHB																			
NW		1	1	0	7	7	7.00	0	0									0	
NW	1994	4	4	0	32	14	8.00	0	0	24	16	0					4.00	0	
MOLINS, Gregory Leo (Ireland) b Dublin 19.3.1975 RHB SLA																			
FC		1	1	0	1	1	1.00	0	0	102	55	2	27.50	2-55	0	0	3.23	0	
BH		3	2	0	10	10	5.00	0	0	114	107	3	35.66	2-44	0	0	5.63	2	
NW		1	1	0	0	0	0.00	0	0	48	39	0					4.87	1	
FC	1996	2	1	0	1	1	1.00	0	0	299	174	6	29.00	3-62	0	0	3.49	0	
MOORE, Declan Martin Patrick (Ireland) b Dublin 5.7.1975 RHB RM																			
BH		1	1	0	0	0	0.00	0	0									0	
FC	1996	1	2	0	68	51	34.00	0	1	36	37	0					6.16	1	

Cmp	Debut	M	I	NO	Runs	HS	Avge	100	50	Balls	Runs	Wkts	Avge	BB	5i	10m	RpO	ct	st
BH	1996	3	3	0	10	10	3.33	0	0	12	11	0					5.50	0	
NW	1996	1	1	0	5	5	5.00	0	0									1	

MORGAN, Peter Gregory (Oxford University) b Johannesburg, South Africa 29.9.1972 RHB

Cmp	Debut	M	I	NO	Runs	HS	Avge	100	50	Balls	Runs	Wkts	Avge	BB	5i	10m	RpO	ct	st
FC		10	18	1	444	63	26.11	0	2									4	

MURPHY, Anthony John (Minor Counties) b Manchester 6.8.1962 RHB RMF (Lancashire 1985-88, Surrey 1989-94)

Cmp	Debut	M	I	NO	Runs	HS	Avge	100	50	Balls	Runs	Wkts	Avge	BB	5i	10m	RpO	ct	st
BH		3	3	2	2	1*	2.00	0	0	180	149	2	74.50	2-39	0	0	4.96	0	
FC	1985	84	86	39	323	38	6.87	0	0	14931	7934	208	38.14	6-97	6	0	3.18	17	
SL	1986	64	15	8	32	9*	4.57	0	0	2851	2241	81	27.66	4-22	1	0	4.71	4	
BH	1989	14	9	5	8	5*	2.00	0	0	828	601	12	50.08	2-23	0	0	4.35	0	
NW	1989	11	3	3	4	3*		0	0	734	439	10	43.90	6-26	1	1	3.58	0	

MYLES, Simon David (Berkshire) b Mansfield 2.6.1966 RHB RM (Sussex 1987, Warwickshire 1988)

Cmp	Debut	M	I	NO	Runs	HS	Avge	100	50	Balls	Runs	Wkts	Avge	BB	5i	10m	RpO	ct	st
NW		1	1	0	25	25	25.00	0	0	72	77	2	38.50	2-77	0	0	6.41	0	
FC	1987	7	11	2	189	59*	21.00	0	1	138	95	0					4.13	4	
SL	1987	9	6	1	57	32	11.40	0	0.	12	20	0					10.00	2	
BH	1987	9	7	1	205	57	34.16	0	2	183	189	3	63.00	2-54	0	0	6.19	3	
NW	1992	6	6	0	246	81	41.00	0	3	154	150	3	50.00	2-77	0	0	5.84	0	

NEWMAN, Paul Geoffrey (Norfolk) b Evington 10.1.1959 RHB RFM (Derbyshire 1980-89)

Cmp	Debut	M	I	NO	Runs	HS	Avge	100	50	Balls	Runs	Wkts	Avge	BB	5i	10m	RpO	ct	st
NW		1	1	0	5	5	5.00	0	0	72	23	4	5.75	4-23	1	0	1.91	1	
FC	1980	135	171	33	2160	115	15.65	1	5	18165	9844	315	31.25	8-29	6	0	3.25	37	
SL	1980	93	58	19	552	52*	14.15	0	1	3926	2914	100	29.14	4-21	3	0	4.45	25	
BH	1981	46	30	11	333	56*	17.52	0	1	2504	1492	46	32.43	4-29	3	0	3.57	3	
NW	1981	23	18	5	219	35	16.84	0	0	1363	766	27	28.37	4-23	1	0	3.37	2	

NICHOLSON, Philip James (Minor Counties) b Jesmond 1.9.1973 RHB WK

Cmp	Debut	M	I	NO	Runs	HS	Avge	100	50	Balls	Runs	Wkts	Avge	BB	5i	10m	RpO	ct	st
BH		5	4	0	15	14	3.75	0	0									5	

OAKES, Simon (Minor Counties, Lincolnshire) b Grantham 9.9.1974 RHB RFM

Cmp	Debut	M	I	NO	Runs	HS	Avge	100	50	Balls	Runs	Wkts	Avge	BB	5i	10m	RpO	ct	st
BH		1	1	0	0	0	0.00	0	0	60	37	3	12.33	3-37	0	0	3.70	1	
NW		1	1	0	4	4	4.00	0	0	30	34	1	34.00	1-34	0	0	6.80	0	
NW	1996	2	2	0	25	21	12.50	0	0	84	53	1	53.00	1-34	0	0	3.78	0	

OWEN, Denzil Malison (Buckinghamshire) b Manchester, Jamaica 16.10.1955 RHB RFM

Cmp	Debut	M	I	NO	Runs	HS	Avge	100	50	Balls	Runs	Wkts	Avge	BB	5i	10m	RpO	ct	st
NW		1									72	81	1	81.00	1-81	0	0	6.75	1	

PASHLEY, David Kent (Staffordshire) b Stoke-on-Trent 24.5.1972 LHB

Cmp	Debut	M	I	NO	Runs	HS	Avge	100	50	Balls	Runs	Wkts	Avge	BB	5i	10m	RpO	ct	st
NW		1	1	0	5	5	5.00	0	0									0	

PATEL, Harshad Vallabhai (Herefordshire) b Nairobi, Kenya 29.1.1964 RHB OB (Worcestershire 1985)

Cmp	Debut	M	I	NO	Runs	HS	Avge	100	50	Balls	Runs	Wkts	Avge	BB	5i	10m	RpO	ct	st
NW		1	1	0	3	3	3.00	0	0									0	
FC	1985	1	1	0	39	39	39.00	0	0									0	
NW	1989	3	3	0	67	63	22.33	0	1									0	

PATTERSON, Andrew David (Ireland) b Belfast 4.9.1975 RHB WK

Cmp	Debut	M	I	NO	Runs	HS	Avge	100	50	Balls	Runs	Wkts	Avge	BB	5i	10m	RpO	ct	st
FC		1	2	0	43	31	21.50	0	0									1	
BH		3	3	1	75	50	37.50	0	1									3	1
NW		1	1	0	0	0	0.00	0	0									1	
FC	1996	2	4	0	88	31	22.00	0	0									1	
NW	1996	2	2	0	2	2	1.00	0	0									2	

PATTERSON, Bruce Mathew Winston (Scotland) b Ayr 29.1.1965 RHB

Cmp	Debut	M	I	NO	Runs	HS	Avge	100	50	Balls	Runs	Wkts	Avge	BB	5i	10m	RpO	ct	st
FC		1	2	0	115	83	57.50	0	1									1	
BH		3	3	0	50	36	16.66	0	0									0	
NW		1	1	0	77	77	77.00	0	1									1	
FC	1988	8	14	0	756	114	54.00	3	4									10	
BH	1989	20	20	0	434	96	21.70	0	3									1	
NW	1988	9	9	0	231	77	25.66	0	2									1	

PEARSON, David John (Cumberland) b Whalley 16.4.1963 LHB WK

Cmp	Debut	M	I	NO	Runs	HS	Avge	100	50	Balls	Runs	Wkts	Avge	BB	5i	10m	RpO	ct	st
NW		1	1	0	3	3	3.00	0	0									1	
NW	1994	4	4	0	43	30	10.75	0	0									2	

PENNETT, David Barrington (Cumberland) b Leeds 26.10.1969 RHB RMF (Nottinghamshire 1992-96)

Cmp	Debut	M	I	NO	Runs	HS	Avge	100	50	Balls	Runs	Wkts	Avge	BB	5i	10m	RpO	ct	st
NW		1	1	0	1	1	1.00	0	0	58	42	3	14.00	3-42	0	0	4.34	0	
FC	1992	31	31	11	196	50	9.80	0	1	4623	2697	60	44.95	5-36	1	0	3.50	7	
SL	1992	37	7	5	20	12*	10.00	0	0	1512	1307	41	31.87	3-27	0	0	5.18	6	
BH	1996	4	2	1	5	4*	5.00	0	0	180	175	2	87.50	2-57	0	0	5.83	3	
NW	1995	2	1	0	1	1	1.00	0	0	130	64	4	16.00	3-42	0	0	2.95	0	

PERCY, Bruce Stephen (Buckinghamshire) b Horsforth 15.6.1966 RHB RM

Cmp	Debut	M	I	NO	Runs	HS	Avge	100	50	Balls	Runs	Wkts	Avge	BB	5i	10m	RpO	ct	st
NW		1	1	0	17	17	17.00	0	0	42	35	1	35.00	1-35	0	0	5.00	0	
NW	1990	5	5	0	33	17	6.60	0	0	126	83	3	27.66	1-2	0	0	3.95	2	

PHILIP, Iain Lindsay (Scotland) b Falkirk 9.6.1958 RHB SLA WK

Cmp	Debut	M	I	NO	Runs	HS	Avge	100	50	Balls	Runs	Wkts	Avge	BB	5i	10m	RpO	ct	st
BH		3	3	0	66	35	22.00	0	0									0	
NW		1	1	0	21	21	21.00	0	0									0	
FC	1986	10	17	1	748	145	46.75	4	2	30	47	0					9.40	10	
BH	1986	36	36	0	1003	95	27.86	0	8									6	
NW	1986	11	11	1	263	102*	26.30	1	1									4	1

Cmp	Debut	M	I	NO	Runs	HS	Avge	100	50	Balls	Runs	Wkts	Avge	BB	5i	10m	RpO	ct	st
PIRIHI, Nicholas Gordon (Oxford University) b Whangarei, New Zealand 19.4.1977 RHB																			
FC		2	3	0	15	15	5.00	0	0									0	
PLUMB, Stephen George (Lincolnshire) b Wimbush 17.1.1954 RHB OB (Essex 1975-77)																			
NW		1	1	0	8	8	8.00	0	0									0	
FC	1975	5	8	1	216	69	30.85	0	1	228	124	3	41.33	2-47	0	0	3.26	2	
SL	1975	2	2	1	4	2*	4.00	0	0									0	
BH	1980	47	45	5	827	63	20.67	0	2	1411	1030	17	60.58	2-3	0	0	4.37	8	
NW	1982	11	11	0	161	57	14.63	0	1	588	355	5	71.00	1-36	0	0	3.62	2	
POTTER, Laurie (Staffordshire) b Bexleyheath 7.11.1962 RHB SLA (Kent 1981-85, Leicestershire 1986-93)																			
NW		1	1	0	19	19	19.00	0	0	24	5	0					1.25	0	
FC	1981	223	354	42	9027	165*	28.93	8	50	14637	6879	177	38.86	5-45	1	0	2.81	190	
SL	1981	135	130	15	2817	105	24.19	1	14	1621	1298	43	30.18	5-28	3	1	4.80	47	
BH	1982	42	38	4	750	112	22.05	1	1	1121	732	19	38.52	4-23	1	0	3.91	17	
NW	1982	21	21	4	511	105*	30.05	1	1	702	446	9	49.55	2-40	0	0	3.81	7	
PUGH, Andrew Joseph (Devon) b Torquay 26.5.1969 RHB																			
NW		1	1	0	29	29	29.00	0	0	36	32	2	16.00	2-32	0	0	5.33	1	
NW	1990	8	8	2	120	33*	20.00	0	0	36	32	2	16.00	2-32	0	0	5.33	6	
RADFORD, Neal Victor (Minor Counties, Herefordshire) b Luanshya, Northern Rhodesia 7.6.1957 RHB RFM (Lancashire 1980-84, Worcestershire 1985-95)																			
BH		4	4	1	37	14	12.33	0	0	234	156	4	39.00	3-52	0	0	4.00	1	
NW		1	1	1	25	25*		0	0	72	64	2	32.00	2-64	0	0	5.33	0	
Test	1986	3	4	1	21	12*	7.00	0	0	678	351	4	87.75	2-131	0	0	3.10	0	
FC	1978	296	298	73	3537	76*	15.72	0	8	50590	26707	994	26.86	9-70	48	7	3.16	130	
Int	1987	6	3	2	0	0*	0.00	0	0	348	230	2	115.00	1-32	0	0	3.96	2	
SL	1980	164	100	42	1141	70	19.67	0	2	6424	4915	215	22.86	5-32	5	2	4.59	39	
BH	1981	57	33	17	424	40	26.50	0	0	3137	1889	78	24.21	4-25	3	0	3.61	14	
NW	1980	36	20	7	176	37	13.53	0	0	2082	1192	51	23.37	7-19	0	1	3.43	14	
RALFS, Dominic Francis (Cambridgeshire) b Hendon 16.12.1971 RHB RM																			
NW		1	1	1	14	14*		0	0	72	69	2	34.50	2-69	0	0	5.75	0	
NW	1994	4	4	2	27	14*	13.50	0	0	246	203	3	67.66	2-69	0	0	4.95	0	
RASHID, Umar Bin Abdul (British Universities) b Southampton 6.2.1976 LHB SLA (Middlesex 1995-96)																			
BH		5	5	0	150	82	30.00	0	1	258	243	4	60.75	1-33	0	0	5.65	2	
FC	1996	1	2	0	15	9	7.50	0	0	36	17	0					2.83	0	
SL	1995	7	4	0	14	8	3.50	0	0	240	235	7	33.57	2-34	0	0	5.87	0	
BH	1995	12	11	2	216	82	24.00	0	1	663	543	9	60.33	2-57	0	0	4.91	3	
RATLEDGE, John (Cambridge University) b Preston 8.8.1974 RHB RM																			
FC		8	12	1	268	100*	24.36	1	0									0	
FC	1994	27	48	1	942	100*	20.04	1	2	124	108	1	108.00	1-16	0	0	5.22	5	
RAWDEN, Paul Anthony (Lincolnshire) b Stamford 15.7.1973 RHB RM																			
NW		1	1	0	0	0	0.00	0	0									0	
NW	1994	3	3	0	21	21	7.00	0	0	24	25	0					6.25	1	
RICHARDSON, Alan (Staffordshire) b Newcastle-under-Lyme 6.5.1975 RHB RM (Derbyshire 1995)																			
NW		1	1	0	0	0	0.00	0	0	54	26	0					2.88	0	
FC	1995	1	1	0	4	4	4.00	0	0	114	60	3	20.00	3-27	0	0	3.15	0	
SL	1995	1								36	41	0					6.83	0	
NW	1996	2	2	0	0	0	0.00	0	0	96	68	0					4.25	0	
ROBERTS, Andrew Richard (Bedfordshire) b Kettering 16.4.1971 RHB LB (Northamptonshire 1989-96)																			
NW		1	1	0	7	7	7.00	0	0	54	40	0					4.44	1	
FC	1989	61	83	18	1173	62	18.04	0	2	9203	4829	107	45.13	6-72	1	0	3.14	23	
SL	1991	11	5	0	42	20	8.40	0	0	263	251	10	25.10	3-26	0	0	5.72	4	
NW	1994	2	1	0	7	7	7.00	0	0	126	63	1	63.00	1-23	0	0	3.00	2	
ROEBUCK, Peter Michael (Devon) b Oxford 6.3.1956 RHB OB (Somerset 1974-91)																			
NW		1	1	0	6	6	6.00	0	0	72	27	2	13.50	2-27	0	0	2.25	0	
FC	1974	335	552	81	17558	221*	37.27	33	93	7606	3540	72	49.16	6-50	1	0	2.79	162	
SL	1975	180	166	23	4191	105	29.30	1	23	707	618	28	22.07	4-11	1	0	5.24	33	
BH	1975	68	64	6	1671	120	28.81	3	9	302	217	8	27.12	2-13	0	0	4.31	28	
NW	1974	43	43	4	1234	102	31.64	1	5	530	334	9	37.11	3-37	0	0	3.78	11	
ROGERS, Carl John (Norfolk) b Norwich 20.10.1970 RHB																			
NW		1	1	0	13	13	13.00	0	0									2	
NW	1991	7	7	0	85	51	12.14	0	1									4	
RUTHERFORD, Alan Thomas (Ireland) b Strabane 2.6.1967 RHB WK																			
FC		1	1	0	19	19	19.00	0	0									1	
NW		1	1	1	4	4*		0	0									2	
FC	1996	2	1	0	19	19	19.00	0	0									4	
BH	1996	4	4	2	60	26	30.00	0	0									3	
NW	1996	2	2	1	6	4*	6.00	0	0									4	

Cmp	Debut	M	I	NO	Runs	HS	Avge	100	50	Balls	Runs	Wkts	Avge	BB	5i	10m	RpO	ct	st

SALMOND, George (Scotland) b Dundee 1.12.1969 RHB

Cmp	Debut	M	I	NO	Runs	HS	Avge	100	50	Balls	Runs	Wkts	Avge	BB	5i	10m	RpO	ct	st
FC		1	2	0	135	89	67.50	0	1									2	
BH		1	1	0	5	5	5.00	0	0									1	
NW		1	1	0	1	1	1.00	0	0									0	
FC	1991	6	10	1	668	181	74.22	2	3									4	
BH	1991	13	13	1	106	26	8.83	0	0									2	
NW	1991	7	6	0	83	52	13.83	0	1									3	

SANDFORD, Gary Don (Bedfordshire) b Stevenage 7.7.1964 RHB WK

NW		1	1	0	16	16	16.00	0	0									0	
NW	1991	3	3	0	17	16	5.66	0	0									1	1

SAWYER, Paul Richard (Buckinghamshire) b High Wycombe 26.12.1979 LHB LB

NW		1	1	1	32	32*		0	0									0	

SCHAFFTER, Prakash Anand (Cambridge University) b Colombo, Ceylon 19.6.1967 RHB RFM

FC		1	1	0	0	0	0.00	0	0	168	77	1	77.00	1-58	0	0	2.75	0	

SCOTHERN, Michael Graeme (Cumberland) b Skipton 19.3.1961 RHB RMF (Worcestershire 1985)

NW		1	1	1	23	23*		0	0	72	50	1	50.00	1-50	0	0	4.16	0	
FC	1985	1								96	42	1	42.00	1-42	0	0	2.62	0	
BH	1995	1	1	0	1	1	1.00	0	0	36	51	0					8.50	1	
NW	1988	6	6	3	54	23*	18.00	0	0	422	352	7	50.28	3-29	0	0	5.00	2	

SCRINI, Alexander Philip (Oxford University) b Sheffield 18.11.1976 RHB WK

FC		11	18	6	253	58*	21.08	0	1									13	

SCRIVEN, Timothy John Adam (Buckinghamshire) b High Wycombe 15.12.1965 RHB SLA (Somerset 1988-89)

NW		1	1	1	3	3*		0	0	72	58	0					4.83	1	
FC	1988	4	3	0	19	8	6.33	0	0	901	446	10	44.60	3-43	0	0	2.97	0	
NW	1988	6	6	1	21	10	4.20	0	0	402	292	5	58.40	2-54	0	0	4.35	2	

SEYMOUR, Stewart Anthony (Berkshire) b Ascot 3.3.1974 RHB

NW		1	1	0	17	17	17.00	0	0									1	

SHARP, Kevin (Shropshire) b Leeds 6.4.1959 LHB OB (Yorkshire 1976-91)

NW		1	1	0	3	3	3.00	0	0									0	
FC	1976	218	361	38	9962	181	30.84	14	47	1262	867	12	73.91	2-13	0	0	4.21	107	
SL	1976	141	135	13	3392	114	27.80	2	20	1	1	0					6.00	45	
BH	1978	51	46	3	1243	105*	28.90	1	7									16	
NW	1978	19	15	2	245	50	18.84	0	1	120	97	4	24.25	4-40	1	0	4.70	7	

SHARP, Marcus Anthony (Minor Counties, Cumberland) b Oxford 1.6.1970 LHB RM (Lancashire 1991)

BH		5	4	1	36	16*	12.00	0	0	282	171	4	42.75	2-17	0	0	3.63	2	
NW		1	1	1	7	7*		0	0	54	27	2	13.50	2-27	0	0	3.00	0	
FC	1991	1								90	21	1	21.00	1-21	0	0	1.40	0	
BH	1995	14	12	6	52	16*	8.66	0	0	738	442	9	49.11	2-17	0	0	3.59	4	
NW	1994	4	3	3	11	7*		0	0	240	114	4	28.50	2-27	0	0	2.85	0	

SHAW, Paul Frank (Staffordshire) b Burton-on-Trent 28.7.1967 LHB RM

NW		1	1	0	18	18	18.00	0	0									0	
NW	1993	5	5	0	105	29	21.00	0	0									1	

SHER, Zaheer Abbas (Bedfordshire) b Slough 13.1.1975 RHB RM

NW		1	1	0	5	5	5.00	0	0	18	42	1	42.00	1-42	0	0	14.00	0	
BH	1996	1	1	0	14	14	14.00	0	0	29	20	3	6.66	3-20	0	0	4.13	0	

SHERIDAN, Keith Lamont Paton (Scotland) b Glasgow 26.3.1971 RHB SLA

FC		1	1	0	0	0	0.00	0	0	228	59	4	14.75	4-43	0	0	1.55	2	
NW		1	1	0	0	0	0.00	0	0	72	69	0					5.75	0	
FC	1992	3	1	0	0	0	0.00	0	0	732	259	7	37.00	4-43	0	0	2.12	2	
BH	1992	1	1	1	3	3*		0	0	60	40	0					4.00	2	
NW	1994	3	3	2	2	1*	2.00	0	0	186	143	2	71.50	1-35	0	0	4.61	1	

SHIMMONS, Adam Mark (Shropshire) b Hillingdon 16.10.1972 LHB RFM

NW		1	1	0	14	14	14.00	0	0	24	27	0					6.75	0	

SKYRME, Richard Philip (Herefordshire) b Hereford 23.12.1960 RHB OB

NW		1	1	0	7	7	7.00	0	0	72	78	2	39.00	2-78	0	0	6.50	2	
NW	1995	2	2	0	17	10	8.50	0	0	72	78	2	39.00	2-78	0	0	6.50	3	

SMITH, Michael Jonathon (Scotland) b Edinburgh 30.3.1966 RHB RM

BH		3	3	0	83	55	27.66	0	1	6	4	0					4.00	1	
NW		1	1	0	73	73	73.00	0	1									0	
FC	1987	3	5	1	145	79	36.25	0	1	138	51	2	25.50	2-30	0	0	2.21	3	
BH	1988	18	18	3	283	55	18.86	0	1	212	187	2	93.50	2-74	0	0	5.29	1	
NW	1988	4	4	0	124	73	31.00	0	1	30	17	1	17.00	1-13	0	0	3.40	1	

SMITH, Timothy Stewart (Cambridgeshire) b Henham 29.12.1953 RHB SLA

NW		1	1	0	9	9	9.00	0	0	72	44	0					3.66	0	
FC	1985	1	1	0	9	9	9.00	0	0	366	137	7	19.57	5-79	1	0	2.24	1	
BH	1984	4	3	2	7	4*	7.00	0	0	150	127	0					5.08	1	
NW	1983	10	10	2	116	36	14.50	0	0	498	306	3	102.00	2-31	0	0	3.68	6	

Cmp	Debut	M	I	NO	Runs	HS	Avge	100	50	Balls	Runs	Wkts	Avge	BB	5i	10m	RpO	ct	st

STANGER, Ian Michael (Scotland) b Glasgow 5.10.1971 RHB RM (Leicestershire 1994)

Cmp	Debut	M	I	NO	Runs	HS	Avge	100	50	Balls	Runs	Wkts	Avge	BB	5i	10m	RpO	ct	st
FC		1	1	0	8	8	8.00	0	0	78	61	1	61.00	1-38	0	0	5.46	0	
NW		1	1	0	21	21	21.00	0	0	60	69	0					6.90	0	
SL	1994	9	6	3	10	6	3.33	0	0	324	294	8	36.75	3-34	0	0	5.44	4	
BH	1993	7	6	1	65	27	13.00	0	0	295	272	1	272.00	1-55	0	0	5.53	5	
NW	1992	4	2	1	33	21	33.00	0	0	216	181	1	181.00	1-35	0	0	5.02	0	

STANLEY, Neil Alfred (Bedfordshire) b Bedford 16.5.1968 RHB RM (Northamptonshire 1988-93)

Cmp	Debut	M	I	NO	Runs	HS	Avge	100	50	Balls	Runs	Wkts	Avge	BB	5i	10m	RpO	ct	st
NW		1	1	0	29	29	29.00	0	0										1
FC	1988	21	35	4	1019	132	32.87	1	7	60	19	0					1.90	9	
SL	1988	12	11	3	90	18	11.25	0	0									2	
BH	1988	3	2	0	13	8	6.50	0	0	6	3	1	3.00	1-3	0	0	3.00	1	
NW	1994	2	2	0	34	29	17.00	0	0									1	

STANWAY, Simon Francis (Buckinghamshire) b Aylesbury 22.4.1966 RHB RFM

Cmp	Debut	M	I	NO	Runs	HS	Avge	100	50	Balls	Runs	Wkts	Avge	BB	5i	10m	RpO	ct	st
NW		1									36	27	0					4.50	1

STEINDL, Peter David (Scotland) b Bundaberg, Australia 14.6.1970 RHB RM

Cmp	Debut	M	I	NO	Runs	HS	Avge	100	50	Balls	Runs	Wkts	Avge	BB	5i	10m	RpO	ct	st
BH		2	1	1	9	9*		0	0	72	82	1	82.00	1-61	0	0	6.83	0	
NW		1	1	0	7	7	7.00	0	0	72	67	1	67.00	1-67	0	0	5.58	0	
BH	1995	5	4	3	27	14*	27.00	0	0	186	174	4	43.50	3-43	0	0	5.61	0	

STOKES, Ian William Edward (Staffordshire) b Solihull 22.2.1964 LHB

Cmp	Debut	M	I	NO	Runs	HS	Avge	100	50	Balls	Runs	Wkts	Avge	BB	5i	10m	RpO	ct	st
NW		1	1	0	18	18	18.00	0	0									0	

SYLVESTER, Jamie Peter John (Minor Counties, Berkshire) b Cardiff 31.7.1971 RHB OB

Cmp	Debut	M	I	NO	Runs	HS	Avge	100	50	Balls	Runs	Wkts	Avge	BB	5i	10m	RpO	ct	st
BH		4	4	0	22	9	5.50	0	0									0	
NW		1	1	0	22	22	22.00	0	0	54	59	2	29.50	2-59	0	0	6.55	0	
BH	1996	6	6	0	63	30	10.50	0	0									0	

THOMAS, David Robert (Norfolk) b Norwich 26.1.1963 LHB RFM

Cmp	Debut	M	I	NO	Runs	HS	Avge	100	50	Balls	Runs	Wkts	Avge	BB	5i	10m	RpO	ct	st
NW		1	1	0	4	4	4.00	0	0	60	38	2	19.00	2-38	0	0	3.80	0	
FC	1990	1	1	0	27	27	27.00	0	0	90	65	0					4.33	0	
BH	1990	8	7	2	90	49*	18.00	0	0	354	286	8	35.75	3-34	0	0	4.84	2	
NW	1984	10	10	1	127	41	14.11	0	0	426	344	13	26.46	3-34	0	0	4.84	1	

THOMAS, Mark Wynne (Norfolk) b Norwich 30.1.1977 RHB RFM

Cmp	Debut	M	I	NO	Runs	HS	Avge	100	50	Balls	Runs	Wkts	Avge	BB	5i	10m	RpO	ct	st
NW		1	1	0	6	6	6.00	0	0	72	50	0					4.16	0	
NW	1996	2	2	0	6	6	3.00	0	0	108	89	0					4.94	0	

THOMSON, Kevin (Scotland) b Dundee 24.12.1971 RHB RMF

Cmp	Debut	M	I	NO	Runs	HS	Avge	100	50	Balls	Runs	Wkts	Avge	BB	5i	10m	RpO	ct	st
FC		1	1	1	9	9*		0	0	204	93	2	46.50	2-41	0	0	2.73	0	
BH		2	1	1	1	1*		0	0	96	73	4	18.25	3-45	0	0	4.56	1	
NW		1	1	1	1	1*		0	0	72	53	0					4.41	0	
FC	1992	2	1	1	9	9*		0	0	360	175	4	43.75	2-41	0	0	2.91	0	
BH	1995	7	5	2	35	17	11.66	0	0	341	251	9	27.88	3-45	0	0	4.41	1	
NW	1996	2	1	1	1	1*		0	0	138	108	1	108.00	1-55	0	0	4.69	0	

TOWNSEND, Gareth Terence John (Devon) b Tiverton 28.6.1968 RHB (Somerset 1990-92)

Cmp	Debut	M	I	NO	Runs	HS	Avge	100	50	Balls	Runs	Wkts	Avge	BB	5i	10m	RpO	ct	st
NW		1	1	0	37	37	37.00	0	0									0	
FC	1990	12	22	2	414	53	20.70	0	1									10	
SL	1991	3	3	0	87	33	29.00	0	0									1	
BH	1992	3	3	0	13	10	4.33	0	0									0	
NW	1994	4	4	0	76	37	19.00	0	0									2	

TREND, Peter Charles (Lincolnshire) b Wolverhampton 26.8.1974 RHB WK

Cmp	Debut	M	I	NO	Runs	HS	Avge	100	50	Balls	Runs	Wkts	Avge	BB	5i	10m	RpO	ct	st
NW		1	1	0	0	0	0.00	0	0									1	

TROTT, Andrew John (Bedfordshire) b Wellingborough 26.9.1968 RHB LB

Cmp	Debut	M	I	NO	Runs	HS	Avge	100	50	Balls	Runs	Wkts	Avge	BB	5i	10m	RpO	ct	st
NW		1	1	0	14	14	14.00	0	0	6	11	0					11.00	0	

WEEKES, Lesroy Charlesworth (Lincolnshire, Leeward Islands) b Montserrat 19.7.1971 RHB RFM (Yorkshire 1994)

Cmp	Debut	M	I	NO	Runs	HS	Avge	100	50	Balls	Runs	Wkts	Avge	BB	5i	10m	RpO	ct	st
NW		1	1	0	8	8	8.00	0	0	36	39	0					6.50	0	
FC	1993	22	32	5	453	46	16.77	0	0	3052	1708	60	28.46	5-83	1	0	3.35	17	

WHITE, Matthew Richard (Bedfordshire) b Bedford 26.9.1968 RHB RF

Cmp	Debut	M	I	NO	Runs	HS	Avge	100	50	Balls	Runs	Wkts	Avge	BB	5i	10m	RpO	ct	st
NW		1	1	1	6	6*		0	0	56	46	0					4.92	0	
NW	1994	2	2	1	8	6*	8.00	0	0	128	97	1	97.00	1-51	0	0	4.54	0	

WHYBORN, Christopher Mark (Cambridgeshire) b Winchester 19.8.1966 RHB RFM

Cmp	Debut	M	I	NO	Runs	HS	Avge	100	50	Balls	Runs	Wkts	Avge	BB	5i	10m	RpO	ct	st
NW		1	1	0	7	7	7.00	0	0	66	62	1	62.00	1-62	0	0	5.63	1	

WILEMAN, Jonathan Ritchie (Lincolnshire) b Sheffield 19.8.1970 RHB RM (Nottinghamshire 1992-96)

Cmp	Debut	M	I	NO	Runs	HS	Avge	100	50	Balls	Runs	Wkts	Avge	BB	5i	10m	RpO	ct	st
NW		1	1	1	1	1		0	0									0	
FC	1992	12	21	6	447	109	29.80	1	0	570	217	4	54.25	2-33	0	0	2.28	9	
SL	1995	16	13	8	226	51*	45.20	0	1	488	476	17	28.00	4-21	2	0	5.85	9	
BH	1995	2	.1	0	0	0	0.00	0	0	18	15	0					5.00	1	
NW	1994	4	3	0	27	14	9.00	0	0	48	55	2	27.50	1-9	0	0	6.87	2	

WILLIAMSON, John Greig (Scotland) b Glasgow 20.12.1968 RHB RM

Cmp	Debut	M	I	NO	Runs	HS	Avge	100	50	Balls	Runs	Wkts	Avge	BB	5i	10m	RpO	ct	st
FC		1	1	0	5	5	5.00	0	0	126	84	2	42.00	1-40	0	0	4.00	0	
BH		3	3	0	60	26	20.00	0	0	124	126	2	63.00	2-61	0	0	6.09	1	
NW		1	1	0	7	7	7.00	0	0	24	28	1	28.00	1-28	0	0	7.00	0	

Cmp	Debut	M	I	NO	Runs	HS	Avge	100	50	Balls	Runs	Wkts	Avge	BB	5i	10m	RpO	ct	st
FC	1994	3	3	0	109	55	36.33	0	1	488	284	4	71.00	2-51	0	0	3.49	0	
BH	1994	11	11	1	180	51*	18.00	0	1	382	353	6	58.83	2-54	0	0	5.54	2	
NW	1989	5	4	0	10	7	2.50	0	0	198	145	2	72.50	1-28	0	0	4.39	0	

WOMBLE, David Robert (Staffordshire) b Stoke-on-Trent 23.2.1977 RHB RM (Derbyshire 1996)

Cmp	Debut	M	I	NO	Runs	HS	Avge	100	50	Balls	Runs	Wkts	Avge	BB	5i	10m	RpO	ct	st
NW		1	1	0	6	6	6.00	0	0	24	17	0					4.25	0	
SL	1996	1								18	29	0					9.66	0	

WRIGHT, Craig McIntyre (Scotland) b Paisley 28.4.1974 RHB RM

Cmp	Debut	M	I	NO	Runs	HS	Avge	100	50	Balls	Runs	Wkts	Avge	BB	5i	10m	RpO	ct	st
FC		1	1	0	0	0	0.00	0	0	188	89	3	29.66	3-66	0	0	2.84	0	

WRIGHT, Gavin James (Oxford University) b Holmfirth 15.12.1973 RHB RM

Cmp	Debut	M	I	NO	Runs	HS	Avge	100	50	Balls	Runs	Wkts	Avge	BB	5i	10m	RpO	ct	st
FC		3	2	1	0	0*	0.00	0	0	276	246	1	246.00	1-60	0	0	5.34	0	
FC	1996	4	2	1	0	0*	0.00	0	0	330	279	1	279.00	1-60	0	0	5.07	0	

YOUNG, Barry James (Bedfordshire) b Luton 12.10.1975 RHB

Cmp	Debut	M	I	NO	Runs	HS	Avge	100	50	Balls	Runs	Wkts	Avge	BB	5i	10m	RpO	ct	st
NW		1	1	1	30	30*		0	0									0	

HOLLAND IN ENGLAND 1997

DE LEEDE, Timotheus Bernardus Maria b Leidschendam 25.1.1968 RHB RM

Cmp	Debut	M	I	NO	Runs	HS	Avge	100	50	Balls	Runs	Wkts	Avge	BB	5i	10m	RpO	ct	st
NW		1	1	0	10	10	10.00	0	0	48	49	1	49.00	1-49	0	0	6.12	2	
Int	1995	5	5	0	90	41	18.00	0	0	162	179	0					6.62	0	
NW	1995	3	3	0	37	19	12.33	0	0	84	82	1	82.00	1-49	0	0	5.85	3	

DULFER, Eric H. b Schiedam 6.4.1961 RHB OB

Cmp	Debut	M	I	NO	Runs	HS	Avge	100	50	Balls	Runs	Wkts	Avge	BB	5i	10m	RpO	ct	st
NW		1	1	0	3	3	3.00	0	0	60	62	1	62.00	1-62	0	0	6.20	1	

GOODWIN, Murray William (Western Australia) b Salisbury, Rhodesia 11.12.1972 RHB LB

Cmp	Debut	M	I	NO	Runs	HS	Avge	100	50	Balls	Runs	Wkts	Avge	BB	5i	10m	RpO	ct	st
NW		1	1	0	4	4	4.00	0	0	30	28	1	28.00	1-28	0	0	5.60	0	
FC	1994	14	25	4	925	127	44.04	1	6									17	

KHAN, Asim b Lahore, Pakistan 14.2.1962 RHB RM

Cmp	Debut	M	I	NO	Runs	HS	Avge	100	50	Balls	Runs	Wkts	Avge	BB	5i	10m	RpO	ct	st
NW		1	1	0	5	5	5.00	0	0	72	59	0					4.91	0	

LEFEBVRE, Roland Philippe b Rotterdam 7.2.1963 RHB RMF (Somerset 1990-92, Glamorgan 1993-95)

Cmp	Debut	M	I	NO	Runs	HS	Avge	100	50	Balls	Runs	Wkts	Avge	BB	5i	10m	RpO	ct	st
NW		1	1	0	4	4	4.00	0	0	72	42	1	42.00	1-42	0	0	3.50	1	
FC	1990	77	89	16	1494	100	20.46	1	3	13485	5399	149	36.23	6-45	3	0	2.40	36	
Int	1995	4	4	1	78	45	26.00	0	0	210	132	3	44.00	1-20	0	0	3.77	1	
SL	1990	76	46	15	439	36*	14.16	0	0	3348	2256	97	23.25	4-23	2	0	4.04	38	
BH	1990	18	13	5	184	37	23.00	0	0	1051	654	18	36.33	3-42	0	0	3.73	5	
NW	1990	14	7	4	69	21*	23.00	0	0	969	395	27	14.62	7-15	0	1	2.44	9	

SCHEWE, Marcelis Michael Catharinus b Waterigen 10.5.1969 RHB WK

Cmp	Debut	M	I	NO	Runs	HS	Avge	100	50	Balls	Runs	Wkts	Avge	BB	5i	10m	RpO	ct	st
NW		1	1	0	10	10	10.00	·0	0									0	
Int	1995	5	4	1	49	20	16.33	0	0									2	1
NW	1996	2	2	0	31	21	15.50	0	0									0	

VAN DIJK, Steven b Rotterdam 23.8.1969 RHB RMF

Cmp	Debut	M	I	NO	Runs	HS	Avge	100	50	Balls	Runs	Wkts	Avge	BB	5i	10m	RpO	ct	st
NW		1	1	1	8	8*		0	0	72	68	1	68.00	1-68	0	0	5.66	0	
NW	1996	2	2	1	13	8*	13.00	0	0	120	125	5	25.00	4-57	1	0	6.25	0	

VAN NOORTWIJK, Klaas-Jan Jeroen b Rotterdam 10.7.1970 RHB

Cmp	Debut	M	I	NO	Runs	HS	Avge	100	50	Balls	Runs	Wkts	Avge	BB	5i	10m	RpO	ct	st
NW		1	1	0	25	25	25.00	0	0									0	
Int	1995	5	5	1	168	64	42.00	0	1									0	
NW	1996	2	2	0	37	25	18.50	0	0									2	

VAN OOSTEROM, Robert Frank b The Hague 16.10.1968 RHB

Cmp	Debut	M	I	NO	Runs	HS	Avge	100	50	Balls	Runs	Wkts	Avge	BB	5i	10m	RpO	ct	st
NW		1	1	0	2	2	2.00	0	0									0	
Int	1995	2	2	2	7	5*		0	0									1	

ZUIDERENT, Bastiaan b Rotterdam 3.3.1977 RHB RM

Cmp	Debut	M	I	NO	Runs	HS	Avge	100	50	Balls	Runs	Wkts	Avge	BB	5i	10m	RpO	ct	st
NW		1	1	0	99	99	99.00	0	1									0	
Int	1995	5	5	1	91	54	22.75	0	1									4	
NW	1996	2	2	0	119	99	59.50	0	1	12	15	0					7.50	1	

ZULFIQAR AHMED b Sialkot, Pakistan 23.2.1966 RHB OB

Cmp	Debut	M	I	NO	Runs	HS	Avge	100	50	Balls	Runs	Wkts	Avge	BB	5i	10m	RpO	ct	st
NW		1	1	0	21	21	21.00	0	0	6	20	0					20.00	0	
NW	1996	2	2	0	48	27	24.00	0	0	48	73	2	36.50	2-53	0	0	9.12	1	

The following contemporary cricketers did not play in domestic English cricket in 1997, but have previously appeared in domestic English limited overs cricket:

AAQIB JAVED (see Pakistan) (Hampshire)

Cmp	Debut	M	I	NO	Runs	HS	Avge	100	50	Balls	Runs	Wkts	Avge	BB	5i	10m	RpO	ct	st
SL	1991	12	2	2	5	4*		0	0	553	423	10	42.30	3-50	0	0	4.58	1	
BH	1991	5	2	1	3	3	3.00	0	0	318	208	9	23.11	3-43	0	0	3.92	0	
NW	1991	5								317	213	8	26.62	4-51	1	0	4.03	2	

ADAMS, J.C. (see West Indies) (Nottinghamshire)

SL	1994	15	15	4	674	93*	61.27	0	7	296	199	6	33.16	2-26	0	0	4.03	5	
BH	1994	3	3	0	133	86	44.33	0	1	18	21	0					7.00	2	
NW	1994	2	2	0	12	11	6.00	0	0									0	

AMBROSE, C.E.L. (see West Indies) (Northamptonshire)

SL	1989	59	28	11	227	37	13.35	0	0	2593	1558	58	26.86	4-20	2	0	3.60	14	
BH	1989	15	8	4	81	17*	20.25	0	0	909	478	25	19.12	4-31	1	0	3.15	9	
NW	1989	21	8	1	96	48	13.71	0	0	1397	513	32	16.03	4-7	1	0	2.20	7	

AZHARUDDIN, M. (see India) (Derbyshire)

SL	1991	25	21	6	807	111*	53.80	1	6	5	5	0					6.00	7	
BH	1991	6	6	1	134	44*	26.80	0	0	96	58	1	58.00	1-17	0	0	3.62	4	
NW	1994	3	3	1	88	74*	44.00	0	1									0	

BAPTISTE, E.A.E. (see South Africa) (Kent, Northamptonshire)

SL	1981	73	62	10	885	60	17.01	0	5	2932	2204	79	27.89	4-22	5	0	4.51	22	
BH	1983	23	20	6	228	43*	16.28	0	0	1237	762	23	33.13	5-30	0	1	3.69	8	
NW	1981	17	14	2	131	34	10.91	0	0	1086	630	23	27.39	5-20	1	1	3.48	7	

BENJAMIN, K.C.G. (see West Indies) (Worcestershire)

SL	1993	7	5	1	35	20	8.75	0	0	349	189	11	17.18	3-25	0	0	3.24	0	
BH	1993	2	1	0	2	2	2.00	0	0	132	65	4	16.25	2-28	0	0	2.95	0	
NW	1993	2								96	49	2	24.50	2-38	0	0	3.06	1	

BEVAN, M.G. (see Australia) (Yorkshire)

SL	1995	29	27	5	1108	103*	50.36	2	7	445	399	23	17.34	5-29	0	1	5.37	9	
BH	1995	10	9	4	544	95*	108.80	0	7	31	25	1	25.00	1-25	0	0	4.83	1	
NW	1995	8	8	2	388	91*	64.66	0	4	114	89	3	29.66	2-47	0	0	4.68	0	

BISHOP, I.R. (see West Indies) (Derbyshire)

SL	1989	15	9	4	119	36*	23.80	0	0	662	480	20	24.00	3-18	0	0	4.35	0	
BH	1992	6	5	1	80	42	20.00	0	0	384	184	10	18.40	4-30	1	0	2.87	0	
NW	1992	2	2	0	6	6	3.00	0	0	132	61	0					2.77	0	

BRYSON, R.E. (see South Africa) (Surrey)

| SL | 1992 | 7 | 3 | 1 | 42 | 20 | 21.00 | 0 | 0 | 271 | 267 | 8 | 33.37 | 2-30 | 0 | 0 | 5.91 | 0 | |
| BH | 1992 | 5 | 2 | 1 | 18 | 18* | 18.00 | 0 | 0 | 312 | 232 | 10 | 23.20 | 4-31 | 2 | 0 | 4.46 | 0 | |

CAIRNS, C.L. (see New Zealand) (Nottinghamshire)

SL	1988	60	50	10	1655	126*	41.37	2	9	2363	1858	86	21.60	6-52	4	2	4.71	17	
BH	1992	12	8	0	112	46	14.00	0	0	617	454	16	28.37	4-47	1	0	4.41	3	
NW	1992	7	7	1	306	77	51.00	0	3	482	279	14	19.92	4-18	1	0	3.47	2	

CAMPBELL, S.L. (see West Indies) (Durham)

SL	1996	15	15	0	455	77	30.33	0	3	33	34	0					6.18	4	
BH	1996	2	2	0	27	27	13.50	0	0									1	
NW	1996	2	2	0	66	39	33.00	0	0	6	17	0					17.00	1	

CUFFY, C.E. (see West Indies) (Surrey)

SL	1994	1								36	43	0					7.16	0	
BH	1994	3								162	154	0					5.70	1	
NW	1994	4	1	1	2	2*		0	0	252	133	6	22.16	4-43	1	0	3.16	1	

CULLINAN, D.J. (see South Africa) (Derbyshire)

SL	1995	12	11	3	365	76*	45.62	0	3									4	
BH	1995	3	3	2	106	101*	106.00	1	0									1	
NW	1995	3	3	2	148	119*	148.00	1	0									2	

DE SILVA, P.A. (see Sri Lanka) (Kent)

SL	1995	15	15	2	473	124	36.38	2	0	342	297	8	37.12	4-28	1	0	5.21	3	
BH	1995	7	6	1	203	112	40.60	1	0	228	128	4	32.00	2-12	0	0	3.36	3	
NW	1995	2	2	0	46	24	23.00	0	0	144	90	3	30.00	2-45	0	0	3.75	1	

DE VILLIERS, P.S. (see South Africa) (Kent)

SL	1990	4	4	0	21	10	5.25	0	0	168	121	3	40.33	1-17	0	0	4.32	0	
BH	1990	1	1	0	0	0	0.00	0	0	60	37	2	18.50	2-37	0	0	3.70	1	
NW	1990	2	2	0	24	14	12.00	0	0	96	57	1	57.00	1-29	0	0	3.56	0	

DODEMAIDE, A.I.C. (see Australia) (Sussex)

SL	1989	40	34	14	572	40*	28.60	0	0	1702	1157	42	27.54	4-40	1	0	4.07	12	
BH	1989	9	5	1	139	38	34.75	0	0	558	333	13	25.61	3-26	0	0	3.58	2	
NW	1989	7	5	2	68	32*	22.66	0	0	472	245	14	17.50	6-9	1	1	3.11	1	

Cmp	Debut	M	I	NO	Runs	HS	Avge	100	50	Balls	Runs	Wkts	Avge	BB	5i	10m	RpO	ct	st
ELWORTHY, S. (see South Africa) (Lancashire)																			
SL	1996	14	9	2	59	15	8.42	0	0	564	477	11	43.36	2-33	0	0	5.07	4	
BH	1996	5	3	0	26	13	8.66	0	0	282	204	10	20.40	4-14	1	0	4.34	0	
NW	1996	2	2	1	13	8	13.00	0	0	108	50	5	10.00	4-40	1	0	2.77	0	
FUSEDALE, N.A. (see South Africa) (Berkshire)																			
NW	1992	2	2	1	32	32*	32.00	0	0	144	138	0					5.75	1	
GIBSON, O.D. (see West Indies) (Glamorgan)																			
SL	1994	29	24	8	362	47*	22.62	0	0	1017	785	22	35.68	2-18	0	0	4.63	8	
BH	1994	4	2	0	105	68	52.50	0	1	202	176	3	58.66	2-50	0	0	5.22	0	
NW	1994	3	3	0	68	44	22.66	0	0	162	116	5	23.20	3-34	0	0	4.29	1	
GIDLEY, M.I. (see South Africa) (Leicestershire)																			
SL	1990	14	12	6	155	55*	25.83	0	1	373	370	8	46.25	3-45	0	0	5.95	2	
BH	1990	3	2	2	21	20*		0	0	72	39	0					3.25	0	
HARPER, R.A. (see West Indies) (Northamptonshire)																			
SL	1985	40	33	9	668	65*	27.83	0	3	1656	1186	40	29.65	4-17	1	0	4.29	24	
BH	1985	8	5	0	118	56	23.60	0	1	456	217	7	31.00	3-48	0	0	2.85	5	
NW	1985	3	3	1	5	4*	2.50	0	0	192	109	4	27.25	3-40	0	0	3.40	1	
HAYNES, D.L. (see South Africa) (Middlesex, Scotland)																			
SL	1989	68	66	6	2445	142*	40.75	3	20	306	287	3	95.66	1-17	0	0	5.62	23	
BH	1983	15	15	1	773	131	55.21	1	7	192	110	3	36.66	1-9	0	0	3.43	7	
NW	1989	14	14	3	838	149*	76.18	2	7	132	66	1	66.00	1-41	0	0	3.00	2	
HOOPER, C.L. (see West Indies) (Kent)																			
SL	1992	65	62	7	2482	145	45.12	4	19	2785	1898	57	33.29	5-41	2	1	4.08	34	
BH	1992	12	12	0	454	98	37.83	0	4	654	385	12	32.08	3-28	0	0	3.53	4	
NW	1992	11	11	1	423	136*	42.30	1	1	651	383	5	76.60	2-12	0	0	3.52	7	
IJAZ AHMED (see Pakistan) (Durham)																			
NW	1991	1	1	0	10	10	10.00	0	0	66	79	0					7.18	0	
JULIAN, B.P. (see Australia) (Surrey)																			
SL	1996	15	11	1	167	41	16.70	0	0	464	449	15	29.93	3-5	0	0	5.83	5	
BH	1996	5	2	0	29	27	14.50	0	0	277	232	7	33.14	3-28	0	0	5.02	4	
NW	1996	4	3	2	37	23	37.00	0	0	221	158	11	14.36	4-46	1	0	4.28	2	
KASPROWICZ, M.S. (see Australia) (Essex)																			
SL	1994	15	12	0	61	17	5.08	0	0	568	458	11	41.63	2-38	0	0	4.83	2	
BH	1994	2								90	76	2	38.00	2-52	0	0	5.06	1	
NW	1994	1	1	0	13	13	13.00	0	0	72	60	5	12.00	5-60	0	1	5.00	0	
KIRSTEN, P.N. (see South Africa) (Derbyshire)																			
SL	1978	69	69	4	1828	102	28.12	1	12	722	582	26	22.38	5-34	1	1	4.83	26	
BH	1978	24	22	3	768	77*	40.42	0	8	312	251	6	41.83	1-6	0	0	4.82	11	
NW	1978	10	10	2	374	110*	46.75	1	2	168	104	4	26.00	2-15	0	0	3.71	4	
KUIPER, A.P. (see South Africa) (Derbyshire)																			
SL	1990	16	16	4	433	62*	36.08	0	3	468	501	19	26.36	3-50	0	0	6.42	9	
BH	1990	4	4	2	185	106*	92.50	1	0	226	235	3	78.33	3-71	0	0	6.23	1	
NW	1990	2	2	0	74	49	37.00	0	0	96	45	1	45.00	1-20	0	0	2.81	0	
KUMBLE, A. (see India) (Northamptonshire)																			
SL	1995	10	3	1	11	8	5.50	0	0	414	347	16	21.68	3-25	0	0	5.02	3	
BH	1995	4	3	0	5	3	1.66	0	0	226	135	3	45.00	2-40	0	0	3.58	1	
NW	1995	5	2	1	8	6*	8.00	0	0	357	203	11	18.45	4-50	1	0	3.41	1	
LARA, B.C. (see West Indies) (Warwickshire)																			
SL	1994	14	14	0	364	75	26.00	0	3									6	
BH	1994	3	3	0	112	70	37.33	0	1									0	
NW	1994	5	5	0	158	81	31.60	0	1									3	
LEE, S. (see Australia) (Somerset)																			
SL	1996	16	15	4	442	71*	40.18	0	5	695	618	25	24.72	4-40	1	0	5.33	7	
BH	1996	5	5	1	63	23	15.75	0	0	242	245	6	40.83	3-60	0	0	6.07	2	
NW	1996	3	3	0	122	104	40.66	1	0	101	83	0					4.93	1	
McMILLAN, B.M. (see South Africa) (Warwickshire)																			
SL	1986	5	5	2	133	78*	44.33	0	1	218	177	7	25.28	3-22	0	0	4.87	3	
BH	1986	4	4	0	170	76	42.50	0	2	252	161	6	26.83	3-51	0	0	3.83	2	
NW	1986	1	1	0	10	10	10.00	0	0	70	54	3	18.00	3-54	0	0	4.62	0	
MORRISON, D.K. (see New Zealand) (Lancashire)																			
SL	1992	4	1	1	0	0*		0	0	180	176	3	58.66	1-41	0	0	5.86	1	
BH	1992	5	2	1	0	0*	0.00	0	0	276	185	5	37.00	2-17	0	0	4.02	1	
NW	1992	2								121	89	5	17.80	3-17	0	0	4.41	0	
NASH, D.J. (see New Zealand) (Middlesex)																			
SL	1995	13	8	0	109	35	13.62	0	0	510	365	16	22.81	3-34	0	0	4.29	4	
BH	1995	6	4	1	97	54	32.33	0	1	336	223	5	44.60	2-31	0	0	3.98	3	
NW	1995	3	3	0	6	4	2.00	0	0	120	93	1	93.00	1-36	0	0	4.65	1	

PATEL, D.N. (see New Zealand) (Worcestershire)

Cmp	Debut	M	I	NO	Runs	HS	Avge	100	50	Balls	Runs	Wkts	Avge	BB	5i	10m	RpO	ct	st
SL	1976	138	131	11	2523	125	21.02	1	6	3478	2841	91	31.21	5-27	0	1	4.90	33	
BH	1976	45	36	4	727	90*	22.71	0	4	1522	886	29	30.55	3-42	0	0	3.49	13	
NW	1978	18	17	2	309	54	20.60	0	1	853	461	16	28.81	4-22	1	0	3.24	4	

PIENAAR, R.F. (see South Africa) (Kent)

Cmp	Debut	M	I	NO	Runs	HS	Avge	100	50	Balls	Runs	Wkts	Avge	BB	5i	10m	RpO	ct	st
SL	1987	21	19	1	510	119	28.33	1	1	474	383	14	27.35	4-34	1	0	4.84	6	
BH	1989	2	2	0	43	36	21.50	0	0									1	
NW	1987	6	4	1	192	90	64.00	0	2	276	120	9	13.33	3-19	0	0	2.60	2	

POLLOCK, S.M. (see South Africa) (Warwickshire)

Cmp	Debut	M	I	NO	Runs	HS	Avge	100	50	Balls	Runs	Wkts	Avge	BB	5i	10m	RpO	ct	st
SL	1996	14	11	2	273	57	30.33	0	2	627	387	25	15.48	3-27	0	0	3.70	3	
BH	1996	7	4	2	98	59*	49.00	0	1	384	277	15	18.46	6-21	0	2	4.32	1	
NW	1996	2	2	0	40	23	20.00	0	0	102	62	4	15.50	4-37	1	0	3.64	0	

PRABHAKAR, M. (see India) (Durham)

Cmp	Debut	M	I	NO	Runs	HS	Avge	100	50	Balls	Runs	Wkts	Avge	BB	5i	10m	RpO	ct	st
SL	1995	12	12	0	324	69	27.00	0	2	522	377	17	22.17	3-30	0	0	4.33	2	
BH	1995	5	5	1	148	69	37.00	0	2	258	187	5	37.40	2-36	0	0	4.34	4	
NW	1995	1	1	0	4	4	4.00	0	0	36	23	0					3.83	1	

PRINGLE, C. (see New Zealand) (Holland)

Cmp	Debut	M	I	NO	Runs	HS	Avge	100	50	Balls	Runs	Wkts	Avge	BB	5i	10m	RpO	ct	st
NW	1996	1	1	0	3	3	3.00	0	0	72	41	0					3.41	0	

PRINGLE, M.W. (see South Africa) (Sussex)

Cmp	Debut	M	I	NO	Runs	HS	Avge	100	50	Balls	Runs	Wkts	Avge	BB	5i	10m	RpO	ct	st
SL	1988	2	1	0	11	11	11.00	0	0	58	46	3	15.33	3-37	0	0	4.75	0	
BH	1988	1	1	1	19	19*		0	0	54	33	1	33.00	1-33	0	0	3.66	0	

RAJPUT, L.S. (see India) (Scotland)

Cmp	Debut	M	I	NO	Runs	HS	Avge	100	50	Balls	Runs	Wkts	Avge	BB	5i	10m	RpO	ct	st
NW	1987	1	1	0	2	2	2.00	0	0	18	12	0					4.00	0	

RICHARDSON, R.B. (see South Africa) (Yorkshire)

Cmp	Debut	M	I	NO	Runs	HS	Avge	100	50	Balls	Runs	Wkts	Avge	BB	5i	10m	RpO	ct	st
SL	1993	21	21	6	740	103	49.33	1	5									5	
BH	1993	2	2	0	59	52	29.50	0	1									0	
NW	1993	5	5	0	194	90	38.80	0	2									0	

SALEEM MALIK (see Pakistan) (Essex)

Cmp	Debut	M	I	NO	Runs	HS	Avge	100	50	Balls	Runs	Wkts	Avge	BB	5i	10m	RpO	ct	st
SL	1991	24	24	2	756	89	34.36	0	5	224	163	4	40.75	3-36	0	0	4.36	10	
BH	1991	8	7	2	218	90*	43.60	0	2	12	7	1	7.00	1-7	0	0	3.50	1	
NW	1991	5	5	1	148	74	37.00	0	1	74	59	4	14.75	4-25	1	0	4.78	5	

SIMMONS, P.V. (see West Indies) (Durham, Leicestershire)

Cmp	Debut	M	I	NO	Runs	HS	Avge	100	50	Balls	Runs	Wkts	Avge	BB	5i	10m	RpO	ct	st
SL	1994	33	33	1	1475	140	46.09	3	10	1103	924	31	29.80	5-37	1	1	5.02	15	
BH	1994	4	4	0	136	64	34.00	0	2	162	134	1	134.00	1-29	0	0	4.96	2	
NW	1989	6	6	0	193	82	32.16	0	1	312	243	8	30.37	3-31	0	0	4.67	3	

SNELL, R.P. (see South Africa) (Somerset)

Cmp	Debut	M	I	NO	Runs	HS	Avge	100	50	Balls	Runs	Wkts	Avge	BB	5i	10m	RpO	ct	st
SL	1992	13	7	2	158	62	31.60	0	1	456	359	12	29.91	2-24	0	0	4.72	1	
BH	1992	4	4	1	60	31	20.00	0	0	257	176	6	29.33	3-47	0	0	4.10	1	
NW	1992	2	1	0	19	19	19.00	0	0	132	99	0					4.50	0	

SRINATH, J. (see India) (Gloucestershire)

Cmp	Debut	M	I	NO	Runs	HS	Avge	100	50	Balls	Runs	Wkts	Avge	BB	5i	10m	RpO	ct	st
SL	1995	6	4	1	13	11	4.33	0	0	263	213	11	19.36	3-27	0	0	4.85	3	
BH	1995	6	6	1	12	6	2.40	0	0	386	176	15	11.73	4-33	1	0	2.73	1	
NW	1995	3	2	1	11	11*	11.00	0	0	152	63	7	9.00	4-38	1	0	2.48	1	

STELLING, W.F. (see South Africa) (Holland)

Cmp	Debut	M	I	NO	Runs	HS	Avge	100	50	Balls	Runs	Wkts	Avge	BB	5i	10m	RpO	ct	st
NW	1995	1	1	0	6	6	6.00	0	0	60	45	0					4.50	0	

STEPHENSON, F.D. (see South Africa) (Gloucestershire, Nottinghamshire, Sussex)

Cmp	Debut	M	I	NO	Runs	HS	Avge	100	50	Balls	Runs	Wkts	Avge	BB	5i	10m	RpO	ct	st
SL	1982	126	107	15	1949	103	21.18	1	6	5733	3969	192	20.67	5-23	7	3	4.15	28	
BH	1988	34	29	7	523	98*	23.77	0	2	2043	1195	56	21.33	5-30	2	1	3.50	4	
NW	1982	21	16	2	255	40	18.21	0	0	1326	706	31	22.77	3-8	0	0	3.19	2	

STREAK, H.H. (see Zimbabwe) (Hampshire)

Cmp	Debut	M	I	NO	Runs	HS	Avge	100	50	Balls	Runs	Wkts	Avge	BB	5i	10m	RpO	ct	st
SL	1995	15	11	5	154	32*	25.66	0	0	672	656	22	29.81	4-56	1	0	5.85	1	
BH	1995	5	4	2	32	18	16.00	0	0	264	171	8	21.37	3-28	0	0	3.88	2	

SYMONDS, A. (see Australia) (Gloucestershire)

Cmp	Debut	M	I	NO	Runs	HS	Avge	100	50	Balls	Runs	Wkts	Avge	BB	5i	10m	RpO	ct	st
SL	1995	29	28	2	756	76	29.07	0	4	312	278	13	21.38	3-34	0	0	5.34	18	
BH	1995	11	11	0	291	95	26.45	0	2	24	23	0					5.75	4	
NW	1995	5	5	0	166	87	33.20	0	1	102	63	1	63.00	1-18	0	0	3.70	0	

TENDULKAR, S.R. (see India) (Yorkshire)

Cmp	Debut	M	I	NO	Runs	HS	Avge	100	50	Balls	Runs	Wkts	Avge	BB	5i	10m	RpO	ct	st
SL	1992	13	13	1	464	107	38.66	1	1	128	102	3	34.00	2-28	0	0	4.78	1	
BH	1992	2	2	0	23	16	11.50	0	0	120	65	3	21.66	2-21	0	0	3.25	1	
NW	1992	2	2	1	53	32*	53.00	0	0									1	

TWOSE, R.G. (see New Zealand) (Devon, Warwickshire)

Cmp	Debut	M	I	NO	Runs	HS	Avge	100	50	Balls	Runs	Wkts	Avge	BB	5i	10m	RpO	ct	st
SL	1989	94	79	13	1880	100	28.48	1	11	1554	1303	37	35.21	3-31	0	0	5.03	26	
BH	1990	17	15	1	465	90	33.21	0	4	228	176	3	58.66	1-23	0	0	4.63	11	
NW	1988	21	18	3	783	110	52.20	2	4	735	496	17	29.17	3-39	0	0	4.04	8	

Cmp	Debut	M	I	NO	Runs	HS	Avge	100	50	Balls	Runs	Wkts	Avge	BB	5i	10m	RpO	ct	st
VAUGHAN, J.T.C. (see New Zealand) (Gloucestershire)																			
SL	1992	6	5	1	34	20	8.50	0	0	189	110	4	27.50	3-31	0	0	3.49	1	
BH	1992	4	3	0	24	12	8.00	0	0	228	177	5	35.40	3-61	0	0	4.65	0	
NW	1992	2	2	1	65	54*	65.00	0	1	96	57	0					3.56	0	
WALSH, C.A. (see West Indies) (Gloucestershire)																			
SL	1984	110	70	11	545	38	9.23	0	0	4484	3023	144	20.99	4-19	3	0	4.04	23	
BH	1985	23	15	5	114	28	11.40	0	0	1367	819	26	31.50	2-19	0	0	3.59	1	
NW	1985	21	14	3	136	37	12.36	0	0	1314	712	42	16.95	6-21	0	2	3.25	2	
WAUGH, M.E. (see Australia) (Essex)																			
SL	1988	63	61	11	2346	112*	46.92	4	15	1297	1234	40	30.85	3-20	0	0	5.70	24	
BH	1989	16	14	1	438	100	33.69	1	2	95	76	4	19.00	3-31	0	0	4.80	5	
NW	1989	8	7	0	145	47	20.71	0	0	252	222	2	111.00	1-45	0	0	5.28	1	
WAUGH, S.R. (see Australia) (Somerset)																			
SL	1988	11	10	2	534	140*	66.75	2	1	120	114	2	57.00	1-27	0	0	5.70	4	
BH	1988	3	3	1	161	79	80.50	0	2	84	63	2	31.50	2-16	0	0	4.50	1	
NW	1988	2	2	0	21	21	10.50	0	0	132	96	4	24.00	2-45	0	0	4.36	1	
WESSELS, K.C. (see South Africa) (Sussex)																			
SL	1977	22	22	0	712	88	32.36	0	6									5	
BH	1977	13	13	1	593	106	49.41	2	4									6	
NW	1978	5	5	0	106	43	21.20	0	0									5	

AUSTRALIA

First First-Class Match: Tasmania v Victoria (Launceston) 1850-51

First First-Class Tour to England: 1878

First Test Match: Australia v England (Melbourne) 1876-77

Present First-Class Teams: New South Wales, Queensland, South Australia, Tasmania, Victoria, Western Australia

First-Class Competition: The Sheffield Shield was instituted for the 1892-93 season for competition between the three leading Australian teams, New South Wales, South Australia and Victoria. Over the years it has been expanded and now includes all six first-class states.

Sheffield Shield Champions 1996-97: Queensland

FIRST-CLASS RECORDS

Highest Team Total: 1107 Victoria v New South Wales (Melbourne) 1926-27
Highest in 1996-97: 560-8d Western Australia v South Australia (Perth); 549 Queensland v New South Wales (Brisbane); 544-4d Australian XI v West Indies (Hobart); 527-6d South Australia v Queensland (Adelaide); 517 Australia v West Indies (Adelaide)

Lowest Team Total: 15 Victoria v MCC (Melbourne) 1903-04
Lowest in 1996-97: 67 Pakistan v Tasmania (Hobart); 84 South Australia v Victoria (Melbourne); 89 New South Wales v Western Australia (Perth); 117 South Australia v New South Wales (Sydney); 122 Australia v West Indies (Melbourne)

Highest Individual Innings: 452* D.G.Bradman New South Wales v Queensland (Sydney) 1929-30
Highest in 1996-97: 274* J.L.Langer Western Australia v South Australia (Perth); 255 D.S.Lehmann South Australia v Queensland (Adelaide); 224 M.L.Hayden Australian XI v West Indies (Hobart); 200 J.Cox Tasmania v Pakistan (Hobart); 187 M.T.G.Elliott Victoria v New South Wales (Sydney)

Most Runs in Season: 1,690 (av 93.88) D.G.Bradman (New South Wales) 1928-29
Most in 1996-97: 1,349 (av 67.45) J.Cox (Tasmania); 960 (av 53.33) D.S.Lehman (South Australia); 960 (av 60.00) R.T.Ponting (Tasmania); 928 (av 46.40) M.E.Hussey (Western Australia); 799 (av 39.95) M.J.di Venuto (Tasmania)

Most Runs in Career: 28,067 (av 95.14) D.G.Bradman (New South Wales, South Australia) 1927-28 to 1948-49
Most by Current Batsman: 20,683 (av 45.52) D.C.Boon (Tasmania, Durham) 1978-79 to date; 19,846 (av 54.07) M.E.Waugh (New South Wales, Essex) 1985-86 to date; 18,555 (av 47.09) T.M.Moody (Western Australia, Warwickshire, Worcestershire) 1985-86 to date; 18,292 (av 51.81) D.M.Jones (Victoria, Durham, Derbyshire) 1981-82 to date; 15,568 (av 51.89) S.R.Waugh (New South Wales, Somerset) 1984-85 to date

Best Innings Analysis: 10-36 T.W.Wall South Australia v New South Wales (Sydney) 1932-33
Best in 1996-97: 7-41 T.M.Moody Western Australia v Tasmania (Hobart); 7-44 I.J.Harvey Victoria v South Australia (Melbourne); 7-48 B.P.Julian Western Australia v Victoria (Melbourne); 7-64 S.Young Tasmania v Pakistan (Hobart); 6-38 A.C.Dale Queensland v Western Australia (Perth)

Most Wickets in Season: 106 (av 13.59) C.T.B.Turner (New South Wales) 1887-88
Most in 1996-97: 48 (av 25.54) M.S.Kasprowicz (Queensland); 42 (av 22.07) A.C.Dale (Queensland); 38 (av 24.36) T.M.Moody (Western Australia)

Most Wickets in Career: 1,424 (av 22.28) C.V.Grimmett (South Australia, Wellington) 1911-12 to 1940-41
Most by Current Bowler: 530 (av 31.83) A.I.C.Dodemaide (Victoria, Sussex) 1983-84 to date; 511 (av 31.45) G.R.J.Matthews (New South Wales) 1982-83 to date; 471 (av 24.44) S.K.Warne (Victoria) 1990-91 to date; 374 (av 27.67) P.R.Reiffel (Victoria) 1987-88 to date; 344 (av 27.49) M.S.Kasprowicz (Queensland, Essex) 1989-90 to date

Record Wicket Partnerships

1st	456	W.H.Ponsford & R.E.Mayne	Victoria v Queensland (Melbourne)	1923-24
2nd	378	L.A.Marks & K.D.Walters	New South Wales v South Australia (Adelaide)	1964-65
3rd	390*	J.M.Wiener & J.K.Moss	Victoria v Western Australia (Melbourne)	1981-82
4th	462*	D.W.Hookes & W.B.Phillips	South Australia v Tasmania (Adelaide)	1986-87
5th	464*	M.E.Waugh & S.R.Waugh	New South Wales v Western Australia (Perth)	1990-91
6th	346	J.H.W.Fingleton & D.G.Bradman	Australia v England (Melbourne)	1936-37
7th	335	C.W.Andrews & E.C.Bensted	Queensland v New South Wales (Sydney)	1934-35

8th	270	V.T.Trumper & E.P.Barbour	New South Wales v Victoria (Sydney)	1912-13
9th	232	C.Hill & E.A.Walkley	South Australia v New South Wales (Adelaide)	1900-01
10th	307	A.F.Kippax & J.E.H.Hooker	New South Wales v Victoria (Melbourne)	1928-29

Highest Partnerships in 1996-97

1st	323	M.L.Hayden & M.T.G.Elliott	Australian XI v West Indies (Hobart)
2nd	207	R.G.Samuels & S.Chanderpaul	West Indies v Western Australia (Perth)
3rd	273	S.R.Waugh & M.E.Waugh	New South Wales v Queensland (Brisbane)
4th	231	J.L.Langer & T.M.Moody	Western Australia v Tasmania (Perth)
5th	209	T.M.Moody & S.M.Katich	Western Australia v Queensland (Brisbane)
6th	290	M.T.G.Elliott & D.S.Berry	Victoria v New South Wales (Sydney)
7th	119	D.J.Marsh & M.N.Atkinson	Tasmania v Victoria (Melbourne)
8th	134	W.A.Seccombe & P.W.Jackson	Queensland v Victoria (Melbourne)
9th	74	C.O.Browne & N.A.M.McLean	West Indies v Australian XI (Hobart)
10th	138*	B.E.McNamara & P.J.S.Alley	New South Wales v Tasmania (Hobart)

Most Wicketkeeping Dismissals in Innings: 8 (8ct) A.T.W.Grout Queensland v Western Australia (Brisbane) 1959-60; 8 (7ct 1st) D.S.Berry Victoria v South Australia (Melbourne) 1996-97
Most in 1996-97: 8 (7ct 1st) D.S.Berry Victoria v South Australia (Melbourne); 6 (5ct 1st) D.S.Berry Victoria v Queensland (Brisbane); 5 (5ct) A.C.Gilchrist Western Australia v Queensland (Perth); 5 (5ct) A.C.Gilchrist Western Australia v New South Wales (Sydney); 5 (5ct) A.C.Gilchrist Western Australia v Queensland (Brisbane)

Most Wicketkeeping Dismissals in Match: 12 (9ct 3st) D.Tallon Queensland v New South Wales (Sydney) 1938-39; 12 (9ct 3st) H.B.Taber New South Wales v South Australia (Adelaide) 1968-69
Most in 1996-97: 11 (10ct 1st) D.S.Berry Victoria v South Australia (Melbourne); 8 (8ct) A.C.Gilchrist Western Australia v Queensland (Perth); 8 (7ct 1st) A.C.Gilchrist Western Australia v Queensland (Brisbane); 8 (8ct) T.J.Nielsen South Australia v Queensland (Brisbane)

Most Wicketkeeping Dismissals in Season: 67 (63ct 4st) R.W.Marsh (Western Australia) 1975-76
Most in 1996-97: 62 (60ct 2st) A.C.Gilchrist (Western Australia); 45 (40ct 5st) D.S.Berry (Victoria); 39 (35ct 4st) W.A.Seccombe (Queensland); 36 (33ct 3st) M.N.Atkinson (Tasmania); 34 (34ct) T.J.Nielsen (South Australia)

Most Wicketkeeping Dismissals in Career: 869 (803ct 66st) R.W.Marsh (Western Australia) 1968-69 to 1983-84
Most by Current Wicketkeeper: 615 (566ct 49st) I.A.Healy (Queensland) 1986-87 to date; 336 (305ct 31st) D.S.Berry (South Australia, Victoria) 1989-90 to date; 332 (297ct 35st) P.A.Emery (New South Wales) 1987-88 to date; 257 (229ct 28st) T.J.Nielsen (South Australia) 1990-91 to date; 231 (220ct 11st) A.C.Gilchrist (New South Wales, Western Australia) 1992-93 to date

Most Catches by Fielder in Innings: 6 J.S.F.Sheppard Queensland v New South Wales (Brisbane) 1914-15
Most in 1996-97: 4 M.W.Goodwin Western Australia v New South Wales (Perth); 4 J.D.Siddons South Australia v England A (Adelaide)

Most Catches by Fielder in Match: 7 J.A.Atkinson Tasmania v Victoria (Melbourne) 1928-29; 7 E.W.Freeman South Australia v Western Australia (Adelaide) 1971-72; 7 G.S.Chappell South Australia v England (Perth) 1974-75; 7 M.A.Taylor New South Wales v Victoria (Melbourne) 1995-96
Most in 1996-97: 5 M.W.Goodwin Western Australia v New South Wales (Perth); 5 C.L.Hooper West Indies v Australia (Melbourne); 5 J.D.Siddons South Australia v England A (Adelaide)

Most Catches by Fielder in Season: 27 I.M.Chappell (South Australia) 1968-69
Most in 1996-97: 19 J.D.Siddons (South Australia); 17 J.P.Maher (Queensland); 15 G.I.Foley (Queensland); 15 S.G.Law (Queensland); 14 T.M.Moody (Western Australia)

Most Catches by Fielder in Career: 383 R.B.Simpson (New South Wales, Western Australia) 1952-53 to 1977-78
Most by Current Fielder: 304 M.E.Waugh (New South Wales, Essex) 1985-86 to date; 300 M.A.Taylor (New South Wales) 1985-86 to date; 258 T.M.Moody (Western Australia, Warwickshire, Worcestershire) 1985-86 to date; 251 D.C.Boon (Tasmania, Durham) 1978-79 to date; 202 S.R.Waugh (New South Wales, Somerset) 1984-85 to date

DOMESTIC LIMITED OVERS RECORDS

Highest Team Totals: 325-6 (50 overs) South Australia v Tasmania (Hobart) 1986-87; 320-4 (50 overs) Queensland v Tasmania (Brisbane) 1993-94; 310-4 (50 overs) New South Wales v South Australia (Sydney) 1981-82; 310-5 (50 overs) New South Wales v Victoria (North Sydney) 1991-92
Highest in 1996-97: 275-5 (50 overs) Queensland v Tasmania (Brisbane)

Lowest Team Totals: 59 (21.3 overs) Western Australia v Victoria (Melbourne) 1969-70; 62 (20.3 overs) Queensland v Western Australia (Perth) 1976-77; 76 (26.1 overs) Western Australia v New Zealand (Melbourne) 1974-75
Lowest in 1996-97: 134 (47.5 overs) South Australia v Queensland (Adelaide)

Highest Individual Innings: 164 R.B.McCosker New South Wales v South Australia (Sydney) 1981-82; 159 S.G.Law Queensland v Tasmania (Brisbane) 1993-94; 142* D.S.Lehmann South Australia v Tasmania (Adelaide) 1994-95
Highest in 1996-97: 129* M.J.di Venuto Tasmania v South Australia (Hobart)
52 centuries have been scored in the competition, D.M.Jones and S.G.Law scoring 4

Most Runs in Season: 421 (av 70.16) D.S.Lehmann (South Australia) 1994-95
Most in 1996-97: 274 (av 68.50) M.J.di Venuto (Tasmania)

Most Runs in Career: 1,844 (av 49.83) D.M.Jones (Victoria) 1981-82 to date; 1,596 (av 53.20) G.R.Marsh (Western Australia) 1981-82 to 1993-94; 1,413 (av 35.32) D.C.Boon (Tasmania) 1978-79 to date

Best Innings Analyses: 7-34 C.G.Rackemann Queensland v South Australia (Adelaide) 1988-89; 6-18 J.R.Thomson Queensland v South Australia (Brisbane) 1978-79; 6-25 B.E.McNamara New South Wales v Tasmania (Sydney) 1996-97
Five wickets in an innings has been achieved on 20 occasions, all by different bowlers.

Most Economical Bowling: 10-4-8-1 G.D.Porter Western Australia v Victoria (Perth) 1986-87
Most Economical in 1996-97: 10-3-12-1 T.M.Moody Western Australia v Victoria (Perth)

Most Expensive Bowling: 10-0-87-2 R.J.Tucker Tasmania v Queensland (Brisbane) 1993-94
Most Expensive in 1996-97: 10-0-63-2 S.Young Tasmania v South Australia (Hobart)

Most Wickets in Season: 18 (av 19.16) S.P.George (South Australia) 1994-95; 18 (av 13.50) K.M.Harvey (Western Australia) 1996-97

Most Wickets in Career: 55 (av 30.01) T.M.Moody (Western Australia) 1985-86 to date; 53 (av 21.98) K.H.MacLeay (Western Australia) 1981-82 to 1991-92; 48 (av 16.89) D.K.Lillee (Western Australia, Tasmania) 1969-70 to 1987-88; 48 (av 26.02) C.G.Rackemann (Queensland) 1979-80 to 1994-95

Record Wicket Partnerships

1st	253	R.B.McCosker & J.Dyson	New South Wales v South Australia (Sydney)	1981-82
2nd	260	M.L.Hayden & S.G.Law	Queensland v Tasmania (Brisbane)	1993-94
3rd	240	S.R.Waugh & M.E.Waugh	New South Wales v Victoria (Sydney)	1991-92
4th	158	S.G.Law & G.I.Foley	Queensland v New South Wales (Brisbane)	1996-97
5th	156	K.J.Roberts & R.Chee Quee	New South Wales v South Australia (Sydney)	1995-96
6th	105	M.G.Bevan & G.R.J.Matthews	New South Wales v Western Australia (Perth)	1990-91
7th	111*	R.W.Marsh & B.Yardley	Western Australia v New South Wales (Sydney)	1973-74
8th	106*	A.C.Gilchrist & B.P.Julian	Western Australia v New South Wales (Sydney)	1995-96
9th	73	R.C.Jordon & R.K.Rowan	Victoria v South Australia (Adelaide)	1970-71
10th	54	B.E.McNamara & G.R.Robertson	New South Wales v South Australia (Adelaide)	1996-97

There were 3 hundred partnerships in 1996-97, the highest being the new 4th wicket record

Most Wicketkeeping Dismissals in Innings: 6 (6ct) K.J.Wadsworth New Zealand v New South Wales (Sydney) 1969-70
Most in 1996-97: 4 (4ct) T.J.Nielsen South Australia v Western Australia (Perth); 4 (4ct) T.J.Nielsen South Australia v New South Wales (Adelaide); 4 (3ct 1st) W.A.Seccombe Queensland v South Australia (Adelaide)

Most Wicketkeeping Dismissals in Season: 14 (12ct 2st) D.S.Berry (Victoria) 1994-95; 14 (12ct 2st) A.C.Gilchrist (Western Australia) 1995-96; 14 (13ct 1st) A.C.Gilchrist (Western Australia) 1996-97

Most Wicketkeeping Dismissals in Career: 54 (41ct 13st) D.S.Berry (South Australia, Victoria) 1989-90 to date; 51 (50ct 1st) R.W.Marsh (Western Australia) 1969-70 to 1983-84; 50 (44ct 6st) P.A.Emery (New South Wales) 1987-88 to date

Most Catches by Fielder in Innings: 4 W.J.Scholes Victoria v New Zealand (Melbourne) 1971-72; 4 I.M.Chappell South Australia v New Zealand (Adelaide) 1972-73
Most in 1996-97: 3 S.K.Warne Victoria v South Australia (Adelaide); 3 S.K.Warne Victoria v Tasmania (Melbourne)

Most Catches by Fielder in Season: 7 G.R.Marsh (Western Australia) 1993-94
Most in 1996-97: 6 S.K.Warne (Victoria)

Most Catches by Fielder in Career: 29 A.R.Border (New South Wales, Queensland) 1977-78 to 1995-96; 24 D.M.Jones (Victoria) 1981-82 to date; 24 J.D.Siddons (Victoria, South Australia) 1985-86 to date

Most Appearances in Competition: 54 T.M.Moody (Western Australia) 1985-86 to date; 49 A.R.Border (New South Wales, Queensland) 1977-78 to 1995-96; 48 D.M.Jones (Victoria) 1981-82 to date

CHAMPION TEAMS

Sheffield Shield

The competition is run on a league basis, but since 1982-83 the two leading teams in the league have met in a final deciding match. In the event of this match being drawn, the team winning the league become winners of the Shield.

1892-93 Victoria	1928-29 New South Wales	1966-67 Victoria
1893-94 South Australia	1929-30 Victoria	1967-68 Western Australia
1894-95 Victoria	1930-31 Victoria	1968-69 South Australia
1895-96 New South Wales	1931-32 New South Wales	1969-70 Victoria
1896-97 New South Wales	1932-33 New South Wales	1970-71 South Australia
1897-98 Victoria	1933-34 Victoria	1971-72 Western Australia
1898-99 Victoria	1934-35 Victoria	1972-73 Western Australia
1899-00 New South Wales	1935-36 South Australia	1973-74 Victoria
1900-01 Victoria	1936-37 Victoria	1974-75 Western Australia
1901-02 New South Wales	1937-38 New South Wales	1975-76 South Australia
1902-03 New South Wales	1938-39 South Australia	1976-77 Western Australia
1903-04 New South Wales	1939-40 New South Wales	1977-78 Western Australia
1904-05 New South Wales	1946-47 Victoria	1978-79 Victoria
1905-06 New South Wales	1947-48 Western Australia	1979-80 Victoria
1906-07 New South Wales	1948-49 New South Wales	1980-81 Western Australia
1907-08 Victoria	1949-50 New South Wales	1981-82 South Australia
1908-09 New South Wales	1950-51 Victoria	1982-83 New South Wales
1909-10 South Australia	1951-52 New South Wales	1983-84 Western Australia
1910-11 New South Wales	1952-53 South Australia	1984-85 New South Wales
1911-12 New South Wales	1953-54 New South Wales	1985-86 New South Wales
1912-13 South Australia	1954-55 New South Wales	1986-87 Western Australia
1913-14 New South Wales	1955-56 New South Wales	1987-88 Western Australia
1914-15 Victoria	1956-57 New South Wales	1988-89 Western Australia
1919-20 New South Wales	1957-58 New South Wales	1989-90 New South Wales
1920-21 New South Wales	1958-59 New South Wales	1990-91 Victoria
1921-22 Victoria	1959-60 New South Wales	1991-92 Western Australia
1922-23 New South Wales	1960-61 New South Wales	1992-93 New South Wales
1923-24 Victoria	1961-62 New South Wales	1993-94 New South Wales
1924-25 Victoria	1962-63 Victoria	1994-95 Queensland
1925-26 New South Wales	1963-64 South Australia	1995-96 South Australia
1926-27 South Australia	1964-65 New South Wales	1996-97 Queensland
1927-28 Victoria	1965-66 New South Wales	

Domestic Limited Overs Competition

For the first ten years the competition was played on a knock-out basis. The six states (including Tasmania) have been regular participants from the outset and the New Zealand national side played until the 1974-75 season. From 1979-80 until 1991-92 two qualifying groups comprised three teams playing a round-robin with the top two teams in each group contesting the semi-finals and final. From 1992-93 a full round-robin was played, with the 2nd and 3rd teams playing off for the right to play the leading team in the final. The overs limit was 40 8-ball overs until 1978-79, and in the following season the present 50 6-ball overs were introduced. The sponsors have changed several times. Results of the finals:

V & G Australasian Knock-Out Competition
1969-70 New Zealand 140-4 (31.4 overs) beat Victoria 129 (34.6 overs) by 6 wkts
1970-71 Western Australia 170 (38.2 overs) beat Queensland 79 (23.5 overs) by 91 runs

Australasian Coca-Cola Competition
1971-72 Victoria 192-2 (33.4 overs) beat South Australia 190 (38.7 overs) by 8 wkts
1972-73 New Zealand 170-9 (35 overs) beat Queensland 132 (31.3 overs) by 38 runs

Gillette Cup
1973-74 Western Australia 151-3 (26.6 overs) beat New Zealand 150 (36.3 overs) by 7 wkts
1974-75 New Zealand 77-2 (17 overs) beat Western Australia 76 (26.1 overs) by 8 wkts
1975-76 Queensland 236-7 (40 overs) beat Western Australia 232 (39 overs) by 4 runs
1976-77 Western Australia 165-9 (39.3 overs) beat Victoria 164 (37.3 overs) by 1 wkt
1977-78 Western Australia 185-3 (37.1 overs) beat Tasmania 184-9 (40 overs) by 7 wkts
1978-79 Tasmania 180-6 (40 overs) beat Western Australia 133 (50 overs) by 47 runs

McDonald's Cup
1979-80 Victoria 199-6 (47.4 overs) beat New South Wales 198-8 (50 overs) by 4 wkts
1980-81 Queensland 188-9 (48 overs) beat Western Australia 116 (32.5 overs) by 72 runs
1981-82 Queensland 224-8 (47 overs) beat New South Wales 197 (44.4 overs) by 27 runs
1982-83 Western Australia 198-6 (49.1 overs) beat New South Wales 195-6 (50 overs) by 4 wkts
1983-84 South Australia 256-6 (49 overs) beat Western Australia 248-9 (49 overs) by 8 runs
1984-85 New South Wales 278-7 (50 overs) beat South Australia 190 (45.5 overs) by 88 runs
1985-86 Western Australia 167 (38 overs) beat Victoria 148 (36.5 overs) by 19 runs
1986-87 South Australia 325-6 (50 overs) beat Tasmania 239-9 (50 overs) by 86 runs
1987-88 New South Wales 219-7 (50 overs) beat South Australia 196-6 (50 overs) by 23 runs

Federated Automobile Insurance Cup
1988-89 Queensland 253-4 (50 overs) beat Victoria 90 (32.4 overs) by 163 runs
1989-90 Western Australia 88-3 (19.1 overs) beat South Australia 87 (34.5 overs) by 7 wkts
1990-91 Western Australia 236-3 (44.5 overs) beat New South Wales 235-7 (50 overs) by 7 wkts
1991-92 New South Wales 199-9 (50 overs) beat Western Australia 130 (40.1 overs) by 69 runs

Mercantile Mutual Cup
1992-93 New South Wales 187-6 (49.4 overs) beat Victoria 186 (50 overs) by 4 wkts
1993-94 New South Wales 264-4 (50 overs) beat Western Australia 218-9 (49 overs) on faster scoring rate
1994-95 Victoria 170-6 (44.5 overs) beat South Australia 169 (46.4 overs) by 4 wkts
1995-96 Queensland 167-6 (44.5 overs) beat Western Australia 166 (49.1 overs) by 4 wkts
1996-97 Western Australia 149-2 (35 overs) beat Queensland 148 (40.1 overs) by 8 wkts

Table of Results 1969-70 to 1996-97

	P	W	L	T	NR	Winner	R-up
Western Australia	103	70	31	1	1	9	8
New South Wales	87	47	37	1	2	5	4
Queensland	82	46	35	0	4	5	3
Victoria	86	37	46	1	2	3	5
South Australia	83	31	51	1	0	2	5
Tasmania	73	18	53	0	1	1	2
New Zealand	10	7	3	0	0	3	1

The original final in 1985-86 which was abandoned after play started and later replayed, is not included in the records or career figures.

1996-97 AND CAREER RECORDS FOR AUSTRALIAN PLAYERS

Cmp	Debut	M	I	NO	Runs	HS	Avge	100	50	Balls	Runs	Wkts	Avge	BB	5i	10m	RpO	ct	st
ADLAM, Warwick James (New South Wales) b Newcastle 16.2.1971 LHB RFM																			
MM		2	1	0	1	1	1.00	0	0	84	58	0					4.14	1	
MM	1993	5	4	0	11	5	2.75	0	0	234	176	2	88.00	1-27	0	0	4.51	1	
ALLANBY, Richard Andrew (Tasmania) b Hobart 26.7.1971 LHB LBG																			
MM		2	2	0	13	7	6.50	0	0									1	
FC	1994	2	3	0	52	29	17.33	0	0	18	10	0					3.33	2	
ALLEN, Jeremy Michael (Western Australia) b Subiaco 11.6.1971 RHB LFM																			
FC		1	1	0	30	30	30.00	0	0	120	87	0					4.35	0	
MM	1994	1	1	1	12	12*		0	0	60	62	3	20.66	3-62	0	0	6.20	0	
ALLEY, Phillip John Sydney (New South Wales) b Orange 26.7.1970 RHB LF																			
FC		8	12	7	228	56	45.60	0	2	1169	641	23	27.86	5-89	1	0	3.28	3	
MM		1	1	0	8	8	8.00	0	0	42	37	2	18.50	2-37	0	0	5.28	0	
FC	1989	30	40	13	445	56	16.48	0	2	4990	2655	90	29.50	5-24	4	0	3.19	19	
MM	1989	7	2	1	16	8*	16.00	0	0	331	230	9	25.55	2-26	0	0	4.16	1	
ANGEL, Jo (Western Australia) b Mount Lawley 22.4.1968 RHB RF																			
FC		8	9	3	117	28	19.50	0	0	1649	685	31	22.09	4-20	0	0	2.49	3	
MM		5	1	1	1	1*		0	0	252	161	6	26.83	3-54	0	0	3.83	0	
Test	1992	4	7	1	35	11	5.83	0	0	748	463	10	46.30	3-54	0	0	3.71	1	
FC	1991	65	83	25	862	84*	14.86	0	2	13368	6844	271	25.25	6-68	11	1	3.07	20	
Int	1994	3	1	0	0	0	0.00	0	0	162	113	4	28.25	2-47	0	0	4.18	0	
MM	1992	25	11	5	60	19*	10.00	0	0	1305	796	29	27.44	3-37	0	0	3.65	0	
ARNBERGER, Jason Lee (New South Wales) b Penrith 18.11.1972 RHB RMF																			
FC		1	2	0	128	71	64.00	0	2									0	
FC	1994	9	17	0	418	71	24.58	0	3									5	
MM	1994	2	2	0	83	73	41.50	0	1									0	
ATKINSON, Mark Neville (Tasmania) b Sydney 11.2.1969 RHB WK																			
FC		11	15	4	328	58	29.81	0	2									33	3
MM		5	5	1	60	15	15.00	0	0									2	1
FC	1991	62	92	39	1883	76*	35.52	0	8									173	18
MM	1992	20	17	6	204	33	18.54	0	0									23	6
ATKINSON, Mark Peter (Western Australia) b Bentley 27.11.1970 RHB RFM																			
FC		1	2	2	88	45*		0	0	162	61	0					2.25	0	
MM		3	2	1	31	31	31.00	0	0	168	119	4	29.75	3-33	0	0	4.25	2	
FC	1992	8	12	6	254	52*	42.33	0	1	1614	918	20	45.90	3-46	0	0	3.41	5	
MM	1992	14	11	3	91	31	11.37	0	0	719	502	16	31.37	3-31	0	0	4.18	6	
AYRES, Warren Geoffrey (Victoria) b Moorabbin 25.10.1965 RHB																			
FC		8	16	1	364	56	24.26	0	3									0	
MM		2	2	0	65	39	32.50	0	0									1	
FC	1987	46	83	6	2611	140	33.90	7	11	56	47	0					5.03	14	
MM	1987	13	12	0	268	53	22.33	0	1									2	
BAKER, Robert Michael (Western Australia) b Osborne Park 24.7.1975 RHB SLA																			
FC		5	9	2	111	48	15.85	0	0	521	245	8	30.62	2-48	0	0	2.82	4	
MM		2	2	0	24	16	12.00	0	0	108	86	1	86.00	1-38	0	0	4.77	1	
FC	1994	12	21	3	433	83	24.05	0	2	1258	552	19	29.05	6-53	1	0	2.63	10	
MM	1995	7	7	1	121	55	20.16	0	1	168	136	1	136.00	1-38	0	0	4.85	2	
BAKKER, Jason Richard (Victoria) b Geelong 12.11.1967 RHB RM																			
FC		1	2	0	39	25	19.50	0	0	72	35	1	35.00	1-27	0	0	2.91	0	
MM		1	1	0	0	0	0.00	0	0									1	
FC	1994	7	12	0	245	75	20.41	0	1	852	393	13	30.23	4-40	0	0	2.76	3	
MM	1994	7	4	0	48	26	12.00	0	0	156	79	6	13.16	4-15	1	0	3.03	5	
BARSBY, Trevor John (Queensland) b Herston 16.1.1964 RHB																			
FC		11	19	1	765	111	42.50	2	5									13	
MM		6	6	0	64	26	10.66	0	0									1	
FC	1984	111	200	7	6913	165	35.81	15	35	96	63	1	63.00	1-8	0	0	3.93	76	
MM	1985	42	41	2	1145	101	29.35	1	10									10	
BAYLISS, Trevor Harley (New South Wales) b Goulburn 21.12.1961 RHB OB WK																			
MM		4	4	1	103	36	34.33	0	0	42	31	0					4.42	2	
FC	1985	58	96	10	3060	163	35.58	5	15	538	212	8	26.50	4-64	0	0	2.36	41	
MM	1986	34	32	4	677	92	24.17	0	2	143	108	5	21.60	2-13	0	0	4.53	7	
BERRY, Darren Shane (Victoria, Australia to England) b Melbourne 10.12.1969 RHB WK																			
FC		11	20	1	590	148	31.05	1	2									40	5
MM		6	4	0	36	18	9.00	0	0									7	5
FC	1989	86	126	17	2212	148	20.29	1	6									305	31
MM	1989	34	25	7	234	34	13.00	0	0									41	13

Cmp	Debut	M	I	NO	Runs	HS	Avge	100	50	Balls	Runs	Wkts	Avge	BB	5i	10m	RpO	ct	st

BEVAN, Michael Gwyl (New South Wales, Australia, Australian XI, Australia to India, Australia to South Africa, Australia to England, Australia to Sri Lanka) b Belconnen 8.5.1970 LHB SLA

Cmp	Debut	M	I	NO	Runs	HS	Avge	100	50	Balls	Runs	Wkts	Avge	BB	5i	10m	RpO	ct	st
Test		4	7	2	275	87*	55.00	0	3	459	265	15	17.66	6-82	1	1	3.46	2	
FC		7	12	3	561	150*	62.33	1	4	585	336	16	21.00	6-82	1	1	3.44	2	
Int		8	7	2	216	79*	43.20	0	1	288	194	6	32.33	3-36	0	0	1.98	3	
Test	1994	17	29	3	773	91	29.73	0	6	1129	629	27	23.29	6-82	1	1	3.34	8	
FC	1989	134	226	38	9750	203*	51.86	31	51	5069	3003	68	44.16	6-82	1	1	3.55	77	
Int	1993	59	53	19	1912	108*	56.23	2	11	1005	810	18	45.00	3-36	0	0	4.83	20	
MM	1989	25	25	10	841	93	56.06	0	7	36	34	2	17.00	2-24	0	0	5.66	7	

BICHEL, Andrew John (Queensland, Australia, Australian XI, Australia to South Africa, Australia to England) b Laidley 27.8.1970 RHB RFM

Cmp	Debut	M	I	NO	Runs	HS	Avge	100	50	Balls	Runs	Wkts	Avge	BB	5i	10m	RpO	ct	st
Test		2	3	0	40	18	13.33	0	0	224	143	1	143.00	1-31	0	0	3.83	0	
FC		6	6	0	103	58	17.16	0	1	1435	650	30	21.66	6-56	4	1	2.71	3	
Int		4	2	1	18	16*	18.00	0	0	212	157	4	39.25	3-17	0	0	4.44	1	
MM		4	1	0	8	8	8.00	0	0	233	157	5	31.40	2-27	0	0	4.04	3	
FC	1992	25	31	3	561	61*	20.03	0	2	4906	2614	103	25.37	6-56	7	1	3.19	15	
Int	1996	8	4	1	35	17	11.66	0	0	446	355	12	29.58	3-17	0	0	4.77	1	
MM	1992	15	7	2	25	8	5.00	0	0	750	523	15	34.86	4-45	1	0	4.18	8	

BLEWETT, Gregory Scott (South Australia, Australia, Australian XI, Australia to South Africa, Australia to England) b Adelaide 29.10.1971 RHB RM

Cmp	Debut	M	I	NO	Runs	HS	Avge	100	50	Balls	Runs	Wkts	Avge	BB	5i	10m	RpO	ct	st
Test		4	7	1	301	99	50.16	0	3	143	64	1	64.00	1-13	0	0	2.68	4	
FC		7	12	2	473	99	47.30	0	5	424	212	7	30.28	5-29	1	0	3.00	7	
Int		8	8	3	172	57*	34.40	0	1	191	123	5	24.60	2-34	0	0	3.86	4	
MM		3	3	0	65	61	21.66	0	1	156	119	2	59.50	1-55	0	0	4.57	0	
Test	1994	22	37	2	1421	214	40.60	4	7	542	277	4	69.25	2-25	0	0	3.06	26	
FC	1991	87	149	11	6438	268	46.65	18	33	4314	2263	55	41.14	5-29	1	0	3.14	62	
Int	1994	24	23	3	459	57*	22.95	0	2	658	551	12	45.91	2-34	0	0	5.02	7	
MM	1992	24	22	4	535	80*	29.72	0	3	954	769	16	48.06	2-30	0	0	4.83	10	

BOON, David Clarence (Tasmania, Durham) b Launceston 29.12.1960 RHB OB

Cmp	Debut	M	I	NO	Runs	HS	Avge	100	50	Balls	Runs	Wkts	Avge	BB	5i	10m	RpO	ct	st
FC		11	17	0	628	118	36.94	1	4	81	52	1	52.00	1-23	0	0	3.85	8	
MM		5	5	0	96	52	19.20	0	1									3	
Test	1984	107	190	20	7422	200	43.65	21	32	36	14	0					2.33	99	
FC	1978	296	496	44	20583	227	45.53	63	95	951	569	12	47.41	2-18	0	0	3.58	251	
Int	1983	181	177	16	5964	122	37.04	5	37	82	86	0					6.29	45	
MM	1978	44	42	2	1413	94	35.32	0	14	24	38	0					9.50	17	

BRAYSHAW, James Antony (South Australia) b Subiaco 11.5.1967 RHB RM

Cmp	Debut	M	I	NO	Runs	HS	Avge	100	50	Balls	Runs	Wkts	Avge	BB	5i	10m	RpO	ct	st
FC		4	8	0	234	96	29.25	0	2									0	
MM		3	3	0	79	37	26.33	0	0									0	
FC	1987	75	130	14	4934	146	42.53	10	29	1169	572	10	57.20	2-15	0	0	2.93	43	
MM	1989	27	23	3	452	101*	22.60	1	0	409	320	8	40.00	2-20	0	0	4.69	10	

CAMPBELL, Ryan John (Western Australia) b Osborne Park 7.2.1972 RHB WK

Cmp	Debut	M	I	NO	Runs	HS	Avge	100	50	Balls	Runs	Wkts	Avge	BB	5i	10m	RpO	ct	st
FC		11	19	1	672	113	37.33	1	6	18	16	0					5.33	13	1
MM		7	7	0	180	50	25.71	0	2									6	
FC	1994	12	21	2	718	113	37.78	1	6	18	16	0					5.33	14	2
MM	1995	11	11	0	217	50	19.72	0	2									8	

CARY, Sean Ross (Western Australia) b Subiaco 10.3.1971 RHB RFM

Cmp	Debut	M	I	NO	Runs	HS	Avge	100	50	Balls	Runs	Wkts	Avge	BB	5i	10m	RpO	ct	st
FC		2	2	1	11	8*	11.00	0	0	330	167	1	167.00	1-8	0	0	3.03	0	
MM		1								30	19	0					3.80	1	
FC	1994	14	15	6	70	12	7.77	0	0	2936	1441	34	42.38	3-35	0	0	2.94	4	
MM	1994	5	2	2	8	7*		0	0	228	163	3	54.33	1-15	0	0	4.28	1	

CASSELL, Jerry Lee (Queensland) b Mona Vale 12.1.1975 RHB SLA

Cmp	Debut	M	I	NO	Runs	HS	Avge	100	50	Balls	Runs	Wkts	Avge	BB	5i	10m	RpO	ct	st
FC		1	1	0	22	22	22.00	0	0									1	

CHEE QUEE, Richard (New South Wales) b Camperdown 4.1.1971 RHB

Cmp	Debut	M	I	NO	Runs	HS	Avge	100	50	Balls	Runs	Wkts	Avge	BB	5i	10m	RpO	ct	st
MM		6	6	0	163	52	27.16	0	1									4	
FC	1992	20	35	1	977	105	28.73	1	6									15	
MM	1993	17	17	1	725	131	45.31	1	5	6	3	0					3.00	8	

CORBETT, Troy Frederick (Victoria) b Ouyen 11.10.1972 RHB LFM

Cmp	Debut	M	I	NO	Runs	HS	Avge	100	50	Balls	Runs	Wkts	Avge	BB	5i	10m	RpO	ct	st
FC		2	2	1	1	1	1.00	0	0	426	238	4	59.50	2-60	0	0	3.35	1	
FC	1994	13	16	7	29	6*	3.22	0	0	2627	1405	34	41.32	6-42	2	0	3.20	4	
MM	1994	8	1	0	9	9	9.00	0	0	423	197	18	10.94	4-30	1	0	2.79	2	

COX, Jamie (Tasmania) b Burnie 15.10.1969 RHB

Cmp	Debut	M	I	NO	Runs	HS	Avge	100	50	Balls	Runs	Wkts	Avge	BB	5i	10m	RpO	ct	st
FC		11	21	1	1349	200	67.45	5	7									5	
MM		5	5	0	50	21	10.00	0	0									2	
FC	1987	91	165	9	6186	200	39.65	16	29	78	77	0					5.92	36	
MM	1988	27	26	1	539	75	21.56	0	4									4	

CRAIG, Shawn Andrew Jacob (Victoria) b Carlton 23.6.1973 LHB LBG

Cmp	Debut	M	I	NO	Runs	HS	Avge	100	50	Balls	Runs	Wkts	Avge	BB	5i	10m	RpO	ct	st
FC		2	4	0	132	90	33.00	0	1	210	161	1	161.00	1-31	0	0	4.60	3	
MM		1	1	0	15	15	15.00	0	0	24	33	2	16.50	2-33	0	0	8.25	0	

Cmp	Debut	M	I	NO	Runs	HS	Avge	100	50	Balls	Runs	Wkts	Avge	BB	5i	10m	RpO	ct	st

CREEVEY, Brendan Neville (Queensland) b Charleville 18.2.1970 RHB RFM

Cmp	Debut	M	I	NO	Runs	HS	Avge	100	50	Balls	Runs	Wkts	Avge	BB	5i	10m	RpO	ct	st
FC		7	10	2	113	48*	14.12	0	0	1189	588	22	26.72	6-70	2	0	2.96	2	
MM		5	3	2	39	19*	39.00	0	0	210	150	6	25.00	2-33	0	0	4.28	0	

DALE, Adam Craig (Queensland, Australia to South Africa) b Ivanhoe 30.12.1968 LHB RFM

Cmp	Debut	M	I	NO	Runs	HS	Avge	100	50	Balls	Runs	Wkts	Avge	BB	5i	10m	RpO	ct	st
FC		10	14	0	180	31	12.85	0	0	2729	927	42	22.07	6-38	2	0	2.03	2	
MM		7	2	1	2	2	2.00	0	0	366	225	9	25.00	4-48	1	0	3.68	0	
Int	1996	7	4	4	38	15*		0	0	390	275	8	34.37	3-18	0	0	4.23	3	
MM	1995	11	4	2	10	6	5.00	0	0	582	307	17	18.05	4-26	2	0	3.16	2	

DALY, Anthony John (Tasmania) b Newcastle 25.7.1969 RHB

Cmp	Debut	M	I	NO	Runs	HS	Avge	100	50	Balls	Runs	Wkts	Avge	BB	5i	10m	RpO	ct	st
FC		3	5	0	90	42	18.00	0	0									0	
FC	1994	13	25	3	579	70	26.31	0	0									7	
MM	1994	4	4	2	45	34*	22.50	0	0									2	

DAVISON, Rodney John (New South Wales) b Kogarah 26.6.1969 LHB LB

Cmp	Debut	M	I	NO	Runs	HS	Avge	100	50	Balls	Runs	Wkts	Avge	BB	5i	10m	RpO	ct	st
FC		7	13	2	464	99	42.18	0	4	19	16	0					5.05	6	
FC	1993	26	48	5	1457	133*	33.88	1	9	91	66	3	22.00	2-15	0	0	4.35	25	
MM	1993	2	2	0	63	51	31.50	0	1									1	

DI VENUTO, Michael James (Tasmania, Australia to South Africa) b Hobart 12.12.1973 LHB

Cmp	Debut	M	I	NO	Runs	HS	Avge	100	50	Balls	Runs	Wkts	Avge	BB	5i	10m	RpO	ct	st
FC		11	20	0	799	130	39.95	2	5	12	9	0					4.50	10	
MM		5	5	1	274	129*	68.50	1	1	12	11	1	11.00	1-11	0	0	5.50	0	
FC	1991	45	80	2	2985	154	38.26	7	15	228	157	0					4.13	32	
Int	1996	5	5	0	150	89	30.00	0	1									1	
MM	1992	22	21	3	671	129*	37.27	1	3	96	86	3	28.66	1-10	0	0	5.37	2	

DIXON, Troy James (Queensland) b Geelong 22.12.1969 LHB RM

Cmp	Debut	M	I	NO	Runs	HS	Avge	100	50	Balls	Runs	Wkts	Avge	BB	5i	10m	RpO	ct	st
FC		5	9	0	271	62	30.11	0	1									0	
FC	1993	7	13	0	427	122	32.84	1	1									0	

DODEMAIDE, Anthony Ian Christopher (Victoria) b Williamstown 5.10.1963 RHB RFM

Cmp	Debut	M	I	NO	Runs	HS	Avge	100	50	Balls	Runs	Wkts	Avge	BB	5i	10m	RpO	ct	st
FC		7	13	5	114	41*	14.25	0	0	1405	618	16	38.62	4-67	0	0	2.63	2	
MM		6	4	3	57	25*	57.00	0	0	354	175	6	29.16	2-28	0	0	2.96	1	
Test	1987	10	15	6	202	50	22.44	0	1	2184	953	34	28.02	6-58	1	0	2.61	6	
FC	1983	181	276	70	5957	123	28.91	5	27	36355	16872	510	31.83	6-58	17	0	2.78	88	
Int	1987	24	16	7	124	30	13.77	0	0	1327	753	36	20.91	5-21	1	1	3.40	7	
MM	1983	36	29	8	452	40	21.52	0	0	1977	1229	35	35.11	3-11	0	0	3.72	5	

EIME, Andrew Barry (South Australia) b North Adelaide 3.7.1971 RHB RFM

Cmp	Debut	M	I	NO	Runs	HS	Avge	100	50	Balls	Runs	Wkts	Avge	BB	5i	10m	RpO	ct	st
FC		1	2	0	7	5	3.50	0	0	136	89	3	29.66	2-58	0	0	3.92	0	

ELLIOTT, Matthew Thomas Gray (Victoria, Australia, Australian XI, Australia to South Africa, Australia to England) b Chelsea 28.9.1971 LHB LM

Cmp	Debut	M	I	NO	Runs	HS	Avge	100	50	Balls	Runs	Wkts	Avge	BB	5i	10m	RpO	ct	st
Test		2	4	1	128	78*	42.66	0	1									1	
FC		5	10	2	577	187	72.12	2	2	78	38	2	19.00	1-13	0	0	2.92	7	
MM		2	2	0	63	59	31.50	0	1									2	
Test	1996	11	19	1	866	199	48.11	2	4									2	
FC	1992	62	115	10	5512	203	52.49	16	27	228	170	3	56.66	1-13	0	0	4.47	67	
Int	1997	1	1	0	1	1	1.00	0	0									0	
MM	1992	21	20	2	475	64	26.38	0	3									12	

EMERY, Philip Allen (New South Wales) b St Ives 25.6.1964 LHB WK

Cmp	Debut	M	I	NO	Runs	HS	Avge	100	50	Balls	Runs	Wkts	Avge	BB	5i	10m	RpO	ct	st
FC		10	17	3	390	100*	27.85	1	0									25	1
MM		6	5	1	64	49	16.00	0	0									7	
Test	1994	1	1	1	8	8*		0	0									5	1
FC	1987	101	144	38	2729	100*	25.74	1	13	17	14	0					4.94	297	35
Int	1994	1	1	1	11	11*		0	0									3	
MM	1987	42	27	11	254	49	15.87	0	0									44	6

FARRELL, Michael Graeme (Tasmania) b Melbourne 24.9.1968 LHB OB

Cmp	Debut	M	I	NO	Runs	HS	Avge	100	50	Balls	Runs	Wkts	Avge	BB	5i	10m	RpO	ct	st
MM		5	4	2	25	12*	12.50	0	0	138	92	5	18.40	2-19	0	0	4.00	0	
FC	1989	25	39	2	730	96	19.72	0	4	2602	1205	22	54.77	3-93	0	0	2.77	31	
MM	1990	23	18	5	147	37	11.30	0	0	1002	696	18	38.66	2-19	0	0	4.16	6	

FAULL, Martin Peter (South Australia) b Darwin 10.5.1968 RHB RM

Cmp	Debut	M	I	NO	Runs	HS	Avge	100	50	Balls	Runs	Wkts	Avge	BB	5i	10m	RpO	ct	st
FC		8	16	0	459	68	28.68	0	6	12	14	0					7.00	6	
MM		3	3	0	52	38	17.33	0	0									1	
FC	1990	17	33	3	929	89	30.96	0	10	120	60	1	60.00	1-22	0	0	3.00	11	
MM	1992	6	6	0	69	38	11.50	0	0									1	

FITZGERALD, David Andrew (South Australia) b Osborne Park 30.11.1972 RHB RM

Cmp	Debut	M	I	NO	Runs	HS	Avge	100	50	Balls	Runs	Wkts	Avge	BB	5i	10m	RpO	ct	st
FC		2	4	0	15	8	3.75	0	0									0	
FC	1993	6	9	2	125	35	17.85	0	0									7	
MM	1994	1	1	0	32	32	32.00	0	0									0	

FLEMING, Damien William (Victoria, Australia to India, Australia to Sri Lanka) b Bentley 24.4.1970 RHB RFM

Cmp	Debut	M	I	NO	Runs	HS	Avge	100	50	Balls	Runs	Wkts	Avge	BB	5i	10m	RpO	ct	st
FC		9	16	6	136	36	13.60	0	0	1912	979	23	42.56	4-66	0	0	3.07	3	
MM		3	1	1	6	6*		0	0	174	101	5	20.20	2-25	0	0	3.48	1	
Test	1994	4	4	0	40	24	10.00	0	0	902	435	17	25.58	4-75	0	0	2.89	2	
FC	1989	64	80	26	786	63*	14.55	0	2	13945	6567	211	31.12	7-90	6	0	2.82	33	

Cmp	Debut	M	I	NO	Runs	HS	Avge	100	50	Balls	Runs	Wkts	Avge	BB	5i	10m	RpO	ct	st
Int	1993	27	9	6	19	5*	6.33	0	0	1356	995	40	24.87	5-36	2	1	4.40	5	
MM	1988	27	14	8	104	21	17.33	0	0	1461	893	32	27.90	3-25	0	0	3.66	7	

FOLEY, Geoffrey Ian (Queensland, MCC) b Jandowae 11.10.1967 LHB RM

Cmp	Debut	M	I	NO	Runs	HS	Avge	100	50	Balls	Runs	Wkts	Avge	BB	5i	10m	RpO	ct	st
FC		11	17	3	483	82*	34.50	0	4	1193	661	9	73.44	2-56	0	0	3.32	15	
MM		7	6	3	238	66	79.33	0	2	318	189	3	63.00	2-33	0	0	3.56	1	
FC	1989	29	48	5	1322	155	30.74	1	7	2985	1566	29	54.00	3-64	0	0	3.14	27	
MM	1989	16	14	4	307	66	30.70	0	2	619	416	12	34.66	4-34	1	0	4.03	4	

FOSTER, Michael Robert (Victoria) b East Melbourne 5.3.1973 RHB LBG

Cmp	Debut	M	I	NO	Runs	HS	Avge	100	50	Balls	Runs	Wkts	Avge	BB	5i	10m	RpO	ct	st
FC		6	12	1	151	32	13.72	0	0	6	0	0					0.00	8	
MM		3	2	1	44	31*	44.00	0	0									2	
FC	1994	7	14	1	160	32	12.30	0	0	6	0	0					0.00	8	

FREEDMAN, David Andrew (New South Wales) b Sydney 19.6.1964 RHB SLC

Cmp	Debut	M	I	NO	Runs	HS	Avge	100	50	Balls	Runs	Wkts	Avge	BB	5i	10m	RpO	ct	st
FC		6	9	2	84	23*	12.00	0	0	870	487	12	40.58	3-92	0	0	3.35	2	
FC	1991	44	49	15	509	54*	14.97	0	2	6967	3570	111	32.16	8-49	4	2	3.07	13	

GARNAUT, Matthew Stuart (Western Australia) b Subiaco 7.11.1973 RHB RFM

Cmp	Debut	M	I	NO	Runs	HS	Avge	100	50	Balls	Runs	Wkts	Avge	BB	5i	10m	RpO	ct	st
FC		10	11	4	40	10*	5.71	0	0	1914	953	23	41.43	4-51	0	0	2.98	3	

GEORGE, Shane Peter (South Australia) b Adelaide 20.10.1970 RHB RF

Cmp	Debut	M	I	NO	Runs	HS	Avge	100	50	Balls	Runs	Wkts	Avge	BB	5i	10m	RpO	ct	st
FC		7	11	2	75	19	8.33	0	0	1259	768	14	54.85	3-70	0	0	3.66	0	
MM		1	1	0	4	4	4.00	0	0	60	64	3	21.33	3-64	0	0	6.40	0	
FC	1987	52	64	14	450	62	9.00	0	2	9998	5903	150	39.35	6-51	2	0	3.54	15	
MM	1991	16	9	3	25	9	4.16	0	0	857	695	27	25.74	4-33	2	0	4.86	1	

GILCHRIST, Adam Craig (Western Australia, Australia, Australia to England, Australia to India, Australia to South Africa) b Bellingen 14.11.1971 LHB WK

Cmp	Debut	M	I	NO	Runs	HS	Avge	100	50	Balls	Runs	Wkts	Avge	BB	5i	10m	RpO	ct	st
FC		12	17	2	591	108*	39.40	1	2									60	2
MM		6	5	1	156	61*	39.00	0	1									13	1
FC	1992	55	84	15	2669	189*	38.68	5	11									220	11
Int	1996	10	9	1	231	77	28.87	0	2									4	1
MM	1992	21	19	3	559	76*	34.93	0	5									34	3

GILLESPIE, Jason Neil (South Australia, Australia, Australian XI, Australia to South Africa, Australia to England, Australia to India, Australia to Sri Lanka) b Darlinghurst 19.4.1975 RHB RFM

Cmp	Debut	M	I	NO	Runs	HS	Avge	100	50	Balls	Runs	Wkts	Avge	BB	5i	10m	RpO	ct	st
Test		2	3	2	22	16*	22.00	0	0	198	94	2	49.00	2-62	0	0	2.84	0	
FC		5	7	2	120	58	24.00	0	1	810	340	9	37.77	5-64	1	0	2.51	2	
Int		1								60	39	2	19.50	2-39	0	0	3.90	0	
MM		1	1	0	2	2	2.00	0	0	60	27	2	13.50	2-27	0	0	2.70	1	
Test	1996	9	14	7	86	28*	12.28	0	0	1370	713	32	22.28	7-37	2	0	3.12	3	
FC	1994	33	45	10	412	58	11.77	0	1	5788	2986	128	23.32	7-34	6	0	3.09	15	
Int	1996	14	8	2	65	26	10.83	0	0	757	607	13	46.69	2-39	0	0	4.81	0	
MM	1995	3	3	1	2	2	1.00	0	0	180	106	9	11.77	4-46	1	0	3.53	1	

GOODWIN, Murray William (Western Australia, Holland) b Salisbury, Rhodesia 11.12.1972 RHB LB

Cmp	Debut	M	I	NO	Runs	HS	Avge	100	50	Balls	Runs	Wkts	Avge	BB	5i	10m	RpO	ct	st
FC		5	9	2	428	127	61.14	1	3									9	
MM		3	2	1	21	13*	21.00	0	0									2	
FC	1994	14	25	4	926	127	44.09	1	6									17	
MM	1994	4	3	1	21	13*	10.50	0	0									2	

HARPER, Laurence Damien (Victoria) b Deniliquin 10.12.1970 LHB RM

Cmp	Debut	M	I	NO	Runs	HS	Avge	100	50	Balls	Runs	Wkts	Avge	BB	5i	10m	RpO	ct	st
FC		10	19	2	543	100*	31.94	1	3	126	68	1	68.00	1-34	0	0	3.23	5	
FC	1992	12	23	2	658	100*	31.33	1	5	126	68	1	68.00	1-34	0	0	3.23	6	

HARRITY, Mark Andrew (South Australia) b Semaphore 9.3.1974 RHB LF

Cmp	Debut	M	I	NO	Runs	HS	Avge	100	50	Balls	Runs	Wkts	Avge	BB	5i	10m	RpO	ct	st
FC		8	11	7	16	7*	4.00	0	0	1384	708	17	41.64	4-61	0	0	3.06	2	
MM		3	2	1	5	4*	5.00	0	0	180	116	5	23.20	3-26	0	0	3.86	0	
FC	1993	31	33	18	63	18	4.20	0	0	5555	3205	81	39.56	5-92	1	0	3.46	11	
MM	1995	4	3	2	7	4*	7.00	0	0	216	141	5	28.20	3-26	0	0	3.91	0	

HARVEY, Ian Joseph (Victoria) b Wonthaggi 10.4.1972 RHB RM

Cmp	Debut	M	I	NO	Runs	HS	Avge	100	50	Balls	Runs	Wkts	Avge	BB	5i	10m	RpO	ct	st
FC		11	21	1	491	88	24.55	0	5	1894	965	35	27.57	7-44	3	0	3.05	9	
MM		6	6	0	72	41	12.00	0	0	341	237	9	26.33	3-29	0	0	4.17	3	
FC	1993	28	50	2	1159	136	24.14	1	9	4110	2186	61	35.83	7-44	3	0	3.19	25	
MM	1993	22	18	2	278	43	17.37	0	0	874	612	23	26.60	3-18	0	0	4.20	5	

HARVEY, Kade Murray (Western Australia) b Subiaco 7.10.1975 RHB RM

Cmp	Debut	M	I	NO	Runs	HS	Avge	100	50	Balls	Runs	Wkts	Avge	BB	5i	10m	RpO	ct	st
FC		4	4	1	22	9	7.33	0	0	678	354	12	29.50	3-30	0	0	3.13	3	
MM		7	3	1	32	14*	16.00	0	0	340	243	18	13.50	4-37	1	0	4.28	0	
FC	1994	6	7	1	150	79	25.00	0	1	884	458	18	25.44	3-30	0	0	3.10	7	
MM	1994	11	5	1	56	20	14.00	0	0	534	391	22	17.77	4-37	1	0	4.39	0	

HATTON, Mark Aaron (Tasmania) b Waverley 24.1.1974 RHB SLA

Cmp	Debut	M	I	NO	Runs	HS	Avge	100	50	Balls	Runs	Wkts	Avge	BB	5i	10m	RpO	ct	st
FC		1	1	1	17	17*		0	0	72	47	1	47.00	1-47	0	0	3.91	1	
FC	1994	14	16	5	186	39*	16.90	0	0	2202	1423	28	50.82	5-113	1	0	3.87	3	
MM	1994	2								60	69	1	69.00	1-46	0	0	6.90	1	

Cmp	Debut	M	I	NO	Runs	HS	Avge	100	50	Balls	Runs	Wkts	Avge	BB	5i	10m	RpO	ct	st

HAYDEN, Matthew Lawrence (Queensland, Australia, Australian XI, Hampshire, Australia to South Africa) b Kingaroy 29.10.1971 LHB RM

Cmp	Debut	M	I	NO	Runs	HS	Avge	100	50	Balls	Runs	Wkts	Avge	BB	5i	10m	RpO	ct	st
Test		3	5	0	177	125	35.40	1	0									3	
FC		8	14	2	648	224	54.00	2	2									9	
MM		4	4	1	184	75*	61.33	0	2									2	
Test	1993	7	12	0	261	125	21.75	1	0									8	
FC	1991	108	194	23	9280	235*	54.26	28	39	371	282	4	70.50	2-17	0	0	4.56	92	
Int	1993	13	12	1	286	67	26.00	0	2									4	
MM	1992	17	17	4	757	121*	58.23	2	6									7	

HAYWOOD, Martin Thomas (New South Wales) b Tamworth 7.10.1969 RHB

Cmp	Debut	M	I	NO	Runs	HS	Avge	100	50	Balls	Runs	Wkts	Avge	BB	5i	10m	RpO	ct	st
MM		2	2	0	38	37	19.00	0	0	20	11	0					3.30	0	
FC	1991	13	20	0	456	97	22.80	0	3	11	6	0					3.27	6	
MM	1993	9	9	0	295	87	32.77	0	3	20	11	0					3.30	2	

HEALY, Ian Andrew (Queensland, Australia, Australia to India, Australia to South Africa, Australia to England, Australia to Sri Lanka) b Spring Hill 30.4.1964 RHB WK

Cmp	Debut	M	I	NO	Runs	HS	Avge	100	50	Balls	Runs	Wkts	Avge	BB	5i	10m	RpO	ct	st
Test		5	9	3	356	161*	59.33	1	0									15	
FC		7	11	3	452	161*	56.50	1	1									23	
Int		8	5	2	44	22*	14.66	0	0									10	5
Test	1988	94	143	19	3470	161*	27.98	3	18									307	22
FC	1986	183	266	56	6717	161*	31.98	3	32	7	2	0					1.71	566	49
Int	1988	168	120	36	1764	56	21.00	0	4									195	39
MM	1987	20	12	2	190	48	19.00	0	0									25	7

HILLS, Dene Fleetwood (Tasmania) b Wynyard 27.8.1970 LHB

Cmp	Debut	M	I	NO	Runs	HS	Avge	100	50	Balls	Runs	Wkts	Avge	BB	5i	10m	RpO	ct	st
FC		11	21	2	701	124*	36.89	2	4	6	2	0					2.00	9	
MM		2	2	0	69	39	34.50	0	0									0	
FC	1991	65	121	6	4743	220*	41.24	12	28	36	17	0					2.83	43	
MM	1992	17	17	1	599	81	37.43	0	5									3	

HODGE, Bradley John (Victoria) b Sandringham 29.12.1974 RHB OB

Cmp	Debut	M	I	NO	Runs	HS	Avge	100	50	Balls	Runs	Wkts	Avge	BB	5i	10m	RpO	ct	st
FC		7	14	0	282	51	20.14	0	2	324	206	4	51.50	2-41	0	0	3.81	7	
MM		5	5	0	103	50	20.60	0	1	42	36	0					5.14	2	
FC	1993	33	63	5	1904	116	32.82	3	11	490	321	8	40.12	2-41	0	0	3.93	17	
MM	1993	19	18	3	349	78*	23.26	0	2	90	62	1	62.00	1-3	0	0	4.13	6	

HOGG, George Bradley (Western Australia, Australian XI, Australia to India, Australia to Sri Lanka) b Narrogin 6.2.1971 LHB SLC

Cmp	Debut	M	I	NO	Runs	HS	Avge	100	50	Balls	Runs	Wkts	Avge	BB	5i	10m	RpO	ct	st
FC		10	11	1	226	59	22.60	0	1	1414	814	16	50.87	3-73	0	0	3.45	6	
MM		5	4	1	37	18	12.33	0	0	36	23	0					3.83	4	
Test	1996	1	2	0	5	4	2.50	0	0	102	69	1	69.00	1-69	0	0	4.05	0	
FC	1993	35	52	10	1093	111*	26.02	2	6	3837	1993	40	49.82	5-59	2	0	3.11	22	
Int	1996	7	7	4	38	11*	12.66	0	0	295	218	3	72.66	1-23	0	0	4.43	2	
MM	1993	19	17	4	233	33	17.92	0	0	293	224	5	44.80	2-46	0	0	4.58	10	

HOLDSWORTH, Wayne John (New South Wales) b Paddington 5.10.1968 RHB RF

Cmp	Debut	M	I	NO	Runs	HS	Avge	100	50	Balls	Runs	Wkts	Avge	BB	5i	10m	RpO	ct	st
MM		2	2	1	5	3	5.00	0	0	96	65	0					4.06	0	
FC	1988	68	67	16	399	34	7.82	0	0	11525	6945	212	32.75	7-41	11	1	3.61	28	
MM	1989	27	11	8	77	49*	25.66	0	0	1295	891	30	29.70	5-28	0	1	4.12	6	

HUSSEY, Michael Edward (Western Australia) b Morley 27.5.1975 LHB LBG

Cmp	Debut	M	I	NO	Runs	HS	Avge	100	50	Balls	Runs	Wkts	Avge	BB	5i	10m	RpO	ct	st
FC		12	22	2	928	147	46.40	2	5	6	2	0					2.00	5	
MM		4	4	0	119	82	29.75	0	1									2	
FC	1994	25	47	3	1889	147	42.93	4	8	6	2	0					2.00	14	

HUTCHISON, Paul James (Tasmania) b Glen Innes 17.2.1968 RHB RFM

Cmp	Debut	M	I	NO	Runs	HS	Avge	100	50	Balls	Runs	Wkts	Avge	BB	5i	10m	RpO	ct	st
FC		1	1	1	6	6*		0	0	84	77	0					5.50	1	
MM		1								60	27	5	5.40	5-27	0	1	2.70	1	
FC	1991	6	9	2	59	14	8.42	0	0	982	598	14	42.71	5-87	1	0	3.65	1	
MM	1992	8	3	3	31	22*		0	0	360	249	8	31.12	5-27	0	1	4.15	2	

JACKSON, Paul William (Queensland) b East Melbourne 1.11.1961 RHB SLA

Cmp	Debut	M	I	NO	Runs	HS	Avge	100	50	Balls	Runs	Wkts	Avge	BB	5i	10m	RpO	ct	st
FC		10	13	6	152	49	21.71	0	0	2108	789	23	34.30	5-85	1	0	2.24	3	
FC	1985	84	96	38	656	49	11.31	0	0	19070	7718	203	38.01	6-55	2	0	2.42	24	
MM	1985	22	12	8	69	17*	17.25	0	0	1180	820	30	27.33	4-26	1	0	4.16	4	

JOHNSON, Benjamin Andrew (South Australia) b Naracoorte 1.8.1973 LHB RM

Cmp	Debut	M	I	NO	Runs	HS	Avge	100	50	Balls	Runs	Wkts	Avge	BB	5i	10m	RpO	ct	st
FC		7	14	1	331	91	25.46	0	2	223	150	2	75.00	2-40	0	0	4.03	5	
MM		4	4	0	54	37	13.50	0	0	77	58	3	19.33	3-46	0	0	4.51	3	
FC	1994	20	38	1	1179	168	31.86	1	8	901	534	16	33.37	3-16	0	0	3.55	11	
MM	1994	6	6	0	65	37	10.83	0	0	149	126	4	31.50	3-46	0	0	5.07	5	

JONES, Dean Mervyn (Victoria, Derbyshire) b Coburg 24.3.1961 RHB RM

Cmp	Debut	M	I	NO	Runs	HS	Avge	100	50	Balls	Runs	Wkts	Avge	BB	5i	10m	RpO	ct	st
FC		7	13	0	521	152	40.07	2	1	90	64	1	64.00	1-26	0	0	4.26	3	
MM		2	2	2	193	100*		1	1									1	
Test	1983	52	89	11	3631	216	46.55	11	14	198	64	1	64.00	1-5	0	0	1.93	34	
FC	1981	234	394	41	18292	324*	51.81	52	83	2704	1533	27	56.77	5-112	1	0	3.40	182	
Int	1983	164	161	25	6068	145	44.61	7	46	106	81	3	27.00	2-34	0	0	4.58	54	
MM	1981	48	46	9	1844	139*	49.83	4	9	342	278	8	34.75	2-30	0	0	4.87	24	

Cmp	Debut	M	I	NO	Runs	HS	Avge	100	50	Balls	Runs	Wkts	Avge	BB	5i	10m	RpO	ct	st

JONES, Neil Richard (New South Wales) b Stourport-on-Severn, England 12.7.1966 RHB RFM

Cmp	Debut	M	I	NO	Runs	HS	Avge	100	50	Balls	Runs	Wkts	Avge	BB	5i	10m	RpO	ct	st
MM		1	1	1	4	4*		0	0	60	44	1	44.00	1-44	0	0	4.40	0	
FC	1994	1	2	1	13	13	13.00	0	0	126	73	0					3.47	0	

JULIAN, Brendon Paul (Western Australia, Australia to England, Australia to South Africa) b Hamilton, New Zealand 10.8.1970 RHB LFM

FC		9	11	2	178	51	19.77	0	1	1908	908	35	25.94	7-48	2	1	2.85	6	
MM		5	4	2	32	15	16.00	0	0	162	131	6	21.83	3-24	0	0	4.85	3	
Test	1993	7	9	1	128	56*	16.00	0	1	1098	599	15	39.93	4-36	0	0	3.27	4	
FC	1989	105	143	24	2785	119	23.40	2	14	18043	10080	330	30.54	7-48	19	2	3.35	65	
Int	1993	3	2	0	11	11	5.50	0	0	174	169	5	33.80	3-50	0	0	5.82	0	
MM	1991	32	24	4	232	48*	11.60	0	0	1568	1124	44	25.54	4-43	1	0	4.30	8	

KASPROWICZ, Michael Scott (Queensland, Australia, Australia to England) b South Brisbane 10.2.1972 RHB RF

Test		2	2	0	27	21	13.50	0	0	288	126	0					2.62	0	
FC		11	15	3	154	26	12.83	0	0	2800	1226	48	25.54	5-64	3	0	2.62	5	
MM		5	2	0	11	7	5.50	0	0	284	156	5	31.20	2-30	0	0	3.29	2	
Test	1996	5	6	0	48	21	8.00	0	0	849	436	14	31.14	7-36	1	0	3.08	2	
FC	1989	88	113	19	1343	49	14.28	0	0	17894	9459	344	27.49	7-36	22	2	3.17	36	
Int	1995	5	2	2	45	28*		0	0	242	208	5	41.60	1-27	0	0	5.15	0	
MM	1989	25	13	2	115	34	10.45	0	0	1278	865	30	28.83	4-21	1	0	4.06	8	

KATICH, Simon Mathew (Western Australia) b Middle Swan 21.8.1975 LHB SLC

FC		2	4	1	131	65*	43.66	0	1									2	
MM		1	1	0	2	2	2.00	0	0									0	
MM	1995	3	3	0	8	5	2.66	0	0									2	

KIMBER, Adam Patrick (South Australia) b North Adelaide 30.9.1969 RHB

| FC | | 2 | 4 | 0 | 54 | 27 | 13.50 | 0 | 0 | | | | | | | | | 3 | |

LANGER, Justin Lee (Western Australia, Australia, Australia to South Africa, Australia to England) b Perth 21.11.1970 LHB RM WK

Test		2	3	0	31	19	10.33	0	0									0	
FC		8	14	4	771	274*	77.10	3	1									2	
MM		4	4	0	101	54	25.25	0	1									2	
Test	1992	8	12	0	272	69	22.66	0	3									2	
FC	1991	77	134	16	5920	274*	50.16	17	23	60	30	0					3.00	59	
Int	1993	8	7	2	160	36	32.00	0	0									2	1
MM	1992	27	26	3	830	93*	36.08	0	7									11	

LARKIN, Rohan Patrick (Victoria) b Seymour 19.10.1969 RHB OB

FC		6	12	0	423	104	35.25	1	3	54	31	0					3.44	4	
MM		4	4	0	76	61	19.00	0	1	6	7	0					7.00	1	
FC	1994	16	30	0	952	116	31.73	2	5	54	31	0					3.44	9	
MM	1992	8	8	0	168	61	21.00	0	1	6	7	0					7.00	4	

LAVENDER, Mark Philip (Western Australia, MCC) b Madras, India 28.8.1967 RHB RM

FC		4	7	0	126	51	18.00	0	1									0	
MM		2	2	0	75	75	37.50	0	1									0	
FC	1990	52	98	8	3079	173*	34.21	6	14	42	15	0					2.14	47	
MM	1991	22	20	0	742	100	37.10	1	6									6	

LAW, Stuart Grant (Queensland, Australian XI, Australia, Essex, Australia to Sri Lanka, Australia to India, Australia to South Africa) b Herston 18.10.1968 RHB RM/LBG

FC		10	16	3	617	144	47.46	1	5	504	220	5	44.00	1-16	0	0	2.61	15	
Int		7	6	0	200	93	33.33	0	1	60	53	2	26.50	2-22	0	0	5.30	2	
MM		4	4	0	149	93	37.25	0	1	66	51	0					4.63	1	
Test	1995	1	1	1	54	54*		0	1	18	9	0					3.00	1	
FC	1988	133	224	23	9522	179	47.37	27	50	6152	2963	64	46.29	5-39	1	0	2.86	135	
Int	1994	44	42	3	1145	110	29.35	1	7	747	572	12	47.66	2-22	0	0	4.59	10	
MM	1988	34	31	4	1107	159	41.00	4	2	572	428	14	30.57	4-33	2	0	4.48	11	

LEE, Shane (New South Wales, Australia to England) b Wollongong 8.8.1973 RHB RM

FC		9	17	2	506	101*	33.73	1	2	767	438	12	26.50	3-15	0	0	3.42	8	
MM		6	6	0	129	63	21.50	0	1	281	211	8	26.37	2-28	0	0	4.50	2	
FC	1992	51	83	16	2968	167*	44.29	9	14	6141	3838	92	41.71	4-20	0	0	3.74	41	
Int	1995	8	6	1	61	39	12.20	0	0	324	207	4	51.75	1-20	0	0	3.83	5	
MM	1992	19	17	3	309	63	22.07	0	1	821	628	24	26.16	4-59	1	0	4.58	7	

LEHMANN, Darren Scott (South Australia, Australian XI, Australia, Yorkshire, Australia to Sri Lanka) b Gawler 5.2.1970 LHB SLA

FC		11	19	1	960	255	53.33	2	3	128	110	0					5.15	7	
Int		1	1	0	10	10	10.00	0	0	12	10	0					5.00	1	
MM		5	5	0	117	65	23.40	0	1	39	46	0					7.07	2	
FC	1987	115	200	11	9792	255	51.80	29	48	1454	730	12	60.83	2-15	0	0	3.01	67	
Int	1996	3	3	0	27	15	9.00	0	0	78	65	1	65.00	1-29	0	0	5.00	2	
MM	1988	41	40	3	1354	142*	36.59	3	8	235	207	3	69.00	1-26	0	0	5.28	14	

LODDING, Brent Andrew (Victoria) b Upper Ferntree Gully 20.3.1973 LHB OB

| FC | | 2 | 4 | 0 | 33 | 18 | 8.25 | 0 | 0 | | | | | | | | | 1 | |

Cmp	Debut	M	I	NO	Runs	HS	Avge	100	50	Balls	Runs	Wkts	Avge	BB	5i	10m	RpO	ct	st
LOVE, Martin Lloyd (Queensland) b Mundubbera 30.3.1974 RHB																			
FC		3	5	0	179	46	35.80	0	0										9	
MM		4	4	1	119	58*	39.66	0	1										0	
FC	1992	46	82	4	3329	187	42.27	9	12										53	
MM	1993	19	18	3	406	58*	27.06	0	1										5	
LOWERY, Daniel Wayne (Victoria) b Geelong 1.6.1974 LHB RMF																			
MM		3								126	97	5	19.40	3-51	0	0	4.61	1	
MacGILL, Stuart Charles Glyndwr (New South Wales, Somerset) b Mount Lawley 25.2.1971 RHB LBG																			
FC		7	10	5	47	11*	9.40	0	0	1143	592	16	37.00	4-72	0	0	3.10	3	
FC	1993	9	14	6	90	25	11.25	0	0	1533	806	20	40.30	4-72	0	0	3.15	3	
McGINTY, Adam David (Victoria) b Melbourne 24.3.1971 LHB RFM																			
FC		1	2	1	1	1*	1.00	0	0	90	67	2	33.50	2-67	0	0	4.46	0	
FC	1995	2	3	1	5	4	2.50	0	0	302	146	4	36.50	2-67	0	0	2.90	2	
MM	1994	1								60	46	0					4.60	0	
McGRATH, Glenn Donald (New South Wales, Australia, Australia to India, Australia to South Africa, Australia to England, Australia to Sri Lanka) b Dubbo 9.2.1970 RHB RFM																			
Test		5	7	2	32	24	6.40	0	0	1205	453	26	17.42	5-50	1	0	2.25	2	
FC		6	9	2	50	24	7.14	0	0	1379	567	29	19.55	5-50	1	0	2.46	2	
Int		6	3	2	1	1	1.00	0	0	342	210	3	70.00	2-45	0	0	3.68	2	
Test	1993	34	40	13	106	24	3.92	0	0	8133	3636	155	23.45	8-38	8	0	2.68	8	
FC	1992	65	64	22	181	24	4.30	0	0	14483	6353	273	23.27	8-38	13	1	2.63	13	
Int	1993	69	23	12	45	10	4.09	0	0	3711	2442	85	28.72	5-52	3	1	3.94	8	
MM	1992	6								342	157	11	14.27	4-17	1	0	2.75	1	
McINTYRE, Peter Edward (South Australia, Australia to India) b Gisborne 27.4.1966 RHB LBG																			
FC		10	17	2	59	23	3.93	0	0	2957	1413	35	40.37	6-64	2	1	2.86	2	
Test	1994	2	4	1	22	16	7.33	0	0	393	194	5	38.80	3-103	0	0	2.96	0	
FC	1988	72	93	25	475	32	6.98	0	0	19125	9417	234	40.24	6-43	8	2	2.95	28	
MM	1993	1								60	53	0					5.30	0	
McNAMARA, Bradley Edward (New South Wales) b Sydney 30.12.1965 RHB RM																			
FC		8	12	2	385	137*	38.50	1	2	1412	741	33	22.45	5-19	3	0	3.14	2	
MM		6	5	2	107	63	35.66	0	1	310	216	11	19.63	6-25	0	1	4.18	2	
FC	1989	53	86	12	2017	137*	27.25	2	10	6058	2813	105	26.79	6-43	5	0	2.78	33	
MM	1989	30	23	8	362	65*	24.13	0	2	1488	937	44	21.29	6-25	0	1	3.77	8	
MAHER, James Patrick (Queensland) b Innistail 27.2.1974 LHB RM																			
FC		11	19	2	532	95	31.29	0	4	132	85	2	42.50	1-17	0	0	3.86	17	
MM		7	7	1	335	111*	55.83	1	1	6	6	0					6.00	2	
FC	1993	44	76	10	2367	122	35.86	3	12	546	300	9	33.33	3-11	0	0	3.29	48	
MM	1993	19	19	6	645	111*	49.61	1	3	91	87	2	43.50	2-43	0	0	5.73	6	
MARQUET, Joshua Phillip (Tasmania) b Melbourne 3.12.1969 RHB RF																			
FC		9	7	5	5	4	2.50	0	0	1736	1028	25	41.12	4-107	0	0	3.55	5	
MM		3	3	1	6	6	3.00	0	0	174	160	1	160.00	1-43	0	0	5.51	1	
FC	1994	20	17	9	20	10	2.50	0	0	4105	2388	57	41.89	5-94	1	0	3.49	8	
MM	1994	8	5	2	7	6	2.33	0	0	468	338	12	28.16	5-23	0	1	4.33	4	
MARSH, Daniel James (Tasmania) b Subiaco 14.6.1973 RHB SLA																			
FC		11	19	5	500	97	35.71	0	3	2112	955	22	43.40	3-55	0	0	2.71	10	
MM		4	4	1	87	30	29.00	0	0	162	119	1	119.00	1-31	0	0	4.40	1	
FC	1993	15	25	7	597	97	33.16	0	3	3078	1435	32	44.84	3-55	0	0	2.79	11	
MM	1993	13	13	5	229	55*	28.62	0	1	666	509	5	101.80	1-31	0	0	4.58	5	
MARTYN, Damien Richard (Western Australia) b Darwin 21.10.1971 RHB RM																			
FC		12	20	1	701	108	36.89	2	3	318	144	3	48.00	1-12	0	0	2.71	11	
MM		7	7	1	219	53	36.50	0	2	48	19	2	9.50	2-19	0	0	2.37	3	
Test	1992	7	12	1	317	74	28.81	0	3	6	0	0					0.00	1	
FC	1990	90	152	18	5959	203*	44.47	17	29	1512	720	13	55.38	3-29	0	0	2.85	65	2
Int	1992	11	10	1	166	51*	18.44	0	1									6	
MM	1991	35	33	6	1016	114*	37.62	1	8	269	205	11	18.63	3-3	0	0	4.57	12	
MASON, Matthew Sean (Western Australia) b Claremont 20.3.1974 RHB RFM																			
FC		1	2	0	5	3	2.50	0	0	138	72	1	72.00	1-72	0	0	3.13	1	
MM		1	1	0	2	2	2.00	0	0	60	42	1	42.00	1-42	0	0	4.20	0	
MATTHEWS, Gregory Richard John (New South Wales) b Newcastle 15.12.1959 LHB OB																			
FC		10	15	1	403	109*	28.78	1	1	1579	620	18	34.44	6-66	1	0	2.35	8	
MM		6	4	1	44	21	14.66	0	0	256	142	3	47.33	1-21	0	0	3.32	1	
Test	1983	33	53	8	1849	130	41.08	4	12	6271	2942	61	48.22	5-103	2	1	2.81	17	
FC	1982	187	277	50	8766	184	38.61	13	48	38389	16073	511	31.45	8-52	22	5	2.51	149	
Int	1983	59	50	13	619	54	16.72	0	1	2808	2004	57	35.15	3-27	0	0	4.28	23	
MM	1982	47	37	9	578	61*	20.64	0	2	2188	1384	47	29.44	3-29	0	0	3.79	13	
MILLER, Colin Reid (Tasmania) b Footscray 6.2.1964 RHB RFM/OB																			
FC		10	13	3	172	41	17.20	0	0	2601	1143	32	35.71	4-48	0	0	2.63	4	
MM		4	4	0	31	20	7.75	0	0	216	160	0					4.44	1	

Cmp	Debut	M	I	NO	Runs	HS	Avge	100	50	Balls	Runs	Wkts	Avge	BB	5i	10m	RpO	ct	st
FC	1985	60	75	14	872	59	14.29	0	1	12937	6420	191	33.61	7-83	5	0	2.97	18	
MM	1988	23	16	3	157	32	12.07	0	0	1273	911	23	39.60	4-48	1	0	4.29	7	

MOODY, Thomas Masson (Western Australia, Australia, Worcestershire) b Adelaide 2.10.1965 RHB RM

Cmp	Debut	M	I	NO	Runs	HS	Avge	100	50	Balls	Runs	Wkts	Avge	BB	5i	10m	RpO	ct	st
FC		9	14	1	621	152	47.76	3	1	2146	926	38	24.36	7-41	1	0	2.58	14	
Int		6	4	1	15	8	5.00	0	0	269	203	5	40.60	2-25	0	0	4.52	1	
MM		7	7	3	232	102*	58.00	1	0	368	178	11	16.18	4-30	1	0	2.90	0	
Test	1989	8	14	0	456	106	32.57	2	3	432	147	2	73.50	1-17	0	0	2.04	9	
FC	1985	258	429	35	18555	272	47.09	56	84	18288	8424	269	31.31	7-38	7	2	2.76	258	
Int	1987	40	36	4	766	89	23.93	0	7	1163	854	21	40.66	3-56	0	0	4.40	11	
MM	1985	54	53	9	1338	102*	30.40	2	7	2546	1651	55	30.01	4-30	1	0	3.89	17	

MOTT, Matthew Peter (Queensland) b Charleville 3.10.1973 LHB RM

Cmp	Debut	M	I	NO	Runs	HS	Avge	100	50	Balls	Runs	Wkts	Avge	BB	5i	10m	RpO	ct	st
FC		6	10	0	590	150	59.00	1	5	54	41	0					4.55	5	
MM		3	2	0	9	6	4.50	0	0	6	5	0					5.00	1	
FC	1994	12	21	0	804	150	38.28	1	6	78	55	0					4.23	11	
MM	1995	4	3	0	32	23	10.66	0	0	6	5	0					5.00	2	

MULDER, Bret (Western Australia) b Subiaco 6.2.1964 RHB OB

Cmp	Debut	M	I	NO	Runs	HS	Avge	100	50	Balls	Runs	Wkts	Avge	BB	5i	10m	RpO	ct	st
FC		7	7	2	52	25*	10.40	0	0	1454	578	23	25.13	6-65	2	1	2.38	4	
FC	1983	21	18	8	90	25*	9.00	0	0	4286	1807	55	32.85	6-65	3	1	2.52	12	

MULLER, Scott Andrew (Queensland) b Herston 11.7.1971 RHB RFM

Cmp	Debut	M	I	NO	Runs	HS	Avge	100	50	Balls	Runs	Wkts	Avge	BB	5i	10m	RpO	ct	st
FC		8	10	3	61	19*	8.71	0	0	1299	645	21	30.71	5-76	1	0	2.97	5	
FC	1995	9	12	4	66	19*	8.25	0	0	1443	730	23	31.73	5-76	1	0	3.03	5	

NICHOLSON, Matthew James (Western Australia) b St Leonards 2.10.1974 RHB RFM

Cmp	Debut	M	I	NO	Runs	HS	Avge	100	50	Balls	Runs	Wkts	Avge	BB	5i	10m	RpO	ct	st
FC		3	3	0	15	10	5.00	0	0	604	323	7	46.14	3-94	0	0	3.20	0	

NIELSEN, Timothy John (South Australia) b Forest Gate, England 5.5.1968 RHB WK OB

Cmp	Debut	M	I	NO	Runs	HS	Avge	100	50	Balls	Runs	Wkts	Avge	BB	5i	10m	RpO	ct	st
FC		11	20	2	521	110*	28.94	1	1									34	
MM		5	4	0	52	35	13.00	0	0									9	
FC	1990	80	134	22	3174	115	28.33	3	14	72	49	1	49.00	1-2	0	0	4.08	229	28
MM	1991	31	25	2	423	57	18.39	0	1									37	1

NIKITARAS, Steven (New South Wales) b Port Kembla 31.8.1970 RHB LFM

Cmp	Debut	M	I	NO	Runs	HS	Avge	100	50	Balls	Runs	Wkts	Avge	BB	5i	10m	RpO	ct	st
FC		2	3	0	13	12	4.33	0	0	288	199	5	39.80	3-76	0	0	4.14	2	
MM		2	1	0	0	0	0.00	0	0	90	72	0					4.80	2	

PARKER, Geoffrey Ross (South Australia) b Malvern 31.3.1968 RHB RM

Cmp	Debut	M	I	NO	Runs	HS	Avge	100	50	Balls	Runs	Wkts	Avge	BB	5i	10m	RpO	ct	st
FC		10	19	2	500	112	29.41	1	3	144	86	2	43.00	1-34	0	0	3.58	7	
MM		5	5	3	114	42*	57.00	0	0	132	93	0					4.22	0	
FC	1985	28	50	5	1139	112	25.31	1	7	405	207	6	34.50	2-30	0	0	3.06	24	
MM	1985	15	15	3	277	83	23.08	0	1	246	194	0					4.73	1	

PEAKE, Clinton John (Victoria) b Geelong 25.3.1977 LHB SLA

Cmp	Debut	M	I	NO	Runs	HS	Avge	100	50	Balls	Runs	Wkts	Avge	BB	5i	10m	RpO	ct	st
MM		1	1	0	2	2	2.00	0	0	30	13	0					2.60	0	
FC	1995	6	11	1	237	46	23.70	0	0	79	71	2	35.50	1-11	0	0	5.39	4	
MM	1995	2	2	1	5	3*	5.00	0	0	30	13	0					2.60	0	

PONTING, Ricky Thomas (Tasmania, Australia, Australia to India, Australia to England, Australia to Sri Lanka) b Launceston 19.12.1974 RHB OB

Cmp	Debut	M	I	NO	Runs	HS	Avge	100	50	Balls	Runs	Wkts	Avge	BB	5i	10m	RpO	ct	st
Test		2	4	0	110	88	27.50	0	1	11	0	1	0.00	1-0	0	0	0.00	2	
FC		10	18	2	960	159	60.00	3	4	107	53	1	53.00	1-0	0	0	2.97	10	
Int		3	3	0	68	44	22.66	0	0									0	
MM		3	3	0	112	64	37.33	0	1	61	58	3	19.33	3-34	0	0	5.70	2	
Test	1995	9	15	0	571	127	38.06	1	3	35	8	2	4.00	1-0	0	0	1.37	10	
FC	1992	67	114	14	5366	211	53.66	18	24	567	345	5	69.00	1-0	0	0	3.65	58	
Int	1994	33	33	3	929	123	30.96	2	5									4	
MM	1992	18	18	2	495	87*	30.93	0	3	121	101	3	33.66	3-34	0	0	5.00	7	

PRESTWIDGE, Scott Arthur (Queensland) b Bankstown 15.5.1968 RHB RFM

Cmp	Debut	M	I	NO	Runs	HS	Avge	100	50	Balls	Runs	Wkts	Avge	BB	5i	10m	RpO	ct	st
FC		1	1	1	22	22*		0	0	102	61	3	20.33	2-16	0	0	3.58	0	
MM		7	3	0	46	28	15.33	0	0	332	232	11	21.09	4-43	1	0	4.19	3	
FC	1991	3	5	2	118	48*	39.33	0	0	510	325	7	46.42	2-16	0	0	3.82	1	
MM	1992	17	12	2	182	33	18.20	0	0	837	633	26	24.34	4-43	2	0	4.53	4	

REIFFEL, Paul Ronald (Victoria, Australia, Australia to India, Australia to South Africa, Australia to England, Australia to Sri Lanka) b Box Hill 19.4.1966 RHB RFM

Cmp	Debut	M	I	NO	Runs	HS	Avge	100	50	Balls	Runs	Wkts	Avge	BB	5i	10m	RpO	ct	st
Test		3	6	0	44	20	7.33	0	0	613	305	12	25.41	5-73	1	0	2.98	2	
FC		6	11	2	115	24*	12.77	0	0	1351	596	20	29.80	5-73	1	0	2.64	3	
Int		4	2	0	4	3	2.00	0	0	183	104	2	52.00	2-26	0	0	3.40	1	
Test	1991	29	41	12	648	56	22.34	0	3	5293	2401	91	26.38	6-71	5	0	2.72	14	
FC	1987	115	137	42	2137	86	22.49	0	8	22623	10349	374	27.67	6-57	14	2	2.74	58	
Int	1991	75	48	19	441	58	15.20	0	1	3898	2526	90	28.06	4-13	5	0	3.88	23	
MM	1987	19	10	3	108	35*	15.42	0	0	998	631	19	33.21	4-14	1	0	3.79	5	

RICCI, Brendan Paul (Victoria) b Fitzroy 24.4.1965 RHB LBG

Cmp	Debut	M	I	NO	Runs	HS	Avge	100	50	Balls	Runs	Wkts	Avge	BB	5i	10m	RpO	ct	st
FC		1	2	0	46	43	23.00	0	0	60	34	0					3.40	1	
MM		3	3	0	67	29	22.33	0	0	13	20	0					9.23	0	

Cmp	Debut	M	I	NO	Runs	HS	Avge	100	50	Balls	Runs	Wkts	Avge	BB	5i	10m	RpO	ct	st
FC	1995	4	8	0	144	55	18.00	0	1	60	34	0					3.40	4	
MM	1995	5	5	0	110	42	22.00	0	0	13	20	0					9.23	1	

RICHARDS, Corey John (New South Wales) b Camden 25.8.1975 RHB RM

Cmp	Debut	M	I	NO	Runs	HS	Avge	100	50	Balls	Runs	Wkts	Avge	BB	5i	10m	RpO	ct	st
FC		6	11	0	292	76	26.54	0	2									5	
MM		5	5	0	159	109	31.80	1	0									0	
FC	1995	11	21	0	468	76	22.28	0	2									7	

RIDGWAY, Mark William (Tasmania) b Warragul 21.5.1961 LHB RFM

Cmp	Debut	M	I	NO	Runs	HS	Avge	100	50	Balls	Runs	Wkts	Avge	BB	5i	10m	RpO	ct	st
FC		8	9	3	50	21	8.33	0	0	1791	978	28	34.92	6-88	1	0	3.27	2	
MM		2	1	0	18	18	18.00	0	0	102	83	5	16.60	4-37	1	0	4.88	0	
FC	1993	23	26	10	209	70	13.06	0	1	5182	2990	87	34.36	6-29	4	0	3.46	9	
MM	1993	11	4	1	58	32	14.50	0	0	642	472	17	27.76	4-37	1	0	4.41	3	

ROACH, Peter John (Victoria) b Kew 19.5.1975 RHB WK

Cmp	Debut	M	I	NO	Runs	HS	Avge	100	50	Balls	Runs	Wkts	Avge	BB	5i	10m	RpO	ct	st
FC		1	2	0	40	28	20.00	0	0									1	1
FC	1995	8	15	5	298	84	29.80	0	2									28	1
MM	1995	3	2	0	39	26	19.50	0	0									4	

ROBERTS. Kevin Joseph (New South Wales) b North Sydney 25.7.1972 RHB RM

Cmp	Debut	M	I	NO	Runs	HS	Avge	100	50	Balls	Runs	Wkts	Avge	BB	5i	10m	RpO	ct	st
FC		7	13	1	424	119	35.33	1	2									5	
MM		5	5	1	156	55*	39.00	0	1									2	
FC	1994	20	36	1	945	119	27.00	1	7									13	
MM	1994	11	11	1	328	101	32.80	1	1									4	

ROBERTSON, Gavin Ron (New South Wales) b Sydney 28.5.1966 RHB OB

Cmp	Debut	M	I	NO	Runs	HS	Avge	100	50	Balls	Runs	Wkts	Avge	BB	5i	10m	RpO	ct	st
MM		4	3	2	58	33*	58.00	0	0	168	102	4	25.50	3-24	0	0	3.64	1	
FC	1987	37	53	8	1134	99	25.20	0	3	7998	3557	75	47.42	6-54	5	0	2.66	18	
Int	1994	4	3	2	7	5*	7.00	0	0	144	127	0					5.29	0	
MM	1989	16	11	6	107	33*	21.40	0	0	792	521	12	43.41	3-24	0	0	3.94	3	

SABALLUS, Andrew William (Tasmania) b Hobart 1.6.1969 RHB RFM

Cmp	Debut	M	I	NO	Runs	HS	Avge	100	50	Balls	Runs	Wkts	Avge	BB	5i	10m	RpO	ct	st
FC		1									120	84	0					4.20	1	
MM		2	2	0	5	5	2.50	0	0	78	76	1	76.00	1-35	0	0	5.84	0	

SAINT, John Michael (Tasmania) b Auburn 31.1.1969 RHB RM

Cmp	Debut	M	I	NO	Runs	HS	Avge	100	50	Balls	Runs	Wkts	Avge	BB	5i	10m	RpO	ct	st
FC		3	5	0	29	10	5.80	0	0	504	270	10	27.00	4-10	0	0	3.21	3	
MM		1	1	0	1	1	1.00	0	0	54	44	2	22.00	2-44	0	0	4.88	0	
FC	1995	4	6	0	35	10	5.83	0	0	767	443	12	36.91	4-10	0	0	3.46	5	
MM	1995	2	2	0	4	3	2.00	0	0	114	75	3	25.00	2-44	0	0	3.94	0	

SAKER, David James (Victoria) b Oakleigh 29.5.1966 RHB RFM

Cmp	Debut	M	I	NO	Runs	HS	Avge	100	50	Balls	Runs	Wkts	Avge	BB	5i	10m	RpO	ct	st
FC		11	20	6	365	66*	26.07	0	2	2556	1210	32	37.81	4-22	0	0	2.84	3	
MM		6	4	1	90	47*	30.00	0	0	252	170	3	56.66	2-56	0	0	4.04	0	
FC	1994	21	34	8	502	66*	19.30	0	2	5044	2325	74	31.41	7-32	1	1	2.76	6	
MM	1994	13	7	3	119	47*	29.75	0	0	672	375	14	26.78	4-35	1	0	3.34	0	

SCUDERI, Joseph Charles (South Australia) b Ingham 24.12.1968 RHB RFM

Cmp	Debut	M	I	NO	Runs	HS	Avge	100	50	Balls	Runs	Wkts	Avge	BB	5i	10m	RpO	ct	st
FC		7	14	2	352	70	29.33	0	3	784	399	23	17.34	5-43	1	0	3.05	4	
MM		4	4	1	35	12	11.66	0	0	186	135	4	33.75	2-41	0	0	4.35	0	
FC	1988	58	95	13	2545	125*	31.03	3	13	11398	5287	154	34.33	7-79	8	1	2.78	20	
MM	1988	33	27	5	498	58	22.63	0	3	1711	1321	31	42.61	3-36	0	0	4.63	2	

SECCOMBE, Wade Anthony (Queensland) b Murgon 30.10.1971 RHB WK

Cmp	Debut	M	I	NO	Runs	HS	Avge	100	50	Balls	Runs	Wkts	Avge	BB	5i	10m	RpO	ct	st
FC		10	14	1	386	103	29.69	1	1	6	0	0					0.00	35	4
MM		7	5	2	71	32	23.66	0	0									9	2
FC	1992	34	50	8	1101	103	26.21	1	3	6	0	0					0.00	162	10
MM	1994	15	12	5	222	64*	31.71	0	1									15	4

SIDDONS, James Darren (South Australia) b Robinvale 25.4.1964 RHB LBG

Cmp	Debut	M	I	NO	Runs	HS	Avge	100	50	Balls	Runs	Wkts	Avge	BB	5i	10m	RpO	ct	st
FC		11	21	0	631	101	30.04	1	5									19	
MM		5	5	0	85	28	17.00	0	0									1	
FC	1984	138	237	19	9968	245	45.72	31	45	522	347	2	173.50	1-8	0	0	3.98	181	
Int	1988	1	1	0	32	32	32.00	0	0									0	
MM	1985	47	45	5	1212	90*	30.30	0	7									24	

SLATER, Michael Jonathon (New South Wales, Australia to India, Australia to England, Australia to Sri Lanka) b Wagga Wagga 21.2.1970 RHB RM

Cmp	Debut	M	I	NO	Runs	HS	Avge	100	50	Balls	Runs	Wkts	Avge	BB	5i	10m	RpO	ct	st
FC		10	19	0	703	102	37.00	1	5	6	2	0					2.00	6	
MM		3	3	0	33	14	11.00	0	0									2	
Test	1993	34	59	3	2655	219	47.41	7	10	7	4	1	4.00	1-4	0	0	3.42	11	
FC	1991	95	167	10	7110	219	45.28	17	41	31	26	1	26.00	1-4	0	0	5.03	47	
Int	1993	42	42	1	987	73	24.07	0	9	12	11	0					5.50	9	
MM	1992	11	11	0	296	96	26.90	0	3									3	

SMITH, Adam Matthew (Victoria) b Greensborough 6.4.1976 RHB SLA

Cmp	Debut	M	I	NO	Runs	HS	Avge	100	50	Balls	Runs	Wkts	Avge	BB	5i	10m	RpO	ct	st
FC		3	6	0	89	36	14.83	0	0	372	151	3	50.33	2-39	0	0	2.43	4	
MM		3	3	1	71	41*	35.50	0	0	18	21	0					7.00	1	

Cmp	Debut	M	I	NO	Runs	HS	Avge	100	50	Balls	Runs	Wkts	Avge	BB	5i	10m	RpO	ct	st

STACEY, Bradley John (Victoria) b Geelong 11.6.1972 RHB LBG

Cmp	Debut	M	I	NO	Runs	HS	Avge	100	50	Balls	Runs	Wkts	Avge	BB	5i	10m	RpO	ct	st
FC		7	12	2	115	32	11.50	0	0	1011	691	12	57.58	4-122	0	0	4.10	4	
FC	1995	8	13	2	117	32	10.63	0	0	1209	814	16	50.87	4-122	0	0	4.03	4	

STEWART, James (Western Australia) b East Fremantle 22.8.1970 RHB SLA

Cmp	Debut	M	I	NO	Runs	HS	Avge	100	50	Balls	Runs	Wkts	Avge	BB	5i	10m	RpO	ct	st
MM		7	2	1	25	13	25.00	0	0	402	246	7	35.14	3-29	0	0	3.67	1	
FC	1992	13	16	4	131	51	10.91	0	1	1914	1016	17	59.76	3-109	0	0	3.18	1	
MM	1992	20	12	7	51	13	10.20	0	0	1134	782	27	28.96	3-29	0	0	4.13	4	

STUART, Anthony Mark (New South Wales, Australian XI, Australia) b Newcastle 2.1.1970 RHB RFM

Cmp	Debut	M	I	NO	Runs	HS	Avge	100	50	Balls	Runs	Wkts	Avge	BB	5i	10m	RpO	ct	st
FC		7	9	0	34	19	3.77	0	0	1117	643	21	30.61	5-63	1	0	3.45	2	
Int		3	1	0	1	1	1.00	0	0	180	109	8	13.62	5-26	0	1	3.63	2	
MM		3	2	0	7	5	3.50	0	0	168	107	8	13.37	4-22	1	0	3.82	0	
FC	1994	15	18	4	90	19	6.42	0	0	2157	1226	50	24.52	5-63	1	0	3.41	6	
MM	1995	5	4	1	10	5	3.33	0	0	276	193	12	16.08	4-22	1	0	4.19	0	

SYMONDS, Andrew (Queensland) b Birmingham, England 9.6.1975 RHB OB

Cmp	Debut	M	I	NO	Runs	HS	Avge	100	50	Balls	Runs	Wkts	Avge	BB	5i	10m	RpO	ct	st
FC		11	18	1	604	111	35.52	1	2	216	116	3	38.66	1-10	0	0	3.22	8	
MM		7	6	0	74	21	12.33	0	0	155	106	4	26.50	2-7	0	0	4.10	3	
FC	1994	59	99	9	3686	254*	40.95	10	16	2046	1113	25	44.52	3-77	0	0	3.26	30	
MM	1993	16	15	0	302	85	20.13	0	1	207	158	6	26.33	2-7	0	0	4.57	7	

TAYLOR, Mark Anthony (New South Wales, Australia, Australia to India, Australia to South Africa, Australia to England) b Leeton 27.10.1964 LHB RM

Cmp	Debut	M	I	NO	Runs	HS	Avge	100	50	Balls	Runs	Wkts	Avge	BB	5i	10m	RpO	ct	st
Test		5	9	0	153	43	17.00	0	0									9	
FC		8	15	0	252	53	16.80	0	1									13	
Int		8	8	0	143	29	17.87	0	0									6	
Test	1988	87	155	9	6116	219	41.89	15	34	42	26	1	26.00	1-11	0	0	3.71	123	
FC	1985	219	377	15	15194	219	41.97	36	82	144	68	2	34.00	1-4	0	0	2.83	300	
Int	1989	113	110	1	3514	105	32.23	1	28									56	
MM	1985	27	27	0	915	84	33.88	0	9	12	3	0					1.50	17	

THOMPSON, Scott Michael (New South Wales) b Bankstown 4.5.1972 RHB RMF

Cmp	Debut	M	I	NO	Runs	HS	Avge	100	50	Balls	Runs	Wkts	Avge	BB	5i	10m	RpO	ct	st
FC		2	3	0	49	26	16.33	0	0	306	223	8	27.87	4-56	0	0	4.37	3	
MM		1	1	0	0	0	0.00	0	0	48	33	1	33.00	1-33	0	0	4.12	1	
FC	1994	13	20	3	335	49*	19.70	0	0	2082	1362	37	36.81	4-56	0	0	3.92	8	
MM	1994	7	7	1	78	24*	13.00	0	0	324	299	5	59.80	1-25	0	0	5.53	1	

VAUGHAN, Jeffrey Mark (South Australia) b Blacktown, Sydney 26.3.1974 RHB RM

Cmp	Debut	M	I	NO	Runs	HS	Avge	100	50	Balls	Runs	Wkts	Avge	BB	5i	10m	RpO	ct	st
FC		2	4	1	16	10*	5.33	0	0									4	

VIMPANI, Graeme Ronald (Victoria) b Herston 27.1.1972 RHB RM

Cmp	Debut	M	I	NO	Runs	HS	Avge	100	50	Balls	Runs	Wkts	Avge	BB	5i	10m	RpO	ct	st
FC		8	15	0	752	161	50.13	3	3									7	
MM		4	4	0	65	35	16.25	0	0									2	
FC	1995	15	29	2	1166	161	43.18	3	7									8	
MM	1995	7	7	0	91	35	13.00	0	0									4	

WARNE, Shane Keith (Victoria, Australia, Australia to South Africa, Australia to England) b Ferntree Gully 13.9.1969 RHB LBG

Cmp	Debut	M	I	NO	Runs	HS	Avge	100	50	Balls	Runs	Wkts	Avge	BB	5i	10m	RpO	ct	st
Test		5	7	0	128	30	18.28	0	0	1303	594	22	27.00	4-95	0	0	2.73	6	
FC		7	10	0	159	30	15.90	0	0	1885	795	27	29.44	4-95	0	0	2.53	8	
Int		8	5	1	38	11	9.50	0	0	454	325	19	17.10	5-33	2	1	4.29	3	
MM		3	2	1	12	12*	12.00	0	0	180	107	9	11.88	5-35	0	1	3.56	6	
Test	1991	58	80	9	1027	74*	14.46	0	2	16642	6323	264	23.95	8-71	11	3	2.27	41	
FC	1990	109	140	20	1874	74*	15.61	0	4	28376	11513	471	24.44	8-71	21	3	2.43	67	
Int	1992	76	43	13	375	55	12.50	0	1	4260	2859	129	22.16	5-33	9	1	4.02	25	
MM	1992	10	6	1	90	32	18.00	0	0	527	360	15	24.00	5-35	0	1	4.09	7	

WAUGH, Dean Parma (New South Wales) b Campsie 3.2.1969 RHB OB

Cmp	Debut	M	I	NO	Runs	HS	Avge	100	50	Balls	Runs	Wkts	Avge	BB	5i	10m	RpO	ct	st
MM		1	1	0	4	4	4.00	0	0	6	4	0					4.00	0	
FC	1995	1	2	0	22	19	11.00	0	0									1	
MM	1995	3	3	0	47	28	15.66	0	0	6	4	0					4.00	0	

WAUGH, Mark Edward (New South Wales, Australia, Australia to India, Australia to South Africa, Australia to England, Australia to Sri Lanka) b Canterbury 2.6.1965 RHB RM

Cmp	Debut	M	I	NO	Runs	HS	Avge	100	50	Balls	Runs	Wkts	Avge	BB	5i	10m	RpO	ct	st
Test		5	9	0	370	82	41.11	0	4	48	31	0					3.87	8	
FC		7	13	0	563	82	43.38	1	4	144	85	2	42.50	2-54	0	0	3.54	12	
Int		7	7	1	358	102	59.66	1	2	51	38	1	38.00	1-11	0	0	4.47	3	
Test	1990	69	112	4	4464	140	41.33	11	28	3174	1489	41	36.31	5-40	1	0	2.81	87	
FC	1985	262	419	52	19846	229*	54.07	64	95	12965	6971	184	37.88	6-68	3	0	3.22	304	
Int	1989	135	130	11	4542	130	38.16	10	28	2643	2124	71	29.91	5-24	1	0	4.82	52	
MM	1985	31	30	3	948	112	35.11	1	6	701	538	16	33.62	3-23	0	0	4.60	15	

WAUGH, Stephen Rodger (New South Wales, Australia, Australia to India, Australia to South Africa, Australia to England, Australia to Sri Lanka) b Canterbury 2.6.1965 RHB RM

Cmp	Debut	M	I	NO	Runs	HS	Avge	100	50	Balls	Runs	Wkts	Avge	BB	5i	10m	RpO	ct	st
Test		4	6	0	188	66	31.33	0	2	151	63	1	63.00	1-15	0	0	2.50	2	
FC		7	12	1	609	186*	55.36	2	3	283	116	1	116.00	1-15	0	0	2.45	8	
Int		6	6	0	159	57	26.50	0	1	18	24	0					8.00	3	
Test	1985	95	148	28	5960	200	49.66	14	34	6515	2894	80	36.17	5-28	3	0	2.66	70	
FC	1984	237	361	61	15568	216*	51.89	45	74	15802	7405	234	31.64	6-51	5	0	2.81	202	

Cmp	Debut	M	I	NO	Runs	HS	Avge	100	50	Balls	Runs	Wkts	Avge	BB	5i	10m	RpO	ct	st
Int	1985	221	201	43	5092	102*	32.22	1	30	7860	5877	172	34.16	4-33	2	0	4.48	79	
MM	1984	28	27	4	1062	131	46.17	2	7	1080	833	33	25.24	4-32	1	0	4.62	9	

WEBBER, Darren Scott (South Australia) b Barnside 18.8.1971 RHB RM

Cmp	Debut	M	I	NO	Runs	HS	Avge	100	50	Balls	Runs	Wkts	Avge	BB	5i	10m	RpO	ct	st
FC		2	4	0	50	41	12.50	0	0									1	
MM		2	2	0	33	18	16.50	0	0									2	
FC	1992	38	69	5	2092	176	32.68	3	8	30	16	0					3.20	30	
MM	1992	21	19	2	340	47	20.00	0	0	4	3	0					4.50	9	

WIGNEY, Bradley Neil (South Australia) b Leongatha 30.6.1965 RHB RFM

Cmp	Debut	M	I	NO	Runs	HS	Avge	100	50	Balls	Runs	Wkts	Avge	BB	5i	10m	RpO	ct	st
FC		1	2	0	3	3	1.50	0	0	228	138	5	27.60	3-76	0	0	3.63	0	
MM		2	2	1	3	2	3.00	0	0	84	58	1	58.00	1-40	0	0	4.14	1	
FC	1992	19	25	11	64	17	4.57	0	0	3817	1896	41	46.24	4-73	0	0	2.98	5	
MM	1992	19	10	5	58	14	11.60	0	0	953	663	22	30.13	3-39	0	0	4.17	3	

WILLIAMS, Brad Andrew (Victoria) b Frankston 20.11.1974 RHB RF

Cmp	Debut	M	I	NO	Runs	HS	Avge	100	50	Balls	Runs	Wkts	Avge	BB	5i	10m	RpO	ct	st
FC		4	5	2	75	37	25.00	0	0	732	432	10	43.20	4-63	0	0	3.54	1	
MM		2									106	82	2	41.00	1-38	0	0	4.64	0	
FC	1994	18	26	10	345	41*	21.56	0	0	3656	2007	55	36.49	6-98	2	0	3.29	4	
MM	1994	6	1	0	16	16	16.00	0	0	286	211	5	42.20	2-45	0	0	4.42	1	

WILSON, Paul (South Australia) b Newcastle 12.1.1972 RHB RFM

Cmp	Debut	M	I	NO	Runs	HS	Avge	100	50	Balls	Runs	Wkts	Avge	BB	5i	10m	RpO	ct	st
FC		5	9	2	28	11*	4.00	0	0	1216	456	18	25.33	3-44	0	0	2.25	1	
MM		4	3	1	13	7	6.50	0	0	240	126	9	14.00	3-18	0	0	3.15	0	
FC	1995	8	13	4	36	11*	4.00	0	0	1732	669	25	26.76	4-50	0	0	2.31	1	
MM	1993	15	8	2	44	16	7.33	0	0	840	499	21	23.76	3-18	0	0	3.56	1	

YOUNG, Bradley Evan (South Australia) b Semaphore 23.2.1973 RHB SLA

Cmp	Debut	M	I	NO	Runs	HS	Avge	100	50	Balls	Runs	Wkts	Avge	BB	5i	10m	RpO	ct	st
FC		9	17	5	475	91*	39.58	0	3	1819	903	23	39.26	4-111	0	0	2.97	6	
MM		5	5	0	52	19	10.40	0	0	210	147	0					4.20	3	

YOUNG, Shaun (Tasmania, Gloucestershire, Australia to England) b Burnie 13.6.1970 LHB RFM

Cmp	Debut	M	I	NO	Runs	HS	Avge	100	50	Balls	Runs	Wkts	Avge	BB	5i	10m	RpO	ct	st
FC		11	18	4	548	113	39.14	2	2	2201	1096	35	31.31	7-64	2	0	2.98	3	
MM		5	5	0	145	64	29.00	0	1	246	207	4	51.75	3-63	0	0	5.04	1	
Test	1997	1	2	1	4	4*	4.00	0	0	48	13	0					1.62	0	
FC	1991	90	147	25	4951	237	40.58	10	30	15125	7300	214	34.11	7-64	8	1	2.89	56	
MM	1990	29	25	3	577	96	26.22	0	3	1318	906	17	53.29	3-63	0	0	4.12	7	

ENGLAND A IN AUSTRALIA 1996-97

BUTCHER, M.A.

Cmp	Debut	M	I	NO	Runs	HS	Avge	100	50	Balls	Runs	Wkts	Avge	BB	5i	10m	RpO	ct	st
FC		3	5	0	264	73	52.80	0	3	36	8	0					1.33	2	

CHAPPLE, G.

FC		2	2	2	43	27*		0	0	405	159	7	22.71	4-43	0	0	2.35	1	

EALHAM, M.A.

FC		3	4	0	137	78	34.25	0	1	216	103	2	51.50	1-16	0	0	2.86	0	

GALLIAN, J.E.R.

FC		1	2	1	38	26	38.00	0	0	84	33	0					2.35	0	

GILES, A.F.

FC		3	4	0	66	29	16.50	0	0	554	199	6	33.16	3-28	0	0	2.15	0	

HARRIS, A.J.

FC		1	2	1	4	4*	4.00	0	0	90	54	0					3.60	0	

HEADLEY, D.W.

FC		3	4	1	71	28	23.66	0	0	613	230	14	16.42	6-60	2	1	2.25	0	

HEGG, W.K.

FC		3	4	0	89	69	22.25	0	1									14	

HOLLIOAKE, A.J.

FC		3	5	0	105	58	21.00	0	1	222	89	3	29.66	1-20	0	0	2.40	2	

McGRATH, A.

FC		3	5	0	52	19	10.40	0	0	24	6	1	6.00	1-6	0	0	1.50	0	

SHAH, O.A.

FC		2	3	0	53	27	17.66	0	0									0	

VAUGHAN, M.P

FC		3	5	0	35	27	7.00	0	0	78	56	0					4.30	3	

WHITE, C.

FC		3	5	1	204	99	51.00	0	2	446	178	11	16.18	6-66	1	0	2.39	3	

PAKISTAN IN AUSTRALIA 1996-97

	M	I	NO	Runs	HS	Avge	100	50	Balls	Runs	Wkts	Avge	BB	5i	10m	RpO	ct	st
AAMER SOHAIL																		
Int	9	9	0	225	67	25.00	0	3	225	161	3	53.66	2-33	0	0	4.29	6	
IJAZ AHMED (b Sialkot)																		
FC	1	2	0	13	13	6.50	0	0	6	18	0					18.00	0	
Int	10	10	1	395	94	43.88	0	4	64	32	1	32.00	1-28	0	0	3.00	4	
IJAZ AHMED (b Lyallpur)																		
Int	2	1	1	3	3*		0	0	30	25	1	25.00	1-9	0	0	5.00	0	
INZAMAM-UL-HAQ																		
FC	1	2	0	15	8	7.50	0	0									0	
Int	9	9	0	181	64	20.11	0	1									1	
MOHAMMAD WASIM																		
FC	1	2	0	52	27	26.00	0	0									0	
Int	9	9	1	282	54	35.25	0	2									4	
MOHAMMAD ZAHID																		
FC	1	1	1	5	5*		0	0	120	96	1	96.00	1-96	0	0	4.80	3	
Int	3	2	1	1	1	1.00	0	0	180	123	3	41.00	2-53	0	0	4.10	0	
MOIN KHAN																		
FC	1	2	0	31	24	15.50	0	0									1	1
Int	10	9	3	192	43	32.00	0	0									9	3
MUJAHID JAMSHED																		
Int	4	3	1	27	23	13.50	0	0	24	6	1	6.00	1-6	0	0	1.50	0	
MUSHTAQ AHMED																		
FC	1	2	0	69	65	34.50	0	1	174	97	4	24.25	4-97	0	0	3.34	0	
Int	6	3	1	10	9	5.00	0	0	330	232	4	58.00	1-32	0	0	4.21	1	
SAQLAIN MUSHTAQ																		
FC	1	2	0	10	10	5.00	0	0	186	84	1	84.00	1-84	0	0	2.70	0	
Int	10	6	1	49	30*	9.80	0	0	528	303	17	17.82	5-29	1	1	3.44	0	
SHAHID KHAN AFRIDI																		
FC	1	2	0	80	80	40.00	0	1	66	26	0					2.36	0	
Int	9	9	0	159	53	17.66	0	1	401	306	11	27.81	3-33	0	0	4.57	3	
SHAHID NAZIR																		
FC	1	2	1	9	9	9.00	0	0	120	61	2	30.50	2-61	0	0	3.05	0	
Int	3	2	1	8	8	8.00	0	0	150	82	3	27.33	3-14	0	0	3.28	0	
WAQAR YOUNIS																		
Int	6	4	2	9	4	4.50	0	0	297	192	11	17.45	4-43	1	0	3.87	0	
WASIM AKRAM																		
FC	1	2	0	29	29	14.50	0	0	60	34	2	17.00	2-34	0	0	3.40	0	
Int	10	9	1	70	33	8.75	0	0	513	270	15	18.00	4-25	1	0	3.15	3	
ZAHOOR ELAHI																		
FC	1	2	0	34	34	17.00	0	0									0	
Int	10	10	1	154	51	17.11	0	1									2	

WEST INDIES IN AUSTRALIA 1996-97

	M	I	NO	Runs	HS	Avge	100	50	Balls	Runs	Wkts	Avge	BB	5i	10m	RpO	ct	st
ADAMS, J.C.																		
Test	5	9	2	140	74*	20.00	0	1	113	59	1	59.00	1-11	0	0	3.13	3	
FC	8	14	3	273	74*	24.81	0	2	406	223	6	37.16	3-53	0	0	3.29	6	
Int	10	9	2	116	34*	16.57	0	0	354	293	9	31.44	5-37	0	1	4.96	8	
AMBROSE, C.E.L.																		
Test	4	6	0	39	15	6.50	0	0	965	444	19	23.36	5-43	2	0	2.76	1	
FC	5	6	0	39	15	6.50	0	0	1038	468	19	24.63	5-43	2	0	2.70	1	
Int	8	4	2	38	31*	19.00	0	0	451	246	9	27.33	2-16	0	0	3.27	1	
BENJAMIN, K.C.G.																		
Test	3	5	0	31	11	6.20	0	0	707	362	9	40.22	3-34	0	0	3.07	1	
FC	5	6	1	33	11	6.60	0	0	1097	577	15	38.46	3-34	0	0	3.15	3	
Int	3	2	0	11	8	5.50	0	0	166	123	2	61.50	1-42	0	0	4.44	0	
BISHOP, I.R.																		
Test	5	8	0	86	48	10.75	0	0	1029	510	20	25.50	3-49	0	0	2.97	1	
FC	7	11	0	111	48	10.09	0	0	1419	726	25	29.04	3-40	0	0	3.06	1	
Int	6	2	2	20	18*		0	0	317	236	6	39.33	4-38	1	0	4.46	0	
BROWNE, C.O.																		
Test	3	5	1	49	25*	12.25	0	0									15	
FC	5	8	2	162	93*	27.00	0	1									23	1

Cmp Debut	M	I	NO	Runs	HS	Avge	100	50	Balls	Runs	Wkts	Avge	BB	5i	10m	RpO	ct	st
CAMPBELL, S.L.																		
Test	5	10	1	291	113	32.33	1	1									3	
FC	7	14	2	523	113	43.58	2	2	12	4	0					2.00	5	
Int	10	10	0	225	52	22.50	0	1									1	
CHANDERPAUL, S.																		
Test	5	9	0	344	82	38.22	0	3	18	2	1	2.00	1-2	0	0	0.66	2	
FC	7	12	1	561	135*	51.00	1	4	90	46	2	23.00	1-2	0	0	3.06	3	
Int	8	7	0	252	72	36.00	0	2	118	101	4	25.25	2-16	0	0	5.13	2	
CUFFY, C.E.																		
Test	1	2	1	5	3*	5.00	0	0	198	116	2	58.00	2-116	0	0	3.51	0	
FC	1	2	1	5	3*	5.00	0	0	198	116	2	58.00	2-116	0	0	3.51	0	
Int	1	1	0	4	4	4.00	0	0	54	33	2	16.50	2-33	0	0	3.66	0	
GRIFFITH, A.F.G.																		
Test	1	2	0	14	13	7.00	0	0									0	
FC	3	6	1	60	23*	12.00	0	0									0	
Int	5	4	1	50	47	16.66	0	0									4	
HOLDER, R.I.C.																		
FC	2	4	1	94	68	31.33	0	1									1	
Int	4	4	0	61	32	15.25	0	0									1	
HOOPER, C.L.																		
Test	5	9	1	362	102	45.25	1	2	696	317	3	105.66	2-86	0	0	2.73	9	
FC	8	14	1	568	102	43.69	1	3	1146	577	11	52.45	4-59	0	0	3.02	10	
Int	9	9	3	234	110*	39.00	1	1	438	293	4	73.25	2-27	0	0	4.01	2	
LARA, B.C.																		
Test	5	9	0	296	132	32.88	1	1									8	
FC	7	13	0	497	132	38.23	1	3									10	
Int	9	9	2	424	103*	60.57	2	1									5	
McLEAN, N.A.M.																		
FC	2	3	1	43	41	21.50	0	0	324	217	6	36.16	5-48	1	0	4.01	0	
Int	6	3	0	8	7	2.66	0	0	204	145	3	48.33	2-33	0	0	4.26	2	
MURRAY, J.R.																		
Test	2	3	0	112	53	37.33	0	1									4	1
FC	3	4	1	142	53	47.33	0	1									4	1
Int	10	10	0	342	86	34.20	0	3									9	2
SAMUELS, R.G.																		
Test	4	8	1	231	76	33.00	0	1									4	
FC	7	14	1	372	96	28.61	0	2									6	
Int	8	5	2	54	36*	18.00	0	0									0	
SIMMONS, P.V.																		
Test	1	1	0	0	0	0.00	0	0	138	67	1	67.00	1-58	0	0	2.91	3	
FC	1	1	0	0	0	0.00	0	0	138	67	1	67.00	1-58	0	0	2.91	3	
Int	2	2	0	0	0	0.00	0	0	84	64	1	64.00	1-30	0	0	4.57	1	
THOMPSON, P.I.C.																		
Test	1	2	1	16	10*	16.00	0	0	96	80	1	80.00	1-80	0	0	5.00	0	
FC	4	5	1	17	10*	4.25	0	0	510	371	5	74.20	2-42	0	0	4.36	0	
Int	2	1	0	2	2	2.00	0	0	114	110	2	55.00	1-46	0	0	5.78	0	
WALSH, C.A.																		
Test	5	8	4	31	18	7.75	0	0	1155	592	19	31.15	5-74	2	0	3.07	2	
FC	6	8	4	31	18	7.75	0	0	1322	688	22	31.27	5-74	2	0	3.12	2	
Int	9	4	2	10	8*	5.00	0	0	492	322	10	32.20	3-40	0	0	3.92	2	

The following current cricketers have played in Australian Domestic limited overs cricket but did not appear in Australian Domestic cricket in 1996-97:

BOWLER, P.D. (see Somerset) (Tasmania)																		
MM 1986	2	2	0	28	21	14.00	0	0									0	
McCAGUE, M.J. (see Kent) (Western Australia)																		
MM 1991	4	2	0	1	1	0.50	0	0	137	89	5	17.80	4-34	1	0	3.89	1	
MILLNS, D.J. (see Leicestershire) (Tasmania)																		
MM 1994	1	1	0	12	12	12.00	0	0	48	41	2	20.50	2-41	0	0	5.12	0	
MULLALLY, A.D. (see Leicestershire) (Western Australia)																		
MM 1988	2								120	95	3	31.66	2-56	0	0	4.75	1	
SMALL, G.C. (see Warwickshire) (South Australia)																		
MM 1985	2	2	2	17	16*		0	0	114	72	3	24.00	3-42	0	0	3.78	0	

Cmp	Debut	M	I	NO	Runs	HS	Avge	100	50	Balls	Runs	Wkts	Avge	BB	5i	10m	RpO	ct	st
STEPHENSON, F.D. (see South Africa) (Tasmania)																			
MM	1981	2	2	0	18	18	9.00	0	0	114	74	2	37.00	2-39	0	0	3.89	0	
WESSELS, K.C. (see South Africa) (Queensland)																			
MM	1979	19	19	2	656	73	38.58	0	6	156	108	7	15.42	4-24	1	0	4.15	11	
WILLIAMS, N.F. (see Essex) (Tasmania)																			
MM	1983	1	1	0	19	19	19.00	0	0	60	38	2	19.00	2-38	0	0	3.80	0	

CANADA

First First-Class Match: USA/Canada v Australians (Toronto) 1913-14. First by Canada v MCC (Toronto) 1951-52.

First First-Class Tour to England: 1954.

First One-Day International Match: India v Pakistan (Toronto) 1996-97

Details of Canada players for 1996-97 appear in the West Indies section, as Canada competed in the Shell-Sandals Trophy.

Cmp Debut	M	I	NO	Runs	HS	Avge	100	50	Balls	Runs	Wkts	Avge	BB	5i	10m	RpO	ct	st

INDIA IN CANADA 1996-97

Cmp Debut	M	I	NO	Runs	HS	Avge	100	50	Balls	Runs	Wkts	Avge	BB	5i	10m	RpO	ct	st
AZHARUDDIN, M.																		
Int	5	5	1	174	88	43.50	0	1									2	
DRAVID, R.S.																		
Int	5	5	0	220	90	44.00	0	1									4	
GANGULY, S.C.																		
Int	3	2	1	23	12	23.00	0	0									1	
JADEJA, A.D.																		
Int	5	4	1	111	47	37.00	0	0	48	58	0					7.25	1	
JOSHI, S.B.																		
Int	5	3	0	34	31	11.33	0	0	263	187	3	62.33	1-27	0	0	4.26	3	
KAMBLI, V.G.																		
Int	4	3	0	38	29	12.66	0	0									1	
KAPOOR, A.R.																		
Int	3	3	0	37	19	12.33	0	0	144	97	2	48.50	2-36	0	0	4.04	0	
KUMBLE, A.																		
Int	5	3	1	26	16	13.00	0	0	264	159	13	12.23	4-12	1	0	3.61	3	
MONGIA, N.R.																		
Int	5	5	0	39	18	7.80	0	0									5	3
SRINATH, J.																		
Int	5	4	0	15	10	3.75	0	0	252	188	8	23.50	3-23	0	0	4.47	2	
TENDULKAR, S.R.																		
Int	5	5	1	137	89*	34.25	0	1	96	86	2	43.00	1-22	0	0	5.37	3	
VENKATESH PRASAD, B.K.																		
Int	5	3	2	19	19	19.00	0	0	276	196	9	21.77	3-22	0	0	4.26	2	

PAKISTAN IN CANADA 1996-97

Cmp Debut	M	I	NO	Runs	HS	Avge	100	50	Balls	Runs	Wkts	Avge	BB	5i	10m	RpO	ct	st
AAMER SOHAIL																		
Int	5	5	0	80	44	16.00	0	0	222	152	2	76.00	1-27	0	0	4.10	4	
AZHAR MAHMOOD																		
Int	3	3	0	17	10	5.66	0	0	108	85	2	42.50	2-38	0	0	4.72	1	
IJAZ AHMED																		
Int	5	5	0	165	90	33.00	0	1									2	
INZAMAM-UL-HAQ																		
Int	4	4	0	83	40	20.75	0	0									1	
MOIN KHAN																		
Int	5	5	0	106	42	21.20	0	0									3	3
MUSHTAQ AHMED																		
Int	4	3	1	10	5*	5.00	0	0	216	145	8	18.12	5-36	0	1	4.11	1	
SAEED ANWAR																		
Int	5	5	0	203	80	40.60	0	1									1	
SALEEM ELAHI																		
Int	2	2	0	5	4	2.50	0	0									2	

Cmp Debut	M	I	NO	Runs	HS	Avge	100	50	Balls	Runs	Wkts	Avge	BB	5i	10m	RpO	ct	st
SALEEM MALIK																		
Int	5	5	1	144	70*	36.00	0	1	50	47	3	15.66	2-6	0	0	5.64	2	
SAQLAIN MUSHTAQ																		
Int	5	5	3	52	22*	26.00	0	0	245	166	9	18.44	3-9	0	0	4.06	2	
SHADAB KABIR																		
Int	2	2	0	0	0	0.00	0	0									0	
WAQAR YOUNIS																		
Int	5	4	4	18	12*		0	0	210	160	3	53.33	2-51	0	0	4.57	0	
WASIM AKRAM																		
Int	5	5	0	56	20	11.20	0	0	239	151	6	25.16	4-35	1	0	3.79	4	

INDIA

First First-Class Match: Europeans v Parsis (Bombay) 1892-93

First First-Class Tour to England: 1911

First Test Match: India v England (Bombay) 1933-34

Present First-Class Teams: Andhra, Assam, Baroda, Bengal, Bihar, Delhi, Gujarat, Goa, Haryana, Himachal Pradesh, Hyderabad, Jammu & Kashmir, Karnataka, Kerala, Madhya Pradesh, Maharashtra, Mumbai (formerly Bombay), Orissa, Punjab, Railways, Rajasthan, Saurashtra, Services, Tamil Nadu, Tripura, Uttar Pradesh, Vidarbha

First-Class Competitions: The National Championship of India for the Ranji Trophy was instituted for the 1934-35 season, and has been India's equivalent of the County Championship since that date. The second major First-Class competition is the Duleep Trophy instituted in 1961-62 and for which India is divided into five zones. The annual match between the Ranji trophy winners and Rest of India played at the start of the season for the Irani Trophy is also first-class.

Ranji Trophy Winners 1996-97: Mumbai

FIRST-CLASS RECORDS

Highest Team Total: 944-6d Hyderabad v Andhra (Secunderabad) 1993-94
Highest in 1996-97: 750-7d Bengal v Bihar (Calcutta); 656 Delhi v Maharashtra (Pune); 647-4 Mumbai v Saurashtra (Rajkot); 630 Mumbai v Delhi (Gwalior); 604-9d Delhi v Punjab (Delhi)

Lowest Team Total: 21 Muslims v Europeans (Poona) 1915-16
Lowest in 1996-97: 65 Tripura v Assam (Agartala); 74 Karnataka v Kerala (Palghat); 76 Andhra v Kerala (Visakhapatnam); 90 Kerala v Punjab (Mohali); 95 Vidarbha v Railways (Delhi)

Highest Individual Innings: 443* B.B.Nimbalkar Maharashtra v Kathiawar (Poona) 1948-49
Highest in 1996-97: 314* W.Jaffer Mumbai v Saurashtra (Rajkot); 254 V.Rathore Punjab v Jammu and Kashmir (Amritsar); 250 R.Lamba Delhi v Punjab (Delhi); 239 S.K.Kulkarni Mumbai v Saurashtra (Rajkot); 230 Jitender Singh Haryanan v Himachal Pradesh (Chamba)

Most Runs in Season: 1,604 (av 64.16) C.G.Borde (Maharashtra) 1964-65
Most in 1996-97: 1,198 (av 99.83) Ajay Sharma (Delhi); 1,034 (av 73.85) R.Lamba (Delhi); 1,003 (av 71.64) H.H.Kanitkar (Maharashtra); 982 (av 57.76) V.Rathore (Punjab); 949 (av 73.00) R.V.Sapru (Uttar Pradesh)

Most Runs in Career: 25,834 (av 51.46) S.M.Gavaskar (Bombay, Somerset) 1966-67 to 1986-87
Most by Current Batsman: 13,584 (av 51.26) M.Azharuddin (Hyderabad, Derbyshire) 1981-82 to date; 9,774 (av 55.53) S.V.Manjrekar (Mumbai) 1984-85 to date; 9,598 (av 56.45) S.R.Tendulkar (Mumbai, Yorkshire) 1988-89 to date; 8,749 (av 70.55) A.K.Sharma (Delhi) 1984-85 to date; 8,625 (av 55.28) R.Lamba (Delhi) 1976-77 to date

Best Innings Analysis: 10-20 P.M.Chatterjee Bengal v Assam (Jorhat) 1956-57
Best in 1996-97: 8-25 B.Ramprakash Kerala v Karnataka (Palghat); 8-64 L.Klusener South Africa v India (Calcutta); 7-50 S.Roy Tripura v Orissa (Agartala); 7-52 R.K.Chauhan Madhya Pradesh v Orissa (Cuttack); 7-54 J.Gokulkrishnan Goa v Karnataka (Panaji)

Most Wickets in Season: 88 (av 15.02) B.S.Bedi (Delhi) 1974-75; 88 (av 19.30) B.S.Bedi (Delhi) 1976-77
Most in 1996-97: 60 (av 26.46) R.K.Chauhan (Madhya Pradesh); 58 (av 24.98) B.Vij (Punjab); 53 (av 21.43) B.Ramprakash (Kerala); 44 (av 19.97) P.Jain (Haryana)

Most Wickets in Career: 1,560 (av 21.69) B.S.Bedi (Northern Punjab, Delhi, Northamptonshire) 1961-62 to 1981-82
Most by Current Bowler: 467 (av 26.02) A.Kumble (Karnataka, Northamptonshire) 1989-90 to date; 466 (av 27.41) N.D.Hirwani (Madhya Pradesh, Bengal) 1984-85 to date; 433 (av 26.05) Chetan Sharma (Haryana, Bengal) 1982-83 to date; 385 (av 28.91) M.Prabhakar (Delhi, Durham) 1982-83 to date; 362 (av 26.74) S.L.Venkatapathy Raju (Hyderabad) 1985-86 to date

Record Wicket Partnerships

1st	464	R.Sehgal & R.Lamba	Delhi v Himachal Pradesh (Delhi)	1994-95
2nd	475	Zahir Alam & L.S.Rajput	Assam v Tripura (Guwahati)	1991-92
3rd	410*	R.S.Modi & L.Amarnath	India v Rest of India (Calcutta)	1946-47
4th	577	Gul Mahomed & V.S.Hazare	Baroda v Holkar (Baroda)	1946-47
5th	391	A.Malhotra & S.Dogra	Delhi v Services (Delhi)	1995-96
6th	371	V.M.Merchant & R.S.Modi	Bombay v Maharashtra (Bombay)	1943-44
7th	460	Bhupinder Singh & P.Dharmani	Punjab v Delhi (Delhi)	1994-95
8th	236	C.T.Sarwate & R.P.Singh	Holkar v Delhi (Delhi)	1949-50
9th	245	V.S.Hazare & N.D.Nagarwala	Maharashtra v Baroda (Poona)	1939-40
10th	233	Ajay Sharma & Maninder Singh	Delhi v Bombay (Bombay)	1991-92

Highest Partnerships in 1996-97

1st	459	W.Jaffer & S.K.Kulkarni	Mumbai v Saurashtra (Rajkot)
2nd	309	S.S.Sugwekar & H.H.Kanitkar	Maharashtra v Punjab (Pune)
3rd	313	A.Dani & Ajay Sharma	Delhi v Mumbai (Gwalior)
4th	220*	R.Shamshad & R.V.Sapru	Central Zone v West Zone (Delhi)
5th	255	S.Sharath & S.Ramesh	South Zone v North Zone (Faridabad)
6th	217	A.Varma & A.K.Das	Bengal v Delhi (Calcutta)
7th	263	N.Bordoloi & Sukhvinder Singh	Assam v Tripura (Agartala)
8th	230	A.A.Muzumdar & P.L.Mhambrey	Mumbai v Gujarat (Mumbai)
9th	103	M.B.Majithia & R.K.Chauhan	Madhya Pradesh v Mumbai (Indore)
10th	100	Sukhvinder Singh & Izaz Hussain	Assam v Bengal (Guwahati)

Most Wicketkeeping Dismissals in Innings: 7 (6ct 1st) S.Benjamin Central Zone v North Zone (Bombay) 1973-74; 7 (7ct) R.W.Taylor England v India (Bombay) 1979-80
Most in 1996-97: 6 (4ct 2st) V.Kamaruddin Kerala v Hyderabad (Secunderabad); 6 (6ct) S.K.Kulkarni Mumbai v Haryana (Mumbai); 6 (6ct) M.S.Mudgal Uttar Pradesh v Hyderabad (Secunderabad)

Most Wicketkeeping Dismissals in Match: 10 (10ct) R.W.Taylor England v India (Bombay) 1979-80; 10 (9ct 1st) A.Ghosh Bihar v Assam (Bhagalpur) 1981-82; 10 (8ct 2st) Z.Parkar Bombay v Maharashtra (Bombay) 1981-82; 10 (10ct) N.R.Mongia Rest of India v Punjab (Ludhiana) 1993-94; 10 (6ct 4st) S.S.Dighe West Zone v Central Zone (Bikaner) 1995-96
Most in 1996-97: 8 (6ct 2st) G.Gopal Orissa v Assam (Guwahati); 8 (8ct) S.M.Kondhalkar Maharashtra v Gujarat (Pune); 8 (8ct) S.K.Kulkarni Mumbai v Baroda (Mumbai); 8 (8ct) S.K.Kulkarni Mumbai v Haryana (Mumbai); 8 (7ct 1st) M.Mehra Punjab v Services (Delhi); 8 (8ct) Z.Zuffri Railways v Uttar Pradesh (Kanpur)

Most Wicketkeeping Dismissals in Season: 55 (47ct 8st) S.S.Dighe (Bombay) 1994-95
Most in 1996-97: 38 (34ct 4st) S.K.Kulkarni (Mumbai); 35 (29ct 6st) M.Mehra (Punjab); 34 (32ct 2st) S.M.Kondhalkar (Maharashtra); 30 (27ct 3st) Z.Zuffri (Railways); 28 (24ct 4st) V.Dhaiya (Delhi)

Most Wicketkeeping Dismissals in Career: 824 (704ct 120st) F.M.Engineer (Bombay, Lancashire) 1958-59 to 1976
Most by Current Wicketkeeper: 351 (289ct 62st) K.S.More (Baroda) 1980-81 to date; 288 (248ct 40st) C.S.Pandit (Bombay, Assam, Madhya Pradesh) 1979-80 to date; 239 (202ct 37st) V.Yadav (Haryana) 1987-88 to date; 222 (179ct 43st) S.S.Karim (Bihar, Bengal) 1982-83 to date; 197 (176ct 21st) N.R.Mongia (Baroda) 1989-90 to date

Most Catches by Fielder in Innings: 6 L.M.R.Deas Europeans v Parsis (Poona) 1898-99
Most in 1996-97: 4 S.Abbas Ali Madhya Pradesh v Orissa (Cuttack); 4 S.S.Bhave Maharashtra v Delhi (Pune); 4 J.Gokulkrishnan Goa v Kerala (Palghat); 4 N.M.Kulkarni Mumbai v Bihar (Jamshedpur); 4 H.J.Parsana Saurashtra v Maharashtra (Rajkot); 4 Tariq-ur-Rehman Bihar v Tripura (Jamshedpur)

Most Catches by Fielder in Match: 8 F.G.Travers Europeans v Parsis (Bombay) 1923-24
Most in 1996-97: 7 S.Abbas Ali Madhya Pradesh v Orissa (Cuttack); 6 A.Deb Burma Tripura v Orissa (Agartala); 6 R.S.Gavaskar Bengal v Assam (Guwahati); 6 N.M.Kulkarni Mumbai v Bihar (Jamshedpur)

Most Catches by Fielder in Season: 28 S.M.Gavaskar (Bombay) 1972-73
Most in 1996-97: 18 R.Puri (Haryana); 18 V.Rathore (Punjab); 17 S.Abbas Ali (Madhya Pradesh); 16 A.A.Muzumdar (Mumbai); 15 D.Gandhi (Bengal)

Most Catches by Fielder in Career: 317 S.Venkataraghavan (Tamil Nadu, Derbyshire) 1963-64 to 1984-85
Most by Current Fielder: 192 M.Azharuddin (Hyderabad, Derbyshire) 1981-82 to date; 103 V.Rathore (Punjab) 1988-89 to date; 90 S.R.Tendulkar (Mumbai, Yorkshire) 1988-89 to date; 89 S.S.Bhave (Maharashtra) 1986-87 to date; 89 S.V.Manjrekar (Mumbai) 1984-85 to date

DOMESTIC LIMITED OVERS RECORDS

Deodhar Trophy

Highest Team Totals: 320-9 (60 overs) West Zone v East Zone (Bombay) 1975-76; 319-6 (50 overs) North Zone v South Zone (Delhi) 1989-90; 309 (48.4 overs) West Zone v North Zone (Sholapur) 1983-84
Highest in 1996-97: 279-9 (50 overs) East Zone v Central Zone (Delhi)

Lowest Team Totals: 68 (20.4 overs) North Zone v South Zone (Surat) 1993-94; 72 (29.5 overs) Central Zone v West Zone (Bombay) 1993-94; 75 (33.1 overs) South Zone v North Zone (Coimbatore) 1992-93
Lowest in 1996-97: 132 (41.2 overs) North Zone v West Zone (Faridabad)

Highest Individual Innings: 140 K.Dubey East Zone v Central Zone (Delhi) 1986-87; 129 T.E.Srinivasan South Zone v West Zone (Madras) 1980-81; 125* R.Lamba North Zone v West Zone (Jullundur) 1989-90; 125 Saurav Ganguly East Zone v West Zone (Pune) 1990-91; 125 S.V.Manjrekar West Zone v East Zone (Jamshedpur) 1994-95
Highest in 1996-97: 102 S.Sharath South Zone v North Zone (Delhi)
30 centuries have been scored in the competition, Saurav Ganguly, S.V.Manjrekar and L.S.Rajput scoring 2

Most Runs in Season: 275 (av 91.66) S.V.Manjrekar (West Zone) 1996-97

Most Runs in Career: 1,022 (av 68.13) S.V.Manjrekar (West Zone) 1986-87 to date; 791 (av 35.95) A.D.Gaekwad (West Zone) 1974-75 to 1987-88; 676 (av 42.25) L.S.Rajput (West Zone, East Zone) 1985-86 to 1993-94

Best Innings Analyses: 6-18 B.K.Venkatesh Prasad South Zone v North Zone (Surat) 1993-94; 6-24 K.D.Ghavri West Zone v North Zone (Pune) 1973-74; 6-29 P.Sharma Central Zone v North Zone (Chandigarh) 1976-77
Best in 1996-97: 4-23 S.A.Ankola West Zone v South Zone (Mohali)
Five wickets in an innings has been achieved 16 times, all by different bowlers.

Most Economical Bowling: 10-4-9-0 D.Meherbaba South Zone v Central Zone (Chandigarh) 1981-82
Most Economical in 1996-97: 10-2-19-1 R.K.Chauhan Central Zone v West Zone (Delhi)

Most Expensive Bowling: 12-1-91-2 R.C.Shukla North Zone v West Zone (Bombay) 1975-76
Most Expensive in 1996-97: 10-0-65-4 M.Suresh Kumar Central Zone v East Zone (Delhi)

Most Wickets in Season: 11 (av 8.72) S.A.Ankola (West Zone) 1995-96
Most in 1996-97: 9 (av 16.44) U.Chatterjee (East Zone)

Most Wickets in Career: 30 (av 19.93) Maninder Singh (North Zone) 1983-84 to 1993-94; 27 (av 23.22) R.J.Shastri (West Zone) 1980-81 to 1993-94; 25 (av 25.88) Madan Lal (North Zone) 1973-74 to 1986-87
Most by Current Bowler: 23 (av 28.26) Avinash Kumar (East Zone) 1985-86 to 1995-96

Record Wicket Partnerships

1st	211	A.D.Gaekwad & G.A.Parkar	West Zone v North Zone (Sholapur)	1983-84
2nd	188	L.S.Rajput & S.V.Manjrekar	West Zone v East Zone (Pune)	1990-91
3rd	154*	D.B.Vengsarkar & A.V.Mankad	West Zone v East Zone (Ahmedabad)	1976-77
4th	179	K.Bhaskar Pillai & Kapil Dev	North Zone v Central Zone (Nagpur)	1988-89
5th	141	H.Gidwani & V.Lamba	North Zone v East Zone (Calcutta)	1975-76
6th	99*	M.L.Jaisimha & S.Abid Ali	South Zone v Central Zone (Madras)	1973-74
7th	133	H.K.Badani & N.A.David	South Zone v West Zone (Mohali)	1996-97
8th	101	Yajuvindra Singh & A.N.Shroff	West Zone v North Zone (Pune)	1977-78
9th	56	V.Sivaramakrishnan & A.Bhattacharjee	East Zone v North Zone (Calcutta)	1975-76
10th	37*	B.A.Burman & Randhir Singh	East Zone v North Zone (Cuttack)	1982-83

There were 5 hundred partnerships in 1996-97, the highest being 159 for the 2nd wicket G.K.Khoda & A.R.Khurasiya Central Zone v West Zone (Delhi)

Most Wicketkeeping Dismissals in Innings: 5 (5ct) S.S.Dighe West Zone v East Zone (Jamshedpur) 1994-95
Most in 1996-97: no wicketkeeper made more than 2

Most Wicketkeeping Dismissals in Season: 8 (5ct 3st) V.Samant (East Zone) 1996-97

Most Wicketkeeping Dismissals in Career: 33 (16ct 17st) S.S.Karim (East Zone) 1982-83 to 1995-96; 21 (17ct 4st) S.M.H.Kirmani (South Zone) 1973-74 to 1991-92; 18 (13ct 5st) V.Yadav (North Zone) 1991-92 to 1995-96

Most Catches by Fielder in Innings: 3 S.Abid Ali South Zone v West Zone (Madras) 1975-76; 3 R.Chadha North Zone v West Zone (Bombay) 1975-76; 3 S.M.Gavaskar West Zone v South Zone (Madras) 1975-76; 3 N.S.Yadav South Zone v West Zone (Chandigarh) 1981-82; 3 A.Bhattacharya East Zone v Central Zone (Vijayawada) 1984-85; 3 Arshad Ayub South Zone v East Zone (Bombay) 1990-91; 3 A.Kumble South Zone v West Zone (Rajkot) 1993-94; 3 R.K.Chauhan Central Zone v West Zone (Delhi) 1996-97; 3 F.Ghayas North Zone v Central Zone (Amritsar) 1996-97; 3 A.D.Jadeja North Zone v South Zone (Delhi) 1996-97; 3 S.Ramesh South Zone v North Zone (Delhi) 1996-97

Most Catches by Fielder in Season: 5 R.K.Chauhan (Central Zone) 1996-97; 5 A.R.Khurasiya (Central Zone) 1996-97; 5 S.Ramesh (South Zone) 1996-97

Most Catches by Fielder in Career: 12 L.S.Rajput (West Zone, East Zone) 1985-86 to 1993-94; 10 Yashpal Sharma (North Zone) 1978-79 to 1987-88; 9 A.K.Sharma (North Zone) 1986-87 to date

Most Appearances in Competition: 25 A.K.Sharma (North Zone) 1986-87 to date; 24 A.D.Gaekwad (West Zone) 1974-75 to 1987-88; 23 S.S.Karim (East Zone) 1982-83 to 1995-96; 23 A.Malhotra (North Zone, East Zone) 1976-77 to 1990-91

Wills Trophy

Highest Team Totals: 379-3 (50 overs) Wills XI v Hyderabad (Rajkot) 1995-96; 299-8 (60 overs) Karnataka v Uttar Pradesh (Bangalore) 1977-78; 299-5 (50 overs) Wills XI v Bengal (Bombay) 1995-96
Highest in 1996-97: 233-4 (47.1 overs) Haryana v Uttar Pradesh (Mohali)

Lowest Team Totals: 73 (41 overs) Rajasthan v Bombay (Delhi) 1980-81; 97 (22.3 overs) Orissa v Wills XI (Secunderabad) 1983-84; 99 (42.1 overs) Delhi v Bombay (Calcutta) 1982-83
Lowest in 1996-97: 187 (49.5 overs) Bengal v Karnataka (Mohali)

Highest Individual Innings: 145 J.Bakrania Gujarat v President's XI (Hyderabad) 1977-78; 136* M.R.Srinivasaprasad Karnataka v Wills XI (Hyderabad) 1983-84; 121* G.K.Khoda Wills XI v Hyderabad (Rajkot) 1995-96; 121 S.R.Tendulkar Wills XI v Hyderabad (Rajkot) 1995-96
Highest in 1996-97: 102* V.G.Kambli Mumbai v Karnataka (Mohali)
29 centuries have been scored in the competition, S.M.Gavaskar and S.R.Tendulkar scoring 3.

Most Runs in Season: 271 (av 135.50) S.M.Gavaskar (Bombay) 1981-82
Most in 1996-97: 166 (av 166.00) S.V.Manjrekar (Mumbai)

Most Runs in Career: 855 (av 61.07) S.V.Manjrekar (Mumbai) 1985-86 to date; 800 (av 40.00) Kirti Azad (Delhi) 1977-78 to 1992-93; 761 (av 54.35) S.J.Kalyani (Maharashtra, Bengal) 1984-85 to 1992-93

Best Innings Analyses: 6-21 R.P.Singh Uttar Pradesh v Bengal (Delhi) 1990-91; 5-30 B.S.Bedi Delhi v President's XI (Ahmedabad) 1978-79; 5-35 R.J.Shastri Bombay v Wills XI (Indore) 1981-82; 5-35 Ajay Sharma President's XI v Karnataka (Calcutta) 1987-88
Best in 1996-97: 4-33 U.Chatterjee Bengal v Karnataka (Mohali)
Five wickets in an innings has been achieved 5 times, twice by R.J.Shastri

Most Economical Bowling: 8-7-2-1 S.Valson Delhi v President's XI (Gauhati) 1982-83; 10-3-13-2 A.R.Kapoor Wills XI v Madhya Pradesh (Bikaner) 1991-92
Most Economical in 1996-97: 10-1-24-2 A.Katti Karnataka v Bengal (Mohali); 10-1-24-2 N.M.Kulkarni Mumbai v President's XI (Jullundur)

Most Expensive Bowling: 10-0-86-0 S.Vishnu Vardhan Hyderabad v Wills XI (Rajkot) 1995-96
Most Expensive in 1996-97: 10-3-65-2 V.Jain Haryana v Uttar Pradesh (Faridabad)

Most Wickets in Season: 10 (av 6.70) M.Prabhakar (Delhi) 1985-86; 10 (av 11.60) Ajay Sharma (President's XI) 1987-88
Most in 1996-97: 7 (av 18.28) S.V.Bahutule (Mumbai)

Most Wickets in Career: 40 (av 17.30) M.Prabhakar (Delhi) 1982-83 to 1995-96; 33 (av 18.57) R.J.Shastri (Bombay) 1980-81 to 1991-92; 26 (av 23.80) Kirti Azad (Delhi) 1977-78 to 1992-93

Record Wicket Partnerships

1st	202	S.V.Manjrekar & S.R.Tendulkar	Bombay v Haryana (Madras)	1994-95
2nd	187	G.K.Khoda & S.V.Manjrekar	Wills XI v Hyderabad (Rajkot)	1995-96
3rd	188*	W.V.Raman & A.Jadeja	Wills XI v Bengal (Delhi)	1990-91
4th	145*	S.V.Manjrekar & A.A.Muzumdar	Mumbai v President's XI (Jullundur)	1996-97
5th	118	V.Jaisimha & Arshad Ayub	Hyderabad v Madhya Pradesh (Indore)	1991-92
6th	123	S.Amarnath & Madan Lal	Delhi v President's XI (Ahmedabad)	1978-79
7th	99*	Saurav Ganguly & S.J.Kalyani	Bengal v Wills XI (Bombay)	1995-96

8th	80*	R.Manchanda & P.Thakur	Haryana v Bombay (Madras)		1994-95
9th	45	Chetan Sharma & A.Sarkar	Bengal v Bombay (Vijayawada)		1994-95
10th	45	Maninder Singh & Randhir Singh	Wills XI v Karnataka (Hyderabad)		1983-84

There were 3 hundred partnerships in 1996-97, the highest being the new 4th wicket record

Most Wicketkeeping Dismissals in Innings: 5 (4ct 1st) S.Viswanath Karnataka v Wills XI (Hyderabad) 1983-84; 5 (3ct 2st) V.Yadav Haryana v Wills XI (Faridabad) 1996-97

Most Wicketkeeping Dismissals in Season: 8 (7ct 1st) S.Viswanath (Karnataka) 1983-84; 8 (5ct 3st) S.S.Dighe (Mumbai) 1996-97

Most Wicketkeeping Dismissals in Career: 33 (26ct 7st) C.S.Pandit (Bombay, Madhya Pradesh) 1982-83 to 1995-96; 23 (20ct 3st) S.C.Khanna (Delhi) 1977-78 to 1986-87; 19 (11ct 8st) K.S.More (Baroda) 1982-83 to 1991-92

Most Catches by Fielder in Innings: 3 A.V.Mankad Wills XI v Bengal (Madras) 1977-78; 3 E.A.S.Prasanna Karnataka v Uttar Pradesh (Bangalore) 1977-78; 3 B.S.Bedi Delhi v President's XI (Ahmedabad) 1978-79; 3 Madan Lal President's XI v Bombay (Kanpur) 1981-82; 3 P.Shastri President's XI v Bengal (Ahmedabad) 1984-85; 3 G.Sharma Wills XI v Delhi (Visakhapatnam) 1988-89; 3 G.K.Pande Uttar Pradesh v Bengal (Baroda) 1989-90; 3 L.Sivaramakrishnan Tamil Nadu v President's XI (Surat) 1989-90; 3 A.D.Jadeja Wills XI v Madhya Pradesh (Bikaner) 1991-92; 3 R.P.Singh Uttar Pradesh v Haryana (Hyderabad) 1994-95
Most in 1996-97: no fielder held more than 2

Most Catches by Fielder in Season: 5 Dhanraj Singh (Haryana) 1994-95
Most in 1996-97: 3 A.A.Muzumdar (Mumbai)

Most Catches by Fielder in Career: 12 S.V.Manjrekar (Mumbai) 1985-86 to date; 12 R.J.Shastri (Bombay) 1980-81 to 1991-92; 11 Arun Lal (Bengal) 1977-78 to 1995-96; 11 A.Malhotra (Haryana, Bengal) 1978-79 to 1992-93

Most Appearances in Competition: 24 Kirti Azad (Delhi) 1977-78 to 1992-93; 22 Arun Lal (Bengal) 1977-78 to date; 21 K.Bhaskar Pillai (Delhi) 1982-83 to 1992-93
Most by Current Player: 19 S.V.Manjrekar (Mumbai) 1985-86 to date

CHAMPION TEAMS

Ranji Trophy

The competing teams were originally divided into four zones, each zone champion being decided on a knock-out basis and the four winners playing semi-finals and a final to decide the ultimate champion. For the 1948-49 season only the zones were abolished and an open draw system used. In 1953-54 a fifth zone was added. Since 1957-58 the zones have been run on a league basis and from 1970-71 each zonal runner-up, as well as the winner, competed in the final knock-out section and from 1992-93 the top three teams in each zone qualified. From 1996-97 the qualifying teams were divided into three groups and a round-robin played to produce a final knock-out section.

1934-35 Bombay	1955-56 Bombay	1976-77 Bombay
1935-36 Bombay	1956-57 Bombay	1977-78 Karnataka
1936-37 Nawanagar	1957-58 Baroda	1978-79 Delhi
1937-38 Hyderabad	1958-59 Bombay	1979-80 Delhi
1938-39 Bengal	1959-60 Bombay	1980-81 Bombay
1939-40 Maharashtra	1960-61 Bombay	1981-82 Delhi
1940-41 Maharashtra	1961-62 Bombay	1982-83 Karnataka
1941-42 Bombay	1962-63 Bombay	1983-84 Bombay
1942-43 Baroda	1963-64 Bombay	1984-85 Bombay
1943-44 Western India	1964-65 Bombay	1985-86 Delhi
1944-45 Bombay	1965-66 Bombay	1986-87 Hyderabad
1945-46 Holkar	1966-67 Bombay	1987-88 Tamil Nadu
1946-47 Baroda	1967-68 Bombay	1988-89 Delhi
1947-48 Holkar	1968-69 Bombay	1989-90 Bengal
1948-49 Bombay	1969-70 Bombay	1990-91 Haryana
1949-50 Baroda	1970-71 Bombay	1991-92 Delhi
1950-51 Holkar	1971-72 Bombay	1992-93 Punjab
1951-52 Bombay	1972-73 Bombay	1993-94 Bombay
1952-53 Holkar	1973-74 Karnataka	1994-95 Bombay
1953-54 Bombay	1974-75 Bombay	1995-96 Karnataka
1954-55 Madras	1975-76 Bombay	1996-97 Mumbai

Duleep Trophy

This competition is run between the five zones into which India is divided for the Ranji Trophy. Originally a knockout competition, it was changed to a league from 1993-94. In 1988-89 the trophy was shared as rain prevented a first-innings decision.

1961-62 West Zone	1973-74 North Zone	1985-86 West Zone
1962-63 West Zone	1974-75 South Zone	1986-87 South Zone
1963-64 West Zone	1975-76 South Zone	1987-88 North Zone
1964-65 West Zone	1976-77 West Zone	1988-89 North Zone, West Zone
1965-66 South Zone	1977-78 West Zone	1989-90 South Zone
1966-67 South Zone	1978-79 North Zone	1990-91 North Zone
1967-68 South Zone	1979-80 North Zone	1991-92 North Zone
1968-69 West Zone	1980-81 West Zone	1992-93 North Zone
1969-70 West Zone	1981-82 West Zone	1993-94 North Zone
1970-71 South Zone	1982-83 North Zone	1994-95 North Zone
1971-72 Central Zone	1983-84 North Zone	1995-96 South Zone
1972-73 West Zone	1984-85 South Zone	1996-97 Central Zone

Domestic Limited Overs Competitions

Deodhar Trophy

This competition is played between the five zonal teams. Originally played on a knockout basis, it was changed to a league from 1993-94. Since 1979-80 the competition has been held in a single zone during one week. The overs limit was 60 between 1973-74 and 1979-80 and thereafter has been reduced to 50. Results of the finals:

1973-74 South Zone 185 (52.1 overs) beat West Zone 101 (38 overs) by 84 runs
1974-75 South Zone 263-5 (60 overs) beat West Zone 255-9 (60 overs) by 8 runs
1975-76 West Zone 185 (55.2 overs) beat South Zone 161 (49 overs) by 24 runs
1976-77 Central Zone 207-7 (56 overs) beat South Zone 206-9 (60 overs) by 3 wkts
1977-78 North Zone 177-0 (38.5 overs) beat West Zone 174 (53 overs) by 10 wkts
1978-79 South Zone 247 (59.4 overs) beat North Zone 218 (56.1 overs) by 29 runs
1979-80 West Zone 246-6 (48 overs) beat North Zone 245-9 (50 overs) by 4 wkts
1980-81 South Zone 275-5 (50 overs) beat West Zone 189-7 (50 overs) by 86 runs
1981-82 South Zone 260-5 (50 overs) beat Central Zone 147 (50 overs) by 113 runs
1982-83 West Zone 198-9 (46 overs) beat North Zone 185-9 (46 overs) by 13 runs
1983-84 West Zone 309 (48.4 overs) beat North Zone 266 (47.2 overs) by 43 runs
1984-85 West Zone 218-4 (37.5 overs) beat North Zone 214-8 (45 overs) by 6 wkts
1985-86 West Zone 227-9 (47 overs) beat North Zone 196 (44.5 overs) by 31 runs
1986-87 North Zone 207-1 (39.5 overs) beat West Zone 206-9 (48 overs) by 9 wkts
1987-88 North Zone 223-3 (45.2 overs) beat West Zone 221-7 (50 overs) by 7 wkts
1988-89 North Zone 243-6 (45 overs) beat South Zone 239-8 (46 overs) by 4 wkts
1989-90 North Zone 319-6 (50 overs) beat South Zone 263-8 (50 overs) by 56 runs
1990-91 West Zone 304-3 (44 overs) beat East Zone 260 (41.4 overs) by 44 runs
1991-92 South Zone 158-7 (35 overs) beat Central Zone 122 (33.2 overs) by 36 runs
1992-93 East Zone 257-9 (50 overs) beat North Zone 254-4 (50 overs) by 1 wkt
1993-94 East Zone
1994-95 Central Zone
1995-96 North Zone
1996-97 East Zone

Table of Results 1973-74 to 1996-97

	P	W	L	T	NR	Winner	R-up
South Zone	52	29	21	0	2	6	6
West Zone	53	29	21	1	2	7	7
North Zone	51	27	22	0	2	6	8
Central Zone	44	17	25	1	1	2	2
East Zone	40	12	25	0	3	3	1

Wills Trophy

This competition is played on a knock-out basis between the five zonal winners of the previous season's Ranji Trophy plus two representative sides, who choose their players from the other Ranji Trophy teams. The overs limit is 50 per side, although in the first two seasons 60 overs per side were played. In 1993-94 Ranji Trophy one-day matches were introduced as qualification for the following season's Wills Trophy. Results of the finals:

1977-78 Wills XI 214-3 (52.3 overs) beat President's XI 213-4 (60 overs) by 7 wkts
1978-79 Delhi 253-7 (60 overs) beat Bombay 253 (56.1 overs) by losing fewer wickets
1979-80 No competition
1980-81 Wills XI 218-7 (49.3 overs) beat President's XI 216-8 (50 overs) by 3 wkts
1981-82 Bombay 225-7 (50 overs) beat President's XI 210-8 (50 overs) by 15 runs
1982-83 Bombay 158 (47.1 overs) beat Delhi 99 (42.1 overs) by 59 runs
1983-84 President's XI 269-6 (42 overs) beat Karnataka 242-9 (42 overs) by 27 runs
1984-85 Wills XI 252-4 (46.1 overs) beat President's XI 249 (49.4 overs) by 6 wkts
1985-86 Bombay 228-9 (46.2 overs) beat Delhi 226-5 (47 overs) by 1 wkt
1986-87 Delhi 258-8 (50 overs) beat Maharashtra 159 (37.4 overs) by 99 runs
1987-88 President's XI 244-5 (47 overs) beat Karnataka 184 (45.5 overs) by 60 runs
1988-89 Delhi 205-2 (44.1 overs) beat Railways 200 (48.2 overs) by 8 wkts
1989-90 Wills XI 265-4 (47.3 overs) beat Delhi 261-9 (49 overs) by 6 wkts
1990-91 Bombay 257-3 (46.5 overs) beat Wills XI 254-9 (49 overs) by 7 wkts
1991-92 President's XI 234-8 (50 overs) beat Wills XI 206-8 (50 overs) by 28 runs
1992-93 President's XI 128 (43.2 overs) beat Delhi 128 (44.4 overs) on scoring rate
1993-94 No competiton
1994-95 Bombay 265-1 (36.4 overs) beat Haryana 263-7 (50 overs) by 9 wkts
1995-96 Wills XI 299-5 (50 overs) beat Bengal 224-6 (50 overs) by 75 runs
1996-97 Mumbai 230-4 (46.1 overs) beat Haryana 229 (50 overs) by 6 wkts

Table of Results 1977-78 to 1996-97

	P	W	L	NR	Winner	R-up
Wills XI	36	22	13	1	5	2
Mumbai	27	21	5	1	6	1
President's XI	34	20	13	1	4	4
Delhi	24	16	8	0	3	4
Karnataka	13	6	6	1	0	2
Bengal	19	5	13	1	0	1
Haryana	11	5	6	0	0	2
Maharashtra	7	3	4	0	0	1
Railways	5	3	2	0	0	1
Madhya Pradesh	4	2	2	0	0	0
Tamil Nadu	6	1	5	0	0	0
Uttar Pradesh	13	1	12	0	0	0
Andhra	1	0	1	0	0	0
Baroda	2	0	2	0	0	0
Bihar	3	0	3	0	0	0
Gujarat	1	0	1	0	0	0
Hyderabad	5	0	4	1	0	0
Orissa	2	0	2	0	0	0
Punjab	1	0	1	0	0	0
Rajasthan	2	0	2	0	0	0

Matches decided on the toss of a coin are included as No Result.

1996-97 AND CAREER RECORDS FOR INDIAN PLAYERS

Cmp	Debut	M	I	NO	Runs	HS	Avge	100	50	Balls	Runs	Wkts	Avge	BB	5i	10m	RpO	ct	st
ABBAS ALI, Syed (Madhya Pradesh) b Indore 20.2.1976 LHB OB																			
FC		10	15	1	761	198	54.35	3	3	144	94	2	47.00	2-19	0	0	3.91	17	
AGARKAR, Ajit Bhalchandra (Mumbai) b Bombay 4.12.1977 RHB SLA																			
FC		3	3	0	72	39	24.00	0	0	420	183	5	36.60	2-45	0	0	2.61	3	
AGASHE, Ashutosh Dnyaneshwar (Maharashtra) b Pune 21.10.1972 RHB RM																			
FC		1	1	0	1	1	1.00	0	0	108	47	0					2.61	1	
AMARJIT KAYPEE (Haryana) b Jullundur 2.10.1960 RHB																			
FC		8	14	4	619	135*	61.90	2	4	30	28	0					5.60	13	
Wlls		2	2	0	52	41	26.00	0	0									1	
FC	1980	93	138	20	6442	210*	54.59	24	26	78	54	1	54.00	1-17	0	0	4.15	79	
Deo	1982	3	3	0	30	19	10.00	0	0	6	7	0					7.00	2	
Wlls	1986	8	7	0	167	59	23.85	0	1									2	
AMRE, Pravin Kalyan (Bengal, East Zone) b Bombay 14.8.1968 RHB LB																			
FC		9	16	1	598	95	39.86	0	6									8	
Deo		4	4	1	147	70*	49.00	0	2									0	
Test	1992	11	13	3	425	103	42.50	1	3									9	
FC	1986	68	103	12	4987	246	54.80	16	21	12	12	0					6.00	45	
Int	1991	37	30	5	513	84*	20.52	0	2	2	4	0					12.00	12	
Deo	1988	17	17	3	425	87*	30.35	0	3									6	
Wlls	1989	8	6	2	147	80*	36.75	0	1	12	9	0					4.50	2	
ANANTH, D.S. (Karnataka)																			
Wlls		2	2	0	48	40	24.00	0	0	114	76	2	38.00	2-30	0	0	4.00	0	
ANANTH, Rangarao (Karnataka) b Calcutta 25.8.1964 RHB OB																			
FC		6	10	1	41	19	4.55	0	0	1296	487	18	27.05	4-72	0	0	2.25	1	
Wlls		2	1	0	1	1	1.00	0	0	112	65	2	32.50	2-28	0	0	3.48	0	
FC	1988	50	57	18	316	30	8.10	0	0	8979	3862	153	25.24	6-56	4	0	2.58	21	
Wlls	1994	3	1	0	1	1	1.00	0	0	118	72	2	36.00	2-28	0	0	3.66	0	
ANKOLA, Salil Ashok (Mumbai, West Zone, President's XI, India to South Africa) b Sholapur 1.3.1968 RHB RMF																			
FC		4	6	0	119	63	19.83	0	1	738	364	11	33.09	3-101	0	0	2.95	2	
Deo		4	3	2	57	43*	57.00	0	0	198	102	6	17.00	4-23	1	0	3.09	0	
Wlls		1								54	46	1	46.00	1-46	0	0	5.11	1	
Test	1989	1	1	0	6	6	6.00	0	0	180	128	2	64.00	1-35	0	0	4.26	0	
FC	1988	54	56	11	707	63	15.71	0	1	8656	4585	181	25.33	6-47	8	0	3.17	22	
Int	1989	20	13	4	34	9	3.77	0	0	807	615	13	47.30	3-33	0	0	4.57	2	
Deo	1988	16	12	4	159	43*	19.87	0	0	747	518	24	21.58	4-22	2	0	4.16	4	
Wlls	1988	8	3	0	30	15	10.00	0	0	360	262	7	37.42	3-11	0	0	4.36	3	
AROTHE, Tushar Bhalchandra (Baroda) b Baroda 17.9.1966 LHB OB																			
FC		7	11	1	470	99	47.00	0	4	884	331	20	16.55	5-38	1	0	2.24	3	
FC	1985	62	95	7	3554	171	40.38	8	17	9050	4514	147	30.70	6-57	9	1	2.99	43	
Deo	1993	6	4	0	79	39	19.75	0	0	270	152	3	50.66	1-17	0	0	3.37	1	
Wlls	1988	2	2	0	60	43	30.00	0	0									0	
ARUNKUMAR, Jagdish (Karnataka) b Bangalore 18.1.1975 RHB OB																			
FC		5	9	0	212	93	23.55	0	1	18	5	1	5.00	1-5	0	0	1.66	5	
Wlls		2	2	0	89	71	44.50	0	1									0	
FC	1993	23	37	2	1535	141	43.85	3	9	30	9	1	9.00	1-5	0	0	1.80	23	
Deo	1994	4	4	0	52	39	13.00	0	0									1	
Wlls	1994	3	3	0	105	71	35.00	0	1									0	
ARVIND KUMAR, Gangashetty (Hyderabad) b Hyderabad 4.10.1973 LHB LBG																			
FC		10	17	0	563	116	33.11	1	3	6	2	0					2.00	5	
FC	1994	18	32	2	948	116	31.60	2	4	12	2	0					1.00	8	
Wlls	1995	1	1	0	0	0	0.00	0	0									0	
ARVIND SINGH (Uttar Pradesh) b Pratapgarh 1.4.1977 RHB RM																			
FC		2	3	1	2	2*	1.00	0	0	204	128	1	128.00	1-76	0	0	3.76	0	
ASHIQUE ALI, Jaffar (Tamil Nadu) b Erode 9.10.1973 RHB LB																			
FC		2	4	1	77	55	25.66	0	1									3	
FC	1995	3	5	1	77	55	19.25	0	1	12	12	0					6.00	3	
ASLAM, Mohammad (Jammu and Kashmir) WK																			
FC		3	6	4	5	3*	2.50	0	0									3	
ASLAM, Mohammad (Rajasthan, Central Zone) b Jaipur 7.8.1974 LHB SLA																			
FC		5	6	1	100	30	20.00	0	0	1439	685	19	36.05	5-95	1	0	2.85	2	
FC	1990	29	44	4	442	39	11.05	0	0	6684	3153	111	28.40	5-42	5	0	2.83	14	
Deo	1995	2	1	0	0	0	0.00	0	0	78	66	3	22.00	3-38	0	0	5.07	1	

Cmp Debut M I NO Runs HS Avge 100 50 Balls Runs Wkts Avge BB 5i 10m RpO ct st

AZHARUDDIN, Mohammad (India, India to South Africa, India to West Indies, India to Canada, India to Sri Lanka, India to Zimbabwe) b Hyderabad 8.2.1963 RHB RM

Cmp	Debut	M	I	NO	Runs	HS	Avge	100	50	Balls	Runs	Wkts	Avge	BB	5i	10m	RpO	ct	st
Test		4	8	2	426	163*	71.00	2	1									6	
FC		4	8	2	426	163*	71.00	2	1									6	
Int		7	7	1	240	94	40.00	0	2									8	
Test	1984	83	120	6	5011	199	43.96	17	16	7	12	0					10.28	88	
FC	1981	199	297	32	13584	226	51.26	47	60	1252	673	12	56.08	2-22	0	0	3.22	192	
Int	1984	245	227	42	6701	108*	36.22	3	39	552	479	12	39.91	3-19	0	0	5.20	106	
Deo	1983	12	12	3	515	101	57.22	1	5	24	16	0					4.00	6	
Wlls	1983	5	4	1	84	47*	28.00	0	0	42	47	1	47.00	1-47	0	0	6.71	3	

BADANI, Hemang Kamal (Tamil Nadu, South Zone, Wills XI) b Madras 14.11.1976 LHB SLA

Cmp	Debut	M	I	NO	Runs	HS	Avge	100	50	Balls	Runs	Wkts	Avge	BB	5i	10m	RpO	ct	st
FC		6	9	2	473	164	67.57	1	3									3	
Deo		4	4	1	127	82*	42.33	0	1									1	
Wlls		1	1	0	17	17	17.00	0	0									1	

BAHUTULE, Sairaj Vasant (Mumbai, West Zone, India A) b Bombay 6.1.1973 LHB LB

Cmp	Debut	M	I	NO	Runs	HS	Avge	100	50	Balls	Runs	Wkts	Avge	BB	5i	10m	RpO	ct	st
FC		10	12	2	253	72	25.30	0	2	3020	1316	39	33.74	4-25	0	0	2.61	3	
Deo		4	3	0	58	40	19.33	0	0	198	140	7	20.00	4-33	1	0	4.24	0	
Wlls		3								180	128	7	18.28	3-29	0	0	4.26	2	
FC	1991	55	71	16	1868	134*	33.96	5	4	12812	5742	180	31.90	7-63	3	0	2.68	31	
Deo	1992	10	8	0	108	40	13.50	0	0	579	400	18	22.22	4-26	2	0	4.14	1	
Wlls	1992	10	3	1	29	28	14.50	0	0	573	354	16	22.12	3-29	0	0	3.70	5	

BAJPAI, Shivdhar (Uttar Pradesh) b Kanpur 25.9.1975 RHB SLA

Cmp	Debut	M	I	NO	Runs	HS	Avge	100	50	Balls	Runs	Wkts	Avge	BB	5i	10m	RpO	ct	st
FC		6	8	3	99	31*	19.80	0	0	965	386	12	32.16	3-49	0	0	2.40	1	

BAKRIWALA, Nimesh Shirishbhai (Gujarat) b Ahmedabad 9.9.1967 RHB RM

Cmp	Debut	M	I	NO	Runs	HS	Avge	100	50	Balls	Runs	Wkts	Avge	BB	5i	10m	RpO	ct	st
FC		1	2	0	17	16	8.50	0	0									0	
FC	1991	11	21	1	551	68	27.55	0	4	72	46	1	46.00	1-29	0	0	3.83	4	

BALAJI RAO, Wandavasi Dorakanti (Tamil Nadu) b Madras 4.3.1978 LHB LBG

Cmp	Debut	M	I	NO	Runs	HS	Avge	100	50	Balls	Runs	Wkts	Avge	BB	5i	10m	RpO	ct	st
FC		5	6	1	30	17	6.00	0	0	788	331	12	27.58	5-47	1	0	2.52	2	
FC	1994	16	19	6	135	26	10.38	0	0	3272	1541	51	30.21	5-47	3	0	2.82	7	

BALASUBRAMANIAM, K.Narayanaiyer (Kerala) b Trivandrum 1.4.1967 RHB OB

Cmp	Debut	M	I	NO	Runs	HS	Avge	100	50	Balls	Runs	Wkts	Avge	BB	5i	10m	RpO	ct	st
FC		9	15	0	326	52	21.73	0	1									10	
FC	1990	17	30	1	650	52*	22.41	0	3	132	50	1	50.00	1-5	0	0	2.27	21'	

BALI, Pradeep (Jammu and Kashmir)

Cmp	Debut	M	I	NO	Runs	HS	Avge	100	50	Balls	Runs	Wkts	Avge	BB	5i	10m	RpO	ct	st
FC		2	4	0	63	29	15.75	0	0	276	144	3	48.00	3-74	0	0	3.13	0	
FC	1991	6	11	1	150	41	15.00	0	0	439	246	6	41.00	3-54	0	0	3.36	1	

BALI, Ranjit (Jammu and Kashmir) b Jammu 22.1.1974 RHB WK

Cmp	Debut	M	I	NO	Runs	HS	Avge	100	50	Balls	Runs	Wkts	Avge	BB	5i	10m	RpO	ct	st
FC		1	2	0	0	0	0.00	0	0									1	
FC	1990	13	23	0	535	68	23.26	0	3									5	

BALJIT SINGH (Orissa) b Sambalpur 18.5.1981 RHB LB

Cmp	Debut	M	I	NO	Runs	HS	Avge	100	50	Balls	Runs	Wkts	Avge	BB	5i	10m	RpO	ct	st
FC		1	1	0	1	1	1.00	0	0	186	98	3	32.66	3-98	0	0	3.16	0	

BANERJEE, Amitava (Bengal) b Calcutta 1.3.1972 RHB RM

Cmp	Debut	M	I	NO	Runs	HS	Avge	100	50	Balls	Runs	Wkts	Avge	BB	5i	10m	RpO	ct	st
FC		1	1	0	5	5	5.00	0	0	30	13	0					2.60	0	

BANERJEE, Souvik (Bengal)

Cmp	Debut	M	I	NO	Runs	HS	Avge	100	50	Balls	Runs	Wkts	Avge	BB	5i	10m	RpO	ct	st
Wlls		1	1	0	2	2	2.00	0	0	30	20	0					4.00	0	

BANERJEE, Subroto (Bengal, East Zone) b Patna 13.2.1969 RHB RMF

Cmp	Debut	M	I	NO	Runs	HS	Avge	100	50	Balls	Runs	Wkts	Avge	BB	5i	10m	RpO	ct	st
FC		6	6	0	86	50	14.33	0	1	738	264	10	26.40	3-23	0	0	2.14	2	
Deo		4	3	0	29	12	9.66	0	0	198	113	4	28.25	3-27	0	0	3.42	0	
Test	1991	1	1	0	3	3	3.00	0	0	108	47	3	15.66	3-47	0	0	2.61	0	
FC	1987	49	62	5	1067	81	18.71	0	7	6720	3283	109	30.11	7-18	6	1	2.93	26	
Int	1991	6	5	3	49	25*	24.50	0	0	240	202	5	40.40	3-30	0	0	5.05	3	
Deo	1988	17	15	5	246	50*	24.60	0	1	793	531	20	26.55	5-40	0	1	4.01	3	
Wlls	1988	8	3	2	25	14*	25.00	0	0	348	217	9	24.11	3-13	0	0	3.74	0	

BANGAR, Sanjay Bapusaheb (Railways, Central Zone, Wills XI) b Beed 11.10.1972 RHB RMF

Cmp	Debut	M	I	NO	Runs	HS	Avge	100	50	Balls	Runs	Wkts	Avge	BB	5i	10m	RpO	ct	st
FC		9	16	2	524	122	37.42	1	2	991	451	14	32.21	3-46	0	0	2.73	3	
Deo		2	2	0	7	7	3.50	0	0	18	15	0					5.00	0	
Wlls		1	1	0	2	2	2.00	0	0	6	11	0					11.00	0	
FC	1993	18	32	4	1221	161	43.60	3	4	1996	964	22	43.81	3-46	0	0	2.89	9	

BARDE, Yeshwant Chandrakant (Goa) b Mapuca 15.2.1973 RHB RM

Cmp	Debut	M	I	NO	Runs	HS	Avge	100	50	Balls	Runs	Wkts	Avge	BB	5i	10m	RpO	ct	st
FC		5	9	2	80	26*	11.42	0	0	534	264	10	26.40	3-60	0	0	2.96	2	
FC	1993	14	27	2	413	42	16.52	9	9	1008	613	15	40.86	4-133	0	0	3.64	7	

BARIK, Ajay (Orissa) b Cuttack 10.1.1976 RHB RM

Cmp	Debut	M	I	NO	Runs	HS	Avge	100	50	Balls	Runs	Wkts	Avge	BB	5i	10m	RpO	ct	st
FC		2	2	0	13	9	6.50	0	0	365	203	3	67.66	3-119	0	0	3.33	0	

BARIK, Alekha (Orissa) b Rourkela 5.2.1976 RHB

Cmp	Debut	M	I	NO	Runs	HS	Avge	100	50	Balls	Runs	Wkts	Avge	BB	5i	10m	RpO	ct	st
FC		3	6	0	120	45	20.00	0	0									2	
FC	1995	4	7	0	132	45	18.85	0	0									2	

BAROT, Dhiren Jayantilal (Gujarat) b Ahmedabad 26.6.1972 LHB SLA

Cmp	Debut	M	I	NO	Runs	HS	Avge	100	50	Balls	Runs	Wkts	Avge	BB	5i	10m	RpO	ct	st
FC		3	6	2	56	16	14.00	0	0	372	242	4	60.50	4-118	0	0	3.90	2	

Cmp	Debut	M	I	NO	Runs	HS	Avge	100	50	Balls	Runs	Wkts	Avge	BB	5i	10m	RpO	ct	st

BEDADE, Atul Chandrakant (Baroda) b Bombay 24.9.1966 LHB RM

Cmp	Debut	M	I	NO	Runs	HS	Avge	100	50	Balls	Runs	Wkts	Avge	BB	5i	10m	RpO	ct	st
FC		7	11	1	289	102*	28.90	1	1	96	45	0					2.81	6	
FC	1990	32	53	2	1911	159	37.47	8	7	165	72	0					2.61	16	
Int	1993	13	10	3	158	51	22.57	0	1									4	
Deo	1993	4	3	0	124	53	41.33	0	1	24	22	0					5.50	1	
Wlls	1988	3	2	0	32	22	16.00	0	0									1	

BEDI, Arun (Punjab) b Hoshiarpur 10.11.1965 RHB RM

Cmp	Debut	M	I	NO	Runs	HS	Avge	100	50	Balls	Runs	Wkts	Avge	BB	5i	10m	RpO	ct	st
FC		1								48	54	0					6.75	0	
FC	1990	22	22	13	97	28*	10.77	0	0	3204	1367	66	20.71	6-26	3	0	2.55	5	
Deo	1995	1	1	0	5	5	5.00	0	0	48	21	1	21.00	1-21	0	0	2.62	0	

BELSARE, Umesh Suresh (Gujarat) b Ahmedabad 11.10.1958 RHB RM

Cmp	Debut	M	I	NO	Runs	HS	Avge	100	50	Balls	Runs	Wkts	Avge	BB	5i	10m	RpO	ct	st
FC		2	4	0	78	48	19.50	0	0									0	
FC	1989	13	23	1	426	72	19.36	0	2	378	282	2	141.00	1-44	0	0	4.47	1	

BHAGWAT, Anshuman (Assam) b Sonitpur 27.12.1978 RHB RM

Cmp	Debut	M	I	NO	Runs	HS	Avge	100	50	Balls	Runs	Wkts	Avge	BB	5i	10m	RpO	ct	st
FC		1	2	1	18	11	18.00	0	0	162	63	2	31.50	2-49	0	0	2.33	0	
FC	1994	5	9	3	88	28	14.66	0	0	559	262	9	29.11	6-49	1	0	2.81	0	

BHARATAN, Krishnamachari (Railways) b Madras 5.1.1963 RHB OB

Cmp	Debut	M	I	NO	Runs	HS	Avge	100	50	Balls	Runs	Wkts	Avge	BB	5i	10m	RpO	ct	st
FC		8	12	1	254	63	23.09	0	1	840	286	5	57.20	2-52	0	0	2.04	8	
FC	1987	44	59	9	1532	140*	30.64	2	8	6980	2771	91	30.45	7-39	5	1	2.38	39	
Wlls	1988	5	5	1	112	32	28.00	0	0	168	100	2	50.00	2-31	0	0	3.57	1	

BHASKAR, Vidya (Jammu and Kashmir) b Jammu 25.4.1965 RHB

Cmp	Debut	M	I	NO	Runs	HS	Avge	100	50	Balls	Runs	Wkts	Avge	BB	5i	10m	RpO	ct	st
FC		2	4	0	148	96	37.00	0	1	48	24	0					3.00	4	
FC	1982	42	75	2	1918	130	26.27	3	11	210	109	1	109.00	1-22	0	0	3.11	25	

BHATIA, Saket (Railways) b Delhi 6.10.1978 RHB RM

Cmp	Debut	M	I	NO	Runs	HS	Avge	100	50	Balls	Runs	Wkts	Avge	BB	5i	10m	RpO	ct	st
FC		2	2	0	22	18	11.00	0	0									3	

BHATT, Prakash Jitendrabhai (Saurashtra) b Bhavnagar 28.1.1970 RHB

Cmp	Debut	M	I	NO	Runs	HS	Avge	100	50	Balls	Runs	Wkts	Avge	BB	5i	10m	RpO	ct	st
FC		3	4	0	242	123	60.50	2	0									1	
FC	1994	8	13	1	455	123	37.91	2	1									7	

BHATT, Zahoor (Jammu and Kashmir)

Cmp	Debut	M	I	NO	Runs	HS	Avge	100	50	Balls	Runs	Wkts	Avge	BB	5i	10m	RpO	ct	st
FC		2	4	0	25	16	6.25	0	0	12	8	0					4.00	1	
FC	1981	25	44	1	675	77	15.69	0	4	270	179	5	35.80	2-29	0	0	3.97	15	

BHATTI, Ajay (Jammu and Kashmir) b Jammu 28.9.1970 LHB

Cmp	Debut	M	I	NO	Runs	HS	Avge	100	50	Balls	Runs	Wkts	Avge	BB	5i	10m	RpO	ct	st
FC		1	2	0	20	20	10.00	0	0									0	
FC	1993	6	9	0	217	69	24.11	0	3									0	

BHAVE, Surendra Shriram (Maharashtra, West Zone) b Poona 30.3.1966 RHB RM

Cmp	Debut	M	I	NO	Runs	HS	Avge	100	50	Balls	Runs	Wkts	Avge	BB	5i	10m	RpO	ct	st
FC		11	16	0	832	168	52.00	2	6	200	130	1	130.00	1-1	0	0	3.90	14	
Deo		3	3	0	63	43	21.00	0	0									2	
FC	1986	74	120	16	6491	292	62.41	22	24	920	487	7	69.57	2-42	0	0	3.17	89	
Deo	1989	17	17	1	521	79	32.56	0	4	42	47	2	23.50	2-47	0	0	6.71	9	
Wlls	1988	5	5	0	182	66	36.40	0	1									0	

BHOHITE, Ajit Prataprao (Baroda) b Baroda 9.10.1976 RHB OB

Cmp	Debut	M	I	NO	Runs	HS	Avge	100	50	Balls	Runs	Wkts	Avge	BB	5i	10m	RpO	ct	st
FC		3	5	1	57	24*	14.25	0	0	6	1	0					1.00	3	

BHUPINDER SINGH (Punjab) b Tarantaran 19.11.1970 RHB

Cmp	Debut	M	I	NO	Runs	HS	Avge	100	50	Balls	Runs	Wkts	Avge	BB	5i	10m	RpO	ct	st
FC		9	13	1	367	68	30.58	0	4	30	23	1	23.00	1-23	0	0	4.60	12	
FC	1989	54	79	10	3210	297	46.52	10	15	84	45	2	22.50	1-21	0	0	3.21	39	
Deo	1994	6	6	0	103	54	17.16	0	1	18	14	1	14.00	1-14	0	0	4.66	2	
Wlls	1992	3	3	0	51	36	17.00	0	0									3	

BHUSHAN, Bharat (Punjab) b Ludhiana 3.9.1973 RHB RMF

Cmp	Debut	M	I	NO	Runs	HS	Avge	100	50	Balls	Runs	Wkts	Avge	BB	5i	10m	RpO	ct	st
FC		7	6	4	41	13*	20.50	0	0	1438	695	26	26.73	5-72	1	0	2.89	3	

BIJENDER SINGH (Uttar Pradesh) b Bulandsaher 1.12.1977 RHB RM

Cmp	Debut	M	I	NO	Runs	HS	Avge	100	50	Balls	Runs	Wkts	Avge	BB	5i	10m	RpO	ct	st
FC		1	1	1	0	0*		0	0	66	29	0					2.63	0	

BISWAL, Ranjib (Orissa) b Cuttack 21.9.1970 RHB OB

Cmp	Debut	M	I	NO	Runs	HS	Avge	100	50	Balls	Runs	Wkts	Avge	BB	5i	10m	RpO	ct	st
FC		1	1	0	0	0	0.00	0	0	370	156	7	22.28	4-109	0	0	2.52	0	
FC	1987	41	59	5	2170	160	40.18	5	13	8562	3647	153	23.83	7-38	13	3	2.55	16	
Deo	1990	12	8	2	136	42	22.66	0	0	256	199	8	24.87	3-31	0	0	4.66	3	

BORA, Deep (Assam) b Gauhati 1.10.1972 RHB

Cmp	Debut	M	I	NO	Runs	HS	Avge	100	50	Balls	Runs	Wkts	Avge	BB	5i	10m	RpO	ct	st
FC		2	3	0	76	50	25.33	0	1									2	
FC	1994	5	9	0	240	102	26.66	1	1									3	

BORA, Rajesh (Assam) b Tezpur 14.11.1967 RHB OB

Cmp	Debut	M	I	NO	Runs	HS	Avge	100	50	Balls	Runs	Wkts	Avge	BB	5i	10m	RpO	ct	st
FC		3	6	0	40	12	6.66	0	0	156	99	1	99.00	1-59	0	0	3.80	0	
FC	1983	53	89	1	2896	235	32.90	5	13	2125	1072	23	46.60	4-110	0	0	3.02	28	
Deo	1983	5	5	0	30	23	6.00	0	0	24	31	0					7.75	2	

BORDOLOI, Nishanta (Assam) b Gauhati 29.12.1977 RHB OB

Cmp	Debut	M	I	NO	Runs	HS	Avge	100	50	Balls	Runs	Wkts	Avge	BB	5i	10m	RpO	ct	st
FC		1	1	1	151	151*		1	0									1	
FC	1994	9	16	1	400	151*	26.66	1	2									11	

Cmp	Debut	M	I	NO	Runs	HS	Avge	100	50	Balls	Runs	Wkts	Avge	BB	5i	10m	RpO	ct	st

BUCH, Valmik Nalinkant (Baroda, West Zone) b Rajkot 29.8.1975 LHB SLA

Cmp	Debut	M	I	NO	Runs	HS	Avge	100	50	Balls	Runs	Wkts	Avge	BB	5i	10m	RpO	ct	st
FC		8	12	2	90	38	9.00	0	0	1403	690	11	62.72	3-62	0	0	2.95	7	
FC	1993	24	37	9	475	94	16.96	0	2	5022	2420	77	31.42	6-75	2	0	2.89	20	
Deo	1995	2	1	0	9	9	9.00	0	0	114	90	4	22.50	3-33	0	0	4.73	0	

BUNDELA, Devendrasingh (Madhya Pradesh) b Indore 22.2.1977 RHB RM

| FC | | 5 | 8 | 2 | 215 | 102* | 35.83 | 1 | 1 | 348 | 206 | 3 | 68.66 | 2-56 | 0 | 0 | 3.55 | 2 | |
| FC | 1995 | 6 | 10 | 2 | 275 | 102* | 34.37 | 1 | 1 | 348 | 206 | 3 | 68.66 | 2-56 | 0 | 0 | 3.55 | 2 | |

BURMAN, Kaushik (Tripura)

| FC | | 4 | 8 | 0 | 195 | 48 | 24.37 | 0 | 0 | | | | | | | | | 3 | |

CHAKRABORTY, Debjit (Assam) b Siliguri 1.6.1968 RHB RM

| FC | | 1 | 2 | 0 | 7 | 7 | 3.50 | 0 | 0 | 30 | 16 | 1 | 16.00 | 1-14 | 0 | 0 | 3.20 | 1 | |
| FC | 1992 | 15 | 26 | 1 | 467 | 72 | 18.68 | 0 | 1 | 581 | 336 | 8 | 42.00 | 2-36 | 0 | 0 | 3.46 | 6 | |

CHAKRABORTY, Devjeet (Bihar) b Patna 8.5.1978 RHB

| FC | | 5 | 9 | 0 | 175 | 111 | 19.44 | 1 | 0 | 126 | 54 | 3 | 18.00 | 2-29 | 0 | 0 | 2.57 | 2 | |

CHAKRABORTY, Satya Gopal (Assam) b Gauhati 12.11.1963 RHB OB

| FC | | 2 | 3 | 1 | 7 | 7* | 3.50 | 0 | 0 | 225 | 80 | 2 | 40.00 | 1-37 | 0 | 0 | 2.13 | 0 | |
| FC | 1982 | 44 | 65 | 23 | 427 | 43* | 10.16 | 0 | 0 | 7034 | 3040 | 77 | 39.48 | 6-35 | 3 | 0 | 2.59 | 9 | |

CHAKRADAR RAO, Konkala (Andhra) b Kurnool 14.11.1963 LHB SLA

| FC | | 5 | 9 | 2 | 35 | 20* | 5.00 | 0 | 0 | 1534 | 572 | 20 | 28.60 | 4-70 | 0 | 0 | 2.23 | 3 | |
| FC | 1988 | 25 | 40 | 8 | 219 | 21 | 6.84 | 0 | 0 | 5585 | 2675 | 90 | 29.72 | 6-92 | 4 | 0 | 2.87 | 14 | |

CHAMAN LAL (Punjab) b Amritsar 20.10.1971 RHB OB

| FC | | 4 | 4 | 1 | 36 | 21* | 12.00 | 0 | 0 | 1153 | 506 | 11 | 46.00 | 3-93 | 0 | 0 | 2.63 | 0 | |
| FC | 1995 | 5 | 5 | 2 | 60 | 24* | 20.00 | 0 | 0 | 1575 | 675 | 15 | 45.00 | 3-75 | 0 | 0 | 2.57 | 2 | |

CHANDA, Timir (Tripura) b Agartala 25.6.1978 RHB RM

| FC | | 1 | 2 | 0 | 46 | 34 | 23.00 | 0 | 0 | | | | | | | | | 0 | |
| FC | 1995 | 3 | 6 | 0 | 73 | 34 | 12.16 | 0 | 0 | 12 | 18 | 0 | | | | | 9.00 | 2 | |

CHANDEL, Sandeep (Himachal Pradesh) b Dharmasala 1.9.1973 LHB SLA

| FC | | 1 | 1 | 1 | 13 | 13* | | 0 | 0 | 199 | 49 | 5 | 9.80 | 5-25 | 1 | 0 | 1.47 | 1 | |
| FC | 1994 | 2 | 1 | 1 | 13 | 13* | | 0 | 0 | 313 | 111 | 5 | 22.20 | 5-25 | 1 | 0 | 2.12 | 1 | |

CHANDURKAR, Yogesh Prakash (Vidarbha) b Kamptee 11.6.1974 LHB SLA

| FC | | 2 | 1 | 33 | 30* | | 33.00 | 0 | 0 | 66 | 19 | 0 | | | | | 1.72 | 0 | |

CHANDRAMOULI, Seetharaman (Tamil Nadu) b Valadi 30.9.1968 OB

| FC | | 5 | 7 | 3 | 48 | 33 | 12.00 | 0 | 0 | 1190 | 478 | 13 | 36.76 | 3-46 | 0 | 0 | 2.41 | 4 | |

CHANDRASEKHAR, Vakkadai Biksheswaran (Goa) b Madras 21.8.1961 RHB WK

FC		5	7	0	364	194	52.00	1	1	12	11	0					5.50	5	
FC	1986	76	115	8	4655	237*	43.50	10	21	150	97	0					3.88	49	2
Int	1988	7	7	0	88	53	12.57	0	1									0	
Deo	1988	8	8	0	189	77	23.62	0	1									2	
Wlls	1988	3	3	0	58	54	19.33	0	1									0	1

CHANDRASEKHARA, Koragappa (Kerala) b Kasargod 2.12.1974 LHB SLA

| FC | | 4 | 4 | 1 | 83 | 72* | 27.66 | 0 | 1 | 168 | 73 | 5 | 14.60 | 3-47 | 0 | 0 | 2.60 | 2 | |
| FC | 1995 | 8 | 11 | 3 | 150 | 72* | 18.75 | 0 | 1 | 636 | 328 | 7 | 46.85 | 3-47 | 0 | 0 | 3.09 | 4 | |

CHATTERJEE, Utpal (Bengal, East Zone) b Calcutta 13.7.1964 LHB SLA

FC		10	14	3	369	120	33.54	1	2	2757	1030	40	25.75	6-115	2	0	2.24	7	
Deo		4	3	1	25	22*	12.50	0	0	219	148	9	16.44	4-24	1	0	4.05	3	
Wlls		1	1	0	5	5	5.00	0	0	60	33	4	8.25	4-33	1	0	3.30	1	
FC	1984	66	80	14	1314	120	19.90	1	5	15440	6164	240	25.68	7-63	12	2	2.39	37	
Int	1994	3	2	1	6	3*	6.00	0	0	161	117	3	39.00	2-35	0	0	4.36	1	
Deo	1993	11	8	1	57	22*	8.14	0	0	596	390	24	16.25	5-26	1	1	3.92	6	
Wlls	1984	13	11	5	110	22*	18.33	0	0	636	468	11	42.54	4-33	1	0	4.41	2	

CHAUHAN, Rajesh Kumar (Madhya Pradesh, Central Zone) b Ranchi 19.12.1966 RHB OB

FC		12	17	6	330	54*	30.00	0	1	4521	1588	60	26.46	7-52	7	2	2.10	12	
Deo		4	4	3	64	45*	64.00	0	0	228	119	4	29.75	2-38	0	0	3.13	5	
Test	1992	15	11	3	65	15*	8.12	0	0	3257	1189	34	34.97	3-8	0	0	2.19	8	
FC	1988	73	98	25	1467	100*	20.09	1	4	18472	7631	258	29.57	7-39	18	4	2.47	53	
Int	1993	21	8	3	73	26*	14.60	0	0	1008	714	21	34.00	3-29	0	0	4.25	5	
Deo	1992	9	8	4	128	55	32.00	0	1	516	270	9	30.00	2-15	0	0	3.13	5	
Wlls	1991	4	3	1	51	24	25.50	0	0	186	92	2	46.00	1-24	0	0	2.96	3	

CHAVADA, Arjunsinh Dolatsinh (Saurashtra) b Bharuch 12.1.1976 RHB RM

| FC | | 4 | 5 | 0 | 47 | 25 | 9.40 | 0 | 0 | 428 | 210 | 4 | 52.50 | 2-57 | 0 | 0 | 2.94 | 1 | |

CHAVAN, Kedar Shankarrao (Baroda) b Baroda 19.10.1963 RHB OB

FC		2	3	0	30	19	10.00	0	0									1	
FC	1986	50	88	8	3507	247	43.83	10	13	30	8	0					1.60	36	
Deo	1991	1	1	0	5	5	5.00	0	0									0	
Wlls	1988	1	1	0	12	12	12.00	0	0									0	

Cmp	Debut	M	I	NO	Runs	HS	Avge	100	50	Balls	Runs	Wkts	Avge	BB	5i	10m	RpO	ct	st

CHITALE, Parag Yeshwant (Maharashtra) b Poona 19.9.1972 RHB SLA

FC		2	2	0	71	48	35.50	0	0	633	233	9	25.88	5-102	1	0	2.20	2	
FC	1993	7	7	2	118	48	23.60	0	0	2113	797	24	33.20	5-102	1	0	2.26	3	
Wlls	1995	1	1	0	17	17	17.00	0	0	33	33	0					6.00	0	

CHOPRA, Nikhil (Delhi) b Allahabad 26.12.1973 RHB OB

| FC | | 9 | 11 | 3 | 357 | 84 | 44.62 | 0 | 3 | 2109 | 961 | 21 | 45.76 | 6-78 | 1 | 0 | 2.73 | 6 | |
| FC | 1993 | 17 | 21 | 5 | 493 | 84 | 30.81 | 0 | 3 | 3438 | 1614 | 44 | 36.68 | 7-66 | 3 | 0 | 2.81 | 10 | |

CHOPRA, Rajneesh (Delhi) b Delhi 30.6.1974 RHB OB

| FC | | 3 | 4 | 0 | 36 | 10 | 9.00 | 0 | 0 | | | | | | | | | 3 | |
| FC | 1995 | 5 | 6 | 1 | 132 | 95 | 26.40 | 0 | 1 | | | | | | | | | 6 | 1 |

CHOWDHURY, Rajarshi (Tripura)

| FC | | 4 | 8 | 0 | 144 | 67 | 18.00 | 0 | 1 | | | | | | | | | 0 | |

CHOWDHURY, Sabul (Tripura)

| FC | | 1 | 2 | 1 | 8 | 8* | 8.00 | 0 | 0 | 84 | 87 | 1 | 87.00 | 1-87 | 0 | 0 | 6.21 | 1 | |
| FC | 1995 | 5 | 10 | 1 | 117 | 31 | 13.00 | 0 | 0 | 596 | 484 | 10 | 48.40 | 5-64 | 1 | 0 | 4.87 | 5 | |

CHUDASAMA, Dharmendra Nankubhai (Saurashtra) b Mahna 2.5.1972 RHB LBG

FC		1								174	128	1	128.00	1-128	0	0	4.41	1	
FC	1992	14	19	5	219	32	15.64	0	0	3162	1681	34	49.44	6-125	1	0	3.18	8	
Deo	1993	2	1	0	2	2	2.00	0	0	72	66	2	33.00	2-26	0	0	5.50	1	

DANI, Ashu (Delhi, North Zone) b Delhi 3.10.1974 RHB RM

FC		10	14	1	696	215	53.53	2	2	12	8	0					4.00	4	
Deo		2	2	0	42	37	21.00	0	0									0	
FC	1994	17	26	1	1206	215	48.24	3	4	12	8	0					4.00	8	

DANI, Amit Pramod (Mumbai) b Bombay 30.6.1973 RHB RM

| FC | | 1 | 1 | 0 | 3 | 3 | 3.00 | 0 | 0 | 102 | 16 | 2 | 8.00 | 2-9 | 0 | 0 | 0.94 | 1 | |
| FC | 1995 | 4 | 3 | 0 | 110 | 88 | 36.66 | 0 | 1 | 318 | 98 | 7 | 14.00 | 5-40 | 1 | 0 | 1.84 | 3 | |

DAS, Abhijit (Assam) b Gauhati 12.4.1976 RHB

| FC | | 2 | 4 | 0 | 55 | 39 | 13.75 | 0 | 0 | | | | | | | | | 2 | |
| FC | 1995 | 4 | 8 | 0 | 92 | 39 | 11.50 | 0 | 0 | | | | | | | | | 3 | |

DAS, Ajay Kumar (Bengal) b Sodepur 5.3.1976 RHB

| FC | | 3 | 5 | 1 | 240 | 81 | 60.00 | 0 | 2 | 30 | 12 | 1 | 12.00 | 1-12 | 0 | 0 | 2.40 | 2 | |
| Wlls | | 1 | 1 | 1 | 19 | 19* | | 0 | 0 | | | | | | | | | 0 | |

DAS, Parag (Assam) b Gauhati 29.10.1976 RHB RM

| FC | | 1 | 1 | 0 | 21 | 21 | 21.00 | 0 | 0 | | | | | | | | | 0 | |
| FC | 1993 | 4 | 7 | 1 | 131 | 50* | 21.83 | 0 | 1 | 66 | 67 | 2 | 33.50 | 2-67 | 0 | 0 | 6.09 | 2 | |

DAS, Pulak (Bengal) WK

| Wlls | | 1 | 1 | 0 | 0 | 0 | 0.00 | 0 | 0 | | | | | | | | | 0 | 3 |

DAS, Pradip Kumar (Orissa) b Cuttack 7.11.1978 RHB OB

| FC | | 3 | 6 | 1 | 202 | 67 | 40.40 | 0 | 2 | 18 | 18 | 0 | | | | | 6.00 | 3 | |

DAS, Sumit Ranjan (Assam) b Tezpur 19.9.1967 RHB OB

| FC | | 1 | 2 | 0 | 2 | 2 | 1.00 | 0 | 0 | 20 | 16 | 0 | | | | | 4.80 | 3 | |

DAS, Shiv Sunder (Orissa, East Zone) b Bhubaneshwar 5.11.1977 RHB

FC		6	12	0	455	85	37.91	0	5	24	7	1	7.00	1-5	0	0	1.75	6	
Deo		1	1	0	1	1	1.00	0	0									1	
FC	1993	20	34	2	1387	178	43.34	2	9	57	21	2	10.50	1-3	0	0	2.21	22	
Deo	1995	4	4	0	81	67	20.25	0	1									2	

DAS GUPTA, Sourav (Tripura) b Amarpur 1.9.1966 RHB RM

FC		4	8	0	97	23	12.12	0	0	48	55	0					6.87	4	
FC	1985	32	64	1	820	76*	13.01	0	2	1047	700	18	38.88	5-51	1	0	4.01	16	
Deo	1994	1	1	0	0	0	0.00	0	0	12	16	0					8.00	0	

DATTA, Brij Jugalkishore (Saurashtra) b Rajkot 9.12.1968 RHB WK

| FC | | 3 | 5 | 0 | 61 | 37 | 12.20 | 0 | 0 | | | | | | | | | 1 | |
| FC | 1987 | 26 | 48 | 3 | 1499 | 139 | 33.31 | 4 | 8 | | | | | | | | | 27 | |

DAVE, Prayan Ramakant (Baroda) b Baroda 17.10.1973 RHB OB

| FC | | 2 | 4 | 0 | 46 | 20 | 11.50 | 0 | 0 | | | | | | | | | 0 | |
| FC | 1993 | 8 | 15 | 2 | 254 | 80 | 19.53 | 0 | 1 | 6 | 8 | 0 | | | | | 8.00 | 6 | |

DAVID, Noel Arthur (Hyderabad, South Zone, India to West Indies) b Hyderabad 26.2.1971 RHB OB

FC		7	11	1	423	105	42.30	1	3	956	337	18	18.72	4-26	0	0	2.11	3	
Deo		4	4	1	84	66	28.00	0	1	174	109	4	27.25	2-23	0	0	3.75	0	
FC	1992	23	37	3	1209	207*	35.55	2	7	2060	814	32	25.43	4-26	0	0	2.37	11	
Int	1996	3	2	2	9	8*		0	0	144	97	4	24.25	3-21	0	0	4.04	0	
Deo	1995	7	6	2	106	66	26.50	0	1	176	113	4	28.25	2-23	0	0	3.85	2	
Wlls	1992	2	2	0	5	5	2.50	0	0	114	110	0					5.78	0	

DEB BURMA, Amitabha (Tripura) b Agartala 11.12.1978 RHB RM

| FC | | 2 | 4 | 0 | 40 | 28 | 10.00 | 0 | 0 | 90 | 85 | 2 | 42.50 | 1-17 | 0 | 0 | 5.66 | 9 | |

Cmp	Debut	M	I	NO	Runs	HS	Avge	100	50	Balls	Runs	Wkts	Avge	BB	5i	10m	RpO	ct	st

DEB BURMAN, Jay Kishore (Tripura) b Agartala 25.7.1972 RHB WK

Cmp	Debut	M	I	NO	Runs	HS	Avge	100	50	Balls	Runs	Wkts	Avge	BB	5i	10m	RpO	ct	st
FC		1	2	0	2	2	1.00	0	0									0	1
FC	1990	15	30	2	343	51	12.25	0	1									9	7

DEB BURMAN, Rajib (Tripura) b Agartala 28.3.1967 RHB RM

| FC | | 4 | 8 | 1 | 88 | 33* | 12.57 | 0 | 0 | 223 | 113 | 4 | 28.25 | 2-43 | 0 | 0 | 3.04 | 0 | |
| FC | 1985 | ·32 | 64 | 3 | 934 | 72 | 15.31 | 0 | 3 | 2277 | 1524 | 20 | 76.20 | 3-63 | 0 | 0 | 4.01 | 21 | |

DEBNATH, Pranab (Tripura) b Agartala 21.6.1974 RHB

| FC | | 1 | 2 | 0 | 47 | 37 | 23.50 | 0 | 0 | | | | | | | | | 0 | |
| FC | 1993 | 12 | 24 | 0 | 372 | 38 | 15.50 | 0 | 0 | 18 | 22 | 1 | 22.00 | 1-22 | 0 | 0 | 7.33 | 4 | |

DESAI, Apurva Subodhbhai (Gujarat) b Surat 6.3.1975 RHB

| FC | | 2 | 4 | 0 | 62 | 41 | 15.50 | 0 | 0 | | | | | | | | | | |

DESAI, Santosh Bipinkumar (Gujarat) b Bulsar 29.1.1971 RHB OB

| FC | | 1 | 2 | 1 | 15 | 10* | 15.00 | 0 | 0 | 36 | 15 | 0 | | | | | 2.50 | 0 | |
| FC | 1992 | 2 | 4 | 2 | 30 | 15* | 15.00 | 0 | 0 | 162 | 107 | 0 | | | | | 3.96 | 0 | |

DEVANAND, Damodaran Kesavapillai (Tamil Nadu) b Ranipet 31.7.1972 LM

| FC | | 5 | 5 | 1 | 20 | 6 | 5.00 | 0 | 0 | 1035 | 445 | 15 | 29.66 | 7-74 | 1 | 0 | 2.57 | 0 | |
| FC | 1995 | 6 | 6 | 1 | 24 | 6 | 4.80 | 0 | 0 | 1179 | 499 | 16 | 31.18 | 7-74 | 1 | 0 | 2.53 | 0 | |

DEY, Chiranjib (Tripura) b Agartala 26.6.1964 RHB OB

FC		2	4	1	33	18*	11.00	0	0	402	219	1	219.00	1-138	0	0	3.26	0	
FC	1988	24	48	9	179	38	4.58	0	0	3962	2126	59	36.03	6-39	6	1	3.21	3	
Deo	1995	1								24	17	0					4.25	0	

DHAIYA, Vijay (Delhi, North Zone, President's XI) b Delhi 10.5.1973 RHB WK

FC		12	17	3	738	134	52.71	1	6									24	4
Deo		3	3	0	21	12	7.00	0	0									2	
Wlls		1	1	0	4	4	4.00	0	0									0	
FC	1993	21	30	3	1100	134	40.74	1	9									49	5

DHANANJAY SINGH (Bihar) b Patna 10.1.1969 RHB RM

FC		2	1	1	34	34*		0	0	272	118	8	14.75	5-24	1	0	2.60	0	
FC	1989	26	28	11	269	39*	15.82	0	0	3691	1766	59	29.93	5-24	4	0	2.87	6	
Deo	1994	1	1	1	2	2*		0	0	24	19	0					4.75	0	

DHANRAJ SINGH (Haryana) b Faridabad 1.6.1968 RHB RM

FC		8	12	1	187	41	17.00	0	0	973	484	14	34.57	4-37	0	0	2.98	7	
Wlls		3	1	1	52	52*		0	1	162	120	3	40.00	2-35	0	0	4.44	0	
FC	1990	35	53	5	887	86	18.47	0	2	2579	1280	40	32.00	4-19	0	0	2.97	29	
Wlls	1994	6	4	1	110	52*	36.66	0	1	291	220	9	24.44	4-44	1	0	4.53	5	

DHARMANI, Pankaj (Punjab, President's XI, Rest of India, India A, India, India to South Africa) b Delhi 27.9.1974 RHB WK

FC		5	8	2	411	130*	68.50	1	2	6	2	0					2.00	6	
Int		1	1	0	8	8	8.00	0	0									0	
Wlls		1	1	0	78	78	78.00	0	1									0	
FC	1992	25	37	8	1674	223*	57.72	5	8	6	2	0					2.00	38	10
Deo	1994	7	7	2	137	44	27.40	0	0									4	1
Wlls	1995	2	2	0	95	78	47.50	0	1									2	1

DHURI, Sandesh Yeshwant (Goa) b Vasco da Gama 26.10.1974 RHB WK

| FC | | 4 | 4 | 0 | 186 | 65 | 46.50 | 0 | 2 | | | | | | | | | 12 | 3 |
| FC | 1993 | 10 | 15 | 1 | 353 | 65 | 25.21 | 0 | 2 | | | | | | | | | 16 | 7 |

DIGHE, Samir Sudhakar (Mumbai, West Zone) b Bombay 8.10.1968 RHB WK

FC		3	4	1	85	44	28.33	0	0									7	1
Deo		4	3	2	82	43*	82.00	0	0									5	·1
Wlls		3	1	1	16	16*		0	0									5	3
FC	1990	48	70	11	2459	153	41.67	8	10	18	9	0					3.00	162	23
Deo	1991	12	11	2	136	43*	15.11	0	0									13	3
Wlls	1992	10	5	2	89	42	29.66	0	0									10	6

DIXIT, Krishan Kumar (Services) b Ghaziabad 19.9.1972 RHB RM

| FC | | 4 | 8 | 1 | 177 | 78 | 25.28 | 0 | 1 | 650 | 327 | 11 | 29.72 | 3-51 | 0 | 0 | 3.01 | 3 | |

DIXIT, Nikhil Anil (Maharashtra) b Pune 20.2.1975 RHB

| FC | | 1 | 1 | 0 | 50 | 50 | 50.00 | 0 | 1 | | | | | | | | | 0 | |

DOEL, Gundeep (Punjab) b Ambala 7.12.1978 RHB LBG

| FC | | 2 | 1 | 0 | 5 | 5 | 5.00 | 0 | 0 | 233 | 143 | 2 | 71.50 | 2-76 | 0 | 0 | 3.68 | 2 | |
| FC | 1995 | 3 | 2 | 1 | 6 | 5 | 6.00 | 0 | 0 | 377 | 220 | 8 | 27.50 | 4-67 | 0 | 0 | 3.50 | 3 | |

DOGRA, Navalkishore (Himachal Pradesh) b Hamirpur 5.10.1973 RHB OB

| FC | | 2 | 0 | 13 | 9 | 6.50 | 0 | 0 | | | | | | | | | | 0 | |

DOGRA, Sumeet (Delhi, North Zone) b Delhi 29.11.1969 RHB OB

FC		8	10	2	259	101*	32.37	1	0	76	44	1	44.00	1-19	0	0	3.47	6	
Deo		4	4	0	137	60	34.25	0	2	102	93	5	18.60	3-47	0	0	5.47	0	
FC	1990	23	28	6	1015	201*	46.13	3	3	242	111	4	27.75	3-14	0	0	2.75	9	

Cmp	Debut	M	I	NO	Runs	HS	Avge	100	50	Balls	Runs	Wkts	Avge	BB	5i	10m	RpO	ct	st

DORAI, Satish (Uttar Pradesh)

Cmp	Debut	M	I	NO	Runs	HS	Avge	100	50	Balls	Runs	Wkts	Avge	BB	5i	10m	RpO	ct	st
Wlls		1	1	0	0	0	0.00	0	0	60	43	0					4.30	0	

DOSHI, Manish Surendra (Vidarbha) b Nagpur 8.3.1973 RHB SLA

Cmp	Debut	M	I	NO	Runs	HS	Avge	100	50	Balls	Runs	Wkts	Avge	BB	5i	10m	RpO	ct	st
FC		3	4	1	80	43	26.66	0	0	409	194	6	32.33	4-64	0	0	2.84	1	
FC	1993	19	28	9	436	89	22.94	0	2	4142	1693	57	29.70	6-42	3	0	2.45	7	
Deo	1995	1								60	21	0					2.10	0	

DRAVID, Rahul Sharad (Karnataka, India, India to South Africa, India to West Indies, India to Canada, India to Sri Lanka) b Indore 11.1.1973 RHB OB WK

Cmp	Debut	M	I	NO	Runs	HS	Avge	100	50	Balls	Runs	Wkts	Avge	BB	5i	10m	RpO	ct	st
Test		4	7	0	215	56	30.71	0	1									4	
FC		5	9	0	235	56	26.11	0	1									7	
Int		10	10	1	381	107	42.33	1	3									2	
Test	1996	14	23	3	1039	148	51.95	1	8									16	
FC	1990	78	126	23	5877	200*	57.05	16	33	156	95	0					3.65	82	1
Int	1995	35	33	3	1065	107	35.50	1	8									18	
Deo	1993	8	7	1	252	79	42.00	0	3	42	31	0					4.42	4	2
Wlls	1994	4	3	1	78	38	39.00	0	0	66	37	0					3.36	0	

DUTTA, Gautam (Assam) b Gauhati 28.10.1973 LHB LM/SLA

Cmp	Debut	M	I	NO	Runs	HS	Avge	100	50	Balls	Runs	Wkts	Avge	BB	5i	10m	RpO	ct	st
FC		3	5	2	154	54*	51.33	0	1	575	260	10	26.00	4-64	0	0	2.71	0	
FC	1989	24	41	8	1058	87	32.06	0	7	3535	1565	67	23.35	9-52	4	1	2.65	8	

DUTTA, Pabitra (Assam) b Sibsagar 27.11.1969 RHB OB

Cmp	Debut	M	I	NO	Runs	HS	Avge	100	50	Balls	Runs	Wkts	Avge	BB	5i	10m	RpO	ct	st
FC		1	2	0	10	7	5.00	0	0	108	77	1	77.00	1-58	0	0	4.27	0	
FC	1987	28	48	2	853	95	18.54	0	4	1642	881	30	29.36	4-30	0	0	3.21	16	

DWEVEDI, Prashant Kashinath (Madhya Pradesh) b Jabalpur 10.1.1967 RHB LBG

Cmp	Debut	M	I	NO	Runs	HS	Avge	100	50	Balls	Runs	Wkts	Avge	BB	5i	10m	RpO	ct	st
FC		7	11	0	428	80	38.90	0	3	187	102	2	51.00	1-5	0	0	3.27	3	
FC	1987	52	83	6	2859	174	37.12	4	15	859	588	8	73.50	1-0	0	0	4.10	56	
Deo	1992	4	4	0	85	40	21.25	0	0	2	4	0					12.00	2	
Wlls	1991	4	4	0	76	40	19.00	0	0	57	43	3	14.33	3-19	0	0	4.52	0	

FAYAZ AHMED (Andhra) b Gurram Konda 26.11.1976 RHB RM

Cmp	Debut	M	I	NO	Runs	HS	Avge	100	50	Balls	Runs	Wkts	Avge	BB	5i	10m	RpO	ct	st
FC		3	6	0	44	20	7.33	0	0	30	18	0					3.60	0	
FC	1995	4	8	0	62	20	7.75	0	0	30	18	0					3.60	0	

FEROZE, Humza (Bengal) b Calcutta 22.2.1974 LHB WK

Cmp	Debut	M	I	NO	Runs	HS	Avge	100	50	Balls	Runs	Wkts	Avge	BB	5i	10m	RpO	ct	st
FC		7	10	2	254	152*	31.75	1	0									17	6
FC	1995	8	11	2	297	152*	33.00	1	0									19	7

FEROZE RASHID KHAN (Kerala) b Ernakulam 23.2.1969 RHB RM

Cmp	Debut	M	I	NO	Runs	HS	Avge	100	50	Balls	Runs	Wkts	Avge	BB	5i	10m	RpO	ct	st
FC		9	14	1	200	63*	15.38	0	1	571	304	6	50.66	1-14	0	0	3.19	2	
FC	1989	42	68	7	1367	91	22.40	0	7	2138	1150	27	42.59	5-29	1	0	3.22	24	

GANDHE, Ulhas Vithal (Vidarbha, Central Zone) b Nagpur 5.10.1974 RHB OB

Cmp	Debut	M	I	NO	Runs	HS	Avge	100	50	Balls	Runs	Wkts	Avge	BB	5i	10m	RpO	ct	st
FC		5	7	0	111	32	15.85	0	0	637	276	10	27.60	4-32	0	0	2.59	5	
FC	1993	16	25	5	557	97	27.85	0	3	1957	852	17	50.11	4-32	0	0	2.61	10	

GANDHI, Devang (Bengal, East Zone) b Bhavnagar 6.9.1971 RHB RM

Cmp	Debut	M	I	NO	Runs	HS	Avge	100	50	Balls	Runs	Wkts	Avge	BB	5i	10m	RpO	ct	st
FC		9	16	0	549	182	34.31	1	3	150	71	1	71.00	1-18	0	0	2.84	15	
Deo		4	4	0	196	75	49.00	0	2									2	
Wlls		1	1	0	47	47	47.00	0	0	30	23	1	23.00	1-23	0	0	4.60	0	
FC	1994	25	41	1	1615	213	40.37	5	6	186	94	1	94.00	1-18	0	0	3.03	27	
Deo	1994	10	10	0	435	104	43.50	1	3									5	
Wlls	1995	4	4	0	118	47	29.50	0	0	30	23	1	23.00	1-23	0	0	4.60	4	

GANESH, Doddanarasiah (Karnataka, South Zone, India A, President's XI, India to South Africa, India to West Indies, India to Zimbabwe) b Bangalore 30.6.1973 RHB RM

Cmp	Debut	M	I	NO	Runs	HS	Avge	100	50	Balls	Runs	Wkts	Avge	BB	5i	10m	RpO	ct	st
FC		7	9	0	52	22	5.77	0	0	1674	961	37	25.97	6-84	4	1	3.44	4	
Test	1996	4	7	3	25	8	6.25	0	0	461	287	5	57.40	2-28	0	0	3.73	0	
FC	1994	23	31	6	300	75*	12.00	0	1	3669	2114	68	31.08	6-84	4	1	3.45	7	
Int	1996	1	1	0	4	4	4.00	0	0	30	20	1	20.00	1-20	0	0	4.00	0	

GANGULY, Prasenjit (Bengal) b Chinsurah 20.4.1976 RHB LB

Cmp	Debut	M	I	NO	Runs	HS	Avge	100	50	Balls	Runs	Wkts	Avge	BB	5i	10m	RpO	ct	st
FC		2	2	0	14	9	7.00	0	0									1	

GANGULY, Saurav Chandidas (India, India to South Africa, India to West Indies, India to Canada, India to Sri Lanka, India to Zimbabwe) b Calcutta 8.7.1972 LHB RM

Cmp	Debut	M	I	NO	Runs	HS	Avge	100	50	Balls	Runs	Wkts	Avge	BB	5i	10m	RpO	ct	st
Test		3	6	1	173	66	34.60	0	1	18	10	0					3.33	0	
FC		3	6	1	173	66	34.60	0	1	18	10	0					3.33	0	
Int		6	6	0	184	62	30.66	0	2	12	11	0					5.50	3	
Test	1996	12	19	1	768	136	42.67	2	3	581	279	10	27.90	3-71	0	0	2.88	2	
FC	1989	75	116	20	4672	200*	48.66	10	28	3938	2326	57	40.80	4-67	0	0	3.54	50	
Int	1991	26	25	2	718	83	31.21	0	5	150	131	0					5.24	6	
Deo	1990	14	14	1	558	125	42.92	2	2	498	357	9	39.66	3-21	0	0	4.30	6	
Wlls	1989	8	8	2	373	104*	62.16	1	2	244	183	9	20.33	4-26	2	0	4.50	3	

GANGULY, Snehasish Chandidas (Bengal) b Calcutta 11.6.1968 LHB OB

Cmp	Debut	M	I	NO	Runs	HS	Avge	100	50	Balls	Runs	Wkts	Avge	BB	5i	10m	RpO	ct	st
FC		2	4	2	38	29	19.00	0	0									0	
FC	1986	59	75	11	2534	158	39.59	6	11	576	313	2	156.50	1-48	0	0	3.26	26	

119

Cmp	Debut	M	I	NO	Runs	HS	Avge	100	50	Balls	Runs	Wkts	Avge	BB	5i	10m	RpO	ct	st
Deo	1989	7	7	0	168	59	24.00	0	1									1	
Wlls	1988	8	8	1	98	37	14.00	0	0									1	

GANI, Usman Iqbal (Vidarbha) b Nagpur 26.3.1964 LHB SLA

| FC | | 4 | 7 | 2 | 75 | 38 | 15.00 | 0 | 0 | 137 | 63 | 3 | 21.00 | 1-5 | 0 | 0 | 2.75 | 3 | |
| FC | 1985 | 33 | 58 | 9 | 1632 | 140 | 33.30 | 1 | 8 | 1172 | 721 | 12 | 60.08 | 5-115 | 1 | 0 | 3.69 | 22 | |

GARSONDIA, Rajesh Raghubhai (Saurashtra) b Rajkot 16.8.1968 LHB LM/SLA

| FC | | 4 | 4 | 3 | 44 | 28* | 44.00 | 0 | 0 | 663 | 221 | 5 | 44.20 | 2-52 | 0 | 0 | 2.00 | 2 | |
| FC | 1987 | 26 | 32 | 13 | 199 | 28* | 10.47 | 0 | 0 | 4571 | 2161 | 43 | 50.25 | 4-37 | 0 | 0 | 2.83 | 12 | |

GAUR, Nischal (Himachal Pradesh) b Mandi 12.5.1971 RHB RM

| FC | | 5 | 9 | 0 | 285 | 128 | 31.66 | 1 | 0 | 619 | 322 | 3 | 107.33 | 1-58 | 0 | 0 | 3.12 | 4 | |
| FC | 1993 | 17 | 30 | 0 | 848 | 128 | 28.26 | 1 | 4 | 812 | 482 | 6 | 80.33 | 2-64 | 0 | 0 | 3.56 | 11 | |

GAVANDE, Mahesh Gangadhar (Goa) b Ponda 15.12.1968 RHB WK

| FC | | 1 | 2 | 0 | 5 | 5 | 2.50 | 0 | 0 | | | | | | | | | 2 | |
| FC | 1990 | 9 | 18 | 3 | 76 | 15 | 5.06 | 0 | 0 | | | | | | | | | 11 | 3 |

GAVASKAR, Rohan Sunil (Bengal, East Zone) b Kanpur 20.2.1976 LHB SLA

FC		10	16	2	648	109	46.28	1	4	174	77	2	38.50	2-51	0	0	2.65	11	
Deo		4	3	0	87	37	29.00	0	0	66	71	3	23.66	2-55	0	0	6.45	2	
Wlls		1	1	0	18	18	18.00	0	0	36	23	1	23.00	1-23	0	0	3.83	1	

GERA, Aman Lajpat (Uttar Pradesh) b Gurgaon 19.4.1969 RHB OB

FC		8	9	2	132	27*	18.85	0	0	1272	532	13	40.92	5-133	1	0	2.50	1	
Wlls		1	1	0	4	4	4.00	0	0	60	40	2	20.00	2-40	0	0	4.00	0	
FC	1995	9	9	2	132	27*	18.85	0	0	1578	631	16	39.43	5-133	1	0	2.39	1	

GHAG, Sudhakar Vishwanath (Services) b Bombay 25.2.1974 RHB RM

| FC | | 2 | 3 | 0 | 33 | 13 | 11.00 | 0 | 0 | 354 | 158 | 5 | 31.60 | 3-44 | 0 | 0 | 2.67 | 0 | |

GHARE, Yogesh Trimbak (Vidarbha) b Nagpur 5.7.1971 RHB RM

| FC | | 3 | 4 | 0 | 78 | 31 | 19.50 | 0 | 0 | | | | | | | | | 0 | |
| FC | 1990 | 27 | 48 | 3 | 1515 | 122 | 33.66 | 5 | 6 | | | | | | | | | 26 | |

GHAYAS, Feroze (Delhi, North Zone) b Delhi 3.5.1973 RHB RFM

FC		7	9	3	81	32	13.50	0	0	1195	664	19	34.94	4-54	0	0	3.33	3	
Deo		4	4	2	13	6	6.50	0	0	178	140	5	28.00	2-42	0	0	4.71	4	
FC	1992	26	32	6	396	47	15.23	0	0	4290	2292	89	25.75	7-53	3	1	3.20	9	
Deo	1995	8	7	3	25	10*	6.25	0	0	376	267	12	22.25	4-30	1	0	4.26	4	
Wlls	1992	3	1	0	1	1	1.00	0	0	102	48	2	24.00	2-17	0	0	2.82	1	

GHOSH, Subhodeep (Assam) b Digboi 13.11.1968 RHB

| FC | | 3 | 4 | 0 | 20 | 16 | 5.00 | 0 | 0 | | | | | | | | | 5 | |
| FC | 1994 | 7 | 8 | 0 | 46 | 24 | 5.75 | 0 | 0 | | | | | | | | | 8 | |

GILL, Rajesh (Jammu and Kashmir)

| FC | | 3 | 6 | 0 | 156 | 79 | 26.00 | 0 | 1 | 11 | 10 | 0 | | | | | 5.45 | 2 | |

GOEL, Nitin Rajinder (Haryana) b Delhi 6.4.1969 LHB

FC		9	16	2	568	135	40.57	1	3	6	0	0					0.00	3	
Wlls		1	1	0	12	12	12.00	0	0									0	
FC	1986	57	89	12	2598	166	33.74	4	11	12	1	0					0.50	40	
Wlls	1988	4	4	0	36	12	9.00	0	0									0	

GOHIL, Virbhadrasinh Dilipsinh (Saurashtra) b Khedoi 14.7.1969 LHB OB

| FC | | 2 | 1 | 0 | 5 | 5 | 5.00 | 0 | 0 | 420 | 179 | 1 | 179.00 | 1-22 | 0 | 0 | 2.55 | 1 | |
| FC | 1987 | 11 | 11 | 2 | 80 | 17 | 8.88 | 0 | 0 | 1728 | 865 | 12 | 72.08 | 4-72 | 0 | 0 | 3.00 | 2 | |

GOKULKRISHNAN, Jayaraman (Goa, South Zone) b Madras 4.1.1973 RHB RM

| FC | | 6 | 8 | 2 | 192 | 104* | 32.00 | 1 | 0 | 1597 | 594 | 28 | 21.21 | 7-54 | 1 | 1 | 2.23 | 7 | |
| FC | 1993 | 12 | 17 | 3 | 306 | 104* | 21.85 | 1 | 0 | 2245 | 871 | 35 | 24.88 | 7-54 | 1 | 1 | 2.32 | 14 | |

GONSALVES, Trevor Aquino (Vidarbha) b Nagpur 4.10.1972 RHB RM

| FC | | 3 | 4 | 1 | 8 | 8* | 2.66 | 0 | 0 | 192 | 117 | 2 | 58.50 | 2-35 | 0 | 0 | 3.65 | 1 | |
| FC | 1992 | 8 | 12 | 3 | 112 | 23 | 12.44 | 0 | 0 | 744 | 499 | 15 | 33.26 | 4-67 | 0 | 0 | 4.02 | 2 | |

GOPAL, Gautam (Orissa) b Delhi 12.7.1972 RHB WK

| FC | | 7 | 11 | 0 | 179 | 48 | 16.27 | 0 | 0 | | | | | | | | | 14 | 4 |
| FC | 1993 | 10 | 17 | 1 | 288 | 78* | 18.00 | 0 | 1 | | | | | | | | | 18 | 4 |

GOTKHINDIKAR, Umesh Gajanan (Maharashtra) b Kolhapur 16.5.1971 RHB SLA

| FC | | 1 | 2 | 1 | 3 | 2 | 3.00 | 0 | 0 | 96 | 51 | 1 | 51.00 | 1-50 | 0 | 0 | 3.18 | 0 | |
| FC | 1995 | 5 | 5 | 2 | 6 | 2 | 2.00 | 0 | 0 | 1177 | 458 | 12 | 38.16 | 4-86 | 0 | 0 | 2.33 | 1 | |

GOWDA, Yere (Railways) b Raichur 27.11.1971 RHB LBG

| FC | | 6 | 9 | 2 | 406 | 100* | 58.00 | 1 | 2 | 114 | 64 | 1 | 64.00 | 1-8 | 0 | 0 | 3.36 | 5 | |
| FC | 1994 | 15 | 23 | 6 | 734 | 100* | 43.17 | 1 | 3 | 162 | 84 | 1 | 84.00 | 1-8 | 0 | 0 | 3.11 | 11 | |

GUDGE, Sunil Chandrakant (Maharashtra) b Poona 31.12.1959 RHB LBG

FC		1	1	1	16	16*		0	0	156	70	1	70.00	1-42	0	0	2.69	0	
FC	1979	55	61	18	1033	125	24.02	1	4	9274	5133	110	46.66	5-46	5	0	3.32	27	
Wlls	1986	3	2	0	21	20	10.50	0	0	156	122	9	13.55	4-31	1	0	4.69	0	

Cmp	Debut	M	I	NO	Runs	HS	Avge	100	50	Balls	Runs	Wkts	Avge	BB	5i	10m	RpO	ct	st

GUPTA, Ashwini (Jammu and Kashmir, North Zone) b Jammu 13.11.1967 RHB OB

FC		4	7	0	233	102	33.28	1	1	900	587	9	65.22	4-199	0	0	3.91	2	
FC	1986	41	75	6	2591	210*	37.55	7	12	5607	3211	75	42.81	5-65	2	0	3.43	32	
Deo	1995	1	1	1	11	11*		0	0	60	46	1	46.00	1-46	0	0	4.60	0	

HALDIPUR, Nikhil (Bengal, East Zone) b Calcutta 19.12.1977 LHB RM

FC		6	11	0	521	113	47.36	1	4	6	9	0					9.00	2	
Deo		1	1	0	69	69	69.00	0	1									1	
Wlls		1	1	0	3	3	3.00	0	0									0	
FC	1994	13	23	0	709	113	30.82	1	4	18	13	0					4.33	6	
Deo	1994	3	3	0	77	69	25.66	0	1									2	
Wlls	1994	2	2	0	3	3	1.50	0	0									1	

HARI KRISHNAN, K.P. (Kerala) b Kalpetta 29.5.1973 WK

| FC | | 4 | 5 | 2 | 13 | 8 | 4.33 | 0 | 0 | | | | | | | | | 5 | 2 |

HARVINDER SINGH (Punjab, Wills XI) b Amritsar 23.12.1977 RHB RFM

FC		5	5	3	73	36	36.50	0	0	930	445	16	27.81	6-36	2	1	2.87	0	
Wlls		1								42	40	0					5.71	0	
FC	1995	10	9	4	95	36	19.00	0	0	1867	915	28	32.67	6-36	2	1	2.94	2	

HAZARE, Sanjay Sukhanand (Baroda) b Baroda 18.2.1961 RHB LBG

FC		4	4	1	15	9	5.00	0	0	834	377	13	29.00	5-29	2	0	2.71	2	
FC	1981	47	65	15	777	65	15.54	0	1	6940	3529	108	32.67	6-46	8	1	3.05	18	
Wlls	1983	1	1	0	10	10	10.00	0	0									1	

HEDAOO, Parimal Kamalkar (Vidarbha) b Nagpur 18.4.1974 LHB OB

| FC | | 4 | 6 | 0 | 140 | 74 | 23.33 | 0 | 1 | 985 | 484 | 16 | 30.25 | 5-115 | 1 | 0 | 2.94 | 0 | |
| FC | 1993 | 15 | 23 | 1 | 640 | 74 | 29.09 | 0 | 4 | 2358 | 1161 | 32 | 36.28 | 6-164 | 2 | 0 | 2.95 | 8 | |

HIRWANI, Narendra Deepchand (Bengal, India, President's XI, Rest of India, East Zone, India to England) b Gorakhpur 18.10.1968 RHB LBG

Test		2	4	2	9	9	4.50	0	0	240	129	2	64.50	2-38	0	0	3.22	0	
FC		11	15	7	63	20	7.87	0	0	2455	1045	41	25.48	6-51	3	0	2.55	3	
Deo		4	3	2	5	5	5.00	0	0	228	176	4	44.00	3-52	0	0	4.63	0	
Test	1987	17	22	12	54	17	5.40	0	0	4298	1987	66	30.10	8-61	4	1	2.77	5	
FC	1984	106	120	48	751	59	10.43	0	1	26935	12776	466	27.41	8-52	37	6	2.84	33	
Int	1987	18	7	3	8	4	2.00	0	0	960	719	23	31.26	4-43	3	0	4.49	2	
Deo	1988	15	9	4	35	14	7.00	0	0	762	605	10	60.50	3-52	0	0	4.76	1	
Wlls	1986	6	4	3	25	25	25.00	0	0	354	223	5	44.60	2-41	0	0	3.77	4	

IDREES GANDROO (Jammu and Kashmir)

| FC | | 1 | 2 | 0 | 65 | 63 | 32.50 | 0 | 1 | 100 | 54 | 3 | 18.00 | 3-54 | 0 | 0 | 3.24 | 1 | |
| FC | 1984 | 14 | 23 | 7 | 279 | 63 | 17.43 | 0 | 2 | 1304 | 907 | 29 | 31.27 | 5-48 | 1 | 0 | 4.17 | 7 | |

IMTIAZ AHMED (Jammu and Kashmir)

| FC | | 1 | 2 | 0 | 14 | 10 | 7.00 | 0 | 0 | | | | | | | | | 1 | |

INAMDAR, Sameer Vijay (Maharashtra) b Phaltan 11.5.1974 RHB RM

FC		2	2	0	14	14	7.00	0	0	450	272	9	30.22	4-163	0	0	3.62	1	
FC	1992	10	12	1	168	55	15.27	0	1	1856	968	27	35.85	4-71	0	0	3.12	4	
Wlls	1995	1	1	0	10	10	10.00	0	0	60	41	1	41.00	1-41	0	0	4.10	1	

INDRAJIT SINGH (Assam) b Gauhati 12.12.1979 RHB LB

| FC | | 2 | 1 | 1 | 4 | 4* | | 0 | 0 | 186 | 85 | 3 | 28.33 | 3-45 | 0 | 0 | 2.74 | 1 | |

INDULKAR, Hemant Ramchandra (Baroda) b Baroda 20.10.1972 RHB LB

| FC | | 2 | 4 | 0 | 29 | 13 | 7.25 | 0 | 0 | | | | | | | | | 0 | |
| FC | 1995 | 5 | 9 | 0 | 189 | 50 | 21.00 | 0 | 1 | | | | | | | | | 2 | |

IQBAL, Mohammad (Jammu and Kashmir)

| FC | | 1 | 2 | 0 | 0 | 0 | 0.00 | 0 | 0 | 6 | 5 | 0 | | | | | 5.00 | 1 | |

IRSHAD HASSAN (Jammu and Kashmir)

| FC | | 1 | 2 | 0 | 4 | 4. | 2.00 | 0 | 0 | | | | | | | | | 0 | |

IYER, Kartik Sadashiv Manian (Vidarbha) b Nagpur 29.12.1972 RHB WK

| FC | | 4 | 5 | 2 | 71 | 40* | 23.66 | 0 | 0 | | | | | | | | | 4 | 1 |
| FC | 1993 | 13 | 21 | 2 | 554 | 89 | 29.15 | 0 | 4 | 6 | 3 | 1 | 3.00 | 1-3 | 0 | 0 | 3.00 | 17 | 1 |

IZAZ HUSSAIN (Assam) b Tezpur 21.6.1975 RHB RM

| FC | | 1 | 2 | 0 | 51 | 36 | 25.50 | 0 | 0 | 102 | 37 | 0 | | | | | 2.17 | 1 | |
| FC | 1992 | 6 | 11 | 6 | 173 | 38* | 34.60 | 0 | 0 | 396 | 203 | 6 | 33.83 | 3-20 | 0 | 0 | 3.07 | 1 | |

JABBAR, Tanveer (Tamil Nadu) b Bangalore 12.7.1974 RHB OB

| FC | | 3 | 4 | 1 | 97 | 59* | 32.33 | 0 | 1 | | | | | | | | | 4 | |
| FC | 1993 | 15 | 20 | 3 | 383 | 59* | 22.52 | 0 | 3 | | | | | | | | | 17 | |

JADEJA, Ajaysinhji Daulatsinhji (Haryana, North Zone, India A, India, India to West Indies, India to Canada, India to Sri Lanka, India to South Africa, India to Zimbabwe) b Jamnagar 1.2.1971 RHB RM

FC		4	7	0	392	154	56.00	1	2	438	195	3	65.00	2-60	0	0	2.67	3	
Int		10	9	3	276	72	46.00	0	2	96	91	3	30.33	2-47	0	0	5.68	3	
Deo		3	3	0	95	49	31.66	0	0	126	116	4	29.00	2-37	0	0	5.52	3	
Test	1992	10	14	1	399	96	30.69	0	3									3	

Cmp	Debut	M	I	NO	Runs	HS	Avge	100	50	Balls	Runs	Wkts	Avge	BB	5i	10m	RpO	ct	st
FC	1988	70	109	10	5187	264	52.39	12	27	3024	1498	36	41.61	4-37	0	0	2.97	48	
Int	1991	90	82	11	2318	104	32.64	1	14	1110	974	14	69.57	2-16	0	0	5.26	23	
Deo	1991	9	9	0	131	49	14.55	0	0	144	126	4	31.50	2-37	0	0	5.25	6	
Wlls	1988	13	13	1	498	104	41.50	1	4	165	156	4	39.00	2-43	0	0	5.67	5	

JADEJA, Bimal Mulabhai (Saurashtra) b Ridaba 22.11.1962 LHB LB

Cmp	Debut	M	I	NO	Runs	HS	Avge	100	50	Balls	Runs	Wkts	Avge	BB	5i	10m	RpO	ct	st
FC		4	7	2	260	132*	52.00	1	0	12	4	0					2.00	4	
FC	1980	63	110	17	3668	190	39.44	8	19	400	278	3	92.66	2-30	0	0	4.17	44	

JADHAV, Himanshu Ramchandra (Baroda) b Baroda 28.10.1972 RHB LB

Cmp	Debut	M	I	NO	Runs	HS	Avge	100	50	Balls	Runs	Wkts	Avge	BB	5i	10m	RpO	ct	st
FC		6	9	1	109	32	13.62	0	0	48	33	0					4.12	3	
FC	1992	10	16	2	259	58	18.50	0	1	127	78	2	39.00	2-19	0	0	3.68	5	

JAFFER, Wasim (Mumbai) b Bombay 16.2.1978 RHB

Cmp	Debut	M	I	NO	Runs	HS	Avge	100	50	Balls	Runs	Wkts	Avge	BB	5i	10m	RpO	ct	st
FC		7	10	4	692	314*	115.33	2	3	12	10	0					5.00	5	
Wlls		3	3	0	138	74	46.00	0	1									0	

JAIN, Anshu (Rajasthan) b Jaipur 19.11.1979 RHB RM

Cmp	Debut	M	I	NO	Runs	HS	Avge	100	50	Balls	Runs	Wkts	Avge	BB	5i	10m	RpO	ct	st
FC		1	1	0	45	45	45.00	0	0									0	

JAIN, Pradeep (Haryana) b Delhi 22.5.1965 LHB SLA

Cmp	Debut	M	I	NO	Runs	HS	Avge	100	50	Balls	Runs	Wkts	Avge	BB	5i	10m	RpO	ct	st
FC		9	13	1	224	48	18.66	0	0	1971	863	44	19.61	7-72	4	1	2.62	10	
Wlls		3	1	0	5	5	5.00	0	0	180	100	4	25.00	2-31	0	0	3.33	1	
FC	1986	70	68	26	650	48	15.47	0	0	15190	6014	259	23.22	8-67	20	5	2.37	45	
Wlls	1988	11	3	2	14	6*	14.00	0	0	592	404	18	22.44	4-51	1	0	4.09	4	

JAIN, Vineet (Haryana) b Malerkotla 16.5.1972 RHB RM

Cmp	Debut	M	I	NO	Runs	HS	Avge	100	50	Balls	Runs	Wkts	Avge	BB	5i	10m	RpO	ct	st
FC		7	8	1	46	15	6.57	0	0	960	430	12	35.83	3-40	0	0	2.68	4	
Wlls		1								60	65	2	32.50	2-65	0	0	6.50	0	
FC	1993	22	23	6	105	16*	6.17	0	0	3307	1692	62	27.29	7-45	4	0	3.06	10	
Wlls	1994	4	1	0	0	0	0.00	0	0	186	157	3	52.33	2-65	0	0	5.06	1	

JAMWAL, Jitender (Himachal Pradesh) b Dharmasala 19.8.1973 RHB LB

Cmp	Debut	M	I	NO	Runs	HS	Avge	100	50	Balls	Runs	Wkts	Avge	BB	5i	10m	RpO	ct	st
FC		3	6	0	63	18	10.50	0	0	384	253	4	63.25	2-78	0	0	3.95	1	
FC	1994	9	16	1	170	42*	11.33	0	0	1351	900	10	90.00	3-174	0	0	3.99	1	

JASMINDER SINGH (Himachal Pradesh)

Cmp	Debut	M	I	NO	Runs	HS	Avge	100	50	Balls	Runs	Wkts	Avge	BB	5i	10m	RpO	ct	st
FC		2	3	0	71	61	23.66	0	1									0	

JASWANT RAI (Himachal Pradesh) b Una 10.6.1968 RHB SLA

Cmp	Debut	M	I	NO	Runs	HS	Avge	100	50	Balls	Runs	Wkts	Avge	BB	5i	10m	RpO	ct	st
FC		5	9	0	133	31	14.77	0	0	1554	681	29	23.48	6-123	2	0	2.62	2	
FC	1986	52	95	5	1388	53	15.42	0	1	10311	5074	110	46.12	6-80	5	0	2.95	28	

JAVED ZAMAN (Railways) b Dhubri 8.8.1976 RHB RM

Cmp	Debut	M	I	NO	Runs	HS	Avge	100	50	Balls	Runs	Wkts	Avge	BB	5i	10m	RpO	ct	st
FC		3	4	2	28	13*	14.00	0	0	533	178	16	11.12	5-45	1	0	2.00	0	
FC	1993	16	23	9	138	26*	9.85	0	0	2998	1310	66	19.84	7-87	5	1	2.62	4	
Deo	1994	1	1	0	1	1	1.00	0	0	42	38	0					5.42	0	

JAYACHANDRA, Pinninti (Orissa) b Bhubaneshwar 3.9.1976 RHB RM

Cmp	Debut	M	I	NO	Runs	HS	Avge	100	50	Balls	Runs	Wkts	Avge	BB	5i	10m	RpO	ct	st
FC		8	16	0	358	84	22.37	0	2	306	109	2	5.40	1-28	0	0	2.13	2	

JAYA SANKAR, Piniti (Andhra) b Ichhapura 30.3.1972 RHB LB

Cmp	Debut	M	I	NO	Runs	HS	Avge	100	50	Balls	Runs	Wkts	Avge	BB	5i	10m	RpO	ct	st
FC		2	4	0	40	23	10.00	0	0	178	109	2	54.50	2-44	0	0	3.67	1	

JEDHE, Santosh Venkatrao (Maharashtra) b Poona 9.6.1966 RHB OB

Cmp	Debut	M	I	NO	Runs	HS	Avge	100	50	Balls	Runs	Wkts	Avge	BB	5i	10m	RpO	ct	st
FC		10	12	1	553	158	50.27	2	2	1793	734	25	29.36	5-47	1	0	2.45	9	
FC	1989	56	83	8	3858	182	51.44	15	12	10066	4539	108	42.02	6-119	4	0	2.70	48	
Deo	1991	4	4	0	30	10	7.50	0	0	114	84	2	42.00	1-36	0	0	4.42	2	
Wlls	1989	4	4	0	88	40	22.00	0	0	174	138	1	138.00	1-48	0	0	4.75	2	

JHA, Chandra Mohan (Bihar) b Dhanbad 23.1.1978 RHB

Cmp	Debut	M	I	NO	Runs	HS	Avge	100	50	Balls	Runs	Wkts	Avge	BB	5i	10m	RpO	ct	st
FC		4	8	0	283	63	35.37	0	3									5	

JHA, Somnath (Bihar) b Jamshedpur 2.1.1970 LHB LM

Cmp	Debut	M	I	NO	Runs	HS	Avge	100	50	Balls	Runs	Wkts	Avge	BB	5i	10m	RpO	ct	st
FC		4	6	0	80	42	13.33	0	0	366	213	4	53.25	2-44	0	0	3.22	4	
FC	1992	5	8	0	80	42	10.00	0	0	480	275	5	55.00	2-44	0	0	3.43	4	

JITENDER SINGH (Haryana, North Zone) b Rohtak 10.1.1976 RHB

Cmp	Debut	M	I	NO	Runs	HS	Avge	100	50	Balls	Runs	Wkts	Avge	BB	5i	10m	RpO	ct	st
FC		10	18	2	807	230	50.43	2	2	24	25	0					6.25	9	
Wlls		3	3	0	99	37	33.00	0	0									0	
FC	1993	28	45	2	1583	230	36.81	3	6	24	25	0					6.25	25	
Deo	1994	1	1	0	10	10	10.00	0	0									0	
Wlls	1994	6	6	0	157	37	26.16	0	0									0	

JOGLEKAR, Manoj Vijay (Mumbai) b Bombay 1.11.1973 LHB OB

Cmp	Debut	M	I	NO	Runs	HS	Avge	100	50	Balls	Runs	Wkts	Avge	BB	5i	10m	RpO	ct	st
FC		2	3	1	98	80	49.00	0	1	30	11	0					2.20	1	
Wlls		3	1	0	4	4	4.00	0	0	132	92	1	92.00	1-48	0	0	4.18	1	
FC	1992	15	22	3	624	114*	32.84	1	5	30	11	0					2.20	18	
Deo	1995	2	2	0	25	23	12.50	0	0									1	

JOHNSON, David Jude (Karnataka, India, South Zone, President's XI, India to South Africa) b Arasikere 16.10.1971 RHB RM

Cmp	Debut	M	I	NO	Runs	HS	Avge	100	50	Balls	Runs	Wkts	Avge	BB	5i	10m	RpO	ct	st
Test		1	1	1	0	0*		0	0	96	52	1	52.00	1-40	0	0	3.25	0	
FC		6	8	1	16	10	2.28	0	0	1199	654	16	40.87	4-82	0	0	3.27	1	

Cmp Debut	M	I	NO	Runs	HS	Avge	100	50	Balls	Runs	Wkts	Avge	BB	5i	10m	RpO	ct	st
Wlls	2	2	1	29	16	29.00	0	0	96	83	0					5.18	0	
Test 1996	2	3	1	8	5	4.00	0	0	240	143	3	47.66	2-52	0	0	3.57	0	
FC 1992	30	36	4	272	39	8.50	0	0	4837	2729	100	27.29	8-55	7	1	3.38	12	
Deo 1995	2								96	57	2	28.50	1-20	0	0	3.56	1	

JOSHI, Pankaj Girish (Delhi) b Delhi 8.10.1980 RHB OB

FC	3	5	2	155	67	51.66	0	1	18	11	0					3.66	3	

JOSHI, Sunil Bandacharya (Karnataka, India, President's XI, South Zone, India to West Indies, India to Canada, India to Sri Lanka, India to South Africa, India to Zimbabwe) b Gadag 6.6.1969 LHB SLA

Test	4	7	0	73	23	10.42	0	0	807	336	10	33.60	4-43	0	0	2.49	2	
FC	7	12	1	206	72*	18.72	0	1	1408	615	27	22.77	6-97	3	1	2.62	6	
Int	10	6	2	34	20	8.50	0	0	545	439	10	43.90	2-32	0	0	4.83	5	
Deo	2	1	0	14	14	14.00	0	0	90	40	3	13.33	2-29	0	0	2.66	0	
Test 1996	9	13	1	181	43	15.08	0	0	1528	667	21	31.76	4-43	0	0	2.61	3	
FC 1992	46	63	11	1719	118	33.05	3	9	9138	3844	156	24.64	7-60	9	2	2.52	30	
Int 1996	22	13	3	127	48	12.70	0	0	1078	812	21	38.66	3-40	0	0	4.51	10	
Wlls 1994	1	1	0	0	0	0.00	0	0									0	

JOSHI, Satyen Dinbandhubhai (Saurashtra) b Rajkot 4.10.1976 RHB WK

FC	4	5	0	32	11	6.40	0	0									8	4

JOSHI, Vilas (Rajasthan) b Jaipur 2.8.1971 LHB RM

FC	4	5	1	302	137	75.50	1	2									6	
FC 1991	21	37	2	1004	137	28.68	1	6	432	241	6	40.16	2-21	0	0	3.34	23	

KADRI, M. (Baroda)

FC	1	2	0	81	81	40.50	0	1	183	104	4	26.00	4-99	0	0	3.40	0	

KAKAD, Bhagwan Dattatraya (Maharashtra) b Nasik 28.10.1974 RM

FC	2	2	1	13	13*	13.00	0	0	300	127	5	25.40	3-35	0	0	2.54	0	

KALE, Abhay Murlidhar (Vidarbha) b Nagpur 31.12.1975 RHB OB

FC	3	5	1	31	22	7.75	0	0	380	154	8	19.25	3-29	0	0	2.43	3	

KALE, Abhijit Vasant (Maharashtra, West Zone, Rest of India) b Ahmednagar 3.7.1973 RHB OB

FC	12	16	1	470	150	31.33	1	2	132	86	0					3.90	14	
FC 1993	30	41	2	2285	209	58.58	8	10	168	104	0					3.71	26	
Deo 1995	2	2	1	66	60*	66.00	0	1										
Wlls 1995	1	1	0	24	24	24.00	0	0									0	

KALEKAR, Netin Sambaji (Goa) b Margao 27.12.1976 RHB OB

FC	4	4	1	2	1	0.66	0	0	974	480	15	32.00	5-104	1	0	2.95	2	

KALYANI, Shrikant Jagannath (Bengal) b Poona 21.8.1964 RHB OB

FC	4	6	1	156	35	31.20	0	0									3	
FC 1983	82	121	14	5144	260	48.07	13	27	440	285	5	57.00	1-0	0	0	3.88	74	
Deo 1984	11	11	2	242	67	26.88	0	2									5	
Wlls 1984	18	17	3	761	99	54.35	0	6	42	45	0					6.42	3	

KAMARUDDIN, V. (Kerala) b Palghat 11.4.1972 RHB WK

FC	5	7	1	44	15*	7.33	0	0									9	2
FC 1993	21	31	12	176	36	9.26	0	0									30	9

KAMAT, Sudin Vinayak (Goa) b Panaji 22.9.1973 RHB RM

FC	5	6	1	40	30	8.00	0	0	732	316	12	26.33	4-36	0	0	2.59	4	
FC 1994	12	18	3	229	53	15.26	0	2	1593	781	27	28.92	4-32	0	0	2.94	1	

KAMBLI, Vinod Ganpat (Mumbai, West Zone, India A, President's XI, India, India to Canada, India to Sri Lanka) b Bombay 18.1.1972 LHB OB

FC	11	13	0	604	111	46.46	1	4	96	72	0					4.50	1	
Int	3	3	1	73	65	36.50	0	1									0	
Deo	4	4	1	100	63*	33.33	0	1									1	
Wlls	3	3	1	148	102*	74.00	1	0	6	3	0					3.00	2	
Test 1992	17	21	1	1084	227	54.20	4	3									7	
FC 1989	71	97	9	5951	262	67.62	22	25	365	279	4	69.75	1-4	0	0	4.58	35	
Int 1991	79	73	19	2076	106	38.44	2	12	4	7	1	7.00	1-7	0	0	10.50	12	
Deo 1991	10	8	2	295	63*	49.16	0	4									2	
Wlls 1989	13	12	5	416	102*	59.42	1	2	6	3	0					3.00	3	

KAMTEKAR, Indrajit Anil (Maharashtra) b Pune 30.10.1976 RHB SLA

FC	8	8	3	303	78*	60.60	0	4	1680	652	8	81.50	2-89	0	0	2.32	5	
FC 1994	10	10	3	322	78*	46.00	0	4	1986	783	10	78.30	2-89	0	0	2.36	6	

KANADE, Rahul Ravindra (Maharashtra) b Poona 8.4.1970 RHB RM

FC	9	11	2	418	81	46.44	0	3	24	10	0					2.50	4	
FC 1995	11	15	2	638	122	49.07	1	3	24	10	0					2.50	4	

KANITKAR, Hrishikesh Hemant (Maharashtra, West Zone, President's XI) b Pune 14.11.1974 LHB OB

FC	11	16	2	1003	205	71.64	5	1	1626	642	21	30.57	3-41	0	0	2.36	9	
Deo	4	3	0	53	32	17.66	0	0	142	83	5	16.60	3-30	0	0	3.50	2	
Wlls	1	1	0	3	3	3.00	0	0	56	45	0					4.82	0	
FC 1994	21	29	4	1699	205	67.96	8	3	3169	1366	31	44.06	3-41	0	0	2.58	17	

Cmp	Debut	M	I	NO	Runs	HS	Avge	100	50	Balls	Runs	Wkts	Avge	BB	5i	10m	RpO	ct	st
Deo	1995	5	4	0	83	32	20.75	0	0	148	89	5	17.80	3-30	0	0	3.60	4	
Wlls	1995	2	2	0	27	24	13.50	0	0	98	70	1	70.00	1-25	0	0	4.28	0	

KANOJIA, Kamal Kant (Uttar Pradesh) b Bareilly 3.3.1975 RHB

Cmp	Debut	M	I	NO	Runs	HS	Avge	100	50	Balls	Runs	Wkts	Avge	BB	5i	10m	RpO	ct	st
FC		3	5	1	54	21*	13.50	0	0									3	
Wlls		1	1	1	38	38*		0	0									1	

KANUNGO, Debabrata (Orissa) b Bhubaneshwar 5.7.1977 LHB SLA

Cmp	Debut	M	I	NO	Runs	HS	Avge	100	50	Balls	Runs	Wkts	Avge	BB	5i	10m	RpO	ct	st
FC		1	2	1	15	14*	15.00	0	0	138	41	0					1.78	0	

KANWALJIT SINGH (Jammu and Kashmir) b Patiala 1.11.1973 RHB

Cmp	Debut	M	I	NO	Runs	HS	Avge	100	50	Balls	Runs	Wkts	Avge	BB	5i	10m	RpO	ct	st
FC		2	4	0	190	97	47.50	0	2	6	2	0					2.00	1	
FC	1990	18	33	0	899	106	27.24	1	5	38	28	0					4.42	9	

KANWALJIT SINGH (Hyderabad) b Secunderabad 15.4.1958 RHB OB

Cmp	Debut	M	I	NO	Runs	HS	Avge	100	50	Balls	Runs	Wkts	Avge	BB	5i	10m	RpO	ct	st
FC		10	13	5	56	25*	7.00	0	0	1848	835	21	39.76	4-72	0	0	2.71	1	
FC	1980	73	75	27	494	50	10.29	0	1	15093	6404	206	31.08	7-33	10	0	2.54	32	
Deo	1994	7	3	1	19	14	9.50	0	0	402	259	12	21.58	4-29	1	0	3.86	1	
Wlls	1991	2	1	1	0	0*		0	0	102	69	1	69.00	1-25	0	0	4.05	0	

KANWAT, Rahul Jagdish (Rajasthan) b Jaipur 21.10.1974 RHB OB

Cmp	Debut	M	I	NO	Runs	HS	Avge	100	50	Balls	Runs	Wkts	Avge	BB	5i	10m	RpO	ct	st
FC		4	5	0	178	68	35.60	0	2	1048	542	8	67.75	2-77	0	0	3.10	6	
FC	1992	17	29	2	643	68	23.81	0	4	2062	1057	19	55.63	3-24	0	0	3.07	14	

KAPOOR, Arvind (Railways) b Jhansi 30.7.1973 RHB

Cmp	Debut	M	I	NO	Runs	HS	Avge	100	50	Balls	Runs	Wkts	Avge	BB	5i	10m	RpO	ct	st
FC		4	6	0	97	45	16.16	0	0	36	16	0					2.66	3	
FC	1992	11	18	1	321	68	18.88	0	1	468	188	2	94.00	1-48	0	0	2.41	6	

KAPOOR, Aashish Rakesh (Punjab, India, India A, President's XI, India to Canada, India to Sri Lanka) b Madras 25.3.1971 RHB OB

Cmp	Debut	M	I	NO	Runs	HS	Avge	100	50	Balls	Runs	Wkts	Avge	BB	5i	10m	RpO	ct	st
Test		2	3	1	39	22	19.50	0	0	318	101	5	20.20	2-19	0	0	1.90	0	
FC		8	10	2	236	53*	29.50	0	1	1632	804	21	38.28	5-94	1	0	2.95	3	
Int		1	1	0	0	0	0.00	0	0	60	32	0					3.20	0	
Deo		4	4	0	51	36	12.75	0	0	240	151	3	50.33	1-36	0	0	3.77	1	
Wlls		1	1	0	14	14	14.00	0	0	54	27	2	13.50	2-27	0	0	3.00	0	
Test	1994	4	6	1	97	42	19.40	0	0	642	255	6	42.50	2-19	0	0	2.38	1	
FC	1989	58	70	9	1982	181	32.49	2	10	11048	5580	182	30.65	7-74	9	2	3.03	46	
Int	1994	15	6	0	43	19	7.16	0	0	816	547	8	68.37	2-33	0	0	4.02	1	
Deo	1991	13	9	0	82	36	9.11	0	0	695	403	13	31.00	3-16	0	0	3.47	4	
Wlls	1991	7	7	0	65	19	9.28	0	0	413	214	5	42.80	2-13	0	0	3.10	1	

KAPOOR, Richie (Himachal Pradesh) b Solan 25.1.1977 RHB RM

Cmp	Debut	M	I	NO	Runs	HS	Avge	100	50	Balls	Runs	Wkts	Avge	BB	5i	10m	RpO	ct	st
FC		2	4	0	33	15	8.25	0	0									1	
FC	1994	4	6	0	56	15	9.33	0	0	18	4	0					1.33	1	

KARIM, Syed Saba (Bengal, East Zone, Rest of India, President's XI, India to South Africa, India to West Indies) b Patna 14.11.1967 RHB WK

Cmp	Debut	M	I	NO	Runs	HS	Avge	100	50	Balls	Runs	Wkts	Avge	BB	5i	10m	RpO	ct	st
FC		6	10	0	407	190	40.70	1	2									16	7
FC	1982	93	133	28	5614	234	53.46	17	23	24	21	0					5.25	179	43
Int	1996	9	8	1	141	55	20.14	0	1									6	2
Deo	1982	23	22	2	393	73	19.65	0	2									16	17
Wlls	1982	9	8	1	143	60*	20.42	0	1									4	2

KARTIK, Murali (Railways) b Madras 11.9.1976 LHB SLA

Cmp	Debut	M	I	NO	Runs	HS	Avge	100	50	Balls	Runs	Wkts	Avge	BB	5i	10m	RpO	ct	st
FC		6	9	0	185	74	20.55	0	1	1053	310	16	19.37	6-28	1	0	1.76	2	

KARUNAMURTHY, Thalaisayanam (Tamil Nadu) b Madras 26.10.1976 RHB

Cmp	Debut	M	I	NO	Runs	HS	Avge	100	50	Balls	Runs	Wkts	Avge	BB	5i	10m	RpO	ct	st
FC		1	2	0	70	39	35.00	0	0									0	
FC	1995	4	8	0	225	57	28.12	0	1									4	

KASHIKAR, Sachin Narayan (Vidarbha) b Nagpur 19.4.1967 RHB RM

Cmp	Debut	M	I	NO	Runs	HS	Avge	100	50	Balls	Runs	Wkts	Avge	BB	5i	10m	RpO	ct	st
FC		1								60	18	0					1.80	0	

KATTI, Anand (Karnataka) b Belgaum 11.7.1972 RHB SLA

Cmp	Debut	M	I	NO	Runs	HS	Avge	100	50	Balls	Runs	Wkts	Avge	BB	5i	10m	RpO	ct	st
FC		6	10	6	80	28*	20.00	0	0	1177	465	21	22.14	4-68	0	0	2.37	4	
Wlls		2	2	1	3	3	3.00	0	0	114	58	3	19.33	2-24	0	0	3.05	0	

KAUL SINGH (Himachal Pradesh) b Gohar 5.6.1975 RHB RM

Cmp	Debut	M	I	NO	Runs	HS	Avge	100	50	Balls	Runs	Wkts	Avge	BB	5i	10m	RpO	ct	st
FC		2	4	0	36	14	9.00	0	0	126	76	1	76.00	1-34	0	0	3.61	2	

KHADSE, Avinash Narayanrao (Vidarbha) b Yavatmal 14.6.1972 RHB RM

Cmp	Debut	M	I	NO	Runs	HS	Avge	100	50	Balls	Runs	Wkts	Avge	BB	5i	10m	RpO	ct	st
FC		1								84	53	0					3.78	0	

KHAKHAR, Piyush Kantilal (Saurashtra) b Rajkot 22.10.1965 RHB SLA

Cmp	Debut	M	I	NO	Runs	HS	Avge	100	50	Balls	Runs	Wkts	Avge	BB	5i	10m	RpO	ct	st
FC		1	2	0	41	29	20.50	0	0	30	33	0					6.60	1	

KHALEEL, Fazal (Karnataka) b Bangalore 6.3.1973 RHB

Cmp	Debut	M	I	NO	Runs	HS	Avge	100	50	Balls	Runs	Wkts	Avge	BB	5i	10m	RpO	ct	st
FC		4	7	0	161	76	23.00	0	1	12	2	0					1.00	10	
Wlls		2	2	0	129	92	64.50	0	1									0	
FC	1995	6	11	1	193	76	19.30	0	1	12	2	0					1.00	12	

KHALID, Saiyed (Goa) b Baroda 21.10.1975 SLA

Cmp	Debut	M	I	NO	Runs	HS	Avge	100	50	Balls	Runs	Wkts	Avge	BB	5i	10m	RpO	ct	st
FC		5	6	1	46	15*	9.20	0	0	1297	473	14	33.78	5-54	1	0	2.18	4	

Cmp	Debut	M	I	NO	Runs	HS	Avge	100	50	Balls	Runs	Wkts	Avge	BB	5i	10m	RpO	ct	st

KHAN, Mansoor Ali (Karnataka) b Bangalore 22.5.1971 RHB RM

Cmp	Debut	M	I	NO	Runs	HS	Avge	100	50	Balls	Runs	Wkts	Avge	BB	5i	10m	RpO	ct	st
Wlls		2	1	1	5	5*		0	0	102	72	5	14.40	3-31	0	0	4.41	1	
FC	1995	1	2	0	6	3	3.00	0	0	90	39	0					2.60	2	

KHAN, Sahid (Orissa) b Rourkela 27.12.1978 RHB LB

Cmp	Debut	M	I	NO	Runs	HS	Avge	100	50	Balls	Runs	Wkts	Avge	BB	5i	10m	RpO	ct	st
FC		4	6	3	29	12*	9.66	0	0	582	276	9	30.66	3-54	0	0	2.84	1	
FC	1995	6	7	3	29	12*	7.25	0	0	951	423	20	21.15	5-42	1	0	2.66	1	

KHATUA, Abakash (Orissa) b Puri 15.2.1967 RHB RM

Cmp	Debut	M	I	NO	Runs	HS	Avge	100	50	Balls	Runs	Wkts	Avge	BB	5i	10m	RpO	ct	st
FC		4	7	0	155	79	22.14	0	1	30	18	0					3.60	1	
FC	1991	24	34	6	956	93*	34.14	0	4	803	432	5	86.40	2-31	0	0	3.22	12	

KHODA, Gagan Kishanlal (Rajasthan, Central Zone, Rest of India, President's XI, Wills XI) b Barmer 24.10.1974 RHB

Cmp	Debut	M	I	NO	Runs	HS	Avge	100	50	Balls	Runs	Wkts	Avge	BB	5i	10m	RpO	ct	st
FC		8	13	0	609	124	46.84	1	6	330	190	2	95.00	1-28	0	0	3.45	8	
Deo		4	4	0	160	79	40.00	0	2	6	10	1	10.00	1-10	0	0	10.00	3	
Wlls		1	1	0	21	21	21.00	0	0									0	
FC	1991	36	64	3	2380	237*	39.01	6	13	599	354	6	59.00	1-6	0	0	3.54	27	
Deo	1993	11	11	0	216	79	19.63	0	2	12	14	1	14.00	1-10	0	0	7.00	5	
Wlls	1995	4	4	1	212	121*	70.66	1	1									1	

KHULLAR, Vinod (Bihar) b Jamshedpur 11.7.1964 RHB

Cmp	Debut	M	I	NO	Runs	HS	Avge	100	50	Balls	Runs	Wkts	Avge	BB	5i	10m	RpO	ct	st
FC		6	11	2	270	75	30.00	0	2	48	20	1	20.00	1-20	0	0	2.50	1	
FC	1990	16	28	2	747	104	28.73	1	5	54	28	1	28.00	1-20	0	0	3.11	3	
Deo	1995	1	1	0	1	1	1.00	0	0									0	

KHURASIYA, Amay Ramsevak (Madhya Pradesh, Central Zone, President's XI) b Jabalpur 18.5.1972 LHB SLA

Cmp	Debut	M	I	NO	Runs	HS	Avge	100	50	Balls	Runs	Wkts	Avge	BB	5i	10m	RpO	ct	st
FC		10	17	0	790	209	46.47	2	2									6	
Deo		4	4	0	188	69	47.00	0	2									5	
Wlls		1	1	0	12	12	12.00	0	0									0	
FC	1989	54	87	6	3655	238	45.12	13	12	6	9	0					9.00	42	
Deo	1993	14	14	0	393	69	28.07	0	3									7	
Wlls	1991	5	5	1	171	89	42.75	0	1									2	

KIRAN KUMAR, Sangani (Hyderabad) b Hyderabad 10.9.1975 RHB

Cmp	Debut	M	I	NO	Runs	HS	Avge	100	50	Balls	Runs	Wkts	Avge	BB	5i	10m	RpO	ct	st
FC		5	7	0	134	59	19.14	0	1									3	
FC	1995	7	11	0	144	59	13.09	0	1	42	22	2	11.00	2-22	0	0	3.14	5	

KOLAMBKAR, Vivekanand Vinayak (Goa) b Margao 8.4.1977 LHB

Cmp	Debut	M	I	NO	Runs	HS	Avge	100	50	Balls	Runs	Wkts	Avge	BB	5i	10m	RpO	ct	st
FC		1	1	0	10	10	10.00	0	0									1	
FC	1995	2	3	0	21	11	7.00	0	0									1	

KONDHALKAR, Sanjay Madhukar (Maharashtra) b Poona 7.12.1965 RHB WK

Cmp	Debut	M	I	NO	Runs	HS	Avge	100	50	Balls	Runs	Wkts	Avge	BB	5i	10m	RpO	ct	st
FC		10	10	1	141	37	15.66	0	0	48	38	0					4.75	32	2
FC	1989	33	38	5	701	121	21.24	1	0	48	38	0					4.75	94	8
Wlls	1995	1	1	0	16	16	16.00	0	0									0	

KOTAK, Shitanshu Hargovindbhai (Saurashtra, West Zone) b Rajkot 19.10.1972 LHB

Cmp	Debut	M	I	NO	Runs	HS	Avge	100	50	Balls	Runs	Wkts	Avge	BB	5i	10m	RpO	ct	st
FC		4	6	1	209	93	41.80	0	2	282	195	5	39.00	2-62	0	0	4.14	2	
Deo		2	1	0	17	17	17.00	0	0	18	6	2	3.00	2-6	0	0	2.00	0	
FC	1992	21	36	3	1290	121	39.09	1	11	353	222	5	44.40	2-62	0	0	3.77	8	
Deo	1994	3	2	0	40	23	20.00	0	0	18	6	2	3.00	2-6	0	0	2.00	1	

KOTECHA, Amrish Suryakant (Gujarat) b Ahmedabad 6.9.1974 LHB SLA

Cmp	Debut	M	I	NO	Runs	HS	Avge	100	50	Balls	Runs	Wkts	Avge	BB	5i	10m	RpO	ct	st
FC		1	2	0	17	10	8.50	0	0	30	9	0					1.80	0	
FC	1995	5	9	0	102	33	11.33	0	0	54	20	0					2.22	2	

KRISHNAKUMAR, Pudiyangum Kesavadasan (Rajasthan, Central Zone, President's XI) b Palghat 1.1.1974 LHB LFM

Cmp	Debut	M	I	NO	Runs	HS	Avge	100	50	Balls	Runs	Wkts	Avge	BB	5i	10m	RpO	ct	st
FC		6	8	0	160	110	20.00	1	0	1185	607	14	43.35	3-43	0	0	3.07	2	
FC	1989	30	49	9	1207	208*	30.17	3	4	5418	2804	91	30.81	6-63	5	1	3.10	9	
Deo	1994	4	3	0	21	18	7.00	0	0	210	136	4	34.00	2-21	0	0	3.88	0	
Wlls	1995	1	1	0	6	6	6.00	0	0	12	10	0					5.00	0	

KUDVA, Ajay Subash (Kerala) b Ernakulum 26.3.1976 RHB RM

Cmp	Debut	M	I	NO	Runs	HS	Avge	100	50	Balls	Runs	Wkts	Avge	BB	5i	10m	RpO	ct	st
FC		9	15	2	393	82	30.23	0	3	1	4	0					24.00	4	
FC	1994	19	33	3	911	162*	30.36	1	3	1	4	0					24.00	8	

KULKARNI, Milind Shripath (Maharashtra) b Koregaon 12.12.1969 RHB RM

Cmp	Debut	M	I	NO	Runs	HS	Avge	100	50	Balls	Runs	Wkts	Avge	BB	5i	10m	RpO	ct	st
FC		8	7	0	90	43	12.85	0	0	1534	746	20	37.30	4-59	0	0	2.91	2	
FC	1992	27	27	8	173	43	9.10	0	0	5021	2537	81	31.32	6-67	4	0	3.03	5	
Deo	1995	1	1	0	8	8	8.00	0	0	60	38	1	38.00	1-38	0	0	3.80	0	
Wlls	1995	1	1	1	4	4*		0	0	30	17	0					3.40	0	

KULKARNI, Nilesh Moreshwar (Mumbai) b Dombivili 3.4.1973 LHB SLA

Cmp	Debut	M	I	NO	Runs	HS	Avge	100	50	Balls	Runs	Wkts	Avge	BB	5i	10m	RpO	ct	st
FC		9	8	0	65	19	8.12	0	0	2661	904	41	22.04	6-51	5	0	2.03	14	
Wlls		2								120	73	3	24.33	2-24	0	0	3.65	1	
FC	1994	26	23	7	174	23	10.87	0	0	6078	2341	100	23.41	6-37	9	2	2.31	34	
Deo	1995	3								126	119	1	119.00	1-49	0	0	5.66	1	
Wlls	1995	3	1	0	2	2	2.00	0	0	150	99	3	33.00	2-24	0	0	3.96	1	

KULKARNI, Sachin Kamlakar (Services) b Nagpur 23.4.1969 RHB LB

Cmp	Debut	M	I	NO	Runs	HS	Avge	100	50	Balls	Runs	Wkts	Avge	BB	5i	10m	RpO	ct	st
FC		3	5	4	19	15	19.00	0	0	402	241	4	60.25	2-74	0	0	3.59	1	

Cmp Debut M I NO Runs HS Avge 100 50 Balls Runs Wkts Avge BB 5i 10m RpO ct st

KULKARNI, Sulkashan Kashinath (Mumbai) b Sadashivgad 15.1.1967 RHB WK

Cmp	Debut	M	I	NO	Runs	HS	Avge	100	50	Balls	Runs	Wkts	Avge	BB	5i	10m	RpO	ct	st
FC		10	12	1	524	239	47.63	2	0									34	4
FC	1985	49	73	7	2810	239	42.57	6	10									86	11
Deo	1986	2	2	1	13	10	13.00	0	0									2	
Wlls	1986	3	3	1	48	22*	24.00	0	0									0	

KUMAR, Ajay (Himachal Pradesh) b Chamba 15.5.1980 RHB RM

Cmp	Debut	M	I	NO	Runs	HS	Avge	100	50	Balls	Runs	Wkts	Avge	BB	5i	10m	RpO	ct	st
FC		2	4	0	31	15	7.75	0	0									1	

KUMAR, Anil (Bihar) b Jamshedpur 6.11.1977 RHB LB

Cmp	Debut	M	I	NO	Runs	HS	Avge	100	50	Balls	Runs	Wkts	Avge	BB	5i	10m	RpO	ct	st
FC		4	6	3	6	4*	2.00	0	0	647	384	7	54.85	4-102	0	0	3.56	2	
FC	1995	6	10	6	23	7	5.75	0	0	899	552	12	46.00	5-74	1	0	3.68	3	

KUMAR, Ashok (Bihar) b Patna 11.12.1975 RHB RM

Cmp	Debut	M	I	NO	Runs	HS	Avge	100	50	Balls	Runs	Wkts	Avge	BB	5i	10m	RpO	ct	st
FC		1	2	0	21	21	10.50	0	0	48	56	0					7.00	0	

KUMAR, Avinash (Bihar, East Zone) b Patna 14.12.1962 RHB SLA

Cmp	Debut	M	I	NO	Runs	HS	Avge	100	50	Balls	Runs	Wkts	Avge	BB	5i	10m	RpO	ct	st
FC		8	11	1	317	139	31.70	1	0	3014	1307	40	32.67	6-42	1	0	2.60	1	
FC	1984	80	99	24	1571	139	20.94	1	5	21910	8548	322	26.54	7-43	22	5	2.34	29	
Deo	1985	18	14	5	95	29*	10.55	0	0	979	650	23	28.26	5-51	1	1	3.98	5	
Wlls	1986	4	3	0	51	35	17.00	0	0	198	156	3	52.00	2-38	0	0	4.72	2	

KUMAR, Chetan (Himachal Pradesh) b Mandi 27.2.1975 RHB LB

Cmp	Debut	M	I	NO	Runs	HS	Avge	100	50	Balls	Runs	Wkts	Avge	BB	5i	10m	RpO	ct	st
FC		5	9	0	257	89	28.55	0	2									8	

KUMAR, Dhiraj (Bihar) b Patna 25.12.1974 RHB RM

Cmp	Debut	M	I	NO	Runs	HS	Avge	100	50	Balls	Runs	Wkts	Avge	BB	5i	10m	RpO	ct	st
FC		3	4	1	43	26*	14.33	0	0	330	183	4	45.75	2-30	0	0	3.32	0	

KUMAR, Pawan (Tripura) b Patna 14.11.1968 RHB RM

Cmp	Debut	M	I	NO	Runs	HS	Avge	100	50	Balls	Runs	Wkts	Avge	BB	5i	10m	RpO	ct	st
FC		4	8	0	47	9	5.87	0	0	570	294	7	42.00	5-85	1	0	3.09	0	
FC	1991	19	38	6	339	42	10.59	0	0	2458	1226	27	45.40	5-85	1	0	2.99	6	

KUMAR, Rajiv (Bihar) b Patna 2.12.1976 RHB

Cmp	Debut	M	I	NO	Runs	HS	Avge	100	50	Balls	Runs	Wkts	Avge	BB	5i	10m	RpO	ct	st
FC		8	13	3	356	129*	35.60	1	1									9	
FC	1994	11	18	3	435	129*	29.00	1	1									12	

KUMAR, Rakesh (Bihar) b Jamshedpur 16.1.1975 RHB OB

Cmp	Debut	M	I	NO	Runs	HS	Avge	100	50	Balls	Runs	Wkts	Avge	BB	5i	10m	RpO	ct	st
FC		1								198	77	1	77.00	1-59	0	0	2.33	0	

KUMAR, Sunil (Bihar) b Muchuatoli 18.2.1971 RHB WK

Cmp	Debut	M	I	NO	Runs	HS	Avge	100	50	Balls	Runs	Wkts	Avge	BB	5i	10m	RpO	ct	st
FC		8	14	1	427	105	32.84	1	1									18	7
FC	1989	28	47	4	1342	105	31.20	1	6	3	8	0					16.00	37	11
Deo	1992	2	2	0	33	27	16.50	0	0									0	

KUMAR, Sunil (Kerala) b Alleppey 9.6.1970 RHB

Cmp	Debut	M	I	NO	Runs	HS	Avge	100	50	Balls	Runs	Wkts	Avge	BB	5i	10m	RpO	ct	st
FC		2	2	0	6	4	3.00	0	0									0	

KUMAR, Tarun (Bihar) b Yarpur 28.12.1974 RHB RM

Cmp	Debut	M	I	NO	Runs	HS	Avge	100	50	Balls	Runs	Wkts	Avge	BB	5i	10m	RpO	ct	st
FC		7	11	2	282	57	31.33	0	1									1	
FC	1992	20	32	5	787	100*	29.14	2	2									5	
Deo	1993	6	6	0	106	61	17.66	0	1									0	

KUMARAN, Thirunavukkarasu (Tamil Nadu) b Madras 30.12.1975 RHB RM

Cmp	Debut	M	I	NO	Runs	HS	Avge	100	50	Balls	Runs	Wkts	Avge	BB	5i	10m	RpO	ct	st
FC		1	1	1	3	3*		0	0	130	94	2	47.00	1-43	0	0	4.33	0	

KUMBLE, Anil (India, India to South Africa, India to West Indies, India to Canada, India to Sri Lanka, India to Zimbabwe) b Bangalore 17.10.1970 RHB LBG

Cmp	Debut	M	I	NO	Runs	HS	Avge	100	50	Balls	Runs	Wkts	Avge	BB	5i	10m	RpO	ct	st
Test		4	7	1	201	88	33.50	0	1	1267	517	22	23.50	5-67	1	0	2.44	2	
FC		4	7	1	201	88	33.50	0	1	1267	517	22	23.50	5-67	1	0	2.44	2	
Int		10	6	1	38	16*	7.60	0	0	576	415	19	21.84	4-25	1	0	4.32	4	
Test	1990	38	46	9	618	88	16.70	0	2	11286	4473	163	27.44	7-59	9	1	2.37	15	
FC	1989	106	133	31	2676	154*	26.23	4	11	27398	11221	467	24.02	8-41	30	6	2.45	51	
Int	1989	120	61	18	398	24	9.25	0	0	6487	4397	167	26.32	6-12	5	2	4.06	44	
Deo	1990	6	3	2	13	7*	13.00	0	0	242	183	9	20.33	3-37	0	0	4.53	5	
Wlls	1989	8	4	3	71	30*	71.00	0	0	426	298	12	24.83	3-55	0	0	4.19	2	

KURUVILLA, Abey (Mumbai, West Zone, India, India to West Indies) b Mannar 8.8.1968 RHB RFM

Cmp	Debut	M	I	NO	Runs	HS	Avge	100	50	Balls	Runs	Wkts	Avge	BB	5i	10m	RpO	ct	st
FC		8	9	4	49	11*	9.80	0	0	1788	852	33	25.81	5-36	1	0	2.85	3	
Int		3	1	0	1	1	1.00	0	0	138	109	3	36.33	2-22	0	0	4.73	0	
Deo		4	1	0	2	2	2.00	0	0	204	142	3	47.33	2-51	0	0	4.17	1	
Test	1996	5	5	0	16	9	3.20	0	0	1032	480	13	36.92	5-68	1	0	2.79	0	
FC	1990	57	59	18	460	76	11.21	0	1	11156	5786	202	28.64	6-61	8	0	3.11	14	
Int	1996	7	3	1	4	3*	2.00	0	0	323	208	7	29.71	3-23	0	0	3.86	1	
Deo	1991	9	3	1	11	9*	5.50	0	0	438	293	7	41.85	2-22	0	0	4.01	1	
Wlls	1992	2	2	1	2	1*	2.00	0	0	92	45	1	45.00	1-22	0	0	2.93	1	

LAHIRI, Satrajit (Tripura) b Murshidabad 26.2.1971 RHB OB

Cmp	Debut	M	I	NO	Runs	HS	Avge	100	50	Balls	Runs	Wkts	Avge	BB	5i	10m	RpO	ct	st
FC		4	8	0	138	54	17.25	0	2									2	
FC	1990	8	16	0	369	54	23.06	0	3									6	

LAHORE, Sunil Shamlal (Madhya Pradesh) b Indore 31.12.1965 LHB SLA

Cmp	Debut	M	I	NO	Runs	HS	Avge	100	50	Balls	Runs	Wkts	Avge	BB	5i	10m	RpO	ct	st
FC		8	9	2	57	19	8.14	0	0	2580	993	27	36.77	4-84	0	0	2.30	1	
FC	1985	62	87	13	1274	89	17.21	0	4	15235	6165	188	32.79	8-100	8	1	2.42	28	

Cmp	Debut	M	I	NO	Runs	HS	Avge	100	50	Balls	Runs	Wkts	Avge	BB	5i	10m	RpO	ct	st
Deo	1986	2	2	1	6	4	6.00	0	0	90	96	0					6.40	0	
Wlls	1991	4	2	0	20	10	10.00	0	0	216	169	6	28.16	4-56	1	0	4.69	0	

LAMBA, Raman (Delhi) b Meerut 2.1.1960 RHB RM

Cmp	Debut	M	I	NO	Runs	HS	Avge	100	50	Balls	Runs	Wkts	Avge	BB	5i	10m	RpO	ct	st
FC		10	14	0	1034	250	73.85	3	4									3	
Test	1986	4	5	0	102	53	20.40	0	1									5	
FC	1978	117	168	12	8625	320	55.28	31	27	816	423	6	70.50	2-9	0	0	3.11	59	
Int	1986	32	31	2	783	102	27.00	1	6	19	20	1	20.00	1-9	0	0	6.33	10	
Deo	1982	11	10	1	362	125*	40.22	1	2	12	25	0					12.50	2	
Wlls	1978	20	17	3	592	116*	42.28	1	4	222	118	2	59.00	2-45	0	0	3.18	4	

LAXMAN, Vangipurappu Venkata Sai (Hyderabad, India, Rest of India, President's XI) b Hyderabad 1.11.1974 RHB OB

Cmp	Debut	M	I	NO	Runs	HS	Avge	100	50	Balls	Runs	Wkts	Avge	BB	5i	10m	RpO	ct	st
Test		2	4	0	77	51	19.25	0	1									1	
FC		8	14	0	441	78	31.50	0	5	64	48	0					4.50	5	
Test	1996	8	13	2	289	64	26.27	0	3	90	49	0					3.26	5	
FC	1992	40	68	10	2766	203*	47.68	7	13	473	212	4	53.00	2-66	0	0	2.68	39	1
Deo	1994	3	3	1	45	30	22.50	0	0	16	10	0					3.75	1	
Wlls	1995	1	1	1	62	62*		0	1									0	

MADHUKAR, Nekkanti (Andhra, South Zone) b Vijayawada 18.5.1976 RHB RMF

Cmp	Debut	M	I	NO	Runs	HS	Avge	100	50	Balls	Runs	Wkts	Avge	BB	5i	10m	RpO	ct	st
FC		4	7	1	40	26	6.66	0	0	318	197	1	197.00	1-43	0	0	3.71	0	
Deo		1								42	32	0					4.57	1	
FC	1995	7	11	1	79	26	7.90	0	0	885	438	15	29.20	5-43	1	0	2.96	1	

MADHUSUDHAN RAJU, Adiraju (Andhra) b Cuddapah 16.6.1971 RHB RM

Cmp	Debut	M	I	NO	Runs	HS	Avge	100	50	Balls	Runs	Wkts	Avge	BB	5i	10m	RpO	ct	st
FC		5	10	1	125	39	13.88	0	0	180	80	0					2.66	2	
FC	1991	14	24	4	277	45	13.85	0	0	900	426	8	53.25	4-38	0	0	2.84	9	

MAGREY, Nazir (Jammu and Kashmir)

Cmp	Debut	M	I	NO	Runs	HS	Avge	100	50	Balls	Runs	Wkts	Avge	BB	5i	10m	RpO	ct	st
FC		1	2	0	18	11	9.00	0	0										

MAHENDRA, Rohit (Kerala) b Cannanore 22.2.1974 RHB RM

Cmp	Debut	M	I	NO	Runs	HS	Avge	100	50	Balls	Runs	Wkts	Avge	BB	5i	10m	RpO	ct	st
FC		4	7	2	15	8	3.00	0	0	579	302	7	43.14	2-38	0	0	3.12	0	

MAHESH, Sadagoppan (Tamil Nadu) b Madras 2.4.1973 RHB RM

Cmp	Debut	M	I	NO	Runs	HS	Avge	100	50	Balls	Runs	Wkts	Avge	BB	5i	10m	RpO	ct	st
FC		5	7	3	158	82*	39.50	0	1	1158	426	12	35.50	3-55	0	0	2.20	5	
FC	1993	14	17	10	175	82*	25.00	0	1	3119	1273	36	35.36	3-40	0	0	2.44	13	

MAITREYA, Pankaj (Services) b Meerut 8.2.1968 LHB SLA

Cmp	Debut	M	I	NO	Runs	HS	Avge	100	50	Balls	Runs	Wkts	Avge	BB	5i	10m	RpO	ct	st
FC		4	7	0	265	78	37.85	0	3	139	70	3	23.33	2-13	0	0	3.02	5	
FC	1992	21	33	3	661	78	22.03	0	3	2333	1098	26	42.23	4-28	0	0	2.82	8	

MAJITHIA, Manish Babulal (Madhya Pradesh) b Bhavnagar 1.9.1971 LHB SLA

Cmp	Debut	M	I	NO	Runs	HS	Avge	100	50	Balls	Runs	Wkts	Avge	BB	5i	10m	RpO	ct	st
FC		9	13	2	157	75	14.27	0	1	2025	727	21	34.61	6-59	1	0	2.15	2	
FC	1991	22	30	4	304	75	11.69	0	2	5150	2100	64	32.81	6-57	2	0	2.44	9	
Deo	1993	3	2	1	10	5*	10.00	0	0	129	100	0					4.65	1	

MALAM, Maqbool (Gujarat) b Rander 2.2.1972 RHB WK

Cmp	Debut	M	I	NO	Runs	HS	Avge	100	50	Balls	Runs	Wkts	Avge	BB	5i	10m	RpO	ct	st
FC		3	6	0	115	47	19.16	0	0									0	
FC	1990	14	28	0	517	71	18.46	0	4									10	

MALHOTRA, Akash (Delhi, North Zone, Wills XI) b Delhi 12.12.1972 RHB RM

Cmp	Debut	M	I	NO	Runs	HS	Avge	100	50	Balls	Runs	Wkts	Avge	BB	5i	10m	RpO	ct	st
FC		10	13	1	409	120	34.08	1	3	156	104	1	104.00	1-6	0	0	4.00	10	
Deo		3	3	0	111	56	37.00	0	1									0	
Wlls		1	1	0	20	20	20.00	0	0	12	8	0					4.00	0	
FC	1993	32	44	5	1777	197	45.56	6	8	651	408	12	34.00	3-7	0	0	3.76	26	
Deo	1995	7	7	0	164	56	23.42	0	1	18	20	1	20.00	1-20	0	0	6.66	2	

MANJREKAR, Sanjay Vijay (Mumbai, India, President's XI) b Mangalore 12.7.1965 RHB OB

Cmp	Debut	M	I	NO	Runs	HS	Avge	100	50	Balls	Runs	Wkts	Avge	BB	5i	10m	RpO	ct	st
Test		1	2	0	39	34	19.50	0	0									1	
FC		11	11	1	675	150	67.50	2	5									12	
Int		1	1	0	7	7	7.00	0	0									0	
Deo		4	4	1	275	93*	91.66	0	3									2	
Wlls		3	3	2	166	86*	166.00	0	2									5	
Test	1987	37	61	6	2043	218	37.14	4	9	17	15	0					5.29	25	1
FC	1984	139	206	30	9774	377	55.53	30	44	383	238	3	79.33	1-4	0	0	3.72	89	2
Int	1987	74	70	10	1994	105	33.23	1	15	8	10	1	10.00	1-2	0	0	7.50	23	
Deo	1986	20	19	4	1022	125	68.13	2	9	2	4	0					12.00	6	
Wlls	1985	19	19	5	855	110*	61.07	2	7									12	

MANKAD, Chetan Chandrakant (Saurashtra) b Delhi 15.3.1964 RHB LFM

Cmp	Debut	M	I	NO	Runs	HS	Avge	100	50	Balls	Runs	Wkts	Avge	BB	5i	10m	RpO	ct	st
FC		1	1	1	32	32*		0	0	144	63	0					2.62	1	
FC	1986	26	37	11	649	65*	24.96	0	4	4713	2234	55	40.61	5-82	1	0	2.84	6	
Deo	1990	3	1	1	5	5*		0	0	174	114	3	38.00	2-40	0	0	3.93	0	
Wlls	1986	2	1	0	0	0	0.00	0	0	120	72	4	18.00	3-36	0	0	3.60	2	

MANOJ, Sivarama Menon (Kerala) b Tripunathura 7.10.1974 RHB OB

Cmp	Debut	M	I	NO	Runs	HS	Avge	100	50	Balls	Runs	Wkts	Avge	BB	5i	10m	RpO	ct	st
FC		8	13	1	202	47	16.83	0	0									5	
FC	1995	12	21	3	309	47	17.16	0	0									6	

Cmp	Debut	M	I	NO	Runs	HS	Avge	100	50	Balls	Runs	Wkts	Avge	BB	5i	10m	RpO	ct	st

MANOJ SINGH (Uttar Pradesh) b Lucknow 1.7.1976 RHB

Cmp	Debut	M	I	NO	Runs	HS	Avge	100	50	Balls	Runs	Wkts	Avge	BB	5i	10m	RpO	ct	st
FC		1	2	1	59	30	59.00	0	0	66	33	1	33.00	1-33	0	0	3.00	0	
Wlls		1	1	0	32	32	32.00	0	0	10	7	0					4.20	0	
FC	1995	3	5	2	73	30	24.33	0	0	90	42	1	42.00	1-33	0	0	2.80	0	

MARTIN, Jacob Joseph (Baroda) b Baroda 11.5.1972 RHB LBG

Cmp	Debut	M	I	NO	Runs	HS	Avge	100	50	Balls	Runs	Wkts	Avge	BB	5i	10m	RpO	ct	st
FC		8	13	1	578	115	48.16	3	2	36	15	0						2.50	7	1
FC	1991	34	56	7	2235	152*	45.61	6	13	498	345	9	38.33	5-51	1	0	4.15	23	1
Deo	1994	2	2	0	47	28	23.50	0	0									0	

MASOOD, Abdul (Bengal) b Calcutta 29.10.1978 RHB RM

Cmp	Debut	M	I	NO	Runs	HS	Avge	100	50	Balls	Runs	Wkts	Avge	BB	5i	10m	RpO	ct	st
FC		1	1	1	. 7	7*		0	0	234	110	3	36.66	3-110	0	0	2.82	0	

MASOOD, C.T.K. (Kerala) b Tellicherry 25.5.1973 LHB SLA

Cmp	Debut	M	I	NO	Runs	HS	Avge	100	50	Balls	Runs	Wkts	Avge	BB	5i	10m	RpO	ct	st
FC		7	8	3	78	16*	15.60	0	0	1151	453	17	26.64	5-53	1	0	2.36	2	
FC	1993	9	12	3	105	22	.11.66	0	0	1438	606	20	30.30	5-53	1	0	2.52	5	

MEDHI, Utpal (Assam) b Gauhati 26.12.1979 RHB RM

Cmp	Debut	M	I	NO	Runs	HS	Avge	100	50	Balls	Runs	Wkts	Avge	BB	5i	10m	RpO	ct	st
FC		2	1	0	0	0	0.00	0	0	168	66	3	22.00	1-5	0	0	2.35	2	

MEHRA, Ajay (Punjab, President's XI) b Delhi 5.1.1969 RHB OB

Cmp	Debut	M	I	NO	Runs	HS	Avge	100	50	Balls	Runs	Wkts	Avge	BB	5i	10m	RpO	ct	st
FC		9	14	2	627	200*	52.25	1	3	54	27	1	27.00	1-8	0	0	3.00	8	
Wlls		1	1	0	16	16	16.00	0	0	12	14	0					7.00	1	
FC	1989	37	58	6	1989	200*	38.25	5	7	391	211	4	52.75	1-0	0	0	3.23	34	
Deo	1995	3	3	0	131	64	43.66	0	2	12	6	1	6.00	1-6	0	0	3.00	3	
Wlls	1990	2	2	0	17	16	8.50	0	0	12	14	0					7.00	2	

MEHRA, Jitender (Himachal Pradesh)

Cmp	Debut	M	I	NO	Runs	HS	Avge	100	50	Balls	Runs	Wkts	Avge	BB	5i	10m	RpO	ct	st
FC		1	1	0	0	0	0.00	0	0	42	19	1	19.00	1-19	0	0	2.71	0	

MEHRA, Manav (Punjab, North Zone) b Jullundur 2.9.1974 RHB WK

Cmp	Debut	M	I	NO	Runs	HS	Avge	100	50	Balls	Runs	Wkts	Avge	BB	5i	10m	RpO	ct	st
FC		9	12	3	388	105	43.11	1	3									29	6
Deo		1	1	0	12	12	12.00	0	0									2	
FC	1993	11	15	3	393	105	32.75	1	3									39	6

MEHTA, Bhavin Niranjan (Gujarat) b Ahmedabad 17.1.1969 RHB OB

Cmp	Debut	M	I	NO	Runs	HS	Avge	100	50	Balls	Runs	Wkts	Avge	BB	5i	10m	RpO	ct	st
FC		4	8	0	169	73	21.12	0	1	1146	538	12	44.83	5-126	1	0	2.81	1	
FC	1993	14	27	1	626	102	24.07	1	2	3330	1621	36	45.02	5-28	3	0	2.92	7	

MEHTA, Kashyap Chandrakant (Saurashtra) b Botad 26.10.1964 RHB OB

Cmp	Debut	M	I	NO	Runs	HS	Avge	100	50	Balls	Runs	Wkts	Avge	BB	5i	10m	RpO	ct	st
FC		1	1	0	8	8	8.00	0	0	180	105	2	52.50	1-46	0	0	3.50	0	

MEHTA, Sudarshan (Jammu and Kashmir)

Cmp	Debut	M	I	NO	Runs	HS	Avge	100	50	Balls	Runs	Wkts	Avge	BB	5i	10m	RpO	ct	st
FC		1	2	0	21	12	10.50	0	0	6	1	0					1.00	0	
FC	1985	13	21	0	334	86	15.90	0	2	6	1	0					1.00	3	

MHAMBREY, Paras Laxmikant (Mumbai, Rest of India) b Bombay 20.6.1972 RHB RM

Cmp	Debut	M	I	NO	Runs	HS	Avge	100	50	Balls	Runs	Wkts	Avge	BB	5i	10m	RpO	ct	st
FC		8	9	0	142	97	15.77	0	1	1366	590	18	32.77	5-34	1	0	2.59	5	
Wlls		3								157	101	6	16.83	3-31	0	0	3.85	0	
Test	1996	2	3	1	58	28	29.00	0	1	258	148	2	74.00	1-43	0	0	3.44	1	
FC	1992	43	49	11	548	97	14.42	0	1	7139	3385	124	27.29	6-47	8	0	2.84	16	
Int	1996	2	1	1	7	7*		0	0	90	98	2	49.00	2-69	0	0	6.53	0	
Deo	1994	5	3	2	27	20*	27.00	0	0	245	149	7	21.28	5-23	0	1	3.64	3	
Wlls	1994	8								385	290	14	20.71	4-46	1	0	4.51	0	

MISQUIN, Balkrishna Kashinath Prabhu (Goa) b Panaji 6.6.1971 RHB OB

Cmp	Debut	M	I	NO	Runs	HS	Avge	100	50	Balls	Runs	Wkts	Avge	BB	5i	10m	RpO	ct	st
FC		4	5	0	158	52	31.60	0	1	47	26	2	13.00	2-23	0	0	3.31	7	
FC	1989	18	31	0	551	107	17.77	1	1	53	31	2	15.50	2-23	0	0	3.50	15	

MODY, Nilesh Dineshbhai (Gujarat) b Nadiad 11.7.1973 RHB WK

Cmp	Debut	M	I	NO	Runs	HS	Avge	100	50	Balls	Runs	Wkts	Avge	BB	5i	10m	RpO	ct	st
FC		4	8	0	303	106	37.87	1	1									4	
FC	1992	15	30	0	764	106	25.46	1	4									19	4

MOHAN SINGH (Rajasthan) b Jaipur 7.7.1972 LHB LMF

Cmp	Debut	M	I	NO	Runs	HS	Avge	100	50	Balls	Runs	Wkts	Avge	BB	5i	10m	RpO	ct	st
FC		2	2	1	17	16*	17.00	0	0	264	106	2	53.00	1-22	0	0	2.40	0	
FC	1995	3	4	1	21	16*	7.00	0	0	375	196	4	49.00	2-71	0	0	3.13	1	

MOHANTY, Bishnu Deb (Orissa) b Cuttack 30.5.1968 RHB WK

Cmp	Debut	M	I	NO	Runs	HS	Avge	100	50	Balls	Runs	Wkts	Avge	BB	5i	10m	RpO	ct	st
FC		2	3	0	39	23	13.00	0	0									4	
FC	1984	29	37	4	655	100*	19.84	1	1	6	6	0					6.00	49	13
Wlls	1985	1	1	0	3	3	3.00	0	0									1	1

MOHANTY, Debasis Sarbeswar (Orissa, East Zone, President's XI) b Bhubaneshwar 20.7.1976 RHB RM

Cmp	Debut	M	I	NO	Runs	HS	Avge	100	50	Balls	Runs	Wkts	Avge	BB	5i	10m	RpO	ct	st
FC		7	11	5	25	7*	4.16	0	0	1614	691	24	28.79	5-52	1	0	2.56	5	
Deo		4	1	1	0	0*		0	0	210	116	6	19.33	4-28	1	0	3.31	1	
Wlls		1	1	1	1	1*		0	0	24	26	0					6.50	1	

MOHANTY, Subash Chandra (Orissa) b Rourkela 24.9.1971 RHB OB

Cmp	Debut	M	I	NO	Runs	HS	Avge	100	50	Balls	Runs	Wkts	Avge	BB	5i	10m	RpO	ct	st
FC		6	10	2	131	56	16.37	0	1	1079	534	18	29.66	4-35	0	0	2.96	1	
FC	1993	8	13	4	141	56	15.66	0	1	1307	671	21	31.95	4-35	0	0	3.08	5	

MOHAPATRA, Prasanta Raghunath (Orissa, East Zone) b Bhubaneshwar 1.9.1973 RHB RM

Cmp	Debut	M	I	NO	Runs	HS	Avge	100	50	Balls	Runs	Wkts	Avge	BB	5i	10m	RpO	ct	st
FC		9	18	2	418	102*	26.12	1	2									10	
FC	1990	32	59	6	1805	157*	34.05	5	9									36	
Deo	1994	1	1	0	16	16	16.00	0	0									0	

Cmp	Debut	M	I	NO	Runs	HS	Avge	100	50	Balls	Runs	Wkts	Avge	BB	5i	10m	RpO	ct	st

MONGIA, Dinesh (Punjab) b Chandigarh 17.4.1977 LHB SLA

| FC | | 8 | 13 | 2 | 521 | 207* | 47.36 | 2 | 0 | 54 | 25 | 0 | | | | | | 2.77 | 8 | |
| FC | 1995 | 9 | 14 | 2 | 542 | 207* | 45.16 | 2 | 0 | 102 | 51 | 0 | | | | | | 3.00 | 8 | |

MONGIA, Nayan Ramlal (India, India to South Africa, India to West Indies, India to Canada, India to Sri Lanka, India to Zimbabwe) b Baroda 19.12.1969 RHB WK

Test		4	8	0	268	152	33.50	1	0										6	2
FC		4	8	0	268	152	33.50	1	0										6	2
Int		10	8	4	106	23*	26.50	0	0										4	3
Test	1993	25	37	2	989	152	28.25	1	3										61	4
FC	1989	77	120	18	4238	165	41.54	9	20	6	4	0						4.00	176	21
Int	1993	74	48	16	661	69	20.65	0	1										61	23
Deo	1991	3	2	0	34	18	17.00	0	0										4	
Wlls	1988	9	4	1	80	37	26.66	0	0										10	3

MORE, Kiran Shankar (Baroda) b Baroda 4.9.1962 RHB WK

FC		8	13	0	714	180	54.92	1	7	11	18	1	18.00	1-18	0	0	9.81	15	2	
Test	1986	49	64	14	1285	73	25.70	0	7	12	12	0					6.00	110	20	
FC	1980	145	196	34	5155	181*	31.82	7	29	239	176	1	176.00	1-18	0	0	4.41	289	62	
Int	1984	94	65	22	563	42*	13.09	0	0									63	27	
Deo	1982	15	8	4	81	26*	20.25	0	0									9	4	
Wlls	1982	13	7	1	86	31	14.33	0	0									11	8	

MORE, Sunil Shankar (Mumbai) b Bombay 24.3.1969 RHB

FC		2	4	1	38	24	12.66	0	0									2		
FC	1992	22	34	4	1354	184	45.13	5	5	36	26	0					4.33	33		
Wlls	1992	1	1	0	9	9	9.00	0	0									0		

MORRIS, Robin Francis (Mumbai) b Bombay 6.11.1976 RHB RM

| Wlls | | 3 | 2 | 0 | 51 | 26 | 25.50 | 0 | 0 | 90 | 73 | 1 | 73.00 | 1-32 | 0 | 0 | 4.86 | 0 | | |
| FC | 1995 | 1 | 1 | 0 | 39 | 39 | 39.00 | 0 | 0 | 138 | 84 | 2 | 42.00 | 2-59 | 0 | 0 | 3.65 | 0 | | |

MOTIVARAS, Jayesh Dhanjibhai (Saurashtra) b Porbandar 7.10.1975 RHB

| FC | | 2 | 4 | 0 | 101 | 52 | 25.25 | 0 | 1 | | | | | | | | | 1 | | |

MUDGAL, Manoj Sitaram (Uttar Pradesh, Central Zone) b Meerut 18.10.1972 RHB WK

FC		8	15	1	555	101	39.64	1	3									17	3	
Deo		3	3	0	59	33	19.66	0	0									1	1	
Wlls		1	1	0	16	16	16.00	0	0									1		
FC	1992	33	54	3	1617	129	31.70	3	9									70	19	
Deo	1993	10	10	0	276	75	27.60	0	2									3	4	
Wlls	1992	3	3	0	29	16	9.66	0	0									3	2	

MUJUMDER, Sumitro (Bengal) b Calcutta 18.6.1973 RHB RM

| FC | | 2 | 2 | 0 | 27 | 18 | 13.50 | 0 | 0 | 408 | 220 | 7 | 31.42 | 4-105 | 0 | 0 | 3.23 | 1 | | |
| Wlls | | 1 | 1 | 0 | 14 | 14 | 14.00 | 0 | 0 | 42 | 35 | 1 | 35.00 | 1-35 | 0 | 0 | 5.00 | 0 | | |

MULLICK, Pravanjan (Orissa) b Bhubaneshwar 12.9.1976 RHB

| FC | | 3 | 6 | 1 | 197 | 66 | 39.40 | 0 | 1 | 18 | 20 | 0 | | | | | 6.66 | 1 | | |

MUZUMDAR, Amol Anil (Mumbai, West Zone, President's XI) b Bombay 11.11.1974 RHB LBG

FC		12	16	2	942	214*	67.28	4	2	30	21	0					4.20	16		
Wlls		3	3	2	102	68*	102.00	0	1									3		
FC	1993	40	61	8	3292	260	62.11	10	17	42	27	0					3.85	47		
Deo	1994	7	7	1	303	82	50.50	0	1									4		
Wlls	1994	6	5	3	117	68*	58.50	0	1									3		

NAIK, Korra Bharat Singh (Andhra) b Guntur 18.9.1973 LHB

FC		5	10	0	299	92	29.90	0	2	36	33	2	16.50	2-20	0	0	5.50	1		
FC	1994	14	28	2	688	103	26.46	1	3	48	38	2	19.00	2-20	0	0	4.75	7		
Deo	1995	1	1	0	10	10	10.00	0	0									1		

NAIK, Rajesh Rama (Goa) b Panaji 20.12.1974 RHB OB

| FC | | 4 | 5 | 0 | 166 | 61 | 33.20 | 0 | 2 | 120 | 85 | 1 | 85.00 | 1-75 | 0 | 0 | 4.25 | 2 | | |
| FC | 1995 | 6 | 9 | 0 | 272 | 61 | 30.22 | 0 | 2 | 180 | 173 | 1 | 173.00 | 1-75 | 0 | 0 | 5.76 | 8 | | |

NAIR, Biju (Services)

| FC | | 2 | 4 | 0 | 30 | 16 | 7.50 | 0 | 0 | | | | | | | | | 1 | 1 | |
| FC | 1990 | 3 | 6 | 0 | 37 | 16 | 6.16 | 0 | 0 | | | | | | | | | 1 | 1 | |

NAND KISHORE, Ammanabrole (Hyderabad) b Warangal 10.7.1970 RHB RM

FC		9	15	1	353	47	25.21	0	0									10		
FC	1994	19	33	2	866	132	27.93	1	2	18	9	0					3.00	24		
Wlls	1995	1	1	0	33	33	33.00	0	0									1		

NARULA, Mukesh Shamsunder (Baroda) b Delhi 2.9.1962 RHB RM

FC		1	2	1	53	44*	53.00	0	0	42	10	0					1.42	1		
FC	1985	57	88	17	2373	176	33.42	5	9	6941	3377	104	32.47	6-80	6	0	2.91	32		
Deo	1990	7	4	2	3	2*	1.50	0	0	292	239	9	26.55	3-37	0	0	4.91	1		

NASIRUDDIN, Thameesdeen (Karnataka) b Mandya 10.8.1969 RHB LM

| FC | | 2 | 3 | 1 | 23 | 12 | 11.50 | 0 | 0 | 96 | 49 | 2 | 24.50 | 1-15 | 0 | 0 | 3.06 | 4 | | |
| FC | 1994 | 3 | 4 | 1 | 24 | 12 | 8.00 | 0 | 0 | 180 | 95 | 2 | 47.50 | 1-15 | 0 | 0 | 3.16 | 4 | | |

Cmp	Debut	M	I	NO	Runs	HS	Avge	100	50	Balls	Runs	Wkts	Avge	BB	5i	10m	RpO	ct	st

NATH, Kartar (Delhi) b Jammu 1.3.1969 LHB SLA

Cmp	Debut	M	I	NO	Runs	HS	Avge	100	50	Balls	Runs	Wkts	Avge	BB	5i	10m	RpO	ct	st
FC		1	2	0	0	0	0.00	0	0	120	85	1	85.00	1-59	0	0	4.25	2	
FC	1992	9	9	1	20	11	2.50	0	0	1740	810	23	35.21	5-53	1	0	2.79	6	

NAWALI, Raghuttam (Karnataka) b Hanumsagar 29.11.1971 RHB WK

Cmp	Debut	M	I	NO	Runs	HS	Avge	100	50	Balls	Runs	Wkts	Avge	BB	5i	10m	RpO	ct	st
FC		1	2	0	22	15	11.00	0	0									1	
FC	1994	4	7	0	139	48	19.85	0	0									5	

NAYYAR, Rajiv (Himachal Pradesh, North Zone, India A) b Delhi 28.3.1970 RHB LBG

Cmp	Debut	M	I	NO	Runs	HS	Avge	100	50	Balls	Runs	Wkts	Avge	BB	5i	10m	RpO	ct	st
FC		8	13	3	717	170	71.70	4	1	330	230	3	76.66	1-3	0	0	4.18	8	
Deo		1	1	1	23	23*		0	0									0	
FC	1986	54	99	9	3756	170	41.73	11	19	3152	1994	39	51.12	7-93	2	0	3.79	33	
Deo	1993	3	3	1	76	52	38.00	0	1	30	24	0					4.80	0	

NEGI, Naveen (Rajasthan) b Sonepat 28.12.1974 RHB WK

Cmp	Debut	M	I	NO	Runs	HS	Avge	100	50	Balls	Runs	Wkts	Avge	BB	5i	10m	RpO	ct	st
FC		4	5	0	260	119	52.00	1	1	6	16	0					16.00	6	
FC	1993	7	10	1	332	119	36.88	1	1	6	16	0					16.00	10	

OASIS, Sunil Chandrasekharan (Kerala, South Zone) b Calicut 3.4.1973 RHB RM

Cmp	Debut	M	I	NO	Runs	HS	Avge	100	50	Balls	Runs	Wkts	Avge	BB	5i	10m	RpO	ct	st
FC		9	15	1	589	135	42.07	1	5	1140	487	19	25.63	4-59	0	0	2.56	6	
Deo		4	3	0	8	8	2.66	0	0	198	136	5	27.20	3-27	0	0	4.12	2	
FC	1993	25	41	4	1441	135	38.94	3	11	2756	1109	40	27.72	4-59	0	0	2.41	26	
Deo	1995	6	3	0	8	8	2.66	0	0	258	188	7	26.85	3-27	0	0	4.37	4	

OBAID, Kamal (Uttar Pradesh, Central Zone) b Allahabad 4.9.1972 RHB RMF

Cmp	Debut	M	I	NO	Runs	HS	Avge	100	50	Balls	Runs	Wkts	Avge	BB	5i	10m	RpO	ct	st
FC		10	13	0	182	55	14.00	0	1	2204	948	39	24.30	7-74	4	0	2.58	1	
Deo		4	3	1	14	8*	7.00	0	0	168	154	3	51.33	1-10	0	0	5.50	1	
Wlls		1	1	0	0	0	0.00	0	0	24	23	0					5.75	0	
FC	1990	40	53	8	691	69	15.35	0	2	8332	3723	140	26.59	7-74	8	0	2.68	12	
Deo	1993	14	8	4	38	12*	9.50	0	0	612	419	16	26.18	4-15	1	0	4.10	2	
Wlls	1990	6	5	2	15	10*	5.00	0	0	306	214	8	26.75	4-38	1	0	4.19	1	

PADMANABHAN, K.Narayanaiyer Anantha (Kerala, South Zone, Wills XI) b Trivandrum 8.9.1969 RHB LBG

Cmp	Debut	M	I	NO	Runs	HS	Avge	100	50	Balls	Runs	Wkts	Avge	BB	5i	10m	RpO	ct	st
FC		11	18	5	615	200	47.30	2	0	2491	1044	32	32.62	6-99	1	0	2.51	12	
Wlls		1	1	0	16	16	16.00	0	0	60	50	2	25.00	2-50	0	0	5.00	0	
FC	1988	56	85	16	1455	200	21.08	2	2	13163	5834	215	27.13	8-57	17	3	2.65	43	
Deo	1993	4	1	1	1	1*		0	0	222	152	4	38.00	2-33	0	0	4.10	1	
Wlls	1992	5	3	0	16	16	5.33	0	0	220	146	8	18.25	4-25	1	0	3.98	2	

PAGNIS, Amit Anil (Mumbai) b Bombay 10.9.1978 LHB RM

Cmp	Debut	M	I	NO	Runs	HS	Avge	100	50	Balls	Runs	Wkts	Avge	BB	5i	10m	RpO	ct	st
FC		1	1	0	5	5	5.00	0	0									1	
FC	1995	2	2	0	5	5	2.50	0	0									1	

PANDA, Sumit (Bihar) b Jamshedpur 3.12.1979 RHB RM

Cmp	Debut	M	I	NO	Runs	HS	Avge	100	50	Balls	Runs	Wkts	Avge	BB	5i	10m	RpO	ct	st
FC		2	3	1	27	22*	13.50	0	0	150	47	2	23.50	1-13	0	0	3.13	1	

PANDE, Gyanendrakumar Kedarnath (Uttar Pradesh, Central Zone) b Lucknow 12.8.1972 LHB SLA

Cmp	Debut	M	I	NO	Runs	HS	Avge	100	50	Balls	Runs	Wkts	Avge	BB	5i	10m	RpO	ct	st
FC		8	12	1	445	101	40.45	1	2	1385	501	11	45.54	3-27	0	0	2.17	5	
Deo		4	4	1	66	34	22.00	0	0	210	183	7	26.14	4-32	1	0	5.22	2	
Wlls		1	1	0	0	0	0.00	0	0	54	43	0					4.77	0	
FC	1988	55	80	13	2584	178	38.56	5	13	7626	3184	76	41.89	7-167	1	0	2.50	34	
Deo	1991	17	15	6	317	89*	35.22	0	2	847	599	27	22.18	4-32	1	0	4.24	8	
Wlls	1989	6	5	1	58	21	14.50	0	0	228	207	5	41.40	3-42	0	0	5.44	3	

PANDEY, Anshuman Vachaspati (Madhya Pradesh) b Chatarpur 26.9.1975 RHB OB

Cmp	Debut	M	I	NO	Runs	HS	Avge	100	50	Balls	Runs	Wkts	Avge	BB	5i	10m	RpO	ct	st
FC		3	6	0	85	24	14.16	0	0									1	
FC	1995	6	11	1	304	209*	30.40	1	0									1	

PANDEY, Jayprakash Nandjee (Services) b Calcutta 16.5.1973 RHB RM

Cmp	Debut	M	I	NO	Runs	HS	Avge	100	50	Balls	Runs	Wkts	Avge	BB	5i	10m	RpO	ct	st
FC		2	4	0	90	52	22.50	0	1	228	111	2	55.50	1-8	0	0	2.92	0	
FC	1993	12	18	5	234	52	18.00	0	1	1834	997	41	24.31	6-64	2	1	3.26	5	

PANDEY, Sanjay (Madhya Pradesh) b Bhopal 14.12.1976 RHB RM

Cmp	Debut	M	I	NO	Runs	HS	Avge	100	50	Balls	Runs	Wkts	Avge	BB	5i	10m	RpO	ct	st
FC		4	5	2	9	8*	3.00	0	0	600	308	8	38.50	4-63	0	0	3.08	1	

PANDEY, Sanjay (Haryana) b Faridabad 2.4.1971 RHB RFM

Cmp	Debut	M	I	NO	Runs	HS	Avge	100	50	Balls	Runs	Wkts	Avge	BB	5i	10m	RpO	ct	st
FC		4	7	3	43	14	10.75	0	0	684	390	10	39.00	5-106	1	0	3.42	2	
Wlls		2	1	0	6	6	6.00	0	0	79	84	1	84.00	1-49	0	0	6.37	0	

PANDEY, Tribhowan Chandra (Services)

Cmp	Debut	M	I	NO	Runs	HS	Avge	100	50	Balls	Runs	Wkts	Avge	BB	5i	10m	RpO	ct	st
FC		1	2	2	23	18*		0	0	126	69	0					3.28	0	

PANDIT, Chandrakant Sitaram (Madhya Pradesh, Central Zone) b Bombay 30.9.1961 RHB WK

Cmp	Debut	M	I	NO	Runs	HS	Avge	100	50	Balls	Runs	Wkts	Avge	BB	5i	10m	RpO	ct	st
FC		12	16	1	873	189	58.20	3	2	12	12	0					6.00	16	3
Deo		1	1	0	26	26	26.00	0	0									0	1
Test	1986	5	8	1	171	39	24.42	0	0									14	2
FC	1979	114	162	24	6986	202	50.62	19	36	331	146	2	73.00	1-26	0	0	2.64	248	40
Int	1985	36	23	9	290	33*	20.71	0	0									15	15
Deo	1983	18	16	4	472	60*	39.33	0	5	4	8	0					12.00	11	6
Wlls	1982	20	17	4	427	57	32.84	0	2									26	7

Cmp	Debut	M	I	NO	Runs	HS	Avge	100	50	Balls	Runs	Wkts	Avge	BB	5i	10m	RpO	ct	st

PANTA, Rahul (Himachal Pradesh) b Taksal 11.3.1977 RHB RM

| FC | | 1 | 1 | 0 | 16 | 16 | 16.00 | 0 | 0 | 84 | 69 | 1 | 69.00 | 1-35 | 0 | 0 | 4.92 | 0 | |
| FC | 1995 | 2 | 2 | 0 | 21 | 16 | 10.50 | 0 | 0 | 169 | 125 | 1 | 125.00 | 1-35 | 0 | 0 | 4.43 | 0 | |

PARANJPE, Jatin Vasudeo (Mumbai) b Bombay 17.4.1972 LHB SLA

FC		8	11	1	541	165	54.10	2	2									4	
FC	1991	33	49	6	1842	218	42.83	6	6	6	0	0						0.00	22
Deo	1993	1																	0
Wlls	1992	2	2	0	84	45	42.00	0	0										0

PARIDA, Kulamani (Railways) b Cuttack 9.3.1977 RHB OB

| FC | | 3 | 4 | 4 | 23 | 9* | | 0 | 0 | 576 | 204 | 15 | 13.60 | 6-121 | 1 | 0 | 2.12 | 0 | |

PARIDA, Rashmi Ranjan (Orissa) b Bhubaneshwar 7.9.1974 RHB WK

| FC | | 8 | 14 | 2 | 447 | 111* | 37.25 | 1 | 2 | 12 | 8 | 0 | | | | | 4.00 | 6 | |
| FC | 1994 | 13 | 22 | 3 | 608 | 111* | 32.00 | 1 | 2 | 12 | 8 | 0 | | | | | 4.00 | 9 | |

PARMAR, Anil Singh (Rajasthan) b Jaipur 27.12.1972 RHB OB

| FC | | 4 | 5 | 0 | 127 | 74 | 25.40 | 0 | 1 | 30 | 32 | 0 | | | | | 6.40 | 3 | |
| FC | 1994 | 13 | 23 | 2 | 727 | 119 | 34.61 | 1 | 4 | 30 | 32 | 0 | | | | | 6.40 | 8 | |

PARMAR, Devendra Vinod (Madhya Pradesh) b Vagra 10.8.1971 RHB OB

| FC | | 1 | 1 | 1 | 1 | 1* | | 0 | 0 | 162 | 46 | 3 | 15.33 | 2-22 | 0 | 0 | 1.70 | 2 | |
| FC | 1993 | 4 | 5 | 4 | 23 | 13* | 23.00 | 0 | 0 | 825 | 341 | 17 | 20.05 | 6-105 | 1 | 0 | 2.48 | 4 | |

PARMAR, Mukund Harishkumar (Gujarat) b Ahmedabad 13.11.1968 RHB SLA

FC		4	8	0	256	134	32.00	1	2	108	65	2	32.50	2-35	0	0	3.61	0	
FC	1987	41	74	6	4050	283	59.55	16	16	2156	1154	19	60.73	4-44	0	0	3.21	20	
Deo	1990	4	2	0	26	19	13.00	0	0	48	65	2	32.50	1-26	0	0	8.12	0	
Wlls	1991	1								60	17	1	17.00	1-17	0	0	1.70	0	

PARSANA, Hitesh Jayarambhai (Saurashtra, West Zone, President's XI) b Rajkot 20.2.1970 RHB OB

FC		6	11	4	466	100*	66.57	1	3	1528	784	19	41.26	5-64	2	0	3.07	7	
Deo		1	1	0	0	0	0.00	0	0	36	26	0					4.33	0	
FC	1988	27	46	10	1066	100*	29.61	1	4	5177	2482	64	38.78	5-64	4	0	2.87	19	
Deo	1995	3	3	1	7	4	3.50	0	0	126	98	4	24.50	3-28	0	0	4.66	1	

PATDIWALA, Kalpesh Rajendrakumar (Gujarat) b Ahmedabad 28.7.1976 RHB

| FC | | 1 | 2 | 0 | 16 | 8 | 8.00 | 0 | 0 | | | | | | | | | 0 | |
| FC | 1993 | 11 | 22 | 1 | 405 | 152 | 19.28 | 1 | 1 | | | | | | | | | 4 | |

PATEL, Dhansukh Thakorbhai (Gujarat) b Rundhmagdalla 3.4.1964 RHB RMF

| FC | | 3 | 5 | 3 | 4 | 3* | 2.00 | 0 | 0 | 490 | 201 | 10 | 20.10 | 4-63 | 0 | 0 | 2.46 | 2 | |
| FC | 1983 | 48 | 71 | 18 | 869 | 63 | 16.39 | 0 | 2 | 8336 | 4947 | 118 | 41.92 | 6-102 | 2 | 0 | 3.56 | 21 | |

PATEL, Hiren Dhanjibhai (Gujarat) b Surat 16.9.1975 LHB SLA

| FC | | 4 | 8 | 0 | 44 | 22 | 5.50 | 0 | 0 | 1029 | 486 | 10 | 48.60 | 3-153 | 0 | 0 | 2.83 | 4 | |
| FC | 1994 | 10 | 19 | 2 | 270 | 81 | 15.88 | 0 | 1 | 2145 | 1066 | 21 | 50.76 | 4-94 | 0 | 0 | 2.98 | 9 | |

PATEL, Jittu (Bihar) b Jamshedpur 16.8.1970 LHB SLA

| FC | | 3 | 5 | 1 | 58 | 22 | 14.50 | 0 | 0 | 264 | 138 | 5 | 27.60 | 3-30 | 0 | 0 | 3.13 | 0 | |

PATEL, Jaimin Jayprakashbhai (Gujarat) b Bhadran 2.2.1973 LHB LMF

| FC | | 2 | 4 | 2 | 8 | 6* | 4.00 | 0 | 0 | 389 | 172 | 0 | | | | | 2.65 | 1 | |

PATEL, Kirti Karshanbhai (Madhya Pradesh) b Indore 27.11.1969 RHB WK

FC		8	12	1	389	79	35.36	0	3									15	3
FC	1987	53	92	8	2948	202	35.09	6	15									100	30
Deo	1992	1	1	0	41	41	41.00	0	0	6	12	0					12.00	0	
Wlls	1991	5	5	0	84	62	16.80	0	1									1	3

PATEL, Manish Prakash (Mumbai) b Bombay 11.3.1971 RHB RM

FC		4	4	3	2	1*	2.00	0	0	807	305	11	27.72	5-65	1	0	2.26	3	
FC	1993	14	11	5	4	1*	0.66	0	0	2241	1033	30	34.43	5-65	2	0	2.76	6	
Wlls	1994	2								120	70	2	35.00	1-24	0	0	3.50	0	

PATEL, Nisrag Ambubhai (Gujarat) b Surat 17.11.1966 RHB OB

| FC | | 2 | 4 | 0 | 63 | 31 | 15.75 | 0 | 0 | 43 | 24 | 1 | 24.00 | 1-5 | 0 | 0 | 3.34 | 2 | |
| FC | 1988 | 23 | 42 | 0 | 934 | 69 | 22.23 | 0 | 6 | 1421 | 876 | 10 | 87.60 | 2-32 | 0 | 0 | 3.69 | 12 | |

PATEL, Pathik Hasmukhbhai (Gujarat) b Ahmedabad 10.9.1972 RHB WK

| FC | | 4 | 8 | 0 | 165 | 51 | 20.62 | 0 | 1 | | | | | | | | | 9 | 2 |
| FC | 1992 | 15 | 29 | 1 | 623 | 68 | 22.25 | 0 | 4 | | | | | | | | | 21 | 5 |

PATEL, Rashid (Baroda) b Sabarkantha 1.6.1964 LHB LFM

FC		1	2	0	11	11	5.50	0	0	54	29	0					3.22	0	
Test	1988	1	2	0	0	0	0.00	0	0	84	51	0					3.64	1	
FC	1986	42	50	7	416	38	9.67	0	0	6748	3933	113	34.80	6-93	3	0	3.49	14	
Int	1988	1								60	58	0					5.80	0	
Deo	1988	1								18	27	0					9.00	0	
Wlls	1986	6	2	1	1	1*	1.00	0	0	221	180	4	45.00	2-32	0	0	4.88	1	

PATEL, Sanjay Kantibhai (Baroda) b Jadeswar 8.4.1966 RHB RM

| FC | | 1 | 1 | 0 | 7 | 7 | 7.00 | 0 | 0 | 186 | 99 | 1 | 99.00 | 1-92 | 0 | 0 | 3.19 | 2 | |
| FC | 1991 | 7 | 8 | 3 | 35 | 10 | 7.00 | 0 | 0 | 1013 | 611 | 14 | 43.64 | 6-106 | 1 | 0 | 3.61 | 4 | |

PATHAK, Amit (Andhra, South Zone) b Visakhapatnam 30.11.1972 RHB RM

Cmp Debut	M	I	NO	Runs	HS	Avge	100	50	Balls	Runs	Wkts	Avge	BB	5i	10m	RpO	ct	st
FC	6	12	0	482	123	40.16	2	3									7	
Deo	2	2	0	11	11	5.50	0	0									0	
FC 1990	31	56	1	2213	145	40.23	8	8	108	74	0					4.11	18	
Deo 1991	4	4	0	35	23	8.75	0	0									1	

PAUL, Reuben (Tamil Nadu, South Zone) b Madras 4.6.1972 RHB WK

Cmp Debut	M	I	NO	Runs	HS	Avge	100	50	Balls	Runs	Wkts	Avge	BB	5i	10m	RpO	ct	st
FC	8	12	0	397	100	33.08	1	1									11	1
Deo	4	4	1	34	19	11.33	0	0									1	2
FC 1995	15	21	1	619	100*	30.95	2	1	6	11	0					11.00	24	3

PAWAR, Rajesh Vithal (Mumbai) b Bombay 6.9.1979 LHB SLA

Cmp Debut	M	I	NO	Runs	HS	Avge	100	50	Balls	Runs	Wkts	Avge	BB	5i	10m	RpO	ct	st
FC	3	3	1	58	29	29.00	0	0	919	463	11	42.09	5-93	1	0	3.02	0	
Wlls	1								60	56	1	56.00	1-56	0	0	5.60	1	

PEERZADA, Asif (Jammu and Kashmir)

Cmp Debut	M	I	NO	Runs	HS	Avge	100	50	Balls	Runs	Wkts	Avge	BB	5i	10m	RpO	ct	st
FC	1	2	1	0	0*	0.00	0	0	114	68	0					3.57	0	
FC 1987	7	10	4	37	16*	6.16	0	0	1105	742	24	30.91	6-144	1	0	4.02	0	

PHATE, Umakant Sewaram (Vidarbha) b Nagpur 13.11.1965 RHB OB

Cmp Debut	M	I	NO	Runs	HS	Avge	100	50	Balls	Runs	Wkts	Avge	BB	5i	10m	RpO	ct	st
FC	3	5	0	72	34	14.40	0	0	6	2	0					2.00	2	
FC 1986	28	51	6	1500	118	33.33	3	6	30	13	0					2.60	10	

POWAR, Kiran Rajaram (Mumbai) b Bombay 6.4.1976 LHB OB

Cmp Debut	M	I	NO	Runs	HS	Avge	100	50	Balls	Runs	Wkts	Avge	BB	5i	10m	RpO	ct	st
FC	1	2	0	16	14	8.00	0	0									1	

PRABHAKAR, Manoj (Delhi) b Ghaziabad 15.4.1963 RHB RM

Cmp Debut	M	I	NO	Runs	HS	Avge	100	50	Balls	Runs	Wkts	Avge	BB	5i	10m	RpO	ct	st
FC	5	6	0	125	44	20.83	0	0	707	271	16	16.93	4-31	0	0	2.29	7	
Test 1984	39	58	9	1600	120	32.65	1	9	7475	3581	96	37.30	6-132	3	0	2.87	20	
FC 1982	154	214	34	7469	229*	41.49	20	30	24116	11134	385	28.91	7-65	10	1	2.77	74	
Int 1983	130	98	21	1858	106	24.12	2	11	6360	4534	157	28.87	5-33	4	2	4.27	27	
Deo 1983	17	14	4	480	117*	48.00	1	3	801	529	23	23.00	4-12	1	0	3.96	7	
Wlls 1982	19	16	5	431	78*	39.18	0	3	1035	692	40	17.30	4-12	2	0	4.01	5	

PRADHAN, Dhiraj (Uttar Pradesh)

Cmp Debut	M	I	NO	Runs	HS	Avge	100	50	Balls	Runs	Wkts	Avge	BB	5i	10m	RpO	ct	st
Wlls	1	1	0	27	27	27.00	0	0									0	

PRAKASH, Anant (Bihar) b Patna 17.9.1979 RHB OB

Cmp Debut	M	I	NO	Runs	HS	Avge	100	50	Balls	Runs	Wkts	Avge	BB	5i	10m	RpO	ct	st
FC	2	4	0	76	30	19.00	0	0	72	47	1	47.00	1-27	0	0	3.91	2	

PRASAD, Mannava Sri Kanth (Andhra, South Zone, Wills XI) b Guntur 24.4.1975 RHB WK

Cmp Debut	M	I	NO	Runs	HS	Avge	100	50	Balls	Runs	Wkts	Avge	BB	5i	10m	RpO	ct	st
FC	6	11	0	206	60	18.72	0	1									11	2
Wlls	1	1	0	17	17	17.00	0	0									1	
FC 1994	16	30	2	661	100*	23.60	1	3									34	8

PRASAD, Raja Vasireddy Chandramouli (Andhra) b Madras 30.5.1974 RHB RM

Cmp Debut	M	I	NO	Runs	HS	Avge	100	50	Balls	Runs	Wkts	Avge	BB	5i	10m	RpO	ct	st
FC	5	10	2	265	141*	33.12	1	1									1	
FC 1995	9	18	3	445	141*	29.66	1	2									3	

PRASANTH, M.V. (Karnataka) b Bangalore 5.8.1975 RHB LB

Cmp Debut	M	I	NO	Runs	HS	Avge	100	50	Balls	Runs	Wkts	Avge	BB	5i	10m	RpO	ct	st
FC	2	3	2	2	1*	2.00	0	0	174	75	2	37.50	1-17	0	0	2.58	0	

PRATAP, Vanka (Hyderabad) b Hyderabad 21.11.1973 RHB RM

Cmp Debut	M	I	NO	Runs	HS	Avge	100	50	Balls	Runs	Wkts	Avge	BB	5i	10m	RpO	ct	st
FC	10	16	1	754	136	50.26	1	7	528	264	8	33.00	2-25	0	0	3.00	5	
FC 1991	37	55	5	1732	136	34.64	2	13	2170	1104	34	32.47	5-100	1	0	3.05	22	
Wlls 1992	2	2	0	22	17	11.00	0	0	48	59	2	29.50	2-59	0	0	7.37	0	

PUJARA, Bipin Shivlal (Saurashtra) b Rajkot 7.10.1963 RHB WK

Cmp Debut	M	I	NO	Runs	HS	Avge	100	50	Balls	Runs	Wkts	Avge	BB	5i	10m	RpO	ct	st
FC	1	2	0	8	6	4.00	0	0									1	
FC 1983	36	62	9	1631	112*	30.77	2	12	6	0	0					0.00	24	9

PURI, Rajesh (Haryana, North Zone) b Simla 28.10.1968 RHB OB

Cmp Debut	M	I	NO	Runs	HS	Avge	100	50	Balls	Runs	Wkts	Avge	BB	5i	10m	RpO	ct	st
FC	9	14	0	414	130	29.57	1	2	24	22	0					5.50	18	
Deo	3	3	0	39	16	13.00	0	0									2	
Wlls	3	3	0	89	45	29.66	0	0									2	
FC 1988	62	90	8	3257	172	39.71	12	11	426	280	3	93.33	2-40	0	0	3.94	65	
Deo 1991	12	12	1	263	52	23.90	0	2	12	9	0					4.50	3	
Wlls 1992	7	7	2	275	68*	55.00	0	2									2	

QAYYUM, Abdul (Jammu and Kashmir, North Zone) b Anantnag 2.3.1967 RHB RM

Cmp Debut	M	I	NO	Runs	HS	Avge	100	50	Balls	Runs	Wkts	Avge	BB	5i	10m	RpO	ct	st
FC	3	6	0	50	26	8.33	0	0	498	284	10	28.40	5-110	1	0	3.42	1	
Deo	1	1	1	4	4*		0	0	42	25	2	13.50	2-25	0	0	3.57	1	
FC 1985	32	57	8	511	46	10.42	0	0	5949	3299	112	29.45	7-57	9	2	3.32	16	
Wlls 1990	1	1	1	1	1*		0	0	60	56	1	36.00	1-56	0	0	5.60	0	

RAGHAVAN, C.Venkatraghavan Kalyanram (Services) b Secunderabad 24.6.1972 RHB

Cmp Debut	M	I	NO	Runs	HS	Avge	100	50	Balls	Runs	Wkts	Avge	BB	5i	10m	RpO	ct	st
FC	2	3	0	26	20	8.66	0	0									0	
FC 1995	6	9	0	84	23	9.33	0	0									3	

RAJ KUMAR (Himachal Pradesh) b Una 2.5.1968 RHB WK

Cmp Debut	M	I	NO	Runs	HS	Avge	100	50	Balls	Runs	Wkts	Avge	BB	5i	10m	RpO	ct	st
FC	5	9	0	95	41	10.55	0	0									4	3
FC 1987	37	69	5	848	57	13.25	0	2									39	10

RAJA ALI (Madhya Pradesh) b Bhopal 5.7.1976 LHB SLA

Cmp Debut	M	I	NO	Runs	HS	Avge	100	50	Balls	Runs	Wkts	Avge	BB	5i	10m	RpO	ct	st
FC	6	9	0	252	70	28.00	0	3	6	14	0					14.00	1	

Cmp	Debut	M	I	NO	Runs	HS	Avge	100	50	Balls	Runs	Wkts	Avge	BB	5i	10m	RpO	ct	st

RAJESH, Padmanabhan (Tamil Nadu) b Bangerpet 26.4.1970 RHB OB

Cmp	Debut	M	I	NO	Runs	HS	Avge	100	50	Balls	Runs	Wkts	Avge	BB	5i	10m	RpO	ct	st
FC		3	5	2	68	34*	22.66	0	0									0	
FC	1995	5	8	2	107	34*	17.83	0	0	6	13	0					13.00	1	

RAJINDER SINGH (Assam) b Gauhati 17.10.1969 RHB RM

Cmp	Debut	M	I	NO	Runs	HS	Avge	100	50	Balls	Runs	Wkts	Avge	BB	5i	10m	RpO	ct	st
FC		3	6	0	80	39	13.33	0	0	108	38	0					2.11	1	
FC	1988	41	75	4	1951	128	27.47	2	9	2742	1356	54	25.11	6-33	2	0	2.96	29	
Deo	1990	3	2	1	60	31*	60.00	0	0	96	116	2	58.00	1-53	0	0	7.25	0	

RAJPUT, Lalchand Sitaram (Vidarbha) b Bombay 18.12.1961 RHB RM/OB

Cmp	Debut	M	I	NO	Runs	HS	Avge	100	50	Balls	Runs	Wkts	Avge	BB	5i	10m	RpO	ct	st
FC		4	7	1	266	123	44.33	1	1	228	108	3	36.00	1-24	0	0	2.84	4	
Test	1985	2	4	0	105	61	26.25	0	1									1	
FC	1981	102	172	18	7557	275	49.07	19	44	5426	2567	54	47.53	5-32	1	0	2.83	75	
Int	1984	4	4	1	9	8	3.00	0	0	42	42	0					6.00	2	
Deo	1985	16	16	0	676	115	42.25	2	4	566	408	9	45.33	2-26	0	0	4.32	12	
Wlls	1982	19	19	1	592	101	32.88	1	4	588	466	11	42.36	2-31	0	0	4.75	2	

RAMAN, Woorkeri Venkat (Tamil Nadu, India, South Zone, India A, India to South Africa) b Madras 23.5.1965 LHB SLA

Cmp	Debut	M	I	NO	Runs	HS	Avge	100	50	Balls	Runs	Wkts	Avge	BB	5i	10m	RpO	ct	st
Test		1	2	0	59	57	29.50	0	1									1	
FC		6	10	0	253	57	25.30	0	2	90	68	1	68.00	1-34	0	0	4.53	3	
Int		1	1	0	29	29	29.00	0	0	36	25	0					4.16	1	
Test	1987	11	19	1	448	96	24.89	0	4	348	129	2	64.50	1-7	0	0	2.22	6	
FC	1982	121	181	19	7661	313	47.29	19	33	6424	3154	84	37.54	6-29	4	1	2.94	88	
Int	1987	27	27	1	617	114	23.73	1	3	162	170	2	85.00	1-23	0	0	6.29	2	
Deo	1986	19	19	0	509	85	26.78	0	3	186	129	3	43.00	2-27	0	0	4.16	3	
Wlls	1987	10	10	2	533	117*	66.62	2	2	161	139	7	19.85	2-12	0	0	5.18	4	

RAMESH, Sandagoppan (Tamil Nadu, South Zone) b Madras 16.10.1975 LHB OB

Cmp	Debut	M	I	NO	Runs	HS	Avge	100	50	Balls	Runs	Wkts	Avge	BB	5i	10m	RpO	ct	st
FC		10	18	1	655	146	38.52	2	3	18	11	0					3.66	4	
Deo		3	3	0	21	19	7.00	0	0									5	
FC	1995	19	33	1	1365	158	42.65	4	7	48	23	0					2.87	17	

RAM KISHEN, Hanumara (Andhra, South Zone, Rest of India) b Vijayawada 29.7.1971 RHB LM/SLA

Cmp	Debut	M	I	NO	Runs	HS	Avge	100	50	Balls	Runs	Wkts	Avge	BB	5i	10m	RpO	ct	st
FC		7	13	6	63	17	9.00	0	0	1841	799	28	28.53	7-126	1	0	2.60	1	
Deo		3	1	1	1	1*		0	0	144	85	3	28.33	3-31	0	0	3.54	0	
FC	1990	25	38	18	132	17	6.60	0	0	5355	2564	88	29.13	7-126	4	0	2.87	7	
Deo	1994	6	3	2	3	2*	3.00	0	0	264	144	5	28.80	3-31	0	0	3.27	1	

RAMPRAKASH, Bhaskaran (Kerala, South Zone) b Madras 18.12.1966 RHB OB

Cmp	Debut	M	I	NO	Runs	HS	Avge	100	50	Balls	Runs	Wkts	Avge	BB	5i	10m	RpO	ct	st
FC		11	16	1	235	60	15.16	0	1	3049	1136	53	21.43	8-25	6	2	2.23	7	
Deo		3	3	2	13	5*	13.00	0	0	156	118	0					4.53	1	
FC	1990	43	72	5	1892	152	28.23	1	12	11767	4457	170	26.21	8-25	14	3	2.27	26	
Deo	1991	8	7	3	54	27*	13.50	0	0	300	196	0					3.92	1	

RANA, Mahendrasinh Pravinsinh (Saurashtra) b Gondal 27.11.1974 RHB RM

Cmp	Debut	M	I	NO	Runs	HS	Avge	100	50	Balls	Runs	Wkts	Avge	BB	5i	10m	RpO	ct	st
FC		1	1	0	7	7	7.00	0	0	180	88	4	22.00	2-28	0	0	2.93	0	
FC	1993	5	8	0	73	42	9.12	0	0	972	467	13	35.92	5-98	1	0	2.88	0	

RANA, Narendrasinh Pravinsinh (Saurashtra) b Gondal 5.9.1970 RHB RM

Cmp	Debut	M	I	NO	Runs	HS	Avge	100	50	Balls	Runs	Wkts	Avge	BB	5i	10m	RpO	ct	st
FC		3	3	0	54	47	18.00	0	0	368	177	4	44.25	2-30	0	0	2.88	0	
FC	1990	19	26	3	261	61	11.34	0	1	2502	1488	27	55.11	3-79	0	0	3.56	3	

RANADE, Atul Anant (Mumbai) b Bombay 19.9.1972 RHB RFM

Cmp	Debut	M	I	NO	Runs	HS	Avge	100	50	Balls	Runs	Wkts	Avge	BB	5i	10m	RpO	ct	st
FC		3	4	1	87	41	29.00	0	0	510	218	6	36.33	2-20	0	0	2.56	1	
Wlls		2								96	70	3	23.33	2-42	0	0	4.37	1	

RANGANATH, Yadalai Sree (Andhra) b Rajahmundry 12.8.1972 RHB OB

Cmp	Debut	M	I	NO	Runs	HS	Avge	100	50	Balls	Runs	Wkts	Avge	BB	5i	10m	RpO	ct	st
FC		2	4	0	27	21	6.75	0	0	467	265	7	37.85	3-67	0	0	3.40	2	

RANJAN, Rajeev (Bihar) b Patna 18.12.1976 RHB LM

Cmp	Debut	M	I	NO	Runs	HS	Avge	100	50	Balls	Runs	Wkts	Avge	BB	5i	10m	RpO	ct	st
FC		1	1	0	8	8	8.00	0	0	180	126	1	126.00	1-126	0	0	4.20	0	

RANJANE, Subash Vasant (Maharashtra) b Poona 1.6.1967 RHB RMF

Cmp	Debut	M	I	NO	Runs	HS	Avge	100	50	Balls	Runs	Wkts	Avge	BB	5i	10m	RpO	ct	st
FC		5	5	1	81	47	20.25	0	0	714	369	10	36.90	4-49	0	0	3.10	2	
FC	1984	28	28	7	346	64*	16.47	0	2	4358	2214	59	37.52	4-49	0	0	3.04	10	
Deo	1987	2								90	61	2	30.50	2-31	0	0	4.06	2	
Wlls	1986	7	5	1	18	8	4.50	0	0	365	247	7	35.28	2-28	0	0	4.06	2	

RAO, Kashireddi Var Prasad (Bihar) b Jamshedpur 21.11.1965 RHB SLA

Cmp	Debut	M	I	NO	Runs	HS	Avge	100	50	Balls	Runs	Wkts	Avge	BB	5i	10m	RpO	ct	st
FC		8	10	1	57	16	6.33	0	0	2629	1095	38	28.81	6-47	2	0	2.49	8	
FC	1987	36	46	10	325	72	9.02	0	1	8226	3165	148	21.38	7-74	11	3	2.30	19	
Deo	1995	2	1	1	1	1*		0	0	90	77	1	77.00	1-50	0	0	5.13	0	
Wlls	1995	1								60	33	0					3.30	0	

RAO, Mutyala Venkatrao (Services) b Parlakhemundi 28.5.1964 RHB RM

Cmp	Debut	M	I	NO	Runs	HS	Avge	100	50	Balls	Runs	Wkts	Avge	BB	5i	10m	RpO	ct	st
FC		4	7	1	198	57	33.00	0	2	630	373	12	31.08	7-59	1	0	3.55	1	
FC	1986	44	70	16	634	57	11.74	0	2	7487	4182	127	32.92	7-59	4	1	3.35	12	

RAO, Sangeet Kishore (Vidarbha) b Jabalpur 27.3.1972 RHB LBG

Cmp	Debut	M	I	NO	Runs	HS	Avge	100	50	Balls	Runs	Wkts	Avge	BB	5i	10m	RpO	ct	st
FC		1	2	1	20	15*	20.00	0	0	6	2	0					2.00	1	
FC	1994	6	10	2	138	49*	17.25	0	0	30	16	0					3.20	6	

Cmp	Debut	M	I	NO	Runs	HS	Avge	100	50	Balls	Runs	Wkts	Avge	BB	5i	10m	RpO	ct	st

RATHORE, Vikram (Punjab, India, North Zone, President's XI, Wills XI, India to South Africa, India to Zimbabwe) b Jullundur 26.3.1969 RHB WK

Cmp	Debut	M	I	NO	Runs	HS	Avge	100	50	Balls	Runs	Wkts	Avge	BB	5i	10m	RpO	ct	st
Test		1	2	0	19	14	9.50	0	0									3	
FC		10	17	0	982	254	57.76	4	2									18	
Wlls		1	1	0	96	96	96.00	0	1									0	
Test	1996	6	10	0	131	44	13.10	0	0									12	
FC	1988	84	143	7	6658	254	48.95	19	31	24	31	0					7.75	103	2
Int	1995	7	7	0	193	54	27.57	0	2									4	
Deo	1993	8	8	0	247	122	30.87	1	0	1	4	0					24.00	1	
Wlls	1994	4	4	1	126	96	42.00	0	1									1	

RAUL, Sanjay (Orissa, East Zone) b Cuttack 6.10.1976 RHB OB

Cmp	Debut	M	I	NO	Runs	HS	Avge	100	50	Balls	Runs	Wkts	Avge	BB	5i	10m	RpO	ct	st
FC		9	17	2	698	173	46.53	1	4	2071	845	38	22.23	6-44	4	1	2.44	8	
Deo		3	3	0	52	43	17.33	0	0	102	72	2	36.00	1-22	0	0	4.23	1	
FC	1993	23	37	3	1368	173	40.23	2	8	2556	1115	44	25.34	6-44	4	1	2.61	24	
Deo	1995	7	5	0	72	43	14.40	0	0	112	82	2	41.00	1-22	0	0	4.39	1	

RAWAT, Prahlad Singh (Railways) b Nagpur 14.10.1970 LHB LMF

Cmp	Debut	M	I	NO	Runs	HS	Avge	100	50	Balls	Runs	Wkts	Avge	BB	5i	10m	RpO	ct	st
FC		5	8	1	170	56	24.28	0	1	24	1	0					0.25	10	
FC	1987	21	34	7	830	140*	30.74	1	5	767	282	5	56.40	2-19	0	0	2.20	20	

RODRIGUES, Peter John (Goa) b Bangalore 11.11.1977 RHB LB

Cmp	Debut	M	I	NO	Runs	HS	Avge	100	50	Balls	Runs	Wkts	Avge	BB	5i	10m	RpO	ct	st
FC		1	2	0	44	29	22.00	0	0	156	88	5	17.60	4-57	0	0	3.38	1	

ROY, Sujit (Tripura) b Agartala 14.3.1973 RHB OB

Cmp	Debut	M	I	NO	Runs	HS	Avge	100	50	Balls	Runs	Wkts	Avge	BB	5i	10m	RpO	ct	st
FC		2	4	0	8	4	2.00	0	0	495	184	11	16.72	7-50	1	0	2.23	1	
FC	1992	14	28	0	342	41	12.21	0	0	1898	830	25	33.20	7-50	1	0	2.62	7	

SABIR, Mohammad (Vidarbha) b Jalgaon 1.1.1976 RHB

Cmp	Debut	M	I	NO	Runs	HS	Avge	100	50	Balls	Runs	Wkts	Avge	BB	5i	10m	RpO	ct	st
FC		4	7	0	174	68	24.85	0	1									3	
FC	1994	8	14	0	344	87	24.57	0	2									5	

SAI, Kasturi Sesha Talpa (Andhra) b Guntur 8.8.1976 LHB RM

Cmp	Debut	M	I	NO	Runs	HS	Avge	100	50	Balls	Runs	Wkts	Avge	BB	5i	10m	RpO	ct	st
FC		3	6	0	138	48	23.00	0	0	12	5	0					2.50	2	
FC	1995	5	9	0	174	48	19.33	0	0	12	5	0					2.50	3	

SAIF, Mohammad (Madhya Pradesh) b Allahabad 21.7.1976 RHB RFM

Cmp	Debut	M	I	NO	Runs	HS	Avge	100	50	Balls	Runs	Wkts	Avge	BB	5i	10m	RpO	ct	st
FC		2	2	0	15	10	7.50	0	0	132	79	0					3.59	1	
FC	1994	5	5	0	79	42	15.80	0	0	242	141	2	70.50	2-48	0	0	3.49	4	
Wlls	1995	2	2	0	21	21	10.50	0	0	39	38	0					5.84	1	

SAIKIA, Subhrajit (Assam, East Zone) b Dibrugarh 9.12.1975 LHB RM

Cmp	Debut	M	I	NO	Runs	HS	Avge	100	50	Balls	Runs	Wkts	Avge	BB	5i	10m	RpO	ct	st
FC		3	6	0	227	59	37.83	0	3									3	
Deo		2	2	1	103	74*	103.00	0	1									0	
FC	1993	13	25	0	825	127	33.00	1	6	18	11	0					3.66	7	
Deo	1995	3	2	1	103	74*	103.00	0	1									0	

SAINI, Narinder (Services) b Bandikul 30.5.1962

Cmp	Debut	M	I	NO	Runs	HS	Avge	100	50	Balls	Runs	Wkts	Avge	BB	5i	10m	RpO	ct	st
FC		4	8	1	164	37	23.42	0	0	12	1	0					0.50	4	

SAINI, Rakesh (Punjab) b Ludhiana 10.12.1975 RHB OB

Cmp	Debut	M	I	NO	Runs	HS	Avge	100	50	Balls	Runs	Wkts	Avge	BB	5i	10m	RpO	ct	st
FC		5	7	1	225	74	37.50	0	2									4	
FC	1995	6	8	1	236	74	33.71	0	2									6	

SAJID, Mohammad (Orissa) b Cuttack 17.1.1977 RHB RM

Cmp	Debut	M	I	NO	Runs	HS	Avge	100	50	Balls	Runs	Wkts	Avge	BB	5i	10m	RpO	ct	st
FC		1	1	1	0	0*		0	0	132	70	1	70.00	1-70	0	0	3.18	0	
FC	1993	2	2	1	0	0*	0.00	0	0	276	209	1	209.00	1-70	0	0	4.54	0	

SAMANT, Vinayak Radhakrishna (Assam, East Zone) b Bombay 25.10.1972 RHB WK

Cmp	Debut	M	I	NO	Runs	HS	Avge	100	50	Balls	Runs	Wkts	Avge	BB	5i	10m	RpO	ct	st
FC		4	7	0	206	89	29.42	0	1									11	2
Deo		4	3	0	46	24	15.33	0	0									5	3
FC	1995	8	14	1	336	89	25.84	0	2	2	4	0					12.00	23	2

SANGHVI, Rahul (Delhi, North Zone, President's XI) b Surat 3.9.1974 LHB SLA

Cmp	Debut	M	I	NO	Runs	HS	Avge	100	50	Balls	Runs	Wkts	Avge	BB	5i	10m	RpO	ct	st
FC		12	14	3	170	41	15.45	0	0	2286	1114	32	34.81	6-75	2	0	2.92	9	
Wlls		1	1	0	1	1	1.00	0	0	48	42	0					5.25	0	
FC	1994	23	27	9	239	41	13.27	0	0	4423	2111	78	27.06	7-42	5	2	2.86	19	

SANJAY SINGH (Bihar) b Jamshedpur 3.2.1976 RHB LBG

Cmp	Debut	M	I	NO	Runs	HS	Avge	100	50	Balls	Runs	Wkts	Avge	BB	5i	10m	RpO	ct	st
FC		1	1	0	10	10	10.00	0	0	66	44	1	44.00	1-22	0	0	4.00	0	
FC	1994	5	6	1	20	10	4.00	0	0	824	335	11	30.45	4-30	0	0	2.43	2	

SANYAL, Chandranath (Tripura)

Cmp	Debut	M	I	NO	Runs	HS	Avge	100	50	Balls	Runs	Wkts	Avge	BB	5i	10m	RpO	ct	st
FC		3	6	1	58	21	11.60	0	0	546	205	4	51.25	3-127	0	0	2.25	0	

SAPRU, Rahul Vijay (Uttar Pradesh, Central Zone) b Kanpur 13.6.1964 RHB OB

Cmp	Debut	M	I	NO	Runs	HS	Avge	100	50	Balls	Runs	Wkts	Avge	BB	5i	10m	RpO	ct	st
FC		10	16	3	949	185*	73.00	5	3	54	31	0					3.44	8	
Deo		4	4	1	110	63*	36.66	0	1	108	88	2	44.00	2-51	0	0	4.88	1	
Wlls		1	1	0	9	9	9.00	0	0	31	28	0					5.41	0	
FC	1982	84	129	20	5531	200*	50.74	17	26	1466	697	18	38.72	5-30	1	0	2.85	70	
Deo	1984	14	14	1	286	63*	22.00	0	1	108	88	2	44.00	2-51	0	0	4.88	8	
Wlls	1983	11	11	1	235	57*	23.50	0	2	67	54	3	18.00	2-10	0	0	4.83	3	

Cmp	Debut	M	I	NO	Runs	HS	Avge	100	50	Balls	Runs	Wkts	Avge	BB	5i	10m	RpO	ct	st
SARABJIT SINGH (Services) b Palampur 15.10.1974 RHB WK																			
FC		4	7	0	116	64	16.57	0	1									6	2
FC	1995	8	14	1	289	64	22.23	0	2									12	3
SARBJIT SINGH (Punjab) b Jullundur 23.8.1977 LHB SLA																			
FC		2	4	1	60	27*	20.00	0	0	126	69	2	34.50	2-35	0	0	3.28	1	
SARKAR, Arindam (Bengal, East Zone) b Calcutta 12.8.1973 LHB RM																			
FC		7	8	3	118	57*	23.60	0	1	1213	618	15	41.20	5-50	1	0	3.05	3	
Deo		4	4	0	52	19	13.00	0	0	151	122	5	24.40	3-36	0	0	4.84	2	
Wlls		1	1	0	5	5	5.00	0	0	42	15	0					2.14	1	
FC	1994	18	18	3	205	57*	13.66	0	1	2991	1380	41	33.65	5-36	2	0	2.76	7	
Deo	1995	7	6	1	75	19	15.00	0	0	319	226	10	22.60	3-27	0	0	4.25	3	
Wlls	1994	5	2	0	17	12	8.50	0	0	258	187	8	23.37	4-32	1	0	4.34	2	
SATPATHY, Sanjay (Orissa) b Bhubaneshwar 15.4.1979 RHB OB																			
FC		1	1	0	0	0	0.00	0	0	143	66	3	22.00	3-66	0	0	2.76	0	
SAWANT, Sangram Suresh (Assam) b Bombay 31.8.1969 RHB SLA																			
FC		3	5	0	218	63	43.60	0	2	324	125	7	17.85	3-44	0	0	2.31	4	
FC	1991	12	19	2	756	121	44.47	1	6	1710	656	25	26.24	4-55	0	0	2.30	11	
SENGUPTA, Moinak (Bengal) b Bhagalpur 30.12.1973 RHB																			
FC		1	2	0	3	3	1.50	0	0									1	
FC	1995	3	4	1	68	65*	22.66	0	1									6	
SENSHARMA, Sagarmoy (Bengal) b Calcutta 8.5.1966 LHB RM																			
FC		2	2	1	14	14	14.00	0	0	192	69	3	23.00	1-8	0	0	2.15	1	
FC	1987	47	41	15	253	38	9.73	0	0	7728	3891	149	26.11	6-33	7	0	3.02	11	
Deo	1989	5	2	0	8	6	4.00	0	0	246	169	3	56.33	1-28	0	0	4.12	1	
Wlls	1991	3	1	0	4	4	4.00	0	0	144	108	5	21.60	3-34	0	0	4.50	0	
SETH, Rajiv (Orissa) b Delhi 5.11.1968 RHB RM																			
FC		6	10	1	134	37	14.88	0	0	660	303	2	151.50	1-25	0	0	2.75	6	
FC	1989	26	30	7	443	45	19.26	0	0	3796	2031	46	44.15	5-107	1	0	3.21	21	
Wlls	1989	3	3	0	2	2	0.66	0	0	90	70.	2	35.00	2-39	0	0	4.66	0	
SHAFIQ KHAN (Haryana) b Faridabad 2.4.1971 RHB RFM																			
FC		8	15	0	530	95	35.33	0	4	72	35	2	17.50	1-7	0	0	2.91	9	
Wlls		3	3	2	116	76*	116.00	0	1	36	36	0					6.00	1	
SHAHANE, Rupesh Dnyaneshwar (Vidarbha) b Nagpur 3.11.1975 RHB OB																			
FC		1	2	0	61	41	30.50	0	0									1	
SHAKTI SINGH (Delhi) b Mandi 19.5.1968 RHB RM																			
FC		1									84	41	2	20.50	1-0	0	0	2.92	0	
FC	1987	37	59	8	943	128	18.49	1	2	5635	3053	106	28.80	7-53	7	1	3.25	7	
Deo	1993	1	1	0	3	3	3.00	0	0	36	14	1	14.00	1-14	0	0	2.33	0	
Wlls	1992	1	1	0	1	1	1.00	0	0	60	40	2	20.00	2-40	0	0	4.00	0	
SHAMSHAD, Rizwan (Uttar Pradesh, Central Zone) b Aligarh 19.11.1972 RHB RMF																			
FC		10	19	5	694	120*	49.57	2	4	66	22	0					2.00	8	
Deo		3	3	0	19	16	6.33	0	0									2	
Wlls		1	1	0	48	48	48.00	0	0	38	32	1	32.00	1-32	0	0	5.05	0	
FC	1990	45	78	10	3690	169	54.26	11	21	489	286	4	71.50	2-59	0	0	3.50	39	
Deo	1993	13	13	2	300	50	27.27	0	1	132	107	3	35.66	1-5	0	0	4.86	7	
Wlls	1992	3	3	0	105	48	35.00	0	0	44	42	2	21.00	1-10	0	0	5.72	0	
SHAMSHER SINGH (Rajasthan) b Hissar 16.10.1972 RHB RMF																			
FC		3	4	2	21	15	10.50	0	0	474	192	5	38.40	2-60	0	0	2.43	0	
FC	1992	14	21	11	7!	15	7.10	0	0	1800	845	21	40.23	5-72	1	0	2.72	5	
SHANKAR, Sivasubramaniyan (Kerala) b Mattancherry 13.2.1971 RHB RM																			
FC		9	15	1	389	62	27.78	0	2	12	1	0					0.50	13	
FC	1993	23	39	3	881	62	24.47	0	6	66	13	0					1.18	39	
SHARATH, Sridharan (Tamil Nadu, South Zone, India A, Wills XI) b Madras 31.10.1972 LHB OB																			
FC		8	12	1	774	151	70.36	3	3									7	
Deo		3	3	1	224	102	112.00	1	1									0	
Wlls		1	1	0	15	15	15.00	0	0	30	25	0					5.00	0	
FC	1992	45	67	15	2823	204*	54.38	7	17	18	9	0					3.00	19	
Deo	1993	12	11	5	402	102	50.25	1	1									1	
Wlls	1995	2	2	0	38	23	19.00	0	0	30	25	0					5.00	1	
SHARMA, Abhay (Railways) b Delhi 30.4.1967 RHB WK																			
FC		4	5	0	64	30	12.80	0	0	72	35	0					2.91	3	
FC	1987	47	65	6	2366	182	40.10	7	9	144	64	0					2.66	77	24
Deo	1991	8	8	0	203	47	25.37	0	0									1	2
Wlls	1992	2	2	0	43	29	21.50	0	0										

Cmp	Debut	M	I	NO	Runs	HS	Avge	100	50	Balls	Runs	Wkts	Avge	BB	5i	10m	RpO	ct	st
SHARMA, Amit (Punjab) b Jullundur 20.11.1974 RHB OB																			
FC		4	5	0	117	63	23.40	0	1	24	13	0					3.25	6	
FC	1992	22	29	3	862	161	33.15	1	5	156	66	1	66.00	1-1	0	0	2.53	16	
Wlls	1995	1	1	0	62	62	62.00	0	1	30	29	1	29.00	1-29	0	0	5.80	0	
SHARMA, Arun (Services) b Jammu 17.9.1976 LHB SLA																			
FC		4	7	0	77	25	11.00	0	0	989	441	9	49.00	3-15	0	0	2.67	1	
FC	1993	13	20	7	178	50*	13.69	0	1	2462	1092	26	42.00	5-28	1	0	2.66	3	
SHARMA, Ajay Kumar (Delhi, North Zone) b Delhi 3.4.1964 RHB SLA																			
FC		10	13	1	1198	220*	99.83	5	5	265	96	2	48.00	1-9	0	0	2.17	8	
Deo		4	4	0	46	25	11.50	0	0	29	33	0					6.82	0	
Test	1987	1	2	0	53	30	26.50	0	0	24	9	0					2.25	1	
FC	1984	107	136	12	8749	259*	70.55	34	31	5502	2315	75	30.86	5-34	1	0	2.52	80	
Int	1987	31	27	6	424	59*	20.19	0	3	1140	875	15	58.33	3-41	0	0	4.60	6	
Deo	1986	25	20	1	641	123*	33.73	1	3	839	716	22	32.54	4-73	1	0	5.12	9	
Wlls	1985	13	10	0	243	71	24.30	0	1	484	369	20	18.45	5-35	0	1	4.57	1	
SHARMA, Chetan (Bengal) b Ludhiana 3.1.1966 RHB RFM																			
FC		1	2	0	75	38	37.50	0	0	72	48	0					4.00	2	
Test	1984	23	27	9	396	54	22.00	0	1	3470	2163	61	35.45	6-58	4	1	3.74	7	
FC	1982	121	145	39	3714	114*	35.03	3	21	19934	11282	433	26.05	7-72	24	1	3.39	71	
Int	1983	65	35	16	456	101*	24.00	1	0	2835	2336	67	34.86	3-22	0	0	4.94	7	
Deo	1983	20	12	4	125	38*	15.62	0	0	782	646	19	34.00	5-16	0	1	4.95	6	
Wlls	1983	11	9	4	175	67*	35.00	0	1	523	400	15	26.66	3-23	0	0	4.58	1	
SHARMA, Chinmoy (Services, North Zone) b Amritsar 22.2.1963 RHB RM																			
FC		4	6	0	438	207	73.00	2	1	431	201	5	40.20	1-0	0	0	2.79	4	
Deo		1	1	0	15	15	15.00	0	0									0	
FC	1985	48	81	7	2741	207	37.04	8	12	2032	951	28	33.96	4-95	0	0	2.80	45	
SHARMA, Nishant (Himachal Pradesh) b Delhi 29.1.1976 RHB RM																			
FC		2	4	2	21	8	10.50	0	0	120	101	0					5.05	0	
SHARMA, Parender (Haryana) b Bhiwani 16.5.1973 RHB RM																			
FC		3	5	0	74	29	14.80	0	0	6	0	0					0.00	2	
Wlls		3	3	0	132	77	44.00	0	1	6	5	0					5.00	0	
FC	1993	5	9	0	185	43	20.55	0	0	6	0	0					0.00	4	
SHARMA, Rajib (Tripura) WK																			
FC		3	6	1	109	92*	21.80	0	1									7	1
SHARMA, Raju (Jammu and Kashmir) b Jammu 18.5.1966 RHB RM																			
FC		1	2	0	39	29	19.50	0	0	84	79	2	39.50	2-79	0	0	5.64	0	
FC	1993	8	15	0	285	60	19.00	0	1	336	210	2	105.00	2-79	0	0	3.75	1	
SHARMA, Rakesh (Uttar Pradesh) b Bulandsaher 1.7.1976 RHB																			
FC		8	15	2	392	98	30.15	0	2									2	
SHARMA, Sandeep (Punjab, North Zone, India A) b Jullundur 14.2.1974 RHB RM																			
FC		10	13	2	324	83	29.45	0	2	2160	908	31	29.29	4-65	0	0	2.52	0	
Deo		2	2	0	11	11	5.50	0	0	48	38	1	38.00	1-14	0	0	4.75	0	
FC	1994	19	22	2	547	98	27.35	0	3	3901	1714	64	26.78	4-26	0	0	2.63	2	1
Wlls	1995	1	1	0	1	1	1.00	0	0	48	47	2	23.50	2-47	0	0	5.87	0	
SHARMA, Sanjay (Jammu and Kashmir) b Jammu 20.12.1968 LHB LM																			
FC		2	4	0	119	55	29.75	0	1	389	209	4	52.25	3-102	0	0	3.22	1	
FC	1988	24	43	7	896	77*	24.88	0	4	4007	1758	44	39.95	6-66	1	0	2.63	15	
SHARMA, Sanjeev (Himachal Pradesh) b Hamirpur 4.7.1970 LHB SLA																			
FC		2	4	0	40	29	10.00	0	0	324	195	2	97.50	2-103	0	0	3.61	1	
SHARMA, Shambhunath (Himachal Pradesh) b Una 28.6.1968 RHB																			
FC		1	2	0	5	5	2.50	0	0	6	8	0					8.00	0	
FC	1987	33	60	4	1034	93*	18.46	0	6	252	171	0					4.07	12	
SHARMA, Sonu (Haryana) b Gurgaon 24.10.1976 LHB SLA																			
FC		2	2	1	44	22*	44.00	0	0	132	27	1	27.00	1-18	0	0	1.22	0	
Wlls		3	1	0	11	11	11.00	0	0	180	146	5	29.20	2-35	0	0	4.86	1	
FC	1994	6	7	1	66	22*	11.00	0	0	500	200	8	25.00	3-35	0	0	2.40	1	
SHARMA, Vijay (Jammu and Kashmir) b Jammu 15.7.1976 RHB RM																			
FC		2	4	1	46	31	15.33	0	0	258	155	3	51.66	2-78	0	0	3.60	1	
FC	1993	5	10	3	140	36	20.00	0	0	636	367	9	40.77	3-75	0	0	3.46	2	
SHARMA, Virender Kumar (Himachal Pradesh) b Hamirpur 11.9.1971 RHB																			
FC		5	9	0	159	45	17.66	0	0	42	18	0					2.57	3	
FC	1990	19	36	0	553	73	15.36	0	2	78	33	0					2.53	7	

Cmp	Debut	M	I	NO	Runs	HS	Avge	100	50	Balls	Runs	Wkts	Avge	BB	5i	10m	RpO	ct	st

SHASHIKANTH, Parambathe Veed (Karnataka) b Mangalore 3.4.1966 RHB RM

FC		6	11	0	214	69	19.45	0	1									2	
FC	1988	51	81	5	2397	160	31.53	4	14	66	28	1	28.00	1-15	0	0	2.54	48	
Wlls	1987	4	4	0	64	25	16.00	0	0									1	

SHETTY, Arun Sheshgiri (Goa) b Bombay 6.1.1969 LHB SLA

| FC | | 2 | 2 | 0 | 66 | 63 | 33.00 | 0 | 1 | 340 | 109 | 4 | 27.25 | 3-79 | 0 | 0 | 1.92 | 1 | |
| FC | 1990 | 27 | 48 | 6 | 834 | 71* | 19.85 | 0 | 4 | 5603 | 2416 | 78 | 30.97 | 6-55 | 3 | 0 | 2.58 | 18 | |

SHOME, Gautam (Bengal) b Calcutta 5.6.1963 RHB RFM

FC		1	1	0	88	88	88.00	0	1									0	
Wlls		1	1	0	36	36	36.00	0	0									0	
FC	1985	22	24	4	526	88	26.30	0	2	3757	2110	47	44.89	4-46	0	0	5.61	13	
Deo	1983	6	6	1	87	49	17.40	0	0	269	223	3	74.33	2-38	0	0	4.97	1	
Wlls	1984	5	4	0	83	36	20.75	0	0	234	169	4	42.25	2-17	0	0	4.33	0	

SHUKLA, Saurabh Anand (Uttar Pradesh, Central Zone) b Lucknow 24.11.1967 RHB LBG

FC		8	12	0	394	145	32.83	1	1	515	273	8	34.12	3-37	0	0	3.18	1	
Deo		3	3	0	62	26	20.66	0	0	36	27	0					4.50	0	
Wlls		1	1	0	41	41	41.00	0	0	6	13	0					13.00	0	
FC	1992	31	43	5	1258	145	33.10	3	4	2777	1632	34	48.00	3-37	0	0	3.52	17	
Deo	1994	9	7	0	134	30	19.14	0	0	150	119	4	29.75	3-45	0	0	4.76	1	
Wlls	1992	3	3	0	76	41	25.33	0	0	54	70	1	70.00	1-41	0	0	7.77	0	

SHUKLA, Sunil Vinubhai (Saurashtra) b Gondal 21.12.1963 LHB SLA

| FC | | 2 | 3 | 0 | 47 | 41 | 15.66 | 0 | 0 | 578 | 259 | 9 | 28.77 | 4-61 | 0 | 0 | 2.68 | 1 | |

SIDDIQUI, Iqbal Rashid (Maharashtra, West Zone) b Aurangabad 26.12.1974 RHB RMF

FC		10	9	2	154	48*	22.00	0	0	2025	960	33	29.09	5-99	2	0	2.84	5	
Deo		4	1	0	6	6	6.00	0	0	156	126	2	63.00	1-21	0	0	4.84	0	
FC	1992	39	45	5	491	76	12.27	0	2	7644	3738	121	30.89	7-139	6	1	2.93	19	
Deo	1993	10	4	0	25	16	6.25	0	0	426	339	5	67.80	3-16	0	0	4.77	0	

SIDHU, Navjot Singh (Punjab, North Zone, India A, Rest of India, India, India to West Indies) b Patiala 20.10.1963 RHB RM

FC		8	10	1	441	132	49.00	1	3	12	14	0					7.00	2	
Int		2	2	0	13	11	6.50	0	0									0	
Test	1983	40	60	2	2363	201	40.74	7	10	6	9	0					9.00	9	
FC	1981	126	184	11	7726	286	44.65	23	38	98	85	0					5.20	43	
Int	1987	111	106	8	3953	134*	40.33	6	31	4	3	0					4.50	16	
Deo	1986	11	11	2	410	104*	45.55	1	3									2	
Wlls	1985	12	12	0	636	93	53.00	0	6									2	

SIGNAPURKAR, Sandeep Anand (Goa) b Panjim 16.6.1975 RHB RM

| FC | | 5 | 6 | 2 | 96 | 33* | 24.00 | 0 | 0 | | | | | | | | | 1 | |

SINGH, Dhrubajyoti (Assam) b Gauhati 17.9.1977 RHB

| FC | | 1 | 1 | 0 | 14 | 14 | 14.00 | 0 | 0 | 48 | 22 | 1 | 22.00 | 1-10 | 0 | 0 | 2.75 | 2 | |

SINGH, Devendra Pal (Rajasthan) b Udaipur 7.8.1975 LHB SLA

| FC | | 2 | 2 | 1 | 21 | 13* | 21.00 | 0 | 0 | 389 | 138 | 4 | 34.50 | 3-51 | 0 | 0 | 2.12 | 0 | |
| FC | 1993 | 9 | 12 | 5 | 118 | 28 | 16.85 | 0 | 0 | 1397 | 611 | 14 | 43.64 | 6-58 | 1 | 0 | 2.62 | 1 | |

SINGH, Narender Pal (Hyderabad, President's XI) b Dehra Dun 10.9.1973 RHB RM

FC		10	15	4	306	74	27.81	0	2	1878	885	24	36.87	3-66	0	0	2.82	5	
Wlls		1	1	0	1	1	1.00	0	0	42	26	0					3.71	0	
FC	1993	24	34	9	429	74	17.16	0	2	4681	2248	68	33.05	6-69	2	0	2.88	9	
Deo	1994	2	1	0	0	0	0.00	0	0	120	73	2	36.50	1-30	0	0	3.65	0	
Wlls	1995	2	2	1	23	22*	23.00	0	0	78	81	0					6.23	0	

SINGH, Rabindra Ramanarayan (Tamil Nadu, South Zone, India, India to West Indies, India to South Africa, India to Zimbabwe) b Princes Town, Trinidad 14.9.1963 LHB RMF

FC		5	7	1	422	150	70.33	1	2	642	295	10	29.50	2-26	0	0	2.75	4	
Int		6	5	0	107	51	21.40	0	1	246	211	8	26.37	2-27	0	0	5.14	2	
Deo		4	4	0	50	15	12.50	0	0	183	122	2	61.00	2-45	0	0	4.00	0	
FC	1982	102	141	25	5799	155	49.99	20	28	8778	4823	131	36.81	7-54	4	1	3.29	81	
Int	1988	20	19	3	378	51	23.62	0	1	683	579	15	38.60	2-18	0	0	5.08	4	
Deo	1988	17	17	3	383	67	27.35	0	3	757	584	19	30.73	3-33	0	0	4.62	3	
Wlls	1987	9	7	3	87	25*	21.75	0	0	384	313	9	34.77	2-35	0	0	4.89	0	

SINGH, Robin (Delhi) b Delhi 1.1.1970 RHB RFM

| FC | | 8 | 8 | 4 | 37 | 15 | 9.25 | 0 | 0 | 1812 | 931 | 30 | 31.03 | 6-80 | 2 | 0 | 3.08 | 0 | |
| FC | 1994 | 12 | 12 | 5 | 46 | 15 | 6.57 | 0 | 0 | 2493 | 1270 | 44 | 28.86 | 7-53 | 3 | 0 | 3.05 | 3 | |

SINGH, Rajinder Pal (Haryana, North Zone) b Amritsar 30.12.1975 RHB RM

FC		4	3	1	6	3	3.00	0	0	444	250	7	35.71	4-64	0	0	3.37	2	
Deo		1	1	0	2	2	2.00	0	0	12	9	0					4.50	0	
FC	1995	8	9	6	10	3*	3.33	0	0	1122	598	18	33.22	4-64	0	0	3.19	2	

SINGH, Shibsagar (Bengal) b Burdwan 15.9.1979 RHB SLA

| FC | | 4 | 5 | 1 | 56 | 25 | 14.00 | 0 | 0 | 966 | 478 | 9 | 53.11 | 3-71 | 0 | 0 | 2.96 | 3 | |

Cmp	Debut	M	I	NO	Runs	HS	Avge	100	50	Balls	Runs	Wkts	Avge	BB	5i	10m	RpO	ct	st

SINHA, Anil Deepnarayan (Rajasthan) b Todaraisingh 13.2.1965 RHB WK

Cmp	Debut	M	I	NO	Runs	HS	Avge	100	50	Balls	Runs	Wkts	Avge	BB	5i	10m	RpO	ct	st
FC		3	4	0	64	35	16.00	0	0	6	3	0					3.00	2	
FC	1990	24	45	3	1181	111	28.11	2	6	7	4	0					3.42	21	2
Wlls	1987	1	1	0	3	3	3.00	0	0									0	

SODHI, Harvinder Singh (Madhya Pradesh) b Agra 17.10.1971 RHB RM

Cmp	Debut	M	I	NO	Runs	HS	Avge	100	50	Balls	Runs	Wkts	Avge	BB	5i	10m	RpO	ct	st
FC		9	13	3	330	120*	33.00	1	1	1349	656	17	38.58	4-46	0	0	2.91	0	
FC	1990	38	55	14	765	120*	18.65	1	2	5386	2762	86	32.11	6-24	3	0	3.07	7	
Deo	1990	5	4	3	45	33*	45.00	0	0	174	113	0					3.89	0	
Wlls	1991	4	2	1	29	25	29.00	0	0	154	93	5	18.60	2-34	0	0	3.62	0	

SODHI, Reetinder Singh (Punjab) b Patiala 18.10.1980 RHB RM

Cmp	Debut	M	I	NO	Runs	HS	Avge	100	50	Balls	Runs	Wkts	Avge	BB	5i	10m	RpO	ct	st
FC		3	5	0	120	55	24.00	0	1	357	130	3	43.33	2-32	0	0	2.18	2	

SOMASHEKAR, Shiraguppi (Karnataka) b Dharwad 14.6.1974 RHB WK

Cmp	Debut	M	I	NO	Runs	HS	Avge	100	50	Balls	Runs	Wkts	Avge	BB	5i	10m	RpO	ct	st
FC		6	11	1	199	62	19.90	0	1									8	1
Wlls		1	1	0	23	23	23.00	0	0									0	1
FC	1994	8	14	2	245	62	20.41	0	1									14	1

SOMASUNDER, Sujith (Karnataka, South Zone, India) b Bangalore 2.12.1972 RHB RM

Cmp	Debut	M	I	NO	Runs	HS	Avge	100	50	Balls	Runs	Wkts	Avge	BB	5i	10m	RpO	ct	st
FC		8	15	0	218	70	14.53	0	1	156	68	1	68.00	1-10	0	0	2.61	8	
Int		2	2	0	16	9	8.00	0	0									0	
Deo		3	3	0	37	21	12.33	0	0									0	
Wlls		2	2	0	14	8	7.00	0	0	24	22	0					5.50	2	
FC	1990	27	45	1	1436	166	32.63	3	9	378	164	7	23.42	3-15	0	0	2.60	27	
Wlls	1994	3	3	0	42	28	14.00	0	0	24	22	0					5.50	2	

SRIDHAR, Maruti Venkat (Hyderabad, South Zone) b Vijayawada 2.8.1965 RHB OB

Cmp	Debut	M	I	NO	Runs	HS	Avge	100	50	Balls	Runs	Wkts	Avge	BB	5i	10m	RpO	ct	st
FC		10	16	1	621	94	41.40	0	6									12	
Deo		2	2	0	71	65	35.50	0	1	6	6	0					6.00	0	
FC	1988	70	113	11	5492	366	53.84	19	20	9	26	0					17.33	64	
Deo	1992	8	8	0	205	78	25.62	0	2	16	14	1	14.00	1-8	0	0	5.25	1	
Wlls	1995	1	1	0	20	20	20.00	0	0									0	

SRIDHAR, Ramakrishnan (Hyderabad, South Zone) b Mysore 16.7.1970 LHB SLA

Cmp	Debut	M	I	NO	Runs	HS	Avge	100	50	Balls	Runs	Wkts	Avge	BB	5i	10m	RpO	ct	st
FC		8	12	0	243	58	20.25	0	1	1314	587	17	34.52	3-155	0	0	2.68	4	
Deo		1	1	1	6	6*		0	0	60	38	1	38.00	1-38	0	0	3.80	0	
FC	1989	25	32	4	440	58	15.71	0	1	5152	2050	74	27.70	6-91	2	0	2.38	18	
Wlls	1992	1	1	1	1	1*		0	0	30	23	0					4.60	0	

SRI HARI RAO, Panuganti (Andhra) b Berhampur 19.6.1975 RHB WK

Cmp	Debut	M	I	NO	Runs	HS	Avge	100	50	Balls	Runs	Wkts	Avge	BB	5i	10m	RpO	ct	st
FC		1	2	0	0	0	0.00	0	0									0	1
FC	1995	3	6	1	86	35	17.20	0	0									1	1

SRINATH, Javagal (India, India to South Africa, India to Canada, India to Sri Lanka) b Mysore 31.8.1969 RHB RFM

Cmp	Debut	M	I	NO	Runs	HS	Avge	100	50	Balls	Runs	Wkts	Avge	BB	5i	10m	RpO	ct	st
Test		3	5	0	45	19	9.00	0	0	765	356	17	20.94	6-21	1	0	2.79	0	
FC		3	5	0	45	19	9.00	0	0	765	356	17	20.94	6-21	1	0	2.79	0	
Int		7	7	2	115	53	23.00	0	1	402	298	3	99.33	2-40	0	0	4.44	0	
Test	1991	27	38	12	432	60	16.61	0	3	6311	2936	92	31.91	6-21	2	0	2.79	11	
FC	1989	82	108	21	1410	60	16.20	0	5	15976	7830	300	26.10	9-76	11	2	2.94	34	
Int	1991	123	64	19	501	53	11.13	0	1	6387	4577	158	28.96	5-24	2	2	4.30	17	
Deo	1992	3	2	1	16	12	16.00	0	0	127	59	3	19.66	2-20	0	0	2.78	1	
Wlls	1989	9	4	0	39	31	9.75	0	0	444	256	9	28.44	3-39	0	0	3.45	4	

SRINATH, Krishnaraj (Tamil Nadu) b Madurai 23.11.1969 RHB OB

Cmp	Debut	M	I	NO	Runs	HS	Avge	100	50	Balls	Runs	Wkts	Avge	BB	5i	10m	RpO	ct	st
FC		2	4	1	95	34	31.66	0	0	18	9	0					3.00	1	
FC	1991	24	37	3	1169	159	34.38	3	5	460	179	6	29.83	2-5	0	0	2.33	26	

SRINIVAS, Gopisetti Nagarao (Andhra) b Vijayawada 18.3.1971 RHB RM/LBG

Cmp	Debut	M	I	NO	Runs	HS	Avge	100	50	Balls	Runs	Wkts	Avge	BB	5i	10m	RpO	ct	st
FC		1	2	0	20	18	10.00	0	0									1	
FC	1993	7	14	1	318	99	24.46	0	1	24	23	0					5.75	7	

SRIRAM, Krishnaraj (Karnataka) b Madurai 15.11.1973 RHB RM/OB

Cmp	Debut	M	I	NO	Runs	HS	Avge	100	50	Balls	Runs	Wkts	Avge	BB	5i	10m	RpO	ct	st
FC		5	9	0	167	54	18.55	0	1									2	
Wlls		2	2	0	6	5	3.00	0	0									0	
FC	1995	10	16	0	534	174	33.37	1	1									5	

SRIRAM, Sridharan (Tamil Nadu) b Madras 21.2.1976 LHB SLA

Cmp	Debut	M	I	NO	Runs	HS	Avge	100	50	Balls	Runs	Wkts	Avge	BB	5i	10m	RpO	ct	st
FC		6	10	0	499	172	49.90	1	3	486	266	3	88.66	3-37	0	0	3.28	3	
FC	1995	7	11	0	521	172	47.36	1	3	600	179	3	118.66	3-37	0	0	3.56	3	

SUBRAMANIAM, Sunil (Tamil Nadu) b Bombay 28.5.1967 RHB SLA

Cmp	Debut	M	I	NO	Runs	HS	Avge	100	50	Balls	Runs	Wkts	Avge	BB	5i	10m	RpO	ct	st
FC		8	10	2	132	40*	16.50	0	0	1566	717	25	28.68	5-84	1	0	2.74	6	
FC	1988	68	73	18	1020	68	18.54	0	4	15716	6347	270	23.50	7-44	18	4	2.42	34	
Deo	1993	6	4	1	38	18	12.66	0	0	293	194	11	17.63	5-22	0	1	3.97	3	
Wlls	1988	5	3	1	9	7	4.50	0	0	274	200	5	40.00	2-55	0	0	4.37	2	

SUDHAKAR, Dharmalingam (Railways) b Madras 20.8.1971 LHB LB

Cmp	Debut	M	I	NO	Runs	HS	Avge	100	50	Balls	Runs	Wkts	Avge	BB	5i	10m	RpO	ct	st
FC		5	9	1	236	69	29.50	0	2									1	

SUGWEKAR, Shantanu Sharad (Maharashtra, President's XI) b Poona 18.12.1966 RHB OB

Cmp	Debut	M	I	NO	Runs	HS	Avge	100	50	Balls	Runs	Wkts	Avge	BB	5i	10m	RpO	ct	st
FC		10	14	1	928	193	71.38	3	4	294	122	3	40.66	2-41	0	0	2.48	2	
Wlls		1	1	0	25	25	25.00	0	0									1	

Cmp	Debut	M	I	NO	Runs	HS	Avge	100	50	Balls	Runs	Wkts	Avge	BB	5i	10m	RpO	ct	st
FC	1987	66	95	15	5513	299*	68.91	16	23	2223	954	18	53.00	2-20	0	0	2.57	32	
Deo	1990	9	8	1	149	39	21.28	0	0	216	149	7	21.28	3-34	0	0	4.13	0	
Wlls	1988	9	8	2	221	44*	36.83	0	0	198	149	3	49.66	2-32	0	0	4.51	2	

SUKHVINDER SINGH (Assam) b Jullundur 23.2.1967 LHB SLA

| FC | | 4 | 7 | 2 | 383 | 167 | 76.60 | 1 | 2 | 1098 | 435 | 31 | 14.03 | 7-99 | 4 | 2 | 2.37 | 4 | |
| FC | 1986 | 8 | 9 | 2 | 424 | 167 | 60.57 | 1 | 2 | 1647 | 610 | 35 | 17.42 | 7-99 | 4 | 2 | 2.22 | 4 | |

SUKHBIR SINGH (Baroda, Wills XI) b Gurudaspur 3.1.1974 RHB RM

FC		7	10	6	24	6*	6.00	0	0	1556	591	27	21.88	4-32	0	0	2.27	1	
Wlls		1	1	1	1	1*		0	0	48	48	1	48.00	1-48	0	0	6.00	1	
FC	1993	20	27	14	65	13*	5.00	0	0	3583	1608	51	31.52	5-90	1	0	2.69	4	
Deo	1995	2	1	1	0	0*		0	0	72	71	1	71.00	1-38	0	0	5.91	0	

SUNIL, Kuriappilly Antony (Kerala) b North Paravoor 8.1.1970 RHB RM

| FC | | 2 | 4 | 0 | 37 | 19 | 9.25 | 0 | 0 | 227 | 122 | 4 | 30.50 | 3-41 | 0 | 0 | 3.22 | 0 | |

SURESH KUMAR, Mani (Railways, Central Zone) b Alleppey 19.4.1973 LHB SLA

FC		7	11	2	129	33	14.33	0	0	1102	415	16	25.93	4-21	0	0	2.25	2	
Deo		4	3	0	14	13	4.66	0	0	192	155	8	19.37	4-65	1	0	4.84	0	
FC	1991	30	39	5	413	42	12.14	0	0	6489	2517	102	24.67	6-34	6	1	2.32	16	

SURINDER SINGH (Himachal Pradesh) b Una 15.1.1973 RHB RM

| FC | | 5 | 9 | 4 | 31 | 13* | 6.20 | 0 | 0 | 588 | 289 | 8 | 36.12 | 5-41 | 1 | 0 | 2.94 | 0 | |
| FC | 1993 | 17 | 31 | 9 | 128 | 23 | 5.81 | 0 | 0 | 2026 | 1086 | 20 | 54.30 | 5-41 | 1 | 0 | 3.21 | 1 | |

SUSHIL, Samir Purshottam (Gujarat) b Ahmedabad 7.3.1970 RHB RM

| FC | | 1 | 2 | 0 | 1 | 1 | 0.50 | 0 | 0 | 114 | 59 | 0 | | | | | 3.10 | 0 | |
| FC | 1995 | 2 | 4 | 2 | 3 | 1* | 1.50 | 0 | 0 | 224 | 110 | 2 | 55.00 | 2-51 | 0 | 0 | 2.94 | 0 | |

SUTHAR, Rajesh (West Zone)

| Deo | | 3 | 3 | 0 | 91 | 54 | 30.33 | 0 | 1 | 24 | 18 | 0 | | | | | 4.50 | 1 | |

SWARUP, Rayapet Arjun (Baroda, West Zone, President's XI) b Secunderabad 20.8.1965 RHB OB

FC		7	12	1	537	134	48.81	1	2	1948	832	29	28.68	6-121	3	0	2.56	9	
Deo		3	2	1	15	11*	15.00	0	0	170	130	5	26.00	3-26	0	0	4.58	0	
Wlls		1	1	0	39	39	39.00	0	0	36	24	1	24.00	1-24	0	0	4.00	1	
FC	1987	44	72	5	2443	140	36.46	6	10	4504	1881	76	24.75	6-121	6	1	2.50	40	
Deo	1993	5	4	1	56	37	18.66	0	0	224	167	9	18.55	4-37	1	0	4.47	0	
Wlls	1991	3	3	0	100	46	33.33	0	0	148	111	1	111.00	1-24	0	0	4.50	1	

TANDON, Ashish Rajendra (Baroda) b Amritsar 2.11.1974 RHB RM

| FC | | 2 | 4 | 0 | 50 | 20 | 12.50 | 0 | 0 | 204 | 95 | 4 | 23.75 | 2-15 | 0 | 0 | 2.79 | 0 | |
| FC | 1995 | 4 | 8 | 2 | 70 | 20 | 11.66 | 0 | 0 | 330 | 192 | 5 | 38.40 | 2-15 | 0 | 0 | 3.49 | 0 | |

TANNA, Sudhir Shantilal (Saurashtra) b Rajkot 17.9.1967 RHB OB

| FC | | 3 | 5 | 0 | 167 | 141 | 33.40 | 1 | 0 | 186 | 71 | 0 | | | | | 2.29 | 3 | |
| FC | 1987 | 37 | 68 | 7 | 2598 | 253* | 42.59 | 6 | 16 | 479 | 228 | 3 | 76.00 | 2-26 | 0 | 0 | 2.85 | 17 | |

TARIQ-UR-REHMAN (Bihar, East Zone) b Darbanga 22.2.1974 LHB SLA

FC		7	12	2	526	118*	52.60	1	5	78	32	0					2.46	6	
Deo		1																0	
FC	1993	16	27	5	1073	122	48.77	3	7	228	106	2	53.00	1-4	0	0	2.78	19	

TENDULKAR, Sachin Ramesh (India, India to South Africa, India to West Indies, India to Canada, India to Sri Lanka, India to Zimbabwe) b Bombay 24.4.1973 RHB RM

Test		4	8	0	176	61	22.00	0	1									1	
FC		4	8	0	176	61	22.00	0	1									1	
Int		10	10	0	557	117	55.70	2	4	217	217	3	72.33	2-61	0	0	6.00	4	
Test	1989	53	80	8	3617	179	50.23	11	18	526	247	4	61.75	2-10	0	0	2.81	42	
FC	1988	126	189	19	9598	179	56.45	26	56	3365	1803	26	69.34	3-60	0	0	3.21	90	
Int	1989	150	147	14	5321	137	40.00	12	32	3358	2723	47	57.93	4-34	1	0	4.86	45	
Deo	1989	7	6	1	149	45*	29.80	0	0	153	153	3	51.00	2-38	0	0	6.00	3	
Wlls	1989	14	14	5	720	121	80.00	3	4	504	397	14	28.35	3-23	0	0	4.72	4	

THAKUR, Iqbal Abubakker (Railways) b Bombay 8.12.1966 RHB RFM

FC		3	3	0	9	5	3.00	0	0	679	303	16	18.93	5-84	1	0	2.67	0	
FC	1992	23	31	11	96	18	4.80	0	0	4153	2161	79	27.35	6-22	5	1	3.12	3	
Deo	1994	5	2	1	4	4*	4.00	0	0	258	156	13	12.00	4-35	1	0	3.62	0	

THAKUR, Pankaj (Haryana) b Jullundur 8.10.1973 RHB OB

FC		9	13	1	175	46	14.58	0	0	2430	1149	47	24.44	6-32	1	1	2.83	3	
Wlls		3	1	0	44	44	44.00	0	0	174	112	4	28.00	3-36	0	0	3.86	1	
FC	1992	27	37	3	547	60	16.08	0	1	6892	3107	111	27.99	7-254	5	1	2.70	11	
Wlls	1994	6	4	2	118	44*	59.00	0	0	342	232	5	46.40	3-36	0	0	4.07	1	

UPADHYAYA, Sachin Shrikant (Goa) b Sangli 16.7.1969 RHB RM

| FC | | 4 | 8 | 3 | 190 | 45 | 38.00 | 0 | 0 | 6 | 4 | 0 | | | | | 4.00 | 8 | |
| FC | 1994 | 9 | 17 | 3 | 271 | 45 | 19.35 | 0 | 0 | 12 | 10 | 0 | | | | | 5.00 | 12 | |

VAIDYA, Avinash (Karnataka) b Hubli 24.1.1969 RHB WK

| FC | | 1 | 2 | 1 | 30 | 22* | 30.00 | 0 | 0 | | | | | | | | | 2 | |
| Wlls | | 1 | 1 | 0 | 24 | 24 | 24.00 | 0 | 0 | | | | | | | | | 1 | |

139

Cmp	Debut	M	I	NO	Runs	HS	Avge	100	50	Balls	Runs	Wkts	Avge	BB	5i	10m	RpO	ct	st
FC	1992	43	59	7	1296	83	24.92	0	8	6	6	0					6.00	106	25
Deo	1992	7	6	2	42	17*	10.50	0	0									6	3
Wlls	1992	3	2	1	27	24	27.00	0	0									5	

VARMA, Ajay (Bengal) b Trivandrum 26.12.1963 RHB

FC		8	12	1	413	162	37.54	1	2	1196	557	20	27.85	4-24	0	0	2.79	4	
Wlls		1	1	0	22	22	22.00	0	0	60	37	2	18.50	2-37	0	0	3.70	2	
FC	1986	17	27	2	956	162	38.24	3	3	1636	745	28	26.60	4-24	0	0	2.73	6	
Wlls	1991	6	6	1	194	82*	38.80	0	2	222	159	4	39.75	2-37	0	0	4.29	2	

VARSANIA, Tejas Narsinhdas (Gujarat) b Bombay 30.9.1971 RHB LM

FC		2	4	1	188	109*	62.66	1	0	42	29	1	29.00	1-21	0	0	4.14	1	
FC	1990	15	26	8	393	109*	21.83	1	0	1821	1178	26	45.30	6-96	1	0	3.88	5	

VASANT KUMAR, R.C. (Tamil Nadu) b Madras 28.4.1976 RHB

FC		4	7	0	134	35	19.14	0	0									4	

VASU, Divakar (Tamil Nadu) b Coonoor 11.12.1967 RHB LM

FC		3	5	0	42	17	8.40	0	0	450	161	3	53.66	2-62	0	0	2.14	1	
FC	1988	59	79	9	2455	132	35.07	2	17	11356	4753	192	24.75	8-114	12	2	2.51	52	
Deo	1990	7	6	0	124	66	20.66	0	1	340	179	7	25.57	2-15	0	0	3.15	1	
Wlls	1988	5	5	1	67	39	16.75	0	0	254	181	7	25.85	2-25	0	0	4.27	1	

VEERABRAHMAM, Nimmakayala (Andhra) b Nellore 28.2.1970 RHB WK

FC		3	6	0	31	13	5.16	0	0									5	1
FC	1990	13	20	2	290	90*	16.11	0	2									10	1

VENKATAPATHY RAJU, Sagi Lakshmi (Hyderabad, President's XI, Rest of India, Wills XI, India to South Africa) b Alamuru 9.7.1969 RHB SLA

FC		9	14	6	146	36*	18.25	0	0	2154	767	28	27.99	6-64	1	0	2.13	4	
Wlls		1	1	0	0	0	0.00	0	0	59	40	0					4.06	0	
Test	1989	24	30	10	229	31	11.45	0	0	6600	2439	85	28.69	6-12	5	1	2.21	5	
FC	1985	106	119	38	1106	54	13.65	0	2	24958	9683	362	26.74	7-82	19	4	2.32	36	
Int	1989	53	16	8	32	8	4.00	0	0	2770	2014	63	31.96	4-46	2	0	4.36	8	
Deo	1989	7	2	1	7	7*	7.00	0	0	354	271	9	30.11	3-23	0	0	4.59	2	
Wlls	1988	8	3	0	0	0	0.00	0	0	413	322	9	35.77	3-35	0	0	4.67	1	

VENKATARAMANA, Margashayam (Tamil Nadu) b Secunderabad 24.4.1966 RHB OB

FC		1	1	0	16	16	16.00	0	0	326	182	6	30.33	5-63	1	0	3.34	1	
Test	1988	1	2	2	0	0*		0	0	70	58	1	58.00	1-10	0	0	4.97	1	
FC	1987	68	77	14	839	60	13.31	0	1	13439	6707	227	29.54	7-94	12	2	2.99	53	
Int	1988	1	1	1	0	0*		0	0	60	36	2	18.00	2-36	0	0	3.60	0	
Deo	1988	4	3	1	25	23	12.50	0	0	174	124	0					4.27	1	
Wlls	1989	4	1	0	22	22	22.00	0	0	210	169	3	56.33	1-32	0	0	4.82	1	

VENKATESH PRASAD, Bapu Krishnarao (India, India to South Africa, India to West Indies, India to Canada, India to Sri Lanka, India to Zimbabwe) b Bangalore 5.8.1969 RHB RMF

Test		4	6	2	17	9	4.25	0	0	699	311	12	25.91	6-104	1	0	2.66	0	
FC		4	6	2	17	9	4.25	0	0	699	311	12	25.91	6-104	1	0	2.66	0	
Int		10	3	1	3	2	1.50	0	0	564	445	15	29.66	4-27	1	0	4.73	2	
Test	1996	15	22	9	67	15	5.15	0	0	3304	1576	55	28.65	6-104	5	1	2.86	2	
FC	1990	60	67	30	322	28	8.70	0	0	10247	4790	180	26.61	7-37	10	2	2.80	27	
Int	1993	67	28	16	72	19	6.00	0	0	3443	2728	79	34.53	4-27	1	0	4.75	22	
Deo	1991	8	3	1	6	3	3.00	0	0	318	180	11	16.36	6-18	0	1	3.39	3	
Wlls	1991	6	2	1	4	4	4.00	0	0	237	177	5	35.40	4-23	1	0	4.48	0	

VERMA, Sanjay (Services)

FC		4	8	0	165	57	20.62	0	1	9	4	0					2.66	2	

VIJ, Bharati (Punjab, North Zone) b Ludhiana 9.1.1967 RHB SLA

FC		10	10	0	112	32	11.20	0	0	3163	1449	58	24.98	7-55	6	3	2.74	5	
Deo		3	3	0	36	30	12.00	0	0	144	121	1	121.00	1-62	0	0	5.04	0	
FC	1987	64	66	16	630	42	12.60	0	0	16197	6780	291	23.29	7-27	23	8	2.51	28	
Deo	1994	10	5	0	43	30	8.60	0	0	552	367	14	26.21	4-29	1	0	3.98	3	
Wlls	1995	1	1	0	2	2	2.00	0	0	60	41	1	41.00	1-41	0	0	4.10	0	

VIJAY, Raghvendrarao (Karnataka, South Zone) b Bangalore 15.8.1975 RHB OB

FC		8	15	0	453	116	30.20	1	3	217	88	3	29.33	1-14	0	0	2.43	15	
Deo		1	1	0	12	12	12.00	0	0	18	16	0					5.33	1	
Wlls		2	2	0	6	6	3.00	0	0	24	27	0					6.75	0	
FC	1994	21	36	4	1179	146	36.84	4	4	277	108	3	36.00	1-14	0	0	2.33	34	

VINAY KUMAR, Devishetty (Hyderabad) b Delhi 21.4.1977 RHB

FC		3	6	1	103	32	20.60	0	0									0	

VINAY KUMAR, Vincent (Andhra) b Guntur 18.5.1969 LHB RM

FC		2	4	0	73	48	18.25	0	0									0	
FC	1989	29	51	1	1184	101	23.68	1	6	1258	760	14	54.28	3-128	0	0	3.62	19	

VISHWAJIT SINGH (Uttar Pradesh) b Ghaziabad 15.9.1974 RHB

FC		1	2	0	11	11	5.50	0	0	36	15	0					2.50	1	

Cmp	Debut	M	I	NO	Runs	HS	Avge	100	50	Balls	Runs	Wkts	Avge	BB	5i	10m	RpO	ct	st

VISHNU VARDHAN, Sankinani (Hyderabad) b Warangal 30.10.1976 LHB LM

Cmp	Debut	M	I	NO	Runs	HS	Avge	100	50	Balls	Runs	Wkts	Avge	BB	5i	10m	RpO	ct	st
FC		6	9	1	131	39	16.37	0	0	1065	486	17	28.58	4-51	0	0	2.73	1	
FC	1995	8	12	3	132	39	14.66	0	0	1443	617	24	25.70	4-51	0	0	2.56	1	
Wlls	1995	1								60	86	0					8.60	0	

WASSAN, Atul Satish (Delhi, North Zone) b Delhi 23.3.1968 RHB RFM

Cmp	Debut	M	I	NO	Runs	HS	Avge	100	50	Balls	Runs	Wkts	Avge	BB	5i	10m	RpO	ct	st
FC		9	11	1	190	48	19.00	0	0	2014	1049	41	25.58	5-48	3	0	3.12	7	
Deo		4	4	0	20	11	5.00	0	0	210	148	2	74.00	2-35	0	0	4.22	0	
Test	1989	4	5	1	94	53	23.50	0	1	712	504	10	50.40	4-108	0	0	4.24	1	
FC	1986	79	82	14	1308	110	19.23	2	1	14402	8065	287	28.10	7-36	17	4	3.35	34	
Int	1989	9	6	2	33	16	8.25	0	0	426	283	11	25.72	3-28	0	0	3.98	2	
Deo	1990	15	11	2	76	32	8.44	0	0	781	496	22	22.54	5-36	1	1	3.81	2	
Wlls	1989	8	5	1	39	18*	9.75	0	0	342	218	9	24.22	4-15	1	0	3.82	2	

WILLIAMS, Connor Cecil (Baroda) b Baroda 7.8.1973 LHB SLA

Cmp	Debut	M	I	NO	Runs	HS	Avge	100	50	Balls	Runs	Wkts	Avge	BB	5i	10m	RpO	ct	st
FC		8	14	1	364	64	28.00	0	3									14	
FC	1995	11	19	1	569	109	31.61	1	4									19	

WILSON, Oniel (Delhi) b Delhi 27.4.1971 RHB RM

Cmp	Debut	M	I	NO	Runs	HS	Avge	100	50	Balls	Runs	Wkts	Avge	BB	5i	10m	RpO	ct	st
FC		1	1	0	19	19	19.00	0	0	222	138	3	46.00	3-85	0	0	3.72	1	
FC	1990	2	1	0	19	19	19.00	0	0	354	195	4	48.75	3-85	0	0	3.30	2	

YADAV, Hemulal (Tripura)

Cmp	Debut	M	I	NO	Runs	HS	Avge	100	50	Balls	Runs	Wkts	Avge	BB	5i	10m	RpO	ct	st
FC		4	8	3	10	4	2.00	0	0	828	422	14	30.14	7-80	1	0	3.05	2	

YADAY, Jai Prakash (Madhya Pradesh, Central Zone) b Bhopal 7.8.1974 RHB RM

Cmp	Debut	M	I	NO	Runs	HS	Avge	100	50	Balls	Runs	Wkts	Avge	BB	5i	10m	RpO	ct	st
FC		12	20	0	825	108	41.25	2	4	198	80	2	40.00	2-14	0	0	2.42	9	
FC	1994	22	35	1	1387	135	40.79	4	4	240	100	2	50.00	2-14	0	0	2.50	16	
Wlls	1995	2	2	0	62	56	31.00	0	1									0	

YADAV, Jyoti Prasad (Uttar Pradesh) b Allahabad 26.9.1977 LHB SLA

Cmp	Debut	M	I	NO	Runs	HS	Avge	100	50	Balls	Runs	Wkts	Avge	BB	5i	10m	RpO	ct	st
FC		5	8	0	442	113	55.25	1	4									3	
FC	1994	13	20	0	992	146	49.60	3	7	30	27	0					5.40	5	
Wlls	1994	1	1	0	16	16	16.00	0	0									0	

YADAV, Monoj (Bihar) b Madhipura 14.1.1971 RHB OB

Cmp	Debut	M	I	NO	Runs	HS	Avge	100	50	Balls	Runs	Wkts	Avge	BB	5i	10m	RpO	ct	st
FC		4	7	1	144	44	24.00	0	0	12	3	0					1.50	3	

YADAV, Pramod (Rajasthan) b Alwar 13.1.1975 RHB RM

Cmp	Debut	M	I	NO	Runs	HS	Avge	100	50	Balls	Runs	Wkts	Avge	BB	5i	10m	RpO	ct	st
FC		1	2	0	0	0	0.00	0	0	24	8	0					2.00	0	

YADAV, Ranjit (Uttar Pradesh) b Gorakhpur 10.6.1978 LHB SLA

Cmp	Debut	M	I	NO	Runs	HS	Avge	100	50	Balls	Runs	Wkts	Avge	BB	5i	10m	RpO	ct	st
FC		2	1	0	2	2	2.00	0	0	114	46	1	46.00	1-31	0	0	2.42	0	

YADAV, Satyendra (Railways) b Meerut 28.1.1970 RHB RM

Cmp	Debut	M	I	NO	Runs	HS	Avge	100	50	Balls	Runs	Wkts	Avge	BB	5i	10m	RpO	ct	st
FC		7	12	1	345	83	31.36	0	3	12	4	0					2.00	3	
FC	1994	17	27	2	867	141	34.68	1	7	156	72	2	36.00	2-40	0	0	2.76	8	
Wlls	1994	1	1	0	42	42	42.00	0	0	30	23	0					4.60	3	

YADAV, Santosh Kumar (Hyderabad) b Secunderabad 17.10.1979 LHB OB

Cmp	Debut	M	I	NO	Runs	HS	Avge	100	50	Balls	Runs	Wkts	Avge	BB	5i	10m	RpO	ct	st
FC		3	5	0	181	70	36.20	0	2	99	61	3	20.33	2-13	0	0	3.69	1	
FC	1995	5	8	0	205	70	25.62	0	2	113	79	3	26.33	2-13	0	0	4.19	1	

YADAV, Vijay (Haryana) b Gonda 14.3.1967 RHB WK

Cmp	Debut	M	I	NO	Runs	HS	Avge	100	50	Balls	Runs	Wkts	Avge	BB	5i	10m	RpO	ct	st
FC		9	13	6	416	80	32.00	0	3	6	1	0					1.00	17	5
Wlls		3	3	2	42	22*	42.00	0	0									4	2
Test	1992	1	1	0	30	30	30.00	0	0									1	2
FC	1987	74	98	5	3442	201	37.01	7	18	15	4	0					1.60	202	37
Int	1992	19	12	2	118	34*	11.80	0	0									12	7
Deo	1991	11	9	2	70	27	10.00	0	0									13	5
Wlls	1987	8	8	2	94	22*	15.66	0	0									8	5

YADAV, Vijendra (Railways) b Zafarpur, Delhi 21.7.1973 RHB RM

Cmp	Debut	M	I	NO	Runs	HS	Avge	100	50	Balls	Runs	Wkts	Avge	BB	5i	10m	RpO	ct	st
FC		6	11	0	153	37	13.90	0	0									8	
FC	1990	29	53	4	1521	157	31.04	2	7	114	75	3	25.00	2-73	0	0	3.94	33	

YALVIGI, Anand Ramrao (Mumbai) b Pune 9.2.1975 RHB OB

Cmp	Debut	M	I	NO	Runs	HS	Avge	100	50	Balls	Runs	Wkts	Avge	BB	5i	10m	RpO	ct	st
FC		3	2	1	15	13*	15.00	0	0	330	181	4	45.25	3-125	0	0	3.29	2	

YUVRAJ SINGH (Hyderabad) b Hyderabad 9.4.1968 RHB WK

Cmp	Debut	M	I	NO	Runs	HS	Avge	100	50	Balls	Runs	Wkts	Avge	BB	5i	10m	RpO	ct	st
FC		10	15	0	129	50	8.60	0	1									22	1
FC	1992	34	46	4	620	50	14.76	0	2									79	6
Deo	1994	1																0	
Wlls	1992	1	1	1	7	7*		0	0									0	

YUVRAJ SINGH (Punjab) b Chandigarh 12.12.1981 LHB LM

Cmp	Debut	M	I	NO	Runs	HS	Avge	100	50	Balls	Runs	Wkts	Avge	BB	5i	10m	RpO	ct	st
FC		1	1	0	0	0	0.00	0	0	6	7	0					7.00	0	

ZAIDI, Ashish Winston (Uttar Pradesh) b Allahabad 16.9.1971 RHB RFM

Cmp	Debut	M	I	NO	Runs	HS	Avge	100	50	Balls	Runs	Wkts	Avge	BB	5i	10m	RpO	ct	st
FC		3	2	0	16	12	8.00	0	0	342	198	2	99.00	1-47	0	0	3.47	0	
FC	1988	44	49	9	509	39	12.72	0	0	7993	4120	124	33.22	8-119	6	1	3.09	7	
Deo	1991	6	5	3	21	12	10.50	0	0	258	142	2	71.00	2-26	0	0	3.30	1	
Wlls	1989	6	3	0	38	18	12.66	0	0	272	203	4	50.75	2-28	0	0	4.47	2	

Cmp	Debut	M	I	NO	Runs	HS	Avge	100	50	Balls	Runs	Wkts	Avge	BB	5i	10m	RpO	ct	st
ZAKIR HUSSAIN (Railways, Central Zone) b Bikaner 26.1.1976 RHB RMF																			
FC		9	13	3	212	97	21.20	0	1	1835	902	32	28.18	5-31	2	0	2.94	1	
Deo		4	2	0	0	0	0.00	0	0	171	110	4	27.50	2-45	0	0	3.85	0	
ZUFFRI, Zakaria (Railways) b Gauhati 12.10.1975 LHB WK																			
FC		8	13	0	327	108	25.15	1	2									27	3
FC	1992	23	40	1	886	108	22.71	1	4	24	23	0					5.75	59	10

AUSTRALIA IN INDIA 1996-97

Cmp	Debut	M	I	NO	Runs	HS	Avge	100	50	Balls	Runs	Wkts	Avge	BB	5i	10m	RpO	ct	st
BEVAN, M.G.																			
Test		1	2	0	59	33	29.50	0	0									0	
FC		2	3	1	159	100*	79.50	1	0	6	13	0					13.00	2	
Int		5	5	0	223	79	44.60	0	2									1	
FLEMING, D.W.																			
FC		1	1	1	4	4*		0	0	66	39	0					3.54	1	
Int		3	1	1	1	1*		0	0	152	129	3	43.00	2-39	0	0	5.09	0	
GILCHRIST, A.C.																			
Int		2	2	0	18	18	9.00	0	0									2	
GILLESPIE, J.N.																			
Int		3	1	0	2	2	2.00	0	0	174	158	2	79.00	1-44	0	0	5.44	0	
HEALY, I.A.																			
Test		1	2	0	29	17	14.50	0	0									1	
FC		2	3	0	78	49	26.00	0	0									2	
Int		3	3	0	21	11	7.00	0	0									1	1
HOGG, G.B.																			
Test		1	2	0	5	4	2.50	0	0	102	69	1	69.00	1-69	0	0	4.05	0	
FC		1	2	0	5	4	2.50	0	0	102	69	1	69.00	1-69	0	0	4.05	0	
Int		5	5	3	25	11*	12.50	0	0	211	159	2	79.50	1-23	0	0	4.52	1	
LAW, S.G.																			
Int		5	5	0	80	52	16.00	0	1	174	145	3	48.33	2-65	0	0	5.00	1	
McGRATH, G.D.																			
Test		1	2	0	6	6	3.00	0	0	216	86	2	43.00	1-30	0	0	2.38	0	
FC		2	2	0	6	6	3.00	0	0	318	120	2	60.00	1-30	0	0	2.26	0	
Int		5	2	1	9	8*	9.00	0	0	275	212	4	53.00	2-42	0	0	4.62	1	
McINTYRE, P.E.																			
Test		1	2	1	22	16	22.00	0	0	228	107	3	35.66	3-103	0	0	2.81	0	
FC		2	3	1	22	16	11.00	0	0	354	169	5	33.80	3-103	0	0	2.86	1	
PONTING, R.T.																			
Test		1	2	0	27	14	13.50	0	0									3	
FC		2	4	1	122	58	40.66	0	1									3	
Int		3	3	0	52	35	17.33	0	0									0	
REIFFEL, P.R.																			
Test		1	2	0	13	7	6.50	0	0	138	59	5	11.80	3-35	0	0	2.56	0	
FC		2	3	0	19	7	6.33	0	0	216	97	7	13.85	3-35	0	0	2.69	0	
Int		4	3	1	15	9	7.50	0	0	240	172	4	43.00	4-35	1	0	4.30	0	
SLATER, M.J.																			
Test		1	2	0	44	44	22.00	0	0									0	
FC		2	4	0	102	56	25.50	0	1									0	
Int		3	3	1	108	53*	54.00	0	2									1	
TAYLOR, M.A.																			
Test		1	2	0	64	37	32.00	0	0									0	
FC		2	4	0	125	41	31.25	0	0									3	
Int		5	5	0	302	105	60.40	1	1									2	
WAUGH, M.E.																			
Test		1	2	0	49	26	24.50	0	0	108	62	1	62.00	1-62	0	0	3.44	2	
FC		2	4	1	76	26	25.33	0	0	209	130	7	18.57	6-68	1	0	3.75	3	
Int		4	4	0	107	50	26.75	0	1	120	86	2	43.00	2-38	0	0	4.30	1	
WAUGH, S.R.																			
Test		1	2	1	67	67*	67.00	0	1	78	25	1	25.00	1-25	0	0	1.92	0	
FC		2	3	1	94	67*	47.00	0	1	78	25	1	25.00	1-25	0	0	1.92	0	
Int		5	5	0	152	41	30.40	0	0	78	76	2	38.00	2-52	0	0	5.84	1	

Cmp Debut	M	I	NO	Runs	HS	Avge	100	50	Balls	Runs	Wkts	Avge	BB	5i	10m	RpO	ct	st

NEW ZEALAND IN INDIA 1996-97

Cmp Debut	M	I	NO	Runs	HS	Avge	100	50	Balls	Runs	Wkts	Avge	BB	5i	10m	RpO	ct	st
ASTLE, N.J.																		
Int	3	3	0	218	117	72.66	1	1	138	105	7	15.00	4-43	1	0	4.56	0	
CAIRNS, C.L.																		
Int	3	3	0	26	17	8.66	0	0	12	12	0					6.00	2	
DAVIS, H.T.																		
Int	2	1	1	0	0*		0	0	66	93	0					8.45	1	
FLEMING, S.P.																		
Int	3	3	0	46	24	15.33	0	0									1	
HARRIS, C.Z.																		
Int	3	3	1	33	26*	16.50	0	0	162	90	0					3.33	3	
HORNE, M.J.																		
Int	3	3	0	109	45	36.33	0	0									0	
LARSEN, G.R.																		
Int	3	3	1	14	12	7.00	0	0	165	115	6	19.16	3-43	0	0	4.18	0	
McMILLAN, C.D.																		
Int	1	1	0	10	10	10.00	0	0									1	
O'CONNOR, S.B.																		
Int	1	1	0	0	0	0.00	0	0	54	44	3	14.66	3-44	0	0	4.88	0	
PARORE, A.C.																		
Int	3	3	1	57	32	28.50	0	0									2	1
PATEL, D.N.																		
Int	3	3	0	19	10	6.33	0	0	162	116	1	116.00	1-49	0	0	4.29	0	
PENN, A.J.																		
Int	2	1	1	7	7*		0	0	87	109	1	109.00	1-50	0	0	7.51	0	
YOUNG, B.A.																		
Int	3	3	0	98	59	32.66	0	1									0	

PAKISTAN IN INDIA 1996-97

Cmp Debut	M	I	NO	Runs	HS	Avge	100	50	Balls	Runs	Wkts	Avge	BB	5i	10m	RpO	ct	st
AAQIB JAVED																		
Int	5	3	1	15	6*	7.50	0	0	258	279	11	25.36	5-35	0	2	6.48	0	
ABDUR RAZZAQ																		
Int	2	1	0	8	8	8.00	0	0	72	86	1	86.00	1-45	0	0	7.16	0	
ARSHAD KHAN																		
Int	1	1	0	0	0	0.00	0	0	60	54	2	27.00	2-54	0	0	5.40	0	
AZHAR MAHMOOD																		
Int	2								54	60	0					6.66	2	
IJAZ AHMED																		
Int	5	5	0	196	55	39.20	0	2									5	
INZAMAM-UL-HAQ																		
Int	4	3	1	91	39*	45.50	0	0									2	
MOHAMMAD HUSSAIN																		
Int	5	5	3	51	18*	25.50	0	0	246	221	3	73.66	2-56	0	0	5.39	1	
MOHAMMAD WASIM																		
Int	1	1	0	20	20	20.00	0	0									0	
MOIN KHAN																		
Int	5	5	2	107	57*	35.66	0	1									2	3
RAMEEZ RAJA																		
Int	5	5	0	200	76	40.00	0	1									0	
SAEED ANWAR																		
Int	5	5	0	267	194	53.40	1	0									0	
SALEEM MALIK																		
Int	5	4	0	127	49	31.75	0	0	252	233	5	46.60	2-46	0	0	5.54	0	
SAQLAIN MUSHTAQ																		
Int	5	3	1	24	18	12.00	0	0	293	252	14	18.00	4-33	1	0	5.16	3	
SHAHID KHAN AFRIDI																		
Int	5	5	0	151	59	30.20	0	2	258	266	2	133.00	1-40	0	0	6.18	1	

SOUTH AFRICA IN INDIA 1996-97

ADAMS, P.R.

Cmp	Debut	M	I	NO	Runs	HS	Avge	100	50	Balls	Runs	Wkts	Avge	BB	5i	10m	RpO	ct	st
Test		3	5	0	14	8	2.80	0	0	471	284	14	20.28	6-55	1	0	3.61	3	
FC		4	5	0	14	8	2.80	0	0	620	392	19	20.63	6-55	2	0	3.79	4	
Int		1	1	0	0	0	0.00	0	0	42	50	2	25.00	2-50	0	0	7.14	0	

BOJE, N.

FC		3	4	0	58	33	14.50	0	0	204	110	1	110.00	1-16	0	0	3.23	2	
Int		5	4	1	25	13*	8.33	0	0	294	209	9	23.22	2-38	0	0	4.26	2	

COMMINS, J.B.

FC		1	1	0	22	22	22.00	0	0									0	

CRONJE, W.J.

Test		3	6	1	152	50*	30.40	0	1	300	83	2	41.50	2-11	0	0	1.66	0	
FC		6	11	2	334	53	37.11	0	2	408	121	5	24.20	2-11	0	0	1.77	1	
Int		8	7	1	178	63*	29.66	0	2	174	147	0					5.06	4	

CROOKES, D.N.

FC		2	3	0	139	76	46.33	0	1	162	77	4	19.25	2-18	0	0	2.85	2	
Int		4	3	0	30	18	10.00	0	0	174	147	4	36.75	2-41	0	0	5.06	2	

CULLINAN, D.J.

Test		3	6	1	270	153*	54.00	1	0									2	
FC		6	10	1	353	153*	39.22	1	0									2	
Int		8	8	2	317	106	52.83	1	1									4	

DE VILLIERS, P.S.

Test		2	4	1	75	67*	25.00	0	1	444	176	5	35.20	2-55	0	0	2.37	2	
FC		4	5	1	77	67*	19.25	0	1	690	305	14	21.78	5-46	1	0	2.65	4	
Int		7	3	2	0	0*	0.00	0	0	369	203	6	33.83	3-32	0	0	3.30	1	

DONALD, A.A.

Test		2	3	0	21	17	7.00	0	0	380	141	10	14.10	4-37	0	0	2.22	1	
FC		3	5	1	34	17	8.50	0	0	548	209	17	12.29	4-37	0	0	2.28	1	
Int		7	1	0	0	0	0.00	0	0	394	294	17	17.29	4-31	1	0	4.47	0	

GIBBS, H.H.

Test		2	4	0	62	31	15.50	0	0									1	
FC		5	9	1	526	200*	65.75	2	1									4	
Int		2	2	0	66	35	33.00	0	0									1	

HUDSON, A.C.

Test		3	6	1	221	146	44.20	1	0									3	
FC		5	10	2	331	146	41.37	1	0									7	
Int		7	7	0	244	68	34.85	0	2									2	

KIRSTEN, G.

Test		3	6	0	322	133	53.66	2	0									2	
FC		5	10	1	404	133	44.88	2	0									6	
Int		8	8	1	308	105*	44.00	1	1									2	1

KLUSENER, L.

Test		2	3	1	53	34*	26.50	0	0	465	258	10	25.80	8-64	1	0	3.32	2	
FC		5	7	3	194	102*	48.50	1	0	845	433	26	16.65	8-64	2	0	3.07	4	
Int		3	2	1	95	88*	95.00	0	1	120	135	3	45.00	2-54	0	0	6.75	0	

McMILLAN, B.M.

Test		3	6	1	61	18	12.20	0	0	534	199	6	33.16	2-40	0	0	2.23	8	
FC		5	9	1	197	130	24.62	1	0	648	247	11	22.45	3-14	0	0	2.28	12	
Int		6	4	1	88	32	29.33	0	0	306	219	4	54.75	3-42	0	0	4.29	3	

RHODES, J.N.

Test		1	2	0	14	14	7.00	0	0									2	
FC		3	5	0	90	46	18.00	0	0									4	
Int		7	6	1	135	54	27.00	0	1									3	

RICHARDSON, D.J.

Test		3	5	1	56	36*	14.00	0	0									4	
FC		5	8	2	98	36*	16.33	0	0									12	
Int		7	5	3	69	43	34.50	0	0									6	2

SYMCOX, P.L.

Test		3	5	1	79	32	19.75	0	0	642	324	6	54.00	2-47	0	0	3.02	0	
FC		4	6	2	87	32	21.75	0	0	750	381	6	63.50	2-47	0	0	3.04	0	
Int		8	4	1	78	46	26.00	0	0	480	314	7	44.85	2-43	0	0	3.92	3	

Cmp Debut	M	I	NO	Runs	HS	Avge	100	50	Balls	Runs	Wkts	Avge	BB	5i	10m	RpO	ct	st

SRI LANKA IN INDIA 1996-97

Cmp Debut	M	I	NO	Runs	HS	Avge	100	50	Balls	Runs	Wkts	Avge	BB	5i	10m	RpO	ct	st
ATAPATTU, M.S.																		
Int	5	5	0	161	53	32.20	0	1									3	
DE SILVA, K.S.C.																		
Int	5	3	1	13	13*	6.50	0	0	234	212	11	19.27	3-40	0	0	5.43	0	
DE SILVA, P.A.																		
Int	5	5	0	189	90	37.80	0	2	162	104	5	20.80	2-22	0	0	3.85	3	
DHARMASENA, H.D.P.K.																		
Int	5	3	0	50	28	16.66	0	0	246	176	5	35.20	2-28	0	0	4.29	1	
JAYASURIYA, S.T.																		
Int	5	5	1	306	151*	76.50	1	2	234	200	5	40.00	2-21	0	0	5.12	0	
KALUWITHARANA, R.S.																		
Int	5	5	1	57	44	14.25	0	0									3	5
LIYANAGE, D.K.																		
Int	1	1	1	1	1*		0	0	36	40	0					6.66	1	
MAHANAMA, R.S.																		
Int	5	4	1	126	54	42.00	0	1									1	
MURALITHARAN, M.																		
Int	5	3	2	16	9*	16.00	0	0	281	213	7	30.42	3-40	0	0	4.54	3	
RANATUNGA, A.																		
Int	5	5	0	229	80	45.80	0	3									0	
TILLAKARATNE, H.P.																		
Int	5	4	0	102	38	25.50	0	0									3	
VAAS, W.P.U.J.C.																		
Int	4	3	0	18	15	6.00	0	0	198	147	5	29.40	2-13	0	0	4.45	0	

The following current cricketers have played in Indian Domestic limited overs cricket but did not appear in Indian Domestic cricket in 1996-97:

Cmp Debut	M	I	NO	Runs	HS	Avge	100	50	Balls	Runs	Wkts	Avge	BB	5i	10m	RpO	ct	st
FRASER, A.R.C. (see Middlesex) (Wills XI)																		
Wlls 1994	2	1	0	19	19	19.00	0	0	118	77	1	77.00	1-41	0	0	3.91	1	
HAYNES, D.L. (see South Africa) (Wills XI)																		
Wlls 1994	2	2	1	51	30	51.00	0	0									2	

KENYA

First First-Class Match: Kenya v Pakistan B (Nairobi) 1996-97. East Africa played first-class matches in Kenya prior to this date. ICC have ruled that from 1997-98 that matches by Kenya will be recognised as first-class.

First One-Day International Match: Kenya v Sri Lanka (Nairobi) 1996-97. Kenya had previously appeared in the 1995-96 World Cup.

Cmp	Debut	M	I	NO	Runs	HS	Avge	100	50	Balls	Runs	Wkts	Avge	BB	5i	10m	RpO	ct	st

1996-97 AND CAREER RECORDS FOR KENYA PLAYERS

ASIF KARIM (Kenya, Kenya to South Africa) b Mombasa 15.12.1963 LHB SLA

Cmp	Debut	M	I	NO	Runs	HS	Avge	100	50	Balls	Runs	Wkts	Avge	BB	5i	10m	RpO	ct	st
Int		3	3	0	25	24	8.33	0	0	162	118	2	59.00	2-44	0	0	4.37	0	
FC	1986	1	1	0	11	11	11.00	0	0	258	119	6	19.83	3-40	0	0	2.76	0	
Int	1995	9	6	1	42	24	8.40	0	0	450	289	6	48.16	2-44	0	0	3.85	0	

BWIBO, Kennedy Shahid (Kenya to South Africa) b Nairobi 15.5.1968 RM
CHUDASAMA, Dipak (Kenya) b Mombasa 20.5.1963 RHB

Cmp	Debut	M	I	NO	Runs	HS	Avge	100	50	Balls	Runs	Wkts	Avge	BB	5i	10m	RpO	ct	st
Int		3	3	0	80	51	26.66	0	1									1	
Int	1995	9	8	0	183	51	22.87	0	1									2	

GUPTA, Sandip Kumar (Kenya) b Nairobi 7.4.1967 RHB WK

Cmp	Debut	M	I	NO	Runs	HS	Avge	100	50	Balls	Runs	Wkts	Avge	BB	5i	10m	RpO	ct	st
Int		3	3	0	43	41	14.33	0	0									0	

MODI, Hitesh S. (Kenya, Kenya to South Africa) b Kisumu 13.10.1971 LHB OB

Cmp	Debut	M	I	NO	Runs	HS	Avge	100	50	Balls	Runs	Wkts	Avge	BB	5i	10m	RpO	ct	st
Int		3	3	1	95	78*	47.50	0	1									0	
Int	1995	9	8	1	179	78*	25.57	0	1									3	

ODOYO, Thomas (Kenya, Kenya to South Africa) b Nairobi 12.5.1978 RHB RMF

Cmp	Debut	M	I	NO	Runs	HS	Avge	100	50	Balls	Runs	Wkts	Avge	BB	5i	10m	RpO	ct	st
Int		3	3	0	41	32	13.66	0	0	150	113	4	28.25	3-25	0	0	4.52	1	
Int	1995	8	7	0	83	32	11.85	0	0	264	225	4	56.25	3-25	0	0	5.11	1	

ODUMBE, Edward Olouch (Kenya) b Kendubay 19.5.1965 RHB RM

Cmp	Debut	M	I	NO	Runs	HS	Avge	100	50	Balls	Runs	Wkts	Avge	BB	5i	10m	RpO	ct	st
Int		2	2	0	7	5	3.50	0	0	36	42	2	21.00	2-29	0	0	7.00	1	
Int	1995	8	7	1	61	20	10.16	0	0	137	137	6	22.83	2-8	0	0	6.00	4	

ODUMBE, Maurice Omondi (Kenya, Kenya to South Africa) b Nairobi 15.6.1969 RHB OB

Cmp	Debut	M	I	NO	Runs	HS	Avge	100	50	Balls	Runs	Wkts	Avge	BB	5i	10m	RpO	ct	st
Int		3	3	0	23	19	7.66	0	0	108	78	2	39.00	1-13	0	0	4.33	0	
Int	1995	9	8	0	135	50	16.87	0	1	365	265	8	33.12	3-15	0	0	4.35	1	

ONYANGO, Lameck (Kenya) b Nairobi 22.9.1973 RHB RM

Cmp	Debut	M	I	NO	Runs	HS	Avge	100	50	Balls	Runs	Wkts	Avge	BB	5i	10m	RpO	ct	st
Int		1	1	0	4	4	4.00	0	0	18	45	1	45.00	1-45	0	0	15.00	0	
Int	1995	2	2	0	27	23	13.50	0	0	42	76	1	76.00	1-45	0	0	10.85	1	

OTIENO, Kennedy (Kenya, Kenya to South Africa) b Nairobi 11.3.1972 RHB WK

Cmp	Debut	M	I	NO	Runs	HS	Avge	100	50	Balls	Runs	Wkts	Avge	BB	5i	10m	RpO	ct	st
Int		3	3	0	27	25	9.00	0	0									1	1
Int	1995	9	8	0	174	85	21.75	0	1									2	1

PATEL, Brijal (Kenya to South Africa) b Nairobi 14.11.1977 RHB SLA
RAJAB ALI (Kenya) b Nairobi 19.11.1965 RHB RMF

Cmp	Debut	M	I	NO	Runs	HS	Avge	100	50	Balls	Runs	Wkts	Avge	BB	5i	10m	RpO	ct	st
Int		1	1	1	1	1*		0	0	24	23	0					5.75	0	
Int	1995	7	3	3	7	6*		0	0	272	213	10	21.30	3-17	0	0	4.69	1	

SUJI, Anthony (Kenya, Kenya to South Africa) b 5.2.1976 RHB RM

Cmp	Debut	M	I	NO	Runs	HS	Avge	100	50	Balls	Runs	Wkts	Avge	BB	5i	10m	RpO	ct	st
Int		2	2	0	14	10	7.00	0	0	62	54	1	54.00	1-16	0	0	5.22	0	

SUJI, Martin A. (Kenya, Kenya to South Africa) b Nairobi 2.6.1971 RHB RMF

Cmp	Debut	M	I	NO	Runs	HS	Avge	100	50	Balls	Runs	Wkts	Avge	BB	5i	10m	RpO	ct	st
Int		3	3	2	6	6*	6.00	0	0	148	137	2	68.50	2-42	0	0	5.55	0	
Int	1995	9	7	4	24	15	8.00	0	0	420	361	6	60.16	2-42	0	0	5.15	3	

TIKOLO, Lazaro Openda (Kenya to South Africa) b Nairobi 27.12.1964 RHB RM

Cmp	Debut	M	I	NO	Runs	HS	Avge	100	50	Balls	Runs	Wkts	Avge	BB	5i	10m	RpO	ct	st
Int		3	2	2	36	25*		0	0	48	55	0					6.87	2	

TIKOLO, Stephen Ogomji (Kenya, Kenya to South Africa) b Nairobi 25.6.1971 RHB OB

Cmp	Debut	M	I	NO	Runs	HS	Avge	100	50	Balls	Runs	Wkts	Avge	BB	5i	10m	RpO	ct	st
Int		3	3	0	20	9	6.66	0	0	18	19	0					6.33	0	
FC	1995	6	10	0	240	64	24.00	0	2									2	
Int	1995	9	8	0	216	96	27.00	0	2	78	102	1	102.00	1-26	0	0	7.84	3	

Cmp Debut	M	I	NO	Runs	HS	Avge	100	50	Balls	Runs	Wkts	Avge	BB	5i	10m	RpO	ct	st

PAKISTAN IN KENYA 1996-97

Cmp Debut	M	I	NO	Runs	HS	Avge	100	50	Balls	Runs	Wkts	Avge	BB	5i	10m	RpO	ct	st
AZHAR MAHMOOD																		
Int	3	3	0	18	15	6.00	0	0	120	143	0					7.15	0	
IJAZ AHMED																		
Int	4	4	0	144	88	36.00	0	1	30	31	0					6.20	1	
MOIN KHAN																		
Int	4	4	1	101	50*	33.66	0	1									3	2
RAMEEZ RAJA																		
Int	3	3	0	10	7	3.33	0	0									1	
SAEED ANWAR																		
Int	4	4	0	175	117	43.75	1	0	12	14	0					7.00	1	
SAEED AZAD																		
Int	3	3	0	46	31	15.33	0	0									1	
SALEEM ELAHI																		
Int	4	4	0	121	54	30.25	0	1									0	
SALEEM MALIK																		
Int	4	4	0	94	43	23.50	0	0	146	133	2	66.50	2-24	0	0	5.46	3	
SAQLAIN MUSHTAQ																		
Int	4	4	3	23	13*	23.00	0	0	240	143	10	14.30	4-33	1	0	3.57	2	
SHAHID KHAN AFRIDI																		
Int	3	2	0	116	102	58.00	1	0	180	123	4	30.75	3-48	0	0	4.10	1	
SHAHID NAZIR																		
Int	3	2	2	11	6*		0	0	108	117	1	117.00	1-31	0	0	6.50	1	
WAQAR YOUNIS																		
Int	4	3	0	43	28	14.33	0	0	221	180	9	20.00	5-52	0	1	4.88	0	
WASIM AKRAM																		
Int	1	1	0	8	8	8.00	0	0	60	42	2	21.00	2-42	0	0	4.20	0	

SOUTH AFRICA IN KENYA 1996-97

Cmp Debut	M	I	NO	Runs	HS	Avge	100	50	Balls	Runs	Wkts	Avge	BB	5i	10m	RpO	ct	st
CRONJE, W.J.																		
Int	4	3	1	89	63*	44.50	0	1	18	29	0					9.66	2	
CROOKES, D.N																		
Int	3	2	0	11	10	5.50	0	0	133	83	5	16.60	3-30	0	0	3.74	3	
CULLINAN, D.J.																		
Int	3	3	0	191	124	63.66	1	1	6	8	0					8.00	2	
DE VILLIERS, P.S.																		
Int	4	3	1	28	20*	14.00	0	0	165	141	5	28.20	2-37	0	0	5.12	0	
DONALD, A.A.																		
Int	4	1	0	0	0	0.00	0	0	210	119	14	8.50	6-23	0	1	3.40	1	
GIBBS, H.H.																		
Int	1	1	0	17	17	17.00	0	0									0	
HUDSON, A.C.																		
Int	4	4	0	78	42	19.50	0	0									0	
KIRSTEN, G.																		
Int	4	4	1	227	118*	75.66	1	1									1	
MCMILLAN, B.M.																		
Int	4	3	1	30	25*	15.00	0	0	168	159	6	26.50	3-17	0	0	5.67	1	
MATTHEWS, C.R.																		
Int	1	1	1	0	0*		0	0	36	44	0					7.33	0	
RHODES, S.J.																		
Int	4	4	1	198	121	66.00	1	1									0	
RICHARDSON, D.J.																		
Int	4	3	1	15	11*	7.50	0	0									4	
SYMCOX, P.L.																		
Int	4	4	0	44	35	11.00	0	0	192	133	4	33.25	2-20	0	0	4.15	1	

Cmp	Debut	M	I	NO	Runs	HS	Avge	100	50	Balls	Runs	Wkts	Avge	BB	5i	10m	RpO	ct	st

SRI LANKA IN KENYA 1996-97

Cmp	Debut	M	I	NO	Runs	HS	Avge	100	50	Balls	Runs	Wkts	Avge	BB	5i	10m	RpO	ct	st
CHANDANA, U.D.U.																			
Int		1								30	22	0					4.40	0	
DE SILVA, K.S.C.																			
Int		3	2	2	4	4*		0	0	126	102	4	25.50	2-27	0	0	4.85	0	
DE SILVA, P.A.																			
Int		3	3	0	180	122	60.00	1	1	84	81	2	40.50	1-23	0	0	5.78	0	
DHARMASENA, H.D.P.K.																			
Int		3	2	1	69	51	69.00	0	1	150	123	2	61.50	1-36	0	0	4.92	2	
GURUSINHA, A.P.																			
Int		3	3	0	23	22	7.66	0	0									3	
JAYASURIYA, S.T																			
Int		3	3	0	52	45	17.33	0	0	132	147	4	36.75	3-94	0	0	6.68	0	
KALUWITHARANA, R.S.																			
Int		3	3	1	146	100*	73.00	1	0									1	1
MAHANAMA, R.S.																			
Int		2	2	0	10	10	5.00	0	0									2	
MURALITHARAN, M.																			
Int		3	1	0	0	0	0.00	0	0	180	126	10	12.60	4-18	2	0	4.20	3	
RANATUNGA, A.																			
Int		3	3	1	88	52	44.00	0	1	18	10	1	10.00	1-10	0	0	3.33	2	
TILLAKARATNE, H.P.																			
Int		3	2	0	16	13	8.00	0	0									0	
VAAS, W.P.U.J.C.																			
Int		3	2	0	29	16	14.50	0	0	132	97	2	48.50	1-13	0	0	4.40	1	

NEW ZEALAND

First First-Class Match: Otago v Canterbury (Dunedin) 1863-64

First First-Class Tour to England: 1927

First Test Match: New Zealand v England (Christchurch) 1929-30

Present First-Class Teams: Auckland, Canterbury, Central Districts, Northern Districts, Otago, Wellington

First-Class Competition: The Plunket Shield was instituted for the 1906-07 season for competition between the first-class teams. It was replaced by the Shell Cup and Trophy from 1975-76, the Shell Cup later becoming a one-day competition.

Shell Trophy Champions 1996-97: Canterbury

FIRST-CLASS RECORDS

Highest Team Total: 777 Canterbury v Otago (Christchurch) 1996-97
Highest in 1996-97: 777 Canterbury v Otago (Christchurch); 586-7d New Zealand v Sri Lanka (Dunedin); 549 Canterbury v Northern Districts (Christchurch); 548-8d Otago v Auckland (Dunedin); 543-8d Canterbury v Central Districts (Rangiora)

Lowest Team Total: 13 Auckland v Canterbury (Auckland) 1877-78
Lowest in 1996-97: 32 Northern Districts v Auckland (Hamilton); 61 Central Districts v Auckland (Auckland); 69 Northern Districts v England (Hamilton); 74 Central Districts v Otago (Invercargill); 107 England v New Zealand A (Wanganui)

Highest Individual Innings: 385 B.Sutcliffe Otago v Canterbury (Christchurch) 1952-53
Highest in 1996-97: 267* B.A.Young New Zealand v Sri Lanka (Dunedin); 251* C.Z.Harris Canterbury v Central Districts (Rangiora); 206 C.Z.Harris Canterbury v Central Districts (Blenheim); 198 C.Z.Harris Canterbury v Otago (Christchurch); 194 C.B.Gaffaney Otago v Auckland (Dunedin)

Most Runs in Season: 1,676 (av 93.11) M.D.Crowe (Central Districts) 1986-87
Most in 1996-97: 843 (av 49.58) M.J.Horne (Otago); 835 (av 139.16) C.Z.Harris (Canterbury); 809 (av 73.54) C.D.McMillan (Canterbury); 722 (av 48.33) M.S.Sinclair (Central Districts); 682 (av 37.58) B.A.Pocock (Northern Districts)

Most Runs in Career: 34,346 (av 49.70) G.M.Turner (Northern Districts, Otago, Worcestershire) 1964-65 to 1982-83
Most by Current Batsman: 15,188 (av 29.95) D.N.Patel (Auckland, Worcestershire) 1976 to date; 9,445 (av 38.08) M.J.Greatbatch (Auckland, Central Districts) 1982-83 to date; 8,213 (av 37.84) R.G.Twose (Northern Districts, Central Districts, Wellington, Warwickshire) 1989 to date; 6,784 (av 35.15) C.L.Cairns (Canterbury, Nottinghamshire) 1988-89 to date. K.R.Rutherford, 11,814 (av 38.10), played for Transvaal but did not appear in New Zealand in 1996-97.

Best Innings Analysis: 10-28 A.E.Moss Canterbury v Wellington (Christchurch) 1889-90
Best in 1996-97: 9-48 A.R.Tait Northern Districts v Auckland (Hamilton); 8-27 J.T.C.Vaughan Auckland v Otago (Alexandra); 8-31 D.G.Sewell Otago v Central Districts (Invercargill); 8-66 P.J.Wiseman Otago v Wellington (Wellington); 7-72 C.J.M.Furlong Central Districts v Northern Districts (Nelson)

Most Wickets in Season: 66 (av 16.48) S.L.Boock (Canterbury) 1977-78
Most in 1996-97: 53 (av 16.32) A.R.Tait (Northern Districts); 40 (av 24.20) P.J.Wiseman (Otago); 36 (av 15.33) A.J.Penn (Central Districts); 36 (av 21.16) D.L.Vettori (Northern Districts); 35 (av 24.31) D.G.Sewell (Otago)

Most Wickets in Career: 1,490 (av 18.11) R.J.Hadlee (Canterbury, Nottinghamshire, Tasmania) 1971-72 to 1990
Most by Current Bowler: 654 (av 33.23) D.N.Patel (Auckland, Worcestershire) 1976 to date; 440 (av 30.22) D.K.Morrison (Auckland, Lancashire) 1985-86 to date; 410 (av 28.93) C.L.Cairns (Canterbury, Nottinghamshire) 1988-89 to date; 275 (av 32.29) M.W.Priest (Canterbury) 1984-85 to date

Record Wicket Partnerships

1st	373	B.Sutcliffe & L.Watt	Otago v Auckland (Auckland)	1950-51
2nd	317	R.T.Hart & P.S.Briasco	Central Districts v Canterbury (New Plymouth)	1983-84
3rd	467	A.H.Jones & M.D.Crowe	New Zealand v Sri Lanka (Wellington)	1990-91
4th	350	Mushtaq Mohammad & Asif Iqbal	Pakistan v New Zealand (Dunedin)	1972-73

149

5th	341	G.R.Larsen & E.B.McSweeney	Wellington v Central Districts (Levin)	1987-88
6th	269	V.T.Trumper & C.Hill	Australia v New Zealand (Wellington)	1904-05
7th	265	J.L.Powell & N.Dorreen	Canterbury v Otago (Christchurch)	1929-30
8th	433	A.Sims & V.T.Trumper	Australians v Canterbury (Christchurch)	1913-14
9th	239	H.B.Cave & I.B.Leggat	Central Districts v Otago (Dunedin)	1952-53
10th	184	R.C.Blunt & W.Hawksworth	Otago v Canterbury (Christchurch)	1931-32

Highest Partnerships in 1996-97

1st	164	R.A.Lawson & C.B.Gaffaney	Otago v Auckland (Dunedin)
2nd	182	M.A.Atherton & A.J.Stewart	England v New Zealand (Auckland)
3rd	150	M.S.Sinclair & L.G.Howell	Central Districts v Wellington (Masterton)
4th	259	G.E.Bradburn & M.E.Parlane	Northern Districts v Canterbury (Christchurch)
5th	290	C.Z.Harris & G.R.Stead	Canterbury v Central Districts (Blenheim)
6th	133	C.Z.Harris & C.L.Cairns	Canterbury v Otago (Christchurch)
7th	169	C.Z.Harris & M.E.L.Lane	Canterbury v Central Districts (Rangiora)
8th	146	M.H.Austen & P.J.Wiseman	Otago v Canterbury (Christchurch)
9th	139	R.G.Hart & A.R.Tait	Northern Districts v Wellington (Gisborne)
10th	106	N.J.Astle & D.K.Morrison	New Zealand v England (Auckland)

Most Wicketkeeping Dismissals in Innings: 7 (7ct) R.M.Schofield Central Districts v Wellington (Wellington) 1964-65; 7 (7ct) Wasim Bari Pakistan v New Zealand (Auckland) 1978-79; 7 (7ct) B.A.Young Northern Districts v Canterbury (Christchurch) 1986-87; 7 (7ct) I.D.S.Smith New Zealand v Sri Lanka (Hamilton) 1990-91
Most in 1996-97: no wicketkeeper took more than 4

Most Wicketkeeping Dismissals in Match: 10 (10ct) C.J.Niven Wellington v Otago (Dunedin) 1995-96
Most in 1996-97: 7 (7ct) C.J.Niven Wellington v Auckland (Wellington)

Most Wicketkeeping Dismissals in Season: 41 (31ct 10st) E.B.McSweeney (Wellington) 1984-85; 41 (35ct 6st) E.B.McSweeney (Wellington) 1989-90
Most in 1996-97: 27 (27ct) J.M.Mills (Auckland); 25 (22ct 3st) A.J.Stewart (England); 24 (24ct) M.G.Croy (Otago); 24 (23ct 1st) R.G.Hart (Northern Districts); 22 (20ct 2st) C.J.Niven (Wellington)

Most Wicketkeeping Dismissals in Career: 453 (417ct 36 st) I.D.S.Smith (Central Districts, Auckland) 1977-78 to 1991-92
Most by Current Wicketkeeper: 261 (235ct 26st) L.K.Germon (Canterbury) 1987-88 to date; 198 (185ct 14st) A.C.Parore (Auckland) 1988-89 to date; 123 (118ct 5st) S.A.Robinson (Otago) 1984-85 to date; 103 (93ct 10st) R.G.Hart (Northern Districts) 1992-93 to date; 57 (55ct 2st) M.G.Croy (Otago) 1994-95 to date

Most Catches by Fielder in Innings: 5 N.T.Williams Auckland v Hawke's Bay (Napier) 1894-95; 5 J.R.Lamason Wellington v Otago (Dunedin) 1937-38; 5 J.R.Lamason North Island Army v South Island Army (Wellington) 1942-43; 5 J.T.Ikin MCC v. Auckland (Auckland) 1946-47; 5 J.F.M.Morrison Wellington v Northern Districts (Wellington) 1980-81; 5 G.K.MacDonald Canterbury v Pakistan (Christchurch) 1984-85; 5 J.J.Crowe Auckland v Canterbury (Christchurch) 1988-89
Most in 1996-97: 4 M.D.Bailey (Northern Districts); 4 P.J.B.Chandler (New Zealand A); 4 C.B.Gaffaney (Otago); 4 N.V.Knight (England); 4 D.S.McHardy (Wellington); 4 R.S.Mahanama (Sri Lanka); 4 D.J.Murray (Canterbury)

Most Catches by Fielder in Match: 7 J.F.M.Morrison Wellington v Northern Districts (Wellington) 1980-81
Most in 1996-97: 6 P.J.B.Chandler New Zealand A v England (Wanganui); 6 D.S.McHardy Wellington v Northern Districts (Hamilton); 5 M.D.Bailey Northern Districts v Otago (Alexandra)

Most Catches by Fielder in Season: 23 B.A.G.Murray (Wellington) 1967-68
Most in 1996-97: 15 N.V.Knight (England); 14 M.J.Horne (Otago); 12 G.E.Bradburn (Northern Districts); 11 M.D.Bell (Northern Districts); 11 R.A.Jones (Auckland)

Most Catches by Fielder in Career: 410 G.M.Turner (Otago, Northern Districts, Worcestershire) 1964-65 to 1982-83
Most by Current Fielder: 193 D.N.Patel (Auckland, Worcestershire) 1976 to date; 138 M.J.Greatbatch (Auckland, Central Districts) 1982-83 to date; 85 G.E.Bradburn (Northern Districts) 1985-86 to date; 74 R.G.Twose (Northern Districts, Central Districts, Wellington, Warwickshire) 1989 to date. K.R.Rutherford, 153, played for Transvaal but did not play in New Zealand in 1996-97.

DOMESTIC LIMITED OVERS RECORDS

Highest Team Totals: 376-3 (50 overs) Central Districts v Otago (New Plymouth) 1996-97; 329-5 (50 overs) Canterbury v Northern Districts (Christchurch) 1995-96; 313-7 (50 overs) Canterbury v Northern Districts (Timaru) 1993-94

Lowest Team Totals: 64 (38.4 overs) Otago v Wellington (Alexandra) 1984-85; 66 (27.4 overs) Wellington v Canterbury (Wellington) 1996-97; 70 (24.3 overs) Auckland v Northern Districts (Pukekohe) 1977-78

Highest Individual Innings: 161 B.R.Hartland Canterbury v Northern Districts (Timaru) 1993-94; 147* B.A.Edgar Wellington v Northern Districts (Gisborne) 1981-82; 143 C.L.Cairns Canterbury v Auckland (Christchurch) 1994-95
Highest in 1996-97: 128* M.H.Richardson Otago v Central Districts (New Plymouth)
63 centuries have been scored in the competition, M.D.Crowe scoring 5.

Most Runs in Season: 687 (av 62.45) N.J.Astle (Canterbury) 1995-96
Most in 1996-97: 467 (av 46.70) B.A.Young (Northern Districts)

Most Runs in Career: 2,206 (av 29.02) R.T.Latham (Canterbury) 1980-81 to 1994-95; 2,171 (av 42.56) M.D.Crowe (Auckland, Central Districts, Wellington) 1980-81 to 1993-94; 2,001 (av 55.58) B.A.Edgar (Wellington) 1976-77 to 1989-90
Most by Current Batsman: : 1,897 (av 29.64) B.A.Young (Northern Districts) 1983-84 to date

Best Innings Analyses: 7-23 W.Watson Auckland v Otago (Auckland) 1984-85; 7-49 E.J.Marshall Otago v Auckland (Dunedin) 1993-94; 6-12 B.J.Barrett Northern Districts v Otago (Gisborne) 1986-87
Best in 1996-97: 6-37 C.L.Cairns Canterbury v Wellington (Christchurch)
Five wickets in an innings has been achieved 35 times, twice by G.N.Cederwall, S.R.McNally and M.L.Su'a

Most Economical Bowling: 10-7-5-2 S.L.Boock Otago v Central Districts (Alexandra) 1986-87
Most Economical in 1996-97: 10-4-16-5 C.M.Brown Auckland v Otago (Auckland)

Most Expensive Bowling: 10-0-93-2 C.M.Presland Northern Districts v Auckland (Gisborne) 1982-83
Most Expensive in 1996-97: 9-0-85-1 R.J.Kennedy Otago v Canterbury (Christchurch); 10-1-85-0 R.J.Kennedy Otago v Central Districts (New Plymouth)

Most Wickets in Season: 25 (av 13.40) J.T.C.Vaughan (Auckland) 1995-96
Most in 1996-97: 21 (av 14.19) G.R.Larsen (Wellington)

Most Wickets in Career: 97 (av 18.14) J.T.C.Vaughan (Auckland) 1990-91 to date; 87 (av 21.63) M.W.Priest (Canterbury) 1987-88 to date; 81 (av 26.03) G.R.Larsen (Wellington) 1984-85 to date

Record Wicket Partnerships

1st	205*	M.W.Douglas & J.M.Aiken	Wellington v Canterbury (Wellington)	1994-95
2nd	189	B.R.Hartland & L.G.Howell	Canterbury v Northern Districts (Timaru)	1993-94
3rd	199*	J.M.Parker & B.G.Cooper	Northern Districts v Auckland (Gisborne)	1982-83
4th	156	S.P.Fleming & C.L.Cairns	Canterbury v Otago (Christchurch)	1995-96
5th	198	C.L.Cairns & L.K.Germon	Canterbury v Wellington (Christchurch)	1992-93
6th	142	C.L.Cairns & S.P.Fleming	Canterbury v Central Districts (Napier)	1993-94
7th	103*	M.H.Richardson & P.A.Campbell	Otago v Central Districts (New Plymouth)	1996-97
8th	98*	B.R.Taylor & R.O.Collinge	Wellington v Central Districts (Lower Hutt)	1971-72
9th	98	L.J.Doull & B.R.Williams	Wellington v Otago (Alexandra)	1993-94
10th	50	C.D.Garner & A.J.Alcock	Central Districts v Otago (Oamaru)	1993-94

There were 23 hundred partnerships in 1996-97, the highest being 179 for the 3rd wicket P.J.B.Chandler & R.G.Twose Wellington v Canterbury (Christchurch)

Most Wicketkeeping Dismissals in Innings: 6 (6ct) E.B.McSweeney Wellington v Auckland (Wellington) 1982-83; 6 (6ct) E.B.McSweeney Wellington v Northern Districts (Wellington) 1988-89; 6 (6ct) G.P.McRae Central Districts v Wellington (Masterton) 1994-95
Most in 1996-97: 4 L.K.Germon (Canterbury) (twice); 4 J.M.Mills (Auckland) (twice); 4 C.J.Niven (Wellington)

Most Wicketkeeping Dismissals in Season: 22 (20ct 2st) C.J.Niven (Wellington) 1996-97

Most Wicketkeeping Dismissals in Career: 123 (97ct 26st) E.B.McSweeney (Central Districts, Wellington) 1980-81 to 1993-94; 87 (69ct 18st) L.K.Germon (Canterbury) 1987-88 to date; 77 (62ct 15st) T.E.Blain (Central Districts) 1982-83 to 1994-95

Most Catches by Fielder in Innings: 5 J.W.Wilson Otago v Auckland (Dunedin) 1993-94
Most in 1996-97: 3 N.J.Astle (Canterbury); 3 H.D.Barton (Auckland); 3 C.M.Brown (Auckland); 3 D.N.Patel (Auckland)

Most Catches by Fielder in Season: 10 N.J.Astle (Canterbury) 1996-97

Most Catches by Fielder in Career: 37 R.T.Latham (Canterbury) 1980-81 to 1994-95; 37 G.E.Bradburn (Northern Districts) 1986-87 to date; 34 M.J.Greatbatch (Central Districts, Auckland) 1982-83 to date

Most Appearances in Competition: 84 R.T.Latham (Canterbury) 1980-81 to 1994-95; 80 G.R.Larsen (Wellington) 1984-85 to date; 78 E.B.McSweeney (Central Districts, Wellington) 1980-81 to 1993-94

CHAMPION TEAMS

Plunket Shield

Until 1920-21, the Shield was run on a challenge basis and the holders were:

Canterbury to Dec 17, 1907; Auckland Dec 17, 1907 to Feb 1, 1911; Canterbury Feb 1, 1911 to Feb 12, 1912; Auckland Feb 12, 1912 to Jan 31, 1913; Canterbury Jan 31, 1913 to Dec 27, 1918; Wellington Dec 27, 1918 to Jan 24, 1919; Canterbury Jan 24, 1919 to Jan 4, 1920; Auckland Jan 4, 1920 to Jan 10, 1921; Wellington from Jan 10, 1921.

From 1921-22 the Shield was run on a League basis, the winners being:

1921-22	Auckland	1938-39	Auckland	1960-61	Wellington
1922-23	Canterbury	1939-40	Auckland	1961-62	Wellington
1923-24	Wellington	1945-46	Canterbury	1962-63	Northern Districts
1924-25	Otago	1946-47	Auckland	1963-64	Auckland
1925-26	Wellington	1947-48	Otago	1964-65	Canterbury
1926-27	Auckland	1948-49	Canterbury	1965-66	Wellington
1927-28	Wellington	1949-50	Wellington	1966-67	Central Districts
1928-29	Auckland	1950-51	Otago	1967-68	Central Districts
1929-30	Wellington	1951-52	Canterbury	1968-69	Auckland
1930-31	Canterbury	1952-53	Otago	1969-70	Otago
1931-32	Wellington	1953-54	Central Districts	1970-71	Central Districts
1932-33	Otago	1954-55	Wellington	1971-72	Otago
1933-34	Auckland	1955-56	Canterbury	1972-73	Wellington
1934-35	Canterbury	1956-57	Wellington	1973-74	Wellington
1935-36	Wellington	1957-58	Otago	1974-75	Otago
1936-37	Auckland	1958-59	Auckland		
1937-38	Auckland	1959-60	Canterbury		

Shell Trophy

Since 1975-76 the first-class Provincial Competition has been sponsored by Shell. For the first four seasons, there were two awards, the Shell Cup for the League winners and the Shell Trophy for winners of a knock-out competition; since 1979-80 however the Shell Trophy only has been awarded to the League winners, the Shell Cup being allocated to the Limited Overs Competition.

1975-76 Canterbury (Cup), Canterbury (Trophy)
1976-77 Northern Districts (Cup), Otago (Trophy)
1977-78 Canterbury (Cup), Auckland (Trophy)
1978-79 Otago (Cup), Otago (Trophy)

1979-80	Northern Districts	1986-87	Central Districts	1992-93	Northern Districts
1980-81	Auckland	1987-88	Otago	1993-94	Canterbury
1981-82	Wellington	1988-89	Auckland	1994-95	Auckland
1982-83	Wellington	1989-90	Wellington	1995-96	Auckland
1983-84	Canterbury	1990-91	Auckland	1996-97	Canterbury
1984-85	Wellington	1991-92	Central Districts,		
1985-86	Otago		Northern Districts		

Domestic Limited Overs Competition

Between 1971-72 and 1979-80 the New Zealand One Day Competition was played on a knock-out basis in a series of five matches each season involving the six provinces. From 1980-81 the competition has been played on a league basis, and from 1993-94 as a double league. From 1980-81 to 1984-85 the top two teams in the league played off in a final and from 1989-90 the top four teams played semi-finals and final. From 1993-94 the top two teams get two chances at the semi-final stage. The overs limit was 40 8-ball overs in the first two seasons, 35 8-ball overs from 1973-74 to 1978-79 (but only 30 in 1977-78), and 50 6-ball overs since 1979-80. Results of the finals:

NZ Motor Corporation Tournament
1971-72 Canterbury 129-3 (33.3 overs) beat Wellington 127 (36.5 overs) by 7 wkts
1972-73 Auckland 209-6 (40 overs) beat Otago 144 (34 overs) by 65 runs
1973-74 Wellington 212-9 (34 overs) beat Auckland 209-7 (35 overs) by 1 wkt

1974-75 Wellington 181-7 (35 overs) beat Northern Districts 165-8 (35 overs) by 16 runs
1975-76 Canterbury 233-6 (35 overs) beat Wellington 153-7 (35 overs) by 80 runs
1976-77 Canterbury 178-7 (34.1 overs) beat Northern Districts 176-7 (35 overs) by 3 wkts

Gillette Cup
1977-78 Canterbury 211-9 (30 overs) beat Northern Districts 154-9 (30 overs) by 57 runs
1978-79 Auckland 156 (34.6 overs) beat Canterbury 143-9 (35 overs) by 13 runs

National Knock-Out Tournament
1979-80 Northern Districts 183-8 (50 overs) beat Otago 182-8 (50 overs) by 2 wkts

Shell Cup
1980-81 Auckland 188-7 (49.1 overs) beat Canterbury 186 (49.3 overs) by 3 wkts
1981-82 Wellington 205-2 (47.5 overs) beat Canterbury 204-7 (50 overs) by 8 wkts
1982-83 Auckland 212-5 (49.1 overs) beat Northern Districts 210 (49.2 overs) by 5 wkts
1983-84 Auckland 130-5 (33.3 overs) beat Wellington 129-6 (35 overs) by 5 wkts
1984-85 Central Districts 156-2 (43.2 overs) beat Wellington 153 (48.2 overs) by 8 wkts
1985-86 Canterbury
1986-87 Auckland
1987-88 Otago
1988-89 Wellington
1989-90 Auckland 198-8 (50 overs) beat Central Districts 176-9 (50 overs) by 22 runs
1990-91 Wellington 214-8 (50 overs) beat Central Districts 140 (42.4 overs) by 74 runs
1991-92 Canterbury 252 (49.4 overs) beat Wellington 249 (49.4 overs) by 3 runs
1992-93 Canterbury 183-8 (50 overs) beat Otago 169-9 (50 overs) by 14 runs
1993-94 Canterbury 240-7 (50 overs) beat Central Districts 215 (49 overs) by 25 runs
1994-95 Northern Districts 256-8 (50 overs) beat Wellington 108 (29.3 overs) by 148 runs
1995-96 Canterbury 329-5 (50 overs) beat Northern Districts 213 (44.4 overs) by 116 runs
1996-97 Canterbury 204-7 (50 overs) beat Wellington 81 (33.5 overs) by 123 runs

Table of Results 1969-70 to 1996-97

	P	W	L	T	NR	Winner	R-up
Wellington	125	75	46	1	3	5	7
Canterbury	123	73	47	0	3	9	4
Auckland	122	64	53	0	5	7	3
Northern Districts	119	49	67	0	3	2	6
Central Districts	115	48	63	0	4	1	3
Otago	114	39	72	1	2	1	3

*The No Result column includes two abandoned knock-out matches which were decided on the toss of a coin.
Auckland and Wellington were joint runners-up in 1985-86. Two original matches which were abandoned and
replayed (in 1993-94 and 1996-97) are not included in the records or averages.*

1996-97 AND CAREER RECORDS FOR NEW ZEALAND PLAYERS

Cmp	Debut	M	I	NO	Runs	HS	Avge	100	50	Balls	Runs	Wkts	Avge	BB	5i	10m	RpO	ct	st
AIKEN, John Maxwell (Wellington) b Sydney, Australia 3.7.1970 LHB																		
FC		5	8	0	107	50	13.37	0	1									6	
SC		4	4	0	20	10	5.00	0	0									2	
FC	1989	31	56	6	1715	170*	34.30	4	7									25	
SC	1989	20	20	1	412	101*	21.68	1	1									7	
ALCOCK, Alistair James (Central Districts) b Napier 20.7.1972 LHB RM																		
SC		2	1	1	5	5*		0	0	111	84	2	42.00	2-31	0	0	4.54	1	
FC	1992	9	14	7	66	29*	9.42	0	0	1199	488	14	34.85	3-43	0	0	2.56	5	
SC	1992	29	13	7	45	11*	7.50	0	0	1564	933	38	24.55	4-33	1	0	3.57	5	
ALLAN, James Matthew (Otago) b Waimate 3.6.1972 RHB																		
FC		1	2	0	6	3	3.00	0	0									4	
FC	1993	13	24	0	427	56	17.79	0	1	12	0	0					0.00	16	
SC	1993	1	1	0	10	10	10.00	0	0									0	
ALLOTT, Geoffrey Ian (Canterbury, New Zealand, New Zealand A) b Christchurch 24.12.1971 RHB LFM																		
Test		2	4	1	12	8*	4.00	0	0	370	197	5	39.40	4-74	0	0	3.19	1	
FC		7	9	2	30	10	4.28	0	0	1344	689	30	22.96	6-60	1	1	3.07	3	
Int		3	2	1	4	3	4.00	0	0	132	110	5	22.00	2-21	0	0	5.00	2	
SC		13	4	2	6	2*	3.00	0	0	515	333	15	22.20	3-13	0	0	3.87	4	
Test	1995	4	6	2	12	8*	3.00	0	0	766	406	9	45.11	4-74	0	0	3.18	1	
FC	1994	16	20	8	67	11*	5.58	0	0	3244	1526	67	22.77	6-60	3	1	2.82	4	
SC	1995	18	4	2	6	2*	3.00	0	0	737	517	23	22.47	3-13	0	0	4.20	4	
ASTLE, Nathan John (Canterbury, New Zealand, Nottinghamshire, New Zealand to Pakistan, New Zealand to Sharjah, New Zealand to India) b Christchurch 15.9.1971 RHB RM																		
Test		5	9	1	251	102*	31.37	1	1	546	213	6	35.50	2-26	0	0	2.34	1	
FC		6	10	1	411	160	45.66	2	1	730	280	12	23.33	6-22	1	0	2.30	1	
Int		7	7	0	268	94	38.28	0	3	183	144	7	20.57	3-9	0	0	4.72	2	
SC		11	11	1	420	114	42.00	1	2	174	119	5	23.80	2-35	0	0	4.10	10	
Test	1995	11	21	1	633	125	31.65	3	2	654	264	8	33.00	2-26	0	0	2.42	8	
FC	1991	48	77	7	2635	191	37.64	8	10	5258	1869	61	30.63	6-22	2	0	2.13	33	
Int	1994	46	46	1	1460	120	32.44	4	8	1523	1130	37	30.54	4-43	1	0	4.45	13	
SC	1991	58	49	11	1672	131	44.00	3	8	2623	1353	55	24.60	4-14	1	0	3.09	26	
AUCKRAM, Craig Laurence (Central Districts) b Levin 9.6.1967 RHB RFM																		
SC		2	2	1	2	2	2.00	0	0	72	71	1	71.00	1-54	0	0	5.91	0	
FC	1989	16	13	9	30	14*	7.50	0	0	1988	1163	33	35.24	7-61	2	0	3.51	2	
SC	1990	4	3	1	3	2	1.50	0	0	138	114	2	57.00	1-23	0	0	4.95	1	
AUSTEN, Michael Hubert (Otago) b Cape Town, South Africa 17.5.1964 RHB LM																		
FC		5	10	1	252	100*	28.00	1	1	354	146	2	73.00	1-13	0	0	2.47	7	
FC	1982	66	120	8	3619	202*	32.31	6	16	3836	1813	55	32.96	5-71	1	0	2.83	48	
SC	1990	44	44	1	1072	95*	24.93	0	7	1211	842	33	25.51	4-47	1	0	4.17	11	
AUSTIN, Eric (Central Districts) b Wanganui 5.4.1974 LHB WK																		
FC		7	9	3	59	24*	9.83	0	0									20	2
SC	1995	5	5	3	18	5*	9.00	0	0									8	
BAILEY, Mark David (Northern Districts) b Hamilton 26.11.1970 RHB RM																		
FC		9	14	0	306	101	21.85	1	0	120	48	1	48.00	1-26	0	0	2.40	9	
SC		12	12	1	287	76	26.09	0	1	287	225	4	56.25	1-17	0	0	4.70	7	
FC	1989	48	70	5	1721	122	26.47	3	8	330	132	3	44.00	2-27	0	0	2.40	42	
SC	1989	54	53	10	1154	76	26.83	0	4	557	424	10	42.40	2-25	0	0	4.56	21	
BARNES, Aaron Craig (Auckland) b Turangi 21.12.1971 RHB RM																		
FC		8	16	1	438	89*	29.20	0	3	579	336	9	37.33	3-37	0	0	3.48	5	
SC		9	9	0	264	77	29.33	0	3	229	159	8	19.87	4-18	1	0	4.16	4	
FC	1993	23	37	3	906	100*	26.64	1	4	1245	700	17	41.17	3-23	0	0	3.37	14	
SC	1993	39	38	3	760	77	21.71	0	4	889	672	25	26.88	4-18	2	0	4.53	14	
BARTLETT, Craig Edward (Central Districts) b Nelson 9.10.1975 RHB RFM																		
FC		1	2	2	0	0*		0	0	108	75	0					4.16	0	
BARTON, Hamish Dymock (Auckland) b Gisborne 16.7.1976 LHB OB																		
FC		7	14	3	198	76*	18.00	0	1	548	261	6	43.50	3-60	0	0	2.85	2	
SC		2	2	1	10	9	10.00	0	0	60	48	0					4.80	3	
FC	1995	9	18	5	286	76*	22.00	0	2	800	387	10	38.70	3-60	0	0	2.88	3	
BELL, Matthew David (Northern Districts) b Dunedin 25.2.1977 RHB OB																		
FC		8	13	1	380	73	31.66	0	3									11	
SC		9	9	1	201	51*	25.12	0	1									2	
FC	1993	22	37	3	1109	83	32.61	0	9									20	
SC	1995	14	14	1	278	51*	21.38	0	1									3	
BENNETT, Dion Rodger Turoa (Northern Districts) b Thames 1.8.1974 RHB RM																		
FC		3	6	5	25	15*	25.00	0	0	426	189	4	47.25	2-55	0	0	2.66	3	

Cmp	Debut	M	I	NO	Runs	HS	Avge	100	50	Balls	Runs	Wkts	Avge	BB	5i	10m	RpO	ct	st
	BLACKMORE, Selwyn John (Wellington) b Whangarei 7.9.1972 RHB RM																		
FC		6	12	1	272	102	24.72	1	1									4	
FC	1991	11	21	2	507	107*	26.68	2	1									8	
	BOND, Shane Edward (Canterbury) b Christchurch 7.6.1975 RHB RFM																		
FC		5	5	3	25	10*	12.50	0	0	1050	530	21	25.23	5-59	1	0	3.02	0	
	BRADBURN, Grant Eric (Northern Districts) b Hamilton 26.5.1966 RHB OB																		
FC		8	12	1	362	148*	32.90	1	1	1253	435	15	29.00	4-12	0	0	2.08	12	
SC		2	2	0	22	19	11.00	0	0	60	44	3	14.66	3-44	0	0	4.40	1	
Test	1990	5	9	2	105	30*	15.00	0	0	615	336	5	67.20	3-134	0	0	3.27	4	
FC	1985	87	142	19	3615	148*	29.39	3	21	14141	6013	178	33.78	6-56	3	0	2.55	85	
Int	1990	7	7	1	57	30	9.50	0	0	234	195	4	48.75	2-18	0	0	5.00	1	
SC	1986	67	61	5	1077	80*	19.23	0	2	2662	1691	42	40.26	3-28	0	0	3.81	37	
	BROWN, Christopher Mark (Auckland) b Rarotonga, Cook Islands 27.3.1973 RHB RFM																		
FC		4	6	0	23	8	3.83	0	0	528	257	12	21.41	5-21	1	0	2.92	0	
SC		8	5	2	31	10*	10.33	0	0	363	229	15	15.26	5-16	1	2	3.78	5	
FC	1993	17	24	7	96	16*	5.64	0	0	2707	1197	63	19.00	6-50	3	1	2.65	2	
SC	1993	19	8	3	45	13	9.00	0	0	903	595	22	27.04	5-16	1	2	3.95	6	
	BULFIN, Carl Edward (Central Districts) b Blenheim 19.8.1973 RHB RFM																		
FC		6	8	2	41	20	6.83	0	0	774	420	17	24.70	5-53	2	1	3.25	3	
SC		7	5	1	32	13	8.00	0	0	356	298	12	24.83	3-15	0	0	5.02	2	
	CAIRNS, Christopher Lance (Canterbury, New Zealand, New Zealand to Pakistan, New Zealand to Sharjah, New Zealand to India) b Picton 13.6.1970 RHB RFM																		
Test		5	9	0	292	70	32.44	0	4	312	146	2	73.00	1-12	0	0	2.80	2	
FC		6	10	0	349	70	34.90	0	5	312	146	2	73.00	1-12	0	0	2.80	2	
Int		7	7	0	191	79	27.28	0	2	24	25	0					6.25	2	
SC		11	9	3	274	113	45.66	1	0	459	276	19	14.52	6-37	0	1	3.60	2	
Test	1989	23	39	0	1084	120	27.79	1	9	3935	2206	60	36.76	6-52	3	0	3.36	11	
FC	1988	141	217	24	6784	120	35.15	7	49	22407	11862	410	28.93	8-47	16	3	3.17	65	
Int	1990	67	63	5	1521	103	26.22	1	7	2472	1883	58	32.46	4-55	1	0	4.57	25	
SC	1988	52	47	7	1505	143	37.62	3	8	2225	1439	64	22.48	6-37	3	2	3.88	12	
	CAMPBELL, Paul Adrian (Otago) b Dunedin 11.2.1968 RHB LM WK																		
SC		7	6	1	81	51*	16.20	0	1									6	
FC	1989	3	6	1	89	37	17.80	0	0	18	9	1	9.00	1-9	0	0	3.00	2	
	CHANDLER, Philip John Barry (Wellington, New Zealand A) b Wellington 6.7.1972 LHB																		
FC		8	15	1	466	177	33.28	1	1									8	
SC		11	11	1	496	106	49.60	1	2									5	
FC	1994	16	30	3	711	177	26.33	1	1									9	
SC	1995	19	19	1	797	106	44.27	1	4									8	
	CLARK, Michael James (Auckland) b Auckland 7.7.1966 LHB																		
FC		2	4	0	62	42	15.50	0	0									2	
FC	1990	6	10	0	158	64	15.80	0	1	36	12	1	12.00	1-5	0	0	2.00	4	
SC	1993	1	1	0	2	2	2.00	0	0									0	
	COOPER, David Mark (Central Districts) b Wanganui 18.2.1972 RHB RSM																		
FC		3	5	1	96	48	24.00	0	0	54	31	0					3.44	0	
SC		1																1	
FC	1993	4	7	1	148	48	24.66	0	0	126	65	1	65.00	1-34	0	0	3.09	0	
SC	1993	7	5	3	56	15*	28.00	0	0	78	82	2	41.00	1-23	0	0	6.30	4	
	CROY, Martyn Gilbert (Otago) b Hamilton 23.1.1974 RHB WK																		
FC		6	12	1	157	35	14.27	0	0									23	
SC		1	1	1	10	10*		0	0									0	
FC	1994	19	33	1	560	104	17.50	1	1									55	2
SC	1994	16	16	3	253	74	19.46	0	1									12	5
	CUMMING, Craig Derek (Canterbury) b Timaru 31.8.1975 RHB																		
FC		6	9	1	287	90*	35.87	0	2	36	24	0					4.00	4	
SC		2	1	0	24	24	24.00	0	0	6	9	0					9.00	2	
FC	1995	11	19	1	507	90*	28.16	0	2	36	24	0					4.00	6	
SC	1993	5	3	0	30	24	10.00	0	0	6	9	0					9.00	3	
	DAVIS, Heath Te-Ihí-O-Te-Rangi (Wellington, New Zealand, New Zealand A, New Zealand to India) b Lower Hutt 30.11.1971 RHB RF																		
Test		3	4	2	19	8*	9.50	0	0	686	304	11	27.63	5-63	1	0	2.65	3	
FC		8	12	4	80	21*	10.00	0	0	1658	769	29	26.51	5-63	1	0	2.78	5	
Int		7	5	3	13	7*	6.50	0	0	330	292	11	26.54	4-35	0	0	5.30	0	
SC		1								60	43	1	43.00	1-43	0	0	4.30	1	
Test	1994	4	6	4	19	8*	9.50	0	0	812	397	12	33.08	5-63	1	0	2.93	3	
FC	1991	49	58	27	390	38*	12.58	0	0	8215	4794	164	29.23	5-32	6	0	3.50	19	
Int	1992	11	6	4	13	7*	6.50	0	0	432	436	11	39.63	4-35	1	0	6.05	2	
SC	1992	13	7	4	45	21	15.00	0	0	582	406	12	33.83	3-44	0	0	4.18	5	

Cmp	Debut	M	I	NO	Runs	HS	Avge	100	50	Balls	Runs	Wkts	Avge	BB	5i	10m	RpO	ct	st

DE SILVA, Pinnaduwage Aravinda (Auckland, Sri Lanka, Sri Lanka to New Zealand, Sri Lanka to West Indies, Sri Lanka to Kenya, Sri Lanka to Sharjah, Sri Lanka to India) b Colombo, Ceylon 17.10.1965 RHB OB

Cmp	Debut	M	I	NO	Runs	HS	Avge	100	50	Balls	Runs	Wkts	Avge	BB	5i	10m	RpO	ct	st
SC		9	9	2	367	106*	52.42	1	1	168	122	6	20.33	2-38	0	0	4.35	1	
Test	1984	61	107	6	3828	267	37.90	11	14	1227	639	17	37.58	3-39	0	0	3.12	27	
FC	1983	163	255	23	10963	267	47.25	31	51	5589	2471	72	34.31	7-24	4	0	2.65	85	
Int	1983	210	204	21	6601	145	36.07	8	45	3206	2586	65	39.78	3-36	0	0	4.83	63	

DOODY, Brad James Kelvin (Canterbury) b Rangiora 17.8.1973 LHB LB

Cmp	Debut	M	I	NO	Runs	HS	Avge	100	50	Balls	Runs	Wkts	Avge	BB	5i	10m	RpO	ct	st
FC		7	11	0	295	93	26.81	0	2									8	
SC		6	6	1	142	83*	28.40	0	1									2	
FC	1995	9	15	0	405	93	27.00	0	3	9	6	0					4.00	10	

DOUGLAS, Mark William (Central Districts) b Nelson 20.10.1968 LHB WK

Cmp	Debut	M	I	NO	Runs	HS	Avge	100	50	Balls	Runs	Wkts	Avge	BB	5i	10m	RpO	ct	st
SC		9	9	0	191	59	21.22	0	2									4	
FC	1987	65	116	16	3386	144	33.86	6	23	72	120	4	30.00	2-29	0	0	10.00	57	
Int	1993	6	6	0	55	30	9.16	0	0									2	
SC	1988	61	60	5	1323	93*	24.05	0	7									24	

DOULL, Simon Blair (New Zealand, Northern Districts, New Zealand to Pakistan, New Zealand to Sharjah) b Pukekohe 6.8.1969 RHB RM

Cmp	Debut	M	I	NO	Runs	HS	Avge	100	50	Balls	Runs	Wkts	Avge	BB	5i	10m	RpO	ct	st
Test		5	8	0	82	26	10.25	0	0	1053	492	21	23.42	5-58	2	0	2.80	5	
FC		5	8	0	82	26	10.25	0	0	1053	492	21	23.42	5-58	2	0	2.80	5	
Int		6	4	1	54	22	18.00	0	0	239	199	6	33.16	2-33	0	0	4.99	3	
SC		9	8	1	50	20*	7.14	0	0	486	313	6	52.16	2-28	0	0	3.86	4	
Test	1992	18	30	5	338	31*	13.52	0	0	3444	1740	64	27.18	5-46	5	0	3.03	14	
FC	1989	60	73	15	978	108	16.86	1	1	9638	4620	178	25.95	6-37	11	1	2.87	24	
Int	1992	22	18	8	136	22	13.60	0	0	959	865	19	45.52	3-42	0	0	5.41	5	
SC	1989	41	33	9	186	20*	7.75	0	0	1945	1306	38	34.36	3-21	0	0	4.02	16	

DRUM, Christopher John (Auckland) b Auckland 10.7.1974 RHB RFM

Cmp	Debut	M	I	NO	Runs	HS	Avge	100	50	Balls	Runs	Wkts	Avge	BB	5i	10m	RpO	ct	st
FC		8	14	4	48	20	4.80	0	0	1192	523	30	17.43	6-47	1	0	2.63	3	

FINDLAY, Craig Owen (Central Districts) b Waipukurau 17.8.1971 RHB RM

Cmp	Debut	M	I	NO	Runs	HS	Avge	100	50	Balls	Runs	Wkts	Avge	BB	5i	10m	RpO	ct	st
FC		3	5	0	91	30	18.20	0	0	492	219	5	43.80	2-57	0	0	2.67	0	
SC		9	7	1	57	43*	9.50	0	0	392	271	3	90.33	1-38	0	0	4.14	4	
FC	1995	8	11	3	224	52	28.00	0	1	1155	520	17	30.58	2-19	0	0	2.70	6	
SC	1995	15	12	1	97	43*	8.81	0	0	739	457	18	25.38	4-21	2	0	3.71	5	

FLEMING, Stephen Paul (Canterbury, New Zealand, New Zealand to Pakistan, New Zealand to Sharjah, New Zealand to India) b Christchurch 1.4.1973 LHB RSM

Cmp	Debut	M	I	NO	Runs	HS	Avge	100	50	Balls	Runs	Wkts	Avge	BB	5i	10m	RpO	ct	st
Test		5	9	0	324	129	36.00	1	3									9	
FC		6	10	0	390	129	39.00	1	4	12	0	0					0.00	10	
Int		7	7	0	182	42	26.00	0	0									3	
SC		11	9	1	292	105*	36.50	1	1									7	
Test	1993	27	47	2	1649	129	36.64	1	13									32	
FC	1991	65	106	9	3847	151	39.65	8	22	90	110	0					7.33	70	
Int	1993	65	64	5	1798	106*	30.47	1	11	29	28	1	28.00	1-8	0	0	5.79	28	
SC	1992	35	31	5	886	105*	34.07	2	4									17	

FORREST, James Cameron (Auckland) b Auckland 16.6.1974 LHB RM

Cmp	Debut	M	I	NO	Runs	HS	Avge	100	50	Balls	Runs	Wkts	Avge	BB	5i	10m	RpO	ct	st
FC		6	12	0	133	34	11.08	0	0									2	

FREW, Robert Mathew (Canterbury) b Darfield 28.12.1970 RHB

Cmp	Debut	M	I	NO	Runs	HS	Avge	100	50	Balls	Runs	Wkts	Avge	BB	5i	10m	RpO	ct	st
FC		2	2	0	11	9	5.50	0	0									1	
FC	1995	7	12	1	277	125	25.18	1	1									3	
SC	1995	9	7	3	114	37*	28.50	0	0									3	

FURLONG, Campbell James Marie (Central Districts) b Napier 16.6.1974 RHB OB

Cmp	Debut	M	I	NO	Runs	HS	Avge	100	50	Balls	Runs	Wkts	Avge	BB	5i	10m	RpO	ct	st
FC		6	9	1	179	39	22.37	0	0	1492	795	16	48.43	7-72	1	0	3.11	7	
FC	1994	14	20	2	332	48	18.44	0	0	3614	1794	41	43.75	7-72	1	0	2.97	14	
SC	1994	4	3	0	83	37	27.66	0	0	150	119	4	29.75	2-41	0	0	4.76	0	

GAFFANEY, Christopher Blair (Otago) b Dunedin 30.11.1975 RHB

Cmp	Debut	M	I	NO	Runs	HS	Avge	100	50	Balls	Runs	Wkts	Avge	BB	5i	10m	RpO	ct	st
FC		9	18	2	642	194	40.12	2	2									10	
SC		10	10	0	191	73	19.10	0	1									2	
FC	1995	13	26	2	761	194	31.70	2	3									18	
SC	1995	20	20	0	415	73	20.75	0	1									4	

GALE, Aaron James (Otago) b Balclutha 8.4.1970 RHB RM

Cmp	Debut	M	I	NO	Runs	HS	Avge	100	50	Balls	Runs	Wkts	Avge	BB	5i	10m	RpO	ct	st
FC		7	11	2	132	44	14.66	0	0	1372	595	20	29.75	4-43	0	0	2.60	3	
SC		4	3	3	14	14*		0	0	208	148	5	29.60	2-42	0	0	4.26	0	
FC	1989	49	76	24	718	60	13.80	0	1	8353	3382	129	26.21	6-42	3	0	2.42	14	
SC	1989	49	35	20	160	18*	10.66	0	0	2578	1706	67	25.46	5-43	2	1	3.97	9	

GARNER, Craig Douglas (Central Districts) b Porirua 12.7.1971 RHB OB

Cmp	Debut	M	I	NO	Runs	HS	Avge	100	50	Balls	Runs	Wkts	Avge	BB	5i	10m	RpO	ct	st
FC		5	8	0	59	25	7.37	0	0	1	4	0					24.00	5	
FC	1992	10	17	1	150	37	9.37	0	0	1	4	0					24.00	9	
SC	1993	7	7	0	159	87	22.71	0	2									3	

Cmp	Debut	M	I	NO	Runs	HS	Avge	100	50	Balls	Runs	Wkts	Avge	BB	5i	10m	RpO	ct	st

GERMON, Lee Kenneth (Canterbury, New Zealand, New Zealand to Pakistan, New Zealand to Sharjah) b Christchurch 4.11.1968 RHB WK

Cmp	Debut	M	I	NO	Runs	HS	Avge	100	50	Balls	Runs	Wkts	Avge	BB	5i	10m	RpO	ct	st
Test		2	4	0	48	14	12.00	0	0									3	1
FC		3	6	0	66	16	11.00	0	0									8	1
Int		5	5	0	44	22	8.80	0	0									4	2
SC		10	6	0	127	60	21.16	0	1									16	1
Test	1995	12	21	3	382	55	21.22	0	1									27	2
FC	1987	93	127	35	2749	160*	29.88	4	8	10	12	1	12.00	1-12	0	0	7.20	235	26
Int	1994	37	31	5	519	89	19.96	0	3									21	9
SC	1987	64	45	14	599	71	19.32	0	2									69	18

GREATBATCH, Mark John (Central Districts, New Zealand Selection XI, New Zealand to Pakistan, New Zealand to Sharjah) b Auckland 11.12.1963 LHB WK

Cmp	Debut	M	I	NO	Runs	HS	Avge	100	50	Balls	Runs	Wkts	Avge	BB	5i	10m	RpO	ct	st
FC		6	10	0	321	141	32.10	1	1									8	
SC		8	8	1	137	57	19.57	0	2									4	
Test	1987	41	71	5	2021	146*	30.62	3	10	6	0	0					0.00	27	
FC	1982	161	278	30	9445	202*	38.08	23	41	153	118	1	118.00	1-23	0	0	4.62	138	
Int	1987	84	83	5	2206	111	28.28	2	13	6	5	0					5.00	35	
SC	1982	57	56	5	1559	84	30.56	0	13	1	4	0					24.00	34	

HAMILTON, Lance John (Central Districts) b Papakura 5.4.1973 RHB LFM

Cmp	Debut	M	I	NO	Runs	HS	Avge	100	50	Balls	Runs	Wkts	Avge	BB	5i	10m	RpO	ct	st
FC		4	5	2	42	23	14.00	0	0	786	429	14	30.64	4-26	0	0	3.27	3	

HARRIS, Chris Zinzan (Canterbury, New Zealand A, New Zealand, New Zealand to Pakistan, New Zealand to Sharjah, New Zealand to India) b Christchurch 20.11.1969 LHB RM

Cmp	Debut	M	I	NO	Runs	HS	Avge	100	50	Balls	Runs	Wkts	Avge	BB	5i	10m	RpO	ct	st
FC		5	7	1	835	251*	139.16	3	2	759	244	10	24.40	4-22	0	0	1.92	10	
Int		7	7	2	160	48*	32.00	0	0	348	171	9	19.00	3-20	0	0	2.94	1	
SC		11	9	3	163	52*	27.16	0	1	495	310	12	25.83	3-23	0	0	3.75	5	
Test	1992	9	18	1	191	56	11.23	0	1	756	375	7	53.57	2-57	0	0	2.97	4	
FC	1989	56	92	24	3309	251*	48.66	7	16	5658	2340	62	37.74	4-22	0	0	2.48	39	
Int	1990	85	76	19	1402	130	24.59	1	3	3824	2738	86	31.83	5-42	0	1	4.29	26	
SC	1989	50	48	14	1302	94*	38.29	0	7	2001	1198	48	24.95	3-7	0	0	3.59	23	

HART, Matthew Norman (Northern Districts, New Zealand to Pakistan) b Hamilton 16.5.1972 LHB SLA

Cmp	Debut	M	I	NO	Runs	HS	Avge	100	50	Balls	Runs	Wkts	Avge	BB	5i	10m	RpO	ct	st
FC		7	12	0	227	61	18.91	0	2	629	205	6	34.16	3-26	0	0	1.95	4	
SC		10	10	1	169	100	18.77	1	0	509	348	14	24.85	3-31	0	0	4.10	5	
Test	1993	14	24	4	175	45	17.65	0	0	3086	1438	29	49.58	5-77	1	0	2.79	9	
FC	1990	77	105	13	1747	87*	18.98	0	6	13037	5852	168	34.83	6-73	6	0	2.69	70	
Int	1993	11	6	0	49	16	8.16	0	0	548	347	13	26.69	5-22	0	1	3.79	7	
SC	1990	41	37	8	626	100	21.58	1	3	1634	1071	34	31.50	3-29	0	0	3.93	21	

HART, Robert Garry (Northern Districts) b Hamilton 2.12.1974 RHB WK

Cmp	Debut	M	I	NO	Runs	HS	Avge	100	50	Balls	Runs	Wkts	Avge	BB	5i	10m	RpO	ct	st
FC		9	13	1	299	78	24.91	0	1									23	1
SC		12	10	4	243	56	40.50	0	2									10	1
FC	1992	33	49	6	939	78	21.83	0	4									93	10
SC	1993	47	32	12	405	56	20.25	0	2									36	9

HARTLAND, Blair Robert (Canterbury) b Christchurch 22.10.1966 RHB

Cmp	Debut	M	I	NO	Runs	HS	Avge	100	50	Balls	Runs	Wkts	Avge	BB	5i	10m	RpO	ct	st
FC		3	3	0	42	30	14.00	0	0									2	
Test	1992	9	18	0	303	52	16.83	0	1									5	
FC	1986	83	150	8	3753	150	26.42	5	19									52	
Int	1992	16	16	1	311	68*	20.73	0	2									5	
SC	1988	42	42	2	1177	161	29.42	2	5	18	22	1	22.00	1-14	0	0	7.33	12	

HASLAM, Mark James (Auckland, New Zealand Selection XI) b Bury, England 26.9.1972 LHB SLA

Cmp	Debut	M	I	NO	Runs	HS	Avge	100	50	Balls	Runs	Wkts	Avge	BB	5i	10m	RpO	ct	st
FC		7	13	1	103	20	8.58	0	0	930	441	8	55.12	2-22	0	0	2.84	1	
SC		6	1	0	2	2	2.00	0	0	324	182	7	26.00	2-26	0	0	3.37	2	
Test	1992	4	2	1	4	3	4.00	0	0	493	245	2	122.50	1-33	0	0	2.98	2	
FC	1991	42	47	16	258	30*	8.32	0	0	6787	3269	76	43.01	4-60	0	0	2.88	15	
Int	1992	1	1	0	9	9	9.00	0	0	30	28	1	28.00	1-28	0	0	5.60	0	
SC	1993	12	6	3	6	3*	2.00	0	0	552	339	10	33.90	2-26	0	0	3.68	2	

HASTINGS, Mark Andrew (Canterbury) b Christchurch 8.5.1968 RHB RM

Cmp	Debut	M	I	NO	Runs	HS	Avge	100	50	Balls	Runs	Wkts	Avge	BB	5i	10m	RpO	ct	st
FC		4	4	1	101	52	33.66	0	1	631	221	10	22.10	4-37	0	0	2.10	1	
FC	1992	6	8	2	137	52	22.83	0	1	925	351	14	25.07	4-30	0	0	2.27	1	
SC	1992	14	11	3	95	31	11.87	0	0	727	350	16	21.87	3-13	0	0	2.88	5	

HAYDEN, Simon Christopher (Auckland) b Ashford, Kent, England 26.10.1970 RHB

Cmp	Debut	M	I	NO	Runs	HS	Avge	100	50	Balls	Runs	Wkts	Avge	BB	5i	10m	RpO	ct	st
FC		1	2	0	3	3	1.50	0	0	2	1	0					3.00	1	
SC		1	1	0	8	8	8.00	0	0									0	

HENRY, Paul James (Otago) b Mataura 16.10.1970 RHB WK

Cmp	Debut	M	I	NO	Runs	HS	Avge	100	50	Balls	Runs	Wkts	Avge	BB	5i	10m	RpO	ct	st
FC		2	2	0	9	9	4.50	0	0									6	

HORE, Andrew John (Otago) b Oamaru 18.6.1969 LHB

Cmp	Debut	M	I	NO	Runs	HS	Avge	100	50	Balls	Runs	Wkts	Avge	BB	5i	10m	RpO	ct	st
FC		2	2	0	10	10	5.00	0	0									2	
SC		3	2	0	37	24	18.50	0	0									0	

Cmp	Debut	M	I	NO	Runs	HS	Avge	100	50	Balls	Runs	Wkts	Avge	BB	5i	10m	RpO	ct	st

HORNE, Matthew Jeffery (Otago, New Zealand, New Zealand A, New Zealand Selection XI, New Zealand to India) b Takapuna 5.2.1970 RHB RM

Test		3	5	0	158	66	31.60	0	1	60	22	0					2.20	2	
FC		10	17	0	843	124	49.58	3	4	180	71	0					2.36	14	
Int		2	2	0	27	14	13.50	0	0									0	
SC		10	10	0	189	40	18.90	0	0	456	317	7	45.28	2-33	0	0	4.17	3	
FC	1992	18	31	0	1302	190	42.00	5	4	240	82	0					2.05	20	
Int	1996	5	5	0	136	45	27.20	0	0									0	
SC	1992	24	23	0	423	67	18.39	0	1	480	341	8	42.62	2-33	0	0	4.26	3	

HOTTER, Stephen John (Wellington) b New Plymouth 2.12.1969 RHB LFM

FC		7	11	1	74	33	7.40	0	0	1379	641	30	21.26	6-69	3	1	2.78	2	
SC		3	1	1	1	1*		0	0	126	121	2	60.50	2-45	0	0	5.76	3	
FC	1988	17	24	5	177	33	9.31	0	0	2971	1522	56	27.17	6-69	3	1	3.07	8	
SC	1995	9	6	4	14	5*	7.00	0	0	420	315	9	35.00	2-14	0	0	4.50	3	

HOWELL, Llorne Gregory (Central Districts, New Zealand A, New Zealand Selection XI) b Napier 8.7.1972 RHB RM

FC		10	19	2	604	91	35.52	0	4	60	42	0					4.20	1	
SC		9	9	2	359	111*	51.28	1	3									1	
FC	1990	57	93	11	2737	181	33.37	3	17	150	110	0					4.40	31	
SC	1991	44	44	10	1292	115*	38.00	3	9	12	9	0					4.50	11	

IRVING, Richard John Robert (Auckland) b Christchurch 19.9.1969 LHB WK

FC		2	3	0	18	15	6.00	0	0									2	1
SC	1995	1	1	1	0	0*		0	0									0	1

JARVIS, Paul William (Wellington, Sussex) b Redcar, England 29.6.1965 RHB RFM

SC		9	8	4	49	13*	12.25	0	0	495	346	18	19.22	3-40	0	0	4.19	1	
Test	1987	9	15	2	132	29*	10.15	0	0	1912	965	21	45.95	4-107	0	0	3.02	2	
FC	1981	201	252	66	3189	80	17.14	0	10	33444	17786	621	28.64	7-55	22	3	3.19	59	
Int	1987	16	8	2	31	16*	5.16	0	0	879	672	24	28.00	5-35	1	1	4.58	1	

JEFFERSON, Mark Robin (Wellington) b Oamaru 28.6.1976 LHB SLA

FC		7	13	5	186	35*	23.25	0	0	1434	575	12	47.91	3-41	0	0	2.40	0	
SC		11	7	4	29	10*	9.66	0	0	498	309	10	30.90	3-42	0	0	3.72	3	

JONAS, Glenn Ralph (Wellington) b Carterton 13.8.1970 RHB RM

FC		4	7	2	10	4	2.00	0	0	683	401	15	26.73	4-49	0	0	3.52	1	
SC		9	3	1	2	2	1.00	0	0	434	357	10	35.70	2-33	0	0	4.93	1	
FC	1993	22	33	8	127	14	5.08	0	0	4279	1967	84	23.41	5-60	1	0	2.75	7	
SC	1993	38	13	8	17	6*	3.40	0	0	1942	1406	60	23.43	4-29	2	0	4.34	12	

JONES, Richard Andrew (Auckland) b Auckland 22.10.1973 RHB

FC		8	16	0	455	99	28.43	0	4									11	
SC		3	3	0	37	26	12.33	0	0									1	
FC	1993	25	46	3	1102	99	25.62	0	8									24	
SC	1992	22	22	2	336	46*	16.80	0	0									5	

KENNEDY, Robert John (Otago, New Zealand A, New Zealand Selection XI, New Zealand to Pakistan) b Dunedin 3.6.1972 RHB RM

FC		8	10	3	50	17*	7.14	0	0	1249	563	25	22.52	4-44	0	0	2.70	4	
SC		7	5	1	19	12	4.75	0	0	414	395	8	49.37	4-47	1	0	5.72	4	
Test	1995	4	5	1	28	22	7.00	0	0	636	380	6	63.33	3-28	0	0	3.58	2	
FC	1993	22	28	7	120	22	5.71	0	0	3383	1669	57	29.28	4-22	0	0	2.96	10	
Int	1995	7	4	3	17	8*	17.00	0	0	312	283	5	56.60	2-36	0	0	5.44	1	
SC	1995	15	11	5	36	12	6.00	0	0	858	709	22	32.22	4-29	3	0	4.95	6	

KERR, Robert James (Wellington) b Wellington 6.4.1966 RHB WK

FC		2	3	0	39	29	13.00	0	0									0	
SC		11	10	0	152	50	15.20	0	1									3	
FC	1993	5	9	0	102	29	11.33	0	0									3	
SC	1993	43	39	12	852	61	31.55	0	3									11	

KING, Richard Terrence (Auckland) b Wellington 23.4.1973 RHB RSM

FC		4	8	0	137	52	17.12	0	1	4	6	0					9.00	3	
FC	1991	15	30	1	513	117*	17.68	1	2	32	16	0					3.00	8	
SC	1994	3	3	0	34	24	11.33	0	0									2	

LAMASON, David William (Central Districts) b Wanganui 23.4.1971 LHB RFM

FC		3	6	2	18	7*	4.50	0	0	541	208	6	34.66	2-62	0	0	2.30	1	
SC		2	1	0	8	8*	8.00	0	0	48	43	0					5.37	1	
FC	1990	5	7	3	20	7*	5.00	0	0	805	363	9	40.33	2-62	0	0	2.70	1	
SC	1993	21	14	4	194	30	19.40	0	0	810	560	17	32.94	3-23	0	0	4.14	5	

LAMONT, Michael James (Otago) b Invercargill 16.1.1967 LHB

FC		3	4	0	17	8	4.25	0	0									2	
SC		10	10	1	227	60	25.22	0	2									1	
FC	1990	29	55	1	1134	127	21.00	1	5	162	128	2	64.00	1-49	0	0	4.74	20	
SC	1990	30	30	3	827	88	30.62	0	8									5	

LANE, Michael Edward Landon (Canterbury) b Blenheim 31.1.1969 RHB WK

Cmp	Debut	M	I	NO	Runs	HS	Avge	100	50	Balls	Runs	Wkts	Avge	BB	5i	10m	RpO	ct	st
FC		6	7	0	121	61	17.28	0	1									13	1
SC		3	2	0	7	7	3.50	0	0									2	
FC	1990	22	34	3	482	84	15.54	0	3									36	2
SC	1995	6	4	2	29	15*	14.50	0	0									7	1

LARSEN, Gavin Rolf (Wellington, New Zealand, New Zealand to Pakistan, New Zealand to Sharjah, New Zealand to India) b Wellington 27.9.1962 RHB RM

Cmp	Debut	M	I	NO	Runs	HS	Avge	100	50	Balls	Runs	Wkts	Avge	BB	5i	10m	RpO	ct	st
FC		3	6	0	211	76	35.16	0	2	347	162	7	23.14	5-33	1	0	2.80	5	
Int		7	6	1	72	26	14.40	0	0	321	187	8	23.37	3-20	0	0	3.49	2	
SC		11	9	2	103	38*	14.71	0	0	610	298	21	14.19	3-21	0	0	2.93	3	
Test	1994	8	13	4	127	26*	14.11	0	0	1967	689	24	28.70	3-57	0	0	2.10	5	
FC	1984	98	150	34	3302	161	28.46	1	17	12387	4536	153	29.64	6-37	5	0	2.19	67	
Int	1989	94	58	22	541	37	15.02	0	0	5020	3096	88	35.18	4-24	1	0	3.70	15	
SC	1984	80	67	16	918	66	18.00	0	1	4174	2109	81	26.03	5-30	1	1	3.03	30	

LAWSON, Robert Arthur (Otago) b Dunedin 14.9.1974 RHB OB

Cmp	Debut	M	I	NO	Runs	HS	Avge	100	50	Balls	Runs	Wkts	Avge	BB	5i	10m	RpO	ct	st
FC		9	18	2	549	98	34.31	0	3									2	
SC		10	10	1	150	63	16.66	0	1	14	5	0					2.14	6	
FC	1992	31	59	4	1493	200	27.14	2	6	24	14	1	14.00	1-13	0	0	3.50	12	
SC	1992	34	34	2	565	63	17.65	0	3	14	5	0					2.14	13	

LEE, Christopher David (Auckland) b Wellington 9.9.1971 RHB RFM

Cmp	Debut	M	I	NO	Runs	HS	Avge	100	50	Balls	Runs	Wkts	Avge	BB	5i	10m	RpO	ct	st
FC		1	2	1	6	6*	6.00	0	0	168	113	0					4.03	0	
FC	1991	9	13	6	174	111*	24.85	1	0	1489	786	18	43.66	3-34	0	0	3.16	0	
SC	1993	5	4	0	19	10	4.75	0	0	245	180	5	36.00	2-23	0	0	4.40	1	

LOVERIDGE, Greg Riaka (Central Districts) b Palmerston North 15.1.1975 RHB LB

Cmp	Debut	M	I	NO	Runs	HS	Avge	100	50	Balls	Runs	Wkts	Avge	BB	5i	10m	RpO	ct	st
FC		5	10	1	158	49*	17.55	0	0	897	472	11	42.90	4-23	0	0	3.15	2	
SC		8	6	2	84	49*	21.00	0	0	373	304	9	33.77	3-37	0	0	4.89	0	
Test	1995	1	1	1	4	4*		0	0									0	
FC	1994	9	15	2	231	49*	17.76	0	0	1479	775	20	38.75	4-23	0	0	3.14	3	
SC	1995	13	11	3	164	50*	20.50	0	1	595	424	16	26.50	4-25	1	0	4.27	0	

LYNCH, Stephen Michael (Auckland) b Auckland 18.2.1976 RHB

Cmp	Debut	M	I	NO	Runs	HS	Avge	100	50	Balls	Runs	Wkts	Avge	BB	5i	10m	RpO	ct	st
FC		8	16	1	536	94	35.73	0	6									5	
SC		9	9	2	258	65	36.85	0	3									1	
FC	1995	14	27	1	837	94	32.19	0	8									12	
SC	1995	19	19	2	426	65	25.05	0	4									2	

McHARDY, David Scott (Wellington) b Blenheim 21.11.1970 RHB LB

Cmp	Debut	M	I	NO	Runs	HS	Avge	100	50	Balls	Runs	Wkts	Avge	BB	5i	10m	RpO	ct	st
FC		3	6	0	96	46	16.00	0	0									8	
SC		1	1	0	9	9	9.00	0	0									1	
FC	1991	18	34	1	845	100	25.60	1	6	102	115	4	28.75	2-78	0	0	6.76	10	
SC	1992	18	17	1	253	48	15.81	0	0									5	

McMILLAN, Craig Douglas (Canterbury, New Zealand, New Zealand to India) b Christchurch 13.9.1976 RHB RM

Cmp	Debut	M	I	NO	Runs	HS	Avge	100	50	Balls	Runs	Wkts	Avge	BB	5i	10m	RpO	ct	st
FC		8	12	1	809	159	73.54	3	2	210	77	1	77.00	1-13	0	0	2.20	5	
SC		13	11	2	203	72*	22.55	0	1	138	129	6	21.50	5-38	0	1	5.60	3	
FC	1994	20	34	4	1435	159	47.83	4	5	534	261	3	87.00	1-0	0	0	2.93	10	
Int	1996	1	1	0	10	10	10.00	0	0									1	
SC	1994	32	30	4	856	114	32.92	2	3	143	133	6	22.16	5-38	0	1	5.58	15	

MATHER, Stephen Robert (Wellington) b Napier 13.8.1973 RHB RM

Cmp	Debut	M	I	NO	Runs	HS	Avge	100	50	Balls	Runs	Wkts	Avge	BB	5i	10m	RpO	ct	st
FC		1	2	0	10	10	5.00	0	0	78	47	1	47.00	1-47	0	0	3.61	0	
FC	1993	19	31	3	570	126	20.35	1	0	606	317	11	28.81	3-9	0	0	3.13	11	
SC	1993	24	21	1	364	40	18.20	0	0	108	71	4	17.75	2-27	0	0	3.94	11	

MAYNARD, Matthew Peter (Otago, Glamorgan) b Oldham, England 21.3.1966 RHB RM

Cmp	Debut	M	I	NO	Runs	HS	Avge	100	50	Balls	Runs	Wkts	Avge	BB	5i	10m	RpO	ct	st
FC		4	6	1	129	47*	25.80	0	0	18	13	0					4.33	2	
SC		10	10	0	177	40	17.70	0	0	180	158	2	79.00	1-20	0	0	5.26	4	
Test	1988	4	8	0	87	35	10.87	0	0									3	
FC	1985	288	473	52	18516	243	43.98	43	101	966	783	6	130.50	3-21	0	0	4.86	274	5
Int	1993	10	10	1	153	41	17.00	0	0									3	
SC	1990	21	21	2	572	101*	30.10	1	0	195	174	2	87.00	1-20	0	0	5.35	10	

MILLS, Jason Martin (Auckland, New Zealand A) b Auckland 12.8.1969 RHB WK

Cmp	Debut	M	I	NO	Runs	HS	Avge	100	50	Balls	Runs	Wkts	Avge	BB	5i	10m	RpO	ct	st
FC		8	14	3	165	40*	15.00	0	0									27	
SC		9	5	1	21	12	5.25	0	0									13	6
FC	1991	24	37	5	568	73*	17.75	0	1									76	1
SC	1992	21	13	5	57	13	7.12	0	0									29	8

MORLAND, Nathan Douglas (Otago) b Dunedin 20.12.1976 RHB OB

Cmp	Debut	M	I	NO	Runs	HS	Avge	100	50	Balls	Runs	Wkts	Avge	BB	5i	10m	RpO	ct	st
FC		3	4	2	37	16	18.50	0	0	597	239	3	79.66	2-163	0	0	2.40	0	
SC		6	4	1	13	8	4.33	0	0	354	238	5	47.60	3-43	0	0	4.03	0	

MORRISON, Daniel Kyle (Auckland, New Zealand, New Zealand Selection XI, New Zealand to Pakistan, New Zealand to Sharjah) b Auckland 3.2.1966 RHB RFM

Cmp	Debut	M	I	NO	Runs	HS	Avge	100	50	Balls	Runs	Wkts	Avge	BB	5i	10m	RpO	ct	st
Test		1	2	1	20	14*		0	0	148	104	3	34.66	3-104	0	0	4.21	0	
FC		7	14	6	150	30	18.75	0	0	1220	574	27	21.25	5-66	1	0	2.82	1	
SC		4	2	0	8	8	4.00	0	0	204	161	4	40.25	2-24	0	0	4.73	0	

Cmp	Debut	M	I	NO	Runs	HS	Avge	100	50	Balls	Runs	Wkts	Avge	BB	5i	10m	RpO	ct	st
Test	1987	48	71	26	379	42	8.42	0	0	10064	5549	160	34.68	7-89	10	0	3.30	14	
FC	1985	142	161	58	1127	46*	10.94	0	0	24896	13298	440	30.22	7-82	19	0	3.20	43	
Int	1987	96	43	24	171	20*	9.00	0	0	4586	3470	126	27.53	5-34	1	1	4.53	19	
SC	1986	37	17	7	100	30*	10.00	0	0	1699	1066	49	21.75	4-21	2	0	3.76	3	

MUIR, Glenn Andrew (Canterbury) b Dunedin 17.11.1971 LHB RM

Cmp	Debut	M	I	NO	Runs	HS	Avge	100	50	Balls	Runs	Wkts	Avge	BB	5i	10m	RpO	ct	st
FC		2	2	0	50	44	25.00	0	0	120	35	0						1.75	0
SC		5	3	1	76	39	38.00	0	0	192	143	7	20.42	3-24	0	0	4.46	0	
FC	1995	4	6	1	99	44	19.80	0	0	298	129	3	43.00	2-54	0	0	2.59	1	
SC	1994	10	5	2	86	39	28.66	0	0	492	349	15	23.26	3-24	0	0	4.25	2	

MURRAY, Darrin James (Canterbury, New Zealand A) b Christchurch 4.9.1967 RHB RM

Cmp	Debut	M	I	NO	Runs	HS	Avge	100	50	Balls	Runs	Wkts	Avge	BB	5i	10m	RpO	ct	st
FC		9	14	0	355	153	25.35	1	1									8	
SC		13	12	2	364	116	36.40	1	2									3	
Test	1994	8	16	1	303	52	20.20	0	1									6	
FC	1990	44	73	5	2555	182	37.57	6	12	90	84	0					5.60	28	
Int	1994	1	1	0	3	3	3.00	0	0									0	
SC	1992	26	25	3	644	116	29.27	1	3	12	13	0					6.50	8	

NASH, Dion Joseph (Northern Districts) b Auckland 20.11.1971 RHB RFM

Cmp	Debut	M	I	NO	Runs	HS	Avge	100	50	Balls	Runs	Wkts	Avge	BB	5i	10m	RpO	ct	st
FC		6	10	0	248	76	24.80	0	1	90	28	1	28.00	1-28	0	0	1.86	5	
Test	1992	14	21	6	236	56	15.73	0	1	2772	1308	44	29.72	6-76	2	1	2.83	7	
FC	1990	73	107	23	1589	76	18.91	0	6	10085	4887	169	28.91	6-30	7	1	2.90	35	
Int	1992	28	18	5	128	40*	9.84	0	0	1284	1024	26	39.38	3-26	0	0	4.78	6	
SC	1991	26	23	2	476	84	22.66	0	1	1346	808	41	19.70	5-44	1	1	3.60	8	

NEVIN, Christopher John (Wellington) b Dunedin 3.8.1975 RHB WK

Cmp	Debut	M	I	NO	Runs	HS	Avge	100	50	Balls	Runs	Wkts	Avge	BB	5i	10m	RpO	ct	st
FC		7	13	2	238	42	21.63	0	0									20	2
SC		11	8	2	63	21	10.50	0	0									20	2
FC	1995	13	23	4	501	86	26.36	0	1									53	3
SC	1995	15	11	4	71	21	10.14	0	0									25	3

O'CONNOR, Shayne Barry (Otago, New Zealand to India) b Hastings 15.11.1973 LHB LFM

Cmp	Debut	M	I	NO	Runs	HS	Avge	100	50	Balls	Runs	Wkts	Avge	BB	5i	10m	RpO	ct	st
FC		7	11	3	196	47	24.50	0	0	1145	602	28	21.50	6-55	2	1	3.15	4	
SC		9	7	2	66	22	13.20	0	0	509	401	16	25.06	4-54	1	0	4.72	1	
FC	1994	14	24	10	285	47	20.35	0	0	2677	1342	48	27.95	6-55	2	1	3.00	6	
Int	1996	1	1	0	0	0	0.00	0	0	54	44	3	14.66	3-44	0	0	4.88	0	
SC	1995	13	10	4	75	22	12.50	0	0	737	563	21	26.80	4-54	1	0	4.58	1	

O'DOWD, Alexander Patrick (Northern Districts) b Auckland 25.2.1967 RHB OB

Cmp	Debut	M	I	NO	Runs	HS	Avge	100	50	Balls	Runs	Wkts	Avge	BB	5i	10m	RpO	ct	st
FC		3	6	1	53	31*	10.60	0	0									6	
FC	1991	17	29	5	604	113	25.16	1	2									12	
SC	1992	9	8	0	85	29	10.62	0	0									5	

O'DOWDA, Karl Robert (Otago) b New Plymouth 8.5.1970 RHB RFM

Cmp	Debut	M	I	NO	Runs	HS	Avge	100	50	Balls	Runs	Wkts	Avge	BB	5i	10m	RpO	ct	st
FC		1	2	0	5	3	2.50	0	0	162	78	4	19.50	3-27	0	0	2.88	0	
SC		1	1	0	10	10	10.00	0	0	30	19	0					3.80	0	
FC	1988	8	11	5	33	19*	5.50	0	0	1197	672	16	42.00	3-27	0	0	3.36	3	
SC	1988	8	6	2	50	22*	12.50	0	0	265	232	8	29.00	3-35	0	0	5.25	1	

PARKER, Mark Moreton (Otago) b Timaru 2.10.1975 RHB

Cmp	Debut	M	I	NO	Runs	HS	Avge	100	50	Balls	Runs	Wkts	Avge	BB	5i	10m	RpO	ct	st
FC		3	6	0	50	14	8.33	0	0									5	

PARLANE, Michael Edward (Northern Districts) b Pukekohe 22.7.1972 RHB WK

Cmp	Debut	M	I	NO	Runs	HS	Avge	100	50	Balls	Runs	Wkts	Avge	BB	5i	10m	RpO	ct	st
FC		9	14	0	489	142	34.92	2	1									6	
SC		11	11	0	241	65	21.90	0	1	3	5	0					10.00	1	
FC	1992	28	49	3	1450	142	31.52	3	5									19	
SC	1992	40	40	1	1149	101	29.46	1	6	3	5	0					10.00	6	

PARLANE, Neal Ronald (Northern Districts) b Whangarei 9.8.1978 RHB

Cmp	Debut	M	I	NO	Runs	HS	Avge	100	50	Balls	Runs	Wkts	Avge	BB	5i	10m	RpO	ct	st
FC		1	2	0	6	5	3.00	0	0									0	
SC		2	2	0	43	28	21.50	0	0									0	

PARORE, Adam Craig (New Zealand, New Zealand Selection XI, Auckland, New Zealand to Pakistan, New Zealand to Sharjah, New Zealand to India) b Auckland 23.1.1971 RHB WK

Cmp	Debut	M	I	NO	Runs	HS	Avge	100	50	Balls	Runs	Wkts	Avge	BB	5i	10m	RpO	ct	st
Test		5	9	0	171	59	19.00	0	1									10	
FC		6	11	0	184	59	16.72	0	1									12	
Int		7	7	0	141	39	20.14	0	0									2	1
SC		8	8	0	191	61	23.87	0	2									1	
Test	1990	34	59	6	1304	100*	24.60	1	7									69	2
FC	1988	95	146	20	4092	155*	32.47	6	22	30	55	0					11.00	185	13
Int	1992	72	68	10	1936	108	33.37	1	10									37	10
SC	1991	34	32	2	696	79*	23.20	0	4									18	1

PATEL, Dipak Narshibhai (New Zealand, Auckland, New Zealand to Pakistan, New Zealand to Sharjah, New Zealand to India) b Nairobi, Kenya 25.10.1958 RHB OB

Cmp	Debut	M	I	NO	Runs	HS	Avge	100	50	Balls	Runs	Wkts	Avge	BB	5i	10m	RpO	ct	st
Test		4	7	1	92	45	15.33	0	0	720	313	6	52.16	2-67	0	0	2.60	4	
FC		4	7	1	92	45	15.33	0	0	720	313	6	52.16	2-67	0	0	2.60	4	
Int		3	3	2	41	24	41.00	0	0	84	72	2	36.00	1-29	0	0	5.14	1	
SC		8	8	0	100	26	12.50	0	0	357	259	8	32.37	2-33	0	0	4.35	7	

Cmp	Debut	M	I	NO	Runs	HS	Avge	100	50	Balls	Runs	Wkts	Avge	BB	5i	10m	RpO	ct	st
Test	1986	37	66	8	1200	99	20.68	0	5	6594	3154	75	42.05	6-50	3	0	2.86	15	
FC	1976	358	558	51	15188	204	29.95	26	66	47767	21737	654	33.23	7-46	27	2	2.73	193	
Int	1986	75	63	10	623	71	11.75	0	1	3251	2260	45	50.22	3-22	0	0	4.17	23	
SC	1986	60	58	1	1291	94	22.64	0	5	2706	1574	60	26.23	4-18	2	0	3.49	26	

PENN, Andrew Jonathan (Central Districts, New Zealand, New Zealand to India) b Wanganui 27.7.1974 RHB RFM

Cmp	Debut	M	I	NO	Runs	HS	Avge	100	50	Balls	Runs	Wkts	Avge	BB	5i	10m	RpO	ct	st
FC		6	11	1	66	17	6.60	0	0	1423	552	36	15.33	6-36	4	1	2.32	1	
Int		1	1	0	1	1	1.00	0	0	12	14	0					7.00	0	
SC		9	7	1	85	63	14.16	0	1	510	420	14	30.00	6-49	0	1	4.94	4	
FC	1994	17	24	6	248	90	13.77	0	1	3361	1576	64	24.62	6-36	4	1	2.81	2	
Int	1996	3	2	1	8	7*	8.00	0	0	99	123	1	123.00	1-50	0	0	7.45	0	
SC	1995	11	8	1	86	63	12.28	0	1	584	519	17	30.52	6-49	0	1	5.33	4	

PETERSON, Simon James (Auckland) b Auckland 17.11.1968 RHB RFM

Cmp	Debut	M	I	NO	Runs	HS	Avge	100	50	Balls	Runs	Wkts	Avge	BB	5i	10m	RpO	ct	st
FC		4	8	1	224	71	32.00	0	1	24	8	1	8.00	1-8	0	0	2.00	5	
SC		8	6	5	87	21*	87.00	0	0									2	
FC	1989	26	46	1	1033	77	22.95	0	5	318	170	5	34.00	2-42	0	0	3.20	26	
SC	1992	18	16	10	203	34*	33.83	0	0	54	39	0					4.33	5	

PETRIE, Richard George (Wellington) b Christchurch 23.8.1967 RHB RFM

Cmp	Debut	M	I	NO	Runs	HS	Avge	100	50	Balls	Runs	Wkts	Avge	BB	5i	10m	RpO	ct	st
FC		7	13	1	347	80	28.91	0	2	1085	458	17	26.94	4-32	0	0	2.53	3	
SC		11	10	0	139	36	13.90	0	0	444	347	14	24.78	3-36	0	0	4.68	1	
FC	1988	41	56	6	1094	100	21.88	1	4	6772	3175	110	28.86	5-23	3	0	2.81	18	
Int	1990	12	8	3	65	21	13.00	0	0	660	449	12	37.41	2-25	0	0	4.08	2	
SC	1988	65	53	7	950	85	20.65	0	5	2726	1972	74	26.64	5-24	2	1	4.34	9	

POCOCK, Blair Andrew (Northern Districts, New Zealand, New Zealand Selection XI) b Papakura 18.6.1971 RHB

Cmp	Debut	M	I	NO	Runs	HS	Avge	100	50	Balls	Runs	Wkts	Avge	BB	5i	10m	RpO	ct	st
Test		5	9	0	292	85	32.44	0	3	12	10	0					5.00	2	
FC		11	18	0	682	137	37.88	1	6	12	10	0					5.00	6	
SC		12	12	0	307	50	25.58	0	1									4	
Test	1993	11	21	0	427	85	20.33	0	3	24	20	0					5.00	3	
FC	1990	60	106	10	2898	139*	30.18	6	15	72	45	0					3.75	31	
SC	1992	27	27	1	732	117	28.15	1	3									8	

PRIEST, Mark Wellings (Canterbury) b Greymouth 12.8.1961 LHB SLA

Cmp	Debut	M	I	NO	Runs	HS	Avge	100	50	Balls	Runs	Wkts	Avge	BB	5i	10m	RpO	ct	st
FC		8	11	3	357	67*	44.62	0	4	2711	1023	41	24.95	6-146	3	0	2.26	8	
SC		13	7	4	115	35*	38.33	0	0	482	308	13	23.69	4-28	1	0	3.83	7	
Test	1990	1	1	0	26	26	26.00	0	0	72	26	1	26.00	1-26	0	0	2.16	0	
FC	1984	90	130	23	3465	119	32.38	4	25	21741	8880	275	32.29	9-95	11	3	2.45	57	
Int	1989	12	10	2	95	24	11.87	0	0	507	419	4	104.75	2-27	0	0	4.95	2	
SC	1987	65	45	14	423	35*	13.64	0	0	3166	1882	87	21.63	5-26	3	1	3.56	26	

PRINGLE, Christopher (Auckland) b Auckland 26.1.1968 RHB RFM

Cmp	Debut	M	I	NO	Runs	HS	Avge	100	50	Balls	Runs	Wkts	Avge	BB	5i	10m	RpO	ct	st
SC		1									36	33	1	33.00	1-33	0	0	5.50	0	
Test	1990	14	21	4	175	30	10.29	0	0	2985	1389	30	46.30	7-52	1	1	2.79	3	
FC	1989	63	75	13	795	47	12.82	0	0	12252	5617	194	28.95	7-52	7	2	2.75	15	
Int	1990	64	41	19	193	34*	8.77	0	0	3314	2459	103	23.87	5-45	2	1	4.45	7	
SC	1989	39	28	9	257	38*	13.52	0	0	1930	1204	56	21.50	4-30	2	0	3.74	8	

RICHARDSON, Mark Hunter (Otago) b Hastings 11.6.1971 LHB SLA

Cmp	Debut	M	I	NO	Runs	HS	Avge	100	50	Balls	Runs	Wkts	Avge	BB	5i	10m	RpO	ct	st
FC		9	16	1	423	98*	28.20	0	2	397	160	3	53.33	2-15	0	0	2.41	6	
SC		10	10	2	442	128*	55.25	2	1	263	200	2	100.00	2-51	0	0	4.56	4	
FC	1989	42	71	13	1899	146	32.74	5	4	3168	1476	28	52.71	5-77	1	0	2.79	20	
SC	1990	32	30	2	868	128*	31.00	2	4	641	469	9	52.11	2-25	0	0	4.39	10	

ROBINSON, Shane Andrew (Otago) b Dunedin 24.8.1967 RHB WK

Cmp	Debut	M	I	NO	Runs	HS	Avge	100	50	Balls	Runs	Wkts	Avge	BB	5i	10m	RpO	ct	st
FC		1	2	0	59	50	29.50	0	1									5	
SC		2	2	0	36	23	18.00	0	0									3	
FC	1984	45	78	10	1427	93	20.98	0	6									118	5
SC	1989	38	36	9	552	44	20.44	0	0									43	2

ROSS, Craig William (Northern Districts) b Papakura 18.10.1970 RHB RM

Cmp	Debut	M	I	NO	Runs	HS	Avge	100	50	Balls	Runs	Wkts	Avge	BB	5i	10m	RpO	ct	st
FC		2	1	0	0	0	0.00	0	0	498	182	6	30.33	3-69	0	0	2.19	0	
SC		4	3	2	2	1*	2.00	0	0	144	105	2	52.50	2-35	0	0	4.37	0	
FC	1989	17	19	5	219	66	15.64	0	1	2777	1337	42	31.83	4-36	0	0	2.88	3	
SC	1994	10	5	4	10	5*	10.00	0	0	481	361	11	32.81	2-35	0	0	4.50	1	

SCRAGG, Richard Steven (Auckland) b Auckland 5.4.1978 RHB LB

Cmp	Debut	M	I	NO	Runs	HS	Avge	100	50	Balls	Runs	Wkts	Avge	BB	5i	10m	RpO	ct	st
FC		1	2	0	25	14	12.50	0	0									0	

SEWELL, David Graham (Otago) b Christchurch 20.10.1977 RHB LFM

Cmp	Debut	M	I	NO	Runs	HS	Avge	100	50	Balls	Runs	Wkts	Avge	BB	5i	10m	RpO	ct	st
FC		8	10	7	35	22*	11.66	0	0	1407	851	35	24.31	8-31	2	1	3.62	4	
SC		4	3	0	9	6	3.00	0	0	198	150	5	30.00	3-36	0	0	4.54	0	
FC	1995	9	11	7	38	22*	9.50	0	0	1605	944	38	24.84	8-31	2	1	3.52	4	

SHARPE, Michael Frank (Canterbury) b Dannevirke 8.10.1966 RHB RM

Cmp	Debut	M	I	NO	Runs	HS	Avge	100	50	Balls	Runs	Wkts	Avge	BB	5i	10m	RpO	ct	st
FC		4	5	2	41	16*	13.66	0	0	624	277	5	55.40	2-48	0	0	2.66	1	
SC		9	3	2	8	4*	8.00	0	0	336	222	10	22.20	4-26	1	0	3.96	1	
FC	1990	21	22	5	199	33	11.70	0	0	3611	1515	55	27.54	4-59	0	0	2.51	4	
SC	1992	30	10	5	41	10*	8.20	0	0	1282	837	41	20.41	4-26	3	0	3.91	6	

Cmp Debut	M	I	NO	Runs	HS	Avge	100	50	Balls	Runs	Wkts	Avge	BB	5i	10m	RpO	ct	st

SINCLAIR, Mathew Stuart (Central Districts) b Katherine, Australia 9.11.1975 RHB RM WK

Cmp Debut	M	I	NO	Runs	HS	Avge	100	50	Balls	Runs	Wkts	Avge	BB	5i	10m	RpO	ct	st
FC	8	16	1	722	189	48.13	1	6									10	
SC	9	8	1	180	62	25.71	0	1									6	
FC 1995	11	20	1	761	189	40.05	1	6									13	
SC 1995	10	9	1	180	62	22.50	0	1									6	

SPEARMAN, Craig Murray (Central Districts, New Zealand A, New Zealand Selection XI, New Zealand to Pakistan, New Zealand to Sharjah) b Auckland 4.7.1972 RHB

Cmp Debut	M	I	NO	Runs	HS	Avge	100	50	Balls	Runs	Wkts	Avge	BB	5i	10m	RpO	ct	st
FC	8	15	1	401	96	28.64	0	3	6	1	0					1.00	8	
SC	8	8	0	229	80	28.62	0	1	6	4	0					4.00	0	
Test 1995	5	10	0	352	112	35.20	1	1									4	
FC 1993	31	59	4	1613	147	29.32	3	6	12	6	0					3.00	28	
Int 1995	24	24	1	485	78	20.20	0	2	3	6	0					12.00	6	
SC 1993	32	32	0	782	80	24.43	0	4	6	4	0					4.00	7	

SPICE, Jason Edward (Northern Districts) b Matamata 7.12.1974 RHB SLA

Cmp Debut	M	I	NO	Runs	HS	Avge	100	50	Balls	Runs	Wkts	Avge	BB	5i	10m	RpO	ct	st
FC	1	1	0	17	17	17.00	0	0	192	65	2	32.50	2-24	0	0	2.03	1	
SC	2	2	0	21	20	10.50	0	0	32	29	0					5.43	0	
FC 1993	5	6	1	77	30*	15.40	0	0	750	336	3	112.00	2-24	0	0	2.68	3	

STEAD, Gary Raymond (Canterbury) b Christchurch 9.1.1972 RHB LB

Cmp Debut	M	I	NO	Runs	HS	Avge	100	50	Balls	Runs	Wkts	Avge	BB	5i	10m	RpO	ct	st
FC	8	12	2	405	124	40.50	1	0	42	37	0					5.28	5	
SC	2	1	0	29	29	29.00	0	0									1	
FC 1991	21	34	3	1011	130	32.61	3	2	726	406	6	67.66	4-58	0	0	3.35	10	
SC 1994	23	20	1	384	61	20.21	0	2	18	23	0					7.66	10	

STEPHENS, Michael James (Auckland) b Auckland 1.11.1967 RHB LFM

Cmp Debut	M	I	NO	Runs	HS	Avge	100	50	Balls	Runs	Wkts	Avge	BB	5i	10m	RpO	ct	st
SC	2	1	0	3	3	3.00	0	0	84	61	3	20.33	2-30	0	0	4.35	0	
FC 1990	7	9	4	79	49*	15.80	0	0	1370	641	22	29.13	5-101	1	0	2.80	3	
SC 1993	8	6	3	19	9	6.33	0	0	354	226	6	37.66	2-27	0	0	3.83	2	

STYRIS, Scott Bernard (Northern Districts) b Brisbane, Australia 10.7.1975 RHB RFM

Cmp Debut	M	I	NO	Runs	HS	Avge	100	50	Balls	Runs	Wkts	Avge	BB	5i	10m	RpO	ct	st
FC	7	11	3	202	56	25.25	0	1	1178	617	18	34.27	6-42	1	0	3.14	1	
SC	10	7	4	48	16	16.00	0	0	396	346	9	38.44	2-26	0	0	5.24	4	
FC 1994	13	19	4	260	56	17.33	0	1	2281	1119	38	29.44	6-42	3	0	2.94	3	
SC 1994	19	13	6	104	20	14.85	0	0	774	653	18	36.27	3-54	0	0	5.06	7	

SULZBERGER, Glen Paul (Central Districts) b Kaponga 14.3.1973 LHB OB

Cmp Debut	M	I	NO	Runs	HS	Avge	100	50	Balls	Runs	Wkts	Avge	BB	5i	10m	RpO	ct	st
FC	8	16	1	212	56	14.13	0	1	636	275	9	30.55	2-62	0	0	2.59	4	
SC	9	9	0	288	71	32.00	0	3	314	281	2	140.50	2-23	0	0	5.36	5	
FC 1995	13	22	1	540	142	25.71	2	1	1120	495	16	30.93	4-19	0	0	2.65	7	

TAIT, Alex Ross (Northern Districts) b Paparoa 13.6.1972 RHB RM

Cmp Debut	M	I	NO	Runs	HS	Avge	100	50	Balls	Runs	Wkts	Avge	BB	5i	10m	RpO	ct	st
FC	9	13	1	268	70	22.33	0	1	2264	865	53	16.32	9-48	4	1	2.29	5	
SC	12	11	2	138	30	15.33	0	0	636	478	20	23.90	3-29	0	0	4.50	4	
FC 1994	16	21	3	502	70	27.88	0	3	3466	1349	73	18.47	9-48	5	1	2.33	6	
SC 1992	46	36	8	531	48	16.59	0	0	2266	1559	64	24.35	3-13	0	0	4.12	9	

THOMSON, Shane Alexander (Northern Districts) b Hamilton 27.1.1969 RHB OB

Cmp Debut	M	I	NO	Runs	HS	Avge	100	50	Balls	Runs	Wkts	Avge	BB	5i	10m	RpO	ct	st
FC	2	1	0	19	19	19.00	0	0	426	148	3	49.33	3-47	0	0	2.08	1	
SC	6	6	1	40	32	8.00	0	0	284	171	6	28.50	2-25	0	0	3.61	2	
Test 1989	19	35	4	958	120*	30.90	1	5	1990	953	19	50.15	3-47	0	0	2.87	7	
FC 1987	90	148	38	4209	167	38.26	6	25	9711	4625	116	39.87	5-49	2	0	2.85	37	
Int 1989	56	52	10	964	83	22.95	0	5	2121	1602	42	38.14	3-14	0	0	4.53	18	
SC 1988	51	49	5	897	70*	20.38	0	7	2188	1359	50	27.18	4-45	1	0	3.72	24	

TUFFEY, Daryl Raymond (Northern Districts) b Milton 11.6.1978 RHB RFM

Cmp Debut	M	I	NO	Runs	HS	Avge	100	50	Balls	Runs	Wkts	Avge	BB	5i	10m	RpO	ct	st
FC	2	1	1	21	21*		0	0	264	175	4	43.75	2-60	0	0	3.97	0	

TWOSE, Roger Graham (Wellington) b Torquay, England 17.4.1968 LHB RM

Cmp Debut	M	I	NO	Runs	HS	Avge	100	50	Balls	Runs	Wkts	Avge	BB	5i	10m	RpO	ct	st
FC	7	13	0	245	63	18.84	0	1	252	82	2	41.00	1-0	0	0	1.95	4	
SC	11	10	3	453	121*	64.71	2	2	294	181	7	25.85	4-31	1	0	3.69	4	
Test 1995	7	11	1	314	94	31.40	0	3	156	80	3	26.66	2-36	0	0	3.07	1	
FC 1989	147	247	30	8213	277*	37.84	16	40	8425	3954	122	32.40	6-28	2	0	2.81	74	
Int 1995	21	20	0	612	92	30.60	0	4	272	237	4	59.25	2-31	0	0	5.22	6	
SC 1989	60	58	4	1754	121*	32.48	4	10	2560	1650	80	20.62	5-30	6	1	3.86	17	

VAUGHAN, Justin Thomas Caldwell (Auckland, New Zealand, New Zealand Selection XI, New Zealand to Pakistan, New Zealand to Sharjah) b Hereford, England 30.8.1967 LHB RM

Cmp Debut	M	I	NO	Runs	HS	Avge	100	50	Balls	Runs	Wkts	Avge	BB	5i	10m	RpO	ct	st
Test	1	2	0	5	3	2.50	0	0	216	57	1	57.00	1-57	0	0	1.58	0	
FC	7	14	0	192	38	13.71	0	0	1070	425	20	21.25	8-27	1	0	2.38	4	
SC	8	6	2	199	67*	49.75	0	2	381	246	13	18.92	3-31	0	0	3.87	1	
Test 1992	6	12	1	201	44	18.27	0	0	1040	450	11	40.90	4-27	0	0	2.59	4	
FC 1989	70	120	20	3159	127	31.59	2	16	8089	3440	132	26.06	8-27	3	0	2.55	66	
Int 1992	18	16	7	162	33	18.00	0	0	696	524	15	34.93	4-33	1	0	4.51	4	
SC 1990	56	53	6	1299	94	27.63	0	7	3000	1760	97	18.14	6-26	5	1	3.52	22	

VETTORI, Daniel Luca (Northern Districts, New Zealand) b Auckland 27.1.1979 RHB SLA

Cmp Debut	M	I	NO	Runs	HS	Avge	100	50	Balls	Runs	Wkts	Avge	BB	5i	10m	RpO	ct	st
Test	4	7	3	70	29*	17.50	0	0	1115	429	18	23.83	5-84	1	0	2.30	2	
FC	7	13	5	100	29*	12.50	0	0	2105	762	36	21.16	5-61	3	0	2.17	3	

Cmp	Debut	M	I	NO	Runs	HS	Avge	100	50	Balls	Runs	Wkts	Avge	BB	5i	10m	RpO	ct	st
Int		1	1	0	4	4	4.00	0	0	12	21	0					10.50	0	
SC		9	6	3	11	4*	3.66	0	0	426	314	5	62.80	1-24	0	0	4.42	4	

WALKER, Matthew David John (Central Districts) b Opunake 17.1.1977 RHB RM

Cmp	Debut	M	I	NO	Runs	HS	Avge	100	50	Balls	Runs	Wkts	Avge	BB	5i	10m	RpO	ct	st
FC		5	9	1	340	84	42.50	0	2	209	100	2	50.00	1-24	0	0	2.87	2	
SC		7	5	1	42	25*	10.50	0	0	175	122	5	24.40	3-41	0	0	4.18	2	
FC	1995	10	15	1	427	84	30.50	0	3	227	115	2	57.50	1-24	0	0	3.03	6	

WALMSLEY, Kerry Peter (Auckland) b Dunedin 23.8.1973 RHB RFM

Cmp	Debut	M	I	NO	Runs	HS	Avge	100	50	Balls	Runs	Wkts	Avge	BB	5i	10m	RpO	ct	st
FC		2	3	0	15	10	5.00	0	0	236	121	6	20.16	3-17	0	0	3.07	0	
SC		4	1	0	4	4	4.00	0	0	198	142	4	35.50	2-28	0	0	4.30	1	
Test	1994	2	3	0	8	4	2.66	0	0	666	344	7	49.14	3-70	0	0	3.09	0	
FC	1994	10	14	3	69	14*	6.27	0	0	1757	945	27	35.00	5-73	1	0	3.22	1	
SC	1994	13	5	2	24	7*	8.00	0	0	660	449	14	32.07	3-36	0	0	4.08	1	

WEENINK, Scott William (Wellington) b Christchurch 1.1.1973 RHB OB

Cmp	Debut	M	I	NO	Runs	HS	Avge	100	50	Balls	Runs	Wkts	Avge	BB	5i	10m	RpO	ct	st
FC		3	5	0	57	40	11.40	0	0	60	42	0					4.20	0	
SC		6	6	0	139	113	23.16	1	0									2	
FC	1995	6	10	0	100	40	10.00	0	0	288	161	4	40.25	4-69	0	0	3.35	3	

WELLS, Jason Douglas (Wellington) b Wellington 25.3.1970 RHB OB

Cmp	Debut	M	I	NO	Runs	HS	Avge	100	50	Balls	Runs	Wkts	Avge	BB	5i	10m	RpO	ct	st
FC		6	11	1	208	69	20.80	0	2	228	138	2	69.00	2-90	0	0	3.63	5	
SC		11	11	1	328	81	32.80	0	3	6	8	0					8.00	3	
FC	1989	55	89	11	1938	102	24.84	1	9	2809	1460	32	45.62	6-59	1	0	3.11	39	
SC	1991	39	37	5	647	81	20.21	0	4	741	478	18	26.55	4-26	1	0	3.87	15	

WEST, Regan Morris (Central Districts) b New Plymouth 27.4.1979 LHB LFM

Cmp	Debut	M	I	NO	Runs	HS	Avge	100	50	Balls	Runs	Wkts	Avge	BB	5i	10m	RpO	ct	st
FC		1								90	38	1	38.00	1-38	0	0	2.53	0	

WILKINSON, Glenn John (Wellington) b Wellington 23.4.1970 RHB RM

Cmp	Debut	M	I	NO	Runs	HS	Avge	100	50	Balls	Runs	Wkts	Avge	BB	5i	10m	RpO	ct	st
FC		1	2	0	173	96	86.50	0	2	15	3	0					1.20	1	

WILSON, Jeffrey William (Otago) b Invercargill 24.10.1973 RHB RFM

Cmp	Debut	M	I	NO	Runs	HS	Avge	100	50	Balls	Runs	Wkts	Avge	BB	5i	10m	RpO	ct	st
FC		2	4	1	135	69*	45.00	0	1	306	151	7	21.57	5-34	1	0	2.96	2	
SC		3	3	0	8	8	2.66	0	0	78	55	1	55.00	1-36	0	0	4.23	0	
FC	1991	26	49	5	980	78	22.27	0	5	5068	2076	93	22.32	5-34	5	0	2.45	23	
Int	1992	4	4	1	80	44*	26.66	0	0	152	135	3	45.00	2-21	0	0	5.32	1	
SC	1991	21	20	2	317	99	17.61	0	1	978	632	21	30.09	3-34	0	0	3.87	16	

WISEMAN, Paul John (Otago, New Zealand A, New Zealand Selection XI) b Auckland 4.5.1970 RHB OB

Cmp	Debut	M	I	NO	Runs	HS	Avge	100	50	Balls	Runs	Wkts	Avge	BB	5i	10m	RpO	ct	st
FC		11	17	2	221	73	14.73	0	1	2191	968	40	24.20	8-66	3	1	2.65	7	
SC		3	3	1	55	19	27.50	0	0	180	100	3	33.33	2-33	0	0	3.33	1	
FC	1991	30	48	6	601	77	14.30	0	2	6352	2741	87	31.50	8-66	5	1	2.58	22	
SC	1993	23	21	4	256	39	15.05	0	0	1152	699	15	46.60	3-11	0	0	3.64	5	

WISNESKI, Warren Anthony (Canterbury) b New Plymouth 19.2.1969 RHB RM

Cmp	Debut	M	I	NO	Runs	HS	Avge	100	50	Balls	Runs	Wkts	Avge	BB	5i	10m	RpO	ct	st
FC		7	8	1	103	40	14.71	0	0	1547	745	27	27.59	4-37	0	0	2.88	4	
SC		10	4	1	30	11	10.00	0	0	429	284	14	20.28	6-43	0	1	3.97	5	
FC	1992	24	32	3	612	86	21.10	0	4	4700	2175	82	26.52	5-21	4	0	2.77	14	
SC	1993	17	10	2	88	37	11.00	0	0	754	541	19	28.47	6-43	0	1	4.30	8	

YOCK, Benjamin Arthur (Canterbury) b Christchurch 8.2.1975 RHB WK

Cmp	Debut	M	I	NO	Runs	HS	Avge	100	50	Balls	Runs	Wkts	Avge	BB	5i	10m	RpO	ct	st
FC		1	1	0	5	5	5.00	0	0									3	

YOUNG, Bryan Andrew (Northern Districts, New Zealand, New Zealand to Pakistan, New Zealand to Sharjah, New Zealand to India) b Whangarei 3.11.1964 RHB WK

Cmp	Debut	M	I	NO	Runs	HS	Avge	100	50	Balls	Runs	Wkts	Avge	BB	5i	10m	RpO	ct	st
Test		5	9	1	504	267*	63.00	1	2									7	
FC		6	11	1	510	267*	51.00	1	2									8	
Int		7	7	0	163	53	23.28	0	1									3	
SC		10	10	0	467	97	46.70	0	6									2	
Test	1993	25	49	2	1700	267*	36.17	2	11									39	
FC	1983	135	227	40	6640	267*	35.50	9	35	48	76	1	76.00	1-76	0	0	9.50	257	11
Int	1990	62	61	4	1360	74	23.85	0	6									26	
SC	1983	72	70	6	1897	101*	29.64	1	12									42	12

YOVICH, Joseph Adam Frank (Northern Districts) b Whangarei 15.12.1976 LHB RFM

Cmp	Debut	M	I	NO	Runs	HS	Avge	100	50	Balls	Runs	Wkts	Avge	BB	5i	10m	RpO	ct	st
FC		4	4	0	87	78	21.75	0	1	364	295	8	36.87	5-66	1	0	4.86	0	

ENGLAND IN NEW ZEALAND 1996-97

ATHERTON, M.A.

Cmp	Debut	M	I	NO	Runs	HS	Avge	100	50	Balls	Runs	Wkts	Avge	BB	5i	10m	RpO	ct	st
Test		3	4	1	325	118	108.33	1	2									1	
FC		6	9	2	354	118	50.57	1	2									7	
Int		4	4	0	94	43	23.50	0	0									1	

Cmp Debut	M	I	NO	Runs	HS	Avge	100	50	Balls	Runs	Wkts	Avge	BB	5i	10m	RpO	ct	st
CADDICK, A.R.																		
Test	2	3	0	39	20	13.00	0	0	527	174	8	21.75	4-45	0	0	1.98	1	
FC	4	6	0	64	20	10.66	0	0	983	340	14	24.28	4-45	0	0	2.07	2	
Int	4	2	1	12	12*	12.00	0	0	204	140	9	15.55	3-35	0	0	4.11	1	
CORK, D.G.																		
Test	3	4	1	121	59	40.33	0	1	593	300	7	42.85	3-96	0	0	3.03	3	
FC	5	6	2	128	59	32.00	0	1	887	441	14	31.50	3-18	0	0	2.98	4	
Int	3	3	1	40	31*	20.00	0	0	168	145	1	145.00	1-52	0	0	5.17	1	
CRAWLEY, J.P.																		
Test	3	4	1	111	56	37.00	0	1									1	
FC	6	8	1	254	65	36.28	0	2									2	
Int	3	2	0	11	11	5.50	0	0									0	
CROFT, R.D.B																		
Test	2	2	0	31	31	15.50	0	0	541	162	10	16.20	5-95	1	0	1.79	2	
FC	4	5	0	84	49	16.80	0	0	913	303	12	25.25	5-95	1	0	1.99	2	
Int	5	4	1	34	20	11.33	0	0	294	180	4	45.00	2-26	0	0	3.67	1	
GOUGH, D.																		
Test	3	3	0	20	18	6.66	0	0	765	361	19	19.00	5-40	1	0	2.83	0	
FC	4	4	0	35	18	8.75	0	0	913	435	25	17.40	5-40	1	0	2.85	0	
Int	5	3	1	21	16	10.50	0	0	275	221	6	36.83	2-29	0	0	4.82	0	
HUSSAIN, N.																		
Test	3	4	0	117	64	29.25	0	1									6	
FC	6	8	0	334	139	41.75	1	2									9	
Int	5	5	2	56	20	18.66	0	0									2	
IRANI, R.C.																		
FC	1	2	0	44	40	22.00	0	0	77	34	2	17.00	2-13	0	0	2.64	0	
Int	3	3	0	4	4	1.33	0	0	114	77	2	38.50	1-23	0	0	4.05	0	
KNIGHT, N.V.																		
Test	3	4	0	56	29	14.00	0	0									9	
FC	6	9	1	180	46	22.50	0	0									15	
Int	4	4	2	132	84*	66.00	0	1									0	
MULLALLY, A.D.																		
Test	1	1	0	21	21	21.00	0	0	318	102	3	34.00	2-47	0	0	1.92	0	
FC	2	2	0	23	21	11.50	0	0	496	160	8	20.00	4-52	0	0	1.93	1	
Int	2									72	57	2	28.50	1-21	0	0	4.75	1	
RUSSELL, R.C.																		
FC	1	2	1	61	61*	61.00	0	1									3	
Int	1	1	0	2	2	2.00	0	0									2	
SILVERWOOD, C.E.W.																		
FC	2	3	0	25	11	8.33	0	0	380	171	11	15.54	6-44	1	0	2.70	2	
Int	2	2	0	16	12	8.00	0	0	90	73	1	73.00	1-53	0	0	4.86	0	
STEWART, A.J.																		
Test	3	4	0	257	173	64.25	1	1									14	2
FC	5	6	1	450	173	90.00	2	1									22	3
Int	5	5	0	188	81	37.60	0	1									7	2
THORPE, G.P.																		
Test	3	4	0	247	119	61.75	2	0	6	0	0					0.00	1	
FC	5	6	0	324	119	54.00	2	1	12	3	0					1.50	7	
Int	5	5	0	203	82	40.60	0	3	36	32	0					5.33	2	
TUFNELL, P.C.R.																		
Test	3	3	2	38	19*	38.00	0	0	792	242	7	34.57	3-53	0	0	1.83	0	
FC	5	5	3	40	19*	20.00	0	0	1194	378	15	25.20	5-58	1	0	1.89	1	
Int	1									60	22	4	5.50	4-22	1	0	2.20	1	
WHITE, C.																		
Test	1	1	0	0	0	0.00	0	0	150	77	2	38.50	2-51	0	0	3.08	0	
FC	4	5	1	60	22*	15.00	0	0	448	232	13	17.84	4-15	0	0	3.10	1	
Int	3	3	0	70	38	23.33	0	0	124	102	6	17.00	4-37	1	0	4.93	2	

SRI LANKA IN NEW ZEALAND 1996-97

Cmp Debut	M	I	NO	Runs	HS	Avge	100	50	Balls	Runs	Wkts	Avge	BB	5i	10m	RpO	ct	st
ATAPATTU, M.S.																		
Test	1	2	0	47	25	23.50	0	0									0	
CHANDANA, U.D.U.																		
Int	2	1	0	3	3	3.00	0	0	24	22	0					5.50	1	

Cmp	Debut	M	I	NO	Runs	HS	Avge	100	50	Balls	Runs	Wkts	Avge	BB	5i	10m	RpO	ct	st
DE SILVA, K.S.C.																			
Test		1	2	1	0	0*	0.00	0	0	150	65	0					2.60	0	
DE SILVA, P.A.																			
Test		2	4	0	9	5	2.25	0	0									2	
Int		2	2	0	102	66	51.00	0	1	12	4	1	4.00	1-4	0	0	2.00	2	
DHARMASENA, H.D.P.K.																			
Test		1	2	1	65	38*	65.00	0	0	276	114	3	38.00	2-75	0	0	2.47	1	
Int		2	1	0	2	2	2.00	0	0	120	73	0					3.65	1	
JAYASURIYA, S.T.																			
Test		2	4	0	73	50	18.25	0	1	54	39	0					4.33	0	
Int		2	2	0	79	79	39.50	0	1	90	56	3	18.66	3-26	0	0	3.73	2	
KALUWITHARANA, R.S.																			
Test		2	4	0	170	103	42.50	1	0									0	1
Int		2	2	0	38	23	19.00	0	0									1	
MAHAMANA, R.S.																			
Test		2	4	0	157	65	39.25	0	1									8	
Int		2	2	0	14	10	7.00	0	0									1	
MURALITHARAN, M.																			
Test		2	4	0	38	26	9.50	0	0	486	241	6	40.16	3-43	0	0	2.97	0	
Int		2	1	0	2	2	2.00	0	0	120	74	4	18.50	2-32	0	0	3.70	1	
RANATUNGA, A.																			
Test		2	4	0	64	33	16.00	0	0	30	29	1	29.00	1-29	0	0	5.80	2	
Int		2	2	1	35	19*	35.00	0	0	30	17	0					3.40	0	
TILLAKARATNE, H.P.																			
Test		2	4	1	75	55*	25.00	0	1									1	
Int		2	2	1	21	13*	21.00	0	0									1	
VAAS, W.P.U.J.C.																			
Test		2	4	0	95	57	23.75	0	1	376	210	6	35.00	4-144	0	0	3.35	0	
Int		2	1	0	0	0	0.00	0	0	98	71	4	17.75	4-26	1	0	4.34	0	
WICKRAMASINGHE, G.P.																			
Test		1	2	0	43	43	21.50	0	0	150	117	1	117.00	1-117	0	0	4.68	1	
ZOYSA, D.N.T.																			
Test		2	4	1	43	16*	14.33	0	0	484	212	7	30.28	3-47	0	0	2.62	1	
Int		2	1	1	3	3*		0	0	102	76	4	19.00	2-29	0	0	4.47	0	

The following current cricketers have played in New Zealand Domestic limited overs cricket but did not appear in New Zealand Domestic cricket in 1996-97:

Cmp	Debut	M	I	NO	Runs	HS	Avge	100	50	Balls	Runs	Wkts	Avge	BB	5i	10m	RpO	ct	st
BROWN, D.R. (see Warwickshire) (Wellington)																			
SC	1995	4	4	0	114	53	28.50	0	1	210	178	6	29.66	2-37	0	0	5.08	1	
HARDEN, R.J. (see Somerset) (Central Districts)																			
SC	1987	12	12	1	502	97	45.36	0	5									4	
HICK, G.A. (see Worcestershire) (Northern Districts)																			
SC	1987	10	10	0	276	100	27.60	1	0	257	142	6	23.66	2-20	0	0	3.31	5	
JAMES, K.D. (see Hampshire) (Wellington)																			
SC	1982	8	5	3	32	23	16.00	0	0	389	236	10	23.60	3-30	0	0	3.64	2	
LEFEBVRE, R.P. (see England other teams) (Canterbury)																			
SC	1990	4	1	0	14	14	14.00	0	0	220	93	5	18.60	3-20	0	0	2.53	1	
NOON, W.M. (see Nottinghamshire) (Northern Districts)																			
SC	1994	11	7	2	49	17	9.80	0	0									15	5
RUTHERFORD, K.R. (see South Africa) (Otago)																			
SC	1983	45	45	1	1381	115*	31.38	2	8	329	246	6	41.00	3-26	0	0	4.48	15	
SPEIGHT, M.P. (see Durham) (Wellington)																			
SC	1992	14	14	0	408	96	29.14	0	3									17	
WHITAKER, P.R. (see Hampshire) (Central Districts)																			
SC	1995	6	6	0	109	50	18.16	0	1	288	175	6	29.16	2-26	0	0	3.64	1	

PAKISTAN

First First-Class Match: Punjab v Sind (Lahore) 1947-48

First First-Class Tour to England: 1954

First Test Match: Pakistan v India (Dacca) 1954-55

Present First-Class Teams: Agricultural Development Bank of Pakistan (ADBP), Allied Bank, Customs, Habib Bank, National Bank, Pakistan International Airlines (PIA), Pakistan National Shipping Corporation (PNSC), United Bank (in Patron's Trophy). Bahawalpur, Faisalabad, Islamabad, Karachi Blues, Karachi Whites, Lahore, Peshawar, Rawalpindi (in Quaid-e-Azam Trophy).

First-Class Competitions: The Quaid-e-Azam trophy was established in 1953-54 and is the premier competition. The Patron's Trophy and Pentangular Tournament are also first-class.

Quaid-e-Azam Trophy winners 1996-97: Lahore

Patron's Trophy winners 1996-97: United Bank

FIRST-CLASS RECORDS

Highest Team Total: 951-7d Sind v Baluchistan (Karachi) 1973-74
Highest in 1996-97: 554 Karachi Whites v Faisalabad (Karachi); 553 Pakistan v Zimbabwe (Sheikhupura); 523 Peshawar v Islamabad (Islamabad); 493 Lahore v Islamabad (Lahore); 479 Karachi Whites v Faisalabad (Karachi)

Lowest Team Total: 27 Dera Ismail Khan v Railways (Lahore) 1964-65
Lowest in 1996-97: 48 Karachi Whites v Bahawalpur (Bahawalpur); 53 Lahore v Peshawar (Peshawar); 76 National Bank v Habib Bank (Multan); 79 PIA v United Bank (Lahore); 82 Karachi Blues v Faisalabad (Faisalabad)

Highest Individual Innings: 499 Hanif Mohammad Karachi v Bahawalpur (Karachi) 1958-59
Highest in 1996-97: 257* Wasim Akram Pakistan v Zimbabwe (Sheikhupura); 207 Iqbal Saleem Karachi Whites v Faisalabad (Karachi); 187 Mujahid Hameed ADBP v PNSC (Karachi); 182 Iqbal Saleem Karachi Whites v Faisalabad (Faisalabad); 167 Nasir Ali Khan Karachi Whites v Faisalabad (Faisalabad)

Most Runs in Season: 1,649 (av 63.42) Saadat Ali (HBFC) 1983-84
Most in 1996-97: 913 (av 57.06) Asif Mujtaba (Karachi Blues, PIA); 911 (av 41.40) Ijaz Ahmed (Faisalabad, Allied Bank); 784 (av 37.33) Basit Ali (Karachi Blues, United Bank); 771 (av 51.40) Mujahid Jamshed (Lahore, Habib Bank); 735 (av 31.95) Aamer Hanif (Karachi Whites, Allied Bank)

Most Runs in Career: 34,843 (av 51.54) Zaheer Abbas (Karachi, PIA, Gloucestershire) 1965-66 to 1986-87
Most by Current Batsman: 15,298 (av 47.50) Saleem Malik (Lahore, Sargodha, Habib Bank, Essex) 1978-79 to date; 13,785 (av 37.87) Mansoor Akhtar (Karachi, United Bank) 1974-75 to date; 13,303 (av 44.34) Rizwan-uz-Zaman (Karachi, PIA) 1976-77 to date; 12,921 (av 41.41) Sajid Ali (Karachi, National Bank) 1982-83 to date; 12,465 (av 50.06) Asif Mujtaba (Karachi, PIA) 1984-85 to date

Best Innings Analysis: 10-28 Naeem Akhtar Rawalpindi B v Peshawar (Peshawar) 1995-96
Best in 1996-97: 9-51 Aaqib Javed Allied Bank v Habib Bank (Lahore); 8-43 Manzoor Elahi Lahore v Karachi Whites (Lahore); 8-70 Kabir Khan Peshawar v Islamabad (Islamabad); 8-109 Inamullah Khan Lahore v Peshawar (Peshawar); 7-36 Rashid Hanif Karachi Whites v Islamabad (Islamabad)

Most Wickets in Season: 107 (av 16.06) Ijaz Faqih (Karachi) 1985-86
Most in 1996-97: 71 (av 19.77) Kabir Khan (Peshawar, Habib Bank); 69 (av 23.66) Shoaib Akhtar (Rawalpindi, ADBP); 64 (av 22.51) Murtaza Hussain (Bahawalpur, PNSC); 59 (av 17.11) Azhar Mahmood (Islamabad, United Bank)

Most Wickets in Career: 1,571 (av 27.67) Intikhab Alam (Karachi, PIA, PWD, Surrey) 1957-58 to 1982
Most by Current Bowler: 829 (av 21.39) Wasim Akram (Lahore, PIA, Lancashire) 1984-85 to date; 690 (av 21.86) Tauseef Ahmed (Karachi, United Bank) 1978-79 to date; 688 (av 21.07) Waqar Younis (Multan, United Bank, Surrey, Glamorgan) 1987-88 to date; 645 (av 23.15) Iqbal Sikander (Karachi, Hyderabad, PIA) 1976-77 to date; 628 (av 24.14) Shahid Mahboob (Karachi, Quetta, Rawalpindi, Islamabad, IDBP, PACO, Allied Bank) 1979-80 to date

Record Wicket Partnerships

1st	561	Waheed Mirza & Mansoor Akhtar	Karachi Whites v Quetta (Karachi)	1976-77
2nd	426	Arshad Pervez & Mohsin Khan	Habib Bank v Income Tax (Lahore)	1977-78
3rd	456	Khalid Irtiza & Aslam Ali	United Bank v Multan (Karachi)	1975-76
4th	346	Zafar Altaf & Majid Khan	Lahore Greens v Bahawalpur (Lahore)	1965-66
5th	355	Altaf Shah & Tariq Bashir	HBFC v Multan (Multan)	1976-77
6th	353	Salahuddin & Zaheer Abbas	Karachi v East Pakistan (Karachi)	1968-69
7th	308	Waqar Hassan & Imtiaz Ahmed	Pakistan v New Zealand (Lahore)	1955-56
8th	313	Wasim Akram & Saqlain Mushtaq	Pakistan v Zimbabwe (Sheikhupura)	1996-97
9th	207	Mahmood Hamid & Athar Laeeq	Karachi Whites v Lahore (Karachi)	1993-94
10th	196*	Nadeem Yousuf & Maqsood Kundi	Muslim C.B. v National Bank (Lahore)	1981-82

Highest Partnerships in 1996-97

1st	281	Zahoor Elahi & Mujahid Jamshed	Lahore v Islamabad (Lahore)
2nd	262	Saeed Anwar & Ijaz Ahmed	Pakistan v New Zealand (Rawalpindi)
3rd	192	Ahmer Saeed & Asif Mujtaba	Karachi Blues v Peshawar (Karachi)
4th	301	Nasir Ali Khan & Iqbal Saleem	Karachi Whites v Faisalabad (Karachi)
5th	240	Iqbal Saleem & Aaley Haider	Karachi Whites v Faisalabad (Karachi)
6th	181	Mujahid Jamshed & Tahir Mahmood	Habib Bank v PIA (Karachi)
7th	131	G.W.Flower & P.A.Strang	Zimbabwe v Pakistan (Sheikhupura)
8th	313	Wasim Akram & Saqlain Mushtaq	Pakistan v Zimbabwe (Sheikhupura)
9th	87	P.A.Strang & B.C.Strang	Zimbabwe v Pakistan (Sheikhupura)
10th	118	Mahmood Hamid & Ali Gauhar	Karachi Blues v Bahawalpur (Karachi)

Most Wicketkeeping Dismissals in Innings: 9 (8ct 1st) Tahir Rasheed Habib Bank v PACO (Gujranwala) 1992-93
Most in 1996-97: 5 Aamer Nazir (Islamabad); 5 Ahsan Raza (Lahore) (twice); 5 Iqbal Saleem (Karachi Whites); 5 Javed Qadeer (PIA); 5 Mohammad Nadeem Hussain (Rawalpindi); 5 Tahir Rasheed (Habib Bank) (twice); 5 Wasim Yousufi (United Bank)

Most Wicketkeeping Dismissals in Match: 10 (8ct 2st) Taslim Arif National Bank v Punjab (Lahore) 1978-79; 10 (9ct 1st) Arif-ud-din United Bank v Karachi B (Karachi) 1978-79; 10 (9ct 1st) Kamal Najamuddin Karachi v Lahore (Multan) 1982-83; 10 (7ct 3st) Azhar Abbas Bahawalpur v Lahore (Bahawalpur) 1983-84; 10 (8ct 2st) Anil Dalpat Karachi v United Bank (Lahore) 1985-86; 10 (10ct) Imran Zia Bahawalpur v Faisalabad (Faisalabad) 1989-90; 10 (10ct) Rifaqat Ali Allied Bank v United Bank (Rawalpindi) 1995-96
Most in 1996-97: 8 (7ct 1st) Javed Qadeer PIA v National Bank (Karachi); 8 (8ct) Wasim Yousufi United Bank v PIA (Lahore)

Most Wicketkeeping Dismissals in Season: 70 (62ct 8st) Ashraf Ali (United Bank) 1986-87
Most in 1996-97: 42 (38ct 4st) Wasim Yousufi (Peshawar, United Bank); 41 (40ct 1st) Tahir Rasheed (Karachi Blues, Habib Bank); 36 (30ct 6st) Javed Qadeer (Karachi Whites, PIA); 30 (30ct) Iqbal Saleem (Karachi Whites, Allied Bank); 30 (30ct) Mohammad Nadeem Hussain (Rawalpindi, ADBP)

Most Wicketkeeping Dismissals in Career: 810 (665ct 145st) Wasim Bari (Karachi, PIA) 1964-65 to 1983-84
Most by Current Wicketkeeper: 464 (406ct 58st) Tahir Rasheed (Karachi, HBFC, IDBP, Habib Bank) 1979-80 to date; 338 (282ct 56st) Bilal Ahmed (Faisalabad, ADBP) 1983-84 to date; 311 (276ct 35st) Moin Khan (Karachi, PIA) 1986-87 to date; 278 (232ct 46st) Wasim Arif (Karachi, National Bank) 1982-83 to date; 278 (238ct 40st) Rashid Latif (Karachi, United Bank, Allied Bank) 1986-87 to date

Most Catches by Fielder in Innings: 6 Gulfraz Khan Railways v Muslim Commercial Bank (Sialkot) 1981-82; 6 Masood Anwar Rawalpindi v Lahore Division (Rawalpindi) 1983-84
Most in 1996-97: 4 Kamran Haider Khan Customs v PNSC (Lahore); 4 Mohammad Nadeem Hussain ADBP v Habib Bank (Lahore); 4 Zeeshan Siddiqi PNSC v PIA (Sahiwal)

Most Catches by Fielder in Match: 8 Masood Anwar Rawalpindi v Lahore Division (Rawalpindi) 1983-84
Most in 1996-97: 6 Kamran Haider Khan Customs v PNSC (Lahore); 6 Naved Ahmed Islamabad v Bahawalpur (Islamabad)

Most Catches by Fielder in Season: 30 Fahim Abbasi (Rawalpindi) 1986-87
Most in 1996-97: 20 Ijaz Ahmed (Faisalabad, Allied Bank); 19 Aaley Haider (Karachi Whites, Allied Bank); 18 Shakeel Ahmed (Peshawar, Habib Bank); 13 Mohammad Asif (Lahore, ADBP); 13 Azhar Mahmood (Islamabad, United Bank)

Most Catches by Fielder in Career: 410 Majid Khan (Lahore, PIA, Rawalpindi, Glamorgan, Queensland) 1961-62 to 1984-85
Most by Current Fielder: 189 Sajid Ali (Karachi, National Bank) 1982-83 to date; 175 Asif Mujtaba (Karachi, PIA) 1984-85 to date; 165 Mansoor Akhtar (Karachi, United Bank) 1974-75 to date; 147 Saleem Malik (Lahore, Sargodha, Habib Bank, Essex) 1978-79 to date; 138 Manzoor Elahi (Multan, Lahore, ADBP) 1982-83 to date

DOMESTIC LIMITED OVERS RECORDS

Highest Team Totals: 341-5 (45 overs) Railways v South Zone (Hyderabad) 1981-82; 338-4 (45 overs) ADBP v Karachi Whites (Faisalabad) 1995-96; 330-2 (50 overs) National Bank v United Bank (Karachi) 1996-97

Lowest Team Totals: 47 (23 overs) Faisalabad v ADBP (Karachi) 1989-90; 48 (16 overs) HBFC v National Bank (Rawalpindi) 1985-86; 52 (19.3 overs) HBFC v United Bank (Lahore) 1989-90
Lowest in 1996-97: 123 (30.3 overs) Peshawar v Islamabad (Peshawar)

Highest Individual Innings: 197* Sajid Ali National Bank v United Bank (Karachi) 1996-97; 184* Sajid Ali National Bank v PNSC (Karachi) 1991-92; 171 Sajid Ali National Bank v Bahawalpur (Bahawalpur) 1991-92
108 centuries have been scored in the competition, Rameez Raja, Sajid Ali and Zahoor Elahi scoring 6

Most Runs in Season: 638 (av 79.75) Sajid Ali (National Bank) 1996-97

Most Runs in Career: 3,442 (av 45.89) Mansoor Akhtar (United Bank) 1980-81 to date; 2,920 (av 37.92) Sajid Ali (National Bank) 1981-82 to date; 2,842 (av 39.47) Shoaib Mohammad (PIA) 1980-81 to date

Best Innings Analyses: 7-20 Anwar Miandad Habib Bank v Karachi (Peshawar) 1988-89; 7-28 Saleem Jaffar United Bank v HBFC (Lahore) 1989-90; 7-32 Saleem Jaffar Karachi v Railways (Karachi) 1985-86
Best in 1996-97: 5-32 Waqar Younis United Bank v Bangladesh (Karachi)
Five wickets in an innings has been achieved on 59 occasions, three times by Nadeem Khan and Wasim Haider

Most Economical Bowling: 10-6-4-1 Nadeem Ghauri Habib Bank v Railways (Faisalabad) 1986-87
Most Economical in 1996-97: 10-3-15-1 Iftikhar Asghar Rawalpindi v Karachi Blues (Lahore)

Most Expensive Bowling: 10-0-94-1 Zahid Ahmed PIA v Lahore (Lahore) 1991-92
Most Expensive in 1996-97: 10-0-90-0 Ali Gauhar United Bank v National Bank (Karachi)

Most Wickets in Season: 19 (av 7.21) Mohammad Hussain (United Bank) 1995-96; 19 (av 5.94) Wasim Akram (PIA) 1995-96
Most in 1996-97: 16 (av 18.87) Mushtaq Ahmed (United Bank)

Most Wickets in Career: 115 (av 21.87) Zahid Ahmed (PIA) 1980-81 to date; 106 (av 22.30) Tauseef Ahmed (United Bank) 1980-81 to date; 98 (av 21.87) Nadeem Ghauri (Habib Bank) 1981-82 to date

Record Wicket Partnerships

1st	297	Sajid Ali & Shahid Anwar	National Bank v Bahawalpur (Bahawalpur)	1991-92
2nd	223	Rizwan-uz-Zaman & Zahid Fazal	PIA v ADBP (Lahore)	1991-92
3rd	202*	Ijaz Ahmed & Saleem Malik	Habib Bank v ADBP (Lahore)	1986-87
4th	172	Saeed Azad & Ameer Akbar	National Bank v PNSC (Karachi)	1995-96
5th	163*	Zaheer Abbas & Hasan Jamil	PIA v Lahore (Lahore)	1981-82
6th	115*	Umar Rasheed & Yahya Toor	Karachi v Muslim CB (Karachi)	1988-89
7th	108*	Shaukat Mirza & Rafat Alam	HBFC v Lahore (Lahore)	1985-86
8th	165	Tariq Alam & Shahzad Ilyas	HBFC v Habib Bank (Karachi)	1993-94
9th	84	Tariq Sarwar & Faisal Elahi	Bahawalpur v Karachi Blues (Karachi)	1996-97
10th	68	Barkatullah Khan & Afzaal Butt	National Bank v PIA (Karachi)	1988-89

There were 30 hundred partnerships in 1996-97, the highest being 221 for the 2nd wicket Sajid Ali & Shahid Anwar National Bank v United Bank (Karachi)

Most Wicketkeeping Dismissals in Innings: 6 (6ct) Tahir Rasheed HBFC v Karachi (Lahore) 1986-87; 6 (5ct 1st) Nadeem Abbasi Rawalpindi v Lahore (Rawalpindi) 1996-97

Most Wicketkeeping Dismissals in Season: 18 (13ct 5st) Tahir Rasheed (Habib Bank) 1993-94
Most in 1996-97: 10 (7ct 3st) Rashid Latif (Allied Bank)

Most Wicketkeeping Dismissals in Career: 113 (71ct 42st) Tahir Rasheed (HBFC, Habib Bank) 1981-82 to date; 79 (58ct 21st) Wasim Arif (National Bank, Karachi) 1982-83 to date; 68 (49ct 19st) Ashraf Ali (United Bank, Lahore) 1981-82 to 1994-95

Most Catches by Fielder in Innings: 4 Mohsin Khan Habib Bank v Railways (Hyderabad) 1981-82; 4 Tariq Baig Multan v ADBP (Gujranwala) 1990-91; 4 Zahir Shah Rawalpindi v Faisalabad (Faisalabad) 1991-92; 4 Maqsood Ahmed Rawalpindi A v Lahore (Rawalpindi) 1994-95; 4 Shahid Hussain Peshawar v National Bank (Lahore) 1995-96
Most in 1996-97: 3 Ijaz Mahmood Faisalabad v Rawalpindi (Lahore)

Most Catches by Fielder in Season: 9 Aleem Dar (Lahore) 1992-93
Most in 1996-97: 7 Ijaz Mahmood (Faislabad)

Most Catches by Fielder in Career: 44 Sajid Ali (National Bank) 1981-82 to date; 43 Akram Raza (Habib Bank) 1985-86 to date; 33 Zahid Ahmed (PIA) 1980-81 to date

Most Appearances in Competition: 92 Rizwan-uz-Zaman (PIA) 1980-81 to date; 88 Mansoor Akhtar (United Bank) 1980-81 to date; 88 Zahid Ahmed (PIA) 1980-81 to date

CHAMPION TEAMS

Quaid-i-Azam Trophy

Until 1978-79 the Trophy was decided by a final knock-out stage. In 1979-80 three teams played a round-robin in the final stages. From 1980-81 the Competition has been run on a league basis, which from 1984-85 has produced qualifiers for a two or four team knockout. The competitions starting in 1964-65 and 1966-67 were spread over two seasons.

1953-54 Bahawalpur	1970-71 Karachi Blues	1984-85 United Bank
1954-55 Karachi	1972-73 Railways	1985-86 Karachi
1956-57 Punjab	1973-74 Railways	1986-87 National Bank
1957-58 Bahawalpur	1974-75 Punjab A	1987-88 PIA
1958-59 Karachi	1975-76 National Bank	1988-89 ADBP
1959-60 Karachi	1976-77 United Bank	1989-90 PIA
1961-62 Karachi Blues	1977-78 Habib Bank	1990-91 Karachi Whites
1962-63 Karachi A	1978-79 National Bank	1991-92 Karachi Whites
1963-64 Karachi Blues	1979-80 PIA	1992-93 Karachi
1964-65 Karachi Blues	1980-81 United Bank	1993-94 Lahore
1966-67 Karachi	1981-82 National Bank	1994-95 Karachi Blues
1968-69 Lahore	1982-83 United Bank	1995-96 Karachi Blues
1969-70 PIA	1983-84 National Bank	1996-97 Lahore

Patron's Trophy

Originally the B.C.C.P. Trophy, it was re-named in 1972-73. The competition was not first-class between 1979-80 and 1982-83 being purely a qualifying competition for the Quaid-i-Azam Trophy. The Trophy was decided by knock-out until 1988-89, since when a league has produced a two or four team knockout.

1970-71 PIA	1979-80 IDBP	1988-89 Karachi
1971-72 PIA	1980-81 Rawalpindi	1989-90 Karachi Whites
1972-73 Karachi Blues	1981-82 Allied Bank	1990-91 ADBP
1973-74 Railways	1982-83 PACO	1991-92 Habib Bank
1974-75 National Bank	1983-84 Karachi Blues	1992-93 Habib Bank
1975-76 National Bank	1984-85 Karachi Whites	1993-94 ADBP
1976-77 Habib Bank	1985-86 Karachi Whites	1994-95 Allied Bank
1977-78 Habib Bank	1986-87 National Bank	1995-96 ADBP
1978-79 National Bank	1987-88 Habib Bank	1996-97 United Bank

Domestic Limited Overs Competition

Wills Cup

This competition consisted of two leagues with the top two teams in each league entering the semi-finals and final, until 1992-93 when four leagues resulted in the top two teams in each qualifying for two further leagues before the final stages. The overs limit was 45 from 1980-81 to 1985-86, 50 from 1986-87 to 1993-94, 45 from 1994-95 to 1995-96 and reverted to 50 from 1996-97. The Emirates Cricket Board took part in the second league in 1995-96 and Bangladesh in 1996-97. Results of the finals:

1980-81 PIA 230 (45 overs) beat United Bank 225 (44.1 overs) by 5 runs
1981-82 PIA 132-3 (32.5 overs) beat Lahore 131 (42.3 overs) by 7 wkts
1982-83 PIA 206-9 (45 overs) beat Habib Bank 173 (43.2 overs) by 33 runs
1983-84 Habib Bank 182-3 (41 overs) beat PIA 181 (39.4 overs) by 7 wkts
1984-85 No competition
1985-86 PIA 257-3 (45 overs) beat United Bank 254-9 (45 overs) by 3 runs
1986-87 Habib Bank 155-7 (49.2 overs) beat United Bank 154 (48.1 overs) by 3 wkts
1987-88 PIA 212-8 (47.4 overs) beat United Bank 206-8 (49 overs) by 2 wkts
1988-89 United Bank 228-6 (45 overs) beat PIA 228 (45 overs) by losing fewer wkts
1989-90 Habib Bank 178-2 (42.4 overs) beat PIA 177 (46.3 overs) by 8 wkts
1990-91 Habib Bank 241-4 (45 overs) beat United Bank 185-9 (45overs) by 6 wkts
1991-92 Habib Bank 254-5 (39 overs) beat PIA 234-4 (43 overs) by 5 wkts
1992-93 National Bank 272-5 (48 overs) beat Habib Bank 269-6 (50 overs) by 5 wkts
1993-94 Habib Bank 249-5 (50 overs) beat Rawalpindi 203-8 (50 overs) by 46 runs
1994-95 National Bank 215-2 (43.2 overs) beat PIA 211 (44.4 overs) by 8 wkts
1995-96 PIA 125-3 (30.5 overs) beat Rawalpindi 124 (42.5 overs) by 7 wkts
1996-97 Allied Bank 252-4 (42.1 overs) beat National Bank 251-9 (50 overs) by 6 wkts

Table of Results 1980-81 to 1996-97

	P	W	L	NR	Winner	R-up
PIA	109	83	22	4	6	5
Habib Bank	99	72	20	7	6	2
United Bank	94	69	21	4	1	5
National Bank	96	52	37	7	2	1
ADBP	64	38	23	3	0	0
PNSC	42	21	21	0	0	0
PACO	44	20	22	2	0	0
Lahore	62	19	40	3	0	1
Karachi	47	18	27	2	0	0
Rawalpindi	47	18	28	1	0	1
HBFC	46	16	27	3	0	0
Allied Bank	26	14	12	0	1	0
Railways	43	14	26	3	0	0
Karachi Blues	33	13	20	0	0	0
Faisalabad	30	9	18	3	0	0
Muslim Commercial Bank	32	9	20	3	0	0
Rawalpindi A	11	7	4	0	0	1
Multan	13	4	9	0	0	0
Peshawar	16	4	12	0	0	0
WAPDA	10	3	7	0	0	0
Karachi Whites	26	3	21	2	0	0
Bahawalpur	20	2	18	0	0	0
Islamabad	15	2	13	0	0	0
Customs	3	1	2	0	0	0
Emirates Cricket Board	4	1	3	0	0	0
IDBP	4	1	3	0	0	0
Sargodha	9	1	8	0	0	0
State Bank	5	1	4	0	0	0
UGC	11	1	10	0	0	0
Bangladesh	4	0	4	0	0	0
North Zone	5	0	4	1	0	0
Rawalpindi B	6	0	6	0	0	0
South Zone	4	0	4	0	0	0

Two Karachi teams took part in 1990-91, 1991-92, 1993-94, 1994-95 and 1995-96 and two Rawalpindi teams took part in 1994-95 and 1995-96.

1996-97 AND CAREER RECORDS FOR PAKISTAN PLAYERS

Cmp	Debut	M	I	NO	Runs	HS	Avge	100	50	Balls	Runs	Wkts	Avge	BB	5i	10m	RpO	ct	st
AALEY HAIDER (Karachi Whites, Allied Bank) b Karachi 4.12.1973 RHB OB																			

AALEY HAIDER (Karachi Whites, Allied Bank) b Karachi 4.12.1973 RHB OB

Cmp	Debut	M	I	NO	Runs	HS	Avge	100	50	Balls	Runs	Wkts	Avge	BB	5i	10m	RpO	ct	st
FC		11	20	0	572	124	28.60	1	2									19	
Wlls		7	5	2	81	36*	27.00	0	0	12	7	0					3.50	0	
FC	1993	54	85	4	2433	124	30.03	3	13	32	17	0					3.18	52	
Wlls	1991	29	25	4	535	85	25.47	0	2	42	26	2	13.00	2-5	0	0	3.71	9	

AAMER BASHIR (United Bank) b Multan 23.2.1972 RHB RM

Cmp	Debut	M	I	NO	Runs	HS	Avge	100	50	Balls	Runs	Wkts	Avge	BB	5i	10m	RpO	ct	st
FC		4	7	0	83	30	11.85	0	0	174	68	1	68.00	1-27	0	0	2.34	6	
Wlls		8	8	1	292	78	41.71	0	3	30	30	0					6.00	3	
FC	1989	76	118	8	2703	95	24.57	0	17	1592	742	16	46.37	3-36	0	0	2.79	44	
Wlls	1990	27	27	5	828	103	37.63	1	6	165	147	4	36.75	1-15	0	0	5.34	7	

AAMER GANGAT (Karachi Whites) b Karachi 28.10.1976 RHB OB

Cmp	Debut	M	I	NO	Runs	HS	Avge	100	50	Balls	Runs	Wkts	Avge	BB	5i	10m	RpO	ct	st
FC		1	1	0	8	8	8.00	0	0									0	

AAMER GUL (Bahawalpur, National Bank) b Lahore 27.12.1974 RHB OB

Cmp	Debut	M	I	NO	Runs	HS	Avge	100	50	Balls	Runs	Wkts	Avge	BB	5i	10m	RpO	ct	st
FC		5	10	0	202	60	20.20	0	1	108	53	1	53.00	1-4	0	0	2.94	2	
Wlls		1	1	1	3	3*		0	0	12	8	0					4.00	0	
FC	1994	13	25	0	460	88	18.40	0	2	288	157	4	39.25	2-56	0	0	3.27	11	

AAMER HANIF (Karachi Whites, Allied Bank) b Karachi 4.10.1971 RHB RM

Cmp	Debut	M	I	NO	Runs	HS	Avge	100	50	Balls	Runs	Wkts	Avge	BB	5i	10m	RpO	ct	st
FC		13	24	1	735	134	31.95	1	5	1175	488	30	16.26	5-57	1	0	2.49	7	
Wlls		8	7	3	172	46	43.00	0	0	258	172	3	57.33	2-19	0	0	4.00	2	
FC	1989	106	164	11	5245	225	34.28	10	25	5376	2599	130	19.99	7-71	7	1	2.90	65	
Int	1993	5	4	2	89	36*	44.50	0	0	130	122	4	30.50	3-36	0	0	5.63	0	
Wlls	1988	43	40	10	1246	108	41.53	2	6	1276	878	20	43.90	2-16	0	0	4.12	12	

AAMER IQBAL (Customs) b Karachi 2.6.1973 RHB WK

Cmp	Debut	M	I	NO	Runs	HS	Avge	100	50	Balls	Runs	Wkts	Avge	BB	5i	10m	RpO	ct	st
FC		6	12	1	181	57	16.45	0	1									3	
Wlls		3	3	2	74	40*	74.00	0	0									2	4
FC	1991	19	27	3	534	94	22.25	0	3									33	3
Wlls	1993	11	11	2	222	60	24.66	0	1									10	9

AAMER MAHMOOD (Peshawar) b Peshawar 16.12.1977 RHB RFM

Cmp	Debut	M	I	NO	Runs	HS	Avge	100	50	Balls	Runs	Wkts	Avge	BB	5i	10m	RpO	ct	st
Wlls		1	1	0	8	8	8.00	0	0	60	59	2	29.50	2-59	0	0	5.90	0	

AAMER MANZOOR (Lahore) b Lahore 5.5.1971 RHB

Cmp	Debut	M	I	NO	Runs	HS	Avge	100	50	Balls	Runs	Wkts	Avge	BB	5i	10m	RpO	ct	st
FC		2	4	1	67	41	22.33	0	0									2	
Wlls		2	2	0	49	46	24.50	0	0									0	
FC	1993	9	15	3	525	127	43.75	1	1	6	2	0					2.00	4	
Wlls	1994	7	7	0	138	46	19.71	0	0	6	10	0					10.00	0	

AAMER NAZIR (Lahore, Allied Bank) b Lahore 2.1.1971 RHB RFM

Cmp	Debut	M	I	NO	Runs	HS	Avge	100	50	Balls	Runs	Wkts	Avge	BB	5i	10m	RpO	ct	st
FC		8	14	6	62	13*	7.75	0	0	1233	767	28	27.39	4-27	0	0	3.73	1	
Wlls		4	2	2	41	24*		0	0	210	225	9	25.00	5-55	0	1	6.42	0	
Test	1992	6	11	6	31	11	6.20	0	0	1057	597	20	28.95	5-46	1	0	3.38	2	
FC	1992	38	53	27	177	18	6.80	0	0	6245	3854	150	25.69	7-54	10	1	3.70	6	
Int	1992	9	3	2	13	9*	13.00	0	0	417	346	11	31.45	3-43	0	0	4.97	0	
Wlls	1993	14	7	5	52	24*	26.00	0	0	636	545	25	21.80	6-16	0	2	5.14	1	

AAMER NAZIR (Islamabad) b Multan 6.4.1966 RHB RM WK

Cmp	Debut	M	I	NO	Runs	HS	Avge	100	50	Balls	Runs	Wkts	Avge	BB	5i	10m	RpO	ct	st
FC		3	5	0	49	20	9.80	0	0	78	34	0					2.61	4	1
FC	1986	22	37	3	872	96	25.64	0	6	186	90	3	30.00	2-27	0	0	2.90	33	6
Wlls	1989	8	8	0	83	20	10.37	0	0	90	79	4	19.75	2-24	0	0	5.26	7	1

AAMER SOHAIL (Allied Bank, Pakistan, Combined XI, Pakistan to Canada, Pakistan to Sharjah, Pakistan to Australia) b Lahore 14.9.1966 LHB SLA

Cmp	Debut	M	I	NO	Runs	HS	Avge	100	50	Balls	Runs	Wkts	Avge	BB	5i	10m	RpO	ct	st
Test		2	3	1	66	46	33.00	0	0	102	34	0					2.00	0	
FC		5	9	1	377	132	47.12	1	1	498	215	8	26.87	4-76	0	0	2.59	1	
Int		1	1	0	55	55	55.00	0	1	36	40	0					6.66	0	
Wlls		8	8	0	217	62	27.12	0	2	384	277	8	34.62	3-33	0	0	4.32	4	
Test	1992	34	62	3	2103	205	35.64	2	13	1613	710	17	41.76	4-54	0	0	2.64	31	
FC	1983	161	276	17	9863	205	38.08	19	46	9862	4899	139	35.24	7-53	2	1	2.98	132	
Int	1990	122	121	2	3919	134	32.93	5	26	4030	3010	70	43.00	4-22	1	0	4.48	39	
Wlls	1983	55	52	4	1508	103	31.41	2	10	1517	1110	51	21.76	4-11	4	0	4.39	22	

AAMER SOHAIL (Bahawalpur, Customs) b Bahawalpur 10.10.1972 LHB SLA

Cmp	Debut	M	I	NO	Runs	HS	Avge	100	50	Balls	Runs	Wkts	Avge	BB	5i	10m	RpO	ct	st
FC		8	15	0	233	93	15.53	0	2	186	95	4	23.75	2-4	0	0	3.06	8	
FC	1989	49	88	6	1502	98	18.31	0	6	1842	960	32	30.00	4-64	0	0	3.12	28	
Wlls	1990	10	10	2	130	38	16.25	0	0	224	164	6	27.33	4-56	1	0	4.39	1	

AAQIB JAVED (Islamabad, Allied Bank, Combined XI, Pakistan to India) b Sheikhupura 5.8.1972 RHB RFM

Cmp	Debut	M	I	NO	Runs	HS	Avge	100	50	Balls	Runs	Wkts	Avge	BB	5i	10m	RpO	ct	st
FC		10	15	4	183	65	16.63	0	1	1695	852	50	17.04	9-51	4	2	3.00	1	
Wlls		2								108	106	5	21.20	4-46	1	0	5.88	0	
Test	1988	21	25	6	100	28*	5.26	0	0	3754	1786	54	33.07	5-84	1	0	2.85	2	
FC	1984	87	89	30	505	65	8.55	0	1	13929	7144	245	29.15	9-51	11	2	3.07	10	

171

Cmp	Debut	M	I	NO	Runs	HS	Avge	100	50	Balls	Runs	Wkts	Avge	BB	5i	10m	RpO	ct	st
Int	1988	139	45	25	252	45*	12.60	0	0	6931	4916	157	31.31	7-37	1	4	4.25	19	
Wlls	1989	17	9	3	54	29	9.00	0	0	780	594	24	24.75	5-26	2	1	4.56	5	

ABDUL BASIT NIAZI (Rawalpindi) b Mianwali 6.11.1968 RHB LB

Cmp	Debut	M	I	NO	Runs	HS	Avge	100	50	Balls	Runs	Wkts	Avge	BB	5i	10m	RpO	ct	st
Wlls		4	4	1	174	100*	58.00	1	1									0	
FC	1988	15	26	1	690	147	27.60	2	3	419	232	7	33.14	3-40	0	0	3.32	11	
Wlls	1990	9	9	1	271	100*	33.87	1	1	14	5	1	5.00	1-5	0	0	2.14	3	

ABDULLAH KHAN (Karachi Whites) b Karachi 15.2.1965 RHB RM

Cmp	Debut	M	I	NO	Runs	HS	Avge	100	50	Balls	Runs	Wkts	Avge	BB	5i	10m	RpO	ct	st
FC		1	1	1	43	43*		0	0	42	8	0					1.14	2	
FC	1986	35	57	6	1886	155*	36.98	3	10	1414	673	16	42.06	4-49	0	0	2.85	11	
Wlls	1988	19	19	1	444	66	24.66	0	5	399	261	7	37.28	3-39	0	0	3.92	3	

ABDUR RAZZAQ (Lahore, Pakistan, Pakistan to India, Pakistan A to England) b Lahore 2.12.1979 RHB RFM

Cmp	Debut	M	I	NO	Runs	HS	Avge	100	50	Balls	Runs	Wkts	Avge	BB	5i	10m	RpO	ct	st
FC		1	2	1	8	6*	8.00	0	0	228	119	9	13.22	7-51	1	0	3.13	1	
Int		2	1	1	0	0*		0	0	75	53	3	17.66	2-29	0	0	4.24	0	
FC	1996	7	11	3	224	62	28.00	0	2	1352	872	32	27.25	7-51	2	0	3.86	1	
Int	1996	4	2	1	8	8	8.00	0	0	147	139	4	34.75	2-29	0	0	5.67	0	

ABDUS SALAM KHAN (Peshawar) b Peshawar 24.9.1974 LHB SLA

Cmp	Debut	M	I	NO	Runs	HS	Avge	100	50	Balls	Runs	Wkts	Avge	BB	5i	10m	RpO	ct	st
FC		4	7	0	229	90	32.71	0	1									4	
Wlls		3	3	0	94	68	31.33	0	1									0	
Wlls	1995	8	8	0	178	68	22.25	0	2									1	

ABID HANIF (Karachi Blues) b Karachi 29.8.1969 RHB OB

Cmp	Debut	M	I	NO	Runs	HS	Avge	100	50	Balls	Runs	Wkts	Avge	BB	5i	10m	RpO	ct	st
Wlls		1	1	0	61	61	61.00	0	1									1	
Wlls	1993	4	4	0	186	63	46.50	0	3									1	

ADNAN JAFRI (Karachi Blues) b Karachi 30.9.1973 RHB LFM

Cmp	Debut	M	I	NO	Runs	HS	Avge	100	50	Balls	Runs	Wkts	Avge	BB	5i	10m	RpO	ct	st
FC		1	2	0	4	4	2.00	0	0	65	84	0					7.75	0	

ADNAN NAEEM (PIA) b Lahore 20.11.1974 RHB RM

Cmp	Debut	M	I	NO	Runs	HS	Avge	100	50	Balls	Runs	Wkts	Avge	BB	5i	10m	RpO	ct	st
FC		3	5	2	43	23	14.33	0	0	318	238	7	34.00	3-75	0	0	4.49	0	
FC	1994	5	7	2	77	23	15.40	0	0	597	479	10	47.90	3-75	0	0	4.81	0	
Wlls	1994	5	2	2	0	0*		0	0	240	218	10	21.80	4-50	2	0	5.45	5	

AFSAR NAWAZ (Customs) b Karachi 16.12.1973 RHB OB

Cmp	Debut	M	I	NO	Runs	HS	Avge	100	50	Balls	Runs	Wkts	Avge	BB	5i	10m	RpO	ct	st
Wlls		3	3	0	63	43	21.00	0	0									0	

AHMED HAYAT (PNSC) b Sargodha 15.3.1969 RHB

Cmp	Debut	M	I	NO	Runs	HS	Avge	100	50	Balls	Runs	Wkts	Avge	BB	5i	10m	RpO	ct	st
Wlls		1	1	0	1	1	1.00	0	0	12	17	0					8.50	1	
FC	1988	13	18	4	148	50	10.57	0	1	756	541	11	49.18	6-142	1	0	4.29	6	
Wlls	1993	7	5	1	3	2	0.75	0	0	312	272	12	22.66	5-31	0	1	5.23	2	

AHMED SHAHAB (Bahawalpur) b Lahore 1.5.1969 RHB OB

Cmp	Debut	M	I	NO	Runs	HS	Avge	100	50	Balls	Runs	Wkts	Avge	BB	5i	10m	RpO	ct	st
FC		1	1	0	8	8	8.00	0	0									0	
Wlls	1995	1	1	0	0	0	0.00	0	0	30	31	0					6.20	0	

AHMED SIDDIQ (Faisalabad) b Lyallpur 11.4.1974 RHB OB

Cmp	Debut	M	I	NO	Runs	HS	Avge	100	50	Balls	Runs	Wkts	Avge	BB	5i	10m	RpO	ct	st
Wlls		5	4	0	41	26	10.25	0	0	72	59	0					4.91	0	
FC	1994	8	12	1	256	45	23.27	0	0									4	
Wlls	1994	8	7	0	84	41	12.00	0	0	72	59	0					4.91	0	

AHMER SAEED (Karachi Blues, Combined XI) b Karachi 21.11.1978 RHB OB

Cmp	Debut	M	I	NO	Runs	HS	Avge	100	50	Balls	Runs	Wkts	Avge	BB	5i	10m	RpO	ct	st
FC		4	7	0	231	74	33.00	0	2	18	11	1	11.00	1-11	0	0	3.66	3	

AHSAN ALI SHAH (Bahawalpur) b Chakwal 7.2.1976 RHB WK

Cmp	Debut	M	I	NO	Runs	HS	Avge	100	50	Balls	Runs	Wkts	Avge	BB	5i	10m	RpO	ct	st
Wlls		1	1	0	4	4	4.00	0	0									1	
FC	1995	2	4	0	18	12	4.50	0	0										

AHSAN RAZA (Lahore) b Lahore 29.10.1975 RHB WK

Cmp	Debut	M	I	NO	Runs	HS	Avge	100	50	Balls	Runs	Wkts	Avge	BB	5i	10m	RpO	ct	st
FC		5	10	2	74	20	9.25	0	0									21	2
FC	1993	13	21	4	128	20	7.52	0	0									40	3

AKHTAR SARFRAZ (Peshawar, National Bank) b Peshawar 20.2.1976 LHB LM

Cmp	Debut	M	I	NO	Runs	HS	Avge	100	50	Balls	Runs	Wkts	Avge	BB	5i	10m	RpO	ct	st
FC		12	22	2	700	135	35.00	2	5	94	74	1	74.00	1-15	0	0	4.72	10	
Wlls		2	2	0	67	61	33.50	0	1	54	47	1	47.00	1-47	0	0	5.22	1	
FC	1994	19	34	3	1024	162	33.03	4	5	94	74	1	74.00	1-15	0	0	4.72	12	
Wlls	1994	8	8	0	257	63	32.12	0	3	66	60	1	60.00	1-47	0	0	5.45	2	

AKHTAR SHAFIQ (Lahore) b Lahore 26.10.1978 RHB OB

Cmp	Debut	M	I	NO	Runs	HS	Avge	100	50	Balls	Runs	Wkts	Avge	BB	5i	10m	RpO	ct	st
FC		1	2	1	0	0*	0.00	0	0	72	45	0					3.75	0	

AKIF ALVI (Karachi Whites) b Karachi 25.12.1971 RHB RM

Cmp	Debut	M	I	NO	Runs	HS	Avge	100	50	Balls	Runs	Wkts	Avge	BB	5i	10m	RpO	ct	st
FC		1	1	0	0	0	0.00	0	0	96	43	1	43.00	1-29	0	0	2.68	1	
Wlls	1993	5	5	1	38	13	12.66	0	0	216	185	6	30.83	2-28	0	0	5.13	1	

AKRAM RAZA (Faisalabad, Habib Bank) b Lahore 22.11.1964 RHB OB

Cmp	Debut	M	I	NO	Runs	HS	Avge	100	50	Balls	Runs	Wkts	Avge	BB	5i	10m	RpO	ct	st
FC		12	16	6	365	77*	36.50	0	1	2241	967	51	18.96	5-49	2	0	2.58	5	
Wlls		3	2	2	98	52*		0	1	180	94	1	94.00	1-23	0	0	3.13	0	
Test	1989	9	12	2	153	32	15.30	0	0	1526	732	13	56.30	3-46	0	0	2.87	8	
FC	1981	155	213	53	4735	145*	29.59	3	26	31250	13331	509	26.19	7-82	25	2	2.55	124	
Int	1989	49	25	14	193	33*	17.54	0	0	2601	1611	38	42.39	3-18	0	0	3.71	19	
Wlls	1985	71	37	14	490	52*	21.30	0	2	3674	2003	90	22.25	4-27	2	0	3.27	43	

Cmp	Debut	M	I	NO	Runs	HS	Avge	100	50	Balls	Runs	Wkts	Avge	BB	5i	10m	RpO	ct	st
ALAMGIR KHAN (Islamabad) b Rawalpindi 17.9.1975 LHB SLA																			
FC		3	4	1	28	13*	9.33	0	0	217	89	2	44.50	1-22	0	0	2.46	2	
Wlls		1								42	44	0					6.28	0	
FC	1994	8	14	6	47	13*	5.87	0	0	961	442	13	34.00	2-15	0	0	2.75	4	
Wlls	1993	8	5	2	31	23	10.33	0	0	379	252	12	21.00	3-26	0	0	3.98	3	
ALEEM MOOSA (National Bank) b Lahore 21.12.1973 RHB RM																			
Wlls		4	1	1	4	4*		0	0	72	75	3	25.00	3-34	0	0	6.25	1	
FC	1992	7	8	3	10	4	2.00	0	0	570	407	8	50.87	3-67	0	0	4.28	4	
ALI GAUHAR (Karachi Blues, United Bank) b Sukkur 25.10.1969 RHB RFM																			
FC		11	14	7	77	40*	11.00	0	0	2493	1244	52	23.92	6-55	3	1	2.99	2	
Wlls		6	4	1	15	11	5.00	0	0	285	241	8	30.12	3-22	0	0	5.07	0	
FC	1993	34	36	16	224	40*	11.20	0	0	6217	3311	146	22.67	7-92	11	4	3.19	6	
Wlls	1994	12	9	2	33	11	4.71	0	0	574	404	18	22.44	3-22	0	0	4.22	0	
ALI HUSSAIN RIZVI (Karachi Whites, Customs, Pakistan A to England) b Karachi 6.1.1974 RHB LB																			
FC		11	20	4	87	25	5.43	0	0	2323	1090	54	20.18	6-123	4	1	2.81	8	
Wlls		3	2	0	5	5	2.50	0	0	180	151	3	50.33	2-47	0	0	5.06	1	
FC	1993	31	44	8	243	28	6.75	0	0	5488	2519	101	24.94	6-77	6	1	2.75	19	
Wlls	1995	7	6	0	9	5	1.50	0	0	366	289	12	24.08	4-19	1	0	4.73	3	
ALI JAFFAR (Karachi Whites) b Karachi 26.1.1976 RHB WK																			
FC		1	1	0	25	25	25.00	0	0									1	1
Wlls		1	1	0	48	48	48.00	0	0									0	
ALI NAQVI (Karachi Blues, Pakistan A to England) b Lahore 19.3.1977 RHB RMF																			
Wlls		1	1	0	10	10	10.00	0	0									0	
FC	1997	8	13	0	362	114	25.85	1	1	36	20	1	20.00	1-11	0	0	3.33	4	
ALI RAZA (Karachi Blues, Karachi Whites) b Karachi 10.12.1974 LHB LFM																			
FC		1	2	1	3	3*	3.00	0	0	108	50	2	25.00	2-46	0	0	2.77	0	
Wlls		2								66	65	1	65.00	1-36	0	0	5.90	0	
AMEEM ABBAS (Lahore) b Lahore 26.4.1975 RHB RFM																			
Wlls		1	1	0	42	42	42.00	0	0	42	41	0					5.85	0	
AMEER AKBAR BABAR (National Bank) b Lahore 18.4.1964 RHB RFM																			
FC		2	4	0	43	28	10.75	0	0									2	
Wlls		4	4	0	54	21	13.50	0	0	6	4	0					4.00	0	
FC	1983	128	211	25	6810	151*	36.61	14	33	2494	1407	38	37.02	4-34	0	0	3.38	83	
Wlls	1983	74	71	10	1967	84	32.24	0	12	984	697	23	30.30	4-7	1	0	4.25	23	
AMJAD ALI (Faisalabad) b Lyallpur 1.6.1973 RHB OB																			
FC		4	8	0	186	77	23.25	0	1									3	
Wlls		3	3	0	9	7	3.00	0	0									0	
FC	1995	7	13	0	353	77	27.15	0	2									6	
ANWAR MIANDAD (Habib Bank) b Karachi 11.3.1960 RHB SLA																			
FC		3	5	0	108	49	21.60	0	0									2	
FC	1978	141	231	25	5018	123	24.35	4	26	3313	2003	51	39.27	4-22	0	0	3.62	82	
Wlls	1980	67	45	12	877	91*	26.57	0	4	840	594	29	20.48	7-20	1	1	4.24	17	
AQEEL AZIZ (Bahawalpur) b Karachi 30.6.1978 RHB OB																			
FC		1	2	0	7	5	3.50	0	0	2	5	0					15.00	2	
Wlls		1	1	0	11	11	11.00	0	0									1	
ARIF BUTT (Rawalpindi) b Attock 10.6.1972 RHB																			
FC		4	6	0	76	37	12.66	0	0									2	
Wlls		3	3	0	47	28	15.66	0	0									1	
FC	1989	22	39	1	886	111	23.31	1	3	1	4	0					24.00	8	
Wlls	1989	22	22	2	351	55*	17.55	0	1									7	
ARIF MAHMOOD (Karachi Blues) b Karachi 19.4.1971 RHB SLA																			
FC		1	2	0	0	0	0.00	0	0	24	9	0					2.25	0	
Wlls		6	5	1	75	27*	18.75	0	0	224	176	5	35.20	2-17	0	0	4.71	2	
Wlls	1993	15	14	1	190	40	14.61	0	0	660	498	14	35.57	3-43	0	0	4.52	4	
ARIF ZAHEER (Karachi Whites) b Karachi RHB RFM																			
Wlls		1	1	0	4	4	4.00	0	0	24	14	0					3.50	0	
ARSHAD KHAN (Peshawar, Allied Bank, Pakistan to India) b Peshawar 22.3.1971 RHB OB																			
FC		12	20	0	222	32	11.10	0	0	2086	878	36	24.38	6-74	2	0	2.52	6	
Wlls		3	1	1	29	29*		0	0	168	95	0					3.39	2	
FC	1988	72	104	20	781	32	9.29	0	0	13164	5573	236	23.61	8-115	14	2	2.54	40	
Int	1992	6	5	3	15	9*	7.50	0	0	293	213	4	53.25	2-54	0	0	4.36	3	
Wlls	1991	15	10 ·	3	70	29*	10.00	0	0	763	435	14	31.07	4-17	1	0	3.42	6	
ASADULLAH BUTT (Habib Bank) b Lahore 15.8.1970 RHB RF																			
FC		8	13	4	291	83	32.33	0	2	1181	647	16	40.43	5-77	1	0	3.28	6	
Wlls		3	3	1	93	50	46.50	0	1	66	46	0					4.18	0	
FC	1991	49	72	14	1214	83	20.93	0	6	8059	4406	167	28.06	7-93	8	1	3.28	25	
Wlls	1990	19	14	2	146	50	12.16	0	1	876	581	23	25.26	4-32	2	0	3.97	5	

173

Cmp	Debut	M	I	NO	Runs	HS	Avge	100	50	Balls	Runs	Wkts	Avge	BB	5i	10m	RpO	ct	st

ASGHAR ALI TABASSAM (Faisalabad) b Lyallpur 10.6.1975 RHB RM

Cmp	Debut	M	I	NO	Runs	HS	Avge	100	50	Balls	Runs	Wkts	Avge	BB	5i	10m	RpO	ct	st
FC		1	2	0	10	9	5.00	0	0									0	

ASIF ALI SAEED (Islamabad) b Rawalpindi 9.9.1973 RHB RFM

Cmp	Debut	M	I	NO	Runs	HS	Avge	100	50	Balls	Runs	Wkts	Avge	BB	5i	10m	RpO	ct	st
FC		7	12	0	183	58	15.25	0	1									8	
Wlls		3	3	1	75	59*	37.50	0	1	24	36	1	36.00	1-36	0	0	9.00	2	
FC	1992	28	43	2	655	72	15.97	0	2	42	29	0					4.14	27	
Wlls	1992	13	13	1	262	59*	21.83	0	2	24	36	1	36.00	1-36	0	0	9.00	4	

ASIF MAHMOOD (Islamabad) b Islamabad 23.3.1979 RHB SLA

Cmp	Debut	M	I	NO	Runs	HS	Avge	100	50	Balls	Runs	Wkts	Avge	BB	5i	10m	RpO	ct	st
FC		2	4	0	46	18	11.50	0	0	48	28	2	14.00	1-13	0	0	3.50	0	
Wlls		1	1	0	31	31	31.00	0	0	60	43	0					4.30	1	

ASIF MAHMOOD (Rawalpindi) b Rawalpindi 18.12.1975 RHB OB

Cmp	Debut	M	I	NO	Runs	HS	Avge	100	50	Balls	Runs	Wkts	Avge	BB	5i	10m	RpO	ct	st
FC		4	6	0	144	62	24.00	0	1									2	
Wlls		6	5	0	139	74	27.80	0	1									2	
FC	1994	12	20	0	453	62	22.65	0	1	1	4	0					24.00	6	
Wlls	1994	14	13	1	410	107*	34.16	1	2	24	13	1	13.00	1-6	0	0	3.25	5	

ASIF MOHAMMAD (PIA) b Karachi 21.12.1965 RHB OB

Cmp	Debut	M	I	NO	Runs	HS	Avge	100	50	Balls	Runs	Wkts	Avge	BB	5i	10m	RpO	ct	st
FC		3	3	0	19	13	6.33	0	0	263	63	5	12.60	2-18	0	0	1.43	3	
FC	1978	109	170	17	4945	183	32.32	7	27	3546	1550	53	29.24	5-54	2	0	2.62	82	
Wlls	1982	75	58	15	1201	70*	27.93	0	5	2132	1296	56	23.14	4-21	3	0	3.64	29	

ASIF MUJTABA (Karachi Blues, PIA, Pakistan to Sri Lanka) b Karachi 4.11.1967 LHB SLA

Cmp	Debut	M	I	NO	Runs	HS	Avge	100	50	Balls	Runs	Wkts	Avge	BB	5i	10m	RpO	ct	st
FC		11	19	3	913	116	57.06	2	7	1191	342	26	13.15	5-60	2	0	1.72	6	
Wlls		1	1	0	5	5	5.00	0	0	59	38	1	38.00	1-38	0	0	3.86	2	
Test	1986	25	41	3	928	65*	24.42	0	8	666	303	4	75.75	1-0	0	0	2.72	20	
FC	1984	197	309	60	12465	208	50.06	37	62	13900	5431	236	23.01	6-19	12	2	2.34	175	
Int	1986	66	55	14	1068	113*	26.04	1	6	756	658	7	94.00	2-38	0	0	5.22	18	
Wlls	1983	73	66	16	1578	80	31.56	0	11	2374	1488	64	23.25	4-27	2	0	3.76	29	

ASIM RIZVI (Karachi Blues) b Karachi 1.9.1971 RHB OB

Cmp	Debut	M	I	NO	Runs	HS	Avge	100	50	Balls	Runs	Wkts	Avge	BB	5i	10m	RpO	ct	st
Wlls		3	2	0	52	29	26.00	0	0									0	
FC	1986	13	20	3	525	110*	30.88	1	3	114	46	2	23.00	2-46	0	0	2.42	4	
Wlls	1993	5	4	0	69	29	17.25	0	0									0	

ASMATULLAH (Peshawar) b Peshawar 16.2.1975 RHB OB

Cmp	Debut	M	I	NO	Runs	HS	Avge	100	50	Balls	Runs	Wkts	Avge	BB	5i	10m	RpO	ct	st
FC		2	3	0	41	33	13.66	0	0									0	
Wlls		2	2	0	13	7	6.50	0	0	24	29	0					7.25	2	
FC	1995	6	9	0	126	50	14.00	0	1									6	
Wlls	1995	6	6	0	68	32	11.33	0	0	24	29	0					7.25	4	

ATA-UR-REHMAN (Lahore, Allied Bank) b Lahore 28.3.1975 RHB RFM

Cmp	Debut	M	I	NO	Runs	HS	Avge	100	50	Balls	Runs	Wkts	Avge	BB	5i	10m	RpO	ct	st
FC		5	7	0	42	15	6.00	0	0	830	431	25	17.24	5-56	2	0	3.11	2	
Wlls		8	2	0	4	4	2.00	0	0	327	275	7	39.28	2-32	0	0	5.04	1	
Test	1992	13	15	6	76	19	8.44	0	0	1973	1071	31	34.54	4-50	0	0	3.25	2	
FC	1990	64	64	13	411	34	8.05	0	0	9179	5376	171	31.43	8-56	5	1	3.51	20	
Int	1992	30	13	6	34	11*	4.85	0	0	1492	1186	27	43.92	3-27	0	0	4.76	0	
Wlls	1991	23	9	1	72	20	9.00	0	0	1013	788	33	23.87	4-17	1	0	4.66	4	

ATHAR LAEEQ (Karachi Blues, National Bank) b Karachi 10.2.1971 RHB RFM

Cmp	Debut	M	I	NO	Runs	HS	Avge	100	50	Balls	Runs	Wkts	Avge	BB	5i	10m	RpO	ct	st
FC		9	14	2	122	22	10.16	0	0	1841	935	38	24.60	6-57	3	1	3.04	2	
Wlls		8	5	2	80	24*	26.66	0	0	370	313	7	44.71	3-26	0	0	5.07	2	
FC	1989	90	106	24	1363	99	16.62	0	4	14933	7702	327	23.55	8-65	19	2	3.09	25	
Wlls	1990	33	24	5	182	24*	9.57	0	0	1449	1132	36	31.44	4-29	3	0	4.68	7	

ATIQ-UR-REHMAN (Lahore) b Lahore 29.12.1978 RHB OB

Cmp	Debut	M	I	NO	Runs	HS	Avge	100	50	Balls	Runs	Wkts	Avge	BB	5i	10m	RpO	ct	st
Wlls		1	1	0	29	29	29.00	0	0									0	

ATIF RAUF (ADBP, Patron's XI) b Lahore 3.3.1964 RHB OB

Cmp	Debut	M	I	NO	Runs	HS	Avge	100	50	Balls	Runs	Wkts	Avge	BB	5i	10m	RpO	ct	st
FC		8	14	2	294	105	24.50	1	0	18	10	0					3.33	6	
Wlls		6	5	2	123	43*	41.00	0	0									2	
Test	1993	1	2	0	25	16	12.50	0	0									0	
FC	1980	115	178	18	6359	200	39.74	14	36	315	290	2	145.00	1-25	0	0	5.52	59	
Wlls	1986	42	37	19	964	80*	53.55	0	6	6	12	0					12.00	9	

ATIQ-UZ-ZAMAN (Customs) b Karachi 20.7.1975 RHB WK

Cmp	Debut	M	I	NO	Runs	HS	Avge	100	50	Balls	Runs	Wkts	Avge	BB	5i	10m	RpO	ct	st
FC		2	4	1	69	26	23.00	0	0									4	1
Wlls	1995	3	2	0	36	25	18.00	0	0									3	2

AZAM KHAN (Karachi Blues, Customs, Pakistan, Combined XI, Pakistan to Sharjah) b Karachi 1.3.1969 RHB

Cmp	Debut	M	I	NO	Runs	HS	Avge	100	50	Balls	Runs	Wkts	Avge	BB	5i	10m	RpO	ct	st
Test		1	1	0	14	14	14.00	0	0									0	
FC		9	17	1	529	70	33.06	0	4									10	
Int		2	1	0	72	72	72.00	0	1									1	
FC	1986	76	131	11	4450	215*	37.08	9	24	24	21	0					5.25	56	
Int	1996	5	4	0	113	72	28.25	0	1									1	
Wlls	1988	16	15	2	318	56*	24.46	0	1									3	

AZEEM HAFEEZ (PIA) b Jhelum 29.7.1963 LHB LFM

Cmp	Debut	M	I	NO	Runs	HS	Avge	100	50	Balls	Runs	Wkts	Avge	BB	5i	10m	RpO	ct	st
FC		2	3	2	12	8*	12.00	0	0	180	117	3	39.00	2-47	0	0	3.90	0	
Test	1983	18	21	5	134	24	8.37	0	0	4351	2204	63	34.98	6-46	4	0	3.03	1	

Cmp	Debut	M	I	NO	Runs	HS	Avge	100	50	Balls	Runs	Wkts	Avge	BB	5i	10m	RpO	ct	st
FC	1982	85	107	26	923	69	11.39	0	1	13793	7832	235	33.32	7-54	9	1	3.40	17	
Int	1983	15	10	7	45	15	15.00	0	0	719	586	15	39.06	4-22	1	0	4.89	3	
Wlls	1982	44	19	11	121	29*	15.12	0	0	1972	1442	49	29.42	5-23	3	1	4.38	1	

AZHAR ABBAS (Bahawalpur) b Khanewal 1.4.1975 RHB RM

FC		1	2	0	8	8	4.00	0	0	78	47	1	47.00	1-41	0	0	3.61	1	
FC	1995	7	13	3	26	8	2.60	0	0	981	535	12	44.58	4-96	0	0	3.27	1	
Wlls	1994	5	3	2	0	0*	0.00	0	0	180	130	7	18.57	3-23	0	0	4.33	0	

AZHAR MAHMOOD (Islamabad, United Bank, Pakistan, Pakistan A to England, Pakistan to Canada, Pakistan to Kenya, Pakistan to India) b Rawalpindi 28.2.1975 RHB RFM

FC		11	19	1	355	69	19.72	0	2	2363	1011	59	17.13	7-65	3	2	2.56	13	
Int		1	1	1	6	6*		0	0	24	17	0					4.25	0	
Wlls		2	1	1	10	10*		0	0	108	94	0					5.22	2	
FC	1993	43	67	11	1321	92	23.58	0	7	7936	3682	179	20.56	7-55	8	2	2.78	33	
Int	1996	9	7	1	41	15	6.83	0	0	306	305	2	152.50	2-38	0	0	5.98	3	
Wlls	1994	12	11	3	102	39	12.75	0	0	516	354	7	50.57	3-15	0	0	4.11	5	

AZHAR SHAFIQ (Bahawalpur, Customs) b Rahim Yar Khan 31.12.1978 LHB RM

FC		14	27	1	689	123	26.50	1	4	1309	756	43	17.58	6-56	4	1	3.46	9	
Wlls		2	2	0	95	90	47.50	0	1	54	41	1	41.00	1-33	0	0	4.55	2	
FC	1994	35	65	2	1534	123	24.34	1	10	3139	1804	89	20.26	7-93	8	2	3.44	14	

BABAR ALI (Lahore) b Lahore 1.6.1977 LHB SLA

FC		1	2	0	0	0	0.00	0	0	111	50	2	25.00	2-50	0	0	2.70	1	
FC	1995	2	4	0	28	17	7.00	0	0	171	82	4	20.50	2-32	0	0	2.87	2	

BABAR ZAMAN (PIA) b Rawalpindi 16.9.1966 RHB RM

FC		2	3	0	41	21	13.66	0	0	18	10	0					3.33	0	
Wlls		2	2	0	72	68	36.00	0	1	36	32	1	32.00	1-14	0	0	5.33	0	
FC	1986	63	109	4	2336	135	22.24	2	13	2529	1441	44	32.75	6-119	2	0	3.41	24	
Wlls	1985	32	29	2	740	110*	27.40	1	3	412	341	7	48.71	2-5	0	0	4.96	13	

BAQAR RIZVI (Karachi Whites) b Karachi 9.2.1968 RHB RFM

FC		5	7	3	54	14	13.50	0	0	713	344	14	24.57	5-33	1	0	2.89	1	
Wlls		2	1	0	0	0	0.00	0	0	54	57	1	57.00	1-45	0	0	6.33	1	
FC	1988	21	31	6	302	45	12.08	0	0	2270	1495	50	29.90	6-75	3	0	3.95	4	
Wlls	1990	21	16	4	121	21*	10.08	0	0	796	621	20	30.05	3-41	0	0	4.68	2	

BASIT ALI (Karachi Blues, United Bank) b Karachi 13.12.1970 RHB OB

FC		12	21	0	784	100	37.33	1	6									10	
Wlls		2	2	0	45	39	22.50	0	0									0	
Test	1992	19	33	1	858	103	26.81	1	5	6	6	0					6.00	6	
FC	1985	125	209	12	7751	157	39.34	20	41	725	399	6	66.50	2-16	0	0	3.30	67	
Int	1992	50	43	6	1265	127*	34.18	1	9	30	21	1	21.00	1-17	0	0	4.20	15	
Wlls	1986	48	47	2	1414	117	31.42	2	8	3	6	0					12.00	14	

BILAL AHMED (Faisalabad, ADBP) b Lyallpur 10.11.1965 RHB OB WK

FC		12	17	1	300	78	18.75	0	3	6	3	0					3.00	25	3
Wlls		1																0	
FC	1983	143	228	14	4435	126	20.72	2	17	132	120	3	40.00	3-47	0	0	5.45	282	56
Wlls	1986	44	31	6	567	89*	22.68	0	3									30	15

BILAL ASAD (Islamabad) b Jhang 17.11.1978 RHB WK

Wlls		3	3	0	70	42	23.33	0	0	18	36	0					12.00	1	
FC	1995	2	3	0	40	38	13.33	0	0									3	
Wlls	1993	8	8	0	104	42	13.00	0	0	18	36	0					12.00	1	

BILAL KHILJI (Bahawalpur, PNSC) b Bahawalpur 10.9.1975 LHB RM

FC		9	17	1	307	83	19.18	0	2	24	19	0					4.75	3	
FC	1994	17	32	1	650	83	20.96	0	5	72	61	2	30.50	2-27	0	0	5.08	6	

BILAL RANA (Islamabad, Allied Bank) b Sahiwal 5.9.1970 RHB SLA

FC		12	20	3	402	69	23.64	0	3	2352	984	36	27.33	6-26	4	1	2.51	7	
Wlls		3	2	0	58	32	29.00	0	0	108	75	1	75.00	1-41	0	0	4.16	1	
FC	1984	81	134	21	3109	121	27.51	3	15	14383	5945	275	21.61	7-57	15	4	2.48	57	
Wlls	1988	34	29	7	669	57*	30.40	0	2	1489	1167	39	29.92	3-20	0	0	4.70	9	

EHSAN BUTT (Islamabad, Allied Bank) b Lahore 30.11.1972 RHB

FC		10	18	1	460	88	27.05	0	4	54	15	0					1.66	6	
FC	1992	33	56	6	1430	136	28.60	1	9	138	56	0					2.43	21	
Wlls	1992	6	6	0	121	36	20.16	0	0	6	2	0					2.00	1	

FAHAD KHAN (Islamabad) b Islamabad 19.2.1978 RHB LB

FC		4	7	3	65	21*	16.25	0	0	360	238	6	39.66	4-63	0	0	3.96	1	
Wlls		2	2	0	9	7	4.50	0	0	111	79	3	26.33	2-35	0	0	4.27	1	
FC	1995	13	18	7	153	49	13.90	0	0	1395	888	24	37.00	4-14	0	0	3.81	5	
Wlls	1995	5	4	1	26	17*	8.66	0	0	237	207	4	51.75	2-35	0	0	5.24	2	

Cmp	Debut	M	I	NO	Runs	HS	Avge	100	50	Balls	Runs	Wkts	Avge	BB	5i	10m	RpO	ct	st

FAISAL ELAHI (Bahawalpur) b Bahawalpur 26.10.1975 LHB SLA

FC		3	6	1	48	42*	9.60	0	0	210	127	5	25.40	2-1	0	0	3.62	2	
Wlls		3	3	0	73	40	24.33	0	0	180	104	4	26.00	2-45	0	0	3.46	3	
FC	1994	13	24	4	280	42*	14.00	0	0	754	435	16	27.18	5-46	1	0	3.46	6	

FAISAL HASHMI (Lahore) b Lahore 15.7.1971 RHB SLA

| Wlls | | 1 | | | | | | | | 23 | 45 | 0 | | | | | 11.73 | 0 | |

FAISAL QURESHI (Karachi Blues, Karachi Whites) b Karachi 15.9.1970 RHB OB

FC		1	2	0	2	2	1.00	0	0									2	
Wlls		1	1	0	4	4	4.00	0	0									0	
FC	1986	54	91	6	2899	107*	24.69	2	12	24	21	0					5.25	64	1
Wlls	1989	16	15	3	300	80*	25.00	0	1	12	6	0					3.00	1	

FARHAN ADIL (Karachi Whites, Pakistan A to England) b Karachi 25.9.1977 RHB OB

| FC | | 1 | 2 | 0 | 16 | 13 | ·8.00 | 0 | 0 | | | | | | | | | 5 | |
| FC | 1996 | 6 | 11 | 0 | 214 | 50 | 19.45 | 0 | 1 | | | | | | | | | 8 | |

FAROOQ HAMEED (Bahawalpur) b Ahmedpur Sharqia 25.7.1978 RHB OB

| Wlls | | 3 | 3 | 3 | 13 | 5* | | 0 | 0 | 174 | 133 | 1 | 133.00 | 1-31 | 0 | 0 | 4.58 | 1 | |

FAZL-E-AKBAR (Peshawar, Pakistan A to England) b Peshawar 20.10.1980 RHB RFM

| FC | | 2 | 4 | 2 | 8 | 4* | 4.00 | 0 | 0 | 336 | 248 | 6 | 41.33 | 3-97 | 0 | 0 | 4.42 | 1 | |
| FC | 1996 | 4 | 7 | 3 | 19 | 6 | 4.75 | 0 | 0 | 606 | 429 | 10 | 42.90 | 3-97 | 0 | 0 | 4.24 | 1 | |

FIDA HUSSAIN (Faisalabad) b Lyallpur 25.11.1975 RHB OB

FC		4	7	1	98	55	16.33	0	1	412	194	3	64.66	2-32	0	0	2.82	5	
Wlls		7	6	1	217	106*	43.40	1	1	306	229	9	25.44	3-23	0	0	4.49	0	
FC	1995	6	10	1	198	83	22.00	0	2	544	233	6	38.83	2-22	0	0	2.56	6	
Wlls	1994	12	11	2	297	106*	33.00	1	1	546	415	15	27.66	3-23	0	0	4.56	2	

GHAFFAR KAZMI (Lahore, ADBP) b Lahore 25.12.1962 RHB LBG

FC		8	13	0	311	76	23.92	0	1	30	13	0					2.60	4	
Wlls		7	7	0	214	64	30.57	0	1	108	90	2	45.00	2-27	0	0	5.00	1	
FC	1981	127	192	19	5241	133	30.29	7	34	7831	4424	140	31.60	7-55	7	2	3.38	107	
Wlls	1985	61	53	8	1221	169	27.13	1	7	825	699	18	38.83	3-18	0	0	5.08	28	

GHAYAS-UD-DIN (Karachi Blues) b Karachi 27.12.1975 RHB OB

| FC | | 1 | 2 | 0 | 14 | 14 | 7.00 | 0 | 0 | | | | | | | | | 0 | |

GHULAM ABBAS (Islamabad) b Rawalpindi 12.10.1976 RHB LM

FC		3	4	1	20	12	6.66	0	0	390	232	12	19.33	4-53	0	0	3.56	0	
Wlls		1	1	0	7	7	7.00	0	0	42	25	2	12.50	2-25	0	0	3.57	0	
FC	1994	7	9	5	26	12	6.50	0	0	792	461	15	30.73	4-53	0	0	3.49	3	
Wlls	1995	3	2	0	7	7	3.50	0	0	108	93	3	31.00	2-25	0	0	5.16	0	

GHULAM ALI (Karachi Blues, PIA) b Karachi 8.9.1966 RHB RM

FC		10	19	5	636	142	45.42	2	2	120	71	1	71.00	1-11	0	0	3.55	11	
Wlls		7	7	0	121	66	17.28	0	1									1	
FC	1989	91	149	15	5415	224	40.41	16	26	847	478	20	23.90	5-43	1	0	3.38	55	
Int	1992	3	3	0	53	38	17.66	0	0									0	
Wlls	1989	50	50	1	1348	131	27.51	1	9	96	95	3	31.66	1-3	0	0	5.93	13	

HAARIS AHMED KHAN (Karachi Blues, Customs) b Karachi 3.9.1964 LHB OB

FC		9	17	4	214	50*	16.46	0	1	1983	836	34	24.58	6-131	2	1	2.52	4	
Wlls		3	3	1	32	18	16.00	0	0	168	112	6	18.66	3-17	0	0	4.00	1	
FC	1983	93	121	37	1443	65*	17.17	0	5	21276	8903	399	22.31	7-44	24	5	2.51	46	
Wlls	1985	38	26	9	174	27*	10.23	0	0	1745	1031	47	21.93	5-14	2	2	3.54	14	

HAIDER ALI (Karachi Blues) b Peshawar 24.12.1970 RHB RM

Wlls		2	1	1	1	1*		0	0	102	83	2	41.50	1-28	0	0	4.88	0	
FC	1995	2	1	0	0		0.00	0	0	384	190	5	38.00	3-68	0	0	2.96	0	
Wlls	1993	3	2	2	6	5*		0	0	150	118	2	59.00	1-28	0	0	4.72	0	

HAIDER NISAR (PIA) b Karachi 7.9.1968 RHB WK

| FC | | 2 | 3 | 1 | 16 | 10 | 8.00 | 0 | 0 | | | | | | | | | 3 | 2 |
| FC | 1986 | 26 | 32 | 8 | 238 | 58 | 9.91 | 0 | 1 | | | | | | | | | 55 | 16 |

HAMEED GUL (Peshawar) b Peshawar 4.11.1977 RHB OB

Wlls		1	1	0	10	10	10.00	0	0									0	
FC	1994	13	21	3	243	52	13.50	0	1	129	81	0					3.76	5	
Wlls	1995	7	7	0	133	54	19.00	0	1	104	104	4	26.00	2-27	0	0	6.00	4	

HAMID IQBAL (Faisalabad) b Gojra 7.6.1970 RHB LB

FC		1	1	0	2	2	2.00	0	0	60	43	0					4.30	0	
Wlls		5	2	1	37	36	37.00	0	0	270	193	4	48.25	1-27	0	0	4.28	0	
FC	1994	5	6	0	86	37	14.33	0	0	660	362	9	40.22	4-83	0	0	3.29	2	
Wlls	1993	8	5	1	111	36	27.75	0	0	342	231	5	46.20	1-25	0	0	4.05	0	

HAMMAD TARIQ (Bahawalpur) b Bahawalpur 22.12.1980 LHB RM

| Wlls | | 3 | 3 | 0 | 42 | 36 | 14.00 | 0 | 0 | 6 | 17 | 0 | | | | | 17.00 | 0 | |

HANIF-UR-REHMAN (Karachi Whites, National Bank) b Karachi 31.3.1976 RHB OB

Cmp	Debut	M	I	NO	Runs	HS	Avge	100	50	Balls	Runs	Wkts	Avge	BB	5i	10m	RpO	ct	st
FC		1	1	0	8	8	8.00	0	0									0	
Wlls		1	1	0	7	7	7.00	0	0									1	
FC	1995	6	11	1	205	76	20.50	0	1									4	

HASAN RAZA (Karachi Blues, Pakistan, Combined XI, Pakistan A to England, Pakistan to Sharjah) b Karachi 11.3.1982 RHB LB

Cmp	Debut	M	I	NO	Runs	HS	Avge	100	50	Balls	Runs	Wkts	Avge	BB	5i	10m	RpO	ct	st
Test		1	1	0	27	27	27.00	0	0									0	
FC		3	5	0	217	96	43.40	0	2									0	
Int		3	2	0	23	12	11.50	0	0									0	
Wlls		1	1	1	13	13*		0	0									1	
FC	1996	9	15	0	566	96	37.73	0	6	114	50	1	50.00	1-36	0	0	2.63	3	
Int	1996	5	4	0	29	12	7.25	0	0									0	

HASNAIN KAZIM (United Bank) b Lahore 11.3.1973 RHB RM

Cmp	Debut	M	I	NO	Runs	HS	Avge	100	50	Balls	Runs	Wkts	Avge	BB	5i	10m	RpO	ct	st
FC		5	9	5	34	22	8.50	0	0	642	369	25	14.76	6-41	2	1	3.44	2	
Wlls		1	1	1	3	3*		0	0	36	37	0					6.16	1	
FC	1992	27	35	18	206	37	12.11	0	0	3000	1602	94	17.04	7-54	6	2	3.20	6	
Wlls	1992	19	10	6	37	19	9.25	0	0	832	624	23	27.13	3-25	0	0	4.50	7	

HUMAYUN FIDA HUSSAIN (Karachi Blues) b Karachi 10.10.1966 LHB RFM

Cmp	Debut	M	I	NO	Runs	HS	Avge	100	50	Balls	Runs	Wkts	Avge	BB	5i	10m	RpO	ct	st
FC		1	1	0	17	17	17.00	0	0	162	116	6	19.33	3-45	0	0	4.29	0	
FC	1991	32	38	12	254	28	9.76	0	0	4045	2303	92	25.03	6-44	3	0	3.41	6	
Wlls	1992	13	7	3	27	10*	6.75	0	0	647	394	19	20.73	4-17	1	0	3.65	2	

IDREES BAIG (Peshawar, Habib Bank) b Lahore 23.6.1972 RHB RM

Cmp	Debut	M	I	NO	Runs	HS	Avge	100	50	Balls	Runs	Wkts	Avge	BB	5i	10m	RpO	ct	st
FC		9	16	0	273	56	17.06	0	2	24	10	0					2.50	4	
Wlls		1	1	0	45	45	45.00	0	0									0	
FC	1991	41	70	7	2102	158	33.36	4	9	138	64	1	64.00	1-18	0	0	2.78	31	
Wlls	1991	8	7	0	116	45	16.57	0	0									2	

IFTIKHAR ASGHAR (Rawalpindi) b Rawalpindi 12.12.1973 LHB SLA

Cmp	Debut	M	I	NO	Runs	HS	Avge	100	50	Balls	Runs	Wkts	Avge	BB	5i	10m	RpO	ct	st
FC		2	3	0	15	8	5.00	0	0	203	110	7	15.71	4-32	0	0	3.25	0	
Wlls		4	3	1	51	25	25.50	0	0	180	105	3	35.00	2-39	0	0	3.50	0	
FC	1994	15	25	4	300	35	14.28	0	0	2302	966	33	29.27	6-59	1	0	2.51	8	
Wlls	1993	13	11	2	143	30	15.88	0	0	582	339	11	30.81	2-15	0	0	3.49	1	

IJAZ AHMED (Pakistan, Habib Bank, Pakistan to Australia, Pakistan to Sri Lanka, Pakistan to Canada, Pakistan to Kenya, Pakistan to Sharjah, Pakistan to India) b Sialkot 20.9.1968 RHB LM

Cmp	Debut	M	I	NO	Runs	HS	Avge	100	50	Balls	Runs	Wkts	Avge	BB	5i	10m	RpO	ct	st
Test		4	5	0	147	125	29.40	1	0									1	
FC		4	5	0	147	125	29.40	1	0									1	
Int		6	6	2	301	117	75.25	1	2	7	6	0					5.14	3	
Wlls		3	2	0	6	6	3.00	0	0	106	92	4	23.00	3-57	0	0	5.20	1	
Test	1986	36	54	2	2034	141	39.11	7	9	84	36	1	36.00	1-9	0	0	2.57	22	
FC	1983	131	212	11	8103	201*	40.31	20	36	1910	1051	33	31.84	5-95	1	0	3.30	90	
Int	1986	176	160	23	4300	124*	31.38	5	25	503	362	4	90.50	2-31	0	0	4.31	67	
Wlls	1983	60	57	7	2104	123*	42.08	4	16	766	484	14	34.57	3-57	0	0	3.79	24	

IJAZ AHMED (Faisalabad, Allied Bank, Pakistan to Australia) b Lyallpur 2.2.1969 RHB OB

Cmp	Debut	M	I	NO	Runs	HS	Avge	100	50	Balls	Runs	Wkts	Avge	BB	5i	10m	RpO	ct	st
FC		13	23	1	911	151	41.40	2	4	610	270	10	27.00	3-36	0	0	2.65	20	
Wlls		8	8	2	324	67*	54.00	0	4	132	94	4	23.50	3-33	0	0	4.27	4	
Test	1995	2	3	0	29	16	9.66	0	0	24	6	0					1.50	3	
FC	1989	77	125	14	4664	202*	42.01	15	16	3665	1636	53	30.86	6-62	2	0	2.67	84	
Int	1996	2	1	1	3	3*		0	0	30	25	1	25.00	1-9	0	0	5.00	0	
Wlls	1989	34	33	4	1194	134	41.17	2	9	831	569	23	24.73	3-30	0	0	4.10	15	

IJAZ ELAHI (Peshawar) b Mardan 15.4.1973 RHB RFM

Cmp	Debut	M	I	NO	Runs	HS	Avge	100	50	Balls	Runs	Wkts	Avge	BB	5i	10m	RpO	ct	st
FC		4	7	2	86	22*	17.20	0	0	472	272	15	18.13	5-27	1	0	3.45	0	
Wlls		2	2	1	17	9	17.00	0	0	102	87	1	87.00	1-49	0	0	5.11	2	
FC	1993	20	32	9	228	22*	9.91	0	0	2284	1432	47	30.46	6-65	3	0	3.76	4	
Wlls	1993	7	6	3	64	20	21.33	0	0	363	297	8	37.12	3-46	0	0	4.90	3	

IJAZ KHAN (Lahore) b Lahore 15.7.1968 RHB RFM

Cmp	Debut	M	I	NO	Runs	HS	Avge	100	50	Balls	Runs	Wkts	Avge	BB	5i	10m	RpO	ct	st
FC		2	3	0	29	23	9.66	0	0	199	90	5	18.00	4-64	0	0	2.71	0	
Wlls		1	1	0	2	2	2.00	0	0	48	40	0					5.00	0	

IJAZ MAHMOOD (Faisalabad) b Lyallpur 3.5.1970 RHB RM

Cmp	Debut	M	I	NO	Runs	HS	Avge	100	50	Balls	Runs	Wkts	Avge	BB	5i	10m	RpO	ct	st
FC		2	4	0	123	56	30.75	0	1	18	8	0					2.66	2	
Wlls		7	7	0	377	101	53.85	1	3	108	79	1	79.00	1-35	0	0	4.38	7	
FC	1994	11	18	0	400	88	22.22	0	3	622	325	6	54.16	3-44	0	0	3.13	7	
Wlls	1991	14	13	0	447	101	34.38	1	3	293	210	2	105.00	1-31	0	0	4.30	8	

IMRAN KHAN (ADBP) b Rawalpindi 10.9.1973 RHB RFM

Cmp	Debut	M	I	NO	Runs	HS	Avge	100	50	Balls	Runs	Wkts	Avge	BB	5i	10m	RpO	ct	st
Wlls		1	1	0	3	3	3.00	0	0									1	
FC	1994	3	5	1	16	7	4.00	0	0	54	44	0					4.88	0	
Wlls	1995	6	5	3	46	34*	23.00	0	0	6	11	0					11.00	4	

IMRAN TAHIR (Lahore) b Lahore 27.3.1979 RHB LBG

Cmp	Debut	M	I	NO	Runs	HS	Avge	100	50	Balls	Runs	Wkts	Avge	BB	5i	10m	RpO	ct	st
FC		1	1	0	0	0	0.00	0	0	192	117	5	23.40	4-83	0	0	3.65	1	

Cmp	Debut	M	I	NO	Runs	HS	Avge	100	50	Balls	Runs	Wkts	Avge	BB	5i	10m	RpO	ct	st

IMRANULLAH (Karachi Blues) b Karachi 12.6.1974 LHB LFM

FC		3	5	1	54	18	13.50	0	0	482	286	13	22.00	6-75	1	0	3.56	0	
FC	1994	10	14	1	93	18	7.15	0	0	1331	807	34	23.73	5-32	3	1	3.63	2	
Wlls	1990	3	1	0	15	15	15.00	0	0	54	76	0					8.44	0	

IMRAN YOUNIS (Islamabad) b Lyallpur 27.1.1973 RHB RFM

FC		1								15	10	0					4.00	0	

INAMULLAH KHAN (Lahore) b Lahore 9.10.1973 RHB RFM

FC		1	2	1	7	6*	7.00	0	0	162	109	8	13.62	8-109	1	0	4.03	0	
Wlls		3	3	0	18	11	6.00	0	0	168	149	7	21.28	4-44	1	0	5.32	1	
FC	1994	8	14	2	226	67*	18.83	0	2	515	414	20	20.70	8-109	3	0	4.82	3	
Wlls	1995	6	6	0	29	11	4.83	0	0	312	318	15	21.20	4-44	2	0	6.11	1	

INTIKHAB ALAM (Lahore) b Lahore 6.10.1974 RHB RM

FC		4	8	1	141	82	20.14	0	1									5	
Wlls		3	3	0	191	86	63.66	0	2	6	11	0					11.00	0	
FC	1994	15	27	3	582	127	24.25	1	2									18	
Wlls	1994	10	9	1	360	86	45.00	0	3	6	11	0					11.00	8	

INZAMAM-UL-HAQ (Faisalabad, United Bank, Pakistan, Pakistan to Australia, Pakistan to Sri Lanka, Pakistan to Canada, Pakistan to Sharjah, Pakistan to India) b Multan 3.3.1970 RHB SLA

Test		2	3	0	15	14	5.00	0	0									1	
FC		4	6	0	82	34	13.66	0	0									1	
Int		3	3	0	23	14	7.66	0	0									0	
Test	1992	37	63	8	2491	148	45.29	5	17									35	
FC	1985	138	221	38	9173	201*	50.12	24	47	2683	1286	37	34.75	5-80	2	0	2.87	112	
Int	1991	137	131	17	4227	137*	37.07	4	29	40	52	2	26.00	1-4	0	0	7.80	33	
Wlls	1988	35	35	9	1092	127	42.00	1	9	292	242	11	22.00	3-18	0	0	4.97	6	

IQBAL IMAM (Karachi Whites, United Bank) b Karachi 17.7.1969 LHB OB

FC		15	25	2	520	88*	22.60	0	2	1315	550	23	23.91	7-71	1	0	2.50	9	
Wlls		6	6	1	104	47*	20.80	0	0	240	207	3	69.00	2-44	0	0	5.17	3	
FC	1989	87	130	10	3330	158	27.75	5	13	5412	2359	82	28.76	7-66	3	0	2.61	83	
Wlls	1990	32	28	4	509	47*	21.20	0	0	1115	810	22	36.81	3-26	0	0	4.35	9	

IQBAL SALEEM (Karachi Whites, Allied Bank, Karachi Blues) b Karachi 25.8.1965 RHB WK

FC		9	14	1	573	207	44.07	2	0									30	
Wlls		6	6	1	169	87*	33.80	0	1									2	1
FC	1986	48	80	6	2015	207	27.22	4	7									105	20
Wlls	1987	22	21	4	691	104	40.64	1	3									14	7

IQBAL SHAIKH (Karachi Whites) b Hyderabad 15.1.1973 RHB LB

Wlls		1	1	0	7	7	7.00	0	0									0	
FC	1995	6	11	0	208	84	18.90	0	1	330	269	7	38.42	3-50	0	0	4.89	1	

IQBAL SIKANDER (Karachi Blues) b Karachi 19.12.1958 RHB LBG

FC		1	2	1	12	9*	12.00	0	0	150	79	2	39.50	2-79	0	0	3.16	0	
FC	1976	183	246	46	4080	111*	20.40	3	22	31776	14934	645	23.15	9-81	44	8	2.81	122	
Int	1991	4	1	1	1	1*		0	0	210	147	3	49.00	1-30	0	0	4.20	0	
Wlls	1980	39	28	5	303	34	13.17	0	0	783	507	19	26.68	3-17	0	0	3.88	13	

IRFAN BHATTI (Rawalpindi) b Peshawar 28.9.1964 RHB RFM

FC		1	2	1	22	18*	22.00	0	0	83	67	2	33.50	1-29	0	0	4.84	0	
Wlls		6	4	0	50	30	12.50	0	0	240	197	8	24.62	3-34	0	0	4.92	2	
FC	1987	9	12	4	182	35	22.75	0	0	671	430	10	43.00	4-16	0	0	3.84	4	
Int	1993	1								48	22	2	11.00	2-22	0	0	2.75	1	
Wlls	1989	25	21	4	281	58	16.52	0	1	1092	759	35	21.68	4-25	1	0	4.17	6	

IRFAN FAZIL (Pakistan A to England) b Lahore 2.11.1981 RHB RFM

FC	1997	3	5	2	43	19	14.33	0	0	336	234	7	33.42	3-51	0	0	4.17	0	

IRFAN HABIB (Karachi Blues) b Karachi 18.4.1968 RHB RFM

FC		1	2	1	0	0*	0.00	0	0	48	41	1	41.00	1-13	0	0	5.12	0	
FC	1987	10	13	5	78	24*	9.75	0	0	986	653	19	34.36	5-78	1	0	3.97	3	
Wlls	1988	10	5	2	8	5*	2.66	0	0	426	398	8	49.75	3-56	0	0	5.60	2	

IRFANULLAH (Karachi Blues) b Karachi 4.10.1966 RHB WK

FC		1	2	0	40	39	20.00	0	0									1	
Wlls		2	2	0	65	40	32.50	0	0									0	
FC	1993	14	22	1	633	128	33.31	1	4									19	1
Wlls	1994	5	5	1	104	40	26.00	0	0									0	

ISHTIAQ AHMED (Karachi Whites) b Karachi 15.3.1962 RHB OB

Wlls		3	3	1	63	54*	31.50	0	1									0	
FC	1986	13	22	4	572	89	31.77	0	4	117	37	2	18.50	2-22	0	0	1.89	10	
Wlls	1989	10	10	1	233	54*	25.88	0	1									2	

JAFFAR QURESHI (Karachi Blues) b Karachi 10.5.1969 LHB SLA

Wlls		2	1	0	0	0	0.00	0	0	113	70	3	23.33	2-23	0	0	3.71	0	
FC	1994	4	5	0	79	46	15.80	0	0	842	401	15	26.73	4-56	0	0	2.85	0	
Wlls	1993	8	7	1	67	20	11.16	0	0	418	259	8	32.37	2-23	0	0	3.71	0	

Cmp	Debut	M	I	NO	Runs	HS	Avge	100	50	Balls	Runs	Wkts	Avge	BB	5i	10m	RpO	ct	st

JAHANGIR BAKHSH (Karachi Blues) b Karachi 27.8.1976 RHB RFM

Cmp	Debut	M	I	NO	Runs	HS	Avge	100	50	Balls	Runs	Wkts	Avge	BB	5i	10m	RpO	ct	st
FC		1	1	0	5	5	5.00	0	0	90	77	1	77.00	1-52	0	0	5.13	1	
FC	1994	6	8	1	105	51	15.00	0	1	768	526	8	65.75	2-43	0	0	4.10	5	
Wlls	1994	4	2	1	2	2	2.00	0	0	198	164	4	41.00	2-24	0	0	4.96	0	

JAHANGIR KHAN, Mohammad (Peshawar, Allied Bank) b Peshawar 1.5.1971 RHB SLA

Cmp	Debut	M	I	NO	Runs	HS	Avge	100	50	Balls	Runs	Wkts	Avge	BB	5i	10m	RpO	ct	st
FC		7	12	0	522	147	43.50	1	2	6	5	0						5.00	1	
Wlls		1	1	0	1	1	1.00	0	0									1	
FC	1990	38	66	1	1874	147	28.83	1	10	92	59	0					3.84	16	
Wlls	1991	13	13	0	253	77	19.46	0	1	72	115	3	38.33	3-61	0	0	9.58	7	

JANNISAR KHAN (Peshawar) b Peshawar 6.10.1981 RHB RM

Cmp	Debut	M	I	NO	Runs	HS	Avge	100	50	Balls	Runs	Wkts	Avge	BB	5i	10m	RpO	ct	st
FC		3	5	1	82	50*	20.50	0	1	174	117	3	39.00	3-44	0	0	4.03	2	
Wlls		1	1	0	2	2	2.00	0	0	6	12	0					12.00	0	

JAVED HAYAT (Lahore, ADBP) b Lahore 25.11.1964 LHB SLA

Cmp	Debut	M	I	NO	Runs	HS	Avge	100	50	Balls	Runs	Wkts	Avge	BB	5i	10m	RpO	ct	st
FC		12	21	7	464	57	33.14	0	1	1567	546	18	30.33	6-49	1	0	2.09	9	
Wlls		4	2	1	83	55*	83.00	0	1	138	101	2	50.50	1-28	0	0	4.39	0	
FC	1984	104	156	27	2968	108	23.00	2	13	16318	7247	253	28.64	7-81	13	0	2.66	56	
Wlls	1985	39	28	7	403	55*	19.19	0	2	1804	1125	43	26.16	5-45	2	1	3.74	14	

JAVED IQBAL (Peshawar) b Peshawar 25.3.1975 RHB OB

Cmp	Debut	M	I	NO	Runs	HS	Avge	100	50	Balls	Runs	Wkts	Avge	BB	5i	10m	RpO	ct	st
Wlls		1	1	0	0	0	0.00	0	0									0	
Wlls	1995	4	4	0	73	51	18.25	0	1									0	

JAVED IQBAL (Faisalabad) b Tandlianwala 22.9.1972 RHB RM

Cmp	Debut	M	I	NO	Runs	HS	Avge	100	50	Balls	Runs	Wkts	Avge	BB	5i	10m	RpO	ct	st
FC		5	9	0	160	60	17.77	0	1	36	31	0					5.16	3	
Wlls		7	7	0	230	96	32.85	0	1									0	
FC	1993	13	21	1	418	101	20.90	1	1	54	48	0					5.33	8	
Wlls	1995	10	10	0	342	96	34.20	0	2									0	

JAVED ISMAIL (Lahore) b Lahore 2.12.1976 RHB OB

Cmp	Debut	M	I	NO	Runs	HS	Avge	100	50	Balls	Runs	Wkts	Avge	BB	5i	10m	RpO	ct	st
Wlls		1	1	0	0	0	0.00	0	0	12	7	0					3.50	0	
FC	1995	1	2	0	6	6	3.00	0	0									0	
Wlls	1995	4	4	1	100	89*	33.33	0	1	12	7	0					3.50	1	

JAVED QADEER (Karachi Whites, PIA, Pakistan A to England) b Karachi 25.8.1976 RHB WK

Cmp	Debut	M	I	NO	Runs	HS	Avge	100	50	Balls	Runs	Wkts	Avge	BB	5i	10m	RpO	ct	st
FC		8	11	1	196	52	19.60	0	1									30	6
FC	1994	27	38	10	578	66*	20.64	0	4									77	9
Int	1994	1	1	0	12	12	12.00	0	0									1	
Wlls	1995	3	1	1	0	0*		0	0									2	1

JAVED SAMI KHAN (Karachi Whites, United Bank) b Karachi 20.11.1975 RHB

Cmp	Debut	M	I	NO	Runs	HS	Avge	100	50	Balls	Runs	Wkts	Avge	BB	5i	10m	RpO	ct	st
FC		5	10	0	197	46	19.70	0	0									3	
Wlls		6	6	0	97	46	16.16	0	0									0	
FC	1993	40	69	7	1585	141*	25.56	2	8	18	10	0					3.33	46	
Wlls	1992	11	11	0	142	46	12.90	0	0	24	35	1	35.00	1-35	0	0	8.75	2	

JOHN, Stephen (Islamabad) b Sialkot 21.6.1974 LHB LMF

Cmp	Debut	M	I	NO	Runs	HS	Avge	100	50	Balls	Runs	Wkts	Avge	BB	5i	10m	RpO	ct	st
FC		3	4	3	12	5*	12.00	0	0	234	162	3	54.00	1-11	0	0	4.15	2	
Wlls		3	2	0	1	1	0.50	0	0	156	117	7	16.71	3-47	0	0	4.50	0	
FC	1995	9	9	6	22	5*	7.33	0	0	1170	676	20	33.80	7-51	1	0	3.46	5	
Wlls	1995	6	4	0	5	4	1.25	0	0	282	199	12	16.58	3-37	0	0	4.23	2	

KABIR KHAN (Peshawar, Habib Bank) b Peshawar 12.4.1974 RHB LFM

Cmp	Debut	M	I	NO	Runs	HS	Avge	100	50	Balls	Runs	Wkts	Avge	BB	5i	10m	RpO	ct	st
FC		15	22	4	171	57	9.50	0	1	2736	1404	71	19.77	8-70	6	0	3.07	6	
Test	1994	4	5	2	24	10	8.00	0	0	655	370	9	41.11	3-26	0	0	3.38	1	
FC	1990	50	70	13	560	57	9.82	0	1	7823	4352	165	26.37	8-70	10	1	3.33	13	
Int	1994	2								116	66	3	22.00	2-32	0	0	3.41	0	
Wlls	1991	22	14	4	51	27	5.10	0	0	993	770	27	28.51	4-35	2	0	4.65	1	

KALEEM AHMED (Faisalabad) b Lyallpur 11.6.1974 LHB SLA

Cmp	Debut	M	I	NO	Runs	HS	Avge	100	50	Balls	Runs	Wkts	Avge	BB	5i	10m	RpO	ct	st
FC		1	2	0	21	16	10.50	0	0	12	12	0					6.00	0	

KAMAL MERCHANT (Faisalabad) b Karachi 2.12.1956 RHB RM

Cmp	Debut	M	I	NO	Runs	HS	Avge	100	50	Balls	Runs	Wkts	Avge	BB	5i	10m	RpO	ct	st
FC		2	4	0	70	33	17.50	0	0	318	114	3	38.00	3-27	0	0	2.15	1	
FC	1974	94	138	30	2860	112	26.48	1	13	7700	2803	118	23.75	6-69	4	0	2.18	37	
Wlls	1980	37	18	6	117	23	9.75	0	0	1679	934	44	21.22	5-11	1	1	3.33	8	

KAMRAN HAIDER KHAN (Karachi Blues, Customs) b Karachi 12.5.1967 RHB

Cmp	Debut	M	I	NO	Runs	HS	Avge	100	50	Balls	Runs	Wkts	Avge	BB	5i	10m	RpO	ct	st
FC		6	12	1	146	47	13.27	0	0									12	
Wlls		1	1	0	5	5	5.00	0	0									0	
FC	1994	12	21	2	390	114	20.52	1	1	17	12	1	12.00	1-8	0	0	4.23	15	
Wlls	1994	10	10	0	296	65	29.60	0	2									2	

KAMRAN HUSSAIN (Karachi Whites) b Karachi 12.4.1974 LHB RM

Cmp	Debut	M	I	NO	Runs	HS	Avge	100	50	Balls	Runs	Wkts	Avge	BB	5i	10m	RpO	ct	st
FC		1	2	1	47	47*	47.00	0	0									2	
FC	1989	13	21	2	585	93	30.78	0	3									15	
Wlls	1991	7	7	0	185	41	26.42	0	0									0	

KAMRAN HUSSAIN (Bahawalpur) b Bahawalpur 5.9.1977 RHB LM

Cmp	Debut	M	I	NO	Runs	HS	Avge	100	50	Balls	Runs	Wkts	Avge	BB	5i	10m	RpO	ct	st
Wlls		3	3	0	49	18	16.33	0	0	168	136	4	34.00	3-50	0	0	4.85	0	
FC	1995	3	6	1	79	35	15.80	0	0	372	212	4	53.00	3-48	0	0	3.41	2	

179

Cmp Debut	M	I	NO	Runs	HS	Avge	100	50	Balls	Runs	Wkts	Avge	BB	5i	10m	RpO	ct	st
KAMRAN KHAN (Lahore) b Lahore 14.12.1969 RHB OB WK																		
FC	1	1	0	1	1	1.00	0	0									2	
Wlls	2	2	0	5	5	2.50	0	0	24	9	1	9.00	1-9	0	0	2.25	0	
FC 1986	54	90	2	2395	152	27.21	5	9	52	44	1	44.00	1-12	0	0	5.07	45	
Wlls 1987	26	25	5	463	105*	23.15	1	2	118	113	1	113.00	1-9	0	0	5.74	6	
KASHAN KHAN (Karachi Whites) b Karachi 30.11.1974 RHB RFM																		
FC	1	1	0	6	6	6.00	0	0	84	45	1	45.00	1-16	0	0	3.21	1	
Wlls 1994	2	1	0	1	1	1.00	0	0	66	61	0					5.54	0	
KASHIF AHMED (Karachi Whites, Customs) b Karachi 17.11.1975 RHB OB																		
FC	8	16	2	303	59	21.64	0	1									11	
Wlls	3	3	0	38	29	12.66	0	0	36	19	0					3.16	1	
FC 1995	20	37	5	801	111*	25.03	1	2	30	26	0					5.20	19	
Wlls 1994	9	9	0	157	57	17.44	0	1	122	76	1	76.00	1-20	0	0	3.73	3	
KASHIF ELAHI (Faisalabad) b Faisalabad 15.3.1979 RHB RFM																		
FC	3	6	2	25	15	6.25	0	0	420	271	10	27.10	3-38	0	0	3.87	4	
KASHIF IBRAHIM (Karachi Whites, Karachi Blues) b Karachi 16.11.1977 RHB RM																		
FC	4	7	0	63	26	9.00	0	0	447	164	15	10.93	5-29	2	0	2.20	1	
Wlls	4	3	2	9	7	9.00	0	0	210	184	4	46.00	2-58	0	0	5.25	0	
KHALID BUTT (Bahawalpur) b Karachi 13.4.1967 LHB SLA																		
FC	2	4	0	65	22	16.25	0	0	108	51	4	12.75	4-27	0	0	2.83	0	
KHALID SALEEM (Islamabad) b Islamabad 1.1.1982 LHB LFM																		
Wlls	1	1	1	1	1*		0	0	48	57	0					7.12	0	
KHALID ZAFAR (Islamabad) b Islamabad 31.1.1977 RHB OB																		
FC	2	4	1	36	15*	12.00	0	0	90	73	0					4.86	1	
Wlls	3	3	0	79	30	26.33	0	0	120	99	8	12.37	4-39	1	0	4.95	2	
Wlls 1995	6	6	1	145	30	29.00	0	0	216	156	11	14.18	4-39	1	0	4.33	2	
LAL FARAZ (Customs) b Peshawar 1.1.1976 RHB RM																		
FC	1	2	1	11	10*	11.00	0	0	84	57	0					4.07	1	
FC 1993	23	27	11	120	24*	7.50	0	0	3680	1986	74	26.83	5-54	4	0	3.23	6	
Wlls 1993	10	6	5	3	2*	3.00	0	0	462	310	7	44.28	2-29	0	0	4.02	1	
MAHMOOD HAMID (Karachi Blues, PIA, Combined XI) b Karachi 19.1.1969 RHB RM																		
FC	11	15	1	474	157	33.85	1	1	132	51	2	25.50	2-26	0	0	2.31	8	
Wlls	5	4	1	141	72	47.00	0	1	174	125	4	31.25	2-30	0	0	4.31	0	
FC 1986	128	199	32	7041	208	42.16	17	36	1101	589	13	45.30	2-26	0	0	3.20	89	
Int 1994	1	1	0	1	1	1.00	0	0									0	
Wlls 1988	44	41	10	769	72	24.80	0	3	740	573	24	23.87	3-30	0	0	4.64	18	
MAISAM HASNAIN (Karachi Whites, PNSC) b Karachi 3.2.1977 RHB																		
FC	5	9	1	136	44	17.00	0	0									6	
FC 1995	6	11	1	141	44	14.10	0	0	1	4	0					24.00	6	
MAJID INAYAT (Combined XI) b Burewala 1.1.1977 RHB WK																		
FC	1	1	1	19	19*		0	0									2	
FC 1995	2	3	1	41	19*	20.50	0	0									2	
MAJID SAEED (PNSC) b Gujranwala 25.2.1973 RHB OB																		
FC	7	12	1	445	115*	40.45	1	2	24	5	1	5.00	1-3	0	0	1.25	4	
Wlls	3	3	0	7	7	2.33	0	0									2	
FC 1993	35	60	5	1861	163*	33.83	2	11	156	43	1	43.00	1-3	0	0	1.65	17	
Wlls 1993	13	12	1	182	36*	16.54	0	0	24	23	2	11.50	2-23	0	0	5.75	2	
MANSOOR AKHTAR (United Bank) b Karachi 25.12.1957 RHB RM																		
FC	8	14	2	260	101*	21.66	1	0	18	9	0					3.00	4	
Wlls	8	8	0	387	115	48.37	1	3	18	18	0					6.00	0	
Test 1980	19	29	3	655	111	25.19	1	3									9	
FC 1974	239	399	35	13785	224*	37.87	28	69	2496	1373	37	37.10	3-24	0	0	3.30	165	2
Int 1980	41	35	1	593	47	17.44	0	0	138	110	2	55.00	1-7	0	0	4.78	14	
Wlls 1980	88	88	13	3442	153*	45.89	4	25	453	356	5	71.20	2-38	0	0	4.71	21	
MANSOOR KHAN (Karachi Whites, Karachi Blues) b Karachi 28.11.1975 RHB OB																		
FC	5	9	0	90	43	10.00	0	0	132	45	3	15.00	2-9	0	0	2.04	5	
Wlls	6	6	1	225	104*	45.00	1	0	90	69	1	69.00	1-24	0	0	4.60	2	
FC 1993	12	21	1	307	43	15.35	0	0	240	103	4	25.75	2-9	0	0	2.57	10	
Wlls 1993	16	16	1	479	104*	31.93	1	3	398	267	9	29.66	3-24	0	0	4.02	7	
MANSOOR RANA (Lahore, ADBP) b Lahore 27.12.1962 RHB OB																		
FC	13	21	3	619	117	34.38	1	3	18	12	0					4.00	6	
Wlls	7	6	3	178	49*	59.33	0	0									1	
FC 1978	169	262	35	10242	207*	45.11	21	62	1117	658	19	34.63	3-31	0	0	3.53	75	
Int 1989	2	2	0	15	10	7.50	0	0	6	7	0					7.00	0	
Wlls 1982	75	66	9	1556	76	27.29	0	8	183	150	7	21.42	2-5	0	0	4.91	26	

180

Cmp	Debut	M	I	NO	Runs	HS	Avge	100	50	Balls	Runs	Wkts	Avge	BB	5i	10m	RpO	ct	st

MANZOOR AKHTAR (Karachi Blues, Allied Bank, Combined XI) b Karachi 16.4.1968 RHB LB

Cmp	Debut	M	I	NO	Runs	HS	Avge	100	50	Balls	Runs	Wkts	Avge	BB	5i	10m	RpO	ct	st
FC		8	15	0	363	124	24.20	1	1	360	197	6	32.82	2-55	0	0	3.28	5	
Wlls		4	3	1	221	127	110.50	1	1	180	174	7	24.85	3-53	0	0	5.80	1	
FC	1988	63	92	11	3232	249	39.90	12	9	4361	2358	64	36.84	6-72	2	1	3.24	50	
Wlls	1991	27	25	6	746	127	39.26	1	5	550	436	20	21.80	3-16	0	0	4.75	13	

MANZOOR ELAHI (Lahore, ADBP) b Sahiwal 15.4.1963 RHB RFM

Cmp	Debut	M	I	NO	Runs	HS	Avge	100	50	Balls	Runs	Wkts	Avge	BB	5i	10m	RpO	ct	st
FC		13	19	3	730	113	45.62	1	4	1577	699	28	24.96	8-43	1	1	2.65	6	
Wlls		5	4	1	116	59*	38.66	0	1	288	176	8	22.00	3-29	0	0	3.66	3	
Test	1984	6	10	2	123	52	15.37	0	1	444	194	7	27.71	2-38	0	0	2.62	7	
FC	1982	174	265	26	7865	163*	32.90	9	45	19057	9937	350	28.39	8-43	15	4	3.12	138	
Int	1984	54	46	13	741	50*	22.45	0	1	1743	1262	29	43.51	3-22	0	0	4.34	21	
Wlls	1983	63	50	9	1147	86	27.97	0	5	2875	1776	64	27.75	5-18	1	1	3.70	23	

MAQSOOD AHMED (Faisalabad) b Faisalabad 31.8.1981 LHB SLA

Cmp	Debut	M	I	NO	Runs	HS	Avge	100	50	Balls	Runs	Wkts	Avge	BB	5i	10m	RpO	ct	st
Wlls		3	1	0	6	6	6.00	0	0	138	95	4	23.75	3-30	0	0	4.13	0	

MAQSOOD RANA (Lahore, National Bank) b Lahore 1.8.1972 RHB RFM

Cmp	Debut	M	I	NO	Runs	HS	Avge	100	50	Balls	Runs	Wkts	Avge	BB	5i	10m	RpO	ct	st
FC		5	7	1	39	17	6.50	0	0	838	483	19	25.42	5-42	2	0	3.45	0	
FC	1987	29	36	11	211	41	8.44	0	0	3805	2309	89	25.94	7-56	6	1	3.64	5	
Int	1989	1	1	0	5	5	5.00	0	0	12	11	0					5.50	0	
Wlls	1991	8	5	0	46	31	9.20	0	0	438	375	12	31.25	3-32	0	0	5.13	1	

MASOOD ANWAR (Faisalabad, United Bank) b Khanewal 12.12.1967 LHB SLA

Cmp	Debut	M	I	NO	Runs	HS	Avge	100	50	Balls	Runs	Wkts	Avge	BB	5i	10m	RpO	ct	st
FC		2	3	0	57	29	19.00	0	0	372	141	6	23.50	5-81	1	0	2.27	0	
Test	1990	1	2	0	39	37	19.50	0	0	161	102	3	34.00	2-59	0	0	3.80	0	
FC	1983	127	168	42	2265	76*	17.97	0	5	30822	12659	581	21.78	8-44	37	9	2.46	46	
Wlls	1981	29	24	7	168	38	8.84	0	0	1498	936	43	21.76	4-40	2	0	3.74	6	

MASOOD MIRZA (Islamabad) b Rawalpindi 15.12.1970 RHB OB

Cmp	Debut	M	I	NO	Runs	HS	Avge	100	50	Balls	Runs	Wkts	Avge	BB	5i	10m	RpO	ct	st
Wlls		2	2	0	23	19	11.50	0	0	36	43	0					7.16	0	
FC	1992	5	6	3	75	38*	25.00	0	0	228	122	2	61.00	2-64	0	0	3.21	0	
Wlls	1992	5	5	0	43	19	8.60	0	0	174	101	2	50.50	2-17	0	0	3.48	1	

MASROOR HUSSAIN (Islamabad, Allied Bank) b Sahiwal 2.7.1972 RHB RM

Cmp	Debut	M	I	NO	Runs	HS	Avge	100	50	Balls	Runs	Wkts	Avge	BB	5i	10m	RpO	ct	st
FC		2	3	0	71	48	23.66	0	0	6	12	0					12.00	3	
Wlls		6	4	1	31	18	10.33	0	0									3	
FC	1988	41	73	6	2035	126	30.37	3	8	114	61	0					3.21	24	
Wlls	1988	28	26	1	433	76	17.32	0	3	6	4	0					4.00	8	

MAZHAR ANSARI (Bahawalpur) b Ahmedpur Sherqia 21.12.1976 RHB RFM

Cmp	Debut	M	I	NO	Runs	HS	Avge	100	50	Balls	Runs	Wkts	Avge	BB	5i	10m	RpO	ct	st
FC		3	5	2	21	13*	7.00	0	0	264	165	2	82.50	2-56	0	0	3.75	0	
FC	1993	10	17	5	69	24	5.75	0	0	932	520	10	52.00	2-23	0	0	3.34	0	
Wlls	1993	1								12	18	0					9.00	0	

MAZHAR QAYYUM (PNSC) b Lahore 29.11.1974 RHB RM

Cmp	Debut	M	I	NO	Runs	HS	Avge	100	50	Balls	Runs	Wkts	Avge	BB	5i	10m	RpO	ct	st
FC		4	6	0	136	52	22.66	0	1	24	22	0					5.50	1	
Wlls		3	3	1	228	118*	114.00	1	2	66	59	2	29.50	2-43	0	0	5.36	2	
FC	1987	46	75	6	2293	200*	33.23	3	14	444	266	1	266.00	1-32	0	0	3.59	14	
Wlls	1992	16	16	3	505	118*	38.84	1	5	252	191	10	19.10	3-21	0	0	4.54	6	

MOHAMMAD AKRAM (Rawalpindi, Allied Bank, Pakistan, Northamptonshire) b Islamabad 10.9.1974 RHB RFM

Cmp	Debut	M	I	NO	Runs	HS	Avge	100	50	Balls	Runs	Wkts	Avge	BB	5i	10m	RpO	ct	st
Test		1	1	1	0	0*		0	0	114	59	0					3.10	0	
FC		5	7	3	29	11	7.25	0	0	1052	621	23	27.00	6-56	2	0	3.54	1	
Wlls		6	1	1	25	25*		0	0	264	202	6	33.66	2-13	0	0	4.59	0	
Test	1995	6	9	3	8	5	1.33	0	0	1033	522	10	52.20	3-39	0	0	3.03	4	
FC	1992	37	47	12	258	28	7.37	0	0	5777	3294	113	29.15	7-51	7	0	3.42	13	
Int	1995	8	5	3	11	7*	5.50	0	0	342	307	9	34.11	2-36	0	0	5.38	2	
Wlls	1992	22	10	5	47	25*	9.40	0	0	1032	750	29	25.86	4-25	1	0	4.36	4	

MOHAMMAD ALI (ADBP) b Bahawalpur 11.9.1973 RHB LFM

Cmp	Debut	M	I	NO	Runs	HS	Avge	100	50	Balls	Runs	Wkts	Avge	BB	5i	10m	RpO	ct	st
FC		5	4	1	26	13	8.66	0	0	1023	543	15	36.20	5-89	1	0	3.18	0	
Wlls		3	2	0	7	6	3.50	0	0	156	127	1	127.00	1-56	0	0	4.88	0	
FC	1993	42	44	16	385	60*	13.75	0	2	7141	4210	134	31.41	6-37	9	1	3.53	17	
Wlls	1993	9	3	1	13	6*	6.50	0	0	432	366	9	40.66	2-29	0	0	5.08	0	

MOHAMMAD ASIF (Lahore, ADBP) b Lahore 13.9.1966 RHB OB

Cmp	Debut	M	I	NO	Runs	HS	Avge	100	50	Balls	Runs	Wkts	Avge	BB	5i	10m	RpO	ct	st
FC		12	15	5	119	31	11.90	0	0	2594	959	53	18.09	5-20	3	1	2.21	13	
Wlls		7	2	0	22	16	11.00	0	0	396	284	10	28.40	4-44	1	0	4.30	0	
FC	1986	106	128	27	1358	70	13.44	0	4	24031	9358	371	25.22	8-58	20	4	2.33	73	
Wlls	1987	54	23	10	113	18	8.69	0	0	2643	1589	65	24.44	4-19	3	0	3.60	16	

MOHAMMAD ASLAM (Peshawar) b Peshawar 4.7.1978 RHB SLA

Cmp	Debut	M	I	NO	Runs	HS	Avge	100	50	Balls	Runs	Wkts	Avge	BB	5i	10m	RpO	ct	st
Wlls		1								60	41	0					4.10	0	

MOHAMMAD BABAR (Karachi Whites) b Karachi 9.2.1976 RHB WK

Cmp	Debut	M	I	NO	Runs	HS	Avge	100	50	Balls	Runs	Wkts	Avge	BB	5i	10m	RpO	ct	st
Wlls		2	2	0	19	19	9.50	0	0									2	

MOHAMMAD FARRUKH (Karachi Blues) b Karachi 27.12.1978 RHB OB

Cmp	Debut	M	I	NO	Runs	HS	Avge	100	50	Balls	Runs	Wkts	Avge	BB	5i	10m	RpO	ct	st
FC		1	2	0	32	19	16.00	0	0									1	
Wlls		3	3	0	68	35	22.66	0	0									1	
Wlls	1995	4	4	0	77	35	19.25	0	0	18	28	1	28.00	1-28	0	0	9.33	1	

Cmp Debut   M   I   NO   Runs   HS   Avge   100   50   Balls   Runs   Wkts   Avge   BB   5i   10m   RpO   ct   st

MOHAMMAD HASNAIN (Karachi Whites) b Karachi 5.12.1973 RHB RFM

Cmp	Debut	M	I	NO	Runs	HS	Avge	100	50	Balls	Runs	Wkts	Avge	BB	5i	10m	RpO	ct	st
FC		2	3	0	10	8	3.33	0	0	318	174	5	34.80	2-43	0	0	3.28	0	
Wlls		1	1	0	8	8	8.00	0	0	54	39	0					4.33	0	
FC	1991	17	23	6	195	34	11.47	0	0	2396	1320	67	19.70	8-61	3	1	3.30	6	
Wlls	1991	6	6	2	26	11	6.50	0	0	298	221	5	44.20	3-58	0	0	4.44	1	

MOHAMMAD HUSSAIN (Lahore, United Bank, Pakistan, Combined XI, Pakistan to India) b Lahore 8.10.1976 LHB SLA

Cmp	Debut	M	I	NO	Runs	HS	Avge	100	50	Balls	Runs	Wkts	Avge	BB	5i	10m	RpO	ct	st
Test		1	1	0	0	0	0.00	0	0	60	21	1	21.00	1-7	0	0	2.10	1	
FC		13	20	4	451	78	28.18	0	3	2689	1015	48	21.14	6-81	3	2	2.26	8	
Wlls		2	2	2	60	53*		0	1	114	103	2	51.50	1-48	0	0	5.42	1	
FC	1994	42	62	10	1299	78	24.98	0	8	9748	3366	166	20.27	7-80	10	4	2.07	24	
Int	1996	5	5	3	51	18*	25.50	0	0	246	221	3	73.66	2-56	0	0	5.39	1	
Wlls	1994	11	10	3	125	53*	17.85	0	0	482	303	24	12.62	6-29	1	2	3.77	3	

MOHAMMAD IJAZ (Bahawalpur) b Karachi 6.12.1972 RHB OB

Cmp	Debut	M	I	NO	Runs	HS	Avge	100	50	Balls	Runs	Wkts	Avge	BB	5i	10m	RpO	ct	st
FC		1	2	0	30	28	15.00	0	0	84	50	3	16.66	2-25	0	0	3.57	0	

MOHAMMAD JAVED (Karachi Whites, National Bank) b Karachi 4.5.1969 RHB RM

Cmp	Debut	M	I	NO	Runs	HS	Avge	100	50	Balls	Runs	Wkts	Avge	BB	5i	10m	RpO	ct	st
FC		8	14	1	168	52	12.92	0	1	1020	534	14	38.14	5-75	1	0	3.14	6	
Wlls		9	7	3	273	62*	68.25	0	3	422	340	13	26.15	4-24	1	0	4.83	4	
FC	1988	78	124	19	3007	169	28.63	4	16	6530	3525	129	27.32	6-62	8	1	3.23	41	
Wlls	1990	50	43	7	1066	91	29.61	0	7	1992	1551	61	25.42	4-22	3	0	4.67	17	

MOHAMMAD MASROOR (Karachi Whites, Customs) b Karachi 6.8.1975 RHB

Cmp	Debut	M	I	NO	Runs	HS	Avge	100	50	Balls	Runs	Wkts	Avge	BB	5i	10m	RpO	ct	st
FC		5	8	1	172	93*	24.57	0	1	18	12	0					4.00	5	
Wlls		1	1	0	8	8	8.00	0	0	24	26	0					6.50	0	
FC	1995	6	10	1	178	93*	19.77	0	1	18	12	0					4.00	5	
Wlls	1994	2	2	0	14	8	7.00	0	0	24	26	0					6.50	0	

MOHAMMAD NADEEM HUSSAIN (Rawalpindi, ADBP) b Rawalpindi 23.10.1975 LHB WK

Cmp	Debut	M	I	NO	Runs	HS	Avge	100	50	Balls	Runs	Wkts	Avge	BB	5i	10m	RpO	ct	st
FC		10	16	0	200	41	12.50	0	0									30	
Wlls		6	3	1	88	43	44.00	0	0									3	1
FC	1993	31	44	1	768	105	17.86	1	2									76	9
Wlls	1994	18	12	3	211	64	23.44	0	1	6	6	0					6.00	10	5

MOHAMMAD NAWAZ (Islamabad, Allied Bank) b Sargodha 10.11.1970 RHB OB

Cmp	Debut	M	I	NO	Runs	HS	Avge	100	50	Balls	Runs	Wkts	Avge	BB	5i	10m	RpO	ct	st
FC		12	22	0	587	83	26.68	0	6	456	220	7	31.42	2-25	0	0	2.89	6	
Wlls		4	4	0	69	38	17.25	0	0	60	53	1	53.00	1-22	0	0	5.30	0	
FC	1985	94	163	7	5237	202*	33.57	8	32	3710	1575	57	27.63	4-41	0	0	2.54	63	
Wlls	1992	15	15	0	299	58	19.93	0	1	493	363	14	25.92	3-33	0	0	4.41	1	

MOHAMMAD NAWAZ (Faisalabad) b Lyallpur 3.10.1974 RHB OB

Cmp	Debut	M	I	NO	Runs	HS	Avge	100	50	Balls	Runs	Wkts	Avge	BB	5i	10m	RpO	ct	st
FC		7	14	2	267	58	22.25	0	1	438	239	7	34.14	3-16	0	0	3.27	3	
Wlls		2	1	0	8	8	8.00	0	0	60	55	0					5.50	1	
FC	1993	33	58	3	1090	94	19.81	0	5	1970	1012	30	33.73	4-37	0	0	3.08	18	
Wlls	1993	9	6	0	40	20	6.66	0	0	282	225	4	56.25	2-30	0	0	4.78	4	

MOHAMMAD RAMZAN (Faisalabad, United Bank) b Lyallpur 25.12.1970 RHB RM

Cmp	Debut	M	I	NO	Runs	HS	Avge	100	50	Balls	Runs	Wkts	Avge	BB	5i	10m	RpO	ct	st
FC		14	25	2	731	112	31.78	1	5	24	21	0					5.25	10	
Wlls		8	8	0	369	121	46.12	1	4									4	
FC	1986	91	150	12	5242	203*	37.98	12	30	213	144	2	72.00	1-8	0	0	4.05	69	
Wlls	1989	33	33	2	905	121	29.19	1	7	66	78	0					7.09	12	

MOHAMMAD RIAZ (Rawalpindi) b Lahore 6.7.1957 LHB SLA

Cmp	Debut	M	I	NO	Runs	HS	Avge	100	50	Balls	Runs	Wkts	Avge	BB	5i	10m	RpO	ct	st
FC		2	3	2	12	8*	12.00	0	0	300	116	4	29.00	4-77	0	0	2.32	0	
FC	1973	103	156	22	3146	134	23.47	4	13	19323	8429	404	20.86	8-66	32	8	2.57	50	
Wlls	1981	36	32	6	328	40	12.61	0	0	1671	971	41	23.68	4-27	1	0	3.48	11	

MOHAMMAD SAEED (Islamabad) b Islamabad 14.12.1974 RHB OB

Cmp	Debut	M	I	NO	Runs	HS	Avge	100	50	Balls	Runs	Wkts	Avge	BB	5i	10m	RpO	ct	st
Wlls		1	1	0	0	0	0.00	0	0									1	

MOHAMMAD SALEEM (Faisalabad) b Faisalabad 11.8.1978 RHB OB

Cmp	Debut	M	I	NO	Runs	HS	Avge	100	50	Balls	Runs	Wkts	Avge	BB	5i	10m	RpO	ct	st
FC		4	8	0	258	107	32.25	1	1									0	
Wlls		1	1	0	4	4	4.00	0	0									1	

MOHAMMAD SARFRAZ (Rawalpindi) b Sargodha 2.2.1975 LHB LFM

Cmp	Debut	M	I	NO	Runs	HS	Avge	100	50	Balls	Runs	Wkts	Avge	BB	5i	10m	RpO	ct	st
Wlls		5	2	1	1	1*	1.00	0	0	264	196	3	65.55	2-44	0	0	4.45	2	
FC	1993	13	16	1	130	36	8.66	0	0	1874	1010	19	53.15	4-59	0	0	3.23	5	
Wlls	1992	14	10	3	35	11*	5.00	0	0	730	504	14	36.00	3-54	0	0	4.14	4	

MOHAMMAD SHEHBAZ (Islamabad) b Mirpurkhas 30.12.1973 RHB WK

Cmp	Debut	M	I	NO	Runs	HS	Avge	100	50	Balls	Runs	Wkts	Avge	BB	5i	10m	RpO	ct	st
FC		1	2	1	19	18*	19.00	0	0									3	1
Wlls		1	1	1	6	6*		0	0									0	

MOHAMMAD TAYYAB (Bahawalpur) b Rahim Yar Khan 6.8.1973 LHB LB

Cmp	Debut	M	I	NO	Runs	HS	Avge	100	50	Balls	Runs	Wkts	Avge	BB	5i	10m	RpO	ct	st
FC		2	4	0	20	9	5.00	0	0									0	
Wlls		1	1	0	6	6	6.00	0	0	12	15	0					7.50	0	
FC	1991	21	36	3	487	43	14.75	0	0	108	87	2	43.50	1-26	0	0	4.83	15	
Wlls	1990	16	15	0	200	35	13.33	0	0	71	63	2	31.50	2-34	0	0	5.32	5	

Cmp	Debut	M	I	NO	Runs	HS	Avge	100	50	Balls	Runs	Wkts	Avge	BB	5i	10m	RpO	ct	st

MOHAMMAD WASIM (Rawalpindi, Pakistan, Combined XI, Pakistan to Australia, Pakistan A to England, Pakistan to Sharjah, Pakistan to India) b Rawalpindi 8.8.1977 RHB LB

Cmp	Debut	M	I	NO	Runs	HS	Avge	100	50	Balls	Runs	Wkts	Avge	BB	5i	10m	RpO	ct	st
Test		2	3	1	114	109*	57.00	1	0									3	
FC		8	14	2	630	109*	52.50	3	3	23	14	2	7.00	2-12	0	0	3.65	8	
Int		1	1	0	8	8	8.00	0	0									0	
FC	1994	27	45	4	1276	155	31.12	4	5	65	35	2	17.50	2-12	0	0	3.23	33	
Int	1996	15	15	1	358	54	25.57	0	2									4	
Wlls	1994	5	5	0	118	43	23.60	0	0									5	

MOHAMMAD YOUNIS (Faisalabad) b Lyallpur 1.7.1975 RHB

Cmp	Debut	M	I	NO	Runs	HS	Avge	100	50	Balls	Runs	Wkts	Avge	BB	5i	10m	RpO	ct	st
FC		1	2	0	76	58	38.00	0	1	60	45	1	45.00	1-45	0	0	4.50	3	
Wlls		6	4	2	86	32*	43.00	0	0									3	
FC	1995	2	4	0	81	58	20.25	0	1	60	45	1	45.00	1-45	0	0	4.50	4	
Wlls	1993	7	5	2	93	32*	31.00	0	0									3	

MOHAMMAD ZAHID (PIA, Pakistan, Combined XI, Pakistan to Australia, Pakistan to Sri Lanka) b Gaggu Mandi 2.8.1976 RHB RFM

Cmp	Debut	M	I	NO	Runs	HS	Avge	100	50	Balls	Runs	Wkts	Avge	BB	5i	10m	RpO	ct	st
Test		1	1	0	0	0	0.00	0	0	246	130	11	11.81	7-66	1	1	3.17	0	
FC		4	3	1	32	28*	16.00	0	0	801	381	31	12.29	7-66	3	2	2.85	0	
Int		1								36	41	0					6.83	0	
Wlls		1	1	1	0	0*		0	0	54	67	1	67.00	1-67	0	0	7.44	0	
Test	1996	3	3	1	6	6*	3.00	0	0	486	278	13	21.38	7-66	1	1	3.43	0	
FC	1995	13	13	8	59	28*	11.80	0	0	2021	1133	56	20.23	7-66	5	2	3.36	6	
Int	1996	4	2	1	1	1	1.00	0	0	216	164	3	54.66	2-53	0	0	4.55	0	
Wlls	1992	3	1	1	0	0*		0	0	114	112	2	56.00	1-25	0	0	5.89	0	

MOHAMMAD ZAHID (Bahawalpur, Allied Bank) b Bahawalpur 12.8.1965 LHB SLA

Cmp	Debut	M	I	NO	Runs	HS	Avge	100	50	Balls	Runs	Wkts	Avge	BB	5i	10m	RpO	ct	st
FC		9	17	6	150	27	13.63	0	0	1803	782	33	23.69	4-44	0	0	2.60	9	
FC	1985	92	134	32	1114	38*	10.92	0	0	16837	7111	325	21.88	8-114	21	3	2.53	77	
Wlls	1991	18	7	4	14	7*	4.66	0	0	978	546	19	28.73	5-50	0	1	3.34	6	

MOHSIN KAMAL (PNSC) b Lyallpur 16.6.1963 RHB RF

Cmp	Debut	M	I	NO	Runs	HS	Avge	100	50	Balls	Runs	Wkts	Avge	BB	5i	10m	RpO	ct	st
FC		4	5	3	23	20	11.50	0	0	590	398	12	33.16	4-43	0	0	4.04	1	
Wlls		1	1	1	0	0*		0	0	24	16	0					4.00	0	
Test	1983	9	11	7	37	13*	9.25	0	0	1348	822	24	34.25	4-116	0	0	3.65	4	
FC	1980	128	154	41	1336	44	11.82	0	0	16859	10361	320	32.37	7-87	9	0	3.68	37	
Int	1984	19	6	3	27	11*	9.00	0	0	881	760	21	36.19	4-47	1	0	5.17	4	
Wlls	1982	45	32	12	185	28	9.25	0	0	2070	1589	62	25.62	5-14	1	2	4.60	8	

MOHTASHIM RASHEED (Karachi Blues) b Karachi 22.9.1968 RHB LB

Cmp	Debut	M	I	NO	Runs	HS	Avge	100	50	Balls	Runs	Wkts	Avge	BB	5i	10m	RpO	ct	st
Wlls		4	3	0	21	11	7.00	0	0	231	127	3	42.33	3-39	0	0	3.29	1	
FC	1993	8	13	1	76	16	6.33	0	0	861	383	11	34.81	4-85	0	0	2.66	2	

MOIN KHAN (Karachi Blues, Pakistan, PIA, Pakistan to Australia, Pakistan to Sri Lanka, Pakistan to Canada, Pakistan to Kenya, Pakistan to Sharjah, Pakistan to India) b Rawalpindi 23.9.1971 RHB WK

Cmp	Debut	M	I	NO	Runs	HS	Avge	100	50	Balls	Runs	Wkts	Avge	BB	5i	10m	RpO	ct	st
Test		4	5	0	175	59	35.00	0	2									7	1
FC		5	6	0	221	59	36.83	0	2									9	2
Int		6	4	0	41	34	10.25	0	0									9	4
Wlls		7	6	1	123	52	24.60	0	1									6	1
Test	1990	26	38	5	1055	117*	31.96	3	5									54	7
FC	1986	113	160	21	3993	129	28.72	7	18	60	81	2	40.50	2-78	0	0	8.10	276	35
Int	1990	82	65	16	1054	61	21.51	0	3									80	32
Wlls	1990	45	26	5	558	84	26.57	0	2									32	22

MOIN-UL-ATIQ (Karachi Whites, Habib Bank) b Karachi 5.8.1964 RHB LB

Cmp	Debut	M	I	NO	Runs	HS	Avge	100	50	Balls	Runs	Wkts	Avge	BB	5i	10m	RpO	ct	st
FC		11	20	3	611	129	35.94	2	2	6	4	0					4.00	6	
Wlls		2	2	0	52	52	26.00	0	1									0	
FC	1984	123	210	17	6384	203*	33.07	13	26	282	178	1	178.00	1-4	0	0	3.78	66	
Int	1987	5	5	0	199	105	39.80	1	0									0	
Wlls	1982	55	53	3	1427	130*	28.54	1	10									15	

MUBASHAR ANWAR (Lahore) b Kamoke Mandi 21.7.1973 RHB RM

Cmp	Debut	M	I	NO	Runs	HS	Avge	100	50	Balls	Runs	Wkts	Avge	BB	5i	10m	RpO	ct	st
FC		1	2	0	17	14	8.50	0	0	132	81	0					3.68	0	
Wlls		1	1	0	1	1	1.00	0	0	18	19	1	19.00	1-19	0	0	6.33	0	

MUBASHIR NAZIR (ADBP) b Gujranwala 29.12.1975 RHB RFM

Cmp	Debut	M	I	NO	Runs	HS	Avge	100	50	Balls	Runs	Wkts	Avge	BB	5i	10m	RpO	ct	st
FC		1	1	1	10	10*		0	0	144	96	4	24.00	3-55	0	0	4.00	2	
FC	1995	3	5	3	20	10*	10.00	0	0	443	263	14	18.78	4-51	0	0	3.56	3	
Wlls	1995	3								126	84	4	21.00	2-26	0	0	4.00	0	

MUFEEZ MURTAZA (Islamabad) b Rawalpindi 30.4.1971 RHB RFM

Cmp	Debut	M	I	NO	Runs	HS	Avge	100	50	Balls	Runs	Wkts	Avge	BB	5i	10m	RpO	ct	st
FC		2	3	0	74	36	24.66	0	0									0	
FC	1992	8	13	0	400	89	30.76	0	2									0	
Wlls	1990	8	8	0	180	58	22.50	0	1									1	

MUJAHID HAMEED (ADBP) b Rawalpindi 23.3.1969 RHB RM WK

Cmp	Debut	M	I	NO	Runs	HS	Avge	100	50	Balls	Runs	Wkts	Avge	BB	5i	10m	RpO	ct	st
FC		5	8	2	291	187	48.50	1	0	6	9	0					9.00	1	
Wlls		3	1	0	31	31	31.00	0	0									0	
FC	1984	99	153	29	3726	187	30.04	3	23	378	219	1	219.00	1-21	0	0	3.47	74	3
Wlls	1987	19	16	5	364	57	33.09	0	2	6	8	0					8.00	3	

Cmp	Debut	M	I	NO	Runs	HS	Avge	100	50	Balls	Runs	Wkts	Avge	BB	5i	10m	RpO	ct	st

MUJAHID JAMSHED (Lahore, Habib Bank, Pakistan A to England, Pakistan to Australia) b Muredke 1.12.1971 RHB OB

Cmp	Debut	M	I	NO	Runs	HS	Avge	100	50	Balls	Runs	Wkts	Avge	BB	5i	10m	RpO	ct	st
FC		10	16	1	771	129	51.40	3	4									4	
FC	1985	77	124	4	4103	196	34.19	11	17	302	239	3	79.66	3-68	0	0	4.74	33	
Int	1996	4	3	1	27	23	13.50	0	0	24	6	1	6.00	1-6	0	0	1.50	0	
Wlls	1991	29	29	2	690	71	25.55	0	3	13	25	0					11.53	10	

MUNAWAR AFTAB ABBASI (Rawalpindi) b Rawalpindi 9.11.1976 RHB RM WK

Cmp	Debut	M	I	NO	Runs	HS	Avge	100	50	Balls	Runs	Wkts	Avge	BB	5i	10m	RpO	ct	st
FC		1	2	0	18	18	9.00	0	0									2	
FC	1995	3	5	0	50	21	10.00	0	0									4	1

MUNIR-UL-HAQ (Karachi Blues) b Karachi 7.1.1961 RHB RM

Cmp	Debut	M	I	NO	Runs	HS	Avge	100	50	Balls	Runs	Wkts	Avge	BB	5i	10m	RpO	ct	st
Wlls		4	4	1	249	105*	83.00	1	1									3	
FC	1981	120	197	20	6992	266	39.50	19	35	1880	1007	18	55.94	3-85	0	0	3.21	59	
Wlls	1982	51	50	4	1479	105*	32.15	1	10	360	306	12	25.50	4-48	1	0	5.10	15	

MURTAZA HUSSAIN (Bahawalpur, PNSC, Combined XI) b Bahawalpur 3.12.1975 RHB OB

Cmp	Debut	M	I	NO	Runs	HS	Avge	100	50	Balls	Runs	Wkts	Avge	BB	5i	10m	RpO	ct	st
FC		13	21	3	302	42*	16.77	0	0	3171	1441	64	22.51	5-43	4	0	2.72	8	
Wlls		2	1	1	6	6*		0	0	120	108	1	108.00	1-50	0	0	5.40	1	
FC	1990	80	118	27	1714	67*	18.83	0	3	16895	7002	311	22.51	9-54	18	3	2.48	34	
Wlls	1990	28	21	5	250	42	15.62	0	0	1230	812	17	47.76	3-42	0	0	3.96	4	

MUSHTAQ AHMED (Lahore, Pakistan, United Bank, Somerset, Pakistan to Australia, Pakistan to Sri Lanka, Pakistan to Canada, Pakistan to Sharjah) b Sahiwal 28.6.1970 RHB LBG

Cmp	Debut	M	I	NO	Runs	HS	Avge	100	50	Balls	Runs	Wkts	Avge	BB	5i	10m	RpO	ct	st
Test		2	3	0	82	42	27.33	0	0	637	282	18	15.66	6-84	2	1	2.65	0	
FC		3	4	0	103	42	25.75	0	0	943	436	28	15.57	6-66	3	2	2.77	1	
Int		3	2	2	8	5*		0	0	174	126	1	136.00	1-35	0	0	4.34	0	
Wlls		8	3	0	16	10	5.33	0	0	453	302	16	18.87	4-50	1	0	4.00	1	
Test	1989	28	42	7	355	42	10.14	0	0	7172	3309	117	28.28	7-56	7	2	2.76	10	
FC	1986	150	189	22	2345	90	14.04	0	7	35086	17052	671	25.41	9-93	47	13	2.91	73	
Int	1988	124	64	27	332	26	8.97	0	0	6431	4638	141	32.89	5-36	2	1	4.32	27	
Wlls	1989	32	17	6	111	19*	10.09	0	0	1509	1077	50	21.54	4-17	3	0	4.28	5	

MUTAHIR SHAH (PNSC) b Karachi 12.2.1971 RHB WK

Cmp	Debut	M	I	NO	Runs	HS	Avge	100	50	Balls	Runs	Wkts	Avge	BB	5i	10m	RpO	ct	st
Wlls		3	3	0	73	60	24.33	0	1									1	
FC	1986	43	64	10	878	68*	16.25	0	2									78	16
Wlls	1988	39	29	5	297	60	12.37	0	1									44	8

MUZAFFAR ABBASI (Customs) b Karachi 5.3.1960 RHB OB

Cmp	Debut	M	I	NO	Runs	HS	Avge	100	50	Balls	Runs	Wkts	Avge	BB	5i	10m	RpO	ct	st
FC		3	6	0	169	68	28.16	0	1									0	
Wlls		2	2	0	25	25	12.50	0	0									0	
FC	1986	6	11	1	271	68	27.10	0	1	6	0	0					0.00	0	

NADEEM ABBASI (Rawalpindi) b Rawalpindi 15.4.1964 RHB WK

Cmp	Debut	M	I	NO	Runs	HS	Avge	100	50	Balls	Runs	Wkts	Avge	BB	5i	10m	RpO	ct	st
FC		4	7	0	85	33	12.14	0	0									9	
Wlls		6	4	1	77	45*	25.66	0	0									7	1
Test	1989	3	2	0	46	36	23.00	0	0									6	
FC	1986	75	121	8	3314	120*	29.32	5	13	414	234	5	46.80	2-27	0	0	3.39	148	25
Wlls	1987	40	38	1	712	57	19.24	0	2	71	65	1	65.00	1-18	0	0	5.49	42	12

NADEEM AFZAL (Faisalabad, PIA) b Lyallpur 28.10.1969 RHB RFM

Cmp	Debut	M	I	NO	Runs	HS	Avge	100	50	Balls	Runs	Wkts	Avge	BB	5i	10m	RpO	ct	st
FC		9	11	4	28	9	4.00	0	0	1434	776	30	25.86	7-70	2	1	3.24	2	
Wlls		6	2	0	8	8	4.00	0	0	318	254	10	25.40	5-38	0	1	4.79	2	
FC	1990	72	95	33	915	100	14.75	1	1	9129	5180	183	28.30	7-51	10	1	3.40	19	
Wlls	1990	29	15	6	51	18	5.66	0	0	1318	892	35	25.48	5-16	0	2	4.06	2	

NADEEM ASHRAF (Customs) b Lyallpur 22.4.1975 RHB RFM

Cmp	Debut	M	I	NO	Runs	HS	Avge	100	50	Balls	Runs	Wkts	Avge	BB	5i	10m	RpO	ct	st
FC		4	8	1	91	26	13.00	0	0	557	310	9	34.44	5-81	1	0	3.33	3	
Wlls		3	2	0	9	8	4.50	0	0	138	111	4	27.75	2-41	0	0	4.82	0	
FC	1995	5	9	1	95	26	11.87	0	0	799	439	19	23.10	5-48	3	1	3.29	3	

NADEEM BABAR (Customs) b Karachi 27.2.1971 RHB RFM

Cmp	Debut	M	I	NO	Runs	HS	Avge	100	50	Balls	Runs	Wkts	Avge	BB	5i	10m	RpO	ct	st
FC		1	2	0	51	28	25.50	0	0	42	29	0					4.14	3	
Wlls		3	3	0	23	13	7.66	0	0	132	76	4	19.00	2-24	0	0	3.45	0	

NADEEM BUTT (Faisalabad) b Lyallpur 9.11.1968 RHB

Cmp	Debut	M	I	NO	Runs	HS	Avge	100	50	Balls	Runs	Wkts	Avge	BB	5i	10m	RpO	ct	st
FC		2	3	1	10	9	5.00	0	0	368	267	9	29.66	5-108	1	0	4.35	0	
FC	1995	3	5	1	35	21	8.75	0	0	368	267	9	29.66	5-108	1	0	4.35	0	

NADEEM GHAURI (Habib Bank) b Lahore 12.10.1962 RHB SLA

Cmp	Debut	M	I	NO	Runs	HS	Avge	100	50	Balls	Runs	Wkts	Avge	BB	5i	10m	RpO	ct	st
FC		7	8	3	31	17	6.20	0	0	1479	639	26	24.57	7-101	1	1	2.18	2	
Wlls		3								174	125	5	25.00	4-22	1	0	4.31	0	
Test	1989	1	1	0	0	0	0.00	0	0	48	20	0					2.50	0	
FC	1977	138	155	59	1108	38	11.54	0	0	33951	13828	618	22.37	8-51	45	12	2.39	53	
Int	1989	6	3	2	14	7*	14.00	0	0	342	230	5	46.00	2-51	0	0	4.03	0	
Wlls	1981	77	24	15	61	11*	6.77	0	0	3732	2144	98	21.87	4-22	5	0	3.44	15	

NADEEM IQBAL (Customs) b Peshawar 5.1.1971 RHB RFM

Cmp	Debut	M	I	NO	Runs	HS	Avge	100	50	Balls	Runs	Wkts	Avge	BB	5i	10m	RpO	ct	st
FC		4	8	1	42	14	6.00	0	0	528	325	7	46.42	4-134	0	0	3.69	2	
FC	1986	31	42	8	238	28	7.00	0	0	4265	2409	71	33.92	5-50	2	0	3.38	12	
Wlls	1992	2	2	0	7	4	3.50	0	0	108	91	3	30.33	2-46	0	0	5.05	0	

Cmp	Debut	M	I	NO	Runs	HS	Avge	100	50	Balls	Runs	Wkts	Avge	BB	5i	10m	RpO	ct	st
NADEEM KHAN (Karachi Blues, PIA) b Rawalpindi 10.12.1969 RHB SLA																			
FC		13	18	1	261	59	15.35	0	1	3315	1308	54	24.22	6-35	3	1	2.36	9	
Wlls		7	3	2	28	23*	28.00	0	0	420	257	7	36.71	2-31	0	0	3.67	2	
Test	1992	1	1	0	25	25	25.00	0	0	312	195	2	97.50	2-147	0	0	3.75	0	
FC	1986	113	138	33	1712	76	16.30	0	3	23166	10386	392	26.49	7-84	26	4	2.68	62	
Int	1992	2	1	0	2	2	2.00	0	0	96	81	0					5.06	0	
Wlls	1990	41	24	12	208	23*	17.33	0	0	2165	1292	63	20.50	6-28	0	3	3.58	13	
NAEEM AKHTAR (Rawalpindi) b Rawalpindi 2.12.1967 RHB RFM																			
FC		6	10	2	232	72	29.00	0	1	1034	428	25	17.12	5-37	2	0	2.48	5	
Wlls		6	4	1	76	32	25.33	0	0	258	162	5	32.40	2-40	0	0	3.76	1	
FC	1990	35	55	5	898	72	17.96	0	3	5159	2616	119	21.98	10-28	8	1	3.04	23	
Wlls	1991	32	30	3	447	71	16.55	0	1	1420	838	49	17.10	5-20	0	1	3.54	6	
NAEEM ASHRAF (Lahore, National Bank) b Lahore 10.11.1972 LHB LFM																			
FC		4	7	0	154	44	22.00	0	0	498	288	8	36.00	4-82	0	0	3.46	4	
Wlls		8	6	2	142	61*	35.50	0	1	366	273	10	27.30	3-28	0	0	4.47	3	
FC	1987	45	69	7	1544	114	24.90	3	5	6501	3494	137	25.50	7-53	7	1	3.22	30	
Int	1994	2	2	1	24	16	24.00	0	0	42	52	0					7.42	0	
Wlls	1988	37	31	8	331	61*	14.39	0	1	1742	1185	40	29.62	3-28	0	0	4.08	11	
NAEEM HAFEEZ (Faisalabad) b Lyallpur 26.2.1976 RHB OB																			
FC		1	2	0	4	2	2.00	0	0									0	
FC	1995	4	7	0	74	45	10.57	0	0									0	
Wlls	1994	2	2	0	6	4	3.00	0	0									1	
NAEEM KHAN (National Bank) b Lahore 10.12.1977 LHB SLA																			
Wlls		4	3	1	64	28	32.00	0	0	194	152	5	30.40	2-29	0	0	4.70	1	
FC	1992	6	8	2	92	33	15.33	0	0	606	389	5	77.80	2-73	0	0	3.85	2	
Wlls	1993	7	5	2	71	28	23.66	0	0	314	219	11	19.90	4-33	1	0	4.18	5	
NAEEM TAYYAB (Karachi Whites, National Bank) b Karachi 10.1.1972 RHB OB																			
FC		9	16	4	173	47*	14.41	0	0	1925	808	31	26.06	6-88	3	0	2.51	8	
Wlls		5	2	1	23	19*	23.00	0	0	228	154	3	51.33	2-34	0	0	4.05	3	
FC	1994	29	41	9	459	71	14.34	0	1	6441	2788	127	21.95	8-112	11	2	2.59	22	
Wlls	1994	10	4	2	35	19*	17.50	0	0	448	331	6	55.16	2-34	0	0	4.43	5	
NASEER AHMED MUGHAL (Rawalpindi) b Rawalpindi 28.6.1971 RHB WK																			
FC		7	12	1	474	89*	43.09	0	4	4	1	1	1.00	1-1	0	0	1.50	12	
Wlls		6	5	1	179	142*	44.75	1	0	7	4	1	4.00	1-1	0	0	3.42	2	
FC	1988	66	105	8	2703	161	27.86	5	14	28	29	1	29.00	1-1	0	0	6.21	78	8
Wlls	1988	37	35	2	816	142*	24.72	1	4	13	13	1	13.00	1-1	0	0	6.00	20	2
NASEER SHAUKAT (Faisalabad) b Lyallpur 24.1.1966 RHB RFM																			
FC		7	12	1	369	72	33.54	0	3	1135	664	30	22.13	6-51	4	1	3.51	4	
Wlls		7	6	2	105	52	26.25	0	1	353	311	10	31.10	3-40	0	0	5.28	4	
FC	1984	39	59	7	1311	89	25.21	0	9	4261	2376	107	22.20	7-42	8	1	3.34	21	
Wlls	1989	23	21	6	331	52	22.06	0	1	1074	802	36	22.27	3-33	0	0	4.48	7	
NASIR ALI KHAN (Karachi Whites) b Karachi 10.1.1970 RHB OB																			
FC		2	3	0	196	167	65.33	1	0									1	
FC	1993	3	5	0	225	167	45.00	1	0	12	12	0					6.00	2	
Wlls	1993	4	3	0	16	14	5.33	0	0	36	24	1	24.00	1-24	0	0	4.00	1	
NASIR JAM (Bahawalpur) b Bahawalpur 25.12.1967 RHB OB																			
FC		7	13	1	159	37	13.25	0	0	3	2	0					4.00	0	
Wlls		3	3	0	104	64	34.66	0	1	6	11	0					11.00	0	
FC	1989	40	65	6	657	53	11.13	0	1	25	18	0					4.32	12	
Wlls	1990	11	10	0	186	64	18.60	0	1	6	11	0					11.00	0	
NASIR KHAN (Karachi Whites) b Karachi 15.11.1968 RHB OB																			
FC		2	3	0	95	45	31.66	0	0	6	2	0					2.00	1	
Wlls		3	3	0	75	38	25.00	0	0	12	14	0					7.00	0	
FC	1986	40	70	8	1735	112*	27.98	1	8	252	146	4	36.50	2-41	0	0	3.47	22	
Wlls	1991	4	4	0	78	38	19.50	0	0	12	14	0					7.00	0	
NASIR SIDDIQ (Lahore) b Lahore 10.8.1976 RHB WK																			
FC		1	1	0	9	9	9.00	0	0									1	
Wlls		3	3	2	2	1*	2.00	0	0									2	
NASIR WASTI (PNSC) b Karachi 6.9.1967 RHB RFM																			
FC		3	5	0	148	84	29.60	0	1									0	
Wlls		3	2	0	6	6	3.00	0	0									0	
FC	1986	71	113	7	3096	134	29.20	3	21	636	479	7	68.42	2-33	0	0	4.51	48	
Wlls	1988	42	39	5	745	55*	21.91	0	2	713	546	16	34.12	4-25	2	0	4.59	13	
NAUMANULLAH (Karachi Whites) b Karachi 20.8.1975 RHB OB																			
Wlls		1	1	0	0	0	0.00	0	0	5	7	0					10.40	0	
FC	1995	4	8	0	226	86	28.25	0	2	408	191	1	191.00	1-73	0	0	2.80	3	
NAUSHAD QAZI (Islamabad) b Islamabad 7.6.1968 RHB OB																			
Wlls		1	1	0	20	20	20.00	0	0	36	49	0					8.16	0	

Cmp	Debut	M	I	NO	Runs	HS	Avge	100	50	Balls	Runs	Wkts	Avge	BB	5i	10m	RpO	ct	st

NAVED AHMED (Islamabad) b Islamabad 22.4.1971 RHB LB

Cmp	Debut	M	I	NO	Runs	HS	Avge	100	50	Balls	Runs	Wkts	Avge	BB	5i	10m	RpO	ct	st
FC		7	12	0	223	72	18.58	0	1									12	
Wlls		3	3	0	76	69	25.33	0	1									1	
FC	1994	10	17	0	239	72	14.05	0	1	18	23	0					7.66	13	
Wlls	1993	7	7	0	143	69	20.42	0	1									3	

NAVED ANJUM (Habib Bank) b Lahore 27.7.1963 RHB RFM

Cmp	Debut	M	I	NO	Runs	HS	Avge	100	50	Balls	Runs	Wkts	Avge	BB	5i	10m	RpO	ct	st
FC		7	11	1	410	92	41.00	0	3	654	294	9	32.66	2-19	0	0	2.69	1	
Wlls		3	2	0	29	16	14.50	0	0	60	45	1	45.00	1-18	0	0	4.50	1	
Test	1989	2	3	0	44	22	14.66	0	0	342	162	4	40.50	2-57	0	0	2.84	0	
FC	1979	141	220	20	5608	159	28.04	6	25	15723	8398	389	21.58	9-35	23	2	3.20	70	
Int	1983	13	12	3	113	30	12.55	0	0	472	344	8	43.00	2-27	0	0	4.37	0	
Wlls	1981	80	62	15	930	65	19.78	0	2	3159	1974	83	23.78	6-30	1	1	3.74	26	

NAVED ASHRAF (Rawalpindi) b Rawalpindi 4.9.1974 RHB RM

Cmp	Debut	M	I	NO	Runs	HS	Avge	100	50	Balls	Runs	Wkts	Avge	BB	5i	10m	RpO	ct	st
FC		6	10	0	139	28	13.90	0	0	114	58	4	14.50	2-17	0	0	3.05	8	
Wlls		6	6	0	110	51	18.33	0	1	310	237	7	33.85	4-38	1	0	4.58	1	
FC	1992	19	33	1	626	86	19.56	0	2	167	89	4	22.25	2-17	0	0	3.19'	13	
Wlls	1994	17	17	1	321	55	20.06	0	3	364	280	9	31.11	4-38	1	0	4.61	2	

NAVED LATIF (Customs) b Sargodha 21.2.1976 RHB

Cmp	Debut	M	I	NO	Runs	HS	Avge	100	50	Balls	Runs	Wkts	Avge	BB	5i	10m	RpO	ct	st
FC		7	14	1	233	62	17.92	0	1	12	13	0					6.50	3	
Wlls		3	3	0	171	127	57.00	1	0									0	
FC	1993	16	27	1	405	70	15.57	0	2	42	65	0					9.28	5	
Wlls	1993	9	9	0	413	127	45.88	1	2	12	20	0					10.00	5	

NAVED NAZEER (Faisalabad, ADBP) b Lyallpur 4.12.1970 RHB SLA

Cmp	Debut	M	I	NO	Runs	HS	Avge	100	50	Balls	Runs	Wkts	Avge	BB	5i	10m	RpO	ct	st
FC		7	11	4	100	53	14.28	0	1	1057	454	14	32.42	4-106	0	0	2.57	2	
Wlls		6	2	1	3	2	3.00	0	0	332	219	7	31.28	2-37	0	0	3.95	4	
FC	1986	68	94	40	448	53	8.29	0	1	13022	5861	208	28.17	9-50	13	3	2.70	25	
Wlls	1989	28	14	8	38	12*	6.33	0	0	1315	860	31	27.74	3-23	0	0	3.92	11	

NIZAMUDDIN (Karachi Whites) b Karachi 15.12.1978 RHB RM

Cmp	Debut	M	I	NO	Runs	HS	Avge	100	50	Balls	Runs	Wkts	Avge	BB	5i	10m	RpO	ct	st
Wlls		1	1	1	31	31*		0	0	24	47	0					11.75	0	

PERVEZ IQBAL (Rawalpindi) b Rawalpindi 26.12.1975 LHB RM

Cmp	Debut	M	I	NO	Runs	HS	Avge	100	50	Balls	Runs	Wkts	Avge	BB	5i	10m	RpO	ct	st
FC		1	1	0	3	3	3.00	0	0	108	73	1	73.00	1-28	0	0	4.05	0	
FC	1993	10	17	1	329	76	20.56	0	3	1206	621	23	27.00	5-59	1	0	3.08	0	
Wlls	1995	8	7	1	76	26	12.66	0	0	318	194	6	32.33	2-26	0	0	3.66	3	

PERVEZ SAFDAR SHAH (Bahawalpur) b Al Khobar, Saudi Arabia 23.9.1960 RHB RFM

Cmp	Debut	M	I	NO	Runs	HS	Avge	100	50	Balls	Runs	Wkts	Avge	BB	5i	10m	RpO	ct	st
FC		1	2	0	5	5	2.50	0	0	30	22	0					4.40	1	
FC	1983	118	197	27	4924	136	28.96	7	20	10706	5561	197	28.22	7-68	7	1	3.11	84	
Wlls	1983	26	22	2	401	46	20.05	0	0	630	495	7	70.71	2-23	0	0	4.71	7	

PERVEZ-UL-HASAN (PNSC) b Karachi 5.9.1967 LHB WK

Cmp	Debut	M	I	NO	Runs	HS	Avge	100	50	Balls	Runs	Wkts	Avge	BB	5i	10m	RpO	ct	st
FC		7	11	7	58	14	14.50	0	0									21	2
FC	1984	67	89	47	413	33	9.83	0	0									154	30
Wlls	1995	2																1	

QAISER MAHMOOD (Islamabad) b Jhang 14.11.1977 RHB WK

Cmp	Debut	M	I	NO	Runs	HS	Avge	100	50	Balls	Runs	Wkts	Avge	BB	5i	10m	RpO	ct	st
FC		6	7	0	119	57	17.00	0	1									15	2
Wlls		2	2	0	15	15	7.50	0	0									4	2
FC	1994	17	23	3	327	57	16.35	0	1									32	3
Wlls	1993	7	7	1	113	33	18.83	0	0									11	2

QAYYUM-UL-HASAN, Rana (Pakistan A to England) b Gujranwala 6.11.1977 RHB OB WK

Cmp	Debut	M	I	NO	Runs	HS	Avge	100	50	Balls	Runs	Wkts	Avge	BB	5i	10m	RpO	ct	st
FC	1993	33	55	3	1205	150*	23.17	2	4									24	
Wlls	1995	3	3	0	87	46	29.00	0	0									6	2

QAZI SHAFIQ (Peshawar) b Peshawar 24.2.1965 LHB LM

Cmp	Debut	M	I	NO	Runs	HS	Avge	100	50	Balls	Runs	Wkts	Avge	BB	5i	10m	RpO	ct	st
Wlls		3	3	0	28	15	9.33	0	0	180	84	0					2.80	2	
FC	1984	19	34	0	392	52	11.52	0	1	307	183	6	30.50	2-8	0	0	3.57	7	

RAEES AHMED (Faisalabad) b Lyallpur 2.9.1972 RHB

Cmp	Debut	M	I	NO	Runs	HS	Avge	100	50	Balls	Runs	Wkts	Avge	BB	5i	10m	RpO	ct	st
FC		1	2	0	13	13	6.50	0	0									0	
Wlls	1995	1	1	0	50	50	50.00	0	1									0	

RAFATULLAH (Peshawar) b Peshawar 6.11.1976 RHB SLA

Cmp	Debut	M	I	NO	Runs	HS	Avge	100	50	Balls	Runs	Wkts	Avge	BB	5i	10m	RpO	ct	st
FC		1	2	0	4	2	2.00	0	0	102	57	0					3.35	1	
Wlls		3	2	0	27	22	13.50	0	0	180	136	7	19.42	3-34	0	0	4.53	1	

RAJ HANS (Islamabad, Allied Bank) b Quetta 27.9.1965 RHB OB

Cmp	Debut	M	I	NO	Runs	HS	Avge	100	50	Balls	Runs	Wkts	Avge	BB	5i	10m	RpO	ct	st
FC		7	12	0	255	106	21.25	1	1	842	421	11	38.27	5-74	1	0	3.00	2	
FC	1983	47	78	5	1829	110*	25.05	3	10	4245	2189	69	31.72	6-90	5	1	3.09	23	
Wlls	1994	3	1	0	1	1	1.00	0	0	24	35	0					8.75	1	

RAJA AFAQ (Rawalpindi, ADBP) b Rawalpindi 15.11.1956 RHB OB

Cmp	Debut	M	I	NO	Runs	HS	Avge	100	50	Balls	Runs	Wkts	Avge	BB	5i	10m	RpO	ct	st
FC		4	5	0	80	52	16.00	0	1	264	92	5	18.40	3-35	0	0	2.09	1	
Wlls		4	1	0	1	1	1.00	0	0	240	156	8	19.50	3-52	0	0	3.90	2	
FC	1976	167	222	40	3800	116*	20.87	1	18	29479	13415	524	25.60	7-55	34	6	2.73	85	
Wlls	1981	63	36	6	332	41	11.06	0	0	2857	1777	77	23.07	4-19	1	0	3.73	13	

Cmp	Debut	M	I	NO	Runs	HS	Avge	100	50	Balls	Runs	Wkts	Avge	BB	5i	10m	RpO	ct	st
RAMEEZ RAJA (Allied Bank, Pakistan to Sri Lanka, Pakistan to Kenya, Pakistan to Sharjah, Pakistan to India) b Lyallpur 14.8.1962 RHB LB																			
FC		7	12	0	405	100	33.75	1	3									6	
Wlls		8	8	1	370	102*	52.85	2	0	6	0	0					0.00	3	
Test	1983	57	94	5	2833	122	31.83	2	22									34	
FC	1977	183	303	20	10382	300	36.68	17	63	485	332	5	66.40	2-2	0	0	4.10	101	
Int	1984	189	188	14	5681	119*	32.64	9	30	6	10	0					10.00	30	
Wlls	1980	73	71	11	2836	131	47.26	6	17	60	43	4	10.75	4-43	1	0	4.30	24	
RASHID HANIF (Karachi Whites) b Karachi 4.1.1978 LHB SLA																			
FC		3	5	2	101	50	33.66	0	1	665	292	15	19.46	7-36	1	0	2.63	2	
Wlls		1	1	1	6	6*		0	0	36	32	0					5.33	0	
RASHID LATIF (Karachi Blues, Allied Bank) b Karachi 14.10.1968 RHB WK																			
FC		7	13	2	200	38	18.18	0	0									23	1
Wlls		8	8	0	164	64	20.50	0	1									7	3
Test	1992	19	29	4	623	68*	24.92	0	3	12	10	0					5.00	58	8
FC	1986	87	122	23	2315	68*	23.38	0	12	118	102	3	34.00	2-17	0	0	5.18	238	40
Int	1992	85	57	16	664	50	16.19	0	1									81	22
Wlls	1990	32	30	6	494	64	20.58	0	2									31	13
REHAN RAFIQ (Bahawalpur) b Bahawalpur 28.10.1976 LHB SLA																			
FC		2	4	0	60	20	15.00	0	0									2	
Wlls		3	3	0	70	58	23.33	0	1									1	
FC	1994	13	24	4	261	34*	13.05	0	0	847	341	12	28.41	4-28	0	0	2.41	9	
Wlls	1993	4	4	1	74	58	24.66	0	1	31	35	0					6.77	1	
RIFAQAT ALI (Allied Bank, Combined XI) b Lahore 20.4.1971 RHB OB WK																			
FC		2	4	1	20	10	6.66	0	0									8	
FC	1986	43	64	5	940	72	15.93	0	6	9	6	0					4.00	120	16
Wlls	1993	10	8	1	66	23	9.42	0	0									9	3
RIZWAN BHATTI (Islamabad) b Islamabad 18.7.1972 RHB RFM																			
FC		1	2	1	6	6*	6.00	0	0	29	35	1	35.00	1-35	0	0	7.24	1	
FC	1994	4	6	2	108	43	27.00	0	0	335	193	8	24.12	4-7	0	0	3.45	2	
Wlls	1993	7	7	0	77	28	11.00	0	0	240	165	6	27.50	2-29	0	0	4.12	1	
RIZWAN QAYYUM (Karachi Whites) b Karachi 8.7.1976 LHB OB																			
FC		1	1	0	8	8	8.00	0	0									1	
RIZWAN-UZ-ZAMAN (PIA) b Karachi 4.9.1961 RHB LBG																			
FC		8	15	1	283	91	20.21	0	2									6	
Wlls		7	7	0	204	112	29.14	1	1	39	36	2	18.00	1-16	0	0	5.53	0	
Test	1981	11	19	1	345	60	19.16	0	3	132	46	4	11.50	3-26	0	0	2.09	4	
FC	1976	184	323	23	13303	217*	44.34	38	66	4901	1877	83	22.61	5-16	2	1	2.29	115	
Int	1981	3	3	0	20	14	6.66	0	0									2	
Wlls	1980	92	92	10	2803	112	34.18	5	21	780	445	17	26.17	3-17	0	0	3.42	20	
SAAD WASIM (Karachi Whites, United Bank) b Karachi 28.7.1975 RHB OB																			
FC		3	3	0	26	24	8.66	0	0									2	
Wlls		1	1	0	11	11	11.00	0	0									1	
FC	1994	9	11	0	168	66	15.27	0	1	30	20	0					4.00	9	
Wlls	1995	2	2	0	13	11	6.50	0	0									1	
SAADAT GUL KHAN (Faisalabad) b Murree 28.8.1967 RHB RFM																			
FC		4	6	0	111	44	18.50	0	0	517	285	14	20.35	5-35	1	0	3.30	2	
Wlls		7	7	3	257	86*	64.25	0	3	278	216	7	30.85	4-22	1	0	4.66	4	
FC	1985	60	93	20	1993	113	27.30	1	10	5802	3187	131	24.32	6-67	5	0	3.29	28	
Wlls	1989	15	13	3	369	86*	36.90	0	3	410	312	9	34.66	4-22	1	0	4.56	4	
SABIH AZHAR (Rawalpindi, ADBP) b Rawalpindi 28.2.1962 RHB RFM																			
FC		8	15	1	304	65	21.71	0	1	66	30	0					2.72	5	
Wlls		4	2	0	13	7	6.50	0	0	174	101	1	101.00	1-41	0	0	3.48	1	
FC	1981	126	197	26	3484	100*	20.37	1	19	9175	4483	165	27.16	7-61	10	1	2.93	50	
Wlls	1985	41	31	5	423	79	16.26	0	1	1336	985	21	46.90	4-19	1	0	4.42	16	
SAEED AJMAL (Faisalabad) b Faisalabad 14.10.1977 RHB OB																			
FC		2	4	4	8	4*		0	0	520	307	11	27.90	7-220	1	0	3.54	1	
Wlls		6	1	1	4	4*		0	0	342	219	4	54.75	2-42	0	0	3.84	1	
Wlls	1995	8	3	2	12	8	12.00	0	0	450	280	6	46.66	2-42	0	0	3.73	1	
SAEED ANWAR (Pakistan, ADBP, Pakistan to Canada, Pakistan to Kenya, Pakistan to Sharjah, Pakistan to India) b Karachi 6.9.1968 LHB SLA																			
Test		4	6	1	339	149	67.80	1	3									3	
FC		4	6 .	1	339	149	67.80	1	3									3	
Int		5	5	1	244	91	61.00	0	2	12	10	0					5.00	0	
Wlls		1	1	0	3	3	3.0ʳ	0	0									1	
Test	1990	21	37	1	1739	176	48.3u	4	13	18	4	0					1.33	12	
FC	1986	97	155	6	6961	221	46.71	21	35	623	393	9	43.66	3-83	0	0	3.78	54	
Int	1988	123	122	11	4402	194	39.65	12	17	174	154	3	51.33	1-9	0	0	5.31	25	
Wlls	1985	54	50	2	1559	108	32.47	5	5	426	273	12	22.75	3-5	0	0	3.84	13	

Cmp	Debut	M	I	NO	Runs	HS	Avge	100	50	Balls	Runs	Wkts	Avge	BB	5i	10m	RpO	ct	st

SAEED AZAD (Karachi Blues, National Bank, Pakistan to Kenya) b Karachi 14.8.1966 RHB RM

Cmp	Debut	M	I	NO	Runs	HS	Avge	100	50	Balls	Runs	Wkts	Avge	BB	5i	10m	RpO	ct	st
FC		5	9	0	235	66	26.11	0	1									0	
Wlls		9	9	2	226	100	32.28	1	1									1	
FC	1984	132	223	14	7189	178	34.39	13	40	30	26	0					5.20	51	
Int	1995	4	4	0	65	31	16.25	0	0									2	
Wlls	1980	79	77	9	1958	112*	28.79	2	12	7	8	0					6.85	18	

SAGHEER ABBAS (PIA) b Karachi 10.12.1964 RHB OB

Cmp	Debut	M	I	NO	Runs	HS	Avge	100	50	Balls	Runs	Wkts	Avge	BB	5i	10m	RpO	ct	st
FC		1	1	0	0	0	0.00	0	0									0	
Wlls		1	1	0	0	0	0.00	0	0	24	18	0					4.50	1	
FC	1979	89	149	16	3532	156*	26.55	5	22	192	159	2	79.50	2-12	0	0	4.96	41	
Wlls	1980	52	50	9	1160	100*	28.29	1	8	44	40	0					5.45	19	

SAIFULLAH (Bahawalpur, United Bank) b Lahore 31.3.1961 RHB WK

Cmp	Debut	M	I	NO	Runs	HS	Avge	100	50	Balls	Runs	Wkts	Avge	BB	5i	10m	RpO	ct	st
FC		7	14	1	256	57	19.69	0	2									16	5
Wlls		6	5	0	57	31	11.40	0	0									3	5
FC	1978	120	204	17	5472	175*	29.26	2	35	36	35	0					5.83	182	28
Wlls	1986	28	24	1	467	73	20.30	0	3									12	10

SAIFULLAH MAGSI (Karachi Whites) b Karachi 2.12.1974 RHB

Cmp	Debut	M	I	NO	Runs	HS	Avge	100	50	Balls	Runs	Wkts	Avge	BB	5i	10m	RpO	ct	st
Wlls		3	3	0	56	49	18.66	0	0	72	51	1	51.00	1-38	0	0	4.25	1	

SAJID ALI (Karachi Blues, National Bank, Pakistan to Sharjah) b Karachi 1.7.1963 RHB OB

Cmp	Debut	M	I	NO	Runs	HS	Avge	100	50	Balls	Runs	Wkts	Avge	BB	5i	10m	RpO	ct	st
FC		11	22	1	479	69	22.80	0	3									12	
Wlls		9	9	1	638	197*	79.75	2	3	79	67	2	33.50	2-45	0	0	5.08	5	
FC	1982	189	323	11	12921	203*	41.41	33	66	472	348	8	43.50	2-15	0	0	4.42	189	
Int	1984	13	12	0	130	28	10.83	0	0									1	
Wlls	1981	81	81	4	2920	197*	37.92	6	11	349	269	9	29.88	2-44	0	0	4.62	44	

SAJID REHMANI (Bahawalpur) b Bahawalpur 2.7.1976 RHB WK

Cmp	Debut	M	I	NO	Runs	HS	Avge	100	50	Balls	Runs	Wkts	Avge	BB	5i	10m	RpO	ct	st
FC		4	8	0	29	12	3.62	0	0									10	
Wlls		2	2	0	22	12	11.00	0	0									3	2
FC	1993	16	29	0	325	39	11.20	0	0									21	
Wlls	1993	5	5	0	119	51	23.80	0	1									3	2

SAJID SHAH (Peshawar, PNSC) b Mardan 19.10.1974 RHB RFM

Cmp	Debut	M	I	NO	Runs	HS	Avge	100	50	Balls	Runs	Wkts	Avge	BB	5i	10m	RpO	ct	st
FC		9	14	1	179	50	13.76	0	1	1464	782	24	32.58	5-89	1	0	3.20	3	
Wlls		3	2	0	87	67	43.50	0	1	168	132	7	18.85	3-39	0	0	4.71	1	
FC	1993	34	51	10	468	50	11.41	0	1	4910	2750	106	25.94	7-63	6	1	3.36	10	
Wlls	1994	5	3	0	114	67	38.00	0	1	264	224	9	24.88	3-39	0	0	5.09	1	

SAJJAD AKBAR (PNSC) b Lahore 1.3.1961 RHB OB

Cmp	Debut	M	I	NO	Runs	HS	Avge	100	50	Balls	Runs	Wkts	Avge	BB	5i	10m	RpO	ct	st
FC		7	12	2	332	110	33.20	1	0	1237	542	20	27.10	4-13	0	0	2.62	5	
Wlls		3	3	1	78	47*	39.00	0	0	180	114	5	22.80	2-28	0	0	3.80	2	
FC	1978	155	237	52	5612	143	30.33	6	24	34776	14958	601	24.88	9-59	37	8	2.58	107	
Int	1989	2	1	0	5	5	5.00	0	0	60	45	2	22.50	2-45	0	0	4.50	0	
Wlls	1982	53	41	14	624	59	23.11	0	2	2649	1763	63	27.98	4-13	3	0	3.99	17	

SAJJAD AKHTAR (Bahawalpur) b Ahmedpur Sharqia 4.8.1980 RHB WK

Cmp	Debut	M	I	NO	Runs	HS	Avge	100	50	Balls	Runs	Wkts	Avge	BB	5i	10m	RpO	ct	st
FC		2	4	0	63	37	15.75	0	0									2	

SAJJAD ALI (PNSC) b Lahore 18.10.1971 RHB RFM

Cmp	Debut	M	I	NO	Runs	HS	Avge	100	50	Balls	Runs	Wkts	Avge	BB	5i	10m	RpO	ct	st
FC		5	8	0	159	40	19.87	0	0	595	339	7	48.42	2-39	0	0	3.41	1	
Wlls		2	1	0	12	12	12.00	0	0	82	66	3	22.00	2-36	0	0	4.82	0	
FC	1990	49	76	4	1145	100	15.90	1	4	6313	3790	109	34.77	6-92	4	0	3.60	18	
Wlls	1990	26	22	6	455	60	28.43	0	3	1063	807	41	19.68	5-47	1	1	4.55	4	

SALEEM ELAHI (United Bank, Pakistan to Sri Lanka, Pakistan A to England, Pakistan to Canada, Pakistan to Kenya) b Sahiwal 21.11.1976 RHB OB

Cmp	Debut	M	I	NO	Runs	HS	Avge	100	50	Balls	Runs	Wkts	Avge	BB	5i	10m	RpO	ct	st
FC		9	16	2	546	78	39.00	0	4									9	
Wlls		2	2	1	171	102*	171.00	1	1									1	
Test	1995	4	7	0	57	17	8.14	0	0									8	1
FC	1995	28	49	2	1446	229	30.76	1	9									33	1
Int	1995	14	14	1	437	102*	33.61	1	3									4	
Wlls	1994	7	7	1	289	102*	48.16	1	1									3	

SALEEM KHAN (Lahore) b Okara 1.4.1974 RHB LFM

Cmp	Debut	M	I	NO	Runs	HS	Avge	100	50	Balls	Runs	Wkts	Avge	BB	5i	10m	RpO	ct	st
FC		1	1	1	0	0*		0	0	186	84	2	42.00	2-84	0	0	2.70	0	

SALEEM KHAN (Peshawar) b Peshawar 5.4.1974 RHB OB

Cmp	Debut	M	I	NO	Runs	HS	Avge	100	50	Balls	Runs	Wkts	Avge	BB	5i	10m	RpO	ct	st
Wlls		1	1	0	2	2	2.00	0	0	54	59	0					6.55	1	

SALEEM MALIK (Pakistan, Habib Bank, Pakistan to Sri Lanka, Pakistan to Canada, Pakistan to Kenya, Pakistan to Sharjah, Pakistan to India) b Lahore 16.4.1963 RHB RM/LB

Cmp	Debut	M	I	NO	Runs	HS	Avge	100	50	Balls	Runs	Wkts	Avge	BB	5i	10m	RpO	ct	st
Test		4	5	0	190	78	38.00	0	2	66	41	0					3.72	5	
FC		4	5	0	190	78	38.00	0	2	66	41	0					3.72	5	
Int		5	4	3	146	73*	146.00	0	2	104	87	3	29.00	1-8	0	0	5.01	2	
Wlls		3	2	0	79	45	39.50	0	0	101	90	3	30.00	2-26	0	0	5.34	1	
Test	1981	96	142	21	5528	237	45.68	15	28	548	321	5	64.20	1-3	0	0	3.51	62	
FC	1978	245	377	55	15298	237	47.50	40	76	5184	2951	84	35.13	5-19	3	0	3.41	152	

Cmp	Debut	M	I	NO	Runs	HS	Avge	100	50	Balls	Runs	Wkts	Avge	BB	5i	10m	RpO	ct	st
Int	1981	259	233	37	6622	102	33.78	5	43	3231	2677	79	33.88	5-35	0	1	4.97	76	
Wlls	1980	64	58	16	2362	129*	56.23	5	17	1000	799	33	24.21	4-39	1	0	4.79	22	

SALEEM YOUSUF (Customs) b Karachi 7.12.1959 RHB WK

Cmp	Debut	M	I	NO	Runs	HS	Avge	100	50	Balls	Runs	Wkts	Avge	BB	5i	10m	RpO	ct	st
FC		1	2	0	25	22	12.50	0	0	1	4	0					24.00	0	
Test	1981	32	44	5	1055	91*	27.05	0	5									91	13
FC	1978	119	183	22	4578	145*	28.43	6	20	19	20	1	20.00	1-16	0	0	6.31	298	41
Int	1981	86	62	19	768	62	17.86	0	4									81	22
Wlls	1980	54	51	2	971	91	19.81	0	5	108	73	4	18.25	2-36	0	0	4.05	42	11

SALMAN FAZAL (Karachi Whites, National Bank) b Karachi 22.10.1975 RHB SLA

Cmp	Debut	M	I	NO	Runs	HS	Avge	100	50	Balls	Runs	Wkts	Avge	BB	5i	10m	RpO	ct	st
FC		11	17	7	64	14*	6.40	0	0	2117	808	39	20.71	6-42	4	0	2.29	5	
Wlls		9	2	2	4	2*		0	0	515	343	9	38.11	3-46	0	0	3.99	4	
FC	1993	27	35	12	219	23*	9.52	0	0	5500	2208	82	26.92	6-42	8	1	2.40	15	
Wlls	1994	20	8	5	24	8	8.00	0	0	966	580	27	21.48	4-32	2	0	3.60	8	

SAQLAIN MUSHTAQ (Pakistan, PIA, Surrey, Pakistan to Australia, Pakistan to Sri Lanka, Pakistan to Canada, Pakistan to Kenya, Pakistan to Sharjah, Pakistan to India) b Lahore 27.11.1976 RHB OB

Cmp	Debut	M	I	NO	Runs	HS	Avge	100	50	Balls	Runs	Wkts	Avge	BB	5i	10m	RpO	ct	st
Test		3	4	1	117	79	39.00	0	1	800	383	11	34.81	4-75	0	0	2.87	0	
FC		3	4	1	117	79	39.00	0	1	800	383	11	34.81	4-75	0	0	2.87	0	
Int		6	3	0	15	10	5.00	0	0	311	255	16	15.93	5-44	1	1	4.91	0	
Wlls		7	5	2	31	18*	10.33	0	0	409	243	12	20.25	4-44	1	0	3.56	5	
Test	1995	9	14	4	256	79	25.60	0	2	3045	1387	38	26.50	5-89	1	0	2.73	4	
FC	1994	41	61	17	716	79	16.27	0	4	9405	4011	172	23.31	7-66	13	3	2.55	21	
Int	1995	56	37	10	255	30*	9.44	0	0	2971	2115	109	19.40	5-29	4	2	4.27	17	
Wlls	1994	21	13	6	52	18*	7.42	0	0	1125	606	35	17.31	4-44	1	0	3.23	10	

SHADAB KABIR (Karachi Blues, Pakistan, Combined XI, Pakistan to Canada) b Karachi 12.11.1977 LHB OB

Cmp	Debut	M	I	NO	Runs	HS	Avge	100	50	Balls	Runs	Wkts	Avge	BB	5i	10m	RpO	ct	st
Test		1	1	0	2	2	2.00	0	0									2	
FC		6	10	0	205	46	20.50	0	0									5	
Test	1996	3	5	0	89	35	17.80	0	0	6	9	0					9.00	4	
FC	1995	25	41	2	957	99	24.53	0	5	30	27	0					5.40	20	
Int	1996	3	3	0	0	0	0.00	0	0									1	
Wlls	1995	6	6	0	221	67	36.83	0	1									4	

SHAFIQ AHMED (Lahore) b Bahawalpur 8.7.1977 LHB LBG

Cmp	Debut	M	I	NO	Runs	HS	Avge	100	50	Balls	Runs	Wkts	Avge	BB	5i	10m	RpO	ct	st
Wlls		2	2	0	4	3	2.00	0	0	120	73	1	73.00	1-27	0	0	3.65	0	
FC	1994	3	4	2	29	15*	14.50	0	0	439	273	11	24.81	8-111	1	1	3.73	1	

SHAHEEN MALIK (Karachi Blues) b Karachi 9.4.1966 RHB WK

Cmp	Debut	M	I	NO	Runs	HS	Avge	100	50	Balls	Runs	Wkts	Avge	BB	5i	10m	RpO	ct	st
FC		1	2	0	30	15	15.00	0	0									1	1
FC	1992	4	7	0	106	52	15.14	0	1									13	3
Wlls	1995	6	5	0	28	12	5.60	0	0									5	7

SHAHID ALI (Customs) b Faisalabad 21.2.1979 RHB LBG

Cmp	Debut	M	I	NO	Runs	HS	Avge	100	50	Balls	Runs	Wkts	Avge	BB	5i	10m	RpO	ct	st
FC		2	4	1	23	9	7.66	0	0	238	129	8	16.12	5-36	1	0	3.25	0	
FC	1994	4	7	3	34	10*	8.50	0	0	436	249	11	22.63	5-36	1	0	3.42	0	
Wlls	1995	1	1	1	2	2*		0	0	54	32	0					3.55	0	

SHAHID ALI KHAN (Lahore) b Lahore 8.3.1968 RHB OB

Cmp	Debut	M	I	NO	Runs	HS	Avge	100	50	Balls	Runs	Wkts	Avge	BB	5i	10m	RpO	ct	st
FC		2	3	2	4	3	4.00	0	0	402	181	8	22.62	3-53	0	0	2.70	1	
Wlls		3	2	0	10	10	5.00	0	0	180	108	4	27.00	3-44	0	0	3.60	1	
FC	1988	43	61	21	311	34*	7.77	0	0	8656	3874	137	28.27	8-123	8	0	2.68	14	
Wlls	1990	19	11	2	48	17	5.33	0	0	1013	661	25	26.44	3-44	0	0	3.91	4	

SHAHID ANWAR (Lahore, National Bank) b Multan 5.7.1968 RHB RM

Cmp	Debut	M	I	NO	Runs	HS	Avge	100	50	Balls	Runs	Wkts	Avge	BB	5i	10m	RpO	ct	st
FC		12	23	1	630	105	28.63	1	5	300	150	10	15.00	6-2	1	0	3.00	2	
Wlls		8	8	1	197	86	28.14	0	2	30	30	0					6.00	1	
FC	1983	152	261	16	9326	195	38.06	19	58	1868	1005	40	25.12	6-2	1	0	3.22	61	
Int	1996	1	1	0	37	37	37.00	0	0									0	
Wlls	1985	69	69	6	1832	117*	29.07	1	13	503	378	12	31.50	3-22	0	0	4.50	18	

SHAHID HUSSAIN (Peshawar, PNSC) b Peshawar 29.12.1970 RHB SLA

Cmp	Debut	M	I	NO	Runs	HS	Avge	100	50	Balls	Runs	Wkts	Avge	BB	5i	10m	RpO	ct	st
FC		7	12	2	142	43	14.20	0	0	1466	715	20	35.75	5-83	1	0	2.92	4	
Wlls		3	2	0	22	14	11.00	0	0	168	118	3	39.33	2-45	0	0	4.21	0	
FC	1986	71	109	24	1101	90	12.95	0	1	12898	5575	214	26.05	6-40	11	0	2.59	32	
Wlls	1991	17	16	2	117	22	8.35	0	0	849	585	19	30.78	3-28	0	0	4.13	8	

SHAHID IQBAL (Karachi Whites, Karachi Blues) b Karachi 9.4.1974 RHB RFM

Cmp	Debut	M	I	NO	Runs	HS	Avge	100	50	Balls	Runs	Wkts	Avge	BB	5i	10m	RpO	ct	st
FC		2	3	0	64	31	21.33	0	0	264	152	7	21.71	3-33	0	0	3.45	0	
Wlls		6	5	3	102	29*	51.00	0	0	240	228	8	28.50	4-48	1	0	5.70	4	
FC	1995	10	18	3	192	31	12.80	0	0	1519	820	33	24.84	6-77	1	0	3.23	2	

SHAHID JAVED (Rawalpindi, Habib Bank) b Rawalpindi 29.8.1968 RHB OB

Cmp	Debut	M	I	NO	Runs	HS	Avge	100	50	Balls	Runs	Wkts	Avge	BB	5i	10m	RpO	ct	st
FC		13	21	4	538	73	31.64	0	4	102	42	0					2.47	10	
Wlls		3	3	1	44	31	22.00	0	0	17	13	0					4.58	0	
FC	1985	151	246	27	7391	207*	33.74	13	43	1001	591	12	49.25	3-52	0	0	3.54	86	
Wlls	1987	30	28	5	731	100*	31.78	1	4	53	50	0					5.66	6	

SHAHID KHAN (Peshawar) b Charsada 5.4.1977 RHB

Cmp	Debut	M	I	NO	Runs	HS	Avge	100	50	Balls	Runs	Wkts	Avge	BB	5i	10m	RpO	ct	st
Wlls		1	1	0	2	2	2.00	0	0									0	

Cmp	Debut	M	I	NO	Runs	HS	Avge	100	50	Balls	Runs	Wkts	Avge	BB	5i	10m	RpO	ct	st

SHAHID KHAN AFRIDI (Karachi Whites, Combined XI, Karachi Blues, Pakistan, Pakistan to Australia, Pakistan to Kenya, Pakistan to Sharjah, Pakistan to India) b Kohat 1.3.1980 RHB LBG

Cmp	Debut	M	I	NO	Runs	HS	Avge	100	50	Balls	Runs	Wkts	Avge	BB	5i	10m	RpO	ct	st
FC		2	4	0	66	30	16.50	0	0	375	219	7	31.28	3-32	0	0	3.50	1	
Int		6	5	0	112	66	22.40	0	1	295	221	6	36.83	2-25	0	0	4.49	3	
Wlls		6	6	0	194	63	32.33	0	1	318	275	7	39.28	4-20	1	0	5.18	3	
FC	1995	8	12	0	221	80	18.41	0	1	1117	594	19	31.26	5-93	1	0	3.19	2	
Int	1996	33	30	0	677	102	22.56	1	5	1599	1194	28	42.64	3-33	0	0	4.48	12	
Wlls	1995	9	9	1	272	63	34.00	0	1	456	404	10	40.40	4-20	1	0	5.31	3	

SHAHID MAHBOOB (Karachi Blues) b Karachi 25.8.1962 RHB RFM

Cmp	Debut	M	I	NO	Runs	HS	Avge	100	50	Balls	Runs	Wkts	Avge	BB	5i	10m	RpO	ct	st
FC		1	2	0	5	5	2.50	0	0	192	95	5	19.00	3-56	0	0	2.96	1	
Test	1989	1								294	131	2	65.50	2-131	0	0	2.67	0	
FC	1979	143	218	17	3229	110	16.06	3	6	28069	15160	628	24.14	8-62	36	7	3.19	80	
Int	1982	10	6	1	119	77	23.80	0	1	540	382	7	54.57	1-23	0	0	4.24	1	
Wlls	1980	48	41	5	596	83*	16.55	0	3	2286	1548	62	24.96	5-52	3	1	4.06	9	

SHAHID MAHMOOD (Habib Bank) b Lahore 25.12.1974 RHB LBG

Cmp	Debut	M	I	NO	Runs	HS	Avge	100	50	Balls	Runs	Wkts	Avge	BB	5i	10m	RpO	ct	st
FC		2	2	0	2	2	1.00	0	0	330	184	6	30.66	3-62	0	0	3.34	1	
FC	1994	18	30	5	401	59	16.04	0	1	3321	1963	51	38.49	4-76	0	0	3.54	10	
Wlls	1992	2	2	1	0	0*	0.00	0	0	84	101	0					7.21	1	

SHAHID NAQI (Rawalpindi) b Karachi 20.10.1972 RHB OB

Cmp	Debut	M	I	NO	Runs	HS	Avge	100	50	Balls	Runs	Wkts	Avge	BB	5i	10m	RpO	ct	st
FC		1	2	0	50	41	25.00	0	0									1	
FC	1990	23	38	1	831	108	22.45	1	4	72	49	0					4.08	11	
Wlls	1993	4	4	1	54	20	18.00	0	0									0	

SHAHID NAWAZ (Lahore) b Lahore 26.8.1970 RHB RM

Cmp	Debut	M	I	NO	Runs	HS	Avge	100	50	Balls	Runs	Wkts	Avge	BB	5i	10m	RpO	ct	st
FC		9	16	0	576	94	36.00	0	4	115	102	3	34.00	2-23	0	0	5.32	12	
Wlls		3	3	1	100	85*	50.00	0	1	90	66	1	66.00	1-42	0	0	4.40	3	
FC	1987	92	146	9	5101	267	37.23	11	27	943	659	18	36.61	3-35	0	0	4.19	59	
Wlls	1988	31	29	1	765	85*	27.32	0	6	223	173	4	43.25	1-17	0	0	4.65	8	

SHAHID NAZIR (Pakistan, Combined XI, Habib Bank, Pakistan to Australia, Pakistan to Sri Lanka, Pakistan to Kenya, Pakistan to Sharjah) b Faisalabad 4.12.1977 RHB RFM

Cmp	Debut	M	I	NO	Runs	HS	Avge	100	50	Balls	Runs	Wkts	Avge	BB	5i	10m	RpO	ct	st
Test		4	5	1	25	13*	6.25	0	0	591	287	13	22.07	5-53	1	0	2.91	0	
FC		5	6	1	27	13*	5.40	0	0	693	339	16	21.18	5-53	1	0	2.93	0	
Int		3	1	1	5	5*		0	0	132	75	4	18.25	2-28	0	0	3.40	1	
Wlls		3	2	2	27	18*		0	0	144	99	5	19.80	2-31	0	0	4.12	1	
Test	1996	6	7	2	27	13*	5.40	0	0	819	435	14	31.07	5-53	1	0	3.18	2	
FC	1995	15	19	7	187	60*	15.58	0	1	2150	1100	51	21.56	6-64	3	0	3.06	4	
Int	1996	12	6	5	25	8	25.00	0	0	534	394	12	32.83	3-14	0	0	4.42	3	
Wlls	1995	6	4	2	62	31	31.00	0	0	300	213	9	23.66	2-26	0	0	4.26	1	

SHAHID SAEED (Lahore) b Lahore 6.1.1966 RHB RM

Cmp	Debut	M	I	NO	Runs	HS	Avge	100	50	Balls	Runs	Wkts	Avge	BB	5i	10m	RpO	ct	st
FC		4	8	0	102	26	12.75	0	0	144	91	4	22.75	2-26	0	0	3.79	4	
Test	1989	1	1	0	12	12	12.00	0	0	90	43	0					2.86	0	
FC	1983	111	190	16	6588	229	37.86	13	33	4311	2604	83	31.37	4-10	0	0	3.62	67	
Int	1989	10	10	0	141	50	14.10	0	1	222	159	3	53.00	2-20	0	0	4.29	2	
Wlls	1985	49	48	5	1475	92*	34.30	0	13	1620	1255	42	29.88	4-21	2	0	4.64	11	

SHAHID TANVIR (National Bank) b Sheikhupura 27.11.1958 RHB OB

Cmp	Debut	M	I	NO	Runs	HS	Avge	100	50	Balls	Runs	Wkts	Avge	BB	5i	10m	RpO	ct	st
FC		2	4	0	81	64	20.25	0	1	30	16	0					3.20	2	
FC	1982	101	165	25	4188	142	29.91	5	23	7391	3892	112	34.75	6-44	4	0	3.15	52	
Wlls	1983	48	40	8	580	82	18.12	0	2	1067	818	37	22.10	4-39	1	0	4.59	11	

SHAKEEL AHMED (Peshawar, Habib Bank) b Daska 12.11.1971 RHB WK

Cmp	Debut	M	I	NO	Runs	HS	Avge	100	50	Balls	Runs	Wkts	Avge	BB	5i	10m	RpO	ct	st
FC		14	25	1	716	123	29.83	1	4									18	
Wlls		3	3	0	63	61	21.00	0	1									3	
Test	1992	3	5	0	74	33	14.80	0	0									4	
FC	1990	97	161	11	5745	200	38.30	11	33	42	19	0					2.71	89	9
Int	1994	2	2	0	61	36	30.50	0	0									0	
Wlls	1991	36	36	2	1317	142	38.73	4	8	6	13	1	13.00	1-13	0	0	13.00	24	2

SHAKEEL AHMED (Rawalpindi) b Kuwait City, Kuwait 12.2.1966 LHB SLA

Cmp	Debut	M	I	NO	Runs	HS	Avge	100	50	Balls	Runs	Wkts	Avge	BB	5i	10m	RpO	ct	st
FC		6	9	2	138	66	19.71	0	1	784	357	15	23.80	4-53	0	0	2.73	1	
Wlls		6	3	0	73	41	24.33	0	0	354	214	12	17.83	4-20	2	0	3.62	4	
FC	1985	61	86	33	674	66	12.71	0	1	10092	4515	203	22.24	7-69	12	3	2.68	31	
Wlls	1987	43	30	14	196	41	12.25	0	0	2153	1280	64	20.00	4-15	5	0	3.56	14	

SHAKEEL KHAN (Habib Bank) b Lahore 28.5.1968 RHB RFM

Cmp	Debut	M	I	NO	Runs	HS	Avge	100	50	Balls	Runs	Wkts	Avge	BB	5i	10m	RpO	ct	st
FC		3	6	1	32	12*	6.40	0	0	561	330	12	27.50	4-80	0	0	3.52	0	
FC	1986	61	76	26	472	43	9.44	0	0	9237	5341	172	31.05	7-46	6	1	3.46	23	
Int	1987	1	1	0	0	0	0.00	0	0	54	50	1	50.00	1-50	0	0	5.55	0	
Wlls	1985	29	10	6	34	7*	8.50	0	0	1204	836	33	25.33	4-33	1	0	4.16	9	

SHAKEEL SAJJAD (Karachi Whites, National Bank) b Karachi 2.4.1964 RHB RFM

Cmp	Debut	M	I	NO	Runs	HS	Avge	100	50	Balls	Runs	Wkts	Avge	BB	5i	10m	RpO	ct	st
FC		1	2	0	18	16	9.00	0	0	12	8	0					4.00	0	
Wlls		1								6	7	0					7.00	0	
FC	1986	54	80	14	1314	105*	19.90	1	4	3800	2147	66	32.53	6-28	1	0	3.39	23	
Wlls	1987	35	28	5	511	58	22.21	0	1	1291	867	24	36.12	4-47	1	0	4.02	10	

Cmp	Debut	M	I	NO	Runs	HS	Avge	100	50	Balls	Runs	Wkts	Avge	BB	5i	10m	RpO	ct	st

SHEHZAD AHMED (Faisalabad) b Gojra 29.10.1977 RHB OB WK

| Wlls | | 7 | 3 | 2 | 34 | 19* | 34.00 | 0 | 0 | | | | | | | | | 4 | 3 |
| FC | 1995 | 4 | 6 | 1 | 55 | 18* | 11.00 | 0 | 0 | | | | | | | | | 12 | 1 |

SHEHZAD BUTT (United Bank) b Lahore 2.4.1973 RHB RFM

FC		7	11	1	188	88	18.80	0	1	949	584	19	30.73	5-42	2	0	3.69	3	
Wlls		1								54	55	2	27.50	2-55	0	0	6.11	0	
FC	1994	21	31	11	276	88	13.80	0	1	2737	1657	61	27.16	5-42	3	0	3.63	14	
Wlls	1994	5	3	2	0	0*	0.00	0	0	237	204	13	15.69	3-38	0	0	5.16	0	

SHEHZAD HANIF (Lahore) b Lahore 21.8.1967 RHB RM

| Wlls | | 1 | 1 | 0 | 0 | 0 | 0.00 | 0 | 0 | | | | | | | | | 0 | |

SHER ALI (Bahawalpur, PNSC) b Lahore 9.4.1970 RHB RM

FC		10	18	1	528	123*	31.05	1	4									6	
FC	1986	91	156	6	4753	201*	31.68	8	28	15	21	0					8.40	45	
Wlls	1989	23	22	1	552	78	26.28	0	5									7	

SHEZAN AHMED (Karachi Whites) b Karachi 4.10.1967 LHB SLA

Wlls		2	1	1	5	5*		0	0	90	61	0					4.06	0	
FC	1989	3	6	0	7	6	1.16	0	0	304	210	3	70.00	2-102	0	0	4.14	0	
Wlls	1991	4	1	1	5	5*		0	0	156	121	0					4.65	0	

SHOAIB AKHTAR (Rawalpindi, ADBP, Pakistan A to England) b Rawalpindi 13.8.1975 RHB RFM

FC		14	16	4	126	23	10.50	0	0	2560	1633	69	23.66	5-58	6	0	3.82	3	
Wlls		5	2	1	10	10*	10.00	0	0	225	229	3	76.33	1-41	0	0	6.10	2	
FC	1994	35	42	15	217	23	8.03	0	0	5318	3409	127	26.84	6-69	10	0	3.84	14	
Wlls	1993	6	2	1	10	10*	10.00	0	0	273	272	4	68.00	1-41	0	0	5.97	2	

SHOAIB KHAN (Peshawar) b Peshawar 27.10.1978 RHB

| Wlls | | 2 | 2 | 0 | 48 | 25 | 24.00 | 0 | 0 | | | | | | | | | 1 | |

SHOAIB MALIK (Pakistan A to England) b Sialkot 1.2.1982 RHB OB

| FC | 1997 | 3 | 4 | 0 | 18 | 9 | 4.50 | 0 | 0 | 738 | 333 | 12 | 27.75 | 3-49 | 0 | 0 | 2.70 | 0 | |

SHOAIB MOHAMMAD (Karachi Blues, PIA) b Karachi 8.1.1961 RHB OB

FC		5	9	2	219	54	31.28	0	2	222	123	2	61.50	1-21	0	0	3.32	2	
Wlls		3	3	0	20	15	6.66	0	0	66	50	0					4.54	2	
Test	1983	45	68	7	2705	203*	44.34	7	13	396	170	5	34.00	2-8	0	0	2.57	22	
FC	1976	183	308	41	10931	208*	40.94	32	51	2505	1151	25	46.04	3-14	0	0	2.75	79	
Int	1984	63	58	6	1269	126*	24.40	1	8	919	725	20	36.25	3-20	0	0	4.73	13	
Wlls	1980	85	85	13	2842	111*	39.47	3	21	602	470	13	36.15	2-6	0	0	4.68	30	

SOHAIL FAZAL (Habib Bank) b Lahore 11.11.1967 RHB RFM

FC		1	1	0	5	5	5.00	0	0	72	32	0					2.66	0	
FC	1985	33	43	7	742	87*	20.61	0	4	1942	1094	26	42.07	3-44	0	0	3.38	21	
Int	1989	2	2	0	56	32	28.00	0	0	6	4	0					4.00	1	
Wlls	1988	23	21	3	473	89*	26.27	0	1	852	699	20	34.95	4-50	1	0	4.92	3	

SOHAIL IDREES (Lahore) b Lahore 3.6.1972 RHB OB

FC		4	8	0	191	55	23.87	0	2									3	
Wlls		2	2	0	27	26	13.50	0	0									1	
FC	1994	12	21	1	464	63	23.20	0	3									11	
Wlls	1995	3	3	0	34	26	11.33	0	0									1	

SOHAIL JAFFAR (Karachi Whites, PIA, Combined XI) b Karachi 17.4.1967 RHB RM

FC		11	17	0	537	72	31.58	0	3	60	36	0					3.60	9	
Wlls		7	6	1	280	64*	56.00	0	3									2	
FC	1986	100	162	10	5473	160	36.00	8	36	1843	1095	24	45.62	3-73	0	0	3.56	52	
Wlls	1990	36	34	1	1133	101	34.33	1	8	12	25	0					12.50	9	

SOHAIL MEHDI (Karachi Whites) b Karachi 1.3.1972 LHB SLA

Wlls		3	3	0	52	34	17.33	0	0	163	102	1	102.00	1-48	0	0	3.75	1	
FC	1989	17	19	8	376	102*	34.18	1	2	2277	1207	41	29.43	5-30	1	0	3.18	10	
Wlls	1990	26	23	4	357	42	18.78	0	0	1196	753	19	39.63	3-11	0	0	3.77	7	

SOHAIL MIANDAD (Habib Bank) b Karachi 10.12.1969 RHB RM

FC		4	7	0	80	24	11.42	0	0									2	
FC	1988	62	106	3	3001	142	28.58	4	16	188	163	2	81.50	1-12	0	0	5.20	25	
Wlls	1988	14	14	3	204	54	18.54	0	1									0	

SULEMAN HUDA (Karachi Whites) b Karachi 14.8.1975 RHB RM

| FC | | 1 | 2 | 0 | 16 | 12 | 8.00 | 0 | 0 | | | | | | | | | 0 | |
| Wlls | | 1 | 1 | 0 | 7 | 7 | 7.00 | 0 | 0 | | | | | | | | | 0 | |

TAHIR BUTT (Lahore, PNSC) b Lahore 26.9.1976 RHB

| FC | | 7 | 12 | 1 | 311 | 52 | 28.27 | 0 | 1 | | | | | | | | | 2 | |
| Wlls | | 3 | 3 | 0 | 72 | 59 | 24.00 | 0 | 1 | | | | | | | | | 2 | |

TAHIR MAHMOOD (PNSC) b Karachi 6.4.1966 RHB OB

| FC | | 4 | 7 | 0 | 101 | 41 | 14.42 | 0 | 0 | 366 | 186 | 5 | 37.20 | 2-29 | 0 | 0 | 2.89 | 2 | |
| Wlls | | 2 | 1 | 0 | 0 | 0 | 0.00 | 0 | 0 | 78 | 56 | 1 | 56.00 | 1-21 | 0 | 0 | 4.30 | 1 | |

Cmp	Debut	M	I	NO	Runs	HS	Avge	100	50	Balls	Runs	Wkts	Avge	BB	5i	10m	RpO	ct	st
FC	1989	40	64	5	1049	90	17.77	0	6	2643	1198	39	30.71	4-28	0	0	2.71	19	
Wlls	1990	25	21	7	426	52	30.42	0	1	607	448	16	28.00	4-44	1	0	4.42	2	

TAHIR RASHEED (Karachi Blues, Habib Bank) b Karachi 21.11.1960 RHB WK

Cmp	Debut	M	I	NO	Runs	HS	Avge	100	50	Balls	Runs	Wkts	Avge	BB	5i	10m	RpO	ct	st
FC		10	15	1	394	73	28.14	0	3									40	1
Wlls		3	2	0	17	13	8.50	0	0									4	2
FC	1979	148	223	34	4988	182	26.39	3	22	72	31	1	31.00	1-11	0	0	2.58	406	58
Wlls	1981	74	52	15	952	115	25.72	1	4									71	42

TAHIR RIAZ (Lahore) b Lahore 22.8.1971 RHB OB

Cmp	Debut	M	I	NO	Runs	HS	Avge	100	50	Balls	Runs	Wkts	Avge	BB	5i	10m	RpO	ct	st
Wlls		2	2	1 .	16	12	16.00	0	0	42	40	0					5.71	1	

TAHIR SHAH (National Bank) b Lahore 27.1.1959 RHB RM

Cmp	Debut	M	I	NO	Runs	HS	Avge	100	50	Balls	Runs	Wkts	Avge	BB	5i	10m	RpO	ct	st
FC		6	12	1	212	43	19.27	0	0	36	23	0					3.83	6	
Wlls		5	5	0	117	77 .	23.40	0	1									0	
FC	1982	141	225	18	6157	150	29.74	6	30	8140	4756	130	36.58	7-65	5	0	3.50	103	1
Wlls	1982	70	64	3	1246	77	20.42	0	6	2100	1163	38	30.60	3-23	0	0	3.32	24	1

TAIMUR ALI KHAN (Islamabad) b Islamabad 7.9.1976 RHB RM

Cmp	Debut	M	I	NO	Runs	HS	Avge	100	50	Balls	Runs	Wkts	Avge	BB	5i	10m	RpO	ct	st
Wlls		2	2	2	9	6*		0	0	90	49	2	24.50	1-17	0	0	3.26	1	
Wlls	1993	3	2	2	9	6*		0	0	132	73	2	36.50	1-17	0	0	3.31	1	

TAIMUR KHAN (Peshawar) b Peshawar 1.5.1975 RHB RFM

Cmp	Debut	M	I	NO	Runs	HS	Avge	100	50	Balls	Runs	Wkts	Avge	BB	5i	10m	RpO	ct	st
FC		4	6	0	53	20	8.83	0	0	18	12	0					4.00	2	
Wlls		3	3	1	153	74*	76.50	0	2	60	58	4	14.50	3-41	0	0	5.80	1	
FC	1994	16	24	1	316	57	13.73	0	1	156	48	1	48.00	1-23	0	0	1.84	22	
Wlls	1995	10	10	2	440	97*	55.00	0	5	216	209	9	23.22	3-22	0	0	5.80	2	

TANVIR SHAUKAT (Faisalabad) b Lyallpur 4.5.1963 RHB RFM

Cmp	Debut	M	I	NO	Runs	HS	Avge	100	50	Balls	Runs	Wkts	Avge	BB	5i	10m	RpO	ct	st
FC		1	2	0	31	20	15.50	0	0	24	18	0					4.50	0	
FC	1983	13	19	4	192	46	12.80	0	0	1379	1008	32	31.50	6-47	1	0	4.38	1	
Wlls	1989	1	1	0	0	0	0.00	0	0	18	19	0					6.33	0	

TARIQ AZIZ (Bahawalpur) b Lahore 5.9.1972 RHB

Cmp	Debut	M	I	NO	Runs	HS	Avge	100	50	Balls	Runs	Wkts	Avge	BB	5i	10m	RpO	ct	st
FC		2	4	0	77	35	19.25	0	0									2	
FC	1993	4	7	0	117	35	16.71	0	0									3	
Wlls	1994	2	2	0	27	15	13.50	0	0									1	

TARIQ MAHMOOD (Lahore) b Lahore 4.10.1968 LHB SLA

Cmp	Debut	M	I	NO	Runs	HS	Avge	100	50	Balls	Runs	Wkts	Avge	BB	5i	10m	RpO	ct	st
FC		2	4	0	92	28	23.00	0	0									1	
FC	1991	28	48	2	1304	206*	28.34	1	7	36	26	0					4.33	27	
Wlls	1993	11	11	1	301	91	30.10	0	1	162	127	5	25.40	2-19	0	0	4.70	4	

TARIQ MOHAMMAD (National Bank) b Karachi 6.9.1971 LHB RM

Cmp	Debut	M	I	NO	Runs	HS	Avge	100	50	Balls	Runs	Wkts	Avge	BB	5i	10m	RpO	ct	st
FC		1	2	0	37	22	18.50	0	0									0	
FC	1993	11	17	2	320	56	21.33	0	1	18	44	0					14.66	4	

TARIQ RASHEED (Lahore) b Lahore 30.11.1970 RHB SLA

Cmp	Debut	M	I	NO	Runs	HS	Avge	100	50	Balls	Runs	Wkts	Avge	BB	5i	10m	RpO	ct	st
FC		1	2	0	7	7	3.50	0	0									0	
FC	1986	15	20	3	360	50*	21.17	0	1	1843	852	22	38.72	4-21	0	0	2.77	11	
Wlls	1993	7	6	2	86	47*	21.50	0	0	276	180	6	30.00	4-18	1	0	3.91	2	

TARIQ SARWAR (Bahawalpur) b Rahim Yar Khan 3.9.1969 RHB RM

Cmp	Debut	M	I	NO	Runs	HS	Avge	100	50	Balls	Runs	Wkts	Avge	BB	5i	10m	RpO	ct	st
Wlls		3	3	1	45	38*	22.50	0	0	159	132	6	22.00	3-40	0	0	4.98	1	
Wlls	1990	8	8	1	125	44	17.85	0	0	346	256	9	28.44	3-40	0	0	4.43	1	

TASSAWAR HUSSAIN (Rawalpindi) b Rawalpindi 12.6.1974 RHB OB

Cmp	Debut	M	I	NO	Runs	HS	Avge	100	50	Balls	Runs	Wkts	Avge	BB	5i	10m	RpO	ct	st
FC		4	8	0	135	75	16.87	0	1									2	
Wlls		6	5	2	162	85	54.00	0	1	28	25	0					5.35	3	
FC	1993	22	39	3	859	89	23.86	0	8	30	39	0					7.80	10	
Wlls	1994	12	11	2	374	85	41.55	0	3	60	64	0					6.40	5	

TAUQEER HUSSAIN (Rawalpindi) b Rawalpindi 30.11.1971 RHB OB

Cmp	Debut	M	I	NO	Runs	HS	Avge	100	50	Balls	Runs	Wkts	Avge	BB	5i	10m	RpO	ct	st
FC		1	2	0	4	3	2.00	0	0	243	106	7	15.14	4-63	0	0	2.61	1	
Wlls		2	1	1	8	8*		0	0	114	102	2	51.00	1-49	0	0	5.36	0	
FC	1990	18	31	8	414	66	12.54	0	1	3149	1446	65	22.24	6-53	4	1	2.75	10	
Wlls	1991	13	10	7	117	38*	39.00	0	0	636	454	14	32.42	3-45	0	0	4.28	1	

TAUSEEF AHMED (United Bank) b Karachi 10.5.1960 RHB OB

Cmp	Debut	M	I	NO	Runs	HS	Avge	100	50	Balls	Runs	Wkts	Avge	BB	5i	10m	RpO	ct	st
FC		8	10	2	99	33	12.37	0	0	1437	438	21	20.85	5-36	1	0	1.82	2	
Wlls		8	4	1	36	30	12.00	0	0	468	249	11	22.63	3-23	0	0	3.19	0	
Test	1979	34	38	20	318	35*	17.66	0	0	7778	2950	93	31.72	6-45	3	0	2.27	9	
FC	1978	171	189	62	1844	77	14.51	0	1	39215	15090	690	21.86	8-52	45	7	2.30	73	
Int	1981	70	25	14	116	27*	10.54	0	0	3250	2247	55	40.85	4-38	1	0	4.14	10	
Wlls	1980	86	47	12	439	49*	12.54	0	0	4259	2364	106	22.30	4-22	1	0	3.33	25	

TAUSEEF MUGHAL (Customs) b Lahore 17.4.1962 RHB LB

Cmp	Debut	M	I	NO	Runs	HS	Avge	100	50	Balls	Runs	Wkts	Avge	BB	5i	10m	RpO	ct	st
FC		1	2	0	17	15	8.50	0	0									0	
Wlls	1989	3	3	1	92	46*	46.00	0	0									1	

UMAIR MUGHAL (Karachi Blues) b Karachi 7.6.1975 RHB RFM

Cmp	Debut	M	I	NO	Runs	HS	Avge	100	50	Balls	Runs	Wkts	Avge	BB	5i	10m	RpO	ct	st
Wlls		4	1	0	22	22	22.00	0	0	218	188	5	37.60	2-39	0	0	5.17	0	

Cmp	Debut	M	I	NO	Runs	HS	Avge	100	50	Balls	Runs	Wkts	Avge	BB	5i	10m	RpO	ct	st

UMAR RASHEED (United Bank) b Karachi 25.12.1962 RHB RM

Cmp	Debut	M	I	NO	Runs	HS	Avge	100	50	Balls	Runs	Wkts	Avge	BB	5i	10m	RpO	ct	st
FC		2	3	0	33	26	11.00	0	0	332	124	9	13.77	3-20	0	0	2.24	1	
Wlls		5	4	3	105	31*	105.00	0	0	138	93	4	23.25	2-19	0	0	4.04	0	
FC	1982	127	207	14	5057	147*	26.20	2	37	7599	3144	125	25.15	7-48	3	2	2.48	100	
Wlls	1981	59	53	9	1134	107*	25.77	1	4	1973	1277	43	29.69	4-25	1	0	3.88	18	

USMAN TARIQ (Bahawalpur) b Bahawalpur 28.12.1983 RHB LB

Cmp	Debut	M	I	NO	Runs	HS	Avge	100	50	Balls	Runs	Wkts	Avge	BB	5i	10m	RpO	ct	st
Wlls		3	3	0	41	18	13.66	0	0	132	95	3	31.66	1-16	0	0	4.31	0	

UZAIR AFAQ (Karachi Blues) b Karachi 25.8.1977 RHB RM

Cmp	Debut	M	I	NO	Runs	HS	Avge	100	50	Balls	Runs	Wkts	Avge	BB	5i	10m	RpO	ct	st
FC		1	2	0	15	15	7.50	0	0									0	

WAHID BAKSH SHIKRANI (Bahawalpur) b Ahmedpur Sherqia 16.9.1967 RHB OB

Cmp	Debut	M	I	NO	Runs	HS	Avge	100	50	Balls	Runs	Wkts	Avge	BB	5i	10m	RpO	ct	st
Wlls		1	1	0	6	6	6.00	0	0	54	41	1	41.00	1-41	0	0	4.55	0	
FC	1995	5	9	3	62	27	10.33	0	0	450	254	5	50.80	5-101	1	0	3.38	1	
Wlls	1993	2	1	0	6	6	6.00	0	0	72	55	1	55.00	1-41	0	0	4.58	0	

WAJAHATULLAH WASTI (Peshawar) b Peshawar 11.11.1974 RHB RFM

Cmp	Debut	M	I	NO	Runs	HS	Avge	100	50	Balls	Runs	Wkts	Avge	BB	5i	10m	RpO	ct	st
FC		7	11	0	345	86	31.36	0	4	12	3	0					1.50	2	
FC	1994	26	44	3	1049	103	25.58	1	6	137	84	2	42.00	2-32	0	0	3.67	22	
Wlls	1994	6	6	0	182	56	30.33	0	1	54	46	0					5.11	1	

WAQAR AHMED (Peshawar) b Peshawar 1.4.1980 LHB LFM

Cmp	Debut	M	I	NO	Runs	HS	Avge	100	50	Balls	Runs	Wkts	Avge	BB	5i	10m	RpO	ct	st
Wlls		3	2	2	6	6*		0	0	171	127	7	18.14	4-41	1	0	4.45	0	

WAQAR YOUNIS (Pakistan, United Bank, Glamorgan, Pakistan to Canada, Pakistan to Kenya, Pakistan to Sharjah, Pakistan to Australia) b Vehari 16.11.1971 RHB RF

Cmp	Debut	M	I	NO	Runs	HS	Avge	100	50	Balls	Runs	Wkts	Avge	BB	5i	10m	RpO	ct	st
Test		3	4	0	26	23	6.50	0	0	588	291	11	26.45	4-48	0	0	2.96	0	
FC		3	4	0	26	23	6.50	0	0	588	291	11	26.45	4-48	0	0	2.96	0	
Int		2	1	0	0	0	0.00	0	0	90	80	4	20.00	2-32	0	0	5.33	0	
Wlls		6	3	1	8	8	4.00	0	0	321	252	15	16.80	5-32	0	1	4.71	1	
Test	1989	44	57	11	429	34	9.32	0	0	9071	4844	227	21.33	7-76	19	4	3.20	6	
FC	1987	151	168	41	1683	55	13.25	0	2	27115	14501	688	21.07	8-17	54	13	3.20	37	
Int	1989	156	78	29	463	37	9.44	0	0	7707	5762	265	21.74	6-26	11	9	4.48	18	
Wlls	1988	24	14	3	45	12	4.09	0	0	1034	839	38	22.07	6-29	1	2	4.86	2	

WAQAS AHMED (Lahore) b Lahore 24.1.1979 RHB RFM

Cmp	Debut	M	I	NO	Runs	HS	Avge	100	50	Balls	Runs	Wkts	Avge	BB	5i	10m	RpO	ct	st
FC		1	1	0	37	37	37.00	0	0	96	52	1	52.00	1-52	0	0	3.25	0	

WASIM AKRAM (Pakistan, PIA, Lancashire, Pakistan to Australia, Pakistan to Canada, Pakistan to Canada, Pakistan to Sharjah) b Lahore 3.6.1966 LHB LF

Cmp	Debut	M	I	NO	Runs	HS	Avge	100	50	Balls	Runs	Wkts	Avge	BB	5i	10m	RpO	ct	st
Test		2	2	1	292	257*	292.00	1	0	430	180	11	16.36	6-48	1	1	2.51	2	
FC		2	2	1	292	257*	292.00	1	0	430	180	11	16.36	6-48	1	1	2.51	2	
Int		6	5	1	132	66	33.00	0	2	290	197	6	32.83	3-43	0	0	4.07	4	
Wlls		6	6	1	82	39*	16.40	0	0	312	162	5	32.40	2-24	0	0	3.11	3	
Test	1984	72	100	13	1944	257*	22.34	2	4	16464	7054	311	22.68	7-119	21	4	2.57	28	
FC	1984	197	271	31	5380	257*	22.41	5	18	39728	17731	829	21.39	8-30	63	15	2.67	67	
Int	1984	232	181	33	2180	86	14.72	0	4	11954	7517	333	22.57	5-15	13	5	3.77	56	
Wlls	1985	33	24	5	418	64	22.00	0	1	1618	926	60	15.43	5-16	4	2	3.43	12	

WASIM ARIF (National Bank) b Karachi 10.10.1964 RHB WK

Cmp	Debut	M	I	NO	Runs	HS	Avge	100	50	Balls	Runs	Wkts	Avge	BB	5i	10m	RpO	ct	st
FC		6	11	1	136	36	13.60	0	0									16	1
Wlls		8	5	0	44	32	8.80	0	0									7	1
FC	1982	89	132	18	2434	105*	21.35	1	12	6	8	0					8.00	232	46
Wlls	1982	54	43	7	527	58	14.63	0	2									58	21

WASIM HAIDER (Faisalabad, PIA) b Lyallpur 6.6.1967 RHB RFM

Cmp	Debut	M	I	NO	Runs	HS	Avge	100	50	Balls	Runs	Wkts	Avge	BB	5i	10m	RpO	ct	st
FC		5	6	1	101	57	20.20	0	1	414	203	9	22.55	4-27	0	0	2.94	2	
Wlls		3	3	1	15	8	7.50	0	0	96	46	1	46.00	1-13	0	0	2.87	0	
FC	1983	102	152	32	3714	184	30.95	4	18	11181	5893	232	25.40	6-46	9	1	3.16	44	
Int	1991	3	2	0	26	13	13.00	0	0	114	79	1	79.00	1-36	0*	0	4.15	0	
Wlls	1985	68	42	12	626	60*	20.86	0	1	2664	1776	70	25.37	6-20	0	3	4.00	24	

WASIM HUSSAIN, Mohammad (Faisalabad) b Gojra 3.3.1974 RHB RM

Cmp	Debut	M	I	NO	Runs	HS	Avge	100	50	Balls	Runs	Wkts	Avge	BB	5i	10m	RpO	ct	st
FC		2	2	0	25	14	12.50	0	0	198	113	1	113.00	1-51	0	0	3.42	1	
Wlls		3	2	0	15	11	7.50	0	0	114	119	2	59.50	2-45	0	0	6.26	0	
FC	1994	13	15	6	234	32	26.00	0	0	2133	1209	44	27.47	6-50	2	0	3.40	6	
Wlls	1995	4	2	0	15	11	7.50	0	0	168	159	2	79.50	2-45	0	0	5.67	0	

WASIM MIR (Lahore) b Lahore 10.5.1969 RHB

Cmp	Debut	M	I	NO	Runs	HS	Avge	100	50	Balls	Runs	Wkts	Avge	BB	5i	10m	RpO	ct	st
Wlls		1	1	0	72	72	72.00	0	1	24	24	0					6.00	0	
Wlls	1993	2	2	0	126	72	63.00	0	2	84	56	3	18.66	3-32	0	0	4.00	2	

WASIM YOUSUFI (Peshawar, United Bank) b Peshawar 3.3.1970 RHB WK

Cmp	Debut	M	I	NO	Runs	HS	Avge	100	50	Balls	Runs	Wkts	Avge	BB	5i	10m	RpO	ct	st
FC		14	23	3	724	100*	36.20	1	4									38	4
Wlls		2																	0	1
FC	1988	75	116	9	2396	101	22.39	2	9									156	15
Wlls	1991	21	16	4	325	77*	27.08	0	3									13	8

YAHYA TAJVEED (Karachi Blues) b Karachi 11.4.1970 RHB OB

Cmp	Debut	M	I	NO	Runs	HS	Avge	100	50	Balls	Runs	Wkts	Avge	BB	5i	10m	RpO	ct	st
Wlls		1	1	0	15	15	15.00	0	0									2	

Cmp	Debut	M	I	NO	Runs	HS	Avge	100	50	Balls	Runs	Wkts	Avge	BB	5i	10m	RpO	ct	st

YASIR HAMEED (Peshawar) b Peshawar 28.2.1978 RHB OB WK

Cmp	Debut	M	I	NO	Runs	HS	Avge	100	50	Balls	Runs	Wkts	Avge	BB	5i	10m	RpO	ct	st
FC		1	2	0	0	0	0.00	0	0	6	14	0					14.00	1	
Wlls		2	2	0	48	24	24.00	0	0									1	
Wlls	1995	3	3	0	57	24	19.00	0	0									3	

YOUSUF AHMED (Karachi Whites) b Karachi 25.10.1976 RHB

Cmp	Debut	M	I	NO	Runs	HS	Avge	100	50	Balls	Runs	Wkts	Avge	BB	5i	10m	RpO	ct	st
Wlls		1	1	1	14	14*		0	0	18	25	0					8.33	0	

YOUSUF YOUHANA (Bahawalpur) b Lahore 27.8.1974 RHB

Cmp	Debut	M	I	NO	Runs	HS	Avge	100	50	Balls	Runs	Wkts	Avge	BB	5i	10m	RpO	ct	st
FC		2	4	0	109	48	27.25	0	0									1	
Wlls		3	3	0	77	55	25.66	0	1									1	

ZAFAR IQBAL (Karachi Blues, National Bank) b Karachi 6.3.1969 RHB RFM

Cmp	Debut	M	I	NO	Runs	HS	Avge	100	50	Balls	Runs	Wkts	Avge	BB	5i	10m	RpO	ct	st
FC		9	17	2	407	79	27.13	0	2	738	469	10	46.90	3-35	0	0	3.81	2	
Wlls		3	1	0	14	14	14.00	0	0	126	105	3	35.00	1-25	0	0	5.00	1	
FC	1990	47	68	8	1626	128	27.10	2	7	5015	3007	111	27.09	7-60	6	0	3.59	21	
Int	1993	8	6	0	48	18	8.00	0	0	198	137	3	45.66	2-37	0	0	4.15	1	
Wlls	1995	35	17	5	239	45*	19.91	0	0	1351	1044	44	23.72	6-22	1	1	4.63	11	

ZAFAR JADOON (Karachi Whites) b Abbotabad 2.5.1976 RHB LB

Cmp	Debut	M	I	NO	Runs	HS	Avge	100	50	Balls	Runs	Wkts	Avge	BB	5i	10m	RpO	ct	st
Wlls		3	3	0	105	60	35.00	0	1	90	50	2	25.00	2-23	0	0	3.33	0	
FC	1995	3	4	0	22	12	5.50	0	0									0	
Wlls	1995	5	5	0	118	60	23.60	0	1	90	50	2	25.00	2-23	0	0	3.33	1	

ZAHEER ABBASI (Islamabad) b Islamabad 10.9.1969 RHB

Cmp	Debut	M	I	NO	Runs	HS	Avge	100	50	Balls	Runs	Wkts	Avge	BB	5i	10m	RpO	ct	st
FC		8	14	2	372	69	31.00	0	4	12	0	0					0.00	4	
Wlls		3	3	0	83	63	27.66	0	1									1	
FC	1994	20	32	4	873	93*	31.17	0	7	12	0	0					0.00	9	
Wlls	1992	9	9	0	207	63	23.00	0	1									1	

ZAHEER AHMED RANA (Faisalabad, National Bank) b Lyallpur 13.6.1974 RHB WK

Cmp	Debut	M	I	NO	Runs	HS	Avge	100	50	Balls	Runs	Wkts	Avge	BB	5i	10m	RpO	ct	st
FC		4	8	1	87	38	12.42	0	0									10	1
Wlls		1																0	
FC	1994	7	11	2	110	38	12.22	0	0									12	4

ZAHID AHMED (PIA) b Karachi 15.11.1961 LHB SLA

Cmp	Debut	M	I	NO	Runs	HS	Avge	100	50	Balls	Runs	Wkts	Avge	BB	5i	10m	RpO	ct	st
FC		4	4	1	83	68	27.66	0	1	587	218	15	14.53	6-71	2	1	2.22	2	
Wlls		1	1	0	0	0	0.00	0	0	48	20	1	20.00	1-20	0	0	2.50	0	
FC	1978	155	242	35	6990	179	33.76	12	39	21416	8934	355	25.16	7-14	18	3	2.50	99	
Int	1987	2	2	1	3	3*	3.00	0	0	96	61	3	20.33	2-24	0	0	3.81	0	
Wlls	1988	88	63	14	1430	88*	29.18	0	8	3717	2516	115	21.87	4-14	6	0	4.06	33	

ZAHID ALI (Karachi Blues) b Karachi 23.12.1965 RHB OB

Cmp	Debut	M	I	NO	Runs	HS	Avge	100	50	Balls	Runs	Wkts	Avge	BB	5i	10m	RpO	ct	st
Wlls		3	2	0	13	13	6.50	0	0									0	
FC	1993	9	14	1	240	45	18.46	0	0	6	2	0					2.00	13	
Wlls	1992	13	12	2	403	102*	40.30	1	3									2	

ZAHID FAZAL (PIA) b Sialkot 10.11.1973 RHB RM/OB

Cmp	Debut	M	I	NO	Runs	HS	Avge	100	50	Balls	Runs	Wkts	Avge	BB	5i	10m	RpO	ct	st
FC		7	12	0	215	62	17.91	0	1									11	
Wlls		6	6	1	284	74	56.80	0	4									3	
Test	1990	9	16	0	288	78	18.00	0	1									5	
FC	1989	73	111	10	3680	199	36.43	8	21	211	168	1	168.00	1-24	0	0	4.77	56	
Int	1990	19	18	3	348	98*	23.20	0	2									2	
Wlls	1989	49	48	5	1626	116	37.81	2	13									17	

ZAHID HUSSAIN (Faisalabad) b Lyallpur 14.8.1976 RHB OB

Cmp	Debut	M	I	NO	Runs	HS	Avge	100	50	Balls	Runs	Wkts	Avge	BB	5i	10m	RpO	ct	st
Wlls		1	1	0	1	1	1.00	0	0									0	

ZAHID JAVED (Lahore) b Rawalpindi 11.5.1958 RHB

Cmp	Debut	M	I	NO	Runs	HS	Avge	100	50	Balls	Runs	Wkts	Avge	BB	5i	10m	RpO	ct	st
FC		1	2	0	23	20	11.50	0	0									1	
FC	1994	10	19	0	373	77	19.63	0	1	6	12	0					12.00	8	
Wlls	1994	5	5	0	60	57	12.00	0	1									2	

ZAHID UMAR (Lahore) b Lahore 5.12.1969 RHB WK

Cmp	Debut	M	I	NO	Runs	HS	Avge	100	50	Balls	Runs	Wkts	Avge	BB	5i	10m	RpO	ct	st
FC		3	5	0	83	30	16.60	0	0									5	1
FC	1986	18	28	1	602	93	22.29	0	4									26	3
Wlls	1987	5	5	0	172	73	34.40	0	1									4	1

ZAHOOR ELAHI (Lahore, Pakistan, Combined XI, ADBP, Pakistan to Australia) b Sahiwal 1.3.1971 RHB RM

Cmp	Debut	M	I	NO	Runs	HS	Avge	100	50	Balls	Runs	Wkts	Avge	BB	5i	10m	RpO	ct	st
Test		2	3	0	30	22	10.00	0	0									1	
FC		8	14	1	571	153	43.92	2	2									7	
Int		4	4	0	143	86	35.75	0	2									0	
Wlls		7	7	2	458	133*	91.60	2	2	6	3	0					3.00	3	
FC	1985	128	217	13	7464	178	36.58	17	41	1899	1067	22	48.50	5-55	1	0	3.37	82	
Int	1996	14	14	1	297	86	22.84	0	3									2	
Wlls	1986	59	59	9	2406	133*	48.12	6	13	72	68	3	22.66	3-43	0	0	5.66	12	

ZAKAULLAH KHAN (Rawalpindi) b Rawalpindi 7.8.1965 RHB OB

Cmp	Debut	M	I	NO	Runs	HS	Avge	100	50	Balls	Runs	Wkts	Avge	BB	5i	10m	RpO	ct	st
FC		1	2	2	2	2*		0	0	84	45	0					3.21	0	
FC	1986	17	23	15	57	21	7.12	0	0	2868	1253	57	21.98	6-48	4	1	2.62	5	

Cmp	Debut	M	I	NO	Runs	HS	Avge	100	50	Balls	Runs	Wkts	Avge	BB	5i	10m	RpO	ct	st
ZEESHAN SIDDIQI (PNSC) b Karachi 26.10.1976 RHB OB WK																		
FC		3	5	0	60	36	12.00	0	0	6	0	0					0.00	5	
Wlls		1	1	0	0	0	0.00	0	0									1	
FC	1995	6	10	0	212	81	21.20	0	1	6	0	0					0.00	6	
Wlls	1995	2	2	0	2	2	1.00	0	0									6	
ZIA-UD-DIN (Customs) b Lahore 10.12.1964 RHB SLA																		
FC		3	6	1	84	44	16.80	0	0	126	33	1	33.00	1-21	0	0	1.57	4	
Wlls		3	3	1	4	3*	2.00	0	0	126	96	4	24.00	2-38	0	0	4.57	1	
FC	1986	12	21	6	349	44	23.26	0	0	1405	636	31	20.51	5-69	1	0	2.71	6	
ZIA-UR-REHMAN (Lahore) b Lahore 28.3.1975 RHB LB																		
FC		1	2	0	1	1	0.50	0	0									0	
ZUBAIR AYUB (Karachi Blues) b Karachi 8.11.1977 RHB OB																		
Wlls		1	1	1	0	0*		0	0	18	11	0					3.66	1	
FC	1995	2	2	2	3	2*		0	0	30	27	0					5.40	0	
ZUBAIR NADEEM (Rawalpindi) b Lahore 21.7.1973 RHB RM																		
FC		1	2	0	52	42	26.00	0	0	30	14	0					2.80	3	
Wlls	1995	4	4	0	216	78	54.00	0	2									0	
ZULFIQAR ALI (Peshawar) b Peshawar 10.4.1974 RHB OB WK																		
FC		2	3	1	57	42*	28.50	0	0									4	
Wlls		3	2	0	0	0	0.00	0	0									3	2

The following runs were conceded by bowlers in first-class matches between 1976-77 and 1979-80 for which full details of overs bowled are not available (these runs are not taken into account when computing the runs per over figure): Iqbal Sikander 44, Mohammad Riaz 122, Nadeem Ghauri 264 and Shahid Mahboob 208.

BANGLADESH IN PAKISTAN 1996-97

Cmp	Debut	M	I	NO	Runs	HS	Avge	100	50	Balls	Runs	Wkts	Avge	BB	5i	10m	RpO	ct	st
ABDUL HALEEM b Dhaka 1.1.1973 RHB OB																		
Wlls		4	4	0	84	34	21.00	0	0	7	7	0					6.00	0	
ATIA-UR-REHMAN b Dhaka 5.1.1976 RHB WK																		
Wlls		4	4	0	25	19	6.25	0	0									4	1
HABIB-UL-BASHAR b Kushtia 17.8.1972 RHB																		
Wlls		4	4	2	174	71	87.00	0	1	10	18	0					10.80	1	
Int	1994	2	2	0	16	16	8.00	0	0									1	
HAROON-UR-RASHEED b Mymensingh 30.11.1968 RHB LB																		
Wlls		4	4	0	76	43	19.00	0	0	12	12	0					6.00	0	
Int	1988	2	2	0	0	0	0.00	0	0									0	
HASAN-UZ-ZAMAN b Jashor 15.1.1975 RHB RFM																		
Wlls		2	2	0	39	22	19.50	0	0									0	
MAFIZ-UR-REHMAN b Madaripur 10.11.1978 RHB RFM																		
Wlls		4	4	0	31	16	7.75	0	0	204	194	6	32.33	3-54	0	0	5.70	1	
MURSHID KHAN b Fareedpur 14.5.1972 LHB LM																		
Wlls		2	2	0	4	3	2.00	0	0	84	87	1	87.00	1-58	0	0	6.21	1	
NAZIMUDDIN CHOWDHURY b Chitakong 14.12.1979 RHB RFM																		
Wlls		1								60	51	0					5.10	0	
PARVEZ AHMED b Sylhat 2.2.1978 RHB																		
Wlls		2	2	0	42	34	21.00	0	0									0	
SAIFULLAH KHAN b Rajshahi 3.6.1973 LHB SLA																		
Wlls		4	2	2	0	0*		0	0	216	178	4	44.50	2-32	0	0	4.94	0	
SHAARIAR HUSSAIN b Narayangang 1.6.1976 RHB																		
Wlls		4	4	0	125	76	31.25	0	1									2	
SHAHNAWAZ KABIR b Chuadanga 31.12.1976 RHB RM																		
Wlls		1	1	1	2	2*		0	0	30	28	0					5.60	0	
SHEIKH SALAHUDDIN b Khulna 10.2.1969 RHB OB																		
Wlls		4	3	1	7	5	3.50	0	0	192	182	3	60.66	2-50	0	0	5.68	0	
ZAKIR HUSSAIN b Mymensingh 1.12.1972 RHB RFM																		
Wlls		4	2	0	9	8	4.50	0	0	210	132	4	33.00	2-24	0	0	3.77	0	

NEW ZEALAND IN PAKISTAN 1996-97

ASTLE, N.J.

Cmp Debut	M	I	NO	Runs	HS	Avge	100	50	Balls	Runs	Wkts	Avge	BB	5i	10m	RpO	ct	st
Test	2	4	0	15	11	3.75	0	0	78	41	2	20.50	1-10	0	0	3.15	1	
FC	3	6	1	46	30*	9.20	0	0	78	41	2	20.50	1-10	0	0	3.15	1	
Int	3	3	0	91	60	30.33	0	1	156	111	3	37.00	2-31	0	0	4.26	1	

CAIRNS, C.L.

Cmp Debut	M	I	NO	Runs	HS	Avge	100	50	Balls	Runs	Wkts	Avge	BB	5i	10m	RpO	ct	st
Test	2	4	0	117	93	29.25	0	1	394	278	7	39.71	5-137	1	0	4.23	2	
FC	2	4	0	117	93	29.25	0	1	394	278	7	39.71	5-137	1	0	4.23	2	
Int	3	3	1	71	36	35.50	0	0	162	129	2	64.50	1-35	0	0	4.77	0	

DOULL, S.B.

Cmp Debut	M	I	NO	Runs	HS	Avge	100	50	Balls	Runs	Wkts	Avge	BB	5i	10m	RpO	ct	st
Test	2	4	3	46	26	46.00	0	0	378	171	10	17.10	5-46	1	0	2.71	1	
FC	3	5	3	57	26	28.50	0	0	480	223	12	18.58	5-46	1	0	2.78	2	
Int	3	2	0	1	1	0.50	0	0	126	116	1	116.00	1-33	0	0	5.52	0	

FLEMING, S.P.

Cmp Debut	M	I	NO	Runs	HS	Avge	100	50	Balls	Runs	Wkts	Avge	BB	5i	10m	RpO	ct	st
Test	2	4	1	182	92*	60.66	0	2									4	
FC	3	6	1	239	92*	47.80	0	2									5	
Int	3	3	1	172	88	86.00	0	1									1	

GERMON, L.K.

Cmp Debut	M	I	NO	Runs	HS	Avge	100	50	Balls	Runs	Wkts	Avge	BB	5i	10m	RpO	ct	st
Test	2	4	0	66	55	16.50	0	1									3	
FC	2	4	0	66	55	16.50	0	1									3	
Int	3	2	0	4	2	2.00	0	0									1	3

GREATBATCH, M.J.

Cmp Debut	M	I	NO	Runs	HS	Avge	100	50	Balls	Runs	Wkts	Avge	BB	5i	10m	RpO	ct	st
Test	2	4	0	40	19	10.00	0	0									0	
FC	3	6	0	47	19	7.83	0	0									0	
Int	1																0	

HARRIS, C.Z.

Cmp Debut	M	I	NO	Runs	HS	Avge	100	50	Balls	Runs	Wkts	Avge	BB	5i	10m	RpO	ct	st
Test	2	4	0	31	16	7.75	0	0	186	80	2	40.00	2-57	0	0	2.58	1	
FC	2	4	0	31	16	7.75	0	0	186	80	2	40.00	2-57	0	0	2.58	1	
Int	3	2	0	42	22	21.00	0	0	150	124	8	15.50	5-42	0	1	4.96	2	

HART, M.N.

Cmp Debut	M	I	NO	Runs	HS	Avge	100	50	Balls	Runs	Wkts	Avge	BB	5i	10m	RpO	ct	st
FC	1	2	1	31	22	31.00	0	0	156	73	2	36.50	2-58	0	0	2.80	0	
Int	1								60	33	2	16.50	2-33	0	0	3.30	0	

KENNEDY, R.J.

Cmp Debut	M	I	NO	Runs	HS	Avge	100	50	Balls	Runs	Wkts	Avge	BB	5i	10m	RpO	ct	st
Int	2	2	2	7	7*		0	0	72	71	1	71.00	1-47	0	0	5.91	0	

LARSEN, G.R.

Cmp Debut	M	I	NO	Runs	HS	Avge	100	50	Balls	Runs	Wkts	Avge	BB	5i	10m	RpO	ct	st
FC	1	2	0	1	1	0.50	0	0	90	44	0					2.93	0	

MORRISON, D.K.

Cmp Debut	M	I	NO	Runs	HS	Avge	100	50	Balls	Runs	Wkts	Avge	BB	5i	10m	RpO	ct	st
FC	1	1	1	9	9*		0	0	66	39	2	19.50	2-39	0	0	3.54	0	

PARORE, A.C.

Cmp Debut	M	I	NO	Runs	HS	Avge	100	50	Balls	Runs	Wkts	Avge	BB	5i	10m	RpO	ct	st
Test	2	4	0	61	37	15.25	0	0									0	
FC	3	6	0	72	37	12.00	0	0									0	
Int	3	3	0	119	47	39.66	0	0									0	

PATEL, D.N.

Cmp Debut	M	I	NO	Runs	HS	Avge	100	50	Balls	Runs	Wkts	Avge	BB	5i	10m	RpO	ct	st
Test	2	4	0	47	26	11.75	0	0	223	93	4	23.25	4-36	0	0	2.50	0	
FC	2	4	0	47	26	11.75	0	0	223	93	4	23.25	4-36	0	0	2.50	0	
Int	1	1	0	0	0	0.00	0	0	18	24	0					8.00	2	

SPEARMAN, C.M.

Cmp Debut	M	I	NO	Runs	HS	Avge	100	50	Balls	Runs	Wkts	Avge	BB	5i	10m	RpO	ct	st
FC	1	2	0	5	5	2.50	0	0	6	5	0					5.00	1	
Int	2	2	0	6	6	3.00	0	0									1	

VAUGHAN, J.T.C.

Cmp Debut	M	I	NO	Runs	HS	Avge	100	50	Balls	Runs	Wkts	Avge	BB	5i	10m	RpO	ct	st
Test	2	4	0	53	27	13.25	0	0	263	147	5	29.40	4-27	0	0	3.35	1	
FC	3	6	0	110	48	18.33	0	0	317	162	6	27.00	4-27	0	0	3.06	1	
Int	2	1	0	13	13	13.00	0	0	114	114	2	57.00	1-55	0	0	6.00	0	

YOUNG, B.A.

Cmp Debut	M	I	NO	Runs	HS	Avge	100	50	Balls	Runs	Wkts	Avge	BB	5i	10m	RpO	ct	st
Test	2	4	0	144	61	36.00	0	1									3	
FC	3	6	0	264	73	44.00	0	2									3	
Int	3	3	0	95	58	31.66	0	1									3	

ZIMBABWE IN PAKISTAN 1996-97

BRENT, G.B.

Cmp Debut	M	I	NO	Runs	HS	Avge	100	50	Balls	Runs	Wkts	Avge	BB	5i	10m	RpO	ct	st
FC	1	1	0	10	10	10.00	0	0	82	53	2	26.50	2-36	0	0	3.87	1	
Int	1	1	0	1	1	1.00	0	0	30	29	0					5.80	0	

Cmp Debut	M	I	NO	Runs	HS	Avge	100	50	Balls	Runs	Wkts	Avge	BB	5i	10m	RpO	ct	st
CAMPBELL, A.D.R.																		
Test	2	4	0	84	52	21.00	0	1									0	
FC	3	6	0	99	52	16.50	0	1									0	
Int	3	2	0	8	7	4.00	0	0	6	4	0					4.00	0	
DEKKER, M.H.																		
Test	2	4	0	46	19	11.50	0	0									1	
FC	3	6	0	74	19	12.33	0	0									4	
Int	2	2	0	29	18	14.50	0	0	24	32	0					8.00	0	
FLOWER, A.																		
Test	2	4	0	113	61	28.25	0	1									5	1
FC	3	6	1	213	100*	42.60	1	1									6	1
Int	3	3	0	134	82	44.66	0	2									1	1
FLOWER, G.W.																		
Test	2	4	0	171	110	42.75	1	0	72	14	1	14.00	1-4	0	0	1.16	0	
FC	3	6	0	258	110	43.00	1	1	240	135	5	27.00	3-84	0	0	3.37	2	
Int	3	3	0	174	91	58.00	0	2	24	17	0					4.25	1	
HOUGHTON, D.L.																		
Test	2	4	0	182	73	45.50	0	2									2	
FC	3	5	0	287	105	57.40	1	2	12	11	0					5.50	2	
Int	3	3	0	31	25	10.33	0	0									3	
MATAMBANADZO, E.																		
Test	1	2	1	7	7	7.00	0	0	96	89	2	44.50	2-62	0	0	5.56	0	
FC	2	2	1	7	7	7.00	0	0	162	114	3	38.00	2-62	0	0	4.22	1	
Int	1	1	1	2	2*		0	0	48	32	4	8.00	4-32	1	0	4.00	0	
MBANGWA, M.																		
Test	1	2	0	2	2	1.00	0	0	144	81	2	40.50	2-67	0	0	3.38	0	
FC	1	2	0	2	2	1.00	0	0	144	81	2	40.50	2-67	0	0	3.38	0	
Int	1	1	0	11	11	11.00	0	0	34	47	0					8.29	0	
OLONGA, H.K.																		
Test	1	1	0	7	7	7.00	0	0	114	60	1	60.00	1-60	0	0	3.15	0	
FC	2	3	1	10	7	5.00	0	0	240	116	2	58.00	1-32	0	0	2.90	1	
RENNIE, G.J.																		
FC	1	2	0	14	12	7.00	0	0	18	19	2	9.50	2-15	0	0	6.33	0	
Int	2	2	0	6	6	3.00	0	0									2	
RENNIE, J.A.																		
Int	3	3	0	34	27	11.33	0	0	138	119	4	29.75	2-37	0	0	5.17	1	
STRANG, B.C.																		
Test	2	3	1	56	42	28.00	0	0	197	107	3	35.66	3-53	0	0	3.25	0	
FC	2	3	1	56	42	28.00	0	0	197	107	3	35.66	3-53	0	0	3.25	0	
Int	1	1	0	6	6	6.00	0	0	24	21	0					5.25	0	
STRANG, P.A.																		
Test	2	4	2	131	106*	65.50	1	0	571	286	6	47.66	5-212	1	0	3.00	0	
FC	2	4	2	131	106*	65.50	1	0	571	286	6	47.66	5-212	1	0	3.00	0	
Int	3	3	1	59	29	29.50	0	0	120	122	0					6.10	2	
WHITTALL, A.R.																		
Test	1	2	1	0	0*	0.00	0	0	272	146	2	73.00	2-146	0	0	3.22	1	
FC	2	4	1	14	10	4.66	0	0	572	335	9	37.22	5-97	1	0	3.51	3	
Int	3	3	2	5	4*	5.00	0	0	138	124	3	41.33	3-36	0	0	5.39	0	
WHITTALL, G.J.																		
Test	2	4	0	41	32	10.25	0	0	192	84	2	42.00	2-73	0	0	2.92	0	
FC	2	4	0	41	32	10.25	0	0	192	84	2	42.00	2-73	0	0	2.92	0	
Int	3	3	0	19	10	6.33	0	0	121	130	3	43.33	2-48	0	0	6.44	0	
WISHART, C.B.																		
Test	2	4	0	17	10	4.25	0	0									0	
FC	3	6	1	101	68*	20.20	0	1									1	
Int	1	1	0	2	2	2.00	0	0									0	

The following current cricketer has played in Pakistan Domestic limited overs cricket but did not appear in Pakistan Domestic Cricket in 1996-97:

SHEERAZ, K.P. (see Gloucestershire) (Rawalpindi B)

| Wlls 1994 | 2 | 1 | 0 | 0 | 0 | 0.00 | 0 | 0 | 66 | 33 | 3 | 11.00 | 2-17 | 0 | 0 | 3.00 | 0 | |

SHARJAH

First One-Day International Match: Pakistan v Sri Lanka 1983-84. Since that date regular one-day International competitions between Test playing countries have taken place, all matches being played at the Sharjah Stadium.

ONE-DAY INTERNATIONAL RECORDS

Highest Team Total: 338-4 (50 overs) New Zealand v Bangladesh 1989-90; 333-7 (50 overs) West Indies v Sri Lanka 1995-96; 332-3 (50 overs) Australia v Sri Lanka 1989-90
Highest in 1996-97: 251-7 (50 overs) Sri Lanka v Pakistan

Lowest Team Total: 55 (28.3 overs) Sri Lanka v West Indies 1986-87; 64 (35.5 overs) New Zealand v Pakistan 1985-86; 87 (32.5 overs) Pakistan v India 1984-85
Lowest in 1996-97: 94 (31.4 overs) Zimbabwe v Pakistan

Highest Individual Innings: 169 B.C.Lara West Indies v Sri Lanka 1995-96; 153 B.C.Lara West Indies v Pakistan 1993-94; 137* Inzamam-ul-Haq Pakistan v New Zealand 1993-94
Highest in 1996-97: 134 P.A.de Silva Sri Lanka v Pakistan

Most Runs in Season: 582 (av 64.66) Saeed Anwar (Pakistan) 1993-94
Most in 1996-97: 462 (av 57.75) P.A.de Silva (Sri Lanka)

Best Innings Analyses: 7-37 Aaqib Javed Pakistan v India 1991-92; 6-14 Imran Khan Pakistan v India 1984-85; 6-26 Waqar Younis Pakistan v Sri Lanka 1989-90
Best in 1996-97: 6-44 Waqar Younis Pakistan v New Zealand

Most Wickets in Season: 21 (av 15.14) Waqar Younis (Pakistan) 1996-97

Record Wicket Partnerships

1st	204	Saeed Anwar & Rameez Raja	Pakistan v Sri Lanka	1992-93
2nd	273	Aamer Sohail & Inzamam-ul-Haq	Pakistan v New Zealand	1993-94
3rd	184	M.S.Atapattu & P.A.de Silva	Sri Lanka v Pakistan	1996-97
4th	172	Saleem Malik & Basit Ali	Pakistan v West Indies	1993-94
5th	119	K.L.T.Arthurton & J.C.Adams	West Indies v Pakistan	1993-94
6th	154	R.B.Richardson & P.J.L.Dujon	West Indies v Pakistan	1991-92
7th	115	A.C.Parore & L.K.Germon	New Zealand v Pakistan	1996-97
8th	81*	Saleem Malik & Aaqib Javed	Pakistan v South Africa	1995-96
9th	45	R.B.Richardson & I.R.Bishop	West Indies v Pakistan	1991-92
10th	29	C.A.Best & C.A.Walsh	West Indies v Pakistan	1989-90

Most Wicketkeeping Dismissals in Innings: 5 (3ct 2st) K.S.More India v New Zealand 1987-88; 5 (5ct) H.P.Tillakaratne Sri Lanka v Pakistan 1990-91; 5 (4ct 1st) R.S.Kaluwitharana Sri Lanka v Pakistan 1994-95
Most in 1996-97: 4 (4ct) L.K.Germon New Zealand v Sri Lanka

Most Wicketkeeping Dismissals in Season: 19 (15ct 4st) Rashid Latif (Pakistan) 1993-94
Most in 1996-97: 14 (10ct 4st) R.S.Kaluwitharana (Sri Lanka)

Most Catches by Fielder in Innings: 4 S.M.Gavaskar India v Pakistan 1984-85; 4 P.V.Simmons West Indies v Sri Lanka 1995-96
Most in 1996-97: 3 R.S.Mahanama Sri Lanka v Zimbabwe

Most Catches by Fielder in Season: 10 R.S.Mahanama (Sri Lanka) 1996-97

CHAMPION TEAMS

The winners of the various Tournaments held in Sharjah have been as follows (the names of the other competing countries are given in brackets):

1983-84 (Asia Cup) India (Pakistan, Sri Lanka)
1984-85 (Rothmans Four Nations Cup) India 140-7 (39.2 overs) beat Australia 139 (42.3 overs) by 3 wkts (Pakistan, England)
1985-86 (Sharjah Cup) West Indies (Pakistan, India)

1985-86 (Australasia Cup) Pakistan 248-9 (50 overs) beat India 245-7 (50 overs) by 1 wkt (New Zealand, Australia, Sri Lanka)

1986-87 (Champions Trophy) West Indies (Sri Lanka, Pakistan, India)

1986-87 (Sharjah Cup) England (India, Australia, Pakistan)

1987-88 (Sharjah Cup) India 250-7 (50 overs) beat New Zealand 198 (45.3 overs) by 52 runs (Sri Lanka)

1988-89 (Champions Trophy) West Indies 235-6 (50 overs) beat Pakistan 224 (49.4 overs) by 11 runs (India)

1988-89 (Sharjah Cup) Pakistan (Sri Lanka)

1989-90 (Champions Trophy) Pakistan (India, West Indies)

1989-90 (Australasia Cup) Pakistan 266-7 (50 overs) beat Australia 230 (46.5 overs) by 36 runs (Sri Lanka, India, New Zealand, Bangladesh)

1990-91 (Sharjah Cup) Pakistan (Sri Lanka)

1991-92 (Wills Trophy) Pakistan 262-6 (50 overs) beat India 190 (46 overs) by 72 runs (West Indies)

1992-93 (Wills Trophy) Pakistan 281-3 (41 overs) beat Sri Lanka 167-7 (41 overs) by 114 runs

1993-94 (Champions Trophy) West Indies 285-4 (45.3 overs) beat Pakistan 284-4 (50 overs) by 6 wickets (Sri Lanka)

1993-94 (Australasia Cup) Pakistan 250-6 (50 overs) beat India 211 (47.4 overs) by 39 runs (Australia, New Zealand, Sri Lanka, United Arab Emirates)

1994-95 (Asia Cup) India 233-2 (41.5 overs) beat Sri Lanka 230-7 (50 overs) by 8 wkts (Pakistan, Bangladesh)

1995-96 (Champions Trophy) Sri Lanka 273 (49.5 overs) beat West Indies 223 (47.3 overs) by 50 runs (Pakistan)

1995-96 (Sharjah Cup) South Africa 287-5 (50 overs) beat India 249-9 (50 overs) by 38 runs (Pakistan)

1996-97 (Singer Cup) Pakistan 160 (48.5 overs) beat New Zealand 119 (36.5 overs) by 41 runs (Sri Lanka)

1996-97 (Singer-Akai Cup) Sri Lanka 215-6 (49.2 overs) beat Pakistan 214 (49.2 overs) by 4 wkts (Zimbabwe)

Table of Results 1983-84 to 1996-97

	P	W	L	T	NR	Winner	R-up
Pakistan	68	46	22	0	0	9	5
India	45	23	22	0	0	4	6
West Indies	27	15	12	0	0	4	1
Sri Lanka	43	14	28	1	0	2	5
Australia	13	6	7	0	0	0	2
South Africa	5	5	0	0	0	1	0
New Zealand	17	5	11	1	0	0	2
England	5	2	3	0	0	1	0
Zimbabwe	6	1	5	0	0	0	0
Bangladesh	5	0	5	0	0	0	0
United Arab Emirates	2	0	2	0	0	0	0

NEW ZEALAND IN SHARJAH 1996-97

	M	I	NO	Runs	HS	Avge	100	50	Balls	Runs	Wkts	Avge	BB	5i	10m	RpO	ct	st
ASTLE, N.J.																		
Int	5	5	0	80	66	16.00	0	1	184	89	6	14.83	2-25	0	0	2.90	1	
CAIRNS, C.L.																		
Int	5	5	0	134	71	26.80	0	1	285	158	11	14.36	3-18	0	0	3.32	1	
DOULL, S.B.																		
Int	4	4	3	18	14	18.00	0	0	146	103	3	34.33	2-39	0	0	4.23	2	
FLEMING, S.P.																		
Int	4	4	0	19	13	4.75	0	0									4	
GERMON, L.K.																		
Int	5	5	1	95	52	23.75	0	1									8	2
GREATBATCH, M.J.																		
Int	5	5	0	120	52	24.00	0	1									3	
HARRIS, C.Z.																		
Int	5	5	1	73	34*	18.25	0	0	246	133	5	26.60	2-28	0	0	3.24	2	
LARSEN, G.R.																		
Int	1	1	0	0	0	0.00	0	0	54	22	1	22.00	1-22	0	0	2.44	0	
MORRISON, D.K.																		
Int	4	2	1	1	1*	1.00	0	0	204	152	9	16.88	5-34	0	1	4.47	1	
PARORE, A.C.																		
Int	5	5	0	193	93	38.60	0	2									1	
PATEL, D.N.																		
Int	5	5	0	13	7	2.60	0	0	276	173	3	57.66	2-30	0	0	3.76	0	
SPEARMAN, C.M.																		
Int	4	4	0	43	39	10.75	0	0	3	6	0					12.00	0	
VAUGHAN, J.T.C.																		
Int	1	1	1	1	1*		0	0	48	33	1	33.00	1-33	0	0	4.12	1	
YOUNG, B.A.																		
Int	2	2	0	7	5	3.50	0	0									0	

PAKISTAN IN SHARJAH 1996-97

	M	I	NO	Runs	HS	Avge	100	50	Balls	Runs	Wkts	Avge	BB	5i	10m	RpO	ct	st
AAMER SOHAIL																		
Int	5	5	0	126	65	25.20	0	1									2	
AZAM KHAN																		
Int	3	3	0	41	22	13.66	0	0									0	
HASAN RAZA																		
Int	2	2	0	6	5	3.00	0	0									0	
IJAZ AHMED																		
Int	9	8	0	150	49	18.75	0	0									7	
INZAMAM-UL-HAQ																		
Int	5	5	0	192	62	38.40	0	2									0	
MOHAMMAD WASIM																		
Int	4	4	0	48	27	12.00	0	0									0	
MOIN KHAN																		
Int	10	10	3	220	61	31.42	0	1									8	3
MUSHTAQ AHMED																		
Int	9	6	4	27	16*	13.50	0	0	498	299	12	24.91	4-27	1	0	3.60	3	
RAMEEZ RAJA																		
Int	4	4	0	85	47	21.25	0	0									2	
SAEED ANWAR																		
Int	5	5	2	278	112*	92.66	2	1									0	
SAJID ALI																		
Int	3	3	0	47	28	15.66	0	0									0	
SALEEM MALIK																		
Int	10	9	0	244	58	27.11	0	2	216	151	7	21.57	2-30	0	0	4.19	3	
SAQLAIN MUSHTAQ																		
Int	10	8	2	35	20	5.83	0	0	545	351	20	17.55	3-31	0	0	3.86	4	

Cmp Debut	M	I	NO	Runs	HS	Avge	100	50	Balls	Runs	Wkts	Avge	BB	5i	10m	RpO	ct	st
SHAHID KHAN AFRIDI																		
Int	10	9	0	139	67	15.44	0	1	465	278	5	55.60	2-14	0	0	3.58	4	
SHAHID NAZIR																		
Int	2	1	1	1	1*		0	0	84	73	2	36.50	2-35	0	0	5.21	0	
WAQAR YOUNIS																		
Int	10	7	2	33	10	6.60	0	0	481	318	21	15.14	6-44	0	1	3.96	5	
WASIM AKRAM																		
Int	9	8	1	76	28*	10.85	0	0	456	302	13	23.23	4-42	1	0	3.97	5	

SRI LANKA IN SHARJAH 1996-97

Cmp Debut	M	I	NO	Runs	HS	Avge	100	50	Balls	Runs	Wkts	Avge	BB	5i	10m	RpO	ct	st
ATAPATTU, M.S.																		
Int	7	7	1	263	94	43.83	0	3	48	37	0					4.62	1	
CHANDANA, U.D.U.																		
Int	4	4	0	18	14	4.50	0	0	162	115	3	38.33	2-41	0	0	4.25	3	
DE SILVA, K.S.C.																		
Int	8	5	2	4	3	1.33	0	0	395	238	14	17.00	3-18	0	0	3.61	5	
DE SILVA, P.A.																		
Int	9	9	1	462	124	57.75	1	3	288	189	3	63.00	2-28	0	0	3.93	2	
DHARMASENA, H.D.P.K.																		
Int	6	5	3	24	10*	12.00	0	0	256	160	6	26.66	3-27	0	0	3.75	0	
GURUSINHA, A.P.																		
Int	2	2	0	59	32	29.50	0	0									0	
JAYASURIYA, S.T.																		
Int	8	8	0	241	67	30.12	0	3	324	240	8	30.00	3-15	0	0	4.44	3	
KALPAGE, R.S.																		
Int	1	1	0	7	7	7.00	0	0	54	38	3	12.66	3-38	0	0	4.22	0	
KALUWITHARANA, R.S.																		
Int	9	9	0	47	16	5.22	0	0									10	4
MAHANAMA, R.S.																		
Int	8	7	1	156	42	26.00	0	0									10	
MURALITHARAN, M.																		
Int	9	6	1	13	4*	2.60	0	0	508	354	18	19.66	3-38	0	0	4.18	3	
PUSHPAKUMARA, K.R.																		
Int	1	1	1	2	2*		0	0	42	34	1	34.00	1-34	0	0	4.85	0	
RANATUNGA, A.																		
Int	9	9	1	136	34	17.00	0	0	30	35	0					7.00	1	
TILLAKARATNE, H.P.																		
Int	9	8	0	174	41	21.75	0	0									6	
VAAS, W.P.U.J.C.																		
Int	8	5	1	32	17*	8.00	0	0	398	205	10	20.50	4-22	1	0	3.09	1	
ZOYSA, D.N.T.																		
Int	1								60	46	1	46.00	1-46	0	0	4.60	0	

ZIMBABWE IN SHARJAH 1996-97

Cmp Debut	M	I	NO	Runs	HS	Avge	100	50	Balls	Runs	Wkts	Avge	BB	5i	10m	RpO	ct	st
BRANDES, E.A.																		
Int	4	4	2	14	10*	7.00	0	0	186	120	4	30.00	2-39	0	0	3.87	1	
CAMPBELL, A.D.R.																		
Int	4	4	0	40	30	10.00	0	0									0	
CARLISLE, S.V.																		
Int	2	2	0	10	6	5.00	0	0									1	
FLOWER, A.																		
Int	4	4	1	129	42	43.00	0	0									3	
FLOWER, G.W.																		
Int	4	4	0	55	28	13.75	0	0	28	15	1	15.00	1-15	0	0	3.21	2	
MATAMBANADZO, E.																		
Int	4	4	2	6	5*	3.00	0	0	168	108	5	21.60	2-25	0	0	3.85	1	

Cmp Debut	M	I	NO	Runs	HS	Avge	100	50	Balls	Runs	Wkts	Avge	BB	5i	10m	RpO	ct	st
STRANG, P.A.																		
Int	4	4	0	83	38	20.75	0	0	222	118	4	29.50	2-16	0	0	3.18	3	
STREAK, H.H.																		
Int	4	4	0	46	20	11.50	0	0	211	89	9	9.88	4-18	1	0	2.53	3	
VILJOEN, D.P.																		
Int	3	3	0	64	25	21.33	0	0									1	
WHITTALL, A.R.																		
Int	4	4	0	7	4	1.75	0	0	168	107	2	53.50	2-38	0	0	3.82	2	
WHITTALL, G.J.																		
Int	3	3	0	45	44	15.00	0	0	168	97	3	32.33	2-37	0	0	3.46	1	
WISHART, C.B.																		
Int	4	4	0	66	32	16.50	0	0									2	

SOUTH AFRICA

First First-Class Match: South Africa v England (Port Elizabeth) 1888-89

First First-Class Tour to England: 1901

First Test Match: South Africa v England (Port Elizabeth) 1888-89

Present First-Class Teams: Boland, Border, Eastern Province, Free State, Griqualand West, Natal, Northern Transvaal, Transvaal, Western Province (Castle Cup); Easterns, North West, Eastern Province B, Natal B, Transvaal B, Western Province B (UCB Bowl).

First-Class Competitions: The Currie Cup was instituted in 1889-90 and has remained the premier Competition since that season, changing to the Castle Cup from 1991-92 and the Supersport Series from 1996-97; in 1951-52 Section B of the Currie Cup (retitled the Castle Bowl in 1977-78 and the UCB Bowl in 1992-93) was instituted as a second first-class Competition.

Supersport Series Champions 1996-97: Natal

UCB Bowl Champions 1996-97: Eastern Province B

FIRST-CLASS RECORDS

Highest Team Total: 676 MCC v Griqualand West (Kimberley) 1938-39
Highest in 1996-97: 628-8d Australia v South Africa (Johannesburg); 541-6d Griqualand West v Northern Transvaal (Kimberley); 529-7d South Africa v India (Cape Town); 509-7d Western Province v Boland (Cape Town); 503-5d Natal v Leicestershire (Durban)

Lowest Team Total: 16 Border v Natal (East London) 1959-60
Lowest in 1996-97: 66 India v South Africa (Durban); 83 Griqualand West v Boland (Paarl); 91 Griqualand West v Natal (Durban); 96 Easterns v Western Province B (Cape Town); 100 India v South Africa (Durban)

Highest Individual Innings: 337* D.J.Cullinan Transvaal v Northern Transvaal (Johannesburg) 1993-94
Highest in 1996-97: 214 G.S.Blewett Australia v South Africa (Johannesburg); 212 P.H.Barnard Griqualand West v Northern Transvaal (Kimberley); 210 A.M.Bacher Transvaal v Griqualand West (Kimberley); 202* D.L.Haynes Western Province v Eastern Province (Port Elizabeth); 201* M.J.Mitchley Easterns v Western Province B (Cape Town)

Most Runs in Season: 1,915 (av 68.39) J.R.Reid (New Zealanders) 1961-62
Most in 1996-97: 1,012 (av 59.52) A.M.Bacher (Transvaal); 859 (av 57.26) L.J.Koen (Eastern Province); 806 (av 57.57) D.M.Benkenstein (Natal); 736 (av 61.33) K.C.Wessels (Eastern Province); 716 (av 47.73) H.H.Dippenaar (Free State)

Most Runs in Career: 28,358 (av 54.74) B.A.Richards (Natal, Gloucestershire, Hampshire, South Australia) 1964-65 to 1982-83
Most by Current Batsman: 23,493 (av 50.41) K.C.Wessels (Orange Free State, Western Province, Northern Transvaal, Eastern Province, Sussex, Queensland) 1973-74 to date; 22,635 (av 44.46) P.N.Kirsten (Western Province, Border, Sussex, Derbyshire) 1973-74 to date; 10,723 (av 34.59) R.F.Pienaar (Transvaal, Western Province, Northern Transvaal, Kent) 1977-78 to date. D.L.Haynes, 26,030 (av 45.90), played for Western Province, R.B.Richardson, 14,204 (av 41.77), played for Northern Transvaal and K.R.Rutherford, 11,814 (av 38.10), played for Transvaal in 1996-97..

Best Innings Analysis: 10-26 A.E.E.Vogler Eastern Province v Griqualand West (Johannesburg) 1906-07
Best in 1996-97: 8-59 V.C.Drakes Border v Natal (Durban); 8-134 A.V.Birrell Eastern Province B v Easterns (Port Elizabeth); 7-34 J.N.Gillespie Australia v Border (East London); 7-58 K.G.Storey Natal v North West (Potchefstroom); 7-114 D.N.Crookes Natal v Free State (Durban)

Most Wickets in Season: 106 (av 19.39) R.Benaud (Australians) 1957-58
Most in 1996-97: 42 (av 26.50) B.N.Schultz (Western Province); 40 (av 22.60) C.E.Eksteen (Tranvaal); 38 (av 19.81) E.A.E.Baptiste (Eastern Province); 38 (av 22.84) G.M.Gilder (Natal); 38 (av 19.50) K.G.Storey (Natal)

Most Wickets in Career: 1,417 (av 19.53) M.J.Procter (Natal, Western Province, Rhodesia, Orange Free State, Gloucestershire) 1965 to 1988-89
Most by Current Bowler: 945 (av 22.39) A.A.Donald (Orange Free State, Warwickshire) 1985-86 to date; 417 (av 29.05) T.G.Shaw (Eastern Province) 1980-81 to date. F.D.Stephenson, 792 (av 24.26), played for Free State, E.A.E.Baptiste, 658 (av 24.69) played for Eastern Province and D.J.Millns, 465 (av 27.89) played for Boland in 1996-97.

Record Wicket Partnerships

1st	424	I.J.Siedle & J.F.W.Nicolson	Natal v Orange Free State (Bloemfontein)	1926-27
2nd	415	A.D.Jadeja & S.V.Manjrekar	Indians v Bowl XI (Springs)	1992-93
3rd	399	R.T.Simpson & D.C.S.Compton	MCC v North Eastern Transvaal (Benoni)	1948-49
4th	342	E.A.B.Rowan & P.J.M.Gibb	Transvaal v N E Transvaal (Johannesburg)	1952-53
5th	385	S.R.Waugh & G.S.Blewett	Australia v South Africa (Johannesburg)	1996-97
6th	259	S.A.Jones & O.Henry	Boland v Border (East London)	1987-88
7th	299	B.Mitchell & A.Melville	Transvaal v Griqualand West (Kimberley)	1946-47
8th	222	S.S.L.Steyn & D.P.B.Morkel	Western Province v Border (Cape Town)	1929-30
9th	217	A.W.Nourse & B.C.Cooley	Natal v Western Province (Johannesburg)	1906-07
10th	174	H.R.Lance & D.Mackay-Coghill	Transvaal v Natal (Johannesburg)	1965-66

Highest Partnerships in 1996-97

1st	220	P.G.Amm & M.G.Beamish	Eastern Province B v Transvaal B (Johannesburg)
2nd	205	D.L.Haynes & J.H.Kallis	Western Province v Eastern Province (Port Elizabeth)
3rd	300*	H.H.Dippenaar & L.J.Wilkinson	Free State v Western Province (Bloemfontein)
4th	241	K.C.Wessels & D.J.Callaghan	Eastern Province v Western Province (Port Elizabeth)
5th	385	S.R.Waugh & G.S.Blewett	Australia v South Africa (Johannesburg)
6th	222	S.R.Tendulkar & M.Azharuddin	India v South Africa (Cape Town)
7th	148	R.E.Veenstra & A.J.Hall	Transvaal v Border (East London)
8th	154	D.L.Haynes & C.R.Matthews	Western Province v Border (Cape Town)
9th	89	N.Pothas & S.Jacobs	Transvaal v Free State (Bloemfontein)
10th	74	B.M.McMillan & A.A.Donald	South Africa v India (Durban)

Most Wicketkeeping Dismissals in Innings: 7 (7ct) M.S.Smith Natal v Border (East London) 1959-60; 7 (6ct 1st) N.Kirsten Border v Rhodesia (East London) 1959-60; 7 (6ct 1st) R.J.East Orange Free State v Western Province B (Cape Town) 1984-85; 7 (7ct) D.J.Richardson Eastern Province v Orange Free State (Bloemfontein) 1988-89; 7 (7ct) P.J.L.Radley Orange Free State v Western Province (Cape Town) 1990-91; 7 (7ct) H.M.de Vos Western Transvaal v Eastern Transvaal (Potchefstroom) 1993-94; 7 (7ct) P.Kirsten Griqualand West v Western Transvaal (Potchefstroom) 1993-94
Most in 1996-97: 5 M.V.Boucher (Border) (twice); 5 U.H.Goedeke (Natal B); 5 I.A.Healy (Australia); 5 P.Kirsten (Western Province); 5 N.R.Mongia (India); 5 I.Pistorius (Northern Transvaal); 5 P.J.L.Radley (Free State)

Most Wicketkeeping Dismissals in Match: 11 (10ct 1st) I.A.Healy Australians v Northern Transvaal (Verwoerdburg) 1993-94; 11 (11ct) R.C.Russell England v South Africa (Johannesburg) 1995-96
Most in 1996-97: 8 (6ct 2st) M.V.Boucher Border v Free State (Bloemfontein); 8 (8ct) N.R.Mongia India v South Africa (Durban)

Most Wicketkeeping Dismissals in Season: 65 (57ct 8st) R.V.Jennings (Transvaal) 1982-83
Most in 1996-97: 41 (39ct 2st) K.A.Forde (Natal); 36 (33ct 3st) M.V.Boucher (Border); 36 (30ct 6st) N.Pothas (Transvaal); 34 (33ct 1st) P.Kirsten (Western Province); 30 (28ct 2st) P.J.L.Radley (Free State)

Most Wicketkeeping Dismissals in Career: 621 (567ct 54st) R.V.Jennings (Transvaal, Northern Transvaal) 1973-74 to 1992-93
Most by Current Wicketkeeper: 585 (549ct 36st) D.J.Richardson (Eastern Province, Northern Transvaal) 1977-78 to date; 179 (165ct 14st) P.J.L.Radley (Free State) 1989-90 to date; 164 (147ct 17st) S.J.Palframan (Eastern Province, Border) 1990-91 to date; 144 (130ct 14st) N.Pothas (Transvaal) 1993-94 to date; 133 (123ct 10st) P.Kirsten (Griqualand West, Western Province) 1992-93 to date

Most Catches by Fielder in Innings: 5 A.D.Nourse Natal v Border (Durban) 1933-34; 5 V.Y.Richardson Australia v South Africa (Durban) 1935-36; 5 C.D.White Border v Griqualand West (Queenstown) 1946-47; 5 P.H.Parfitt MCC v SA Universities (Pietermaritzburg) 1964-65; 5 A.H.Jordaan Northern Transvaal v Border (East London) 1972-73; 5 A.Barrow Transvaal B v Northern Transvaal B (Pietersburg) 1982-83; 5 P.J.R.Steyn Griqualand West v Western Province B (Kimberley) 1985-86; 5 D.N.Crookes Natal v Northamptonshire (Durban) 1991-92
Most in 1996-97: 4 N.Boje Free State v Eastern Province (Bloemfontein); 4 V.V.S.Laxman India v Free State (Bloemfontein); 4 E.Liebenberg Boland v Transvaal (Johannesburg); 4 B.M.White Border v Natal (Durban)

Most Catches by Fielder in Match: 7 S.P.de Vigne North Eastern Transvaal v Orange Free State (Benoni) 1950-51; 7 A.Barrow Transvaal B v Northern Transvaal B (Pietersburg) 1982-83; 7 C.B.Lambert Northern Transvaal v Boland (Paarl) 1994-95
Most in 1996-97: 5 N.Boje Free State v Eastern Province (Bloemfontein); 5 L.J.Koen Eastern Province v Free State (Bloemfontein); 5 D.B.Rundle Western Province B v North West (Cape Town); 5 B.M.White Border v Natal (Durban); 5 S.Nicholson North West v Western Province B (Cape Town)

Most Catches by Fielder in Season: 21 M.J.Procter (Rhodesia) 1972-73; 21 A.J.Kourie (Transvaal) 1984-85
Most in 1996-97: 16 L.J.Koen (Eastern Province); 16 B.M.White (Border); 15 N.C.Johnson (Natal); 14 E.L.R.Stewart (Natal); 13 K.R.Rutherford (Transvaal)

Most Catches by Fielder in Career: 401 C.E.B.Rice (Transvaal, Natal, Nottinghamshire) 1969-70 to 1993-94
Most by Current Fielder: 258 K.C.Wessels (Orange Free State, Western Province, Northern Transvaal, Eastern Province, Sussex, Queensland) 1973-74 to date; 190 P.N.Kirsten (Western Province, Border, Sussex, Derbyshire) 1973-74 to date. R.B.Richardson, 203, played for Northern Transvaal, D.L.Haynes, 202, played for Western Province and P.V.Simmons, 197, played for Easterns in 1996-97.

DOMESTIC LIMITED OVERS RECORDS

Highest Team Totals: 341-3 (50 overs) Transvaal v Western Transvaal (Potchefstroom) 1994-95; 319-6 (45 overs) Natal v Western Transvaal (Fochville) 1995-96; 316-4 (45 overs) Transvaal v North West (Fochville) 1996-97

Lowest Team Totals: 47 (32.1 overs) Border v Western Province (East London) 1991-92; 58 (37 overs) Griqualand West v Northern Transvaal (Kimberley) 1995-96; 61 (15.4 overs) Transvaal v Eastern Transvaal (Johannesburg) 1994-95
Lowest in 1996-97: 84 (26 overs) Border v Natal (East London)

Highest Individual Innings: 146* N.C.Johnson Natal v Griqualand West (Kimberley) 1996-97; 146 R.P.Snell Transvaal v Western Transvaal (Potchefstroom) 1994-95; 140 A.M.Bacher Transvaal v North West (Fochville) 1996-97
100 centuries have been scored in the competition, K.C.Wessels scoring 6

Most Runs in Season: 766 (av 58.92) M.J.R.Rindel (Northern Transvaal) 1996-97

Most Runs in Career: 3,725 (av 51.73) K.C.Wessels (Eastern Province) 1986-87 to date; 3,555 (av 37.42) P.N.Kirsten (Western Province, Border) 1981-82 to date; 3,350 (av 31.90) R.F.Pienaar (Western Province, Northern Transvaal, Transvaal) 1981-82 to date

Best Innings Analyses: 6-22 B.N.Schultz Eastern Province v Transvaal (Johannesburg) 1995-96; 6-30 M.W.Pringle Western Province v Border (East London) 1989-90; 5-10 S.T.Jefferies Western Province v Transvaal (Cape Town) 1983-84; 5-10 F.D.Stephenson Orange Free State v Western Province (Cape Town) 1992-93
Best in 1996-97: 5-33 D.J.van Zyl Northern Transvaal v Transvaal (Johannesburg)
Five wickets in an innings has been achieved 33 times, twice by R.J.McCurdy and M.W.Pringle

Most Economical Bowling: 9-5-4-1 G.R.Dilley Natal v Impalas (Pietermaritzburg) 1985-86
Most Economical in 1996-97: 9-2-11-1 D.B.Rundle Western Province v Easterns (Cape Town); 9-3-11-3 P.L.Symcox Natal v Boland (Paarl)

Most Expensive Bowling: 9-0-84-3 L.B.Taylor Natal v Western Province (Cape Town) 1983-84; 10-1-84-1 L.Botes Western Transvaal v Transvaal (Potchefstroom) 1994-95
Most Expensive in 1996-97: 9-0-75-2 C.W.Henderson Boland v Northern Transvaal (Centurion)

Most Wickets in Season: 30 (av 13.50) E.O.Simons (Western Province) 1996-97

Most Wickets in Career: 154 (av 19.92) E.O.Simons (Northern Transvaal, Western Province) 1983-84 to date; 113 (av 24.13) T.G.Shaw (Eastern Province) 1984-85 to date; 106 (av 21.93) A.P.Kuiper (Western Province, Boland) 1981-82 to date

Record Wicket Partnerships

1st	222	N.C.Johnson & D.J.Watson	Natal v Easterns (Benoni)	1996-97
2nd	211*	H.R.Fotheringham & R.F.Pienaar	Transvaal v Orange Free State (Johannesburg)	1988-89
3rd	243	A.M.Bacher & N.D.McKenzie	Transvaal v North West (Fochville)	1996-97
4th	178	J.H.Kallis & H.D.Ackerman	Western Province v Free State (Bloemfontein)	1995-96
5th	132*	R.G.Pollock & K.A.McKenzie	Transvaal v N Transvaal (Johannesburg)	1982-83
	132	P.G.Amm & D.J.Richardson	E Province v W Province (Cape Town)	1989-90
6th	158	D.R.Laing & N.Pothas	Transvaal v Eastern Province (Johannesburg)	1995-96
7th	126	D.R.Laing & A.J.Hall	Transvaal v Eastern Province (Port Elizabeth)	1996-97
8th	88	F.J.C.Cronje & I.L.Howell	Border v Boland (Stellenbosch)	1993-94
9th	76	A.P.Kuiper & C.R.Matthews	Western Province v Impalas (Cape Town)	1987-88
10th	59	A.P.Kuiper & M.W.Pringle	W Province v E Province (Cape Town)	1990-91

There were 33 hundred partnerships in 1996-97, the highest being the new 3rd wicket record

Most Wicketkeeping Dismissals in Innings: 6 (6ct) W.Bossenger Griqualand West v Northern Transvaal (Centurion) 1996-97

Most Wicketkeeping Dismissals in Season: 27 (27ct) P.Kirsten (Western Province) 1996-97

Most Wicketkeeping Dismissals in Career: 128 (123ct 5st) R.J.Ryall (Western Province) 1982-83 to 1994-95; 87 (81ct 6st) D.J.Richardson (Eastern Province, Northern Transvaal) 1981-82 to 1995-96; 81 (73ct 8st) R.V.Jennings (Transvaal, Northern Transvaal) 1981-82 to 1992-93

Most Catches by Fielder in Innings: 5 K.C.Jackson Boland v Natal (Durban) 1995-96
Most in 1996-97: 3 N.C.Johnson Natal v Transvaal (Durban); 3 J.H.Kallis Western Province v Natal (Durban); 3 L.J.Wilkinson Free State v Natal (Bloemfontein)

Most Catches by Fielder in Season: 13 D.B.Rundle (Western Province) 1995-96
Most in 1996-97: 9 H.D.Ackerman (Western Province)

Most Catches by Fielder in Career: 43 P.N.Kirsten (Western Province, Border) 1981-82 to date; 43 D.B.Rundle (Western Province) 1984-85 to date; 42 D.J.Cullinan (Western Province, Transvaal, Border, Impalas) 1984-85 to date

Most Appearances in Competition: 118 R.F.Pienaar (Western Province, Northern Transvaal, Transvaal) 1981-82 to date; 116 A.P.Kuiper (Western Province, Boland) 1981-82 to date; 107 P.N.Kirsten (Western Province, Border) 1981-82 to date

PROVINCIAL CHAMPIONS

Supersport Series

1889-90 Transvaal	1936-37 Natal	1974-75 Western Province
1890-91 Kimberley	1937-38 Natal, Transvaal	1975-76 Natal
1892-93 Western Province	1946-47 Natal	1976-77 Natal
1893-94 Western Province	1947-48 Natal	1977-78 Western Province
1894-95 Transvaal	1950-51 Transvaal	1978-79 Transvaal
1896-97 Western Province	1951-52 Natal	1979-80 Transvaal
1897-98 Western Province	1952-53 Western Province	1980-81 Natal
1902-03 Transvaal	1954-55 Natal	1981-82 Western Province
1903-04 Transvaal	1955-56 Western Province	1982-83 Transvaal
1904-05 Transvaal	1958-59 Transvaal	1983-84 Transvaal
1906-07 Transvaal	1959-60 Natal	1984-85 Transvaal
1908-09 Western Province	1960-61 Natal	1985-86 Western Province
1910-11 Natal	1962-63 Natal	1986-87 Transvaal
1912-13 Natal	1963-64 Natal	1987-88 Transvaal
1920-21 Western Province	1965-66 Natal, Transvaal	1988-89 Eastern Province
1921-22 Natal, Transvaal,	1966-67 Natal	1989-90 Eastern Province,
Western Province	1967-68 Natal	Western Province
1923-24 Transvaal	1968-69 Transvaal	1990-91 Western Province
1925-26 Transvaal	1969-70 Transvaal,	1991-92 Eastern Province
1926-27 Transvaal	Western Province	1992-93 Orange Free State
1929-30 Transvaal	1970-71 Transvaal	1993-94 Orange Free State
1931-32 Westen Province	1971-72 Transvaal	1994-95 Natal
1933-34 Natal	1972-73 Transvaal	1995-96 Western Province
1934-35 Transvaal	1973-74 Natal	1996-97 Natal

UCB Bowl

1977-78 Northern Transvaal	1985-86 Boland	1991-92 Eastern Transvaal
1978-79 Northern Transvaal	1986-87 Transvaal B	1992-93 Boland
1979-80 Natal B	1987-88 Boland	1993-94 Transvaal B,
1980-81 Western Province B	1988-89 Border	Western Province B
1981-82 Boland	1989-90 Border,	1994-95 Natal B
1982-83 Western Province B	Western Province B	1995-96 Griqualand West
1983-84 Western Province B	1990-91 Border,	Natal B
1984-85 Transvaal B	Western Province B	1996-97 Eastern Province B

Domestic Limited Overs Competition

This competition is played at night under floodlights. In 1981-82 it was played on a knockout basis with an overs limit of 50 per side, but from 1982-83 to 1995-96 it was played as a round-robin followed by the top four teams contesting semi-finals (since 1986-87 over the best of three legs) and a final. In 1996-97 the sponsors changed from Benson and Hedges to Standard Bank and the top six teams in the round-robin were joined by Kenya and Mashonaland for a knockout with only the final being best of three legs. The over limit is 45, except for 1993-94 and 1994-95 when it was 50. The Impalas side was made up of players from the provinces not playing in the competition. Results of the finals:

Benson and Hedges Series
1981-82 Transvaal 265-7 (47.3 overs) beat Natal 263 (49.3 overs) by 3 wkts
1982-83 Transvaal 277-4 (42.1 overs) beat Western Province 275-9 (45 overs) by 6 wkts
1983-84 Natal 125-3 (29.2 overs) beat Eastern Province 124 (37.3 overs) by 7 wkts
1984-85 Transvaal 179-3 (36.2 overs) beat Northern Transvaal 176 (43.1 overs) by 7 wkts
1985-86 Western Province 265-4 (45 overs) beat Northern Transvaal 253-9 (45 overs) by 12 runs
1986-87 Western Province 205-6 (45 overs) beat Transvaal 164 (41.4 overs) by 41 runs
1987-88 Western Province 190-5 (44 overs) beat Transvaal 189 (44.3 overs) by 5 wkts
1988-89 Orange Free State 213 (45 overs) beat Western Province 152 (39.4 overs) by 61 runs
1989-90 Eastern Province 205-9 (45 overs) beat Natal 202 (44.5 overs) by 1 wkt
1990-91 Western Province 168-4 (39.3 overs) beat Natal 164-8 (45 overs) by 6 wkts
1991-92 Eastern Province 246-4 (44.1 overs) beat Western Province 244-2 (45 overs) by 6 wkts
1992-93 Transvaal 193-7 (45 overs) beat Natal 192-8 (45 overs) by 1 run
1993-94 Orange Free State 108-3 (28.1 overs) beat Natal 103 (36.2 overs) by 7 wkts
1994-95 Orange Free State 291-8 (50 overs) beat Eastern Province 178-8 (50 overs) by 113 runs
1995-96 Free State 290-6 (45 overs) beat Transvaal 148 (37.4 overs) by 142 runs

Standard Bank Cup
1996-97 Natal beat Western Province 2-1

Table of Results 1981-82 to 1996-97

	P	W	L	T	NR	Winner	R-up
Western Province	142	90	44	0	8	4	4
Transvaal	134	73	49	1	11	4	3
Eastern Province	128	65	51	0	12	2	2
Natal	126	64	47	1	14	2	5
Free State	91	48	32	1	10	4	0
Northern Transvaal	115	48	55	1	11	0	2
Border	69	20	39	0	10	0	0
Boland	43	17	22	0	4	0	0
Impalas	69	13	52	0	4	0	0
Griqualand West	32	9	20	0	3	0	0
Easterns	30	5	19	0	6	0	0
North West	30	4	25	0	1	0	0
Mashonaland	2	1	1	0	0	0	0
Kenya	1	0	1	0	0	0	0

1996-97 AND CAREER RECORDS FOR SOUTH AFRICAN PLAYERS

Cmp	Debut	M	I	NO	Runs	HS	Avge	100	50	Balls	Runs	Wkts	Avge	BB	5i	10m	RpO	ct	st

ABRAHAMS, Shafiek (Eastern Province B, Eastern Province) b Port Elizabeth 4.3.1968 RHB OB

Cmp	Debut	M	I	NO	Runs	HS	Avge	100	50	Balls	Runs	Wkts	Avge	BB	5i	10m	RpO	ct	st
FC		1	2	0	21	21	10.50	0	0	288	101	3	33.66	3-81	0	0	2.10	0	
SB		4	1	1	3	3*		0	0	126	96	0					4.57	0	
FC	1992	23	27	7	478	58*	23.90	0	2	4776	1901	59	32.22	5-49	1	0	2.38	14	
SB	1992	30	14	10	87	17*	21.75	0	0	1396	867	21	41.09	3-47	0	0	3.70	3	

ACKERMAN, Hylton Deon (Western Province, Western Province to Zimbabwe) b Cape Town 14.2.1973 RHB RM

Cmp	Debut	M	I	NO	Runs	HS	Avge	100	50	Balls	Runs	Wkts	Avge	BB	5i	10m	RpO	ct	st
FC		9	14	3	573	122	52.09	2	2	60	36	0					3.60	9	
SB		15	15	2	405	62*	31.15	0	3									9	
FC	1993	45	71	7	2578	154	40.28	5	16	90	46	0					3.06	34	
SB	1993	39	37	4	1025	81	31.06	0	8									14	

ACKERMANN, Sean (Boland) b Cape Town 6.6.1977 LHB OB

Cmp	Debut	M	I	NO	Runs	HS	Avge	100	50	Balls	Runs	Wkts	Avge	BB	5i	10m	RpO	ct	st
FC		1	2	0	31	18	15.50	0	0	18	14	0					4.66	0	
SB		8	8	2	67	26*	11.16	0	0	24	17	2	8.50	2-17	0	0	4.25	2	

ADAMS, Paul Regan (Western Province, South Africa, South Africa to India) b Cape Town 20.1.1977 RHB SLC

Cmp	Debut	M	I	NO	Runs	HS	Avge	100	50	Balls	Runs	Wkts	Avge	BB	5i	10m	RpO	ct	st
Test		4	5	1	23	15	5.75	0	0	938	496	13	38.15	3-45	0	0	3.17	3	
FC		5	5	1	23	15	5.75	0	0	1232	618	18	34.33	4-68	0	0	3.00	5	
Int		2								90	63	1	63.00	1-31	0	0	4.20	0	
SB		6								170	125	6	20.83	2-11	0	0	4.41	1	
Test	1995	9	13	2	66	29	6.00	0	0	2052	1011	35	28.88	6-55	1	0	2.95	8	
FC	1995	21	21	7	133	29	9.50	0	0	4994	2465	90	27.38	6-55	5	0	2.96	14	
Int	1995	9	4	1	10	10	3.33	0	0	420	296	13	22.76	3-26	0	0	4.22	1	
SB	1995	11	2	1	1	1	1.00	0	0	374	244	10	24.40	2-11	0	0	3.91	2	

ALBANIE, James Daniel (Boland) b Touwsrivier 1.5.1968 RHB RFM

Cmp	Debut	M	I	NO	Runs	HS	Avge	100	50	Balls	Runs	Wkts	Avge	BB	5i	10m	RpO	ct	st
FC		2	3	2	3	3	3.00	0	0	372	149	6	24.83	4-37	0	0	2.40	0	
FC	1995	6	8	2	34	17	5.66	0	0	858	375	17	22.05	4-37	0	0	2.62	0	

AMM, Philip Geoffrey (Eastern Province, Eastern Province B) b Grahamstown 2.4.1964 RHB LB

Cmp	Debut	M	I	NO	Runs	HS	Avge	100	50	Balls	Runs	Wkts	Avge	BB	5i	10m	RpO	ct	st
FC		5	8	1	340	105	48.57	1	2									6	
SB		2	1	0	1	1	1.00	0	0									1	
FC	1981	115	205	14	6834	214	35.78	12	39	182	84	0					2.76	72	
SB	1984	92	91	1	2730	136	30.33	2	17									29	

ARTHUR, John Michael (Griqualand West) b Johannesburg 17.5.1968 RHB

Cmp	Debut	M	I	NO	Runs	HS	Avge	100	50	Balls	Runs	Wkts	Avge	BB	5i	10m	RpO	ct	st
FC		8	16	1	539	86	35.93	0	3									7	
SB		12	12	1	427	84	38.81	0	4									1	
FC	1986	82	153	7	4780	131	32.73	7	29	6	0	0					0.00	53	
SB	1987	84	82	4	1946	126*	24.94	1	9	6	2	0					2.00	20	

BACHER, Adam Marc (Transvaal, South Africa) b Johannesburg 29.10.1973 RHB RM

Cmp	Debut	M	I	NO	Runs	HS	Avge	100	50	Balls	Runs	Wkts	Avge	BB	5i	10m	RpO	ct	st
Test		5	10	0	302	96	30.20	0	2	6	4	0					4.00	4	
FC		10	19	2	1012	210	59.52	4	3	24	8	0					2.00	8	
Int		7	7	0	123	45	17.57	0	0									1	
SB		11	11	1	605	140	60.50	2	3	78	71	1	71.00	1-19	0	0	5.46	5	
FC	1993	30	56	5	2095	210	41.07	6	9	24	8	0					2.00	43	
SB	1994	31	30	3	1238	140	45.85	4	6	78	71	1	71.00	1-19	0	0	5.46	11	

BADAT, Mehood (Natal B) b Durban 13.5.1970 RHB WK

Cmp	Debut	M	I	NO	Runs	HS	Avge	100	50	Balls	Runs	Wkts	Avge	BB	5i	10m	RpO	ct	st
FC		3	6	0	107	45	17.83	0	0									1	
FC	1991	9	16	2	282	54*	20.14	0	1									11	1

BADENHORST, Alan (Eastern Province, Eastern Province B, MCC) b Cape Town 10.7.1970 RHB RF

Cmp	Debut	M	I	NO	Runs	HS	Avge	100	50	Balls	Runs	Wkts	Avge	BB	5i	10m	RpO	ct	st
FC		5	6	2	4	4*	1.00	0	0	1027	472	19	24.84	4-39	0	0	2.75	4	
SB		2	1	0	11	11	11.00	0	0	84	82	2	41.00	2-52	0	0	5.85	1	
FC	1993	24	27	10	86	21*	5.05	0	0	4397	2134	76	28.07	5-49	2	0	2.91	7	
SB	1995	9	3	1	16	11	8.00	0	0	270	250	6	41.66	2-52	0	0	5.55	1	

BAGULEY, Bryan Christopher (Boland) b Pinelands 25.3.1971 RHB

Cmp	Debut	M	I	NO	Runs	HS	Avge	100	50	Balls	Runs	Wkts	Avge	BB	5i	10m	RpO	ct	st
FC		3	6	0	134	77	22.33	0	1									2	
FC	1991	16	29	3	731	133*	28.11	1	4	6	5	0					5.00	14	
SB	1995	3	3	0	25	17	8.33	0	0									0	

BAIRD, Ferdinand (North West) b Potchefstroom 19.3.1974 LHB LFM

Cmp	Debut	M	I	NO	Runs	HS	Avge	100	50	Balls	Runs	Wkts	Avge	BB	5i	10m	RpO	ct	st
FC		2	4	1	14	8	4.66	0	0	257	167	7	23.85	4-33	0	0	3.89	1	
SB		7	3	0	0	0	0.00	0	0	282	272	4	68.00	2-58	0	0	5.78	3	
FC	1993	13	19	5	103	18	7.35	0	0	1261	834	23	36.26	5-72	1	0	3.96	2	
SB	1994	14	9	1	9	5	1.12	0	0	540	502	14	35.85	4-31	1	0	5.57	4	

BAKKES, Herman Charles (Free State, Free State to West Indies) b Port Elizabeth 24.12.1969 RHB RFM

Cmp	Debut	M	I	NO	Runs	HS	Avge	100	50	Balls	Runs	Wkts	Avge	BB	5i	10m	RpO	ct	st
FC		7	11	0	202	43	18.36	0	0	990	492	17	28.94	6-43	1	0	2.98	3	
SB		7	4	0	61	36	15.25	0	0	312	272	4	68.00	1-31	0	0	5.23	1	
FC	1991	34	49	14	906	68	25.88	0	3	5229	2357	70	33.67	6-28	2	0	2.70	17	
SB	1991	29	16	6	158	36	15.80	0	0	1370	953	32	29.78	3-12	0	0	4.17	4	

Cmp	Debut	M	I	NO	Runs	HS	Avge	100	50	Balls	Runs	Wkts	Avge	BB	5i	10m	RpO	ct	st
BAPTISTE, Eldine Ashworth Elderfield (Eastern Province) b Liberta, Antigua 12.3.1960 RHB RFM																		
FC		8	11	2	201	50	22.33	0	1	1965	753	38	19.81	5-37	3	1	2.29	3	
SB		9	5	1	54	24	13.50	0	0	438	318	7	45.42	2-17	0	0	4.35	4	
Test	1983	10	11	1	233	87*	23.30	0	1	1362	563	16	35.18	3-31	0	0	2.48	2	
FC	1981	217	302	38	7309	136*	27.68	3	42	36805	16249	658	24.69	8-76	32	4	2.64	107	
Int	1983	43	16	4	184	31	15.33	0	0	2214	1511	36	41.97	2-10	0	0	4.09	14	
SB	1991	59	45	14	457	56	14.74	0	1	2913	1866	73	25.56	3-15	0	0	3.84	19	
BARNARD, Pieter Hendrik (Griqualand West) b Nelspruit 8.5.1970 RHB WK																		
FC		8	15	0	652	212	43.46	1	4									3	
SB		12	11	2	194	48*	21.55	0	0									3	
FC	1990	42	79	5	2320	212	31.35	4	12	6	2	0					2.00	23	
SB	1992	29	26	3	739	82	32.13	0	5									4	
BASTOW, Jonathan Edward (Natal B) b Pietermaritzburg 12.2.1974 RHB RFM																		
FC		3	2	1	24	12*	24.00	0	0	378	181	5	36.20	2-67	0	0	2.87	3	
BEAMISH, Michael Gwynne (Eastern Province, Eastern Province B) b King William's Town 30.7.1969 RHB																		
FC		8	15	0	633	164	42.20	3	1									6	
FC	1993	25	47	1	1516	164	32.95	5	5	32	24	0					4.50	16	
BENFIELD, Mark Rowland (Transvaal, Transvaal B) b Potgietersrus 3.12.1976 RHB RM																		
FC		9	17	0	459	122	27.00	1	1									6	
FC	1995	14	27	1	749	122	28.80	1	4									8	
BENKENSTEIN, Brett Norman (Griqualand West) b Salisbury, Rhodesia 14.4.1971 RHB SLA																		
FC		7	13	3	232	68	23.20	0	2	1369	711	10	71.10	3-35	0	0	3.11	3	
SB		12	9	2	89	52	12.71	0	1	552	358	9	39.77	2-26	0	0	3.89	3	
FC	1994	15	23	7	373	68	23.31	0	2	2780	1286	27	47.62	4-23	0	0	2.77	4	
SB	1995	22	16	6	125	52	12.50	0	1	990	662	18	36.77	2-19	0	0	4.01	4	
BENKENSTEIN, Dale Martin (Natal) b Salisbury, Rhodesia 9.6.1974 RHB RM/OB																		
FC		10	15	1	806	129	57.57	4	3	618	303	8	37.87	2-33	0	0	2.94	8	
SB		15	15	6	374	64	41.55	0	2	326	248	13	19.07	4-23	1	0	4.56	5	
FC	1993	41	54	6	2285	203*	47.60	6	13	1306	600	17	35.29	2-26	0	0	2.75	23	
SB	1993	44	40	9	901	64	29.06	0	3	326	248	13	19.07	4-23	1	0	4.56	12	
BIRRELL, Adrian Victor (Eastern Province, Eastern Province B) b Grahamstown 8.12.1960 RHB LB																		
FC		6	8	2	125	34	20.83	0	0	1516	812	32	25.37	8-134	2	1	3.21	4	
FC	1984	43	72	6	1347	105	20.40	1	7	3989	2203	73	30.17	8-134	2	1	3.31	33	
SB	1985	4	4	2	43	24*	21.50	0	0									0	
BLAKE, Theo (Easterns) b Port Elizabeth 1.9.1972 RHB																		
FC		2	3	1	82	64*	41.00	0	1									2	
SB		3	2	0	10	8	5.00	0	0									1	
SB	1995	4	3	0	11	8	3.66	0	0									1	
BODI, Goolam Hussain (Transvaal, Transvaal B) b Hathuran, India 4.1.1979 LHB SLC																		
FC		2	3	1	51	33	25.50	0	0	108	82	2	41.00	2-39	0	0	4.55	1	
BOJE, Nico (Free State, South Africa to India) b Bloemfontein 20.3.1973 LHB SLA																		
FC		6	11	0	189	34	17.18	0	0	1128	532	11	48.36	3-60	0	0	2.82	10	
SB		3	3	1	45	30	22.50	0	0	156	130	2	65.00	1-36	0	0	5.00	0	
FC	1990	56	77	14	1685	102	26.74	1	9	11928	5277	146	36.14	6-100	5	0	2.65	31	
Int	1995	7	5	2	27	13*	9.00	0	0	378	263	9	29.22	2-38	0	0	4.17	2	
SB	1993	35	25	10	330	79*	22.00	0	1	1669	1058	33	32.06	4-18	2	0	3.80	13	
BOSCH, Tertius (Natal) b Vereeniging 14.3.1966 RHB RF																		
FC		7	8	1	37	31	5.28	0	0	1309	470	20	23.50	5-15	1	0	2.15	4	
SB		8	3	2	6	3*	6.00	0	0	306	243	9	27.00	3-39	0	0	4.76	1	
Test	1991	1	2	2	5	5*		0	0	237	104	3	34.66	2-61	0	0•	2.63	0	
FC	1986	64	75	29	352	31	7.65	0	0	11194	5513	199	27.70	7-75	7	1	2.95	18	
Int	1991	2								51	66	0					7.76	0	
SB	1987	55	22	12	64	19*	6.40	0	0	2515	1626	70	23.22	3-21	0	0	3.87	7	
BOSSENGER, Wendell (Griqualand West) b Cape Town 23.10.1976 RHB WK																		
FC		8	15	2	236	82	18.15	0	1									19	2
SB		12	7	4	63	24*	21.00	0	0									15	3
BOTES, Louis (North West) b Tzaneen 29.3.1969 RHB RFM																		
FC		1	2	0	29	23	14.50	0	0	96	34	2	17.00	2-3	0	0	2.12	0	
SB		5	3	2	5	5*	5.00	0	0	252	162	6	27.00	3-43	0	0	3.85	0	
FC	1992	16	25	5	514	64	25.70	0	2	2138	1113	30	37.10	3-63	0	0	3.12	2	
SB	1992	32	26	14	300	38	25.00	0	0	1598	1154	22	52.45	3-43	0	0	4.33	12	
BOTHA, Andre Cornelius (Griqualand West) LHB RM																		
SB		1	1	0	17	17	17.00	0	0	24	28	0					7.00	0	
BOTHA, Anthony Greyvensteyn (Natal, Natal B) b Pretoria 17.11.1976 LHB SLA																		
FC		7	9	3	122	41*	20.33	0	0	1033	464	21	22.09	4-52	0	0	2.69	5	
SB		7	2	0	10	5	5.00	0	0	156	113	2	56.50	2-50	0	0	4.34	2	
FC	1995	9	12	3	143	41*	15.88	0	0	1228	553	23	24.04	4-52	0	0	2.70	6	

Cmp	Debut	M	I	NO	Runs	HS	Avge	100	50	Balls	Runs	Wkts	Avge	BB	5i	10m	RpO	ct	st

BOTHA, Henk (Free State, Free State to West Indies) b Bloemfontein 16.1.1976 RHB RFM

Cmp	Debut	M	I	NO	Runs	HS	Avge	100	50	Balls	Runs	Wkts	Avge	BB	5i	10m	RpO	ct	st
FC		2	2	0	0	0	0.00	0	0	187	118	4	29.50	3-31	0	0	3.78	0	
SB		1	1	1	0	0*		0	0	12	14	0					7.00	0	
FC	1995	8	9	3	55	31	9.16	0	0	807	449	17	26.41	4-31	0	0	3.33	1	

BOTHA, Lodewikus Daniel (Eastern Province, Eastern Province B) b Elsburg 11.4.1968 RHB RFM

Cmp	Debut	M	I	NO	Runs	HS	Avge	100	50	Balls	Runs	Wkts	Avge	BB	5i	10m	RpO	ct	st
FC		5	6	1	25	9	5.00	0	0	1061	545	17	32.05	6-59	1	0	3.08	2	
SB		5								204	145	2	72.50	1-23	0	0	4.26	1	
FC	1991	29	38	6	374	50	11.68	0	1	4226	2337	83	28.15	6-59	3	0	3.31	9	
SB	1991	37	17	7	69	25*	6.90	0	0	1674	1286	36	35.72	5-30	0	1	4.60	6	

BOTHA, Pierre (Eastern Province B) b Roodepoort 14.7.1975 RHB RMF

Cmp	Debut	M	I	NO	Runs	HS	Avge	100	50	Balls	Runs	Wkts	Avge	BB	5i	10m	RpO	ct	st
FC		1	2	1	52	40	52.00	0	0	84	52	3	17.33	3-43	0	0	3.71	0	

BOTHA, Peterus Johannes (Border) b Vereeniging 28.9.1966 RHB RFM

Cmp	Debut	M	I	NO	Runs	HS	Avge	100	50	Balls	Runs	Wkts	Avge	BB	5i	10m	RpO	ct	st
FC		9	17	1	636	136	39.75	1	3	1701	698	33	21.15	5-35	2	0	2.46	5	
SB		9	9	3	174	57*	29.00	0	1	441	266	13	20.46	3-11	0	0	3.61	0	
FC	1987	77	135	11	3410	136	27.50	5	15	8303	3682	121	30.42	5-35	3	0	2.66	38	
SB	1989	54	45	7	909	73	23.92	0	5	2177	1425	50	28.50	3-8	0	0	3.92	13	

BOUCHER, Mark Verdon (Border) b East London 3.12.1976 RHB WK

Cmp	Debut	M	I	NO	Runs	HS	Avge	100	50	Balls	Runs	Wkts	Avge	BB	5i	10m	RpO	ct	st
FC		9	17	5	566	71	47.16	0	5									33	3
SB		9	9	0	85	46	9.44	0	0									5	1
FC	1995	14	24	6	689	71	38.27	0	5	18	20	0					6.66	39	5
SB	1995	13	12	1	128	46	11.63	0	0									9	1

BRADFIELD, Carl Crispin (Eastern Province, Eastern Province B) b Grahamstown 18.1.1975 LHB RM

Cmp	Debut	M	I	NO	Runs	HS	Avge	100	50	Balls	Runs	Wkts	Avge	BB	5i	10m	RpO	ct	st
FC		7	13	2	371	163	33.72	1	1	12	7	0					3.50	8	
FC	1993	13	23	3	555	163	27.75	1	2	12	7	0					3.50	10	

BRINK, Mechiel Matthys (Boland) b Barberton 10.6.1975 RHB WK

Cmp	Debut	M	I	NO	Runs	HS	Avge	100	50	Balls	Runs	Wkts	Avge	BB	5i	10m	RpO	ct	st
FC		4	7	0	81	34	11.57	0	0									13	1
SB		5	5	0	62	35	12.40	0	0									3	
FC	1994	15	28	2	556	77	21.38	0	1									43	4
SB	1994	14	9	0	82	35	9.11	0	0									15	2

BROOKER, Finley Clint (Griqualand West) b Kimberley 26.12.1972 RHB RM

Cmp	Debut	M	I	NO	Runs	HS	Avge	100	50	Balls	Runs	Wkts	Avge	BB	5i	10m	RpO	ct	st
FC		4	7	0	143	45	20.42	0	0									5	
SB		2	2	0	37	22	18.50	0	0									1	
FC	1992	30	49	4	1182	89	26.26	0	5	54	74	0					8.22	18	
SB	1993	30	26	1	300	28	12.00	0	0									6	

BROPHY, Gerard Louis (Transvaal B) b Welkom 26.11.1975 RHB WK

Cmp	Debut	M	I	NO	Runs	HS	Avge	100	50	Balls	Runs	Wkts	Avge	BB	5i	10m	RpO	ct	st
FC		5	7	0	116	68	16.57	0	1									16	

BRUCE, Philip Paul (Eastern Province B) b Durban 17.8.1971 RHB RFM

Cmp	Debut	M	I	NO	Runs	HS	Avge	100	50	Balls	Runs	Wkts	Avge	BB	5i	10m	RpO	ct	st
FC		1									144	87	3	29.00	3-55	0	0	3.62	0	

BRUYNS, Mark Lloyd (Natal, Natal B) b Pietermaritzburg 8.11.1973 RHB WK

Cmp	Debut	M	I	NO	Runs	HS	Avge	100	50	Balls	Runs	Wkts	Avge	BB	5i	10m	RpO	ct	st
FC		9	15	0	490	105	32.66	2	1									10	
SB		8	6	3	64	18*	21.33	0	0									2	
FC	1993	36	53	3	1624	105	32.48	2	10	78	30	1	30.00	1-7	0	0	2.30	78	3
SB	1993	35	31	10	712	85*	33.90	0	3									20	5

BRYANT, James Douglas Campbell (Eastern Province B) b Durban 4.2.1976 RHB

Cmp	Debut	M	I	NO	Runs	HS	Avge	100	50	Balls	Runs	Wkts	Avge	BB	5i	10m	RpO	ct	st
FC		1	1	1	48	48*		0	0									1	

BRYSON, Rudi Edwin (Northern Transvaal, South Africa) b Springs 25.7.1968 RHB RFM

Cmp	Debut	M	I	NO	Runs	HS	Avge	100	50	Balls	Runs	Wkts	Avge	BB	5i	10m	RpO	ct	st
FC		7	12	4	137	22	17.12	0	0	1334	642	23	27.91	5-84	1	0	2.88	3	
Int		7	4	3	32	17*	32.00	0	0	378	323	7	46.14	2-34	0	0	5.12	1	
SB		14	7	3	24	13	6.00	0	0	562	419	24	17.45	4-17	2	0	4.47	4	
FC	1987	77	100	21	1453	100	18.39	1	4	13060	6879	251	27.40	7-68	14	3	3.16	19	
SB	1988	71	31	10	228	44*	10.85	0	0	3377	2433	94	25.88	4-17	5	0	4.32	7	

BUXTON-FORMAN, Jon (Natal B) b Pietermaritzburg 15.11.1974 RHB WK

Cmp	Debut	M	I	NO	Runs	HS	Avge	100	50	Balls	Runs	Wkts	Avge	BB	5i	10m	RpO	ct	st
FC		4	7	0	213	70	30.42	0	2									2	
FC	1995	5	9	0	258	70	28.66	0	2									4	

CALLAGHAN, David John (Eastern Province) b Queenstown 1.2.1965 RHB RM

Cmp	Debut	M	I	NO	Runs	HS	Avge	100	50	Balls	Runs	Wkts	Avge	BB	5i	10m	RpO	ct	st
FC		9	16	2	445	102	31.78	1	2	792	291	12	24.25	2-11	0	0	2.20	3	
SB		10	8	2	105	38*	17.50	0	0	402	324	6	54.00	2-13	0	0	4.83	4	
FC	1983	100	161	21	5335	171	38.10	12	27	5041	2243	67	33.47	4-17	0	0	2.66	79	
Int	1992	27	24	6	478	169*	26.55	1	0	444	365	10	36.50	3-32	0	0	4.93	6	
SB	1984	82	77	17	1984	86	33.06	0	13	1925	1566	48	32.62	3-13	0	0	4.88	22	

CHELLAN, Jesse Mark (Natal B) b Durban 28.10.1964 RHB RM

Cmp	Debut	M	I	NO	Runs	HS	Avge	100	50	Balls	Runs	Wkts	Avge	BB	5i	10m	RpO	ct	st
FC		2	2	1	21	21*	21.00	0	0									1	
FC	1991	3	4	1	63	30	21.00	0	0									2	

CILLIERS, Sarel Arnold (Free State) b Klerksdorp 6.6.1971 RHB RFM

Cmp	Debut	M	I	NO	Runs	HS	Avge	100	50	Balls	Runs	Wkts	Avge	BB	5i	10m	RpO	ct	st
FC		8	11	5	63	28*	10.50	0	0	1304	672	27	24.88	5-69	1	0	3.09	6	
SB		3	2	2	10	10*		0	0	132	137	3	45.66	2-46	0	0	6.22	0	
FC	1991	18	23	9	193	32*	13.78	0	0	2722	1560	54	28.88	5-69	1	0	3.43	9	

Cmp	Debut	M	I	NO	Runs	HS	Avge	100	50	Balls	Runs	Wkts	Avge	BB	5i	10m	RpO	ct	st

COMMINS, John Brian (Western Province, South Africa to India, Western Province to Zimbabwe) b East London 19.2.1965 RHB RM

Cmp	Debut	M	I	NO	Runs	HS	Avge	100	50	Balls	Runs	Wkts	Avge	BB	5i	10m	RpO	ct	st
FC		7	10	4	598	200*	99.66	2	3									0	
SB		8	8	3	296	84*	59.20	0	3									3	
Test	1994	3	6	1	125	45	25.00	0	0									2	
FC	1984	81	142	18	5200	200*	41.93	13	29	323	170	4	42.50	2-28	0	0	3.15	30	
SB	1987	42	39	7	1061	93	33.15	0	10	18	27	0					9.00	10	

COOKE, Gavin Peter (Easterns) b Johannesburg 7.9.1971 RHB RFM

Cmp	Debut	M	I	NO	Runs	HS	Avge	100	50	Balls	Runs	Wkts	Avge	BB	5i	10m	RpO	ct	st
FC		3	5	0	85	36	17.00	0	0	174	82	1	82.00	1-17	0	0	2.82	2	
SB		6	6	0	140	72	23.33	0	2	105	103	2	51.50	2-32	0	0	5.88	1	
FC	1993	16	21	1	305	49	15.25	0	0	1988	925	31	29.83	4-68	0	0	2.79	7	
SB	1993	16	14	1	235	72	18.07	0	3	459	438	13	33.69	4-38	1	0	5.72	4	

COOKE, Jonathan Leicester (Natal B) b Johannesburg 21.7.1973 RHB WK

Cmp	Debut	M	I	NO	Runs	HS	Avge	100	50	Balls	Runs	Wkts	Avge	BB	5i	10m	RpO	ct	st
FC		1	1	1	1	1*		0	0									2	
FC	1994	2	2	1	30	29	30.00	0	0									4	1

CRAVEN, Christiaan Frans (Free State, Free State to West Indies) b Dundee 6.12.1970 RHB RM

Cmp	Debut	M	I	NO	Runs	HS	Avge	100	50	Balls	Runs	Wkts	Avge	BB	5i	10m	RpO	ct	st
FC		5	7	0	263	109	37.57	1	2	318	127	5	25.40	2-8	0	0	2.39	4	
SB		9	7	2	81	23	16.20	0	0	156	166	4	41.50	1-23	0	0	6.38	0	
FC	1990	33	53	6	1614	152	34.34	3	9	2622	1103	44	25.06	6-25	1	0	2.52	20	
SB	1990	43	35	9	479	59*	18.42	0	1	772	609	25	24.36	3-9	0	0	4.73	6	

CRONJE, Frans Johannes Cornelius (Border) b Bloemfontein 15.5.1967 RHB RM

Cmp	Debut	M	I	NO	Runs	HS	Avge	100	50	Balls	Runs	Wkts	Avge	BB	5i	10m	RpO	ct	st
FC		4	7	0	145	67	20.71	0	1	126	71	1	71.00	1-38	0	0	3.38	0	
SB		10	10	2	234	93*	29.25	0	2	120	105	4	26.25	2-18	0	0	5.25	4	
FC	1986	56	93	9	2503	152*	29.79	4	9	4264	2132	67	31.82	5-22	2	0	3.00	28	
SB	1988	44	38	9	899	93*	31.00	0	7	652	520	20	26.00	3-28	0	0	4.78	14	

CRONJE, Schalk Grove (Free State to West Indies) b Bloemfontein 6.9.1970 RHB SLA

Cmp	Debut	M	I	NO	Runs	HS	Avge	100	50	Balls	Runs	Wkts	Avge	BB	5i	10m	RpO	ct	st
FC	1993	17	25	9	302	50*	18.87	0	1	2899	1399	44	31.79	5-43	1	0	2.89	6	
SB	1995	1								42	40	0					5.71	0	

CRONJE, Wessel Johannes (Free State, South Africa, Ireland, South Africa to India, South Africa to Kenya) b Bloemfontein 25.9.1969 RHB RM

Cmp	Debut	M	I	NO	Runs	HS	Avge	100	50	Balls	Runs	Wkts	Avge	BB	5i	10m	RpO	ct	st
Test		6	11	1	344	79*	34.40	0	2	472	173	7	24.71	2-21	0	0	2.19	2	
FC		9	17	2	520	79*	34.66	0	3	760	267	8	33.37	2-21	0	0	2.10	5	
Int		15	13	6	525	87*	75.00	0	4	545	423	11	38.45	2-34	0	0	4.65	4	
SB		2	2	0	96	94	48.00	0	1	54	46	0					5.11	1	
Test	1991	36	63	7	2012	135	35.92	5	7	2411	768	17	45.17	2-11	0	0	1.91	12	
FC	1987	128	226	23	8496	251	41.85	22	39	7000	2816	70	40.22	4-47	0	0	2.41	83	
Int	1991	115	107	20	3473	112	39.91	2	22	3554	2559	69	37.08	5-32	1	1	4.32	46	
SB	1988	52	49	8	1675	120	40.85	4	12	804	545	19	28.68	2-8	0	0	4.06	15	

CROOKES, Derek Norman (Natal, South Africa, South Africa to India, South Africa to Kenya) b Mariannhill 5.3.1969 RHB OB

Cmp	Debut	M	I	NO	Runs	HS	Avge	100	50	Balls	Runs	Wkts	Avge	BB	5i	10m	RpO	ct	st
FC		7	10	1	453	128*	50.33	2	2	1374	625	25	25.00	7-114	2	0	2.72	5	
Int		5	4	1	39	18	13.00	0	0	216	156	1	156.00	1-42	0	0	4.33	6	
SB		8	8	0	190	72	23.75	0	1	343	265	11	24.09	2-12	0	0	4.63	1	
FC	1989	52	76	7	2940	155*	42.60	7	18	8095	3767	123	30.62	7-114	6	0	2.79	45	
Int	1994	18	14	1	190	54	14.61	0	1	673	527	10	52.70	3-30	0	0	4.69	13	
SB	1990	52	47	8	740	72	18.97	0	2	1916	1383	66	20.95	4-32	4	0	4.33	11	

CROSOER, Martin James (Western Province B) b Durban 22.5.1977 RHB

Cmp	Debut	M	I	NO	Runs	HS	Avge	100	50	Balls	Runs	Wkts	Avge	BB	5i	10m	RpO	ct	st
FC		1	1	0	0	0	0.00	0	0									0	

CULLINAN, Daryll John (Transvaal, South Africa, South Africa to India, South Africa to Kenya) b Kimberley 4.3.1967 RHB OB

Cmp	Debut	M	I	NO	Runs	HS	Avge	100	50	Balls	Runs	Wkts	Avge	BB	5i	10m	RpO	ct	st
Test		6	12	2	413	122*	41.30	1	2									6	
FC		8	15	2	512	122*	39.38	1	3	12	0	0					0.00	10	
Int		15	14	2	634	89	52.83	0	7	6	7	1	7.00	1-7	0	0	7.00	10	
SB		2	2	0	35	25	17.50	0	0									1	
Test	1992	28	49	5	1778	153*	40.40	3	11									21	
FC	1983	145	255	35	8827	337*	40.12	19	48	150	70	3	23.33	2-27	0	0	2.80	126	
Int	1992	77	75	11	2528	124	39.50	3	17	24	22	1	22.00	1-7	0	0	5.50	35	
SB	1984	77	74	10	1718	111*	26.84	2	6	12	12	0					6.00	42	

DAVIDS, Faiek (Western Province, Western Province B, Western Province to Zimbabwe) b Cape Town 1.9.1964 RHB RM

Cmp	Debut	M	I	NO	Runs	HS	Avge	100	50	Balls	Runs	Wkts	Avge	BB	5i	10m	RpO	ct	st
FC		6	7	1	233	65	38.83	0	2	486	251	6	41.83	2-29	0	0	3.09	2	
SB		6	5	1	36	27	9.00	0	0	60	58	1	58.00	1-6	0	0	5.80	1	
FC	1991	29	43	2	1196	146	29.17	1	7	1757	1009	32	31.53	4-24	0	0	3.44	16	
SB	1991	17	13	4	162	32*	18.00	0	0	236	194	8	24.25	3-23	0	0	4.93	1	

DAVIS, Mark Jeffrey Gronow (Northern Transvaal) b Port Elizabeth 10.10.1971 RHB OB

Cmp	Debut	M	I	NO	Runs	HS	Avge	100	50	Balls	Runs	Wkts	Avge	BB	5i	10m	RpO	ct	st
FC		7	13	3	149	38*	14.90	0	0	1335	622	17	36.58	6-80	1	0	2.79	7	
SB		14	9	4	59	16*	11.80	0	0	642	481	14	34.35	2-29	0	0	4.49	5	
FC	1990	47	79	13	1128	71	17.09	0	4	7354	3251	95	34.22	8-37	2	1	2.65	29	
SB	1993	34	17	5	180	35	15.00	0	0	1596	1118	26	43.00	2-29	0	0	4.20	10	

Cmp	Debut	M	I	NO	Runs	HS	Avge	100	50	Balls	Runs	Wkts	Avge	BB	5i	10m	RpO	ct	st

DAWSON, Alan Charles (Western Province, Western Province B, Western Province to Zimbabwe) b Cape Town 27.11.1969 RHB RM

Cmp	Debut	M	I	NO	Runs	HS	Avge	100	50	Balls	Runs	Wkts	Avge	BB	5i	10m	RpO	ct	st
FC		5	7	2	230	64	46.00	0	2	1137	494	19	26.00	5-30	1	0	2.60	5	
SB		12	6	2	81	27*	20.25	0	0	534	396	17	23.29	3-30	0	0	4.44	4	
FC	1992	36	53	10	897	64	20.86	0	6	5835	2506	91	27.53	6-18	4	0	2.57	23	
SB	1993	35	20	7	308	44*	23.69	0	0	1588	1129	50	22.58	5-39	1	1	4.26	11	

DE BRUYN, Zander (Transvaal, Transvaal B) b Johannesburg 5.7.1975 RHB RFM

Cmp	Debut	M	I	NO	Runs	HS	Avge	100	50	Balls	Runs	Wkts	Avge	BB	5i	10m	RpO	ct	st
FC		6	11	1	215	70*	21.50	0	1	576	386	11	35.09	6-120	1	0	4.02	4	
SB		3	3	1	28	16*	14.00	0	0	5	10	1	10.00	1-10	0	0	12.00	0	
FC	1995	11	20	6	605	126*	43.21	1	3	576	386	11	35.09	6-120	1	0	4.02	4	
SB	1995	5	5	1	59	22	14.75	0	0	5	10	1	10.00	1-10	0	0	12.00	1	

DE KOCK, Grant (Western Province) b Bellville 18.11.1976 LHB LFM

Cmp	Debut	M	I	NO	Runs	HS	Avge	100	50	Balls	Runs	Wkts	Avge	BB	5i	10m	RpO	ct	st
FC		5	7	0	187	67	26.71	0	2	585	288	15	19.20	3-8	0	0	2.95	3	
FC	1995	6	7	0	187	67	26.71	0	2	729	356	17	20.94	3-8	0	0	2.93	4	

DE VILLIERS, Michael Craig (Western Province B, Western Province, Western Province to Zimbabwe) b Cape Town 10.5.1970 RHB RM

Cmp	Debut	M	I	NO	Runs	HS	Avge	100	50	Balls	Runs	Wkts	Avge	BB	5i	10m	RpO	ct	st
FC		2	2	0	20	16	10.00	0	0	12	10	0					5.00	3	
SB		3	3	1	23	11	11.50	0	0									0	
FC	1993	8	11	2	382	88	42.44	0	4	28	47	0					10.07	6	

DE VILLIERS, Petrus Stephanus (Northern Transvaal, South Africa to India, South Africa to Kenya) b Vereeniging 13.10.1964 RHB RFM

Cmp	Debut	M	I	NO	Runs	HS	Avge	100	50	Balls	Runs	Wkts	Avge	BB	5i	10m	RpO	ct	st
FC		2	2	0	20	19	10.00	0	0	342	148	4	37.00	2-39	0	0	2.59	1	
SB		6	3	0	17	11	5.66	0	0	240	205	6	34.16	3-41	0	0	5.12	0	
Test	1993	16	23	6	305	67*	17.94	0	2	4453	1909	75	25.45	6-43	4	2	2.57	10	
FC	1985	95	128	37	1550	67*	17.03	0	4	19057	8845	380	23.27	6-43	20	2	2.78	47	
Int	1992	79	34	15	163	20*	8.57	0	0	4200	2481	90	27.56	4-27	2	0	3.54	13	
SB	1985	51	32	14	220	23*	12.22	0	0	2281	1544	61	25.31	4-16	2	0	4.06	2	

DE VOS, Dirk Johannes Jacobus (Northern Transvaal) b Pretoria 15.6.1975 RHB OB

Cmp	Debut	M	I	NO	Runs	HS	Avge	100	50	Balls	Runs	Wkts	Avge	BB	5i	10m	RpO	ct	st
FC		4	7	1	67	31*	11.16	0	0	330	140	0					2.54	2	
SB		11	9	2	143	58	20.42	0	1	180	143	3	47.66	3-15	0	0	4.76	7	
FC	1992	17	29	4	448	77	17.92	0	1	1808	849	22	38.59	4-34	0	0	2.81	13	
SB	1995	13	10	2	150	58	18.75	0	1	258	179	6	29.83	3-15	0	0	4.16	7	

DE VOS, Hendrik Moller (North West) b Klerksdorp 5.10.1969 RHB WK

Cmp	Debut	M	I	NO	Runs	HS	Avge	100	50	Balls	Runs	Wkts	Avge	BB	5i	10m	RpO	ct	st
FC		1	2	0	28	20	14.00	0	0									0	
SB		2	2	0	10	7	5.00	0	0									1	
FC	1991	29	53	3	1270	115	25.40	1	4									35	2
SB	1994	21	20	0	469	91	23.45	0	2									8	2

DIPPENAAR, Hendrik Human (Free State, Free State to West Indies) b Kimberley 14.6.1977 RHB OB

Cmp	Debut	M	I	NO	Runs	HS	Avge	100	50	Balls	Runs	Wkts	Avge	BB	5i	10m	RpO	ct	st
FC		9	16	1	716	151*	47.73	1	5	6	8	0					8.00	5	
SB		9	8	2	173	69*	28.83	0	1									2	
FC	1995	15	25	1	1033	151*	43.04	2	5	7	12	0					10.28	8	
SB	1995	15	14	4	255	69*	25.50	0	1	6	2	0					2.00	4	

DONALD, Allan Anthony (South Africa, Free State, Warwickshire, South Africa to India, South Africa to Kenya) b Bloemfontein 20.10.1966 RHB RF

Cmp	Debut	M	I	NO	Runs	HS	Avge	100	50	Balls	Runs	Wkts	Avge	BB	5i	10m	RpO	ct	st
Test		6	9	1	80	26	10.00	0	0	1448	644	31	20.77	5-36	2	0	2.66	0	
FC		6	9	1	80	26	10.00	0	0	1448	644	31	20.77	5-36	2	0	2.66	0	
Int		15	1	0	6	6	6.00	0	0	840	603	27	22.33	4-37	2	0	4.30	4	
SB		2								102	93	5	18.60	4-33	1	0	5.47	0	
Test	1991	33	44	18	334	33	12.84	0	0	7609	3621	155	23.36	8-71	8	2	2.85	7	
FC	1985	241	279	107	2126	46*	12.36	0	0	44768	21160	945	22.39	8-37	51	8	2.83	92	
Int	1991	87	21	10	40	7*	3.63	0	0	4710	3211	147	21.84	6-23	5	2	4.09	12	
SB	1985	65	21	10	64	19*	5.81	0	0	3018	1850	83	22.28	4-18	4	0	3.67	9	

DRAKES, Vasbert Conniel (Border, Barbados, Sussex) b St James, Barbados 5.8.1969 RHB RF

Cmp	Debut	M	I	NO	Runs	HS	Avge	100	50	Balls	Runs	Wkts	Avge	BB	5i	10m	RpO	ct	st
FC		6	8	2	127	41	21.16	0	0	1209	552	22	25.09	8-59	1	1	2.73	1	
SB		10	7	0	153	104	21.85	1	0	426	309	15	20.60	3-33	0	0	4.35	1	
FC	1991	63	100	15	2048	180*	24.09	4	6	10463	6027	198	30.43	8-59	6	1	3.45	17	
Int	1994	5	2	0	5	4	2.50	0	0	239	204	3	68.00	1-36	0	0	5.12	1	

DREYER, Jan Nicolaas (North West) b Amanzimtoti 9.9.1976 RHB RM

Cmp	Debut	M	I	NO	Runs	HS	Avge	100	50	Balls	Runs	Wkts	Avge	BB	5i	10m	RpO	ct	st
FC		2	2	0	15	14	7.50	0	0	270	158	4	39.50	3-64	0	0	3.51	0	
SB		5	2	0	12	12	6.00	0	0	205	219	3	73.00	2-60	0	0	6.40	1	
SB	1995	8	4	2	30	16*	15.00	0	0	265	273	3	91.00	2-60	0	0	6.18	1	

DROS, Gerald (Northern Transvaal) b Pretoria 2.4.1973 RHB RM

Cmp	Debut	M	I	NO	Runs	HS	Avge	100	50	Balls	Runs	Wkts	Avge	BB	5i	10m	RpO	ct	st
FC		1	2	0	59	54	29.50	0	1									1	
SB		2	1	0	2	2	2.00	0	0									0	
FC	1993	18	34	4	745	83*	24.83	0	4	456	200	3	66.66	1-29	0	0	2.63	18	
SB	1993	5	4	0	45	28	11.25	0	0	24	32	0					8.00	1	

Cmp	Debut	M	I	NO	Runs	HS	Avge	100	50	Balls	Runs	Wkts	Avge	BB	5i	10m	RpO	ct	st

DRY, Willem Moolman (Griqualand West) b Vryburg 9.1.1971 RHB RM

FC		6	11	0	280	74	25.45	0	2	42	34	0					4.85	5	
SB		10	9	1	218	66*	27.25	0	2	60	69	1	69.00	1-17	0	0	6.90	3	
FC	1993	22	37	4	1157	99	35.06	0	8	654	406	8	50.75	2-39	0	0	3.72	15	
SB	1994	23	21	3	463	66*	25.72	0	2	66	89	1	89.00	1-17	0	0	8.09	7	

DU PLESSIS, Clint Norton (Eastern Province B) b Cape Town 12.12.1975 LHB LM

| FC | | 4 | 6 | 1 | 145 | 46 | 29.00 | 0 | 0 | 168 | 81 | 0 | | | | | 2.89 | 2 | |
| FC | 1995 | 7 | 9 | 1 | 200 | 46 | 25.00 | 0 | 0 | 174 | 85 | 0 | | | | | 2.93 | 3 | |

DU PLESSIS, Petrus Bouwer (Border) b Somerset East 13.10.1969 RHB RM

FC		3	6	1	40	33	8.00	0	0	204	93	4	23.25	2-25	0	0	2.73	1	
SB		3	2	0	20	15	10.00	0	0	102	94	1	94.00	1-27	0	0	5.52	1	
FC	1988	8	13	5	289	104*	36.12	2	0	634	398	15	26.53	3-49	0	0	3.76	2	
SB	1995	7	5	1	78	33*	19.50	0	0	126	124	1	124.00	1-27	0	0	5.90	1	

EKSTEEN, Clive Edward (Transvaal) b Johannesburg 2.12.1966 RHB SLA

FC		9	12	3	187	32	20.77	0	0	2360	904	40	22.60	5-83	1	0	2.29	5	
SB		11	6	2	37	10	9.25	0	0	563	324	13	24.92	3-19	0	0	3.45	8	
Test	1993	6	10	2	87	22	10.87	0	0	1458	447	8	55.87	3-12	0	0	1.83	4	
FC	1985	86	114	31	1170	58	14.09	0	1	21330	8217	282	29.13	7-29	11	1	2.31	66	
Int	1991	6	2	2	6	6*		0	0	222	181	2	90.50	1-26	0	0	4.89	3	
SB	1989	69	34	10	244	26	10.16	0	0	3169	1989	60	33.15	5-13	1	1	3.76	18	

ELLIOTT, Grant David (Transvaal B) b Johannesburg 21.3.1979 RHB RFM

| FC | | 1 | 1 | 0 | 67 | 67 | 67.00 | 0 | 1 | 36 | 30 | 0 | | | | | 5.00 | 0 | |

ELWORTHY, Steven (Northern Transvaal) b Bulawayo, Rhodesia 23.2.1965 RHB RFM

FC		8	15	0	314	51	20.93	0	1	1550	804	24	33.50	4-71	0	0	3.11	5	
SB		14	13	4	285	86*	31.66	0	1	570	377	21	17.95	4-23	1	0	3.96	5	
FC	1987	79	129	20	2224	88	20.40	0	7	14194	7896	257	30.72	7-65	8	1	3.33	30	
SB	1988	67	54	18	983	116*	27.30	1	2	3035	2019	74	27.28	4-23	2	0	3.99	10	

EMSLIE, Peter Arthur Norman (Border) b Grahamstown 21.10.1968 RHB OB

FC		5	7	3	67	13*	16.75	0	0	590	289	8	36.12	3-36	0	0	2.93	2	
SB		10	5	5	24	8*		0	0	390	250	5	50.00	2-38	0	0	3.84	1	
FC	1993	25	29	14	184	20*	12.26	0	0	3885	1819	59	30.83	5-103	1	0	2.80	10	
SB	1993	24	11	8	68	18*	22.66	0	0	1020	672	18	37.33	3-49	0	0	3.95	4	

ENGELKE, Justin Marc (Transvaal B) b Cape Town 3.4.1976 RHB RMF

| FC | | 4 | 3 | 1 | 27 | 11* | 13.50 | 0 | 0 | 465 | 251 | 7 | 35.85 | 2-30 | 0 | 0 | 3.23 | 1 | |

ENGLISH, Cedric Vaughan (Griqualand West) b Kimberley 13.9.1973 RHB RFM

FC		8	15	0	326	51	21.73	0	1	1103	668	18	37.11	5-65	1	0	3.63	3	
SB		8	7	2	45	18	9.00	0	0	288	242	5	48.40	1-27	0	0	5.04	2	
FC	1990	27	40	7	700	108	21.21	1	2	3705	2043	56	36.48	5-65	1	0	3.30	9	
SB	1993	22	13	3	101	21	10.10	0	0	904	761	20	38.05	3-24	0	0	5.05	4	

ENSLIN, Christian Thinus (North West) b Klerksdorp 16.9.1975 RHB RM

SB		1								12	17	0					8.50	0	
FC	1995	3	2	1	35	19	35.00	0	0	204	106	5	21.20	4-46	0	0	3.11	2	
SB	1995	8	6	1	79	43*	15.80	0	0	299	287	10	28.70	3-34	0	0	5.75	1	

ERASMUS, Marais (Boland) b George 27.2.1964 RHB RFM

FC		1	2	0	0	0	0.00	0	0	105	57	1	57.00	1-21	0	0	3.25	0	
SB		1	1	0	5	5	5.00	0	0	54	39	0					4.33	0	
FC	1988	53	89	24	1913	103*	29.43	1	7	8402	3692	131	28.18	6-22	7	0	2.63	35	
SB	1989	47	35	9	226	18	8.69	0	0	2256	1580	39	40.51	3-25	0	0	4.20	14	

ESTERHUYSEN, Barend Daniel (North West) b Vereeniging 4.7.1972 RHB OB

FC		3	5	0	106	58	21.20	0	1	24	22	1	22.00	1-9	0	0	5.50	2	
SB		2	1	1	48	48*		0	0	30	33	1	33.00	1-33	0	0	6.60	1	
FC	1992	6	11	0	192	58	17.45	0	1	72	55	1	55.00	1-9	0	0	4.58	4	
SB	1994	13	11	2	273	67	30.33	0	1	54	64	2	32.00	1-9	0	0	7.11	3	

FERREIRA, Lloyd Douglas (Boland) b Parktown, Johannesburg 6.5.1974 RHB LM

FC		8	16	0	409	127	25.56	1	1	3	2	0					4.00	3	
SB		9	9	1	354	125*	44.25	2	0									3	
FC	1993	25	49	0	958	127	19.55	1	4	3	2	0					4.00	9	
SB	1994	33	33	1	1131	125*	35.34	2	7									8	

FERREIRA, Quentin (Eastern Province, Eastern Province B) b East London 28.12.1972 RHB RFM

| FC | | 7 | 5 | 1 | 33 | 9 | 8.25 | 0 | 0 | 1188 | 593 | 18 | 32.94 | 3-64 | 0 | 0 | 2.99 | 2 | |
| SB | | 10 | 4 | 2 | 49 | 27* | 24.50 | 0 | 0 | 457 | 353 | 15 | 23.53 | 3-40 | 0 | 0 | 4.63 | 2 | |

FORDE, Keith Adrian (Natal) b Pietermaritzburg 12.7.1969 RHB LB WK

FC		10	12	2	231	38	23.10	0	0									39	2
SB		15	8	5	115	41*	38.33	0	0									19	5
FC	1989	29	43	3	1333	150	33.32	4	2	162	52	3	17.33	3-52	0	0	1.92	62	2
SB	1989	24	17	6	210	41*	19.09	0	0									23	6

Cmp	Debut	M	I	NO	Runs	HS	Avge	100	50	Balls	Runs	Wkts	Avge	BB	5i	10m	RpO	ct	st

FOURIE, Brenden Craig (Border) b East London 13.4.1970 RHB RFM

FC		1	2	0	17	16	8.50	0	0	144	77	2	38.50	2-55	0	0	3.20	0	
SB		2	2	1	10	8	10.00	0	0	36	55	1	55.00	1-55	0	0	9.16	0	
FC	1988	49	70	21	556	34	11.34	0	0	9649	4312	160	26.95	6-74	7	0	2.68	14	
SB	1988	60	26	11	203	32	13.53	0	0	2778	1963	77	25.49	4-24	4	0	4.23	15	

FOURIE; Shaun Eddie (Border) b East London 28.8.1973 RHB RFM

| FC | | 1 | 1 | 1 | 0 | 0* | | 0 | 0 | 54 | 48 | 2 | 24.00 | 2-48 | 0 | 0 | 5.33 | 0 | |
| FC | 1993 | 11 | 13 | 3 | 215 | 52 | 21.50 | 0 | 1 | 1356 | 886 | 22 | 40.27 | 4-71 | 0 | 0 | 3.92 | 4 | |

FUSEDALE, Neil Andrew (Transvaal B, Transvaal) b Hendon, England 11.11.1967 RHB SLA

FC		3	3	1	97	44*	48.50	0	0	618	312	8	39.00	3-59	0	0	3.02	3	
SB		2	2	1	8	8*	8.00	0	0	79	46	1	46.00	1-18	0	0	3.49	0	
FC	1994	9	7	2	120	44*	24.00	0	0	1845	791	21	37.66	4-23	0	0	2.57	10	
SB	1994	10	7	3	39	14	9.75	0	0	424	277	8	34.62	2-30	0	0	3.91	3	

GAIN, Douglas Robert (Transvaal, Transvaal B) b Johannesburg 29.12.1976 RHB RM

| FC | | 6 | 11 | 1 | 408 | 88 | 40.80 | 0 | 3 | 42 | 34 | 0 | | | | | 4.85 | 2 | |

GIBBS, Herschelle Herman (Western Province, South Africa, South Africa to India, South Africa to Kenya) b Green Point, Cape Town 23.2.1974 RHB RFM/LB

Test		2	4	0	63	31	15.75	0	0									0	
FC		6	11	1	553	163*	55.30	2	1									0	
Int		6	6	0	122	33	20.33	0	0									2	
SB		8	8	0	210	53	26.25	0	1									3	
Test	1996	4	8	0	125	31	15.62	0	0									1	
FC	1990	57	100	6	4059	200*	43.18	10	17	132	74	3	24.66	2-14	0	0	3.36	33	
Int	1996	9	9	0	205	35	22.77	0	0									3	
SB	1990	42	35	4	871	101	28.09	1	5									19	

GIDLEY, Martyn Ian (Griqualand West) b Leicester, England 30.9.1968 LHB OB

FC		8	16	2	559	117	39.92	1	4	940	526	11	47.81	3-59	0	0	3.35	2	
SB		12	12	2	431	108*	43.10	2	1	450	311	8	38.87	4-11	1	0	4.14	2	
FC	1989	46	76	12	2409	160	37.64	5	13	6000	2873	57	50.40	5-48	1	0	2.87	22	
SB	1994	32	31	2	939	108*	32.37	2	4	1206	868	15	57.86	4-11	1	0	4.31	6	

GILDER, Gary Michael (Natal, Natal B) b Salisbury, Rhodesia 6.7.1974 RHB LFM

FC		10	10	1	54	17	6.00	0	0	1889	868	38	22.84	5-57	2	0	2.75	2	
SB		8	5	2	8	7	2.66	0	0	204	175	6	29.16	2-18	0	0	5.14	1	
FC	1994	18	19	2	114	23	6.70	0	0	3027	1389	70	19.84	8-22	5	2	2.75	3	

GOEDEKE, Udo Herbert (Natal B) b Pietermaritzburg 10.11.1968 RHB WK

FC		5	8	2	275	102*	45.83	1	1									12	
FC	1990	28	37	9	858	137	30.64	2	1	12	0	0					0.00	68	6
SB	1992	11	9	4	65	14	13.00	0	0									20	2

GRACE, Graham Vernon (Eastern Province B) b Salisbury, Rhodesia 16.8.1975 LHB

| FC | | 1 | 2 | 0 | 30 | 29 | 15.00 | 0 | 0 | | | | | | | | | 0 | |

GRAINGER, Chad (Northern Transvaal) b Johannesburg 23.9.1972 RHB

SB		2	2	0	4	4	2.00	0	0									1	
FC	1991	19	32	1	1298	233	41.87	2	9	72	34	2	17.00	2-23	0	0	2.83	10	
SB	1995	11	11	0	324	89	29.45	0	4	137	121	4	30.25	2-45	0	0	5.29	4	

GRIFFITHS, Andrew Vaughan (Transvaal B) b East London 22.12.1967 LHB SLA

| FC | | 1 | 1 | 1 | 0 | 0* | | 0 | 0 | 173 | 72 | 5 | 14.40 | 3-61 | 0 | 0 | 2.49 | 2 | |
| FC | 1988 | 4 | 6 | 2 | 33 | 16 | 8.25 | 0 | 0 | 789 | 344 | 15 | 22.93 | 5-78 | 1 | 0 | 2.61 | 2 | |

HALL, Andrew James (Transvaal, Transvaal B) b Johannesburg 31.7.1975 RHB RFM

FC		8	13	2	322	78	29.27	0	2	1001	455	21	21.66	4-29	0	0	2.72	4	
SB		9	5	3	165	68	82.50	0	2	338	277	6	46.16	1-13	0	0	4.91	4	
FC	1995	11	15	3	338	78	28.16	0	2	1439	649	24	27.04	4-29	0	0	2.70	4	
SB	1994	24	17	9	263	68	32.87	0	2	1033	766	21	36.47	3-32	0	0	4.44	7	

HAYNES, Desmond Leo (Western Province) b Holders Hill, Barbados 15.2.1956 RHB RM

FC		8	13	1	600	202*	50.00	1	4									4	
SB		11	11	0	284	94	25.81	0	1									1	
Test	1977	116	202	25	7487	184	42.29	18	39	18	8	1	8.00	1-2	0	0	2.66	65	
FC	1976	376	639	72	26030	255*	45.90	61	138	536	279	8	34.87	1-2	0	0	3.12	202	1
Int	1977	238	237	28	8648	152*	41.37	17	57	30	24	0					4.80	59	
SB	1994	26	26	0	896	106	34.46	3	3									5	

HAYWARD, Mornantau (Eastern Province) b Uitenhage 6.3.1977 RHB RF

FC		6	4	1	10	9*	3.33	0	0	1212	680	12	56.66	2-62	0	0	3.36	0	
SB		10	3	3	30	19*		0	0	492	385	24	16.04	5-40	1	1	4.69	1	
FC	1995	8	4	1	10	9*	3.33	0	0	1464	783	16	48.93	2-50	0	0	3.20	3	
SB	1995	13	3	3	30	19*		0	0	645	483	27	17.88	5-40	1	1	4.49	1	

HEARLE, Philip Kenyon (Transvaal B) b Johannesburg 31.5.1978 LHB

| FC | | 1 | 1 | 0 | 16 | 16 | 16.00 | 0 | 0 | | | | | | | | | 1 | |

Cmp	Debut	M	I	NO	Runs	HS	Avge	100	50	Balls	Runs	Wkts	Avge	BB	5i	10m	RpO	ct	st

HENDERSON, Claude William (Boland) b Worcester 14.6.1972 RHB SLA

Cmp	Debut	M	I	NO	Runs	HS	Avge	100	50	Balls	Runs	Wkts	Avge	BB	5i	10m	RpO	ct	st
FC		7	14	3	191	29	17.36	0	0	1934	779	25	31.16	5-107	1	0	2.41	1	
SB		9	5	3	29	15*	14.50	0	0	432	370	9	41.11	2-57	0	0	5.13	4	
FC	1990	54	77	24	752	53*	14.18	0	1	13038	5625	193	29.14	7-57	6	0	2.58	16	
SB	1990	47	23	13	100	15*	10.00	0	0	2167	1501	51	29.43	4-30	1	0	4.15	15	

HENDERSON, James Michael (Transvaal B) b Worcester 6.8.1975 LHB OB

Cmp	Debut	M	I	NO	Runs	HS	Avge	100	50	Balls	Runs	Wkts	Avge	BB	5i	10m	RpO	ct	st
FC		4	7	0	112	30	16.00	0	0	120	92	1	92.00	1-44	0	0	4.60	1	
FC	1994	8	15	1	291	122*	20.78	1	0	150	110	1	110.00	1-44	0	0	4.40	1	
SB	1994	1	1	0	12	12	12.00	0	0									0	

HEWITT, Glen Michael (North West) b Johannesburg 16.4.1973 RHB OB

Cmp	Debut	M	I	NO	Runs	HS	Avge	100	50	Balls	Runs	Wkts	Avge	BB	5i	10m	RpO	ct	st
FC		5	10	0	107	52	10.70	0	1									6	
SB		9	9	1	377	108	47.12	1	3	42	63	1	63.00	1-21	0	0	9.00	5	
FC	1993	8	15	0	186	52	12.40	0	1									8	
SB	1995	13	13	1	489	108	40.75	1	4	42	63	1	63.00	1-21	0	0	9.00	6	

HOFMEYR, Simon (Western Province B) b Cape Town 24.2.1978 LHB LM

Cmp	Debut	M	I	NO	Runs	HS	Avge	100	50	Balls	Runs	Wkts	Avge	BB	5i	10m	RpO	ct	st
FC		4	6	0	119	51	19.83	0	1									1	

HORAN, Brendan Patrick (Border) b Cape Town 17.9.1974 RHB RMF

Cmp	Debut	M	I	NO	Runs	HS	Avge	100	50	Balls	Runs	Wkts	Avge	BB	5i	10m	RpO	ct	st
FC		2	1	0	11	11	11.00	0	0	324	191	3	63.66	2-41	0	0	3.53	1	
SB		4	1	0	10	10	10.00	0	0	60	60	0					6.00	2	
FC	1995	9	9	5	71	28	17.75	0	0	1079	589	18	32.72	4-43	0	0	3.27	1	
SB	1995	12	4	1	25	10	8.33	0	0	366	297	6	49.50	3-40	0	0	4.86	2	

HOWELL, Ian Lester (Border) b Port Elizabeth 20.5.1958 LHB LM

Cmp	Debut	M	I	NO	Runs	HS	Avge	100	50	Balls	Runs	Wkts	Avge	BB	5i	10m	RpO	ct	st
FC		8	9	5	300	102*	75.00	1	0	1487	571	11	51.90	3-46	0	0	2.30	3	
SB		10	6	1	52	25*	10.40	0	0	441	286	6	47.66	2-26	0	0	3.89	1	
FC	1981	112	175	43	3685	115*	27.91	5	13	21933	8387	236	35.53	6-38	5	0	2.29	68	
SB	1981	84	57	10	575	50	12.23	0	1	3903	2384	53	44.98	3-23	0	0	3.66	15	

HUDSON, Andrew Charles (Natal, South Africa, South Africa to India, South Africa to Kenya) b Eshowe, Zululand 17.3.1965 RHB RM

Cmp	Debut	M	I	NO	Runs	HS	Avge	100	50	Balls	Runs	Wkts	Avge	BB	5i	10m	RpO	ct	st
Test		4	8	0	255	80	31.87	0	3									6	
FC		6	12	1	398	80	36.18	0	3									6	
Int		6	6	0	68	26	11.33	0	0									3	
SB		6	6	0	91	37	15.16	0	0									1	
Test	1991	32	58	3	1920	163	34.90	4	13									33	
FC	1984	123	225	17	7438	184*	35.75	14	43	24	5	0					1.25	119	
Int	1991	85	84	1	2530	161	30.48	2	18									16	
SB	1985	55	55	2	1649	109	31.11	1	12	6	3	0					3.00	12	

JACKSON, Kenneth Conrad (Boland) b Kitwe, Northern Rhodesia 16.8.1964 RHB RM

Cmp	Debut	M	I	NO	Runs	HS	Avge	100	50	Balls	Runs	Wkts	Avge	BB	5i	10m	RpO	ct	st
FC		8	16	1	542	120	36.13	1	3	120	48	2	24.00	1-18	0	0	2.40	6	
SB		9	9	0	215	95	23.88	0	1									2	
FC	1988	51	95	3	2615	150	28.42	4	15	520	269	7	38.42	2-18	0	0	3.10	35	
SB	1990	58	58	3	1723	105*	31.32	1	10	96	78	1	78.00	1-0	0	0	4.87	24	

JACOBS, Stefan (Transvaal, Transvaal B) b Virginia 11.3.1966 RHB RFM

Cmp	Debut	M	I	NO	Runs	HS	Avge	100	50	Balls	Runs	Wkts	Avge	BB	5i	10m	RpO	ct	st
FC		7	9	2	178	85	25.42	0	1	1322	527	19	27.73	5-63	1	0	2.39	5	
SB		9	6	0	31	11	5.16	0	0	396	324	10	32.40	3-28	0	0	4.90	2	
FC	1987	55	86	19	1378	102*	20.56	2	4	9648	3651	154	23.70	6-35	5	0	2.27	37	
SB	1989	68	45	12	674	61	14.42	0	1	2963	2278	62	36.74	3-23	0	0	4.61	16	

JAMAL, Tahir (Easterns) b Johannesburg 12.3.1972 RHB OB

Cmp	Debut	M	I	NO	Runs	HS	Avge	100	50	Balls	Runs	Wkts	Avge	BB	5i	10m	RpO	ct	st
FC		1	2	0	22	19	11.00	0	0	24	12	0					3.00	2	
SB		7	6	1	104	63	20.80	0	1	54	47	1	47.00	1-18	0	0	5.22	2	
FC	1993	10	16	0	428	114	26.75	1	1	210	168	1	168.00	1-19	0	0	4.80	5	
SB	1993	17	14	1	170	63	13.07	0	1	54	47	1	47.00	1-18	0	0	5.22	3	

JOHNSON, Neil Clarkson (Natal, Leicestershire) b Salisbury, Rhodesia 24.1.1970 LHB RFM

Cmp	Debut	M	I	NO	Runs	HS	Avge	100	50	Balls	Runs	Wkts	Avge	BB	5i	10m	RpO	ct	st
FC		10	15	1	356	69	25.42	0	3	1233	575	20	28.75	3-52	0	0	2.79	15	
SB		15	15	2	509	146*	39.15	2	1	395	262	14	18.71	4-19	1	0	3.97	6	
FC	1989	64	97	14	2777	150	33.45	4	18	6608	3308	110	30.07	5-79	2	0	3.00	73	
SB	1989	49	44	5	1093	146*	28.02	2	5	1247	934	34	27.47	4-19	2	0	4.49	26	

JORDAAN, Deon (Free State, Free State to West Indies) b Bloemfontein 3.12.1970 LHB RM

Cmp	Debut	M	I	NO	Runs	HS	Avge	100	50	Balls	Runs	Wkts	Avge	BB	5i	10m	RpO	ct	st
FC		9	16	0	703	117	43.93	1	6	222	79	1	79.00	1-26	0	0	2.13	11	
SB		8	8	0	147	57	18.37	0	1									2	
FC	1991	50	92	5	2982	123	34.27	6	15	385	201	1	201.00	1-26	0	0	3.13	55	
SB	1992	39	38	0	997	116	26.23	1	7	182	153	6	25.50	1-5	0	0	5.04	13	

JORDAAN, Lucas Cornelius Rudolph (North West) b Johannesburg 20.7.1963 RHB SLA

Cmp	Debut	M	I	NO	Runs	HS	Avge	100	50	Balls	Runs	Wkts	Avge	BB	5i	10m	RpO	ct	st
FC		4	6	5	30	11*	30.00	0	0	816	354	8	44.25	3-78	0	0	2.60	0	
SB		4	3	2	1	1*	1.00	0	0	186	146	2	73.00	2-35	0	0	4.70	0	
FC	1990	36	39	19	165	19*	8.25	0	0	7427	3033	122	24.86	6-59	7	1	2.45	7	
SB	1994	17	9	5	13	6	3.25	0	0	838	500	12	41.66	2-15	0	0	3.57	3	

Cmp	Debut	M	I	NO	Runs	HS	Avge	100	50	Balls	Runs	Wkts	Avge	BB	5i	10m	RpO	ct	st

JOUBERT, Pierre (Northern Transvaal) b Pretoria 2.5.1978 RHB RFM

FC		4	8	2	28	9	4.66	0	0	621	286	10	28.60	3-52	0	0	2.76	2	
SB		1								54	37	1	37.00	1-37	0	0	4.11	0	
FC	1995	7	12	3	59	31*	6.55	0	0	1211	565	20	28.25	3-52	0	0	2.79	2	

KALLIS, Jacques Henry (Western Province, South Africa, Middlesex) b Pinelands 16.10.1975 RHB RM

Test		3	5	0	49	39	9.80	0	0	352	134	5	26.80	3-29	0	0	2.28	0	
FC		10	16	2	656	143	46.85	2	2	860	414	17	24.35	4-46	0	0	2.88	4	
Int		11	11	2	425	82	47.22	0	5	348	297	4	74.25	2-23	0	0	5.12	3	
SB		14	13	0	541	86	41.61	0	6	360	256	12	21.33	3-42	0	0	4.26	6	
Test	1995	5	7	0	57	39	8.14	0	0	376	136	5	27.20	3-29	0	0	2.17	1	
FC	1993	54	80	8	3271	186*	45.43	8	19	4523	2079	76	27.35	5-54	2	0	2.75	36	
Int	1995	25	24	6	700	82	38.88	0	6	570	459	8	57.37	3-21	0	0	4.83	5	
SB	1994	31	30	3	1026	116*	38.00	2	7	813	582	20	29.10	3-42	0	0	4.29	9	

KATZ, Gareth Sam (Natal B) b Pietermaritzburg 4.7.1971 LHB LF

| FC | | 3 | 5 | 0 | 168 | 58 | 33.60 | 0 | 2 | 6 | 17 | 0 | | | | | 17.00 | 2 | |
| FC | 1995 | 4 | 7 | 1 | 171 | 58 | 28.50 | 0 | 2 | 24 | 29 | 0 | | | | | 7.25 | 2 | |

KEMP, Justin (Eastern Province B) b Queenstown 2.10.1977 RHB RFM

| FC | | 1 | 2 | 1 | 45 | 35* | 45.00 | 0 | 0 | 120 | 79 | 1 | 79.00 | 1-67 | 0 | 0 | 3.95 | 0 | |

KIDWELL, Errol Wayne (Transvaal, Transvaal B) b Vereeniging 6.6.1975 RHB RF

FC		10	12	6	70	27*	11.66	0	0	1924	1044	32	32.62	4-54	0	0	3.25	2	
SB		9	4	4	4	2*		0	0	402	296	20	14.80	5-36	1	1	4.41	1	
FC	1995	16	16	8	99	27*	12.37	0	0	2971	1521	63	24.14	6-23	2	1	3.07	3	
SB	1995	13	5	4	5	2*	5.00	0	0	522	413	22	18.77	5-36	1	1	4.74	1	

KIP, Sven (North West) b Johannesburg 18.6.1970 RHB WK

SB		2	2	0	0	0	0.00	0	0									1	2
FC	1995	5	7	3	116	50*	29.00	0	1									7	
SB	1995	7	6	0	47	34	7.83	0	0									4	3

KIRSTEN, Gary (Western Province, South Africa, South Africa to India, South Africa to Kenya) b Cape Town 23.11.1967 LHB OB

Test		6	12	0	219	103	18.25	1	0									2	
FC		8	16	0	305	103	19.06	1	0	54	41	0					4.55	4	
Int		8	8	1	298	82	42.57	0	4									2	
SB		8	8	0	296	63	37.00	0	3									2	
Test	1993	29	53	2	1806	133	35.41	4	9	325	135	2	67.50	1-0	0	0	2.49	22	
FC	1987	109	196	19	7594	244	42.90	20	35	1625	779	20	38.95	6-68	1	0	2.87	83	
Int	1993	66	66	8	2723	188*	46.94	7	14	30	23	0					4.60	21	1
SB	1988	58	57	3	1299	104*	24.05	1	6	78	52	2	26.00	1-25	0	0	4.00	19	

KIRSTEN, Paul (Western Province, Western Province to Zimbabwe) b Cape Town 30.10.1969 RHB WK

FC		8	10	2	153	50	19.12	0	1									33	1
SB		16	11	7	103	19*	25.75	0	0									27	
FC	1992	37	53	6	932	87	19.82	0	5									123	10
SB	1990	38	24	10	307	40	21.92	0	0									49	3

KIRSTEN, Peter Noel (Border) b Pietermaritzburg 14.5.1955 RHB OB

FC		9	17	1	666	173*	41.62	2	2									3	
SB		10	10	2	218	68*	27.25	0	1									2	
Test	1991	12	22	2	626	104	31.30	1	4	54	30	0					3.33	8	
FC	1973	327	568	59	22635	271	44.46	57	107	10287	4682	117	40.01	6-48	2	0	2.73	190	
Int	1991	40	40	6	1293	97	38.02	0	9	183	152	6	25.33	3-31	0	0	4.98	11	
SB	1981	107	104	9	3555	134*	37.42	2	29	1264	859	24	35.79	3-7	0	0	4.07	43	

KLUSENER, Lance (Natal, South Africa, South Africa to India) b Durban 4.9.1971 LHB RFM

Test		5	9	2	229	102*	32.71	1	0	862	426	11	38.72	3-75	0	0	2.96	4	
FC		6	11	3	300	102*	37.50	1	0	1166	536	16	33.50	4-61	0	0	2.75	5	
Int		11	8	1	175	92	25.00	0	1	550	438	17	25.76	5-42	0	1	4.77	3	
SB		8	7	0	96	36	13.71	0	0	324	289	8	36.12	2-31	0	0	5.35	2	
Test	1996	7	12	3	282	102*	31.33	1	0	1327	684	21	32.57	8-64	1	0	3.09	6	
FC	1993	45	64	20	1563	105	35.52	3	5	7347	3804	161	23.62	8-34	6	1	3.10	28	
Int	1995	15	11	2	270	92	30.00	0	2	694	592	20	29.60	5-42	0	1	5.11	3	
SB	1993	27	23	5	657	91	36.50	0	5	1114	882	34	25.94	4-19	1	0	4.75	10	

KOEN, Louis Johannes (Eastern Province, South Africa) b Paarl 28.3.1967 RHB

FC		9	16	1	859	186	57.26	2	5	6	1	0					1.00	16	
Int		2	2	0	22	22	11.00	0	0									0	
SB		10	9	1	277	70	34.62	0	2									5	
FC	1987	60	103	11	3872	202*	42.08	7	22	6	1	0					1.00	82	
SB	1990	60	58	6	1671	107	32.13	2	8									23	

KOENIG, Sven Gaetan (Western Province, Western Province to Zimbabwe) b Durban 9.12.1973 LHB OB

FC		8	13	0	496	119	38.15	1	2	78	44	0					3.38	4	
SB		5	5	0	40	27	8.00	0	0									1	
FC	1993	40	68	3	2300	149*	35.38	3	13	98	53	0					3.24	25	
SB	1994	13	13	0	219	43	16.84	0	0									1	

Cmp	Debut	M	I	NO	Runs	HS	Avge	100	50	Balls	Runs	Wkts	Avge	BB	5i	10m	RpO	ct	st

KOORTZEN, Pieter Petrus Johannes (Griqualand West) b Kimberley 24.9.1979 RHB OB

| FC | | 1 | 2 | 0 | 44 | 28 | 22.00 | 0 | 0 | 96 | 78 | 2 | 39.00 | 2-78 | 0 | 0 | 4.87 | 1 | |

KOSTER, Ralph Alexander (Griqualand West) b Beaufort West 21.10.1968 RHB RM

FC		5	10	0	284	74	28.40	0	1									1	
SB		12	11	1	281	63	28.10	0	2									2	
FC	1992	18	31	3	1010	95	36.07	0	6	133	74	3	24.66	1-8	0	0	3.33	5	
SB	1992	27	25	4	599	77*	28.52	0	6									3	

KRUIS, Gideon Jacobus (Northern Transvaal) b Pretoria 9.5.1974 RHB RFM

| FC | | 3 | 6 | 3 | 7 | 6* | 2.33 | 0 | 0 | 375 | 233 | 2 | 116.50 | 1-72 | 0 | 0 | 3.72 | 0 | |
| FC | 1993 | 14 | 19 | 8 | 65 | 20 | 5.90 | 0 | 0 | 2120 | 984 | 32 | 30.75 | 5-36 | 1 | 0 | 2.78 | 3 | |

KUIPER, Adrian Paul (Boland) b Johannesburg 24.8.1959 RHB RM

FC		7	14	1	514	117*	39.53	1	3	586	259	5	51.80	3-56	0	0	2.65	3	
SB		9	9	2	309	79*	44.14	0	4	96	85	3	28.33	3-50	0	0	5.31	2	
Test	1991	1	2	0	34	34	17.00	0	0									1	
FC	1977	156	259	30	7597	161*	33.17	9	46	11757	5628	189	29.77	6-55	4	0	2.87	101	
Int	1991	25	23	7	539	63*	33.68	0	3	588	518	18	28.77	3-33	0	0	5.28	3	
SB	1981	116	109	17	2964	118	32.21	2	20	3301	2325	106	21.93	4-28	3	0	4.22	40	

LAING, Dean Ralph (Transvaal) b Durban 18.9.1970 RHB RM

FC		7	13	1	410	128	34.16	1	2	186	100	1	100.00	1-32	0	0	3.22	2	
SB		11	10	2	232	77	29.00	0	1	236	204	8	25.50	4-16	1	0	5.18	1	
FC	1989	61	99	10	2354	128	26.44	3	14	6082	2762	69	40.02	3-18	0	0	2.72	26	
SB	1989	69	56	7	1047	85	21.36	0	4	2548	1722	44	39.13	4-16	1	0	4.05	10	

LAVINE, Mark John (North West) b Barbados 4.3.1973 RHB RF

FC		5	9	0	227	107	25.22	1	0	900	434	18	24.11	4-58	0	0	2.89	6	
SB		8	6	0	104	58	17.33	0	1	364	344	5	68.80	2-58	0	0	5.67	4	
FC	1992	7	12	0	284	107	23.66	1	0	1002	482	19	25.36	4-58	0	0	2.88	6	

LEES, Patrick John (Easterns) b Johannesburg 15.3.1971 RHB OB

| FC | | 3 | 6 | 0 | 50 | 24 | 8.33 | 0 | 0 | 348 | 204 | 3 | 68.00 | 1-4 | 0 | 0 | 3.51 | 2 | |
| SB | | 3 | 2 | 0 | 7 | 6 | 3.50 | 0 | 0 | 84 | 78 | 0 | | | | | 5.57 | 1 | |

LERM, Johan Stephen (Easterns) b Boksburg 30.1.1968 RHB LM

FC		3	6	0	142	38	23.66	0	0	12	13	0					6.50	1	
SB		2	2	0	23	22	11.50	0	0									0	
FC	1993	6	12	0	245	56	20.41	0	1	18	23	0					7.66	2	
SB	1994	8	7	2	64	22*	12.80	0	0									3	

LIEBENBERG, Elmar (Boland) b Paarl 28.3.1973 LHB RM

| FC | | 3 | 6 | 0 | 61 | 20 | 10.16 | 0 | 0 | | | | | | | | | 7 | |
| FC | 1995 | 4 | 8 | 0 | 149 | 62 | 18.62 | 0 | 1 | | | | | | | | | 7 | |

LIEBENBERG, Gerhardus Frederick Johannes (Free State, Free State to West Indies) b Upington 7.4.1972 RHB RFM WK

FC		9	16	1	618	133*	41.20	1	3									7	
SB		10	8	2	300	85*	50.00	0	3									4	
FC	1989	85	148	8	5040	229	36.00	13	21	36	11	1	11.00	1-10	0	0	1.83	75	4
Int	1995	1	1	0	12	12	12.00	0	0									0	
SB	1989	62	54	10	1168	85*	26.54	0	9		.							42	4

LIGHT, Craig (Griqualand West) b Randburg 23.9.1972 RHB OB

FC		2	4	0	63	38	15.75	0	0	6	7	0					7.00	1	
SB		10	10	1	169	46	18.77	0	0	72	61	1	61.00	1-23	0	0	5.08	3	
FC	1993	19	34	1	966	121*	29.27	2	4	462	305	4	76.25	2-76	0	0	3.96	12	
SB	1994	11	11	1	46	46	17.90	0	0	72	61	1	61.00	1-23	0	0	5.08	3	

LOON, Gavin Ian (Western Province B) b Port Elizabeth 16.8.1970 LHB RM

| FC | | 1 | 2 | 0 | 7 | 5 | 3.50 | 0 | 0 | | | | | | | | | 0 | |

LOVE, Geoff Terry (Eastern Province, Eastern Province B) b Port Elizabeth 19.9.1976 RHB OB

| FC | | 6 | 4 | 2 | 53 | 25 | 26.50 | 0 | 0 | 1509 | 521 | 16 | 32.56 | 4-38 | 0 | 0 | 2.07 | 2 | |
| FC | 1995 | 10 | 8 | 3 | 129 | 35 | 25.80 | 0 | 0 | 1797 | 738 | 17 | 43.41 | 4-38 | 0 | 0 | 2.46 | 2 | |

LYLE, Rowan Andrew (Transvaal, Transvaal B) b Kokstad 1.12.1968 RHB RFM

FC		3	3	2	19	10	19.00	0	0	372	203	5	40.60	3-40	0	0	3.27	1	
SB		2	1	1	2	2*		0	0	64	55	1	55.00	1-47	0	0	5.15	1	
FC	1988	40	55	23	288	35*	9.00	0	0	6864	3329	105	31.70	6-63	2	1	2.90	8	
SB	1989	28	10	4	32	13	5.33	0	0	1345	946	25	37.84	3-48	0	0	4.22	6	

McDONALD, Duncan Iain (Natal B) b Pietermaritzburg 25.6.1972 RHB RM

| FC | | 1 | 2 | 0 | 7 | 6 | 3.50 | 0 | 0 | 36 | 44 | 0 | | | | | 7.33 | 2 | |
| FC | 1995 | 2 | 3 | 0 | 7 | 6 | 2.33 | 0 | 0 | 96 | 85 | 1 | 85.00 | 1-29 | 0 | 0 | 5.31 | 2 | |

MacHELM, Dean Quinton (Western Province, Western Province B) b Kuils River 18.4.1971 LHB SLA

| FC | | 6 | 7 | 2 | 48 | 15* | 9.60 | 0 | 0 | 1021 | 490 | 14 | 35.00 | 3-76 | 0 | 0 | 2.87 | 3 | |
| FC | 1992 | 31 | 35 | 15 | 122 | 15* | 6.10 | 0 | 0 | 5811 | 2477 | 86 | 28.80 | 7-85 | 3 | 1 | 2.55 | 11 | |

McKENZIE, Neil Douglas (Transvaal) b Johannesburg 24.11.1975 RHB RM

| FC | | 9 | 17 | 2 | 511 | 139 | 34.06 | 1 | 3 | 18 | 14 | 0 | | | | | 4.66 | 4 | |
| SB | | 11 | 10 | 1 | 356 | 118 | 39.55 | 2 | 1 | | | | | | | | | 4 | |

Cmp	Debut	M	I	NO	Runs	HS	Avge	100	50	Balls	Runs	Wkts	Avge	BB	5i	10m	RpO	ct	st
FC	1994	19	34	3	1127	150*	36.35	3	7	78	32	1	32.00	1-11	0	0	2.46	13	
SB	1995	24	21	2	632	118	33.26	2	3	84	79	1	79.00	1-17	0	0	5.64	6	

McMILLAN, Brian Mervin (Western Province, South Africa, South Africa to India, South Africa to Kenya) b Welkom 22.12.1963 RHB RFM

Cmp	Debut	M	I	NO	Runs	HS	Avge	100	50	Balls	Runs	Wkts	Avge	BB	5i	10m	RpO	ct	st
Test		5	10	4	415	103*	69.16	1	4	565	250	7	35.71	2-27	0	0	2.65	5	
FC		7	13	5	490	103*	61.25	1	5	733	330	8	41.25	2-27	0	0	2.70	7	
SB		5	5	1	106	33	26.50	0	0	84	54	4	13.50	2-24	0	0	3.85	3	
Test	1992	31	51	11	1702	113	42.55	3	11	5340	2238	73	30.65	4-65	0	0	2.51	41	
FC	1984	124	197	34	6554	140	40.20	13	36	17901	7960	289	27.54	5-35	4	0	2.66	134	
Int	1991	68	46	16	788	127	26.26	1	0	3179	2268	62	36.58	4-32	1	0	4.28	38	
SB	1985	71	60	19	1320	75	32.19	0	7	2587	1702	59	28.84	4-36	2	0	3.94	27	

MacQUEEN, Robert Bruce (Natal B, Natal) b Durban 6.9.1977 RHB OB

Cmp	Debut	M	I	NO	Runs	HS	Avge	100	50	Balls	Runs	Wkts	Avge	BB	5i	10m	RpO	ct	st
FC		2	4	1	63	42	21.00	0	0	363	231	8	28.87	4-44	0	0	3.81	4	
SB		1								48	46	0					5.75	0	

MALL, Ashraf (Natal B) b Durban 8.10.1978 LHB

Cmp	Debut	M	I	NO	Runs	HS	Avge	100	50	Balls	Runs	Wkts	Avge	BB	5i	10m	RpO	ct	st
FC		2	4	0	23	14	5.75	0	0									0	

MANACK, Hussein Ahmed (Transvaal, Transvaal B) b Pretoria 10.4.1968 RHB RM

Cmp	Debut	M	I	NO	Runs	HS	Avge	100	50	Balls	Runs	Wkts	Avge	BB	5i	10m	RpO	ct	st
FC		7	13	2	414	173	37.63	2	0									2	
FC	1991	24	43	5	1218	173	32.05	3	4	108	62	1	62.00	1-17	0	0	3.44	11	
SB	1991	2	2	0	28	15	14.00	0	0									0	

MARON, Ryan (Western Province, Western Province B, Western Province to Zimbabwe) b Cape Town 24.2.1975 LHB SLA

Cmp	Debut	M	I	NO	Runs	HS	Avge	100	50	Balls	Runs	Wkts	Avge	BB	5i	10m	RpO	ct	st
FC		6	10	1	257	65*	28.55	0	1	23	21	1	21.00	1-4	0	0	5.47	2	
FC	1995	8	14	1	312	65*	24.00	0	1	53	46	2	23.00	1-4	0	0	5.20	2	

MARSH, Terence Alan (Easterns) b Benoni 19.5.1970 RHB LFM

Cmp	Debut	M	I	NO	Runs	HS	Avge	100	50	Balls	Runs	Wkts	Avge	BB	5i	10m	RpO	ct	st
FC		5	10	2	269	61	33.62	0	2	518	302	5	60.40	2-71	0	0	3.49	1	
SB		9	9	2	161	72*	23.00	0	1	320	286	8	35.75	4-34	1	0	5.36	2	
FC	1991	32	49	9	1084	106	27.10	1	8	2890	1503	47	31.97	4-22	0	0	3.12	29	
SB	1991	38	35	8	702	91	26.00	0	5	1384	1162	30	38.73	4-34	1	0	5.03	5	

MARTIN, Nico (Northern Transvaal) b Umtali, Rhodesia 4.2.1972 RHB RM

Cmp	Debut	M	I	NO	Runs	HS	Avge	100	50	Balls	Runs	Wkts	Avge	BB	5i	10m	RpO	ct	st
FC		1	2	0	6	6	3.00	0	0	48	23	0					2.87	0	
SB		8	8	0	107	35	13.37	0	0	59	42	4	10.50	4-19	1	0	4.27	6	
FC	1991	16	27	4	658	89*	28.60	0	5	1284	732	14	52.28	4-67	0	0	3.42	17	
SB	1993	12	11	2	164	36*	18.22	0	0	161	114	5	22.80	4-19	1	0	4.24	8	

MARTYN, Aubrey (Western Province, Western Province to Zimbabwe) b Pretoria 23.6.1972 LHB LFM

Cmp	Debut	M	I	NO	Runs	HS	Avge	100	50	Balls	Runs	Wkts	Avge	BB	5i	10m	RpO	ct	st
FC		3	3	0	23	17	7.66	0	0	735	317	13	24.38	4-76	0	0	2.58	0	
SB		8	1	0	0	0	0.00	0	0	378	264	11	24.00	2-22	0	0	4.19	1	
FC	1992	27	32	4	153	20	5.46	0	0	5798	2492	108	23.07	6-22	4	0	2.57	11	
SB	1993	27	8	6	35	14*	17.50	0	0	1281	857	43	19.93	4-52	1	0	4.01	4	

MASIKAZANA, Lulama (Eastern Province, Eastern Province B) b Port Elizabeth 6.2.1973 RHB WK

Cmp	Debut	M	I	NO	Runs	HS	Avge	100	50	Balls	Runs	Wkts	Avge	BB	5i	10m	RpO	ct	st
FC		5	5	0	75	26	15.00	0	0									14	2
SB		1	1	0	1	1	1.00	0	0									1	
FC	1993	20	21	2	285	49	15.00	0	0									50	8

MATTHEWS, Craig Russell (Western Province, South Africa, South Africa to Kenya) b Cape Town 15.2.1965 RHB RFM

Cmp	Debut	M	I	NO	Runs	HS	Avge	100	50	Balls	Runs	Wkts	Avge	BB	5i	10m	RpO	ct	st
FC		6	5	2	183	96	61.00	0	2	1003	564	15	37.60	4-44	0	0	3.37	4	
Int		2								31	35	0					6.77	0	
SB		8	4	2	8	6*	4.00	0	0	278	202	4	50.50	1-17	0	0	4.35	3	
Test	1992	18	25	6	348	62*	18.31	0	1	3980	1502	52	28.88	5-42	2	0	2.26	4	
FC	1986	89	100	27	1403	105	19.21	1	3	15549	6318	262	24.11	6-22	9	0	2.43	45	
Int	1991	56	22	9	141	26	10.84	0	0	3003	1975	79	25.00	4-10	3	0	3.94	10	
SB	1987	65	26	14	186	31*	15.50	0	0	3141	1920	81	23.70	4-24	2	0	3.66	15	

MEYER, Esias Engelbertus (Easterns) b Bethal 18.4.1978 RHB WK

Cmp	Debut	M	I	NO	Runs	HS	Avge	100	50	Balls	Runs	Wkts	Avge	BB	5i	10m	RpO	ct	st
SB		5	5	1	42	19*	10.50	0	0									1	

MEYER, Jonathan Reid (Easterns) b Kroonstad 23.6.1965 RHB RFM

Cmp	Debut	M	I	NO	Runs	HS	Avge	100	50	Balls	Runs	Wkts	Avge	BB	5i	10m	RpO	ct	st
FC		4	6	3	11	5	3.66	0	0	446	197	11	17.90	6-43	1	0	2.65	0	
SB		9	6	1	11	9	2.20	0	0	368	256	12	21.33	4-12	1	0	4.17	2	
FC	1990	24	30	4	234	32	9.00	0	0	2770	1423	61	23.32	6-43	1	0	3.08	4	
SB	1994	26	18	6	71	19*	5.91	0	0	1050	746	25	29.84	4-12	1	0	4.26	5	

MILLNS, David James (Boland, Leicestershire, Leicestershire to South Africa) b Clipstone, England 27.2.1965 LHB RF

Cmp	Debut	M	I	NO	Runs	HS	Avge	100	50	Balls	Runs	Wkts	Avge	BB	5i	10m	RpO	ct	st
FC		5	10	1	193	44	21.44	0	0	708	399	10	39.90	4-64	0	0	3.38	0	
SB		7	5	2	52	25	17.33	0	0	345	247	6	41.16	2-30	0	0	4.29	1	
FC	1988	145	171	51	2455	121	20.45	3	6	22747	12973	465	27.89	9-37	21	4	3.42	64	

MITCHELL, Timothy John (Western Province B) b Cape Town 24.8.1968 RHB RM

Cmp	Debut	M	I	NO	Runs	HS	Avge	100	50	Balls	Runs	Wkts	Avge	BB	5i	10m	RpO	ct	st
FC		1	2	0	5	4	2.50	0	0	30	20	0					4.00	2	
FC	1989	29	48	12	1192	90	33.11	0	9	2996	1185	42	28.21	3-0	0	0	2.37	13	
SB	1994	6	5	1	42	19	14.00	0	0	288	202	4	50.50	2-38	0	0	4.20	0	

Cmp	Debut	M	I	NO	Runs	HS	Avge	100	50	Balls	Runs	Wkts	Avge	BB	5i	10m	RpO	ct	st

MITCHLEY, Mark John (Easterns) b Johannesburg 15.3.1967 LHB RM

Cmp	Debut	M	I	NO	Runs	HS	Avge	100	50	Balls	Runs	Wkts	Avge	BB	5i	10m	RpO	ct	st
FC		5	10	1	462	201*	51.33	2	1									0	
SB		8	8	0	236	65	29.50	0	2									0	
FC	1986	40	70	7	1999	201*	31.73	4	8	308	139	2	69.50	1-5	0	0	2.70	33	
SB	1986	25	24	3	546	65	26.00	0	4	48	21	0					2.62	3	

MOLEON, Eugene Owen (Western Province B) b Cape Town 2.3.1977 RHB RFM

Cmp	Debut	M	I	NO	Runs	HS	Avge	100	50	Balls	Runs	Wkts	Avge	BB	5i	10m	RpO	ct	st
FC		2	3	2	29	10*	29.00	0	0	276	173	3	57.66	2-51	0	0	3.76	0	

MOODLEY, Sagren (Natal B) b Pietermaritzburg 16.7.1971 RHB SLA

Cmp	Debut	M	I	NO	Runs	HS	Avge	100	50	Balls	Runs	Wkts	Avge	BB	5i	10m	RpO	ct	st
FC		1	2	1	14	8	14.00	0	0	30	14	0					2.80	0	

MORGAN, Grant (Eastern Province, Eastern Province B) b Port Elizabeth 19.5.1971 RHB WK

Cmp	Debut	M	I	NO	Runs	HS	Avge	100	50	Balls	Runs	Wkts	Avge	BB	5i	10m	RpO	ct	st
FC		8	11	2	273	65*	30.33	0	2									18	2
SB		9	4	0	115	56	28.75	0	1									11	3
FC	1993	27	43	11	800	65*	25.00	0	3									51	5
SB	1993	25	17	4	236	56	18.15	0	1									27	6

MYBURGH, George Wayne (Easterns) b Cape Town 1.2.1977 RHB RM

Cmp	Debut	M	I	NO	Runs	HS	Avge	100	50	Balls	Runs	Wkts	Avge	BB	5i	10m	RpO	ct	st
FC		5	10	0	221	45	22.10	0	0									5	
SB		7	7	1	154	33	25.66	0	0									0	

MYERS, Jodi Henre (Griqualand West) b Cape Town 6.9.1973 RHB WK

Cmp	Debut	M	I	NO	Runs	HS	Avge	100	50	Balls	Runs	Wkts	Avge	BB	5i	10m	RpO	ct	st
FC		1	2	0	4	4	2.00	0	0									1	
FC	1994	3	6	0	55	37	9.16	0	0									3	3

NASH, Brandon Aubrey (Natal B) b Durban 26.7.1969 RHB OB

Cmp	Debut	M	I	NO	Runs	HS	Avge	100	50	Balls	Runs	Wkts	Avge	BB	5i	10m	RpO	ct	st
FC		3	4	0	168	64	42.00	0	2	18	16	0					5.33	1	
FC	1991	14	24	2	673	129*	30.59	1	3	1099	581	13	44.69	3-38	0	0	3.17	7	
SB	1991	6	6	1	109	60*	21.80	0	1	18	31	0					10.33	0	

NEL, Andre (Easterns) b Germiston 15.7.1977 RHB RFM

Cmp	Debut	M	I	NO	Runs	HS	Avge	100	50	Balls	Runs	Wkts	Avge	BB	5i	10m	RpO	ct	st
FC		2	3	2	13	11*	13.00	0	0	258	121	3	40.33	1-30	0	0	2.81	1	

NICOLSON, Shawn (North West) b Virginia 2.7.1972 RHB OB

Cmp	Debut	M	I	NO	Runs	HS	Avge	100	50	Balls	Runs	Wkts	Avge	BB	5i	10m	RpO	ct	st
FC		5	10	0	215	70	21.50	0	2	66	28	1	28.00	1-19	0	0	2.54	10	
SB		9	8	2	185	91*	30.83	0	1	258	231	9	25.66	3-33	0	0	5.37	2	
FC	1993	20	34	2	900	117*	28.12	3	4	189	90	3	30.00	1-4	0	0	2.85	20	
SB	1995	19	18	4	335	91*	23.92	0	2	426	377	10	37.70	3-33	0	0	5.30	7	

NORRIS, Craig Reginald (Easterns) b Johannesburg 11.9.1963 LHB LM

Cmp	Debut	M	I	NO	Runs	HS	Avge	100	50	Balls	Runs	Wkts	Avge	BB	5i	10m	RpO	ct	st
FC		5	10	0	331	75	33.10	0	4	762	363	18	20.16	4-14	0	0	2.85	1	
SB		9	8	0	204	87	25.50	0	1	204	160	2	80.00	1-28	0	0	4.70	1	
FC	1982	71	123	16	3451	132*	32.25	5	18	4930	2579	102	25.28	7-31	2	0	3.13	47	
SB	1984	30	26	3	511	87	22.21	0	2	342	287	7	41.00	3-42	0	0	5.03	5	

NTINI, Makhaya (Border) b Zwelitsha 6.7.1977 RHB RF

Cmp	Debut	M	I	NO	Runs	HS	Avge	100	50	Balls	Runs	Wkts	Avge	BB	5i	10m	RpO	ct	st
FC		9	9	2	16	5	2.28	0	0	1333	847	25	33.88	6-49	1	0	3.81	0	
SB		1								18	17	0					5.66	0	
FC	1995	17	22	4	85	19*	4.72	0	0	2473	1477	42	35.16	6-49	1	0	3.58	0	
SB	1995	3	1	1	3	3*		0	0	102	86	0					5.05	0	

OOSTHUIZEN, Riaan Carel (Boland) b Cape Town 3.5.1972 RHB WK

Cmp	Debut	M	I	NO	Runs	HS	Avge	100	50	Balls	Runs	Wkts	Avge	BB	5i	10m	RpO	ct	st
FC		4	8	1	88	32*	12.57	0	0									6	2
SB		4	3	0	47	41	15.66	0	0									3	1
FC	1991	5	10	1	98	32*	10.88	0	0									9	2

OUTRAM, Gary (North West) b Johannesburg 13.2.1976 RHB

Cmp	Debut	M	I	NO	Runs	HS	Avge	100	50	Balls	Runs	Wkts	Avge	BB	5i	10m	RpO	ct	st
SB		3	3	0	16	14	5.33	0	0	6	10	0					10.00	1	

PALFRAMAN, Steven John (Border) b East London 12.5.1970 RHB WK

Cmp	Debut	M	I	NO	Runs	HS	Avge	100	50	Balls	Runs	Wkts	Avge	BB	5i	10m	RpO	ct	st
FC		2	3	0	65	30	21.66	0	0									4	
SB		9	9	1	183	73	22.87	0	1									6	3
FC	1990	53	82	7	1560	123	20.80	1	5									147	17
Int	1995	7	4	0	55	28	13.75	0	0									9	
SB	1991	46	38	7	856	90*	27.61	0	6									50	10

PANGARKER, Hassan (Western Province B) b Elsies River, Cape Town 31.8.1968 LHB

Cmp	Debut	M	I	NO	Runs	HS	Avge	100	50	Balls	Runs	Wkts	Avge	BB	5i	10m	RpO	ct	st
FC		4	6	0	345	144	57.50	1	1									4	
FC	1991	9	16	0	508	144	31.75	1	1									8	

PARSONS, Nigel John (Natal B) b Durban 10.9.1968 RHB

Cmp	Debut	M	I	NO	Runs	HS	Avge	100	50	Balls	Runs	Wkts	Avge	BB	5i	10m	RpO	ct	st
FC		2	4	0	100	84	25.00	0	1									1	

PAYNE, Dean Geoffrey (Western Province B) b Claremont, Cape Town 13.1.1969 LHB RFM

Cmp	Debut	M	I	NO	Runs	HS	Avge	100	50	Balls	Runs	Wkts	Avge	BB	5i	10m	RpO	ct	st
FC		5	7	3	131	41*	32.75	0	0	1097	434	24	18.08	5-20	2	0	2.37	2	
FC	1988	32	35	18	259	41*	15.23	0	0	5766	2637	105	25.11	7-63	3	0	2.74	6	
SB	1991	5	2	2	2	2*		0	0	285	155	11	14.09	5-40	0	1	3.26	3	

PIENAAR, Roy Francois (Northern Transvaal) b Johannesburg 17.7.1961 RHB RM/OB

Cmp	Debut	M	I	NO	Runs	HS	Avge	100	50	Balls	Runs	Wkts	Avge	BB	5i	10m	RpO	ct	st
FC		6	11	0	367	95	33.36	0	3									0	
SB		11	11	1	252	54	25.20	0	1									1	
FC	1977	194	337	27	10723	153	34.59	18	60	10388	5079	153	33.19	5-24	3	0	2.93	78	
SB	1981	118	114	9	3350	124*	31.90	2	27	1208	1076	28	38.42	4-37	1	0	5.34	15	

PISTORIUS, Ivan (Northern Transvaal) b Durban 8.7.1970 LHB WK

Cmp	Debut	M	I	NO	Runs	HS	Avge	100	50	Balls	Runs	Wkts	Avge	BB	5i	10m	RpO	ct	st
FC		8	15	3	151	33	12.58	0	0									24	
FC	1990	22	41	6	634	84	18.11	0	4									53	1
SB	1995	6	3	3	24	22*		0	0									10	1

PLAYER, Bradley Todd (Free State) b Benoni 18.1.1967 RHB RFM

Cmp	Debut	M	I	NO	Runs	HS	Avge	100	50	Balls	Runs	Wkts	Avge	BB	5i	10m	RpO	ct	st
FC		7	10	2	221	133*	27.62	1	0	1227	588	24	24.50	4-41	0	0	2.87	4	
SB		10	10	2	148	39*	18.50	0	0	491	391	11	35.54	3-31	0	0	4.77	1	
FC	1984	63	92	20	1442	133*	20.02	2	1	9121	4451	135	32.97	6-43	2	0	2.92	27	
SB	1986	78	52	13	724	83	18.56	0	2	3495	2348	80	29.35	5-27	3	1	4.03	8	

POLLOCK, Andrew Graeme (Easterns) b Port Elizabeth 14.11.1969 LHB RFM

Cmp	Debut	M	I	NO	Runs	HS	Avge	100	50	Balls	Runs	Wkts	Avge	BB	5i	10m	RpO	ct	st
FC		5	9	3	187	56*	31.16	0	1	705	333	12	27.75	4-52	0	0	2.83	2	
SB		8	6	2	23	14	5.75	0	0	282	198	3	66.00	1-10	0	0	4.21	1	
FC	1991	20	23	10	292	56*	22.46	0	1	2957	1459	53	27.52	4-52	0	0	2.96	4	

POLLOCK, Graeme Anthony (Transvaal B) b Port Elizabeth 7.4.1973 LHB OB

Cmp	Debut	M	I	NO	Runs	HS	Avge	100	50	Balls	Runs	Wkts	Avge	BB	5i	10m	RpO	ct	st
FC		5	9	0	199	115	22.11	1	0									1	
FC	1991	24	43	4	1254	115	32.15	3	5	119	69	3	23.00	3-21	0	0	3.47	10	
SB	1991	14	12	3	162	94*	18.00	0	1									3	

POLLOCK, Shaun Maclean (Natal, South Africa) b Port Elizabeth 16.7.1973 RHB RFM

Cmp	Debut	M	I	NO	Runs	HS	Avge	100	50	Balls	Runs	Wkts	Avge	BB	5i	10m	RpO	ct	st
Test		5	10	3	211	79	30.14	0	1	804	342	14	24.42	3-25	0	0	2.55	1	
FC		9	17	3	471	79	33.64	0	3	1614	660	36	18.33	5-48	1	0	2.45	4	
Int		15	10	4	273	75	45.50	0	1	828	562	21	26.76	4-33	1	0	4.07	1	
SB		12	11	2	85	23	9.44	0	0	515	372	15	24.80	3-30	0	0	4.33	3	
Test	1995	10	16	4	344	79	28.66	0	1	1703	719	30	23.96	5-32	1	0	2.53	3	
FC	1991	51	73	12	1875	150*	30.73	2	7	9670	3987	182	21.90	7-33	7	1	2.47	20	
Int	1995	33	21	10	433	75	39.36	0	2	1813	1209	47	25.72	4-33	2	0	4.00	6	
SB	1992	42	25	6	185	23	9.73	0	0	1758	1135	48	23.64	3-25	0	0	3.87	9	

POOLE, Ezra Glynn (North West) b Cape Town 10.2.1975 RHB WK

Cmp	Debut	M	I	NO	Runs	HS	Avge	100	50	Balls	Runs	Wkts	Avge	BB	5i	10m	RpO	ct	st
FC		5	9	2	112	43	16.00	0	0									12	3
SB		5																	4	

POPE, Steven Charles (Border) b East London 15.11.1972 RHB RM WK

Cmp	Debut	M	I	NO	Runs	HS	Avge	100	50	Balls	Runs	Wkts	Avge	BB	5i	10m	RpO	ct	st
FC		8	13	3	417	103	41.70	1	1	198	147	2	73.50	1-35	0	0	4.45	6	
SB		5	4	0	92	42	23.00	0	0	24	20	0					5.00	1	
FC	1992	33	57	6	1233	103	24.17	1	4	1146	747	28	26.67	7-62	2	0	3.91	34	
SB	1992	24	21	4	336	42*	19.76	0	0	60	62	1	62.00	1-42	0	0	6.20	11	1

POTHAS, Nic (Transvaal) b Johannesburg 18.11.1973 RHB WK

Cmp	Debut	M	I	NO	Runs	HS	Avge	100	50	Balls	Runs	Wkts	Avge	BB	5i	10m	RpO	ct	st
FC		9	15	2	344	100*	26.46	1	1									30	6
SB		11	10	3	160	44	22.85	0	0									10	3
FC	1993	41	66	10	1849	147	33.01	2	9	6	5	0					5.00	130	14
SB	1993	38	32	9	694	101	30.17	1	3									33	7

PRETORIUS, Nicolaas Willem (Free State, Free State to West Indies) b Ventersdorp 8.3.1969 RHB RFM

Cmp	Debut	M	I	NO	Runs	HS	Avge	100	50	Balls	Runs	Wkts	Avge	BB	5i	10m	RpO	ct	st
FC		5	10	3	38	14	5.42	0	0	745	405	16	25.31	4-26	0	0	3.26	4	
SB		5	1	0	20	20	20.00	0	0	240	226	5	45.20	2-44	0	0	5.65	2	
FC	1986	53	71	25	546	33	11.86	0	0	9581	5531	161	34.35	5-60	4	0	3.46	17	
SB	1993	22	10	5	53	20	10.60	0	0	989	856	26	32.92	3-33	0	0	5.19	8	

PRINCE, Ashwell Gavin (Eastern Province, Eastern Province B) b Port Elizabeth 28.5.1977 LHB

Cmp	Debut	M	I	NO	Runs	HS	Avge	100	50	Balls	Runs	Wkts	Avge	BB	5i	10m	RpO	ct	st
FC		6	10	1	333	125*	37.00	1	2									5	
SB		3	1	0	12	12	12.00	0	0									0	
FC	1995	11	17	1	498	125*	31.12	1	3									6	

PRINGLE, Meyrick Wayne (Western Province, Western Province to Zimbabwe) b Adelaide 22.6.1966 RHB RFM

Cmp	Debut	M	I	NO	Runs	HS	Avge	100	50	Balls	Runs	Wkts	Avge	BB	5i	10m	RpO	ct	st
FC		8	6	0	9	6	1.50	0	0	2071	1057	30	35.23	4-26	0	0	3.06	7	
SB		10	6	2	30	14*	7.50	0	0	490	369	14	26.35	3-32	0	0	4.51	1	
Test	1991	4	6	2	67	33	16.75	0	0	652	270	5	54.00	2-62	0	0	2.48	0	
FC	1985	92	118	21	1671	105	17.22	1	6	17986	8529	332	25.68	7-60	14	2	2.84	27	
Int	1991	17	8	3	48	13*	9.60	0	0	870	604	22	27.45	4-11	1	0	4.16	2	
SB	1987	74	36	12	270	31	11.25	0	0	3636	2491	99	25.16	6-30	2	2	4.11	14	

PRYKE, David John (Natal) b Welkom 26.11.1970 RHB RFM

Cmp	Debut	M	I	NO	Runs	HS	Avge	100	50	Balls	Runs	Wkts	Avge	BB	5i	10m	RpO	ct	st
SB		5	2	1	11	11*	11.00	0	0	156	106	4	26.50	3-21	0	0	4.07	1	
FC	1990	20	17	10	211	48	30.14	0	0	2858	1188	55	21.60	6-27	2	0	2.49	9	
SB	1991	14	7	4	29	14*	9.66	0	0	612	393	7	56.14	3-21	0	0	3.85	1	

RADFORD, Glen (North West) b Luanshya, Northern Rhodesia 27.2.1962 LHB RFM

Cmp	Debut	M	I	NO	Runs	HS	Avge	100	50	Balls	Runs	Wkts	Avge	BB	5i	10m	RpO	ct	st
FC		1	2	0	12	12	6.00	0	0	210	119	1	119.00	1-59	0	0	3.40	1	
FC	1991	16	18	2	154	40*	9.62	0	0	2146	1103	40	27.57	6-70	2	0	3.08	6	
SB	1993	5	4	0	31	15	7.75	0	0	192	212	4	53.00	1-25	0	0	6.62	1	

RADFORD, Wayne Reginald (Easterns) b Luanshya, Northern Rhodesia 29.8.1958 RHB LB

Cmp	Debut	M	I	NO	Runs	HS	Avge	100	50	Balls	Runs	Wkts	Avge	BB	5i	10m	RpO	ct	st
FC		1	2	0	30	28	15.00	0	0	101	46	0					2.73	0	
SB		3	3	0	81	44	27.00	0	0									1	
FC	1977	18	32	1	859	157	27.70	2	1	797	417	6	69.50	4-119	0	0	3.13	8	
SB	1993	28	27	0	626	101	23.18	1	3	24	29	0					7.25	10	

	Cmp	Debut	M	I	NO	Runs	HS	Avge	100	50	Balls	Runs	Wkts	Avge	BB	5i	10m	RpO	ct	st

RADLEY, Philip Johannes Lourens (Free State, Free State to West Indies) b Bloemfontein 7.2.1969 RHB WK

	Cmp	Debut	M	I	NO	Runs	HS	Avge	100	50	Balls	Runs	Wkts	Avge	BB	5i	10m	RpO	ct	st
FC			9	13	5	261	58*	32.62	0	1									28	2
SB			10	7	3	88	43*	22.00	0	0									11	3
FC		1989	59	80	22	1108	58*	19.10	0	1	6	0	0					0.00	165	14
SB		1990	50	28	10	232	43*	12.88	0	0									55	6

REDDY, Desigan (Natal B) b Durban 13.12.1979 LHB RM

	Cmp	Debut	M	I	NO	Runs	HS	Avge	100	50	Balls	Runs	Wkts	Avge	BB	5i	10m	RpO	ct	st
FC			1								87	39	2	19.50	2-39	0	0	2.68	0	

RHODES, Jonathan Neil (Natal, South Africa, South Africa to India, South Africa to Kenya) b Pietermaritzburg 27.7.1969 RHB RM

	Cmp	Debut	M	I	NO	Runs	HS	Avge	100	50	Balls	Runs	Wkts	Avge	BB	5i	10m	RpO	ct	st
Test			1	2	0	30	22	15.00	0	0									0	
FC			7	11	2	589	156*	65.44	3	0									7	
Int			15	14	5	420	83*	46.66	0	3									10	
SB			8	8	1	219	85	31.28	0	1	12	3	0					1.50	3	
Test		1992	29	47	5	1267	101*	30.16	1	7	12	5	0					2.50	16	
FC		1988	96	153	15	4839	156*	35.06	8	26	126	56	1	56.00	1-13	0	0	2.66	69	
Int		1991	110	102	19	2639	121	31.79	1	11									42	
SB		1988	55	53	9	1240	86*	28.18	0	8	36	16	2	8.00	1-2	0	0	2.66	23	

RICHARDSON, David John (Eastern Province, South Africa, South Africa to India, South Africa to Kenya) b Johannesburg 16.9.1959 RHB WK

	Cmp	Debut	M	I	NO	Runs	HS	Avge	100	50	Balls	Runs	Wkts	Avge	BB	5i	10m	RpO	ct	st
Test			6	10	2	211	72*	26.37	0	1									23	1
FC			7	11	2	252	72*	28.00	0	1									25	1
Int			15	7	3	39	15*	9.75	0	0									13	
Test		1991	37	56	7	1273	109	25.97	1	8									134	1
FC		1977	189	295	48	6772	134	27.41	6	36									549	36
Int		1991	108	69	28	793	53	19.34	0	1									131	15
SB		1981	86	77	18	1301	94	22.05	0	4									81	6

RICHARDSON, Richard Benjamin (Northern Transvaal) b Five Islands, Antigua 12.1.1962 RHB RM

	Cmp	Debut	M	I	NO	Runs	HS	Avge	100	50	Balls	Runs	Wkts	Avge	BB	5i	10m	RpO	ct	st
FC			6	11	0	254	69	23.09	0	3	24	11	1	11.00	1-11	0	0	2.75	5	
SB			11	11	0	194	55	17.63	0	1									2	
Test		1983	86	146	12	5949	194	44.39	16	27	66	18	0					1.63	90	
FC		1981	223	369	29	14204	194	41.77	37	67	510	249	7	35.57	5-40	1	0	2.92	203	
Int		1983	224	217	30	6248	122	33.41	5	44	58	46	1	46.00	1-4	0	0	4.75	74	

RINDEL, Michael John Raymond (Northern Transvaal) b Durban 9.2.1963 LHB LFM

	Cmp	Debut	M	I	NO	Runs	HS	Avge	100	50	Balls	Runs	Wkts	Avge	BB	5i	10m	RpO	ct	st
FC			6	12	0	230	60	19.16	0	1	426	221	6	36.83	2-45	0	0	3.11	3	
SB			14	14	1	766	121	58.92	3	4	294	237	6	39.50	2-26	0	0	4.83	5	
FC		1983	91	169	15	5662	174	36.76	11	29	2779	1438	36	39.94	2-13	0	0	3.10	58	
Int		1994	8	8	1	215	106	30.71	1	0	114	89	3	29.66	2-15	0	0	4.68	4	
SB		1986	79	74	12	2344	133*	37.80	5	16	1038	837	25	33.48	4-28	1	0	4.83	21	

ROE, Garth Anthony (Griqualand West) b Port Elizabeth 9.7.1973 RHB RFM

	Cmp	Debut	M	I	NO	Runs	HS	Avge	100	50	Balls	Runs	Wkts	Avge	BB	5i	10m	RpO	ct	st
FC			8	13	5	71	21*	8.87	0	0	1797	901	21	42.90	4-74	0	0	3.00	4	
SB			12	4	4	12	8*		0	0	558	452	14	32.28	5-49	0	1	4.86	1	
FC		1993	28	36	14	149	21*	6.77	0	0	4706	2101	60	35.01	4-42	0	0	2.67	6	
SB		1994	27	6	5	18	8*	18.00	0	0	1269	965	26	37.11	5-49	1	1	4.56	2	

ROSSOUW, Daniel (North West) b Port Elizabeth 30.4.1970 RHB RM

	Cmp	Debut	M	I	NO	Runs	HS	Avge	100	50	Balls	Runs	Wkts	Avge	BB	5i	10m	RpO	ct	st
FC			4	7	1	118	49	19.66	0	0	630	332	17	19.52	5-61	1	0	3.16	0	
SB			6	4	1	4	4*	1.33	0	0	215	237	4	59.25	2-19	0	0	6.61	2	
FC		1994	13	19	5	292	68*	20.85	0	1	2111	1116	51	21.88	5-57	2	0	3.17	3	
SB		1994	11	5	2	5	4*	1.66	0	0	415	368	9	40.88	2-19	0	0	5.32	2	

ROTHMAN, Grant Justin (Easterns) b Grahamstown 6.9.1972 RHB WK

	Cmp	Debut	M	I	NO	Runs	HS	Avge	100	50	Balls	Runs	Wkts	Avge	BB	5i	10m	RpO	ct	st
FC			4	6	2	69	29	17.25	0	0									13	1
SB			8	7	3	49	17*	12.25	0	0									3	1

RUNDLE, David Bryan (Western Province, Western Province B, Western Province to Zimbabwe) b Cape Town 25.9.1965 RHB OB

	Cmp	Debut	M	I	NO	Runs	HS	Avge	100	50	Balls	Runs	Wkts	Avge	BB	5i	10m	RpO	ct	st
FC			7	9	1	134	81*	16.75	0	1	1386	720	14	51.42	3-42	0	0	3.11	11	
SB			9	8	2	179	73	29.83	0	1	360	202	7	28.85	2-32	0	0	3.36	7	
FC		1984	96	141	30	2597	116	23.39	2	7	19415	8025	250	32.10	6-37	9	2	2.48	76	
Int		1993	2	2	0	6	6	3.00	0	0	96	95	5	19.00	4-42	1	0	5.93	3	
SB		1984	84	56	23	838	75	25.39	0	2	3951	2369	84	28.20	4-19	1	0	3.59	43	

RUSHMERE, Mark Weir (Eastern Province) b Port Elizabeth 7.1.1965 RHB RM

	Cmp	Debut	M	I	NO	Runs	HS	Avge	100	50	Balls	Runs	Wkts	Avge	BB	5i	10m	RpO	ct	st
FC			9	15	4	521	89*	47.36	0	4	6	0	0					0.00	5	
SB			10	6	3	249	64	83.00	0	3									2	
Test		1991	1	2	0	6	3	3.00	0	0									0	
FC		1983	119	211	34	7367	188	41.62	18	35	108	41	2	20.50	1-0	0	0	2.27	62	
Int		1991	4	4	0	78	35	19.50	0	0									1	
SB		1985	95	89	15	2784	121	37.62	2	22									27	

RUTHERFORD, Kenneth Robert (Transvaal) b Dunedin, New Zealand 26.10.1965 RHB RM

	Cmp	Debut	M	I	NO	Runs	HS	Avge	100	50	Balls	Runs	Wkts	Avge	BB	5i	10m	RpO	ct	st
FC			8	14	1	322	126*	24.76	1	0	6	7	0					7.00	13	
SB			11	11	1	259	100	25.90	1	0									3	
Test		1984	56	99	8	2465	107*	27.08	3	18	256	161	1	161.00	1-38	0	0	3.77	32	

Cmp	Debut	M	I	NO	Runs	HS	Avge	100	50	Balls	Runs	Wkts	Avge	BB	5i	10m	RpO	ct	st
FC	1982	194	337	27	11814	317	38.10	27	59	1715	1007	22	45.77	5-72	1	0	3.52	153	
Int	1984	121	115	9	3143	108	29.65	2	18	389	323	10	32.30	2-39	0	0	4.98	41	
SB	1995	24	23	1	600	100	27.27	1	3									9	

SCHONEGEVEL, Wayne Edward (Griqualand West) b Bloemfontein 25.8.1962 RHB RM

Cmp	Debut	M	I	NO	Runs	HS	Avge	100	50	Balls	Runs	Wkts	Avge	BB	5i	10m	RpO	ct	st
FC		2	4	0	57	32	14.25	0	0									2	
FC	1980	44	79	3	1937	153*	25.48	1	9	228	176	3	58.66	2-41	0	0	4.63	25	
SB	1993	20	19	1	524	103	29.11	1	2	17	22	0					7.76	1	

SCHULTZ, Brett Nolan (Western Province, Western Province B, South Africa) b East London 26.8.1970 LHB LF

Cmp	Debut	M	I	NO	Runs	HS	Avge	100	50	Balls	Runs	Wkts	Avge	BB	5i	10m	RpO	ct	st
Test		1	1	0	2	2	2.00	0	0	222	91	6	15.16	4-52	0	0	2.45	1	
FC		9	8	2	27	13	4.50	0	0	2112	1113	42	26.50	5-49	3	0	3.16	1	
SB		8	2	1	1	1*	1.00	0	0	345	275	13	21.15	4-19	1	0	4.78	0	
Test	1992	8	7	2	8	6	1.60	0	0	1643	691	36	19.19	5-48	2	0	2.52	2	
FC	1989	55	51	14	285	36*	7.70	0	0	11329	5339	213	25.06	7-70	11	0	2.82	10	
Int	1992	1								54	35	1	35.00	1-35	0	0	3.88	0	
SB	1989	54	10	7	12	5	4.00	0	0	2662	1734	93	18.64	6-22	5	1	3.90	10	

SCOTT, Gareth (Natal B) b Durban 8.8.1970 LHB RMF

Cmp	Debut	M	I	NO	Runs	HS	Avge	100	50	Balls	Runs	Wkts	Avge	BB	5i	10m	RpO	ct	st
FC		2	4	0	29	11	7.25	0	0	202	107	1	107.00	1-49	0	0	3.17	0	
FC	1993	3	5	0	30	11	6.00	0	0	322	188	1	188.00	1-49	0	0	3.50	1	

SEPTEMBER, Junaid (Eastern Province B) b Port Elizabeth 19.11.1975 RHB RFM

Cmp	Debut	M	I	NO	Runs	HS	Avge	100	50	Balls	Runs	Wkts	Avge	BB	5i	10m	RpO	ct	st
FC		3	2	0	18	18	9.00	0	0	426	240	5	48.00	2-65	0	0	3.38	1	
FC	1995	6	4	0	26	18	6.50	0	0	654	347	6	57.83	2-65	0	0	3.18	1	

SEYMORE, Andre Johan (Northern Transvaal) b Rustenburg 16.2.1975 RHB

Cmp	Debut	M	I	NO	Runs	HS	Avge	100	50	Balls	Runs	Wkts	Avge	BB	5i	10m	RpO	ct	st
FC		8	15	0	409	132	27.26	1	1									6	
SB		5	4	0	150	101	37.50	1	0									4	
FC	1993	27	52	0	1302	132	25.03	2	7									25	
SB	1993	17	16	1	457	101	30.46	1	2									8	

SHAW, Timothy Gower (Eastern Province) b Empangeni, Zululand 5.7.1959 LHB SLA

Cmp	Debut	M	I	NO	Runs	HS	Avge	100	50	Balls	Runs	Wkts	Avge	BB	5i	10m	RpO	ct	st
FC		9	9	3	178	40	29.66	0	0	2148	807	19	42.47	4-67	0	0	2.25	6	
SB		5	3	0	22	12	7.33	0	0	252	183	7	26.14	3-16	0	0	4.35	2	
FC	1980	138	190	51	3215	105	23.12	1	9	33256	12118	417	29.05	7-79	15	2	2.18	107	
Int	1991	9	6	4	26	17*	13.00	0	0	504	298	9	33.11	2-19	0	0	3.54	2	
SB	1984	100	66	22	677	56*	15.38	0	1	4800	2727	113	24.13	4-31	2	0	3.40	28	

SHUTTE, Jonathan William (Eastern Province B) b Cape Town 6.6.1977 RHB LM

Cmp	Debut	M	I	NO	Runs	HS	Avge	100	50	Balls	Runs	Wkts	Avge	BB	5i	10m	RpO	ct	st
FC		3	3	2	7	5*	7.00	0	0	274	139	3	46.33	2-29	0	0	3.04	0	

SIMMONS, Philip Verant (Easterns, Trinidad, West Indies to Australia) b Arima, Trinidad 18.4.1963 RHB RM

Cmp	Debut	M	I	NO	Runs	HS	Avge	100	50	Balls	Runs	Wkts	Avge	BB	5i	10m	RpO	ct	st
FC		4	8	0	220	102	27.50	1	0	449	209	6	34.83	3-43	0	0	2.79	3	
SB		7	7	0	190	87	27.14	0	1	312	256	3	85.33	2-39	0	0	4.92	1	
Test	1987	25	45	2	1000	110	23.25	1	4	612	248	4	62.00	2-34	0	0	2.43	26	
FC	1982	169	289	13	10297	261	37.30	22	55	10309	4779	161	29.68	6-14	4	0	2.78	197	
Int	1987	119	117	7	3242	122	29.47	5	17	3034	2185	62	35.24	4-3	2	0	4.32	51	
SB	1992	9	9	0	275	87	30.55	0	1	420	317	6	52.83	3-32	0	0	4.52	1	

SIMONS, Eric Owen (Western Province) b Cape Town 9.3.1962 RHB RFM

Cmp	Debut	M	I	NO	Runs	HS	Avge	100	50	Balls	Runs	Wkts	Avge	BB	5i	10m	RpO	ct	st
FC		7	9	1	278	80	34.75	0	3	954	371	7	53.00	2-14	0	0	2.33	3	
SB		16	16	5	362	59*	32.90	0	1	657	405	30	13.50	4-17	2	0	3.69	5	
FC	1982	109	171	37	3725	102*	27.79	1	24	17897	7700	284	27.11	6-26	5	0	2.58	70	
Int	1993	23	18	4	217	24	15.50	0	0	1212	810	33	24.54	4-42	1	0	4.00	6	
SB	1983	104	85	31	1308	74*	24.22	0	5	4735	3068	154	19.92	4-3	11	0	3.88	32	

SMITH, Dennis James (Northern Transvaal) b Durban 26.11.1971 RHB WK

Cmp	Debut	M	I	NO	Runs	HS	Avge	100	50	Balls	Runs	Wkts	Avge	BB	5i	10m	RpO	ct	st
SB		14	11	3	102	30*	12.75	0	0									11	1
FC	1993	10	16	1	257	88*	17.13	0	1									20	1
SB	1995	16	12	3	103	30*	11.44	0	0									15	1

SMITH, Gregory James (Northern Transvaal) b Pretoria 30.10.1971 RHB LFM

Cmp	Debut	M	I	NO	Runs	HS	Avge	100	50	Balls	Runs	Wkts	Avge	BB	5i	10m	RpO	ct	st
FC		2	3	0	42	23	14.00	0	0	358	165	4	41.25	2-68	0	0	2.76	0	
SB		1	1	1	0	0*		0	0	36	20	1	20.00	1-20	0	0	3.33	0	
FC	1993	29	40	15	301	68	12.04	0	1	4768	2397	87	27.55	5-24	3	0	3.01	6	
SB	1993	13	4	2	13	9	6.50	0	0	650	503	22	22.86	5-11	0	1	4.64	2	

SNELL, Richard Peter (Transvaal B, Transvaal) b Durban 12.9.1968 RHB RFM

Cmp	Debut	M	I	NO	Runs	HS	Avge	100	50	Balls	Runs	Wkts	Avge	BB	5i	10m	RpO	ct	st
FC		3	5	1	192	52	48.00	0	1	276	152	4	38.00	2-54	0	0	3.30	1	
SB		8	7	0	39	15	5.57	0	0	42	65	0					9.28	4	
Test	1991	5	8	1	95	48	13.57	0	0	1025	538	19	28.31	4-74	0	0	3.14	1	
FC	1987	81	107	17	1892	105	21.02	1	8	14261	7052	248	28.43	6-33	9	1	2.96	22	
Int	1991	42	28	8	322	63	16.10	0	2	2095	1574	44	35.77	5-40	2	1	4.50	7	
SB	1988	64	52	7	1086	146	24.13	2	3	2575	1905	70	27.21	4-28	2	0	4.43	14	

SOLOMONS, Mario Theodore (Western Province, Western Province B) b Kuils River 24.2.1971 RHB WK

Cmp	Debut	M	I	NO	Runs	HS	Avge	100	50	Balls	Runs	Wkts	Avge	BB	5i	10m	RpO	ct	st
FC		6	8	0	125	32	15.62	0	0									17	1
FC	1995	10	12	1	219	67	19.90	0	1									26	4

Cmp	Debut	M	I	NO	Runs	HS	Avge	100	50	Balls	Runs	Wkts	Avge	BB	5i	10m	RpO	ct	st

SOMMERVILLE, Blaise Justin (Northern Transvaal) b Pretoria 25.5.1967 RHB RM/OB

FC		3	6	0	125	62	20.83	0	1									4	
SB		1	1	0	13	13	13.00	0	0										0
FC	1990	29	56	3	1416	138	26.71	1	6	642	331	2	165.50	1-22	0	0	3.09	28	
SB	1991	18	18	1	422	107	24.82	1	1	136	111	2	55.50	2-26	0	0	4.89	3	

SONTUNDU, Mtimkulu Derrick Cicelo (Eastern Province B) b Port Elizabeth 3.12.1973 RHB

| FC | | 1 | 2 | 0 | 53 | 47 | 26.50 | 0 | 0 | | | | | | | | | 1 | |

STELLING, William Frederick (Boland) b Johannesburg 30.6.1969 RHB RFM

FC		2	4	0	49	23	12.25	0	0	156	94	1	94.00	1-13	0	0	3.61	2	
SB		8	7	2	150	58	30.00	0	1	378	302	2	151.00	1-17	0	0	4.79	3	
FC	1991	17	28	2	475	53	18.26	0	1	2203	980	28	35.00	4-12	0	0	2.66	8	
SB	1991	30	24	12	393	58	32.75	0	1	1337	982	29	33.86	3-41	0	0	4.40	12	

STEPHENSON, Franklyn Dacosta (Free State) b Halls, Barbados 8.4.1959 RHB RFM

FC		4	5	0	87	36	17.40	0	0	546	213	11	19.36	4-21	0	0	2.34	3	
SB		10	10	1	263	97	29.22	0	1	486	392	16	24.50	4-36	1	0	4.83	3	
FC	1981	219	342	34	8622	166	27.99	12	43	40303	19218	792	24.26	8-47	44	10	2.86	100	
SB	1991	60	56	5	1458	108	28.58	1	6	3009	1660	101	16.43	5-10	7	1	3.31	17	

STEWART, Errol Leslie Rae (Natal) b Durban 30.7.1969 RHB RM WK

FC		10	17	1	576	138	36.00	1	2									14	
SB		13	12	2	302	53	30.20	0	2									6	
FC	1988	54	92	8	2939	207*	34.98	7	10	90	45	0					3.00	100	2
Int	1992	5	5	1	57	23*	14.25	0	0									3	
SB	1990	55	47	7	1006	86*	25.15	0	5	6	6	0					6.00	28	2

STEYN, Philippus Jeremia Rudolf (Natal, Natal B) b Kimberley 30.6.1967 RHB RM WK

FC		4	7	1	222	100*	37.00	1	0									2	
SB		7	5	0	55	21	11.00	0	0									2	
Test	1994	3	6	0	127	46	21.16	0	0									0	
FC	1985	95	174	11	4733	178	29.03	6	23	54	24	1	24.00	1-22	0	0	2.66	44	1
Int	1995	1	1	0	4	4	4.00	0	0									0	
SB	1986	76	71	7	1888	117	29.50	2	12									16	

STIGANT, Bruce Gordon (Eastern Province B) b Cape Town 17.10.1975 RHB SLA

| FC | | 3 | 3 | 0 | 18 | 17 | 6.00 | 0 | 0 | 198 | 60 | 1 | 60.00 | 1-24 | 0 | 0 | 1.81 | 1 | |

STOREY, Keith Graham (Natal, Natal B) b Salisbury, Rhodesia 25.1.1969 RHB RFM

| FC | | 9 | 8 | 3 | 55 | 34* | 11.00 | 0 | 0 | 1684 | 741 | 38 | 19.50 | 7-58 | 2 | 0 | 2.64 | 6 | |
| FC | 1993 | 22 | 19 | 7 | 159 | 34* | 13.25 | 0 | 0 | 3866 | 1761 | 85 | 20.71 | 7-58 | 4 | 1 | 2.73 | 16 | |

STRYDOM, Morne (North West) b Port Elizabeth 20.2.1974 RHB OB

FC		5	10	1	464	129	51.55	1	2	822	401	15	26.73	6-55	1	0	2.92	7	
SB		6	6	0	231	92	38.50	0	2	300	203	10	20.30	3-34	0	0	4.06	3	
FC	1995	9	14	1	536	129	41.23	1	3	1218	593	19	31.21	6-55	1	0	2.92	7	
SB	1995	7	7	0	231	92	33.00	0	2	300	203	10	20.30	3-34	0	0	4.06	3	

STRYDOM, Pieter Coenraad (Border) b Somerset East 10.6.1969 RHB SLA

FC		9	16	3	442	100	34.00	1	3	250	129	7	18.42	4-52	0	0	3.09	6	
SB		10	10	1	179	69*	19.88	0	1	102	91	0					5.35	1	
FC	1987	48	80	6	2322	127	31.37	4	13	1472	656	24	27.33	4-52	0	0	2.67	28	
SB	1992	47	42	5	1025	80	27.70	0	7	381	291	8	36.37	3-28	0	0	4.58	10	

SUGDEN, Craig Brian (Natal, Natal B) b Durban 7.3.1974 RHB

FC		7	10	3	265	85*	37.85	0	2	60	33	2	16.50	2-24	0	0	3.30	10	
SB		1																	0
FC	1993	20	30	4	850	106	32.69	1	4	120	59	2	29.50	2-24	0	0	2.95	24	
SB	1995	2																	0

SWANEPOEL, Adriaan Johannes (Griqualand West) b Kimberley 19.3.1972 LHB LFM

FC		4	5	0	27	14	5.40	0	0	642	310	7	44.28	3-31	0	0	2.89	0	
SB		7	3	0	26	19	8.66	0	0	319	227	11	20.63	3-29	0	0	4.26	2	
FC	1991	26	31	11	143	27	7.15	0	0	3850	1909	57	33.49	5-29	2	1	2.97	10	
SB	1994	22	10	1	60	19	6.66	0	0	996	695	27	25.74	3-29	0	0	4.18	4	

SYMCOX, Patrick Leonard (Natal, South Africa, South Africa to India, South Africa to Kenya) b Kimberley 14.4.1960 RHB OB

Test		1	1	0	16	16	16.00	0	0	252	111	3	37.00	2-49	0	0	2.64	0	
FC		6	9	4	175	45*	35.00	0	0	1478	678	22	30.81	4-26	0	0	2.75	3	
Int		8	2	1	26	26	26.00	0	0	438	390	9	43.33	2-38	0	0	5.34	0	
SB		8	7	1	63	40	10.50	0	0	414	203	14	14.50	3-11	0	0	2.94	1	
Test	1993	10	13	1	259	50	21.58	0	1	1883	861	18	47.83	3-75	0	0	2.74	0	
FC	1977	94	145	19	3191	107	25.32	1	17	14455	6256	193	32.41	7-93	4	0	2.59	54	
Int	1993	47	30	4	382	61	14.69	0	1	2424	1635	46	35.54	3-20	0	0	4.04	10	
SB	1985	36	29	12	405	53*	23.82	0	1	1357	733	33	22.21	3-11	0	0	3.24	15	

TALJARD, Dion (Border) b East London 7.1.1970 RHB RM

| FC | | 3 | 4 | 0 | 41 | 32 | 10.25 | 0 | 0 | 671 | 320 | 11 | 29.09 | 3-33 | 0 | 0 | 2.86 | 2 | |
| FC | 1993 | 12 | 13 | 4 | 103 | 32 | 11.44 | 0 | 0 | 2273 | 959 | 24 | 39.95 | 4-47 | 0 | 0 | 2.53 | 5 | |

Cmp	Debut	M	I	NO	Runs	HS	Avge	100	50	Balls	Runs	Wkts	Avge	BB	5i	10m	RpO	ct	st

TELEMACHUS, Roger (Boland) b Stellenbosch 27.3.1973 RHB RFM

Cmp	Debut	M	I	NO	Runs	HS	Avge	100	50	Balls	Runs	Wkts	Avge	BB	5i	10m	RpO	ct	st
FC		3	6	0	107	29	17.83	0	0	597	222	12	18.50	6-21	1	0	2.23	1	
SB		7	5	1	49	26*	12.25	0	0	338	236	15	15.73	5-54	0	1	4.18	1	
FC	1994	25	34	6	379	59	13.53	0	1	3676	1818	70	25.97	6-21	3	0	2.96	5	
SB	1994	22	14	6	103	26*	12.87	0	0	1080	733	37	19.81	5-54	0	1	4.07	5	

TERBRUGGE, David John (Transvaal, Transvaal B) b Ladysmith 31.1.1977 RHB RFM

Cmp	Debut	M	I	NO	Runs	HS	Avge	100	50	Balls	Runs	Wkts	Avge	BB	5i	10m	RpO	ct	st
FC		3	4	1	43	20	14.33	0	0	411	166	8	20.75	4-54	0	0	2.42	1	
FC	1994	4	6	1	49	20	9.80	0	0	579	234	10	23.40	4-54	0	0	2.42	1	

TOUZEL, Frank Barry (Western Province B) b Pinelands 8.10.1963 LHB

Cmp	Debut	M	I	NO	Runs	HS	Avge	100	50	Balls	Runs	Wkts	Avge	BB	5i	10m	RpO	ct	st
FC		5	8	1	124	52*	17.71	0	1									6	
FC	1984	57	105	10	2815	132	29.63	3	12									43	
SB	1992	6	6	0	133	66	22.16	0	1									1	

TOYANA, Geoffrey (Transvaal B) b Soweto 27.2.1974 LHB RM

Cmp	Debut	M	I	NO	Runs	HS	Avge	100	50	Balls	Runs	Wkts	Avge	BB	5i	10m	RpO	ct	st
FC		4	4	0	26	17	6.50	0	0									2	
FC	1995	8	9	1	90	29	11.25	0	0									6	

TRUTER, Wayne Stoney (Boland) b Cape Town 27.6.1965 RHB RM

Cmp	Debut	M	I	NO	Runs	HS	Avge	100	50	Balls	Runs	Wkts	Avge	BB	5i	10m	RpO	ct	st
FC		7	14	0	276	95	19.71	0	1	317	141	3	47.00	1-31	0	0	2.66	4	
SB		4	4	0	78	34	19.50	0	0									1	
FC	1987	58	105	5	2637	141	26.37	5	11	779	388	7	55.42	4-59	0	0	2.98	41	
SB	1989	44	42	2	827	74	20.67	0	5	27	42	0					9.33	9	

VAN DER MERWE, Casparus Cornelius (Free State, Free State to West Indies) b Johannesburg 11.7.1973 RHB RM

Cmp	Debut	M	I	NO	Runs	HS	Avge	100	50	Balls	Runs	Wkts	Avge	BB	5i	10m	RpO	ct	st
SB		3	2	0	16	11	8.00	0	0	66	73	1	73.00	1-28	0	0	6.63	1	
FC	1994	10	18	2	317	67	19.81	0	2	1020	544	10	54.40	3-43	0	0	3.20	7	
SB	1995	6	4	0	56	39	14.00	0	0	138	127	4	31.75	3-36	0	0	5.52	4	

VAN DER WATH, Johannes Jacobus (Easterns) b Newcastle 10.1.1978 RHB RF

Cmp	Debut	M	I	NO	Runs	HS	Avge	100	50	Balls	Runs	Wkts	Avge	BB	5i	10m	RpO	ct	st
FC		2	4	0	38	31	9.50	0	0	96	64	2	32.00	2-57	0	0	4.00	0	
SB		5	4	1	10	4	3.33	0	0	137	138	2	69.00	1-42	0	0	6.04	0	
SB	1995	6	4	1	10	4	3.33	0	0	191	168	2	84.00	1-42	0	0	5.27	0	

VAN DEVENTER, Andre Jean (North West) b Strand 1.8.1969 RHB

Cmp	Debut	M	I	NO	Runs	HS	Avge	100	50	Balls	Runs	Wkts	Avge	BB	5i	10m	RpO	ct	st
SB		4	4	0	52	31	13.00	0	0									1	
FC	1991	25	45	4	1429	117*	34.85	1	9	6	4	0					4.00	17	
SB	1992	32	32	3	571	63*	19.68	0	2									6	

VAN JAARSVELD, Martin (Northern Transvaal) b Klerksdorp 18.6.1974 RHB RM

Cmp	Debut	M	I	NO	Runs	HS	Avge	100	50	Balls	Runs	Wkts	Avge	BB	5i	10m	RpO	ct	st
FC		7	13	0	301	109	23.15	1	0	186	120	1	120.00	1-28	0	0	3.87	4	
SB		12	11	0	366	123	33.27	1	0									7	
FC	1994	16	28	0	767	109	27.39	1	4	198	130	1	130.00	1-28	0	0	3.93	18	
SB	1995	14	13	0	369	123	28.38	1	0									8	

VAN REENEN, Adriaan (Western Province B) b Somerset West 3.11.1975 LHB LF

Cmp	Debut	M	I	NO	Runs	HS	Avge	100	50	Balls	Runs	Wkts	Avge	BB	5i	10m	RpO	ct	st
FC		1	1	1	6	6*		0	0	222	113	2	56.50	2-61	0	0	3.05	0	
FC	1995	4	2	1	10	6*	10.00	0	0	635	401	10	40.10	5-47	1	0	3.78	0	

VAN RENSBURG, Petrus (Free State) b Virginia 28.3.1977 RHB SLA

Cmp	Debut	M	I	NO	Runs	HS	Avge	100	50	Balls	Runs	Wkts	Avge	BB	5i	10m	RpO	ct	st
FC		1	1	0	26	26	26.00	0	0	132	88	0					4.00	0	
SB		2	1	0	18	18	18.00	0	0	108	90	0					5.00	1	

VAN SCHALKWYK, Morne (North West) b Cape Town 8.1.1975 RHB RMF

Cmp	Debut	M	I	NO	Runs	HS	Avge	100	50	Balls	Runs	Wkts	Avge	BB	5i	10m	RpO	ct	st
FC		2	3	1	36	31*	18.00	0	0	168	80	6	13.33	4-17	0	0	2.85	1	
SB		2								90	54	0					3.60	1	

VAN WYK, Morne Nico (Free State) b Bloemfontein 20.3.1979 RHB WK

Cmp	Debut	M	I	NO	Runs	HS	Avge	100	50	Balls	Runs	Wkts	Avge	BB	5i	10m	RpO	ct	st
FC		2	3	0	104	49	34.66	0	0										

VAN ZYL, Daniel Jacobus (Northern Transvaal) b Pretoria 8.1.1971 RHB OB

Cmp	Debut	M	I	NO	Runs	HS	Avge	100	50	Balls	Runs	Wkts	Avge	BB	5i	10m	RpO	ct	st
FC		5	10	0	249	57	24.90	0	1	451	301	5	60.20	2-73	0	0	4.00	2	
SB		13	12	4	163	44*	20.37	0	0	580	406	19	21.36	5-33	0	1	4.20	4	
FC	1992	25	48	3	1232	78	27.37	0	7	2018	995	26	38.26	3-15	0	0	2.95	17	
SB	1992	35	30	9	467	52*	22.23	0	1	1574	1186	38	31.21	5-33	0	1	4.52	8	

VEENSTRA, Ross Edward (Transvaal) b Estcourt 22.4.1972 RHB LFM

Cmp	Debut	M	I	NO	Runs	HS	Avge	100	50	Balls	Runs	Wkts	Avge	BB	5i	10m	RpO	ct	st
FC		8	12	3	252	135*	28.00	1	0	1437	680	33	20.60	5-36	1	0	2.83	2	
SB		4	3	0	33	16	11.00	0	0	204	134	6	22.33	2-26	0	0	3.94	1	
FC	1990	49	63	10	1234	135*	23.28	1	2	7874	3409	143	23.83	6-38	3	0	2.59	18	
SB	1990	30	17	2	193	33*	13.00	0	0	1456	979	34	28.79	3-25	0	0	4.03	8	

VENTER, Jacobus Francois (Free State, Free State to West Indies) b Bloemfontein 1.10.1969 LHB OB

Cmp	Debut	M	I	NO	Runs	HS	Avge	100	50	Balls	Runs	Wkts	Avge	BB	5i	10m	RpO	ct	st
FC		9	14	1	464	101	35.69	1	4	1539	718	25	28.72	6-96	1	1	2.79	5	
SB		9	7	0	195	50	27.85	0	1	316	272	10	27.20	4-38	1	0	5.16	4	
FC	1989	56	93	8	2476	193	29.12	2	18	6278	3343	89	37.56	6-96	3	1	3.19	38	
SB	1989	44	38	6	920	60	28.75	0	4	856	671	27	24.85	5-21	1	1	4.70	14	

VENTER, Martin Colin (North West) b East London 12.12.1968 RHB RM

Cmp	Debut	M	I	NO	Runs	HS	Avge	100	50	Balls	Runs	Wkts	Avge	BB	5i	10m	RpO	ct	st
FC		5	10	1	126	46	14.00	0	0									2	
SB		8	7	2	247	95*	49.40	0	2									2	

Cmp	Debut	M	I	NO	Runs	HS	Avge	100	50	Balls	Runs	Wkts	Avge	BB	5i	10m	RpO	ct	st
FC	1988	54	96	6	2287	129	25.41	6	5	102	94	1	94.00	1-42	0	0	5.52	26	
SB	1990	43	41	4	843	95*	22.78	0	4									9	

VICTOR, Gavin Charles (Eastern Province, Eastern Province B) b Port Elizabeth 11.8.1966 RHB

Cmp	Debut	M	I	NO	Runs	HS	Avge	100	50	Balls	Runs	Wkts	Avge	BB	5i	10m	RpO	ct	st
FC		6	12	1	439	95	39.90	0	5	24	17	1	17.00	1-17	0	0	4.25	4	
SB		10	9	1	387	78	48.37	0	4									1	
FC	1988	52	93	5	3022	139*	34.34	5	20	67	38	2	19.00	1-10	0	0	3.40	42	
SB	1987	58	55	4	1282	100	25.13	1	6	6	1	0					1.00	12	

VILJOEN, Andre Willie (Natal B) b Durban 12.10.1971 RHB RM

Cmp	Debut	M	I	NO	Runs	HS	Avge	100	50	Balls	Runs	Wkts	Avge	BB	5i	10m	RpO	ct	st
FC		1	1	0	0	0	0.00	0	0	138	67	2	33.50	2-28	0	0	2.91	0	

VORSTER, Christiaan Jakobus (Boland) b Paarl 17.8.1976 RHB RMF

Cmp	Debut	M	I	NO	Runs	HS	Avge	100	50	Balls	Runs	Wkts	Avge	BB	5i	10m	RpO	ct	st
FC		4	7	0	99	49	14.14	0	0	697	362	14	25.85	3-44	0	0	3.11	4	

VORSTER, Johan (Transvaal B) b Roodepoort 28.10.1977 RHB LF

Cmp	Debut	M	I	NO	Runs	HS	Avge	100	50	Balls	Runs	Wkts	Avge	BB	5i	10m	RpO	ct	st
FC		1	2	0	0	0	0.00	0	0	126	103	0					4.90	0	

VORSTER, Louis Phillippus (North West) b Potchefstroom 2.11.1966 LHB OB

Cmp	Debut	M	I	NO	Runs	HS	Avge	100	50	Balls	Runs	Wkts	Avge	BB	5i	10m	RpO	ct	st
FC		5	9	0	206	69	22.88	0	1									2	
SB		9	8	4	392	92	98.00	0	5									3	
FC	1985	85	148	17	4137	188	31.58	6	24	69	41	1	41.00	1-10	0	0	3.56	57	
SB	1986	59	53	11	1435	92	34.16	0	10									18	

WALSH, Vaughn Anthony (Griqualand West) b Liberta, Antigua 2.12.1964 RHB RF

Cmp	Debut	M	I	NO	Runs	HS	Avge	100	50	Balls	Runs	Wkts	Avge	BB	5i	10m	RpO	ct	st
FC		8	13	6	49	13*	7.00	0	0	1806	1002	19	52.73	3-58	0	0	3.32	3	
SB		10	5	2	19	14*	6.33	0	0	485	415	18	23.05	4-37	1	0	5.13	3	
FC	1991	27	37	14	268	51	11.65	0	1	5277	2747	92	29.85	6-52	2	0	3.12	9	
SB	1995	20	11	4	61	18*	8.71	0	0	950	747	31	24.09	4-37	1	0	4.71	5	

WANDRAG, Vaughan (North West) b Potchefstroom 9.5.1974 RHB OB

Cmp	Debut	M	I	NO	Runs	HS	Avge	100	50	Balls	Runs	Wkts	Avge	BB	5i	10m	RpO	ct	st
SB		2	2	0	11	11	5.50	0	0	96	97	1	97.00	1-42	0	0	6.06	1	
FC	1995	3	3	0	58	34	19.33	0	0	210	96	1	96.00	1-42	0	0	2.74	2	
SB	1994	16	14	0	120	19	8.57	0	0	762	539	11	49.00	2-27	0	0	4.24	3	

WATSON, Douglas James (Natal) b Pietermaritzburg 15.5.1973 RHB

Cmp	Debut	M	I	NO	Runs	HS	Avge	100	50	Balls	Runs	Wkts	Avge	BB	5i	10m	RpO	ct	st
FC		10	16	3	571	200*	43.92	1	3	3	6	0					12.00	9	
SB		12	12	0	624	93	52.00	0	8									2	
FC	1993	30	46	4	1555	200*	37.02	2	11	3	6	0					12.00	22	
SB	1993	16	16	0	685	93	42.81	0	8									2	

WEBSTER, Trevor Craig (Transvaal) b Johannesburg 4.10.1969 RHB RFM

Cmp	Debut	M	I	NO	Runs	HS	Avge	100	50	Balls	Runs	Wkts	Avge	BB	5i	10m	RpO	ct	st
FC		2	1	0	2	2	2.00	0	0	372	184	5	36.80	2-31	0	0	2.96	1	
SB		7	2	0	1	1	0.50	0	0	334	278	9	30.88	3-34	0	0	4.99	1	
FC	1990	17	19	11	224	42*	28.00	0	0	2402	1408	40	35.20	6-65	2	0	3.51	7	
SB	1994	14	6	1	29	12*	5.80	0	0	640	541	17	31.82	3-34	0	0	5.07	2	

WEINSTEIN, Mark Steven (Transvaal B) b Johannesburg 21.12.1973 RHB OB

Cmp	Debut	M	I	NO	Runs	HS	Avge	100	50	Balls	Runs	Wkts	Avge	BB	5i	10m	RpO	ct	st
FC		1	2	0	6	6	3.00	0	0	103	115	1	115.00	1-35	0	0	6.69	0	

WESSELS, Andrew (Boland) b Pietermaritzburg 13.5.1974 RHB

Cmp	Debut	M	I	NO	Runs	HS	Avge	100	50	Balls	Runs	Wkts	Avge	BB	5i	10m	RpO	ct	st
FC		3	6	1	103	56*	20.60	0	1									6	
SB		2	1	0	1	1	1.00	0	0									0	
FC	1991	9	15	2	294	65	22.61	0	3									9	
SB	1995	6	5	0	32	24	6.40	0	0									0	

WESSELS, Kepler Christoffel (Eastern Province) b Bloemfontein 14.9.1957 LHB RM

Cmp	Debut	M	I	NO	Runs	HS	Avge	100	50	Balls	Runs	Wkts	Avge	BB	5i	10m	RpO	ct	st
FC		9	14	2	736	179	61.33	2	6	30	18	1	18.00	1-18	0	0	3.60	6	
SB		10	9	3	271	91	45.16	0	2	54	32	2	16.00	2-32	0	0	3.55	3	
Test	1982	40	71	3	2788	179	41.00	6	15	90	42	0					2.80	30	
FC	1973	300	512	46	23493	254	50.41	62	126	1416	574	13	44.15	2-25	0	0	2.43	258	
Int	1982	109	105	7	3367	107	34.35	1	26	749	666	18	37.00	2-16	0	0	5.33	49	
SB	1986	85	84	12	3725	124	51.73	6	29	133	101	4	25.25	2-32	0	0	4.55	37	

WHITE, Brad Middleton (Border) b Johannesburg 15.5.1970 LHB RM

Cmp	Debut	M	I	NO	Runs	HS	Avge	100	50	Balls	Runs	Wkts	Avge	BB	5i	10m	RpO	ct	st
FC		9	17	0	312	63	18.35	0	2	396	176	3	58.66	1-5	0	0	2.66	16	
SB		7	7	0	90	59	12.85	0	1	143	106	7	15.14	2-9	0	0	4.44	0	
FC	1988	47	90	5	2557	180*	30.08	6	9	1340	675	17	39.70	2-3	0	0	3.02	46	
SB	1990	25	25	1	582	84	24.25	0	4	185	165	7	23.57	2-9	0	0	5.35	3	

WHITE, Gareth (Easterns) b Witbank 13.5.1975 RHB WK

Cmp	Debut	M	I	NO	Runs	HS	Avge	100	50	Balls	Runs	Wkts	Avge	BB	5i	10m	RpO	ct	st
FC		1	2	0	12	7	6.00	0	0									1	

WIBLIN, Wayne (Border) b Grahamstown 13.2.1969 RHB RM

Cmp	Debut	M	I	NO	Runs	HS	Avge	100	50	Balls	Runs	Wkts	Avge	BB	5i	10m	RpO	ct	st
SB		1	1	0	1	1	1.00	0	0									0	
FC	1995	3	4	0	205	160	51.25	1	0	12	6	0					3.00	0	
SB	1995	5	4	0	76	50	19.00	0	1									1	

WILKINSON, Louis Johannes (Free State) b Vereeniging 19.11.1966 RHB RM

Cmp	Debut	M	I	NO	Runs	HS	Avge	100	50	Balls	Runs	Wkts	Avge	BB	5i	10m	RpO	ct	st
FC		5	7	1	396	139*	66.00	1	2									2	
SB		7	5	0	68	23	13.60	0	0									6	
FC	1986	85	147	6	4397	226*	31.18	7	21	888	513	6	85.50	1-13	0	0	3.46	78	
SB	1987	72	65	8	1577	83	27.66	0	10	372	319	10	31.90	4-48	1	0	5.14	30	

WILLIAMS, Elton Charl (Boland) b Stellenbosch 19.9.1973 RHB

Cmp	Debut	M	I	NO	Runs	HS	Avge	100	50	Balls	Runs	Wkts	Avge	BB	5i	10m	RpO	ct	st
FC		1	2	0	5	5	2.50	0	0									1	

WILLIAMS, Henry Smith (Boland) b Pniel 11.6.1967 RHB RFM

Cmp	Debut	M	I	NO	Runs	HS	Avge	100	50	Balls	Runs	Wkts	Avge	BB	5i	10m	RpO	ct	st
FC		7	12	4	87	22*	10.87	0	0	1323	511	25	20.44	6-57	2	0	2.31	5	
SB		4	2	0	2	1	1.00	0	0	216	151	12	12.58	4-35	1	0	4.19	0	
FC	1992	37	52	15	315	24	8.51	0	0	6646	2662	107	24.87	6-57	3	0	2.40	13	
SB	1992	37	14	6	23	6*	2.87	0	0	1854	1285	45	28.55	4-35	1	0	4.15	2	

WILLOUGHBY, Charl Myles (Boland) b Cape Town 3.12.1974 LHB LFM

Cmp	Debut	M	I	NO	Runs	HS	Avge	100	50	Balls	Runs	Wkts	Avge	BB	5i	10m	RpO	ct	st
FC		4	7	4	14	5*	4.66	0	0	594	197	7	28.14	3-28	0	0	1.98	1	
SB		9	4	1	21	11	7.00	0	0	454	357	9	39.66	4-39	1	0	4.71	0	
FC	1994	17	29	14	62	11	4.13	0	0	2694	1250	38	32.89	4-43	0	0	2.78	2	
SB	1994	19	5	2	22	11	7.33	0	0	904	691	21	32.90	4-39	1	0	4.58	0	

WILSON, Craig Rhys (Border) b Cradock 24.3.1974 LHB

Cmp	Debut	M	I	NO	Runs	HS	Avge	100	50	Balls	Runs	Wkts	Avge	BB	5i	10m	RpO	ct	st
FC		2	4	0	60	24	15.00	0	0									4	
FC	1994	6	11	0	289	101	26.27	1	0									4	

WYLIE, Andrew Robert (Boland) b Pietermaritzburg 31.12.1971 RHB OB

Cmp	Debut	M	I	NO	Runs	HS	Avge	100	50	Balls	Runs	Wkts	Avge	BB	5i	10m	RpO	ct	st
FC		5	10	0	210	74	21.00	0	2									9	
SB		4	4	1	81	35*	27.00	0	0									1	
FC	1992	22	42	1	799	108*	19.48	1	4									17	
SB	1994	21	20	3	457	90	26.88	0	2									4	

YATES, Graeme Clive (Transvaal B) b Johannesburg 23.11.1970 RHB LF

Cmp	Debut	M	I	NO	Runs	HS	Avge	100	50	Balls	Runs	Wkts	Avge	BB	5i	10m	RpO	ct	st
FC		1									216	115	2	57.50	2-69	0	0	3.19	1	
FC	1991	9	7	1	118	50	19.66	0	1	1695	858	31	27.67	5-46	2	0	3.03	4	
SB	1991	4	3	2	16	12*	16.00	0	0	204	162	2	81.00	1-34	0	0	4.76	0	

ZONDI, Linda Eugene (Natal B) b Durban 24.4.1976 RHB WK

Cmp	Debut	M	I	NO	Runs	HS	Avge	100	50	Balls	Runs	Wkts	Avge	BB	5i	10m	RpO	ct	st
FC		1	1	1	20	20*		0	0									0	

AUSTRALIA IN SOUTH AFRICA 1996-97

BEVAN, M.G.

Cmp	M	I	NO	Runs	HS	Avge	100	50	Balls	Runs	Wkts	Avge	BB	5i	10m	RpO	ct	st
Test	3	5	1	72	37*	18.00	0	0	372	176	9	19.55	4-32	0	0	2.83	0	
FC	6	8	1	135	52	19.28	0	1	814	407	19	21.42	4-32	0	0	3.00	4	
Int	7	6	1	297	103	59.40	1	2	222	203	1	203.00	1-33	0	0	5.48	1	

BICHEL, A.J.

Cmp	M	I	NO	Runs	HS	Avge	100	50	Balls	Runs	Wkts	Avge	BB	5i	10m	RpO	ct	st
FC	2	2	1	24	14*	24.00	0	0	378	206	10	20.60	5-62	1	0	3.26	0	
Int	4	2	0	17	17	8.50	0	0	234	198	8	24.75	3-43	0	0	5.07	0	

BLEWETT, G.S.

Cmp	M	I	NO	Runs	HS	Avge	100	50	Balls	Runs	Wkts	Avge	BB	5i	10m	RpO	ct	st
Test	3	5	0	271	214	54.20	1	0	141	74	1	74.00	1-13	0	0	3.14	2	
FC	5	8	1	517	214	73.85	2	1	231	162	3	54.00	2-35	0	0	4.20	4	
Int	7	6	0	148	53	24.66	0	1	186	167	3	55.66	1-18	0	0	5.38	2	

DALE, A.C.

Cmp	M	I	NO	Runs	HS	Avge	100	50	Balls	Runs	Wkts	Avge	BB	5i	10m	RpO	ct	st
Int	7	4	4	38	15*		0	0	390	275	8	34.37	3-18	0	0	4.23	3	

DI VENUTO, M.J.

Cmp	M	I	NO	Runs	HS	Avge	100	50	Balls	Runs	Wkts	Avge	BB	5i	10m	RpO	ct	st
Int	5	5	0	150	89	30.00	0	1									1	

ELLIOTT, M.T.G.

Cmp	M	I	NO	Runs	HS	Avge	100	50	Balls	Runs	Wkts	Avge	BB	5i	10m	RpO	ct	st
Test	3	5	0	182	85	36.40	0	1									2	
FC	6	10	1	406	85	45.11	0	2	24	30	0					7.50	9	

GILCHRIST, A.C.

Cmp	M	I	NO	Runs	HS	Avge	100	50	Balls	Runs	Wkts	Avge	BB	5i	10m	RpO	ct	st
Int	6	5	1	127	77	31.75	0	1									2	1

GILLESPIE, J.N.

Cmp	M	I	NO	Runs	HS	Avge	100	50	Balls	Runs	Wkts	Avge	BB	5i	10m	RpO	ct	st
Test	3	4	3	7	6*	7.00	0	0	622	287	14	20.50	5-54	1	0	2.76	0	
FC	6	6	4	15	6*	7.50	0	0	1065	534	32	16.68	7-34	2	0	3.00	1	
Int	6	4	1	48	26	16.00	0	0	330	247	8	30.87	2-39	0	0	4.49	0	

HAYDEN, M.L.

Cmp	M	I	NO	Runs	HS	Avge	100	50	Balls	Runs	Wkts	Avge	BB	5i	10m	RpO	ct	st
Test	3	5	0	64	40	12.80	0	0									4	
FC	6	10	1	215	112	23.88	1	0									6	

HEALY, I.A.

Cmp	M	I	NO	Runs	HS	Avge	100	50	Balls	Runs	Wkts	Avge	BB	5i	10m	RpO	ct	st
Test	3	5	1	57	19	14.25	0	0									11	
FC	6	9	2	146	41*	20.85	0	0									24	1
Int	4	4	2	56	25	28.00	0	0									2	1

JULIAN, B.P.

Cmp	M	I	NO	Runs	HS	Avge	100	50	Balls	Runs	Wkts	Avge	BB	5i	10m	RpO	ct	st
Int	1	1	0	0	0	0.00	0	0	48	53	2	26.50	2-53	0	0	6.62	0	

Cmp Debut	M	I	NO	Runs	HS	Avge	100	50	Balls	Runs	Wkts	Avge	BB	5i	10m	RpO	ct	st
LANGER, J.L.																		
FC	2	3	1	66	31*	33.00	0	0									0	
LAW, S.G.																		
Int	7	7	0	145	50	20.71	0	1	51	52	1	52.00	1-36	0	0	6.11	2	
McGRATH, G.D.																		
Test	3	3	0	11	11	3.66	0	0	670	289	13	22.23	6-86	1	0	2.58	2	
FC	4	4	1	12	11	4.00	0	0	924	401	16	25.06	6-86	1	0	2.60	2	
REIFFEL, P.R.																		
FC	3	2	1	40	40*	40.00	0	0	276	104	5	20.80	2-15	0	0	2.26	1	
Int	4	3	0	17	10	5.66	0	0	234	170	1	170.00	1-44	0	0	4.35	1	
TAYLOR, M.A.																		
Test	3	5	0	80	38	16.00	0	0									3	
FC	5	8	0	186	85	23.25	0	1									3	
Int	2	2	0	24	17	12.00	0	0									0	
WARNE, S.K.																		
Test	3	5	0	42	18	8.40	0	0	798	282	11	25.63	4-43	0	0	2.12	3	
FC	5	7	0	101	44	14.42	0	0	1014	397	16	24.81	4-43	0	0	2.34	4	
Int	6	5	1	45	23	11.25	0	0	325	272	10	27.20	2-36	0	0	5.02	3	
WAUGH, M.E.																		
Test	3	5	0	209	116	41.80	1	0	48	38	1	38.00	1-34	0	0	4.75	3	
FC	5	7	0	395	124	56.42	2	1	120	68	1	68.00	1-34	0	0	3.40	5	
Int	4	3	1	118	115*	59.00	1	0	21	16	0					4.57	2	
WAUGH, S.R.																		
Test	3	5	1	313	160	78.25	1	2	51	20	1	20.00	1-4	0	0	2.35	3	
FC	5	7	1	404	160	67.33	1	3	165	94	2	47.00	1-4	0	0	3.41	5	
Int	7	7	1	301	91	50.16	0	4	30	25	0					5.00	3	

INDIA IN SOUTH AFRICA 1996-97

	M	I	NO	Runs	HS	Avge	100	50	Balls	Runs	Wkts	Avge	BB	5i	10m	RpO	ct	st
ANKOLA, S.A.																		
Int	5	5	0	20	9	4.00	0	0	240	201	2	100.50	1-32	0	0	5.02	1	
AZHARUDDIN, M.																		
Test	3	6	0	160	115	26.66	1	0									3	
FC	4	7	0	180	115	25.71	1	0									3	
Int	8	8	0	279	60	34.87	0	3									3	
DHARMANI, P.																		
FC	1	2	0	15	11	7.50	0	0									0	
DRAVID, R.S.																		
Test	3	6	1	277	148	55.40	1	1									6	
FC	5	10	3	419	148	59.85	1	2	6	3	0					3.00	9	
Int	8	8	0	280	84	35.00	0	3									3	
GANESH, D.																		
Test	2	4	2	4	2*	2.00	0	0	257	165	1	165.00	1-38	0	0	3.85	0	
FC	4	5	3	12	8*	6.00	0	0	590	384	3	128.00	2-89	0	0	3.90	0	
GANGULY, S.C.																		
Test	3	6	0	202	73	33.66	0	2	216	85	3	28.33	2-36	0	0	2.36	0	
FC	5	10	1	323	97	35.88	0	3	348	179	4	44.75	2-36	0	0	3.08	0	
Int	8	8	0	227	83	28.37	0	1	12	11	0					5.50	1	
JADEJA, A.D.																		
Int	8	8	1	187	56*	26.71	0	1	24	25	0					6.25	4	
JOHNSON, D.J.																		
Test	1	2	0	8	5	4.00	0	0	144	91	2	45.50	2-52	0	0	3.79	0	
FC	3	2	0	8	5	4.00	0	0	478	313	8	39.12	5-78	1	0	3.92	0	
JOSHI, S.B.																		
Int	3	1	1	3	3*		0	0	120	88	4	22.00	3-40	0	0	4.40	1	
KARIM, S.S.																		
FC	1	2	1	61	53*	61.00	0	1									1	
Int	6	6	1	121	55	24.20	0	1									2	1
KUMBLE, A.																		
Test	3	6	1	66	29	13.20	0	0	932	384	8	48.00	3-40	0	0	2.47	0	
FC	4	7	2	77	29	15.40	0	0	1034	435	8	54.37	3-40	0	0	2.52	1	
Int	8	6	1	38	11*	7.60	0	0	390	297	10	29.70	2-45	0	0	4.56	4	

Cmp	Debut	M	I	NO	Runs	HS	Avge	100	50	Balls	Runs	Wkts	Avge	BB	5i	10m	RpO	ct	st
LAXMAN, V.V.S.																			
Test		2	3	2	40	35*	40.00	0	0									0	
FC		3	5	4	142	56*	142.00	0	1									4	
MONGIA, N.R.																			
Test		3	6	0	86	50	14.33	0	1									14	
FC		4	7	0	86	50	12.28	0	1									15	
Int		2	1	0	7	7	7.00	0	0									1	
RAMAN, W.V.																			
Test		2	4	0	22	16	5.50	0	0	90	63	0					4.20	0	
FC		4	8	0	64	18	8.00	0	0	119	78	0					3.93	0	
RATHORE, V.																			
Test		2	4	0	66	44	16.50	0	0									4	
FC		4	8	0	366	115	45.75	1	3									4	
SINGH, R.R.																			
Int		8	8	2	178	48	29.66	0	0	321	252	6	42.00	2-18	0	0	4.71	1	
SRINATH, J.																			
Test		3	5	0	63	41	12.60	0	0	889	517	18	28.72	5-104	1	0	3.48	0	
FC		3	5	0	63	41	12.60	0	0	889	517	18	28.72	5-104	1	0	3.48	0	
Int		8	6	0	58	37	9.66	0	0	427	287	7	41.00	3-35	0	0	4.03	0	
TENDULKAR, S.R.																			
Test		3	6	0	241	169	40.16	1	0	28	18	0					3.85	3	
FC		4	7	0	303	169	43.28	1	1	88	57	1	57.00	1-39	0	0	3.88	3	
Int		8	8	0	243	104	30.37	1	0	90	85	1	85.00	1-19	0	0	5.66	1	
VENKATAPATHY RAJU, S.L.																			
FC		2	1	0	1	1	1.00	0	0	312	197	1	197.00	1-85	0	0	3.78	0	
VENKATESH PRASAD, B.K.																			
Test		3	6	2	23	15	5.75	0	0	732	425	17	25.00	5-60	2	1	3.48	0	
FC		4	6	2	23	15	5.75	0	0	822	457	18	25.38	5-60	2	1	3.33	0	
Int		8	5	5	15	10*		0	0	432	349	10	34.90	3-49	0	0	4.84	2	

KENYA IN SOUTH AFRICA 1996-97

Cmp	Debut	M	I	NO	Runs	HS	Avge	100	50	Balls	Runs	Wkts	Avge	BB	5i	10m	RpO	ct	st
ASIF KARIM																			
SB		1	1	0	13	13	13.00	0	0	54	35	0					3.88	0	
BWIBO, K.S.																			
SB		1	1	1	2	2*		0	0	12	13	0					6.50	1	
MODI, H.S.																			
SB		1	1	0	19	19	19.00	0	0									1	
ODOYO, T.																			
SB		1	1	0	21	21	21.00	0	0	48	41	1	41.00	1-41	0	0	5.12	0	
ODUMBE, M.O.																			
SB		1	1	0	8	8	8.00	0	0	54	51	0					5.66	2	
OTIENO, K.																			
SB		1	1	0	16	16	16.00	0	0									0	
PATEL, B.																			
SB		1	1	0	4	4	4.00	0	0	18	19	3	6.33	3-19	0	0	6.33	0	
SUJI, A.																			
SB		1	1	0	9	9	9.00	0	0	30	25	0					5.00	0	
SUJI, M.A.																			
SB		1	1	0	15	15	15.00	0	0	54	46	1	46.00	1-46	0	0	5.11	1	
TIKOLO, L.O.																			
SB		1	1	0	1	1	1.00	0	0									0	
TIKOLO, S.O.																			
SB		1	1	0	2	2	2.00	0	0									0	
SB	1995	6	6	0	151	104	25.16	1	0	36	36	0					6.00	0	

Cmp	Debut	M	I	NO	Runs	HS	Avge	100	50	Balls	Runs	Wkts	Avge	BB	5i	10m	RpO	ct	st

LEICESTERSHIRE IN SOUTH AFRICA 1996-97

BRIMSON, M.T.

Cmp	Debut	M	I	NO	Runs	HS	Avge	100	50	Balls	Runs	Wkts	Avge	BB	5i	10m	RpO	ct	st
FC		1	2	1	22	12*	22.00	0	0	204	104	2	52.00	2-104	0	0	3.05	0	

DAKIN, J.M.

| FC | | 1 | 2 | 0 | 35 | 23 | 17.50 | 0 | 0 | 60 | 39 | 1 | 39.00 | 1-39 | 0 | 0 | 3.90 | 1 | |

MADDY, D.L.

| FC | | 1 | 2 | 0 | 52 | 50 | 26.00 | 0 | 1 | 42 | 31 | 0 | | | | | 4.42 | 0 | |

MILLNS, D.J. (Boland - see main section)

| FC | | 1 | 2 | 0 | 18 | 17 | 9.00 | 0 | 0 | 108 | 90 | 0 | | | | | 5.00 | 0 | |

NIXON, P.A.

| FC | | 1 | 2 | 0 | 66 | 51 | 33.00 | 0 | 1 | | | | | | | | | 1 | |

PARSONS, G.J.

| FC | | 1 | 2 | 1 | 30 | 16 | 30.00 | 0 | 0 | 132 | 57 | 0 | | | | | 2.59 | 1 | |

PIERSON, A.R.K.

| FC | | 1 | 2 | 0 | 28 | 27 | 14.00 | 0 | 0 | 156 | 121 | 1 | 121.00 | 1-121 | 0 | 0 | 4.65 | 0 | |

SMITH, B.F.

| FC | | 1 | 2 | 0 | 32 | 27 | 16.00 | 0 | 0 | | | | | | | | | 0 | |

SUTCLIFFE, I.J.

| FC | | 1 | 2 | 0 | 1 | 1 | 0.50 | 0 | 0 | | | | | | | | | 0 | |

WELLS, V.J.

| FC | | 1 | 2 | 0 | 69 | 61 | 34.50 | 0 | 1 | 90 | 54 | 1 | 54.00 | 1-54 | 0 | 0 | 3.60 | 0 | |

WHITAKER, J.J.

| FC | | 1 | 2 | 0 | 115 | 105 | 57.50 | 1 | 0 | | | | | | | | | 1 | |

MASHONALAND IN SOUTH AFRICA 1996-97

BRANDES, E.A.

Cmp	Debut	M	I	NO	Runs	HS	Avge	100	50	Balls	Runs	Wkts	Avge	BB	5i	10m	RpO	ct	st
SB		2	2	1	35	32*	35.00	0	0	102	100	3	33.33	3-51	0	0	5.88	0	

CAMPBELL, A.D.R.

| SB | | 2 | 2 | 1 | 78 | 55* | 78.00 | 0 | 1 | 24 | 32 | 0 | | | | | 8.00 | 3 | |

CAMPBELL, D.J.R.

| SB | | 1 | 1 | 0 | 12 | 12 | 12.00 | 0 | 0 | | | | | | | | | 2 | |

CARLISLE, S.V.

| SB | | 1 | 1 | 0 | 13 | 13 | 13.00 | 0 | 0 | | | | | | | | | 1 | |

ERASMUS, D.N.

| SB | | 1 | 1 | 0 | 12 | 12 | 12.00 | 0 | 0 | | | | | | | | | 0 | |

EVANS, C.N.

| SB | | 2 | 2 | 0 | 37 | 29 | 18.50 | 0 | 0 | 60 | 73 | 2 | 36.50 | 2-24 | 0 | 0 | 7.30 | 0 | |

FLOWER, A.

| SB | | 1 | 1 | 0 | 24 | 24 | 24.00 | 0 | 0 | | | | | | | | | 0 | |

FLOWER, G.W.

| SB | | 1 | 1 | 0 | 100 | 100 | 100.00 | 1 | 0 | 24 | 20 | 1 | 20.00 | 1-20 | 0 | 0 | 5.00 | 0 | |

HOUGHTON, D.L.

| SB | | 1 | 1 | 0 | 28 | 28 | 28.00 | 0 | 0 | | | | | | | | | 0 | |

KIRTLEY, R.J.

| SB | | 1 | | | | | | | | 48 | 62 | 2 | 31.00 | 2-62 | 0 | 0 | 7.75 | 1 | |

MATAMBANADZO, E.

| SB | | 1 | | | | | | | | 36 | 61 | 1 | 61.00 | 1-61 | 0 | 0 | 10.16 | 1 | |

MURPHY, B.A.

| SB | | 1 | | | | | | | | 48 | 49 | 2 | 24.50 | 2-49 | 0 | 0 | 6.12 | 1 | |

OMARSHAH, A.H.

| SB | | 1 | 1 | 0 | 3 | 3 | 3.00 | 0 | 0 | 18 | 20 | 1 | 20.00 | 1-20 | 0 | 0 | 6.66 | 1 | |

STRANG, B.C.

| SB | | 2 | 2 | 1 | 0 | 0* | 0.00 | 0 | 0 | 102 | 69 | 1 | 69.00 | 1-34 | 0 | 0 | 4.05 | 0 | |

STRANG, P.A.

| SB | | 1 | 1 | 0 | 4 | 4 | 4.00 | 0 | 0 | 54 | 43 | 2 | 21.50 | 2-43 | 0 | 0 | 4.77 | 1 | |

VILJOEN, D.P.

| SB | | 1 | 1 | 1 | 20 | 20* | | 0 | 0 | | | | | | | | | 0 | |

WISHART, C.B.

| SB | | 2 | 2 | 0 | 14 | 11 | 7.00 | 0 | 0 | | | | | | | | | 1 | |

NOTTINGHAMSHIRE IN SOUTH AFRICA 1996-97

AFFORD, J.A.

Cmp	M	I	NO	Runs	HS	Avge	100	50	Balls	Runs	Wkts	Avge	BB	5i	10m	RpO	ct	st
FC	1	1	0	13	13	13.00	0	0	67	39	3	13.00	3-39	0	0	3.49	0	

AFZAAL, U.

FC	1	2	0	41	37	20.50	0	0	168	67	3	22.33	3-62	0	0	2.39	0	

ARCHER, G.F.

FC	1	2	0	47	25	23.50	0	0	60	29	1	29.00	1-6	0	0	2.90	1	

BOWEN, M.N.

FC	1	1	1	28	28*		0	0	180	99	7	14.14	4-56	0	0	3.30	0	

JOHNSON, P.

FC	1	2	1	101	88*	101.00	0	1									0	

METCALFE, A.A.

FC	1	2	0	13	12	6.50	0	0									0	

NOON, W.M.

FC	1	1	0	0	0	0.00	0	0									5	

PICK, R.A.

FC	1	1	0	17	17	17.00	0	0	156	58	1	58.00	1-34	0	0	2.23	0	

POLLARD, P.R.

FC	1	1	0	79	79	79.00	0	1									1	

ROBINSON, R.T.

FC	1	2	0	14	10	7.00	0	0									0	

TOLLEY, C.M.

FC	1	2	1	73	51*	73.00	0	1	210	85	1	85.00	1-49	0	0	2.42	0	

ZIMBABWE IN SOUTH AFRICA 1996-97

BRANDES, E.A.

Cmp	M	I	NO	Runs	HS	Avge	100	50	Balls	Runs	Wkts	Avge	BB	5i	10m	RpO	ct	st
Int	6	3	2	11	8*	11.00	0	0	317	262	12	21.83	5-41	0	1	4.95	0	

CAMPBELL, A.D.R.

Int	6	6	0	207	86	34.50	0	2	12	8	1	8.00	1-8	0	0	4.00	5	

CARLISLE, S.V.

Int	1	1	0	3	3	3.00	0	0									1	

EVANS, C.N.

Int	4	4	1	119	43	39.66	0	0	126	107	2	53.50	1-25	0	0	5.09	1	

FLOWER, A.

Int	6	6	0	80	35	13.33	0	0									3	1

FLOWER, G.W.

Int	6	6	0	248	80	41.33	0	2	49	42	0					5.14	3	

HOUGHTON, D.L.

Int	6	6	1	149	57	29.80	0	2									0	

MATAMBANADZO, E.

Int	1								51	53	1	53.00	1-53	0	0	6.23	0	

RENNIE, J.A.

Int	5	1	1	0	0*		0	0	222	158	7	22.57	2-28	0	0	4.27	0	

STRANG, P.A.

Int	6	6	2	174	47	43.50	0	0	306	228	2	114.00	1-43	0	0	4.47	3	

STREAK, H.H.

Int	6	5	2	39	12	13.00	0	0	336	285	4	71.25	2-51	0	0	5.08	0	

WALLER, A.C.

Int	5	5	0	61	52	12.20	0	1									1	

WHITTALL, G.J.

Int	6	6	1	113	41	22.60	0	0	258	215	4	53.75	1-20	0	0	5.00	2	

WISHART, C.B.

Int	2	2	0	32	24	16.00	0	0									0	

The following current cricketers have played in South African Domestic limited overs cricket but did not appear in South African Domestic cricket in 1996-97:

AUSTEN, M.H. (see New Zealand) (Western Province)

SB 1987	4	4	0	64	54	16.00	0	1									1	

BARNETT, K.J. (see Derbyshire) (Impalas)

SB 1984	6	6	0	70	31	11.66	0	0	54	25	1	25.00	1-25	0	0	2.77	1	

BOON, T.J. (see England other teams) (Natal)

SB 1991	2	2	0	3	3	1.50	0	0									2	

CAPEL, D.J. (see Northamptonshire) (Eastern Province)

SB 1985	9	9	2	192	44	27.42	0	0	409	249	9	27.66	3-36	0	0	3.65	2	

CURRAN, K.M. (see Northamptonshire) (Natal, Boland)

SB 1988	23	22	2	734	71	36.70	0	6	631	461	17	27.11	3-26	0	0	4.38	10	

DE FREITAS, P.A.J. (see Derbyshire) (Boland)

SB 1993	9	8	1	125	30	17.85	0	0	468	249	13	19.15	3-22	0	0	3.19	3	

EMBUREY, J.E. (see Northamptonshire) (Western Province)

SB 1982	10	6	1	31	20	6.20	0	0	357	221	7	31.57	3-6	0	0	3.71	5	

FAIRBROTHER, N.H. (see Lancashire) (Transvaal)

SB 1994	8	8	4	347	123*	86.75	1	2									3	

GIBSON, O.D. (see West Indies) (Border)

SB 1992	17	11	1	233	41	23.30	0	0	925	656	28	23.42	4-35	2	0	4.25	3	

GOOCH, G.A. (see Essex) (Western Province)

SB 1993	11	11	0	546	106	49.63	1	3	354	293	7	41.85	3-31	0	0	4.96	3	

LAMBERT, C.B. (see West Indies) (Northern Transvaal)

SB 1993	24	24	0	421	76	17.54	0	1									12	

LARA, B.C. (see West Indies) (Northern Transvaal)

SB 1992	3	3	0	102	48	34.00	0	0									0	

METCALFE, A.A. (see Nottinghamshire) (Orange Free State)

SB 1988	9	9	1	326	71	40.75	0	1									4	

MOLES, A.J. (see Warwickshire) (Impalas)

SB 1986	7	7	0	128	47	18.28	0	0									4	

MOORES, P. (see Sussex) (Orange Free State)

SB 1988	4	4	0	50	20	12.50	0	0									7	

MORRIS, J.E. (see Durham) (Impalas)

SB 1988	5	4	0	170	68	42.50	0	2									4	

NEWPORT, P.J. (see Worcestershire) (Northern Transvaal)

SB 1992	2	2	0	21	18	10.50	0	0	108	72	2	36.00	1-26	0	0	4.00	1	

SMITH, R.A. (see Hampshire) (Natal)

SB 1981	12	10	0	206	98	20.60	0	1									3	

STEPHENSON, J.P. (see Hampshire) (Impalas)

SB 1988	4	4	0	41	27	10.25	0	0									1	

VAN TROOST, A.P. (see Somerset) (Griqualand West)

SB 1994	3	2	0	0	0	0.00	0	0	138	119	3	39.66	2-30	0	0	5.17	0	

SRI LANKA

First First-Class Match: Dr J.Rockwood's Ceylon XI v W.E.Lucas' Bombay XI (Colombo) 1925-26

First First-Class Tour to England: 1975

First Test Match: Sri Lanka v England (Colombo) 1981-82

Present First-Class Teams: Antonians Sports Club, Bloomfield Cricket and Athletic Club, Burgher Recreation Club, Colombo Cricket Club, Colts Cricket Club, Galle Sports Club, Kalutara Town Cricket Club, Kurunegala Youth Cricket Club, Nondescripts Cricket Club, Panadura Sports Club, Police Sports Club, Sebastianites Cricket and Athletic Club, Singha Sports Club, Sinhalese Sports Club, Tamil Union Cricket and Athletic Club in 1996-97. Clubs compete in a non-first-class qualifying competition, so that different clubs may play in first-class matches each season. The BCCSL has ruled that domestic matches are first-class from 1988-89 onwards. Only Sri Lankan teams against overseas first-class teams were considered first-class up to 1987-88.

Sara Trophy Champions 1996-97: Bloomfield

FIRST-CLASS RECORDS

Highest Team Total: 549-8d West Indies v Ceylon (Colombo) 1966-67
Highest in 1996-97: 523-9d West Indies A v Sri Lanka A (Matara); 470-9d West Indies A v Sri Lanka A (Kurunegala); 458-4d Colts v Antonians (Colombo); 453-5d Colts v Galle (Colombo); 453-4d Sinhalese v Sebastianites (Colombo)

Lowest Team Total: 31 Kurunegala Youth v Sinhalese (Colombo) 1993-94
Lowest in 1996-97: 54 Antonians v Bloomfield (Colombo); 57 Police v Colts (Colombo); 63 Police v Bloomfield (Colombo); 64 Singha v Burgher (Colombo); 70 Kurunegala Youth v Antonians (Wattala)

Highest Individual Innings: 285 F.M.M.Worrell Commonwealth v Ceylon (Colombo) 1950-51
Highest in 1996-97: 200* A.Ranatunga Sinhalese v Sebastianites (Colombo); 183 A.Jayasinghe Tamil Union v Burgher (Colombo); 179 R.S.Kaluwitharana Colts v Kurunegala Youth (Colombo); 178* S.I.Fernando Colts v Galle (Colombo); 176 R.S.Mahanama Bloomfield v Kalutara Town (Colombo)

Most Runs in Season: 1,475 (av 70.23) R.P.Arnold (Nondescripts) 1995-96
Most in 1996-97:1,270 (av 70.55) R.S.Kaluwitharana (Colts); 1,032 (av 43.00) S.K.L.de Silva (Kurunegala Youth); 954 (av 47.70) S.T.Jayasuriya (Bloomfield); 913 (av 41.50) E.M.I.Galagoda (Burgher); 887 (av 49.27) S.I.Fernando (Colts)

Most Runs in Career: 10,963 (av 47.25) P.A.de Silva (Nondescripts, Kent) 1983-84 to date
Most by Current Batsman: see de Silva above, then 8,860 (av 42.80) A.Ranatunga (Sinhalese) 1981-82 to date; 7,169 (av 43.71) A.P.Gurusinha (Sinhalese, Nondescripts) 1984-85 to date; 6,939 (av 47.52) H.P.Tillakaratne (Nondescripts) 1984-85 to date; 6,361 (av 35.53) U.C.Hathurusingha (Tamil Union) 1988-89 to date

Best Innings Analysis: 10-41 G.P.Wickramasinghe Sinhalese v Kalutara Physical Culture (Colombo) 1991-92
Best in 1996-97: 9-15 M.Villavaryan Bloomfield v Police (Colombo); 9-29 A.D.B.Ranjith Singha v Antonians (Colombo); 8-29 U.C.Hathurusingha Tamil Union v Burgher (Colombo); 8-50 A.D.B.Ranjith Singha v Galle (Galle); 8-77 C.D.U.S.Weerasinghe Nondescripts v Colts (Colombo); 8-78 C.N.Bandaratilleke Tamil Union v Galle (Colombo)

Most Wickets in Season: 81 (av 14.33) K.P.J.Warnaweera (Galle) 1989-90
Most in 1996-97: 70 (av 16.40) A.D.B.Ranjith (Singha); 66 (av 14.42) M.Muralitharan (Tamil Union); 61 (av 20.13) R.S.Kalpage (Bloomfield); 58 (av 17.25) C.N.Bandaratilleke (Tamil Union); 57 (av 17.42) K.G.Perera (Antonians)

Most Wickets in Career: 395 (av 20.16) S.D.Anurasiri (Panadura) 1984 to date
Most by Current Bowler: see Anurasiri above, then 375 (av 21.24) M.Muralitharan (Tamil Union) 1989-90 to date; 287 (av 19.96) K.P.J.Warnaweera (Galle, Singha) 1985-86 to date; 284 (av 23.43) A.W.Ekanayake (Kurunegala Youth) 1990-91 to date; 259 (av 24.19) R.S.Kalpage (Bloomfield) 1988-89 to date

Record Wicket Partnerships

1st	255	H.Premasiri & W.M.J.Kumudu	Singha v Moratuwa (Moratuwa)	1995-96
2nd	289	W.A.M.P.Perera & T.P.Kodikara	Antonians v Rio (Colombo)	1992-93
3rd	315	S.T.Perera & R.S.Kalpage	Bloomfield v Antonians (Colombo)	1995-96
4th	278	R.P.A.H.Wickramaratne & M.S.Atapattu		
			Sinhalese v Tamil Union (Colombo)	1994-95
5th	317*	A.Ranatunga & R.P.A.H.Wickramaratne		
			Sinhalese v Sebastianites (Colombo)	1996-97
6th	246*	J.J.Crowe & R.J.Hadlee	New Zealand v Sri Lanka (Colombo)	1986-87
7th	153	P.A.de Silva & A.G.D.Wickremasinghe		
			Nondescripts v Sinhalese (Colombo)	1993-94
8th	222	D.Arnolda & S.Madanayake	Burgher v Galle (Galle)	1996-97
9th	153	R.Wickramaratne & S.Munaweera	Colts v Singha (Colombo)	1989-90
10th	118	A.W.Ekanayake & D.Amarasinghe	Kurunegala Youth v Antonians (Colombo)	1991-92

Highest Partnerships in 1996-97

1st	188	D.P.Samaraweera & M.C.Mendis	Colts v Panadura (Colombo)
2nd	175	D.Maiarachchi & S.Ranatunga	Nondescripts v Antonians (Katunayake)
3rd	277	S.I.Fernando & R.S.Kaluwitharana	Colts v Galle (Colombo)
4th	229	G.Wijekoon & A.Jayasinghe	Tamil Union v Burgher (Colombo)
5th	317*	A.Ranatunga & R.P.A.H.Wickramaratne	
			Sinhalese v Sebastianites (Colombo)
6th	239*	A.Gunawardene & H.P.Tillakarante	Nondescripts v Galle (Colombo)
7th	111	I.Amirthakeerthi & I.Gallage	Panadura v Burgher (Panadura)
8th	222	D.Arnolda & S.Madanayake	Burgher v Galle (Galle)
9th	118	W.C.Labrooy & H.M.L.Sagara	Burgher v Sinhalese (Colombo)
10th	102	S.Attanayake & B.Perera	Colts v Sinhalese (Colombo)

Most Wicketkeeping Dismissals in Innings: 7 (7ct) H.H.Devapriya Colts v Sinhalese (Colombo) 1995-96
Most in 1996-97: 6 (4ct 2st) M.Y.Kudagodage Police v Panadura (Panadura); 6 (2ct 4st) S.T.Perera Bloomfield v Antonians (Colombo)

Most Wicketkeeping Dismissals in Match: 10 (10ct) K.L.R.Fernando Moratuwa v Panadura (Moratuwa) 1989-90
Most in 1996-97: 8 (8ct) P.B.Dassanayake Bloomfield v Kurunegala Youth (Kurunegala); 8 (3ct 5st) N.C.Mendis Panadura v Kurunegala Youth (Moratuwa); 8 (6ct 2st) M.Perera Sinhalese v Kurunegala Youth (Colombo); 8 (4ct 4st) S.T.Perera Bloomfield v Antonians (Colombo)

Most Wicketkeeping Dismissals in Season: 57 (49ct 8st) A.G.D.Wickremasinghe (Nondescripts) 1990-91
Most in 1996-97: 45 (39ct 6st) S.K.L.de Silva (Kurunegala Youth); 40 (35ct 5st) E.M.I.Galagoda (Burgher); 38 (34ct 4st) C.I.Dunusinghe (Nondescripts); 36 (30ct 6st) T.M.Dilshan (Kalutara Town); 35 (31ct 4st) R.S.Kaluwitharana (Colts)

Most Wicketkeeping Dismissals in Career: 247 (214ct 33st) A.G.D.Wickremasinghe (Nondescripts) 1984-85 to 1995-96
Most by Current Wicketkeeper: 157 (139ct 18st) R.S.Kaluwitharana (Colts) 1988-89 to date; 155 (132ct 23st) U.N.K.Fernando (Sinhalese) 1989-90 to date; 149 (128ct 21st) C.I.Dunusinghe (Antonians, Nondescripts) 1990-91 to date; 140 (112ct 28st) P.B.Dassanayake (Colts, Bloomfield) 1989-90 to date; 125 (105ct 20st) S.K.L.de Silva (Kurunegala Youth) 1991-92 to date

Most Catches by Fielder in Innings: 6 C.M.Wickremasinghe Sebastianites v Police (Colombo) 1995-96
Most in 1996-97: 4 R.S.Mahanama Sri Lanka v Zimbabwe (Colombo); 4 K.C.Silva Panadura v Bloomfield (Panadura); 4 M.N.C.Silva Police v Galle (Galle); 4 Saleem Elahi Pakistan v Sri Lanka (Colombo)

Most Catches by Fielder in Match: 7 H.P.Tillakaratne Sri Lanka v New Zealand (Colombo) 1992-93
Most in 1996-97: 5 R.S.Mahanama Sri Lanka v Zimbabwe (Colombo); 5 K.C.Silva Panadura v Bloomfield (Panadura); 5 M.N.C.Silva Police v Galle (Galle)

Most Catches by Fielder in Season: 23 U.C.Hathurusingha (Tamil Union) 1994-95; 23 M.P.Silva (Panadura) 1995-96
Most in 1996-97: 20 S.N.Liyanage (Panadura); 18 R.S.Mahanama (Bloomfield); 18 M.N.Nawaz (Bloomfield); 17 J.Kulatunga (Colts)

Most Catches by Fielder in Career: 119 R.S.Mahanama (Colombo, Bloomfield) 1984-85 to date
Most by Current Fielder: see Mahanama above, then 102 R.P.A.H.Wickramaratne (Sinhalese) 1990-91 to date; 92 U.C.Hathurusingha (Tamil Union) 1988-89 to date; 89 A.P.Gurusinha (Sinhalese, Nondescripts) 1984-85 to date; 86 A.Ranatunga (Sinhalese) 1981-82 to date

CHAMPION TEAMS

Sara Trophy

Many teams compete in a preliminary round to decide which will qualify for the final stages, which have been ruled first-class since 1988-89. The winners were awarded the Lakspray Trophy in 1988-89 and 1989-90, and the Sara Trophy (sponsored by J and B) from 1990-91. The winners have been:

1988-89	Nondescripts,
	Sinhalese
1989-90	Sinhalese
1990-91	Sinhalese
1991-92	Colts
1992-93	Sinhalese
1993-94	Nondescripts
1994-95	Bloomfield,
	Sinhalese
1995-96	Colombo
1996-97	Bloomfield

Singer Trophy

The Inter-Provincial tournament currently competed for by Western Province South, North and City, Southern Province, Central Province and North Western Province. The winners have been:

1989-90	Western Province
1990-91	Western Province City
1991-92	Western Province North
1992-93	No competition
1993-94	Western Province City
1994-95	Western Province City
1995-96	No competition
1996-97	No competition

1996-97 AND CAREER RECORDS FOR SRI LANKAN PLAYERS

Cmp	Debut	M	I	NO	Runs	HS	Avge	100	50	Balls	Runs	Wkts	Avge	BB	5i	10m	RpO	ct	st

ABEYASEKERA, D. (Kalutara Town) RHB

| FC | | 2 | 4 | 1 | 4 | 2 | 1.33 | 0 | 0 | | | | | | | | | 0 | |

ABEYNAIKE, Sajeeka (Bloomfield) b Colombo 28.4.1974 RHB

| FC | | 2 | 3 | 1 | 79 | 62 | 39.50 | 0 | 1 | | | | | | | | | 1 | |

ABEYWARDENE, Widara Don Justus (Sebastianites) b Moratuwa 7.3.1975 RHB RFM

| FC | | 8 | 13 | 0 | 216 | 75 | 16.61 | 0 | 1 | 108 | 95 | 1 | 95.00 | 1-28 | 0 | 0 | 5.27 | 1 | |
| FC | 1993 | 21 | 38 | 1 | 882 | 91 | 23.83 | 0 | 6 | 598 | 458 | 5 | 91.60 | 1-20 | 0 | 0 | 4.59 | 6 | |

ABEYWICKREME, B. (Panadura) RHB RM

| FC | | 1 | 2 | 2 | 23 | 15* | | 0 | 0 | 6 | 14 | 0 | | | | | 14.00 | 0 | |

ACHINATH, Thusara (Singha) b Balapitiya 21.8.1977 LHB WK

| FC | | 12 | 23 | 2 | 358 | 47 | 17.04 | 0 | 0 | | | | | | | | | 19 | 3 |

ADIKARAM, Naresh (Sinhalese) b Colombo 17.9.1970 RHB

| FC | | 1 | 1 | 0 | 7 | 7 | 7.00 | 0 | 0 | | | | | | | | | 1 | |
| FC | 1995 | 7 | 11 | 1 | 259 | 55* | 25.90 | 0 | 1 | | | | | | | | | 9 | |

ALEXANDER, Suchitra (Colts) b Colombo 14.10.1972 RHB RM

| FC | | 6 | 8 | 2 | 53 | 21 | 8.83 | 0 | 0 | 282 | 213 | 5 | 42.60 | 1-15 | 0 | 0 | 4.53 | 6 | |
| FC | 1993 | 29 | 36 | 10 | 609 | 83 | 23.42 | 0 | 3 | 2810 | 1721 | 55 | 31.29 | 5-26 | 1 | 0 | 3.67 | 19 | |

ALLES, Surath Hemantha (Colts) b Colombo 10.11.1976 RHB RM

| FC | | 2 | 1 | 0 | 1 | 1 | 1.00 | 0 | 0 | 156 | 133 | 2 | 66.50 | 1-34 | 0 | 0 | 5.11 | 1 | |
| FC | 1995 | 10 | 10 | 5 | 159 | 53* | 31.80 | 0 | 2 | 420 | 294 | 7 | 42.00 | 2-44 | 0 | 0 | 4.20 | 1 | |

AMITHAKEERTHI, Indika (Panadura) b Colombo 18.10.1976 RHB OB

| FC | | 11 | 16 | 4 | 547 | 137* | 45.58 | 2 | 0 | 795 | 380 | 16 | 23.75 | 5-6 | 1 | 0 | 2.86 | 7 | |

AMUGODA, Nilantha (Antonians) RHB WK

| FC | | 4 | 4 | 0 | 15 | 7 | 3.75 | 0 | 0 | | | | | | | | | 13 | 2 |

AMUNUGAMA, Rajith Krishnantha Bandara (Kurunegala Youth) b Mawanella 22.4.1969 LHB RM

| FC | | 7 | 11 | 3 | 201 | 39 | 25.12 | 0 | 0 | 742 | 420 | 17 | 24.70 | 5-61 | 1 | 0 | 3.39 | 3 | |
| FC | 1988 | 61 | 79 | 22 | 828 | 52* | 14.52 | 0 | 1 | 6669 | 4107 | 161 | 25.50 | 8-60 | 6 | 1 | 3.69 | 28 | |

ANUPAMA, Gayan (Kalutara Town) b Kalutara 22.2.1977 LHB

| FC | | 4 | 7 | 0 | 13 | 7 | 1.85 | 0 | 0 | | | | | | | | | 2 | |

ANURASIRI, Sangarange Don (Panadura) b Panadura 25.2.1966 RHB SLA

FC		9	11	0	189	37	17.18	0	0	1955	474	39	12.15	7-84	5	1	1.45	2	
Test	1985	17	21	4	88	24	5.17	0	0	3697	1442	37	38.97	4-71	0	0	2.34	3	
FC	1984	110	131	30	1270	74	12.57	0	1	23090	7964	395	20.16	8-53	32	9	2.06	48	
Int	1990	45	18	12	62	11	10.33	0	0	2100	1464	32	45.75	3-40	0	0	4.18	10	

ARNOLD, Russel Premakumaran (Nondescripts, Sri Lanka, Sri Lanka A, Sri Lanka to West Indies) b Colombo 25.10.1973 LHB OB

Test		2	4	0	126	50	31.50	0	1	78	31	0					2.38	3	
FC		17	24	-1	813	131	35.34	3	3	1934	941	41	22.95-	7-84	1	0	2.91	16	
Test	1996	3	6	0	138	50	23.00	0	1	78	31	0					2.38	4	
FC	1993	49	74	7	3202	217*	47.79	9	12	·5208	2439	107	22.79	7-84	4	0	2.80	51	

ARNOLDA, Duncan (Burgher) b Kandy 17.1.1975 RHB RM

| FC | | 10 | 17 | 4 | 359 | 129* | 27.61 | 1 | 1 | 830 | 490 | 15 | 32.66 | 3-55 | 0 | 0 | 3.54 | 4 | |
| FC | 1994 | 12 | 19 | 4 | 367 | 129* | 24.46 | 1 | 1 | 872 | 519 | 15 | 34.60 | 3-55 | 0 | 0 | 3.57 | 5 | |

ASSALARACHCHI, Don Aruna (Panadura) b Panadura 13.3.1977 RHB LM

| FC | | 5 | 6 | 1 | 63 | 27 | 12.60 | 0 | 0 | 378 | 256 | 7 | 36.57 | 2-18 | 0 | 0 | 4.06 | 1 | |
| FC | 1995 | 9 | 11 | 5 | 80 | 27 | 13.33 | 0 | 0 | 720 | 467 | 12 | 38.91 | 2-18 | 0 | 0 | 3.89 | 2 | |

ATAPATTU, Marvan Samson (Sinhalese, Sri Lanka, Sri Lanka A, Sri Lanka to New Zealand, Sri Lanka to West Indies, Sri Lanka to Sharjah, Sri Lanka to India) b Kalutara 22.11.1970 RHB LB

Test		2	4	0	43	25	10.75	0	0	24	9	1	9.00	1-9	0	0	2.25	2	
FC		13	19	4	721	135*	48.06	3	3	42	14	2	7.00	1-3	0	0	2.00	10	
Int		1																	0
Test	1990	7	14	0	108	25	7.71	0	0	24	9	1	9.00	1-9	0	0	2.25	4	
FC	1988	103	140	32	6170	253*	57.12	22	24	1254	652	19	34.31	3-19	0	0	3.11	77	
Int	1990	22	21	4	478	94	28.11	0	4	51	41	0					4.82	7	

ATTANAYAKE, Sanjaya (Colts) b Colombo 5.3.1973 RHB RM WK

| FC | | 4 | 7 | 4 | 153 | 46* | 51.00 | 0 | 0 | | | | | | | | | 10 | 1 |
| FC | 1994 | 21 | 30 | 6 | 519 | 75 | 21.62 | 0 | 1 | 18 | 5 | 0 | | | | | 1.66 | 26 | 2 |

BALAGALLA, M. (Kalutara Town) b Kalutara 19.3.1978 RHB

| FC | | 1 | 2 | 1 | 7 | 4 | 7.00 | 0 | 0 | | | | | | | | | 0 | |

BANDARA, Malinga (Kalutara Town) b Kalutara 31.12.1979 RHB LB

| FC | | 4 | 8 | 3 | 29* | 24 | 5.80 | 0 | 0 | 418 | 280 | 8 | 35.00 | 3-57 | 0 | 0 | 4.01 | 2 | |

BANDARANAYAKE, Ananda Hulugalle (Kurunegala Youth) b Kurunegala 31.10.1971 LHB OB

Cmp	Debut	M	I	NO	Runs	HS	Avge	100	50	Balls	Runs	Wkts	Avge	BB	5i	10m	RpO	ct	st
FC		4	7	0	84	34	12.00	0	0	192	110	2	55.00	2-32	0	0	3.43	4	
FC	1989	36	60	3	977	83	17.14	0	5	2996	1738	52	33.42	5-74	2	0	3.48	31	

BANDARATILLEKE, Chandima Niroshan (Tamil Union) b Colombo 16.5.1975 RHB SLA

FC		13	16	5	245	77	22.27	0	1	2361	1001	58	17.25	8-78	4	0	2.54	12	
FC	1993	43	47	11	737	77	20.47	0	1	6612	2992	156	19.17	8-78	11	1	2.71	39	

BATUWITARACHCHI, Indika Prabath Priyankara (Bloomfield) b Colombo 3.11.1974 RHB RA

FC		5	9	1	325	109	40.62	1	2	6	1	0					1.00	3	
FC	1994	20	34	3	1097	144	35.38	2	6	6	1	0					1.00	10	

BODIYABADUGE, Dharshana (Sebastianites) b Moratuwa 6.8.1975 RHB SLA

FC		7	13	2	246	55	22.36	0	1	60	47	0					4.70	3	
FC	1994	19	34	4	980	111	32.66	1	4	911	547	15	36.46	3-38	0	0	3.60	8	

BOPAGE, Nilantha Sanjeewa (Bloomfield) b Colombo 11.1.1972 RHB RM

FC		8	12	0	278	81	23.16	0	2									5	
FC	1989	33	50	1	1220	145	24.89	2	6	132	82	0					3.72	32	

BOTEJU, Hemantha (Bloomfield) b Colombo 3.11.1977 RHB RM

FC		3	4	2	26	11	13.00	0	0	246	112	7	16.00	3-29	0	0	2.73	2	
FC	1995	7	9	2	207	74	29.28	0	2	972	472	21	22.47	4-32	0	0	2.91	6	

BOTEJU, Thusitha Martinus Chaminda (Sinhalese) b Gampaha 6.8.1975 RHB RM

FC		6	5	1	69	53*	17.25	0	1	768	449	15	29.93	3-41	0	0	3.50	1	
FC	1995	18	16	3	123	53*	9.46	0	1	2176	1168	41	28.48	4-33	0	0	3.22	3	

CHANDANA, Kapila (Panadura) b Panadura 30.7.1974

FC		1	1	0	6	6	6.00	0	0	96	43	0					2.68	0	

CHANDANA, K. (Singha) RHB

FC		1	2	0	5	4	2.50	0	0	18	7	0					2.33	0	

CHANDANA, Ruwan (Kalutara Town) RHB RFM

FC		8	15	7	63	16*	7.87	0	0	743	604	17	35.52	3-41	0	0	4.87	4	

CHANDANA, Umagiliya Durage Upul (Tamil Union, Sri Lanka, Sri Lanka to Kenya, Sri Lanka to Sharjah, Sri Lanka to New Zealand) b Galle 7.5.1972 RHB LB

FC		9	12	1	537	104*	48.81	2	4	1331	707	29	24.37	6-25	1	0	3.18	7	
Int		3	1	1	14	14*		0	0	156	121	7	17.28	4-35	1	0	4.65	4	
FC	1991	66	81	8	2719	163	37.24	7	15	5492	2750	115	23.91	6-25	3	0	3.00	56	
Int	1993	17	11	1	99	26	9.90	0	0	510	393	11	35.72	4-35	1	0	4.62	12	

CHRISHANTHA, Wellage Chaminda (Singha) b Galle 10.6.1976 RHB SLA

FC		6	12	4	54	24*	6.75	0	0	387	253	8	31.62	4-106	0	0	3.92	2	

DABARE, Niranjan (Colombo) b Colombo 22.10.1971 RHB OB

FC		2	3	3	22	20*		0	0	329	121	7	17.28	3-40	0	0	2.20	0	
FC	1992	30	30	18	193	24*	16.08	0	0	4380	1982	102	19.43	7-28	7	0	2.71	11	

DALUGODA, Amal Prasantha (Colombo, Sebastianites) b Colombo 5.12.1973 RHB SLA

FC		10	15	1	498	116	35.53	1	4	1888	711	19	37.42	4-31	0	0	2.25	5	
FC	1994	26	42	5	1158	116	31.29	1	9	5060	1927	71	27.14	5-45	1	0	2.28	13	

DAMMIKA, Tharanga (Antonians) b Colombo 6.1.1977 LHB

FC		2	4	1	24	21*	8.00	0	0	126	113	0					5.38	1	

DASSANAYAKE, Pubudu Bathiya (Bloomfield) b Kandy 11.7.1970 RHB WK

FC		11	16	1	566	119	37.73	1	3									18	3
Test	1993	11	17	2	196	36	13.06	0	0									19	5
FC	1989	67	100	8	2724	144	29.60	4	14									112	28
Int	1993	16	10	2	85	20*	10.62	0	0									9	4

DE ALWIS, Mahesh Priyanka (Sebastianites) b Moratuwa 26.4.1975 LHB OB

FC		1	2	0	2	1	1.00	0	0	48	34	0					4.25	0	
FC	1994	13	25	3	389	61	17.68	0	1	641	382	7	54.57	3-96	0	0	3.57	7	

DE SARAM, Samantha Indika (Tamil Union, Sri Lanka A) b Matara 2.9.1973 RHB WK

FC		8	12	0	348	105	29.00	1	1									8	2
FC	1990	48	74	4	2798	237	39.97	6	13	7	3	0					2.57	62	7

DESHAPRIYA, Miniwampitiyage Vijith (Panadura) b Panadura 6.9.1961 RHB LBG

FC		2	2	0	4	4	2.00	0	0	136	115	1	115.00	1-59	0	0	5.07	1	
FC	1987	63	81	10	1631	121*	22.97	2	5	4701	2675	110	24.31	7-41	5	1	3.41	37	

DE SILVA, Bathesha (Bloomfield) b Colombo 11.7.1976 RHB OB

FC		7	9	0	209	66	23.22	0	2	463	260	19	13.68	6-22	2	1	3.36	6	
FC	1995	19	26	3	599	101*	26.04	1	5	1973	1132	65	17.41	8-79	7	2	3.44	18	

DE SILVA, Daminda (Bloomfield) b Colombo 10.10.1973 RHB

FC		1	1	1	4	4*		0	0	96	72	1	72.00	1-72	0	0	4.50	0	

DE SILVA, Ellawalankanamge Asoka Ranjit (Nondescripts) b Kalutara 28.3.1956 LHB LBG

FC		7	6	0	67	36	11.16	0	0	630	251	10	25.10	3-39	0	0	2.39	8	
Test	1985	10	16	4	185	50	15.41	0	1	2328	1032	8	129.00	2-67	0	0	2.65	4	

Cmp	Debut	M	I	NO	Runs	HS	Avge	100	50	Balls	Runs	Wkts	Avge	BB	5i	10m	RpO	ct	st
FC	1983	84	103	13	1900	82*	21.11	0	8	11729	4551	186	24.46	6-48	7	0	2.32	48	
Int	1986	28	20	6	138	19*	9.85	0	0	1374	967	17	56.88	3-38	0	0	4.22	6	

DE SILVA, Karunakalage Sajeewa Chanaka (Nondescripts, Sri Lanka, Sri Lanka to New Zealand, New Zealand to West Indies, Sri Lanka to Kenya, Sri Lanka to Sharjah, Sri Lanka to India) b Kalutara 11.1.1971 LHB LFM

Cmp	Debut	M	I	NO	Runs	HS	Avge	100	50	Balls	Runs	Wkts	Avge	BB	5i	10m	RpO	ct	st
Test		1	1	0	0	0	0.00	0	0	260	158	5	31.60	5-85	1	0	3.64	0	
FC		10	6	4	11	8*	5.50	0	0	1558	755	38	19.86	6-48	2	0	2.90	5	
Test	1996	4	7	4	13	6	4.33	0	0	722	422	8	52.75	5-85	1	0	3.50	1	
FC	1990	50	70	17	473	31	8.92	0	0	7529	4067	179	22.72	7-73	11	2	3.24	28	
Int	1996	17	10	5	21	13*	4.20	0	0	797	610	30	20.33	3-18	0	0	4.59	5	

DE SILVA, Malaka Mahendra (Galle) b Galle 29.1.1975 RHB SLA

Cmp	Debut	M	I	NO	Runs	HS	Avge	100	50	Balls	Runs	Wkts	Avge	BB	5i	10m	RpO	ct	st
FC		13	21	3	239	53	13.27	0	1	2228	1270	46	27.60	6-27	4	1	3.42	7	
FC	1994	31	48	9	570	83	14.61	0	2	4632	2300	91	25.27	6-27	6	1	2.97	17	

DE SILVA, Nilan (Tamil Union) b Colombo 28.6.1971 RHB WK OB

Cmp	Debut	M	I	NO	Runs	HS	Avge	100	50	Balls	Runs	Wkts	Avge	BB	5i	10m	RpO	ct	st
FC		11	14	1	261	52	20.07	0	1									25	8
FC	1990	36	57	3	1411	124*	26.12	1	6	134	138	3	46.00	2-105	0	0	6.17	76	13

DE SILVA, Pinnaduwage Aravinda (Sri Lanka, Auckland, Sri Lanka to New Zealand, Sri Lanka to West Indies, Sri Lanka to Kenya, Sri Lanka to Sharjah, Sri Lanka to India) b Colombo 17.10.1965 RHB OB

Cmp	Debut	M	I	NO	Runs	HS	Avge	100	50	Balls	Runs	Wkts	Avge	BB	5i	10m	RpO	ct	st
Test		4	6	2	483	168	120.75	3	0	78	34	0					2.61	2	
FC		4	6	2	483	168	120.75	3	0	78	34	0					2.61	2	
Int		4	4	4	334	127*		1	2	72	67	0					5.58	1	
Test	1984	61	107	6	3828	267	37.90	11	14	1227	639	17	37.58	3-39	0	0	3.12	27	
FC	1983	163	255	23	10963	267	47.25	31	51	5589	2471	72	34.31	7-24	4	0	2.65	85	
Int	1983	210	204	21	6601	145	36.07	8	45	3206	2586	65	39.78	3-36	0	0	4.83	63	

DE SILVA, Sunesh Amila (Antonians) b Anuradhapura 30.9.1974 RHB RFM

Cmp	Debut	M	I	NO	Runs	HS	Avge	100	50	Balls	Runs	Wkts	Avge	BB	5i	10m	RpO	ct	st
FC		1	2	0	36	20	18.00	0	0									0	
FC	1992	21	37	3	435	48	12.79	0	0	360	279	8	34.87	4-37	0	0	4.65	9	

DE SILVA, Sanjeewa Kumara Lanka (Kurunegala Youth, Sri Lanka A) b Kurunegala 29.7.1975 RHB WK OB

Cmp	Debut	M	I	NO	Runs	HS	Avge	100	50	Balls	Runs	Wkts	Avge	BB	5i	10m	RpO	ct	st
FC		14	25	1	1032	109	43.00	4	5									39	6
FC	1991	52	91	10	3393	183*	41.88	9	19	6	0	1	0.00	1-0	0	0	0.00	105	20

DE SILVA, Wali Thushira (Tamil Union) b Colombo 28.5.1970 RHB WK

Cmp	Debut	M	I	NO	Runs	HS	Avge	100	50	Balls	Runs	Wkts	Avge	BB	5i	10m	RpO	ct	st
FC		2	3	0	43	16	14.33	0	0									4	1
FC	1991	38	58	8	1154	94	23.08	0	6									44	8

DEVARAJAN, Nalliah (Antonians) b Jaffna 24.8.1965 RHB OB

Cmp	Debut	M	I	NO	Runs	HS	Avge	100	50	Balls	Runs	Wkts	Avge	BB	5i	10m	RpO	ct	st
FC		9	16	3	252	53*	19.38	0	2	78	38	0					2.92	0	
FC	1988	45	72	8	1562	125*	24.40	2	9	1166	731	24	30.45	5-78	1	0	3.76	22	

DHANASINGHE, Hidda Marakkala Nishan Chandrajith (Singha) b Ambalangoda 16.8.1966 RHB RM

Cmp	Debut	M	I	NO	Runs	HS	Avge	100	50	Balls	Runs	Wkts	Avge	BB	5i	10m	RpO	ct	st
FC		1								18	11	0					3.66	0	
FC	1989	35	59	1	1193	215	20.56	3	2	2422	1386	39	35.53	4-17	0	0	3.43	47	

DHARMASENA, Handunnettige Deepthi Priyantha Kumara (Bloomfield, Sri Lanka, Sri Lanka to New Zealand, Sri Lanka to West Indies, Sri Lanka to Kenya, Sri Lanka to Sharjah, Sri Lanka to India) b Colombo 24.4.1971 RHB RM/OB

Cmp	Debut	M	I	NO	Runs	HS	Avge	100	50	Balls	Runs	Wkts	Avge	BB	5i	10m	RpO	ct	st
Test		2	3	2	54	42*	54.00	0	0	455	135	3	45.00	1-19	0	0	1.78	2	
FC		7	9	4	405	155*	81.00	1	2	1001	327	18	18.16	5-27	1	0	1.96	4	
Int		3								144	141	4	35.25	2-33	0	0	5.87	0	
Test	1993	15	27	4	503	62*	21.86	0	2	3607	1423	34	41.85	6-99	1	0	2.36	8	
FC	1988	61	82	14	2076	155*	30.52	1	11	10382	4160	188	22.12	7-111	12	3	2.40	35	
Int	1996	57	35	15	505	51*	25.25	0	3	2752	2022	57	35.47	4-37	1	0	4.40	14	

DHARMASENA, Krishan (Antonians) b Colombo 29.11.1966 RHB OB

Cmp	Debut	M	I	NO	Runs	HS	Avge	100	50	Balls	Runs	Wkts	Avge	BB	5i	10m	RpO	ct	st
FC		12	20	4	191	37*	11.93	0	0	1100	523	17	30.76	3-41	0	0	2.85	8	
FC	1988	44	66	10	1168	99*	20.85	0	5	4841	2189	94	23.28	6-72	1	0	2.71	33	

DILSHAN, Tuwan Mohamed (Kalutara Town) b Kalutara 14.10.1976 RHB RM WK

Cmp	Debut	M	I	NO	Runs	HS	Avge	100	50	Balls	Runs	Wkts	Avge	BB	5i	10m	RpO	ct	st
FC		13	26	0	606	111	23.30	1	4	6	12	0					12.00	30	6
FC	1993	19	37	1	887	126	24.63	2	4	6	12	0					12.00	38	6

DISSANAYAKE, Kolitha (Kalutara Town) b

Cmp	Debut	M	I	NO	Runs	HS	Avge	100	50	Balls	Runs	Wkts	Avge	BB	5i	10m	RpO	ct	st
FC		1	2	1	3	3	1.50	0	0									2	

DISSANAYAKE, Shanuka (Bloomfield) LHB RA

Cmp	Debut	M	I	NO	Runs	HS	Avge	100	50	Balls	Runs	Wkts	Avge	BB	5i	10m	RpO	ct	st
FC		2	2	0	39	39	19.50	0	0	162	99	8	12.37	4-26	0	0	3.66	5	
FC	1995	4	5	2	39	39	20.66	0	0	234	167	9	18.55	4-26	0	0	4.28	8	

DODANWELA, Samantha Bandara (Sinhalese) b Kandy 15.9.1970 RHB RM

Cmp	Debut	M	I	NO	Runs	HS	Avge	100	50	Balls	Runs	Wkts	Avge	BB	5i	10m	RpO	ct	st
FC		9	7	4	74	22	24.66	0	0	1044	526	29	18.13	5-39	1	0	3.02	2	
FC	1993	28	22	9	133	22	10.23	0	0	3367	1734	103	16.83	6-44	5	1	3.08	7	

DUNUSINGHE, Chamara Iroshan (Nondescripts, Sri Lanka A, President's XI) b Colombo 19.10.1970 RHB WK

Cmp	Debut	M	I	NO	Runs	HS	Avge	100	50	Balls	Runs	Wkts	Avge	BB	5i	10m	RpO	ct	st
FC		13	16	3	278	50*	21.38	0	1									34	4
Test	1994	5	10	0	160	91	16.00	0	1									13	2
FC	1990	54	78	7	1444	91	20.33	0	8									128	21
Int	1994	1	1	0	1	1	1.00	0	0									1	1

Cmp	Debut	M	I	NO	Runs	HS	Avge	100	50	Balls	Runs	Wkts	Avge	BB	5i	10m	RpO	ct	st
DUNUWILA, Ramesh (Burgher)																			
FC		1	1	0	11	11	11.00	0	0	48	27	0					3.37	2	
EDIRIWEERA, Prince Bradmon (Colombo, Bloomfield) b Colombo 19.9.1975 LHB RM																			
FC		6	9	0	292	82	32.44	0	3	36	18	0					3.00	1	
FC	1995	19	28	0	1054	106	37.64	1	9	36	18	0					3.00	4	
EKANAYAKE, Ajith Wijeratne (Kurunegala Youth) b Kurunegala 3.10.1965 RHB SLA																			
FC		11	19	1	323	82	17.94	0	2	2171	1075	47	22.87	5-41	3	0	2.97	5	
FC	1990	68	97	11	1251	82	14.54	0	6	15094	6656	284	23.43	8-39	22	3	2.64	43	
EKANAYAKE, Dushantha (Burgher) b 8.6.1969 RHB RFM																			
FC		6	8	1	· 58	29*	8.28	0	0	612	317	12	26.41	5-33	1	0	3.10	4	
FC	1992	8	12	3	68	29*	7.55	0	0	934	527	22	23.95	7-129	2	0	3.38	4	
FAUMI, Shihabdeen Mohamed (Galle) b Matara 6.5.1966 RHB RM																			
FC		12	19	2	398	46	·23.41	0	0	1678	924	27	34.22	4-111	0	0	3.30	10	
FC	1989	67	102	8	1716	95	18.25	0	4	6773	3897	127	30.68	6-52	2	0	3.45	51	
FERNANDO, Asela (Sebastianites) b Moratuwa 12.7.1970 RHB																			
FC		13	19	2	461	113	27.11	1	2									4	
FC	1989	33	56	5	1081	113	21.19	1	3	18	11	1	11.00	1-11	0	0	3.66	36	
FERNANADO, Chaminda Nishantha (Sinhalese) b Colombo 31.10.1969 RHB LMF																			
FC		7	8	1	317	107	45.28	1	2	308	151	8	18.87	5-25	1	0	2.94	6	
FC	1988	51	54	6	1364	131*	28.41	2	8	3531	1792	70	25.60	5-25	3	0	3.04	39	
FERNANDO, Charinda Roshan (Antonians) b Colombo 3.11.1977 RHB OB																			
FC		1	1	1	17	17*		0	0	84	29	0					2.07	0	
FC	1995	3	5	1	84	33	21.00	0	0	174	89	0					3.06	0	
FERNANDO, Edirappulige Felician Mahinda Upul (Colombo, Antonians) b Colombo 8.6.1973 RHB RM WK																			
FC		11	18	1	610	105	35.88	1	4									13	10
FC	1991	42	66	2	1812	112	28.31	2	9	54	36	1	36.00	1-22	0	0	4.00	67	13
FERNANDO, Sajith Ian (Colts, President's XI) b Kandy 27.9.1972 LHB OB																			
FC		14	21	3	887	178*	49.27	2	4	1174	528	19	27.78	5-45	1	0	2.69	8	
FC	1993	40	68	8	2346	178*	39.10	3	13	4354	2032	68	29.88	6-114	3	0	2.80	22	
FERNANDO, Ungamandadige Nisal Kumudusiri (Sinhalese) b Colombo 10.3.1970 RHB WK																			
FC		10	12	0	357	92	29.75	0	3	12	5	0					2.50	17	4
FC	1989	68	83	10	2730	160	37.39	3	17	12	5	0					2.50	132	23
Int	1993	2	2	2	22	20*		0	0									0	
FONSEKA, Hewafonsekage Saman Surendra (Kalutara Town) b Kalutara 8.7.1969 RHB OB																			
FC		13	26	0	612	91	23.53	0	3	686	435	15	29.00	3-30	0	0	3.80	13	
FC	1988	69	119	3	2644	190	22.79	2	12	1085	683	21	32.52	4-55	0	0	3.77	63	
FONSEKA, Shantha Roshan (Burgher) b Colombo 28.9.1975 LA																			
FC		1	1	1	4	4*		0	0	48	25	0					3.12	1	
GALAGODA, Ekanayake Mudiyansalage Indika (Burgher) b Colombo 29.7.1974 RHB WK																			
FC		13	23	1	913	117	41.50	1	5	12	3	0					1.50	35	5
FC	1994	26	42	2	1232	117	30.80	1	7	12	3	0					1.50	55	6
GALAPPATHY, Rohan Chaminda (Panadura) b Panadura 14.8.1974 RHB																			
FC		9	15	0	273	69	18.20	0	1									10	
FC	1992	12	21	0	310	69	14.76	0	1									15	
GALLAGE, Indika Sanjeewa (Panadura) b Panadura 22.11.1975 RHB RM																			
FC		12	14	1	140	38	10.76	0	0	1556	899	36	24.97	5-72	2	0	3.46	2	
FC	1995	24	30	4	313	40	12.03	0	0	2574	1609	57	28.22	5-72	2	0	3.75	6	
GAMAGE, Janaka Champika (Galle) b Matara 17.4.1964 RHB RFM																			
FC		5	6	1	68	32	13.60	0	0	414	140	10	14.00	4-34	0	0	2.02	6	
FC	1988	44	54	14	442	49	11.05	0	0	5947	2993	124	24.13	7-69	6	1	3.01	24	
Int	1994	4	2	2	8	7*		0	0	132	104	3	34.66	2-17	0	0	4.72	2	
GUNARATNE, Pulasthi Waruna (Bloomfield) b Colombo 27.9.1973 RHB RFM																			
FC		13	8	1	103	22	14.71	0	0	1492	765	32	23.90	6-71	1	1	3.07	9	
FC	1993	38	29	6	349	34	15.17	0	0	5099	2601	112	23.22	6-31	4	2	3.06	27	
GUNASENA, Lasitha Yasakula (Nondescripts) b Colombo 9.5.1974 LHB WK																			
FC		2	3	0	4	4	1.33	0	0									3	3
GUNAWARDENE, Avishka (Nondescripts) b Colombo 26.5.1977 LHB																			
FC		13	16	2	552	120*	39.42	2	1									11	
GUNAWARDENE, Aruna Alwis Wijesiri (Sinhalese) b Colombo 31.3.1969 RHB RM																			
FC		10	14	3	599	158*	54.45	2	1	66	35	2	17.50	1-8	0	0	3.18	6	
FC	1988	76	114	14	3325	158*	33.25	6	16	497	241	10	24.10	2-2	0	0	2.90	72	
Int	1993	1	1	0	2	2	2.00	0	0									0	
GUNAWARDENE, Arachchige Chintaka (Bloomfield) b Colombo 12.12.1977 RHB																			
FC		1								72	66	2	33.00	1-27	0	0	5.50	0	

Cmp	Debut	M	I	NO	Runs	HS	Avge	100	50	Balls	Runs	Wkts	Avge	BB	5i	10m	RpO	ct	st
GUNAWARDENE, Ishan Deepak (Police) b Colombo 21.10.1969 LHB RM																			
FC		13	22	2	402	93	20.10	0	2	900	454	13	34.92	3-8	0	0	3.02	7	
FC	1995	23	38	3	750	94	21.42	0	4	2016	1165	36	32.36	4-72	0	0	3.46	14	
GURUGE, Sudharshana Samanthika (Kurunegala Youth) b Hikkaduwa 23.7.1962 LHB RM																			
FC		6	8	0	211	66	26.37	0	1	306	149	5	29.80	2-42	0	0	2.92	1	
FC	1989	24	37	3	765	66	22.50	0	5	696	341	11	31.00	3-35	0	0	2.93	6	
GURUSINHA, Asanka Pradeep (Sri Lanka, Sri Lanka to Kenya, Sri Lanka to Sharjah) b Colombo 16.9.1966 LHB RM																			
Test		2	2	0	140	88	70.00	0	2	30	7	0					1.40	3	
FC		2	2	0	140	88	70.00	0	2	30	7	0					1.40	3	
Int		4	3	0	60	29	20.00	0	0	12	17	0					8.50	0	
Test	1985	41	70	7	2452	143	38.92	7	8	1408	681	20	34.05	2-7	0	0	2.90	33	
FC	1984	124	183	19	7169	162	43.71	20	32	5142	2298	107	21.47	5-54	1	0	2.68	89	
Int	1985	147	143	5	3902	117*	28.27	2	22	1585	1354	26	52.07	2-25	0	0	5.12	49	
HANDUNETTIGE, Chaminda P. (Colombo, Kurunegala Youth) b Colombo 19.10.1970 RHB RM																			
FC		6	10	0	166	82	16.60	0	1	258	135	3	45.00	1-20	0	0	3.13	3	
FC	1988	37	57	4	1613	172*	30.45	2	12	276	142	3	47.33	1-20	0	0	3.08	36	
HANDUNETTIGE, Ranesh (Sebastianites) b Colombo 4.4.1977 RHB RA																			
FC		3	4	0	56	43	14.00	0	0	6	6	0					6.00	1	
HATHURUSINGHA, Chaminda Mangala (Tamil Union) b Colombo 9.10.1971 RHB RM																			
FC		13	15	4	75	13	6.81	0	0	1580	852	23	37.04	6-72	1	0	3.23	5	
FC	1992	51	48	22	227	22	8.73	0	0	5968	3440	121	28.42	8-40	5	1	3.45	14	
HATHURUSINGHA, Upul Chandika (Tamil Union) b Colombo 13.9.1968 RHB RMF																			
FC		6	9	0	264	121	29.33	1	1	1505	700	36	19.44	8-29	4	1	2.79	7	
Test	1990	24	42	1	1260	83	30.73	0	8	1704	668	16	41.75	4-66	0	0	2.35	6	
FC	1988	124	192	13	6361	143	35.53	10	37	11254	4874	196	24.86	8-29	7	1	2.59	92	
Int	1991	32	30	1	648	66	22.34	0	4	840	614	14	43.85	4-57	1	0	4.38	5	
HERATH, Rangana (Kurunegala Youth) b Kurunegala 19.3.1978 LHB LA																			
FC		5	9	4	70	29	14.00	0	0	620	293	14	20.92	5-96	1	0	2.83	1	
HERATHGE, Sapumal P. (Tamil Union) b Colombo 21.4.1972 RHB																			
FC		8	10	0	310	60	31.00	0	2									11	
FC	1991	17	25	0	555	81	22.20	0	3	54	64	2	32.00	2-47	0	0	7.11	15	
HETTIARACHCHI, Chitraka Nilanga (Kalutara Town) b Kalutara 8.9.1976 RHB OB																			
FC		12	24	0	473	68	19.70	0	2	528	303	13	23.30	5-51	1	0	3.44	9	
HETTIARACHCHI, Dinuka (Colts) b Colombo 15.7.1976 RHB SLA																			
FC		5	3	1	8	4*	4.00	0	0	659	286	12	23.83	3-51	0	0	2.60	3	
FC	1994	27	28	12	157	35	9.81	0	0	4511	2233	79	28.26	8-102	3	1	2.97	10	
HETTIARACHCHI, Udaya (Burgher) b Colombo 14.1.1968 LHB LB																			
FC		10	14	2	188	41	15.66	0	0	96	95	0					5.93	2	
FC	1988	35	53	8	1196	125	26.57	2	4	1374	862	21	41.04	4-76	0	0	3.76	22	
HEWAGAMMA, Kalpa Ruwan (Galle) b Galle 21.6.1977 RHB LM																			
FC		2	3	0	7	5	2.33	0	0	60	29	0					2.90		
HEWAGE, Pradeep Randy (Nondescripts) b Colombo 7.12.1978 RHB RM																			
FC		3	3	2	19	11	19.00	0	0	276	121	6	20.16	2-15	0	0	2.63	1	
FC	1995	7	9	2	152	39	21.71	0	0	894	418	20	20.90	4-56	0	0	2.80	2	
HEWAMANNE, Chithragupta Kariyawasam (Galle) b Galle 1.12.1969 RHB WK OB																			
FC		12	19	1	282	54	15.66	0	1	6	8	0					8.00	16	4
FC	1990	31	47	5	818	85*	19.47	0	3	12	13	1	13.00	1-5	0	0	6.50	45	10
HUNUKUMBURA, Damitha (Kurunegala Youth) LHB WK																			
FC		5	10	0	150	54	15.00	0	1									5	
INDIKA, Tharanga (Singha) b Galle 4.3.1975 LHB RM																			
FC		4	8	1	48	14	6.85	0	0	30	26	0					5.20	1	
FC	1995	5	9	1	53	14	6.62	0	0	96	71	0					4.43	2	
JABBAR, Mohamed Hassan Abdul (Sebastianites) b Colombo 21.9.1964 RHB OB																			
FC		6	9	7	23	11	11.50	0	0	522	282	9	31.33	3-97	0	0	3.24	2	
FC	1990	37	61	34	198	21*	7.33	0	0	4972	2598	101	25.72	6-66	2	0	3.13	30	
JANAKA, Sujith (Colts) b Colombo 22.9.1976 RHB																			
FC		7	12	1	560	148	50.90	1	5									4	
JAYAKODY, Lalin Kumara (Police) b Colombo 1.6.1970 RHB RA																			
FC		4	6	1	46	22	9.20	0	0	6	2	0					2.00	2	
FC	1995	8	12	4	68	22	8.50	0	0	36	30	2	15.00	2-28	0	0	5.00	4	
JAYALATH, Warusawitharan Kusumsiri (Singha) b Galle 7.12.1968 LHB SLA																			
FC		10	18	7	88	13*	8.00	0	0	1478	653	28	23.32	4-26	0	0	2.65	6	
FC	1989	24	39	13	246	26	9.46	0	0	3360	1594	51	31.25	4-26	0	0	2.84	8	
JAYANTHA, Saman (Singha, Sri Lanka A, President's XI) b Ambalangoda 26.1.1974 RHB OB																			
FC		12	23	1	726	97	33.00	0	6	612	304	9	33.77	3-79	0	0	2.98	12	
FC	1992	48	82	4	2876	212*	36.87	4	17	3265	1436	43	33.39	3-24	0	0	2.63	34	

Cmp	Debut	M	I	NO	Runs	HS	Avge	100	50	Balls	Runs	Wkts	Avge	BB	5i	10m	RpO	ct	st

JAYARATNE, Sanjeewa (Nondescripts) b Colombo 13.11.1975 LHB LM

FC		4	6	1	81	33	16.20	0	0	564	388	17	22.82	5-106	1	0	4.12	5	

JAYASEKERA, Saman Thushara Rubasing (Galle) b Galle 9.8.1971 LHB RM

FC		4	7	5	19	5*	9.50	0	0	246	238	7	34.00	3-67	0	0	5.80	3	
FC	1989	12	18	10	64	13	8.00	0	0	1134	855	24	35.62	4-64	0	0	4.52	6	

JAYASINGHE, Asela Sudharsha (Tamil Union) b Ragama 23.8.1974 LHB RM

FC		13	19	1	773	183	42.94	2	2	288	169	2	84.50	1-31	0	0	3.52	14	
FC	1994	17	24	1	852	183	37.04	2	2	366	208	3	69.33	1-24	0	0	3.40	15	

JAYASINGHE, Chaminda Prasad (Tamil Union) b Colombo 22.2.1974 RHB RM

FC		8	10	2	236	46	29.50	0	0	54	55	0					6.11	3	
FC	1995	18	23	4	669	102*	35.21	1	2	198	128	4	32.00	2-19	0	0	3.87	8	

JAYASINGHE, Chinthaka Umesh (Burgher) b Kalutara 19.5.1978

FC		2	3	0	48	38	16.00	0	0	36	13	1	13.00	1-13	0	0	2.16	2	

JAYASUNDERA, S. (Burgher) RHB

FC		1	2	0	34	31	17.00	0	0	6	8	0					8.00	0	

JAYASURIYA, Sathiya Prasanna Weeraratne (Burgher) b Colombo 1.9.1962 LHB OB

FC		2	3	2	18	13	18.00	0	0	12	3	0					1.50	1	
FC	1988	19	27	5	384	64*	17.45	0	1	343	219	14	15.64	4-18	0	0	3.83	12	

JAYASURIYA, Sanath Teran (Bloomfield, Sri Lanka, Sri Lanka to New Zealand, Sri Lanka to Kenya, Sri Lanka to Sharjah, Sri Lanka to India) b Matara 30.6.1969 LHB SLA

Test		4	7	1	337	113	56.16	1	2	84	32	2	16.00	2-16	0	0	2.28	1	
FC		13	21	1	954	129	47.70	2	6	697	242	13	18.61	4-54	0	0	2.08	9	
Int		4	4	1	196	120*	65.33	1	0	210	163	3	54.33	2-43	0	0	4.65	2	
Test	1990	25	42	6	1373	113	38.13	2	9	816	482	6	80.33	2-15	0	0	3.54	21	
FC	1988	117	172	22	5927	207*	39.51	12	30	4531	2098	60	34.96	4-44	0	0	2.77	76	
Int	1989	133	125	4	3178	151*	26.26	4	18	4599	3706	110	33.69	6-29	2	2	4.83	53	

JAYAWARDENE, Denagamage Proboth Mahela (Sinhalese, Sri Lanka A, President's XI) b Colombo 27.5.1977 RHB RM

FC		12	17	3	644	106*	46.00	2	5	596	310	13	23.84	5-72	1	0	3.12	11	
FC	1995	15	23	3	858	160	42.90	3	5	638	336	13	25.84	5-72	1	0	3.15	11	

JAYAWARDENE, Namal (Panadura) RHB WK

FC		1	2	0	14	14	7.00	0	0									2	
FC	1994	7	12	0	274	47	22.83	0	0									9	4

JAYAWARDENE, Rochana (Sinhalese) b Colombo 12.5.1964 RHB OB

FC		9	13	2	335	89	30.45	0	3	600	284	9	31.55	3-29	0	0	2.84	4	
FC	1983	46	49	5	1049	89	23.84	0	7	3377	1644	66	24.90	7-39	3	0	2.92	23	

JAYAWARDENE, Sarath (Antonians) b Panadura 22.7.1969 RHB RM

FC		12	21	0	408	120	19.42	1	0	1184	684	19	36.00	5-40	1	0	3.46	5	
FC	1988	77	131	9	2533	120	20.76	2	13	6826	4014	122	32.90	6-40	5	1	3.52	38	

JAYMON, Nilam (Kurungegala Youth) b Kurunegala 27.10.1978 RHB

FC		6	10	2	45	13	5.62	0	0									2	

JAYMON, Raden Jehan (Kurunegala Youth) b Kurunegala 16.1.1971 LHB RM

FC		9	15	0	269	74	17.93	0	2	6	7	0					7.00	6	
FC	1989	53	91	4	2304	247	26.48	2	11	608	340	11	30.90	2-29	0	0	3.35	59	

JAYMON, Raden Roshan (Kurunegala Youth) b Anuradhapura 8.2.1973 RHB OB

FC		12	22	0	507	102	23.04	1	2	96	91	1	91.00	1-4	0	0	5.68	11	
FC	1991	52	91	4	2108	147	24.22	2	10	894	676	12	56.33	2-32	0	0	4.53	40	

KALPAGE, Ruwan Senani (Bloomfield, Sri Lanka, Sri Lanka A, President's XI, Sri Lanka to Sharjah) b Kandy 19.2.1970 LHB OB

Test		1	1	0	5	5	5.00	0	0	258	102	0					2.37	0	
FC		15	22	6	731	160*	45.68	1	5	2980	1228	61	20.13	7-37	3	2	2.47	9	
Test	1993	9	15	1	270	63	19.28	0	2	1175	507	6	84.50	2-27	0	0	2.58	6	
FC	1988	97	132	24	3649	160*	33.78	8	18	15588	6266	259	24.19	7-37	9	4	2.41	57	
Int	1991	76	62	27	757	51	21.62	0	1	3510	2586	70	36.94	4-36	2	0	4.42	24	

KALUWITHARANA, Romesh Shantha (Colts, Sri Lanka, Sri Lanka to New Zealand, Sri Lanka to West Indies, Sri Lanka to Kenya, Sri Lanka to Sharjah, Sri Lanka to India) b Colombo 24.11.1969 RHB WK

Test		4	5	0	194	71	38.80	0	2									9	1
FC		13	18	0	1270	179	70.55	6	3									31	4
Int		4	4	0	131	58	32.75	0	2									3	5
Test	1992	14	23	1	762	132*	34.63	2	4									27	2
FC	1988	69	104	7	4543	179	46.83	12	29									139	18
Int	1990	75	71	5	1089	100*	16.50	1	5									51	32

KAPILARATNE, Asela (Sinhalese) b Colombo 16.3.1974 LHB

FC		3	4	0	62	58	15.50	0	1									2	

KARIYAWASAM, Ruwan (Kurunegala Youth) b Colombo 5.11.1972 LHB SLA

FC		12	22	1	377	87	17.95	0	1	900	513	15	34.20	4-95	0	0	3.42	12	
FC	1993	37	65	4	1290	177	21.14	1	3	1138	670	18	37.22	4-95	0	0	3.53	27	

KARUNARATNE, Lanka (Kurungala Youth) b Kuruegala 8.2.1978 RHB RFM

| FC | | 9 | 14 | 2 | 114 | 32 | 9.50 | 0 | 0 | 6 | 4 | 0 | | | | | 4.00 | 5 | |
| FC | 1991 | 26 | 42 | 5 | 437 | 53 | 11.81 | 0 | 1 | 6 | 4 | 0 | | | | | 4.00 | 11 | |

KODAGODA, Roshan Indika (Burgher) b Colombo 2.8.1975

| FC | | 1 | 1 | 0 | 1 | 1 | 1.00 | 0 | 0 | 54 | 39 | 2 | 19.50 | 2-32 | 0 | 0 | 4.33 | 0 | |

KODIKARA, Thusara Prabath (Antonians) b Kandy 17.11.1969 RHB RM

| FC | | 13 | 23 | 1 | 479 | 88 | 21.77 | 0 | 3 | 588 | 428 | 6 | 71.33 | 2-32 | 0 | 0 | 4.36 | 0 | |
| FC | 1990 | 48 | 79 | 5 | 2059 | 236* | 27.82 | 3 | 8 | 2940 | 1627 | 45 | 36.15 | 5-78 | 1 | 0 | 3.32 | 20 | |

KODITUWAKKU, Samantha (Galle) b Colombo 21.11.1971 LHB RM

| FC | | 10 | 17 | 1 | 332 | 74 | 20.75 | 0 | 2 | 37 | 30 | 0 | | | | | 4.86 | 2 | |
| FC | 1988 | 42 | 66 | 6 | 1171 | 74 | 19.51 | 0 | 5 | 574 | 296 | 11 | 26.90 | 6-73 | 1 | 0 | 3.09 | 19 | |

KOTTACHCHI, Rohitha Dharmakeerthi (Kalutara Town) b Kalutara 9.8.1971 LHB SLA

| FC | | 10 | 20 | 3 | 341 | 52 | 20.05 | 0 | 1 | 743 | 440 | 16 | 27.50 | 5-60 | 1 | 0 | 3.55 | 10 | |

KUDAGODAGE, Manohara Yasas (Police) b Galle 30.10.1972 RHB WK

| FC | | 5 | 9 | 1 | 59 | 26 | 7.37 | 0 | 0 | | | | | | | | | 11 | 5 |
| FC | 1995 | 10 | 17 | 4 | 238 | 41* | 18.30 | 0 | 0 | | | | | | | | | 24 | 10 |

KULATUNGA, Jeevantha (Colts) b Colombo 2.11.1973 RHB RMF

| FC | | 12 | 18 | 2 | 634 | 118 | 39.62 | 1 | 4 | 36 | 13 | 0 | | | | | 2.16 | 17 | |
| FC | 1990 | 48 | 73 | 5 | 2077 | 118 | 30.54 | 1 | 15 | 734 | 390 | 12 | 32.50 | 3-15 | 0 | 0 | 3.18 | 48 | |

KUMARA, Amugoda Kankanamge Don Aruna Saman (Panadura) b Galle 2.1.1963 LHB OB WK

| FC | | 1 | 1 | 0 | 23 | 23 | 23.00 | 0 | 0 | | | | | | | | | 0 | |
| FC | 1988 | 48 | 73 | 5 | 1982 | 119 | 29.14 | 3 | 8 | 106 | 94 | 0 | | | | | 5.32 | 45 | 9 |

KUMARA, Gange Asoka (Singha) b Ambalangoda 11.7.1960 RHB RA WK

| FC | | 2 | 4 | 0 | 21 | 13 | 5.25 | 0 | 0 | | | | | | | | | 1 | |
| FC | 1989 | 8 | 15 | 1 | 262 | 81* | 18.71 | 0 | 1 | 6 | 4 | 0 | | | | | 4.00 | 12 | |

KUMARA, Halambage Wasantha (Singha) b Galle 31.1.1972 RHB LB

| FC | | 2 | 4 | 0 | 31 | 16 | 7.75 | 0 | 0 | 24 | 23 | 0 | | | | | 5.75 | 0 | |
| FC | 1989 | 14 | 21 | 1 | 386 | 50 | 14.84 | 0 | 1 | 252 | 178 | 3 | 59.33 | 2-34 | 0 | 0 | 4.23 | 7 | |

KUMARA, Manel Wasantha (Kurungala Youth) b Kurunegala 13.7.1964 RHB RFM

| FC | | 13 | 20 | 7 | 141 | 35 | 10.84 | 0 | 0 | 1859 | 982 | 31 | 31.67 | 6-64 | 1 | 0 | 3.16 | 7 | |
| FC | 1990 | 51 | 73 | 24 | 546 | 50* | 11.14 | 0 | 1 | 6077 | 3239 | 100 | 32.39 | 6-64 | 2 | 0 | 3.19 | 28 | |

KUMARA, Sagara (Tamil Union)

| FC | | 4 | 7 | 1 | 68 | 17 | 11.33 | 0 | 0 | 330 | 186 | 5 | 37.20 | 2-37 | 0 | 0 | 3.38 | 4 | |

KUMARA, Sugath (Kurungala Youth) b Kurunegala 17.7.1978

| FC | | 1 | 2 | 0 | 0 | 0 | 0.00 | 0 | 0 | | | | | | | | | 0 | |

KUMARA, Sunendra (Panadura) RHB OB

| FC | | 11 | 17 | 1 | 589 | 142 | 36.81 | 1 | 4 | 1699 | 608 | 21 | 28.95 | 3-37 | 0 | 0 | 2.14 | 7 | |
| FC | 1991 | 47 | 76 | 8 | 2080 | 142 | 30.58 | 2 | 11 | 3346 | 1441 | 50 | 28.82 | 4-41 | 0 | 0 | 2.58 | 41 | |

KUMUDU, Wadu Mestri Janaka (Singha) b Colombo 2.5.1969 LHB RA

| FC | | 12 | 24 | 0 | 318 | 48 | 13.25 | 0 | 0 | | | | | | | | | 2 | |
| FC | 1989 | 68 | 115 | 5 | 2912 | 161 | 26.47 | 4 | 11 | 24 | 13 | 0 | | | | | 3.25 | 33 | |

LABROOY, Wendell Cleophus (Colombo, Burgher, Sri Lanka A) b Negombo 25.9.1971 LHB RM

| FC | | 10 | 18 | 3 | 262 | 65* | 17.46 | 0 | 1 | 1366 | 1089 | 28 | 38.89 | 5-90 | 1 | 0 | 4.78 | 7 | |
| FC | 1991 | 49 | 67 | 13 | 1034 | 65* | 19.14 | 0 | 4 | 6851 | 4930 | 161 | 30.62 | 7-147 | 8 | 1 | 4.31 | 21 | |

LALITH, D. (Kurunegala Youth)

| FC | | 1 | 2 | 1 | 0 | 0* | 0.00 | 0 | 0 | | | | | | | | | 0 | |

LIYANAGE, Dulip Kapila (Colts, Sri Lanka to West Indies, Sri Lanka to India) b Kalutara 6.6.1972 LHB RFM

FC		10	14	3	269	60*	24.45	0	1	1368	800	37	21.62	5-26	2	0	3.50	3	
Test	1992	8	8	0	66	23	8.25	0	0	1271	622	17	36.58	4-56	0	0*	2.93	0	
FC	1991	54	63	9	1107	95	20.50	0	5	6101	3429	135	25.40	6-36	6	1	3.29	12	
Int	1992	11	8	2	100	43	16.66	0	0	462	358	7	51.14	3-49	0	0	4.64	4	

LIYANAGE, Hiran (Kurungala Youth) b Kurunegala 7.8.1975 LHB OB

| FC | | 9 | 16 | 3 | 380 | 82 | 29.23 | 0 | 3 | 168 | 147 | 0 | | | | | 5.25 | 6 | |
| FC | 1993 | 25 | 41 | 4 | 983 | 82 | 26.56 | 0 | 6 | 439 | 320 | 4 | 80.00 | 2-55 | 0 | 0 | 4.37 | 17 | |

LIYANAGE, Ravi Chaminda (Police) b Kurunegala 22.8.1970 RHB WK

| FC | | 12 | 22 | 2 | 741 | 86 | 37.05 | 0 | 6 | | | | | | | | | 24 | 3 |
| FC | 1991 | 28 | 51 | 5 | 1407 | 115* | 30.58 | 1 | 9 | | | | | | | | | 51 | 8 |

LIYANAGE, Sham Nishantha (Panadura) b Panadura 21.3.1978 RHB RMF

| FC | | 12 | 19 | 1 | 385 | 77 | 21.38 | 0 | 2 | 378 | 250 | 4 | 62.50 | 2-49 | 0 | 0 | 3.96 | 20 | |
| FC | 1994 | 30 | 42 | 2 | 746 | 77 | 18.65 | 0 | 6 | 906 | 535 | 10 | 53.50 | 2-49 | 0 | 0 | 3.54 | 33 | |

MADANAYAKE, Suwanji (Burgher) LHB SLA

| FC | | 10 | 14 | 0 | 229 | 110 | 16.35 | 1 | 0 | 843 | 540 | 26 | 20.76 | 5-36 | 2 | 0 | 3.84 | 8 | |
| FC | 1991 | 17 | 22 | 3 | 344 | 110 | 18.10 | 1 | 1 | 1473 | 798 | 33 | 24.18 | 5-36 | 2 | 0 | 3.25 | 11 | |

MADURAPPERUMA, Devinda Deepal (Burgher) b Colombo 24.8.1963 RHB LB

| FC | | 13 | 21 | 1 | 414 | 59* | 23.00 | 0 | 1 | 1259 | 712 | 26 | 27.38 | 6-45 | 1 | 0 | 3.39 | 10 | |
| FC | 1988 | 31 | 47 | 3 | 1036 | 59* | 23.54 | 0 | 6 | 2502 | 1406 | 49 | 28.69 | 6-45 | 2 | 0 | 3.37 | 14 | |

MADURASINGHE, Madurasinghe Arachchige Wijayasiri Ranjith (Kurunegala Youth) b Kurunegala 30.1.1961 LHB OB

Cmp	Debut	M	I	NO	Runs	HS	Avge	100	50	Balls	Runs	Wkts	Avge	BB	5i	10m	RpO	ct	st
FC		11	17	3	219	35	15.64	0	0	1951	753	34	22.14	5-49	1	0	2.31	5	
Test	1988	3	6	1	24	11	4.80	0	0	396	172	3	57.33	3-60	0	0	2.60	0	
FC	1988	91	120	29	1418	83*	15.58	0	3	14163	6303	245	25.72	7-85	8	1	2.67	49	
Int	1988	12	6	4	21	8*	10.50	0	0	480	358	5	71.60	1-11	0	0	4.47	3	

MAGESH, T. (Antonians)

Cmp	Debut	M	I	NO	Runs	HS	Avge	100	50	Balls	Runs	Wkts	Avge	BB	5i	10m	RpO	ct	st
FC		1	1	0	0	0	0.00	0	0	6	1	0					1.00	0	

MAHANAMA, Roshan Siriwardene (Bloomfield, Sri Lanka, Sri Lanka to New Zealand, Sri Lanka to West Indies, Sri Lanka to Kenya, Sri Lanka to Sharjah, Sri Lanka to India) b Colombo 31.5.1966 RHB

Cmp	Debut	M	I	NO	Runs	HS	Avge	100	50	Balls	Runs	Wkts	Avge	BB	5i	10m	RpO	ct	st
Test		2	3	1	19	12*	9.50	0	0									8	
FC		9	13	3	520	176	52.00	2	1									18	
Int		3	1	0	50	50	50.00	0	1									2	
Test	1985	43	74	1	2086	153	28.57	3	10	36	30	0					5.00	44	
FC	1984	119	184	18	5677	176	34.19	9	27	36	30	0					5.00	119	
Int	1985	168	156	18	4136	119*	29.97	4	27	2	7	0					21.00	89	

MAHINDARATNE, Jayasinghe Arachchige (Burgher) b Hamdantota 11.11.1973 LHB LA

Cmp	Debut	M	I	NO	Runs	HS	Avge	100	50	Balls	Runs	Wkts	Avge	BB	5i	10m	RpO	ct	st
FC		3	4	2	24	12	12.00	0	0	636	260	13	20.00	4-29	0	0	2.45	2	
FC	1990	4	4	2	24	12	12.00	0	0	762	302	16	18.87	4-29	0	0	2.37	2	

MAIARACHCHI, Damith (Nondescripts) b Colombo 17.9.1976 RHB RM

Cmp	Debut	M	I	NO	Runs	HS	Avge	100	50	Balls	Runs	Wkts	Avge	BB	5i	10m	RpO	ct	st
FC		4	7	0	243	79	34.71	0	2	186	151	3	50.33	3-32	0	0	4.87	1	

MALMEEWALA, Senadi (Kurunegala Youth) RHB

Cmp	Debut	M	I	NO	Runs	HS	Avge	100	50	Balls	Runs	Wkts	Avge	BB	5i	10m	RpO	ct	st
FC		5	9	0	132	32	14.66	0	0	18	11	0					3.66	6	

MANJULA, Ramesh (Kalutara Town) LHB

Cmp	Debut	M	I	NO	Runs	HS	Avge	100	50	Balls	Runs	Wkts	Avge	BB	5i	10m	RpO	ct	st
FC		1	2	0	9	6	4.50	0	0	17	9	0					3.17	0	

MANSOOR, Mohamed (Galle) b Galle 3.2.1979

Cmp	Debut	M	I	NO	Runs	HS	Avge	100	50	Balls	Runs	Wkts	Avge	BB	5i	10m	RpO	ct	st
FC		1	2	2	1	1*		0	0	6	17	0					17.00	0	

MENDIS, Manimeldura Chaminda (Colts, Sri Lanka A, President's XI) b Galle 28.12.1968 RHB OB

Cmp	Debut	M	I	NO	Runs	HS	Avge	100	50	Balls	Runs	Wkts	Avge	BB	5i	10m	RpO	ct	st
FC		13	20	0	714	131	35.70	2	2	30	15	0					3.00	9	
FC	1988	82	126	11	4328	200*	37.63	11	18	1014	512	12	42.66	5-155	1	0	3.02	55	
Int	1994	1	1	1	3	3*		0	0									2	

MENDIS, Manoj Shyam (Sebastianites) b Colombo 13.11.1974 RHB

Cmp	Debut	M	I	NO	Runs	HS	Avge	100	50	Balls	Runs	Wkts	Avge	BB	5i	10m	RpO	ct	st
FC		11	17	1	530	100	33.12	1	4	96	56	0					3.50	9	
FC	1995	14	22	1	659	100	31.38	1	4	96	56	0					3.50	10	

MENDIS, Nisala Charaka (Panadura) b Panadura 16.7.1976 RHB WK

Cmp	Debut	M	I	NO	Runs	HS	Avge	100	50	Balls	Runs	Wkts	Avge	BB	5i	10m	RpO	ct	st
FC		9	11	2	144	23*	16.00	0	0									12	7
FC	1995	23	34	6	432	63*	15.42	0	2									35	12

MUDALIGE, Chamikara Ravinda Bentota (Galle) b Galle 5.7.1976 RHB OB

Cmp	Debut	M	I	NO	Runs	HS	Avge	100	50	Balls	Runs	Wkts	Avge	BB	5i	10m	RpO	ct	st
FC		9	14	3	56	13	5.09	0	0	872	510	10	51.00	2-26	0	0	3.50..	6	
FC	1995	12	18	6	64	13	5.33	0	0	974	574	15	38.26	5-61	1	0	3.53	10	

MURALITHARAN, Muttiah (Tamil Union, Sri Lanka, Sri Lanka to New Zealand, Sri Lanka to West Indies, Sri Lanka to Kenya, Sri Lanka to Sharjah, Sri Lanka to India) b Kandy 17.4.1972 RHB OB

Cmp	Debut	M	I	NO	Runs	HS	Avge	100	50	Balls	Runs	Wkts	Avge	BB	5i	10m	RpO	ct	st
Test		3	3	2	9	8*	9.00	0	0	951	293	20	14.65	6-98	2	0	1.84	1	
FC		11	11	4	39	11	5.57	0	0	2334	972	66	14.72	7-55	6	2	2.49	6	
Int		4								222	147	4	36.75	2-41	0	0	3.97	2	
Test	1992	30	43	20	262	26	11.39	0	0	8124	3526	123	28.66	6-98	9	0	2.60	15	
FC	1989	78	95	33	658	36	10.61	0	0	16880	7118	335	21.24	8-8	25	3	2.53	48	
Int	1993	70	31	15	85	9*	5.31	0	0	3798	2652	95	27.91	4-18	3	0	4.18	35	

NADARAJAH, Damien Nithyananthan (Tamil Union) b Jaffna 4.3.1968 RHB OB

Cmp	Debut	M	I	NO	Runs	HS	Avge	100	50	Balls	Runs	Wkts	Avge	BB	5i	10m	RpO	ct	st
FC		13	17	3	415	102*	29.54	1	2									8	
FC	1988	76	110	15	3057	170	32.17	5	15	41	43	1	43.00	1-11	0	0	6.29	33	

NADEEKA, Marapathirage Gayan (Singha) b Ambalangoda 18.2.1977 LHB RFM

Cmp	Debut	M	I	NO	Runs	HS	Avge	100	50	Balls	Runs	Wkts	Avge	BB	5i	10m	RpO	ct	st
FC		6	11	1	82	17	8.20	0	0	419	188	3	62.66	2-30	0	0	2.69	1	
FC	1994	7	12	1	84	17	7.63	0	0	419	188	3	62.66	2-30	0	0	2.69	1	

NANAYAKKARA, Duminda (Police) b Moratuwa 21.3.1969 RHB OB

Cmp	Debut	M	I	NO	Runs	HS	Avge	100	50	Balls	Runs	Wkts	Avge	BB	5i	10m	RpO	ct	st
FC		7	13	4	101	24	11.22	0	0	234	125	4	31.25	2-9	0	0	3.20	4	
FC	1995	9	17	4	156	24	12.00	0	0	294	165	4	41.25	2-9	0	0	3.36	4	

NAWALAGE, Tushara (Tamil Union) b Colombo 4.4.1972 RHB WK

Cmp	Debut	M	I	NO	Runs	HS	Avge	100	50	Balls	Runs	Wkts	Avge	BB	5i	10m	RpO	ct	st
FC		1	2	0	15	8	7.50	0	0	36	31	0					5.16	0	
FC	1994	2	4	0	21	8	5.25	0	0	36	31	0					5.16	0	

NAWAZ, Mohamed Naveed (Bloomfield, Sri Lanka A) b Colombo 20.9.1973 LHB OB

Cmp	Debut	M	I	NO	Runs	HS	Avge	100	50	Balls	Runs	Wkts	Avge	BB	5i	10m	RpO	ct	st
FC		12	20	1	758	124	39.89	2	3	48	24	1	24.00	1-0	0	0	3.00	18	
FC	1993	34	50	4	1733	152*	37.67	3	9	322	180	9	20.00	5-16	1	0	3.35	31	

NILANJANA, Raigamacharige Madhumal (Kalutara Town) b Colombo 20.3.1975 LHB LB

Cmp	Debut	M	I	NO	Runs	HS	Avge	100	50	Balls	Runs	Wkts	Avge	BB	5i	10m	RpO	ct	st
FC		7	14	1	80	17	6.15	0	0	54	37	0					4.11	1	

PALLIAYAGE, Ruwan Janaka (Police) b Colombo 12.9.1972 RHB																		
FC	7	11	0	94	27	8.54	0	0										5	
FC 1995	14	23	1	265	44	12.04	0	0										10	
PEIRIS, Gorakanage Ruwin Prasantha (Nondescripts, President's XI) b Colombo 9.8.1970 LHB SLA																		
FC	11	14	1	640	125	49.23	2	3	90	73	1	73.00	1-47	0	0	4.86	7	
FC 1992	51	72	2	2653	139	37.90	5	14	750	361	10	36.10	2-10	0	0	2.88	55	
PEIRIS, Marlon (Sebastianites) b Colombo 10.12.1975 RHB RM																		
FC	11	18	1	345	43	20.29	0	0	795	477	11	43.36	2-40	0	0	3.60	6	
FC 1995	20	32	2	552	65	18.40	0	2	1161	742	22	33.72	3-52	0	0	3.83	11	
PERERA, Anura (Sebastianites) b Colombo 8.7.1969 RHB RM																		
FC	12	17	7	88	27	8.80	0	0	1507	937	31	30.22	6-87	2	0	3.73	3	
FC 1995	17	24	8	135	32	8.43	0	0	1876	1205	35	34.42	6-87	2	0	3.85	3	
PERERA, Anusha (Sebastianites) b Colombo 5.11.1974 RHB OB																		
FC	12	18	1	483	90	28.41	0	3	777	393	12	32.75	4-40	0	0	3.03	5	
FC 1993	35	59	3	1321	143*	23.58	1	5	2125	1103	32	34.46	4-40	0	0	3.11	17	
PERERA, Bathia (Colts) b Colombo 28.4.1977 RHB																		
FC	6	5	4	90	59	90.00	0	1	679	534	27	19.77	4-21	0	0	4.71	6	
PERERA, Buddika Pradeep (Panadura) b Panadura 31.5.1975 RHB RM																		
FC	12	19	0	498	110	26.21	1	1.	6	10	0					10.00	7	
FC 1994	31	51	0	1033	110	20.25	1	2	668	462	9	51.33	4-58	0	0	4.14	22	
PERERA, Chetaka Rajkumar (Burgher) b Colombo 23.10.1967 RHB RM																		
FC	11	18	1	335	74	19.70	0	1	215	117	1	117.00	1-14	0	0	3.26	5	
FC 1988	22	35	2	574	74	17.39	0	1	686	364	10	36.40	4-37	0	0	3.18	10	
PERERA, Chamath Sarnath (Burgher) b Moratuwa 13.5.1969 RHB RM																		
FC	4	6	1	30	25	6.00	0	0	407	218	8	27.25	3-30	0	0	3.21	2	
FC 1989	35	61	6	1086	56	19.74	0	1	3233	1944	48	40.50	6-55	1	0	3.60	21	
PERERA, Gomasge Ruwan Manoj Anthony (Sebastianites) b Colombo 12.6.1971 RHB SLA																		
FC	7	9	2	115	28	16.42	0	0	1247	473	14	33.78	5-49	1	0	2.27	0	
FC 1990	40	51	12	666	77	17.07	0	2	4931	1868	77	24.25	6-61	4	0	2.25	12	
PERERA, Himal (Sinhalese SC) RHB RM																		
FC	1	1	0	1	1	1.00	0	0	144	75	3	25.00	3-61	0	0	3.12	1	
FC 1994	11	8	2	50	23	8.33	0	0	994	671	18	37.27	3-61	0	0	4.05	9	
PERERA, Indika (Police)																		
FC	1	1	0	5	5	5.00	0	0	48	23	1	23.00	1-13	0	0	2.87	2	
PERERA, Kahawelage Gamini (Antonians) b Colombo 22.5.1964 RHB SLA																		
FC	13	19	6	130	26	10.00	0	0	2814	993	57	17.42	7-49	3	1	2.11	5	
FC 1983	64	90	21	723	52	10.47	0	1	12546	5255	189	27.80	8-60	12	2	2.51	33	
Int 1985	1								12	15	0					7.50	0	
PERERA, Malintha (Sinhalese) b Colombo 20.10.1974 RHB WK																		
FC	8	12	1	310	106	28.18	1	1									25	5
PERERA, Nimesh R.G. (Colombo, Sri Lanka A, President's XI) b Colombo 5.9.1977 LHB LB																		
FC	3	4	1	38	21	12.66	0	0	450	318	3	106.00	2-150	0	0	4.24	1	
FC 1995	9	11	2	203	63	22.55	0	1	1302	768	20	38.40	5-34	1	0	3.53	6	
PERERA, Pathmanath (Kalutara Town) b Kalutara 4.5.1972 LHB RM																		
FC	12	24	0	496	133	20.66	1	2	1753	824	35	23.54	6-41	3	0	2.82	3	
FC 1991	39	72	4	1271	133	18.69	2	5	4843	2112	96	22.00	7-46	6	0	2.61	10	
PERERA, Pahalage Manahara Chaminda (Tamil Union) b Colombo 18.5.1970																		
FC	1	1	1	2	2*		0	0									1	
FC 1992	2	2	1	18	16	18.00	0	0									2	
PERERA, Randika (Kurunegala Youth) b Kurunegala 11.10.1975																		
FC	1	2	1	0	0*	0.00	0	0									0	
PERERA, Ramesh Clement (Kalutara Town) b Aluthgama 25.11.1973 RHB RM																		
FC	6	12	1	161	55	14.63	0	1	312	194	3	64.66	2-25	0	0	3.73	2	
PERERA, Ruchira Laksiri (Bloomfield) b Colombo 27.10.1976																		
FC	7	6	2	71	26	17.75	0	0	720	427	15	28.46	5-26	1	0	3.55	6	
PERERA, Suranga Kumara (Bloomfield) b Colombo 28.12.1974 RHB RA																		
FC	3	5	0	113	46	22.60	0	0									0	
FC 1994	23	37	4	976	115	29.57	1	4	30	21	0					4.20	13	
PERERA, Sampath Thevada (Bloomfield) b Colombo 17.9.1974 RHB WK																		
FC	13	21	3	700	102*	38.88	1	5									17	6
FC 1993	39	62	3	2081	164	35.27	4	15	18	15	0					5.00	49	8
PERERA, Wewalage Augustus Melvin Priyantha (Antonians) b Colombo 3.9.1966 RHB OB WK																		
FC	7	13	2	204	57	18.54	0	1	18	10	0					3.33	8	
FC 1990	43	71	6	1685	116	25.92	1	9	48	16	0					2.00	33	8

PHILIPS, Ravi (Kalutara Town) RA

Cmp	Debut	M	I	NO	Runs	HS	Avge	100	50	Balls	Runs	Wkts	Avge	BB	5i	10m	RpO	ct	st
FC		1	2	0	14	8	7.00	0	0	48	30	0					3.75	1	

PRADEEP, Demunhewage Susantha (Kalutara Town) b Kalutara 5.5.1980 RHB

| FC | | 2 | 4 | 0 | 35 | 19 | 8.75 | 0 | 0 | | | | | | | | | 1 | |

PRADEEP, Janaka (Nondescripts) b Colombo 6.12.1975

| FC | | 2 | 4 | 0 | 60 | 37 | 15.00 | 0 | 0 | | | | | | | | | 0 | |

PRADEEP CHANDANA, Malavige (Singha) b Ambalangoda 17.4.1976 RHB LB

| FC | | 3 | 5 | 0 | 83 | 32 | 16.60 | 0 | 0 | 54 | 20 | 2 | 10.00 | 2-12 | 0 | 0 | 2.22 | 1 | |
| FC | 1994 | 18 | 27 | 4 | 329 | 64* | 14.30 | 0 | 1 | 560 | 381 | 12 | 31.75 | 3-35 | 0 | 0 | 4.08 | 13 | |

PRASANGA, Manoj (Antonians) b Colombo 5.6.1974 RHB LB

| FC | | 9 | 16 | 0 | 213 | 73 | 13.31 | 0 | 1 | 138 | 80 | 0 | | | | | 3.47 | 6 | |
| FC | 1994 | 25 | 43 | 1 | 905 | 109 | 21.54 | 1 | 4 | 925 | 439 | 18 | 24.38 | 4-22 | 0 | 0 | 2.84 | 21 | |

PRASANNA, Dulip (Panadura) b Colombo 3.7.1973 RHB WK

| FC | | 9 | 14 | 5 | 169 | 33* | 18.77 | 0 | 0 | | | | | | | | | 11 | 2 |
| FC | 1992 | 26 | 42 | 10 | 566 | 84 | 17.68 | 0 | 2 | | | | | | | | | 22 | 3 |

PREMASIRI, Halambage (Singha) b Colombo 24.2.1964 RHB OB

| FC | | 12 | 23 | 0 | 457 | 71 | 19.86 | 0 | 2 | | | | | | | | | 9 | |
| FC | 1990 | 55 | 98 | 3 | 2776 | 147 | 29.22 | 6 | 13 | 85 | 45 | 1 | 45.00 | 1-21 | 0 | 0 | 3.17 | 40 | |

PRIYADARSHANA, Rasika Suranga (Tamil Union) b Galle 23.11.1975 RHB RFM

| FC | | 3 | 3 | 1 | 14 | 14 | 7.00 | 0 | 0 | 228 | 83 | 2 | 42.50 | 2-40 | 0 | 0 | 2.18 | 1 | |
| FC | 1993 | 13 | 17 | 2 | 210 | 34 | 14.00 | 0 | 0 | 1652 | 1013 | 36 | 28.13 | 8-85 | 2 | 0 | 3.67 | 6 | |

PRIYANTHA, Aruna (Police) b Colombo 4.2.1973 RHB LM

| FC | | 13 | 22 | 0 | 484 | 79 | 22.00 | 0 | 3 | 956 | 401 | 26 | 15.42 | 6-30 | 1 | 0 | 2.51 | 7 | |
| FC | 1995 | 22 | 38 | 0 | 679 | 79 | 17.86 | 0 | 3 | 1465 | 673 | 37 | 18.18 | 6-30 | 1 | 0 | 2.75 | 15 | |

PUSHPAKUMARA, Karuppiahyage Ravindra (Nondescripts, Sri Lanka, Sri Lanka A, Sri Lanka to West Indies, Sri Lanka to Sharjah) b Panadura 21.7.1975 RHB RFM

Test		1	1	0	23	23	23.00	0	0	114	58	2	29.00	1-24	0	0	3.05	0	
FC		10	10	0	114	24	11.40	0	0	1461	858	43	19.95	6-43	6	3	3.52	4	
Int		2								72	50	2	25.00	2-27	0	0	4.16	0	
Test	1994	10	16	6	77	23	7.70	0	0	1520	971	30	32.36	7-116	2	0	3.83	4	
FC	1992	41	46	12	348	27	10.23	0	0	5795	3494	130	26.87	7-116	10	3	3.61	11	
Int	1993	23	7	5	36	14*	18.00	0	0	1076	870	18	48.33	3-25	0	0	4.85	4	

RAJAPAKSE, Dhammika (Burgher) b Dehiwala 15.5.1971 RHB LB

| FC | | 13 | 22 | 1 | 743 | 101* | 35.38 | 1 | 5 | 816 | 383 | 12 | 31.91 | 3-33 | 0 | 0 | 2.81 | 14 | |
| FC | 1989 | 16 | 28 | 1 | 872 | 101* | 32.29 | 1 | 6 | 816 | 383 | 12 | 31.91 | 3-33 | 0 | 0 | 2.81 | 15 | |

RAJAPAKSE, Hasitha (Galle) b Galle 8.3.1971 RHB OB

| FC | | 12 | 19 | 3 | 293 | 45 | 18.31 | 0 | 0 | 771 | 447 | 13 | 34.38 | 3-69 | 0 | 0 | 3.47 | 5 | |
| FC | 1990 | 47 | 71 | 15 | 1218 | 80 | 21.75 | 0 | 4 | 3829 | 2023 | 63 | 32.11 | 6-90 | 1 | 0 | 3.17 | 23 | |

RAJAPAKSE, Mahesh (Burgher) b Colombo 7.12.1974 LHB

| FC | | 9 | 16 | 0 | 376 | 66 | 23.50 | 0 | 2 | 12 | 4 | 0 | | | | | 2.00 | 0 | |
| FC | 1994 | 13 | 24 | 1 | 600 | 87* | 26.08 | 0 | 3 | 12 | 4 | 0 | | | | | 2.00 | 2 | |

RAJAPAKSE, Priyantha Kamal (Nondescripts) b Colombo 10.6.1971 RHB

| FC | | 10 | 13 | 1 | 255 | 88 | 21.25 | 0 | 1 | | | | | | | | | 10 | |
| FC | 1995 | 16 | 23 | 2 | 620 | 108 | 29.52 | 1 | 3 | | | | | | | | | 14 | |

RAJAPAKSE, Suminda Deepal (Nondescripts) b Matara 3.2.1970 RHB OB

| FC | | 7 | 10 | 0 | 174 | 46 | 17.40 | 0 | 0 | 12 | 11 | 0 | | | | | 5.50 | 5 | |
| FC | 1995 | 19 | 32 | 0 | 599 | 53 | 18.71 | 0 | 2 | 102 | 63 | 0 | | | | | 3.70 | 10 | |

RAMBUKWELLA, Prageeth Jayashantha (Tamil Union) b Moratuwa 22.1.1976 WK

| FC | | 1 | 2 | 0 | 7 | 6 | 3.50 | 0 | 0 | | | | | | | | | 6 | |
| FC | 1995 | 4 | 5 | 1 | 35 | 26 | 8.75 | 0 | 0 | | | | | | | | | 13 | |

RANASINGHE, Lasantha (Singha) b Ambalangoda 20.4.1959 LHB SLA

| FC | | 3 | 6 | 3 | 26 | 8* | 8.66 | 0 | 0 | 108 | 75 | 2 | 37.50 | 1-14 | 0 | 0 | 4.16 | 1 | |
| FC | 1992 | 28 | 40 | 16 | 198 | 25 | 8.25 | 0 | 0 | 4912 | 2381 | 78 | 30.52 | 6-48 | 3 | 0 | 2.90 | 18 | |

RANATUNGA, Arjuna (Sinhalese, Sri Lanka, Sri Lanka to New Zealand, Sri Lanka to West Indies, Sri Lanka to Kenya, Sri Lanka to Sharjah, Sri Lanka to India) b Colombo 1.12.1963 LHB RM

Test		4	6	0	258	75	43.00	0	3	43	13	0					1.81	5	
FC		11	13	2	680	200*	61.81	1	4	103	34	0					1.98	11	
Int		4	3	1	59	39*	29.50	0	0	30	22	1	22.00	1-22	0	0	4.40	1	
Test	1981	69	118	7	3933	135*	35.43	4	27	2235	984	15	65.60	2-17	0	0	2.64	32	
FC	1981	162	231	24	8860	238*	42.80	19	46	6874	3002	91	32.98	5-45	2	0	2.62	86	
Int	1981	213	202	38	5791	102*	35.31	2	38	4674	3716	79	47.03	4-14	1	0	4.77	45	

RANATUNGA, Nishantha (Colts) b Gampaha 22.1.1966 RHB RMF

FC		11	13	2	233	57	21.18	0	1	696	395	12	32.91	3-42	0	0	3.40	7	
FC	1988	87	109	8	3011	212*	29.81	3	18	9670	4764	217	21.95	7-22	10	1	2.92	48	
Int	1992	2	1	0	0	0	0.00	0	0	102	82	1	82.00	1-33	0	0	4.82	0	

RANATUNGA, Sanjeeva (Nondescripts, Sri Lanka A, Sri Lanka to West Indies) b Colombo 25.4.1969 LHB OB

Cmp	Debut	M	I	NO	Runs	HS	Avge	100	50	Balls	Runs	Wkts	Avge	BB	5i	10m	RpO	ct	st
FC		17	25	4	805	97	38.33	0	6	104	65	3	21.66	3-38	0	0	3.75	13	
Test	1994	9	17	1	531	118	33.18	2	2									2	
FC	1988	95	140	15	4249	147*	33.99	6	26	1606	688	33	20.84	5-37	1	0	2.57	48	
Int	1994	13	11	0	253	70	23.00	0	2									2	

RANAWEERA, Ashan Priyanka (Burgher) b Colombo 1.12.1973 RHB RM

Cmp	Debut	M	I	NO	Runs	HS	Avge	100	50	Balls	Runs	Wkts	Avge	BB	5i	10m	RpO	ct	st
FC		6	11	1	228	61*	22.80	0	2	765	361	10	36.10	3-66	0	0	2.83	3	

RANAWEERA, Vajira Hemantha Kumara (Police) b Colombo 18.12.1968 RHB RM

Cmp	Debut	M	I	NO	Runs	HS	Avge	100	50	Balls	Runs	Wkts	Avge	BB	5i	10m	RpO	ct	st
FC		13	18	9	39	11	4.33	0	0	1766	936	41	22.82	5-39	2	0	3.18	5	
FC	1995	27	38	16	58	11	2.63	0	0	3356	1878	77	24.38	5-39	2	0	3.35	7	

RANGANA, Wasantha (Kalutara Town) b Colombo 5.9.1977 LHB

Cmp	Debut	M	I	NO	Runs	HS	Avge	100	50	Balls	Runs	Wkts	Avge	BB	5i	10m	RpO	ct	st
FC		2	4	1	63	27	21.00	0	0	12	23	0					11.50	2	

RANGA YASALAL, G.G. (Sebastianites) b Colombo 6.1.1975 RHB RM

Cmp	Debut	M	I	NO	Runs	HS	Avge	100	50	Balls	Runs	Wkts	Avge	BB	5i	10m	RpO	ct	st
FC		7	11	4	283	139	40.42	1	1	444	333	6	55.50	2-48	0	0	4.50	2	
FC	1992	21	29	8	696	139	33.14	1	3	1548	906	23	39.39	3-46	0	0	3.51	11	

RANJITH, Arachchige Don Bandula (Singha) b Balapitiya 11.12.1969 RHB RFM

Cmp	Debut	M	I	NO	Runs	HS	Avge	100	50	Balls	Runs	Wkts	Avge	BB	5i	10m	RpO	ct	st
FC		11	19	0	156	41	8.21	0	0	2214	1148	70	16.40	9-29	7	3	3.11	9	
FC	1990	25	40	1	551	69*	14.12	0	3	4666	2170	119	18.23	9-29	12	5	2.79	16	

RANJITH, Hitiya Mudiyanselage Rohitha (Singha) b 20.4.1962 RHB RFM

Cmp	Debut	M	I	NO	Runs	HS	Avge	100	50	Balls	Runs	Wkts	Avge	BB	5i	10m	RpO	ct	st
FC		1	2	0	4	4	2.00	0	0	48	34	1	34.00	1-34	0	0	4.25	0	
FC	1989	10	17	1	482	124	30.12	1	3	1414	860	31	27.74	5-61	2	0	3.64	6	

RATHNAWEERA, Kalzim Priyadarshana (Panadura) b Panadura 16.9.1976 RHB OB

Cmp	Debut	M	I	NO	Runs	HS	Avge	100	50	Balls	Runs	Wkts	Avge	BB	5i	10m	RpO	ct	st
FC		6	8	4	43	12*	10.75	0	0	1270	667	20	33.35	4-59	0	0	3.15	2	
FC	1995	8	10	6	47	12*	11.75	0	0	1504	759	22	34.50	4-59	0	0	3.02	4	

RATNASIRI, Anura (Police) b Colombo 23.4.1969 LHB LM

Cmp	Debut	M	I	NO	Runs	HS	Avge	100	50	Balls	Runs	Wkts	Avge	BB	5i	10m	RpO	ct	st
FC		9	15	5	106	27	10.60	0	0	79	44	2	22.00	1-7	0	0	6.28	5	
FC	1988	20	27	11	116	27	7.25	0	0	1391	834	33	25.27	6-26	2	0	3.59	8	

REGINALD, Prasanna John (Burgher) b Colombo 28.9.1973 LHB LFM

Cmp	Debut	M	I	NO	Runs	HS	Avge	100	50	Balls	Runs	Wkts	Avge	BB	5i	10m	RpO	ct	st
FC		1	2	1	0	0*	0.00	0	0	54	48	1	48.00	1-32	0	0	5.33	1	
FC	1994	8	13	4	98	28	10.88	0	0	606	436	10	43.60	3-85	0	0	4.31	3	

RIDEEGAMMANAGEDERA, Anil (Galle) b Galle 23.6.1976 RHB LB

Cmp	Debut	M	I	NO	Runs	HS	Avge	100	50	Balls	Runs	Wkts	Avge	BB	5i	10m	RpO	ct	st
FC		13	22	1	572	100	27.23	1	3	2353	1017	46	22.10	5-54	2	0	2.59	7	
FC	1995	28	47	2	1202	100	26.71	1	9	4377	1784	82	21.75	5-26	3	0	2.44	14	

RILLEGODAGE, Sujith Kumara (Galle) b Galle 23.3.1975 RHB WK

Cmp	Debut	M	I	NO	Runs	HS	Avge	100	50	Balls	Runs	Wkts	Avge	BB	5i	10m	RpO	ct	st
FC		4	6	3	20	9	6.66	0	0									9	

RUWAN, Sellaperumage Earl Dilip (Panadura) b Kalutara 10.3.1977 LHB

Cmp	Debut	M	I	NO	Runs	HS	Avge	100	50	Balls	Runs	Wkts	Avge	BB	5i	10m	RpO	ct	st
FC		13	21	2	528	61*	27.78	0	2									7	
FC	1995	15	24	2	552	61*	25.09	0	2									8	

SAGARA, Hewa Madinage Lalith (Burgher) b Colombo 9.8.1962 RHB SLA

Cmp	Debut	M	I	NO	Runs	HS	Avge	100	50	Balls	Runs	Wkts	Avge	BB	5i	10m	RpO	ct	st
FC		9	14	5	169	48	18.77	0	0	1854	976	22	44.36	4-131	0	0	3.15	4	
FC	1992	32	43	10	603	74	18.27	0	1	5726	2519	102	24.69	6-40	4	1	2.63	13	

SALGADO, Piyal (Kalutara Town) b Colombo 22.2.1974 RHB OB

Cmp	Debut	M	I	NO	Runs	HS	Avge	100	50	Balls	Runs	Wkts	Avge	BB	5i	10m	RpO	ct	st
FC		5	10	1	100	32	11.11	0	0	310	149	5	29.80	2-21	0	0	2.88	2	
FC	1995	14	25	4	186	32	8.85	0	0	1630	839	26	32.26	4-25	0	0	3.08	4	

SALGADO, Primal (Sebastianites) b Colombo 26.9.1971 RHB LB

Cmp	Debut	M	I	NO	Runs	HS	Avge	100	50	Balls	Runs	Wkts	Avge	BB	5i	10m	RpO	ct	st
FC		12	18	0	201	47	11.16	0	0	1075	585	22	26.59	5-42	1	0	3.26	4	
FC	1990	47	79	5	1132	64	15.29	0	2	3594	1986	59	33.66	5-42	1	0	3.31	20	

SAMARASINGHE, Dinesh (Nondescripts) b Colombo 1.1.1974 RHB RM

Cmp	Debut	M	I	NO	Runs	HS	Avge	100	50	Balls	Runs	Wkts	Avge	BB	5i	10m	RpO	ct	st
FC		9	8	1	39	11	5.57	0	0	756	412	14	29.42	4-47	0	0	3.26	4	
FC	1990	35	50	9	720	106*	17.56	1	2	3245	2070	62	33.38	7-87	2	0	3.82	23	

SAMARAWEERA, Dulip Prasanna (Colts, Sri Lanka A) b Colombo 12.2.1972 RHB OB WK

Cmp	Debut	M	I	NO	Runs	HS	Avge	100	50	Balls	Runs	Wkts	Avge	BB	5i	10m	RpO	ct	st
FC		13	21	1	664	100	33.20	1	3	84	42	1	42.00	1-4	0	0	3.00	15	
Test	1993	7	14	0	211	42	15.07	0	0									5	
FC	1991	74	116	8	4011	250*	37.13	7	21	1727	762	35	21.77	5-78	1	0	2.64	63	
Int	1993	5	4	0	91	49	22.75	0	0									3	

SAMARAWEERA, Thilan Thusara (Colts) b Colombo 22.9.1976 RHB OB

Cmp	Debut	M	I	NO	Runs	HS	Avge	100	50	Balls	Runs	Wkts	Avge	BB	5i	10m	RpO	ct	st
FC		12	16	8	476	117	59.50	1	3	1562	743	38	19.55	5-8	2	0	2.85	11	
FC	1995	14	18	9	513	117	57.00	1	3	1694	798	38	21.00	5-8	2	0	2.82	12	

SAMARAWICKREME, Haren Udesh Gamini (Galle) b Galle 7.9.1969 RHB WK

Cmp	Debut	M	I	NO	Runs	HS	Avge	100	50	Balls	Runs	Wkts	Avge	BB	5i	10m	RpO	ct	st
FC		4	7	0	149	66	21.28	0	1									4	4

SAMARAWICKREME, Namal Sadikeen (Antonians) b Colombo 8.9.1975 RHB RM

Cmp	Debut	M	I	NO	Runs	HS	Avge	100	50	Balls	Runs	Wkts	Avge	BB	5i	10m	RpO	ct	st
FC		3	4	1	11	6	3.66	0	0	234	187	3	62.33	2-22	0	0	4.79	0	
FC	1995	13	21	5	176	31	11.00	0	0	1256	843	26	32.42	4-82	0	0	4.02	5	

SAMPATH, M. (Kalutara Town) RHB RM

Cmp	Debut	M	I	NO	Runs	HS	Avge	100	50	Balls	Runs	Wkts	Avge	BB	5i	10m	RpO	ct	st
FC		1	2	0	46	38	23.00	0	0	36	13	2	6.50	2-11	0	0	2.16	0	

SAMPATH, Manage Thusara (Colts) b Galle 19.11.1974 RHB RM

Cmp	Debut	M	I	NO	Runs	HS	Avge	100	50	Balls	Runs	Wkts	Avge	BB	5i	10m	RpO	ct	st
FC		8	10	1	164	50	18.22	0	1									7	
FC	1990	26	40	5	1088	190	31.08	3	4	854	472	14	33.71	6-51	1	0	3.31	21	

SANDANAYAKE, C. (Panadura) RHB OB

Cmp	Debut	M	I	NO	Runs	HS	Avge	100	50	Balls	Runs	Wkts	Avge	BB	5i	10m	RpO	ct	st
FC		1	2	0	23	22	11.50	0	0	24	24	0					6.00	1	

SANJEEWA, Suraj (Singha) b Balapitiya 17.2.1972 RHB RFM

Cmp	Debut	M	I	NO	Runs	HS	Avge	100	50	Balls	Runs	Wkts	Avge	BB	5i	10m	RpO	ct	st
FC		11	21	1	262	72*	13.10	0	2	1315	822	15	54.80	3-67	0	0	3.75	3	
FC	1992	19	36	3	499	72*	15.12	0	4	2137	1417	32	44.28	5-86	1	0	3.97	3	

SANJEEWA, Sawanawadu Chaturan (Singha) b Balapitiya 6.6.1980 RHB

Cmp	Debut	M	I	NO	Runs	HS	Avge	100	50	Balls	Runs	Wkts	Avge	BB	5i	10m	RpO	ct	st
FC		1	2	0	18	17	9.00	0	0									1	

SARANASEKERA, Buddhi Nishantha (Nondescripts) b Galle 23.11.1968 LHB SLA

Cmp	Debut	M	I	NO	Runs	HS	Avge	100	50	Balls	Runs	Wkts	Avge	BB	5i	10m	RpO	ct	st
FC		8	9	5	63	16*	15.75	0	0	872	471	13	36.23	4-22	0	0	3.24	5	
FC	1988	29	28	12	195	29	12.18	0	0	1642	1642	72	22.80	7-74	3	1	2.77	20	

SEEMAN, Pradeep Chandika (Kalutara Town) b Kalutara 10.11.1977 RHB

Cmp	Debut	M	I	NO	Runs	HS	Avge	100	50	Balls	Runs	Wkts	Avge	BB	5i	10m	RpO	ct	st
FC		6	12	0	146	45	12.16	0	0									4	

SENASINGHE, Ajantha Vipula (Police) RHB RM

Cmp	Debut	M	I	NO	Runs	HS	Avge	100	50	Balls	Runs	Wkts	Avge	BB	5i	10m	RpO	ct	st
FC		7	10	0	93	36	9.30	0	0	12	4	0					2.00	4	

SENEVIRATNE, Asanga Chandana (Colombo) b Colombo 21.5.1965 LHB SLA

Cmp	Debut	M	I	NO	Runs	HS	Avge	100	50	Balls	Runs	Wkts	Avge	BB	5i	10m	RpO	ct	st
FC		1	1	0	26	26	26.00	0	0	24	15	0					3.75	0	
FC	1988	31	40	2	1139	141	29.97	1	5	444	193	7	27.57	3-16	0	0	2.60	11	

SERASINGHE, Pushpakumara (Police) b Colombo 8.4.1963 RHB SLA

Cmp	Debut	M	I	NO	Runs	HS	Avge	100	50	Balls	Runs	Wkts	Avge	BB	5i	10m	RpO	ct	st
FC		13	19	4	136	20*	9.06	0	0	2410	996	53	18.79	7-55	3	0	2.47	7	
FC	1993	31	46	9	365	43	9.86	0	0	5190	2080	102	20.39	7-55	6	1	2.40	19	

SHAMAN, Akmeemana Palliyaguruge Ruchira (Bloomfield) b Matara 22.1.1968 RHB RM

Cmp	Debut	M	I	NO	Runs	HS	Avge	100	50	Balls	Runs	Wkts	Avge	BB	5i	10m	RpO	ct	st
FC		12	18	4	510	117	36.42	1	2	881	434	20	21.70	4-45	0	0	2.95	8	
FC	1989	49	68	11	1473	117	25.84	1	9	4215	2301	80	28.76	5-47	1	0	3.27	36	

SHIROMAN, Nuwan (Galle) b Galle 14.9.1974 RHB RA

Cmp	Debut	M	I	NO	Runs	HS	Avge	100	50	Balls	Runs	Wkts	Avge	BB	5i	10m	RpO	ct	st
FC		10	18	1	486	103	28.58	1	2									4	
FC	1995	16	27	1	689	103	26.50	1	2	253	180	10	18.00	4-78	0	0	4.26	10	

SILVA, Chasun Randeera Priyankara (Kalutara Town) b Kalutara 26.7.1976 RHB RFM

Cmp	Debut	M	I	NO	Runs	HS	Avge	100	50	Balls	Runs	Wkts	Avge	BB	5i	10m	RpO	ct	st
FC		12	24	7	86	16	5.05	0	0	1420	1176	28	42.00	4-68	0	0	4.96	2	

SILVA, Kapila Chandana (Panadura) b Kalutara 30.7.1974 RHB RMF

Cmp	Debut	M	I	NO	Runs	HS	Avge	100	50	Balls	Runs	Wkts	Avge	BB	5i	10m	RpO	ct	st
FC		10	12	0	141	27	11.75	0	0	751	511	18	28.38	5-41	1	0	4.08	9	
FC	1992	26	34	3	325	37	10.48	0	0	1417	886	32	27.68	5-41	1	0	3.75	15	

SILVA, Kelaniyage Jayantha (Sinhalese, Sri Lanka, Sri Lanka A) b Kalutara 2.6.1973 RHB SLA

Cmp	Debut	M	I	NO	Runs	HS	Avge	100	50	Balls	Runs	Wkts	Avge	BB	5i	10m	RpO	ct	st
Test		3	2	0	0	0	0.00	0	0	737	262	16	16.37	4-16	0	0	2.13	1	
FC		17	12	2	18	11	1.80	0	0	2942	1287	56	22.98	6-42	3	0	2.62	14	
Test	1995	4	4	1	6	6*	2.00	0	0	947	382	17	22.47	4-16	0	0	2.42	1	
FC	1991	44	42	14	87	22	3.10	0	0	9326	3650	175	20.85	6-7	14	2	2.34	27	
Int	1994	1	1	1	1	1*		0	0	48	55	0					6.87	0	

SILVA, Manjula Nishantha Chamara (Police) b Balapitiya 25.1.1972 RHB SLA

Cmp	Debut	M	I	NO	Runs	HS	Avge	100	50	Balls	Runs	Wkts	Avge	BB	5i	10m	RpO	ct	st
FC		13	21	1	357	58*	17.85	0	1	521	259	11	23.54	3-4	0	0	2.98	6	
FC	1995	26	43	5	652	58*	17.15	0	1	994	524	18	29.11	3-4	0	0	3.16	15	

SILVA, Manjula Priyanganath (Panadura) b Panadura 26.5.1975 RHB OB

Cmp	Debut	M	I	NO	Runs	HS	Avge	100	50	Balls	Runs	Wkts	Avge	BB	5i	10m	RpO	ct	st
FC		1	2	0	15	13	7.50	0	0									2	
FC	1994	18	29	1	630	96	22.50	0	4	60	38	0					3.80	28	

SILVA, Prageeth Chamara (Panadura) b Panadura 14.12.1979

Cmp	Debut	M	I	NO	Runs	HS	Avge	100	50	Balls	Runs	Wkts	Avge	BB	5i	10m	RpO	ct	st
FC		2	3	0	24	24	8.00	0	0	12	8	0					4.00	1	

SILVA, Sanjeewa (Colombo, Sebastianites) b Colombo 9.4.1975 RHB RM WK

Cmp	Debut	M	I	NO	Runs	HS	Avge	100	50	Balls	Runs	Wkts	Avge	BB	5i	10m	RpO	ct	st
FC		9	13	0	581	135	44.69	2	1	48	30	0					3.75	2	
FC	1993	26	42	1	1844	201*	44.97	5	9	291	178	3	59.33	1-7	0	0	3.67	20	1

SILVA, Sanjeewa Gayan Sameera (Singha) b Balapitiya 14.1.1974 LHB WK

Cmp	Debut	M	I	NO	Runs	HS	Avge	100	50	Balls	Runs	Wkts	Avge	BB	5i	10m	RpO	ct	st
FC		13	25	1	406	58	16.91	0	2									16	1
FC	1992	46	82	6	1742	95	22.92	0	9									64	14

SILVA, Sella Hannadige Suranjith Mudushan Kanchana (Sinhalese) b Colombo 4.3.1975 RHB LB

Cmp	Debut	M	I	NO	Runs	HS	Avge	100	50	Balls	Runs	Wkts	Avge	BB	5i	10m	RpO	ct	st
FC		8	7	0	148	44	21.14	0	0	951	459	18	25.50	4-35	0	0	2.89	1	
FC	1993	39	43	9	832	53*	24.47	0	1	6939	3769	135	27.91	8-130	4	1	3.25	19	

SILVA, Sujith Kumara (Sebastianites) b Colombo 28.4.1968 LHB WK

Cmp	Debut	M	I	NO	Runs	HS	Avge	100	50	Balls	Runs	Wkts	Avge	BB	5i	10m	RpO	ct	st
FC		10	16	0	524	111	32.75	1	4									19	7
FC	1991	43	71	0	2280	144	32.11	2	15									88	20

SILVA, S.S. (Singha)

Cmp	Debut	M	I	NO	Runs	HS	Avge	100	50	Balls	Runs	Wkts	Avge	BB	5i	10m	RpO	ct	st
FC		1	1	0	0	0	0.00	0	0									1	

SITTAMIGE, Vipula (Antonians) b Colombo 30.4.1968 RHB OB WK

Cmp	Debut	M	I	NO	Runs	HS	Avge	100	50	Balls	Runs	Wkts	Avge	BB	5i	10m	RpO	ct	st
FC		12	19	0	369	62	19.42	0	2	132	84	6	14.00	2-14	0	0	3.81	16	
FC	1988	53	84	5	2300	155	29.11	3	12	690	342	15	22.80	2-14	0	0	2.97	50	1

SOORIYARACHCHI, Samantha (Kalutara Town) b Kalutara 31.3.1967 RHB RA

Cmp	Debut	M	I	NO	Runs	HS	Avge	100	50	Balls	Runs	Wkts	Avge	BB	5i	10m	RpO	ct	st
FC		1	2	0	34	23	17.00	0	0	24	14	0					3.50	0	
FC	1989	42	67	7	1578	148	26.30	2	5	691	334	8	41.75	2-67	0	0	2.90	48	

SOYSA, Iddadura Chamara (Singha) b Telwatta 12.10.1978 RHB RM

| FC | | 3 | 5 | 3 | 60 | 25* | 30.00 | 0 | 0 | 108 | 40 | 0 | | | | | 2.22 | 1 | |
| FC | 1994 | 7 | 8 | 4 | 131 | 29* | 32.75 | 0 | 0 | 450 | 246 | 6 | 41.00 | 3-37 | 0 | 0 | 3.28 | 2 | |

SOYSA, S. (Singha)

| FC | | 1 | 2 | 0 | 8 | 6 | 4.00 | 0 | 0 | 6 | 11 | 0 | | | | | 11.00 | 0 | |

SOYSA, Wijesekera Nihil Mahinda (Police) b Colombo 9.4.1970 LHB SLA

| FC | | 13 | 23 | 1 | 438 | 73 | 19.90 | 0 | 3 | 1666 | 805 | 23 | 35.00 | 5-44 | 1 | 0 | 2.89 | 9 | |
| FC | 1988 | 41 | 69 | 8 | 1202 | 170 | 19.70 | 2 | 4 | 4957 | 2146 | 91 | 23.58 | 6-22 | 5 | 1 | 2.59 | 22 | |

SUDARSHANA, Dhammika (Galle) b Galle 19.6.1976 RHB RM

| FC | | 13 | 22 | 1 | 569 | 91 | 27.09 | 0 | 5 | 642 | 459 | 7 | 65.57 | 1-10 | 0 | 0 | 4.28 | 14 | |
| FC | 1995 | 24 | 39 | 1 | 836 | 91 | 22.00 | 0 | 5 | 876 | 593 | 14 | 42.35 | 4-30 | 0 | 0 | 4.06 | 24 | |

SURENDRA, Dhammika (Antonians) LHB SLA

| FC | | 7 | 10 | 5 | 32 | 16 | 6.40 | 0 | 0 | 696 | 342 | 12 | 28.50 | 5-95 | 1 | 0 | 2.94 | 1 | |
| FC | 1993 | 10 | 13 | 6 | 35 | 16 | 5.00 | 0 | 0 | 1004 | 508 | 20 | 25.40 | 5-95 | 1 | 0 | 3.03 | 5 | |

TENNEKOON, Sidath Keerthi Banda (Burgher) b Colombo 10.9.1971 RHB

| FC | | 10 | 16 | 1 | 428 | 62 | 28.53 | 0 | 3 | | | | | | | | | 9 | |
| FC | 1994 | 17 | 29 | 1 | 615 | 62 | 21.96 | 0 | 3 | | | | | | | | | 13 | |

THALERATNE, Irantha Sajan (Nondescripts) b Colombo 25.2.1977 RM

| FC | | 1 | 1 | 0 | 0 | 0 | 0.00 | 0 | 0 | 108 | 31 | 1 | 31.00 | 1-25 | 0 | 0 | 1.72 | 0 | |
| FC | 1995 | 2 | 1 | 0 | 0 | 0 | 0.00 | 0 | 0 | 186 | 88 | 1 | 88.00 | 1-25 | 0 | 0 | 2.83 | 0 | |

THENUWARA, Nalin Tharanga (Singha) b Galle 21.4.1978 RHB

| FC | | 2 | 4 | 1 | 33 | 21 | 11.00 | 0 | 0 | | | | | | | | | 1 | |

THITHAGALA, Saman (Antonians) RHB OB

| FC | | 4 | 7 | 1 | 53 | 12 | 8.83 | 0 | 0 | 30 | 17 | 0 | | | | | 3.40 | 3 | |
| FC | 1995 | 7 | 13 | 1 | 178 | 54 | 14.83 | 0 | 1 | 36 | 20 | 0 | | | | | 3.33 | 4 | |

TILLAKARATNE, Hashan Prasantha (Nondescripts, Sri Lanka, Sri Lanka to New Zealand, Sri Lanka to West Indies, Sri Lanka to Kenya, Sri Lanka to Sharjah, Sri Lanka to India) b Colombo 14.7.1967 LHB RM WK

Test		4	6	2	337	126*	84.25	2	1	12	3	0					1.50	2	
FC		13	14	4	840	143	84.00	5	2	234	159	1	159.00	1-51	0	0	4.07	9	
Int		4	2	1	35	34*	35.00	0	0									1	
Test	1989	43	72	12	2579	126*	42.98	6	14	34	14	0					2.47	72	
FC	1984	134	190	44	6939	176*	47.52	22	30	1327	698	19	36.73	4-37	0	0	3.15	171	5
Int	1986	158	135	31	2935	104	28.22	2	9	124	92	4	23.00	1-3	0	0	4.45	70	5

TILLAKARATNE, Nilantha (Kalutara Town) b Kalutara 16.3.1977 RHB RM

| FC | | 12 | 24 | 0 | 569 | 78 | 23.70 | 0 | 4 | 204 | 133 | 4 | 33.25 | 2-45 | 0 | 0 | 3.91 | 3 | |

TILLAKARATNE, Yasas Nilantha (Colombo, Antonians) b Colombo 15.9.1972 LHB LB

| FC | | 10 | 16 | 1 | 470 | 135* | 31.33 | 1 | 1 | 594 | 310 | 8 | 38.75 | 4-65 | 0 | 0 | 3.13 | 7 | |
| FC | 1992 | 26 | 38 | 5 | 1160 | 135* | 35.15 | 2 | 5 | 1601 | 873 | 33 | 26.45 | 6-47 | 2 | 0 | 3.27 | 20 | |

UPASHANTHA, Kalutarage Eric Amila (Colts, President's XI) b Kurunegala 10.6.1972 RHB RFM

FC		12	12	2	181	35	18.10	0	0	1321	769	32	24.03	4-48	0	0	3.49	14	
FC	1990	50	61	6	1235	77	22.45	0	10	4937	2996	107	28.00	4-28	0	0	3.52	40	
Int	1995	3	2	1	8	8*	11.00	0	0	114	91	3	30.33	2-24	0	0	4.78	1	

VAAS, Warnakulasooriya Patabendige Ushantha Joseph Chaminda (Colts, Sri Lanka, Sri Lanka to New Zealand, Sri Lanka to Kenya, Sri Lanka to Sharjah, Sri Lanka to India) b Mattumagala 27.1.1974 LHB LFM

Test		4	5	0	77	34	15.40	0	0	873	347	13	26.69	4-60	0	0	2.38	5	
FC		10	11	2	146	34	16.22	0	0	2171	945	51	18.52	6-12	2	0	2.61	8	
Int		3								126	87	2	43.50	2-23	0	0	4.14	1	
Test	1994	18	30	2	492	57	17.57	0	2	4050	1674	67	24.98	6-87	4	1	2.48	6	
FC	1990	46	53	10	732	58*	17.02	0	3	8785	3871	186	20.81	6-12	12	1	2.60	13	
Int	1993	72	40	15	328	33	13.12	0	0	3464	2259	89	25.38	4-20	3	0	3.91	11	

VILLAVARAYAN, Mario (Colombo, Bloomfield, Sri Lanka A, President's XI) b Colombo 22.8.1969 RHB RM

| FC | | 9 | 9 | 1 | 136 | 61 | 17.00 | 0 | 1 | 1102 | 521 | 29 | 17.96 | 9-15 | 1 | 1 | 2.83 | 2 | |
| FC | 1992 | 33 | 31 | 6 | 466 | 61 | 18.64 | 0 | 1 | 4836 | 2382 | 105 | 22.68 | 9-15 | 4 | 1 | 2.85 | 14 | |

VISWANATH, Prasanna (Sinhalese) b Colombo 12.10.1974 RHB RM

| FC | | 2 | 3 | 1 | 63 | 61* | 31.50 | 0 | 1 | 6 | 0 | 0 | | | | | 0.00 | 0 | |

VITHANAGE, Harshana Primal Warakagoda (Kalutara Town) b Kalutara 28.10.1975 RHB

| FC | | 6 | 11 | 2 | 78 | 24* | 8.66 | 0 | 0 | 6 | 10 | 0 | | | | | 10.00 | 4 | |

WANASINGHE, Pasan Nirmitha (Antonians) b Colombo 30.10.1970 RHB RFM

| FC | | 13 | 23 | 1 | 389 | 110 | 17.68 | 1 | 2 | 1749 | 1017 | 35 | 29.05 | 6-42 | 2 | 0 | 3.48 | 2 | |
| FC | 1990 | 35 | 60 | 2 | 1351 | 136 | 23.29 | 2 | 6 | 3792 | 2184 | 68 | 32.11 | 6-42 | 2 | 0 | 3.45 | 13 | |

Cmp	Debut	M	I	NO	Runs	HS	Avge	100	50	Balls	Runs	Wkts	Avge	BB	5i	10m	RpO	ct	st

WARANGODA, Varuna S.K. (Colombo, Tamil Union, Sri Lanka A) b Colombo 18.2.1971 LHB RA

Cmp	Debut	M	I	NO	Runs	HS	Avge	100	50	Balls	Runs	Wkts	Avge	BB	5i	10m	RpO	ct	st
FC		8	11	0	539	138	49.00	1	4									7	
FC	1990	42	57	3	2881	204	53.35	10	12	16	8	0					3.00	26	

WARNAWEERA, Kahakatchchi Patabandige Jayananda (Singha) b Matara 23.11.1960 LHB RM/OB

FC		4	3	0	14	8	4.66	0	0	450	218	7	31.14	3-43	0	0	2.90	0	
Test	1985	10	12	3	39	20	4.33	0	0	2333	1021	32	31.90	4-25	0	0	2.62	0	
FC	1985	68	76	33	265	24*	6.16	0	0	12953	5729	287	19.96	7-16	22	6	2.65	10	
Int	1990	6	3	3	1	1*		0	0	294	200	6	33.33	2-24	0	0	4.08	2	

WEERAPPULI, Ajantha Thushara (Nondescripts) b Colombo 3.12.1976

| FC | | 2 | 4 | 1 | 167 | 65 | 55.56 | 0 | 2 | | | | | | | | | 1 | |

WEERASINGHE, Colombage Don Udesh Sanjeewa (Nondescripts) b Colombo 1.3.1968 RHB LBG

FC		8	11	0	110	27	10.00	0	0	1057	683	33	20.69	8-77	4	2	3.87	8	
Test	1985	1	1	0	3	3	3.00	0	0	114	36	0					1.89	0	
FC	1984	44	58	11	845	112*	17.97	1	2	4593	2476	103	24.03	8-77	6	2	3.23	39	

WEERASINGHE, Krishantha Chaminda (Panadura) b Panadura 15.5.1975 RHB RM

| FC | | 3 | 4 | 1 | 20 | 10 | 6.66 | 0 | 0 | 174 | 153 | 4 | 38.25 | 2-23 | 0 | 0 | 5.27 | 2 | |

WEERASINGHE, Mahesh (Antonians)

| FC | | 3 | 4 | 0 | 34 | 19 | 8.50 | 0 | 0 | | | | | | | | | 1 | |

WEWALWALA, Asela Sampath (Singha) b Colombo 11.5.1975 RHB RFM

FC		12	24	3	667	74	31.76	0	4	830	540	19	28.42	5-40	1	0	3.90	5	
FC	1994	23	41	5	954	74	26.50	0	5	1598	1105	30	36.83	5-40	1	0	4.14	8	

WICKRAMARATNE, Ranasinghe Pattikirikoralalage Aruna Hemantha (Sinhalese, President's XI) b Colombo 21.2.1971 LHB SLA WK

FC		12	15	3	688	130	57.33	2	4	192	156	3	52.00	2-56	0	0	4.87	16	
FC	1990	76	93	14	3739	209	47.32	6	28	731	390	9	43.33	2-7	0	0	3.20	102	
Int	1993	3	2	0	4	3	2.00	0	0									0	

WICKRAMASINGHE, Duminda Dharmin (Galle) b Galle 1.10.1968 RHB

FC		13	21	1	532	103*	26.60	1	3									9	
FC	1990	45	71	8	2340	127*	37.14	5	13	18	12	1	12.00	1-1	0	0	4.00	40	

WICKRAMASINGHE, Gallage Pramodya (Sinhalese, Sri Lanka A, Sri Lanka, Sri Lanka to New Zealand) b Matara 14.8.1971 RHB RFM

FC		11	10	2	97	48	12.12	0	0	1582	913	39	23.41	6-82	1	0	3.46	6	
Int		1								54	33	1	33.00	1-33	0	0	3.66	0	
Test	1991	24	39	4	323	43	9.22	0	0	4505	2337	47	49.72	5-73	1	0	3.11	9	
FC	1988	77	85	13	824	55*	11.44	0	1	12161	6218	220	28.26	10-41	7	2	3.06	31	
Int	1990	85	31	12	140	21*	7.36	0	0	3638	2689	60	44.81	3-28	0	0	4.43	15	

WICKRAMASINGHE, Prasad Priyankara (Bloomfield) b Colombo 12.5.1977

| FC | | 9 | 7 | 5 | 138 | 39 | 69.00 | 0 | 0 | 816 | 355 | 18 | 19.72 | 5-26 | 1 | 0 | 2.61 | 9 | |

WICKREMASINGHE, Chandana Mahesh (Sebastianites) b Colombo 23.9.1965 RHB OB

FC		7	8	0	199	59	24.87	0	1	78	47	0					3.61	5	
FC	1988	61	92	5	2106	131	24.20	3	7	4023	1724	73	23.61	5-43	1	0	2.57	53	1

WIJEGUNAWARDENE, Vajira (Sinhalese) b Colombo 29.7.1970 RHB RM

| FC | | 3 | 5 | 0 | 168 | 74 | 33.60 | 0 | 1 | 156 | 79 | 2 | 39.50 | 1-12 | 0 | 0 | 3.03 | 0 | |

WIJEKOON, Gayan Ramya Kumara (Tamil Union) b Gampaha 21.12.1976 LHB LM

| FC | | 11 | 14 | 2 | 552 | 117 | 46.00 | 1 | 4 | 372 | 226 | 6 | 37.66 | 3-22 | 0 | 0 | 3.64 | 11 | |

WIJENAYAKE, Warakagoda Gamage Suranga (Bloomfield) b Colombo 27.10.1976 LHB SLA

FC		7	10	4	118	22*	19.66	0	0	494	258	12	21.50	5-38	1	0	3.13	3	
FC	1995	9	11	4	119	22*	17.00	0	0	716	354	14	25.28	5-38	1	0	2.96	3	

WIJESIRI, Saluka (Tamil Union) b Colombo 1.1.1973 RHB RM

FC		6	9	1	88	25	11.00	0	0									2	
FC	1989	24	36	4	803	127	25.09	1	5	462	148	5	29.60	2-34	0	0	1.92	15	

WIJETUNGE, Chethiya (Sebastianites) b Colombo 5.3.1974 RHB WK

FC		1	1	0	4	4	4.00	0	0									0	
FC	1992	8	14	0	145	26	10.35	0	0									5	1

WIMALASENA, Roshan Ruwan Kumara (Panadura) b Panadura 17.12.1977 RHB

| FC | | 2 | 4 | 1 | 54 | 30* | 18.00 | 0 | 0 | 12 | 10 | 0 | | | | | 5.00 | 1 | |

WIMALASIRI, Raja Ravindra (Police) b Colombo 19.8.1969 RHB LB

FC		13	22	2	480	66*	24.00	0	2	342	192	7	27.42	3-22	0	0	3.36	14	
FC	1990	31	53	6	1076	82	22.89	0	6	1185	734	22	33.36	3-22	0	0	3.71	22	

WITHANAGE, Chanaka Mawalle (Galle) b Galle 26.6.1976 LHB RM

| FC | | 6 | 10 | 0 | 167 | 60 | 16.70 | 0 | 1 | 12 | 10 | 1 | 10.00 | 1-10 | 0 | 0 | 5.00 | 3 | |

ZOYSA, Demuni Nuwan Tharanga (Sinhalese, Sri Lanka, Sri Lanka A, Sri Lanka to New Zealand, Sri Lanka to Sharjah) b Colombo 13.5.1978 LHB LFM

Test		1	1	0	0	0	0.00	0	0	60	55	0					5.50	0	
FC		10	9	4	82	32*	16.40	0	0	1638	811	42	19.30	7-58	2	0	2.97	2	
Test	1996	3	5	1	43	16*	10.75	0	0	544	267	7	38.14	3-47	0	0	2.94	1	

Cmp	Debut	M	I	NO	Runs	HS	Avge	100	50	Balls	Runs	Wkts	Avge	BB	5i	10m	RpO	ct	st
FC	1996	12	13	5	125	32*	15.62	0	0	2122	1023	49	20.87	7-58	2	0	2.89	3	
Int	1996	3	1	1	3	3*		0	0	162	122	5	24.40	2-29	0	0	4.51	0	

The following runs were conceded by bowlers in first-class matches in 1992-93 for which full details of overs bowled are not available (these runs are not taken into account when computing the runs per over figure): J.C.Gamage 8, D.K.Liyanage 80, G.R.M.A.Perera 11, N.Ranatunga 54, K.E.A.Upashantha 93, W.P.U.J.C.Vaas 57, M.Villavarayan 83

AUSTRALIA IN SRI LANKA 1996-97

BEVAN, M.G.

Cmp	M	I	NO	Runs	HS	Avge	100	50	Balls	Runs	Wkts	Avge	BB	5i	10m	RpO	ct	st
Int	4	4	1	84	56	28.00	0	1	42	32	2	16.00	2-14	0	0	4.57	2	

FLEMING, D.W.

Cmp	M	I	NO	Runs	HS	Avge	100	50	Balls	Runs	Wkts	Avge	BB	5i	10m	RpO	ct	st
Int	4	2	1	4	3	4.00	0	0	168	128	5	25.60	3-26	0	0	4.57	0	

GILLESPIE, J.N.

Cmp	M	I	NO	Runs	HS	Avge	100	50	Balls	Runs	Wkts	Avge	BB	5i	10m	RpO	ct	st
Int	1	1	0	6	6	6.00	0	0	36	27	0					4.50	0	

HEALY, I.A.

Cmp	M	I	NO	Runs	HS	Avge	100	50	Balls	Runs	Wkts	Avge	BB	5i	10m	RpO	ct	st
Int	4	4	0	37	20	9.25	0	0									4	

HOGG, G.B.

Cmp	M	I	NO	Runs	HS	Avge	100	50	Balls	Runs	Wkts	Avge	BB	5i	10m	RpO	ct	st
Int	2	2	1	13	11*	13.00	0	0	84	59	1	59.00	1-26	0	0	4.21	1	

LAW, S.G.

Cmp	M	I	NO	Runs	HS	Avge	100	50	Balls	Runs	Wkts	Avge	BB	5i	10m	RpO	ct	st
Int	4	4	0	131	67	32.75	0	1	12	23	0					11.50	1	

LEHMANN, D.S.

Cmp	M	I	NO	Runs	HS	Avge	100	50	Balls	Runs	Wkts	Avge	BB	5i	10m	RpO	ct	st
Int	2	2	0	17	15	8.50	0	0	66	55	1	55.00	1-29	0	0	5.00	1	

McGRATH, G.D.

Cmp	M	I	NO	Runs	HS	Avge	100	50	Balls	Runs	Wkts	Avge	BB	5i	10m	RpO	ct	st
Int	4	2	1	8	8*	8.00	0	0	197	125	7	17.85	3-33	0	0	3.80	0	

PONTING, R.T.

Cmp	M	I	NO	Runs	HS	Avge	100	50	Balls	Runs	Wkts	Avge	BB	5i	10m	RpO	ct	st
Int	4	4	1	116	53	38.66	0	1									1	

REIFFEL, P.R.

Cmp	M	I	NO	Runs	HS	Avge	100	50	Balls	Runs	Wkts	Avge	BB	5i	10m	RpO	ct	st
Int	3	2	1	13	12	13.00	0	0	90	103	4	25.75	2-23	0	0	6.86	0	

SLATER, M.J.

Cmp	M	I	NO	Runs	HS	Avge	100	50	Balls	Runs	Wkts	Avge	BB	5i	10m	RpO	ct	st
Int	4	4	0	96	50	24.00	0	1									0	

WAUGH, M.E.

Cmp	M	I	NO	Runs	HS	Avge	100	50	Balls	Runs	Wkts	Avge	BB	5i	10m	RpO	ct	st
Int	4	4	0	100	50	25.00	0	1	132	130	4	32.50	3-24	0	0	5.90	2	

WAUGH, S.R.

Cmp	M	I	NO	Runs	HS	Avge	100	50	Balls	Runs	Wkts	Avge	BB	5i	10m	RpO	ct	st
Int	4	4	0	214	82	53.50	0	3	150	111	3	37.00	1-24	0	0	4.44	3	

INDIA IN SRI LANKA 1996-97

AZHARUDDIN, M.

Cmp	M	I	NO	Runs	HS	Avge	100	50	Balls	Runs	Wkts	Avge	BB	5i	10m	RpO	ct	st
Int	3	3	1	101	58	50.50	0	1									2	

DRAVID, R.S.

Cmp	M	I	NO	Runs	HS	Avge	100	50	Balls	Runs	Wkts	Avge	BB	5i	10m	RpO	ct	st
Int	3	2	1	20	13	20.00	0	0									1	

GANGULY, S.C.

Cmp	M	I	NO	Runs	HS	Avge	100	50	Balls	Runs	Wkts	Avge	BB	5i	10m	RpO	ct	st
Int	3	3	0	111	59	37.00	0	1	30	34	0					6.80	0	

JADEJA, A.D.

Cmp	M	I	NO	Runs	HS	Avge	100	50	Balls	Runs	Wkts	Avge	BB	5i	10m	RpO	ct	st
Int	3	3	0	74	68	24.66	0	1	68	51	0					4.50	0	

JOSHI, S.B.

Cmp	M	I	NO	Runs	HS	Avge	100	50	Balls	Runs	Wkts	Avge	BB	5i	10m	RpO	ct	st
Int	2	1	0	48	48	48.00	0	0	114	60	4	15.00	2-23	0	0	3.15	1	

KAMBLI, V.G.

Cmp	M	I	NO	Runs	HS	Avge	100	50	Balls	Runs	Wkts	Avge	BB	5i	10m	RpO	ct	st
Int	3	3	1	48	29*	24.00	0	0									0	

KAPOOR, A.R.

Cmp	M	I	NO	Runs	HS	Avge	100	50	Balls	Runs	Wkts	Avge	BB	5i	10m	RpO	ct	st
Int	1								60	51	0					5.10	0	

KUMBLE, A.

Cmp	M	I	NO	Runs	HS	Avge	100	50	Balls	Runs	Wkts	Avge	BB	5i	10m	RpO	ct	st
Int	3	1	0	0	0	0.00	0	0	171	109	6	18.16	4-33	1	0	3.82	1	

MONGIA, N.R.

Cmp	M	I	NO	Runs	HS	Avge	100	50	Balls	Runs	Wkts	Avge	BB	5i	10m	RpO	ct	st
Int	3	1	0	38	38	38.00	0	0									1	2

SRINATH, J.

Cmp	M	I	NO	Runs	HS	Avge	100	50	Balls	Runs	Wkts	Avge	BB	5i	10m	RpO	ct	st
Int	3	2	1	3	2	3.00	0	0	144	107	1	107.00	1-42	0	0	4.45	0	

Cmp Debut	M	I	NO	Runs	HS	Avge	100	50	Balls	Runs	Wkts	Avge	BB	5i	10m	RpO	ct	st
TENDULKAR, S.R.																		
Int	3	3	0	157	110	52.33	1	0	108	87	1	87.00	1-29	0	0	4.83	2	
VENKATESH PRASAD, B.K.																		
Int	3	1	1	6	6*		0	0	136	142	4	35.50	2-42	0	0	6.26	1	

PAKISTAN IN SRI LANKA 1996-97

Cmp Debut	M	I	NO	Runs	HS	Avge	100	50	Balls	Runs	Wkts	Avge	BB	5i	10m	RpO	ct	st
ASIF MUJTABA																		
Test	2	3	0	76	49	25.33	0	0	360	145	2	72.50	1-23	0	0	2.41	2	
IJAZ AHMED																		
Test	2	3	0	164	113	54.66	1	0	30	18	0					3.60	0	
INZAMAM-UL-HAQ																		
Test	2	3	1	109	54*	54.50	0	1									0	
MOHAMMAD ZAHID																		
Test	2	2	1	6	6*	6.00	0	0	240	148	2	74.00	1-44	0	0	3.70	0	
MOIN KHAN																		
Test	2	2	0	98	98	49.00	0	1									1	2
MUSHTAQ AHMED																		
Test	2	2	0	27	26	13.50	0	0	829	420	10	42.00	3-94	0	0	3.03	1	
RAMEEZ RAJA																		
Test	2	3	0	86	50	28.66	0	1									2	
SALEEM ELAHI																		
Test	2	3	0	14	14	4.66	0	0									7	1
SALEEM MALIK																		
Test	2	3	0	237	155	79.00	1	1	54	33	0					3.66	0	
SAQLAIN MUSHTAQ																		
Test	2	3	1	86	58	43.00	0	1	1171	512	14	36.57	5-89	1	0	2.62	1	
SHAHID NAZIR																		
Test	2	2	1	2	2	2.00	0	0	228	148	1	148.00	1-61	0	0	3.89	2	

WEST INDIES A IN SRI LANKA 1996-97

Cmp Debut	M	I	NO	Runs	HS	Avge	100	50	Balls	Runs	Wkts	Avge	BB	5i	10m	RpO	ct	st
CUFFY, C.E.																		
FC	4	4	3	7	6*	7.00	0	0	632	336	18	18.66	7-84	1	1	3.18	3	
FORD, S.G.B.																		
FC	3	4	1	60	27	20.00	0	0									10	
FRANCIS, N.B.																		
FC	3	4	1	37	20	12.33	0	0	264	176	5	35.20	4-32	0	0	4.00	2	
GIBSON, O.D.																		
FC	3	4	1	72	39	24.00	0	0	406	178	4	44.50	2-51	0	0	2.63	0	
HARPER, R.A.																		
FC	3	4	1	109	51	36.33	0	1	679	205	17	12.05	5-61	1	0	1.81	5	
JACOBS, R.D.																		
FC	1	1	1	100	100*		1	0									3	
JOSEPH, D.R.E.																		
FC	4	5	0	150	93	30.00	0	1									5	
LEWIS, R.N.																		
FC	4	4	0	17	8	4.25	0	0	678	327	14	23.35	4-23	0	0	2.89	3	
POWELL, T.O.																		
FC	4	5	0	244	87	48.80	0	2									4	
REIFER, F.L.																		
FC	4	5	0	184	96	36.80	0	2	30	16	0					3.20	2	
SAMAROO, A.																		
FC	2	1	0	13	13	13.00	0	0	214	98	1	98.00	1-3	0	0	2.74	1	
WALLACE, P.A.																		
FC	4	6	1	407	125	81.40	2	2									5	
WILLIAMS, L.R.																		
FC	1	1	0	5	5	5.00	0	0	96	31	1	31.00	1-26	0	0	1.93	1	

Cmp Debut	M	I	NO	Runs	HS	Avge	100	50	Balls	Runs	Wkts	Avge	BB	5i	10m	RpO	ct	st
WILLIAMS, S.C.																		
FC	4	6	1	305	170	61.00	1	1									7	

ZIMBABWE IN SRI LANKA 1996-97

Cmp Debut	M	I	NO	Runs	HS	Avge	100	50	Balls	Runs	Wkts	Avge	BB	5i	10m	RpO	ct	st
BRANDES, E.A.																		
Int	1	1	0	17	17	17.00	0	0	60	47	2	23.50	2-47	0	0	4.70	0	
CAMPBELL, A.D.R.																		
Test	2	4	0	78	36	19.50	0	0									0	
Int	3	3	0	73	54	24.33	0	1	24	24	0					6.00	2	
DEKKER, M.H.																		
Test	2	4	0	52	20	13.00	0	0									0	
Int	2	2	1	11	8*	11.00	0	0	18	17	0					5.66	0	
EVANS, C.N.																		
Test	1	2	0	10	9	5.00	0	0	36	27	0					4.50	1	
Int	3	3	1	115	96*	57.50	0	1	48	33	1	33.00	1-19	0	0	4.12	0	
FLOWER, A.																		
Test	2	4	0	36	31	9.00	0	0									3	1
Int	3	3	0	89	78	29.66	0	1									1	
FLOWER, G.W.																		
Test	2	4	0	92	52	23.00	0	1	36	29	0					4.83	0	
Int	3	3	0	33	26	11.00	0	0	54	48	0					5.33	0	
JAMES, W.R.																		
Int	1																0	
OLONGA, H.K.																		
Test	2	4	1	7	3*	2.33	0	0	280	155	2	77.50	2-57	0	0	3.32	1	
Int	1								36	47	2	23.50	2-47	0	0	7.83	1	
OMARSHAH, A.H.																		
Test	1	2	0	63	62	31.50	0	1									0	
Int	2	2	0	47	41	23.50	0	0	12	18	0					9.00	0	
STRANG, B.C.																		
Test	1	2	0	5	3	2.50	0	0	120	63	3	21.00	3-63	0	0	3.15	1	
Int	1	1	1	1	1*		0	0	47	52	0					6.63	2	
STRANG, P.A.																		
Test	2	4	1	66	50	22.00	0	1	453	185	9	20.55	5-106	1	0	2.45	2	
Int	3	3	0	52	24	17.33	0	0	174	163	2	81.50	1-41	0	0	5.62	1	
STREAK, H.H.																		
Test	1	2	2	3	3*		0	0	120	54	3	18.00	3-54	0	0	2.70	1	
Int	3	2	0	2	2	1.00	0	0	168	120	2	60.00	1-46	0	0	4.28	0	
WHITTALL, A.R.																		
Test	2	4	0	27	12	6.75	0	0	264	115	0					2.61	1	
Int	1								60	30	1	30.00	1-30	0	0	3.00	0	
WHITTALL, G.J.																		
Test	2	4	0	55	39	13.75	0	0	173	91	1	91.00	1-48	0	0	3.15	0	
Int	3	3	1	27	15*	13.50	0	0	144	108	3	36.00	3-53	0	0	4.50	1	
WISHART, C.B.																		
Test	2	4	0	81	51	20.25	0	1									2	
Int	3	3	0	60	53	20.00	0	1									1	

WEST INDIES

First First-Class Match: Barbados v Demerara (Bridgetown) 1864-65

First First-Class Tour to England: 1906

First Test Match: West Indies v England (Bridgetown) 1929-30

Present First-Class Teams: Barbados, Guyana, Jamaica, Leeward Islands, Trinidad and Tobago, Windward Islands.

First-Class Competition: The Shell Shield was instituted for the 1965-66 season for competition between the first-class teams, and this was the first regular competition for all the countries in the West Indies. It was replaced by the Red Stripe Cup from 1987-88.

Red Stripe Cup Champions 1996-97: Barbados

FIRST-CLASS RECORDS

Highest Team Total: 849 England v West Indies (Kingston) 1929-30
Highest in 1996-97: 453 Jamaica v India (Kingston); 448-4d Barbados v Guyana (Georgetown); 446 Windward Islands v Guyana (Tanteen); 436 India v West Indies (Port of Spain); 434 Barbados v Windward Islands (Bridgetown)

Lowest Team Total: 16 Trinidad v Barbados (Bridgetown) 1941-42
Lowest in 1996-97: 77 Jamaica v Windward Islands (Castries); 81 India v West Indies (Bridgetown); 82 and 95 Leeward Islands v Trinidad (Port of Spain); 97 Leeward Islands v Jamaica (St Catherine)

Highest Individual Innings: 375 B.C.Lara West Indies v England (St John's) 1993-94
Highest in 1996-97: 218 J.R.Murray Windward Islands v Guyana (St Georges); 201 N.S.Sidhu India v West Indies (Port of Spain); 200 F.L.Reifer Barbados v Windward Islands (Bridgetown); 159 C.B.Lambert Guyana v Trinidad (Albion); 158 R.P.Arnold Sri Lanka v Leeward Islands (St Johns)

Most Runs in Season: 1,765 (av 135.76) E.H.Hendren (MCC) 1929-30
Most in 1996-97: 965 (av 43.86) B.C.Lara (Trinidad); 964 (av 38.56) S.C.Williams (Leeward Islands); 940 (av 40.86) F.L.Reifer (Barbados); 908 (av 37.83) R.I.C.Holder (Barbados); 815 (av 58.21) S.Chanderpaul (Guyana)

Most Runs in Career: 37,354 (av 45.88) C.G.Greenidge (Barbados, Hampshire) 1970 to 1992
Most by Current Batsman: 14,689 (av 44.78) C.L.Hooper (Guyana, Kent) 1983-84 to date; 10,978 (av 54.07) B.C.Lara (Trinidad, Warwickshire) 1987-88 to date; 10,297 (av 37.30) P.V.Simmons (Trinidad, Leicestershire, Easterns) 1982-83 to date; 7,494 (av 43.06) J.C.Adams (Jamaica) 1984-85 to date. D.L.Haynes, 26,030 (av 45.90), played for Western Province and R.B.Richardson, 14,204 (av 41.77) played for Northern Transvaal but did not appear in West Indies in 1996-97.

Best Innings Analysis: 10-36 D.C.S.Hinds A.B.St.Hill's XII v Trinidad (Port of Spain) 1901-02 (12 a side match); 10-175 E.E.Hemmings International XI v West Indies XI (Kingston) 1982-83
Best in 1996-97: 7-58 C.A.Davis Windward Islands v Jamaica (Discovery Bay); 7-82 R.D.King Guyana v India (Georgetown); 7-84 N.C.McGarrell Guyana v Trinidad (Port of Spain); 7-104 W.D.Phillip Leeward Islands v Jamaica (St Catherine); 6-15 T.E.Rollock Barbados v Trinidad (Bridgetown)

Most Wickets in Season: 80 (av 12.46) E.M.Dowson (R.A.Bennett's XI) 1901-02
Most in 1996-97: 71 (av 18.39) F.A.Rose (Jamaica); 46 (av 21.52) O.D.Gibson (Barbados); 43 (av 23.39) I.R.Bishop (Trinidad); 40 (av 20.30) W.E.Reid (Barbados); 39 (av 22.64) C.A.Walsh (Jamaica)

Most Wickets in Career: 1,637 (av 19.02) M.D.Marshall (Barbados, Hampshire, Natal) 1977-78 to date
Most by Current Bowler: 1,465 (av 22.24) C.A.Walsh (Jamaica, Gloucestershire) 1981-82 to date; 800 (av 26.53) C.E.L.Ambrose (Leeward Islands, Northamptonshire) 1985-86 to date; 567 (av 25.97) R.A.Harper (Guyana, Northamptonshire) 1979-80 to date; 492 (av 22.02) I.R.Bishop (Trinidad, Derbyshire) 1986-87 to date. F.D.Stephenson, 792 (av 24.26), played for Orange Free State and E.A.E.Baptiste, 658 (av 24.69), for Eastern Province but did not appear in West Indies in 1996-97.

Record Wicket Partnerships

1st	390	G.L.Wight & G.L.Gibbs	British Guiana v Barbados (Georgetown)	1951-52
2nd	446	C.C.Hunte & G.S.Sobers	West Indies v Pakistan (Kingston)	1957-58
3rd	434	J.B.Stollmeyer & G.E.Gomez	Trinidad v British Guiana (Port of Spain)	1946-47
4th	574*	C.L.Walcott & F.M.M.Worrell	Barbados v Trinidad (Port of Spain)	1945-46

5th	327	P.Holmes & W.E.Astill	MCC v Jamaica (Kingston)	1925-26
6th	487*	G.A.Headley & C.C.Passailaigue	Jamaica v Tennyson's XI (Kingston)	1931-32
7th	347	D.S.Atkinson & C.C.Depeiaza	West Indies v Australia (Bridgetown)	1954-55
8th	255	E.A.V.Williams & E.A.Martindale	Barbados v Trinidad (Bridgetown)	1935-36
9th	168	L.G.Crawley & F.B.Watson	MCC v Jamaica (Kingston)	1925-26
10th	167	A.W.F.Somerset & W.C.Smith	MCC v Barbados (Bridgetown)	1912-13

Highest Partnerships in 1996-97

1st	186	S.C.Williams & J.Mitchum	Leeward Islands v Windward Islands (Arnos Vale)
2nd	242	R.P.Arnold & M.S.Atapattu	Sri Lanka v Leeward Islands (St Johns)
3rd	275	P.A.Wallace & F.L.Reifer	Barbados v Windward Islands (Bridgetown)
4th	167	C.B.Lambert & A.R.Percival	Guyana v Barbados (Bridgetown)
5th	97	J.R.Murray & K.Martin	Windward Islands v Guyana (St Georges)
6th	104	F.L.Reifer & T.E.Rollock	Barbados v Guyana (Bridgetown)
7th	93	S.Chanderpaul & V.Nagamootoo	Guyana v India (Georgetown)
8th	101	N.C.McGarrell & M.V.Nagamootoo	Guyana v India (Georgetown)
9th	124	M.D.Ventura & F.A.Rose	Jamaica v Leeward Islands (Anguilla)
10th	78*	L.R.Williams & C.A.Walsh	Jamaica v India (Kingston)

Most Wicketkeeping Dismissals in Innings: 6 (3ct 3st) A.P.Binns Jamaica v British Guiana Georgetown) 1952-53; 6 (4ct 2st) R.A.Pinnock Jamaica v Trinidad (Port of Spain) 1969-70; 6 (3ct 3st) T.M.Findlay Windward Islands v Leeward Islands (Roseau) 1971-72; 6 (6ct) M.C.Worrell Barbados v Leeward Islands (Bridgetown) 1984-85; 6 (5ct 1st) T.R.O.Payne Barbados v England (Bridgetown) 1985-86; 6 (6ct) M.V.Simon Leeward Islands v Jamaica (St John's) 1986-87; 6 (5ct 1st) L.L.Harris Leeward Islands v Trinidad (Pointe-a-Pierre) 1987-88; 6 (6ct) R.D.Jacobs Leeward Islands v Barbados (Bridgetown) 1991-92; 6 (5ct 1st) R.D.Jacobs Leeward Islands v Jamaica (Kingston) 1993-94
Most in 1996-97: 5 (5ct) C.O.Browne Barbados v Jamaica (Discovery Bay); 5 (5ct) S.G.B.Ford Jamaica v Barbados (Discovery Bay); 5 (5ct) R.L.Hoyte Barbados v Trinidad (Port of Spain); 5 (5ct) P.A.Wallace Barbados v Windward Islands (St Georges)

Most Wicketkeeping Dismissals in Match: 9 (7ct 2st) T.M.Findlay Combined Islands v Guyana (Berbice) 1973-74
Most in 1996-97: 7 (7ct) S.G.B.Ford Jamaica v Leeward Islands (St Catherine); 7 (6ct 1st) J.R.Murray Windward Islands v Guyana (Tanteen); 7 (5ct 2st) D.Williams Trinidad v Windward Islands (Port of Spain); 7 (6ct 1st) D.Williams Trinidad v Jamaica (Kingston)

Most Wicketkeeping Dismissals in Season: : 42 (40ct 2st) C.O.Browne (Barbados) 1996-97
Most in 1996-97: 42 (40ct 2st) C.O.Browne (Barbados); 36 (35ct 1st) S.G.B.Ford (Jamaica); 27 (20ct 7st) D.Williams (Trinidad); 26 (21ct 5st) R.D.Jacobs (Leeward Islands); 19 (16ct 3st) J.R.Murray (Windward Islands)

Most Wicketkeeping Dismissals in Career: 848 (740ct 108st) D.L.Murray (Trinidad, Nottinghamshire, Warwickshire) 1960-61 to 1980-81
Most by Current Wicketkeeper: 281 (234ct 47st) D.Williams (Trinidad) 1982-83 to date; 240 (218ct 22st) C.O.Browne (Barbados) 1990-91 to date; 228 (210ct 18st) J.R.Murray (Windward Islands) 1986-87 to date; 133 (120ct 13st) R.D.Jacobs (Leeward Islands) 1991-92 to date; 84 (72ct 12st) S.G.B.Ford (Jamaica) 1993-94 to date

Most Catches by Fielder in Innings: 5 T.N.M.Peirce Barbados v Trinidad (Bridgetown) 1941-42; 5 O.M.Durity Trinidad v Guyana (Georgetown) 1970-71; 5 O.M.Durity South Trinidad v North Trinidad (Pointe-a-Pierre) 1971-72; 5 G.S.Camacho Demerara v Berbice (Georgetown) 1971-72; 5 I.V.A. Richards Leeward Islands v Barbados (Basseterre) 1981-82; 5 R.C.Haynes Jamaica v Barbados (Bridgetown) 1991-92; 5 T.O.Powell Jamaica v Trinidad (Port of Spain) 1993-94; 5 B.C.Lara Trinidad v Leeward Islands (Port of Spain) 1996-97
Most in 1996-97: 5 B.C.Lara Trinidad v Leeward Islands (Port of Spain)

Most Catches by Fielder in Match: 7 T.N.M.Peirce Barbados v Trinidad (Bridgetown) 1941-42
Most in 1996-97: 5 C.E.L.Ambrose Leeward Islands v Jamaica (St Catherine); 5 T.M.Dowlin Guyana v Windward Islands (Tanteen); 5 B.C.Lara Trinidad v Leeward Islands (Port of Spain)

Most Catches by Fielder in Season: 23 B.C.Lara (Trinidad) 1993-94
Most in 1996-97: 17 B.C.Lara (Trinidad); 16 S.C.Williams (Leeward Islands); 14 R.I.C.Holder (Barbados); 12 M.Azharuddin (India); 12 C.L.Hooper (Guyana); 12 D.Ramnarine (Trinidad)

Most Catches by Fielder in Career: 516 C.G.Greenidge (Barbados, Hampshire) 1970 to 1992
Most by Current Fielder: 262 R.A.Harper (Guyana, Northamptonshire) 1979-80 to date; 260 C.L.Hooper (Guyana, Kent) 1983-84 to date; 197 P.V.Simmons (Trinidad, Leicestershire, Easterns) 1982-83 to date; 161 B.C.Lara (Trinidad, Warwickshire) 1987-88 to date. R.B.Richardson, 203, played for Northern Transvaal and D.L.Haynes, 202, for Western Province but did not play in West Indies in 1996-97.

DOMESTIC LIMITED OVERS RECORDS

Highest Team Totals: 327-7 (50 overs) Guyana v Leeward Islands (St John's) 1979-80; 304-5 (50 overs) Leeward Islands v Canada (St Catherine) 1996-97; 296-5 (50 overs) Guyana v Leeward Islands (Blairmont) 1995-96

Lowest Team Totals: 68 (20.4 overs) Jamaica v Barbados (Bridgetown) 1981-82; 71 (33.4 overs) Barbados v Trinidad (Port of Spain) 1979-80; 74 (39 overs) Canada v Leeward Islands (Kingston) 1996-97

Highest Individual Innings: 145* E.A.Lewis Leeward Islands v Barbados (Bridgetown) 1984-85; 137* C.A.Best Barbados v Trinidad (Bridgetown) 1986-87; 133* D.S.Morgan Jamaica v Canada (Montego Bay) 1996-97
27 centuries have been scored in the competition, B.C.Lara scoring 3

Most Runs in Season: 384 (av 64.00) B.C.Lara (Trinidad) 1996-97

Most Runs in Career: 1,127 (av 40.25) J.C.Adams (Jamaica) 1984-85 to date; 1,090 (av 49.54) B.C.Lara (Trinidad) 1987-88 to date; 1,049 (av 32.78) D.L.Haynes (Barbados) 1976-77 to 1994-95

Best Innings Analyses: 7-15 H.A.G.Anthony Leeward Islands v Barbados (St John's) 1994-95; 5-16 A.C.Cummins Barbados v Leeward Islands (Bridgetown) 1993-94; 5-17 M.D.Marshall Barbados v Guyana (Bridgetown) 1990-91
Best in 1996-97: 5-35 R.Dhanraj Trinidad v Canada (Kingston)
Five wickets in an innings has been achieved on 26 occasions, twice by A.C.Cummins, R.Dhanraj, M.D.Marshall and F.D.Stephenson

Most Economical Bowling: 10-6-5-4 D.R.Parry Leeward Islands v Barbados (St John's)
Most Economical in 1996-97: 10-4-16-1 K.L.T.Arthurton Leeward Islands v Canada (Kingston)

Most Expensive Bowling: 10-0-87-1 N.F.Williams Windward Islands v Leeward Islands (St John's) 1989-90
Most Expensive in 1996-97: 8-1-66-3 C.A.Davis Windward Islands v Barbados (Blairmont); 10-1-66-0 D.Joseph Canada v Trinidad (Montego Bay)

Most Wickets in Season: 19 (av 9.47) R.Dhanraj (Trinidad) 1996-97

Most Wickets in Career: 56 (av 21.37) R.C.Haynes (Jamaica) 1984-85 to date; 53 (av 22.62) R.A.Harper (Guyana) 1979-80 to date; 52 (av 23.00) C.A.Walsh (Jamaica) 1981-82 to date

Record Wicket Partnerships

1st	172	S.C.Williams & L.A.Harrigan	Leeward Islands v Barbados (Bridgetown)	1993-94
2nd	162	R.S.Gabriel & H.A.Gomes	Trinidad v Jamaica (Pointe-a-Pierre)	1981-82
	162	L.D.John & L.A.Lewis	Windward Islands v Jamaica (Kingston)	1986-87
3rd	173	C.A.Best & R.I.C.Holder	Barbados v Windward Islands (Bridgetown)	1991-92
4th	131	H.A.Gomes & T.Cuffy	Trinidad v Windward Islands (Bridgetown)	1985-86
5th	121	D.R.E.Joseph & R.Powell	Leeward Islands v Guyana (Georgetown)	1994-95
6th	129	C.L.Hooper & A.R.Percival	Guyana v Windward Islands (Enmore)	1994-95
7th	102	F.R.Redwood & L.R.Williams	Jamaica v Trinidad (Kingston)	1992-93
8th	69*	B.M.Watt & N.A.M.McLean	Windward Islands v Barbados (Hampton Court)	1996-97
9th	67*	K.F.Semple & B.S.Browne	Guyana v Leeward Islands (Albion)	1995-96
10th	58	D.A.Murray & W.W.Daniel	Barbados v Trinidad (Bridgetown)	1980-81

There were 10 hundred partnerships in 1996-97, the highest being 139 for the 2nd wicket D.S.Morgan & J.C.Adams Jamaica v Canada (Montego Bay)

Most Wicketkeeping Dismissals in Innings: 6 (5ct 1st) S.N.Mohammed Guyana v Barbados (Bridgetown) 1990-91
Most in 1996-97: 3 (3ct) C.O.Browne Barbados v Guyana (Blairmont); 3 (1ct 2st) D.Williams Trinidad v Jamaica (Kingston); 3 (1ct 2st) D.Williams Trinidad v Guyana (Georgetown)

Most Wicketkeeping Dismissals in Season: 13 (6ct 7st) D.Williams (Trinidad) 1996-97

Most Wicketkeeping Dismissals in Career: 48 (29ct 19st) D.Williams (Trinidad) 1984-85 to date; 40 (38ct 2st) R.D.Jacobs (Leeward Islands) 1991-92 to date; 39 (33ct 6st) P.J.L.Dujon (Jamaica) 1975-76 to 1992-93

Most Catches by Fielder in Innings: 4 K.G.D'Heurieux Trinidad v Barbados (Port of Spain) 1979-80; 4 R.A.Harper Guyana v Windward Islands (Castries) 1991-92
Most in 1996-97: 3 R.O.Hurley Barbados v Windward Islands (Blairmont); 3 B.C.Lara Trinidad v Leeward Islands (Kingston); 3 B.E.A.Rajadurai Canada v Trinidad (Kingston); 3 S.C.Williams Leeward Islands v Canada (St Catherine)

Most Catches by Fielder in Season: 7 S.L.Campbell (Barbados) 1993-94; 7 D.A.Joseph (Windward Islands) 1993-94; 7 P.V.Simmons (Trinidad) 1996-97

Most Catches by Fielder in Career: 27 R.A.Harper (Guyana) 1979-80 to date; 26 P.V.Simmons (Trinidad) 1982-83 to date; 23 D.A.Joseph (Windward Islands) 1986-87 to date

Most Appearances in Competition: 47 R.A.Harper (Guyana) 1979-80 to date; 40 R.C.Haynes (Jamaica) 1984-85 to date; 39 C.A.Walsh (Jamaica) 1981-82 to date

CHAMPION TEAMS

From 1891-92 to 1938-39 Barbados, Demerara (British Guiana) and Trinidad competed in the inter-colonial tournament. Because of distance, Jamaica did not participate. The winners of the tournament were:

1891-92 Barbados	1909-10 Trinidad	1929-30 British Guiana
1893-94 Barbados	1910-11 Barbados	1931-32 Trinidad
1895-96 Demerara	1911-12 Barbados	1933-34 Trinidad
1897-98 Barbados	1921-22 No result	1934-35 British Guiana
1899-00 Barbados	1922-23 Barbados	1935-36 British Guiana
1901-02 Trinidad	1923-24 Barbados	1936-37 Trinidad
1903-04 Trinidad	1924-25 Trinidad	1937-38 British Guiana
1905-06 Barbados	1925-26 Trinidad	1938-39 Trinidad
1907-08 Trinidad	1926-27 Barbados	
1908-09 Barbados	1928-29 Trinidad	

Shell Shield

The Shell Shield for Caribbean Regional Cricket Tournament began in 1965-66, there having been several one-off tournaments between 1938-39 and the founding of the Shell Shield. The Shield winners were:

1965-66 Barbados	1974-75 Guyana	1981-82 Barbados
1966-67 Barbados	1975-76 Barbados,	1982-83 Guyana
1968-69 Jamaica	Trinidad	1983-84 Barbados
1969-70 Trinidad	1976-77 Barbados	1984-85 Trinidad
1970-71 Trinidad	1977-78 Barbados	1985-86 Barbados
1971-72 Barbados	1978-79 Barbados	1986-87 Guyana
1972-73 Guyana	1979-80 Barbados	
1973-74 Barbados	1980-81 Combined Islands	

Red Stripe Cup

Following a change in sponsorship, the Red Stripe Cup was instituted in 1987-88. The winners have been:

1987-88 Jamaica	1991-92 Jamaica	1995-96 Leeward Islands
1988-89 Jamaica	1992-93 Guyana	1996-97 Barbados
1989-90 Leeward Islands	1993-94 Leeward Islands	
1990-91 Barbados	1994-95 Barbados	

Domestic Limited Overs Competition

The competition was played on a zonal basis with three teams in each zone playing a round-robin with the winners contesting the final up to 1991-92. From 1992-93 (and also in 1981-82) a complete round-robin was played with the top two contesting the final. From 1994-95 the teams were split into two groups playing a double round-robin before the final. From 1996-97 Bermuda and Canada took part. The overs limit per innings has remained at 50 throughout. Results of the finals:

Gillette Cup
1975-76 Barbados 191 (49.3 overs) beat Trinidad 148 (39.5 overs) by 43 runs
1976-77 Barbados 97-2 (27 overs) beat Trinidad 95 (33.3 overs) by 8 wkts

Geddes Grant/Harrison Line Trophy
1977-78 Jamaica and Leeward Islands shared the trophy as the final was abandoned
1978-79 Trinidad 214-9 (50 overs) beat Barbados 158 (47.1 overs) by 56 runs
1979-80 Guyana 327-7 (50 overs) beat Leeward Islands 224 (41.1 overs) by 103 runs
1980-81 Trinidad 128-6 (42 overs) beat Barbados 127 (49 overs) by 4 wkts
1981-82 Leeward Islands 95-5 (29.3 overs) beat Barbados 94 (37.5 overs) by 5 wkts
1982-83 Guyana 211-8 (41 overs) beat Jamaica 83 (25 overs) by 128 runs
1983-84 Jamaica 213-7 (41.2 overs) beat Leeward Islands 212-9 (42 overs) by 3 wkts
1984-85 Guyana 140-5 (41 overs) beat Jamaica 139 (46.1 overs) by 5 wkts
1985-86 Jamaica 173-4 (34.3 overs) beat Leeward Islands 169-8 (39 overs) by 6 wkts
1986-87 Jamaica 252-6 (46 overs) beat Barbados 249-3 (49 overs) by 4 wkts
1987-88 Barbados 219-9 (46 overs) beat Jamaica 218-8 (46 overs) by 1 wkt

Geddes Grant Shield
1988-89 Windward Islands 155-9 (49.3 overs) beat Guyana 154-9 (50 overs) by 1 wkt
1989-90 Trinidad 180-5 (44.2 overs) beat Barbados 178-9 (47 overs) by 5 wkts
1990-91 Jamaica 232-6 (49.5 overs) beat Leeward Islands 228-8 (50 overs) by 4 wkts
1991-92 Trinidad 167-2 (37.3 overs) beat Barbados 163 (49.3 overs) by 8 wkts
1992-93 Guyana and Leeward Islands shared the shield as the final was abandoned
1993-94 Leeward Islands 289-6 (50 overs) beat Barbados 255 (46.1 overs) by 34 runs

Shell/Sandals Trophy
1994-95 Leeward Islands 188 (49 overs) beat Barbados 110 (31 overs) by 78 runs
1995-96 Guyana and Trinidad shared the trophy as the final was abandoned
1996-97 Trinidad 236-4 (50 overs) beat Guyana 227 (49.3 overs) by 9 runs

Table of Results 1975-76 to 1996-97

	P	W	L	NR	Winner	R-Up
Barbados	73	39	30	4	3	8
Leeward Islands	70	37	25	8	5	4
Trinidad	70	35	30	5	6	2
Guyana	69	34	25	10	5	2
Jamaica	70	33	33	4	5	3
Windward Islands	62	16	41	5	1	0
Canada	6	0	4	2	0	0
Bermuda	6	0	6	0	0	0

For the three finals abandoned both teams are shown as winners. Two matches abandoned and replayed in 1995-96 are not included in the above or in career figures.

1996-97 AND CAREER RECORDS FOR WEST INDIAN PLAYERS

Cmp	Debut	M	I	NO	Runs	HS	Avge	100	50	Balls	Runs	Wkts	Avge	BB	5i	10m	RpO	ct	st
ADAMS, Fabian (Leeward Islands) b The Valley, Anguilla 7.1.1975 RHB OB																		
FC		3	6	2	153	69*	38.25	0	2									3	
ADAMS, James Clive (Jamaica, West Indies, West Indies to Australia) b Port Maria, Jamaica 9.1.1968 LHB SLA WK																		
FC		8	15	2	572	73	44.00	0	6	444	158	5	31.60	2-40	0	0	2.13	3	
Int		4	2	1	44	35*	44.00	0	0	48	30	1	30.00	1-8	0	0	3.75	1	
SS		6	6	1	319	84	63.80	0	4	156	143	7	20.42	3-34	0	0	5.50	3	
Test	1991	29	46	11	1991	208*	56.88	5	9	1233	654	15	43.60	5-17	1	0	3.18	30	
FC	1984	127	212	38	7494	208*	43.06	16	38	5623	2432	67	36.29	5-17	1	0	2.59	115	
Int	1992	74	57	20	1038	81*	28.05	0	7	834	668	22	30.36	5-37	0	1	4.80	48	5
SS	1984	32	31	3	1127	112	40.25	1	8	385	298	15	19.86	3-34	0	0	4.64	15	1
AMBROSE, Curtly Elconn Lynwall (Leeward Islands, West Indies, West Indies to Australia) b Swetes Village, Antigua 21.9.1963 LHB RF																		
Test		7	9	3	175	37	29.16	0	0	1205	464	21	22.09	5-37	2	0	2.31	0	
FC		10	13	3	189	37	18.90	0	0	1611	575	29	19.82	5-37	2	0	2.14	6	
Int		5	3	1	26	13	13.00	0	0	249	143	7	20.42	4-36	1	0	3.44	2	
SS		6	3	1	10	9	5.00	0	0	263	·101	6	16.83	3-6	0	0	2.30	0	
Test	1987	72	102	22	1064	53	13.30	0	1	16489	6566	306	21.45	8-45	18	3	2.38	14	
FC	1985	201	257	61	2909	78	14.84	0 ›	4	40967	16431	800	20.53	8-45	44	8	2.40	78	
Int	1987	146	77	32	513	31*	11.40	0	0	7805	4518	200	22.59	5-17	6	4	3.47	36	
SS	1985	29	16	7	110	18*	12.22	0	0	1452	722	34	21.23	3-6	0	0	2.98	5	
ANTHONY, Hamish Arbeb Gervais (Leeward Islands, MCC) b Urlings Village, Antigua 16.1.1971 RHB RFM																		
FC		6	9	1	117	29	14.62	0	0	828	401	12	33.41	3-32	0	0	2.90	2	
SS		6	3	0	11	7	3.66	0	0	264	183	4	45.75	2-54	0	0	4.15	2	
FC	1989	74	108	9	1707	91	17.24	0	7	11344	6303	222	28.39	6-22	6	1	3.33	28	
Int	1995	3	3	0	23	21	7.66	0	0	156	143	3	47.66	2-47	0	0	5.50	0	
SS	1989	28	22	5	203	32	11.94	0	0	1243	931	31	30.03	7-15	0	1	4.49	7	
ANTOINE, Eugene Clifford (Trinidad) b Trinidad 8.4.1967 RHB RFM																		
FC		1	1	0	10	10	10.00	0	0	114	79	2	39.50	1-31	0	0	4.15	0	
SS		7	3	1	24	15	12.00	0	0	304	171	5	34.20	2-28	0	0	3.37	0	
FC	1990	25	33	14	167	34*	8.78	0	0	4227	2277	74	30.77	6-49	4	0	3.23	7	
SS	1990	27	12	7	41	15	8.20	0	0	1230	717	30	23.90	4-43	2	0	3.49	4	
ARMSTRONG, Sean Hussain (Barbados) b Barbados 11.5.1973 RHB RM																		
FC		3	6	1	62	21	12.40	0	0									2	
FC	1995	7	13	1	233	92	19.41	0	1	12	15	0					7.50	2	
ARTHURTON, Keith Lloyd Thomas (Leeward Islands, MCC, Buckinghamshire) b Charlestown, Nevis 21.2.1965 LHB SLA																		
FC		9	15	1	488	95	34.85	0	4	488	144	5	28.80	2-3	0	0	1.77	5	
SS		5	5	1	239	118	59.75	1	1	216	105	7	15.00	4-25	1	0	2.91	1	
Test	1988	33	50	5	1382	157*	30.71	2	8	473	183	1	183.00	1-17	0	0	2.32	22	
FC	1985	115	180	25	7171	200*	46.26	19	39	2242	926	27	34.29	3-14	0	0	2.47	61	
Int	1988	86	76	15	1652	84	27.08	0	9	797	666	22	30.27	3-31	0	0	5.01	21	
SS	1985	31	31	5	919	118	35.34	1	5	744	431	19	22.68	4-25	2	0	3.47	9	
AUSTIN, Henry Adrian (Barbados) b Barbados 31.10.1972 RHB RFM																		
FC		1	1	0	0	0	0.00	0	0	60	35	0					3.50	0	
BALLIRAM, Anil (Trinidad) b Trinidad 27.2.1974 RHB OB																		
FC		2	4	1	73	24*	24.33	0	0									2	
FC	1993	14	26	2	608	76	25.33	0	6	72	50	0					4.18	9	
SS	1993	3	3	0	8	6	2.66	0	0	18	6	0					2.00	0	
BASDEO, Amarnath (Trinidad) b Trinidad 13.4.1977 RHB WK																		
FC		1	1	0	0	0	0.00	0	0									4	1
BASS, A. (Leeward Islands)																		
FC		1	1	0	0	0	0.00	0	0	222	139	1	139.00	1-59	0	0	3.75	0	
BENJAMIN, Kenneth Charlie Griffith (Leeward Islands, West Indies, West Indies to Australia) b St John's, Antigua 8.4.1967 RHB RF																		
FC		1	1	0	5	5	5.00	0	0	30	8	2	4.00	2-8	0	0	1.60	0	
SS		5	2	0	8	4	4.00	0	0	228	136	7	19.42	4-33	1	0	3.57	1	
Test	1991	24	32	7	215	43*	8.60	0	0	4754	2619	89	29.42	6-66	4	1	3.30	2	
FC	1988	86	102	26	885	52*	11.64	0	1	14713	7443	294	25.31	7-51	13	1	3.03	17	
Int	1992	26	13	7	65	17	10.83	0	0	1319	923	33	27.96	3-34	0	0	4.19	4	
SS	1988	24	12	3	73	15	8.11	0	0	1076	695	30	23.16	4-33	1	0	3.87	3	
BISHOP, Ian Raphael (Trinidad, West Indies, West Indies to Australia) b Port of Spain, Trinidad 24.10.1967 RHB RF																		
Test		6	7	0	67	24	9.57	0	0	928	447	17	26.29	4-22	0	0	2.89	2	
FC		13	17	0	315	111	18.52	1	1	2163	1006	43	˙ 23.39	5-82	1	0	2.79	3	
Int		2	1	0	31	31	31.00	0	0	66	72	1	72.00	1-37	0	0	6.54	0	
Test	1988	37	54	9	509	48	11.31	0	0	7699	3522	154	22.87	6-40	6	0	2.74	7	
FC	1986	135	180	36	2164	111	15.02	2	2	22976	10835	492	22.02	7-34	22	1	2.82	38	

Cmp	Debut	M	I	NO	Runs	HS	Avge	100	50	Balls	Runs	Wkts	Avge	BB	5i	10m	RpO	ct	st
Int	1988	83	43	18	390	33*	15.60	0	0	4302	3085	117	26.36	5-25	7	2	4.30	12	
SS	1986	18	9	5	68	22*	17.00	0	0	927	644	26	24.76	3-10	0	0	4.16	6	

BISHOP, Renwick John (Trinidad) b Toco, Trinidad 10.9.1965 RHB OB

SS		5	4	2	42	24*	21.00	0	0	72	44	2	22.00	1-15	0	0	3.66	0	
FC	1986	11	21	0	229	50	10.90	0	1	233	93	6	15.50	3-29	0	0	2.39	4	
SS	1986	20	17	2	287	44	19.13	0	0	366	221	8	27.62	3-33	0	0	3.62	7	

BLACK, Marlon Ian (Trinidad) b Trinidad 7.6.1975 RHB RFM

FC		1								60	33	0					3.30	0	
FC	1993	2	2	1	7	7*	7.00	0	0	222	132	3	44.00	3-69	0	0	3.56	0	
SS	1993	1	1	0	0	0	0.00	0	0	12	9	0					4.50	0	

BODOE, Mahadeo (Trinidad) b Chaguanas, Trinidad 3.12.1966 RHB SLA

FC		4	6	0	121	49	20.16	0	0	366	155	2	77.50	2-73	0	0	2.54	1	
FC	1984	20	31	4	673	65	24.92	0	4	1841	873	16	54.56	3-65	0	0	2.84	12	
SS	1984	4	4	1	67	40	22.33	0	0	36	18	0					3.00	4	

BREESE, Gareth Rohan (Jamaica) b Montego Bay, Jamaica 9.1.1976 RHB OB

FC		2	3	0	1	1	0.33	0	0	156	61	2	30.50	1-29	0	0	2.34	3	
SS		1	1	0	11	11	11.00	0	0									0	
FC	1995	5	9	2	246	124	35.14	1	1	198	86	2	43.00	1-29	0	0	2.60	7	

BROOMES, Henderson Glenroy (Barbados) b Barbados 24.11.1968 RHB RFM

SS		3	2	2	12	9*		0	0	132	138	3	46.00	2-49	0	0	6.27	0	
SS	1994	8	4	3	16	9*	16.00	0	0	432	306	8	38.25	2-16	0	0	4.25	0	

BROWNE, Barrington St Aubyn (Guyana) b Georgetown, Guyana 16.9.1967 RHB RF

FC		1	2	0	8	5	4.00	0	0	138	83	1	83.00	1-83	0	0	3.60	1	
FC	1987	43	53	20	209	29	6.33	0	0	5868	3411	117	29.15	6-51	5	0	3.48	10	
Int	1994	4	3	2	8	8*	8.00	0	0	180	156	2	78.00	2-50	0	0	5.20	0	
SS	1986	27	11	6	45	26*	9.00	0	0	1113	775	26	29.80	2-9	0	0	4.17	3	

BROWNE, Courtney Oswald (Barbados, West Indies, West Indies to Australia) b Lambeth, England 7.12.1970 RHB WK

Test		5	7	2	64	39*	12.80	0	0									21	
FC		12	20	4	245	78	15.31	0	1									40	2
Int		4	2	1	17	10*	17.00	0	·0									3	
SS		6	5	2	69	25	23.00	0	0									6	3
Test	1994	13	20	6	250	39*	17.85	0	0									59	1
FC	1990	65	101	21	2079	102*	25.98	2	8	12	16	0					8.00	218	22
Int	1995	24	18	4	172	26	12.28	0	0									30	5
SS	1990	31	22	7	411	60*	27.40	0	3									30	7

BRYAN, Henderson Ricardo (Barbados) b Barbados 21.3.1970 RHB RFM

FC		11	16	5	239	42*	21.72	0	0	1597	820	37	22.16	5-39	1	0	3.08	7	
FC	1994	16	24	6	289	42*	16.05	0	0	2203	1214	46	26.39	5-39	1	0	3.30	9·.	
SS	1994	9	3	1	10	9*	5.00	0	0	414	329	16	20.56	4-42	1	0	4.76	4	

BURTON, Shimei Nathaniel (Jamaica) b Manchester, Jamaica 3.2.1975 LHB LF

SS		1								30	26	0					5.20	0	
FC	1995	2	2	1	4	4*	4.00	0	0	204	118	0					3.47	1	

BYAM, Denis F.A. (Windward Islands) b St Vincent RHB RM

FC		3	6	0	52	17	8.66	0	0									2	

CAMPBELL, Sherwin Legay (Barbados, West Indies, West Indies to Australia) b Belleplaine, Barbados 1.11.1970 RHB RM

Test		7	11	0	311	79	28.27	0	2									1	
FC		15	25	1	790	109	32.91	1	4									6	
SS		4	4	0	62	46*	20.66	0	0	6	2	0					2.00	0	
Test	1994	23	39	2	1487	208	40.18	2	9									17	
FC	1990	80	139	7	5268	208	39.90	13	28	124	67	1	67.00	1-38	0	0	3.24	71	
Int	1994	36	36	0	835	86	23.19	0	3									10	
SS	1989	16	15	3	448	80*	37.33	0	3	6	2	0					2.00	11	

CHANDERPAUL, Shivnarine (Guyana, West Indies, West Indies to Australia) b Unity Village, Guyana 16.8.1974 LHB LB

Test		5	8	2	443	137*	73.83	1	3	390	156	1	156.00	1-56	0	0	2.40	1	
FC		11	18	4	815	176*	58.21	2	5	582	238	5	47.60	2-18	0	0	2.45	9	
Int		4	4	1	209	109*	69.66	1	1	48	36	1	36.00	1-36	0	0	4.50	1	
SS		7	6	4	314	88	157.00	0	3	231	152	12	12.66	3-18	0	0	3.94	2	
Test	1993	21	33	6	1454	137*	53.85	1	14	1026	490	4	122.50	1-2	0	0	2.86	9	
FC	1991	65	104	23	4409	303*	54.43	10	29	3244	1680	41	40.97	4-48	0	0	3.10	48	
Int	1994	42	39	2	1210	109*	32.70	1	9	466	414	8	51.75	2-16	0	0	5.33	10	
SS	1991	26	24	8	800	88	50.00	0	7	683	496	33	15.03	4-22	2	0	4.35	9	

CHINSAMMY, Matthew Nathaniel (Guyana) b Guyana 25.9.1974 RHB RFM

FC		1	1	0	2	2	2.00	0	0	98	26	1	26.00	1-26	0	0	1.59	0	

COLLINS, Pedro Tyrone (Barbados) b Boscobelle, Barbados 12.8.1976 RHB LFM

FC		7	8	3	12	4	2.40	0	0	685	423	16	26.43	4-36	0	0	3.70	1	

258

CUFF, Wayne Everton (Jamaica) b Kingston, Jamaica 26.12.1971 LHB WK

Cmp	Debut	M	I	NO	Runs	HS	Avge	100	50	Balls	Runs	Wkts	Avge	BB	5i	10m	RpO	ct	st
FC		2	4	0	52	36	13.00	0	0									1	
FC	1995	3	6	0	83	36	13.83	0	0									3	
SS	1995	4	4	0	51	25	12.75	0	0									3	

CUFFY, Cameron Eustace (Windward Islands, West Indies to Australia, West Indies A to Sri Lanka) b South Rivers, St Vincent 8.2.1970 RHB RF

Cmp	Debut	M	I	NO	Runs	HS	Avge	100	50	Balls	Runs	Wkts	Avge	BB	5i	10m	RpO	ct	st
FC		2	4	1	3	2	1.00	0	0	222	116	1	116.00	1-68	0	0	3.13	2	
SS		5	2	1	7	6*	7.00	0	0	246	116	6	19.33	3-33	0	0	2.82	2	
Test	1994	3	5	2	6	3*	2.00	0	0	512	306	7	43.71	3-80	0	0	3.58	1	
FC	1990	50	68	29	177	15	4.53	0	0	7812	3874	141	27.47	7-80	6	1	2.97	14	
Int	1994	11	7	3	25	17*	6.25	0	0	547	352	9	39.11	2-19	0	0	3.86	3	
SS	1990	24	10	6	27	8*	6.75	0	0	1140	663	31	21.38	4-29	2	0	3.48	6	

DARLINGTON, Kevin Godfrey (Guyana) b Guyana 26.4.1972 RHB RFM

Cmp	Debut	M	I	NO	Runs	HS	Avge	100	50	Balls	Runs	Wkts	Avge	BB	5i	10m	RpO	ct	st
FC		2	3	2	10	6*	10.00	0	0	234	177	3	59.00	3-105	0	0	4.53	0	
SS		6	1	1	0	0*		0	0	216	110	5	22.00	2-14	0	0	3.05	0	
FC	1994	6	10	5	20	7	4.00	0	0	561	409	8	51.12	3-105	0	0	4.37	3	
SS	1995	8	1	1	0	0*		0	0	228	131	5	26.20	2-14	0	0	3.44	0	

DAVIS, Casper Andre (Windward Islands) b St Vincent 14.3.1966 RHB RF

Cmp	Debut	M	I	NO	Runs	HS	Avge	100	50	Balls	Runs	Wkts	Avge	BB	5i	10m	RpO	ct	st
FC		9	18	7	175	27*	15.90	0	0	1213	613	29	21.13	7-58	3	0	3.03	2	
SS		5	3	1	11	6	5.50	0	0	216	157	8	19.62	3-34	0	0	4.36	1	
FC	1991	31	55	16	657	43*	16.84	0	0	4234	2207	81	27.24	7-58	4	0	3.12	16	
SS	1991	20	12	2	79	20	7.90	0	0	962	649	30	21.63	4-22	1	0	4.04	8	

DE GROOT, Nicholas Alexander (Guyana) b Guyana 22.10.1975 RHB OB

Cmp	Debut	M	I	NO	Runs	HS	Avge	100	50	Balls	Runs	Wkts	Avge	BB	5i	10m	RpO	ct	st
FC		8	15	1	328	63	23.42	0	3	6	1	0					1.00	5	
SS		1	1	0	28	28	28.00	0	0									0	
FC	1994	15	26	1	531	78	21.24	0	4	6	1	0					1.00	7	

DHANIRAM, Sudesh (Guyana) b Albion, Guyana 14.1.1967 RHB OB

Cmp	Debut	M	I	NO	Runs	HS	Avge	100	50	Balls	Runs	Wkts	Avge	BB	5i	10m	RpO	ct	st
SS		6	6	1	118	63*	23.60	0	1	12	2	1	2.00	1-2	0	0	1.00	1	
FC	1986	46	72	2	2040	131	29.14	4	10	398	243	4	60.75	2-55	0	0	3.66	22	
SS	1986	35	34	1	631	63*	19.12	0	2	113	73	5	14.60	3-29	0	0	3.87	6	

DHANRAJ, Rajindra (Trinidad) b Barrackpore, Trinidad 6.2.1969 RHB LBG

Cmp	Debut	M	I	NO	Runs	HS	Avge	100	50	Balls	Runs	Wkts	Avge	BB	5i	10m	RpO	ct	st
FC		5	7	3	42	24*	10.50	0	0	984	417	18	23.16	4-18	0	0	2.54	2	
SS		7	3	1	9	4*	4.50	0	0	278	180	19	9.47	5-35	2	1	3.88	1	
Test	1994	4	4	0	17	9	4.25	0	0	1087	595	8	74.37	2-49	0	0	3.28	1	
FC	1987	70	89	32	467	47	8.19	0	0	15021	7518	277	27.14	9-97	14	3	3.00	26	
Int	1994	6	2	1	8	8	8.00	0	0	264	170	10	17.00	4-26	1	0	3.86	1	
SS	1989	27	15	5	75	17*	7.50	0	0	1226	807	50	16.14	5-26	5	2	3.94	5	

DILLON, Mervyn (Trinidad, West Indies) b Toco, Trinidad 5.6.1974 RHB RFM

Cmp	Debut	M	I	NO	Runs	HS	Avge	100	50	Balls	Runs	Wkts	Avge	BB	5i	10m	RpO	ct	st
Test		2	3	1	21	21	10.50	0	0	324	148	4	37.00	3-92	0	0	2.74	0	
FC		12	16	6	76	21	7.60	0	0	1945	1068	36	29.66	4-94	0	0	3.29	3	
SS		3	2	1	1	1*	1.00	0	0	84	61	2	30.50	1-20	0	0	4.35	1	

DOWLIN, Travis Montague (Guyana) b Georgetown, Guyana 24.2.1977 RHB OB

Cmp	Debut	M	I	NO	Runs	HS	Avge	100	50	Balls	Runs	Wkts	Avge	BB	5i	10m	RpO	ct	st
FC		1	2	0	32	30	16.00	0	0									5	

DRAKES, Vasbert Conniel (Barbados, Border, Sussex) b St James, Barbados 5.8.1969 RHB RF

Cmp	Debut	M	I	NO	Runs	HS	Avge	100	50	Balls	Runs	Wkts	Avge	BB	5i	10m	RpO	ct	st
FC		1									186	88	1	88.00	1-45	0	0	2.83	1	
FC	1991	63	100	15	2048	180*	24.09	4	6	10463	6027	198	30.43	8-59	6	1	3.45	17	
Int	1994	5	2	0	25	16	12.50	0	0	239	204	3	68.00	1-36	0	0	5.12	1	
SS	1991	17	8	1	136	46*	19.42	0	0	812	508	26	19.53	3-15	0	0	3.75	5	

FELIX, Brian (Windward Islands) b Dominica

Cmp	Debut	M	I	NO	Runs	HS	Avge	100	50	Balls	Runs	Wkts	Avge	BB	5i	10m	RpO	ct	st
FC		1	2	0	2	2	1.00	0	0									0	

FORD, Shane George Bancroft (Jamaica, West Indies A to Sri Lanka) b Kingston, Jamaica 8.9.1969 RHB WK

Cmp	Debut	M	I	NO	Runs	HS	Avge	100	50	Balls	Runs	Wkts	Avge	BB	5i	10m	RpO	ct	st
FC		10	15	2	231	44	17.75	0	0									35	1
SS		6	4	1	59	46*	19.66	0	0									3	1
FC	1993	25	38	8	652	56*	21.73	0	2									72	12
SS	1994	13	9	2	110	46*	15.71	0	0									8	4

FRANCIS, Nigel Bernard (Trinidad, MCC, West Indies A to Sri Lanka) b Trinidad 6.9.1971 RHB RF

Cmp	Debut	M	I	NO	Runs	HS	Avge	100	50	Balls	Runs	Wkts	Avge	BB	5i	10m	RpO	ct	st
FC		6	9	1	60	16	7.50	0	0	775	436	13	33.53	2-37	0	0	3.37	3	
SS		1	1	0	3	3	3.00	0	0	48	21	1	21.00	1-21	0	0	2.62	0	
FC	1992	25	34	3	251	26	8.09	0	0	3067	1863	50	37.26	4-32	0	0	3.64	12	
SS	1992	6	6	2	23	10	5.75	0	0	254	162	5	32.40	2-35	0	0	3.82	0	

GANGA, Darren (Trinidad) b Trinidad 14.1.1979 RHB

Cmp	Debut	M	I	NO	Runs	HS	Avge	100	50	Balls	Runs	Wkts	Avge	BB	5i	10m	RpO	ct	st
FC		6	11	2	137	54	15.22	0	1									3	

GARRICK, Leon Vivian (Jamaica) b St Ann, Jamaica 11.11.1976 RHB WK

Cmp	Debut	M	I	NO	Runs	HS	Avge	100	50	Balls	Runs	Wkts	Avge	BB	5i	10m	RpO	ct	st
FC		10	20	1	640	138	33.68	2	2									11	
SS		2	2	0	42	23	21.00	0	0									0	

Cmp	Debut	M	I	NO	Runs	HS	Avge	100	50	Balls	Runs	Wkts	Avge	BB	5i	10m	RpO	ct	st
GIBBS, Marlon Christopher (Jamaica) b Jamaica 30.3.1971 RHB OB																		
SS		6	4	4	4	1*		0	0	246	157	1	157.00	1-31	0	0	3.82	1	
FC	1995	5	6	1	46	14	9.20	0	0	1177	460	15	30.66	4-35	0	0	2.34	1	
SS	1995	9	4	4	4	1*		0	0	420	229	8	28.62	3-22	0	0	3.27	1	
GIBSON, Ottis Delroy (Barbados, West Indies, West Indies A to Sri Lanka) b Sion Hill, Barbados 16.3.1969 RHB RF																		
FC		11	17	0	268	49	15.76	0	0	1936	990	46	21.52	5-57	1	0	3.06	11	
Int		2	1	0	3	3	3.00	0	0	108	109	5	21.80	4-61	1	0	6.05	0	
SS		5	4	0	16	9	4.00	0	0	276	190	8	23.75	4-36	1	0	4.13	3	
Test	1995	1	2	0	43	29	21.50	0	0	204	132	2	66.00	2-81	0	0	3.88	0	
FC	1990	93	137	19	2619	101*	22.19	1	14	16241	9328	319	29.24	7-55	12	3	3.44	40	
Int	1995	15	11	1	141	52	14.10	0	1	739	621	34	18.26	5-40	2	2	5.04	3	
SS	1991	19	13	5	181	41*	22.62	0	0	970	668	33	20.24	5-25	2	1	4.13	8	
GRIFFITH, Adrian Frank Gordon (Barbados, West Indies to Australia) b Bridgetown 19.11.1971 LHB RM																		
FC		8	13	0	339	123	26.07	1	1									6	
SS		5	5	0	142	57	28.40	0	1									1	
Test	1996	1	2	0	14	13	7.00	0	0									0	
FC	1992	25	43	2	1323	145	32.26	4	6	30	29	0					5.80	16	
Int	1996	5	4	1	50	47	16.66	0	0									4	
SS	1992	14	14	0	349	57	24.92	0	1									3	
HANIFF, Azeemul (Guyana) b Guyana 24.10.1977 LHB																		
FC		3	5	0	128	62	25.60	0	1									3	
HANIFF, Zaheer Abbass (Guyana) b Guyana 13.4.1974 LHB																		
FC		4	7	0	229	71	32.71	0	3	18	11	0					3.66	1	
FC	1994	8	14	1	307	71	23.61	0	3	18	11	0					3.66	4	
SS	1994	1	1	0	4	4	4.00	0	0									1	
HARPER, Roger Andrew (Guyana, West Indies A to Sri Lanka) b Georgetown, Guyana 17.3.1963 RHB OB																		
SS		7	4	1	96	44	32.00	0	0	312	115	3	38.33	2-12	0	0	2.21	4	
Test	1983	25	32	3	535	74	18.44	0	3	3615	1291	46	28.06	6-57	1	0	2.14	36	
FC	1979	200	263	43	7480	234	34.00	10	36	37825	14726	567	25.97	6-24	28	3	2.33	262	
Int	1983	105	73	20	855	45*	16.13	0	0	5175	3431	100	34.31	4-40	3	0	3.97	55	
SS	1979	47	41	9	760	53	23.75	0	1	2342	1199	53	22.62	5-37	3	1	3.07	27	
HAYNES, Robert Christopher (Jamaica) b Kingston, Jamaica 2.11.1964 LHB LBG																		
SS		6	5	0	89	25	17.80	0	0	312	194	6	32.33	4-38	1	0	3.73	1	
FC	1981	65	104	4	2166	98	21.66	0	10	14616	6327	221	28.62	6-53	10	1	2.59	55	
Int	1989	8	6	1	26	18	5.20	0	0	270	224	5	44.80	2-36	0	0	4.97	5	
SS	1984	40	35	5	546	83	18.20	0	1	2073	1197	56	21.37	4-22	4	0	3.46	16	
HAZEL, Kenneth Clayton (Trinidad) b Trinidad 6.8.1971 RHB SLA																		
SS		6	2	0	5	3	2.50	0	0	168	128	2	64.00	1-9	0	0	4.57	1	
FC	1994	1	1	0	25	25	25.00	0	0	264	99	2	49.50	1-45	0	0	2.25	0	
SS	1993	17	10	2	51	20*	6.37	0	0	654	445	7	63.57	2-29	0	0	4.08	2	
HINDS, Wavell Wayne (Jamaica) b Kingston, Jamaica 7.9.1976 LHB RM																		
FC		1	2	0	84	84	42.00	0	1									0	
FC	1995	2	4	0	120	84	30.00	0	1									1	
HOLDER, Roland Irwin Christopher (Barbados, West Indies, West Indies to Australia) b Port of Spain, Trinidad 22.12.1967 RHB RM																		
Test		7	11	2	290	91	32.22	0	2									7	
FC		15	26	2	908	111	37.83	2	7									14	
Int		5	3	2	57	41*	28.50	0	0									0	
SS		6	6	1	191	65	38.20	0	3									0	
FC	1985	68	110	11	3947	162*	39.86	13	16									37	
Int	1993	35	29	6	597	65	25.95	0	2									8	
SS	1985	36	31	5	984	111	37.84	1	7	12	0	0					0.00	13	
HOOPER, Carl Llewellyn (Guyana, West Indies, West Indies to Australia) b Georgetown, Guyana 15.12.1966 RHB OB																		
Test		7	12	2	393	129	39.30	1	1	886	318	9	35.33	5-26	1	0	2.15	6	
FC		12	20	2	791	129	43.94	3	2	1549	539	15	35.93	5-26	2	0	2.08	12	
Int		5	4	1	96	48	32.00	0	0	199	136	1	136.00	1-40	0	0	4.10	5	
SS		7	5	3	109	72*	54.50	0	1	330	175	9	19.44	2-9	0	0	3.18	4	
Test	1987	64	108	10	3303	178*	33.70	7	15	7648	3307	63	52.49	5-26	3	0	2.59	72	
FC	1983	229	363	35	14689	236*	44.78	37	73	29997	13179	367	35.91	5-26	12	0	2.63	260	
Int	1986	155	139	33	3600	113*	33.96	1	20	6263	4536	134	33.85	4-34	1	0	4.34	76	
SS	1984	29	26	7	997	104	52.47	1	8	1345	789	33	23.90	3-30	0	0	3.51	16	
HOYTE, Ricardo Lawrence (Barbados) b Bridgetown, Barbados 15.10.1969 LHB WK																		
FC		5	8	2	167	50*	27.83	0	1									13	
SS		2	2	0	76	50	38.00	0	1									1	
FC	1989	18	31	6	564	75	22.56	0	4									30	3
HURLEY, Ryan O'Neal (Barbados) b Barbados 13.9.1975 RHB OB																		
FC		4	6	0	176	112	29.33	1	0	265	109	5	21.80	5-66	1	0	2.46	1	
SS		6	5	0	47	17	9.40	0	0	336	205	4	51.25	1-18	0	0	3.66	5	
FC	1995	8	9	1	261	112	32.62	1	0	475	249	7	35.57	5-66	1	0	3.14	3	

IRISH, Lesroy (Leeward Islands) b Montserrat

Cmp	Debut	M	I	NO	Runs	HS	Avge	100	50	Balls	Runs	Wkts	Avge	BB	5i	10m	RpO	ct	st
FC		4	5	2	3	2	1.00	0	0	696	282	9	31.33	2-14	0	0	2.43	4	

JACOBS, Ridley Detamore (Leeward Islands, West Indies A to Sri Lanka) b Antigua 26.11.1967 LHB WK

Cmp	Debut	M	I	NO	Runs	HS	Avge	100	50	Balls	Runs	Wkts	Avge	BB	5i	10m	RpO	ct	st
FC		10	15	3	464	107	38.66	1	2									21	5
SS		6	4	1	37	22	12.33	0	0									7	
FC	1991	41	65	15	2125	119*	42.50	5	12									120	13
Int	1995	4	3	0	13	10	4.33	0	0									1	1
SS	1991	28	25	4	538	85	25.61	0	4									38	2

JOSEPH, Dawnley Alister (Windward Islands) b Stubbs, St Vincent 20.8.1966 RHB RM/OB

Cmp	Debut	M	I	NO	Runs	HS	Avge	100	50	Balls	Runs	Wkts	Avge	BB	5i	10m	RpO	ct	st
FC		5	10	0	92	25	9.20	0	0									5	
SS		6	6	0	165	67	27.50	0	1									6	
FC	1986	60	109	3	3408	149	32.15	5	17	422	198	5	39.60	2-29	0	0	2.81	50	
SS	1986	33	32	3	888	108	30.62	1	4	627	430	15	28.66	4-55	1	0	4.11	23	

JOSEPH, David Rolston Emmanuel (Leeward Islands, West Indies A to Sri Lanka) b Antigua 15.11.1969 RHB

Cmp	Debut	M	I	NO	Runs	HS	Avge	100	50	Balls	Runs	Wkts	Avge	BB	5i	10m	RpO	ct	st
FC		10	16	2	248	66	17.71	0	1									5	
SS		6	6	2	169	51	42.25	0	1									4	
FC	1990	32	49	4	1501	131	33.35	4	7									35	
SS	1990	17	15	3	452	94	37.66	0	3									5	

JOSEPH, Jenson Eugene Simon (Leeward Islands) b Antigua 7.10.1966 LHB RFM

Cmp	Debut	M	I	NO	Runs	HS	Avge	100	50	Balls	Runs	Wkts	Avge	BB	5i	10m	RpO	ct	st
FC		1	1	0	8	8	8.00	0	0	216	168	4	42.00	3-122	0	0	4.66	2	
FC	1994	11	15	0	218	44	14.53	0	0	1733	1001	39	25.66	5-59	1	0	3.46	11	
SS	1994	7	5	2	50	20*	16.66	0	0	260	236	6	39.33	2-15	0	0	5.44	1	

JOSEPH, Sylvester Cleofoster (Leeward Islands) b St Johns, Antigua 5.9.1978 RHB OB

Cmp	Debut	M	I	NO	Runs	HS	Avge	100	50	Balls	Runs	Wkts	Avge	BB	5i	10m	RpO	ct	st
FC		7	12	0	197	49	16.41	0	0									6	
SS		2	2	0	46	41	23.00	0	0	6	9	1	9.00	1-9	0	0	9.00	0	

KING, Reon Dane (Guyana) b Guyana 6.10.1975 RHB RFM

Cmp	Debut	M	I	NO	Runs	HS	Avge	100	50	Balls	Runs	Wkts	Avge	BB	5i	10m	RpO	ct	st
FC		5	8	0	52	30	6.50	0	0	1114	542	26	20.84	7-82	3	0	2.91	1	
SS		2								66	65	1	65.00	1-32	0	0	5.90	0	
FC	1995	9	14	0	90	30	6.42	0	0	1690	812	31	26.19	7-82	3	0	2.88	2	
SS	1994	4	1	0	1	1	1.00	0	0	120	136	1	136.00	1-32	0	0	6.80	0	

LAMBERT, Clayton Benjamin (Guyana) b New Amsterdam, Guyana 10.2.1962 LHB OB

Cmp	Debut	M	I	NO	Runs	HS	Avge	100	50	Balls	Runs	Wkts	Avge	BB	5i	10m	RpO	ct	st
FC		4	8	1	454	159	64.85	2	1	4	4	0					6.00	1	
SS		7	7	2	295	91	59.00	0	3									5	
Test	1991	1	2	0	53	39	26.50	0	0	4	4	1	4.00	1-4	0	0	6.00	2	
FC	1983	98	174	15	7166	263*	45.06	18	32	217	119	4	29.75	2-33	0	0	3.29	132	
Int	1989	5	5	0	132	66	26.40	0	1									0	
SS	1984	28	28	3	817	111*	32.68	1	5	84	56	2	28.00	2-30	0	0	4.00	17	

LARA, Brian Charles (Trinidad, West Indies, West Indies to Australia) b Santa Cruz, Trinidad 2.5.1969 LHB LBG

Cmp	Debut	M	I	NO	Runs	HS	Avge	100	50	Balls	Runs	Wkts	Avge	BB	5i	10m	RpO	ct	st
Test		7	12	0	511	115	42.58	2	2	18	16	0					5.33	6	
FC		13	22	0	965	135	43.86	3	5	48	39	1	39.00	1-14	0	0	4.87	17	
Int		5	4	1	125	67	41.66	0	1									2	
SS		7	7	1	384	127	64.00	1	4									5	
Test	1990	45	76	2	4004	375	54.10	10	20	60	28	0					2.80	59	
FC	1987	128	209	6	10978	501*	54.07	31	48	383	307	2	153.50	1-14	0	0	4.80	161	
Int	1990	118	116	12	4881	169	46.93	11	31	24	22	2	11.00	2-5	0	0	5.50	59	
SS	1987	28	25	3	1090	127	49.54	2	9	22	15	0					4.09	13	

LAWRENCE, Andre (Trinidad) b Trinidad 4.5.1969 RHB RM

Cmp	Debut	M	I	NO	Runs	HS	Avge	100	50	Balls	Runs	Wkts	Avge	BB	5i	10m	RpO	ct	st
FC		3	5	0	35	28	7.00	0	0	108	33	2	16.50	1-6	0	0	1.83	3	
SS		7	7	1	189	81	31.50	0	1	72	54	4	13.50	2-10	0	0	4.50	2	
FC	1993	6	11	0	118	44	10.72	0	0	192	64	3	21.33	1-6	0	0	2.00	6	
SS	1993	9	9	1	200	81	25.00	0	1	150	119	4	29.75	2-10	0	0	4.76	2	

LEWIS, Rawl Nicholas (Windward Islands, West Indies A to Sri Lanka) b Grenada 5.9.1974 RHB LBG

Cmp	Debut	M	I	NO	Runs	HS	Avge	100	50	Balls	Runs	Wkts	Avge	BB	5i	10m	RpO	ct	st
FC		9	18	5	366	55*	28.15	0	1	1718	899	27	33.29	5-160	1	0	3.13	10	
SS		6	5	1	31	15*	7.75	0	0	246	189	4	47.25	2-28	0	0	4.60	1	
FC	1991	34	56	14	748	55*	17.80	0	3	6095	3082	100	30.82	7-66	5	0	3.03	21	
SS	1992	14	12	3	89	23*	9.88	0	0	480	401	8	50.12	2-28	0	0	5.01	2	

LIBURD, Merlin Dave (Leeward Islands) b Nevis 15.12.1969 RHB

Cmp	Debut	M	I	NO	Runs	HS	Avge	100	50	Balls	Runs	Wkts	Avge	BB	5i	10m	RpO	ct	st
FC		4	6	0	134	40	22.33	0	0									4	
SS		6	6	0	167	77	27.83	0	1									2	
FC	1994	10	15	0	379	77	25.26	0	1									12	
SS	1994	15	15	0	425	77	28.33	0	3									4	

McGARRELL, Neil Christopher (Guyana) b Guyana 12.7.1972 RHB SLA

Cmp	Debut	M	I	NO	Runs	HS	Avge	100	50	Balls	Runs	Wkts	Avge	BB	5i	10m	RpO	ct	st
FC		8	14	3	279	73	25.36	0	1	2324	924	27	34.22	7-84	1	1	2.38	7	
SS		5	1	0	1	1	1.00	0	0	122	53	0					2.60	1	
FC	1995	12	18	3	339	73	22.60	0	1	2780	1107	31	35.70	7-84	1	1	2.38	17	
SS	1995	8	3	1	42	22*	21.00	0	0	236	162	0					4.11	1	

McKENZIE, Denville St Delmo (Jamaica) b Little London, Jamaica 4.12.1975 RHB RF

Cmp	Debut	M	I	NO	Runs	HS	Avge	100	50	Balls	Runs	Wkts	Avge	BB	5i	10m	RpO	ct	st
FC		5	8	2	25	8	4.16	0	0	456	292	10	29.20	4-35	0	0	3.84	0	
FC	1995	7	10	3	47	16	6.71	0	0	624	422	11	38.36	4-35	0	0	4.05	0	

McLEAN, Nixon Alexei McNamara (Windward Islands, West Indies to Australia) b Stubbs, St Vincent 28.7.1973 LHB RF

Cmp	Debut	M	I	NO	Runs	HS	Avge	100	50	Balls	Runs	Wkts	Avge	BB	5i	10m	RpO	ct	st
SS		6	5	1	87	41*	21.75	0	0	252	189	7	27.00	2-32	0	0	4.50	3	
FC	1992	11	19	8	248	49*	22.54	0	0	1325	829	21	39.47	5-48	1	0	3.75	1	
Int	1996	6	3	0	8	7	2.66	0	0	204	145	3	48.33	2-33	0	0	4.26	2	
SS	1992	14	11	3	140	41*	17.50	0	0	500	398	11	36.18	2-18	0	0	4.77	4	

MARSHALL, Dave Kerwin (Barbados) b Barbados 24.5.1972 RHB LBG

Cmp	Debut	M	I	NO	Runs	HS	Avge	100	50	Balls	Runs	Wkts	Avge	BB	5i	10m	RpO	ct	st
FC		5	6	3	81	42	27.00	0	0	601	295	15	19.66	6-62	1	0	2.94	3	
FC	1992	8	10	3	100	42	14.28	0	0	787	365	17	21.47	6-62	1	0	2.78	5	

MARSHALL, Roy Ashworth (Windward Islands) b St Joseph, Dominica 1.4.1965 RHB SLA

Cmp	Debut	M	I	NO	Runs	HS	Avge	100	50	Balls	Runs	Wkts	Avge	BB	5i	10m	RpO	ct	st
FC		9	18	0	295	46	16.38	0	0	1642	654	30	21.80	3-15	0	0	2.38	8	
SS		6	6	0	83	44	13.83	0	0	312	190	7	27.14	2-25	0	0	3.65	0	
FC	1984	37	67	1	1141	112	17.28	1	2	6841	2553	98	26.05	7-99	3	1	2.23	26	
SS	1991	18	17	4	404	77*	31.07	0	1	941	592	19	31.15	2-25	0	0	3.77	6	

MARTIN, Kenroy (Windward Islands) b St Vincent LHB

Cmp	Debut	M	I	NO	Runs	HS	Avge	100	50	Balls	Runs	Wkts	Avge	BB	5i	10m	RpO	ct	st
FC		4	8	0	129	65	16.12	0	1									1	

MASON, Keno (Trinidad) b Trinidad 13.11.1972 RHB WK

Cmp	Debut	M	I	NO	Runs	HS	Avge	100	50	Balls	Runs	Wkts	Avge	BB	5i	10m	RpO	ct	st
FC		5	7	0	110	49	15.71	0	0	13	8	0					3.69	4	
FC	1992	26	42	1	968	84	23.60	0	5	13	8	0					3.69	27	
SS	1992	14	13	0	187	68	14.38	0	1									6	

MAYNARD, John Carl (Leeward Islands) b Nevis 18.5.1969 RHB RF

Cmp	Debut	M	I	NO	Runs	HS	Avge	100	50	Balls	Runs	Wkts	Avge	BB	5i	10m	RpO	ct	st
FC		4	5	2	41	19*	13.66	0	0	370	206	7	29.42	3-41	0	0	3.34	1	
FC	1991	10	13	5	65	19*	8.12	0	0	1183	641	24	26.70	4-19	0	0	3.25	2	
SS	1991	7	2	1	1	1	1.00	0	0	282	196	11	17.81	3-21	0	0	4.17	0	

MILLS, Michael (Leeward Islands) b Nevis

Cmp	Debut	M	I	NO	Runs	HS	Avge	100	50	Balls	Runs	Wkts	Avge	BB	5i	10m	RpO	ct	st
FC		2	3	0	4	2	1.33	0	0	342	138	10	13.80	5-33	1	0	2.42	0	

MITCHUM, Junie (Leeward Islands) b St Kitts 22.11.1973 RHB

Cmp	Debut	M	I	NO	Runs	HS	Avge	100	50	Balls	Runs	Wkts	Avge	BB	5i	10m	RpO	ct	st
FC		5	10	1	224	89	24.88	0	2	54	42	1	42.00	1-42	0	0	4.66	6	
SS		1	1	0	39	39	39.00	0	0	36	30	0					5.00	0	
FC	1994	6	11	1	266	89	26.60	0	2	54	42	1	42.00	1-42	0	0	4.66	6	

MORGAN, Delroy Simeon (Jamaica) b Rollington Town, Jamaica 4.3.1967 RHB OB

Cmp	Debut	M	I	NO	Runs	HS	Avge	100	50	Balls	Runs	Wkts	Avge	BB	5i	10m	RpO	ct	st
FC		9	15	1	343	63	24.50	0	3	48	27	0					3.37	11	
SS		4	4	1	155	133*	51.66	1	0									2	
FC	1986	60	105	6	2826	122	28.54	3	14	498	199	5	39.80	4-31	0	0	2.39	57	
SS	1986	32	32	2	984	133*	32.80	1	7	408	273	9	30.33	2-24	0	0	4.01	21	

MORGAN, McNeil Junior (Windward Islands) b St Vincent 18.10.1970 RHB RFM

Cmp	Debut	M	I	NO	Runs	HS	Avge	100	50	Balls	Runs	Wkts	Avge	BB	5i	10m	RpO	ct	st
FC		9	18	2	127	35	7.93	0	0	1082	628	24	26.16	4-32	0	0	3.48	5	
FC	1994	10	20	2	129	35	.7.16	0	0	1130	648	25	25.92	4-32	0	0	3.44	6	

MORTON, Runako Shaku (Leeward Islands) b Nevis 22.7.1968 RHB OB

Cmp	Debut	M	I	NO	Runs	HS	Avge	100	50	Balls	Runs	Wkts	Avge	BB	5i	10m	RpO	ct	st
FC		2	3	0	31	31	10.33	0	0									3	

MURPHY, Brian Samuel (Jamaica) b Jamaica 7.4.1973 RHB LBG

Cmp	Debut	M	I	NO	Runs	HS	Avge	100	50	Balls	Runs	Wkts	Avge	BB	5i	10m	RpO	ct	st
FC		10	17	5	299	43*	24.91	0	0	1220	496	21	23.61	5-85	1	0	2.43	7	
FC	1993	20	33	9	485	47	20.20	0	0	2722	1314	45	29.20	5-35	3	0	2.89	11	

MURRAY, Junior Randalph (Windward Islands, West Indies, West Indies to Australia) b St Georges, Grenada 20.1.1968 RHB WK

Cmp	Debut	M	I	NO	Runs	HS	Avge	100	50	Balls	Runs	Wkts	Avge	BB	5i	10m	RpO	ct	st
Test		2	3	1	24	12*	12.00	0	0									2	
FC		8	15	1	547	218	39.07	2	1									16	3
Int		1	1	0	2	2	2.00	0	0									0	
SS		5	5	3	109	40	54.50	0	0									2	
Test	1992	28	37	4	848	101*	25.69	1	3									92	3
FC	1986	93	149	20	3749	218	29.06	6	11									210	18
Int	1992	49	30	6	557	86	23.20	0	4									44	7
SS	1987	26	21	5	307	42	19.18	0	0									14	5

NAGAMOOTOO, Mahendra Veeren (Guyana) b Guyana 9.10.1975 LHB LBG

Cmp	Debut	M	I	NO	Runs	HS	Avge	100	50	Balls	Runs	Wkts	Avge	BB	5i	10m	RpO	ct	st
FC		7	11	1	154	56	15.40	0	1	1931	872	29	30.05	4-59	0	0	2.70	3	
SS		7	2	1	0	0*	0.00	0	0	414	239	16	14.93	3-29	0	0	3.46	2	
FC	1994	19	31	3	368	56	13.14	0	1	4129	1898	67	28.32	7-76	1	0	2.75	10	
SS	1995	8	2	1	0	0*	0.00	0	0	414	239	16	14.93	3-29	0	0	3.46	2	

NAGAMOOTOO, Vishal (Guyana) b Guyana 7.1.1977 RHB WK

Cmp	Debut	M	I	NO	Runs	HS	Avge	100	50	Balls	Runs	Wkts	Avge	BB	5i	10m	RpO	ct	st
FC		7	11	1	186	36	18.60	0	0									10	4
FC	1995	8	11	1	186	36	18.60	0	0									10	4

NEBLETT, Jermaine Cleavon (Guyana) b Guyana 15.9.1974 RHB RFM

Cmp	Debut	M	I	NO	Runs	HS	Avge	100	50	Balls	Runs	Wkts	Avge	BB	5i	10m	RpO	ct	st
FC		1	1	1	1	1*		0	0	30	36	0					7.20	0	

Cmp	Debut	M	I	NO	Runs	HS	Avge	100	50	Balls	Runs	Wkts	Avge	BB	5i	10m	RpO	ct	st

NEDD, Gavin Hilton (Guyana) b Guyana 21.7.1972 RHB OB

| FC | | 1 | 2 | 1 | 0 | 0* | 0.00 | 0 | 0 | 66 | 37 | 0 | | | | | 3.36 | 0 | |
| FC | 1994 | 8 | 13 | 2 | 58 | 22 | 5.27 | 0 | 0 | 1105 | 518 | 10 | 51.80 | 3-42 | 0 | 0 | 2.81 | 0 | |

PERCIVAL, Andre Ricardo (Guyana) b New Amsterdam, Guyana 5.1.1975 LHB RM

FC		4	8	1	182	91	26.00	0	1									6	
SS		7	3	0	51	42	17.00	0	0	12	3	1	3.00	1-3	0	0	1.50	1	
FC	1991	12	20	2	471	91	26.16	0	3									13	
SS	1993	15	10	2	155	45	19.37	0	0	12	3	1	3.00	1-3	0	0	1.50	5	

PERRY, Nehemiah Odolphus (Jamaica) b Jamaica 16.6.1968 RHB OB

FC		5	9	0	115	41	12.77	0	0	780	287	9	31.88	2-18	0	0	2.20	0	
SS		3	2	0	44	34	22.00	0	0	132	76	2	38.00	2-34	0	0	3.45	1	
FC	1986	60	88	10	1532	160	19.64	1	8	11185	4499	176	25.56	8-45	8	1	2.41	32	
SS	1991	16	11	0	169	56	15.36	0	1	702	494	11	44.90	4-45	1	0	4.22	7	

PERSAD, Mukesh (Trinidad) b Trinidad 1.5.1970 RHB OB

| FC | | 3 | 5 | 2 | 12 | 8* | 4.00 | 0 | 0 | 552 | 225 | 7 | 32.14 | 4-55 | 0 | 0 | 2.44 | 1 | |
| FC | 1994 | 8 | 11 | 6 | 36 | 10* | 7.20 | 0 | 0 | 1747 | 725 | 26 | 27.88 | 5-63 | 1 | 0 | 2.48 | 2 | |

PHILLIP, Warrington Dexter (Leeward Islands) b Nevis 23.7.1968 LHB SLA

FC		9	13	2	73	14	6.63	0	0	2714	1024	35	29.25	7-104	3	0	2.26	5	
SS		2								108	49	3	16.33	2-22	0	0	2.72	0	
FC	1990	32	45	13	406	41*	12.68	0	0	7372	2981	117	25.47	8-92	8	2	2.42	27	
SS	1994	4	1	1	1	1*		0	0	210	99	7	14.14	3-25	0	0	2.82	0	

PIERRE, Andrew Jones (Windward Islands) b Goodwill, Dominica 5.10.1963 RHB

FC		3	6	0	60	24	10.00	0	0									1	
SS		6	6	0	245	69	40.83	0	2									4	
FC	1987	16	32	2	632	73	21.06	0	3									8	
SS	1988	12	10	1	274	69	30.44	0	2									7	

POPE, Uzzah (Windward Islands) b St Vincent 3.1.1971 LHB WK

FC		6	12	0	161	34	13.41	0	0									12	3
SS		5	5	0	102	30	20.40	0	0									3	
FC	1991	30	55	2	966	91	18.22	0	5									60	9
SS	1991	21	18	2	276	54	17.25	0	1									8	1

POWELL, Kirk Howard (Jamaica) b Jamaica 17.6.1972 RHB RFM

| SS | | 5 | 4 | 1 | 44 | 20 | 14.66 | 0 | 0 | 192 | 145 | 5 | 29.00 | 4-33 | 1 | 0 | 4.53 | 1 | |

POWELL, Ronald Malcolm (Leeward Islands) b Nevis 5.3.1968 RHB OB

FC		7	10	0	228	51	22.80	0	1	1698	655	23	28.47	3-31	0	0	2.31	4	
SS		6	4	2	75	42	37.50	0	0	156	97	4	24.25	2-15	0	0	3.73	2	
FC	1995	8	12	0	285	51	23.75	0	1	1926	742	27	27.48	3-31	0	0	2.31	5	
SS	1994	13	8	2	142	48	23.66	0	0	468	318	8	39.75	2-13	0	0	4.07	4	

POWELL, Tony Orlando (Jamaica, West Indies A to Sri Lanka) b Jamaica 22.12.1972 LHB RM

FC		8	15	0	317	76	21.13	0	1									5	
SS		6	6	0	145	45	24.16	0	0									1	
FC	1991	26	45	1	1219	125*	27.70	1	8									29	
SS	1992	23	21	2	519	76	27.31	0	3									4	

PROVERBS, Ahmed Edward (Barbados) b Barbados 28.1.1970 RHB RM WK

SS		3	2	0	60	47	30.00	0	0	36	48	0					8.00	0	
FC	1990	5	8	0	110	50	13.75	0	1	36	14	0					2.33	3	
SS	1991	5	3	0	63	47	21.00	0	0	39	52	0					8.00	0	

PROVERBS, Stanton Nathaniel (Barbados) b Barbados 6.3.1968 RHB RM

FC		5	9	2	210	112*	30.00	1	0	66	35	0					3.18	4	
FC	1989	10	19	2	394	112*	23.17	1	1	90	47	0					3.13	6	
SS	1989	4	3	0	106	92	35.33	0	1									0	

QUINN, Whitmoore Kenneth Lyndon (Leeward Islands) b All Saints, Antigua 30.5.1971 RHB RFM

| FC | | 4 | 5 | 2 | 27 | 11 | 9.00 | 0 | 0 | 741 | 283 | 14 | 20.21 | 4-39 | 0 | 0 | 2.29 | 1 | |
| FC | 1993 | 11 | 15 | 6 | 95 | 48 | 10.55 | 0 | 0 | 1882 | 937 | 42 | 22.30 | 7-65 | 1 | 0 | 2.98 | 2 | |

RAGOONATH, Suruj (Trinidad) b Trinidad 22.3.1968 RHB

FC		8	14	3	625	128	56.81	2	2									1	
SS		7	7	0	199	75	28.42	0	2									1	
FC	1988	42	74	6	2147	128	31.57	2	13	11	6	0					3.27	19	
SS	1990	28	26	0	522	75	20.07	0	3									4	

RAMNARINE, Dinanath (Trinidad, West Indies) b Trinidad 4.6.1975 RHB LBG

FC		10	14	2	151	43	12.58	0	0	2191	848	38	22.31	5-69	1	0	2.32	12	
Int		1								60	52	2	26.00	2-52	0	0	5.20	0	
SS		6	1	0	1	1	1.00	0	0	264	137	8	17.12	4-23	1	0	3.11	0	
FC	1993	17	25	3	226	43	10.27	0	0	3315	1412	57	24.77	5-48	2	0	2.55	15	
SS	1993	12	7	1	39	14	6.50	0	0	538	316	14	22.57	4-23	1	0	3.52	0	

RAMPERSAD, Denis (Trinidad) b Trinidad 22.9.1974 RHB OB

| FC | | 1 | 2 | 0 | 22 | 15 | 11.00 | 0 | 0 | 60 | 22 | 5 | 4.40 | 3-13 | 0 | 0 | 2.20 | 0 | |

	Cmp Debut	M	I	NO	Runs	HS	Avge	100	50	Balls	Runs	Wkts	Avge	BB	5i	10m	RpO	ct	st

REID, Winston Emmerson (Barbados) b Bank Hall, Barbados 29.9.1962 LHB SLA

		M	I	NO	Runs	HS	Avge	100	50	Balls	Runs	Wkts	Avge	BB	5i	10m	RpO	ct	st
FC		10	17	5	240	54*	20.00	0	1	2088	812	40	20.30	4-72	0	0	2.33	6	
SS		6	4	1	56	23	18.66	0	0	354	167	13	12.84	4-20	2	0	2.83	1	
FC	1985	40	62	12	668	78	13.36	0	2	7991	3302	127	26.00	6-73	1	0	2.47	26	
SS	1986	27	10	3	86	23	12.28	0	0	1370	821	29	28.31	4-20	2	0	3.59	9	

REIFER, Floyd Lamonte (Barbados, West Indies, West Indies A to Sri Lanka) b Parish Land, Barbados 23.7.1972 LHB RM WK

		M	I	NO	Runs	HS	Avge	100	50	Balls	Runs	Wkts	Avge	BB	5i	10m	RpO	ct	st
Test		2	4	0	48	29	12.00	0	0									3	
FC		14	25	2	940	200	40.86	2	5	24	22	1	22.00	1-19	0	0	5.50	11	
Int		1	1	0	9	9	9.00	0	0									1	
SS		6	6	2	127	47	31.75	0	0	72	62	1	62.00	1-22	0	0	5.16	2	
FC	1991	37	63	8	2172	200	39.49	4	12	54	38	1	38.00	1-19	0	0	4.22	21	
SS	1991	22	21	3	445	82	24.72	0	1	84	77	1	77.00	1-22	0	0	5.50	6	

ROBERTS, Lincoln Abraham (Trinidad) b Tobago 4.9.1974 RHB RM

		M	I	NO	Runs	HS	Avge	100	50	Balls	Runs	Wkts	Avge	BB	5i	10m	RpO	ct	st
FC		8	13	1	319	65	26.58	0	2	72	41	0					3.41	4	
SS		7	6	1	167	52	33.40	0	1									2	
FC	1995	13	21	2	402	65	21.15	0	2	72	41	0					3.41	7	
SS	1995	13	10	1	303	55	33.66	0	2	6	4	0					4.00	2	

ROLLOCK, Terry Euclyn (Barbados) b Barbados 25.9.1969 RHB LBG

		M	I	NO	Runs	HS	Avge	100	50	Balls	Runs	Wkts	Avge	BB	5i	10m	RpO	ct	st
FC		7	11	1	137	53	13.70	0	1	546	266	13	20.46	6-15	1	0	2.92	4	

ROSE, Franklyn Albert (Jamaica, West Indies) b Chalk Hill, Jamaica 1.2.1972 RHB RF

		M	I	NO	Runs	HS	Avge	100	50	Balls	Runs	Wkts	Avge	BB	5i	10m	RpO	ct	st
Test		7	7	2	64	34	12.80	0	0	1069	545	23	23.69	6-100	1	0	3.05	1	
FC		16	20	3	263	96	15.47	0	1	2525	1306	71	18.39	6-63	4	1	3.10	4	
Int		5	3	0	21	9	7.00	0	0	246	175	5	35.00	3-25	0	0	4.26	1	
FC	1992	32	44	10	558	96	16.41	0	1	5037	2757	118	23.36	6-63	5	1	3.28	8	
SS	1992	13	10	2	49	27	6.12	0	0	540	399	10	39.90	3-35	0	0	4.43	5	

SAMAROO, Avidesh (Trinidad, West Indies A to Sri Lanka) b Trinidad 22.1.1978 RHB SLC

		M	I	NO	Runs	HS	Avge	100	50	Balls	Runs	Wkts	Avge	BB	5i	10m	RpO	ct	st
FC		1	1	1	1	1*		0	0	77	36	2	18.00	2-32	0	0	2.80	0	
FC	1995	9	12	4	93	25	11.62	0	0	1140	702	25	28.08	4-44	0	0	3.69	4	

SAMUELS, Marlon Nathaniel (Jamaica) b Kingston, Jamaica 5.1.1981 RHB OB

		M	I	NO	Runs	HS	Avge	100	50	Balls	Runs	Wkts	Avge	BB	5i	10m	RpO	ct	st
FC		1	2	0	3	2	1.50	0	0	90	34	1	34.00	1-18	0	0	2.26	0	

SAMUELS, Robert George (Jamaica, West Indies to Australia) b Jamaica 13.3.1971 LHB

		M	I	NO	Runs	HS	Avge	100	50	Balls	Runs	Wkts	Avge	BB	5i	10m	RpO	ct	st
FC		8	16	2	417	90*	29.78	0	3									7	
SS		6	6	0	134	60	22.33	0	1									2	
Test	1995	6	12	2	372	125	37.20	1	1									8	
FC	1988	59	111	8	3594	159	34.89	5	19									35	
Int	1995	8	5	2	54	36*	18.00	0	0									0	
SS	1990	27	27	1	793	103	30.50	1	5									10	

SANFORD, Adam (Windward Islands) b Dominica 12.7.1976 RHB

		M	I	NO	Runs	HS	Avge	100	50	Balls	Runs	Wkts	Avge	BB	5i	10m	RpO	ct	st
FC		1	1	1	30	30*		0	0	150	55	2	27.50	1-5	0	0	2.20	0	

SARJOO, R. (Guyana)

		M	I	NO	Runs	HS	Avge	100	50	Balls	Runs	Wkts	Avge	BB	5i	10m	RpO	ct	st
FC		1	2	0	24	21	12.00	0	0									0	
SS		1	1	0	22	22	22.00	0	0									0	

SARWAN, Ramnaresh (Guyana) b Wakeanam, Guyana 23.6.1980 RHB LB

		M	I	NO	Runs	HS	Avge	100	50	Balls	Runs	Wkts	Avge	BB	5i	10m	RpO	ct	st
FC		7	12	0	210	77	17.50	0	2	102	44	1	44.00	1-21	0	0	2.58	5	
SS		1	1	0	0	0	0.00	0	0									0	
FC	1995	8	12	0	210	77	17.50	0	2	162	53	2	26.50	1-9	0	0	1.96	7	

SEMPLE, Keith Fitzpatrick (Guyana) b Georgetown, Guyana 21.8.1970 RHB RM

		M	I	NO	Runs	HS	Avge	100	50	Balls	Runs	Wkts	Avge	BB	5i	10m	RpO	ct	st
FC		4	7	1	94	29	15.66	0	0	54	30	0					3.33	2	
SS		6	5	0	123	71	24.60	0	1	228	132	0					3.47	0	
FC	1989	30	49	5	1225	142	27.84	1	9	120	59	1	59.00	1-8	0	0	2.95	33	
SS	1992	25	23	4	503	71	26.47	0	3	396	226	2	113.00	2-30	0	0	3.42	6	

SIMMONS, Philip Verant (Trinidad, Easterns, West Indies to Australia) b Arima, Trinidad 18.4.1963 RHB RM

		M	I	NO	Runs	HS	Avge	100	50	Balls	Runs	Wkts	Avge	BB	5i	10m	RpO	ct	st
FC		4	6	1	200	116	40.00	1	1	426	173	5	34.60	2-17	0	0	2.43	3	
SS		4	3	2	118	80*	118.00	0	1	192	142	5	28.40	2-32	0	0	4.43	7	
Test	1987	25	45	2	1000	110	23.25	1	4	612	248	4	62.00	2-34	0	0	2.43	26	
FC	1982	169	289	13	10297	261	37.30	22	55	10309	4779	161	29.68	6-14	4	0	2.78	197	
Int	1987	119	117	7	3242	122	29.47	5	17	3034	2185	62	35.24	4-3	2	0	4.32	51	
SS	1982	35	32	3	1017	125	35.06	1	9	1044	729	24	30.37	5-36	0	1	4.18	26	

SMITH, Richard Andrew Mortimer (Trinidad) b Trinidad 17.7.1971 RHB

		M	I	NO	Runs	HS	Avge	100	50	Balls	Runs	Wkts	Avge	BB	5i	10m	RpO	ct	st
FC		9	14	1	277	62	21.30	0	1	84	31	1	31.00	1-28	0	0	2.21	8	
SS		3	2	0	32	22	16.00	0	0									0	
FC	1990	32	52	2	923	99	18.46	0	3	144	66	1	66.00	1-28	0	0	2.75	18	
SS	1991	18	16	0	286	77	17.87	0	1	9	5	1	5.00	1-5	0	0	3.33	2	

STEPHEN, Lee (Windward Islands) b St Lucia 29.10.1975 RHB

		M	I	NO	Runs	HS	Avge	100	50	Balls	Runs	Wkts	Avge	BB	5i	10m	RpO	ct	st
FC		2	4	0	39	17	9.75	0	0									2	
SS		2	2	0	44	31	22.00	0	0									0	

STUART, Colin Ellsworth Laurie (Guyana) b Guyana 28.9.1973 RHB RFM

Cmp	Debut	M	I	NO	Runs	HS	Avge	100	50	Balls	Runs	Wkts	Avge	BB	5i	10m	RpO	ct	st
FC		7	10	6	33	19	8.25	0	0	1062	616	13	47.38	2-29	0	0	3.48	4	
FC	1994	13	20	13	51	19	7.28	0	0	1598	988	26	38.00	3-43	0	0	3.70	5	

SYLVESTER, John Anthony Rodney (Windward Islands) b Grenada 6.10.1969 RHB

Cmp	Debut	M	I	NO	Runs	HS	Avge	100	50	Balls	Runs	Wkts	Avge	BB	5i	10m	RpO	ct	st
FC		7	14	0	332	70	23.71	0	3	36	10	1	10.00	1-10	0	0	1.66	3	
SS		2	2	1	33	19*	33.00	0	0									0	
FC	1992	14	26	1	522	70	20.88	0	4	36	10	1	10.00	1-10	0	0	1.66	11	
SS	1992	10	8	1	58	19*	8.28	0	0									6	

SYLVESTER, Kester Kenneth (Windward Islands) b Grenada 5.12.1973 RHB WK

Cmp	Debut	M	I	NO	Runs	HS	Avge	100	50	Balls	Runs	Wkts	Avge	BB	5i	10m	RpO	ct	st
FC		6	12	0	108	56	9.00	0	1	3	10	0					20.00	4	
SS		2	2	0	9	9	4.50	0	0									0	
FC	1992	22	43	0	635	77	14.76	0	3	3	10	0					20.00	19	
SS	1992	12	11	0	139	33	12.63	0	0									1	

THOMAS, Dennison (Windward Islands) b Grenada 3.3.1968 RHB RF

Cmp	Debut	M	I	NO	Runs	HS	Avge	100	50	Balls	Runs	Wkts	Avge	BB	5i	10m	RpO	ct	st
FC		6	12	2	119	33*	11.90	0	0	850	328	15	21.86	3-21	0	0	2.31	0	
SS		6	6	1	44	21	8.80	0	0	278	158	6	26.33	3-18	0	0	3.41	0	
FC	1993	15	28	4	488	70	20.33	0	2	1779	803	32	25.09	4-42	0	0	2.70	4	
SS	1993	16	14	1	216	54	16.61	0	1	542	390	11	35.45	3-18	0	0	4.31	2	

THOMAS, Preston (Windward Islands)

Cmp	Debut	M	I	NO	Runs	HS	Avge	100	50	Balls	Runs	Wkts	Avge	BB	5i	10m	RpO	ct	st
FC		2	4	0	23	18	5.75	0	0									3	

THOMPSON, Patterson Ian Chesterfield (Barbados, West Indies to Australia) b Barbados 26.9.1971 RHB RFM

Cmp	Debut	M	I	NO	Runs	HS	Avge	100	50	Balls	Runs	Wkts	Avge	BB	5i	10m	RpO	ct	st
FC		6	8	3	35	15	7.00	0	0	666	447	11	40.63	3-27	0	0	4.02	1	
SS		6	4	2	6	3*	3.00	0	0	282	230	4	57.50	2-51	0	0	4.89	3	
Test	1995	2	3	1	17	10*	8.50	0	0	228	215	5	43.00	2-58	0	0	5.65	0	
FC	1994	20	25	8	59	15	3.47	0	0	2594	1743	53	32.88	5-105	1	0	4.03	5	
Int	1996	2	1	0	2	2	2.00	0	0	114	110	2	55.00	1-46	0	0	5.78	0	

TUCKETT, Carl McArthur (Leeward Islands) b Nevis 18.5.1970 RHB RFM

Cmp	Debut	M	I	NO	Runs	HS	Avge	100	50	Balls	Runs	Wkts	Avge	BB	5i	10m	RpO	ct	st
FC		2	4	1	60	20*	20.00	0	0	240	90	5	18.00	3-57	0	0	2.25	1	
SS		4	2	0	7	7	3.50	0	0									2	
FC	1994	7	14	3	246	63	22.36	0	1	360	153	7	21.85	3-57	0	0	2.55	1	

VENTURA, Mario Dimitri (Jamaica) b Jamaica 21.4.1974 LHB

Cmp	Debut	M	I	NO	Runs	HS	Avge	100	50	Balls	Runs	Wkts	Avge	BB	5i	10m	RpO	ct	st
FC		6	10	1	229	96	25.44	0	1									2	
SS		2	2	1	32	20	32.00	0	0									0	
FC	1992	17	29	2	631	102	23.37	1	2									6	
SS	1994	10	10	4	304	73*	50.66	0	2									1	

WALDRON, Earl (Leeward Islands) b All Saints, Antigua 31.8.1966 RHB OB

Cmp	Debut	M	I	NO	Runs	HS	Avge	100	50	Balls	Runs	Wkts	Avge	BB	5i	10m	RpO	ct	st
FC		1	2	0	50	43	25.00	0	0									3	

WALLACE, Philo Alphonso (Barbados, West Indies A to Sri Lanka) b Around-the-town, Barbados 2.8.1970 RHB RM

Cmp	Debut	M	I	NO	Runs	HS	Avge	100	50	Balls	Runs	Wkts	Avge	BB	5i	10m	RpO	ct	st
FC		12	21	0	787	121	37.47	1	5									14	
SS		4	4	0	165	87	41.25	0	1									0	
FC	1989	52	91	1	3438	135	38.20	6	21									33	
Int	1991	12	12	0	217	52	18.08	0	1									3	
SS	1989	31	30	2	790	87	28.21	0	6									3	

WALSH, Courtney Andrew (Jamaica, West Indies, West Indies to Australia) b Kingston, Jamaica 30.10.1962 RHB RF

Cmp	Debut	M	I	NO	Runs	HS	Avge	100	50	Balls	Runs	Wkts	Avge	BB	5i	10m	RpO	ct	st
Test		6	6	1	26	21	5.20	0	0	1118	468	11	42.54	4-73	0	0	2.51	4	
FC		12	15	6	97	25*	10.77	0	0	2192	883	39	22.64	6-39	2	0	2.41	7	
Int		5	2	1	3	3	3.00	0	0	242	130	4	32.50	2-26	0	0	3.22	0	
SS		6	4	0	19	10	4.75	0	0	289	139	6	23.16	3-40	0	0	2.88	1	
Test	1984	93	122	37	769	30*	9.04	0	0	19851	8798	339	25.95	7-37	13	2	2.65	18	
FC	1981	357	452	115	4148	66	12.30	0	8	68868	32593	1465	22.24	9-72	86	16	2.83	98	
Int	1984	176	66	28	291	30	7.65	0	0	9288	5936	196	30.28	5-1	5	1	3.83	26	
SS	1981	39	23	6	127	32*	7.47	0	0	2021	1196	52	23.00	5-27	2	1	3.55	8	

WATT, Balthazar Michael (Windward Islands) b Dominica 12.4.1975 RHB RM

Cmp	Debut	M	I	NO	Runs	HS	Avge	100	50	Balls	Runs	Wkts	Avge	BB	5i	10m	RpO	ct	st
FC		9	18	0	422	64	23.44	0	3	53	27	2	13.50	2-5	0	0	3.05	4	
SS		4	4	2	40	23*	20.00	0	0	58	45	0					4.65	2	

WEEKES, Lesroy Charlesworth (Leeward Islands, Lincolnshire) b Montserrat 19.7.1971 RHB RFM

Cmp	Debut	M	I	NO	Runs	HS	Avge	100	50	Balls	Runs	Wkts	Avge	BB	5i	10m	RpO	ct	st
FC		6	9	2	150	38*	21.42	0	0	809	393	13	30.23	3-46	0	0	2.91	3	
SS		5	3	2	9	4*	9.00	0	0	246	160	4	40.00	3-18	0	0	3.90	0	
FC	1993	22	32	5	453	46	16.77	0	0	3052	1708	60	28.46	5-83	1	0	3.35	17	
SS	1990	13	5	2	19	5	6.33	0	0	558	418	17	24.58	4-33	1	0	4.49	0	

WILLIAMS, David (Trinidad) b San Fernando, Trinidad 4.11.1963 RHB WK LB

Cmp	Debut	M	I	NO	Runs	HS	Avge	100	50	Balls	Runs	Wkts	Avge	BB	5i	10m	RpO	ct	st
FC		9	13	1	360	55	30.00	0	2									20	7
SS		7	6	2	66	18	16.50	0	0									6	7
Test	1991	3	6	0	21	15	3.50	0	0									15	1
FC	1982	105	151	15	2643	112	19.43	2	7	60	42	0					4.20	234	47
Int	1987	29	17	6	119	32*	10.81	0	0									33	8
SS	1984	37	30	9	372	53	17.71	0	1	24	20	0					5.00	29	19

Cmp	Debut	M	I	NO	Runs	HS	Avge	100	50	Balls	Runs	Wkts	Avge	BB	5i	10m	RpO	ct	st

WILLIAMS, Joseph Henderson (Barbados) b Barbados 1.9.1974 RHB RFM

Cmp	Debut	M	I	NO	Runs	HS	Avge	100	50	Balls	Runs	Wkts	Avge	BB	5i	10m	RpO	ct	st
FC		1	1	0	10	10	10.00	0	0	138	57	3	19.00	3-57	0	0	2.47	0	
SS		4	3	0	10	7	3.33	0	0	173	154	4	38.50	3-33	0	0	5.34	1	
FC	1995	2	1	0	10	10	10.00	0	0	138	57	3	19.00	3-57	0	0	2.47	0	

WILLIAMS, Laurie Rohan (Jamaica, West Indies, West Indies A to Sri Lanka) b Jamaica 12.12.1968 RHB RM

Cmp	Debut	M	I	NO	Runs	HS	Avge	100	50	Balls	Runs	Wkts	Avge	BB	5i	10m	RpO	ct	st
FC		10	17	4	331	102*	25.46	1	0	1515	648	33	19.63	6-26	1	0	2.56	7	
Int		1	1	0	14	14	14.00	0	0	48	56	3	18.66	3-56	0	0	7.00	1	
SS		6	6	1	76	35*	15.20	0	0	204	176	6	29.33	3-55	0	0	5.17	1	
FC	1989	25	42	7	783	102*	22.37	1	4	3967	1758	81	21.70	6-26	4	0	2.65	15	
Int	1995	5	3	0	20	14	6.66	0	0	155	141	8	17.62	3-16	0	0	5.45	3	
SS	1992	17	15	2	208	36	16.00	0	0	804	585	23	25.43	5-46	0	1	4.36	1	

WILLIAMS, Stuart Clayton (Leeward Islands, West Indies, West Indies A to Sri Lanka) b Government Road, Nevis 12.8.1969 RHB

Cmp	Debut	M	I	NO	Runs	HS	Avge	100	50	Balls	Runs	Wkts	Avge	BB	5i	10m	RpO	ct	st
Test		7	12	0	413	128	34.41	1	1	18	19	0					6.33	5	
FC		16	26	1	964	141	38.56	4	2	132	55	1	55.00	1-25	0	0	2.50	16	
Int		5	5	1	261	90	65.25	0	3									2	
SS		6	6	1	163	50	32.60	0	1	60	62	2	31.00	2-62	0	0	6.20	5	
Test	1993	19	31	2	799	128	27.55	1	2	18	19	0					6.33	19	
FC	1988	83	138	7	4814	170	36.74	13	16	180	85	1	85.00	1-25	0	0	2.83	69	
Int	1994	33	33	3	999	90	33.30	0	8									7	
SS	1988	30	30	1	951	105	36.57	1	7	60	62	2	31.00	2-62	0	0	6.20	13	

WONG, Kenneth Arthur (Guyana) b Guyana 22.5.1973 RHB WK

Cmp	Debut	M	I	NO	Runs	HS	Avge	100	50	Balls	Runs	Wkts	Avge	BB	5i	10m	RpO	ct	st
FC		1	2	0	15	14	7.50	0	0									1	
SS		7	1	0	0	0	0.00	0	0									3	3
FC	1992	22	31	4	237	25	8.77	0	0									39	7
SS	1993	16	4	1	10	8	3.33	0	0									4	6

BERMUDA IN WEST INDIES 1996-97

BLADES, Roger W. b Barbados 25.5.1963 RHB

Cmp	Debut	M	I	NO	Runs	HS	Avge	100	50	Balls	Runs	Wkts	Avge	BB	5i	10m	RpO	ct	st
SS		4	4	0	24	15	6.00	0	0	126	79	4	19.75	4-30	1	0	3.76	0	

BRATHWAITE, B.A.

SS		4	4	3	11	10	11.00	0	0	102	103	2	51.50	1-16	0	0	6.05	1	

DOUGLAS, Allan Craig b Somersall Road, Bermuda 17.2.1958 RHB WK

SS		2	2	0	12	8	6.00	0	0									0	1

FOX, Kameron Shaun b St Davids, Bermuda 16.11.1977 RHB SLA

SS		4	2	1	1	1*	1.00	0	0	108	114	0					6.33	0	

MANDERS, Willard Arnold E. b Bermuda 26.4.1959 RHB OB

SS		6	6	1	45	23	9.00	0	0	293	224	3	74.66	2-34	0	0	4.58	0	

MARSHALL, Charles MacDonald b Baileys Bay, Bermuda 10.5.1961 LHB LM

SS		6	6	0	194	86	32.33	0	1	224	155	7	22.14	3-46	0	0	4.15	0	

MINORS, Dean Anthony b Hamilton, Bermuda 6.1.1970 LHB WK

SS		6	6	0	110	36	18.33	0	0									2	

PERINCHIEF, Bruce Dwayne b Paget, Bermuda 27.11.1960 RHB LBG

SS		3	3	3	11	8*		0	0	120	92	0					4.60	0	

RICHARDSON, Jeff A. RHB

SS		4	3	0	39	29	13.00	0	0									1	

SMITH, Clay James b Bermuda 15.1.1971 RHB OB

SS		6	6	0	151	69	25.16	0	2	259	176	4	44.00	2-31	0	0	4.07	1	

SMITH, Glen Shane b Baileys Bay 22.1.1973 LHB

SS		1	1	0	54	54	54.00	0	1									0	

STEEDE, Albert B. b Bermuda 17.5.1968 RHB

SS		6	6	0	124	47	20.66	0	0									3	

TROTT, Roger Lee b Paget, Bermuda 25.6.1963 RHB WK

SS		5	5	0	52	27	10.40	0	0									2	

TUCKER, Janeiro J. b Bermuda 15.3.1975 RHB RM

SS		6	6	1	82	43	16.40	0	0	239	189	2	94.50	1-23	0	0	4.74	2	

WADE, Clevie P. RHB RM

SS		3	2	2	29	25*		0	0	48	54	0					6.75	0	

Cmp	Debut	M	I	NO	Runs	HS	Avge	100	50	Balls	Runs	Wkts	Avge	BB	5i	10m	RpO	ct	st

CANADA IN WEST INDIES 1996-97

BHANSINGH, Latchman b Guyana 26.11.1966 LHB SLA

Cmp	Debut	M	I	NO	Runs	HS	Avge	100	50	Balls	Runs	Wkts	Avge	BB	5i	10m	RpO	ct	st
SS		6	5	1	89	45	22.25	0	0	14	20	0					8.57	0	
FC	1985	2	4	0	36	18	9.00	0	0	30	25	0					5.00	2	

ETWAROO, Derick b Guyana 6.1.1964 OB

Cmp	Debut	M	I	NO	Runs	HS	Avge	100	50	Balls	Runs	Wkts	Avge	BB	5i	10m	RpO	ct	st
SS		3	1	1	7	7*		0	0	96	73	1	73.00	1-43	0	0	4.56	0	

GARDNER, T.

Cmp	Debut	M	I	NO	Runs	HS	Avge	100	50	Balls	Runs	Wkts	Avge	BB	5i	10m	RpO	ct	st
SS		4	2	0	32	21	8.00	0	0	156	118	4	29.50	2-42	0	0	4.53	0	

GLEGG, Alex b Zimbabwe 9.8.1971 WK

Cmp	Debut	M	I	NO	Runs	HS	Avge	100	50	Balls	Runs	Wkts	Avge	BB	5i	10m	RpO	ct	st
SS		4	4	0	85	37	21.25	0	0									2	

JOSEPH, Davis b Grenada 31.7.1963 RMF

Cmp	Debut	M	I	NO	Runs	HS	Avge	100	50	Balls	Runs	Wkts	Avge	BB	5i	10m	RpO	ct	st
SS		6	2	0	2	2	1.00	0	0	282	248	3	82.66	1-33	0	0	5.27	1	

KISSOON, D.

Cmp	Debut	M	I	NO	Runs	HS	Avge	100	50	Balls	Runs	Wkts	Avge	BB	5i	10m	RpO	ct	st
SS		5	2	2	16	14*		0	0	146	123	1	123.00	1-27	0	0	5.05	0	

LIBURD, Ingleton b Trinidad 27.4.1961 LHB RM

Cmp	Debut	M	I	NO	Runs	HS	Avge	100	50	Balls	Runs	Wkts	Avge	BB	5i	10m	RpO	ct	st
SS		6	5	0	149	78	29.80	0	2	78	78	1	78.00	1-40	0	0	6.00	2	

MAXWELL, Don b Barbados 23.2.1971

Cmp	Debut	M	I	NO	Runs	HS	Avge	100	50	Balls	Runs	Wkts	Avge	BB	5i	10m	RpO	ct	st
SS		6	4	0	47	30	11.75	0	0	168	164	6	27.33	2-41	0	0	5.85	0	

PRASHAD, M.

Cmp	Debut	M	I	NO	Runs	HS	Avge	100	50	Balls	Runs	Wkts	Avge	BB	5i	10m	RpO	ct	st
SS		2	2	2	10	9*		0	0	12	11	0					5.50	0	

PRASHAD, Paul

Cmp	Debut	M	I	NO	Runs	HS	Avge	100	50	Balls	Runs	Wkts	Avge	BB	5i	10m	RpO	ct	st
SS		6	4	0	70	48	17.50	0	0	48	60	1	60.00	1-46	0	0	7.50	0	

RAJADURAI, Brian Eric Anton b Colombo, Ceylon 24.8.1965 RHB LBG

Cmp	Debut	M	I	NO	Runs	HS	Avge	100	50	Balls	Runs	Wkts	Avge	BB	5i	10m	RpO	ct	st
SS		5	5	1	30	15	7.50	0	0	163	111	5	22.20	4-20	1	0	4.08	5	
FC	1988	31	31	7	381	65	15.87	0	1	2884	1234	56	22.03	5-53	3	0	2.75	25	

RANA, Sukhjinder b Punjab, India 17.2 1969 LM

Cmp	Debut	M	I	NO	Runs	HS	Avge	100	50	Balls	Runs	Wkts	Avge	BB	5i	10m	RpO	ct	st
SS		4	1	0	9	9	9.00	0	0	150	130	3	43.33	2-23	0	0	5.20	1	

SEEBARAN, Barry b Vancouver, Canada 12.9.1972 SLA

Cmp	Debut	M	I	NO	Runs	HS	Avge	100	50	Balls	Runs	Wkts	Avge	BB	5i	10m	RpO	ct	st
SS		4	1	0	10	10	10.00	0	0	124	79	1	79.00	1-23	0	0	3.82	2	

SEERAM, Shivnauth b Guyana 25.9.1963 RM WK

Cmp	Debut	M	I	NO	Runs	HS	Avge	100	50	Balls	Runs	Wkts	Avge	BB	5i	10m	RpO	ct	st
SS		5	2	0	12	12	6.00	0	0									3	
FC	1985	1	2	0	12	12	6.00	0	0									1	

FREE STATE IN WEST INDIES 1996-97

BAKKES, H.C.

Cmp	Debut	M	I	NO	Runs	HS	Avge	100	50	Balls	Runs	Wkts	Avge	BB	5i	10m	RpO	ct	st
FC		1	1	0	4	4	4.00	0	0	168	66	2	33.00	2-9	0	0	2.35	0	

BOTHA, H.

Cmp	Debut	M	I	NO	Runs	HS	Avge	100	50	Balls	Runs	Wkts	Avge	BB	5i	10m	RpO	ct	st
FC		1	1	1	0	0*		0	0	162	88	2	44.00	1-42	0	0	3.25	1	

CRAVEN, C.F.

Cmp	Debut	M	I	NO	Runs	HS	Avge	100	50	Balls	Runs	Wkts	Avge	BB	5i	10m	RpO	ct	st
FC		1	1	0	25	25	25.00	0	0	48	37	0					4.62	0	

CRONJE, S.G.

Cmp	Debut	M	I	NO	Runs	HS	Avge	100	50	Balls	Runs	Wkts	Avge	BB	5i	10m	RpO	ct	st
FC		1	1	0	0	0	0.00	0	0	222	105	7	15.00	5-43	1	0	2.83	0	

DIPPENAAR, H.H.

Cmp	Debut	M	I	NO	Runs	HS	Avge	100	50	Balls	Runs	Wkts	Avge	BB	5i	10m	RpO	ct	st
FC		1	1	0	111	111	111.00	1	0									2	

JORDAAN, D.

Cmp	Debut	M	I	NO	Runs	HS	Avge	100	50	Balls	Runs	Wkts	Avge	BB	5i	10m	RpO	ct	st
FC		1	1	0	4	4	4.00	0	0									2	

LIEBENBERG, G.F.J.

Cmp	Debut	M	I	NO	Runs	HS	Avge	100	50	Balls	Runs	Wkts	Avge	BB	5i	10m	RpO	ct	st
FC		1	1	0	131	131	131.00	1	0									0	

PRETORIUS, N.W.

Cmp	Debut	M	I	NO	Runs	HS	Avge	100	50	Balls	Runs	Wkts	Avge	BB	5i	10m	RpO	ct	st
FC		1	1	0	0	0	0.00	0	0	144	111	2	55.50	1-39	0	0	4.62	1	

RADLEY, P.J.L.

Cmp	Debut	M	I	NO	Runs	HS	Avge	100	50	Balls	Runs	Wkts	Avge	BB	5i	10m	RpO	ct	st
FC		1	1	0	14	14	14.00	0	0									1	1

VAN DER MERWE, C.C.

Cmp	Debut	M	I	NO	Runs	HS	Avge	100	50	Balls	Runs	Wkts	Avge	BB	5i	10m	RpO	ct	st
FC		1	1	0	0	0	0.00	0	0	6	9	0					9.00	1	

VENTER, J.F.

Cmp	Debut	M	I	NO	Runs	HS	Avge	100	50	Balls	Runs	Wkts	Avge	BB	5i	10m	RpO	ct	st
FC		1	1	0	11	11	11.00	0	0	198	89	1	89.00	1-89	0	0	2.69	1	

INDIA IN WEST INDIES 1996-97

AZHARUDDIN, M.

Cmp Debut	M	I	NO	Runs	HS	Avge	100	50	Balls	Runs	Wkts	Avge	BB	5i	10m	RpO	ct	st
Test	5	5	0	63	31	12.60	0	0									9	
FC	7	7	0	121	57	17.28	0	1									12	
Int	4	3	0	67	40	22.33	0	0									0	

DAVID, N.A.

	M	I	NO	Runs	HS	Avge	100	50	Balls	Runs	Wkts	Avge	BB	5i	10m	RpO	ct	st
FC	2	3	0	14	5	4.66	0	0	390	166	5	33.20	2-40	0	0	2.55	0	
Int	3	2	2	9	8*		0	0	144	97	4	24.25	3-21	0	0	4.04	0	

DRAVID, R.S.

	M	I	NO	Runs	HS	Avge	100	50	Balls	Runs	Wkts	Avge	BB	5i	10m	RpO	ct	st
Test	5	7	2	360	92	72.00	0	4									5	
FC	7	10	2	468	92	58.50	0	5	54	28	0					3.11	5	
Int	4	3	0	121	74	40.33	0	1									1	

GANESH, D.

	M	I	NO	Runs	HS	Avge	100	50	Balls	Runs	Wkts	Avge	BB	5i	10m	RpO	ct	st
Test	2	3	1	21	8	10.50	0	0	204	122	4	30.50	2-28	0	0	3.58	0	
FC	4	5	1	26	8	6.50	0	0	540	298	10	29.80	3-25	0	0	3.31	1	

GANGULY, S.C.

	M	I	NO	Runs	HS	Avge	100	50	Balls	Runs	Wkts	Avge	BB	5i	10m	RpO	ct	st
Test	4	4	0	78	42	19.50	0	0	120	59	1	59.00	1-3	0	0	2.95	2	
FC	7	9	2	414	90	59.14	0	4	228	144	2	72.00	1-3	0	0	3.78	3	
Int	3	3	1	122	79	61.00	0	1	72	51	0					4.25	1	

JADEJA, A.D.

	M	I	NO	Runs	HS	Avge	100	50	Balls	Runs	Wkts	Avge	BB	5i	10m	RpO	ct	st
Test	2	2	0	104	96	52.00	0	1									0	
FC	4	5	0	292	106	58.40	1	2	6	0	0					0.00	0	
Int	4	3	0	96	68	32.00	0	1	16	6	0					2.25	0	

JOSHI, S.B.

	M	I	NO	Runs	HS	Avge	100	50	Balls	Runs	Wkts	Avge	BB	5i	10m	RpO	ct	st
Test	4	4	1	84	43	28.00	0	0	721	331	11	30.09	3-57	0	0	2.75	1	
FC	7	7	1	97	43	16.16	0	0	1391	688	24	28.66	5-98	1	0	2.96	2	
Int	1	1	0	8	8	8.00	0	0	24	19	0					4.75	0	

KARIM, S.S.

	M	I	NO	Runs	HS	Avge	100	50	Balls	Runs	Wkts	Avge	BB	5i	10m	RpO	ct	st
FC	2	4	2	39	17*	19.50	0	0									2	1
Int	3	2	0	20	14	10.00	0	0									4	1

KUMBLE, A.

	M	I	NO	Runs	HS	Avge	100	50	Balls	Runs	Wkts	Avge	BB	5i	10m	RpO	ct	st
Test	5	5	2	58	23*	19.33	0	0	1204	576	19	30.31	5-104	2	0	2.87	2	
FC	6	6	2	67	23*	16.75	0	0	1468	663	21	31.57	5-104	2	0	2.70	2	
Int	4	3	1	21	13	10.50	0	0	197	124	4	31.00	2-22	0	0	3.77	2	

KURUVILLA, A.

	M	I	NO	Runs	HS	Avge	100	50	Balls	Runs	Wkts	Avge	BB	5i	10m	RpO	ct	st
Test	5	5	0	16	9	3.20	0	0	1032	480	13	36.92	5-68	1	0	2.79	0	
FC	8	8	1	30	11	4.28	0	0	1488	753	17	44.29	5-68	1	0	3.03	4	
Int	4	2	1	3	3*	3.00	0	0	185	99	4	24.75	3-23	0	0	3.21	1	

LAXMAN, V.V.S.

	M	I	NO	Runs	HS	Avge	100	50	Balls	Runs	Wkts	Avge	BB	5i	10m	RpO	ct	st
Test	4	6	0	172	64	28.66	0	2	90	49	0					3.26	4	
FC	7	11	0	365	98	33.18	0	3	289	136	2	68.00	2-66	0	0	2.82	8	

MONGIA, N.R.

	M	I	NO	Runs	HS	Avge	100	50	Balls	Runs	Wkts	Avge	BB	5i	10m	RpO	ct	st
Test	5	5	0	140	78	28.00	0	1									13	
FC	6	6	0	157	78	26.16	0	1									13	
Int	1	1	0	29	29	29.00	0	0									0	

SIDHU, N.S.

	M	I	NO	Runs	HS	Avge	100	50	Balls	Runs	Wkts	Avge	BB	5i	10m	RpO	ct	st
Test	4	6	0	276	201	46.00	1	0									1	
FC	7	11	1	426	201	42.60	2	0									3	
Int	2	1	0	5	5	5.00	0	0									1	

SINGH, R.R.

	M	I	NO	Runs	HS	Avge	100	50	Balls	Runs	Wkts	Avge	BB	5i	10m	RpO	ct	st
FC	2	4	1	73	53	24.33	0	1	150	97	0					3.88	0	
Int	3	3	0	35	29	11.66	0	0	84	78	1	78.00	1-46	0	0	5.57	1	

TENDULKAR, S.R.

	M	I	NO	Runs	HS	Avge	100	50	Balls	Runs	Wkts	Avge	BB	5i	10m	RpO	ct	st
Test	5	6	1	289	92	57.80	0	3	12	9	0					4.50	5	
FC	6	7	1	295	92	49.16	0	3	68	46	0					4.05	5	
Int	4	4	1	119	65*	39.66	0	1	72	50	1	50.00	1-13	0	0	4.16	0	

VENKATESH PRASAD, B.K.

	M	I	NO	Runs	HS	Avge	100	50	Balls	Runs	Wkts	Avge	BB	5i	10m	RpO	ct	st
Test	5	5	2	10	10*	3.33	0	0	1018	465	11	42.27	5-82	1	0	2.74	2	
FC	6	6	2	11	10*	2.75	0	0	1168	529	13	40.69	5-82	1	0	2.71	2	
Int	4	2	0	5	5	2.50	0	0	204	155	5	31.00	2-22	0	0	4.55	2	

SRI LANKA IN WEST INDIES 1996-97

ARNOLD, R.P.

	Cmp	Debut	M	I	NO	Runs	HS	Avge	100	50	Balls	Runs	Wkts	Avge	BB	5i	10m	RpO	ct	st
Test			1	2	0	12	12	6.00	0	0									1	
FC			2	4	0	184	158	46.00	1	0									1	

ATAPATTU, M.S.

			M	I	NO	Runs	HS	Avge	100	50	Balls	Runs	Wkts	Avge	BB	5i	10m	RpO	ct	st
Test			1	2	0	17	10	8.50	0	0									2	
FC			2	4	0	146	118	36.50	1	0									3	
Int			1	1	0	1	1	1.00	0	0									1	

DE SILVA, K.S.C.

			M	I	NO	Runs	HS	Avge	100	50	Balls	Runs	Wkts	Avge	BB	5i	10m	RpO	ct	st
Test			2	4	3	13	6	13.00	0	0	312	199	3	66.33	1-46	0	0	3.82	1	
FC			2	4	3	13	6	13.00	0	0	312	199	3	66.33	1-46	0	0	3.82	1	
Int			1								42	58	1	58.00	1-58	0	0	8.28	0	

DE SILVA, P.A.

			M	I	NO	Runs	HS	Avge	100	50	Balls	Runs	Wkts	Avge	BB	5i	10m	RpO	ct	st
Test			2	4	0	160	78	40.00	0	1									0	
FC			3	6	0	246	80	41.00	0	2									0	
Int			1	1	0	7	7	7.00	0	0	18	20	1	20.00	1-20	0	0	6.66	0	

DHARMASENA, H.D.P.K.

			M	I	NO	Runs	HS	Avge	100	50	Balls	Runs	Wkts	Avge	BB	5i	10m	RpO	ct	st
Test			2	4	0	77	31	19.25	0	0	282	128	5	25.60	2-62	0	0	2.72	1	
FC			3	5	1	85	31	21.25	0	0	362	174	7	24.85	2-37	0	0	2.88	2	
Int			1	1	1	51	51*		0	1	60	41	0					4.10	2	

JAYASURIYA, S.T.

			M	I	NO	Runs	HS	Avge	100	50	Balls	Runs	Wkts	Avge	BB	5i	10m	RpO	ct	st
Test			2	4	0	192	90	48.00	0	2	30	25	0					5.00	3	
FC			2	4	0	192	90	48.00	0	2	30	25	0					5.00	3	
Int			1	1	0	44	44	44.00	0	0	60	58	5	11.60	5-58	0	1	5.80	0	

KALUWITHARANA, R.S.

			M	I	NO	Runs	HS	Avge	100	50	Balls	Runs	Wkts	Avge	BB	5i	10m	RpO	ct	st
Test			2	4	0	48	23	12.00	0	0									6	
FC			3	5	0	76	28	15.20	0	0									7	2
Int			1	1	0	9	9	9.00	0	0									1	

LIYANAGE, D.K.

			M	I	NO	Runs	HS	Avge	100	50	Balls	Runs	Wkts	Avge	BB	5i	10m	RpO	ct	st
FC			1								84	77	2	38.50	2-44	0	0	5.50	0	
Int			1	1	0	43	43	43.00	0	0	54	36	0					4.00	2	

MAHANAMA, R.S.

			M	I	NO	Runs	HS	Avge	100	50	Balls	Runs	Wkts	Avge	BB	5i	10m	RpO	ct	st
Test			2	4	0	72	29	18.00	0	0									2	
FC			3	6	0	150	65	25.00	0	1									2	
Int			1	1	0	14	14	14.00	0	0									0	

MURALITHARAN, M.

			M	I	NO	Runs	HS	Avge	100	50	Balls	Runs	Wkts	Avge	BB	5i	10m	RpO	ct	st
Test			2	4	1	10	6*	3.33	0	0	588	247	16	15.43	5-34	2	0	2.52	1	
FC			3	4	1	10	6*	3.33	0	0	726	315	20	15.75	5-34	2	0	2.60	2	
Int			1	1	1	5	5*		0	0	60	58	0					5.80	1	

PUSHPAKUMARA, K.R.

			M	I	NO	Runs	HS	Avge	100	50	Balls	Runs	Wkts	Avge	BB	5i	10m	RpO	ct	st
Test			2	3	0	9	8	3.00	0	0	328	222	10	22.20	5-41	1	0	4.06	0	
FC			3	3	0	9	8	3.00	0	0	430	290	12	24.16	5-41	1	0	4.04	0	

RANATUNGA, A.

			M	I	NO	Runs	HS	Avge	100	50	Balls	Runs	Wkts	Avge	BB	5i	10m	RpO	ct	st
Test			2	4	1	140	72*	46.66	0	1									0	
FC			3	5	1	175	72*	43.75	0	1									0	
Int			1	1	0	53	53	53.00	0	1									0	

RANATUNGA, S.

			M	I	NO	Runs	HS	Avge	100	50	Balls	Runs	Wkts	Avge	BB	5i	10m	RpO	ct	st
Test			1	2	0	9	9	4.50	0	0									0	
FC			1	2	0	9	9	4.50	0	0									0	

TILLAKARATNE, H.P.

			M	I	NO	Runs	HS	Avge	100	50	Balls	Runs	Wkts	Avge	BB	5i	10m	RpO	ct	st
Test			1	1	1	1	1*		0	0									0	
FC			2	3	3	43	23*		0	0	6	8	0					8.00	1	
Int			1	1	0	2	2	2.00	0	0									0	

The following current cricketers have played in West Indian Domestic limited overs cricket but did not appear in West Indian Domestic cricket in 1996-97:

BAPTISTE, E.A.E. (see South Africa) (Leeward Islands)

	Cmp	Debut	M	I	NO	Runs	HS	Avge	100	50	Balls	Runs	Wkts	Avge	BB	5i	10m	RpO	ct	st
	SS	1981	19	11	2	102	32	11.33	0	0	903	657	27	24.33	5-45	0	1	4.36	6	

LAVINE, M.J. (see South Africa) (Barbados)

	Cmp	Debut	M	I	NO	Runs	HS	Avge	100	50	Balls	Runs	Wkts	Avge	BB	5i	10m	RpO	ct	st
	SS	1992	3	2	0	64	53	32.00	0	1	147	114	5	22.80	2-22	0	0	4.65	0	

Cmp	Debut	M	I	NO	Runs	HS	Avge	100	50	Balls	Runs	Wkts	Avge	BB	5i	10m	RpO	ct	st
LYNCH, M.A. (see Gloucestershire) (Guyana)																			
SS	1982	3	3	0	169	129	56.33	1	0	72	47	5	9.40	3-41	0	0	3.91	0	
RICHARDSON, R.B. (see South Africa) (Leeward Islands)																			
SS	1981	28	27	0	648	84	24.00	0	4	30	39	1	39.00	1-25	0	0	7.80	7	
STEPHENSON, F.D. (see South Africa) (Barbados)																			
SS	1982	6	4	0	43	21	10.75	0	0	274	199	14	14.21	5-26	0	2	4.35	2	
WALSH, V.A. (see South Africa) (Leeward Islands)																			
SS	1991	7	4	3	6	2*	6.00	0	0	328	224	9	2.48	3-22	0	0	4.09	1	
WILLIAMS, N.F. (see Essex) (Windward Islands)																			
SS	1982	7	6	4	129	38	64.50	0	0	318	286	13	22.00	5-60	0	1	5.39	1	

ZIMBABWE

First First-Class Match: Rhodesia v H.D.G.Leveson-Gower's XI (Bulawayo) 1909-10. Rhodesia had previously played one first-class match in the 1904-05 Currie Cup at Johannesburg.

First First-Class Tour to England: 1982 (formerly Rhodesian players were part of the South African touring teams)

First Test Match: Zimbabwe v India (Harare) 1992-93

Present First-Class Teams: Mashonaland, Matabeleland. No domestic matches were considered first-class until 1993-94.

Logan Cup Champions 1996-97: Mashonaland

FIRST-CLASS RECORDS

Highest Team Total: 600-6d Sri Lankans v Mashonaland Country Districts (Harare) 1994-95
Highest in 1996-97: 503-4d Mashonaland v Matabeleland (Harare); 477-6d Mashonaland v Matabeleland (Bulawayo); 448 Matabeleland v Mashonaland (Harare); 406 England v Zimbabwe (Bulawayo); 376 Zimbabwe v England (Bulawayo)

Lowest Team Total: 56 Zimbabwe v Leicestershire (Salisbury) 1980-81
Lowest in 1996-97: 110 England v Mashonaland (Harare); 118 Matabeleland v Mashonaland (Bulawayo); 145 Worcestershire v Matabeleland (Bulawayo); 156 England v Zimbabwe (Harare); 180 England v Mashomaland (Harare)

Highest Individual Innings: 266 D.L.Houghton Zimbabwe v Sri Lanka (Bulawayo) 1994-95
Highest in 1996-97: 243* G.W.Flower Mashonaland v Matabeleland (Harare); 159 G.J.Whittall Matabeleland v Mashonaland (Harare); 131 S.V.Carlisle Mashonaland v Matabeleland (Bulawayo); 114 N.V.Knight England v Matabeleland (Bulawayo); 113 N.Hussain England v Zimbabwe (Bulawayo)

Most Runs in Season: 983 (av 57.82) G.W.Flower (Mashonaland Under 24) 1994-95
Most in 1996-97: 477 (av 53.00) G.W.Flower (Mashonaland); 370 (av 61.66) A.D.R.Campbell (Mashonaland); 328 (av 65.60) J.P.Crawley (England); 328 (av 41.00) N.V.Knight (England); 324 (av 46.28) A.J.Stewart (England)

Most Runs in Career: 27,453 (av 39.96) B.F.Davison (Rhodesia, Leicestershire, Gloucestershire, Tasmania) 1967-68 to 1987-88
Most by Current Batsman: 7,317 (av 39.76) D.L.Houghton (Mashonaland) 1978-79 to date; 4,501 (av 42.06) G.W.Flower (Mashonaland) 1986-87 to date; 3,912 (av 46.57) A.Flower (Mashonaland) 1989-90 to date; 3,168 (av 33.00) A.D.R.Campbell (Mashonaland) 1990-91 to date; 2,327 (av 27.37) G.J.Whittall (Matabaleland) 1990-91 to date

Best Innings Analysis: 9-71 M.J.Procter Rhodesia v Transvaal (Bulawayo) 1972-73
Best in 1996-97: 6-64 D.Gough England v Matabeleland (Bulawayo); 5-45 P.A.Strang Mashonaland v Matabeleland (Bulawayo); 5-50 B.C.Strang Mashonaland v Matabeleland (Bulawayo); 5-53 R.J.Kirtley Mashonaland v England (Harare); 5-56 R.J.Kirtley Mashonaland v Matabeleland (Bulawayo)

Most Wickets in Season: 53 (av 13.98) J.T.Partridge (Rhodesia) 1961-62
Most in 1996-97: 36 (av 25.16) P.A.Strang (Mashonaland); 19 (av 19.31) D.Gough (England); 17 (av 27.93) H.H.Streak (Matabeleland); 16 (av 21.81) R.D.B.Croft (England); 15 (av 30.53) H.K.Olonga (Matabeleland)

Most Wickets in Career: 1,417 (av 19.53) M.J.Procter (Rhodesia, Natal, Western Province, Orange Free State, Gloucestershire) 1965 to 1988-89
Most by Current Bowler: 200 (av 32.00) P.A.Strang (Mashonaland, Kent) 1992-93 to date; 178 (av 27.09) H.H.Streak (Matabeleland, Hampshire) 1992-93 to date; 151 (av 31.02) E.A.Brandes (Mashonaland) 1985 to date; 134 (av 23.64) B.C.Strang (Mashonaland) 1994-95 to date; 88 (av 32.50) G.J.Whittall (Matabeleland) 1990-91 to date

Record Wicket Partnerships

1st	261	D.J.McGlew & T.L.Goddard	Natal v Rhodesia (Bulawayo)	1958-59
2nd	317*	R.G.Twose & Asif Din	Warwickshire v Mashonaland XI (Harare)	1993-94
3rd	299	S.Ranatunga & P.A.de Silva	Sri Lanka v Mashonaland Country Dists (Harare)	
				1994-95
4th	301	T.E.Bailey & P.B.H.May	MCC v Rhodesia (Salisbury)	1956-57
5th	233*	G.W.Flower & G.J.Whittall	Zimbabwe v Pakistan (Harare)	1994-95
6th	217*	H.P.Tillakaratne & A.G.D.Wickremasinghe		
			Sri Lanka B v Zimbabwe (Harare)	1987-88

7th	193	A.Flower & D.H.Brain	Mashonaland v Matabeleland (Harare)	1994-95
8th	175	I.P.Butchart & P.A.Strang	Mashonaland Country v Matabeleland (Harare)	
				1994-95
9th	268	J.B.Commins & N.Boje	South Africa A v Mashonaland (Harare)	1994-95
10th	81	M.Prabhakar & R.R.Kulkarni	Young Indians v Zimbabwe (Harare)	1983-84

Highest Partnerships in 1996-97

1st	231	G.W.Flower & S.V.Carlisle	Mashonaland v Matabeleland (Harare)
2nd	233	G.W.Flower & A.C.Waller	Mashonaland v Matabeleland (Harare)
3rd	184	S.V.Carlisle & C.B.Wishart	Mashonaland v Matabeleland (Bulawayo)
4th	116	D.L.Houghton & C.B.Wishart	Mashonaland v England (Harare)
5th	148	N.Hussain & J.P.Crawley	England v Zimbabwe (Bulawayo)
6th	66	M.H.Dekker & M.Ranchod	Matabeleland v Mashonaland (Bulawayo)
7th	161*	A.Flower & P.A.Strang	Mashonaland v Matabeleland (Bulawayo)
8th	24	A.D.R.Campbell & E.R.Marillier	Mashonaland v Western Province (Harare)
9th	49	M.Ranchod & H.K.Olonga	Matabeleland v Mashonaland (Bulawayo)
10th	52	R.D.B.Croft & P.C.R.Tufnell	England v Mashonaland (Harare)

Most Wicketkeeping Dismissals in Innings: 9 (7ct 2st) W.R.James Matabeleland v Mashonaland Country Districts (Bulawayo) 1995-96
Most in 1996-97: 4 (4ct) D.J.R.Campbell Mashonaland v England (Harare); 4 (4ct) W.R.James Matabeleland v England (Bulawayo); 4 (4ct) P.Kirsten Western Province v Mashonaland (Harare); 4 (3ct 1st) S.J.Rhodes Worcestershire v Matabeleland (Bulawayo)

Most Wicketkeeping Dismissals in Match: 13 (11ct 2st) W.R.James Matabeleland v Mashonaland Country Districts (Bulawayo) 1995-96
Most in 1996-97: 7 (7ct) D.J.R.Campbell Mashonaland v England (Harare); 7 (7ct) P.Kirsten Western Province v Mashonaland (Harare)

Most Wicketkeeping Dismissals in Season: 27 (26ct 1st) W.R.James (Matabeleland) 1994-95; 27 (25ct 2st) W.R.James (Matabeleland) 1995-96
Most in 1996-97: 10 (10ct) D.J.R.Campbell (Mashonaland); 10 (10ct) A.Flower (Mashonaland); 10 (9ct 1st) W.R.James (Matabeleland); 8 (8ct) A.J.Stewart (England); 7 (7ct) P.Kirsten (Western Province)

Most Wicketkeeping Dismissals in Career: 179 (163ct 16st) D.L.Houghton (Mashonaland) 1978-79 to date
Most by Current Wicketkeeper: 121 (111ct 10st) A.Flower (Mashonaland) 1986-87 to date; 108 (101ct 7st) W.R.James (Matabeleland) 1986-87 to date; 83 (76ct 7st) D.J.R.Campbell (Mashonaland) 1992-93 to date

Most Catches by Fielder in Innings: 4 S.J.Bezuidenhout Eastern Province v Rhodesia (Bulawayo) 1972-73; G.R.J.Roope International Wanderers v Rhodesia (Bulawayo) 1975-76; 4 E.J.Barlow Western Province v Rhodesia (Bulawayo) 1976-77; 4 I.P.Butchart President's XI v Young West Indies (Harare) 1986-87; 4 A.J.Traicos Zimbabwe v Lancashire (Harare) 1988-89; 4 M.H.Dekker Zimbabwe v Sri Lanka (Harare) 1994-95
Most in 1996-97: 3 A.D.R.Campbell Mashonaland v Matabeleland (Bulawayo); 3 P.C.R.Tufnell England v Matabeleland (Bulawayo); 3 A.R.Whittall Matabeleland v Worcestershire (Bulawayo); 3 and 3 G.J.Whittall Matabeleland v England (Bulawayo))

Most Catches by Fielder in Match: 7 I.P.Butchart President's XI v Young West Indies (Harare) 1986-87
Most in 1996-97: 6 G.J.Whittall Matabeleland v England (Bulawayo); 5 A.D.R.Campbell Mashonaland v Matabeleland (Bulawayo)

Most Catches by Fielder in Season: 16 G.W.Flower (Mashonaland Under 24) 1994-95
Most in 1996-97: 15 A.D.R.Campbell (Mashonaland); 11 J.P.Crawley (England); 10 G.W.Flower (Mashonaland); 8 G.J.Whittall (Matabeleland)

Most Catches by Fielder in Career: 338 B.F.Davison (Rhodesia, Leicestershire, Gloucestershire, Tasmania) 1967-68 to 1987-88
Most by Current Fielder: 57 G.W.Flower (Mashonaland) 1989-90 to date; 51 A.D.R.Campbell (Mashonaland) 1990-91 to date; 50 P.A.Strang (Mashonaland, Kent) 1992-93 to date; 41 M.H.Dekker (Matabeleland) 1990-91 to date; 34 C.B.Wishart (Mashonaland) 1992-93 to date

CHAMPION TEAMS

Logan Cup

| 1993-94 | Mashonaland Under 24 | 1995-96 | Matabeleland |
| 1994-95 | Mashonaland | 1996-97 | Mashonaland |

1996-97 AND CAREER RECORDS FOR ZIMBABWE PLAYERS

Cmp	Debut	M	I	NO	Runs	HS	Avge	100	50	Balls	Runs	Wkts	Avge	BB	5i	10m	RpO	ct	st
ABRAMS, Mark Desmond (Matabeleland) b Gatooma 26.4.1972 RHB RM																			
FC		5	9	0	134	45	14.88	0	0									2	
FC	1993	20	33	1	582	71	18.18	0	4	150	126	0					5.04	12	
BRANDES, Eddo Andre (Mashonaland, Zimbabwe, Zimbabwe to Sharjah, Zimbabwe to Sri Lanka, Zimbabwe to South Africa, Mashonaland to South Africa) b Port Shepstone, South Africa 5.3.1963 RHB RFM																			
Test		1	1	0	9	9	9.00	0	0	222	80	0					2.16	0	
FC		2	1	0	9	9	9.00	0	0	438	187	4	46.75	4-107	0	0	2.56	0	
Int		4	2	1	8	8*	8.00	0	0	192	115	9	12.77	5-28	0	1	3.59	0	
Test	1992	9	13	2	111	39	10.09	0	0	1870	886	22	40.27	3-45	0	0	2.84	4	
FC	1985	52	74	12	1040	165*	16.77	1	2	8557	4685	151	31.02	7-38	7	1	3.28	25	
Int	1987	44	31	8	245	55	10.65	0	1	2190	1755	59	29.74	5-28	1	2	4.80	8	
BRENT, Gary Bazil (Mashonaland, Zimbabwe to Pakistan) b Sinoia 13.1.1976 RHB RMF																			
FC		4	2	1	14	13*	14.00	0	0	354	135	6	22.50	4-22	0	0	2.28	4	
FC	1994	11	13	3	182	40	18.20	0	0	1258	652	20	32.60	4-22	0	0	3.10	6	
Int	1996	1	1	0	1	1	1.00	0	0	30	29	0					5.80	0	
CAMPBELL, Alistair Douglas Ross (Mashonaland, Zimbabwe, Zimbabwe to Pakistan, Zimbabwe to Sri Lanka, Zimbabwe to Sharjah, Zimbabwe to South Africa, Mashonaland to South Africa) b Salisbury 23.9.1972 LHB OB																			
Test		2	3	0	135	84	45.00	0	1									7	
FC		5	8	2	370	84	61.66	0	4	18	16	0					5.33	15	
Int		4	4	2	150	80*	75.00	0	1									3	
Test	1992	22	38	1	1116	99	30.16	0	9	30	7	0					1.40	17	
FC	1990	61	111	15	3168	135*	33.00	3	22	1160	665	17	39.11	4-82	0	0	3.43	51	
Int	1991	57	54	4	1205	131*	24.12	1	7	165	116	3	38.66	2-22	0	0	4.21	23	
CAMPBELL, Donald James Ross (Mashonaland, Matabeleland Invitation XI, Mashonaland to South Africa) b Salisbury 24.6.1974 RHB WK																			
FC		2	3	0	83	46	27.66	0	0									10	
FC	1992	26	45	3	655	60*	15.59	0	1									76	7
CARLISLE, Stuart Vance (Mashonaland, Zimbabwe, Zimbabwe to Sharjah, Zimbabwe to South Africa, Mashonaland to South Africa) b Salisbury 10.5.1972 RHB RM																			
Test		1	2	0	4	4	2.00	0	0									2	
FC		4	6	0	243	131	40.50	1	1									4	
Test	1994	6	10	1	175	58	19.44	0	1									10	
FC	1993	25	44	4	1459	147	36.47	3	8	6	0	0					0.00	23	
Int	1994	8	8	1	79	28	11.28	0	0									4	
CRAIG, James Ross (Matabeleland) b Bulawayo 11.6.1971 RHB																			
FC		1	2	0	16	11	8.00	0	0	24	11	0					2.75	2	
FC	1993	16	28	1	414	63	15.33	0	2	78	29	1	29.00	1-10	0	0	2.23	8	
DEKKER, Mark Hamilton (Matabeleland, Zimbabwe, Zimbabwe to Pakistan, Zimbabwe to Sri Lanka) b Gatooma 5.12.1969 LHB LM/SLA																			
Test		1	1	0	2	2	2.00	0	0									1	
FC		4	6	0	309	104	51.50	1	2	6	16	0					16.00	2	
Test	1993	14	22	1	333	68*	15.85	0	2	60	15	0					1.50	12	
FC	1990	43	72	4	1761	162*	25.89	2	10	1750	862	15	57.46	2-4	0	0	2.95	41	
Int	1992	23	22	2	379	79	18.95	0	2	347	290	9	32.22	2-16	0	0	5.01	5	
ERASMUS, Daniel Nicolaas (Mashonaland to South Africa) b Salisbury 7.7.1973 RHB LB																			
FC	1992	27	48	2	1072	97	23.30	0	4	140	84	2	42.00	2-43	0	0	3.60	19	
EVANS, Craig Neil (Mashonaland, Zimbabwe, Zimbabwe to Sri Lanka, Zimbabwe to South Africa, Mashonaland to South Africa) b Salisbury 29.11.1969 RHB RM																			
FC		1	1	0	4	4	4.00	0	0	48	15	1	15.00	1-15	0	0	1.87	1	
Int		4	3	0	34	32	11.33	0	0	60	26	1	26.00	1-20	0	0	2.60	1	
Test	1996	1	2	0	10	9	5.00	0	0	36	27	0		*			4.50	1	
FC	1990	24	44	2	954	112	22.71	2	5	1291	660	18	36.66	2-28	0	0	3.06	13	
Int	1992	24	22	4	406	96*	22.55	0	1	246	172	5	34.40	1-6	0	0	4.19	3	
FELLOWS, Gary Matthew (Matabeleland) b Halifax, England 3.7.1978 RHB RM																			
FC		2	3	0	66	50	22.00	0	1	6	5	0					5.00	0	
FLOWER, Andrew (Mashonaland, Zimbabwe, MCC, Zimbabwe to Pakistan, Zimbabwe to Sri Lanka, Zimbabwe to Sharjah, Zimbabwe to South Africa, Mashonaland to South Africa) b Cape Town, South Africa 28.4.1968 LHB OB WK																			
Test		2	3	0	132	112	44.00	1	0									3	
FC		5	6	2	270	112	67.50	1	2									10	
Int		4	3	0	108	63	36.00	0	1									10	2
Test	1992	22	37	5	1330	156	46.57	3	9	1	0	0					0.00	50	4
FC	1986	63	103	19	3912	156	46.57	10	24	390	163	4	40.75	1-1	0	0	2.50	111	10
Int	1991	65	63	4	1711	115*	29.00	1	12	30	23	0					4.60	52	10

FLOWER, Grant William (Mashonaland, Zimbabwe, MCC, Zimbabwe to Pakistan, Zimbabwe to Sri Lanka, Zimbabwe to Sharjah, Zimbabwe to South Africa, Mashonaland to South Africa) b Salisbury 20.12.1970 RHB SLA

Cmp	Debut	M	I	NO	Runs	HS	Avge	100	50	Balls	Runs	Wkts	Avge	BB	5i	10m	RpO	ct	st
Test		2	3	0	116	73	38.66	0	1	132	65	0					2.95	3	
FC		7	11	2	477	243*	53.00	1	1	440	204	3	68.00	2-30	0	0	2.78	10	
Int		4	4	1	141	62	47.00	0	2	60	37	1	37.00	1-17	0	0	3.70	2	
Test	1992	22	38	1	1175	201*	31.75	2	6	672	322	3	107.33	1-4	0	0	2.87	11	
FC	1989	65	116	9	4501	201*	42.06	8	29	3890	1834	43	42.65	3-20	0	0	2.82	57	
Int	1992	55	53	3	1526	91	30.52	0	11	863	719	16	44.93	3-15	0	0	4.99	27	

GRIPPER, Trevor Raymond (Matabeleland) b Salisbury 28.12.1975 RHB OB

Cmp	Debut	M	I	NO	Runs	HS	Avge	100	50	Balls	Runs	Wkts	Avge	BB	5i	10m	RpO	ct	st
FC		1	2	0	45	45	22.50	0	0									1	

HOUGHTON, David Laud (Mashonaland, Zimbabwe, Zimbabwe to Pakistan, Zimbabwe to South Africa, Mashonaland to South Africa) b Bulawayo 23.6.1957 RHB OB WK

Cmp	Debut	M	I	NO	Runs	HS	Avge	100	50	Balls	Runs	Wkts	Avge	BB	5i	10m	RpO	ct	st
Test		2	3	0	100	37	33.33	0	0									2	
FC		6	7	0	311	110	44.42	1	1									5	
Int		4	3	0	26	19	8.66	0	0									2	
Test	1992	20	32	2	1395	266	46.50	4	4	5	0	0					0.00	15	
FC	1978	117	197	13	7317	266	39.76	17	35	149	59	2	29.50	2-7	0	0	2.37	163	16
Int	1983	60	57	2	1485	142	27.00	1	12	12	19	1	19.00	1-19	0	0	9.50	29	2

JAMES, Wayne Robert (Matabeleland, Zimbabwe to Sri Lanka) b Bulawayo 27.8.1965 RHB WK

Cmp	Debut	M	I	NO	Runs	HS	Avge	100	50	Balls	Runs	Wkts	Avge	BB	5i	10m	RpO	ct	st
FC		4	7	1	255	74	42.50	0	3									9	1
Test	1993	4	4	0	61	33	15.25	0	0									16	
FC	1986	40	70	6	2442	215	38.15	3	16									101	7
Int	1991	11	8	1	101	29	14.42	0	0									6	

KIRTLEY, Robert James (Mashonaland, Sussex, Mashonaland to South Africa) b Eastbourne, England 10.1.1975 RHB RFM

Cmp	Debut	M	I	NO	Runs	HS	Avge	100	50	Balls	Runs	Wkts	Avge	BB	5i	10m	RpO	ct	st
FC		2	1	0	2	2	2.00	0	0	427	172	14	12.28	5-53	2	0	2.41	0	
FC	1995	23	31	13	76	15*	4.22	0	0	3475	2125	74	28.71	6-60	4	0	3.66	11	

LOCK, Alan Charles Ingram (Mashonaland) b Marandellas 10.9.1962 RHB RFM

Cmp	Debut	M	I	NO	Runs	HS	Avge	100	50	Balls	Runs	Wkts	Avge	BB	5i	10m	RpO	ct	st
FC		1	1	1	15	15*		0	0	120	62	1	62.00	1-48	0	0	3.10	0	
Test	1995	1	2	1	8	8*	8.00	0	0	180	105	5	21.00	3-68	0	0	3.50	0	
FC	1987	10	12	5	74	16	10.57	0	0	1455	767	29	26.44	6-59	1	0	3.16	3	
Int	1995	8	3	2	8	5	8.00	0	0	289	219	8	27.37	5-44	0	1	4.54	1	

MADONDO, Trevor Nyasha (Matabeleland) b Mount Darwin 22.11.1976 RHB WK

Cmp	Debut	M	I	NO	Runs	HS	Avge	100	50	Balls	Runs	Wkts	Avge	BB	5i	10m	RpO	ct	st
FC		1	2	0	5	5	2.50	0	0									1	
FC	1994	2	4	0	89	48	22.25	0	0									4	

MARILLIER, Eian Robert (Mashonaland) b Scotland 19.9.1976 RHB WK

Cmp	Debut	M	I	NO	Runs	HS	Avge	100	50	Balls	Runs	Wkts	Avge	BB	5i	10m	RpO	ct	st
FC		1	1	1	14	14*		0	0									5	

MATAMBANADZO, Darlington (Mashonaland) b Salisbury 13.4.1976 RHB RMF

Cmp	Debut	M	I	NO	Runs	HS	Avge	100	50	Balls	Runs	Wkts	Avge	BB	5i	10m	RpO	ct	st
FC		1	1	1	3	3*		0	0	36	34	1	34.00	1-34	0	0	5.66	1	
FC	1993	10	13	3	85	21	8.50	0	0	1289	797	27	29.51	4-52	0	0	3.70	6	

MATAMBANADZO, Everton (Mashonaland, Zimbabwe, Zimbabwe to Pakistan, Zimbabwe to Sharjah, Zimbabwe to South Africa, Mashonaland to South Africa) b Salisbury 13.4.1976 RHB RMF

Cmp	Debut	M	I	NO	Runs	HS	Avge	100	50	Balls	Runs	Wkts	Avge	BB	5i	10m	RpO	ct	st
FC		2	1	0	0	0	0.00	0	0	253	167	6	27.83	3-76	0	0	3.96	1	
Test	1996	1	2	1	7	7	7.00	0	0	96	89	2	44.50	2-62	0	0	5.56	0	
FC	1993	11	14	7	69	32*	9.85	0	0	1399	819	23	35.60	3-20	0	0	3.51	5	
Int	1996	6	5	3	8	5*	4.00	0	0	267	193	10	19.30	4-32	1	0	4.33	1	

MBANGWA, Mpumelelo (Matabeleland, Zimbabwe to Pakistan) b Plumtree 26.6.1976 RHB RFM

Cmp	Debut	M	I	NO	Runs	HS	Avge	100	50	Balls	Runs	Wkts	Avge	BB	5i	10m	RpO	ct	st
FC		5	7	1	21	8	3.50	0	0	642	339	7	48.42	2-16	0	0	3.16	1	
Test	1996	1	2	0	2	2	1.00	0	0	144	81	2	40.50	2-67	0	0	3.37	0	
FC	1995	16	18	5	52	14*	4.00	0	0	2088	1091	27	40.40	2-16	0	0	3.13	7	
Int	1996	1	1	0	11	11	11.00	0	0	34	47	0					8.29	0	

MURPHY, Brian Andrew (Mashonaland to South Africa) b Salisbury 1.12.1976 RHB LBG

Cmp	Debut	M	I	NO	Runs	HS	Avge	100	50	Balls	Runs	Wkts	Avge	BB	5i	10m	RpO	ct	st
FC	1995	1								42	21	0					3.00	0	

OATES, Jason Mark (Mashonaland) b Salisbury 11.7.1974 LHB SLA

Cmp	Debut	M	I	NO	Runs	HS	Avge	100	50	Balls	Runs	Wkts	Avge	BB	5i	10m	RpO	ct	st
FC		1	2	0	27	27	13.50	0	0									1	
FC	1995	2	4	0	142	115	35.50	1	0									1	

OLONGA, Henry Khaaba (Matabeleland, Zimbabwe, Zimbabwe to Pakistan, Zimbabwe to Sri Lanka) b Lusaka, Zambia 3.7.1976 RHB RFM

Cmp	Debut	M	I	NO	Runs	HS	Avge	100	50	Balls	Runs	Wkts	Avge	BB	5i	10m	RpO	ct	st
Test		2	3	0	0	0	0.00	0	0	246	160	5	32.00	3-90	0	0	3.90	0	
FC		5	9	1	94	33	11.75	0	0	750	458	15	30.53	3-38	0	0	3.66	3	
Test	1994	7	9	1	14	7	1.75	0	0	802	487	10	48.70	3-90	0	0	3.64	4	
FC	1993	26	38	8	270	41	9.00	0	0	3672	2134	66	32.33	5-80	1	0	3.48	18	
Int	1995	3	1	0	6	6	6.00	0	0	120	138	5	46.00	2-47	0	0	6.90	1	

OMARSHAH, Ali Hassimshah (Zimbabwe to Sri Lanka, Mashonaland to South Africa) b Salisbury 7.8.1959 LHB RM

Cmp	Debut	M	I	NO	Runs	HS	Avge	100	50	Balls	Runs	Wkts	Avge	BB	5i	10m	RpO	ct	st
Test	1992	3	5	0	122	62	24.40	0	1	186	125	1	125.00	1-46	0	0	4.03	0	
FC	1979	45	74	5	1766	200*	25.59	3	5	3816	1710	35	48.85	4-113	0	0	2.68	21	
Int	1983	28	28	2	437	60*	16.80	0	1	1077	812	18	45.11	3-33	0	0	4.52	6	

Cmp	Debut	M	I	NO	Runs	HS	Avge	100	50	Balls	Runs	Wkts	Avge	BB	5i	10m	RpO	ct	st

PECK, Graeme (Matabeleland) b Bulawayo 5.2.1975 RHB OB

Cmp	Debut	M	I	NO	Runs	HS	Avge	100	50	Balls	Runs	Wkts	Avge	BB	5i	10m	RpO	ct	st
FC		2	4	0	26	17	6.50	0	0	18	4	1	4.00	1-4	0	0	1.33	1	
FC	1994	11	17	3	244	51	17.42	0	1	678	305	7	43.57	2-56	0	0	2.69	6	

RANCHOD, Manish (Matabeleland) b Bulawayo 1.6.1971 RHB

Cmp	Debut	M	I	NO	Runs	HS	Avge	100	50	Balls	Runs	Wkts	Avge	BB	5i	10m	RpO	ct	st
FC		4	7	3	109	56*	27.25	0	1									0	
FC	1993	12	20	4	327	56*	20.43	0	1									6	

RENNIE, Gavin James (Mashonaland, Zimbabwe to Pakistan) b Fort Victoria 12.1.1976 LHB SLA

Cmp	Debut	M	I	NO	Runs	HS	Avge	100	50	Balls	Runs	Wkts	Avge	BB	5i	10m	RpO	ct	st
FC		2	4	0	33	10	8.25	0	0	36	15	3	5.00	3-15	0	0	2.50	2	
FC	1993	24	41	1	807	76	20.17	0	4	1437	843	21	40.14	3-15	0	0	3.51	12	
Int	1996	2	2	0	6	6	3.00	0	0									2	

RENNIE, John Alexander (Matabeleland, Zimbabwe, Zimbabwe to Pakistan, Zimbabwe to South Africa) b Fort Victoria 29.7.1970 RHB RMF

Cmp	Debut	M	I	NO	Runs	HS	Avge	100	50	Balls	Runs	Wkts	Avge	BB	5i	10m	RpO	ct	st
FC		5	8	2	153	57*	25.50	0	1	731	379	7	54.14	2-44	0	0	3.11	1	
Int		4	1	0	0	0	0.00	0	0	150	102	3	34.00	3-27	0	0	4.08	2	
Test	1993	3	4	1	24	19*	8.00	0	0	658	256	3	85.33	2-22	0	0	2.33	0	
FC	1992	31	46	12	684	67*	20.11	0	3	5291	2621	67	39.11	6-34	3	0	2.97	8	
Int	1993	21	11	6	81	27	16.20	0	0	892	731	18	40.61	3-27	0	0	4.91	6	

STRANG, Bryan Colin (Mashonaland, Zimbabwe, Zimbabwe to Pakistan, Zimbabwe to Sri Lanka, Mashonaland to South Africa) b Bulawayo 9.6.1972 RHB LMF

Cmp	Debut	M	I	NO	Runs	HS	Avge	100	50	Balls	Runs	Wkts	Avge	BB	5i	10m	RpO	ct	st
Test		1	2	1	7	4*	7.00	0	0	102	54	0					3.17	1	
FC		6	5	1	79	68	19.75	0	1	1042	436	12	36.33	5-50	1	0	2.51	3	
Test	1994	9	15	5	117	42	11.70	0	0	1776	661	24	27.54	5-101	1	0	2.23	6	
FC	1994	34	50	11	540	68	13.84	0	2	7364	3169	134	23.64	7-64	9	1	2.58	12	
Int	1994	12	8	4	17	6	4.25	0	0	488	347	10	34.70	4-36	1	0	4.26	7	

STRANG, Paul Andrew (Mashonaland, Zimbabwe, Kent, Zimbabwe to Pakistan, Zimbabwe to Sri Lanka, Zimbabwe to Sharjah, Zimbabwe to South Africa, Mashonaland to South Africa) b Bulawayo 28.7.1970 RHB LBG

Cmp	Debut	M	I	NO	Runs	HS	Avge	100	50	Balls	Runs	Wkts	Avge	BB	5i	10m	RpO	ct	st
Test		2	3	1	104	47*	52.00	0	0	700	259	10	25.90	5-123	1	0	2.22	2	
FC		7	7	2	236	103*	47.20	1	0	2193	906	36	25.16	5-45	3	1	2.47	3	
Int		4	3	0	14	13	4.66	0	0	155	76	5	15.20	3-24	0	0	2.94	0	
Test	1994	13	21	5	505	106*	31.56	1	1	2894	1278	32	39.93	5-106	3	0	2.64	6	
FC	1992	61	91	19	2050	106*	28.47	2	11	13777	6424	200	32.12	7-75	15	2	2.79	50	
Int	1994	38	34	10	603	47	25.12	0	0	1872	1355	37	36.62	5-21	1	1	4.34	12	

STREAK, Heath Hilton (Matabeleland, Zimbabwe, Zimbabwe to Sri Lanka, Zimbabwe to Sharjah, Zimbabwe to South Africa) b Bulawayo 16.3.1974 RHB RFM

Cmp	Debut	M	I	NO	Runs	HS	Avge	100	50	Balls	Runs	Wkts	Avge	BB	5i	10m	RpO	ct	st
Test		2	3	1	34	19	17.00	0	0	535	240	8	30.00	4-43	0	0	2.69	0	
FC		6	9	2	204	67	29.14	0	1	1080	475	17	27.94	4-20	0	0	2.63	0	
Int		4	2	1	54	43*	54.00	0	0	215	153	11	13.90	5-32	0	1	4.26	2	
Test	1993	15	22	5	225	53	13.23	0	1	3641	1551	69	22.47	6-90	3	0	2.55	5	
FC	1992	59	85	15	1586	131	22.65	2	7	10545	4823	178	27.09	7-69	4	0	2.74	24	
Int	1993	44	35	10	423	43*	16.92	0	0	2287	1604	58	27.65	5-32	3	1	4.20	9	

VAGHMARIA, Darshan (Matabeleland) b Bulwayo 17.6.1971 LHB SLA

Cmp	Debut	M	I	NO	Runs	HS	Avge	100	50	Balls	Runs	Wkts	Avge	BB	5i	10m	RpO	ct	st
FC		4	6	0	51	18	8.50	0	0	501	318	8	39.75	3-44	0	0	3.80	2	
FC	1995	6	9	3	94	26*	15.66	0	0	765	512	15	34.13	4-108	0	0	4.01	2	

VILJOEN, Dirk Peter (Mashonaland, Matabeleland Invitation XI, Zimbabwe to Sharjah, Mashonaland to South Africa) b Salisbury 11.3.1977 LHB SLA

Cmp	Debut	M	I	NO	Runs	HS	Avge	100	50	Balls	Runs	Wkts	Avge	BB	5i	10m	RpO	ct	st
FC		5	8	0	155	47	19.37	0	0	18	10	0					3.33	3	
FC	1994	8	14	1	208	47	16.00	0	0	18	10	0					3.33	4	
Int	1996	3	3	0	64	25	21.33	0	0									1	

WALLER, Andrew Christopher (Mashonaland, Zimbabwe, Zimbabwe to South Africa) b Salisbury 25.9.1959 RHB RM

Cmp	Debut	M	I	NO	Runs	HS	Avge	100	50	Balls	Runs	Wkts	Avge	BB	5i	10m	RpO	ct	st
Test		2	3	0	69	50	23.00	0	1									1	
FC		3	4	0	173	104	43.25	1	1	102	42	0					2.47	1	
Int		4	4	0	92	48	23.00	0	0									1	
FC	1984	39	65	4	1653	104	27.09	1	11	546	255	5	51.00	1-1	0	0	2.80	24	
Int	1987	39	38	3	818	83*	23.37	0	4									10	

WHITTALL, Andrew Richard (Matabeleland, Zimbabwe to Pakistan, Zimbabwe to Sri Lanka, Zimbabwe to Sharjah) b Mutare 28.3.1973 RHB OB

Cmp	Debut	M	I	NO	Runs	HS	Avge	100	50	Balls	Runs	Wkts	Avge	BB	5i	10m	RpO	ct	st
FC		5	8	1	65	23	9.28	0	0	756	455	7	65.00	3-119	0	0	3.61	5	
Test	1996	3	6	1	27	12	5.40	0	0	536	261	2	130.50	2-146	0	0	2.92	2	
FC	1993	43	55	9	691	91*	15.02	0	2	8841	4930	85	58.00	6-46	3	1	3.34	24	
Int	1996	8	7	2	12	4*	2.40	0	0	366	261	6	43.50	3-36	0	0	4.27	2	

WHITTALL, Guy James (Matabeleland, Zimbabwe, Zimbabwe to Pakistan, Zimbabwe to Sri Lanka, Zimbabwe to Sharjah, Zimbabwe to South Africa) b Chipinga 5.9.1972 RHB RM

Cmp	Debut	M	I	NO	Runs	HS	Avge	100	50	Balls	Runs	Wkts	Avge	BB	5i	10m	RpO	ct	st
Test		2	3	0	64	56	21.33	0	1	252	69	5	13.80	4-18	0	0	1.64	1	
FC		6	10.	0	316	159	31.60	1	1	642	270	8	33.75	4-18	0	0	2.58	8	
Int		4	4	1	47	19*	15.66	0	0	138	87	5	17.40	2-11	0	0	3.78	2	
Test	1993	18	30	2	642	113*	22.92	1	3	2213	919	27	34.03	4-18	0	0	2.49	7	
FC	1990	52	92	7	2327	180*	27.37	6	9	5682	2860	88	32.50	6-34	2	0	3.02	33	
Int	1993	45	45	5	694	70	17.35	0	2	1569	1287	34	37.85	3-46	0	0	4.92	13	

WISHART, Craig Brian (Mashonaland, Zimbabwe, Zimbabwe to Pakistan, Zimbabwe to Sri Lanka, Zimbabwe to Sharjah, Zimbabwe to South Africa, Mashonaland to South Africa) b Salisbury 9.1.1974 RHB RM

Cmp	Debut	M	I	NO	Runs	HS	Avge	100	50	Balls	Runs	Wkts	Avge	BB	5i	10m	RpO	ct	st
FC		5	8	3	250	110	50.00	1	1	78	30	2	15.00	2-30	0	0	2.30	2	
Test	1995	6	12	1	154	51	14.00	0	1									3	
FC	1992	44	81	8	1819	110	24.91	1	12	1203	730	23	31.73	5-24	1	0	3.64	34	
Int	1996	10	10	0	160	53	16.00	0	1									3	

ENGLAND IN ZIMBABWE 1996-97

ATHERTON, M.A.

	M	I	NO	Runs	HS	Avge	100	50	Balls	Runs	Wkts	Avge	BB	5i	10m	RpO	ct	st
Test	2	4	0	34	16	8.50	0	0									2	
FC	4	8	0	102	55	12.75	0	1									3	
Int	3	3	0	66	25	22.00	0	0									2	

CADDICK, A.R.

	M	I	NO	Runs	HS	Avge	100	50	Balls	Runs	Wkts	Avge	BB	5i	10m	RpO	ct	st
FC	2	3	1	57	28	28.50	0	0	252	127	3	42.33	2-38	0	0	3.02	1	

CRAWLEY, J.P.

	M	I	NO	Runs	HS	Avge	100	50	Balls	Runs	Wkts	Avge	BB	5i	10m	RpO	ct	st
Test	2	3	1	166	112	83.00	1	0									6	
FC	4	6	1	328	112	65.60	1	2									11	
Int	3	3	0	83	73	27.66	0	1									1	

CROFT, R.D.B.

	M	I	NO	Runs	HS	Avge	100	50	Balls	Runs	Wkts	Avge	BB	5i	10m	RpO	ct	st
Test	2	2	0	21	14	10.50	0	0	552	178	8	22.25	3-39	0	0	1.93	2	
FC	4	5	1	112	80*	28.00	0	1	926	349	16	21.81	4-65	0	0	2.26	2	
Int	3	3	2	40	30*	40.00	0	0	138	119	4	29.75	2-33	0	0	5.17	2	

GOUGH, D.

	M	I	NO	Runs	HS	Avge	100	50	Balls	Runs	Wkts	Avge	BB	5i	10m	RpO	ct	st
Test	2	3	1	7	3*	3.50	0	0	384	171	7	24.42	4-40	0	0	2.67	1	
FC	4	6	1	27	12	5.40	0	0	746	367	19	19.31	6-64	2	1	2.95	3	
Int	3	3	1	18	9	9.00	0	0	173	116	7	16.57	4-43	1	0	4.02	0	

HUSSAIN, N.

	M	I	NO	Runs	HS	Avge	100	50	Balls	Runs	Wkts	Avge	BB	5i	10m	RpO	ct	st
Test	2	4	0	130	113	32.50	1	0									2	
FC	4	8	0	249	113	31.12	1	0									4	
Int	3	3	1	56	49*	28.00	0	0									1	

IRANI, R.C.

	M	I	NO	Runs	HS	Avge	100	50	Balls	Runs	Wkts	Avge	BB	5i	10m	RpO	ct	st
FC	1	2	1	15	10*	15.00	0	0	56	33	0					3.53	1	
Int	3	3	0	12	7	4.00	0	0	131	79	1	79.00	1-39	0	0	3.61	0	

KNIGHT, N.V.

	M	I	NO	Runs	HS	Avge	100	50	Balls	Runs	Wkts	Avge	BB	5i	10m	RpO	ct	st
Test	2	4	0	197	96	49.25	0	2									2	
FC	4	8	0	328	114	41.00	1	2									3	
Int	3	3	0	16	13	5.33	0	0									1	

MULLALLY, A.D.

	M	I	NO	Runs	HS	Avge	100	50	Balls	Runs	Wkts	Avge	BB	5i	10m	RpO	ct	st
Test	2	2	0	4	4	2.00	0	0	384	150	3	50.00	1-32	0	0	2.34	1	
FC	3	4	0	9	4	2.25	0	0	492	210	5	42.00	2-18	0	0	2.56	1	
Int	3	2	0	20	20	10.00	0	0	174	92	6	15.33	3-29	0	0	3.17	1	

SILVERWOOD, C.E.W.

	M	I	NO	Runs	HS	Avge	100	50	Balls	Runs	Wkts	Avge	BB	5i	10m	RpO	ct	st
Test	1	1	0	0	0	0.00	0	0	150	71	4	17.75	3-63	0	0	2.84	1	
FC	1	1	0	0	0	0.00	0	0	150	71	4	17.75	3-63	0	0	2.84	1	
Int	3	2	0	1	1	0.50	0	0	126	84	2	42.00	2-27	0	0	4.00	0	

STEWART, A.J.

	M	I	NO	Runs	HS	Avge	100	50	Balls	Runs	Wkts	Avge	BB	5i	10m	RpO	ct	st
Test	2	4	1	241	101*	80.33	1	1									5	
FC	4	8	1	324	101*	46.28	1	1									8	
Int	3	3	0	96	41	32.00	0	0									8	

THORPE, G.P.

	M	I	NO	Runs	HS	Avge	100	50	Balls	Runs	Wkts	Avge	BB	5i	10m	RpO	ct	st
Test	2	4	1	70	50*	23.33	0	1									1	
FC	4	8	1	187	65	26.71	0	2	22	9	1	9.00	1-3	0	0	2.45	1	
Int	1	1	0	1	1	1.00	0	0	12	5	0					2.50	0	

TUFNELL, P.C.R.

	M	I	NO	Runs	HS	Avge	100	50	Balls	Runs	Wkts	Avge	BB	5i	10m	RpO	ct	st
Test	2	2	1	11	9	11.00	0	0	497	192	7	27.42	4-61	0	0	2.31	1	
FC	4	5	2	29	10	9.66	0	0	945	407	14	29.07	5-78	1	0	2.58	5	

WHITE, C.

	M	I	NO	Runs	HS	Avge	100	50	Balls	Runs	Wkts	Avge	BB	5i	10m	RpO	ct	st
Test	1	1	0	9	9	9.00	0	0	96	41	1	41.00	1-41	0	0	2.56	0	
FC	1	1	0	9	9	9.00	0	0	96	41	1	41.00	1-41	0	0	2.56	0	
Int	2	2	0	4	4	2.00	0	0	102	78	1	78.00	1-39	0	0	4.58	0	

INDIA IN ZIMBABWE 1996-97

Player	Cmp	M	I	NO	Runs	HS	Avge	100	50	Balls	Runs	Wkts	Avge	BB	5i	10m	RpO	ct	st
AZHARUDDIN, M.	Int	1	1	0	24	24	24.00	0	0									1	
GANESH, D.	Int	1	1	0	4	4	4.00	0	0	30	20	1	20.00	1-20	0	0	4.00	0	
GANGULY, S.C.	Int	1	1	0	2	2	2.00	0	0	12	10	0					5.00	0	
JADEJA, A.D.	Int	1	1	0	0	0	0.00	0	0									0	
JOSHI, S.B.	Int	1	1	0	0	0	0.00	0	0	12	19	0					9.50	0	
KUMBLE, A.	Int	1	1	0	21	21	21.00	0	0	36	18	1	18.00	1-18	0	0	3.00	0	
MONGIA, N.R.	Int	1	1	0	4	4	4.00	0	0									0	
RATHORE, V.	Int	1	1	0	34	34	34.00	0	0									0	
SINGH, R.R.	Int	1	1	0	45	45	45.00	0	0	24	31	0					7.75	0	
TENDULKAR, S.R.	Int	1	1	0	13	13	13.00	0	0									0	
VENKATESH PRASAD, B.K.	Int	1	1	1	0	0*		0	0	41	35	0					5.12	0	

WESTERN PROVINCE IN ZIMBABWE 1996-97

Player	Cmp	M	I	NO	Runs	HS	Avge	100	50	Balls	Runs	Wkts	Avge	BB	5i	10m	RpO	ct	st
ACKERMAN, H.D.	FC	1	2	0	7	7	3.50	0	0									0	
COMMINS, J.B.	FC	1	2	0	106	104	53.00	1	0									1	
DAVIDS, F.	FC	1	2	0	26	26	13.00	0	0	54	53	0					5.88	0	
DAWSON, A.C.	FC	1	2	2	47	30*		0	0	117	62	1	62.00	1-56	0	0	3.17	0	
DE VILLIERS, M.C.	FC	1	2	1	86	84	86.00	0	1									0	
KIRSTEN, P.	FC	1	2	0	23	18	11.50	0	0									7	
KOENIG, S.G.	FC	1	2	0	116	67	58.00	0	1									0	
MARON, R.	FC	1	2	0	23	22	11.50	0	0	18	7	1	7.00	1-7	0	0	2.33	0	
MARTYN, A.	FC	1	2	0	6	6	3.00	0	0	186	58	6	9.66	4-46	0	0	1.87	0	
PRINGLE, M.W.	FC	1	2	0	23	14	11.50	0	0	216	102	3	34.00	2-26	0	0	2.83	0	
RUNDLE, D.B.	FC	1	2	0	55	41	27.50	0	0	120	50	0					2.50	0	

WORCESTERSHIRE IN ZIMBABWE 1996-97

Player	Cmp	M	I	NO	Runs	HS	Avge	100	50	Balls	Runs	Wkts	Avge	BB	5i	10m	RpO	ct	st
CHAPMAN, R.J.	FC	1	1	1	7	7*		0	0	138	67	2	33.50	2-40	0	0	2.91	0	
CURTIS, T.S.	FC	1	2	0	7	7	3.50	0	0									3	
HAYNES, G.R.	FC	1	2	0	40	29	20.00	0	0	126	40	1	40.00	1-21	0	0	1.90	1	

Cmp	Debut	M	I	NO	Runs	HS	Avge	100	50	Balls	Runs	Wkts	Avge	BB	5i	10m	RpO	ct	st
HICK, G.A.																			
FC		1	2	0	54	32	27.00	0	0	112	76	6	12.66	4-59	0	0	4.07	1	
ILLINGWORTH, R.K.																			
FC		1	2	1	28	14*	28.00	0	0	212	62	4	15.50	2-30	0	0	1.75	2	
LAMPITT, S.R.																			
FC		1	2	1	35	22*	35.00	0	0	138	64	2	32.00	1-20	0	0	2.78	1	
LEATHERDALE, D.A.																			
FC		1	2	0	62	44	31.00	0	0									0	
NEWPORT, P.J.																			
FC		1	2	0	10	5	5.00	0	0	150	55	3	18.33	2-21	0	0	2.20	0	
RHODES, S.J.																			
FC		1	2	0	68	46	34.00	0	0									4	1
SOLANKI, V.S.																			
FC		1	2	0	61	61	30.50	0	1	12	19	0					9.50	2	
WESTON, W.P.C.																			
FC		1	2	0	11	10	5.50	0	0									0	

CORRECTIONS TO 1997 YEAR BOOK

Page 25   A.E.Warner FC career bwg av 31.45
Page 36   W.S.Kendall FC balls 114, RC 82, av 41.00, RpO 4.31
Page 40   N.H.Fairbrother BH bttg av 72.00
Page 42   V.P.Clarke FC bwg av 42.00
Page 44   I.J.Sutcliffe FC balls 120, RC 86, av 28.66, RpO 4.30
Page 67   M.Azharuddin FC ct (not st) 3
Page 74   S.Gourlay BH bttg av 20.00
Page 77   S.J.O'Shaughnessy FC career BB 4-66
Page 78   G.N.Reifer FC career bttg av 20.42
Page 112   U.S.Belsare FC R 40, av 10.00
Page 114   R.Deb Burman FC NO 2, R 120, av 20.00
Page 120   P.K.Krishnakumar FC balls 1034, RC 530, av 29.44, RpO 3.07
Page 123   A.Mehra FC ct 9
Page 124   B.Nath FC NO 0, R 0, HS 0, av 0.00
Page 126   N.A.Patel FC R 127, av 18.14, A.Pathak FC ct 4,
           J.Paul FC R 7, HS 4, av 1.75, FC career R 31, av 3.87
Page 128   R.P.Rathore FC balls 330, RC 145, av 24.16, RpO 2.63, FC career balls 5672, RC 2670,
           av 30.34, RpO 2.82
Page 129   A.Saha FC R 35, av 5.00, FC career R 399, av 6.54
Page 130   Shamsher Singh FC RC 137, av 68.50, BB 1-18, RpO 3.91
Page 131   Sandeep Sharma FC ct 0
Page 144   M.D.Crowe Int career I 140, NO 18
Page 146   C.D.Ingham SC career 50 3, ct 4
Page 160   Aamer Ishaq FC R 245, av 30.62, FC career R 2011, av 26.46
Page 161   Abdul Qadir Int career RC 3454, av 26.16
Page 162   Akram Raza FC RC 357, av 25.50, RpO 2.39
Page 163   Asif Mujtaba FC RC 333, av 23.78, RpO 1.93
Page 164   Azam Khan FC R 1281, av 44.17
Page 165   Basit Ali add Pakistan to Singapore
Page 169   Javed Iqbal (Peshawar) Wlls mt 3, I 3, R 73, av 24.33, delete Javed Khan (Peshawar)
Page 171   Mansoor Akhtar add Karachi Blues,
           Manzoor Akhtar FC balls 1340, RC 748, av 34.00, RpO 3.34
Page 181   Shahid Anwar FC RC 9, RpO 1.50
Page 183   Taimur Khan (b Peshawar 1.5.1975) played, not Taimur Ali Khan
Page 184   Waheed Niazi FC career Balls 7717
Page 187   N.V.Knight FC ct 8, D.P.Ostler FC ct 5
Page 194   Aamer Sohail Int 4-4-1-162-54.00, Aaqib Javed Int mt 4, Ijaz Ahmed Int 4-3-1-89-44.50,
           Inzamam-ul-Haq Int 4-3-0-106-35.33, Mohammad Akram Int mt 2, Rashid Latif Int mt 4
           Saeed Anwar Int 4-4-0-126-31.50, Saleem Malik Int 4-4-2-126-63.00,
           Saqlain Mushtaq Int mt 4, Waqar Younis Int mt 4, add Basit Ali Int mt 1, ct 0
Page 195   P.A.de Silva Int mt 4, H.D.P.K.Dharmasena Int mt 3, bwg 114-94-3-31.33, RpO 4.94, ct 3,
           A.P.Gurusinha Int mt 3, S.T.Jayasuriya Int mt 4, R.S.Kaluwitharana Int mt 4, ct 4,
           R.S.Mahanama Int mt 4, M.Muralitharan Int mt 4,
           A.Ranatunga Int mt 4, bwg 24-28-1-28.00-1/8-0-0-7.00, H.P.Tillakaratne Int mt 4,
           W.P.U.J.C.Vaas Int mt 4, bwg 172-131-9-14.55, RpO 4.56, ct 1,
           G.P.Wickramasinghe Int mt 4, bwg 150-146-2-73.00, RpO 5.84
Page 201   F.Abderouf (not Aberdouf)
Page 231   C.D.Fernando FC career 8-15-335-22.33, 198-103-2-51.50, RpO 3.12
Page 234   D.Kanchana FC ct 7, FC career ct 9
Page 237   R.Pushpakumara FC career balls 3522, RpO 2.79
Page 255   O.R.Richards FC BB 1-48
Page 258   J.E.R.Gallian FC BB 2-33, G.Keedy FC BB 2-73
Page 265   S.G.Peall Int career mt 21
Page 273   Asif Karim Int mt 6, D.Chudasama Int mt 6, H.S.Modi Int mt 6, T.Odoyo Int mt 5,
           bwg 114-112-0, RpO 5.89, E.O.Odumbe Int mt 6, bwg 101-95-4-23.75-2/8, RpO 5.64,
           ct 3, M.O.Odumbe Int mt 6, ct 1, K.Otieno Int mt 6, Rajab Ali Int mt 6,
           bwg 248-190-10-19.00, RpO 4.59, M.A.Suji Int mt 6, bwg 272-224-4-56.00, RpO 4.94,
           Tariq Iqbal Int mt 3, S.O.Tikolo Int mt 6
Page 277   A.D.R.Campbell Int 6-6-0-114-19.00, C.N.Evans Int mt 6, A.Flower Int 6-6-1-51-10.20,
           G.W.Flower Int 6-6-1-150-30.00, A.C.I.Lock Int mt 6, S.G.Peall Int mt 5,
           B.C.Strang Int mt 4, P.A.Strang Int mt 6, H.H.Streak Int mt 6,
           A.C.Waller Int 6-6-0-162-27.00, G.J.Whittall Int 6-6-0-83-13.83

CORRECTIONS TO 1996 YEAR BOOK

Page 68   J.N.Batty BH st 0, R.A.Bunting FC career I 40
Page 117   Kapil Dev Int career mt 225
Page 177   Rizwan Sattar FC career 50 6
Page 181   Taimur Khan (b Peshawar 1.5.1975) played, not Taimur Ali Khan
Page 207   R.C.Ontong FC career balls 53697, RC 26487
Page 225   P.B.Dassanayake Int mt 9
Page 226   P.A.de Silva Int mt 10, C.Devinda delete, H.D.P.K.Dharmasena Int mt 6
Page 227   C.Fernando (Moratuwa) FC 2-4-117-29.25, 30-12-0, RpO 2.40
Page 228   J.C.Gamage FC Balls 1468, RpO 2.93
Page 229   S.T.Jayasuriya Int mt 10, R.S.Kalpage Int mt 10
Page 231   R.S.Mahanama Int mt 8
Page 233   A.Ranatunga Int mt 10
Page 234   S.Ranatunga Int mt 7
Page 235   H.P.Tillakaratne Int mt 9
Page 236   W.P.U.J.C.Vaas Int mt 9, bwg 335-210-5-42.00, RpO 3.76
Page 237   G.P.Wickramasinghe Int mt 10, bwg 346-245-9-27.22, RpO 4.24
Page 238   M.Azharuddin Int mt 4, A.C.Bedade Int mt 4, R.K.Chauhan Int mt 4,
           V.G.Kambli Int mt 4, Kapil Dev Int mt 4, A.Kumble Int mt 4, N.R.Mongia Int mt 4,
           M.Prabhakar Int 4-4-1-47-15.66, N.S.Sidhu Int mt 4, J.Srinath Int mt 2,
           S.R.Tendulkar Int 4-4-1-127-42.33

CORRECTIONS TO 1995 YEAR BOOK

Page 117   Maninder Singh Int career RC 2066, av 31.30
Page 125   G.Sharma FC career Balls 24773
Page 146   C.Pringle Int RC 310, av 25.83, RpO 4.36
Page 149   A.D.Jadeja Int R 201, av 50.25
Page 254   R.Pushpakumara FC balls 1062, RpO 2.94

CORRECTIONS TO 1994 YEAR BOOK

Page 38   I.D.Austin BH ct 2
Page 40   P.J.Martin BH ct 2
Page 125   K.Srikkanth Int career R 4091, av 29.01
Page 159   Hasnain Kazim FC ct 2
Page 168   Shahid Ali Khan FC ct 1
Page 241   D.Sultan FC career bwg av 41.57

CORRECTIONS TO 1993 YEAR BOOK

Page 140   R.E.W.Mawhinney FC career bttg av 23.54
Page 157   Imran Khan Int career RC 4844, av 26.61
Page 185   L.J.Barnard FC career balls 4831, RC 2276, av 37.31, RpO 2.82

CORRECTIONS TO 1992 YEAR BOOK

Page 222   A.F.D.Jackman FC career bttg av 37.93

CORRECTIONS TO 1991 YEAR BOOK

Page 70   S.J.Malone FC career 10m 1
Page 72   P.R.Oliver FC career 50 9
Page 147   H.R.Fotheringham BH career R 1707, av 36.31
Page 150   Abdul Qadir Int RC 13, av 13.00, BB 1-13, RpO 3.90
Page 155   Imran Khan Int RC 28, av 5.60, RpO 3.11
Page 164   Saleem Malik Int R 29, HS 29, av 29.00
Page 168   Wasim Akram Int RC 41, av 20.50, BB 2-25, RpO 3.72
Page 169   R.Lamba Int R 17, HS 10, av 8.50, Maninder Singh Int RC 41, av 13.66, RpO 3.41
Page 170   K.Srikkanth Int R 48, av 24.00, N.S.Sidhu Int R 3, av 1.50

CORRECTIONS TO 1988 YEAR BOOK

Page 70   Rizwan Sattar FC 50 2
Page 77   L.J.Barnard FC RC 47, av 15.66
Page 81   R.C.Ontong FC RC 679, av 33.95

Unless otherwise stated all corrections refer to figures for the appropriate season. Corrections to career figures are only noted if the player concerned does not appear in the 1998 Year Book, and then against the latest yearbook in which the player appears.